Berlitz®

Ocean Cruising
& Cruise Ships 2005

by Douglas Ward
President
The Maritime Evaluations Group

Editorial

Written by
Douglas Ward
Editorial Director
Brian Bell

Editorial address
Berlitz Publishing
PO Box 7910, London SE1 1WE
United Kingdom
Fax: (44) 20-7403 0290
berlitz@apaguide.co.uk

Distribution
United States
Langenscheidt Publishers, Inc.
46–35 54th Road, Maspeth, NY 11378
Fax: (718) 784 0640
Canada
Thomas Allen & Son Ltd
390 Steelcase Road East
Markham, Ontario L3R 1G2
Fax: (1) 905 475 6747
UK & Ireland
GeoCenter International Ltd
The Viables Centre, Harrow Way
Basingstoke, Hants RG22 4BJ
Fax: (44) 1256 817988
Worldwide
Apa Publications GmbH & Co.
Verlag KG (Singapore branch)
38 Joo Koon Road, Singapore 628990
Tel: (65) 6865 1600. Fax: (65) 6861 6438

Printing
Insight Print Services (Pte) Ltd
38 Joo Koon Road, Singapore 628990
Tel: (65) 6865-1600. Fax: (65) 6861-6438

©2005 Apa Publications GmbH & Co.
Verlag KG (Singapore branch)
All Rights Reserved

*Berlitz Trademark Reg. U.S. Patent Office
and other countries. Marca Registrada.
Used under licence from the Berlitz
Investment Corporation*

First Edition 1985
Fifteenth Edition 2005

CONTACTING THE AUTHOR
Although every effort is made to
provide accurate information, we live
in a fast-changing world and would
appreciate it if readers would call our
attention to any outdated information by
writing to Douglas Ward at:
The Maritime Evaluations Group
Canada House, 1 Carrick Way
New Milton, Hampshire BH25 6UD
United Kingdom
dw@berlitzcruising.com
www.berlitzcruising.com

www.berlitzpublishing.com

FROM THE AUTHOR

The main purpose of this book is to help you choose the right ship, for the right reasons. It is a comprehensive source of information about cruising and the ships that offer to take you away from the pressures, stresses, and confines of daily life ashore.

When you first look into taking a cruise, you will be confronted by an enormous, often bewildering choice. Reading this book will simplify that choice and you will leave for your cruise as well informed as most specialists in the industry.

From time to time, the media reports on criminal aspects of the cruise industry, such as rape and environmental pollution. The international cruise industry, which consists of more than 70 ocean-going cruise operators carrying more than 12½ million passengers a year, provides an extremely safe and hassle-free way to take a vacation. Indeed, with fewer than 100 cases of alleged rape among more than 12½ million passengers, life ashore seems perilous by comparison.

After the terrorist attacks on the US on September 11, 2001, life got tougher for cruise companies as many passengers developed a temporary aversion to travel. But, as in many industries, the financially strong survived and prospered. Standards did suffer from cost-cutting as the major cruise lines tried to recover from the deep dis-counting that plagued the marketplace, led by lines based in North America. Nevertheless, the cruise industry provides vacation experiences seldom matched in product delivery, cleanliness and friendliness by land-based resorts. And the value for money is certainly better today than it has been for 20 years.

Some things that used to be included in the price of a cruise now cost extra, the resulting "onboard revenue" helping to compensate the industry for the fact that basic prices are as low now as in 1980. Discounted pricing has done one thing, however, and that is to open up cruising to a much wider socio-economic base than ever before, including younger people and more families with children.

The above changes have necessarily affected the ratings of some cruise ships. I am pleased to report, however, that other ships have significantly improved their product and standing in the international cruise industry; these changes are also reflected in this book.

In welcoming new readers to this edition, I should mention my qualifications for assessing cruise ships on your behalf. Passenger ships and the sea have captivated me ever since my very first transatlantic crossing, in July 1965, aboard Cunard Line's 83,673-ton ocean liner *RMS Queen Elizabeth* (then the largest passenger ship in

HOW TO USE THIS BOOK

This book is divided into two main parts, followed by a short section of practical information and useful addresses. The first part (Questions and Answers, The Cruising Experience, Choosing the Right Cruise) helps you define what you are looking for in a cruise vacation and advises you on how to find it. It provides a wealth of information, including a look at life aboard ship and how to get the best from it; the cuisine, dining and "alternative" dining rooms; nautical terminology; how the ship's hierarchy works; and advice about going ashore. Specialist cruises are discussed, too, culminating with that ultimate travel experience: the around-the-world cruise.

The book's main section profiles 256 ocean-going cruise vessels. From large to small, from unabashed luxury and exclusivity to ships for the budget-minded, new and old, they are all here.

Cutting edge: the author assesses the quality of a ship's silverware.

travel agents. This book is a tribute to everyone who has made my seafaring experiences possible, and I would like to thank the cruise lines for their cooperation and assistance during the complex scheduling, sailing, inspection, evaluation and rating processes.

And the winner is...

The cruise industry's marketing men are quick to advertise the fact that they have won this award or that award (Readers' Choice Poll is a favorite) from travel magazines, as the "Best Ship in the World," or "Best Cruise Line in the World," or "Best Large Cruise Ship" and so on. In truth, these polls are only as good as the number of people who vote in them, the criteria established and its regulation and tabulation. For example, if a magazine in the United States initiates a readers' poll and no readers have cruised aboard a British or Japanese or German or Spanish-speaking cruise ship, that ship will get no votes. It stands to reason that the votes will go to the most traveled ships. The magazines never state the criteria for their decisions. At Berlitz, we do. That's why *Berlitz Ocean Cruising and Cruise Ships* is the most authoritative guide you can buy.

— *Douglas Ward*

the world). To date, I have completed over 5,000 days at sea, participating in more than 900 cruises, 150 transatlantic crossings, and countless Panama Canal transits, shipyard visits, ship christenings, and numerous maiden voyages.

This book is a special one for me. This is its 20th year of publication. The first edition came out in 1985, when I introduced 120 cruise ships to people who had never heard of cruising as an alternative to land-based vacations. Since then, the book has become the most sought after, highly regarded source of comparative material not only for cruise purchasers, but also for cruise industry executives, crew members, and

---

The ratings and evaluations are a painstaking documentation of the author's personal work. He travels constantly throughout the world, and is at sea for approximately nine months each year. All evaluations have been made objectively, without bias, partiality, or prejudice. In almost all instances, the ships have been visited recently by the author or one of his team members in order to update or adjust earlier ratings or to assess current status. Passenger comments are also taken into account in the final evaluations *(see form on page 656)*. Please note that, although I have supplied price indicators for such things as alternative restaurants, spa treatments and other items, the prices may have changed since I completed this book.

Most of the statistical information contained in the ship profiles was supplied and checked by the cruise lines and ship owners. Any errors or updated information should be sent to the author at the address shown on the facing page.

Please note that the author's constant cruise and ship inspection schedule means that he is seldom on land, and regrets that he is therefore no longer able to answer letters. However, every comment received will be studied and will help maintain the authority of the next edition for the benefit of all.

Introduction

The Cruising Experience

Different Kinds of Cruises

Choosing the Right Cruise

The Ships and their Ratings

Practical Information

Maps

Tables and Charts

Introduction

WHY TAKE A CRUISE?

We answer the questions about ocean cruising most frequently asked

both by those new to this type of vacation and by regulars

Compared to most land vacations, cruises offer so much more value for money. For a start, your initial fare includes your accommodation, main meals and in-between snacks, entertainment, lectures, social functions, participation events, movies, and use of the ship's facilities, including the fitness center, casino (no entry charge, and you don't have to be a member), and perhaps air tickets and transfers to get to and from your cruise ship. The hassles of an ordinary land-based vacation are completely eliminated in one very neat package – and you have to pack and unpack only once.

With the outstanding choice of cruises, ships and itineraries available for every budget, a cruise represents almost unlimited potential. More than 260 ocean-going cruise ships carrying from 50 to just under 4,000 passengers visit almost 2,000 destinations throughout the world, and new ships are being constantly introduced. Cruising is a year-round vacation for singles, couples, families with children, and those of senior years. You are transported from place to place in a highly civilized manner. You can be as active, or as relaxed and pampered as you like. Most cruise ships have a well equipped medical center.

Early booking means greater savings, and a better choice of accommodation. Many lines allow you to extend your vacation and have special pre- and post-cruise hotel/resort or safari game-park extra stay packages available at appealing rates.

Why are cruises so popular?

More than 12½ million people throughout the world took an ocean (or sea) cruise last year. Cruising is popular today because it takes you away from the pressures and strains of contemporary life by offering an escape from reality. Cruise ships are really self-contained resorts, without the crime, which can take you to several destinations in the space of just a few days.

The sea has always been a source of adventure, excitement, romance, and wonder. It is beneficial and therapeutic, and, because you pay in advance, you know what you will spend on your vacation without any hidden surprises. There is no traffic (except when you go ashore in ports of call), and no pollution. The hassles of ordinary travel are almost eliminated in one pleasant little package. And, you can save a substantial amount of money over a regular land-based vacation.

Then there are the sights. Some of the world's most beautiful places are seen best from the decks of cruise ships. Indeed, there's simply no other way to see the dramatic, awe-inspiring beauty of Antarctica, Alaska's Inside Passage and its glaciers, the Galápagos Islands, the Panama Canal, or Vietnam's haunting Halong Bay. Up-close and personal is just one of the reasons that cruising is such a valuable experience. It's no wonder that 85 percent of passengers want to go again. And again. And again. Cruising is addictive.

Has terrorism had an effect?

Yes. In the weeks after the September 11, 2001, attacks on the United States, several cruise lines went out of business or filed for bankruptcy protection. Seven ocean-going and one river cruise lines, and 22 ocean-going ships were affected (plus three river cruise vessels). Among them were: American Hawaii Cruises (1 ship), Delta Queen Coastal Cruises (1 ship), Dreamline Cruises (1 ship), Renaissance Cruises (10 ships), United States Lines (1 ship), Valtur Tourism (1 ship).

In addition, the Delta Queen Steamboat Company suspended sailings aboard two of its three Mississippi riverboats: *American Queen, Delta Queen* and *Mississippi Queen* (although all are now back in operation). In 2001, before September 11, several small cruise lines also ceased operations: Great Lakes Cruises (1 ship), Hyundai Cruises (3 ships), Marine Expeditions (3 ships).

Many cruise lines had to redeploy their ships, while others saw passenger numbers drop dramatically. With fixed operating costs, several had cash flow problems as new bookings dried up. Thus the effect of the attacks and the subsequent 2003 war against Iraq translated to a lack of confidence (particularly in North Americans) in traveling by air. But, as deep discounts were introduced, many passengers decided to start cruising again. A more recent result has been the increase in popularity of "homeland" cruising.

Has quality declined as a result?

Yes, unfortunately it has. In the mass market, a cruise aboard the ships of the "Big 7" cruise lines (Carnival Cruise Lines, Celebrity Cruises, Costa Cruises, Holland America Line, Norwegian Cruise Line, Princess

Far from the stress and strain of life ashore.

Cruises, and Royal Caribbean International) has become a "not so inclusive" product, and passengers are asked to pay extra for all sorts of things that were formerly included. The cruise lines have also raised their prices for many items, including drinks and spa treatments, among others. While it's still an excellent value for the money vacation, the quality is going down, particularly among the large resort ships.

To ensure better quality, you will need to pay more money. Indeed, there is more distance now between the cruise ships belonging to the "Big 7" cruise lines and the (generally smaller) more upscale ships, particularly in terms of crew, food, service and training.

Other effects of cost cutting include the withdrawal of hospitality services such as stewards and stewardesses who show you to your cabin when you first embark. Examples of large lines that have dispensed with this service include Princess Cruises and Royal Caribbean International, whose meager staff on duty at the ship side of the gangway, now merely point you in the direction of your deck, or to the ship's elevators.

However, despite the cost cutting, cruise fares remain at pre-1980 levels, an indication of the incredible value of a cruise when compared to a land-based vacation.

I've never been on a cruise. Where do I start?

First, think about where you want to go, how long a cruise you would like, and how much money you want to spend. You'll need to think about how large a ship you'd like to cruise aboard. Then, find a good travel agent who specializes in cruises and is interested in matching your needs, requirements, lifestyle, and personality. Be sure to ask these 10 questions:

1. What size cruise ship would you recommend?
2. What should I budget for the cruise?
3. What is included in the cruise price?
4. What additional costs can I expect to pay?
5. Which destinations are included?
6. What kind of accommodation would you recommend for my tastes and budget?
7. What is the ship's onboard ambiance like?
8. What facilities does the ship have?
9. What kind of food and service does it provide?
10. What kind of entertainment should I expect?

You can also research the internet, although you won't be able to ask those all-important questions.

What is "homeland" cruising?

The term stems from cruise ships sailing out of an increased number of ports in the United States (as many as 18 at last count). While some, like Miami and Fort Lauderdale, have good facilities for checking in, many do not, and long lines are the result, particularly when 50 motorcoaches arrive at virtually the same time. However, "homeland" cruising does have great appeal for people who can drive themselves to a local (regional) port of embarkation. The result, however, is that one ship sailing out of, say, Philadelphia, will attract many other people from the surrounding area, and that might make it hard to get away from your neighbors, who had the same idea as you – to take a cruise to get away from it all. It also makes for particularly strong regional dialects aboard any given ship, and can even change the ways that cruise consumers act and dress.

What exactly *is* a cruise?

A cruise is a vacation. It is an antidote to (and escape from) the stress and strain of life ashore. It offers you a chance to relax and unwind in comfortable surroundings, with attentive service, good food, and a ship that changes the scenery for you. It is virtually a hassle-free, and, more importantly, a crime-free vacation. You never have to make blind choices. Everything's close to hand, and there are always polite people to help you. A cruise provides great value for money, variety (in ship size, destinations, facilities, cuisine, entertainment, activities and shore excursions), a chance to explore new places, meet new people, make friends, and, above all, provides the ingredients for a wonderful vacation.

How long does one last?

It can be as short or as long as you want. Cruise lines offer cruises from as little as three nights to more than six months (there are even passengers who stay aboard some ships all year round, and disembark only when the ship has to go into dry dock for refits).

Aren't all ships and cruises similar?

Far from it. Look through this book and you will see that ships range from under 200 ft (60 meters) to over 1,000 ft (300 meters) in length. They carry from under 100 to almost 4,000 passengers; facilities, food, and service vary according to the size of the ship. Ambience ranges from ultra-casual to very formal (starchy and reserved). Entertainment ranges from amateur dramatics to full-fledged high-tech production shows, from the corner cabaret to a world-famous headliner, and everything in between.

Isn't cruising just for old people?

Far from it – the average age of passengers gets younger each year. Although those of silver years have found cruising to be a very safe way to travel the world, the average age of first-time passengers is now well under 40. Remember also that even old people can have fun, too, and many have more get-up-and-go than many people under the age of 40.

On a typical cruise you'll meet singles, couples, families with children of all ages (including single

It's not only the ship that's moving…

parents and grandparents), honeymooners, second- or third-time honeymooners, groups of friends, and college buddies are all passengers. In fact, today's passengers are likely to be your next-door neighbors.

Won't I get bored?

Usually, it's the men who ask this question, but get them aboard and often there's not enough time in the day to do all the things they want to do – as long as you choose the right ship, for the right reasons. There are more things to do aboard today's ships than there is on almost any Caribbean island. So, whether you want to lie back and be pampered, or go nonstop, you can do it on a cruise vacation, and you will only have to pack and unpack once. Just being at sea provides a sense of freedom that few other places can offer.

Where can I go on a cruise?

There are over 30,000 different cruises to choose from each year, and almost 2,000 cruise destinations in the world. A cruise can also take you to places inaccessible by almost any other means, such as Antarctica, the North Cape, the South Sea islands, and so on. In fact, if you close your eyes and think of almost anywhere in the world where there's water, there's probably a cruise ship or river vessel to take you there.

Isn't cruising expensive?

Compare what it would cost on land to have all your meals and entertainment provided, as well as transportation, fitness and sports facilities, social activities, educational talks, parties, and other functions, and you will soon realize the incredible value of a cruise. Further, a ship is a destination in itself, which moves to other destinations. No land-based resort could ever do that. Simply give yourself a vacation budget, and go to your professional travel supplier with it. The rest, as they say, will be taken care of.

A seven-day cruise is advertised for $400 a person. Is there a catch?

As a rule, yes. A decent hotel room in New York costs at least $200 per night (plus taxes) without meals or entertainment, so it stands to reason that something is not quite as it seems. Before booking, read the fine print. Look at all the additional costs such as tips to cabin and dining room stewards, shore excursions, drinks (plus a 15 percent gratuity), plus getting to and from the ship. That $400 per person could well be for a four-berth cabin adjacent to the ship's laundry or above the disco, but in any event, not in a desirable location (just like a $50 hotel room in New York).

European and Far East cruises cost more than in the Caribbean. Why?

There are several reasons:
● Almost all aspects of operations, including fuel costs, port charges, air transportation, supplying food to the ships, are much higher in Europe. (An advan-

Family cruising is the industry's biggest growth sector.

tage with European-sourced food is that there will probably be more taste – eggs with real yellow yolks, and food free from the chemical additives, coloring and flavoring – than is found in the processed foods that cruise lines often purchase from US suppliers.)
● Companies can make more money (called yield) than in the cut-price Caribbean, where sun, sea, and sand are the principal attractions, whereas sightseeing, architecture, culture, and other things are part of a more enriching cruise experience.
● The price of shore excursions in Europe is high. For example, in 2002 the price of admission to the Acropolis in Greece was more than doubled.

How inclusive is "all-inclusive"?

That's like asking how much sand is on the beach! It typically means that transportation (often including flights), accommodation, food, and entertainment are wrapped up in one neat package. Today on land, however, "super clubs" offer everything "all-in" including drinks (although low-quality brands are often provided, with a much smaller selection than on board most cruise ships). While that concept works better aboard small ships (those carrying less than 500 passengers), large cruise ships (those carrying more than 1,000 passengers) provide more facilities and more reasons for you to spend money on board, so "mostly inclusive" might be a better term.

How does a cruise compare with an all-inclusive land vacation?

When compared realistically, a cruise is by far the better bargain. In general, aboard any cruise ship, service levels are higher, staff are friendlier and

better trained, there is more variety of food and drinks, and a cruise can take you to several destinations (a land-based resort can't do that).

Does cruising suit singles?

Yes, indeed. A cruise vacation is ideal for those traveling alone (over 25 percent of all passengers are solo travelers – worldwide, that's over 3 million), because it is easy to meet other people in a noncompetitive environment. Many ships also have dedicated cabins for singles as well as special add-on rates for single occupancy of double cabins. Some cruise lines will even find a cabin mate for you to share with, if you so desire.

However, you should be aware that in cabins that have three or four berths, personal privacy will be non-existent. Also, some companies sell two-bed cabins at a special single rate, but don't bother to think about the fact that many people who cruise solo do so because their spouse or partner has passed on, so the last thing they want to do is to be in a cabin with two beds.

Why is it so expensive for singles to travel alone?

Because it's a couples world Almost all cruise lines base their rates on double occupancy, as do hotels. Thus, when you travel alone, the cruise (cabin) portion of your fare reflects an additional supplement. While almost all new ships are built with cabins for double occupancy, some older ships do have single occupancy cabins (as an example, *Queen Elizabeth 2* has 151 single-occupancy cabins, while *Queen Mary 2* has none).

A cruise is ideal in many ways for honeymooners.

Do cruises suit honeymooners?

Absolutely. A cruise is the ideal setting for romance, for shipboard weddings (these can be arranged in some ports, depending on local regulations), receptions, and honeymoons. Most decisions are already made for you, so all you have to do is show up. Most ships have double-, queen- or king-sized beds, too. And for those on a second honeymoon, many ships now perform a "renewal of vows" ceremony (some charge for this).

And what about children?

A cruise provides families with more quality time than any other type of vacation (family cruising is the largest growth segment in the cruise industry). Activities are tailored to various age groups (Disney has cruise ships dedicated to families and children). In addition, a cruise is educational, allows children to interact in a safe, crime-free environment, and takes them to destinations in comfortable and familiar surroundings. In fact, children have such a good time aboard ship and ashore, you may have difficulty getting them home after the cruise (if you choose the right ship). And you as parents (or single parent) will get time to enjoy life, too. While children don't like organized clubs, they will probably find they make new friends quickly. Note that if you cruise aboard one of the Big 7 cruise lines, you may have tips for your children automatically added to your onboard account. NCL, for example, requests $5 per day from each child of 3–12 years, while those over 13 pay the adult rate of $10 per day.

Can I find a quiet, serene cruise, away from children and noise?

If you don't like crowds, noise, long lines, there are some beautiful small ships. Perhaps a sail-cruise vessel or a river or barge cruise could also provide the right atmosphere. Companies with ships that are totally child-free include P&O Cruises (*Adonia*), Saga Cruises (*Saga Rose*), Swan Hellenic Discovery Cruises (*Minerva II*).

Can I go cruising if I'm pregnant?

Yes, but most cruise lines will not allow a mother-to-be to cruise past her 28th week of pregnancy. You may need to produce a doctor's certificate.

It's even possible to play mini-golf at sea.

Do ships have spas?

The newest, and largest (resort) ships tend to have more space allotted to spas, with a wide range of mollycoddling, body pampering treatments (often marketed as "rituals") designed to promote your feeling of well-being – at a price. Aboard some ships, whole spa packages, some lasting days, are available (at great extra cost), perhaps leaving you without enough time to go ashore.

What about showers and personal hygiene?

Anyone concerned about personal hygiene should note that some ships have fixed shower heads. Better are those that have a removeable shower and hose, for washing those parts that fixed head showers simply can't reach. Check with your cruise booking agent or the cruise line *before* you book.

Can I take my bicycle?

Most cruise lines will let you take your bike (preferably of the folding variety due to a lack of in-cabin storage space). If you use a flight case, however, it may not be easy to find storage space for it. Airlines will also charge you to transport your bike. Ask your travel provider to contact the cruise line to ascertain their rules.

How about bringing golf clubs?

Yes, you can. However, although cruise lines do not charge for carrying them, some airlines do.

Is there a cruise with no ports of call?

Yes, but it isn't really a cruise. It's a transatlantic *crossing*, from New York to Southampton, England, aboard Cunard Line's *Queen Mary 2*. While I have been advising cruise lines for years that a ship doing occasional three-, four-, or seven-day cruises to nowhere would be welcomed by many repeat passengers, no cruise line has yet taken the initiative. Many passengers are so "allergic" to places that are really tourist rip-off destinations that they really want nothing more than to be aboard a ship at sea, with all the creature comforts of home.

Will I need a passport?

Yes, you will, particularly in these days of heightened security checks, when some form of government-issued photo ID is needed almost everywhere. You can usually apply for a passport at your local post office. In capital cities, and, possibly, other major cities, there will be a passport office where you can apply in person, or at short notice.

What size of ship is best?

Ships really come in four discernable sizes: Boutique, Small, Mid-Size, and Large.
● Choose a Large Resort Ship (these carry over 1,200 passengers up to almost 4,000) if you like lots of people, big-city facilities and entertainment.
● Choose a Mid-Sized ship (500–1,200 passengers) for a small-town atmosphere, with some entertainment and a small choice of facilities.
● Choose a Small Ship (these carry 200 to 500 passengers) if you are seeking a quiet, serene vacation, probably without children, and you don't need much entertainment – just really good food and relaxation.
● Choose a Boutique Ship (these carry 50 to 200 passengers) if you are seeking a very relaxing, private and totally unstructured yacht-style vacation to escape it all.

See "Selecting the Right Ship" (*page 134*).

What is expedition cruising?

Expedition cruises are operated with small ships that have ice-strengthened hulls or with specially constructed ice-breakers that enable them to reach areas that are totally inaccessible to "normal" cruise ships. The ships are typically converted to carry passengers in some degree of basic comfort, with comfortable accommodation and a relaxed, informal atmosphere, with expert lecturers and expedition leaders accompanying every cruise. These cruises really are for small groups, and much care and attention is placed on minimizing the impact on the environment.

Should I book early?

The further you book ahead, the greater will be any discount applied by the cruise line. You'll also get the cabin you want, in the location you want, and you may also be upgraded. When you book late (close to the sailing date), you may get a low price, but you typically won't get the cabin or location you might like, or (worse still), in ships with two seatings for dinner, you won't be able to choose early or late seating.

Can I dine when I want to?

Yes, you can – well, almost. Several major cruise lines have introduced "flexible dining" which allows you to choose (with some limitations) when you want to eat, and with whom you dine. Just like going out to restaurants ashore, reservations may be required (you may also have to wait), and occupants of the most expensive suites get priority. Aboard large cruise ships (1,000-plus passengers) the big evening entertainment shows typically are staged twice, so you end up with the equivalent of two-seating dining anyway.

What is "alternative" dining?

Some ships now have alternative dining spots other than the main restaurant. These usually cost extra – typically between $15 and $25 a person, but the food quality is decidedly better, as is presentation, service, and ambiance. Most alternative dining spots are also typically more intimate, and much quieter than the main dining rooms.

Are hygiene standards acceptable?

Occasionally, the news media focuses on the question of hygiene and sanitation aboard cruise ships, particularly when an "outbreak" of gastrointestinal disease has been reported in the confines of a cruise ship (particularly a large one). In the 1980s, the North American cruise industry agreed with the Centres for Disease Control (CDC) that hygiene and sanitation inspections should be carried out once or twice yearly aboard all cruise ships carrying American passengers, and the Vessel Sanitation Program (VSP) was born. The original intention of the VSP was to achieve and maintain a level of sanitation that would lower the risk of gastrointestinal disease outbreaks and assist the cruise industry to provide a healthy environment for passengers and crew.

It is a voluntary, not a mandatory inspection, for which the cruise lines pay handsomely for each inspection. However, the 42 inspection points are judged to be a good system for all to adhere to. The inspections cover two main areas:

❶ Water sanitation (including free chlorine residuals in the potable water system, swimming pool and hot tub filters).

"Rock climbing" on the *Voyager of the Seas*' funnel.

❷ Food sanitation (food storage, preparation and serving areas, including bars and passenger service pantries.

The industry's ships score extremely well (the ones that undergo inspections, that is; but some ships that don't call on U.S. ports would possibly not pass the inspections every time). Older ships with outdated galley equipment and poor storage would have a harder time complying with the USPH inspection standards (some other countries also have strict health inspection standards).

I must tell you, however, that if the same USPH inspection standards were applied to restaurants and hotels ashore, it is estimated that at least 90 percent or more would fail, *consistently*.

Small luxury ships offer varied watersports.

What about the Norwalk virus?

This (temporary) illness occurs worldwide. Humans are the only known hosts, and only the common cold is reported more frequently than viral gastroenteritis as a cause of illness in the USA, for example. In 2002, 23 million Americans were diagnosed with the effects of the Norwalk-like virus (NLV gastroenteritis). It is more prevalent in adults and older children than in the very young.

Norwalk is part of a family of virus called "calicivirus". The name derives from the chalice or calyx, meaning cuplike; this refers to the indentations of the surface of the virus. The disease itself is self-limiting, is mild, and is characterised by nausea, vomiting, diarrhoea, and abdominal pain. Although it can be transmitted by person-to-person contact, Norwalk gastroenteritis is more likely to be transmitted by the fecal-oral route via contaminated foods and water (so make sure you wash your hands thoroughly after using the toilet). Shellfish (most notably clams and oysters), salad ingredients and fruits are the foods most often implicated in Norwalk outbreaks.

Water can also be a common source of outbreaks (water aboard cruise ships stored in tanks, etc). A mild and brief illness typically occurs 24 to 48 hours after contaminated food or water has been consumed, and lasts for 24 to 60 hours. The virus can also be brought on board when passengers are ashore in foreign ports, where hygiene and sanitation may be questionable.

Should I worry about security?

Cruise lines are subject to stringent international safety and security standards. A cruise ship provides a secure, controlled environment with limited access (far different to resort hotels on land); it's rather like having a building with 24-hour security. Passengers and crew can embark or disembark only by passing through a security checkpoint. Cruise ships maintain zero tolerance for onboard crime or offences against the person. Trained security professionals are employed aboard all cruise ships. In the case of the USA (where more than 60 percent of cruise passengers reside), you will be far more secure aboard a cruise ship than almost anywhere on land.

How about accidents at sea?

Cruising presents the travel industry's best safety record, with no passenger fatalities during the past 20 years due to a maritime accident.

Do ships have different classes?

Not really. Gone are the class distinctions and the pretensions of formality of the past. Differences are now found mainly in the type of accommodation chosen; in the price you pay for a larger cabin (or suite), the location of your cabin (or suite), and whether or not you have butler service. Some cruise lines (Holland America Line, for example) provide a "concierge lounge" which can be used only by occupants of accommodation designated as suites (thus, in effect, re-creating a two-class system). Celebrity Cruises goes further, in essence creating three classes: 1) for those accommodated in Suite categories; 2) for those accommodated in Concierge

Class (middle-level) mini-suites/cabins; 3) for those accommodated in standard (exterior view and interior-no view) cabins. I prefer to differentiate it aboard today's large cruise ships as "Balcony Class" and "Non-Balcony Class." For an explanation of the difference between degrees of comfort, food and service, see "The Oatmeal Factor" in the "What the Descriptions Mean" panel on Page 150.

What is a category guarantee?

It means you have purchased a specific grade of accommodation (just as in a hotel), although the *actual* cabin may not have been assigned to your booking yet. Your cabin may be assigned before you go, or when you arrive for embarkation.

What's the difference between an "outside" and an "interior" cabin?

An "outside" (or "exterior") cabin doesn't mean it's outside the ship; it simply means that it has a window (or porthole) with a view of the outside, or there is a private balcony for you to physically be (or look) outside. An "interior" cabin means that it does not have a view of the outside, but it will have artwork or curtains on one wall instead of a window or patio-like (balcony) door.

Isn't it hard to find one's way around large resort ships?

Well, it can take at least a few hours, or a day or so. However, in general, remember that decks are horizontal, while stairs are vertical. The rest comes naturally, with practice.

How do you escape from the noise aboard large resort ships?

I understand your problem. Simply contact the hotel manager and let him (or her) know that volume levels are unacceptable and to please do something about it. If enough people do this, things will have to change for the better. Or you could take earplugs!

Can I send and receive e-mails on board?

Aboard most ships, e-mail facilities have now been added to some degree or other. Several ships have an Internet café, or Internet Center, where you can "log on" for about 50¢ per minute. However, you should note that connections and downloads are often very slow compared to land-based services (shipboard e-mails must link through satellite systems). For many companies, e-mail has now become an important revenue generator. Receiving an e-mail from ashore can be expensive; aboard *Adonia*'s Grand Voyage in 2004, for example, each incoming e-mail cost £2.50 ($4.50). For many companies, e-mail has now become an important revenue generator. One cruise ship, *Europa* (Hapag-Lloyd Cruises) even has a *full*

personal computer in *every* cabin with 24 hour internet/e-mail connectivity (e-mails are free), while some other ships put computers in their most expensive suites.

Are computer courses available?

Yes. Crystal Cruises, Cunard Line and Seabourn Cruise Line are just three examples of cruise lines that provide computers and learning classes. Indeed, the Computer Learning Centers aboard *Crystal Harmony, Crystal Serenity, Crystal Symphony, QE2* and *QM2*, each have almost two-dozen computer workstations or laptops for class use.

Can I go shopping in ports of call?

Yes, you can. Many passengers with a black belt in shopping engage in "retail therapy" when visiting ports of call such as Dubai, Hong Kong, Singapore, St. Maarten, and St. Thomas, among so many others. Just remember you will have to carry all your purchases home at the end of your cruise.

Do I have to leave the ship in each port of call?

Absolutely not. In fact, many repeat passengers enjoy being aboard "their" ships when there are virtually no other passengers board. Also, if you have a spa treatment, it could be less expensive during this period than when the ship is at sea (some ships have price differentials for sea days/port days – *Queen Mary 2* is one example.

The ocean as viewed from a glass elevator.

Venice is a port of call for *Costa Victoria*.

Can I fly in the night before or stay an extra day after the cruise?

Cruise lines often do offer pre- and post-cruise stay packages at an additional cost. The advantage is that you don't have to do anything else. All will be taken care of, as they say. If you book a hotel on your own, however, you may have to pay an "air deviation" fee (payable if you do not take the cruise line's air arrangements, or you want to change them).

Can I pre-book seats on flights?

With packaged vacations such as cruises, it is normally not possible to reserve airline seats prior to check-in, and, although the cruise line will typically forward your requests for preferred seating, these may not be guaranteed.

Where did all the money go?

Apart from the cruise fare itself, there could be other incidentals such as government taxes, port charges, air ticket tax. On board, extra costs may include drinks, mini-bar items, cappuccino and espresso coffees, shore excursions, surfing the internet, sending or receiving e-mails, health spa treatments, casino gaming, photographs, laundry and dry-cleaning, babysitting services, wine tasting, bottled water placed in your cabin, and medical services.

A cruise aboard a ship belonging to one of the "Big 7" cruise lines (Carnival Cruise Lines, Celebrity Cruises, Costa Cruises, Holland America Line, Norwegian Cruise Line, Princess Cruises, Royal Caribbean International) could be compared to buying a car, whereby motor manufacturers offer a basic model at a set price, with optional extras. These cruise lines will tell you that income generated on board helps to keep the basic cost of a cruise reasonable.

What are cruising's downsides?

Much anticipated ports of call can be aborted, or changed due to poor weather or other conditions. Some popular ports (particularly in the Caribbean) can become extremely crowded – up to 12 ships in St. Thomas, or six in St. Maarten. It's as if you've invited 10,000 others to join your vacation. Onboard expenses can mount up aboard the large resort ships. So can the cost of shore excursions (particularly those involving flights in Alaska). Fellow passengers, and those lacking social manners and etiquette can also be irritating to many (particularly in the dining room where you may have to share a table with strangers).

So what if I don't like my cruise?

Given today's standards, it's almost certain that you *will* enjoy your cruise vacation. One company – Carnival Cruise Lines – has a Vacation Guarantee that states that if you do not like the cruise, the ship, or other aspect of the vacation, you can disembark in the first port of call, and the line will return all your money. Now, that's an excellent guarantee that less than one-tenth of 1 percent of its passengers take up. Other lines would do well to follow this example. ❏

WHAT'S NEW FOR 2005

Look out for more internet access, larger health spas, entertaining architecture, more dining choices – and the world's biggest ever ocean liner

The cruise industry is still growing, and the introduction of new ships continues, albeit at a slower pace than in the past few years. Some 13 new ships are scheduled for delivery between January 2005 and December 2007, at a cost of about $5 billion, fueled by the continuing increase in demand for high-value cruise vacations.

New ships incorporate the latest in sophisticated high-tech electronic navigation and safety equipment, recent advances in propulsion technology and the best in advanced ship design and construction, offering passengers an ocean full of options, choice of facilities, and dining and entertainment experiences.

The world's largest ever cruise ship made its debut in early 2004: *Queen Mary 2*, measuring a whopping 148,528 tons. The next largest ships are Royal Caribbean International's *Adventure of the Seas, Explorer of the Seas, Mariner of the Seas, Navigator of the Seas,* and *Voyager of the Seas*, introduced between 1999 and 2003 – all measuring around 137,300 tons and carrying 3,114 passengers; these ships are floating leisure playgrounds aimed at the standard cruise marketplace. Is bigger better? That's up to the individual, but it can be rather like being in a large shopping mall environment as opposed to a smaller boutique environment, or "almost all-exclusive" versus "almost all-inclusive" cruising.

Propulsion

The latest ships are powered by gas turbines, or by diesel-electric or diesel-mechanical propulsion or a mix of diesel and gas turbine systems that propel them at speeds of up to 28 knots (only Cunard Line's *QE2 and QM2,* with a top speed of more than 30 knots, are faster).

A new technology is now incorporated into propulsion design, the "pod" system. Briefly, pods, which resemble huge outboard motors, replace internal electric propulsion motors, shaft lines, rudders and their machinery, and are compact, self-contained units that typically weigh about 170 tons each. Pod units *pull,* rather than *push,* a ship through the water. When going ahead, pod units face with the propeller forward (ships can go astern either by rotating the pods 180 degrees or by reversing the thrust). A vessel's turning circle diameter is reduced considerably, and vibration at the ship's stern is virtually eliminated.

New ships will incorporate everything viewed as environmentally friendly, such as "enviro-engines" that provide power without visible smoke, "enviro-laundries," – maybe even "enviro-entertainment"! How about recruiting some "enviro-passengers?"

Exteriors

The indented, cascading (flowing) after-decks of ships such as *Aurora, Oriana, Norwegian Dawn, Norwegian Spirit, Norwegian Star, Oosterdam, SuperStar Virgo, Westerdam* and *Zuiderdam* are both stunning and practical – overlooking aft pool areas. Other cruise ships take the "block" approach and fill in stern areas with cabins that have an aft-facing view (*Carnival Destiny, Carnival Triumph, Carnival Victory,* for example), or multilevel dining rooms with huge expanses of glass windows (*Century, Constellation, Galaxy, Infinity, Mercury, Millennium,* and *Summit*), or other public rooms and facilities.

The most instantly recognizable exteriors are those of *AIDAaura, AIDABlu, AIDAcara* and *AIDAvita,* with huge bold red lips and brown eyes adorning their prows. Yet other ships now have huge slogans painted on their white sides (Royal Caribbean international's slogan "Like No Vacation On Earth" for example).

Some ships are not at all handsome, no matter how you look at them (examples: *Constellation, Infinity, Millennium, Summit*), and display designers gone mad with trying to create a "yacht-like" exterior – to a ship of 90,000 tons.

Interiors

Both "retro" and "contemporary" are "in," as interior designers try to create luxurious, welcoming interiors reminiscent of Europe's grand hotels.

Large ships have interiors that include such things as multi-deck-high atriums, large theaters complete with revolving stages, hydraulic orchestra pits, huge scenery stowage spaces, internet cafes, computer learning centers, and in-cabin interactive television – not to mention billiard (pool) tables that self-correct aboard a moving ship. Some ships have two atrium lobbies instead of one (*Carnival Destiny, Carnival Triumph, Carnival Victory, Galaxy,* and *Mercury*), while the industry's largest group – *Adventure of the Seas, Explorer of the Seas, Mariner of the Seas, Navigator of the Seas* and *Voyager of the Seas* – feature a large *horizontal,* rather than a *vertical* atrium, rather reminiscent of a city shopping mall, and extremely popular (particularly among North Americans).

As for contemporary, among the most stunning, bold, and graphic interiors are those that are found in the ships of Carnival Cruise Lines. Somehow,

1. Minnows Pool
2. Terrace Pool
3. Grand Duplex & Duplex Apartments
4. Kennels
5. Boardwalk Café
6. Fairways – Golf Simulators
7. The Pavilion
8. Splash Pool
9. Sports Centre
10. The Lookout – Observation Deck
11. Atlantic Room
12. Commodore Club Lounge
13. Library & Bookshop
14. Royal Suites with private lift access
15. Illuminations – Theatre & Auditorium
16. Canyon Ranch SpaClub

lilac neon, fiber optics, mosaics, and multicolored carpeting go together here although they never would in *any* setting other than a Las Vegas hotel. It is all a feast for the eyes and mind (entertainment architecture, as the interior designer calls it), but for many (especially for European passengers) it could be sensory overload.

Ships have become instant floating art museums (some are better than others), with collections of artwork costing several million dollars per ship. For example: $12 million (*Voyager of the Seas*); $6 million (*Vision of the Seas*); $5.3 million (*Serenade of the Seas*); $4 million (*Enchantment of the Seas*); $3.8 million (*Century*); $3 million (*Galaxy*); $2.5 million (*Sun Princess*); $2 million (*Veendam*); $1 million (*AIDAcara, Inspiration*). However, it is not the money spent that's important; it is the fact that artwork now forms a more important integral part of the interior decor than ever before, and particularly so with large resort ships, with ever larger wall spaces to cover.

Computer-Driven Cruising

Can you send and/or receive emails when aboard your cruise ship? Yes, you can, at least aboard some ships – but at a price. As an example, Crystal Cruises imposes a set-up charge of $5, plus $3 for each page of email messages. Many ships have now introduced internet cafés, where you can "do" coffee and email – typically at a cost of 50 cents to $1 per minute.

Most cruise lines have web sites on the internet (*see listing at the end of the book*). Computers link almost all departments and functions aboard the latest ships, and (somewhat inflexible) interactive television systems let you order wine, arrange shore excursions, play casino games, go shopping, and order pay-per-view movies, all from your cabin.

Computers cannot yet pour you a drink, although you can order one, accompanied by a light snack. But, order a croissant with your breakfast and the "point and select" system won't bother to ask whether you'd like it warm or cold. Oh, well, that's technology for you; as long as you are a "standard" photofit passenger, it'll work for you. Otherwise, call room service (sort of defeats the purpose, doesn't it?).

Spas: The Ultimate Pampership

Health and fitness spas are among the hottest passenger (revenue) facilities in the latest cruise ships,

QUEEN MARY 2
An anatomy of the world's largest cruise ship

- ⑰ Cunard ConneXions
- ⑱ Royal Court Theatre
- ⑲ Winter Garden Lounge
- ⑳ Grand Lobby
- ㉑ Empire Casino
- ㉒ King's Court Alternative Dining Venues
- ㉓ Champagne Bar
- ㉔ Golden Lion Pub
- ㉕ Chart Room Bar and Lounge
- ㉖ Britannia Restaurant
- ㉗ Queen's Grill Lounge
- ㉘ Todd English Restaurant
- ㉙ Queen's Room – Ballroom
- ㉚ Queen's Grill
- ㉛ Children's Facilities
- ㉜ G32 Nightclub

with more space than ever devoted to them. The basic sauna, steam room, and massage facility has evolved into huge, specially designed spas that include the latest in high-tech muscle exercising, aerobic and weight-training machines, and relaxation treatments, such as: hydrotherapy and thalassotherapy baths, jet blitz, rasul (graduated steam and all-over body mud cleansing), seaweed wraps, and hot and cold stone massage. *(See pages 42–44 for more details).*

Ships with large spas locate them on the uppermost decks of the latest ships, and feature large floor-to-ceiling ocean-view windows. Treatment rooms (some will have integral showers) are flexible and can be adapted to incorporate the latest trends, gimmicks, and themes.

Traditional Japanese and Indonesian design elements have been included, with rock gardens, running water, shoji screens and hot tea help to create a serene environment in some spas. Among the ships with such designs and features: *Century, Constellation, Galaxy, Mercury, Millennium, Star Princess,* and *Summit.* There are large co-ed saunas (holding as many as 30 persons), with large glass walls and exterior views (*AIDAaura, AIDAcara, AIDAvita*).

For Smokers

Cigar smoking is still in vogue, and special cigar bars and lounges have been created aboard several ships, including: *Adventure of the Seas, Brilliance of the Seas, Century, Crystal Harmony, Crystal Serenity, Crystal Symphony, Europa, Explorer of the Seas, Galaxy, Horizon, Mercury, Mistral, Mariner of the Seas, Navigator of the Seas, Norwegian Dawn, Norwegian Star, Norwegian Sun, Queen Mary 2, Radiance of the Seas, Serenity of the Seas, Seven Seas Mariner, Seven Seas Voyager, SuperStar Virgo, Voyager of the Seas,* and *Zenith.* Note however, that ships starting or ending their cruises in a US port are not permitted to carry real Cuban cigars (instead, most cigars will be made in the Dominican Republic).

For Non-smokers

Carnival Cruise Lines' *Paradise* was the first and only cruise ship to be totally non-smoking (even the shipyard workers who built the ship were not allowed to smoke – officially anyway). However, its non-smoking status was extinguished in September 2004 when the ship was moved to a new itinerary. Meanwhile, non-smokers will be pleased to know that many ships now have totally non-smoking dining rooms and show lounges.

Dining and Service

What's really in vogue are what are termed *"alternative"* restaurants – particularly aboard the new large resort ships (older ships – those built before 1980 – rarely have them). These are typically à la carte restaurants where you *must* make a reservation, and pay for the privilege of dining in small, intimate places with the best in food and service.

Some ships, such as *Norwegian Dawn, Norwegian Star, Norwegian Spirit* and *SuperStar Virgo* feature as many as 10 different restaurants and eateries, some of which incur an extra charge – just like going out ashore. But getting a reservation in some of them can be very difficult.

Several ships now pay homage to past transatlantic liners of the past in the décor of their dining rooms or alternative restaurants; examples include the Normandie Restaurant aboard *Carnival Pride*, the Ocean Liners Restaurant aboard *Constellation*, the Olympic Restaurant aboard *Millennium,* the United States Restaurant aboard *Infinity*, and the Normandie Restaurant aboard *Summit*. Many ships now charge extra for better dining experiences.

Many new ships have flexible dining and 24-hour casual eateries, so you can eat (or snack) when you want. Although the concept is good, the delivery often is not (it is typically self-service eating, and not the *dining* experience most passengers envisage).

Also hot (in culinary-speak) is the fact that several cruise lines have aligned themselves with well-known chefs and brand names ashore in order to provide an "authenticity" to their product, and to produce even more of a "wow" effect, at least in terms of marketing. Examples include Crystal Cruises (Wolfgang Puck); Cunard Line (Daniel Boulud); Seven Seas Cruises (Le Cordon Bleu); Seabourn Cruise Lines (Charlie Palmer); Silversea Cruises (Relais & Châteaux).

Two-deck-high dining rooms are back in vogue: *Amsterdam, Century, Carnival Legend, Carnival Pride, Carnival Spirit, Costa Atlantica, Costa fortuna, Costa Mediterranea, Dawn Princess, Galaxy, Legend of the Seas, Infinity, Maasdam, Mercury, Millennium, Nordic Empress, Oosterdam, Rotterdam, Ryndam, Splendour of the Seas, Statendam, Summit, Sun Princess, Veendam, Volendam* and *Zuiderdam* have them. Not to be outdone, *Adventurer of the Seas, Explorer of the Seas, Mariner of the Seas, Navigator of the Seas, Queen Mary 2* and *Voyager of the Seas* have dining halls that are three decks high.

What's Not So Hot in 2005

● The large floating resorts that travel by night and are in port during the day provide little connection to nature and the sea, the ship being the destination

Glitzy production shows, no longer fashionable on dry land, remain alive and kicking in the cruise industry.

(small town takes to water). Almost everything is designed to keep you *inside* the ship – to spend money, thus increasing onboard revenue and shareholder dividends.

● Entertainment – either production shows or cabaret acts – it's all so much the same no matter what ship you are aboard. It's time for more creative thinking.

● Aggressive, young, so-called "cruise directors" who insist on interposing themselves into every part of your cruise, day and night. Public address systems are *consistently* overused by these bouncy youngsters, and are too loud, and too intrusive, which hardly makes for a restful cruise. Some of these cruise directors may make excellent cheerleaders, but seem unable to communicate with anyone over 25.

● Homogenous accommodation. As identically sized standard cabins are the same shape and layout (good for incentive planners, but not for individual passengers), they also tend to be the same colors: eggshell white, off-white, or computer-colored beige. Although such colors are welcome after days in the sun, they quickly become tedious on voyages over long stretches of water. Only bold bedspreads or the occasional color prints that adorn a spare wall bring relief. Plain ceilings are also boring. Close to useless are wall-mounted hairdryers (which have poor directed pressure) in modular bathrooms; they should, instead, be located in the vanity desk or dressing area.

A disadvantage of large ships is that the lines are long for embarkation and disembarkation.

● Calling passengers "guests" is becoming widespread. It is confusing, however, and nautically incorrect (a guest in one's house doesn't pay). Further, the word "guest" cannot be translated into some languages. Passengers *pay* to be aboard ship. Ships are different from hotels, and should remain so. They provide a nautical experience and move through water; passengers have cabins and suites, and decks, not floors. However, several cruise lines prefer to think they think they are in the hotel business – but that's because hoteliers, ex-airline people, and accountants run them, not shipping people.

● The use of "hotel-speak" is further invading the industry. Royal Caribbean International, for example, now calls its in-cabin refrigerators "Automatic Refreshment Centers."

● Two things that have almost disappeared: streamers and free champagne, formerly provided at bon voyage parties on deck on sailing day (exception: world cruises and Japanese-registered cruise ships). Instead, waiters hustle you to buy a "bon voyage" cocktail, or some "Bahamaramamaslammer" in a plastic or polystyrene sports cup. The little goodies, such as travel bags, and extensive personal amenity kits, have been taken away by the bean counters of many of the world's cruise lines, believing that passengers won't notice. Believe me, they *do*.

● As for food, you should note that ships that feature 7-day cruises repeat menu cycles each week. If, for example, you take two, back-to-back 7-day Eastern and Western Caribbean cruises, the menu will probably be repeated for the second week (so will the whole entertainment program and the cruise director's spiel, jokes, and activities).

Cruise ship food and service standards have suffered more lately as a result of deep discounting. Ships carrying more than 1,000 passengers cannot seem to deliver what is portrayed in the cruise brochures consistently. Also, because of the acute shortage of waiters who speak good English (the majority of passengers being North American), many cruise lines have had to train personnel from Caribbean basin, Central American countries and eastern Europe; their command of the English language is often less than adequate.

One thing that *should* go into deep waters is the amateurish, intrusive "Baked Alaska Parade." Popular with first-time passengers, it is old hat for many. It's time the cruise lines were more creative. The industry should also find a better way to sing "Happy Birthday" than the present waiter-induced chant that usually sounds like a funeral dirge.

● In the seven-day cruise market (particularly from US ports) disembarkation is still an untidy and hostile process. Passengers are unceremoniously dumped ashore, with little help after the trying procedures of locating their luggage and going through customs inspection. Poor representation once they get to their respective airports for check-in may be an added ordeal. Of particular concern is the fact that the same procedure applies to all passengers, whether they are in the finest penthouse suite or the smallest interior (no-view) cabin. The final impression of these seven-day cruises, therefore, is poor. The worst disembarkation ports: Fort Lauderdale, Los Angeles, Miami, and San Juan.

Environmental Concerns

Cruise ships refine oil, treat human waste, and incinerate garbage, but that's not enough today, as pressure continues to mount for clean oceans. Engine emissions are now subject to the provisions of Marpol Annexe VI.

Cruise ships and their operating companies also have a unique position among all shipping interests. They are not likely to damage the ocean environment as compared with oil tankers, although spillage of any kind is regrettable.

Other environmental concerns involve the condition of the air aboard ships. A ship's air-conditioning system can provide an ideal site for mold growth such as that found in the aerospora group (including *Cladosporium sp.*). Thus it is vital that cruise lines not skimp on maintenance, and the replacement of filters and other items in air-conditioning systems is very important. ❑

CRUISING'S IRRESISTIBLE GROWTH

Outpaced by jet aircraft, passenger liners seemed destined for the scrapyard.

Then they began transforming themselves into floating resorts

In 1835, a curious advertisement appeared in the first issue of the *Shetland Journal*. Headed "To Tourists" it proposed an imaginary cruise from Stromness in Scotland, round Iceland and the Faroe Islands, and hinted at the pleasures of cruising under the Spanish sun in winter. Thus, it is said, the journal's founder, Arthur Anderson, invented the concept of cruising. Just two years later, Anderson, along with his partner Brodie Wilcox, founded the great Peninsular Steam Navigation Company (later to become P&O).

Soon after, Samuel Cunard started his transatlantic sailings, from Liverpool to Halifax, across the most dangerous ocean in the world, the North Atlantic, with a steam-powered sailing vessel, *Britannia*, on July 4, 1840. Every year since then, a Cunard ship has operated scheduled transatlantic liner service between the old and new worlds.

Sailing for leisure soon caught on. Even writers

such as William Makepeace Thackeray and Charles Dickens boarded ships for the excitement of the voyage, not just to reach a destination. The Victorians, having discovered tourism, promoted the idea widely. Indeed, Thackeray's account of his legendary voyage in 1844, from Cornhill to Grand Cairo by means of the P&O ships of the day, makes fascinating reading, as does the account by Dickens of his transatlantic crossing aboard a Cunard ship in 1842. P&O's *Tagus*, which journeyed from London to the Black Sea in 1843, was the subject of Mark Twain's *The Innocents Abroad*, published in 1869.

In the 1920s, cruising became the thing to do for the world's well-to-do. Being pampered in such grand style was fashionable – and is still the underlying concept of cruising. The ship took you and your belongings anywhere, and fed you, accommodated you, relaxed you, and entertained you. At the same time, it even catered for your servants – who, of course, accompanied you.

The First Booze Cruises

Cruising for Americans was helped greatly by Prohibition in the 1930s. After all, just a few miles out at sea, you were free to consume as much liquor as you wanted. And cheap three- and four-day weekend "booze cruises" out of New York were preferable to "bathtub gin." Then came short cruises, with destinations as well as alcohol. In time, the short cruise was to become one of the principal sources of profit for the steamship companies of the day.

In the 1930s a battle raged between the giant cruising companies of the world, as Britain, France, Germany, and the United States built liners of unprecedented luxury, elegance, glamour, and comfort. Each country was competing to produce the biggest and best afloat. For a time, quality was somehow related to smokestacks: the more a ship had the better. Although speed had always been a factor, particularly on the transatlantic run, it now became a matter of national ambition.

The first ship designed specifically for cruising from the US after World War II was *Ocean Monarch* (Furness Withy & Company Ltd), which was awarded a gold medal by the US Academy of Designing for "outstanding beauty and unusual design features of a cruise ship." Its maiden voyage was from New York to Bermuda in 1951. I worked aboard the ship for a short time.

One of the most renowned cruise liners of all time was Cunard's *Caronia* (34,183 tons), conceived in 1948. It was designed and built to offer a transatlantic service in the peak summer months only and then spend the rest of the year doing long, expensive cruises. One outstanding feature was a single giant mast and one smokestack, the largest of its time. The hull was painted four shades of green, supposedly for the purposes of heat resistance and easy identification. Known as the "Green Goddess" and "the Millionaires' Ship," it was one of the first vessels to provide a private adjoining bathroom for every cabin – a true luxury.

The Birth of Modern Cruising

In June 1958, the first commercial jet aircraft flew across the Atlantic and forever altered the economics of transatlantic travel. It was the last year in which more passengers crossed the North Atlantic by sea than by air.

In the early 1960s, passenger-shipping directories listed over 100 passenger lines. Until the mid-1960s, it was cheaper to cross the Atlantic by ship than by plane, but the appearance of the jet aircraft changed that rapidly, particularly with the introduction of the Boeing 747 in the early 1970s. In 1962, more than 1 million people crossed the North Atlantic by ship; in 1970, that number was down to 250,000.

The success of the jumbo jets created a fleet of unprofitable and out-of-work passenger liners that appeared doomed for the scrap heap. Even the famous big "Queens," noted for their regular weekly transatlantic service, were at risk. Cunard White Star Line's *Queen Mary* (80,774 tons) was withdrawn in September 1967. Cunard Line's sister ship *Queen*

Elizabeth, at 83,673 tons the largest passenger liner ever built (until 1996), made its final crossing in October 1968.

Ships were sold for a fraction of their value. Many lines went out of business and ships were scrapped. Those that survived attempted to mix transatlantic crossings with voyages south to the sun. The Caribbean (including the Bahamas) became appealing, cruising became an alternative, and an entire new industry was born, with new lines being formed exclusively for cruising.

Then came smaller, more specialized ships, capable of getting into the tiny ports of developing Caribbean islands (there were no commercial airlines taking vacationers to the Caribbean then, and few hotels). Instead of cruising long distances south from more northerly ports such as New York, companies established their headquarters in Florida. This not only avoided the cold weather, choppy seas, and expense of the northern ports but also saved fuel costs with shorter runs to the Caribbean. Cruising was reborn. California became the base for cruises to the Mexican Riviera, and Vancouver on Canada's west coast became the focus for summer cruises to Alaska.

Flying passengers to embarkation ports was the next logical step, and soon a working relationship emerged between the cruise lines and the airlines. Air/sea and "sail and stay" packages thrived – joint cruise and hotel vacations with inclusive pricing. Some of the old liners came out of mothballs, purchased by emerging cruise lines and refurbished for warm-weather cruising operations, often with their interiors redesigned and refitted. During the late 1970s, the modern cruise industry grew at a rapid rate.

Cruising Today

Today's cruise concept hasn't changed much from that of earlier days, although it has been improved, refined, expanded, and packaged for ease of consumption. No longer the domain of affluent, retired people, the cruise industry today, is vibrant and alive with passengers of *every* age and socio-economic background. Cruising is no longer the shipping business, but the hospitality industry (although some cruise ship personnel appear to be in the hostility industry).

New ships are generally larger than their counterparts of yesteryear, yet cabin size has become "standardized" to provide more space for entertainment and other public facilities. Today's ships boast air conditioning to keep out heat and humidity; stabilizers to keep the ship on an even keel; a high level of maintenance, safety, and hygiene; and more emphasis on health and fitness facilities.

Cruise ship design has moved from the traditional, classic, rounded profiles of the past (example: *Queen Elizabeth 2*) to the extremely boxy shapes with squared-off sterns and towering superstructures today (examples: *Constellation, Infinity, Millennium, Summit*). Although ship lovers lament these design changes, they have resulted from the need to squeeze as much as possible in the space provided (you can squeeze more in a square box than you can in a round one, though it may be less aesthetically appealing). Form follows function, and ships have changed from ocean transportation to floating vacation resorts.

Although ships have long been devoted to eating and relaxation in comfort (promulgating the maxim "Traveling slowly unwinds you faster"), ships today offer more activities, and more learning and life-enriching experiences than before. And there are many more places you can visit on a cruise:

from Antarctica to Acapulco, Bermuda to Bergen, Dakar to Dominica, Shanghai to St. Thomas, or if you prefer, perhaps nowhere at all.

The cruise industry is a $15 billion business worldwide and still growing. It provides employment to a growing number, both directly (there are over 100,000 shipboard officers, staff and crew, as well as about 15,000 employees in cruise company offices), and indirectly (suppliers of foodstuffs and mechanical and electrical parts, port agents, transport companies, destinations, airlines, railways, hotels, car rental companies). In 2002, over 12 million people worldwide took a cruise, packaged and sold by cruise lines through tour operators and travel agents.

Building a Modern Cruise Ship

More than any other type of vessel, a cruise ship has to fulfill fantasies and satisfy exotic imaginations. It is the job of the shipyard to take those fantasies and turn them into a steel ship without unduly straining the laws of naval architecture and safety regulations, not to mention budgets.

Although no perfect cruise ship exists, turning owners' dreams and concepts into ships that embody those ideals is the job of specialized marine architects and shipyards, as well as consultants, interior designers, and a mass of specialist suppliers. Computers have simplified this complex process, although shipboard management and operations personnel often become frustrated with designers who are more idealistic than they are practical. Ships represent a compromise between ideals and restrictions of space and finance, the solution being to design ships for specific areas and conditions of service.

Ships used to be constructed in huge building docks, from the keel (backbone) up. Today, ships are built in huge sections, then joined together in an assembly area (typically as many as 100 or more sections for a resort ship such as *Carnival Miracle*, each section weighing up to 450 tons, most of which are extensively pre-outfitted). The sections may not even be constructed in the shipyard, although they will be assembled there. The design of today's ships is completely computer-based.

Formerly, passenger spaces were slotted in wherever there was space within a given hull. Today, computers provide highly targeted ship design, enabling a new ship to be built within two years instead of within the four or five years it took in the 1950s.

The maximum noise and vibration levels allowable in the accommodation spaces and recreational areas are stipulated in any owner's contract with the shipyard. Vibration tests are carried out once a ship is built and launched, using a finite method element of evaluation; this embraces analyses of prime sources of noise and excitation, namely the ship's propellers and main engines.

DID YOU KNOW?

● that the first vessel built exclusively for cruising was Hamburg-Amerika Line's two-funnel yacht, the 4,409-ton *Princessin Victoria Luise*? This luxury ship even included a private suite for the German kaiser.

● that the first ship to be fitted with real stabilizers (not an autogyro device) was the Peninsular & Oriental Steam Navigation Company's 1949-built 24,215-ton *Chusan*?

● that the first consecrated oceangoing Roman Catholic chapel aboard a passenger ship was in Compagnie Generale Transatlantique's *Ile de France* of 1928?

● that the latest life rafts called Hydrostatic Release Units (HRU), designed in Britain and approved by the Royal Navy, are now compulsory on all British-registered ships? Briefly, an HRU is capable of automatically releasing a life raft from its mountings when a ship sinks (even after it sinks) but can also be operated manually at the installation point, saving precious time in an emergency.

Previous pages and above: classic cruising posters

Prefabricated cabin modules, including *in situ* bathrooms complete with toilets and all plumbing, are used today. When the steel structure of the relevant deck is ready, with main lines and insulation installed, cabin modules are then affixed to the deck, and power lines and sanitary plumbing are swiftly connected. All waste and power connections, together with hot/cold water mixing valves, are arranged in the service area of the bathroom and can be reached from the passageway outside the cabin for maintenance.

Cruising Tomorrow

Current thinking in ship design is increasingly following two quite distinct paths: large resort ships or smaller ships.

● Large ships, where "economy of scale" helps the operator to keep the cost per passengers down. Five companies (Carnival Cruise Lines, Costa cruises, Cunard Line, Princess Cruises, and Royal Caribbean International) have ships measuring over 100,000 tons, accommodating over 3,000 passengers, with the "bigger is better" principle being pursued for all it's worth. These ships are, however, too wide to transit the Panama Canal (non-Panamax) unless they take a more circuitous route (perhaps to the Mediterranean via South America or Southeast Asia and the Suez Canal).

● Small ships, where the "small is beautiful" concept has taken hold, particularly in the exclusive and luxury categories. Cruise lines offer high-quality ships of low capacity, which can provide a highly personalized range of quality services.

Other cruise lines have expanded by "stretching" their ships. This is accomplished literally by cutting a ship in half, and inserting a newly constructed midsection, thus instantly increasing capacity, adding more accommodation and public rooms, while maintaining the same draft.

"Stretched" ships include: *Black Watch* (ex-*Royal Viking Star*), *Costa Europa* (ex-*Westerdam*), *Enchantment of the Seas*, *Norwegian Dream* (ex-*Dreamward*), *Norwegian Majesty* (ex-*Royal Majesty*) and *Norwegian Wind* (ex-*Windward*).

Whatever direction the design of cruise vessels takes in the future, ships are becoming increasingly environmentally friendly. With growing concern, particularly in eco-sensitive areas such as Alaska and the South Pacific, better safeguards against environmental pollution and damage are being built into the vessels.

The cruise industry is fast approaching "zero discharge," which means that nothing is discharged into the world's oceans at any time. This is an easier objective for the latest batch of ships to attain, since older ships usually have a more difficult time achieving this ambitious target because of their outdated equipment. ❏

At the helm of the *Queen Mary*, withdrawn in 1967.

A Chronology of Modern Cruising

1960 Passenger shipping directories listed more than 30 companies operating transatlantic voyages. Many ships were laid up from 1960 to 1970, and most were sold for a fraction of their value. *Britannic,* the last passenger ship to wear the White Star Line colors, went out of service.
1962 Compagnie Générale Transatlantique's liner *France*, at 1,035 ft the longest passenger ship ever built, entered service from Le Havre to New York.
1963 Cunard Line's RMS *Queen Elizabeth* made an experimental cruise from New York to the West Indies. As a result, full air conditioning was fitted in 1965–66 to facilitate more extensive cruising.
1965 The Orient Steam Navigation Company was absorbed into the P&O Group. The new company became known as the Peninsular & Oriental Steam Navigation Company. Stanley B. McDonald founded Princess Cruises.
1966 Soviet transatlantic service was reopened with the Black Sea Shipping Company's *Aleksandr Pushkin* inaugurating service between Montreal and Leningrad (now St. Petersburg) for the first time since 1949. The Norwegian company Klosters Reederei joined Miami businessman Ted Arison in marketing Caribbean cruises from Miami. Sanford Chobol founded Commodore Cruise Line.

1967 Cunard withdrew the transatlantic liner *Queen Mary* from service.
1968 Cunard's *Queen Elizabeth* withdrawn. Cunard refused delivery of *Queen Elizabeth 2* from its builder, John Brown, in December, because of unacceptable turbine vibration levels. Repairs led to a five-month delay to its maiden transatlantic crossing. Boise Cascade purchased Princess Cruises from its founder, Stanley B. McDonald, who bought back the line two years later.
1969 Lars-Eric Lindblad's *Lindblad Explorer,* designed for close-in expedition cruising, was launched. Royal Caribbean Cruise Line was set up by a consortium of Norwegian shipping companies. The loss-making *United States* was laid up.
1970 Royal Viking Line was founded by three partners (Bergen Line, A.F. Klaveness, and Nordenfjeldske) who each contributed one ship (*Royal Viking Sea*, *Royal Viking Sky*, and *Royal Viking Star*). Germany's Norddeutscher Lloyd and Hapag (Hamburg American Line) merged as Hapag-Lloyd.
1971 Cunard Line was sold to Trafalgar House Investments. Royal Cruise Line was founded.
1972 Ted Arison founded Carnival Cruise Lines. It began with just one ship, *Mardi Gras* (ex-*Empress of Canada*). It ran aground on its first voyage. Sitmar Cruises began operations with *Fairsea* (and later added *Fairstar* and *Fairwind*) from Los Angeles.

1974 P&O bought Princess Cruises. Compagnie Générale Transatlantique laid up the loss-making *France*. The Port Authority of New York and New Jersey opened its Passenger Ship Terminal. Royal Cruise Lines' first ship, *Golden Odyssey*, built to accommodate the equivalent load of a Boeing 747 aircraft (425 passengers), was introduced.
1975 *Island Princess* and *Pacific Princess* (Princess Cruises) become the "stars" in the American television show *The Love Boat*.
1976 The Italian Line and Lloyd Triestino ceased transatlantic passenger operations.
1977 World Explorer Cruises was founded with a single ship, *Universe*. Holland America Line absorbed Monarch Cruise Lines.
1978 Richard Hadley founded United States Cruises.
1979 American Hawaii Cruises was formed. In June, SS *France* was purchased by Lauritz Kloster, rebuilt for Caribbean cruises, renamed *Norway* and transferred to Norwegian Caribbean Lines.
1980 Sea Goddess Cruises was founded by Helge Naarstad. Denmark's United Steamship Company (DFDS) founded Scandinavian World Cruises to operate one-day cruises from Miami (the company subsequently became SeaEscape). Two Royal Caribbean ships were "stretched" by the addition of a mid-section (the first time this technique had been applied in the cruise industry).
1981 Transatlantic service provided by Soviet-registered ships was discontinued because of a US embargo. Astor Cruises was formed in the UK.
1982 The British government chartered Cunard's *Queen Elizabeth 2* and P&O Cruises' *Canberra* for use as troop carriers during the Falklands War between Argentina and Britain.
1983 P&O appointed Jeffrey Sterling as chairman

in order to fend off an unwanted takeover bid by Cunard Line's owners, Trafalgar House, which purchased Norwegian America Cruises (NAC), together with *Sagafjord* and *Vistafjord*. Premier Cruise Lines was founded. Salen-Lindblad Cruising's *Lindblad Explorer* became the first passenger ship to successfully navigate the Northwest Passage, sailing 4,790 miles (7,700 km) from Saint John's, Newfoundland, to Point Barrow, Alaska.
1984 Sundance Cruises was founded by Stanley B. McDonald with a single ship, *Sundancer*. Also founded were Dolphin Cruise Line, Premier Cruise Lines, and Regency Cruises. Windstar Sail Cruises re-launched the age of commercial sail. Network TV advertising was used in the US for the first time, by Carnival Cruise Lines.
1985 The Chandris Group of Companies acquired Fantasy Cruises from GoGo Tours, renaming it Chandris Fantasy Cruises in the US and Chandris Cruises in the UK.
1986 Signet Cruise Line was founded in Norway. Owing to a lawsuit brought by an American who claimed the right to the name Signet, the company changed its name in 1988 to Seabourn Cruise Line. Eastern Cruise Lines, Western Cruise Lines, and Sundance Cruises merged to become Admiral Cruises. Cunard acquired Sea Goddess Cruises, together with *Sea Goddess I* and *Sea Goddess II*.
1987 Carnival Cruise Lines made its first public stock offering. Cunard's *Queen Elizabeth 2* was converted at a German shipyard from steam turbine to diesel-electric power, the largest conversion in maritime history. Ocean Cruise Lines merged with Pearl Cruises. Princess Cruises

The *Canberra* is escorted back into Southampton after having been a troop carrier in the 1982 Falklands War.

replaced almost 500 unionized British hotel and catering staff aboard its five ships.

1988 Commodore Cruise Lines sold its *Bohème* to the Church of Scientology; it was renamed *Freewinds*. Crystal Cruises was formed as a wholly-owned division of Japan's Nippon Yusen Kaisha (NYK). Royal Caribbean Cruise Line merged with Admiral Cruises to form Royal Admiral Cruises (later Royal Caribbean Cruises). Carnival Cruise Lines acquired Holland America Line, including its land-based hotel/transport operations and Windstar Cruises. Seabourn Cruise Line's first ship, *Seabourn Pride*, entered service.

1989 American Cruise Lines, which operated small vessels for intracoastal cruising, went into bankruptcy. The Chandris Group of Companies announced the creation of Celebrity Cruises. Ocean Quest International was formed to provide seven-day cruises for scuba diving enthusiasts; the venture failed after a diver died in a hyperbaric decompression chamber. Renaissance Cruises was formed by Fearnley & Eger (a 120-year-old Oslo-based shipping concern) to build and market eight small premium cruise vessels. The Panama Canal celebrated its 75th birthday. Lars-Eric Lindblad's Lindblad Travel company went into bankruptcy.

1990 Starlite Cruises (part of the Piraeus-based Lelakis Group) was formed to provide ships for one-day and seven-day cruises. Ocean Cruise Lines was purchased by Croisières Paquet, itself owned by the French giant Accor leisure company. Japan Cruise Line entered the cruise market in Japan with its new 606-passenger *Orient Venus* for charters and incentive cruises for Japanese companies. At the start of the Gulf War, the US government chartered *Cunard Princess* for six months for use as a rest and relaxation center for US service personnel in the Persian Gulf.

1991 Carnival Cruise Lines acquired a 25 percent stake in Seabourn Cruise Line. Renaissance Cruises was sold to an international group of investors. Effjohn International purchased Crown Cruise Line. Seawind Cruise Line commenced cruise operations. Nippon Yusen Kaisha (NYK) purchased Salen Lindblad Cruising.

1992 Costa Cruise Lines introduced its new Euro-Luxe cruise concept with the debut of *CostaClassica*. Admiral Cruises ceased operations. Carnival Cruise Lines deployed *Mardi Gras* to accommodate 600 staff members made homeless by the Hurricane Andrew. The Chandris Group of Companies and Overseas Shipholding Group (OSG) signed an agreement to form a joint venture company called Celebrity Cruise Lines, Inc. Chargeurs and Accor, the French property and leisure industries group that own Paquet Cruises and Ocean Cruise Lines, purchased a 23 percent stake in Costa Crociere, the parent company of Costa Cruises.

1993 Carnival Cruise Lines formed Fiesta Marina Cruises for the Spanish-speaking Latin American market; it was phenomenally unsuccessful. George Poulides founded Festival Cruises. SeaQuest Cruises ceased operations. *Frontier Spirit* was returned to its Japanese owners and was chartered as *Bremen* to Germany's Hanseatic Tours.

1994 Delta Queen Steamboat Company changed its corporate name to American Classic Voyages Company; it owns American Hawaii Cruises and the Delta Queen Steamboat Company. Trafalgar House, Cunard's parent company, signed an agreement to purchase the rights to the name Royal Viking Line, together with *Royal Viking Sun*. *Royal Viking Queen* went to Royal Cruise Line, becoming *Queen Odyssey* and later *Seabourn Legend*. Radisson Diamond Cruises and Seven Seas Cruise Line merged to become Radisson Seven Seas Cruises. Star Cruises was founded.

1995 British company Airtours purchased *Southward* from Norwegian Cruise Line and *Nordic Prince* from Royal Caribbean Cruises.

1996 Kloster Cruise (the parent company of Norwegian Cruise Line and Royal Cruise Line) announced the closure of its Royal Cruise Line division. *Crown Odyssey* and *Royal Odyssey* went to Norwegian Cruise Line as *Norwegian Crown* and *Norwegian Star*, respectively. *Queen Odyssey* went to Seabourn Cruise Line and renamed *Seabourn*

WHO GOES CRUISING

Cruising's popularity continues to increase. The Maritime Evaluations Group has analyzed by nationality the breakdown of passengers choosing to take an oceangoing cruise vacation:

United States	9,000,000
UK	960,000
Asia (not including Japan)	600,000
Germany	429,000
Canada	300,000
Italy	250,000
Australasia	250,000
France	250,000
Rest of Europe	250,000
Japan	200,000
Cyprus *	75,000
Freighter Passengers	3,000
Total	12,567,000

* Local Cyprus market only.

Note: The above numbers do not include the approximately 1 million passengers who took a river/inland waterway cruise, nor the 300,000 passengers who took a coastal cruise aboard the ships of Norwegian Coastal Voyages. All figures are for 2003.

Legend. Star Odyssey was sold to Fred Olsen Cruise Lines and renamed *Black Watch*. Baltic Line and Sunshine Cruise Lines ceased cruise operations. Cunard (together with parent company Trafalgar House) was purchased by Kvaerner.

David's Supper Club in *Carnival Pride*: the style and décor of some recent vessels emulates Las Vegas.

1997 Hapag-Lloyd acquired Hanseatic Tours, together with its expedition ship, *Hanseatic*. Carnival Corporation, jointly with Airtours, purchased the shares of Costa Cruises. Celebrity Cruises was bought by Royal Caribbean International for $1.3 billion. P&O Cruises' *Canberra* was withdrawn from service and sent to Pakistan for scrap.

1998 Australia repealed its cabotage laws, allowing international cruise ships to dock and operate from Australian ports without restrictions. Kvaerner sold Cunard for $500 million to a consortium that included Carnival Corporation.

1999 Crown Cruise Line was reintroduced as an upscale division of Commodore Cruise Line. The company chartered *Crown Dynasty* and later purchased the ship for $86.2 million.

2000 Star Cruises took full control of Norwegian Cruise Line (including Orient Lines) after purchasing the outstanding shares held by the Carnival Corporation. The P&O Group separated its cruising activities from the rest of the group, placing more emphasis on what it sees as its core business; it has four cruise divisions – Aida Cruises, P&O Cruises, P&O Cruises (Australia), and Princess Cruises. Costa Cruises became 100% owned by the Carnival Corporation.

2001 Spain's Pullmantur bought *Oceanic* (formerly Premier Cruise Lines' *Big Red Boat I*) and *Seawind Crown* (formerly operated by Premier Cruise Lines) for the Spanish-speaking market. The Carnival Corporation sold its 25.1% shareholding in Airtours. Renaissance Cruises ceased operations after the September 11 terrorist attacks on the US. So did American Hawaii Cruises, United States Lines and Delta Queen Coastal Cruises all ceased operations.

2002 Valtur Tourism ceased its cruise operations; the Italian company had one ship (*Valtur Prima*). SeaDream Yacht Club began operations with two ships, *SeaDream I* and *SeaDream II*. Golden Sun Cruises became Golden Star Cruises and started operating *Aegean I*.

2003 The Carnival Corporation and P&O Princess Cruises merged to become the world's largest cruise company, with more than 60 ships and 13 brands (A'Rosa Cruises, Aida Cruises, Carnival Cruise Lines, Costa Cruises, Cunard Line, Holland America Line, Ocean Village, P&O Cruises, P&O Cruises Australia, Princess Cruises, Seabourn Cruise Line, Swan Hellenic Cruises and Windstar Cruises). Oceania Cruises was founded by Frank del Rio and Joe Watters, with two ships, *Insignia* and *Regatta* (the former Renaissance Cruises' *R1* and *R2*). Regal Cruises ceased operations; the company had one ship (*Regal Empress*). Mauritius Island Cruises was founded with two ships, *Island Sky* and *Island Sun* (the former Renaissance Cruises' *R7* and *R8)*.

2004 Festival Cruises had its ships impounded, the company went out of business, and its ships were sold at auction. Royal Olympia Cruises also suffered the same fate (but recovered, albeit with a smaller fleet), a victim of high ship and operating costs against a backdrop of a discount marketplace.

2005 Sun Cruises (My Travel) ceases operations; its three vessels are sold to other operators. ❑

LIFE ABOARD

This A to Z survey covers the astonishing range of facilities that modern

cruise ships offer and tells you how to make the most of them

Air-Conditioning

Cabin temperature can be regulated by an individually controlled thermostat, so you can adjust it to suit yourself. Public room temperatures are controlled automatically. Air temperatures are often kept cooler than you may be used to.

Art Auctions

Aboard many large and mid-size ships, art auctions form part of the entertainment. They are fun participation events, but don't expect to purchase an heirloom, as most of the art pieces are rubbish. It's funny how so many identical pieces can be found aboard so many ships (as frequent cruise passengers are finding out). Also, the charges for getting art pieces framed and sent to your home (from centralized warehouses) can be a rip-off.

Baby-Sitting

In some ships, stewards, stewardesses, and other staff may be available as babysitters for an hourly charge. Make arrangements at the reception desk/purser's office. Note that aboard some ships, evening baby-sitting services may not start until late in the evening (it is wise to check times and availability *before* you book your cruise).

Beauty Salon/Barber Shop

Make appointments as soon after boarding as possible (particularly on short cruises). Appointment times fill up rapidly, especially before social events such as a captain's cocktail party. Charges are comparable to those ashore. Typical services: haircut for men and women, styling, permanent waving, coloring, manicure, pedicure, leg waxing.

Bridge Visits

Check the *Daily Program* for navigation bridge visits. In most large resort ships, bridge visits are not allowed for insurance and security reasons. In others, although personal visits are forbidden, a *Behind the Scenes* video on how the ship is run may be shown on the cabin television system.

Cashless Cruising

It is now the norm to cruise cash-free, and to settle your account with one payment (by cash or credit card) prior to disembarking on the last day. Often an imprint of your credit card is taken at embarkation, permitting you to sign for everything. Before the end of the cruise, a detailed statement is delivered to your cabin. Some cruise lines may discontinue their "cashless" system for the last day of the cruise, which can be most irritating.

Be warned that something of a rip-off for non-US credit card holders has recently emerged. When you charge your onboard account to your MasterCard or Visa card, if it is a non-US issued and denominated credit card, US-based companies such as Celebrity Cruises and Royal Caribbean International convert the amount to be charged into the currency of your credit card – but they then add a "currency conversion service charge" to your conversion account.

Ships visiting a "private island" on a Bahamas/Caribbean itinerary will probably ask you to pay cash for beverages, water sports and scuba diving gear, and other items that you purchase ashore.

Casino Gaming

While most passengers do not choose a cruise in order to gamble, many cruise ships have casinos, where a range of table games is played (typically blackjack or 21, Caribbean stud poker, roulette, craps, and baccarat). Playing chips and cash change are available from the cashier or from banknote acceptance machines. Children under 18 are not allowed in the casino. The casino will be closed in port due to international customs regulations, and taking photographs in the casino is usually forbidden. German- and Japanese-registered ships are not permitted to operate casinos that give cash prizes.

Most cruise lines have videos showing how to play the various table games, as well as free lessons to entice players. Remember that casinos provide entertainment rather than a hard-core gambling environment, and there is no charge to enter any shipboard casino (all you need is luck).

Slot machines can also be found (whether casino ashore or cruise line casino, more than half of the profits are from slot machines). They provide entertainment, although they don't require any human interaction.

Comment Cards

On the last day of the cruise you will be asked to fill out a company "comment card." Some lines

LEFT: Keeping track of time – an elaborate astrological clock in the atrium lobby of the *Amsterdam*.

Low stakes on the high seas: many ships have casinos.

offer "incentives" such as a bottle of champagne. Be truthful, as the form serves as a means of communication between you and the cruise line. Pressure from staff to write "excellent" for everything is rampant aboard cruise ships. But if there *have* been problems, do say so.

Communications

Most ships now have a direct-dial satellite telephone system. In addition, all ships are given an internationally recognized call sign, made up of a combination of several letters and digits. When the ship is at sea, you can call from your cabin (or the ship's radio room) to anywhere in the world:
● via radiotelephone (a slight/moderate background noise might be noticed).
● via satellite (which will be as clear as your own home phone).

Direct dial satellite calls (this service started in 1986) are more expensive, but are completed instantly. Some ships also have credit card telephones located in public areas; these also connect instantly, via satellite. Satellite calls can also be made when the ship is in port (radiotelephone calls cannot). Satellite telephone calls cost between US$5 and $15 per minute, depending on the type of communications equipment the ship carries (the latest systems are digital). Calls are charged to your onboard account.

Your relatives and friends can reach you by calling the High Seas Operator in most countries (in the United States, dial 1-800-SEA-CALL). The operator will need the name of the ship, together with the ocean code (Atlantic is 871; Pacific is 872; and the Indian Ocean is 873).

Cruisespeak

The following terminology is used aboard today's cruise ships. The correct nautical terminology is given, while the words that follow are what many cruise lines now use:
Cabin: Penthouse Suite, Junior Suite, Stateroom, or Room
Cabin Service: Room Service
Passenger: Guest
Purser's Office: Guest Relations Desk or Front Office

Customs Regulations

All countries vary in the duty-free allowances granted by their own customs service, but you will be informed aboard your cruise ship of the allowable amounts for your nationality and residency.

Daily Program

The *Daily Program* contains a useful list of the day's activities, entertainment, and social events. It is normally delivered to your cabin the evening before the day that it covers.

Death at Sea

What happens if someone dies at sea? Typically, it happens more on long cruises, where passengers are generally older. Bodies are put in a special refrigeration unit for removal at the port of disembarkation, or the body can be flown home from a wayward port of call (more complicated, owing to the paperwork). Note that flying a body home usually involves a large expense. A burial at sea can also be arranged aboard ship (some people have a body cremated at home, return to their favorite cruise ship, and have the ashes scattered at sea).

Departure Tax

If you are disembarking in a foreign port and flying home, be advised that there could be a departure tax to pay (in local currency) at the airport.

Disembarkation

During the final part of your cruise, the cruise director will give an informal talk on customs, immigration, and disembarkation (sometimes called "debarkation") procedures. The night before your ship reaches its final destination, you will be given a customs form to fill out. Any duty-free items bought from the shop on board must be included in your allowance (save the receipts in case a customs officer wishes to see them).

The night before arrival, place your main baggage outside your cabin on retiring (or before 4am). It will be collected and off-loaded on arrival. Leave out fragile items, liquor, and the clothes you intend to wear for disembarkation and onward travel (it is amazing just how many people pack everything, only to find they are in an embarrassing position on disembarkation day). Anything left in your cabin will be considered hand luggage to be hand-carried off when you leave.

On disembarkation day, breakfast will probably be early. It might be better to miss breakfast and sleep later, providing announcements on the ship's public address system do not wake you (it may be possible to turn off such announcements). Even worse than early breakfast, is the fact that you will be commanded (requested, if you are lucky) to leave your cabin early, only to wait in crowded public rooms – sometimes for hours. To add insult to injury, your cabin steward (after he has received his tip, of course) will knock on the door to take the sheets off the bed so the cabin can be made up for the incoming passengers. Cruise aboard the smaller "upscale" ships and this will not happen.

Before leaving the ship, remember to claim any items you have placed in the ship's safety deposit boxes and leave your cabin key in your cabin. Passengers cannot go ashore until all baggage has been offloaded, and customs and/or immigration inspections or pre-inspections have been carried out. In most ports, this takes two to three hours after arrival. It is wise to leave at least three hours from the time of arrival to catch a connecting flight or other transportation. Once off the ship, you will identify your baggage on the pier before going through customs inspection (delays are usually minimal). Porters may be there to assist you.

Engine Room

In almost all passenger ships, the engine room is off-limits to passengers, and visits are not allowed, for insurance and security reasons. In some ships, a technical information leaflet may be available. Aboard others, a Behind the Scenes video may be shown on the cabin television system. For more specific or detailed information, contact a member of the ship's engineering staff via the purser's office.

Gift Shops

The gift shop/boutique/drugstore will offer souvenirs, gifts, toiletries, and duty-free items, as well as a basic stock of essential items. You will find duty-free items, such as perfumes and watches, very competitively priced. Opening hours are posted at the store and in the Daily Program.

Health and Fitness Facilities

The latest ships have elaborate spas where (for an extra fee) whole days of treatments are on offer.

Most ships provide plenty of opportunity for exercise.

Stress reducing and relaxation treatments are practiced combined with the use of seawater, which contains minerals, micronutrients, and vitamins. Massages might include Swedish remedial massage, shiatsu, and aromatherapy treatments. You can even get a massage on your private balcony aboard some ships. More details: page 43. The latest "con" in the extra charge game is to have separate charges for days at sea compared to days in port.

Launch (Tender) Services

Enclosed or open motor launches ("tenders") are used when your cruise ship is unable to berth at a port or island. In such cases, a regular launch service is operated between ship and shore for the duration of the port call. Details of the launch service will be provided in the Daily Program. When stepping on or off a tender, remember to extend "forearm to forearm" to the person assisting you. Do not grip their hands because this simply has the effect of immobilizing the helper.

Launderette

Some ships are fitted with self-service launderettes, equipped with washers, dryers, and ironing facilities. There is sometimes a charge for washing powder and for use of the machines.

Laundry and Dry Cleaning

Most ships offer a full laundry and pressing service. Some ships may also offer dry-cleaning

The *Oriana's* library contains a table made by Britain's Lord Linley, son of the late Princess Margaret.

facilities. A detailed list of services (and prices) can be found in your cabin. Your steward will collect and deliver your laundry or dry cleaning.

Library

Most cruise ships have a library offering a good selection of books, reference material, and periodicals. A small deposit (refundable on return of the book) is sometimes required when you borrow a book. Note that aboard the small luxury ships, the library is open 24 hours a day, and no deposit is required. Aboard the large resort ships, you may find that the library is open only a couple of hours each morning and afternoon. *Aurora, Orian, QE2* and *QM2* are examples of ships with full-time, qualified librarians (aboard most other ships a member of the cruise staff or entertainment staff – with little knowledge of books or authors – staffs the library). The library is typically where you will find board games such as Scrabble, backgammon, and chess.

Lifeboat Drill

There have been few recent incidents requiring the evacuation of passengers, although two cruise ships have been lost following collisions (*Jupiter,* 1988, and *Royal Pacific,* 1992). Travel by ship, however, remains one of the safest means of transportation. Even so, it cannot be stressed enough that attendance at lifeboat drill is not only required but makes sense, and participation is mandatory. You must, at the very least, know your boat station and how to get to it in the event of an emergency.

If other passengers are lighthearted about the

Those who've seen *Titanic* don't mind lifeboat drills.

drill, do not let that affect your seriousness of purpose. Be sure to note your exit and escape pathways and learn how to put on your lifejacket correctly. The drill takes no more than 15 minutes of your time and is a good investment in playing safe (the *Royal Pacific* sank in just 16 minutes following a collision).

A Passenger Lifeboat Drill must be conducted on board within 24 hours of leaving the embarkation port (within 6 hours would be more desirable). You will hear an announcement from the bridge, which goes something like this: "Ladies and Gentlemen, may I have your attention, please. This is the captain speaking to you from the bridge. In 15 minutes' time, the ship's alarm bells will signal emergency lifeboat drill for all passengers. This is a mandatory drill, conducted in accordance with the requirements of the Safety of Life at Sea Convention. There are no exceptions."

Here is an example of an announcement from the navigation bridge: "The emergency signal is a succession of seven or more short blasts followed by one long blast of the ship's whistle, supplemented by the ringing of the electric gongs throughout the ship. On hearing this signal, you should make your way quickly but quietly to your cabin, put on warm clothing and your lifejacket, then follow the signs to your emergency boat station, where you will be kept fully informed over the loudspeakers through which I am speaking to you now."

Lost Property

Contact the reception desk/purser's office immediately if you lose or find something on the ship.

Notices regarding lost and found property may be posted on the bulletin boards.

Mail

You can buy stamps and mail letters aboard most ships. Some ships use the postal privileges and stamps of their flag of registration, while others buy local stamps at ports of call. Mail is usually taken ashore by the ship's port agent just before the ship sails. You will receive a list of port agents and mailing addresses with your tickets and documents, so you can advise friends and family how they can send mail to you.

Massage

Make appointments for a massage as soon after embarkation as possible, in order to obtain the time and day of your choice. Larger ships have more staff and offer more flexibility in appointment times. The cost averages about $2 a minute. In some ships, a massage service is available in your cabin (or on your private balcony), if it is large enough to accommodate a portable massage table.

Medical Services

Except for ships registered in England or Norway, there are no mandatory international maritime requirements for cruise lines to carry a licensed physician or to have hospital facilities aboard. However, in general, all ships carrying over 50 passengers do have hospital facilities and do carry at least one licensed doctor aboard ship (ships

There are plenty of organized diversions.

registered in England and Norway have both, without exception). Usually, there is a reasonably equipped hospital in miniature, although the standard of medical practice and of the physicians themselves may vary from line to line. Most shipboard doctors are generalists; there are no cardiologists or neurosurgeons. Doctors are often employed as outside contractors and therefore will charge for use of their services, including seasickness shots (except for Russian and Ukrainian registered vessels, where medical services are free). UK passengers should note that ships fall outside the UK National Health Service scheme.

Regrettably, many cruise lines place a low priority on providing medical services (there are, however, some exceptions). Most shipboard physicians are not certified in trauma treatment or medical evacuation procedures, for example. Most ships that cater to North American passengers tend to carry doctors licensed in the United States, Canada, or Britain, but aboard many other ships, doctors come from a variety of countries and disciplines. Some medical organizations, such as the American College of Emergency Physicians, have created a special division for cruise medicine.

Cunard Line's *QE2*, with 2,921 passengers and crew, has a fully equipped hospital with one surgeon, one doctor, a staff of six nurses, and two medical orderlies; contrast this with Carnival's *Sensation*, which carries up to 3,514 passengers and crew, with just one doctor and two nurses.

Standards and equipment vary widely. Obviously, any ship that features long-distance cruises, with several days at sea, should have better medical facilities and a better qualified staff than one engaged in a standard seven-day Caribbean cruise, with a port of call to make almost every day.

There is no agreed industry-wide standard relating to the medical certification required by cruise ships. Most ship doctors are general practitioners, but often short-term contracts can mean poor continuity and differing standards.

Ideally, a ship's medical staff should be certified in Advanced Cardiac Life Support. The minimal standard medical equipment should include an examination room, isolation ward/bed, X-ray machine (to verify the existence of broken or fractured bones), cardiac monitor (EKG) and defibrillator, oxygen-saturation monitor (to determine a patient's blood-oxygen level), external pacemaker, oxygen, suction and ventilators, hematology analyzer, culture incubator, and a mobile trolley intensive care unit.

Any *existing* health problems that require treatment on board must be reported at the time of booking. If you do have to use the services of a ship's doctor, note that, aboard some ships, you may be charged for filling a prescription in addition to the cost of any prescribed drugs. There may also be a charge if you are unwell, have to cancel a shore excursion and need a doctor's letter to prove it.

Movies

In most cruise ships a dedicated movie theater is an essential part of the ship's public-room facilities. The movies are recent, often selected by the cruise line from a special licensed film- or video-leasing service. Many of the latest ships have replaced or supplemented the ship's movie theater with television sets and video players in each cabin.

News and Sports Bulletins

The world's news and sports results are reported in the ship's newspaper or placed on the bulletin board that is normally located near the purser's office or in the library. For sports results not listed, ask at the purser's office; it may be possible for the results to be obtained for you.

Passenger Lists

All ships of yesteryear provided passenger lists with each passenger's name and hometown or region. Today, only a handful of companies carry on the tradition (perhaps some passengers are traveling with someone they should not!).

Photographs

Professional photographers take pictures (increasingly digital) of passengers throughout the cruise, including their arrival on board. They cover all the main events and social functions, such as the captain's cocktail party. The pictures can be viewed without any obligation to purchase, but the prices may surprise. The cost is now likely to exceed $10 for a postcard-sized color photograph, and a 10 x 8-inch embarkation photo aboard *Queen Mary 2,* for example, is now a whopping $27.50.

Postcards and Writing Paper

These are available from the writing room, library, purser's office, or your room steward. Aboard many ships, they are available for a modest sum.

Purser's Office

This is also known as the Reception Office, guest relations, or information desk. Centrally located, it is the nerve center of the ship for general passenger information and problems. Opening hours (in some ships, 24 hours a day) are posted outside the office and given in the *Daily Program.*

Religious Services

Interdenominational services are conducted on board, usually by the captain or staff captain. A few older ships (and Costa Cruises' ships) have a small private chapel. Denominational services

---

TOP 30 PET PEEVES – MINE AND OTHER PASSENGERS'

● Passengers who do not possess a credit card (particularly older Asian passengers) are made to feel inferior at the check-in/embarkation desks, particularly in the United States. Some cruise lines have the temerity to ask for a $500 deposit in cash, just for the "privilege" of securing an onboard charge card. No hotel on land does this. Simply refuse, and say that if you cannot trust me, then refund my cruise fare.

● Aboard the large, high-tech ships, getting Cabin Services, or the "Guest Relations Desk," or the Operator to answer the telephone can be an exercise in frustration, patience, and gross irritation.

● Aboard many ships, 15 percent is automatically added to wine bills. Thus, a wine waiter makes much more money on a more expensive bottle of wine, whether he knows anything about that wine (or how to decant and serve it, for example) or not. For doing just the same job for a wine costing $125 as for a wine costing $15 he makes a lot more. Therefore, insist on adding your own gratuity, and politely refuse to be told how much you have to tip.

● Cruise brochures that use models, and provide the anticipation of an onboard product that a ship cannot deliver; the result is disappointment for passengers.

● Cruise brochures that state that their ship has a "small ship feel, big ship choice" when it really caters to more than 1,000 passengers (often more than 2,000).

● Constant, irritating, and repetitive announcements for bingo, horse racing, art auctions, and the latest gizmos for sale in the shops.

● "Elevator" music playing continuously in passageways and on open decks (even worse: rock music).

● Any announcement that is repeated. Any announcement that is repeated.

● Flowers in one's cabin that, are not watered or refreshed by the steward.

● Bathrobes provided but never changed for the duration of the cruise.

● Skimpy towels.

● Mini-bar/refrigerators that do not provide limes and lemons for drink mixes.

● Remote control units that need an instruction manual to understand their operation for turning on the television and getting a video player to work.

● In-cabin announcements at any time, except for emergencies (they are completely unnecessary for programmed events and shore excursions).

● Garnishes, when "parsley with everything" seems to be the rule of the seagoing entree experience.

● Baked Alaska parades.

● Paper, plastic, or polystyrene plastic cups for drinks of any kind.

● Paper napkins for meals or informal buffets (they should be linen or cotton).

● Plastic plates (often too small) for buffets.

● Buffets where only cold plates are available, even for hot food items.

● Repetitive breakfast and luncheon buffets and uncreative displays.

● Artwork placed aboard ships, but with the cruise line not caring or knowing enough about it to place the name of the artist and the year of creation alongside, whether it be a painting or a sculpture.

● Shopping lecturers, shopping videos, art auctions, and carpet auctions.

● Shore-side porters who take your bags when you get off the bus, or out of your car, then stand there until you tip them before they move your bags or drop them (worst ports: Ft. Lauderdale and Miami).

● Cabin stewards/stewardesses who place small folded pieces of paper in cabin door frames to show when their passengers have left their cabins.

● Audiovisual technicians who think that the volume level of the show should equal that for a rock concert for 250,000 people.

● Bands scheduled to play in a lounge that do not start playing until passengers walk in and sit down.

● Private island days, when the tender ride to get to the island is longer than the flight to get to the ship.

● Ships that ask you to settle your shipboard account before the morning of disembarkation.

● Long lines and waiting periods for disembarkation.

may be offered by specially invited or fellow-passenger members of the clergy.

Room Service

Beverages and snacks are available at most times. Liquor is normally limited to the opening hours of the ship's bars. Your room steward will advise you of the services. There's no charge for room service.

Safety First

In an increasingly regulated world, the importance of safety cannot be overplayed. The training of crew in relation to safety and security has become extremely important – so much so that new international regulations will soon require all crew to undergo basic safety training *before* they are allowed to join and work aboard any cruise ship. No longer will crew be recruited with the intention of providing on-the-job training.

Safeguards for passengers include lifeboats and life rafts. Since the introduction of the 1983 amendments to Chapter III of the *Safety of Life at Sea* (SOLAS) *Convention 1974* (which came into effect in 1980), much attention has been given to safety. The SOLAS conventions are subscribed to by all member countries of the United Nations, under the auspices of the International Maritime Organization (IMO).

All cruise ships built since July 1, 1986, must have either totally enclosed or partially enclosed lifeboats (only ships built before this date can have open lifeboats). These have diesel engines that will still operate when the lifeboat is inverted.

The 1990 SOLAS standards on stability and fire protection (mandating the enclosing of all stairways and the installation of sprinkler and smoke detection systems and "low-location" lighting) for all new ship construction took effect on October 1, 1997. Existing ships were given another five years to comply (the retrofitting of sprinkler systems in particular is an expensive measure that may not be considered viable by owners of older ships).

October 1, 1997, was the deadline whereby all cruise ships were required to:
● Fit smoke detectors and smoke alarms in all passenger cabins, corridors, stairway enclosures, and other public spaces.
● Have and use low-level lighting showing routes of escape (such as in corridors and stairways).
● Make all fire doors throughout the ship controllable from the ship's navigation bridge, and their status displayed thereon.
● Make all fire doors that are held open by hinges capable of release from a remote location.
● Fit a general emergency alarm that is audible in all cabins.
In 2010, the use of combustible materials in cruise ship construction (allowed under the previous SOLAS 60 regulations) will be forbidden.

The crew attends frequent emergency drills, the lifeboat equipment is regularly tested, and the fire-detecting devices, and alarm and fire-fighting systems are checked throughout the ship. If you spot fire or smoke, use the nearest fire alarm box, alert a member of staff, or contact the bridge.

Since July 1, 2002, all ocean-going cruise ships on international voyages have been required to carry voyage data recorders (VDRs – similar to black boxes carries by aircraft).

Sailing Time

In each port of call, sailing and all-aboard times are posted at the gangway. The all-aboard time is usually half an hour before sailing (ships cannot wait for passengers who are delayed).

Seasickness

The French term *mal de mer* may sound quaint, but the malady has been nauseating to seafarers since the Phoenicians. Fortunately, seasickness is rare these days, even in rough weather (less than 3 percent of all passengers become seasick). Ships have stabilizers – large underwater "fins" on each side of the hull – to counteract any rolling motion. Nevertheless, it is possible to develop some symptoms – anything from slight nausea to vomiting.

Seasickness occurs when the brain receives confusing messages from the body's sensory organs, causing an imbalance of receptors in the inner ear. The mind and brain are accustomed to our walking or riding on a nonmoving surface. If the surface itself moves in another direction, a signal is sent to the brain that something's wrong. Continuous mixed signals result in headaches, clammy skin, dizziness, paleness, and yawning, soon followed by nausea and vomiting. There is still no explanation for the great difference in individual susceptibility to seasickness.

Both old-time sailors and modern physicians have their own remedies, and you can take your choice or try them all (but not at the same time):
● When you notice the first movement of a ship, go out on deck and walk back and forth. You will find that your knees, which are our own form of stabilizer, will start getting their feel of balance and counteraction. This is the sign that you are "getting your sea legs."
● Get the fresh sea breeze into your face (arguably the best antidote of all), and if nauseated, suck an orange or a lemon.
● When on deck, focus on a steady point, such as the horizon.
● Eat lightly. Do not make the mistake of thinking a heavy meal will keep your stomach well anchored. It will not.

Senior officers have become more security-conscious.

● Dramamine (dimenhydrinate, an anti-histamine and sedative introduced just after World War II) will be available aboard in tablet (chewable) form.
● Scopoderm (also known as Transderm Scop), known as "The Patch" (manufactured by Ciba-Geigy), has an ingredient known as scopolamine, which has proven effective. It was reintroduced in 1997 after being taken off the market for several years. Possible side effects are dry mouth, blurred vision, drowsiness and problems with urinating.
● If you are really distressed, the ship's doctor can give you an injection to alleviate discomfort. It may make you drowsy, but the last thing on your mind will be staying awake at the movie.
● Try applying Travel Oil, an aromatherapy oil made by Borealis Healthcare in the UK, to the temples and across the forehead. It is a natural alternative to drug-based medications and has no side effects.
● Another natural preventive is ginger in powder form. Mix half a teaspoon in a glass of warm water or milk, and drink it before sailing. This is said to settle any stomach for up to eight hours.
● "Sea Bands" (or "Aquastraps") are a drug-free method of controlling motion sickness. These are slim bands (in varying colors) that are wrapped around the wrist, with a circular "button" that presses against the acupressure point Pericardium 6 (*nei kuan*) on the lower arm. Attach them a few minutes before you step aboard and wear on both wrists throughout the cruise.
● Another drug-free remedy can be found in ReliefBand, a watch-like device worn on the wrist. It is said to 'emit gentle electrical signals that interfere with nerves that cause nausea.'

All this being said, bear in mind that in addition to stabilizers in the hull, most cruises are in warm, calm waters and most cruise ships spend much time along the coast or pull into port regularly. The odds are very much against being seasick.

Security

A recognized standard of passenger ship protection exists, following the hijacking of *Achille Lauro* in 1985, and the terrorist atrocities that occurred in New York and Washington in September 2001. You will be required to go through metal detection devices at the gangway, and your baggage will be inspected more stringently.

All cabins can be locked, and it is recommended that you keep your cabin locked at all times when you are not there. Old-style keys are made of metal and operate a mechanical lock; most will be plastic key cards that operate electronically coded locks. Cruise lines do not accept responsibility for any money or valuables left in cabins and suggest that you store them in a safety deposit box at the purser's office, or, if one is supplied, in your in-cabin personal safe.

You will be issued a personal boarding pass when you embark (the latest high-tech passes may include your photo, lifeboat station, restaurant seating, and other pertinent information). This serves as identification and must be shown at the gangway each time you board (you may also be asked for a separate photo ID, such as a driver's license). The system of boarding passes is one of many ways in which cruise lines ensure passenger safety.

Shipboard Etiquette

Cruise lines want you to have a good vacation, but there are some rules to be observed.

● In public rooms, smoking and nonsmoking sections are available. In the dining room, however, cigar and pipe smoking are not permitted at all.

● If you take a video camera with you, be aware that you are not allowed to tape any of the professional entertainment shows and cabarets because of regulations designed to prevent international copyright infringement.

It is all right to be casual when on vacation, but not to enter a ship's dining room in just a bathing suit. Bare feet, likewise, are not permitted. If you are uncomfortable eating with the typical 10-piece dining room cutlery setting, some cruise lines have introduced etiquette classes to help you.

Shipboard Injury

Slipping, tripping, and falling are the major sources of shipboard injury. This does not mean that ships are unsafe, but there are some things you can do to minimize the chance of injury. If you *do* suffer from injury aboard ship, feel it is the cruise line's fault, and want to take some kind of legal action against the company, you should be aware of the following:

In the United States, Appendix 46, Section 183(b) of the US Civil Code requires that "the injured passenger notify the cruise line in writing within six months from the date of the injury to file a claim and suit must be filed within one year from the date of injury." So, if you file a claim after the one-year period, the cruise line will probably seek a summary judgment for dismissal.

It is imperative that you first *read your ticket*. The passenger ticket is a *legal contract* between passenger and cruise line. It will invariably state that you must file suit in the state (or country) designated in the ticket. Thus, if a resident of California buys a cruise, and the cruise line is based in Florida, then the lawsuit must be filed in Florida. If you reside in the US and you purchase a cruise in the Mediterranean and the cruise line is based in Italy, then you would have to file suit in Italy. This is known as the Forum Clause. (Part of a typical contract is reproduced on page 603.)

One area in which passengers may not be able to sue a cruise line is in the event of injury or accident when they are on a shore excursion advertised and sold aboard ship. This is because the tour operators are independent contractors. So, when you buy your shore excursion, ask if the ship's insurance fully covers you under the terms of the passenger ticket contract.

In your cabin: Note that aboard many ships, particularly older vessels, there are raised lips separating the bathroom from the sleeping area.

Do not hang anything from the fire sprinkler heads located on most cabin ceilings.

On older ships, it is wise to note how the door lock works. Some require a key on the inside in order to unlock the door. Leave the key in the lock, so that in the event of a real emergency, you do not have to hunt for the key.

On deck: Aboard older ships, watch for raised lips in doorways leading to open deck areas. Be alert and do not trip over them.

Wear sensible shoes with rubber soles (not crepe) when walking on deck or going to pool and lido areas. Do not wear high heels.

Walk with caution when the outer decks are wet after being washed, or if they are wet after rain. This applies especially to metal decks – falling onto a solid steel deck is really painful.

Do not throw a lighted cigarette or cigar butt, or knock out your pipe, over the ship's side. They can easily be sucked into an opening in the ship's side or onto an aft open deck area, and cause a fire.

Shore Excursions

These used to be limited to city tours and venues that offered folkloric dances by local troupes. Today's excursions are almost limitless, and include flight-seeing, floatplane rides, cross-country four-wheel drive trips, mountain biking, and even overland safaris. Indeed, be careful or you could end up spending far more on shore excursions than the price of your cruise.

Cruise lines plan and oversee shore excursions assuming that you have not seen a place and aim to show you its highlights in a comfortable manner and at a reasonable price. Buses, rather than taxis or private cars, are often used. This cuts costs and allows the tour operator to narrow the selection of guides to only those most competent, knowledgeable, and fluent in whatever language the majority of passengers speak, while providing some degree of security and control.

Brochure descriptions of shore excursions include artistic license, often written by personnel who haven't visited the port of call. All cruise lines should adopt the following definitions in their descriptive literature and for their lectures and presentations: The term "visit" should mean actually entering the place or building concerned. The term "see" should mean viewing from the outside (as from a bus, for example).

Shore excursions are timed to be most convenient for the greatest number of participants, taking into account the timing of meals on board (these may be altered according to excursion times). Departure times are listed in the descriptive literature and in the *Daily Program*, and may or may not be announced over the ship's public address system. There are no refunds if you miss

Shopping ashore at Charlotte Amalie, US Virgin Islands.

the excursion. If you are hearing-impaired, therefore, arrange for the shore excursion manager to assist you in meeting the correct times.

The ship's representative supervising the shore excursion program is the eyes and ears of the cruise line, and can recommend to the head office that any excursion be suspended if it is not up to standard. Shore excursion staff will be dockside dispatching the excursions in each port.

Most excursions give little in-depth history, and the general knowledge of guides is often limited. City excursions are basically superficial. To get to know a city intimately, go alone or with a small group. Take a taxi or bus, or walk directly to the places that are of most interest to you.

Many ships operate diving excursions at a reasonable price that includes all equipment. Instruction is offered on board, and underwater cameras can often be rented, too.

When you buy a shore excursion from the cruise line, you are fully covered by the ship's insurance; arrange it on your own and you are not covered when you step off the ship.

Shore excursion booking forms should be forwarded with your cruise tickets and documents. In some ships, they can be booked via the interactive television system in your cabin.

Book early, particularly those listed as "limited participation." This means that places are restricted, sold on a first-come, first-served basis. Where shore excursions can be booked before the sailing date, they are often sold out.

For cancellations, most ships require a minimum of 24 hours' notice before the advertised shore excursion departure time. Refunds are at the discretion of the cruise line.

Take along only what is necessary; leave any valuables aboard ship, together with any money and credit cards you do not plan to use. Groups of people are often targets for pickpockets in popular sightseeing destinations and major cities. Also, beware of excursion guides who give you a colored disk to wear for "identification." He may be marking you as a "rich" tourist for local shopkeepers.

Going solo? If you hire a taxi for sightseeing, negotiate the price in advance, and don't pay until you get back to the ship or to your final destination. If you are with friends, hiring a taxi for a full- or half-day sightseeing trip can often work out far cheaper than renting a car, and you also avoid the hazards of driving. Naturally, prices vary according to destination, but if you can select a driver who speaks your language, and the taxi is comfortable, even air-conditioned, you are ahead.

Shopping

Many cruise lines operating in Alaska, the Bahamas, the Caribbean, and the Mexican Riviera engage a company that provides the services of a "shopping lecturer." This person promotes selected shops, goods, and services heavily, fully authorized by the cruise line (which receives a commission). This relieves the cruise director of responsibility, together with any questions concerning his involvement, credibility, and financial remuneration.

Shopping maps, with "selected" stores highlighted, are placed in your cabin. Often, they come with a "guarantee" such as: "Shop with confidence at each of the recommended stores. Each merchant listed on this map has been carefully selected on the basis of quality, fair dealing, and value. These merchants have given Cruise Line X a guarantee of satisfaction valid for 30 days after purchase, excluding passenger negligence and buyers' regret, and have paid a promotional fee for inclusion as a guaranteed store."

When shopping time is included in shore excursions, be wary of stores recommended by tour guides; the guides are likely to be receiving commissions from the merchants. Shop around before you buy. Good shopping hints and recommendations are often given in the port lecture at the start of your cruise. When buying local handicrafts, make sure they have indeed been made locally.

Be wary of "bargain-priced" name brands, as they may well be counterfeit and of dubious quality. For watches, check the guarantee. Some shopping information may be available in information literature about the port and this should be available at the ship's shore excursion office.

Remember that the ship's shops are also duty free and, for the most part, competitive in price. The shops on board are closed while in port, however, due to international customs regulations.

Working out on *Carnival Triumph*.

Spas (shipboard)

Land-based health spas have long provided a range of body treatments and services for those who wanted to hide away at a venue in the countryside (often called health farms). With the increase in awareness of the body beautiful and the importance of well-being has come a whole new array of shipboard spas to rival those on land, particularly in the range of body-pampering treatments available.

Having body-pampering treatments aboard a cruise ship can be wonderful, as the ship can provide a serene environment in itself, and when enhanced by something like a massage or facial the benefits can be doubly therapeutic. Or half as therapeutic, as the case may be. For example, ship interior designers get it so wrong by placing massage treatment rooms directly underneath a basketball court! They need to pay more attention to soundproofing so that facilities can be used at all hours (lighting dimmers are also essential – it's surprising how often this simple, but essential, item is overlooked). Sadly, treatments seem to be available only until dinnertime, whereas I would welcome being able to have a massage late at night before retiring to bed (the problem is that most shipboard spas are run by concessions, who seem to treat well-being as a daytime-only event).

A typical large resort ship spa will include a gymnasium (probably with ocean-view windows and the latest in muscle-pumping equipment (universal stations, treadmills, bicycles), saunas, steam rooms, several body treatment rooms, thalasso-therapy pool, relaxation area, changing rooms, and beauty salon. The gymnasiums are all open rooms, with no privacy between you and the next person.

The latest fad for sea-going spas is for Asian-themed decor as an aid to relaxation, with warm woods and gently flowing water to provide a natural aesthetic environment aimed to caress and soothe, with therapy staff dressed in Eastern attire.

● MASSAGE
A whole range of treatments and styles has evolved from the standard Swedish massage. These include, but are not limited to, the following:
Swedish Massage: There are two main effects of massage – a reflex effect and a mechanical effect. There are four basic movements in this general massage: effleurage (the stroking movements that benefit the circulation of lymphatic fluids and drainage), petrissage (the picking, kneading, rolling and wringing movements), friction (the application of circular pressure) and tapotement (the percussive tapping, flicking and hacking movements that stimulate circulation).
Shiatsu Massage: This literally means "finger pressure" and in Japan for thousands of years has been applied to the pressure points of the body as

Shipboard spas cater for bodies that need pampering.

a preventative measure. It typically promotes a peaceful awareness of both body and mind, and is administered in a calm, relaxing environment.

Hot Stone Massage: The therapist places in a special oven 36 volcanic basalt (smooth) stones of varying sizes (from Arizona), and applies them to various key energy points of the body, using the stones to gently massage specific areas and muscles. The therapist then leaves the heated stones in place while working on other parts of the body. The heat from the stones will help the body to achieve a deep sense of relaxtion.

Well-being Massage: This is really another term for general Swedish Massage but with more emphasis on efflurage movements, the use of complementary aromatic (aromatherapy) oils and four-hand massage (two therapists working rhythmically in unison).

Aboard some ships, having a massage just before the sun goes down is a rare treat that more people are discovering. Today, many ships have suites and cabins with a "private" balcony, although you'll need a balcony with plenty of space in order to set up a proper portable massage table and allow the masseur/masseuse room to walk around it and work from all sides). It can be a real stress-busting experience, but if it's not right it can prove frustrating, and expensive.

As a *shipstester* (as the Germans called me in a television documentary which Nord Deutscher Runddfunk made about me in 2001), I have tried (in some cases endured at great expense) massages in some exotic locations both aboard and ashore. Here are some favourites (always taken in the late afternoon or early evening, preferably just before the sun goes down):

➤ Aboard *Constellation, Infinity, Millennium, Summit* (on the balcony of a Sky Suite).

➤ Aboard *Royal Clipper* (on the deck outside, but in a private massage hut).

➤ Aboard *SuperStar Virgo* (on the bedroom floor of the junior suites).

➤ In a beach cabana ashore on Castaway Cay in the Bahamas, or as part of the beach, caviar and champagne experience of ships such as *SeaDream I* and *II* in the British Virgin Islands.

● BODY WRAP

Often called a body mask, this treatment typically includes the use of algae and seaweeds applied to the whole body. The body is then wrapped (covered) in aluminium foil and blankets. There are many variations on this theme, using mud from the Dead Sea or Mediterranean Sea, or sea salt and ginger, or cooling cucumber and aloe, or other combinations that leave you feeling a warm glow afterwards. The aim of this treatment is to detoxify, firm and tone the skin, and reduce cellulite.

● BODY SCRUB

The aim of this treatment is to cleanse and soften the skin, and to draw out impurities from within, using aromatic oils, creams and lotions.

● FACIAL

Aromatherapy facial. Typically this treatment uses aromatic oils such as lavender, sandalwood and geranium plus a rejuvenating mask, creams and essences to "lift" the skin and facial muscles. **Rejuvenation Facial**. Typically a classic French facial which utilizes the latest skin care products that may include essential plant and vitamin-rich oils. This facial aims to reduce lines and wrinkles.

● RASUL CHAMBER

This is a room that is typically fully tiled and with Moorish decor. When you enter, you paste yourself or your partner (it's a much better experience with a partner) with three types of mud, and sit down while gentle steam surrounds you. The various muds become heated and then you're in a mud bath, after which you rub yourself (or each other) with large crystals of rock salt. Then shower, sit, and relax – all in the privacy of the chamber. Your skin will feel wonderful afterwards. Then it's time for a nap.

● COMMENTS

A word of warning: it's easy to telephone and make an appointment for a massage or facial or two (some cruise lines let you do this online), but do watch the cost. When you charge treatments to your onboard account, remember that gratuities are often added automatically (usually 10–15%).

Elixirs of youth, lotions and potions, creams and scrubs – all are sold by therapists, typically at the end of your treatment, as an ongoing recommendation for when you get home. But be warned, these are expensive items, and you could easily go over your vacation budget by such impetuous decisions when feeling relaxed (and vulnerable to sales talk).

● FITNESS CENTERS

Virtual-reality exercise machines are often found in the gymnasiums aboard the latest cruise ships, and state-of-the-art equipment is provided for body strengthening and toning, and cardiovascular workouts. Gymnasiums aboard many ships have personal trainers, as well as body fat analysis and other measurement items available at extra cost (example: $149 aboard *Queen Mary 2* on sea days).

Exercise classes typically include aerobics (aqua-robics, chair-obics), kick-boxing, group exercycling, yoga, and pilates. While many classes are free, some specialist classes cost extra.

Sports facilities might include basketball and paddle tennis (a sort of downsized tennis court), and electronic golf simulators. In addition, aboard some of the small "luxury" ships, facilities include kayaking, water-skiing, jet skiing, wake boarding, all included in the cruise fare. In reality, however, the watersports equipment is typically only used on one or two days during a 7-day cruise.

Sports Facilities

The variety of sports facilities on board depends on the size of the ship. Facilities typically include: badminton, basketball practice area, golf driving cage, horseshoes, jogging track, miniature putting green, paddle tennis, quoits, ring toss, shuffleboard, skeet shooting, squash (rarely), table tennis, and volleyball.

Sun

Cruising to the sun? Note that the closer you get to the equator the more potent and penetrating are the rays. They are most harmful when the sun is directly overhead. Use a protective sun lotion (15–30 factor), and reapply it every time you go for a swim or soak in the pool or ocean. Start with just 15 minutes' exposure and gradually work your way up to an hour or so. It is better to go home with a suntan than sunburn.

Surviving a Shipboard Fire

Shipboard fires generate heat, smoke, and often panic. In the unlikely event that you are in one, try to remain calm and think logically and clearly.

When you board the ship and get to your cabin, check the way to the nearest emergency exits fore and aft. Count the number of cabin doorways and other distinguishing features to the exits in case you have to escape without the benefit of lighting, or in case the passageway is filled with smoke and you cannot see clearly. New ships will use the "low location" lighting systems more and more, which are either the electroluminescent or photoluminescent type.

Exit signs are located just above floor level, but aboard older vessels the signs may be above your head, which is virtually useless, as smoke and flames always rise. Note the nearest fire alarm location and know how to use it in case of dense smoke and/or no lighting. In future, it is likely that directional sound evacuation beacons will be mandated; these will direct passengers to exits, escape-ways and other safe areas and appear to be better than the present inadequate visual aids.

If you are in your cabin and there is fire in the passageway outside, first put on your lifejacket and feel the cabin door. If the door handle is hot, soak a towel in water and use it to turn the handle of the door. If there is a raging fire in the passageway, cover yourself in wet towels and go through the flames. It may be your only means of escape, unless you have a balcony cabin.

Check the passageway. If there are no flames, or if everything looks clear, walk to the nearest emergency exit or stairway. If there is smoke in the passageway, crawl to the nearest exit. If the exit is blocked, then go to an alternate one. It may take considerable effort to open a heavy fire door to the exit. Don't use the elevators: they may stop at a deck that's on fire or full of smoke.

If there's a fire in your cabin, report it immediately by telephone. Then get out of your cabin if

A nursery pool to keep kids cool

you can and close the door behind you to prevent smoke or flames from entering the passageway. Finally, sound the alarm and alert your neighbors.

Swimming Pools

Most ships have outdoor or indoor swimming pools, or both. They may be closed in port owing to local health regulations and/or cleaning. Opening hours will be listed in the *Daily Program*. Diving is not allowed, since pools are shallow. Parents should note that most pools are unsupervised. Be aware that some ships use excessive chlorine or bleaching agents for cleaning; these could cause bathing suit colors to run.

Television

Television programming is obtained from a mixture of satellite feeds and onboard videos. Some ships can lock on to live international news programs (such as CNN or BBC World News), or to text-only news services. Satellite television reception is sometimes poor because ships constantly move out of the narrow beam transmitted from the satellite and they therefore cannot "track" the signal as accurately as a land-based facility.

Tipping (Gratuities)

Many travelers feel that the ship should host its passengers, and that the passengers should not host the crew by means of tips, so the question of tipping is awkward and embarrassing. In some ships, there are subtle suggestions made regarding tips; in others, cruise directors get carried away and are simply dictatorial regarding tipping.

Some ships offer hints on tipping via the in-cabin video system. Some cruise brochures state "tipping is not required." They may not be required, but will definitely be expected by the staff. Here are the accepted industry guidelines: **Dining room waiter**: $3–$4 per person per day; **Busboy**: $1.50–$2 per day; **Cabin steward or stewardess**: $3–$3.50 per person per day; **Butler**: $5–$6 per person per day.

Aboard many ships, a gratuity of 10 or 15 percent is automatically added to your bar check, whether you get good service or not.

Tips are normally given on the last evening of a cruise of up to 14 days' duration. For longer cruises, you would extend half of the tip halfway through and the rest on your last evening. *Note*: Aboard some Greek-flagged ships, gratuities are pooled and given to the chief steward, who gives them out at the end of each cruise ($8–$10 per person per day is the norm).

Gratuities are included in the cruise fare aboard a small number of ships (principally those in the luxury end of the market), where no extra tipping is permitted (in theory). Gratuities (at a rate of about $10 per person, per day) are increasingly being added automatically to onboard accounts by most of the major cruise lines.

Origin of the word "tip": Before postage

When show business goes to sea: the Las Vegas-like grand atrium of Carnival Cruise Lines' *Fascination.*

stamps were introduced in 1840, coachmen who transported passengers were often asked to carry a letter or other package. A small recompense was given for this service, called a "tip" – which stands for "to insure personal service." Hence, when in the future some special service was provided, particularly in the hospitality industry, tips became an accepted way of saying thank-you for services rendered.

Valuables

Many ships now have a small personal safe installed in each cabin. However, items of special value should be kept in a safety deposit box in the purser's office. You will then have simple and convenient access to your valuables during the cruise.

Visitors

Passes to enable friends and relations to see you on board prior to sailing must always be arranged in advance, preferably when you book. Clear announcements will be made when it is time for all visitors to go ashore. Unfortunately, bon voyage parties are virtually a thing of the past. They are no longer possible (with the exception of ships operating around-the-world cruises) owing to security concerns and insurance regulations.

Water Sports

Some small ships have a water sports platform that is lowered from the ship's stern or side. These ships carry windsurfers, waterski boats, jet skis, water skis, and scuba and snorkel equipment, usually at no extra charge. Some may also have an enclosed swimming "cage" for areas of the world where unpleasant fish might be lurking.

Although such facilities look good in the cruise brochures, in many cases ships seem reluctant to use them. This is because many itineraries have too few useful anchor ports. Also, the sea must be in an almost flat calm condition, which is seldom the case. Another more prosaic reason is simply because of strict insurance regulations.

Wine and Liquor

The cost of drinks on board is generally lower than on land, since ships have access to duty-free liquor. Drinks may be ordered in the dining room, at any of the ship's bars or from room service. Some lines charge "corkage," a fee to deter passengers from bringing their own wines into the dining room.

In the dining room, you can order wine with your meals from an extensive and reasonably priced wine list. For wine with your dinner, it's worth placing your order at lunchtime, as wine waiters are very busy during the evening meal.

In some ships, a duty-free sales point allows you to buy wine and liquor to drink in your cabin. You will not normally be permitted to bring these purchases into the dining room or public rooms, nor indeed any duty-free wine or liquor bought in port. These regulations are made to protect bar sales, a substantial source of onboard revenue. ❑

CUISINE

*Anyone wanting to eat 24 hours a day could do so aboard many ships,
and the variety of food would keep boredom at bay*

Dining is the single most talked- and written-about aspect of the cruise experience. There is a thrill of anticipation that comes with dining out in a fine restaurant – although the latest trend on land is towards less than thrilling "bistro" style eateries. The same is true aboard ship, where dining in elegant, friendly, and comfortable surroundings stimulates an appetite sharpened by the bracing sea air.

Attention to presentation, quality, and choice of menu in the honored tradition of the transatlantic luxury liners has made cruise ships justly famous. Cruise lines know that you will spend more time eating on board than doing anything else, so their intention is to cater well to your palate, within the confines of a predetermined budget. People enjoy the ceremony of dining and to feel that they are part of a performance. Presenting food has a show business element and some ships even have open or "show" kitchens in their specialty restaurants (examples: *Constellation, Infinity, Millennium, Queen Mary 2, Seven Seas Voyager, Summit*).

The "intelligent standardization" of the food operation and menus translates, of course, to cost-effectiveness in the process of food budgeting for any cruise line (the cost of such things as beef, fish and seafood went up by over 10 percent in 2003–4). Being able to rationalize expenditure *and* provide maximum passenger satisfaction is, therefore, quite a science today. Quite simply, *you get what you pay for*. Aboard low-priced cruises, you will get portion-controlled frozen food that has been reheated. To get fresh food (particularly fresh fish and the best cuts of meats), cruise lines must pay significantly more, adding to the cruise price. Unfortunately, the "fresh" fish (often described as "Catch of the Day") aboard some ships haven't had any contact with the sea for quite a long time.

Sushi bars have become the latest fad but, in 90% of cases, the sushi is cooked, and raw (sashimi-style) fish is not available, as storage and preparation facilities are inadequate. The *only* ships with authentic sushi bars and authentic sushi/sashimi are *Asuka* and *Crystal Serenity*.

Cruise lines boast about their food, but not all meals aboard all ships are gourmet affairs by any means. In general, cruise cuisine compares favorably with "banquet" food in a standard hotel or family restaurant – in other words, almost tasteless (unless it has been "enhanced" by chemical additives and food flavorings). Remember that high-quality food ingredients cost money, and therefore you should not expect low-cost cruises to offer anything other than low-cost food items.

Most ships cannot offer a real "gourmet" experience because the galley (ship's kitchen) may be striving to turn out hundreds of meals at the same time. What you *will* find is a good selection of palatable, pleasing, and complete meals served in comfortable surroundings, in the company of friends – and *you* do not have to do the cooking. Maybe you will even dine by candlelight, a pleasant way to spend any evening.

Food from hell

Experienced passengers have seen it, smelled it, and tasted it all before aboard ship: real rubber duck-foul (fowl) food, fit only to be stuffed, painted, and used as children's toys in their bathtubs. Talk about rock-hard lobster, fish with the elasticity of a baseball bat, inedible year-old shrimp, veterinarian-rejected chicken, and grenade-quality meats. Not to mention

Asian stir-fry aboard *Crystal Symphony*.

Fine dining is offered by the best ships – at a price.

teary-eyed or hammer-proof cheese, soggy salty crackers, unripe fruits, and coffee that looks (and tastes) like army surplus paint. Or yellow-green leaves that could be either garnish or an excuse for salad. Sadly, it is all there, in cruising's global cafeteria.

Most ships have self-serve buffets for breakfast and luncheon, one of the effects of discounted fares (and less staff are required). Strangely, passengers do not seem to mind lining up for self-service food (this somehow reminds me of school lunches). But while buffets look fine when they are fresh, after a few minutes of passengers serving themselves, they do not. And, one learns soon enough that otherwise sweet little old ladies can become ruthlessly competitive at buffet opening time. Passengers should not have to play guessing games when it comes to food, but many cruise lines forget to put labels on food items; this slows down any buffet line. Labels on salad dressings, sauces, and cheeses would be particularly useful.

Passengers have different tastes. Some like their food plain, while some like it spicy; some like *nouvelle cuisine*, some like meat and potatoes (and lots of it). Some try new things, some stick with the same old stuff. It is all a matter of personal taste. Cruise lines tend to cater to general tastes.

The best ships offer food cooked more or less individually to your liking. Some people are accustomed to drinking coffee out of polystyrene plastic cups and eating food off paper plates at home. Others wouldn't dream of doing that and expect fine dining, with food correctly served on fine china, just as they do at home.

If you are *left-handed*, tell your waiter at your first meal exactly how you want your cutlery placed and to make sure that tea or coffee cup handles are turned in the correct direction (this is impossible with a fish knife, of course). It would be better if right- or left-hand preferences were established when you book, and let the cruise line inform the ship.

Menus are typically displayed outside the dining room each day so that you can preview each meal. Suite occupants have menus delivered to their suite. When looking at the menu, you don't have to consider the price: it is all included.

Healthy Eating

With today's emphasis on low-cholesterol and low-salt diets, most ships have "spa" menus, with calorie-filled sauces replaced by spa cuisine. Some include basic nutritional information, such as the calorie count and fat, protein, and carbohydrate content, on their "spa" menus, or for selected "light" items on regular menus (mostly for dinner, seldom for breakfast or luncheon).

If you are vegetarian, vegan, macrobiotic, counting calories, want a salt-free, sugar-restricted, low-fat, low-cholesterol, or any other diet, advise your travel agent at the time of booking, and get the cruise line to confirm that the ship can actually handle your dietary requirements. Note that cruise ship food does tend to be liberally sprinkled with salt, and that vegetables are often cooked with sauces containing dairy products, salt, and sugar.

The Dining Room

Many ships contract the running and staffing of dining rooms to a specialist maritime catering organization. Ships that cruise far from their home country find that professional catering companies do an excellent job. However, ships that control their own catering staff and food often go to great lengths to ensure that their passengers are satisfied.

Which Seating?

Open Seating: It's also called Freestyle Dining (Norwegian Cruise Line), or Personal Choice Dining (Princess Cruises), this simply means that you can sit at *any* available table, with whomever *you* wish, at *whatever time* you choose (within dining room opening hours). So, just turn up, and you'll be seated – just like going out to a restaurant ashore. However, this is a little bit of an anomaly aboard large resort ships, as the principal entertainment program is typically set at two shows each night, which, in effect, limits your choice of dining times if you wish to catch a show.

Single Seating: you can choose *when* you wish to eat (within dining room hours) but have an assigned table for the cruise.

Two Seatings: you are assigned (or choose) one of two seatings, early or late. Typical meal times for two-seating ships are: Breakfast: 6.30am–8.30am; Lunch: 12 noon–1.30pm; Dinner: 6.30pm–8.30pm

Some ships operate two seatings only for dinner, while others operate on a two-seating arrangement for all meals.

Four Seatings: you choose the time, although once you decide you can't change it. Only Carnival Cruise Lines and Holland America Line currently operate four seatings, with dinner at 5.30pm, 6.45pm, 7.30pm or 8.45pm. However, two seatings apply aboard *Carnival Legend, Carnival Miracle, Carnival Pride* and *Carnival Spirit*.

Some ships that operate in Europe (the Mediterranean) or South America may have later meal times. Dinner hours may also vary when the ship is in port to allow for the timing of shore excursions.

Smoking/Nonsmoking

Many ships have totally nonsmoking dining rooms, while some provide smoking (cigarettes only, not cigars or pipes) and nonsmoking sections. Those wishing to sit in a no-smoking area should tell the restaurant manager when reserving a table. At open seating breakfasts and luncheons in the dining room (or informal buffet dining area), smokers and nonsmokers may be seated close together.

The Captain's Table

The captain usually occupies a large table in or near the center of the dining room on "formal" nights. The table seats eight or more people picked from the passenger or "commend" list by the hotel manager. If you are invited to the captain's table, it is gracious to accept, and you will have the chance to ask all the questions you like about shipboard life.

The Big 7 Cruise Lines: How They Score on Cuisine and Service

Food	Carnival Cruise Lines	Celebrity Cruises	Costa Cruises	Holland America Line	Norwegian Cruise Line	Princess Cruises	Royal Caribbean Int.
Dining Room/Cuisine	6.3	8.0	6.4	7.2	6.2	7.2	7.1
Buffets/Informal Dining	6.0	7.6	5.7	6.1	5.7	6.5	6.4
Quality of Ingredients	6.0	8.6	6.2	7.1	6.3	6.9	6.9
Afternoon Tea/Snacks	4.2	6.8	5.1	5.6	4.8	5.9	5.4
Wine List	7.8	8.2	5.6	6.0	6.1	6.6	6.1
Overall Food Score	6.06	7.84	5.8	6.4	5.82	6.62	6.38
Service							
Dining Rooms	5.8	8.3	6.1	7.0	6.7	7.3	7.2
Bars	6.8	8.0	6.4	7.1	6.8	7.5	7.3
Cabins	6.6	8.1	6.8	7.4	6.4	7.5	7.3
Open Decks	6.0	7.6	5.8	6.6	6.2	6.8	6.4
Wines	5.7	8.0	5.3	6.1	6.4	6.2	6.1
Overall Service Score	6.18	8.00	6.08	6.84	6.50	7.06	6.80
Combined food/service score	**6.12**	**7.92**	**5.94**	**6.62**	**6.16**	**6.84**	**6.59**

Dining Room Staff

The restaurant manager (also known as the Maître d' Hotel – not to be confused with the ship's Hotel Manager) is an experienced host, with shrewd perceptions about compatibility. It is his responsibility to seat you with compatible fellow passengers. If a reservation has been arranged prior to boarding, you will find a table assignment/ seating card in your cabin when you embark. If not, make your reservation with the restaurant manager or one of his assistants immediately after you embark.

Unless you are with your own family or group of friends, you will be seated next to strangers. Tables for two are a rarity; most tables seat four, six, or eight. It is a good idea to ask to be seated at a larger table, because if you are a couple seated at a table for four and you do not get along with your table partners, there is no one else to talk to. And remember, if the ship is full, it may be difficult to change tables once the cruise has started.

If you are unhappy with any aspect of the dining room operation, the sooner you tell someone the better. Don't wait until the cruise is over to send a scathing letter to the cruise line – it's too late then to do anything positive.

The best waiters are those trained in European hotels or hotel/catering schools. They excel in fine service and will learn your likes and dislikes quickly. They normally work aboard the best ships, where dignified professionalism is expected and living conditions are good.

A Typical Day

From morning till night (and beyond), food is offered to the point of overkill, even aboard the most modest cruise ship.

6am: hot coffee and tea on deck for early risers.
Full breakfast: typically with as many as 60 different items, in the main dining room. For a more casual meal, you can serve yourself buffet-style at an indoor/outdoor deck café (the choice may be more restricted than in the main dining room, yet adequate).

Lunchtime: with service in the dining room, buffet-style at an informal café, or at a separate grill for hot dogs and hamburgers, and a pizzeria, where everything is cooked right in front of you.

4pm: Afternoon tea, in the British tradition, complete with finger sandwiches and cakes. This may be served in one of the main lounges to the accompaniment of live music (it may even be a "tea-dance") or recorded classical music.

Dinner: the main event of the evening, and apart from the casualness of the first and last nights, it is formal in style.

Midnight Buffet: This is without a doubt the most famous of all shipboard meals. They are grand spreads, often based around a different theme each night, (seafood, Oriental, tropical fruit fantasy, chocoholic, etc.). There may be a Gala Midnight Buffet (usually on the penultimate evening), for which the chefs pull out all the stops.

Plate Service vs. Silver Service

Plate Service: When the food is presented as a complete dish, it is as the chef wants it to look; color combinations, the size of the component parts, and their positioning on the plate. All are important. In most cruise ships, "plate service" is now the norm. It works well and means that most people seated at a table will be served at the same time and can eat together, rather than let their food become cold, as can be the case with silver service.

Silver Service: When the component parts are brought to the table separately, so that the diner, not the chef, can choose what goes on the plate and in what proportion. Silver service is best when there is plenty of time (few cruise ships provide silver service today). What some cruise lines class as silver service is actually silver service of vegetables only, with the main item, be it fish, fowl, or meat, already positioned on the plate.

DID YOU KNOW?

● that there is an unwritten rule called "Ward's Third Law of Gluttony," which states that passengers will take precisely twice as much food as they need from breakfast and luncheon buffets, then add a lettuce leaf or two at dinner in order to justify the guilt complex brought about by over-consumption?

● that the liner *Amerika* in 1938 was the first ship to have an alternative restaurant open separately from the dining saloons? It was named the Ritz Carlton.

● that the first à la carte restaurant aboard a passenger ship was in the German ship *Amerika* of 1905?

● that the longest bar aboard any cruise ship can be found aboard *AIDAcara*? It is 195 feet (59.5 meters) long.

● that a whole county in Iowa raises all its beef cattle for Carnival Cruise Lines?

● that *Legend of the Seas* was christened with the world's largest bottle of champagne? It had to be specially made, and was a "Sovereign-size" bottle (the equivalent of 34 bottles) of Moët & Chandon champagne.

● that the United States Line's *Manhattan* in 1931 was the first ship to have a cocktail named after it – perhaps the only ship with that distinction?

● that 2,000 Methuselah-sized bottles (the equivalent of 12 bottles) of Cristal champagne were made specially for Crystal Cruises' passengers to purchase for the eve of the year 2000 (the millennium)? The cost: $2,000 each.

National Differences

The different nationalities among passengers present their own special needs and requirements. Here are some necessarily generalized examples:

Asian, British, German, and other European passengers like boiled eggs served in real china eggcups for breakfast. North Americans rarely eat boiled eggs, and most often put the eggs into a bowl and eat them with a fork.

German passengers tend to prefer breads (especially dark breads) and a wide variety of cheeses for breakfast and lunch. They tend to like yellow (not white) potatoes. They also have an obvious liking for German draught or bottled beers rather than American canned beers.

The French like soft – not flaky – croissants, and may request brioches and confitures.

Japanese passengers like "bento box" breakfasts of salmon and eel, and vegetable pickles, as well as Japanese rice (very different from Chinese rice).

Southern Italians like to have red sauce with just about everything, while northern Italians like less of the red sauces and more white sauces and flavorings, such as garlic, with their pasta.

Australian passengers like to have "vegemite" to spread on bread and toast.

North Americans like weak coffee with everything – often before, during, and after a meal. This is why, even on the most upscale ships, sugar is placed on tables (also for iced tea). North Americans tend to eat and run, whereas Europeans dine in a more leisurely fashion, treating mealtimes as a social occasion.

Most passengers agree that cruise coffee is

Inspirational dining experience aboard the Inspiration.

appalling, but often it is simply the chlorinated water that gives it a different taste. Europeans prefer strong coffee, usually made from the coffee beans of African countries such as Kenya. North Americans usually drink the coffee from Colombia or Jamaica.

European tea drinkers prefer teacups, not coffee or sports mugs (very few cruise ships know how to make a decent cup of tea, so British passengers in particular should be aware of this).

Alternative Dining

A number of ships now have "alternative" dining rooms, for which reservations are needed (make them early aboard large ships). These typically incur an extra charge ($20–$25 a person), for which you get much better food, presentation and service than in the ship's main dining room(s), which tend to be large and noisy. The costs can quickly add up, just as when you dine out ashore. As an example, take David's Supper Club aboard *Carnival Pride*. The food is excellent (but the portions are large), and the ambiance is quiet and refined, but if you are a couple and you have just two glasses of wine each (Grgich Hills Chardonnay, for example, at $12.50 a glass), and pay the cover charge, that's $100 for dinner (if you want caviar, add $29 for a 1-ounce serving).

The Executive Chef

The executive chef plans the menus, orders the food, organizes his staff, and arranges all the meals on the menus. He makes sure that menus are not repeated, even on long cruises. On some cruises, he works with guest chefs from restaurants ashore to offer tastes of regional cuisine. He may also purchase fish, seafood, fruit, and various other local produce in "wayside" ports and incorporate them into the menu with a "special of the day" announcement.

The Galley

The galley ("kitchen") is the heart of all food preparation on board. At any time of the day or night, there is plenty of activity, whether it is baking fresh bread at 2am, making meals and snacks for passengers and crew around the clock, or decorating a special birthday cake. The staff, from executive chef to pot-washer, all work together as a team, each designated a specific role, with little room for error.

The galley and preparation areas consist of the following sections (the names in parentheses are the French names given to the person who is the specialist in the area of expertise):

Fish Preparation Area (Poisonnier): This area contains freezers and a fully equipped preparation room, where fish is cleaned and cut to size before it is sent to the galley.

Meat Preparation Area (Butcher/Rotisseur): This area contains separate freezers for meat and poultry. Their temperatures are kept at around 10°F (–17°C). There are also defrosting areas kept at 35°–40°F (2°–4°C). Meat and poultry are sliced and portioned before being sent to the galley.

Vegetable Preparation Area (Entremetier): Vegetables are cleaned and prepared in this area.

Sauce Preparation Area (Saucier): This is where the sauces are prepared.

What's on the Menu

HEALTHY CHOICE MENU
Our Healthy Choice Menu reflects today's awareness of lighter, more balanced diets. In response to these nutritional needs, Princess Cruises offers dishes that are low in cholesterol, fat, and sodium but high in flavor.
USA: Fresh Fruit Cup California Style
China: Won Ton and Vegetable Soup
New Zealand: John Dory Fillet Maori Style
Austria: Kranz Cake, Warm Vanilla Custard Sauce

VEGETARIAN MENU
USA: Fresh Fruit Cup California Style
Greece: Greek Salad, Mediterranean Dressing
Italy: Risotto with Asparagus
France: Puff Pastry Vegetable Roll with Tomato Sauce
Switzerland: Vacherin Suisse
Assorted International Cheese and Crackers

ALWAYS AVAILABLE
Classic Caesar Salad
Broiled North Sea Silver Salmon Fillet
Grilled Skinless Chicken Breast
Grilled Black Angus Sirloin Steak
Baked Potato and French Fries can be requested in addition to the daily vegetable selection.

APPETIZERS
Italy: Cocktail di Granseola Costa Esmeralda
Crabmeat Served in Half Cantaloupe Melon with Aurora Sauce
France: Smoked Breast of Strasbourg Duckling

England: Cured York Rolls on a Bed of Fresh Baby Leaves
USA: Fresh Fruit Cup California Style

SOUPS
China: Won Ton and Vegetable Soup
Scotland: Mutton and Barley Soup
Polynesia: Chilled Tropical Fresh Fruit Cream Soup

SALAD
Greece: Greek Salad, Mediterranean Dressing

PRINCESS FAVORITE
Italy: Risotto con Pollo e Asparagi
A Combination of Italian Carnaroli Rice with Green Asparagus Tips and Strips of Chicken Finished with Freshly Grated Parmesan Cheese and Herbs

ENTRÉES
New Zealand: John Dory Fillet Maori Style
Norway: Rainbow Trout Seven Sisters Fjord Fashion
Poached and Served with a Delicate Dill Sauce. Potatoes au Gratin
Holland: Glazed Milk-Fed Veal Leg Ancienne
Sliced and Served with a Mushroom Morel Cream Sauce, Hollandaise Potatoes
Australia: Oven-Baked Spring Leg of Lamb Aussie Style
Coated with Mustard and Aromatic Herbs Flavored with Mint
USA: Surf and Turf
Filet Mignon and Jumbo Shrimp from the Grill with Browned Red New Potatoes and Bâtonnet Vegetables

The main dining room aboard *Adventure of the Seas.*

Soup Preparation Area (Potagier): Soups are made in huge tureens.

Cold Kitchen (Garde Manger): This is the area where all cold dishes and salads are prepared, from the simplest sandwich (for room service, for example) to the works of art that grace the buffets. The area is well equipped with mixing machines, slicing machines, and refrigeration cabinets where prepared dishes are stored until required.

Bakery and Pastry Shop (Baker): This area provides the raw ingredients for preparing food, and contains dough mixers, refrigerators, proving ovens, ovens, and containers in all shapes and sizes. Dessert items, pastries, sweets, and other confectionery are prepared and made here.

Pantry: This is where cheese and fruits are prepared, and where sandwiches are made.

Dishwashing Area: This area contains huge conveyor-belt dishwashing machines. Wash and rinse temperatures are carefully controlled to comply with public health regulations. This is where all cooking utensils are scrubbed and cleaned, and where the silverware is scrupulously polished.

Hygiene Standards

Galley equipment is in almost constant use, and regular inspections and maintenance help detect potential problems. There is continual cleaning of equipment, utensils, bulkheads, floors, and hands.

Cruise ships sailing from or visiting US ports are subject to in-port sanitation inspections. These are voluntary, not mandatory inspections, based on 42 inspection items, undertaken by the United States Public Health (USPH) Department of Health and Human Services, under the auspices of the Centers for Disease Control. The cruise line pays for each ship inspection. A similar process takes place in Britain under the Port Health Authority, which has even more stringent guidelines and requirements.

A tour of the galley proves to be a highlight for some passengers, when a ship's insurance company permits. A video of *Behind the Scenes*, for use on in-cabin television, may be provided instead.

In accordance with internationally accepted standards, all potable water brought on board, or produced by distillation aboard cruise ships, should contain a free chlorine or bromine residual equal to or greater than 0.2 ppm (parts per million). This is why drinking water served in the dining room often tastes of chlorine.

Waste Disposal

Cruise ships must be capable of efficient handling of garbage and waste materials, as trash generated by passengers and crew must be managed, stored, and disposed of efficiently and economically. The larger the ship, the more waste is created, and the greater the need for reliable disposal systems.

Trash includes bottles, cans, corrugated cartons, fabrics, foodstuffs, paper products, plastic containers, as well as medical waste, sludge oil, wet waste, and so on. The sheer magnitude of waste materials can be highly problematic, especially on long cruises. If solid waste is not burnable, or cannot be disposed of overboard (this must be biodegradable), it must be stored for later off-loading and disposal on land.

The latest breed of cruise ships is equipped with "zero-discharge" facilities. These include incinerators and food waste handling systems that include vacuum transportation from feeding station in all galleys and food preparation areas, recycling and storage systes for ash, glass, metal and paper. But many older cruise ships still have a way to go when it comes to garbage handling. One method of dealing with food waste is to send it to a waste-pulping machine that has been partially filled with water. Cutting mechanisms reduce the waste and allow it to pass through a special sizing ring to be pumped directly overboard or into a holding tank or an incinerator when the ship is within three-mile limits.

Whichever method of waste disposal is chosen, it, as well as the ship, must meet the extremely stringent demands of Annex V of MARPOL 73/78 international regulations.

Caviar

This has been valued for thousands of years: in 40 BC Marc Anthony's wife in Rome received word of the banquets her husband enjoyed with Cleopatra, queen of Egypt, at Alexandria. "We feast on the finest fresh sturgeon and golden caviar from the Caspian Sea…" Although it might seem like it from menu descriptions, most ships do not serve Beluga caviar (the best and most sought after), but the less expensive and more widely available Sevruga and Sevruga Malossol (low-salt) caviar. Even more widely served aboard the large, standard cruise ships is Norwegian lumpfish "caviar." If you are partial to the best caviar, you might want to know that Cunard Line is reputed to be the world's largest single buyer of caviar (spending about $500,000 a year), after the Russian and the Ukrainian governments.

Those who have not tasted good caviar may find it very salty. That's because the eggs are taken fresh from a sleeping female sturgeon (it takes about 20 years for a female beluga sturgeon to mature, and caviar is taken from onlh three of 29 varieties of female sturgeon). The eggs are then passed through a screen to separate them from other fibrous matter, then mixed with salt, which acts as a preservative and also promotes the taste. The more salt added, the better the caviar is preserved; the less salt added the finer the taste.

The process is done by highly skilled labor, which adds to its cost. The two countries that produce most of the world's caviar are Iran and Russia (both countries produce farmed sturgeon stock, which is released into the Caspian Sea continually to replenish dwindling stocks). In general, Russian caviar is more highly salted than caviar from Iran. And just as each vineyard produces different wines, so each fishery will produce different-tasting caviar. Additionally, there are about 400 species of sturgeon, so grades can differ.

The Caspian Sea is the spawning ground for 90 percent of the world's caviar-producing sturgeon. There are three types that are sought:

● The giant beluga is hardest to find and the most expensive. It can weigh 1,500 pounds (680 kg) or more. One fish can yield up to 20 pounds (9 kg) of caviar, and its smoky-gray eggs are the largest (they are also the most delicate).

● The ossetra this takes about 13 years to mature, and weighs up to 40 pounds (18 kg). These are the most durable eggs (they are also smaller) and range in color from a darkish brass to olive green.

● The sevruga weighs about six pounds. It also has small eggs, ranging in color from soft gray to dark gray.

There is also a fourth type of sturgeon, known as a sterlet, which produces a translucent golden egg, although it is hard to find (before 1917 all the golden caviar was sent to the Tsar in Russia).

There was a time when sturgeon was found in abundance. So much so that caviar was often placed on the bars of London and New York as a snack to promote the sale of beer and ale. Caviar is a natural accompaniment for good champagne, but good champagne (like anything else of high quality) doesn't come cheap. What most ships use as champagne, for the Captain's Welcome Aboard Cocktail Party, for example, just about passes as champagne. Some ships feature a caviar and champagne bar on board, offering several varieties of caviar at extra cost.

Champagne

Champagne making is a real art (in France itself the production of Champagne is restricted to a very small geographic area). Unlike wine, it is bottled in many sizes, ranging from the minute to the

What Wine Costs		
CELLAR MASTER SUGGESTIONS		
	Glass	Bottle
Fumé Blanc Robert Mondavi,		
Napa Valley	$5.50	$21.00
Chardonnay Cuvaison,		
Napa Valley		$34.00
Cabernet Sauvignon Wente		
Estate, Livermore Valley	$5.50	$22.00
Cabernet Sauvignon Guenoc		
Estate, Lake County		$24.00

ridiculously huge, and with a confusing variety of names to match:

Quarter bottle	18.7 centiliters
Half bottle (split)	37.5 centiliters
Bottle	75 centiliters
Magnum	2 bottles
Jeroboam	4 bottles
Rehoboam	6 bottles
Methuselah	8 bottles
Salmanazar	12 bottles
Balthazar	16 bottles
Nebuchadnezzar	20 bottles

The three main grape-growing districts in Champagne are: the Montagne de Reims, to the south and east of Reims; the Vallée de la Marne, surrounding the river; and the Côtes des Blancs, south of Epernay. The first two mainly grow the dark pinot-noir and pinot-meunier grapes; the latter grows the white chardonnay variety (all are used in making champagne). Removing the husks before full fermentation prevents the dark grapes from coloring the wine red. For pink champagne, the skins are left in the grape mix for a longer time to add color.

Although the Champagne area has been producing wines of renown for a long time, its vintners were unable to keep their bubbles from fizzling out until Dom Perignon, a monk in the Abbey of Hautvilliers, came up with the solution. The bubbles – escaping carbonic acid gas – had always escaped, until Dom Perignon devised a bottle capable of containing the champagne without it exploding from the bottle, a common occurrence in local cellars.

The legacy of this clever monk is that the

A cruise is a good way to celebrate an anniversary.

champagne bottle is the strongest bottle made today. Its thickness is concentrated around the bottle's base and shoulders. Dom Perignon's bottle was aided by the coincidental development of the cork.

Even after his work, champagne was not the perfect elixir enjoyed today. It was rather cloudy due to residual sediment (dead yeast cells). Its bubbles, therefore, could not be truly relished visually until la Veuve Cliquot (the Widow Cliquot) devised the system of *remuage* in the 19th century. Rather than laying the bottles down horizontally for their period of aging, she put them in a special rack, called a pupitre, which held them at a 45-degree angle, with the neck of the bottle facing down. Each day, the bottles are given a short, sharp, quarter turn so as to shake the sediment, which gradually settles in the neck of the bottle.

Once this is complete, a process called *dégorgement* freezes the neck of the bottle. It is then uncorked and internal pressure ejects the ice containing the sediment. Obviously, this means that the bottle is a little less than totally full, so the champagne is topped up with what is called the *dosage*, which is a sweet champagne liqueur.

The degree of sweetness of this addition depends on the tastes of the market to which the champagne is ultimately destined. After the *dosage* is added, the permanent cork is forced in and wired up. The bottles then remain in the cellar of the winery until they are ordered. Each bottle is then washed and labeled prior to being shipped for sale. ❏

ENTERTAINMENT ABOARD

After food, the most subjective part of any mainstream cruise is the
entertainment, which has to be diversified and innovative but never controversial

Ask 1,000 people what they'd like to see as part of any evening entertainment program, and you'll get 1,000 different answers. It's all a matter of personal taste and choice. Whatever one expects, the days are gone when you would have been entertained by waiters doubling as singers, although a few bar waiters are still known to perform tray-spinning effects to boost their tips.

Many passengers, despite having paid so little for their cruise, expect to see top-notch entertainment, "headline" marquee-name cabaret artists, the world's most "popular" singers, and the most dazzling shows with slick special effects, just as one would find in the best venues in Las Vegas, London, or Paris. There are many reasons why it is not exactly so. International star acts invariably have an entourage that accompanies them to any venue: their personal manager, their musical director (often a pianist or conductor), a rhythm section (with bass player and drummer), even their hairdresser. On land, one-night shows are possible, but with a ship, an artist cannot always disembark after just one night, especially when it involves moving equipment, costumes,

Some of the larger ships mount spectacular shows.

and baggage. This makes the whole matter logistically and financially unattractive for all but the very largest ships on fixed itineraries, where a marquee-name act might be a marketing plus.

When you are at home you can bring the world's top talent into your home via television. Cruise ships are a different matter. Most entertainers don't like to be away from their "home base" for long periods, as they rely on telephone contact. Most don't like the long contracts that the majority of ships must offer in order to amortize the cost.

So many acts working aboard cruise ships are interchangeable with so many other acts also working aboard cruise ships. Ever wonder why? Entertainers aboard ship must also *live* with their audiences for several days (sometimes weeks) – something unheard-of on land – as well as work on stages aboard older ships that weren't designed for live performances. However, there is no question that cruise ships are the new location for vaudeville acts, where a guaranteed audience is a bonus for many former club-date acts, as well as fresh acts trying to break in to the big time on land.

Many older (pre-1980) ships have extremely limited entertainment spaces, and very few ships provide proper dressing rooms and backstage

facilities for the storage of costumes, props, or effects, not to mention the extensive sound and lighting equipment most live "name" artists demand or need. Only the latest ships provide the extensive facilities needed for presenting the kind of high-tech shows one would find in Las Vegas, London, or New York, for example. These feature elaborate electronic backdrops, revolving stages, orchestra pits, multi-slide projection, huge stage-side video screens, pyrotechnic capabilities, and the latest light-mover and laser technology. Even the latest ships often lack enough dressing room and hanging space for the 150 costumes required in a single typical ship production show.

However, more emphasis has been placed on entertainment since the mid-1970s. Entertainment in today's large resort ships is market-driven. In other words, it is directed toward that segment of the industry that the cruise line's marketing department is specifically targeting (discounting notwithstanding). This is predominantly a family audience, so the fare must appeal to as broad an age range as possible – a tall order for any cruise line's director of entertainment.

A cruise line with several ships in its fleet will normally employ an entertainment department comprising an entertainment director and several assistants, and most cruise lines have contracts with one or more entertainment agencies that specialize in entertainment for cruise ships.

It is no use, for example, in a company booking a juggler who needs a floor-to-ceiling height of 12 feet but finds that the ship has a show lounge with a height of just 7 feet (although I did overhear one cruise director ask if the act "couldn't he juggle sideways"); or an acrobatic knife-throwing act (in a moving ship?); or a concert pianist when the ship only has an upright honky-tonk piano; or a singer who sings only in English when the passengers are German-speaking.

Indeed, the hardest audience to cater to is one of mixed nationalities (each of whom will expect entertainers to cater exclusively to their particular linguistic group). Given that cruise lines are now marketing to more international audiences in order to fill ships, the problem of finding the right entertainment is far more acute.

The more upscale cruise lines (typically those operating small ships) offer more classical music, even some light opera, more guest lecturers and top authors than the seven-day package cruises heading for warm-weather destinations.

Part of the entertainment experience aboard large cruise ships is the glamorous "production show," the kind of show you would expect to see in any good Las Vegas show palace, with male and female lead singers and Marilyn Monroe look-alike dancers, a production manager, lavish backdrops, extravagant sets, grand lighting, special effects, and stunning custom-designed costumes. Unfortunately, many cruise line executives, who know little or nothing about entertainment, still regard plumes and huge feather boas paraded by showgirls who *step*, but don't *dance*, as being desirable. Some cruise ships have coarse shows that are not becoming to either

DID YOU KNOW?

● that Roy, of the famous Siegfried & Roy (Siegfried Fischbacher and Roy Uwe Ludwig Horn) illusion act, used to be a steward aboard the German liner *Bremen*? Siegfried was a bartender aboard the same ship. That's how they met.

● that musical instruments of some of the stars of rock and pop can be found aboard Holland America Line's *Zaandam*? They were acquired from the "Pop and Guitars" auction at Christie's in London, and a Fender Squire Telecaster guitar signed by Mick Jagger, Keith Richards, Charlie Watts, Ronnie Wood and Bill Wyman of The Rolling Stones; A Conn Saxophone signed on the mouthpiece by former US President Bill Clinton; an Ariana acoustic guitar signed by David Bowie and Iggy Pop; a Fender Stratocaster guitar signed in silver ink by the members of the rock band Queen; a Bently "Les Paul" style guitar signed by various artists, including Carlos Santana, Eric Clapton, BB King, Robert Cray, Keith Richards and Les Paul.

● that the Cunard White Star Line's *Queen Mary* was the first ship to have a system of colored lights that varied according to music (chromsonics)?

● that Verdi wrote an opera to commemorate the opening of the Suez Canal? Its name is *Aïda*.

● that the 212-passenger *Seabourn Legend* was the star of the film *Speed 2: Cruise Control*, released in 1997 in the US? The film was shot on location in Marigot, the capital of the French side of the tiny two-nation Caribbean island of St. Martin/St. Maarten. The filming called for the building of almost a complete "town" at Marigot, into which the ship crashes.

● that *Titanic*, the stage musical, cost $10 million to mount in New York in 1997? That's $2.5 million more than it cost to build the original ship that debuted in 1912. The play debuted at the Lunt-Fontanne Theater in April 1997 (the ship sank on April 14, 1912).

● that the Hollywood film that cost the most money – but also made the most – was based aboard a passenger liner? The film, *Titanic*, was released in 1997.

● that the cruise ship used in the 1974 movie *Juggernaut*, in which seven bombs in oil drums were placed aboard, was *Maxim Gorkiy*? The film starred Richard Harris, Omar Sharif, David Hemmings, and Anthony Hopkins.

dancer or passenger. Such things went out of vogue about 20 years ago. Shows that offer more creative costuming and real dancing win more votes today.

Book back-to-back seven-day cruises (on alternating eastern and western Caribbean itineraries, for example), and you should note that entertainment is generally geared to seven-day cruises. Thus, you will probably find the same two or three production shows and the same acts on the second week of your cruise. The way to avoid seeing everything twice is to pace yourself. Go to some shows during the first week and save the rest for the second week.

Regular passengers will notice that they seem to see the same acts time after time on various ships. For the reasons given above (and more), the criteria narrow the field even though there are many fine land-based acts. In addition, ship entertainers need to enjoy socializing. Successful shipboard acts tend to be good mixers, are presentable when in public, do not do drugs or take excess alcohol, are not late for rehearsals, and must cooperate with the cruise director and his or her staff as well as with the band.

Sadly, with cruise lines forever looking for ways to cut costs, entertainment has of late been a major target for some companies (particularly the smaller operators). Cutting costs translates to

Music aboard cruise ships caters for many tastes.

bringing on, for example, lower-cost singers (who often turn out to be non-reading, vocally-challenged persons) and bands that cannot read charts (musician-speak for musical arrangements) brought on board by cabaret acts.

Show Biz at Sea

In today's high-tech world, staging a lavish 45 to 50-minute production show involves the concerted efforts of a range of experienced people, and a cost of $500,000 to $1 million a show isn't unheard-of. Weekly running costs (performers' salaries, costume cleaning and repair, royalties, replacement audio and videotapes, and so on) all add up to an expensive package for what can be a largely unappreciative and critical audience.

Other Entertainment

Most cruise ships organize acts that, while perhaps not nationally recognized "names," can provide two or three different shows during a seven-day cruise. These will be male/female singers, illusionists, puppeteers, hypnotists, and even circus acts, with wide age-range appeal.

There are comedians and comedy duos who perform "clean" material and who may find employment year-round on what is now known as the "cruise ship circuit." These popular comics enjoy good accommodation, are stars while on board, and often go from ship to ship on a standard rotation every few days. There are raunchy, late-night "adults only" comedy acts in some of the ships with younger, "hip" audiences, but few have enough material for several shows.

The larger a ship, the larger the entertainment program will be. In some ships, the cruise director may "double" as an act, but most companies prefer him/her to be strictly an administrative and social director, allowing more time to be with passengers. Most passengers find that being entertained "live" is an experience far superior to that of sitting at home in front of a television set, watching its clinical presentation.

Playing the game

Television game shows should be the next audience participation event aboard the large resort ships with the huge showlounges. Disney Cruise Line has "Who Wants to be a Mouseketeer?" These professionally produced game shows, licensed from television companies, involve all passengers seated in the show lounge because interactive buttons are wired into every seat. They are great fun, and provide good entertainment. While they are quite expensive to mount, they provide something different from the costumed production show extravaganzas that cost the cruise lines millions to produce. ❏

THE SHIP'S COMPANY

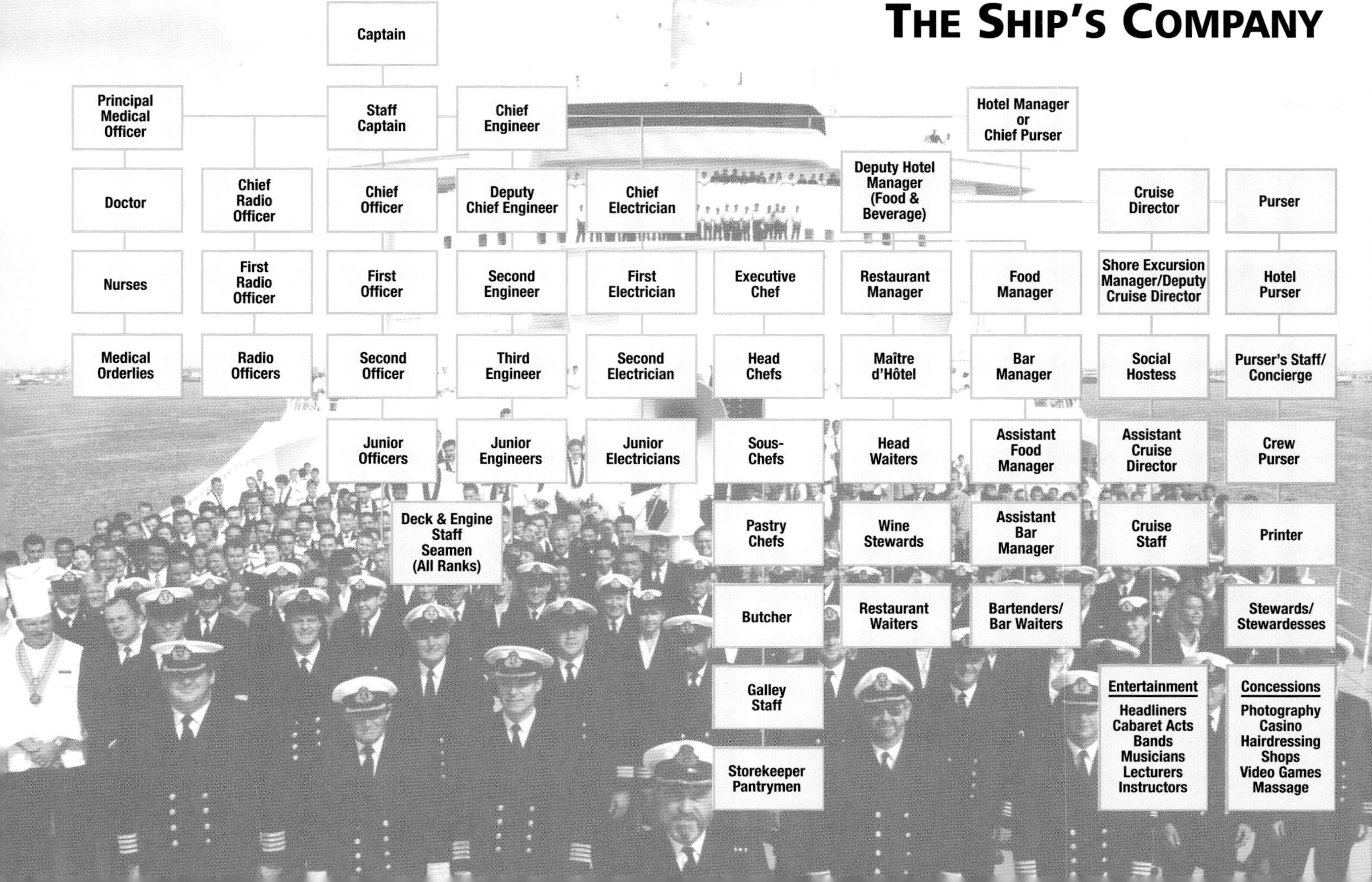

Medical

- Principal Medical Officer
  - Doctor
  - Nurses
  - Medical Orderlies

Command / Deck

- Captain
  - Staff Captain
    - Chief Officer
    - First Officer
    - Second Officer
    - Junior Officers
      - Deck & Engine Staff Seamen (All Ranks)

Radio

- Chief Radio Officer
  - First Radio Officer
  - Radio Officers

Engineering

- Chief Engineer
  - Deputy Chief Engineer
  - Second Engineer
  - Third Engineer
  - Junior Engineers

Electrical

- Chief Electrician
  - First Electrician
  - Second Electrician
  - Junior Electricians

Hotel

- Hotel Manager or Chief Purser
  - Deputy Hotel Manager (Food & Beverage)
    - Executive Chef
      - Head Chefs
      - Sous-Chefs
      - Pastry Chefs
      - Butcher
      - Galley Staff
      - Storekeeper Pantrymen
    - Restaurant Manager
      - Maître d'Hôtel
      - Head Waiters
      - Wine Stewards
      - Restaurant Waiters
    - Food Manager
      - Assistant Food Manager
    - Bar Manager
      - Assistant Bar Manager
      - Bartenders/Bar Waiters

Cruise

- Cruise Director
  - Shore Excursion Manager/Deputy Cruise Director
  - Social Hostess
  - Assistant Cruise Director
  - Cruise Staff
  - **Entertainment**
    - Headliners
    - Cabaret Acts
    - Bands
    - Musicians
    - Lecturers
    - Instructors

Purser

- Purser
  - Hotel Purser
  - Purser's Staff/Concierge
  - Crew Purser
  - Printer
  - Stewards/Stewardesses
  - **Concessions**
    - Photography
    - Casino
    - Hairdressing
    - Shops
    - Video Games
    - Massage

Western Mediterranean

Eastern Mediterranean

The Baltic and Northern Europe

While *Crystal Symphony* contains a cinema, Sydney provides an opera house.

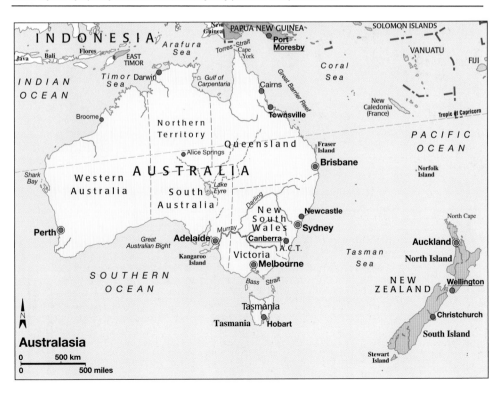

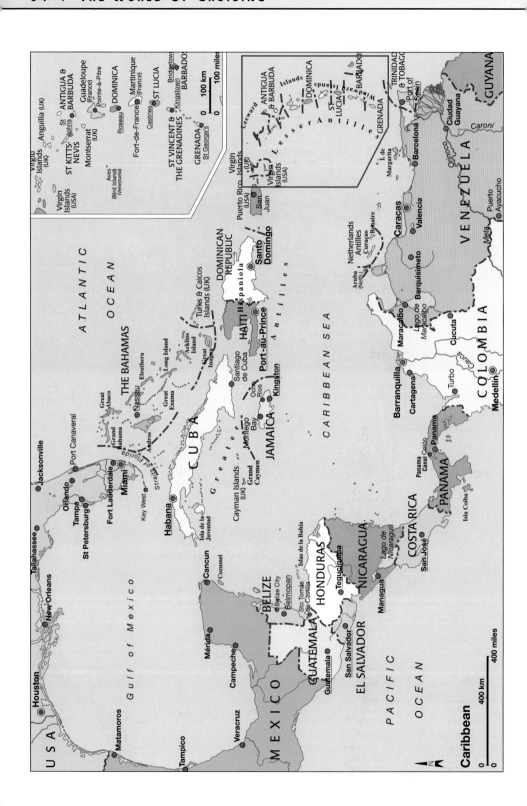

Caribbean

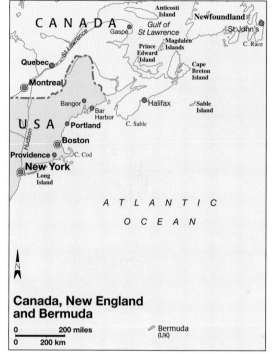

Canada, New England and Bermuda

CANADA

Anticosti Island
Newfoundland
Gulf of St Lawrence
St John's
C. Race
Gaspe
Prince Edward Island
Magdalen Islands
Quebec
St Lawrence
Montreal
Cape Breton Island
Bangor
Bar Harbor
Halifax
Sable Island
USA
Portland
C. Sable
Hudson
Boston
Providence
C. Cod
New York
Long Island

ATLANTIC OCEAN

0   200 miles
0   200 km

Bermuda (UK)

United Kingdom

0   200 km
0   200 miles

NORTH SEA

Portree
Scotland
Dundee
Greenock
Kirkcaldy
Edinburgh (Leith)
Glasgow
N. Ireland
Newcastle-upon-Tyne
Belfast
IRELAND
Irish Sea
UNITED
Liverpool
Hull
Dublin
Holyhead
England
KINGDOM
Cobh
Wales
Birmingham
Harwich
Celtic Sea
Cardiff
London
Southampton
Fowey
Dover
Penzance
Falmouth
Plymouth
Dartmouth
Weymouth
Poole
English Channel
FRANCE

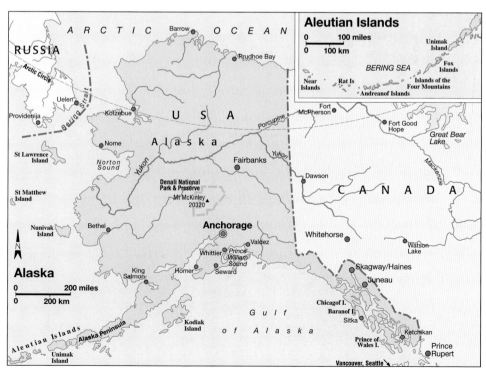

Aleutian Islands

0   100 miles
0   100 km

Unimak Island
BERING SEA
Fox Islands
Near Islands
Rat Is
Islands of the Four Mountains
Andreanof Islands

Alaska

ARCTIC OCEAN
Barrow
RUSSIA
Prudhoe Bay
Arctic Circle
Uelen
Fort McPherson
Fort Good Hope
Providenija
Kotzebue
USA
Porcupine
Great Bear Lake
Bering Strait
Alaska
Mackenzie
Nome
Norton Sound
Yukon
Fairbanks
Yukon
Dawson
St Lawrence Island
St Matthew Island
Denali National Park & Preserve
Mt McKinley 20320
CANADA
Nunivak Island
Bethel
Anchorage
Whitehorse
Watson Lake
Valdez
Whittier
Prince William Sound
King Salmon
Homer
Seward
Skagway/Haines
Juneau
0   200 miles
0   200 km
Gulf
Chicagof I.
Baranof I.
Sitka
Kodiak Island
of Alaska
Ketchikan
Aleutian Islands
Alaska Peninsula
Prince of Wales I.
Prince Rupert
Unimak Island
Vancouver, Seattle

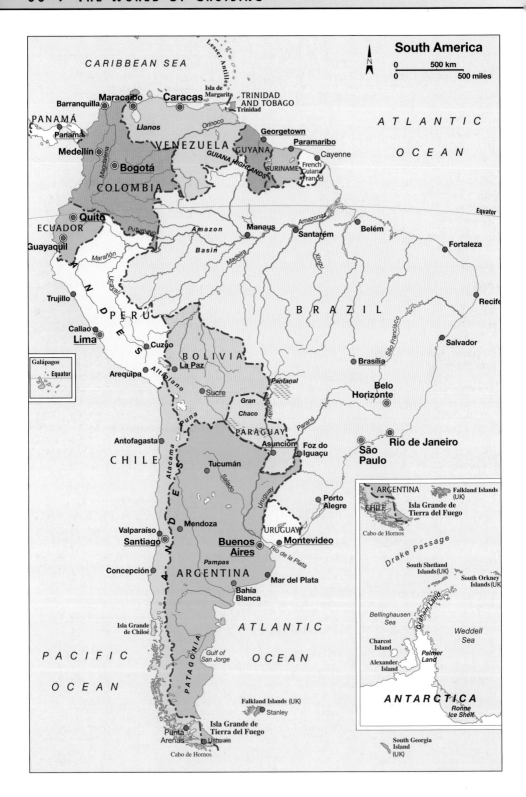

WHERE TO?

Cruise lines currently visit just under 2,000 destinations, so there's almost certainly a ship to take you where you want to go

Because itineraries vary widely, depending on each ship and cruise, it is wise to make as many comparisons as you can by reading the cruise brochures for descriptions of the ports of call. Several ships may offer the same or similar itineraries simply because these have been tried and tested. Narrow the choice further by noting the time spent at each port, and whether the ship actually docks in port or lies at anchor. Then, compare the size of each vessel and its facilities.

Caribbean Cruises

There are over 7,000 islands in the Caribbean Sea, although many are small or uninhabited. Caribbean cruises are usually destination-intensive cruises in a warm, sunny climate that cram between four and eight ports into one week, depending on whether you sail from a Florida port or from a port already in the Caribbean, such as Barbados or San Juan. This means you could be visiting at least one port a day, with little time at sea for relaxation. This kind of island-hopping leaves little time to explore a destination. Although you see a lot of places in a week, by the end of the cruise you may need another week to unwind. *Note*: June to November is hurricane season in the Caribbean (including the Bahamas and Florida).

● **Eastern Caribbean** cruises include ports such as Barbados, Dominica, Martinique, Puerto Rico, St. Croix, St. Kitts, St. Martin, and St. Thomas.
● **Western Caribbean** cruises typically include ports such as Calica, Cozumel, Grand Cayman, and Playa del Carmen.
● **Southern Caribbean** cruises typically include ports such as Antigua, Aruba, Barbados, La Guaira (Venezuela), and Grenada.

Private Islands

Several cruise lines with Bahamas/Caribbean itineraries feature a "private island" (also called an "out-island"). This is a small island close to Nassau in the Bahamas outfitted with all the ingredients to make an all-day beach party a "nice day out." Also available are water sports, scuba, snorkeling, crystal-clear waters, warm sands, even a hammock or two, and, possibly, massage in a beach cabana. There are no reservations to make, no tickets to buy, and no hassles with taxis. But be aware that you may be sharing your private island with more than 2,000 others from a large ship anchored for a "beach barbecue."

One bonus is that a "private island" will not be cluttered with hawkers and hustlers, as are so many Caribbean beaches. And, because they *are* private, there is security, and no fear of passengers being mugged, as occurs in some islands.

Private island beach days are not all-inclusive, however, and attract high prices for snorkel gear (and mandatory swim vest), pleasure craft, and "banana" boat fun rides; it has become yet another way for cruise lines to increase revenue. However, it costs a lot of money to develop a private island. Examples: Disney Cruise Line spent $25 million developing and outfitting Castaway Cay (formerly known as Gorda Cay), while Holland America Line spent $16 million developing Half Moon Cay.

Europe/Mediterranean Cruises

Traveling within Europe (including the Baltic, Black Sea, Mediterranean, and Norwegian fjord areas) makes economic sense. Although no single cruise covers every port, cruise ships do offer a comfortable way of exploring the area's rich mix of cultures, his-

Private Islands

Cruise Line	Name of Island	Location	First Used	Berlitz Rating (out of 10)
Celebrity Cruises	Catalina Island	Dominican Republic	1995	5.7
Costa Cruises	Serena Cay	Dominican Republic	1996	5.7
Disney Cruise Line	Castaway Cay	Bahamas	1998	8.5
Holland America Line	Half Moon Cay	Bahamas	1997	8.6
Norwegian Cruise Line	Great Stirrup Cay	Bahamas	1977	7.5
Princess Cruises	Princess Bay	Mayreau, Genadines	1986	7.3
Princess Cruises	Princess Cays	Eleuthera, Bahamas	1992	7.5
Royal Caribbean International	Coco Cay	Bahamas	1990	6.4
Royal Caribbean International	Labadee	Haiti	1986	7.2

Greece and its islands – a classic cruise destination.

tory, traditions, architecture, lifestyles and cuisines. For some, the appeal is mainly the educational experience of sampling unfamilar cultures and the chance to sail the Mediterranean's azure waters that have inspired writers ever since Homer ("To dream and dream…" he wrote in *The Iliad*). For others, it is the chance to have a safe, crime-free holiday – something that cannot always be guaranteed on land.

European and Mediterranean cruises are popular because:
● So many of Europe's major cosmopolitan cities – Amsterdam, Barcelona, Copenhagen, Genoa, Helsinki, Lisbon, London, Monte Carlo, Nice, Oslo, St. Petersburg, Stockholm, and Venice – are on the water. It is far less expensive to take a cruise than to fly and stay in decent hotels (and have to pay for food and transport).
● You will not have to try to speak or understand different languages when you are aboard ship as you would ashore (if you choose the right ship).
● Aboard ship you use a single currency (typically US dollars or euros).
● A wide variety of shore excursions are offered.
● Lecture programs provide insights before you step ashore. Small ships are arguably better than large resort ships, as they can obtain better berthing space (the large resort ships may have to anchor in more of the smaller ports, so it can take time to get to and from shore). Many Greek islands are accessible only by shore tender. Some companies allow more time ashore than others, so compare itineraries in the brochures.

Alaska Cruises
These are especially popular because:
● They offer the best way to see the state's magnificent shoreline and glaciers.
● Alaska is a vast, relatively unexplored region.
● There is a wide range of shore excursions, including many floatplane and helicopter tours.
● There are many excursions. These include "dome car" rail journeys to Denali National Park to see North America's highest peak, Mt. McKinley.
● Pre- and post-cruise journeys to Banff and Jasper National Parks can be made from Vancouver.

There are two popular cruise routes:
The Inside Passage Route, a 1,000-mile (1,600-km) stretch of protected waterways carved a million years ago by Ice Age glaciers. This usually includes visits to tidewater glaciers, such as those in Glacier Bay's Hubbard Glacier or Tracy Arm (just two of the 15 active glaciers along the 60-mile/100-km Glacier Bay coastline). Typical ports of call might include Juneau, Ketchikan, Skagway, and Haines.
The Glacier Route, which usually includes the Gulf of Alaska during a one-way cruise between Vancouver and Anchorage. Typical ports of call might include Seward, Sitka, and Valdez.

Two major lines, Holland America Line and Princess Cruises, have such comprehensive facilities ashore (hotels, tour buses, even trains) that they are committed to Alaska for many years. Between them, they have invested more than $300 million in the state; indeed, Holland America Line-Westours is Alaska's largest private employer. In 2002, Holland America Line took 115,000 passengers to Alaska, while Princess Cruises took 180,000 (both are owned by Carnival Corporation). Other lines depend on what's left of the local transportation for their land tours.

In ports where docking space is limited, some ships anchor rather than dock. Many cruise brochures unfortunately do not indicate which ports are known to be anchor (tender) ports.

With 700,000 cruise passengers a year visiting

DID YOU KNOW?

● that Alaska has two time zones? Most of Alaska is one hour behind Pacific Standard Time, whereas the Aleutian Islands are two hours behind Pacific Standard Time.
● that the Pacific Ocean has a tide of 22 feet (6.7 meters) and the Atlantic Ocean has a tide of only 8 inches (20.3 centimeters)?
● that the Wallace Line is not a new cruise company, but the scientific demarcation separating Asia and Oceania?
● that the average time for a ship to pass through the Panama Canal is eight hours? The fastest transit time was set by the uss Manley at 4 hours and 38 minutes.

Regal Princess in Gaillard Cut, the Panama Canal.

Alaska and several large resort ships likely to be in port on any given day, there's so much congestion in many of the small ports that avoiding crowded streets can be difficult. Even nature is retreating; with more people around, wildlife is harder to spot. And some of the same shops are now found in Alaska as well as in the Caribbean. The more adventurous might consider one of the more unusual Alaska cruises to the far north, around the Pribilof Islands (superb for bird watching) and into the Bering Sea.

Transcanal Cruises

These take you through the Panama Canal, constructed by the United States after the failure of a French effort which began in 1882 with a labor force of over 10,000 but was plagued by disease and financial problems (over 22,000 people died). The US took over the building effort in 1904 and the waterway opened on August 15, 1914, shaving over 7,900 nautical miles off the distance between New York and San Francisco. The cost was an astonishing $387 million (in 1914 terms). The Panama Canal runs from *northwest* to *southeast* (not west to east), covering 51 miles (82 km) of locks and gates and dams, and the best way to experience this engineering wonder is from the deck of a cruise ship.

Control of the canal passed from the US to Panama in 2000. A proposed $4 billion widening of the canal and new locks, to be built by 2010, will enable the latest generation of large cruise ships to use it (at present they are too large).

Between the Caribbean and the Pacific, a ship is lifted 85 ft (26 meters) in a continuous flight of three steps at Gatun Locks to Gatun Lake through which it travels to Gaillard Cut where the Canal slices through the Continental Divide. It is lowered at Pedro Miguel Locks 31 ft (9.4 meters) in one step to Miraflores Lake, then the remaining two steps to sea level at Miraflores Locks before passing into the Pacific. Ships move through the locks under their own power, guided by towing locomotives. The 50-mile (80-km) trip across the Isthmus of Panama takes 8–9 hours.

Panama Canal cruises typically depart from Fort Lauderdale or San Juan, calling at one or two Caribbean islands before entering the canal and ending in Acapulco, Los Angeles, or San Francisco.

Australasia and Orient Cruises

If you like the idea of cruising in Australasia, Southeast Asia, or the Orient and you live in Europe or North America, be aware that the flying time to get to your port of embarkation and ship will be long. It's advisable to arrive at least two days before the cruise, as time changes and jet lag can be severe. The area has so much to offer that it's worth taking a cruise of at least 14 days.

Choose an itinerary, then read about the proposed destinations. Your cruise or travel agent will provide essential background, as will the wide range of Berlitz Pocket Guides. Australia, New Zealand, the islands of the South Pacific, Hong Kong, China, Japan, Indonesia, Malaysia, Singapore, Thailand, and Vietnam are all fascinating destinations. ❏

CRUISING FOR ROMANTICS

With more and more people taking solo trips, the possibility of a shipboard romance has a special attraction for many

Back in 1932, Warner Bros. released the film *One Way Passage*, a bittersweet story starring Kay Francis and William Powell. Remember the shipboard romance between Bette Davis and Paul Henreid in the film *Now, Voyager*? Or Irene Dunne and Charles Boyer in *An Affair to Remember*? All involved oceangoing passenger ships and romance. Then there was *Gentlemen Prefer Blondes*, in which Marilyn Monroe and Jane Russell starred. In the early 1950s, Howard Hughes presented Jane Russell in an RKO movie called *The French Line*, which depicted life on board one of the great ocean liners of the time – the SS *Liberté* – as being exciting, frivolous, promiscuous, and romantic. The movie was, in fact, made on board the great ship.

Today that same romantic attraction is still very much in vogue. In 1997, in the Hollywood blockbuster *Titanic*, Kate Winslet and Leonardo Di Caprio wooed aboard the stricken ocean liner on its maiden voyage across the North Atlantic.

While you may not believe in mermaids, romance does happen. More than 3 million cruise passengers (more than 25 percent of all cruise passengers) traveled as singles in 2003. About 25 percent of all calls to travel agents are made by singles and single parents. Cruise lines are just waking up to this fact and are providing special programs for singles. Some cruise lines or tour operators advertise special cruises for singles, but remember that the age range could be anything from 7 to 70.

Make no mistake about it: the world of cruising is made for couples. Singles are an expensive afterthought. Indeed, many singles are prejudiced against cruising because most cruise lines charge a single occupancy supplement for anyone traveling alone. The reason is that the most precious commodity aboard any cruise ship is space. Since a single cabin is often as large as a double and uses the same wiring, plumbing, and fixtures – and thus is just as expensive to build – cruise lines naturally feel justified in charging supplements or premiums for those who are occupying single cabins.

Single cabins are often among the most expensive, when compared with the per-person rates for double occupancy cabins. From the point of view of the crew, it takes as much time to clean a single cabin as it does a double. And, of course, there is only one tip instead of two. Note, however, that in most cabins built for double occupancy, there is typically only one personal safe.

Single Supplements

If you want to travel alone and not share a cabin, you can pay either a flat rate for the cabin or a single "supplement" if you occupy a double cabin. Some lines charge a fixed amount – $250, for instance – as a supplement, no matter what the cabin category, ship, itinerary, or length of cruise. Single supplements, or solo occupancy rates, vary between lines, and sometimes between ships. Check with your travel agent for the latest rates.

Guaranteed Singles Rates

Although some singles travel with friends or family, many others like to travel alone. For this reason, cruise lines have established several programs to accommodate them. One is the "Guaranteed Single" rate, which provides a set price without having to be concerned about which cabin

LEFT: fountain in the atrium of the *Statendam*.
RIGHT: fun activities bring singles together.

Getting together in the hot tub aboard *Imagination.*

to choose. Some cruise lines have guaranteed singles' rates, but the line and *not* the passenger picks the cabin. If the line does not find a roommate, the single passenger may get the cabin to himself/herself at no extra charge.

Guaranteed Share Programs

A "Guaranteed Share" program allows you to pay the normal double-occupancy rate, but the cruise line will find another passenger of the same sex to share the double cabin with you. Some cruise lines do not advertise a guaranteed-share program in their brochures but will often try to accommodate such bookings, particularly when demand for space is light. You could book a guaranteed share basis cabin only to find that you end up with a cabin to yourself. As cruise lines are apt to change such things at short notice, check with your travel agent for the latest rates, and read the fine print.

Cruising for Single Women

Any single woman can take a cruise knowing she is going to be as safe – if not safer – than she would be in any major vacation destination, but that does not mean that a cruise ship is a totally safe, completely hassle-free environment. Common sense should be the rule. Undoubtedly though, cruising is a great way to relax, and if you are seeking that special someone, cruising somehow brings people closer together.

There is always someone to talk to, be they couples or other singles, and cruising is not a "meat market" where you are always under observation. The easiest way to meet other singles, however, is to participate in scheduled activities. Be a little assertive, and get the cruise director or cruise staff to introduce you to other singles.

In the dining room, ask the restaurant manager to seat you with other singles, or a mix of singles and couples. Single black women should note that there is often a dearth of single black men for dancing or socializing with (they simply have not discovered cruising yet).

If you *are* looking for romance, however, beware of the lure of the uniform, of an easy affair or fling with a ship's officer (or member of the crew). They get to see new faces every week (or every cruise), and thus the possible risk of sexually transmitted diseases should be borne in mind.

Gentlemen Cruise Hosts

The female-to-male passenger ratio is high (as much as eight-to-one on world cruises and long voyages), especially for those of middle to senior years, so some cruise lines provide male social hosts, specially recruited as dance and bridge partners, and company during social functions. First used to good effect aboard Cunard Line's *QE2* in the late 1970s, gentlemen hosts are now employed by a number of cruise lines (particularly those carrying a large number of elderly passengers).

They generally host a table in the dining room, appear as dance partners at all cocktail parties and dance classes, and accompany women on shore excursions. These gentlemen, usually over 55 years of age and/or retired, are outgoing, mingle easily, are well groomed, and enjoy cruise ships and traveling around the world almost free.

If you think you would like such a job, do remember that you'll have to dance for several hours most nights, and dance just about every kind of dance well! Crystal Cruises, Cunard Line, Holland America Line, and Silversea Cruises, among others, provide gentlemen hosts.

The *Love Boat* Connection

Two famous TV shows, *The Love Boat* (US) and *Traumschiff* (Germany), boosted the concept of cruising as the ultimate romantic vacation, although what is screened may not quite correspond to reality. Indeed, the real captain of one ship, when asked the difference between his job and that of the captain of *The Love Boat*, remarked: "On TV they can do a retake if things are not right the first time around, whereas I have to get it right the first time!"

Getting Married Aboard Ship

As in all those old black-and-white movies, a ship's captain can indeed marry you when at sea (unless the ship's country of registry prohibits, or does not recognize, such marriages). In practice, however, this service is rarely offered by cruise lines today. You would need to inquire in your country of domicile (or residence) whether such a marriage is legal, and ascertain what paperwork and blood tests are required.

The onus to provide the *validity* of such a marriage is yours. The captain could be sued and perhaps held criminally liable if he marries a couple that are not legally entitled to be married (for example, an underage male or female who do not have the consent of a parent or guardian, or if one or both parties are not legally divorced).

Arranging to get married aboard almost any cruise ship when it is alongside in port is simple, provided you take along your own registered minister. Carnival Cruise Lines, Holland America Line, and Princess Cruises, among others offer special wedding packages. These include the services of a minister to marry you, wedding cake, champagne, bridal bouquet and matching boutonniere for the bridal party, a band to perform at the ceremony, and an album of wedding photos.

Carnival Cruise Lines' program includes a marriage ceremony on a beach in Grand Cayman or St. Thomas. Princess Cruises offers weddings on a beach in St. Thomas (prices range from $525 to $1175 per package). Or you could arrange a romantic wedding Disney-style on its private island, *Castaway Cay*.

Princess Cruises offers weddings aboard *Caribbean Princess*, *Coral Princess*, *Diamond Princess*, *Golden Princess*, *Grand Princess* (which

introduced the first oceangoing wedding chapel aboard a contemporary cruise vessel), *Island Princess*, *Sapphire Princess* and *Star Princess*. The ceremonies are performed by the captain, and are legal because of the ships' registry, Bermuda.

The basic Wedding At Sea package costs $1,800, plus $400 for licensing fees. Harborside or shoreside packages vary according to the port. A Wedding Coordinator at the line handles all the details, enabling you to be married aboard ship *and* honeymoon aboard, too.

Even if you can't get married aboard ship, you could have your wedding reception aboard one. Many cruise lines offer outstanding facilities and provide complete services to help you plan your reception. Contact the Director of Hotel Services at the cruise line of your choice. The cruise line should go out of its way to help, especially if you follow the reception with a honeymoon cruise.

UK-based passengers should know that P&O Cruises hosts a series of cruises called the "Red-Letter Anniversary Collection" for those celebrating 10, 15, 20, 25, 30, 35, 40, 45, 50, 55, or 60 years of marriage. Gifts you will receive with the compliments of P&O Cruises include a brass carriage clock, leather photograph album, free car parking at Southampton, or free first-class rail travel from anywhere in the UK (check with your travel agent for the latest details).

A cruise also makes a fine, no-worry honey-

Sea, sky, and opportunities for easy sociability.

moon vacation, and a delightful belated honeymoon getaway if you had no time to spare when you were married. You may feel you are on a movie set as you sail away to fairy-tale places, though actually, the ship is a destination in itself.

Renewal of Vows

There has recently been an upsurge in cruise lines performing "renewal of vows" ceremonies. A cruise is a wonderful setting for reaffirming to one's partner the strength of commitment. A handful of ships have a small chapel where this ceremony can take place; otherwise it can be anywhere aboard ship (a most romantic time is at sunrise or sunset on the open deck). The renewal of vows ceremony is conducted by the ship's captain and a nondenominational text reaffirms the love and trust between "partners, lifetime friends, and companions."

Although some companies, such as Carnival Cruise Lines, Celebrity Cruises, Holland America Line, and Princess Cruises, have complete packages for purchase, which include music, champagne, hors d'oeuvres, certificate, corsages for the women, and so on, most other companies do not charge (yet).

Cruising for Honeymooners

Cruising is popular as a honeymoon vacation. The advantages are obvious: you pack and unpack only once; it is a hassle-free and crime-free environment; and you get special attention, if you want it. It is also easy to budget in advance, as one price often includes airfare, cruise, food, entertainment, several destinations, shore excursions, and pre- and post-cruise hotel stays.

Once you are married, some cruise lines make a point of offering discounts to entice you to book a future (anniversary) cruise. Just think, no cooking meals, everything will be done for you.

Although no ship as yet provides bridal suites (hint, hint), many ships do provide cabins with

queen-sized or double beds. Some, but by no means all, also provide tables for two in the dining room should you wish to dine together without having to make friends with others.

Some cruise ships feature Sunday departures, so couples can plan a Saturday wedding and reception before traveling to their ship. Pre- and post-cruise hotel accommodation can also be arranged.

Most large resort ships accommodate honeymoon couples well; however, if you want to plan a more private, intimate honeymoon, it would be a good idea to try one of the smaller, yacht-like cruise vessels such as those of Seabourn Cruise Line, Seven Seas Cruises, Silversea Cruises, or Windstar Cruises.

And what could be more romantic for honeymooners than to stroll, by themselves on deck, to the forward part of the ship, above the ship's bridge. This is the quietest (except perhaps for some wind noise) and most dimly lit part of the ship, and an ideal spot for stargazing and romancing.

Cruise lines offer a variety of honeymoon packages, just as hotels and resorts on land do. Although not all cruise lines provide all services, typically they might include:

❤ Private captain's cocktail party for honeymooners.

❤ Tables for two in the dining room.

❤ Set of crystal champagne or wine glasses.

❤ Honeymoon photograph with the captain, and photo album.

❤ Complimentary champagne (imported or domestic) or wine.

❤ Honeymoon cruise certificate.

❤ Champagne and caviar for breakfast.

❤ Flowers in your suite or cabin.

❤ Complimentary cake.

❤ Special T-shirts.

Finally, remember to take a copy of your marriage license or certificate, for immigration (or marriage) purposes, as your passports will not yet have been amended.

Also, remember to allow extra in your budget for things like shipboard gratuities (tips), shore excursions, and spending money ashore.

If your romance includes the desire to sleep in a large bed next to your loved one, check with your travel agent and cruise line to make sure the cabin you have booked has such a bed. Better still, book a suite. But check and double-check to avoid disappointment.

If you need to take your wedding gown aboard for a planned wedding somewhere along the way – in Hawaii or Bermuda, for example – there is usually space to hang it in the dressing room next to the stage in the main showlounge, especially aboard the large resort ships. ❑

DID YOU KNOW?

● that motion pictures' most famous on-screen odd couple, Jack Lemmon and Walter Matthau, played gentlemen dance hosts intent on defrauding rich widows aboard a Caribbean cruise ship? Called *Out to Sea,* the 1997 Martha Coolidge film also starred Gloria DeHaven, Dyan Cannon, Hal Linden, Elaine Stritch, and Brent Spiner. The "cruise ship" interior was filmed at Raleigh Studios in Hollywood.
● that Epirotiki Line's *Jupiter* was used to carry the 61 finalists of the Miss Universe contest in 1976 (Epirotiki Line is now part of Royal Olympia Cruises)?
● that on Valentine's Day, 1998, some 5,000 couples renewed their vows aboard the ships of Princess Cruises?

CRUISING FOR FAMILIES

When parents decide to take their children with them on a cruise,

it's important to choose a ship with the right facilities

Yes, you *can* take your children on a cruise. In fact, once you get them aboard, you will hardly see them at all, if you choose the right ship and cruise. Family cruises can give parents a welcome break; no one has to cook, or do the dishes, make the beds, drive, or find a place to park. Families can do different things on a cruise, and parents don't have to be concerned about the whereabouts of their children. Where else can you go out for a night on the town without having to drive, and be home in a moment should the babysitter need you? Dad can sleep in. Mom can go swimming and join an aerobics class.

The children can join in the organized activities that go on all day long. While they may not like organized clubs (too reminiscent of school), they will probably make new friends quickly in the surroundings of a cruise ship. Whether you share a cabin with them or whether they have their own separate but adjoining cabin, there will be plenty to keep them occupied.

Some cruise lines have token family programs, with limited activities and only a couple of general staff allocated to look after children, even though their brochures might claim otherwise. But cruise lines that are really serious about family cruise programs dedicate complete teams of kids', "tweens and teens" counselors, who run special programs that are off-limits to adults. They also have facilities such as high chairs in the dining room, cots, and real playrooms. Most entertainment for children is designed to run simultaneously with adult programs; few ships have dedicated children's entertainers. For those cruising with very young children, baby-sitting services may also be available. For example, *QE2 and QM2* have real children's nurses and even trained English National Nursing Examination Board-qualified nannies. *Aurora, Oceana* and *Oriana* have a "night nursery" for two- to five-year-olds.

Parents, of course, have long realized that children cost more as they age. For example, children under two years travel free on most cruise lines (and airlines). If older, they cost money.

There's no better vacation for families than a ship cruise, especially at holiday time. Active parents can have the best of all worlds, family togetherness, social contact, and privacy. Cruise ships provide a very safe, crime-free, encapsulated environment, and give junior passengers a lot of free-

dom without parents having to be concerned about where their children are at all times. Because the days aboard are long, youngsters will be able to spend time with their parents or grandparents, as well as with their peers. They can also tour the ship's bridge, meet senior officers and learn about the navigation, radar, and communications equipment. They will be exposed to different environments, experience many types of food, travel to and explore new places, and participate in any number of exciting activities.

Many cruise lines, recognizing the needs of families, have added a whole variety of children's programs to their daily activities. Some ships have separate swimming pools and play areas for children, as well as junior discos, video rooms, and teen centers. Not to be outdone by Disney, Carnival Cruise Lines has "Fun Ship Freddy" – a lifesized mascot with a head in the shape of the company's distinctive funnels. He mingles with children of all ages (adults, too), providing plenty of photo ops.

In some ships, stewards, stewardesses, and other staff may be available as private babysitters for an

Cruising increasingly provides activities for children.

The water slide aboard *Disney Magic*.

hourly charge (otherwise, *group* babysitting may be available). Make arrangements at the reception desk/purser's office. Aboard some ships, evening baby-sitting services may not start until late in the evening (check details *before* booking your cruise).

Cruise lines serious about children divide them into five distinct age groups, with various names to match, according to cruise line and program: Toddlers (ages 2–4); Juniors (ages 5–7); Intermediate (ages 8–10); Tweens (ages 11–13); and Teens (ages 14–17). It often seems to be children under 12 who get the most from a cruise.

Disney Goes Cruising

In 1998, Disney Cruise Line entered the family cruise market with a big splash. The giant enter-

tainment and theme park company introduced the first of two large resort ships (each has two funnels) to cater specifically to families with children, with cruises of 3, 4 and 7 days. *Disney Magic* and *Disney Wonder* are family ships that cater to 1,750 adults and up to 1,000 children, with the whole of the Disney organization to support the shipboard entertainment program. Disney has its own passenger terminal (designed after the original Art Deco-inspired Ocean Terminal of the 1930s in Southampton, England) and facilities at Port Canaveral, Florida, as well as a fleet of specially constructed motorcoaches. For more details, see *Disney Magic* and *Disney Wonder* in the listings section.

General Information

Selected baby foods are stocked by ships that cater to children (along with cribs and high chairs, but do ask your travel agent to check first). If you need that special brand of baby food, or a high chair in the restaurant, a crib, baby bathtub, baby stroller (few ships have them available for rent), or monitoring service, let your travel agent know *well in advance*, and get them and the cruise line to *confirm in writing* that the facilities and items will be available. Given enough notice, most cruise lines will do their best to obtain what is needed.

Parents using organic baby foods, such as those obtained from health food stores, should be aware that cruise lines buy their supplies from major general food suppliers and not the smaller specialized food houses.

Although many ships have full programs for children during days at sea, these may be limited

---

DID YOU KNOW?

● that the French liner *Ile de France* was the first, and only, ship to have a real carousel in the children's playroom? This was also the ship used in the 1960 movie *The Last Voyage*, with Robert Stack and Dorothy Malone.

● that a 15-foot-high Goofy hangs upside down over the stern of *Disney Magic*? What is he doing? Why, painting the ship, of course!

● that Carnival Cruise Lines and Mattel teamed up to produce a nautical-themed Barbie Doll? She can be found in the gift shops aboard all the company's ships.

● that Carnival Cruise Lines carried more than 400,000 children aboard its ships in 2003?

when the ship is in port. Ships expect you to take your children with you on organized excursions, and sometimes (though not always) there are special prices for children. If the ship has a playroom, it might be wise to find out if it is open and supervised on all days of the cruise.

When going ashore, remember that if you want to take your children swimming or to the beach, it is wise to phone ahead to a local hotel with a beach or pool. Most hotels will be happy to show off their property to you, hoping for your future business.

Some cruise ships in the Caribbean have the use of a "private" island for a day. A lifeguard will be on duty, and there will be water sports and snorkeling equipment you can rent. Remember, however, that the beaches on some "private" islands are fine for 200 passengers, but with 2,000 they become crowded, and standing in line for beach barbecues and changing and toilet facilities becomes a necessary part of the experience.

Although the sun and warm sea might attract juniors to the Caribbean, children aged seven and over will find a Baltic, Black Sea, or Mediterranean cruise a delight. They will have a fine introduction to history, languages, and different cultures.

Children's Rates

Most cruise lines offer special rates for children sharing their parents' cabin. The cost is often lower than third and fourth person share rates. To get the best possible rates, however, it is wise to book early. And do not overlook booking an interior (no-view) cabin; you will rarely be in it anyway.

Although many adult cruise rates include airfare, most children's rates don't. Also, although some lines say children sail "free," they must pay port taxes as well as airfare. The cruise line will get the airfare at the best rate, so there is no need to shop around. If you have very young children and can get to your ship without having to fly, you'll save yourself the hassles of struggling though airports (with security creating longer lines) with pushchairs, strollers, and other paraphernalia.

Single Parents

Only a handful of cruise lines so far have introduced their versions of the "Single Parent Plan." This offers an economical way for single parents to take their children on a cruise, with parent and child sharing a two-berth cabin, or parent and children sharing a three-berth cabin. Single parents will pay approximately one-third the normal single-person rate for their children, and there will be plenty of activities for both parent and child(ren) to enjoy.

Family Reunions

A cruise can provide the ideal place for a family reunion (either with or without children). Here are some tips to take into account when planning one.

Let your travel agent do the planning and make all the arrangements (ask for a group discount if the total in your group adds up to more than 15). Make sure that together you choose the right cruise line, for the right reasons.

Book 12 months in advance if possible so that you can arrange cabins adjacent or close to each other (you may also wish to arrange for everyone to be at the same dinner seating, if the ship operates two seatings).

If anyone in the group has a birthday or anniversary, tell your travel agent to arrange a special cake (most cruise lines do not charge extra for this). Special private parties can also be arranged, although there will be an additional cost. If the group is not too large, you may be able to request to dine at the captain's table. Kids can be given "unlimited use" soft drinks cards so they don't have to come looking for you.

Arrange shore excursions as a group (in some ports, private arrangements may prove unbeatable). Finally, get everything in writing (particularly cabin assignments and locations). ❑

THE BEST CHOICE FOR CHILDREN

These cruise lines and ships have been selected by the author for their excellent children programs and care (not all ships of a particular cruise line have been chosen):

Aida Cruises (*AIDAcara, AIDAaura, AIDAvita*)
Carnival Cruise Lines (*Carnival Conquest, Carnival Destiny, Carnival Glory, Carnival Legend, Carnival Liberty, Carnival Pride, Carnival Spirit, Carnival Triumph, Carnival Valor, Carnival Victory, Ecstasy, Elation, Fantasy, Fascination, Imagination, Inspiration, Paradise, Sensation*)
Celebrity Cruises (*Century, Constellation, Galaxy, Infinity, Mercury, Millennium, Summit*)
Cunard (*Queen Elizabeth 2, Queen Mary 2*)
Disney Cruise Line (*Disney Magic, Disney Wonder*)
Norwegian Cruise Line (*Norwegian Dawn, Norwegian Spirit, Norwegian Star, Norwegian Sun*)
P&O Cruises (*Aurora, Oceana, Oriana*)
Princess Cruises (*Diamond Princess, Golden Princess, Grand Princess, Sapphire Princess, Star Princess*)
Royal Caribbean International (*Adventure of the Seas, Brilliance of the Seas, Explorer of the Seas, Jewel of the Seas. Mariner of the Seas, Navigator of the Seas, Radiance of the Seas, Serenade of the Seas, Voyager of the Seas*)
Star Cruises (*Star Pisces, SuperStar Virgo*)
Thomson Cruises (*The Emerald, Thomson Celebration, Thomson Spirit*)

Note that *Aurora, Disney Magic, Disney Wonder, Oceana, Oriana, QE2* and *QM2* cater to children and babies of all ages particularly well, while most other ships in this list do not generally provide good facilities (or individual babysitting services for children under 3 years old).

CRUISING FOR THE PHYSICALLY CHALLENGED

A relaxed environment, lots of social contact and organized entertainment
are the attractions. But it's important to choose the right ship

Cruising for the physically challenged offers one of the most hassle-free vacations possible, with a wide choice of ships and itineraries, a clean environment, and almost all of the details taken care of before you go. In the past 15 years, cruise ships have become significantly more accessible for people with most types of disabilities. Many new ships also have text telephones, listening device kits for the hearing-impaired (including show lounges and theaters aboard some ships). Special dietary needs can also be accommodated by most cruise lines, and many cruise ships have cabins with refrigerators (useful for those with diabetes who need to keep supplies of insulin cool). There are even cruises organized for dialysis patients, those who need oxygen reglarly. However, not all cruise ships are the same (some insurance companies may prohibit smaller ships from accepting passengers with severe disabilites).

The advantages of a cruise for the physically challenged are many, apart from the obvious ones of no packing and unpacking:

● Good place for relaxation and self-renewal.
● Pure air at sea (no smog, pollen or pollution).
● Spacious public rooms.
● Excellent medical facilities close by.
● Specialized dietary requirements can be met.
● The staff will generally be very helpful.
● Varied entertainment, including gambling (but no wheelchair-accessible gaming tables or slot machines).
● Security (no crime on board).
● Different ports of call.

But there are also significant disadvantages:

● Although some of the newest and largest ships have been well designed, none are barrier-free, and it can be hard to access some areas such as self-serve buffets.
● Very few ships have access-help lifts installed at swimming pools (exception: P&O Cruises) or angled steps with handrail, or thalassotherapy pools or shore tenders (exception: Holland America Line).
● Unless cabins are specifically designed for the physically challenged, problem areas include the entrance, furniture configuration, closet hanging rails, and beds.
● Cabin bathrooms: doors that open inward are useless; the grab bars, wheel-in shower stall, toiletries cabinet should be at an accessible height.
● Elevators: the width of the door is important for wheelchair passengers; controls often cannot be reached from a wheelchair (except in the newer ships).

● Sometimes having to wait at elevators behind hordes of able-bodied passengers who really don't need them.
● Access to outside decks is usually provided through doors that must be opened manually rather than via electric-eye doors that open and close automatically.
● Cruise lines, port authorities, airlines, and various allied services are slowly improving their facilities. But few cruise lines show photographs of passengers in wheelchairs (Princess Cruises is an exception).

The design of ships has traditionally worked against the mobility-limited. To keep water out or to prevent water escaping from a flooded cabin or public area, raised edges (known as "coamings" or "lips") are often placed in doorways and across exit pathways. Also, cabin doorways are often not wide enough to accommodate even a standard wheelchair. A "standard" cabin door is about 24 inches (60 cm) wide.

Cabins designed for the mobility-limited typically have doors that are about 30 inches (76 cm) wide. "Standard" bathroom doors are normally only about 22 inches (56 cm) wide, whereas those designed for wheelchairs are about 28–30 inches (71–76 cm) wide. Ask your travel agent to confirm the width of cabin and

Author Douglas Ward checks out a ship's facilities.

bathroom doors. Allow for the fact that your knuckles on either side of a wheelchair can add to the width of your wheelchair. Beds in cabins for the physically challenged aboard most ships are not equipped with a "panic" button, adjacent to a bedside light switch (*Carnival Destiny*, *Carnival Triumph* and *Carnival Victory* are examples of ships that have them installed).

Bathroom doors are a particular problem, and the door itself, whether it opens outward into the cabin or inward into the bathroom, hinders maneuverability. Four cabins for the physically challenged in *QE2*, however, have electrically operated sliding doors into the bathroom, a completely level entrance into both cabin and bathroom, and remote-controlled lights, curtains, and doors, as well as a door intercom and alarm.

Bathrooms in many older ships are small and full of plumbing fixtures, often at odd angles, awkward when moving about in a wheelchair. The bathrooms aboard new ships are more accessible, but the plumbing is often located beneath the complete prefabricated module, making the floor higher than that in the cabin, which means a ramp must be fitted in order to wheel in.

Some cruise lines will, if given advance notice, remove a bathroom door and hang a fabric curtain in its place. Many lines will provide ramps for the bathroom doorway, where a sill or "lip" is encountered.

Almost all cruise lines used to discourage the mobility-limited from traveling by ship for reasons of safety, insurance, and legal liability. But a cruise is the ideal holiday for such people, as it provides a relaxed environment with plenty of social contact, organized entertainment, and activities. Despite most brochures declaring that they accept wheelchairs, few ships are well fitted to accommodate them. Some cruise lines openly state that all public restrooms and cabin bathrooms are inaccessible to wheelchair-bound passengers.

What about safety? At present, only four cruise ships currently provide direct access ramps to the lifeboats; they are *Crystal Harmony*, *Crystal Serenity*, *Crystal Symphony* and *Europa*.

It's not as easy to provide facilities for wheelchair-bound passengers as you might think. Specially trained crew members must be assigned to assist all wheelchair-bound passengers, which translates to two crew members per eight-hour shift (thus, *six* crew members would be required according to the latest safety and evacuation regulations solely to provide support for *one* wheelchair-bound passenger – a big drain on labor resources).

The list overleaf provides a guide to the accessibility of ships reviewed in this book (the author, or one of his staff, personally wheels around each ship to check).

Once you've decided on your ship and cruise, the next step is to select your accommodation. Choose a cruise line that permits you to choose a specific cabin, rather than one that merely allows you to select a price category, then assigns you a cabin just before your departure date or, worse, at embarkation.

What Cabins Should Include:

● No "lip" or threshold at the cabin door, which should be a minimum of 35 inches wide (89 cm).
● Bedside "panic" button linked to the navigation bridge (which is staffed 24 hours a day).
● Enough space to maneuver a wheelchair between entrance, bed, closet, and bathroom.
● Closet with "pull down" clothes rail.
● Telephone mounted at wheelchair height (not high up on wall).
● Mirrors that can be used when seated in a wheelchair (full-length).
● Safe or lockable drawer that is reachable at wheelchair height.
● Convenient electrical outlet for battery charger (for electronic wheelchair users)

What Bathrooms Should Include:

● Outward opening door.
● No "lip" at bathroom door.
● No "lip" into shower stall.
● Shower stall (with detachable showerhead located at head height when seated in a wheelchair).
● Shower chair that folds up when not in use.
● Grab rails for shower and toilet.
● Toilet with electric automatic seat pad cleaner.
● Sink low enough for wheelchair to move up close.
● Emergency red (panic) button or pull-cord in or adjacent to shower (for falls).
The following tips will help you choose wisely:

Bathrooms aboard newer ships are more accessible.

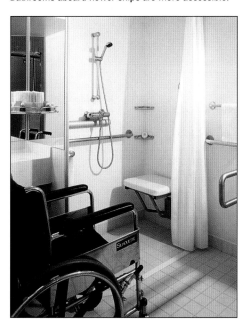

● If the ship does not have any specially equipped cabins, book the best outside cabin in your price range or choose another ship. However, be careful as you may find that even cruise brochures that state that a ship has "wheelchair accessible" cabins fail to say whether the wheelchair will fit through the *bathroom* door, or whether there is a "lip" at the door. Find out whether the wheelchair can fit into the shower area. Get your travel agent to check, and recheck the details. Do not take "I think so" as an answer. Get specific measurements.

● Choose a cabin close to an elevator. Not all elevators go to all decks, so check the deck plan carefully. Smaller and older vessels may not even have elevators, making access to even the dining room difficult.

● Avoid, at all costs, a cabin down a little alleyway shared by several other cabins, even if the price is attractive. Entering a cabin in a wheelchair from a narrow alleyway is likely to be difficult.

● Cabins located amidships are less affected by vessel motion, so choose something in the middle of the ship if you are concerned about rough seas, no matter how infrequently they might occur.

● The larger (and therefore more expensive) the cabin, the more room you will have to maneuver in. This is particularly important in the bathroom.

● If your budget allows, pick a cabin with a bath rather than just a shower, because there will be considerably more room, especially if you can't stand comfortably.

● Meals in some ships may be served in your cabin, on special request. This is a decided advantage should you wish to avoid dressing for every meal. But few ships have enough space in the cabin for dining tables.

Which Ships Best Cater for the Physically Challenged

Ship		Ship		Ship		Ship	
Adonia	B	Carnival Spirit	B	Enchantment of		Le Diamant	D
Adventure of the Seas	A	Carnival Triumph	B	the Seas	B	Le Levant	D
Aegean I	D	Carnival Valor	B	Endeavour	D	Le Ponant	D
AIDAaura	B	Carnival Victory	B	Europa	B	Legacy	D
AIDAblu	B	Celebration	C	Explorer II	B	Legend of the Seas	B
AIDAcara	B	Celebrity Xpedition	D	Explorer of the Seas	A	MSC Armonia	B
AIDAvita	B	Century	B	Fantasy	C	MSC Lirica	B
Akademik Sergey		Clipper Adventurer	D	Fascination	C	MSC Melody	C
Vavilov	D	Clipper Odyssey	C	Flying Cloud	D	MSC Monterey	D
Albatros	C	Club Med 2	D	Fuji Maru	D	MSC Opera	B
American Eagle	D	C. Columbus	C	Funchal	D	MSC Rhapsody	D
American Glory	D	Constellation	A	Galapagos Explorer II	D	MSC Sinfonia	B
American Spirit	D	Coral Princess	B	Galaxy	B	Maasdam	B
Amsterdam	B	Costa Allegra	D	Golden Princess	A	Majesty of the Seas	C
Andrea	D	Costa Atlantica	B	Grand Latino	C	Mandalay	D
Arcadia	B	Costa Classica	B	Grand Princess	A	Marco Polo	C
Arion	D	Costa Europa	C	Grand Voyager	B	Mariner of the Seas	A
Astor	C	Costa Fortuna	B	Grande Caribe	D	Maxim Gorkiy	D
Astoria	C	Costa Magica	B	Grande Mariner	D	Mercury	B
Asuka	C	Costa Marina	D	Grandeur of the Seas	B	Millennium	A
Atalante	D	Costa Mediterranea	B	Hanseatic	D	Minerva II	B
Aurora	A	Costa Romantica	B	Hebridean Princess	D	Mona Lisa	C
Ausonia	D	Costa Tropicale	D	Hebridean Spirit	D	Monarch of the Seas	C
Black Prince	D	Costa Victoria	B	Holiday	D	Monet	D
Black Watch	C	Crystal Harmony	A	Holiday Dream	C	Nantucket Clipper	D
Bolero	D	Crystal Serenity	A	Horizon	B	Navigator of the Seas	A
Braemar	C	Crystal Symphony	A	Imagination	C	New Flamenco	D
Bremen	D	Dawn Princess	B	Infinity	A	Niagara Prince	D
Brilliance of the Seas	B	Delphin Renaissance	B	Insignia	B	Nippon Maru	C
Calypso	D	Deutschland	C	Inspiration	C	Norwegian Crown	B
Caribbean Princess	B	Diamond Princess	B	Island Escape	D	Norwegian Dawn	A
Carnival Conquest	B	Discovery	C	Island Princess	B	Norwegian Dream	C
Carnival Destiny	B	Disney Magic	B	Island Sky	D	Norwegian Majesty	D
Carnival Glory	B	Disney Wonder	B	Island Sun	D	Norwegian Sea	D
Carnival Legend	B	easyCruise I	D	Jewel of the Seas	B	Norwegian Spirit	B
Carnival Liberty	B	Ecstasy	C	Kapitan Dranitsyn	D	Norwegian Star	A
Carnival Miracle	B	Elation	C	Kapitan Khlebnikov	D	Norwegian Sun	B
Carnival Pride	B	Empress of the Seas	C	Kristina Regina	D	Norwegian Wind	C

● If you want to join other passengers in the dining room and your ship offers two fixed-time seatings for meals, choose the second. Then you can linger over your dinner, secure in the knowledge that the waiter will not try to rush you.

● Space at dining room tables is limited in many ships. When making table reservations, tell the restaurant manager that you would like a table that leaves plenty of room for your wheelchair, so that it leaves plenty of room for waiters – and other passengers – to get past.

● Find a travel agent who knows your needs and understands your requirements, but follow up on all aspects of the booking yourself so that there will be no last-minute slip-ups.

● Make sure that the cabin you booked is so stated on the final passenger ticket contract. Also make sure that the contract specifically states that if, for any reason, the cabin is not available, that you will get a full refund *and* transportation back home as well as a refund on any hotel bills incurred.

● Take your own wheelchair with you, as ships carry only a limited number of wheelchairs; these are provided for emergency hospital use only. An alternative is to rent an electric wheelchair, which can be delivered to the ship on your sailing date.

● If you live near the port of embarkation, arrange to visit the ship yourself to check its suitability for your accessibility requirements (most cruise lines will be helpful in this regard).

● Hanging rails in the closets on most ships are positioned too high for someone in a wheelchair to reach (even the latest ships seem to repeat this basic error).

Ship		Ship		Ship		Ship	
Ocean Majesty	D	Ryndam	C	Silver Whisper	B	The Jasmine	D
Ocean Monarch	D	Saga Ruby	C	Silver Wind	C	Thomson Celebration	C
Ocean Village	B	Saga Rose	C	Sovereign of the Seas	C	Thomson Destiny	C
Oceana	B	Sapphire	D	Spirit of '98	D	Thomson Spirit	C
Oceanic	C	Sapphire Princess	B	Spirit of Alaska	D	Triton	D
Odysseus	D	Seabourn Legend	D	Spirit of Columbia	D	Van Gogh	D
Oosterdam	B	Seabourn Pride	D	Spirit of Discovery	D	Veendam	C
Oriana	B	Seabourn Spirit	D	Spirit of Endeavour	D	Vision of the Seas	B
Orient Venus	D	SeaDream I	D	Spirit of Glacier Bay	D	Vistamar	D
Orion	D	SeaDream II	D	Spirit of Oceanus	D	Volendam	B
Pacific Princess	B	Sea Bird	D	Splendour of the Seas	B	Voyager of the Seas	A
Pacific Sky	C	Sea Cloud	D	Star Clipper	D	Westerdam	B
Pacific Sun	C	Sea Cloud II	D	Star Flyer	D	Wilderness Adventurer	D
Pacific Venus	C	Sea Lion	D	Star Pisces	D	Wind Spirit	D
Paloma I	D	Sensation	C	Star Princess	A	Wind Star	D
Paradise	C	Serenade	D	Statendam	C	Wind Surf	D
Paul Gauguin	C	Serenade of the Seas	A	Summit	A	World Renaissance	D
Polaris	D	Seven Seas Mariner	A	Sun Princess	B	Yamal	D
Polynesia	D	Seven Seas Navigator	B	SuperStar Gemini	C	Yankee Clipper	D
Pride of America	B	Seven Seas Voyager	A	SuperStar Virgo	B	Yorktown Clipper	D
Pride of Aloha	B	Silver Cloud	C	Tahitian Princess	B	Zaandam	B
Princesa Marissa	D	Silver Shadow	B	The Emerald	D	Zenith	B
Princess Danae	D	Silver Star	D	The Iris	D	Zuiderdam	B
Prinsendam	A						
Professor Molchanov	D						
Professor Multanovskiy	D						
Queen Elizabeth 2	B						
Queen Mary 2	A						
Radiance of the Seas	B						
Radisson Diamond	C						
Regal Empress	D						
Regal Princess	B						
Regatta	B						
Rhapsody of the Seas	B						
Rotterdam	A						
Royal Clipper	D						
Royal Princess	B						
Royal Star	D						

KEY
A) Recommended as most suitable for wheelchair passengers
B) Reasonably accessible for wheelchair passengers
C) Moderately accessible for wheelchair passengers
D) Not suitable for wheelchair passengers

● The following ships of Carnival Cruise Lines have double-width entertainment deck promenades that are good for wheelchair passengers, but the public restrooms are not accessible. In addition, although the cabin bathrooms are equipped with shower stalls and grab rails, the bathrooms have a steel "lip" and are therefore neither suitable nor accessible when stepping out of a wheelchair: *Celebration, Ecstasy, Elation, Fantasy, Fascination, Holiday, Imagination, Inspiration, Paradise, Sensation.*

● *Crystal Harmony, Crystal Serenity* and *Crystal Symphony* (Crystal Cruises) are the only ships presently in operation that provide special access ramps from an accommodation deck directly to the ship's lifeboats.

● *Regal Princess* (Princess Cruises) has large outside cabins for the physically challenged, although they have lifeboat-obstructed views.

Many cruise ships, however, have cabins specially fitted out to suit the mobility-limited. They are typically fitted with roll-in closets and have a pull-down facility to bring your clothes down to any height you want.

● Elevators are a constant source of difficulty for wheelchair passengers. Often the control buttons, especially those for upper decks, are far too high to reach.

● Doors on upper decks that open onto a Promenade or Lido Deck are very strong, are difficult to handle, and have high sills. Unless you can get out of your wheelchair, these doors can be a source of annoyance, even if help is at hand, as they open inward or outward (they should ideally be electrically operated sliding doors).

● Advise your airline with of any special needs well ahead of time so that arrangements can be made to accommodate you without last-minute problems.

● Advise the cruise line repeatedly of the need for proper transfer facilities, in particular buses or vans with wheelchair ramps.

Embarkation

Even if you've alerted the airline and arranged your travel according to your needs, there is still one problem to surmount when you arrive at the cruise embarkation port to join your ship: the actual boarding. If you embark at ground level, the gangway to the ship may be level or inclined. It will depend on the embarkation deck of the ship and/or the tide in the port.

Alternatively, you may be required to embark from an upper level of a terminal, in which case the gangway could well be of the floating loading-bridge type, like those used at major airports. Some have flat floors; others may have raised lips spaced every three feet (awkward to negotiate in a wheelchair, especially if the gangway is made steeper by a rising tide).

Tendering Ashore

Cruise lines should (but don't always) provide an anchor emblem in brochures for those ports of call where a ship will be at anchor instead of alongside. If the ship is at anchor, be prepared for an interesting but safe experience. The crew will lower you and your wheelchair into a waiting tender (ship-to-shore launch) and then, after a short boat-ride, lift you out again onto a rigged gangway or integral platform. If the sea is calm, this maneuver proceeds uneventfully; if the sea is choppy, it could vary from exciting to harrowing.

Fortunately (or not) this type of embarkation is rare unless you are leaving a busy port with several ships all sailing the same day. Holland America Line is one of the few companies that have made shore tenders accessible to wheelchair passengers, with a special boarding ramp and scissor lift so that wheelchair passengers can see out of the shore tender's windows.

Wheelchairs

Wheelchair passengers with limited mobility should use a collapsible wheelchair (which could be rented from specialist providers at your port of embarkation if you don't want to bring your own). By limited mobility, I mean a person able to get out of the wheelchair and step over a sill or walk with a cane, crutches, or other walking device.

The chart on the preceding pages indicates the best cruise ships for wheelchair accessibility. Remember to ask questions before you make a booking. Examples:

● Does the cruise line's travel insurance (with a cancellation/trip interruption) cover you for any injuries while you are aboard ship?

● Are any public rooms or public decks aboard the ship inaccessible to wheelchairs (for instance, it is sometimes difficult to obtain access to the outdoor swimming pool deck)?

● Will you be guaranteed a good viewing place in the main showroom from where you can see the shows if seated in a wheelchair?

● Will special transportation be provided to transfer you from airport to ship?

● If you need a collapsible wheelchair, can this be provided by the cruise line?

● Do passengers have to sign a medical release?

● Do passengers need a doctor's note to qualify for a cabin for the physically challenged?

● Will crew be on hand to help, or must the passengers rely on their own traveling companions for help?

● Are the ship's tenders accessible to wheelchairs?

● How do you get from your cabin to the lifeboats (which may be up or down several decks) in an emergency if the elevators are out of action?

Waivers

Passengers who do not require wheelchairs but are challenged in other ways, such as those who have impaired sight, hearing, or speech, present their own particular requirements. Many of these can be avoided if the person is accompanied by an able-bodied companion experienced in attending to their special needs. In any event, some cruise lines require physically challenged passengers to sign a waiver.

Hearing Impaired

Those affected should be aware of problems aboard ship: hearing the announcements on the public address system; use of the telephone; and poor acoustics in key areas (for example, boarding shore tenders).

Take a spare battery for your hearing aid. More new ships have cabins specially fitted with colored signs to help those who are hearing impaired. Crystal Cruises' *Crystal Harmony, Crystal Serenity* and *Crystal Symphony*, and Celebrity Cruises' *Century, Galaxy,* and *Mercury* have movie theaters that are fitted with special headsets for the hearing impaired.

Finally, when going ashore, particularly on organized excursions, be aware that most destinations, particulalry in Europe and Southeast Asia, are simply not equipped to handle the hearing impaired. ❑

ALTERNATIVE CRUISES

The choice includes river cruises, nature expeditions, sail-cruise ships,
freighter travel, ocean crossings, and round-the-world trips

Coastal Cruises

Europe

There is year-round coastal cruising along the shores of Norway to the Land of the Midnight Sun aboard the ships of Norwegian Coastal Voyages (known locally as the Hurtig-Ruten, or "Highway 1"). The fleet consists of small, comfortable, working express coastal packet steamers and contemporary cruise vessels that deliver mail, small packaged goods, and foodstuffs, and take passengers, to the communities spread on the shoreline.

This is a 2,500-mile (4,000-km) journey from Bergen in Norway to Kirkenes, close to the Russian border (half of which is north of the Arctic Circle) and takes 12 days. You can join it at any of the 34 ports of call and stay as long as you wish (the ships sail every day of the year). In 2003, the company carried over 300,000 passengers.

The service started in 1893 and is now run as a joint effort by two companies. The ships can accommodate between 144 and 674 passengers.

Exploring Norway's fjords at close quarters.

The newest ships in the fleet have an elevator that can accommodate a wheelchair passenger.

Archipelago hopping can be done along Sweden's eastern coast, too, by sailing in the daytime and staying overnight in one of the many small hotels. One vessel sails from Norrtalje, north of Stockholm, to Oskarshamn, near the Baltic island of Öland, right through the spectacular Swedish archipelago. You can also cruise from the Finnish city of Lappeenranta to the Estonian city of Viborg without a visa, thanks to perestroika. Point-to-point coastal transportation between neighboring countries, major cities, and commercial centers is big business in Northern Europe.

Scotland

The fishing town of Oban, two hours west of Glasgow by road, perhaps seems an unlikely point to start a cruise, but it is the base for one of the world's finest cruise experiences. *Hebridean Princess* is an absolute gem, with Laura Ashley-style interiors. This ship carries passengers around some of Scotland's most magnificent coastline and islands. Take lots of warm clothing, however (layers are ideal), as the weather can be somewhat unkind. As an alternative, there's *Lord of the*

Glens, another treat for small ship lovers, cruising in style through the lakes and canals of Scotland.

United States

Coastal vessels flying the American flag offer a change of style from oceangoing cruise ships. Informality is the order of the day. Accommodating up to 226 passengers, the ships are more like private parties – there's no pretentiousness. Unlike large cruise ships, these small vessels are rarely out of sight of land. Their operators seek out lesser-known areas, offering in-depth visits to destinations inaccessible to larger ships, both along the eastern coast and in Alaska. If you are the sort of person who prefers a small country inn to a larger resort, this type of cruise might appeal.

The ships, measuring under 2,500 tons and classified as "D-class" vessels, are subject neither to the bureaucratic regulations nor to the union rules that sounded the death knell for large US-registered ships. They are restricted to cruising no more than 20 miles (32 km) offshore, at a comfortable 12 knots. Public room facilities are limited, and because the vessels are of American registry, there is no casino. For entertainment, passengers are usually left to their own devices. Most vessels are in port during the evening, so you can easily go ashore for the local nightlife.

Accommodation is in outside-view cabins (some open directly onto the deck, not convenient when it rains), each with a picture window and small bathroom. The cabins are small but cozy, and closet space is very limited. There's no room service, and you turn your own bed down. Cabins are closer to the engines and generators so noise can be considerable at night. The quietest cabins are at the bow, and most cruising is done by day so passengers can sleep better at night. Tall passengers should note that the overall length of beds rarely exceeds 6 feet (1.82 meters).

The principal evening event is dinner in the dining room, which accommodates all passengers at once. This can be a family-style affair, with passengers at long tables, and the food passed around. The cuisine is decidedly American, with fresh local specialties featured.

These vessels usually have three or four decks, and no elevators. Stairs can be on the steep side and are not recommended for people with walking difficulties. This kind of cruise is good for those who do enjoy a family-type cruise experience in pleasant surroundings. The maxim "You just relax, we'll move the scenery" is very appropriate in this case. A small selection of coastal and inland cruise vessels is featured in the profiles in Part Two, since they are small and specialized and have limited facilities.

River and Barge Cruising

Whether you want to cruise down the Nile, along the mighty Amazon or the lesser Orinoco, the stately Volga or the primal Sepik, the magnificent Rhine or the "blue" Danube, along the mystical Ayeyarwady (formerly the Irrawaddy) or the "yellow" Yangtze – to say nothing of the Don and the Dnieper, the Elbe, or Australia's Murray – there's a river vessel and cruise to suit you.

What sort of person enjoys cruising aboard river vessels? Well, anyone who survives well without dressing up, bingo, casinos, discos, or entertainment, and those who want a totally unstructured lifestyle. In 2003, more than *1 million* people took a river/inland waterway cruise.

European River Cruising

Cruising down one of Europe's great waterways is a soothing experience – different from sailing on an open sea, where wave motion is a factor. These cruises provide a constant change of scenery, often passing through several countries, each with its own history and architecture, in a week-long journey. River vessels are always close to land and provide a chance to visit cities and areas inaccessible to the large resort ships. A cruise along the Danube, for example, will take you through four countries and from the Black Forest to the Black Sea.

The new Rhine-Main-Danube waterway, at 2,175 miles (3,500 km), is the longest waterway in Europe. It connects 14 countries, from Rotterdam on the North Sea to Sulina and Izmail on the Black Sea, and offers river travelers some of the most fascinating sights anywhere.

River vessels are long and low in the water, and their masts fold down in order to negotiate low bridges. Although small when compared to oceangoing cruise ships, they have a unique and friendly international atmosphere. The most modern are air-conditioned and offer the discreet luxury of a small floating hotel, with several public rooms

Norwegian Coastal Voyages Ships

Ship	Tonnage	Built	Berths
Finnmarken	12,000	2002	675
Kong Harald	11,200	1993	490
Midnatsol	16,053	2003	650
Narvik	4,073	1982	314
Nordkapp	11,386	1996	490
Nordlys	11,200	1994	490
Nordnorge	11,386	1997	490
Polarlys	12,000	1996	490
Richard With	11,205	1993	490
Trollfjord	12,000	2002	674
Vesterålen	6,261	1983	314

Coastal Cruise Vessels (more than 10 cabins)

Ship	Cruise Line	Cabins	Region	Built
Ambassador I	Marco Polo Cruises	45	Galapagos Islands	1959
American Eagle	American Cruise Lines	27	USA Coastal Cruises	2000
American Glory	American Cruise Lines	27	USA Coastal Cruises	2002
Aranui 3*	Campagnie Polynesienne de Transport Maritime	63	Tahiti/Marquesas	2003
Callisto	Travel Dynamics International	17	Greek Isles	
Coral Princess	Coral Princess Cruises	27	Australia (Great Barrier Reef)	1988
Coral Princess II	Coral Princess Cruises	25	Australia (Great Barrier Reef)	1987
Corinthian	Ecoventura/Galapagos Network	45	Galapagos Islands	1967
Executive Explorer	Glacier Bay Cruises	25	Alaska	1986
Grande Caribe	American Canadian Caribbean Line	48	USA Coastal Cruises	1997
Grande Mariner	American Canadian Caribbean Line	50	USA Coastal Cruises	1999
Halcyon	Various operators	24	Greek Islands, Mediterranean	1990
Haumana	Bora Bora Cruises	19	Tahiti and Islands	1997
Isabela II	Metropolitan Touring	21	Galapagos Islands	1989
Lycianda	Blue Lagoon Cruises	21	Yasawa Islands (Fiji)	1984
Mare Australis	Cruceros Australis	63	Patagonia	2002
Mystique Princess	Blue Lagoon Cruises	36	Yasawa Islands (Fiji)	1996
Nantucket Clipper	Clipper Cruise Line	51	USA Coastal Cruises	1984
Nanuya Princess	Blue Lagoon Cruises	25	Yasawa Islands (Fiji)	1987
Niagara Prince	American Canadian Caribbean Line	42	USA Coastal Cruises	1994
Pegasus	Classical Cruises	23	Greek Islands, Mediterranean	1992
Reef Endeavour	Captain Cook Cruises	75	Australia (Great Barrier Reef)	1995
ReefEscape	Captain Cook Cruises	60	Australia	1987
Santa Cruz	Metropolitan Touring	43	Galapagos Islands	1979
Sea Bird	Lindblad Expeditions	35	Alaska, Baja	1981
Sea Lion	Lindblad Expeditions	35	Alaska, Baja	1982
Sea Voyager	Lindblad Expeditions	33	Central America	1982
Shearwater	Various operators	40	Worldwide	1962
Spirit of '98	Cruise West	48	Alaska	1984
Spirit of Alaska	Cruise West	39	Alaska	1980
Spirit of Columbia	Cruise West	39	Alaska	1979
Spirit of Discovery	Cruise West	25	Alaska	1982
Spirit of Endeavor	Cruise West	51	Alaska	1983
Spirit of Glacier Bay	Cruise West	43	Alaska	1971
Spirit of Oceanus	Cruise West	50	Alaska/South Pacific	1991
Sydney 2000	Captain Cook Cruises	60	Australia	1979
Temptress Explorer	Temptress Adventure Cruises	50	Central America	1970
Tia Moana	Bora Bora Cruises	37	Tahitian Islands	2003
Tu Moana	Bora Bora Cruises	37	Tahitian Islands	2003
Tropic Sun	Aquanaut Cruise Lines	18	Galapagos Islands	1967
Wilderness Adventurer	Glacier Bay Cruises	38	Alaska	1983
Wilderness Discoverer	Glacier Bay Cruises	43	Alaska	1992
Wilderness Explorer	Glacier Bay Cruises	18	Alaska	1969
Yasawa Princess	Blue Lagoon Cruises	33	Yasawa Islands (Fiji)	1984
Yorktown Clipper	Clipper Cruise Line	69	USA Coastal Cruises	1988

KEY * = Coastal Freighter

including a dining room, observation lounge, bar, heated swimming "dip" pool (some even have a heated indoor pool), sauna, solarium, whirlpool, gymnasium, massage, hairdresser, and shop kiosk.

Although the cabins may be small, with limited closet space (take casual clothing, as informality is the order of the day), they are functional. Almost all have an outside view (facing the river), with a private bathroom, and will prove very comfortable for a one-week journey. Romantics should note that twin beds are the norm (they can seldom be pushed together). Many cabins in the latest vessels have a personal safe, a mini-bar, a TV set, and an alarm clock/radio. The ceilings are rather low, and the beds are short.

River cruising in Europe has reached quite a sophisticated level, and you can be assured of good service and meals of a consistently high European standard. Dining is a pleasant although not always a gourmet experience (the best food is that catered by Austrian, German or Swiss companies). While lunch is generally a buffet affair, dinners feature a set menu consisting of three or four courses.

Typical rates for river cruises are from $800 to over $3,000 per person for a one-week cruise, including meals, cabin with private facilities, side trips, and airport/railway transfers. If you are already in Europe, many cruises can be purchased "cruise-only" for greater flexibility.

Tip: It is best to go for a cabin on a deck that doesn't have a promenade deck walkway outside it. Normally, cabins on the lowest deck have a four-berth configuration. It does not matter which side of the vessel you are on, as you will see a riverbank and scenery on both sides.

River Cruising: Russia

Often referred to as the "Waterways of the Tsars," the country benefits from a well-developed network of rivers, lakes, and canals. Geographically, river routes for tourists are divided into three main areas: Central European Russia, Northwestern European Russia, and Asian Russia.

In the days before privatization, Rechtflot was the Russian government's management overlord, with 21 shipping companies and a combined fleet of more than 5,000 vessels, which together carried more than 20 million passengers and about 500 million tons of cargo each year. Today, there are about 80 river cruise vessels that carry international tourists.

In the Central Basin, Moscow is the hub of river tourism, and the newly opened waterways between Moscow and St. Petersburg allow a seven-day cruise link between the present and former capitals. The best-known Russian rivers are the Don, Moskva, Neva, and Volga, but the lesser known Belaya, Dvina (and North Dvina) Irtysh, Kama, Ob (longest river in Siberia), Oka, Svir, Tura, and Vyatka connect the great system of rivers and lakes in the vast Russian hinterland.

Many Russian vessels are chartered to foreign cruise wholesalers and tour packagers. The vessels do vary quite a lot in quality and facilities. Some are air-conditioned and most are clean.

One unusual Russian river vessel worth mentioning, *Rossiya*, is used for state visits and is extremely elegant and fitted throughout with exceptionally fine materials. Cruises include the services of a cruise manager and lecturers. Some companies also specialize in pre- or post-cruise "home stays" as part of a cultural package.

River Cruising: The Nile

A journey along the Nile is a journey back in time, to over 4,000 years before the birth of Christ, when one of the greatest civilizations in history lived along the river's banks. The scenery has changed remarkably little in over 2,000 years. The best way to see it, of course, is by riverboat.

In all, there are over 7,000 departures every year aboard 300 or so Nile cruise vessels, which offer standards of comfort, food, and service that vary between very good and extremely poor. Most have a swimming pool, lounge, piano bar, and disco. A specialist lecturer in ancient Egyptian history accompanies almost all sailings, which cruise the 140 miles (220 km) between Aswân and Luxor in four or five days. Extended cruises, typically of seven or eight days, cover about 295 miles (475 km) and visit Dendera and Abydos. The longest cruises, of 10 to 12 days, cover 590 miles (950 km) and include visits to Sohâg, El Amarna, Tuna El Gabal, and Ashmuneim, ending in Cairo.

Most Nile cruises include sight-seeing excursions, which are accompanied by experienced, trained guides who may reside on board, or who may meet the boat at each call. Security in Egypt generally has been much improved in recent years, though it's wise to be vigilant.

River Cruising: China

About 60 rivercruise vessels offer cruises along the Yangtze, the world's third-longest river, particularly through the area known as the Three Yangtze River Gorges, a 100-mile (160-km) stretch between Nanjin Pass in the east and White King City in the west.

The Yangtze stretches 3,900 miles (6,300 km) from Shanghai through the very heartland of China. The Three Gorges include the 47-mile-long (76-km) Xiling Gorge, the 25-mile-long (40-km) Wu Gorge, and the 28-mile-long (45-km) Qutang Gorge (known locally as "Wind Box Gorge"). The Lesser Three Gorges (or Three Small Gorges) are also an impressive sight, often part of the main

Exploring the Yangtze, the world's third longest river.

cruise but also reached by small vessels from Wushan. If possible, take a cabin with a balcony. It is worth the extra money, and the view is better.

Standards of hygiene are generally far lower than you may be used to at home. In China, rats and rivers often go together, and rat poison may well be found under your bed. Some vessels have Chinese- and western-style restaurants, a beauty salon, a small health club with sauna, and private mah-jong and karaoke rooms. Fine Asian hospitality and service prevail, and cabins are kept supplied with fresh towels and hot tea.

There are several other operators, but do check on the facilities, meet-and-greet service, and the newness of the vessels before booking. The best time of the year to go is May–June, and late August–October (July and early August are extremely hot and humid).

The new $60 billion hydroelectric Sanxia (Three Gorges) Dam, will create, when completed in 2009, a reservoir 375 miles long (600 km), and 575 ft deep (175 meters), with an average width of 3,600 ft (1,100 meters). It will submerge 13 cities, 140 towns, 1,352 villages, 657 factories and 66 million acres of cultivated land (more than 1½ million people will be relocated). The new Three Gorges Dam locks (larger than the Panama Canal locks) are in full operation.

The dam will eventually raise the River only 150 ft (45 meters) against the backdrop of the Three Gorges, which rise majestically some 3,280 ft (1,000 meters). Cruise vessels of up to 10,000 tons will be able to sail up the Yangtze from the Pacific Ocean, and the dam will reduce flooding in the region.

Ayeyarwady (Irrawaddy) River (Myanmar)

How about the *Road to Mandalay*? Orient Express Hotels operates a fine river cruise vessel in Myanmar (formerly known as Burma). The river vessel *Road to Mandalay* operates weekly between Mandalay and Pagan, along the Ayeyarwady (formerly Irrawaddy) River. Or there are two smaller vessels: *Pandaw*, a stern-wheeler built in Scotland in 1947, and *Pandaw II*, a slightly larger replica, introduced in 2001.

River Murray (Australia)

The fifth-largest river in the world, the Murray, was the lifeblood of the pioneers who lived on the driest continent on earth. Today, the river flows for more than 1,250 miles (2,760 km) across a third of Australia, its banks forming protected lagoons for an astonishing variety of bird and animal life. Paddlewheel boats such as *Murray Princess* offer most of the amenities found aboard America's *Mississippi Queen*. There are even six cabins for the physically disabled.

Barge Cruising: Europe

Smaller and more intimate than river vessels, and more accurately called boats, "cruise barges" ply the inland waterways and canals of Europe from spring to fall, when the weather is best. Barge cruises (usually of 3 to 13 days' duration) offer a completely informal atmosphere, and a slow pace of life, for up to a dozen passengers. They chug along slowly in the daytime, and moor early each evening, giving you time to pay a visit to a local village and get a restful night's sleep. The inland waterways of Europe all adhere to the CEVNI regulations (Code Européan des Voies de la Navigation Intérieur), a United Nations instrument with international authority and relevance.

Most cruise barges are comfortable and beautifully fitted out with rich wood paneling, full carpeting, custom-built furniture and tastefully chosen fabrics. Each has a dining room/lounge-bar. Captains take pride in their vessel, often displaying some rare memorabilia.

Locally grown fresh foods are usually purchased and prepared each day, allowing you to live well and feel like a houseguest. Most cruise barges can also be chartered exclusively so you can just take your family and friends, for example.

The waterways of France especially offer beauty, tranquility, and a diversity of interests, and barge cruising is an excellent way of exploring an area not previously visited. Most cruises include a visit to a famous vineyard and wine cellar, as well as side trips to places of historic, architectural, or scenic interest. Shopping opportunities are limited, and evening entertainment is impromptu. You

A cruise barge is a convenient way to see Europe.

will be accompanied by a crew member familiar with the surrounding countryside. You can even go hot-air ballooning over the local countryside (an expensive extra) and land to a glass of champagne and your flight certificate.

How you dine on board a barge will depend on the barge and area; dining ranges from home-style cooking to outstanding nouvelle cuisine, with all the trimmings. Often, the barge's owner, or spouse, turns out to be the cook.

Barging on the canals often means going through a constant succession of locks. Nowhere is this more enjoyable and entertaining than in the Burgundy region of France where, between Dijon and Mâcon, for example, a barge can negotiate as many as 54 locks during a six-day cruise. Interestingly, all lockkeepers in France are women.

Rates range from $600 to more than $3,000 per person for a six-day cruise. I do not recommend taking children. Rates include a cabin with private facilities, all meals, good wine with lunch and dinner, other beverages, use of bicycles, side trips, and airport/railway transfers. Some operators provide a hotel the night before or after the cruise. Clothing is totally casual – but, at the beginning and end of the season, take sweaters and rain gear.

Steamboating: United States

The most famous of all American river cruises are those aboard the steamboats of the mighty Mississippi River. Mark Twain, a fan of such travel, at one time said: "When man can go 700 miles an hour, he'll want to go seven again."

The grand traditions of the steamboat era are maintained by the *American Queen*, and by the older, smaller *Delta Queen* and *Mississippi Queen*

The *American Queen* steamboat on the Mississippi.

(Delta Queen Steamboat Company), all of which are powered by steam engines that drive huge wooden paddlewheels at the stern. The smallest and oldest of the three boats, the 174-passenger *Delta Queen*, was built on Scotland's Clydeside in 1926, and was placed on the US National Register of Historic Places in 1989. President Carter spent a week aboard the vessel in 1979.

Half a century younger, the $27-million, 400-passenger *Mississippi Queen* was constructed in Jefferson, Indiana, where nearly 5,000 steamboats were built during the 19th century. *Mississippi Queen* was designed by James Gardner of London (creator of Cunard's *QE2*).

Traveling aboard one of the steamboats is like stepping into the past. There's a certain charm and old-world graciousness as well as delightful woods, brass, and flowing staircases. And, once a year, boats challenge one another in the Great Steamboat Race, a 10-day extravaganza.

Steamboat cruises, up and down the Mississippi and Ohio rivers, last from 2 to 12 days, and during the year there are several theme cruises, with big bands and lively entertainment. The food is American fare, which means steak, and shrimp, Creole sauces, fried foods, and few fresh vegetables.

Expedition/Nature Cruises

There are countless virtually untouched areas to be visited by the more adventurous, whose motto might be "see it before it is spoiled." Such passengers tend to be more self-reliant and more interested in doing or learning than in being entertained. Passengers become "participants" and take an active role in almost every aspect of the voyage, which is destination-, exploration-, and nature-intensive. Naturalists, historians, and lecturers (rather than entertainers) are aboard each ship to provide background information and observations about wildlife. Each participant receives a personal logbook, illustrated and written by the wildlife artists and writers who accompany each cruise. The logbook documents the entire voyage and serves as a great source of information as well as a diary of your cruise. Adventure cruise companies provide expedition parka and waterproof boots, but you will need to take waterproof trousers (for Antarctica and the Arctic).

You can walk on pack ice in the islands in the Arctic Ocean and Arctic Circle, explore a gigantic penguin rookery on an island in the Antarctic Peninsula, the Falkland Islands or South Georgia, or search for "lost" peoples in Melanesia. Or you can cruise close to the source of the Amazon, gaze at species of flora and fauna in the Galápagos Islands (Darwin's laboratory), or watch a genuine dragon on the island of Komodo (from a comfortable distance, of course).

Briefings and lectures bring cultural and intellectual elements to expedition cruise vessels. There is no formal entertainment as such; passengers enjoy this type of cruise more for the camaraderie and learning experience, and being close to nature. The ships are designed and equipped to sail in ice-laden waters, yet they have a shallow enough draft to glide over coral reefs.

Expedition cruise vessels can, nevertheless, provide comfortable and even elegant surroundings for up to 200 passengers, and offer first-class food and service. Without traditional cruise ports at which to stop, a ship must be self-sufficient, capable of long-range cruising, and totally environmentally friendly.

Lars-Eric Lindblad pioneered expedition cruising in the late 1960s. A Swedish American, he was determined to turn travel into adventure by opening up parts of the world tourists had not visited. After chartering several vessels for cruises to Antarctica (which he started in 1966), he organized the design and construction of a ship capable of going almost anywhere in comfort and safety. In 1969, *Lindblad Explorer* was launched, and soon earned an enviable reputation in adventure travel. Lindblad sold it to Salen-Lindblad Cruising in 1982. They subsequently resold it to Society Expeditions, which renamed it *Society Explorer* (the ship was withdrawn from service in October 2003).

Specialist adventure and expedition cruise companies provide in-depth expertise and specially constructed vessels, usually with ice-hardened hulls that are capable of going into the vast reaches of the Arctic and Antarctica.

Expedition/Nature Cruise Areas

Buddha was once asked to express verbally what life meant to him. He waited a moment – then, without speaking, held up a single rose. Several "destinations" on our planet cannot be adequately described by words. Like the rose, they have to be experienced. The principal adventure cruise areas of the world are Alaska and the Aleutians, the Amazon and the Orinoco, Antarctica, Australasia and the Great Barrier Reef, the Chilean fjords, the Galápagos Archipelago, Indonesia, Melanesia, the Northwest Passage, Polynesia, and the South Pacific. Baja California and the Sea of

A close-up look at Alaska.

Cortez, Greenland, the Red Sea, East Africa, the Réunion Islands and the Seychelles, West Africa and the Ivory Coast, and the South China Seas and China Coast are other adventure cruise destinations growing in popularity.

To put together cruise expeditions, companies turn to knowledgeable sources and advisors. Scientific institutions are consulted; experienced world explorers and naturalists provide up-to-date reports on wildlife sightings, migrations, and other natural phenomena. Although some days are scheduled for relaxation, participants are kept physically and mentally active. Speaking of physical activity, it is unwise to consider such an adventure cruise if you are not completely ambulatory.

Antarctica

This is the ultimate place to chill-out. It was first sighted only in 1820 by the American sealer Nathaniel Palmer, British naval officer Edward Bransfield, and Russian captain Fabian Bellingshausen. For most, it is just a wind-swept frozen wasteland (it has been calculated that the ice mass contains almost 90 percent of the world's snow and ice). For others, it represents the last pristine place on earth, empty of people, commerce, and pollution, yet offering awesome icescape scenery and a truly wonderful abundance of marine and bird life. There are no germs and not a single tree.

More than 12,000 people visited the continent – the only smoke-free continent on earth – in 2001, yet the first human to come here did so within a

---

Passenger Ships through the Northwest Passage

1984 *Lindblad Explorer* (Capt. Hasse Nilsson)
1985 *World Discoverer* (Capt. Heinz Aye)
1988 *Society Explorer* (Capt. Heinz Aye)
1991 *Frontier Spirit* Ship returned at Flaxman Island – trip cancelled (Capt. Heinz Aye)
1992 *Frontier Spirit* (Capt. Hainz Aye)
1994 *Kapitan Khlebnikov*
1995 *Hanseatic* (Capt. Hartwig von Harling)
1995 *Kapitan Khlebnikov* (Capt. Hartwig von Harling)
1996 *Hanseatic* Grounded Simpson Street for 10 days – passengers taken aboard *Kapitan Dranitsyn* (Capt. Hartwig von Harling)
1997 *Hanseatic* (Capt. Heinz Aye)
1998 *Kapitan Khlebnikov*
1998 *Hanseatic* (Capt. Heinz Aye)

generation of man landing on the moon. There is not a single permanent inhabitant of the continent, whose ice is as much as 2 miles thick. Its total land mass equals more than all the rivers and lakes on earth and exceeds that of China and India combined. Icebergs can easily be the size of Belgium. The continent has a raw beauty and an ever-changing landscape, but do take sunscreen, as there is no pollution and it is easy to get sunburned when the weather is good.

Once part of the ancient land mass known as Gondwanaland (which also included Africa, South America, India, Australasia, and Madagascar), it is, perhaps, the closest thing on earth to another planet, and it has an incredibly fragile ecosystem that needs international protection.

Although visited by "soft" expedition cruise ships and even "normal"-sized cruise ships with ice-hardened hulls, the more remote "far side" – the Oates and Scott Coasts, McMurdo Sound, and the famous Ross Ice Shelf – can be visited only by real icebreakers such as *Kapitan Dranitsyn, Kapitan Khlebnikov* and *Yamal* (they carry 100 passengers or fewer), as the winds can easily reach more than 100 mph (160 km/h).

There are no docks in Antarctica, so venturing "ashore" is done by Zodiacs – rubber inflatable craft, an integral part of the Antarctica experience. Be aware that you *can* get stuck even aboard these specialized expedition ships, as did *Clipper Adventurer* in February 2000, in an ice field – it had to be rescued by an Argentine Navy icebreaker.

Note to photographers: take plastic bags to cover your camera, so that condensation forms inside the bag and not on your camera when changing from the cold of the outside Antarctic air to the warmth of your expedition cruise vessel. Make sure you know how to operate your camera with gloves on (taking them off even for a short time could induce frostbite in poor weather conditions).

The Arctic

Want some Northern Exposure? Try the Arctic. The Arctic is an ocean surrounded by continents, whereas Antarctica is an ice-covered continent surrounded by ocean. The Arctic Circle is located at 66 degrees, 33 minutes, and 3 seconds north, although this really designates where 24-hour days and nights begin. The Arctic is best defined as that region north of which no trees grow, and where water is the primary feature of the landscape. It is technically a desert (receiving less than 10 inches of rainfall a year) but actually teems with wildlife, including polar bears, walruses, seals, and Arctic birds. It has short, cool summers; long, cold winters; and frequent high winds. Canada's Northwest Territories, which cover 1.3 million square miles, is part of the Arctic region, as are some of Russia's northernmost islands such as Franz Josef Land. Photographers should note the practical advice given for Antarctica.

Galápagos

A word of advice about the Galápagos Islands: do not even think about taking a cruise with a "non-Ecuadorian flag" ship; the Ecuadorians jealously guard their islands and prohibit the movement of almost all non-Ecuadorian-registered cruise vessels within its boundaries. The best way to see this place that Darwin loved is to fly to Quito and cruise aboard an Ecuadorian-registered vessel.

DID YOU KNOW?

● that passengers once asked the operations director of a well-known expedition cruise ship where the best shops were in Antarctica? His reply: "On board, madam!"

● that Quark Expeditions had the good fortune of making maritime history in July/August 1991, when its chartered Russian icebreaker, *Sovetskiy Soyuz*, made a spectacular 21-day voyage to negotiate a passage from Murmansk, Russia, to Nome, Alaska, across the North Pole? The ship followed the trail that had been set in 1909 by Admiral Peary, who crossed the North Pole with 56 Eskimos, leaving by sled from Ellesmere Island. Although the polar ice cap had been navigated by the US nuclear submarines *Skate* and *Nautilus*, as well as by dirigible and airplane, this was the first passenger ship to make the hazardous crossing (planning for it took over two years).

● that in 1984, Salen Lindblad Cruising made maritime history by successfully negotiating a westbound voyage through the Northwest Passage, a 41-day epic that started from St. John's, Newfoundland, in Canada, and ended at Yokohama, Japan? The expedition cruise had taken two years of planning and was sold out just days after it was announced. The search for a Northwest Passage to the Orient attracted brave explorers for more than four centuries. Despite numerous attempts and loss of life, including Henry Hudson in 1610, a "white passage" to the East remained an elusive dream. Amundsen's 47-ton ship *Gjoa* eventually navigated the route in 1906, taking three years to do so. It was not until 1943 that a Canadian ship, *St. Roch*, became the first vessel in history to make the passage in a single season. *Lindblad Explorer* became the 34th vessel, and the first cruise vessel, to complete the Northwest Passage.

● that the most expensive expedition cruise excursion was a cruise/dive to visit the resting place of RMS *Titanic* aboard the two deep-ocean submersibles *Mir I* and *Mir II* used in James Cameron's Hollywood blockbuster. Just 60 participants went as up-close-and-personal observers in 1998, and another 60 were taken in 1999.

The government of Ecuador set aside most of the islands as a wildlife sanctuary in 1934, while uninhabited areas were declared national parks in 1959. The national park includes approximately 97 per cent of the islands' landmass, together with 20,000 sq. miles (50,000 sq. km) of ocean. The Charles Darwin Research Station was established in 1964, and the government created the Galápagos Marine Resources Reserve in 1986.

Note that the Galápagos National Park tax is presently about $100 per person. Smoking is prohibited on the islands of the Galápagos, and visitors are limited to 50,000 a year.

Greenland

The world's largest island, Greenland, in the Northern Hemisphere's Arctic Circle, is technically a desert 82 percent covered with ice (actually compressed snow) up to 11,000 feet thick. Greenland's rocks are among the world's oldest (the 3.8

billion-year-old Isukasia formations), and its ecosystem is one of the newest.

Forget Alaska – the glacier at Jacobshavn (also known as Ilulissat) is the fastest moving in the world and creates a new iceberg every five minutes. Greenland is said to have more dogs than people, and these provide the principal means of transport for the Greenlanders.

The Environment

Since the increase in environmental awareness, adventurers have banded together to protect the environment from further damage. In the future, only ships capable of meeting new "zero discharge" standards, such as those introduced in the Arctic by the Canadian Coast Guard, will be allowed to proceed through environmentally sensitive areas. Expedition cruise companies are very concerned about the environment (none more than Hapag-Lloyd Cruises and Quark Expeditions),

How Berlitz Rates the Expedition Vessels

Research Vessels/ True Expedition Vessels	Rating (Ship/ Facilities)	Rating (Expedition Experience)	Company/Operator [1]
Akademik Ioffe	Basic (46)	55	Various Tour Operators
Akademik Sergey Vavilov	Basic (47)	58	Poseidon Arctic Voyages
Akademik Sholaskiy	Basic (43)	54	Various Tour Operators
Grigoriy Mikheev	Basic (46)	55	Oceanwide Expeditions
Kapitan Dranitsyn	Better (49)	62	Poseidon Arctic Voyages
Kapitan Khlebnikov	Better (51)	70	Quark Expeditions
Polar Pioneer	Basic (45)	60	Aurora Expeditions/ Peregrine Expeditions
Professor Molchanov	Basic (44)	64	Oceanwide Expeditions
Professor Multanovskiy	Basic (44)	64	Quark Expeditions
Yamal [2]	Better (75)	75	Quark Expeditions
More Luxurious Vessels			
Andrea	Basic (41)	43	Elegant Cruises & Tours
Bremen	Better (76)	77	Hapag-Lloyd Cruises
Clipper Adventurer	Better (56)	61	Clipper Cruise Line
Endeavour	Better (51)	64	Lindblad Expeditions
Explorer II	Better (54)	63	Abercrombie & Kent
Hanseatic	Best (85)	86	Hapag-Lloyd Cruises
Marco Polo	Better (54)	64	Orient Lines
Orion	Better (76)	78	Travel Dynamics International
Orlova	Better (63)	65	Quark Expeditions
Polar Star	Better (55)	58	Karlsen Shipping/ Polar Star Expeditions
World Discoverer	Better (62)	68	Society Expeditions

NOTES
(1) = most expedition ships are sold by multiple expedition companies, or operate

and they spend much time and money in educating both crews and passengers about safe environmental procedures.

An "Antarctic Traveler's Code" has been created, the rules of which are enforced by all expedition cruise companies. It is based on the Antarctic Conservation Act of 1978, designed to protect and preserve the ecosystem, flora, and fauna of the Antarctic continent, as well as Recommendation XVIII-1, adopted at the Antarctic Treaty Meeting in Kyoto in 1994.

Briefly, the Act makes it unlawful, unless authorized by regulation or permit, to take native animals or birds, to collect any special native plant or introduce species, to enter certain special areas (SPAs), or to discharge or dispose of any pollutants. To "take" means to remove, harass, molest, harm, pursue, hunt, shoot, kill, trap, capture, restrain, or tag any native mammal or bird, or to attempt to do so. Violators are subject to civil penalties, including a fine of up to $10,000 and one year imprisonment for each violation. The Act is found in the library of each adventure/expedition ship that visits the continent.

Will large cruise ships ever cruise in Antarctica? Not in the foreseeable future. Ships are limited to a maximum of 400 passengers, so the likelihood of a mega-ship zooming in on the penguins with 2,000-plus passengers is unlikely (nor would it be possible to rescue passengers and crew in the event of an emergency).

The Companies

Abercrombie & Kent operates *Explorer II*.

Aurora Expeditions charters and operates the 56-passenger *Polar Pioneer*, a small Russian icebreaker, and includes camping and sea kayaking as options in Antarctica.

Clipper Cruise Lines operates *Clipper Adventurer*, a small ship with a hull that is ice-hardened.

Built	Tonnage	Registry	Length (m)	Pass. Cabins	Max No. Passengers	Former Names
1988	6,460	Russia	117.10	55	110	*Marine Adventurer, Akademik Ioffe*
1988	6,231	Russia	117.80	40	110	
1982	2,140	Russia	71.56	22	44	
1990	2,000	Russia	70.00	22	44	
1980	10,471	Russia	131.00	53	113	
1981	12,288	Russia	132.49	54	114	
1985	2,140	Russia	71.60	26	54	*Marine Spirit, Akademik Shuleykin*
1983	1,753	Russia	71.60	29	52	
1983	1,753	Russia	71.60	29	49	
1992	23,445	Russia	150.00	50	100	
1960	2,568	Norway	87.40	57	112	*Harald Jarl*
1990	6,752	The Bahamas	111.51	82	184	*Frontier Spirit*
1976	5,750	The Bahamas	100.01	61	122	*Alla Tarasova*
1966	3,132	The Bahamas	89.20	62	110	*Caledonian Star North Star, Lindmar, Marburg*
1996	12,500	The Bahamas	133.00	178	474	*Minerva, Okean*
1993	8,378	The Bahamas	122.80	92	194	*Society Adventurer*
1965	22,080	The Bahamas	176.28	425	915	*Alexandr Pushkin*
2003	4,050	The Bahamas	102.70	53	139	
1976	4,251	Yugoslavia	90.91	62	124	*Marine Discovery, Lyubov Orlova*
1969	4,998	Barbados	86.50	45	105	*Njord*
1989	6,000	The Bahamas	108.20	82	164	*Dream 21, Baltic Clipper, Sally Clipper, Delfin Clipper*

under sole charter conditions   (2) = nuclear powered

Bremen in Lamaire Channel, Antarctic Peninsula.

Hapag-Lloyd Cruises operates *Bremen* and *Hanseatic*, small, high-tech expedition cruise vessels. Both ships have fine, rather luxurious appointments (*Bremen* is less luxurious than *Hanseatic*) and are marketed to both English- and German-speaking passengers.

Lindblad Expeditions operates *Polaris*, a small expedition vessel operating in the Galápagos Islands, which offers welcome creature comforts (see listings section for details). In addition, two small vessels, *Sea Bird* and *Sea Lion* (former Exploration Cruise Lines vessels) operate "soft" coastal cruises in protected coastal areas in the United States, including Alaska.

Quark Expeditions charters Russian-owned nuclear- or diesel-powered icebreakers fitted with some outstanding amenities and decent creature comforts for up to 100 passengers. The operator, a pioneer in this specialized segment of the cruise industry, concentrates on itineraries to the Antarctic, the Arctic, and North Polar regions. Among the vessels chartered are the superb *Kapitan Khlebnikov, Professor Molchanov, Orlova, Professor Multanovskiy,* and *Yamal*.

Sail-powered Cruise "Yachts"

Thinking of a cruise but really want to be free as the wind? Think about cruising under sail, with towering masts, the creak of taut ropes and washing-powder-white sails to power you along. There is simply nothing that beats the thrill of being aboard a multi-mast tall ship, sailing under thousands of square feet of canvas through waters that mariners have sailed for centuries. This is cruising in the traditional manner, aboard authentic sailing ships, contemporary copies of clipper ships, or aboard the latest high-tech cruise-sail ships.

There are no rigid schedules, and life aboard equates to an unstructured lifestyle, apart from meal times. Weather conditions may often dictate whether a scheduled port visit will be made or not, but passengers sailing on these vessels are usually unconcerned. They would rather savor the thrill of being one with nature, albeit in a comfortable, civilized setting, and without having to do the work themselves.

Real Tall Ships

While we have all been dreaming of adventure, a pocketful of designers and yachtsmen committed pen to paper, hand in pocket and rigging to mast, and came up with a potpourri of stunning vessels to delight the eye and refresh the spirit.

Look in the listings section for these true, working tall ships: *Royal Clipper, Sea Cloud, Sea Cloud II, Star Clipper,* and *Star Flyer*. Of these, *Sea Cloud* has a history that spans over 70 years – a true veteran working sailing ship that still is at the height of luxury under sail.

In the Caribbean, Windjammer Barefoot Cruises also operates a fleet of five tall ships offering very basic fun-and-sun cruises: *Flying Cloud, Legacy, Mandalay, Polynesia,* and *Yankee Clipper*. Only shorts and T-shirts are needed. Although cabin towels are provided, you'll need to take your own beach towels. Only one vessel is certified by the US Coast Guard, the others are not, although they do comply with most international safety regulations.

Contemporary Sail-Cruise Ships

To combine sailing with push-button automation, try *Club Med 2* (Club Mediterranée) or *Wind Surf* (Windstar Cruises) – with five tall aluminum masts, they are the world's largest sail-cruise ships – and *Wind Song*, *Wind Spirit*, and *Wind Star* (Windstar Cruises), with four masts. Not a hand touches the sails; they are computer-controlled from the navigation bridge. Indeed, these ships are contemporary oceangoing robots. A drawback for some people is that there's little sense of sailing because the computer controls keep the ship on a steady, even keel.

From a yachtsman's viewpoint, the sail-to-power ratio is poor. That's why these cruise ships with sails have engine power to get them into and out of port. (The Star Clipper ships, by contrast, do it by sail alone, except when there is no wind, which is infrequent.). On some itineraries, when there is little wind, you could well be under motor power for most of the cruise, with only a few hours spent under sail. The four Windstar Cruises' vessels and one Club Med ship are typically under sail for about 40 percent of the time.

It was a Norwegian living in New York, Karl Andren, who first turned the concept of a cruise vessel with sails into reality. "Boyhood dream stuff," he said. The shipyard (Société Nouvelle des Ateliers et Chantiers du Havre – or ACH, as it is known locally), enjoyed the challenge of building these most unusual vessels, having had much experience in the design and construction of cable-laying ships using the hydraulic power of servomechanisms.

The Windstar ships carry mainly North American passengers, whereas the Club Med vessel caters primarily to French-speaking passengers.

Another slightly smaller but very chic vessel is the sleek *Le Ponant*. This three-mast ship caters to just 64 French-speaking passengers in elegant, yet casual, high-tech surroundings, developing the original Windstar concept to an advanced state of contemporary technology.

Freighter Travel

More than 3,000 passengers travel by freighter each year, and the number is growing as passengers become further disenchanted with the large resort ships that dominate the cruise industry. Traveling by freighter is also the ultimate way to travel for those seeking a totally unstructured voyage without entertainment or other diversions.

There are about 250 cargo ships (freighters and container vessels) offering berths, with German operators accounting for about more than half of them. True freighters – the general breakbulk carrier ships and feeder container vessels – carry up to 12 passengers. Freighter schedules change constantly, depending on the whim of the owner and the cargo to be carried, whereas container ships travel on regular schedules. For the sake of simplicity, they are all termed freighters.

Star Clippers' superb *Royal Clipper* under full sail.

Wind Spirit, one of three similar vessels.

Freighters have changed dramatically over the past few years, as cost management and efficiency have become vital. Container ships are operated as passenger liners used to be – running line voyages on set schedules, or name-day voyages, as they are presently termed.

Passengers opting for this type of travel typically include independent types (anyone allergic to traveling in groups), retirees, relocating executives, people with family connections in other countries, graduates returning home from an overseas educational establishment, or professors on sabbatical. Because there are no medical facilities, maximum age limits are imposed by most freighter companies and anyone over the age of 65 must produce a medical certificate of good health.

What do you get when you book a freighter voyage? You get a cabin with double or twin beds, a small writing table, and a private bathroom. You also get good company, cocktails with conversation, hearty food (you'll eat in one seating with the ship's officers), an interesting voyage, a lot of water, and the allure of days at sea. What don't you get? Entertainment, bingo, horse racing, and other mindless parlor games (unless you take them with you). You will certainly have time to relax and unwind completely, read books (some freighters have a small library), or play card games or board games with the few other passengers who may be on board.

The accommodation will typically consist of a spacious and well-equipped outside-view cabin high above the water line, with a large window rather than a porthole, comfortable lounge/sitting area, and private facilities – generally far larger than most standard cruise ship cabins.

While freighter travel can be less expensive than regular cruise ship travel on a per day basis ($75–$150), remember that voyages last much longer – typically 30 days or more – so the cost can be considerable. Most are sold out far in advance (often more than a year ahead), so plan

THE LOWDOWN ON FREIGHTERS

Freighters that take passengers

The following lines offer regular passenger voyages year-round:
American President Lines, Australia New Zealand Direct Lines, Bank Line, Blue Star Line, Canada Maritime, Chilean Lines, Cho Yang Shipping, Columbus Line, Egon Oldendorff, Great Lakes Shipping, Hamburg-Sud, Hanseatic Shipping Company, Hapag-Lloyd, Ivaran Lines, Lykes Brothers Steamship Company, Mediterranean Shipping Company, Nauru Pacific Line, Safmarine Cruises, and United Baltic Corporation.

Books and Information

Traveltips Cruise & Freighter Association
P.O. Box 580188, Flushing, NY 11358, USA
Freighter World Cruises
180 South Lake Avenue, Suite 335, Pasadena, CA 91101, USA
The Cruise People
88 York Street, London W1H 1DP, England
Strand Voyages
Charing Cross Shopping Concourse, Strand, London WC2N 4HZ, England
Sydney International Travel Centre
75 King Street, Level 8, Sydney 2000, Australia

ahead, and purchase trip cancellation insurance.

What to take with you? Casual clothing (do check with the freighter line, as some require a jacket and tie for dinner), all medication, cosmetics, and toiletry items, hairdryer, multi-voltage converter plug, washing powder, and other sundry items. There may be a small "shop" on board (for the crew) carrying bare essentials like toothpaste. Bring along some extra photos of yourself in case the ship makes unannounced port stops and visas are required. The only gratuities needed are for the waiter and cabin steward, at about $1–$2 per day, per person.

Freighters sometimes have to cancel port calls for various reasons. So if you are initially attracted by a particular itinerary or a certain port, bear in mind that the details are subject to change.

Crossings

By "crossings," I mean crossings 3,000 miles (4,800 km) or so that constitute the North Atlantic, although the term might include any other major stretches of water, such as the Pacific Ocean or the Indian Ocean.

The North Atlantic

Crossing the North Atlantic by passenger vessel should really be considered an art form. I have done it myself 149 times and always enjoy it immensely. I consider crossings as rests in musical parlance, for both are described as "passages." Indeed, musicians do often "hear" rests in between notes. So if ports of call are the musical notes of a voyage, then the rests are the days at sea – a temporary interlude, when the indulgence of the person and psyche are of paramount importance.

Experienced mariners will tell you that a ship only behaves like a ship when it is doing a crossing, for that's what a real ship is built for. Yet the days when ships were built specifically for crossings are almost gone. The only ship offering a regularly scheduled transatlantic service (a "crossing") is Cunard's *Queen Mary 2*, a 148,151-grt ship, built with an incredibly thick hull, designed to hold well against the worst weather the North Atlantic has to offer. Indeed, captains work harder on an Atlantic crossing than on regular cruising schedules.

The most unpredictable weather in the world, together with fog off the Grand Banks of Newfoundland, can mean that the captain will spend torturous hours on the bridge, with little time for socializing. When it is foggy, the crew of *QM2* are often pestered by passengers wanting to know if the ship has yet approached latitude 41°46' north, longitude 50°14' west – where White Star Line's *Titanic* (43,326-tons) struck an Arctic iceberg on that fateful April night in 1912.

There is something magical in "doing a crossing." It takes you back to the days when hordes of passengers turned up at the piers of the ports of New York, Southampton, Cherbourg, or Hamburg, accompanied by chauffeurs and steamer trunks, jewels and finery, ablaze in a show of what they thought was best in life. Movie stars of the 1920s, '30s, and '40s often traveled abroad on the largest liners of the day, to arrive refreshed and ready to dazzle European fans.

Excitement and anticipation precede a cross-

Queen Mary 2 sails out of New York.

ing. First there is the hubbub and bustle of check-in, then the crossing of the threshold on the gangway before being welcomed into the calmness aboard, and finally escorted to one's accommodation for the next several days.

Once the umbilical cord of the gangway is severed, bow and stern mooring lines are cast off, and with three long blasts on the ship's deep whistle, the *QM2* is pried gently from its berth. The ship sails silently down the waterway, away from the world, as serene as a Rolls-Royce. Passengers on deck often observe motorboats trying to keep up with the giant liner as it edges down the Hudson River, past Battery Park City, the Statue of Liberty, the restored Ellis Island, then out toward the Verrazano-Narrows Bridge, and out to the open sea.

Coming westbound, arriving in New York by ship is one of the world's thrilling travel experiences. Following a six-day crossing aboard the *QM2*, where five of the days are 25 hours long (but only 23 hours long on an eastbound crossing), everything else is an anticlimax.

The *QM2* has year-round scheduled crossings, whereas other cruise ships crossing the Atlantic are little more than repositioning cruises – a way of moving ships that cruise the Mediterranean in summer to the Caribbean in winter, and vice versa – they offer more chances to experience the romance and adventure of a crossing, usually in the spring and in the fall. These are particularly

London is a popular port of call on European cruises.

good for those wanting uninterrupted days at sea and plenty of leisure time.

Most cruise ships operating repositioning crossings cross the Atlantic using the "sunny southern route" – departing from southern ports such as Ft. Lauderdale, San Juan, or Barbados, and ending the journey in Lisbon, Genoa, or Copenhagen via the Azores or the Canary Islands off the coast of northern Africa. In this way, they avoid the more difficult weather often encountered in the North Atlantic. The crossings take longer, however: between eight and 12 days.

World Cruises

The ultimate classic voyage for any experienced traveler is a round-the-world cruise, which first gained popularity in the 1920s and is defined as the *complete* circumnavigation of the earth in a continuous one-way voyage. Ports of call are carefully planned for their interest and diversity, and the entire voyage can last six months or longer.

Such a trip is for some the cultural, social, and travel experience of a lifetime – and, for the few who can afford it, an annual event, perhaps enabling them to exchange the northern winter for the southern sun. Most passengers who regularly sail on the around-the-world voyages take them in a westbound direction, thus gaining time instead of losing it (one hour for each 25 degrees that the ship crosses). Ships occasionally make their around-the-world cruises in an *eastbound* direction, so those days get progressively shorter by one

The Caribbean offers sun during the northern winter.

hour each time you go through a time zone.

A world cruise aboard a modern ship means experiencing stabilized, air-conditioned comfort in luxury cabins, and extraordinary sight-seeing and excursions on shore and overland. In some ships, every passenger will get to dine with the captain at least once.

Although at first the idea of such a cruise may sound extravagant, but fares can be as low as $100 a day – though they can be more than $3,000 a day. Alternately, you can book just a segment of the cruise if that fits your pocket and interest. There is a difference in what you get for your money, however. For example, aboard ships rated at four stars or more, shuttle buses from your ship to the center of town (or attraction) will probably be included; this is not so aboard ships rated three stars or less.

Needless to say, most passengers prefer the *westbound* direction. Do check brochures and itineraries carefully. Some ships offering world cruises spend little time in port (on the 2003 world cruise of *Aurora*, for example, there were no overnight stays, even in some of the most desirable port cities such as San Francisco, Sydney, Hong Kong, Tokyo, or Singapore).

Some of the special events planned for a world cruise will typically include celebrity entertainers, world-renowned lecturers, themed formal balls and parties, an Equator crossing ceremony, an International Dateline crossing ceremony, overnight and multi-day overland excursions, and personalized stationery

Planning and Preparation

Few enterprises can match the complexity of planning and preparing for a world cruise. For example, more than 675,000 main meals will be prepared in the galleys during a typical *QE2* world cruise. Several hundred professional entertainers, lecturers, bands, and musicians must all be booked about a year in advance. Crew changeovers during the cruise must be organized. A ship the size of the *QE2* needs two major crew changes during the three-month-long voyage.

Because a modern world cruise ship has to be totally self-contained, a warehouse-full of spare parts (electrical, plumbing, and engineering supplies, for example) must be ordered, loaded, and stored somewhere aboard ship prior to sailing. For just about every shipboard department, the same basic consideration will apply: once at sea, it will be impossible to pick up a replacement projector bulb, air-conditioning belt, table tennis ball, saxophone reed, or anything else that the ship might run out of.

The cruise director will have his/her hands full planning entertainment and social events for a long voyage. It is not like the "old days" when an occasional game of bingo, horse racing, or the daily tote would satisfy passengers.

A cruise line must give advance notice of the date and time that pilots will be needed, together with requirements for tugs, docking services, customs and immigration authorities, or meetings with local dignitaries and the press. Then there is the organization of dockside labor and stevedoring services at each port of call, plus planning and contracting of bus or transportation services for shore excursions. Other preparations include reserving fuel at various ports on the itinerary.

World Cruise Segments

Cruises to exotic destinations – China, the Orient, the South Pacific, around Africa, the Indian Ocean, and around South America – offer all the delights associated with a world cruise, but you may not have the time or funds to see everything in one trip. Taking a segment of a world cruise is shorter and hence less expensive, yet it offers the same elegance and comfort, splendid food, delightful ambience, and well-traveled fellow passengers.

An exotic voyage can be a totally self-contained cruise to a specific destination, lasting anywhere from 30 days to more than 200 days (*Europa*'s 2003 world cruise lasted for an astonishing 239 days, though the 2005 itinerary is less ambitious). Or you can book a segment of a world cruise to begin at one of its ports of call, getting off at another port. "Segmenting" is ideal for those who wish to be a part of a world cruise but have neither the time nor the money for the prolonged extravagance of a three- to six-month vacation.

Segment cruising involves flying either to or from your cruise (or both). You can travel to join your exotic cruise at one of the principal ports

Europa's world cruise lasts more than six months.

such as Genoa, Rio de Janeiro, Acapulco, Honolulu, Sydney, Hong Kong, Singapore, Bangkok, Colombo, Mumbai (Bombay), Mombasa, or Athens, depending on the ship and the itinerary.

Ships that roam worldwide during the year offer

Around the World Cruises 2005

Ship	Company	Days	Date	From (Start)
Astor	Transocean Tours	118	December 22, 2004	Nice
Asuka	NYK Cruises	99	April 6, 2005	Yokohama
Aurora *	P&O Cruises	103	January 9, 2005	Southampton
Black Watch	Fred Olsen Cruise Lines	102	January 5, 2005	Southampton
Columbus	Hapag-Lloyd Cruises	129	December 19, 2004	La Guaira
Crystal Serenity	Crystal Cruises	101	January 15, 2005	Los Angeles
Delphin Renaissance	Delphin Seereisen	148	December 4, 2004	Barcelona
Europa	Hapag-Lloyd Cruises	282	September 14, 2004	Hamburg
Maxim Gorkiy	Phoenix Seereisen	139	December 19, 2004	Bremerhaven
Oriana	P&O Cruises	82	January 7, 2005	Southampton
Prinsendam	Holland America Line	115	January 13, 2005	Fort Lauderdale
Queen Elizabeth 2	Cunard Line	103	January 3, 2005	New York
Saga Rose	Saga Cruises	108	January 7, 2005	Southampton
Seven Seas Voyager	Seven Seas Cruises	108	January 5, 2005	Los Angeles
Silver Whisper **	Silversea Cruises	100	January 12, 2005	San Diego

* *Grand Voyage to Australia and back and not a complete around-the-world cruise*

P&O's *Aurora* pays a visit to Istanbul.

the most experienced world cruises or segments. Most of these world cruise ships operate at about 75 percent capacity, thus providing considerably more space for passengers than they would normally have.

Going P.O.S.H.

This colloquialism for "grand" or "first-rate" has its origin in the days of ocean steamship travel between England and India. Wealthy passengers would, at considerable cost, book round-trip passage as "Port Outward, Starboard Home." They would thus secure a cabin on the cooler side of the ship while crossing the unbearably hot Indian Ocean under the sun. *(Brewers Dictionary of Phrase and Fable).*

However, the reality is that the monsoon winds that blow in and out of the Asian area shift between winter and summer, so that the sheltered side of a ship would change according to the season. Further, in looking at deck plans of ships of the period, most cabins were located *centrally*, with indoor promenades or corridors along each side, so the actual definition of the origin of P.O.S.H. could be said to be taken as artistic license.

Around the World Cruises 2005–6

Fancy taking a cruise lasting three or four months? This table below shows the 15 ships scheduled to operate a true around-the-world cruise in 2005–6. This is the smallest number for many years, and is partly an after-effects of the ship redeployment after 2001's terrorist attacks depressed business.

Note that the number of ports visited varies from a low of 24 (P&O Cruises' *Oriana*) to a high of 117 (Hapag-Lloyd Cruises' *Europa*). ❏

Date (Finish)	To	Direction	Number of Ports
May 18, 2005	Bremerhaven	Westbound	63
July 15, 2005	Kobe	Westbound	27
April 22, 2005	Southampton	East/West	33
April 18, 2005	Southampton	Eastbound	35
April 27, 2005	Venice	Westbound	73
April 27, 2005	London	Westbound	41
April 30, 2005	Nice	Westbound	68
June 24, 2005	Hamburg	Westbound	117
May 7, 2005	Bremerhaven	Eastbound	64
March 29, 2005	Southampton	Westbound	24
April 14, 2005	New York	Westbound	42
April 16, 2005	Southampton	Westbound	36
April 26, 2005	Southampton	Westbound	39
April 23, 2005	Fort Lauderdale	Westbound	44
April 22, 2005	Venice	Westbound	60

DID YOU KNOW?

● that the Dollar Steamship Line featured a round-the-world cruise that started October 15, 1910, from New York, aboard the ss *Cleveland?* The cruise was advertised as "one-class, no overcrowding" voyage. The cost was "$650 and up," according to an advertisement placed by the Frank Clark Travel Agency, of the Times Building in New York.

● that a round-the-world cruise was made in 1922–23 by Cunard's *Laconia* (19,680 grt), a three-class ship that sailed from New York? The itinerary included many ports of call that are still popular with world cruise travelers today. The vessel accommodated 350 persons in each of its first two classes, and 1,500 in third class, giving a total capacity of 2,200 passengers, more than many ships of today.

● about the lady who went to her travel agent, who asked if she had enjoyed her cruise around the world? The lady replied, "Yes, but next year I want to go somewhere different."

What the Brochures Really Mean

There are ships and cruises to suit every taste, but the variety can be bewildering. Below, we help you make the right decisions

Despite constant cruise company claims that theirs has been named the "Best Cruise Line" or "Best Cruise Ship," *there really is no such thing* – only what's good, and right, for you. Most ship owners want to be a "luxury" cruise operator, and most passengers want to sail aboard one of the top-rated "luxury" ships. But *few* operators can really deliver a ship, product, and crew worthy of five Berlitz stars.

What a Cruise Is

A cruise is a vacation. It offers you a chance to relax and unwind in comfortable surroundings, with attentive service, good food, and a ship that changes the scenery for you. It is a virtually hassle-free and crime-free vacation. You never have to make blind choices. Everything's close at hand, and there are always polite people to help you.

What a Cruise Is Not

Some cruises simply aren't relaxing despite cruise brochure claims that "you can do as much or as little as you want to." For example, the large resort ships carrying more than 1,200 passengers, and particularly those with 3,000 or more, cram lots of people into small cabins and provide nonstop activities that insult the intelligence and assault the wallet.

Price is, of course, the key factor for most people. The cost of a cruise provides a useful guideline to a ship's ambience, type of passengers, and degree of luxury, food, and service. The amount you are prepared to spend will determine the size, location, and style of accommodation you get. Be wary of huge discounts – it either means that the product was unrealistically priced at source or that quality will be reduced somewhere. Ships are as individual as fingerprints: each can change its "personality" from cruise to cruise, depending on the mix of passengers (and crew).

Passengers encompass all types of personalities and lifestyles, from affluent, reserved, and mature to active, athletic, fun-loving, and youthful, or family-oriented, or conservation-minded, or adventurous, or wild fun seekers. They may be well traveled, or honeymooners on their first cruise, or veteran passengers who cruise several times a year.

How Long?

The standard of luxury, comfort, and service is generally in direct proportion to the length of the cruise. To operate long, low-density voyages, cruise lines

must charge high rates to cover the extensive preparations, high food and transportation costs, port operations, fuel, and so on. The length of cruise you choose will depend on the time and money at your disposal and the degree of comfort you are seeking.

The popular standard length of a cruise is seven days, although cruises can vary from two-day party cruises to a slow exotic voyage around the world of up to 180 days. If you are new to cruising and want to "get your feet wet," try a short cruise first.

Which Ship?

There's something to suit virtually all tastes, so take into account your own personality and tastes.

Ships are measured (not weighed) in gross tons (gt) and come in four principal size categories:
Boutique Ships: for up to 200 passengers (typically measure 1,000–5,000 tons)
Small Ships: for 200–500 passengers (typically measure 5,000–25,000 tons)
Mid-Size Ships: for 500–1,200 passengers (typically measure 25,000–50,000 tons)
Large Resort Ships: for over 1,200 passengers (typically measure 50,000–150,000 tons)

Whatever the physical dimensions, all cruise ships provide the same basic ingredients: accommodation, activities, entertainment, plenty of food, good service, and ports of call, although some do it much better than others (and charge more).

Space

To get an idea of the amount of the space around you, look at the Passenger Space Ratio given for each ship in the listings section (tonnage divided by number of passengers). A Passenger Space Ratio of **50 and above** is the ultimate; **30 to 50** is very spacious; **20 to 30** is reasonably spacious; **10 to 20** is moderate to high density; and **10 or below** is extremely cramped.

Boutique Ships (50–200 Passengers) and Small Ships (200–500 Passengers)
Choose a boutique or small ship for an intimate cruise experience and a small number of passengers. Some of the most exclusive cruise ships in the world belong in this group (but so do most of the coastal vessels with basic, unpretentious amenities, sail-cruise ships, and the expedition-style cruise vessels that take passengers to see nature). Choose this size ship if you do not need much entertainment, large resort ship facilities, gambling casinos, several restaurants, and if you don't like to wait in lines for anything. If you

---

Left: planning the next cruise.

want to swim in the late evening, or have champagne in the Jacuzzi at midnight, it is easier aboard boutique or small ships than aboard larger ships, where more rigid programs lead to inflexible, passenger-unfriendly thinking.

Boutique/Small Ships: Advantages
● More like small inns than mega-resorts.
● Easy to find your way around, and signage is usually clear and concise.
● At their best in warm weather areas.
● Capable of true culinary excellence, with fresh foods cooked individually to order.
● Most provide an "open seating" in the dining room; this means that you can sit with whomever you wish, whenever you wish, for all meals.
● Provide a totally unstructured lifestyle, offering a level of service not found aboard most of the larger ships, and no or almost no announcements.
● Provide an "open bridge" policy, allowing passengers to go to the navigational bridge at almost any time (except during difficult maneuvers and in cases of difficult weather conditions).
● Some small ships have a hydraulic marina water sports platform located at the stern and carry equipment such as jet skis, windsurfers, a water ski powerboat, and scuba and snorkeling gear.
● Go to the more off-beat ports of call that larger ships can't get into.
● When the ship is at anchor, going ashore is easy and speedy, with a continuous tender service.
● Less crowded ports mean a more exclusive cruise experience.

Boutique/Small Ships: Disadvantages
● Do not have the bulk, length, or beam to sail well in open seas in inclement weather conditions.
● Do not have the range of public rooms or open spaces that the large resort ships can provide. Options for entertainment, therefore, are limited.

Mid-Size Ships (500–1,200 Passengers)
These are well suited to the smaller ports of the Aegean and Mediterranean, and are more maneuverable than larger ships. Several operate around-the-world cruises and other long-distance itineraries to exotic destinations not really feasible aboard many of the ships in the small or large resort ship categories.

There is a big difference in the amount of space available. Accommodation varies from large "penthouse suites" complete with butler service to tiny interior (no-view) cabins. These ships will generally be more stable at sea than "small ships", due to their increased size and draft. They provide more facilities, more entertainment, and more dining options. There is some entertainment, and more structured activities than aboard small ships, but less than aboard the large resort ships.

Mid-Size Ships: Advantages
● They are neither too large, nor too small; their size and facilities often strike a happy balance.
● It is an easy matter to find one's way around.
● They generally sail well in areas of bad weather, being neither high-sided like the large resort ships, nor of too shallow draft like some of the small ships.
● Lines seldom form (except for ships that are approaching 1,200 passengers), but if they do, they are likely to be short.
● They appear more like traditional ships than most of the larger vessels, which tend to be more "boxy" in shape and profile.

Mid-Size Ships: Disadvantages
● They do not offer as wide a range of public rooms and facilities as do the large resort ships.
● Few have large show lounges for large-scale production shows; hence entertainment tends to be more of the cabaret variety.

Large Resort Ships (1,200–4,000 Passengers)
Choose a large resort ship if you enjoy being with lots of other people, in a big-city environment, you enjoy being sociable, and like to experience plenty of entertainment and dining (no, make that *eating*) options. These ships provide a well packaged standard or premium cruise vacation experience, usually in a seven-day cruise. Aboard large cruise ships, it is the interaction between passengers and crew that determines the quality of the experience.

Large resort ships have extensive facilities and programs for families with children of all ages. But if you meet someone on the first day and want to meet them again, make sure you appoint a place and time, or you may not see them again (apart from the size of the ship, they may be at a different meal seating). These ships have a highly structured array of activities and passenger participation events each day, together with large entertainment venues, and the most lavish production shows at sea. It is in the standard of service, entertainment, lecture programs, level of communication, and finesse in dining services that really can move these ships into high rating categories, but they must be exceptional to do so. Choose higher-priced suite accommodation and the service improves.

Large resort ships are highly programmed. It is difficult, for example, to go swimming in the late evening, or after dinner (decks are cleaned and pools are often netted over by 6pm). Having champagne delivered to outdoor hot tubs late at night is virtually impossible. They have lost the flexibility for which cruise ships were once known, and have become victims of company "policy" legislation and insurance regulations. There can be a feeling of "conveyor-belt" cruising.

Large Resort Ships: Advantages
● Have the widest range of public rooms and facili-

Ships like *Voyager of the Seas* have a big-city feel.

ties, often a wraparound promenade deck outdoors, and more space (but more passengers).
● Generally better flexibility in dining options.
● The newest ships have state-of-the-art electronic interactive entertainment facilities (good if you like computers and high-tech gadgetry).
● Generally sail well in open seas in inclement weather conditions.
● There are more facilities and activities for people of all ages, particularly for families with children.

Large Resort Ships: Disadvantages
● Trying to find your way around the ship can prove frustrating.
● Lines to wait in: for embarkation, the purser's office (information desk), elevators, informal buffet meals, fast food grills, shore tenders, shore excursions, security checkpoint (when returning to the ship), immigration, and disembarkation.
● They resemble floating hotels (but with constant announcements), and so many items cost extra. They are like retail parks surrounded by cabins.
● No matter how big your suite is, or how many public rooms the ship has, you can't help feeling like just one of the crowd, and the individual attention or recognition is missing. You also have to mingle with all the other (lesser paying) passengers in the public rooms.
● The itineraries may be limited by ship size, and there are typically too many tender ports.
● Signage is often confusing; there will be a lack of elevators at peak times.
● The larger the ship, the more impersonal the service

(except for "butler" service in a penthouse suite).
● You will probably have to use a sign-up sheet to use gymnasium equipment such as treadmills or exercise bicycles.
● There are too many announcements (they could be in several languages).
● Dining room staff is so programmed to provide speedy service, it is almost impossible to sit and dine in leisurely fashion.
● Food may well be bland (cooking for 3,000 is not quite the same as cooking for a dinner party of 20).
● Telephoning room service can be frustrating, particularly in those ships with automatic telephone answering systems that state "your call will be answered by room service personnel in the order it was received."
● Room service breakfast is not generally available on the day of disembarkation.
● In early evening, some take the deck chairs away, or strap them up so they can't be used.
● The in-cabin music aboard the latest ships is supplied through the television set, and it may be impossible to turn off the picture (so much for quiet, romantic late-night music, and darkened cabins).
● When the ship is at anchor (few ports can accept the large resort ships alongside their docking facilities), you will need to stand in line, or wait in a lounge, for a "tender ticket" – then wait until your ticket number is called – to go ashore by ship-to-shore craft. This can take an hour or more. Getting back on board could take some time, too, and you could be standing out in the hot sun for a long time.
● Some of the large resort ships have only two main passenger staircases. In an emergency, the evacuation of more than 3,000 passengers could be difficult. ❑

THE BIG 7 CRUISE LINES

Is big necessarily beautiful? We compare what the world's largest

cruise companies have to offer when it comes to cuisine, service and ambiance

Seven cruise lines dominate the industry: Carnival Cruise Lines, Celebrity Cruises, Costa Cruises, Holland America Line, Norwegian Cruise Line, Princess Cruises, Royal Caribbean International. But cruising's consolidation is even more dramatic than it seems because these Big 7 lines are actually owned by just *three* corporations:
● *Carnival Corporation* (based in Miami, Florida) owns Carnival Cruise Lines, Costa Cruises, Holland America, and Princess Cruises.
● *Royal Caribbean Cruises* (based in Miami, Florida) owns Celebrity Cruises, and Royal Caribbean International.
● *Star Cruises Group* (based in Kuala Lumpur, Malaysia) owns NCL America, Norwegian Cruise Line, Orient Lines, and Star Cruises.
Carnival Corporation also owns Aida Cruises, Cunard Line, Ocean Village, P&O Cruises, P&O Cruises (Australia), Seabourn Cruise Line and Windstar Cruises. Norwegian Cruise Line/NCL America also owns Orient Lines.

Holland America Line and Princess Cruises virtually control Alaska large ship cruising, and own hotels, lodges, tour companies and much land-based transportation (other operators have to buy their services). This virtual monopoly came about in 2002–3 when Princess Cruises' parent company, P&O Group, sold its cruising division to Holland America's owner, Carnival Corporation. But this is no more monopolistic than some tour operators in Europe that own a chain of travel agencies, hotels, an airline, and cruise ships in a vertical integration that provides them with great efficiency in terms of overall control and management.

So how does one choose between the companies? To help lure customers, each of the Big 7 has its own marketing tag: Carnival Cruise Lines (We've Got the Fun); Celebrity Cruises (Premium with a Touch of Luxury); Costa Cruises (Cruising Italian Style); Holland America Line (Signature of Excellence); Norwegian Cruise Line (Freestyle Cruising); Princess Cruises: (Where I Belong); and Royal Caribbean International (Get Out There).

What the Big 7 have in common

All offer one thing: a well-packaged cruise vacation (generally of seven days), with interesting itineraries, plenty of food, reasonable service, and a good array of entertainment including large-scale production shows and cabaret acts, plus large casinos, shopping malls, and extensive spa and fitness facilities. All offer a variety of "drive to" embarkation ports within the United States (known as "homeland cruising").

The Big 7's ships have a lot in common as well. All have art auctions, bingo, horse racing, shopping talks for ports of call (which promote "recommended" stores), programs for children and teens, wedding vows renewal programs, and "internet connect" centers (chargeable, typically at about 50 cents per minute). All feature the "Peppermill Routine" (the waiter brings a huge peppermill to your table before you've even tasted the food), but none offer tableside carving or flambée items. Standing in line for embarkation, disembarkation, shore tenders and for self-serve buffet meals is an inevitable aspect of cruising aboard all Big 7 large cruise ships.

Additional costs include port taxes, insurance, gratuities to staff, and use of washer/ dryers in self-serve launderettes.

The ships do, however, differ in their facilities, maintenance, space, crew-to-passenger ratio, food and service, and other aspects, and these variations are noted in our listings. Bear in mind that changes, upgrading and downgrading of products and services may have occurred since this book was completed.

Who does what best

● **Carnival Cruise Lines** is best for all-round fun and activities for the lively youth market (although most passengers are typically over 45).
● **Celebrity Cruises** has the best food and most elegant ships and spas.
● **Costa Cruises** has the edge on European style and lively ambiance, but the ships are full of noisy children in peak holiday periods (when they invade the swimming pools).
● **Holland America Line** has all the right touches for seniors and retirees, smiling service staff, and lots of flowers.
● **Norwegian Cruise Line** is good for a first cruise for families with children, choice of restaurants and eateries, and consistently good entertainment.
● **Princess Cruises** is also good for its consistent product delivery, although the ships have décor that is rather bland, and passengers of an upper age range.
● **Royal Caribbean International** is good for the Caribbean (naturally), for first time cruisers and families with children, with a good variety of entertainment, and consistently interesting programs for families with children.

Carnival Victory cruises out of Miami, Florida.

1 CARNIVAL CRUISE LINES

Ships

Carnival Conquest (2002), *Carnival Destiny* (1996), *Carnival Glory* (2003), *Carnival Legend* (2002), *Carnival Liberty* (2005), *Carnival Miracle* (2004), *Carnival Pride* (2002), *Carnival Spirit* (2001), *Carnival Triumph* (1999), *Carnival Valor* (2004), *Carnival Victory* (2000), *Celebration* (1987), *Ecstasy* (1991), *Elation* 1998), *Fantasy* (1990), *Fascination* (1994), *Holiday* (1985), *Imagination* (1995), *Inspiration* (1996), *Paradise* (1998), *Sensation* (1993).

About the company

Carnival Cruise Lines is a brilliantly organized company whose large resort ships provide opportunities for active fun. It is the world's largest and most successful single cruise line. More than 20 new ships have debuted since the line was founded in 1972.

Carnival does not sell itself as a "luxury" or "upscale" cruise line and consistently delivers exactly what its brochures say, for which there is a huge and growing first-time cruise market. The company provides a well-packaged cruise vacation, with smart ships that have the latest high-tech entertainment facilities and features, and extra-cost alternative dining spots.

Suitable For

Carnival Cruise Lines' ships are best suited to active, rather than passive, first-time young (and young-at-heart) couples, single passengers, tots, children and teenagers (anyone under 21 must be accompanied by a parent, relative or guardian). Its customers enjoy big-city nightlife and expect contemporary, upbeat surroundings, the latest in facilities, plenty of entertainment lounges and bars – all in one neat, highly programmed, well packaged cruise vacation. Carnival ships are also good for whole ship charters and incentive groups, for multi-generational passengers and for family reunions.

So what's it really like?

It's an all-American experience – exciting, loud, challenging in many ways, but blood pressure-raising fun. The ships are great floating playgrounds for young, active adults who enjoy constant stimulation, close contact with lots of others, as well as the three Gs – glitz, glamour and gambling – a real "life on the ocean rave." Like life in the fast lane, this is cruising in theme-park fantasyland, with constant upbeat music, and passenger participation games typically found in a jolly, summer camp atmosphere. While the fastidious might view some participation events as almost degrading, they are nevertheless well liked by passengers who associate such activities with "fun" – the line's theme. Forget relaxation, you can do that when you go home!

The dress code is decidedly casual – indeed, the waiters are typically better dressed than most passengers (particularly during youth-heavy holiday seasons and spring break, when clothes appear to be optional). Fun squeezed out fashion. Although Carnival is all about "happy," it's an impersonal cruise experience, overseen by young cruise directors who deliver the same jokes and banter every cruise. Perhaps it doesn't matter so much because this will be the first cruise for most passengers. Repeat passengers, however, have a distinct sense of *déja vu*.

Although open deck space may look adequate when you first board (with mouth open, going "wow"), on days at sea you can expect your plastic deck chair, if you can find one that's free, to be kissing its neighbour (it's probably tied to it). There are topless sunbathing areas around the base of the ship's funnel for those seeking that (almost) all-over tan. There are no cushioned pads for the deck lounge chairs, which are hard to sit on with just a towel for any length of time.

You may well encounter lots of smokers, and masses of fellow passengers walking around in unsuitable clothing (passengers dress better on longer cruises such as Panama Canal sailings) clutching plastic sport drinks bottles at any time of the day or night. Expect to be subjected to a stream of flyers advertising daily art auctions, "designer" watches, "inch of gold/silver" and other promotions, while "artworks" for auction are strewn throughout the ships. Also, expect intrusive announcements (particularly for activities that bring revenue), and waiters hustling you to have drinks.

Carnival Capers, the ship's daily program, is among the industry's poorest information sheets (in layout and print quality), and always includes big text blocks designed to persuade you to spend money. The decibel level is high: it is difficult to escape from noise and loud music, and background music is played even in cabin hallways and elevators 24 hours a day. There are libraries but few or no books, and bookshelves are always locked by 6pm, because you are expected to be out in the (revenue-earning) public areas each evening.

As for accommodation, the balconies in many of the cabins with "private" balconies aren't so private, and most can be overlooked from other cabins located on the deck above and from various public locations. You may have to carry a credit card to operate the personal safes (inconvenient).

Embarkation and disembarkation can be a bothersome procedure (depending on the port). When you do finally walk across the gangway after check-in, the few staff members on duty will merely point you in the direction of your deck or to the ship's elevators instead of escorting you to your cabin. There is little finesse and not enough attention to individuals.

Carnival operates from many "drive to" embarkation ports within the United States, and the company features a "vacation guarantee program" that makes it user-friendly for anyone not familiar with cruising. If you are not satisfied, you must notify Carnival before arrival in the *first* port of call (you must then disembark at the *first* non-U.S. port of call); Carnival will then refund the unused portion of your cruise fare and pay your flight back. The guarantee is void where prohibited (it is not applicable in Alaska, Hawaii, Panama Canal itineraries, and cruises to nowhere); so, in effect, it's really only useful for Bahamas and Caribbean cruises. Actually, fewer than 1 percent of Carnival's passengers ever use the facility.

Decor

The decor aboard the ships is stunningly creative, although you probably wouldn't want to let the ship's interior designer loose in your home. But there's no denying that Joe Farcus, the designer (born

Carnival Conquest: geometric seating for sun lovers.

Carnival tempts cruisegoers with calories.

in the "neon-lithic" age), is a color genius. In dramatic manner, he manages to place *every* color under – and over – the rainbow (including some colors not before seen by man) into the melting pot that is the inside of a cruise ship. And it all works. It's pure magic, whimsical, and very entertaining. Carpets have a licence to thrill, and sensory perception overload is practiced exquisitely. So, if you *love* color, you'll be fine, but if you don't, take sunglasses. Public toilets, however, are something else; they are so clinical and sad, and need some cheering up (the designer clearly hasn't been in one lately).

Cuisine/Dining

All Carnival ships have one or two main dining rooms (all dining venues are non-smoking), and dinner is in either two or four seatings (depending on the ship and configuration). Menus are standardized across the fleet.

Don't even *think* about a quiet table for two, or a candlelight dinner on deck – it's not Carnival's style. Dining aboard a Carnival ship is all about table mates and social chat. Tables are, however, nicely set with white tablecloths, plenty of silverware, and iced water/iced tea whenever you want it. Oh, and the peppermill routine (where the waiter brings a huge peppermill to your table before you've even tasted the food) is all part of the show – delivered with friendly service that lacks polish but invites extra gratuities. The waiters also sing and dance (be prepared for Simply the Best, Hot, Hot, Hot, the Macarena, and other popular hits of yesteryear), and there are constant waiter parades. The dining room marries food and show business, all in the name of fun – and gaining positive passenger comments.

Taste-filled food is not the company's strong point, but quantity, not quality, is. Although the company does strive to improve its cuisine and menu choices look good, the actual food delivered is really adequate banquet-style catering, with its attendant standardization and production cooking. Meats are of a decent quality, but poultry, fish and seafood items are questionable. Sauces and gravies are used well as disguises, and there are few garnishes. The selection of fresh green vegetables, breads, rolls, cheese and ripe fruit is limited, and there is much use of canned fruit and jellied desserts, not to mention packets of jam, marmalade, butter, sugar – the same stuff you'd find in Denny's or IHOP, for example. It is difficult to obtain anything remotely unusual or off-menu. Vegetarian menus and children's menus are available, although they wouldn't get many marks for their nutritional content.

The wine list, however, is excellent and quite varied (it includes some fine Bordeaux reds of good vintage), but there are no wine waiters or decent-sized wine glasses. Waiters have to serve both food and wine, which doesn't work at all well (they pour wine like soft drinks – too fast).

Alternative (Extra Charge) Dining Spots (Reservations Required)

Carnival Conquest, Carnival Destiny, Carnival Glory, Carnival Liberty, Carnival Miracle, Carnival Triumph, Carnival Valor:

Fine table settings, china and silverware are featured, as well as leather-bound menus. Menu favourites include prime American steaks such as filet mignon (9 ounces), porterhouse steak (24 ounces) and New York strip loin (be prepared for huge cuts of meat – shown to you at your table before you order), and broiled lobster tail, as well as stone crab claws from Joe's Stone Crabs of South Miami Beach. Reservations are necessary, and a cover charge of $25 per person (for service and gratuity) applies. A connoisseur's wine list is impressive (it includes such names as Opus One and Château Lafite-Rothschild). The

Having a ball on the open deck.

food is extremely good, and the ambiance is reasonably quiet. But if you are a couple and you have just two glasses of wine each (Grgich Hills Chardonnay or Merlot, for example, at $12.50 a glass), and pay the cover charge, that's $100 for dinner (caviar is an extra $29 for a 1-ounce serving); it's worth it.

Casual Eateries: In addition to the main dining rooms, all ships have large food court-style spaces for casual food, fast food items, grilled meats, pizzas (each ship serves over 800 pizzas in a typical day), stir fry, deli and salad items. There are self-help beverage stands, coffee that looks like rusty water, and tea provided in paper cups with a teabag (tea dust is a more accurate description), plastic or wooden stirrers (no teaspoons and no saucers), and packets of chemical "milk" or "creamer." But some people are happy to have it that way, and it's actually better than what is offered aboard competitor Royal Caribbean International's ships.

The Coffee/Tea Factor: Regular coffee is weak and poor, scoring 1 out of 10 (paper/foam cups in buffet areas). Espresso/cappuccino coffees score 2 out of 10 (paper/foam cups, in buffet areas).

For Children:

Children are provided with very good facilities. "Camp Carnival", the line's extensive child/youth program, is well organized and extensive. There are four categories: Toddlers (ages 2–5); Juniors (6–8); Intermediate (9–11); and Teens (12–15). Soft-drinks packages can be purchased for children (adults, too). Note: Babysitting service is not available after 10pm.

Best ships for children: *Carnival Conquest, Carnival Destiny, Carnival Glory, Carnival Legend, Carnival Miracle, Carnival Pride, Carnival Spirit, Carnival Triumph, Carnival Valor, Ecstasy, Elation, Fantasy, Fascination, Holiday, Imagination, Inspiration, Paradise, Sensation* (but not *Celebration* or *Holiday*).

Gratuities

$9.75 per person per day (the amount charged when this book was completed) is added to your onboard account. You can have this amount adjusted, although you'll have to visit the information desk to do so. Additionally, 15% is added to your account for all bar, wine and spa charges. The onboard currency is the US dollar.

Entertainment

Carnival ships have big showlounges (all non-smoking), and big production shows. On a typical 7-day cruise, there will be two large-scale, trend-setting production shows, with male and female lead singers and a clutch of dancers, backed by a 10-piece live orchestra (supported by "click" tracks). They are ritzy-glitzy, razzle-dazzle, Las Vegas-style revues with little or no story line or flow (lots of running around on stage and stepping in place, but little dancing). However, the skimpy costumes are very colorful, as is the lighting (with extensive use of "color mover" lights).

They are, for the most part, loud, and I mean *loud* (think hearing-impaired audio controllers), in-your-face shows, with colourful skimpy costumes (lots of bare flesh), and stage "smoke" that seems to be a theme central to all shows (grossly overdone to the annoyance and irritation of anyone silly enough to be seated in the front few rows). But, hey, this is Splash Vegas, remember, so what else could you expect?

Specialty acts (Carnival rotates entertainers aboard its ships, so passengers see different acts each night) take center stage on nights when there is no production show. There's also live music in just about every bar and lounge (during the evenings), and always smutty late-night adults-only comedy, in addition to cabaret acts such as vocalists, magic acts, ventriloquists, and comedy jugglers. Each cruise features karaoke nights, and a Passenger Talent show. Additionally, each ship has a discotheque with ear-splitting volumes and megaphones so you can have a conversation with your date.

Spa/Fitness Facilities

Spa/Fitness facilities are operated by Steiner Leisure, a specialist concession, whose young, hungry (for revenue) staff do tend to push (sell) you Steiner's own-brand beauty products (spa girls have sales targets). Some fitness classes are free, while some, such as yoga and kick-boxing, cost extra (typically $10 per class). Treatments include massage (including Hot Stone massage, Chakra Balancing massage and other well-being massages), facials, pedicures, and beauty salon treatments cost extra (massage, for example, costs about $2 per minute, plus tip). Make appointments early, as treatment time slots can go quite quickly.

The Spa Carnival layout spaces and facilities are identical to other ships in the same 'class,' as follows:
● *Carnival Legend, Carnival Miracle, Carnival Pride, Carnival Spirit*
SpaCarnival spans two decks, is located directly above the navigation bridge in the forward part of the ship and has 13,700 sq. ft (1,272 sq. meters) of space. Facilities on the lower level include a solarium, eight treatment rooms, lecture rooms, sauna and steam rooms for men and women, and a beauty parlor; the upper level consists of a large gymnasium with floor-to-ceiling windows on three sides, including forward-facing ocean views (with a large array of the latest in muscle-pumping electronic machines), and an aerobics room with instructor-led classes (the aerobics room and gymnasium together measure almost 6,000 sq. ft/560 sq. meters).
● *Carnival Conquest, Carnival Destiny, Carnival Glory, Carnival Miracle, Carnival Triumph, Carnival Valor*
SpaCarnival spans two decks (with a total area of 13,700 sq. ft/1,272 sq. meters), and is located directly above the navigation bridge in the forward part of the ship (accessible from the forward stairway). Facilities on the lower level include a solarium, eight treatment rooms, lecture rooms, sauna and steam rooms for men and women, and a beauty parlor; the upper level consists of a large gymnasium with floor-to-ceiling windows on three sides, including forward-facing ocean views (with a large array of the latest in muscle-pumping electronic machines), and an aerobics room with instructor-led classes (some at extra cost)
● *Ecstasy, Elation, Fantasy, Fascination, Holiday, Imagination, Inspiration, Paradise, Sensation*
SpaCarnival is located on Sports Deck, forward of the ship's mast, and accessed from the forward stairway. It consists of a gymnasium with ocean-view windows that look out over the ship's bow (you could 'cycle' your way to the next port of call if you so wish), complete with a good array of the latest in muscle-pumping electronic machines, an aerobics exercise room, men's and women's changing rooms (towels are provided), sauna and steam rooms, and beauty salon.

2 CELEBRITY CRUISES

Ships

Century (1995), *Constellation* (2002), *Galaxy* (1996), *Horizon* (1990), *Infinity* (2001), *Mercury* (1997), *Millennium* (2000), *Summit* (2001), *Zenith* (1992).

About the company

Celebrity Cruises was founded in 1989. In the 1990s (its formative years), it established an outstanding reputation for its cuisine, particularly in the main dining rooms, with its formal presentation and service. It advertises itself as being a premium line with a taste of luxury, and that, in a nutshell, sums it up rather nicely (the product delivery on board being far superior to that of parent company Royal Caribbean International).

Suitable For:

The ships are best suited to well educated adult couples (both young and not so young), families with older children and teenagers, and singles that like to mingle in a large ship setting with sophisticated surroundings, reasonably decent entertainment, and food and service that are extremely good, at a price that represents outstanding value for money.

So what's it really like?

The ships are spotlessly clean and extremely well maintained. There are always lots of flowers and flower displays (some ships have flower shops, where you can purchase fresh flowers and artistic creations for special occasions).

There is a lot of fine artwork aboard Celebrity's ships (some you'll like, some you won't, but at least it will make you think), and is probably the most remarkable collection of contemporary art in the cruise industry. The company provides a lot of the niceties that other lines in the Big 7 set have long forgotten (although some are now playing "catch up"): being escorted to your cabin on arrival by a steward; waiters that carry your trays when you obtain food from buffets or casual eateries; water spritzes on the pool deck.

There really are three different "classes" aboard Celebrity ships: those in accommodation designated as suites; those in standard exterior-view and interior (no view) cabins; and a third that comes between the two, known as "Concierge Class." Concierge Class adds another dimension and items that bring added value to passengers. Enhanced facilities include priority embarkation, disembarkation, tender tickets, alternative dining and spa reservations; European duvet; double bed overlay (no more falling "between the cracks" for couples); choice of four pillows (goose down pillow, isotonic pillow, body pillow, conformance pillow); eight-vial flower vase on vanity desk; throw pillows on sofa; fruit basket; binoculars; golf umbrella; leather telephone notepad; larger beach towels; hand-held hairdryer. Balconies get better furniture. In the bathrooms: plusher Frette bathrobe; larger towels in sea green and pink (alternating days); flower in silver vase in bathroom. It all adds up to excellent value for money, as well as better recognition from staff.

Regardless of the accommodation grade chosen, Celebrity Cruises delivers a well-defined North American cruise experience at a very modest price. Book a suite-category cabin for the extra benefits it brings – it's worth it. Strong points include the many European staff and the high level of service, fine

Primary colors dominate *Millennium*'s Fun Factory.

spas with a good range of facilities and treatments, taste-filled food attractively presented and served in fine European dining tradition, the provision of many intimate spaces, a fine collection of artwork, a "zero announcement policy" (which means little intrusion), cloth towels in public restrooms instead of paper towels (as aboard most of the other Big 7 companies). On days at sea (in warm weather areas) if you are sunbathing on deck, someone will bring you a cold towel, and a sorbet, ice water or iced tea. Little touches like this differentiate Celebrity Cruises from others.

Celebrity Cruises' ships have many more staff than other ships of comparable size and capacity. This is particularly noticeable in the housekeeping and food and beverage departments, and results in a superior product.

The company appeals to a slightly younger, affluent and more upmarket set of passengers, who want things to be better than standard issue. Even so, such things as topless sunbathing spaces are now available aboard all ships. Meanwhile, what were formerly cigar smoking lounges are slowly being turned into cosy jazz/piano lounges. Some cruises aboard some ships are designated as child-free.

Embarkation: When you first embark, a member of staff, dressed in a crisp white uniform (or black butler's uniform if you are in one of the more expensive suites) will escort you (and carry your hand luggage) directly to your cabin, with white glove service and a smile.

So, what's the difference between Celebrity Cruises and parent company Royal Caribbean International? Although Royal Caribbean owns Celebrity Cruises, there are many differences in the onboard product. Here are a few differences concerning food items, for example:

● **Royal Caribbean International** (*Brilliance of the Seas*)
Café: Seattle Coffee Company coffee served in paper cups
Dining Room Food: overcooked, poor quality (think leather briefcase) meat
Dining Room: no tables for 2
In the Windjammer Cafe, waiters *do not* help passengers to tables with trays; melamine (plastic) plates are used, cutlery is wrapped in paper napkins, melamine mugs for coffee/tea, tea selection poor, and poor quality (Lipton) teas.
Public Restrooms feature paper towels.
● **Celebrity Cruises** (*Mercury*):
Cova Café: Coffees/teas served in china cups/saucers, with doily and chocolate
Dining Room Food: Good standard of food and presentation
Dining Room: Tables for 2 are available
In the Lido Cafe, Waiters line up to help pax with trays to tables. Real china, white cloth napkins, pol-

Celebrity Cruises' *Century* approaches Valletta, Malta.

ished cutlery, and a decent selection of teas are provided

Public Restrooms feature cloth (not paper) towels.

Decor

The decor is elegant – Greek, classical, minimalist, although it could be said to be a little antiseptic and cool in places. Celebrity Cruises has some of the most eclectic original artwork (from Picasso to Warhol) and sculptures found at sea – a magnificent collection that is thought provoking. The colors do not jar the senses, and cannot be said to be glitzy (the casinos are the exception – they are mostly vulgar), and subtle is the word for the way in which each public room invites you to move along to the next. The ships absorb people well, and the flow is, for the most part, good, except for entrances to showlounges and around photo galleries.

For Children:

Junior passengers are divided into four groups: Shipmates (3–6 years), Cadets (7–9 years), Ensigns (10–12 years), Teens (13–17 years).

Best ships for children: *Constellation, Infinity, Millennium, Summit*. Almost as good: *Century, Galaxy, Mercury*. But not *Horizon* or *Zenith*.

Cuisine/Dining

The dining rooms aboard all ships are non-smoking areas. There are two seatings for dinner (open seating for breakfast and lunch). Table settings are excellent, with fine quality linen, china and glassware. Tables for two are available (there are far more than most of the other Big 7). What sets Celebrity apart from any other Big 7 cruise line is the superior training and supervision of dining room waiters, and the service.

The food represents a wide range of culinary influences; it is based on classical French cuisine, modified to appeal to North Americans and European alike. Menus are standardized across the fleet, and have recently been completely refreshed in 2004. The menu variety in the main dining rooms is good (overseen by consultant chef Michel Roux); the food has taste, and it is very attractively presented and served in a well orchestrated operation that displays fine European traditions and training.

Full service in-cabin dining is also available for all meals (including dinner).

The food is made fresh from high quality ingredients – no pre-made sauces, soups, or croissants here, thank you very much. Take croissants, for example. Those found aboard Celebrity ships are made fresh each morning, while aboard most other ships in the Big 7 they are purchased from ashore. There is a big difference in their taste and consistency, depending on what kind of dough, and butter, are used.

Celebrity Cruises also has real sommeliers and wine waiters – they also know their wines. The four largest ships (*Constellation, Infinity, Millennium, Summit*) have special wine rooms in their 'alternative' restaurants that you can actually have dinner in, and fine wines that cost anything up to (and even beyond) $10,000 per bottle (but also wines that start at about $20 per bottle).

Casual Eateries: Casual self-serve buffets are found aboard all Celebrity Cruises' ships. Most are laid-out in continuous lines, which does mean – lines form at peak times (when morning shore excursions return, for example, by lunchtime). However,

Celebrity is trying to be more creative with these buffets, and, like other cruise lines, has stations for pasta, sushi, salads, grilled and rotisserie items, and hot food items. When you have chosen your food, a waiter will take your tray to a table for you. A bar trolley service for drinks and wines is provided at lunchtime, and wine waiters are always on hand to discuss and take wine orders for dinner. All the ships make great martinis (best of the Big 7).

The Coffee/Tea Factor: Regular Coffee: Weak and poor. Score: 2 out of 10. Espresso/Cappuccino coffees: Score: 3 out of 10. Note that if you order espresso/cappuccino coffees in the dining room, there is a charge (treated like a bar item).

Cova Cafe: All ships feature a Cova Café (featuring strong Italian coffee made from Arabica beans). This is a signature item aboard all Celebrity ships, and is a seagoing version of the original Cafe di Milano that was located next to La Scala Opera House in Milan. The shipboard cafes are in prominent locations, and several display cases show off the extensive range of Cova coffee, chocolates and alcoholic digestives, available for purchase. Cova Cafes provide a fine setting for those who appreciate fine Italian coffees (espresso, espresso macchiato, cappuccino, and latte), pastries and superb cakes. Breakfast pastries are to die for (favourites include the Italian pane con cioccolata – chocolate pastry, and superb almond croissants). Cova coffee is presented in a proper china cup, with a Cova

chocolate on the side (and tablecloths on tables). It costs extra, but it's worth it, and Cova Cafes are real (civilized) coffee houses, staffed by servers in Cova Café uniforms.

Gratuities: Suggested gratuity rates, per person, per day: Waiter, $3.50; Assistant Waiter, $2.00; Maitre d', $0.75; Butler (suites only), $3.50; $3.50 Cabin Steward(ess); Chief Housekeeper, $0.50. Additionally, 15 percent is added for all bar, wine purchases; 10 percent for spa treatments. The onboard currency is the US dollar.

Entertainment

All showlounges are non-smoking venues. The company has little cohesive policy regarding big production shows, and cannot seem to get them right. With different standards of productions aboard its ships, there is no consistency. However, while some are quite decent, with good costuming and lighting, they are, for the most part, dated and are served up without story line, flow or connectivity. Each ship carries its own resident troupe of singers/dancers and audio-visual support staff.

Production shows are not nearly as lavish as the showlounge they play in. In fact, compared to some of the other major cruise lines, the shows are a letdown, and not in keeping with the elegant nature of the interior decor. Most consist mainly of running, jumping, smoke, colored laser lighting, loud music and click tracks, and very little story line intelligence. Bar service, supplied throughout shows, disrupts concentration.

At present there is absolutely nothing to distinguish Celebrity Cruises in the entertainment department. While some cabaret acts are good, they are the same ones seen aboard many ships of the Big 7. The ships have a variety of bands and small musical units, although there is very little music for social dancing, other than disco and pop music.

Then there are those silly (summer camp-style) audience participation events and activities that are unbecoming to Celebrity's quality of food and service, and degrade the product. There are the usual culprits, such as "The Newlywed Game" or "King of the Ship" (poolside games), and a Passenger Talent show. It's time for some new ones; how about "I'm a Celebrity Passenger – Get Me *Out* of Here?" There are also the inevitable country line dances, and playschool-style "Pass the spoon down your dress and up your trousers" routines. It may be fun stuff for those that haven't grown up (or don't want to) or seen it yet, but otherwise, it's amateurish? On days at sea the daily program is crammed with activities, and revenue-enhancing activities (such as art auctions, giant jackpot bingo, and horse racing) featured in larger type size.

As this book was being completed, Celebrity Cruises announced a six-year alliance with Cirque

The grand entrance to *Century*'s main restaurant.

Costa Atlantica's glass stairway to the stars.

du Soleil that is expected to bring benefits to Celebrity's entertainment shows and programs, and to help differentiate the company in the race for brand recognition (perhaps it could market itself as Celebrity Circus Cruises?).

Spa/Fitness Facilities

Celebrity Cruises has realized that spas and fitness facilities are in, and has been busy making its facilities better. Spa/fitness programs are staffed and operated by Steiner Leisure, a specialist concession, whose enthusiastic staff will try to and sell you Steiner's own-brand beauty products (spa girls have sales targets). Some fitness classes are free, while some, such as yoga, and kickboxing, cost $10 per class. However, being aboard will give you an opportunity to try some of the more exotic treatments (particularly some of the massages available).

Massage (including exotic massages such as Aroma Stone massage, Chakra Balancing massage and other well-being massages), facials, pedicures, and beauty salon treatments are at extra cost. Examples of treatment costs: massage at $109 (50 minutes), facial at $109, seaweed wrap (75 minutes) $190 – all plus a gratuity of 10 percent. Personal training sessions in the gymnasium cost $83 for one hour. Do make appointments as early as possible, perhaps even on your first day aboard – aboard a ship so large, time slots go quickly.

3 COSTA CRUISES

Ships

Costa Allegra (1992), *Costa Atlantica* (2000), *Costa Classica* (1992(, *Costa Europa* (1986), *Costa Fortuna* (2003), *Costa Marina* (1990), *Costa Magica* (2004), *Costa Mediterranea* (2003), *Costa Romantica* (1993), *Costa Tropicale* (1982), *Costa Victoria* (1996).

About the company

Costa Crociere (parent company of Costa Cruises) was founded in 1860. Costa specializes in cruises for Europeans (or passengers with European tastes), and particularly Italians (during the summer European season). Costa has undertaken an aggressive newbuild policy in recent years, in order to modernise the company's previously ageing fleet of different sized ships.

Most ships are well maintained, although there are inconsistencies throughout the fleet; the same is true of cleanliness – some are extremely clean, while others are, how to say it kindly, a little dusty around the edges, as are its shore tenders. The ships have a distinctive European "feel" to them, in their decor and manner of product delivery, which is very laidback. Carnival Corporation, parent company of Costa Cruises, purchased part of the company in 1997 and the rest in 2000.

Costa offers a wide range of massages.

Suitable For

Costa Cruises' ships are best suited to young (and young at heart) couples and singles (plus families with children) that enjoy big city life, piazzas and outdoor cafes, constant activity accompanied by lots of noise (some call it ambience), late nights, entertainment that is loud, and food that is more notable for quantity rather than quality.

So what's it really like?

Costa Cruises is noted for its "Italian" style, ambiance and spirit. To be truthful, however, there are few Italian crew members on board its ships (although many of the officers *are* Italian). The lifestyle on board is, however, perceived to be Italian – lively, noisy, with lots of love for life and a love of the casual to the nth degree.

Although the "spit and polish" of fine service is missing, the staff are friendly and lively. The dress code is very casual, even on formal nights. Most passengers are Italian, with a generous sprinkling of other Europeans. One night (at the end of each cruise) is reserved for a "Roman Bacchanal", and passengers dress up toga-style for dinner and beyond. Costa Cruises does a good job of providing first-time cruise passengers with a well-packaged holiday that is a mix of sophistication and basic fare, albeit accompanied by rather loud music.

The cabins tend to be on the mean side in size, but the décor is fresh and upbeat, and the bathrooms are very practical units (some ships have cabin bathrooms with sliding doors), an excellent alternative to those that open inward, using up space).

There is extensive smoking on board. No-smoking zones and signs are often ignored to the frustration of non-smoking passengers, and ashtrays are moved at whim; many of the officers and crew also smoke (even when moving through public rooms), so they don't bother to enforce the no-smoking zones.

All printed materials (room service folio, menus, etc.) are in six languages (Italian, English, French, German, Portuguese, and Spanish). Announcements are made in at least two languages (Caribbean itineraries) and at least four languages (Europe/Mediterranean itineraries).

On Europe/Mediterranean cruises, English will be the language least spoken, as most passengers will be Italian, Spanish, French and German. On Caribbean itineraries there will be a great percentage of passengers will be speaking Spanish, as the ships carry passengers from several Latin American countries in addition to passengers from North America. Expect to cruise with a *lot* of children of all ages during peak holiday cruises (and in Europe schoolchildren at certain times such as Easter have longer holidays, so you *could* book the wrong week if you don't want to cruise with lots of kids - check with your travel agent or the cruise line). Without doubt, this is a cruise line for those who like to enjoy life and party. If you want quiet, take earplugs (good ones).

Embarkation: Few staff members are on duty at the gangway when you arrive, and they will merely point you in the direction of your deck, or to the ship's elevators instead of escorting you to your cabin.

Decor

Older Ships: *Costa Allegra, Costa Classica, Costa Europa, Costa Marina, Costa Romantica, Costa Tropicale, Costa Victoria* - have a fairly sophisticated, distinctively European feel to them – lively without being brash, or pastel-toned without being boring, depending on the ship you choose.

Newer (larger) ships (*Costa Atlantica, Costa Classica, Costa Fortuna, Costa Magica, Costa Mediterranea*) have this "in-your-face" brashness that competes with the ships of Carnival Cruise Lines, with digital artwork on walls, panels - even inside elevators, that is grainy and unflattering. There is also an abundance of fine or grotesque sculptures (depending on your point of view) and huge murals that are both stunning and mind-numbing. "Entertainment architecture," as a certain Joe Farcus quite correctly calls it. It certainly will knock your socks off, or make you want to wear your knickers back to front.

Cuisine/Dining

Dining rooms aboard all Costa ships are smoke-free (in theory). Main dining rooms have one-deck high ceilings (exceptions: *Costa Atlantica, Costa Fortuna, Costa Magica, Costa Mediterranea*). All ships feature two seatings for dinner; dining times on Europe/Mediterranean and South America cruises are typically later than those in the Caribbean – because Europeans and Latin passengers eat much later than North Americans. Few tables for two are available, most being for four, six, or eight.

The cuisine is best described as continental, with many regional Italian dishes included, and much emphasis on pasta. The presentation and food quality is not memorable (exception: pasta dishes, made fresh on board, and cream sauces are good), and is the subject of many negative comments from passengers. So, although there is plenty of food, its quality and presentation often prove disappointing to those who expect better. While the quality of meats is adequate, it is often disguised with gravies and rich sauces. Fish and seafood tend to lack taste, and are typically overcooked. Green vegetables are hard to come by. Breads and bread rolls are usually good, but the desserts are of supermarket quality and tend to have little taste.

Although you might expect to find jovial Italian waiters serving you in the dining rooms, you won't find any (as you might expect aboard the ship of an Italian company), although the maitre d's (restaurant managers) could be Italian. While service (from waiters of an international mix) is adequate, it is inconsistent across the fleet (sloppy in some ships, good in others). There is a wine list, although there are no wine waiters (table waiters are expected to serve both food and wine, which does not work well), and almost all wines are young – very young.

Alternative Dining

If you opt for one of the 'alternative' restaurants (aboard the larger ships), note that a cover charge applies: Euros 20 per person + 10% service charge (Europe/Mediterranean cruises), or $20 per person + 15% service charge (Caribbean cruises).

Casual Eateries

All ships have self-serve lido buffets. Most are of the line (move along with your tray) type, although the latest ships have more active stations and individual islands. The items available are quite basic. All ships except *Costa Europa* also have a pizzeria.

The Coffee/Tea Factor

Regular Coffee: Decent and quite strong (Score: 5 out of 10).

Espresso/Cappuccino coffees (Lavazza) are among the best of the Big 7 cruise lines (the main competition is the slightly better Cova Coffee from Milan – found aboard the ships of Celebrity Cruises, and served more elegantly). All ships feature coffee machines in most lounges/bars. Score: 8 out of 10)

Children

Costa Kids Club is a program that is variable by ship, itinerary and season for children aged 3–17. Group babysitting is available each evening from 6.30 to 11pm. During port days, babysitting is available generally 8.30am–12.30pm and 2.30–6.30pm. Junior passengers are in four groups: Kids Club is for 3–6; Junior Club is for 7–12; Teen Club is for 13–17.

Best ships for children: *Costa Atlantica, Costa*

Costa pays tribute to Christopher Columbus.

Fortuna, Costa Magica, Costa Mediterranea. But not: *Costa Classica, Costa, Europa, Costa Romantica, Costa Tropicale, Costa Victoria.*

Gratuities

$53 per 7-day cruise per person (Caribbean cruises), or Euro 32 per 7-day cruise per person (Europe/Mediterranean cruises) is charged to your onboard account, while 15% is added to all bar and wine orders (Caribbean Cruises) or 10% (Europe/Mediterranean cruises). You can have this amount adjusted, although you'll have to visit the information desk to do so. The onboard currency is the Euro (Europe/Mediterranean cruises), or US dollar (Caribbean cruises), depending on ship and itinerary.

Entertainment

Each ship carries its own resident troupe of singers/dancers and audio-visual support staff. Costa Cruises is not known for its entertainment. What it does present tends to be of the "no finesse" variety, with revue-style shows (performed by a small troupe of resident onboard singers/ dancers) that have little story line, poor choreography and execution, and fast moving action (this is more stepping in place than dancing), but lots of volume. Cabaret acts (typically singers, magicians, comedy jugglers, ventriloquists, and so on) are entertaining but rather ho-hum, and are more based on price than coherent themes.

Each Costa cruise has a "Toga Night" (the toga is supplied) for an evening of Bacchanal (Caribbean cruises), or Venetian Carnival night (Europe/Mediterranean cruises). Other passenger participation activities include poolside games, including such things as a "Belly Flop" competition; election of the "Ideal Couple." There are also dance classes, and the inevitable "Fine Art Auction."

Spa/Fitness Facilities

Spa/fitness facilities vary according to ship and size the newest and largest ships (*Costa Atlantica, Costa Fortuna, Costa Magica, Costa Mediterranea*) have more space and better facilities, while the others have only basic facilities.

Spa/fitness facilities are staffed and operated by Steiner Leisure, a specialist concession, whose young staff will try to sell you Steiner's own-brand beauty products. Some fitness classes are free, while some, such as yoga, and kick-boxing, cost $10 per class. However, being aboard will give you an opportunity to try some of the more exotic treatments (particularly some of the massages available). Massage (including exotic massages such as Aroma Stone massage, Chakra Balancing massage and other well-being massages), facials, pedicures, and beauty salon treatments are at extra cost (massage, for example, costs about $2 per minute, plus gratuity). Do make appointments early as time slots can go quickly.

Holland America Line offers sports at sea level...

4 HOLLAND AMERICA LINE

Ships:

Amsterdam (2000), *Maasdam* (1993), *Oosterdam* (2003), *Prinsendam* (1988), *Rotterdam* (1997), *Ryndam* (1994), *Statendam* (1993), *Veendam* (1996), *Volendam* (1999), *Westerdam* (2004), *Zaandam* (2000), *Zuiderdam* (2002).

About the company

Holland America Line (owned by Carnival Corporation) was founded in 1873, and today is a leftover from the days of transatlantic travel between Holland and the United States. Its newest ships get larger and larger as the line moves towards catering to (multi-generational) families with children. All ships have teakwood outdoors promenade decks, whereas most rivals have artificial grass or some other form of indoor-outdoor carpeting. The ships are very clean and well maintained. The cruise line features many theme cruises, and each cruise features a crew show.

Suitable For

Holland America Line ships are best suited to older couples and singles (and their grandchildren), who like to mingle in a large ship, in an unhurried setting with fine quality surroundings, with plenty of

... or to take to the air by parachute.

eclectic antique artwork, decent (though not gourmet) food and service from a smiling Indonesian/Filipino crew that likes to serve, but that lacks the finesse many passengers would expect from a "premium "product.

So what's it really like?

The company has lived on its "tradition of excellence" maxim for so many years, that everyone in the company believed it. However, the truth is that the onboard product delivery was, for many years, well below what it advertised. However, things have changed for the better in the past year, and the onboard product and its delivery have been put through the hoop to improve the onboard cruise experience, the result of fresh management with updated ideas, and the latest "signature of excellence" slogan.

There are two distinct types of ships in the brand, appealing to different types of people. Families with children and grandchildren are best suited to the new, larger ships such as *Oosterdam*, *Westerdam*, and *Zuiderdam*, whereas adults of senior years (HAL's traditional audience of repeat passengers from alumni groups) are typically attracted to ships that are smaller and less glitzy, such as *Amsterdam*, *Maasdam*, *Prinsendam*, *Rotterdam*, *Ryndam*, *Statendam*, *Veendam*, and *Zaandam*. All the ships are well maintained and cleaning takes place constantly.

In what is seen as an effort to catch up to Celebrity Cruises' Concierge Class, HAL introduced a raft of "value-added" items in 2004 covering dining, service, accommodation, and activities. These include "Premium-Plus" Euro-Top mattresses, 100 percent cotton bed linens or duvets (top suites only), massage showerheads, fruit basket, VCRs or DVD players. Suite passengers also get access to the Neptune Lounge (a concierge lounge only available to suite occupants), thus creating, in effect, a two-class system.

Holland America Line has its own training school in Jakarta, Indonesia, and so is able to "pre-train" crew members who have never been to sea before. However, in the past few years, the company has promoted so many crew members to supervisory positions due to a host of new ships introduced, but few of those promoted have the formal training, professional or management skills, or experience to do the job properly. Better trained middle management is needed to improve the standard of product delivery and communication. Internal promotion is fine, but, decreased professionalism is not the price that passengers should pay. Few crew members can carry on a conversation with the majority of HAL's American passengers for more than a couple of minutes before having to excuse themselves. However, crew members *are* willing, polite, and smile a lot (particularly if extra tips are forthcoming), which is more than can be said for service staff on land today.

HAL is one of only two of the Big 7 cruise lines with proper dedicated cinemas built into all its ships (the other is Princess Cruises, while Celebrity Cruises has them aboard all but two ships – *Horizon* and *Zenith*). HAL also operates lots of theme-related cruises, and has an extensive "University at Sea" program of (life enrichment) lecturers.

HAL has established smoking and no-smoking areas throughout its ships, although in practice there seem to be many more smokers than you would expect (depending on ship and itinerary). The hotel service crew is mainly Indonesian, but they do nothing to remind passengers that they may be smoking in a non-smoking area, or not to smoke where food is being served. So, if you are a non-smoker, be aware. **Embarkation**: When you first embark, a member of staff, dressed in a crisp white uniform (or black butler's uniform if you are in one of the top suites) will escort you directly to your cabin (and carry your hand luggage). Early embarkation and leisurely disembarkation is now available aboard all HAL ships.

Decor

Aboard *Amsterdam, Maasdam, Prinsendam, Rotterdam, Ryndam, Statendam, Veendam, Volendam, Zaandam*, the décor is rather bland and dark (restful), with eclectic artwork that is focused on Dutch artefacts mainly from the 16th and 17th centuries. However, aboard the newest ships (*Oosterdam, Westerdam, Zuiderdam*) the décor is – wow – showy, lively and glitzy - a shock to the regulars, but acceptable for families with children who like bright things like large wall panels with digital "in-your-face" artwork that present an *Alice in Wonderland* look. You wouldn't go for it in your living room, but aboard these large ships it *almost* works, although not when there are few children aboard and most of the passengers are older. It is important, therefore, to choose the right ship for your personality type, and for the right reasons.

Cuisine/Dining

Like Carnival, HAL has now opted to have four seatings in its main dining rooms (all ships). You must choose your preferred time and stick with it. Although some tables for two are available, most are for four, six, or eight persons. Fine Rosenthal china and cutlery are used. Live music is provided for dinner each evening; once each cruise, a Dutch Dinner is featured (hats are provided), as is an Indonesian Lunch. "Lighter option" meals are always available for the nutrition-conscious and the weight-conscious.

Holland America Line food is, unfortunately, not as nice as the china it's placed on, and doesn't match the standard found aboard other ships in the premium segment of the industry. While the USDA beef is good, poultry and most fish are often overcooked and dry (except when the ships are in Alaska, when the halibut and salmon are excellent). What are also definitely not luxurious (or even premium) are the

---

Venice is on Holland America Line's itinerary.

endless packets of sugar, and packets (instead of glass jars) of supermarket brand breakfast jams, marmalade and honey, and poor quality teas. While these may be suitable for a family diner with tablecloth service, they do not belong aboard a ship that claims to have "award-winning cuisine."

Dessert and pastry items are of a reasonable quality (specifically suited to American tastes), but there is much use of canned fruit and jellied desserts, and packets of jam, marmalade, butter, sugar – the same stuff you find in Denny's or IHOP, for example. Forget the selection of "international" cheeses, most of it is highly colored processed "cheese" from Wisconsin (none of those tasty small producer cheeses from states such as Vermont and Virginia). Holland America Line can and does provide Kosher meals; these are prepared ashore, frozen, and brought to your table sealed in their original containers (there is no Kosher kitchen on board).

The company also offers complimentary cappuccino/espresso coffees and free ice cream during certain hours of the day aboard its ships, as well as hot hors d'oeuvres in all bars – something other major lines seem to have dropped, or charge extra for. Cabin service breakfasts are very basic, with only Continental breakfast available and a few hot food items.

The wine list is heavily reliant on wines from California and Washington State, with few decent wines from France or Germany, other than those found in a typical supermarket.

Alternative Dining

All HAL ships now feature an "alternative dining" spot (some ships are being retrofitted with this facility through 2006) called the "Pinnacle Grill," which serves "Pacific Northwest Cuisine" (little more than surf n' turf dining) in a more intimate restaurant with tablecloths, linen napkins and decent size wine glasses (although more refinement is, fortunately, taking place). The food is far better than in the main dining rooms (there is a cover charge, and reservations are required). Bulgari china, Frette linens, and Reidel glasses are part of this "enhanced" dining experience.

Casual Eateries

All ships feature a Lido Deck self-serve buffet. Most are of the line (move along with your tray) type, although the latest ships feature more active stations and individual islands, and include decent salad bars, dessert bars, regional specialties and fast food (grilled) items such as hamburgers, salmon burgers, hot dogs and French fries.

The Coffee/Tea Factor

Regular Coffee: Half decent, but weak (Score: 3 out of 10).Espresso/cappuccino coffees (Javanese) are adequate, served in proper china, but not quite up to the standard of Celebrity or Costa. Score: 6 out of 10. However, both in the main dining rooms and the Java Cafes aboard all HAL ships, espresso/cappuccinos do not cost extra (unlike other Big 7 lines).

New Holland America Line ships near completion.

For Children:

Club HAL: Junior passengers are divided into three age-appropriate groups: 3–8, 9–12, and teens. Programming is based on the number of children booked on any given sailing, and children's counsellors are provided accordingly. HAL's children's programs are not as extensive as those of Carnival Cruise Lines, for example, although they are improving with the latest breed of large ships.

Best ships for children: *Oosterdam, Westerdam, Zuiderdam*, but not: *Amsterdam, Maasdam, Prinsendam, Rotterdam, Ryndam, Statendam, Veendam, Zaandam*.

Gratuities: $10 per person per day (the amount charged when this book was completed) is added to your onboard account. You can have this amount adjusted, but you'll need to visit the information desk to do so. Additionally, 15% is added to bar and wine accounts. The onboard currency is the US dollar.

Entertainment

Holland America Line is not known for its fine entertainment (the budgets aren't high enough). The production shows, while a good attempt, fall short on story line, choreography and performance, with colorful costuming and lighting hiding the weak spots. Each ship carries its own resident troupe of singers/dancers and audio-visual support staff. HAL also offers a consistently good, tried and tested array of cabaret acts that constantly pop up on the cruise ship circuit. All show lounges are nonsmoking venues.

A number of bands, a string ensemble and solo musicians present live music for dancing and listening in many of the lounges and bars throughout the ship. Each ship has a Crows Nest Lounge (by day an observation lounge) for social dancing, and there is always serenading string music in the Explorer's Lounge and dining room.

Each cruise includes a Crew Show. These can be naff to decent, depending on your viewpoint. Passengers always seem enthusiastic, because they like connecting staff that they know and have seen during their cruise. Yes, they might be able to sing a song or two, but they probably wouldn't ever make it in the real world because they have no musical charts (orchestra/band charts), more than 15 minutes of material, and, most important, a manager or business sense. Still, they enjoy themselves, and are proud of what they have achieved, and that's what it's all about in the world of cruise ships.

Spa/Fitness Facilities

The Greenhouse Spa, beauty and fitness facilities (named after the Texas-based facility of the same name) aboard all HAL ships (some of which will be retrofitted between 2005–06) are staffed and operated by Steiner Leisure, a specialist concession, whose staff will try to sell you Steiner's own-brand beauty products (spa personnel have sales targets). Some fitness classes are free, while some, such as yoga, kickboxing or Pilates essentials, cost $11 per class (a special price is offered for unlimited classes). Massages (including exotic massages such as Aroma Stone massage, Chakra Balancing massage and other well-being massages), facials, pedicures, and beauty salon treatments are extra cost items. Examples: Well-being massage $99 for 50 minutes; Hot Stone therapy massage $158 for 75 minutes; Reflexology $99 for 50 minutes; Japanese Silk Booster facial 129 for 75 minutes; personal fitness instruction $75 for 60 minutes (course of three for $191). Do make appointments as early as possible (on embarkation day), as time slots can go quickly.

5 NORWEGIAN CRUISE LINE / NCL AMERICA

Ships
Norwegian Crown (1998), *Norwegian Dawn* (2002), *Norwegian Dream* (1992), *Norwegian Jewel* (2005), *Norwegian Majesty* (1992), *Norwegian Sea* (1988), *Norwegian Spirit* (1998), *Norwegian Star* (2002), *Norwegian Sun* (2001), *Norwegian Wind* (1993); *Pride of Aloha* (2004), *Pride of America* (2005).

About the company
Norwegian Cruise Line, the originator of contemporary cruising, was founded in 1966 by three Norwegian shipping companies as Norwegian Caribbean Line. The line was bought by Star Cruises in 2000, and has been replacing its older, smaller ships with

NCL provides balloons to keep the kids occupied.

brand new, larger vessels. NCL also operates NCL America, with all-American crews and a base in Hawaii (most comments apply to both brands).

NCL's fleet is diverse, so the cruise experience varies (there is more standardization aboard the larger, newer ships). The senior officers are the only thing Norwegian (except aboard NCL America vessels, where they are American). Choose this line for a good all-round family cruise, interesting itineraries, and plenty of dining choices, particularly aboard the largest ships. NCL provides a good product for a youthful, active, sports-minded audience (all its ships have sports bars and memorabilia). For the most part, standard cabins are small, although they have reasonably attractive decor and are functional. Closet and drawer space is very limited in the newest ships.

Suitable For
Norwegian Cruise Line ships are best suited to first-time young (and young at heart) couples, single passengers, tots, children and teenagers who enjoy big city nightlife, who want contemporary, upbeat, color-rich surroundings, and the latest in facilities, plenty of entertainment lounges and bars and high-tech sophistication – all in one neat, highly programmed, well packaged cruise vacation. There's plenty of lively music, constant activity, entertainment, and food that is mainstream and acceptable but nothing more (unless you pay extra to eat in the "alternative" dining spots). All this is delivered by a smiling, friendly service staff that lacks polish but is willing.

So what's it really like?
If this is your first cruise, you should have a decent overall vacation in an upbeat setting. The onboard lifestyle is contemporary, fresh, with a casualness typical of youthful city dwellers, and with its "eat when

Tributes to showbusiness in *Pride of Aloha.*

you want" philosophy, the shipboard ambiance is casual. So is the dress code – indeed, the waiters may be better dressed than many passengers. The staff is in the main, congenial, and you'll find a high percentage of females in cabin and restaurant service departments (more than most other Big 7 cruise lines).

All ships can provide an almost full-size newspaper from a wide choice of US and European titles on the Multicast satellite delivery system (the cost: $3.95 per newspaper, per day). You can also make a special request for your favourite newspaper that's not in the list, although it may cost more.

Embarkation: Few staff members are on duty at the gangway when you first arrive, and they will merely point you in the direction of your deck, or to the ship's elevators instead of escorting you to your cabin.

NCL's Private Island (Great Stirrup Cay): Drinks: Only coffee and ice-water are free (there's no iced tea), and everything else is charged.

Cuisine/Dining

NCL has recognized the increasing trend in the USA away from formal restaurants (for dining) into bistros (for eating faster). For cruising, NCL has championed more choices in dining than any other cruise line (except parent company Star Cruises) with its "Freestyle Dining," giving you the opportunity to try different types of cuisine, in different settings, when you want. In practice, however, it means that you have to make reservations (this can prove frustrating), and getting it just right takes a bit of planning. Freestyle Dining works best aboard the newest ships, which have been purposely designed for it (*Norwegian Dawn, Norwegian Spirit, Norwegian Star, Pride of Aloha, Pride of America*) while the others have

been modified and massaged to accommodate the concept, which tends to create food outlets instead of restaurants. On Formal Nights and other major production show presentation nights, most people want to eat at the same time (to see the shows), and this can cause prime-time congestion and frustration. Make reservations at least one day ahead, so you don't get caught in the "sorry, you'll have to wait 30-60 minutes" routine that many experience.

After-dinner espresso/cappuccino coffees are available in the dining rooms without extra charge –a nice feature. Once each cruise, NCL features a Chocoholics Buffet (for which you'll be given paper plates and plastic cutlery).

The wine list aboard NCL ships is quite good, with many excellent wines in the $20–$30 range. Wine is typically served by table waiters, whose knowledge of wines and their correct service is zero.

Cabin service breakfasts are very basic, with only Continental breakfast available and no hot food items (for those you'll need to go to one of the restaurants or the self-serve buffet. The (non-breakfast) Room Service menu has only two hot items available throughout the day: Oriental soup and pizza, the rest is cold (salads and sandwiches).

Casual Eateries: All NCL ships have self-serve buffet-style eateries. Most are of the move-along-with-your-tray type, although the newest ships have more active stations and individual islands.

The Coffee/Tea Factor: Regular Coffee: Weak and poor. Score: 2 out of 10. Espresso/Cappuccino coffees: Score: 4 out of 10. Some bars have espresso/cappuccino machines, which are extra charge items.

For Children:

NCL's Junior Cruisers program divides children into three groups, according to age: Junior sailors (ages

2–5); First Mates and Navigators (ages 6–12); Teens (ages 13–17). Babysitting services are available (group only, not individual), at an extra change.

Best ships for children: *Norwegian Dawn, Norwegian Star, Norwegian Sun.* But not: *Norwegian Crown, Norwegian Dream, Norwegian Majesty, Norwegian Sea, Norwegian Wind.*

Gratuities:

Starting in May 2005, a non-adjustable $10 per person per day service charge is added to your onboard account. Children over 13 pay the adult rate of $10 per day while those aged 3-12 pay $5 per day (those under age 3 pay nothing). A 15% gratuity is added to all bar, wine and spa charges. The onboard currency is the US dollar.

Entertainment

All showlounges are non-smoking venues. Of the Big 7 cruise lines, NCL has always had consistently good production shows that provided lots of color and spectacle in a predictable (though now a little dated) format. Each ship carries its own resident troupe of singers/dancers and audio-visual support staff. There are two or three production shows in a typical 7-day cruise (all provided by the Jean Ann Ryan Company).

They are all very colorful, high-energy, razzle-dazzle shows, with much use of pyrotechnics, laser and color-mover lights, and so much happening on stage that by the end of the evening, if you are a typical passenger, you will be tired and unable to remember much about the shows, which are, however, very entertaining.

Activities and passenger participation events tend to range from the extremely naff to the naff.

Spa/Fitness Facilities

The spas are staffed and operated by the Hawaii-based Mandara Spa, owned by Steiner Leisure). Many of the staff are quite young, and will try to sell you Steiner's own-brand beauty products (spa girls have sales targets). Some fitness classes are free, while some, such as yoga and kick-boxing, cost $10 per class. However, being aboard will give you an opportunity to try some of the more exotic treatments (particularly some of the massages available). Massage (including Aroma Stone massage, Chakra Balancing massage and other well-being massages), facials, pedicures, and beauty salon treatments cost extra. Examples: Lomi Lomi Massage ($99 for 50 minutes/$140 for 80 minutes); Hot Stone Massage ($185 for 80 minutes); Mandara Four Hands Massage ($180 for 50 minutes); Aromapure Facial ($99 for 50 minutes); Coconut Rub/Milk Body Wrap ($115 for 55 minutes); Jasmine Flower Hydrotherapy Bath ($40 for 25 minutes). You need to book early because the most convenient time slots go quickly.

Serving yourself at Princess Cruises' buffets.

6 PRINCESS CRUISES

Ships

Caribbean Princess (2004), *Coral Princess* (2002), *Dawn Princess* (1997), *Diamond Princess* (2004), *Golden Princess* (2001), *Grand Princess* (1998), *Island Princess* (2003), *Pacific Princess* (1999), *Regal Princess* (1991), *Royal Princess* (1984) (withdrawn in May 2005, to be replaced by *Sea Princess*), *Sapphire Princess* (2005), *Star Princess* (2002), *Sun Princess* (1995), *Tahitian Princess* (1999).

About the company

Princess Cruises was founded in 1965. Today it is part of the Carnival Corporation. Its ships that are well designed, and passenger flow (particularly aboard the latest ships) is very good (exception: *Regal Princess*). Although they are large ships, they really do absorb people well, and there is little sense of crowding (pool decks notwithstanding), although areas around photo galleries do present bottlenecks, particularly at feeding times when more people are milling about. The ships have a higher-than-average Passenger Space Ratio than competitors Carnival or RCI.

Suitable For

The ships of Princess Cruises are best suited to couples (both young and not so young), families with children and teenagers, and older singles who like

Princess Cruises offers the latest video games.

to mingle in a large ship setting with pleasing, sophisticated surroundings and lifestyle, reasonably good entertainment and fairly decent food and service, all wrapped up in one affordable package.

So what's it really like?

Princess Cruises' ships are very clean and well maintained at all times, and the promenade decks of some ships have teak deck lounge chairs (others are plastic). Princess Cruises also has a nice balance of officers, staff and crew members, and the line's British connections help it to achieve the feeling of calmness aboard its ships that some other lines don't have. Choose Princess Cruises if you enjoy being with families and fellow passengers of mid-50s and upwards, who want a well-organized cruise experience with unpretentious middle-of-the-road cuisine, a good range of entertainment, and an excellent shore excursion programme (arguably the best run of any of the Big 7 companies).

Princess Cruises is one of only three cruise lines in the Big 7 with proper cinemas aboard all its ships (the other is Holland America Line, while Celebrity Cruises has them aboard all but two ships – *Horizon* and *Zenith*). Passenger niggles include the fact that your name is placed outside your cabin adjacent to the "mailbox," and that cabin stewards still knock even when you have placed a "do not disturb" sign on it.

All passengers receive turndown service and chocolates on pillows each night, as well as bathrobes (on request) and toiletry amenity kits (larger, naturally, for suite/mini-suite occupants) that typically include soap, shampoo, conditioner, and hand/body lotion. A hairdryer is typically provided in all cabins, sensibly located at a lounge area vanity desk unit. BBC World, CNN, CNBC, ESPN and TNT can be found on the in-cabin color TV system (when available, depending on cruise area).

Lines can form at peak times for elevators, the purser's (information) office, and for open-seating breakfast and lunch in the main dining rooms. Lines for shore excursions and shore tenders are also a fact of life aboard large ships.

Countless pieces of questionable "art" are encountered in almost every foyer and public room – an annoying reminder that today, cruising aboard large ships is like living in a bazaar of paintings surrounded by a ship. Now, what am I bid for this piece of art that is really worth only $10? Let's hear it: $1,200? Do I hear $1,400? Or will someone actually imagine it to be worth even more? There's also a charge for using washers and dryers in self-service launderettes.

Princess Cruises has the most extensive wedding program of any of the Big 7, with its "Tie the Knot" wedding packages. The ship's captain can *legally* marry (American) couples at sea aboard its ships registered in Bermuda (by special dispensation, which should be verified when in the planning stage, and may vary according to where you reside). The basic Wedding At Sea package costs $1,800, plus $400 for licensing fees. Harborside or (shore-side) packages vary according to the port. For the latest rates, see the Princess Cruises website or your travel agent.

The dress code is either formal (typically one formal night per 7-day cruise), or smart casual (which seems to be translated by many as jeans or tracksuits and trainers). The onboard product (particularly the food and entertainment) is totally geared to the North American market, however British and other European nationalities should feel at home, as long as they realize that this is all about highly organized, packaged cruising, food and service, with an increasing emphasis on onboard revenue. Expect to be subjected to a stream of flyers advertising daily art auctions, "designer" watches, specialized classes (Princess Cruises' "ScholarShip@Sea" programs), and the like.

You'll also have to live with many extra charge items (such as ice cream, non-standard coffees and pastry item taken in venues other than the restaurants, $4 per hour for group babysitting services, and $40 for an "introduction to pottery" class – the ship has its own kiln).

Embarkation: There are few staff members on duty at the gangway when you first arrive, and they will merely point you in the direction of your deck, or to the ship's elevators instead of escorting you to your cabin. An "express check-in" option is available by completing certain documentation 40 days in advance of your cruise.

Decor

If Carnival's ships have the brightest décor imaginable, the décor aboard Princess Cruises' ships is almost the opposite – perhaps a little bland in places, with much use of neutral tones, calm colors and pastels. But it really does suit the passengers that cruise with Princess, and nothing (we're talking about the décor) is garish or too bright.

Cuisine/Dining

Traditional shipboard dining (assigned tables and the same waiter each night in one of two seating times) is featured aboard *Regal Princess* and *Royal Princess.* "Personal Choice Dining" – a mixture of both traditional and "your choice" – where you choose when you want to eat, and with whom, aboard *Caribbean Princess, Coral Princess, Dawn Princess, Diamond Princess, Golden Princess, Grand Princess, Island Princess, Pacific Princess, Sapphire Princess, Star Princess, Sun Princess, Tahitian Princess.* All dining rooms and restaurants are smoke-free.

Although portions are generous, the food and its presentation are somewhat disappointing, and lack taste. Fish is often disguised by crumb or batter coating, the selection of fresh green vegetables is limited, and few garnishes are used. However, do remember that this is big-ship banquet catering, with all its attendant standardization and production cooking. Meats are of a decent quality, although often disguised by gravy-based sauces, and pasta dishes

The end of another day on the *Sun Princess.*

are acceptable (though voluminous), and are typically served by section headwaiters that may also make "something special just for you" – in search of gratuities and good comments.

If you like desserts, order a sundae at dinner, as most other desserts are just so-so. While ice cream ordered in the dining room is included, but costs extra elsewhere (Hagen Dazs can be found at poolside).

Specially designed dinnerware and good quality linens and silverware are featured, such as Dudson of England (dinnerware), Frette Egyptian cotton table linens, and silverware by Hepp of Germany. Themed dinners are a feature. On a 7-day cruise, a typical menu cycle will include a Sailaway Dinner, Captain's Welcome Dinner, Chef's Dinner, Italian Dinner, French Dinner, Captain's Gala Dinner, and Landfall Dinner.

The wine list is reasonable, but not good, but there are no wine waiters (table waiters or section head waiters serve the wine).

Casual Eateries: For casual eating, each ship has a Horizon Buffet (open round the clock), and, at night, provides an informal dinner setting with sit-down waiter service; a small (limited) bistro menu is also available. The buffet displays are, for the most part, quite repetitious, but far better than they have been in the past few years (there is no finesse in presentation, however, as plastic plates are provided, instead of trays). The cabin service menu is very limited, and presentation of food items featured is poor.

The Coffee/Tea Factor: Regular Coffee: Weak and poor. Score: 2 out of 10. Espresso/Cappuccino coffees: Score: 3 out of 10. Except for beverage station at the serve-yourself buffets, coffees/teas in bars are available at extra charge.

For Children:

Children are divided into four age groups: Princess Pelicans: (ages 2–5); Princess Pirateers, (ages 8–12); Off Limits, (ages 13–17). The groups are split into age-related activities, and Princess Cruises has very good children's counsellors and supervised activities.

Best Ships for children: *Caribbean Princess, Coral Princess, Dawn Princess, Diamond Princess, Golden Princess, Grand Princess, Island Princess, Sapphire Princess, Star Princess, Sun Princess.* But not: *Regal Princess, Royal Princess, Tahitian Princess.*

Gratuities:

Gratuities to staff are added to your account, at $10 per person, per day (gratuities for children are charged at the same rate). If you want to pay less, you'll need to go to the reception desk to have these charges adjusted (that could mean lining up with many other passengers wanting to do the same). Additionally, 15% is added to all bar and wine bills. The onboard currency is the US dollar.

The disco aboard *Grand Princess*.

Entertainment

All showlounges are non-smoking venues. Princess Cruises' production shows have always been aimed at its slightly older, more elegant passengers who liked the traditional, with elegant costuming and Hollywood image.

For entertainment, Princess Cruises prides itself on its glamorous all-American production shows, and the shows aboard this ship should not disappoint (there are typically two or three shows each 7-day cruise). Each ship carries its own resident troupe of singers/dancers and audio-visual support staff.

Passenger participation events always appear to be put on by cruise staff that is waiting for a bit part in an episode of *The Love Boat*. Most lounges and bars have live music. Musical units range from solo pianists, to string quartets, to a cappella singers, to bands that can provide music for ballroom dancing. Princess Cruises also provides a number of male hosts as dance partners for women traveling alone.

Spa/Fitness Facilities

You can now make online reservations for any spa treatments before your cruise – so you can obtain the time you want, instead of all that frustration often encountered when aboard, although careful planning will need to be made so as not to clash with shore excursions and other diversions (days at sea are easiest to make online, and hardest to obtain on board).

● *Caribbean Princess, Sapphire Princess:*
Spa/beauty treatments and fitness facilities are staffed and operated by Princess Cruises' own in-

house department (Princess Cruises was the first of the Big 7 cruise lines to operate its own spa services, starting in 2004). Many of the staff is young, however. The spa features beauty treatment products by the French specialist well-being company Phytomer, and hair products are by Carita of Paris.

● *Coral Princess, Dawn Princess, Diamond Princess, Golden Princess, Grand Princess, Island Princess, Royal Princess, Star Princess, Sun Princess:*
Spa/beauty treatments and fitness facilities are staffed and operated by Steiner Leisure, a concession, whose young staff will also try to sell you Steiner's own-brand beauty products (spa girls have sales targets).

Some fitness classes are free (Stepexpress, Power Walk, Total Body Conditioning, Xpress Circuit are examples), while some, such as yoga and kick-boxing, cost extra. However, being aboard will give you an opportunity to try some of the more exotic treatments (particularly some of the massages available). Massage, including Aromatherapy massage, Hot Stone massage, Chakra Balancing massage, Asian Lotus ritual (featuring massage with reflexology, reiki and shiatsu massage), deep-tissue sports therapy massage, and other well-being massages, lime and ginger salt glow, wild strawberry back cleanse, and seaweed mud wraps, among others devised to make you feel good (and also to part you from your money), facials, pedicures, and beauty salon treatments are at extra cost (massage, for example, costs about $2 per minute, plus gratuity). Do make appointments as early as possible (the day you board is the best time to book your preferred treatments).

The billiards table is gyroscopically controlled.

7 ROYAL CARIBBEAN INTERNATIONAL

Ships

Adventure of the Seas (2001), *Brilliance of the Seas* (2002), *Empress of the Seas* (1990), *Enchantment of the Seas* (1997), *Explorer of the Seas* (2000), *Grandeur of the Seas* (1996), *Jewel of the Seas* (2004), *Legend of the Seas* (1995), *Majesty of the Seas* (1992), *Mariner of the Seas* (2004), *Monarch of the Seas* (1991), *Navigator of the Seas* (2003), *Radiance of the Seas* (2001), *Rhapsody of the Seas* (1997), *Sovereign of the Seas* (1988), *Vision of the Seas* (1998), *Voyager of the Seas* (1999).

About the company

Royal Caribbean International (owned and founded in 1969 by Royal Caribbean Cruises Ltd.) started out as a highly creative cruise line in the late 1960s. However, since it now has shareholders controlled by Wall Street, the onboard product has slipped to equal that of Carnival Cruise Lines (whose ships, in general, have larger standard cabins).

The ships are shapely, with well-rounded sterns, and interesting design profiles that make them instantly recognizable. Large, brightly lit casinos are provided, as are shopping galleries that passengers have to walk through to get almost anywhere else. It is all cleverly designed to extract maximum revenue.

Suitable For

Royal Caribbean International ships are best suited to active, young-minded couples and singles of all ages, families with toddlers, children, and teenagers who like to mingle in a large ship setting with plenty of life and high-energy entertainment, with food that is acceptable in quantity rather than quality unless you are prepared to pay extra for dining in the "alternative" restaurant (not all ships have them), all delivered with friendly service that lacks polish.

So what's it really like?

RCI provides a well organized, but rather homogenous cruise experience. It is a well-integrated, fine-tuned, comfortable and well-liked product that is consistent. This is cruising for mainstream America). The ships are all quite pleasing, and some have really comfortable public rooms, lounges, bars, and some innovative gimmicks such as ice-skating rinks. The company competes directly with Carnival Cruise Lines and Princess Cruises in terms of what's offered on board, and the way it is delivered, as well as the hard sell for onboard revenue (the result of highly discounted pricing in the marketplace).

There's really nothing "royal" about it, except in the name. The ships' senior officers are Norwegian or Scandinavian (there *is* a difference), but the service staff are an eclectic mix of many nationalities. There is a big difference between the largest ships – termed the *Voyager*-class ships (*Adventure of the Seas, Explorer of the Seas, Mariner of the Seas, Navigator of the Seas, Voyager of the Seas*) and others (mainly in the internal layout) which sport a large mall-like high street – the focal point for most passengers. Many of the public rooms, lounges and bars are located as adjuncts to the mall. It's rather like a mall with a ship built around it.

The next group of ships (*Brilliance of the Seas, Jewel of the Seas, Radiance of the Seas, Serenade of the Seas*) have lots of balcony cabins, and large expanses of glass, which help to provide more of a connection with the sea, while *Enchantment of the Seas, Grandeur of the Seas, Legend of the Seas, Rhapsody of the Seas, Splendour of the Seas, Vision of the Seas* also have large expanses of glass in the public areas, but not so many balcony cabins.

The oldest ships (*Majesty of the Seas, Monarch of the Seas, Sovereign of the Seas*), innovative in the late 1980s, are looking decidedly dated. They have small cabins, and tiny tub chairs in public rooms, for example, when most passengers have become larger.

The onboard product is dedicated to those with an active, contemporary lifestyle (rather like Ocean Drive on South Beach, Miami). All ships have a 30-ft (9 meters) high rock-climbing wall, with five separate climbing tracks. You'll need to plan what you want to take part in wisely as almost everything requires you to sign-up in advance.

All lobby foyers are named Centrum – as in many cities in Europe. There are few quiet places to sit and read – almost everywhere there is intrusive background music – played even in elevators and all passenger hallways, and many, many intrusive announcements. Bars also have very loud music.

Captains and senior officers are Scandinavian. Service personnel are quite friendly, but only a small percentage offer a greeting when passing you in the corridors (this includes the officers), so the hospitality factor could be better. The elevators talk to you ("going up/going down" is informative, but monotonous, although the illuminated picture displays of decks is good). Standing in line for embarkation, the reception desk, disembarkation, for port visits, shore tenders and for the self-serve buffet stations in the Windjammer Cafe is an inevitable aspect of cruising aboard large ships. There are no cushioned pads for the deck lounge chairs (they have plastic webbing and, even with a towel placed on them, soon become uncomfortable).

Take lots of extra pennies – you'll need them to pay for all the additional-cost items. Expect to be subjected to a stream of flyers advertising daily art auctions, "designer" watches, "inch of gold/silver" and other promotions, while "artworks" for auction are strewn throughout the ship. Expect intrusive announcements for activities that bring revenue, such as art auctions and bingo.

Embarkation: There are few staff members on duty at the gangway when you first arrive, and they will merely point you in the direction of your deck, or to the ship's elevators instead of escorting you to your cabin. Lines for check-in, embarkation and disembarkation (if you are a non-US resident and stay at an RCI-booked hotel, all formalities can be completed there and then you'll simply walk on board to your cabin, after going through security checks, of course) are a bit daunting, but the company does well in making it all flow as smoothly as possible.

Decor

The interior décor of all ships is bright and contemporary, but not as neon-intensive and glitzy as Carnival's ships. There is much Scandinavian design influence, with some interesting pieces of sculpture and artwork that some might call eclectic. The ("you are here") signage and deck plans are excellent, so finding your way around should be easy. Much of the furniture in public lounges tends to feature small "tub" chairs that are constantly being broken by passengers who are simply too large for them.

Cuisine/Dining

Most ships have dining rooms two or three decks high, giving a sense of space and grandeur. Few tables for two are available, most being for four, six, or eight persons. All dining rooms and eateries are non-smoking. The efficient dining operation emphasizes highly programmed (insensitive), extremely hurried service that many find intrusive.

The cuisine in the main dining rooms is typical of mass banquet catering with standard fare comparable to that found in American family-style restaurants ashore – mostly disappointing and lacking in taste (the food costs per passenger are well below those for sister company Celebrity Cruises, so you should not expect the same food quality). Dinner menus typically include a Welcome-Aboard Dinner, French Dinner, Italian Dinner, International Dinner, and Captain's Gala Dinner, and all offer plenty of choice. There's plenty of food, and, although it is basically well prepared, it is all rather homogenous. While menu descriptions sound tempting, what's delivered appears to be lost in translation, and is non-memo-

The chairman's Morgan aboard *Voyager of the Seas*.

Rock climbing at sea is available aboard all RCI ships.

rable. A decent selection of light meals is provided, however, and there is a vegetarian menu.

While the USDA prime beef supplied is very good, other meats may not be (they are often disguised with gravies or heavy sauces). Most fish (except salmon) and seafood items tend to be overcooked and lack taste. Green vegetables are scarce, although salad items are plentiful. Rice is often used as a source of carbohydrates (potatoes being more expensive). Breads and pastry items are generally good (although some items, such as croissants, may not be made on board). Dessert items are standardized, and the cheese selection is poor, as is the choice of accompanying (typically salted) crackers. The selection of breads, rolls, and fruit could be better. Caviar (once a standard menu item) incurs a hefty extra charge.

Each cruise, a "Galley Buffet" allows passengers to go through a section of the galley collecting food while noting its spotless, stainless steel backdrop (cleaner than almost any land-based dining facility).

Although prices are moderate, the wine list is not extensive, and almost all wines are extremely young (only small glasses are provided). The waiters tend to be overly friendly for some tastes – particularly on the last night of the cruise, when tips are expected.

Alternative Dining Venues: All new ships now feature two additional dining venues: *Chops Grill Steakhouse* (for premium veal chops and steaks), and *Portofino* (for Italian-American cuisine). Both venues feature food that is of a much higher quality than in the main dining room. An additional charge of $20 per person (including gratuities) applies, and reservations are required. Typically open for dinner between 6pm and 11pm, you should be prepared to eat a lot of food (perhaps this justifies the cover

charge), from Texas-sized portions presented on large plates. Note that menus do not change throughout the cruise. The dress code is smart casual.

Casual Eateries: All RCI ships have casual eateries called Windjammer Café for fast food items, salads, and other casual meals. Most are of the single line (move along with your tray) type, although the newest ships feature more active stations and individual islands for more variety and less lines. However, the actual quality of food items is extremely poor, as are the tacky counter dressings. Breakfast buffet items are virtually the same each day, monotonous and even below the standards of diner food. The same is true of lunchtime salad items, which have little or no taste. The beverage stations have only the most basic items. Hamburgers and hot dogs in self-serve buffet locations are generally left in bain-maries (steam tables), and are steamed rather than grilled, although you can ask for one to be grilled in front of you.

Drinks packages are available in bars, in the form of cards or stickers, so you can pre-pay for a selection of standard soft drinks and alcoholic drinks. The packages are not user-friendly, however.

The Coffee/Tea Factor: Regular Coffee: Weak and poor. Score: 1 out of 10. Espresso/Cappuccino coffees (Seattle's Best): Score: 4 out of 10 (but it comes in paper cups)

For Children:

Adventure Ocean is RCI's "edutainment" area. Junior passengers are divided into four age-appropriate groups: Aquanaut Center (ages 3–5); Explorer Center (ages 6–8); Voyager Center (ages 9–12); and Optix Teen Center (ages 13–17).

Best ships for children: *Adventure of the Seas, Explorer of the Seas, Mariner of the Seas, Navigator of the Seas, Voyager of the Seas.* Ships that are acceptable, but with fewer facilities: *Brilliance of the Seas, Enchantment of the Seas, Grandeur of the Seas, Jewel of the Seas, Legend of the Seas, Radiance of the Seas, Rhapsody of the Seas, Serenade of the Seas, Splendour of the Seas, Vision of the Seas.* Ships with minimal facilities for children: *Empress of the Seas, Majesty of the Seas, Monarch of the Seas, Sovereign of the Seas.*

Gratuities

Gratuities can be paid in cash or added to your onboard account daily at the suggested rate of $9 per person. Also, 15% is added to all bar, wine and spa charges. The onboard currency is the US dollar.

Entertainment

All showlounges are non-smoking venues. The entertainment throughout is upbeat (in fact, it is difficult to get away from music and noise), but is typical of the kind of resort hotel found in Las Vegas. Royal Caribbean's production shows are colorful, fast-paced, high volume razzle-dazzle spectaculars, but they have little or no storyline, poor linkage between themes and scenes, and choreography that is more stepping in place than dancing. However, they do entertain and provide a change to the world outside the showlounge. The shows are accompanied by a live band and "click" tracks to make it all sound like a big, professional orchestra. Each ship carries its own resident troupe of singers and dancers.

Then there are silly audience participation (summer camp-style, but often funny) events and activities – something that RCI has always done well. These include such things as "How Deep is Your Love" or "The Newlywed Game," line dances, and the inevitable kindergarten-style "Pass the spoon down your dress and up your trousers" routines. Perhaps the Cruise Staff still do the "If I were not upon the Sea…" routine that cruise lines did in the 1960s. Still, it's fun stuff for those that haven't grown up (or don't want to). At least the daily programs are easy to read.

Spa/Fitness Facilities

All RCI ships: The Spa facilities are operated by Steiner Leisure, a specialist concession, whose young, hungry (for revenue) staff do tend to sell you Steiner's own-brand beauty products. Some fitness classes are free, while some, such as yoga and kick-boxing, cost $10 per class. Massage (including exotic massages such as Aroma Stone massage, Chakra Balancing massage and other well-being massages), facials, pedicures, and beauty salon treatments cost extra (massage, for example, costs about $2 per minute, plus tip). Make appointments early – aboard large ships, treatment time slots go quickly.

For the more sporting, there is activity galore – and all RCI ships now feature a rock-climbing wall, with several separate climbing tracks. There is a 30-minute instruction period before anyone is allowed to climb, and this is done in pairs. It's free, and all safety gear is included, but you'll need to sign up. ❑

● *For how the Big 7 cruise lines scored on cuisine and service, see the chart on page 49.*

The Biggest of the Big: Cruise Ships over 100,000 tons

Ship Name	Cruise Line	Tonnage	
Queen Mary 2	Cunard Line	148,528	
Explorer of the Seas	Royal Caribbean International	137,308	
Voyager of the Seas	Royal Caribbean International	137,280	
Adventure of the Seas	Royal Caribbean International	137,276	
Mariner of the Seas	Royal Caribbean International	137,276	
Navigator of the Seas	Royal Caribbean International	137,276	
Caribbean Princess	Princess Cruises	116,000	
Diamond Princess	Princess Cruises	113,000	
Sapphire Princess	Princess Cruises	113,000	
Carnival Conquest	Carnival Cruise Lines	110,319	
Carnival Glory	Carnival Cruise Lines	110,000	
Carnival Liberty	Carnival Cruise Lines	110,000	
Carnival Valor	Carnival Cruise Lines	110,000	
Star Princess	Princess Cruises	108,977	
Golden Princess	Princess Cruises	108,865	
Costa Fortuna	Costa Cruises	105,000	
Costa Magica	Costa Cruises	105,000	
Carnival Triumph	Carnival Cruise Lines	101,509	
Carnival Victory	Carnival Cruise Lines	101,509	
Carnival Destiny	Carnival Cruise Lines	101,353	Biggest of all: *Queen Mary 2.*

Biggest of all: *Queen Mary 2.*

The Big 7 cruise lines

KEY
(1) = Selected suites only
(2) = On request only
(3) = In the shower unit only: *CostaVictoria*
(4) = On back-to-back cruises only (turnaround day)

A look at this chart shows just what cruise lines do (or do not) provide in your cabin and bathroom

CRUISE LINE	Carnival Cruise Lines		Celebrity Cruises		
	Standard Cabins	Suites	Standard Cabins	Concierge Class	Suites
CABIN					
Bed Linen: Duvets (not sheets/blankets)	No	No	No	Yes	Yes
Bed Linen: 100% Cotton	No	No	No	Yes	Yes
Bed Linen: 50% Cotton/50% Polyester	Yes	Yes	Yes	No	No
Pillowcases: 100% Cotton	No	No	No	Yes	Yes
Towels: 100% Cotton	No	No	Yes	Yes	Yes
Towels: 86% Cotton/14% Polyester	Yes	Yes	No	No	No
Non-Allergenic Pillows	No	No	No	Yes	Yes
Fresh Fruit Bowl	No	No	No	Yes	Yes
Fresh Flowers	No	No	No	Yes	Yes
Telephone	Yes	Yes	Yes	Yes	Yes
Personal Safe	Yes	Yes	Yes	Yes	Yes
Personalized Stationery	No	No	No	Yes	Yes
Television	Yes	Yes	Yes	Yes	Yes
VCR Player	No	Yes	No	No	Yes
CD Player	No	No	No	No	Yes (7)
MP3 Player	No	No	No	Yes	No
Shoe Shine	No	No	No	Yes	Yes
Continental Breakfast	Yes	Yes	Yes	Yes	Yes
Full In-Cabin Breakfast/Lunch/Dinner Service	No	No	Yes	Yes	Yes
Complimentary Espresso/Cappuccino Coffees	Yes	Yes	No	Yes	Yes
Free Local Newspaper in Port (when available)	No	No	No	Yes	Yes
Complimentary Pressing Service (First 24 Hours)	No	No	No	No	Yes
CABIN BATHROOM					
Real Glasses in Bathroom	Yes	Yes	Yes	Yes	Yes
Soap/Shampoo Dispenser Unit	No	No	Yes	Yes	Yes
Soap	Yes	Yes	Yes	Yes	Yes
Shampoo	No	No	No	Yes	No
Conditioner	No	No	No	Yes	No
Combined Shampoo/Conditioner	Yes	Yes	Yes	Yes	Yes
Foaming Bath Oil	No	No	No	No	Yes
Hand Lotion	No	Yes	Yes	Yes	Yes
Mouthwash	No	No	No	No	Yes
Shower Cap	No	No	No	Yes	Yes
Loofah Sponge	No	No	No	No	Yes
Hairdryer	Yes (10)	Yes (10)	Yes	Yes	Yes
Weight Scale	No	No	No	No	Yes
Bathrobes	Yes (10)	Yes	Yes	Yes	Yes
Shaving/Make-Up Mirror	No	Yes (10)	No	No	Yes

(5) = Deluxe cabins only

(6) = Royal Suite only

(7) = Penthouse Suite only

(8) = All outside-view suites and cabins (all ships)

(9) = *Brilliance of the Seas, Jewel of the Seas, Radiance of the Seas* and *Serenade of the Seas* only

(10) = Not all ships

Costa Cruises		Holland America Line		Norwegian Cruise Line		Princess Cruises		Royal Caribbean International	
Cabins	Suites	Standard Cabins	Suites	Standard Cabins	Suites	Standard Cabins	Suites	Standard Cabins	Suites
No	No	No	No	No	No	No	No	No	No
Yes	Yes	No	No	On request	On request	No	Yes	Yes (9)	No
No	No	Yes	Yes	Yes	Yes	Yes	No	Yes	Yes
No	No	No	No	No	No	No	Yes	Yes (9)	No
Yes	Yes	No	No	Yes	Yes	Yes	Yes	Yes	Yes
No	No	Yes	Yes	No	No	No	No	No	No
Yes (2)	Yes (2)	No	No	No	No	Yes	Yes	Yes	Yes
Yes (2)	Yes (2)	Yes	Yes	Yes (2)	Yes	Yes	Yes	No	No
Yes (2)	Yes (2)	Yes	Yes	No	Yes	No	Yes	No	No
Yes	Yes	Yes	Yes	Yes	Yes	Yes	Yes	Yes	Yes
Yes	Yes	No	Yes	No	Yes	Yes	Yes	Yes	Yes
No	No	No	Yes	No	No	No	No	No	No
Yes	Yes	Yes	Yes	Yes	Yes	Yes	Yes	Yes	Yes
No	No	No	Yes	No	Yes (1)	No	No	No	Yes (6)
No	No	No	No	No	Yes (1)	No	No	No	Yes (6)
No	No	No	No	No	No	No	No	No	No
Yes	Yes	No	No	No	No	No	Yes	No	No
Yes	Yes	Yes	Yes	Yes	Yes	Yes	Yes	Yes	Yes
Yes	Yes	Yes	Yes	Yes	Yes	Yes	Yes	Yes	Yes
No	No	Yes	Yes	No	No	No	No	No	No
No	No	No	No	No	No	Yes (4)	Yes (4)	No	No
No	Yes	No	Yes	No	No	No	Yes	No	No
Yes	Yes	Yes	Yes	Yes	Yes	Yes	Yes	Yes	Yes
Yes (3)	Yes (3)	No	No	No	No	No	No	No	No
Yes	Yes	Yes	Yes	Yes	Yes	Yes	Yes	Yes	Yes
Yes	Yes	No	No	No	No	Yes	Yes	Yes	Yes
Yes	Yes	No	No	No	No	Yes	Yes	No	Yes (5)
No	No	Yes	No	Yes	Yes	No	No	No	No
No	No	No	Yes	No	Yes (1)	No	No	No	No
Yes	Yes	Yes	Yes	Yes	Yes	Yes	Yes	No	Yes (5)
No	No	No	No	No	No	No	No	No	No
Yes	Yes	Yes	Yes	Yes	Yes	Yes (2)	Yes (2)	Yes	Yes
No	No	No	No	No	No	No	No	No	No
Yes	Yes	Yes	Yes	Yes	Yes	Yes	Yes	No	No
No	No	No	No	No	Yes (1)	No	No	No	No
No	Yes	No	Yes	No	Yes	Yes	Yes	No	Yes
No	No	No	No	No	No	No	No	No	No

SELECTING THE RIGHT SHIP

Are new ships better than old? Should you consider a maiden voyage?

Is corporate cruising good value? Are theme cruises fun?

A ship built before 1980 is considered old. How-ever, this really depends on the level of main-tenance it has received, and whether it has operated on short or longer cruises (short cruises get more passenger throughput, and so more wear and tear). Yet many passengers do like older ships, as they tend to have fewer synthetic materials in their interior decor. Although it is inevitable that some older tonnage cannot match the latest in high-tech ships, it should be noted that ships today are not constructed to the same high standards, or with the same loving care, as in the past.

New Ships: Advantages

● Incorporate the latest in high-tech electronic equip-ment and in advanced ship design and construction.
● Meet the latest safety and operating standards as laid down by international maritime conventions.
● Have more public room space, with public rooms and lounges built out to the sides of the hull (enclosed promenade decks are no longer seen as essential).
● Offer more standardized cabin layouts and fewer categories.
● Are more fuel-efficient.
● Have a shallower draft, which makes it easier for them to enter and leave ports.
● Have bow and stern thrusters, so they seldom require tug assistance in many ports, thus reducing operating costs.
● Have plumbing and air-conditioning systems that are new and work.
● Have diesel engines mounted on rubber to mini-mize vibration.
● Usually have the latest submersible lifeboats.

New Ships: Disadvantages

● Do not "take the weather" as well as older ships (the experience of sailing across the North Atlantic in November on one of the new large resort ships can be unforgettable). Because of their shallow draft, these ships roll, even when there's the slightest puff of wind.
● Tend to have smaller standard cabins, which can mean narrow, short beds.
● Have thin hulls and do not withstand the bangs and dents as well as older, more heavily plated vessels.
● Have décor made mostly from synthetic materials (due to stringent regulations) and therefore could cause problems for those passengers who are sensi-tive to such materials.
● Have toilets of the powerful vacuum suction "bark-ing dog" type.

● Are powered mainly by diesel (or diesel-electric) engines, which inevitably cause some vibration; although on the latest vessels, the engines are mounted on pliable, floating rubber cushions and are, therefore, virtually vibration-free.
● Have cabin windows that are completely sealed instead of portholes that can be opened.

Pre-1980 Ships: Advantages

● Have strong, plated hulls (often riveted) that can withstand tremendously hard wear and tear; they "take the weather" well.
● Have large cabins with long, wide beds/berths, because passengers needed more space in the days when voyages were much longer.
● Have a wide range of cabin sizes, shapes, and grades more suited to families with children.
● Have toilets that are of the "gentle flush" variety instead of the powerful "barking dog" vacuum toi-lets found aboard newer ships.
● Are powered by steam turbines, which are virtually free of vibration or noise and are considerably quieter and smoother than modern vessels.
● Have portholes that sometimes actually open.
● Have interiors that are built from more traditional materials such as wood and brass, with less use of synthetic fibers (less likely to affect anyone who is allergic to synthetics).
● Have deep drafts that help them to achieve a smooth ride in the open seas.

Pre-1980 Ships: Disadvantages

● They are not so fuel-efficient and, therefore, are more expensive to operate than the new ships.
● Need a larger crew, because of the more awkward, labor-intensive layouts of the ships.
● Have a deep draft (necessary for a smooth ride) but need tugs to negotiate ports and tight berths.
● Have tougher job complying with the current inter-national fire, safety, and environmental regulations.
● Are usually fitted with older-type open lifeboats.
● If 10 years or older, plumbing and air-conditioning problems in cabins and public areas are commoner.

The Crew

You can estimate the standard of service by looking at the crew-to-passenger ratio (provided in the ship pro-files in this book). The best service levels are aboard ships that have a ratio of one crew member to every two passengers, or higher. The best ships in the world, from the point of view of crew living and working con-

Modern ships have extensive spa facilities

ditions, also tend to be the most expensive ones (the adage "you get what you pay for" tends to be true).

Most ships now have multinational crews, with one or two exceptions. The crew mixture gives the impression of a ship being like a miniature United Nations. If the crew is happy, the ship will be happy, too, and passengers will sense it.

Corporate Cruising

Corporate, incentive organizations and seagoing conferences provide a growing market for cruise companies. Ships of all sizes, types and styles can provide an exciting venue for between 50 and 3,000 participants. Corporate organizers realize the benefits when they don't have to deal with such things as accommodation, food or entertainment for their delegates or participants, as these items are already in place.

Cruise companies have specialized departments and personnel to deal with all the details. Corporate organizers don't even have to think about car rentals either. Many larger ships have almost identical cabin sizes and configurations, a bonus for incentive houses.

Once you have signed the contract and paid the deposit for a charter, there is no refund (thus insurance is essential). Although you may need only 70% of the capacity of a ship, you will have to pay for the whole ship if you want an *exclusive* charter.

If you want to charter a whole ship (popular among corporations and association), where you have complete control over the utilization of public areas, do the following:

● Decide which part of the world you want to be in.
● Decide how long you want to cruise for.
● Estimate how many will be in your group.
● Make arrangements as early as possible (at least

one year ahead, preferably more).
● Although you can contact the cruise line direct, I would recommend contacting the Miami-based cruise charter specialist organizer Landry & Kling, which has many years' experience in this field.

Maiden/Inaugural Voyages

There is an element of excitement in taking the maiden voyage of a new cruise ship, or in joining the inaugural voyage of a recently refurbished, reconstructed, or stretched vessel.

If you have a degree of tolerance and you are not bothered by some inconvenience, slow or nonexistent service in the dining room, fine; otherwise, wait until the ship has been in service for at least three months. Then again, if you book a cruise on the third or fourth voyage, and the ship's introduction is delayed, you could find yourself on the maiden voyage.

One thing is certain — any maiden voyage is a collector's item, but Murphy's Law prevails: "If anything can go wrong, it will." For example:

● A strike, a fire, or a shipyard bankruptcy, are some of the possible causes of delay to a new ship.
● Service aboard new or recently refurbished ships (or a new cruise line) is likely to be uncertain at best and could be a complete disaster. An existing cruise line may use experienced crew from its other vessels to help "bring out" a new ship, but they may be unfamiliar with the ship's layout and may have problems training other staff.
● Plumbing and electrical items tend to cause the most problems, particularly aboard reconstructed and refurbished vessels. Examples: toilets that don't flush or don't stop flushing; faucets incorrectly marked, where "hot" really means "cold"; room thermostats mistakenly fitted with reverse wiring; televisions, audio channels, lights, and electronic card key locks

that don't work; electrical outlets wrongly indicated; and "automatic" telephones that refuse to function.
● The galley (kitchen) of a new ship causes perhaps the most consternation. Even if everything works and the executive chef has ordered the right supplies, they could be anywhere other than where they should be. Imagine if they forgot to load the seasoning, or if the eggs arrived shell-shocked.
● Items such as menus, postcards, writing paper, or TV remote control units, door keys, towels, pillow-cases, glassware, and even toilet paper may be lost in the bowels of the ship, or simply not ordered.
● In the entertainment department, items such as spare spotlight bulbs may not be in stock. Or there may be no hooks in the dressing rooms to hang cos-tumes on (many older ships do not even have dress-ing rooms). Or what if the pianos arrived damaged, or "flip" charts for the lecturers didn't show up? Manu-als for high-tech sound and lighting equipment may be in a foreign language.

Theme Cruises

Each year, an ever richer variety of theme cruises is available, with many cultural, ecological, and educa-tional subjects. Typical topics include: Adventure, Antiques, Archaeological, Art Lovers, Astronomy, Backgammon, Ballroom and Latin Dancing, Big Band, Bridge, Chess Tournament, Classical Music, Computer Science, Diet and Nutrition, Educational, Exploration, Fashion, Film Festival, Food and Wine, Gardening, Holistic Health, Gay/Lesbian, Jazz Festi-val, Movie Buffs, Murder Mystery, Naturalist/Nude, Octoberfest, Ornithology, Photography, Scottish Dancing, Sequence Dancing, Singles, Steamboat Race, Superbowl, Theatrical, and Wine Tasting.

Signs You've Chosen the Wrong Ship

● When, just after you've embarked, a waiter hands you a drink in a tall plastic glass from a tray of drinks of identical color and froth, then gives you a bill to sign without even saying "Welcome Aboard."
● When your "luxury" cabin has walls so thin you can hear your neighbors combing their hair.
● When the brochure's "full bathtub" turns out to be "a large sink" located at floor level.
● When you wanted a quiet, restful cruise, but your travel agent booked you aboard a ship with 300 base-ball fans and provided them all with signed baseball bats and boom boxes for their use on deck (solution: read this book thoroughly first).
● When you packed your tuxedo, but other passen-gers take "formal" attire to mean clean cut-off jeans and a less stained T-shirt.
● When the "medical facility" is located in the purser's office and consists of a box of adhesive ban-dages with instructions in a foreign language.
● When the gymnasium equipment is kept in the restaurant manager's office.

● When you have a cabin with an "obstructed view" (usually there is a lifeboat hanging outside it), and it is next to or below the disco. Or the laundry. Or the garbage disposal facility. Or the anchor.
● When "fresh selected greens" means a sprig of parsley on the entrée plate, at every lunch and dinner seating (boring even on a three-day cruise).
● When the cruise director tries to sell passengers a watch, or an artwork, over the public address system.
● When front-row seats at a rock concert would be quieter than a poolside deck chair at midday.
● When you hear the same pop song 10 times during the first day.
● When you have to buy shin pads to prevent injury from the 600 children chasing through passageways.
● When the cruise brochure shows your cabin with flowers and champagne, but you get neither.
● When the bottled water on your dining room table incurs a bill as soon as you open the bottle.
● When the brochure says "Butler Service," but you have to clean your own shoes, get your own ice, and still tip twice the amount you would for an "ordi-nary" cabin steward.
● When the Beer Drinking or Hog Calling Contest, Knobby Knees Contest, and Pajama Bingo are listed as "enrichment lectures."
● When the "fresh-squeezed orange juice" you just ordered means fresh-squeezed, but last week, or the week before that, on land, and then poured into indus-trial-size containers, before transfer to your poly-styrene plastic cup on deck.
● When the brochure says tipping is not required, but your waiter and cabin steward insist otherwise.
● When the cruise director thoughtfully telephones you at 2.30am to tell you that the bingo jackpot is up to $1,000 and that an art auction is about to start.
● When, on the final day, the words "early break-fast" means 5am, and "vacate your cabin by 7.30am" means you must spend about three hours sitting in the show lounge waiting for disembarkation, with 500 available seats, your hand luggage, and 2,000 other passengers, probably playing bingo.
● When on deck, you notice a large hole in the bot-tom of one or more of the ship's lifeboats.
● When the cabin steward tries to sell you a cut-price time-share in his uncle's coal mine.
● When the proclaimed "five-course gourmet meal" in the dining room turns out to be four courses of salty chicken soup and a potato.
● When the "Deck Buffet" means that there are no tables and chairs, only the deck, to eat off.
● When the brochure shows photos of smiling young couples, but you and your spouse/partner are the only passengers under 80.
● When the library is located in the engine room.
● When the captain tells you he is really a concert pianist and his professiional diploma is really for the piano, not navigation. ❑

CHOOSING THE RIGHT CABIN

Does cabin size count? Are suites sweeter than cabins?

Is a balcony desirable? What about location?

Ideally, you should feel at home when at sea, so it is important to choose the right accommodation. Like houses ashore, all cabins have good and not-so-good points. Choose wisely, for if you find your cabin (incorrectly called a "stateroom" by some companies) is too small when you get to the ship, it may be impossible to change it or to upgrade, as the ship could very well be completely full.

Cruise lines designate cabins only when deposits have been received (they may, however, guarantee the grade and rate requested). If this is not done automatically, or if you find a disclaimer such as "All cabin assignments are confirmed upon embarkation of the vessel", get a guarantee in writing that your cabin will *not* be changed on embarkation.

There are three main types of accommodation, but many variations on each theme:

● **Suites**: (the largest living spaces, typically with a private balcony); and "junior" suites (with or without private balcony).

● **Outside-view cabins**: a large picture window or one or more portholes (with or without private balcony).

● **Interior (no-view) cabins**: so called because there is no window or porthole.

Private Balconies

Once you've had one, you won't be able to do without one on your next cruise. A private balcony (or "veranda," or "terrace") is just that. It is a balcony (or mini-terrace) adjoining your cabin where you can sit, enjoy the view, dine, or even have a massage. There's something very civilized (if slightly antisocial) about sitting on one's balcony sipping champagne, or having breakfast "à la deck" in some exotic place. It is also pleasant to get fresh air and to escape cold (air-conditioned) cabins. The value of a private balcony, for which you pay a premium, comes into its own in warm weather areas. Balconies are like cruises: they're addictive. Indeed, some ships have enough private balconies for more than 900 budding Juliets to be wooed by their Romeos.

Some private balconies are not so private, however. Balconies not separated by full floor-to-ceiling partitions (examples: *Carnival Destiny, Carnival Triumph, Carnival Victory, Maasdam, Norway, Oriana, Queen Mary 2, Ryndam, Seven Seas Mariner, Seven Seas Voyager, Statendam*, and *Veendam*) don't quite cut it. You could get noise or smoke from your neighbor. Some ships have balconies with full floor-to-ceiling privacy partitions *and* an outside light (examples: *Century, Galaxy, Mercury,* and *Radisson Diamond*). Some par-

Zodiac Suite bedroom aboard *Norwegian Spirit.*

titions in *Century, Galaxy,* and *Mercury* are of the full type, while some are of the partial type. Another downside of private balconies is that you can't escape the loud music being played on the open swimming pool deck atop the ship – annoying when "island night" goes on until the early morning hours. Note that many of the large resort ships have balconies too small to accommodate even two reclining chairs.

Some suites with forward-facing private balconies may not be so good, as the wind speed can make them all but unusable. And when the ship drops anchor in ports of call, the noise pollution can be deafening (examples, *Silver Cloud, Silver Wind*).

All private balconies (except French balconies – *see below*) have railings to lean on, but the balconies in some ships have solid steel plates between railing and deck, so you cannot look out to sea when seated (examples: *Costa Classica, Costa Romantica, Dawn Princess, Sea Princess,* and *Sun Princess*). Better are those ships with balconies that have clear glass (examples: *Aurora, Brilliance of the Seas, Century, Galaxy, Mercury, Empress of the Seas, Radiance of the Seas,* and *Serenade of the Seas*) or horizontal bars.

Don't be fooled by brochure-speak. A French bal-

Typical Cabin Layouts

The following rates are typical of those you can expect to pay for ❶ a seven-day and ❷ a 10-day Caribbean cruise aboard a modern cruise ship. The rates are per person and include free roundtrip airfare or low-cost air add-ons from principal North American gateways

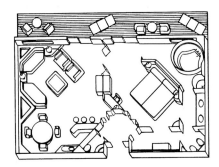

Luxury outside suite with private verandahh, separate lounge area, vanity area, extra-large double or queen-sized bed, bathroom with tub, shower, and extensive closet and storage space.

❶ **$2,250** ❷ **$4,000**

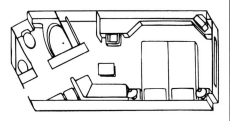

Large outside double with bed and convertible daytime sofabed, bathroom with shower, and good closet space.

❶ **$1,750** ❷ **$2,450**

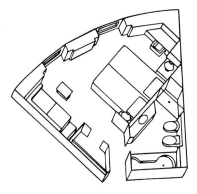

Deluxe outside cabin with lounge area, double or twin beds, bathroom with tub, shower, and ample closet and storage space.

❶ **$2,250** ❷ **$2,850**

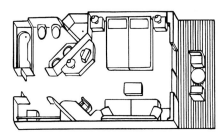

Standard outside double with twin beds (plus a possible upper third/fourth berth), small sitting area, bathroom with shower, and reasonable closet space.

❶ **$1,450** ❷ **$1,975**

■ Note that in some ships, third- and fourth-person berths are available for families or friends wishing to share. The upper Pullman berths, not shown on these cabin layouts, are recessed into the wall above the lower beds.

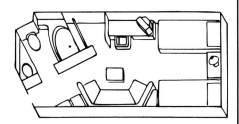

Inside double with two lower beds that may convert into daytime sofabeds (plus a possible upper third/fourth berth), bathroom with shower, and fair closet space.

❶ **$1,250** ❷ **1,750**

cony is one where the doors open to fresh air, but there's no balcony for you to step onto unless your feet are less than six inches long.

How Much?

The amount you pay for accommodation is directly related to the size of the cabin, its location, and the facilities and services provided.
● Each line implements its own system according to ship size, age, construction, and profit potential.
● Many cruise lines still do not give accurate cabin sizes in their brochures, but you will find the size range in the ship profiles in this book.
● If this is your first cruise, choose the most expensive cabin you can afford.
● It may be better to book a low-grade cabin on a good ship than a high-grade cabin on a poor ship.
● If you are in a party of three or more and do not mind sharing a cabin, you will achieve a substantial saving per person, so you may be able to book a higher-grade cabin without paying extra.

Cabin Sizes

Cabins provide more or less the same facilities as hotel rooms, except space. Viewed by most owners as little more than a convenient place for passengers to sleep, shower, and change, cabin space is often compromised in favor of large public rooms. In some smaller interior (no-view) and outside cabins, changing clothes is a major challenge.

The latest ships have more standardized cabin sizes, because they are made in modular form (I consider 170 sq. ft/15.7sq. meters to be the *minimum* acceptable size for a "standard" cruise ship cabin today). They all have integrated bathrooms (mostly made from noncombustible phenolic-glass-reinforced plastics) fitted during the ships' construction.

Older (pre-1980) ships had more spacious cabins (there were more days at sea, fewer ports of call, and fewer entertainment rooms). This encouraged many to spend a great deal of time in their cabins, often entertaining other passengers. Ask your travel agent for the dimensions of the cabin you have selected.

Cabin Location

● An "outside-view" cabin is recommended for first-time passengers: an "interior (no-view)" cabin has no portholes or windows, making it more difficult to orient you or to gauge the weather or time.
● Cabins in the center of a ship are more stable and tend to be noise and vibration-free. Ships powered by diesel engines (i.e. most modern vessels) create and transmit some vibration, especially at the stern.
● Take into account personal habits when choosing the cabin location. If you like to go to bed early, avoid a cabin close to the disco. If you have trouble walking, choose a cabin close to the elevator.
● Generally, the higher the deck, the higher the cabin

price, and the better the service. This is an inheritance from transoceanic times, when upper-deck cabins and suites were sunnier and warmer.
● Cabins at the front of a ship are slightly crescent-shaped, given that the outer wall follows the curvature of the ship's hull. But they can be exposed to early-morning noises, such as the anchor being dropped at ports where the ship is too big to dock.
● Cabins with interconnecting doors are fine for families or close friends, but the dividing wall is usually so thin you can hear the conversation next door.
● Many brochures indicate cabins with "obstructed-views." Cabins on lower decks are closer to engine noise and heat, especially at the aft of the vessel and around the engine casing. In many older ships, elevators may not operate to the lowermost decks.

Facilities

Cabins provide some, or all, of the following:
● Private bathroom (generally small and compact) fitted with shower, washbasin, and toilet. Higher-grade cabins and suites may have full-size bathtubs. Some even have a whirlpool bath and/or bidet, a hairdryer, and more space.
● Electrical outlets for personal appliances, usually 110 and/or 220 volts.
● Multi-channel radio, TV (regular satellite channels or closed circuit), and VCR or DVD player.
● Two beds or a lower and upper berth (possibly, another one or two upper berths) or a double-, queen- or king-size bed. In some ships, twin beds can be pushed together to form a double.

DID YOU KNOW?

● that the first "en suite" rooms (with private bathroom in cabin) were on board Cunard Line's *Campania* of 1893?
● that the first single-berth cabins built as such were also aboard the *Campania*?
● that the first liner to offer private terraces with their first-class suites was *Normandie* in 1935 (the Trouville Suite had four bedrooms as well as a private terrace)?
● that the first ships to feature private balconies were the *Saturnia* and *Vulcania* in the early 1900s?
● that the first ship to be fitted with interior plumbing was the 6,283-ton *Normandie* of 1883?
● that the first ship to be fitted with an internal electric lighting system was aboard the Inman liner *City of Berlin* in 1879?
● that cruising today is not the same as it was in the 19th century? On the first cruise ships there was little entertainment, and passengers had to clean their own cabins. Orders enforced on all ships sailing from Great Britain in 1849, for example, instructed all passengers to be in their beds by 10pm.
● that Carnival Cruise Lines places more than 10 million chocolates on passenger pillows each year?

A luxury cabin aboard *SeaDream I.*

● Telephone, for inter-cabin or ship-to-shore communication.
● Depending on cabin size, a chair, or chair and table, or sofa and table, or even a separate lounge/ sitting area (higher accommodation grades).
● Refrigerator and bar (higher grades).
● Vanity/desk unit with chair or stool.
● Personal safe.
● Closet space, some drawer space, plus storage room under beds for suitcases.
● Bedside night stand/table unit.
● Towels, soap, shampoo, and conditioner. (Many ships, particularly the "upscale" ones, provide a greater selection of items.)

Many first-time passengers are surprised to find their cabin has twin beds. Double beds are a comparative rarity except in the higher-priced suites. Aboard some ships you will find upper and lower berths. A "berth" is a nautical term for a bed held in a wooden or metal frame. A "Pullman berth" tucks away out of sight during the day, usually into the bulkhead or ceiling. You climb up a short ladder at night to get into an upper berth.

The Suite Life

Suites are the most luxurious and spacious of all shipboard accommodation, and typically come with butler service. A suite (literally a "suite of rooms") is a place where you could almost get lost in. It should measure a *minimum* 400 sq.ft. (37 sq. meters), and comprise a lounge or sitting room separated from a bedroom by a solid door (not just a curtain); a bedroom with a large bed; one or more bathrooms, and an abundance of closet, drawer, and other storage space. Many cruise lines inaccurately describe some accommodation as suites, when they are nothing more than a large cabin with a curtain that divides sitting and sleeping areas.

Suites are best on long voyages with several days at sea. Be aware that in the large resort ships (those carrying more than 1,200 passengers), there may be a whole deck or two devoted to penthouses and suites, but you will have to share the rest of the ship with those in lower-priced accommodation. That means there is no preferential seating in the showroom, the dining rooms, or on sunbathing decks. You may, however, get separate check-in facilities and preferential treatment upon disembarkation, but your luggage will be lumped together with everyone else's.   ❑

The 10 Largest Suites Afloat

Ship	Cruise Line	Total (sq. ft)	Total (sq. m)
Norwegian Dawn *	Norwegian Cruise Line	5,350.0	497.0
Norwegian Star *	Norwegian Cruise Line	5,350.0	497.0
Constellation	Celebrity Cruises	2,530.0	235.0
Infinity	Celebrity Cruises	2,530.0	235.0
Millennium	Celebrity Cruises	2,530.0	235.0
Summit	Celebrity Cruises	2,530.0	235.0
Seven Seas Mariner	Seven Seas Cruises	1,580.0	146.7
Century	Celebrity Cruises	1,535.0	142.5
Galaxy	Celebrity Cruises	1,535.0	142.5
Mercury	Celebrity Cruises	1,535.0	142.5

Note: The spaces shown include balconies.   * = including a large garden.
(This list does not include the suites aboard ships such as The World, which is for residents and not normal cruise passengers)

Ocean-going Ships to Debut: 2005–2007

Notes

This chart shows ships under firm contract. It is given in alphabetical order according to cruise line.

Delivery/debut dates may be subject to change. tba = to be announced

CRUISE LINE	NAME OF SHIP	TONS	COST	LENGTH (feet)	LENGTH (meters)	PASSENGERS (lower bed capacity)	BUILDER	MONTH
2005 (5 Ships)								
American Cruise Lines	American Spirit	99	n/a	220	67	97	Chesapeake Shipyard (USA)	July
Carnival Cruise Lines	Carnival Liberty	110,000	$460 million	951.4	290	2,974	Fincantieri (Italy)	July
P&O Cruises	Arcadia	85,700	$400 million	957	291.7	1,968	Fincantieri (Italy)	April
NCL America	Pride of America	81,000	$350 million	921.9	281	2,100	Lloyd Werft (Germany)	July
Norwegian Cruise Line	Norwegian Jewel	93,000	$390 million	967.8	295	2,376	Meyer Werft (Germany)	August
2006 (6 Ships)								
Costa Cruises	tba	112,000	€450 million	951.4	290	3,004	Fincantieri (Italy)	June
Holland America Line	Noordam	85,700	$400 million	957	291.7	1,800	Fincantieri (Italy)	January
MSC Italian Cruises	tba	90,000	$360 million	964.5	294	2,568	Fincantieri (Italy)	June
NCL America	Pride of Hawaii	93,000	$390 million	967.8	295	2,376	Meyer Werft (Germany)	August
Princess Cruises	tba	116,000	$500 million	951.4	290	3,110	Fincantieri (Italy)	May
Royal Caribbean International	tba	160,000	$720 million	1115.4	340	3,600	Kvaerner Masa-Yards (Finland)	May
2007 (2 Ships)								
Cunard Line	Queen Victoria	85,000	€390 million	957	291.7	1,968	Fincantieri (Italy)	January
MSC Italian Cruises	tba	90,000	$360 million	964.5	294	2,568	Fincantieri (Italy)	Spring

THIS YEAR'S WORLD BEATERS

Having reviewed 256 cruise ships, Berlitz names the best performers for 2005

and explains why they scored as highly as they did

BERLITZ FIVE-STARS-PLUS CLUB (★★★★★+)

For this 2005 edition, only one ship has achieved the score required for it to be awarded membership in this most exclusive club.

Europa   (Hapag Lloyd Cruises)   1,858 points   ★★★★★+

Why? Because there is outstanding cuisine and attentive, friendly, very attentive, yet unobtrusive personal service from a staff dedicated to working aboard the world's finest cruise ship. But it's not just the ship itself and its facilities and appointments that contribute to the ship's high rating – it's also in the extensive array of details and personal attention from a fine, dedicated crew. It all adds up to the very best and most luxurious cruise ship and cruise experience available today – unless you have your own private motor yacht. Additionally, thanks to the pod propulsion system, there is absolutely no vibration anywhere.

BERLITZ FIVE-STARS CLUB (★★★★★)

For this 2005 edition, only 19 ships have achieved the score required for them to be awarded membership in the prestigious Berlitz Five-Stars Club.

	points
SeaDream I	1,790
SeaDream II	1,790
Seabourn Legend	1,786
Seabourn Pride	1,785
Seabourn Spirit	1,785
Queen Mary 2 (Grill Class)	1,764
Silver Shadow	1,757
Silver Whisper	1,757
Hanseatic	1,740
Silver Cloud	1,717
Silver Wind	1,717
Sea Cloud II	1,709
Hebridean Spirit	1,707
Sea Cloud	1,704
Crystal Serenity	1,702
Crystal Symphony	1,701
Hebridean Princess	1,701
Seven Seas Mariner	1,701
Seven Seas Voyager	1,701

This year's runners-up: *SeaDream I* (above) and *SeaDream II*.

Almost all the ships feature one seating or open-seating dining, extremely comfortable accommodation, the very best in terms of seagoing cuisine, and highly personal service. There may be ships that have larger penthouse suites, balconies, showlounges, health spas and other appointments, but aboard the ships in the *Berlitz Five-Stars Club*, what counts is the cuisine and service, and the attention to detail. At a time when many cruise lines are making economies, these criteria are more important than ever.

LEFT: 2005's winning ship, *Europa*, operated by Hapag Lloyd Cruises, explores the Caribbean.

HOW WE EVALUATE THE SHIPS

The facilities count, of course, but just as important are the standards of food, service, staff and hospitality

I have been evaluating and rating cruise ships and the onboard product professionally since 1980. In addition, I am provided with regular reports from a small team of trained professional passengers. The ratings are conducted with *total objectivity*, from a set of predetermined criteria and a modus operandi designed to work *globally*, not just regionally, across the entire spectrum of ocean-going cruise ships today, in all segments of the marketplace.

As I have stressed earlier in this book, there really is no "best cruise line in the world" or "best cruise ship" – only the ship and cruise that is *right for you*. Therefore, different criteria are applied to ships of different sizes, styles, and market segments throughout the world. Since so many new ships are of similar dimensions, but with different decor, more emphasis is placed on the standard of the dining experience, and the service and hospitality aspects of the cruise.

This section includes 256 oceangoing cruise ships in service (or due to enter service) and chosen by the author for inclusion when this book was completed. Almost all except the newest ships have been carefully evaluated, taking into account more than 400 separate inspection points based on personal cruises, visits and revisits to ships, as well as observations and comments from my reporting team. These are channeled into 20 major areas, each with a possible 100 points. The maximum possible score for any ship is therefore 2,000 points.

For the sake of clarity and at-a-glance user-friendliness, these are provided in the five main sections (Ship, Accommodation, Food, Service, Cruise Operation).

Cruise lines, ship owners, and operators should note that ratings, like stocks and shares, can go *down* as well as *up* each year, due to increased competition, the introduction of newer ships with more custom-designed facilities, and other market- or passenger-driven factors.

The ratings more reflect the *standards* of the cruise product delivered to passengers (the software), and less the physical plant (the hardware). Thus, although a ship may be the latest, most stunning vessel in the world in terms of design and decor, if the food, service, staff, and hospitality are not so good, the scores and ratings will reflect these aspects more clearly.

The stars beside the name of the ship at the top of each page relate directly to the Overall Rating. The highest number of stars awarded is **five stars** (★★★★★), and the lowest is one star. This system is universally recognized throughout the hospitality industry. A plus (+) indicates that a ship deserves just that little bit more than the number of stars attained. However, I must emphasize that it is the number of points achieved rather than the number of stars attained that perhaps is more meaningful to anyone comparing ships.

WHAT MAKES A FIVE-STAR SHIP

During the past 20 years of the life of this book, passengers' lifestyles and personal tastes have changed. It would now be difficult to build and market almost any cruise ship (except for niche-market expedition ships or tall ships) without balcony cabins, for example. Passengers now expect, and want different things. As life ashore has become ever faster, passengers seek refuge at sea, and want to be able to relax on their vacation, without the constraints of rigid structures, such as choosing one of two seatings for dinner (or shows), features typically experienced aboard most large cruise ships today. Dining choices are now at the forefront of those changing tastes. Multiple dining venues with open seating or single/one seating dining are now expected.

After many discussions between cruise industry executives and myself, and much thought about the change in affluence and taste of passengers, for the first time the scores and ratings now reflect these changing tastes, and the requirements of a more youthful cruise industry. Complaints from passengers aboard the large cruise ships are at an all time high, particularly with regard to standing in line for security checks in ports of call (standing outside when it's raining in Alaska is not pleasant, for example). Although the cruise lines do their very best to minimize such lines, sometimes they are at the mercy of local regulations, customs and immigration officials and other authoritarian units.

The perception of luxury is not about brand names, but exclusivity. Likewise, plastic deck furniture, packets of jams, conserves and condiments, and paper towels in public restrooms aboard an "upscale" ship help ruin the perception of luxury. It's all in the details, you see.

Sea Dream I and *Sea Dream II* nestling in Nice, France.

The Star System

★★★★★+	1,851–2,000 points
★★★★★	1,701–1850 points
★★★★+	1,551–1,700 points
★★★★	1,401–1,550 points
★★★+	1,251–1,400 points
★★★	1,101–1,250 points
★★+	951–1,100 points
★★	801–950 points
★+	650–800 points
★	601–650 points

What The Ratings Mean

1,851–2,000 points ★★★★★ +

You can expect an outstanding luxury cruise experience – in fact, it doesn't get any better than this. It should be truly memorable, and with the highest attention to detail, finesse, and highly personal service (how important you are made to feel is critical). The decor must be elegant and tasteful, measured by restraint and not flashiness, with fresh flowers and other decorative touches in abundance, and the layout of the public rooms might well be in accordance with the principles of *feng shui*.

Any ship with this rating must be just about unsurpassable in the cruise industry, and it has to be very, very special, with service and hospitality levels to match. There must be the very highest quality surroundings, comfort and service levels, the finest and freshest quality foods, including all breads and rolls baked on board. Highly creative menus, regional cuisine, and dining alternatives should provide maximum choice and variety, and special orders will be part of the dining ritual.

Dining room meals (particularly dinners) are expected to be grand, memorable affairs, correctly served on the finest china, with a choice of wines of suitable character and vintage available, and served in the correct-sized sommelier glasses of the highest quality (Reidel or Schott).

The service staff will take pleasure in providing you with the ultimate personal, yet unobtrusive, attention with the utmost of finesse, and the word "no" should definitely not be in their vocabulary. This really is the very best of the best in terms of refined, unstructured living at sea, but it may cause serious damage to your bank statement.

1,701–1,850 points ★★★★★

You can expect a truly excellent and memorable cruise experience, with the finesse and attention to detail commensurate with the amount of money paid. The service and hospitality levels will be extremely high from all levels of officers and staff, with strong emphasis on fine hospitality training (all service personnel members *must* make you feel important).

The food will be commensurate with the high level expected from what is virtually the best possible, while the service should be very attentive yet unobtrusive. The cuisine should be memorable, with ample taste. Special orders should never be a problem, with a creative cuisine of a very high standard. There must be a varied selection of wines, which should be served in glasses of the correct size (not simply a standard size glass for white and one for red wines).

Entertainment is expected to be of prime quality and variety. Again, the word "no" should not be in the vocabulary of any member of staff aboard a ship with this rating. A cruise aboard a ship with this high rating may well cause damage to your bank statement, particularly if you choose the most spacious grades of accommodation. Few things will cost extra once you are on board, and brochures should be more "truthful" than those for ships with a lower rating.

1,551–1,700 points ★★★★ +

You should expect to have a high-quality cruise experience that will be quite memorable, and just a little short of being excellent in all aspects. Perhaps the personal service and attention to detail could be slightly better, but, nonetheless, this should prove to be a fine all-round cruise experience, in a setting that is extremely clean and comfortable, with few lines anywhere, a caring attitude from service personnel, and a good standard of entertainment that appeals to a mainstream market. The cuisine and service will be well rounded, with mostly fresh ingredients and varied menus that should appeal to almost anyone, served on high quality china.

All in all, this should prove to be an extremely well rounded cruise experience, probably in a ship that is new or almost new. There will probably be less "extra cost" items than ships with a slightly lower rating, but you get what you pay for these days.

1,401–1,550 points ★★★★

You should expect to have a very good quality all-round cruise experience, most probably aboard a modern, highly comfortable ship that will provide a good range of facilities and services. The food and service will be quite decent overall, although decidedly not as "gourmet" and fanciful as the brochures with the always-smiling faces might have you believe.

The service on board will be well organized, although it will perhaps be a little robotic and impersonal at times, and only as good as the cruise line's training program allows. You may notice a lot of things cost extra once you are on board, although the typically vague brochure tells you that the things are "available" or are an "option." However, you should have a good time, and your bank account will be only moderately damaged.

1,251–1,400 points ★★★ +

You should expect to have a decent quality cruise experience, from a ship where the service levels should be good, but perhaps without the finesse that could be expected from a more upscale environment. The crew aboard any ship achieving this score should reflect a positive attitude with regard to hospitality, and a willingness to accommodate your needs, up to a point. Staff training will probably be in need of more attention to detail and flexibility.

Food and service levels in the dining room(s) should be reasonably good, although special orders or anything out of the ordinary might prove more difficult. There will probably be a number of extra-cost items you thought were included in the price of your cruise – although the brochure typically is vague and tells you that the things are "available" or are an "option."

1,101–1,250 points ★★★

You can expect a reasonably decent, middle-of-the-road cruise experience, with a moderate amount of space and quality in furnishings, fixtures, and fittings. The cabins are likely to be a little on the small side (dimensionally challenged). The food and service levels will be quite acceptable, although not at all memorable, and somewhat inflexible with regard to special orders, as almost everything is standardized.

Crew attitude could certainly be improved, the level of hospitality and cleanliness will be moderate but little more, and entertainment will probably be weak. A good option, however, for those looking for the reasonable comforts of home without pretentious attitudes, and little damage to their bank statement.

951–1,100 points ★★

You should expect to have a cruise experience that will be below the average in terms of accommodation (typically with cabins that are dimensionally challenged), quality of the ship's facilities, food, wine list, service, and hospitality levels, in surroundings that are completely unpretentious. In particular, the food and its service will probably prove to be most disappointing and rather typical of roadside café standards.

There will be little flexibility in the levels of service, hospitality and staff training, which will be no better than poor. Thus, the overall experience will be commensurate with the small amount of money you paid for the cruise.

801–950 points ★★

You should expect to have a cruise experience of modest quality aboard a ship that is probably in need of more attention to maintenance and service levels, not to mention hospitality. The food is likely to be quite tasteless and homogenized, and of low quality, and service will leave much to be desired in terms of attitude, which will tend to be mediocre at best. Staff training is likely to be minimal, and turnover will probably be high. The "end-of-pier" entertainment could well leave you wanting to read a good book.

651–800 points ★ +

You can expect to have only the most basic cruise experience, with little or no attention to detail, from a poorly trained staff that is probably paid low wages and to whom you are just another body. The ship will, in many cases, probably be in need of much maintenance and upgrading, and will probably have few facilities.

Cleanliness and hygiene may well be questionable, and there will be absolutely no finesse in personal service levels, with poor attitude from the crew, and dismal entertainment as significant factors in the low score and rating. On the other hand, the price of a cruise is probably alluringly low.

A relatively spacious balcony aboard *Costa Atlantica*.

601–650 points ★

You can expect to have a cruise experience that is the absolute bottom of the barrel, with almost nothing in terms of hospitality or finesse. You can forget about attention to detail – there won't be any. This will be the kind of experience that would equal a stay in the most basic motel, with few facilities, a poorly trained, uncaring staff, most of whom will have undergone a hospitality bypass, and a ship that is in need of better maintenance and upgrading.

The low cost of a cruise aboard any cruise ship with this rating should provide a clue to the complete lack of any quality. This will be particularly true in the areas of food, service, and entertainment. In other words, this could well be a totally forgettable cruise experience.

Distribution of points

These are the percentage of the total points available which are allocated to each of the main areas evaluated:

- The Ship — 25%
- Accommodation — 15%
- Cuisine — 15%
- Service — 20%
- Entertainment — 7.5%
- The Cruise Experience — 17.5%

The Ship

Hardware/Maintenance/Safety

This score reflects the general profile and condition of the ship as hardware, its age and maintenance, hull condition, exterior paint, decking and caulking, swimming pool and surrounds, deck furniture, shore tenders, lifeboats, life rafts, and other safety items. It also reflects interior cleanliness (public restrooms, elevators, floor coverings, wall coverings, stairways, passageways, and doorways), food preparation areas, refrigerators, garbage handling, compacting, and incineration, and waste disposal facilities.

Outdoor Facilities/Space

This score reflects the overall space per passenger on open decks, crowding, swimming pools/ whirlpools and their surrounds, lido deck areas, number and type of deck lounge chairs (with or without cushioned pads) and other deck furniture, outdoor sports facilities, shower enclosures and changing facilities, towels, and quiet areas (those without music).

Interior Facilities/Space/Flow

This score reflects the use of common interior public spaces, including enclosed promenades; passenger flow and points of congestion; ceiling height; lobby areas, stairways, and all passenger hallways; elevators; public restrooms and facilities; signage, lighting, air-conditioning and ventilation; and degree of comfort and density.

Decor/Furnishings/Artwork

This score reflects the overall interior decor and color scheme; hard and soft furnishings, wood (real, imitation, or veneer) paneling, carpeting (tuft density, color, and practicality), fit and finish (seams and edging), chairs (comfort, height, and support), ceilings and decor treatments, reflective surfaces, artwork (paintings, sculptures, and atrium centerpieces), and lighting.

Spa/Fitness Facilities

This score reflects any health spa, wellness center, and fitness facilities; location and accessibility; lighting and flooring materials; fitness and muscle-training machines and other equipment; fitness programs; sports and games facilities; indoor swimming pools; whirlpools; grand baths; aqua-spa pools; saunas and steam rooms; rasul, the various types of massage (Swedish Remedial, Shiatsu, Ayurvedic, Reflexology), and other treatment rooms; changing facilities; jogging and walking tracks; and promenades.

Accommodation

Cabins: Suites and Deluxe Grades

This score reflects the design and layout of all grades of suites and deluxe grade cabins, private balconies (whether full floor-to-ceiling partition or part partitions, balcony lighting, balcony furniture). Also beds/berths, furniture (its placement and practicality), and other fittings; closets and other hanging space, drawer space, and bedside tables; vanity unit, bathroom facilities, washbasin, cabinets, and toiletries storage; lighting, air-conditioning, and ventilation; audiovisual facilities; quality and degree of luxury; artwork; bulkhead insulation, noise, and vibration levels. Suites should not be so designated unless the sleeping room is completely separate from the living area.

Note that some large cruise ships now have whole decks devoted to superior grade accommodation, with a significant difference between this accommodation and that of "standard" cabins.

Also the soft furnishings and details such as the information manual (list of services); paper and postcards (including personalized stationery); telephone directory; laundry lists; tea- and coffee-making equipment; flowers (if any); fruit (if any); bathroom personal amenities kits, bathrobes, slippers, and the size, thickness, quality, and material content of towels.

Cabins: Standard Sizes

This score reflects the design and layout (whether outside or inside), beds/berths, furniture (its placement and practicality), and other fittings. Also taken into account: closets and other hanging space, drawer space, bedside tables, and vanity unit; bathroom facilities, washbasin, cabinets, and toiletries storage; lighting, air-conditioning and ventilation; audiovisual facilities; quality and degree of fittings and furnishings; artwork; bulkhead insulation, noise, and vibration levels.

In addition, we have taken into account the usefulness of the information manual (directory of services); paper and postcards (including stationery); telephone directory; laundry lists; tea- and coffee-making equipment; flowers (if any); fruit (if any); and bathroom amenities kits, bathrobes, slippers, and the size, thickness, quality, and material content of towels.

Cuisine

This section forms 15 percent of the whole rating system and is very important, as food is often the main feature of today's cruises. Cruise lines put maximum emphasis on promising passengers how good their food will be, often to the point of being unable to deliver what is promised. Generally, the standard of food is good. The rule of thumb is: if you were to eat out in a good restaurant, what would you expect? Does the ship meet your expectations? Would you come back again for the food?

There are perhaps as many different tastes as there are passengers. The "standard" market cruise lines cater to a wide range of tastes, while the more exclusive cruise lines can offer better quality food, cooked individually to your taste. As in any good restaurant, you get what you pay for.

Dining Room/Cuisine

This score reflects the physical structure of dining rooms; window treatments; seating (alcoves and individual chairs, with or without armrests); lighting and ambience; table set-ups; the quality and condition of linen, china, and cutlery; and table centerpieces (flowers). It also reflects menus, food quality, presentation, food combinations, culinary creativity, variety, design concepts, appeal, taste, texture, palatability, freshness, color, balance, garnishes, and decorations; appetizers, soups, pastas, flambeaus, tableside cooking; fresh fruit and cakes; the wine list (and connoisseur wine list), price range, and wine service. Alternative dining venues are also checked for menu variety, food and service quality, décor and noise levels.

Informal Dining/Buffets

This score reflects the hardware (including the provision of hot and cold display units, sneeze guards, tongs, ice containers and ladles, and serving utensils); buffet displays (which have become quite disappointing and institutionalized); presentation; trays and set-ups; correct food temperatures; food labeling; breakfast, luncheon, deck buffets, midnight buffets, and late-night snacks; decorative elements such as ice carvings; and staff attitude, service, and communication skills.

Quality of Ingredients

This score reflects the overall quality of ingredients used, including consistency and portion size; grades of meat, fish, and fowl; and the price paid by the cruise line for its food product per passenger per day. It is the quality of ingredients that most dictates the eventual presentation and quality of the finished product as well as its taste. Also included is the quality of tea and coffee (better quality ships are expected to provide more palatable tea and coffee).

Tea/Coffee/Bar Snacks

This score reflects the quality and variety of teas and coffees available (including afternoon teas/coffees and their presentation); whether mugs or cups and saucers are presented or available; whether milk is served in the correct open containers or in sealed packets; whether self-service or graciously served. The quality of such items as cakes, scones, and pastries, as well as bar/lounge snacks, hot and cold canapés, and hors d'oeuvres also forms part of this section.

A quiet spot aboard P&O Cruises' *Oriana*.

Service

Dining Room

This score reflects the professionalism of the restaurant staff: the maître d'hotel, dining room managers, head section waiters, waiters and assistant waiters (busboys), and sommeliers and wine waiters. It includes place settings and correct service (serving, taking from the correct side), communication skills, attitude, flair, dress sense (uniform), and finesse. Waiters should note whether passengers are right- or left-handed and, aboard ships with assigned table places, make sure that the cutlery and glasses are placed on the side of preference. Cutlery and wine glasses are also included.

Bars

This score reflects the lighting and ambience; overall service in bars and lounges; noise levels; communication skills (between bartenders and bar staff and passengers); staff attitude, personality, flair and finesse; correct use of glasses (and correct size of glasses); billing and attitude when presenting the bill (aboard those ships where a charge is made).

Cabins

This score reflects the cleaning and housekeeping staff, butlers (for penthouse and suite passengers), cabin stewards/stewardesses and their supervisory staff, attention to detail and cleanliness, in-cabin food service, linen and bathrobe changes, and language and communication skills.

Open Decks

This score reflects steward/stewardess service for beverages and food items around the open decks; service for placement and replacement of towels on deck lounge chairs, self-help towels, and emptying of used towel bins; general tidiness of all associated deck equipment; and the availability of service at nonstandard times (in the evening or early morning, for example).

Gratuities

In the Other Comments section at the end of each rating, all gratuities are usually at extra cost unless specifically included in the price. Likewise, insurance and port taxes are also at extra cost unless they are specifically stated as included.

Entertainment

On specialist ships, such as those featuring expedition cruises, or tall ships, where entertainment is not a feature, it is the lecture program that forms this portion of the evaluations.

The score reflects the overall entertainment program and content as designed and targeted to specific passenger demographics. Cruise ship entertainment has to appeal to passengers of widely varying ages and types. Included is the physical plant (stage/bandstand) of the main showlounge; technical support, lighting, follow spotlight operation and set/backdrop design; sound and light systems (including laser shows); recorded click-tracks and all special effects; variety and quality of large-scale production shows (including story, plot, content, cohesion, creativeness of costumes, relevancy, quality, choreography, and vocal content); cabaret; variety shows; game shows, singers; visual acts; bands and solo musicians.

The Cruise Experience

Activities Program

This score reflects the variety, quality, and quantity of daytime activities and events. It includes the cruise director and staff (their visibility, availability, ability, and professionalism), sports programs, participation games, special interest programs, port and shopping lecturers, and mind-enrichment lecturers.

This score also reflects the extent and quality of any water sports equipment carried), instruction programs, overall staff supervision, the marina or side-retractable water sports platforms, and any enclosed swimming area (if applicable).

Movies/Television Programming

This score reflects movies screened in onboard theaters, including screen, picture and sound quality; videos screened in the in-cabin system; other televised programming, including a ship's own television station programming; content; and entertainment value. Cabin TV audio channels are included.

Hospitality Standard

This score reflects the level of hospitality of the crew and their attention to detail and personal satisfaction. It includes the professionalism of senior officers, middle management, supervisors, cruise staff, and general crew; social contact, appearance, and dress codes or uniforms; atmosphere and ambience; motivation; communication skills (most important); the general ambience and the attention to detail.

Overall Product Delivery

This score reflects the quality of the overall cruise as a vacation experience – what the brochure states

---

WHAT THE DESCRIPTIONS MEAN

Ship Size

● Boutique Ship (50–200 passengers)
● Small Ship (200–500 passengers)
● Mid-Size Ship (500–1,200 passengers)
● Large Resort Ship (1,200–4,000 passengers)

Lifestyle

Designated as Standard, Premium, Luxury, or Utterly Exclusive, according to a general classification into which segment of the market the ship falls. This should help you choose the right size ship and cruise experience to fit your lifestyle.

● **Standard**: the least expensive.
● **Premium**: more expensive than Standard, have generally better food, service, and facilities.
● **Luxury**: more expensive than Premium or Standard, and provide more personal comfort, space, and better food, staff and training.
● **Utterly Exclusive**: the best in facilities, food, and service, and the finest cruise experience available at present, but are more expensive than Luxury, Premium or Standard.

The Oatmeal Factor: Luxury by Degree

As defined by the author of this book, The Oatmeal Factor shows how various cruise ships will provide a passenger with a basic item such as a bowl of oatmeal. The difference can be found in its presentation. In the cruise industry, there are ships that provide one of four levels of oatmeal presentation, as follows.

Standard (D): Hot oatmeal (such as supermarket brand oats) mixed with water, with little or no chance of obtaining tahini to add taste to the oatmeal. You get it from a soup tureen at the buffet, and put it into a plastic or inexpensive china bowl yourself (or it may be served in the dining room by a waiter/waitress); it is eaten with plastic or basic canteen cutlery. In other words, it's basic, basic, basic.

Premium (C): Hot oatmeal, water, salt and little olive oil; served in a higher quality bowl, by a waiter or wait-

ress, with hotel-quality (or better) cutlery. It's possible that the ship will have tahini, to add taste and creaminess. It's also possible that the waiter/waitress will ask if you'd like hot or cold milk with your oatmeal. There may even be a doily between the oatmeal bowl and base plate.

Luxury (B): Hot oatmeal (medium or large flakes), water, salt, tahini, a little (extra virgin) olive oil and nutmeg, with a dash of blended Scotch (whisky); served in a high quality brand name bowl (Versace), with base plate and doily, and Hepp- or Robbe & Berking-quality silverware. Naturally, the waiter/waitress will ask if you'd like hot or cold milk with your oatmeal.

Utterly Exclusive (A): Hot Scottish (large flakes, hand ground) oatmeal, water, sea salt, tahini, and nutmeg (grated at the table), high-quality cold-pressed olive oil and a layer of rare single malt Scotch whisky; served in small production hand-made china, with base plate and doily, and sterling silver cutlery. Of course, the waiter/waitress will ask if you'd like hot or cold milk (or anything else) with your oatmeal.

Naturally, there are variations on the theme, and some crossover depending on the cruise ship, supplies available, staff training and other considerations. Also, the setting and presentation also play a large part in determining quality. Noise level, decor, chairs, table height, table settings, and overall comfort are all part of the total equation, and, ultimately, the evaluation process.

Cruise Line

The cruise line and the operator may be different if the company that owns the vessel does not market and operate it (tour operators often charter cruise ships for their exclusive use – Thomson Cruises is one example).

First Entered Service

Where two dates are given, the first is the ship's maiden passenger voyage when new, and the second is the date it began service for the current operator.

and promises (real or implied), which reflects on the level of expectation versus the onboard product delivery of hospitality and services received.

Notes on the Rating Results

Cruise ship evaluations and ratings have become tougher and much more complex. Although a ship may be the newest, with all the latest high-tech facilities possible, passengers reiterate that it is the onboard food and service that often disappoints.

Cruise companies say that food quality is a trade-off against lower prices. However, this attitude only results in a downward spiral that affects food quality, freshness, variety, creativity, and presentation, as well as service, quality of personnel, crew training, safety, maintenance, and other related items.

Cuts in food quality, crew wages and detail items are typically made by cruise companies in the hope that passengers will not notice them. However, in the final analysis, it is the little things that add to points lost on the great scorecard.

The ratings are intended to help the cruise companies to take note of their product, listen to their income-generating passengers, and return some of the items and the finesse currently missing in the overall cruise vacation experience, while adjusting fares to better reflect long-term growth of this good value-for-money vacation. ❑

Pod Propulsion

The azimuthing pod propulsion system is a relatively recent high-tech installation. It replaces conventional propeller shafts, propellers and rudders, negates the need for stern thrusters, and saves valuable machinery space. The "pods" (typically two for most ships, although some ships have three, or even four pods), which resemble huge outboard motors with an externally mounted propeller, replace shaft lines, rudders and their machinery, and are compact, self-contained units powered by an internal electric propulsion motor. Each pod typically weighs about 170 tons each (the four pods attached to *Queen Mary 2* weigh 250 tons each – more than an empty Boeing 747 jumbo jet; two are fixed, two are of the azimuthing variety). Although they are at the stern, pod units *pull*, rather than *push*, a ship through the water, thanks to their forward facing propellers that can be turned through 360°), and provide greater maneuvrability. Ships with a pod propulsion system will have little or no noticeable vibration or engine noise at the stern, unlike ships with conventional propulsion systems. Different manufacturers have different names for their pod systems (examples: Azipod, Mermaid).

Propulsion

The type of propulsion is given (i.e. gas turbine, diesel, diesel-electric, or steam turbine), together with the output (at 100 percent), expressed as MW (megawatts) or kW (kilowatts) generated.

Propellers

Number of propellers or azimuthing pods *(see above)*.

Passenger Capacity

The number of passengers is based on:
● Two lower beds/berths per cabin, plus all cabins for single occupancy.
● All available beds/berths filled (Note: This figure may not always be accurate, as cruise lines often make changes by adding or taking away third/fourth berths according to demand).

Passenger Space Ratio (Tons Per Passenger)

Achieved by dividing the gross tonnage by the number of passengers.

Crew to Passenger Ratio

Achieved by dividing the number of passengers by the number of crew (lower beds/all possible beds and berths filled).

Cabin Size Range

From the smallest cabin to the largest suite (including "private" balconies/verandahs), these are provided in square feet and square meters, rounded up to the nearest number.

Wheelchair-accessible Cabins

Cabins designed to accommodate passengers with mobility problems.

Dedicated Cinema/seats

A "yes" means that there is a separate cinema dedicatedly solely to showing large-screen movies throughout the day and during the evening. This is distinct from a show lounge that may be used to screen movies during the day (afternoon) and live shows in the evening. The number of seats is provided where known.

A Note About Prices

Some price examples are given throughout the ship reviews (for massage, the cover price for "alternative" restaurants, for internet access, or gratuities added to your onboard account, for example), but please note that these are provided *only* as a guideline, and may have changed since this book was completed. Always check with the cruise line, onboard concession or your travel provider for the latest prices.

Adonia
★★★★

Large (Resort) Ship: ....77,690 tons	Total Crew: 850	Cabins (with private balcony): 410
Lifestyle: ....Standard	Passengers	Cabins (wheelchair accessible): 19
Cruise Line: ....P & O Cruises	(lower beds/all berths): 2,016/2,272	Cabin Current: ....110 and 220 volts
Former Names: ....Sea Princess	Passenger Space Ratio	Elevators: 11
Builder: ....Fincantieri (Italy)	(lower beds/all berths): 39.3/34.1	Casino (gaming tables): ....Yes
Original Cost: ....$300 million	Crew/Passenger Ratio	Slot Machines: ....Yes
Entered Service: .... Dec 1998/May 2003	(lower beds/all berths): 2.2/2.5	Swimming Pools (outdoors): 4
Registry: ....Great Britain	Navigation Officers: ....British	Swimming Pools (indoors): 0
Length (ft/m): 857.2/261.3	Cabins (total): 1,008	Whirlpools: 5
Beam (ft/m): 105.6/32.2	Size Range (sq ft/m): 158.2–610.3/	Self-Service Launderette: ....Yes
Draft (ft/m): 26.5/8.1	14.7–56.7	Dedicated Cinema/Seats: ....No
Propulsion/Propellers: .....diesel-electric	Cabins (outside view): 603	Library: ....Yes
(46,080kW)/2	Cabins (interior/no view): 405	Classification Society: ....Lloyds Register
Passenger Decks: 10	Cabins (for one person): 0	

OVERALL SCORE: 1,537 (OUT OF A POSSIBLE 2,000 POINTS)

OVERVIEW. Although large (and an identical twin to *Oceana*), this all-white ship has a profile that is well balanced by a large, stylish, swept-back buff-colored funnel, which contains a deck tennis/basketball/ volleyball court in its sheltered aft base. Originally built for Princess Cruises as *Sea Princess*, the ship, after some modification, is now marketed to British passengers as part of the P&O Cruises fleet. There is a wide, teak wrap-around promenade deck outdoors, some real teak steamer-style deck chairs (with royal blue cushioned pads), and 93,000 sq. ft (8,640 sq. meters) of outdoors space. A large glazed area on the upper decks provides plenty of light and connection with the outside world.

Adonia absorbs passengers quite well (and has a decent passenger space ratio for a large ship, although this is not quite as much as P&O Cruises' more traditional ships *Aurora* and *Oriana*), and some areas have quite an intimate feel to them, which is what the interior designers intended. The interiors are very attractive, with warm colors and welcoming decor that includes countless wall murals and other artwork. The signs around the ship could be better designed, however.

The main public entertainment rooms are located under three decks of cabins. There is a wide range of public rooms to choose from (including 13 bars), with several intimate rooms and spaces so that you aren't overwhelmed by large spaces. The decor is tasteful, with fairly attractive (but rather bland) color combinations that are warm and don't clash (nothing is brash). The interior focal point is a large four-deck-high atrium lobby with winding, double stairways, complete with two panoramic glass-walled elevators.

BERLITZ'S RATINGS

	Possible	Achieved
Ship	500	428
Accommodation	200	162
Food	400	266
Service	400	291
Entertainment	100	84
Cruise	400	306

The library is a very warm room and has several large buttery leather chairs for listening to compact audio discs, with ocean-view windows. The collection of artwork is good, particularly on the stairways, and helps make the ship feel smaller than it is, although in places it doesn't always seem coordinated. The Monte Carlo Club Casino is not really in the main passenger flow and so it does not generate the "walk-through" factor found aboard so many ships.

Perhaps the most popular drinking room can be found in the All That Jazz lounge, with decor that is a pleasing mix of traditional and modern (it may remind you of a gentleman's club, complete with wood paneling and comfortable seating). With a bandstand and dance floor, a wide range of live music is presented here during the day, with light jazz each evening.

A very pleasant place to spend time is in the Easy Like a Sunday ("lifestyle") lounge, located at the aft end of Deck 12, and adjacent to both the pool deck and the Ocean Spa. In this lounge, life is easy and totally relaxed (remember the song *Easy Like a Sunday Morning*?). Created from what was formerly a children's area, it has ocean views from its position on the starboard side (although it doesn't accommodate many users); part of the lounge area features 6 internet computer terminals, although there is no privacy. The room is rectangular in shape and has several sections designed to flow into each other, except for one small section looking out to the swimming pools which has four lounge chairs set around a stone slab with Chinese symbols that mean "wind" and "water" (or feng shui in the translation into English). Take a leisurely breakfast or casual lunch, read a magazine, or lounge in one of seven very comfortable cream leather deck lounge chairs and do nothing except watch the water go by.

At the end of the day – as is the case aboard most large ships – you will be well attended if you live in the top-grade cabins; if you do not, you will merely be one of a very large number of passengers. One nice feature is the captain's cocktail party – normally held in the four-deck-high main atrium, so you can come and go as you please – and there's no standing in line to have your photograph taken with the captain if you don't want to.

However, note that in the quest for increased onboard revenue (and shareholder value), even birthday cakes are now an extra-cost item, as are espressos and cappuccinos (fake ones, made from instant coffee, are available in the dining rooms). Also at extra cost are ice cream (except in the restaurant), and bottled water (these can add up to a considerable amount on a long cruise). For gratuities (which are optional), you should typically allow £3.50 per person, per day.

Adonia was transferred from the Princess Cruises fleet (its previous name was *Sea Princess*) to the UK-based parent company P&O Cruises, and began cruising in May 2003. *Adonia* replaced *Arcadia*, which was placed into a new cruise brand named Ocean Village (targeted at a younger audience). *Adonia* was introduced as a child-free ship, catering to an adults-only clientele (no under 18s), with a "dress to impress" (your fellow passengers, that is) dress code (evenings have a formal or smart casual dress code), and many of the public rooms underwent a name change to better reflect the tastes of P&O's mainly British passengers, many of whom smoke. In May 2005 *Adonia* will be transferred back to Princess Cruises, renamed *Sea Princess*, and marketed to both British and North American passengers. *Sea Princess* will then operate from the UK in summer, and in the Caribbean in winter.

Note that there are a number of dead ends in the interior layout, so it's not as user-friendly as it could be. Standing in line for embarkation, disembarkation, shore tenders and for self-serve buffet meals is an inevitable aspect of cruising aboard all large ships. The swimming pools are quite small considering the number of passengers carried, and the pool deck can become cluttered with plastic deck lounge chairs. The digital voice announcing lift deck stops is annoying for many.

SUITABLE FOR: *Adonia* is best suited to couples and singles who enjoy cruising in a child-free environment, with facilities and entertainment geared specifically for them in a comfortable, contemporary large ship setting with plenty of public rooms.

ACCOMMODATION. There are 19 different cabin price grades, designated as: suites (with private balcony), mini-suites (with private balcony), outside-view twin-bedded cabins with balcony, outside-view twin-bedded cabins, and interior (no view) twin-bedded cabins. The price you pay will depend on the grade, size, and location you choose. Although the standard outside-view and interior (no view) cabins are a little small, they are well designed and func-

tional in layout, and have earth tone colors accentuated by splashes of color from the bedspreads. Proportionately, there are quite a lot of interior (no view) cabins.

Many of the outside-view cabins have private balconies, and all seem to be quite well soundproofed, although the balcony partition is not of the floor to ceiling type, so you can hear your neighbors clearly (or smell their smoke). The balconies are very narrow, and only just large enough for two small chairs, and there is no dedicated outdoor balcony lighting. Some cabins have third- and fourth-person upper bunk beds – these are good for families with children. Tea and coffee making facilities are provided in all cabins – a comforting addition.

There is a reasonable amount of closet space and abundant drawer and other storage space in all cabins; although this is adequate for a 7-night cruise, it could prove to be quite tight for longer. Also provided are a color television, and refrigerator, and each night a chocolate will appear on your pillow. The cabin bathrooms are practical units, and come complete with all the facilities one needs, although again, they really are tight spaces, best described as one person at-a-time units. Fortunately, they have a shower enclosure of a decent size, a small amount of shelving for your personal toiletries, real glasses, and a hairdryer.

Suites: The largest cabins can be found in six suites (Orcades, Orion, Orissa, Oronsay, Orsova, Orontes), two on each of three decks located at the stern of the ship, each with its own large private balcony. These suites are well laid out, and have large bathrooms with two basins, a Jacuzzi bathtub, and a separate shower enclosure. The bedroom features generous amounts of wood accenting and detailing, indented ceilings, and television sets in both bedroom and lounge areas. The suites also have a dining table and four chairs.

Mini-Suites: These typically have two lower beds that convert into a queen-sized bed. There is a separate bedroom/sleeping area with vanity desk, and a lounge with sofa and coffee table, indented ceilings with generous amounts of wood accenting and detailing, a walk-in closet, and a larger bathroom with Jacuzzi bathtub and separate shower enclosure.

Standard Outside-view/Interior (No View) Cabins: The cabin bathrooms are practical, and come with all the details one needs, although they really are tight spaces, best as one-person-at-a-time units. They do, however, have a decent shower enclosure, a small amount of shelving for personal toiletries, real glasses, and a hairdryer.

P&O Cruises features the BBC World channel on the in-cabin color television system (when available, depending on cruise area), as well as movies (there is no dedicated theater aboard this ship). The cabin numbering system is quite illogical, however, with numbers going through several hundred series on the same deck.

CUISINE/DINING. There are two main, asymmetrically designed dining rooms (each seating about 500), Rigoletto and Traviata, located adjacent to the two lower levels of the four-deck high atrium lobby. Both dining rooms are non-smoking, as are the dining rooms aboard all ships of P & O Cruises, and which one you are assigned to will depend on the location of your cabin. Each has its own galley and each is split into multi-tier sections, which help create a feeling of intimacy, although there is a lot of noise from the waiter stations. Breakfast and lunch are provided in an open seating arrangement; dinner is in two seatings.

The cuisine is decidedly British – a little adventurous at times, but always there will be plenty of curry dishes and other standard British items. You should not expect exquisite dining – this is British hotel standard catering that does not pretend to offer gourmet food. However, what the company does present is attractive and tasty, with some excellent gravies and sauces to accompany meals. In keeping with the Britishness of P&O Cruises, the desserts are always varied and quite enjoyable. A statement in the on-board cruise folder states that P&O Cruises does not knowingly purchase genetically modified foods (how about all those cereals, then?). The service is provided by a team of friendly stewards – most of whom are from Goa – with which P&O has had a long relationship.

The wine list is quite reasonable. Note that 15% is added to all beverage bills, including wines (whether you order a £10 bottle or a £100 bottle of wine, even though it takes the same amount of service to open and pour the wine).

The Pavilion is the ship's casual, self-serve buffet. Open 24 hours a day, it is located above the navigation bridge in the forward section of the ship, and has some commanding wrap-around views. At night, this large room (there are two food lines – one each on port and starboard sides), which resembles a food court, can be transformed into an informal bistro dinner setting with waiter service (reservations are necessary and there may be a cover charge).

Outdoors on deck, with a sheltered view over the Riviera Pool, the Horizon Grill features fast-food items for those who don't want to change from their sunbathing attire. In the evening, the grill offers steaks, seafood, and "white sisters" mixed grill (a cover charge applies for dining under the stars).

For informal eats, try Cafe Corniche for pizzas and light snacks; it is located on the uppermost level of the four-deck-high atrium lobby. In addition, there's also a patisserie (for cappuccino/espresso coffees and pastries), and a champagne/caviar bar called Premier Cru (a 28-gram portion of Sevruga costs £18.95, while Osetra is £21), and special caviar and champagne combinations are available.

The cabin service menu is very limited, and presentation of the food items featured is poor. If you have coffee or tea at any of the ship's bars, there is a charge.

ENTERTAINMENT. There are two showlounges (Limelight Theater, and Spotlights), one at each end of the ship. The Limelight, located at the forward part of the ship, is a superb 550-seat, theater-style showlounge, for production shows and theater events (movies can also be shown here), while Spotlights is a 480-seat cabaret-style lounge with bar.

P&O Cruises prides itself on a decent quality of entertainment. To this end, the ship has the Stadium Theater Company, a resident group of actors, singers and dancers. They provide theater-style presentations such as mini versions of well-known musicals, "book" shows, revues, and drama presentations. In addition, the ship features a whole array of cabaret acts. Although many of the cabaret acts are not what you would call headliners, they regularly travel the cruise ship circuit. Classical concerts are scheduled for many of the cruises throughout the year.

Ballroom dance aficionados will be pleased to note that there are several good-sized wooden dance floors aboard this ship, and P&O Cruises normally carries a professional dance couple as hosts and teachers (there is plenty of dancing time included in the entertainment programming).

SPA/FITNESS. The Oasis Spa has facilities that are contained in a glass-walled complex which is located on Lido Deck – one of the highest decks, at the aft section of the ship. It includes a gymnasium with ocean views aft and to the port side, with all the associated high-tech muscle-pumping and body toning equipment, and a combination aerobics/exercise room. Other facilities include a sauna and steam room, and several well-being treatment rooms. There is no extra chanrge for most fitness and exercise classes.

The spa is operated by Harding Brothers, a UK concession that provides the staff and a wide range of beauty and wellness treatments. Examples of treatments and prices: Full Body Massage (£45 for 50 minutes); Indian Head Massage (£35); Marine Algae Body Wrap (£40 for 60 minutes); Collagen Velvet Facial Mask or Hydrodermie Facial (£45 for 75 minutes). A shampoo and blow dry will cost you £22, while a manicure (reshape and repolish) is £25 for 45 minutes. If you want to book spa treatments (massage, facial, hair styling), it is wise to do so as soon after you embark as possible, as time slots do fill up quickly aboard large ships such as this.

Forming part of the outside area of the spa complex, one swimming pool is "suspended" aft between two decks (two other pools are located in another area in the center of the ship), although they are not large for the size of the ship. Sports facilities are located in an open-air sports deck positioned inside the ship's funnel and adaptable for basketball, volleyball, badminton, or paddle tennis. Joggers can exercise on the wrap-around open Promenade Deck. There's also an electronic golf simulator (no need to bring your own clubs).

Adventure of the Seas
★★★★

Large (Resort) Ship: . . . . . . .137,276 tons	Passenger Decks: 14	Cabins (for one person): 0
Lifestyle: . . . . .Standard	Total Crew: .1,185	Cabins (with private balcony): 765
Cruise Line: . . . . .Royal Caribbean	Passengers	Cabins (wheelchair accessible): 26
International	(lower beds/all berths): 3,114/3,838	Cabin Current: . . . . .110 volts
Former Names: . . . . .none	Passenger Space Ratio	Elevators: . . . . .14 (6 glass-enclosed)
Builder: . . .Kvaerner Masa-Yards (Finland)	(lower beds/all berths): 44.0/35.7	Casino (gaming tables): . . . . .Yes
Original Cost: . . . .$500 million	Crew/Passenger Ratio	Slot Machines: . . . . .Yes
Entered Service: . . . . .Nov 2001	(lower beds/all berths): 2.6/3.2	Swimming Pools (outdoors): 3
Registry: . . . . .The Bahamas	Navigation Officers: . . . . . . .Scandinavian	Swimming Pools (indoors): 0
Length (ft/m): 1,020.6/311.1	Cabins (total): 1,557	Whirlpools: 6
Beam (ft/m): 155.5/47.4	Size Range (sq ft/m): 151.0–1,358.0/	Self-Service Launderette: . . . . .No
Draft (ft/m): 28.8/8.8	14.0–126.1	Dedicated Cinema/Seats: . . . . .No
Propulsion/Propellers: . . . . .diesel-electric	Cabins (outside view): 939	Library: . . . . .Yes
(75,600kW)/3 azimuthing pods	Cabins (interior/no view): 618	Classification Society: Det Norske Veritas

OVERALL SCORE: 1,537 (OUT OF A POSSIBLE 2,000 POINTS)

OVERVIEW. *Adventure of the Seas* is a stunning, large, floating leisure resort (sister to *Explorer of the Seas, Mariner of the Seas, Navigator of the Seas,* and *Voyager of the Seas*, which debuted between 1999 and 2004). The exterior design is not unlike an enlarged version of the company's Vision-class ships. The *Voyager*-class ships are, at present, the largest cruise vessels in the world in terms of tonnage measurement, except for Cunard Line's ocean liner, *Queen Mary 2*.

Adventure of the Seas was named in New York City by Mayor Giuliani on November 10, 2001, together with representatives from the Fire Department of New York, New York Police Department, and the Port Authority Police Department in a moving ceremony at the New York Passenger Terminal at Pier 88. At that time, Royal Caribbean International made a $50,000 contribution to the Twin Towers Relief Fund, in the aftermath of the terrorist atrocities inflicted on the city.

The propulsion is derived from three pod units, powered by electric motors (two azimuthing, and one fixed at the centerline) instead of conventional rudders and propellers, in the latest configuration of high-tech systems.

With large proportions, the ship provides more facilities and options, and caters to more passengers than any other Royal Caribbean International ship has in the past, and yet the ship manages to have a healthy passenger space ratio (the amount of space per passenger). Being a "non-Panamax" ship, it is simply too large to go through the Panama Canal, thus limiting its itineraries almost exclusively to the Caribbean (where only a few islands can accept it), or for use as a floating island resort. Spend the first few hours

BERLITZ'S RATINGS

	Possible	Achieved
Ship	500	431
Accommodation	200	160
Food	400	252
Service	400	294
Entertainment	100	83
Cruise	400	317

exploring all the many facilities and public spaces aboard this vessel and it will be time well spent.

Although *Adventure of the Seas* is a large ship, the cabin hallways are warm and attractive, with artwork cabinets and wavy lines to lead you along and break up the monotony. In fact, there are plenty of colorful, even whimsical, decorative touches to help you avoid what would otherwise be a very clinical environment.

Embarkation and disembarkation take place through two stations/access points, designed to minimize the inevitable lines (that's over 1,500 people for each access point). Once inside the ship, you'll need good walking shoes, particularly when you want to go from one end to the other – it really is quite a long way.

The four-decks-high Royal Promenade, which is 393.7 ft (120 meters) long, is the main interior focal point (it's a good place to hang out, to meet someone, or to arrange to meet someone). The length of two football fields (American football, that is), it has two internal lobbies (atria) that rise through 11 decks. Restaurants, shops, and entertainment locations front this winding street and interior "with-view" cabins look into it from above. It is designed loosely in the image of London's fashionable Burlington Arcade – although there's not a real brick in sight, and I wonder if the designers have ever visited the real thing. It is, however, an imaginative piece of design work, and most passengers (particularly those who enjoy shopping malls) enjoy it immensely.

The super-atrium houses a "traditional" pub, with draft beer and plenty of "street-front" seating (North American passengers always seem to sit down, while British passengers prefer to stand at the bar). There is also a Champagne Bar, a Sidewalk Cafe (for continental breakfast, all-day pizzas, speciality coffees, and desserts), Sprinkles (for round-the-clock ice cream and yoghurt), and a sports bar. There are also several shops – jewelry shop, gift shop, liquor shop and the logo souvenir shop. Altogether, the Royal Promenade is a nice place to see and be seen, and it sees action throughout the day and night. Comedy art has its place here, too, for example in the trompe l'oeil painter climbing up the walls). The Guest Reception and Shore Excursion counters are located at the aft end of the promenade, as is an ATM machine. Things to watch for: look up to see the large moving, asteroid-like sculpture (constantly growing and contracting). At times, street entertainers appear, and parades are staged, while at other (carefully orchestrated) times it's difficult to walk through the area as it is filled to the brim with shopping items – like a cheap bazaar.

Arched across the promenade is a captain's balcony. Meanwhile, in the center of the promenade is a stairway that connects you to the deck below, where you'll find the Schooner Bar (a piano lounge that is a feature of all RCI ships) and the colorful Casino Royale. This is naturally large and full of flashing lights and noises. Gaming includes blackjack, Caribbean stud poker, roulette, and craps, as well as 300 slot machines.

Aft of the casino is the Aquarium Bar, while close by are some neat displays of oceanographic interest. Royal Caribbean International has teamed up with the University of Miami's Rosenstiel School of Marine and Atmospheric Science to study the ocean and the atmosphere. A small onboard laboratory is part of the project.

There's also a regulation-size ice-skating rink (Studio B), featuring real, not fake, ice, with "bleacher" seating for up to 900, and the latest in broadcast facilities. Ice Follies shows are presented here. Slim pillars obstruct clear-view arena stage sight lines, however. If ice-skating in the Caribbean doesn't appeal, you may enjoy the stunning two-deck library (open 24 hours a day). A grand $12 million was spent on permanent artwork. Drinking places include a neat Aquarium Bar, complete with 50 tons of glass and water in four large aquariums (whose combined value is over $1 million).

Other drinking places include the small and intimate Champagne Bar, Crown & Anchor Pub, and Connoisseur Club – for cigars and cognacs. Lovers of jazz might appreciate Blue Moon, an intimate room for cool music atop the ship in the Viking Crown Lounge, or the Schooner Bar piano lounge. Golfers might enjoy the 19th Hole – a golf bar, as they play the Adventure Links.

There is a large television studio, located adjacent to rooms that can be used for trade show exhibit space, with conference center that seats 400 and a multi-media screening room that seats 60. Lovers could tie the knot in a wedding chapel in the sky, the Skylight Chapel (located on the upper level of the Viking Crown Lounge, it has wheelchair access via an electric stairlift). Outdoors, the pool and open deck areas provide a resort-like environment.

Families with children are also well catered for, as facil-

ities for children and teenagers are quite extensive. "Aquanauts" is for 3–5 year olds; "Explorers" is for 6–8 year olds; "Voyagers" is for 9–12 year olds. Optix is a dedicated area for teenagers, including a daytime club (with several computers), soda bar, and dance floor. "Challenger's Arcade" features an array of the latest video games. Paint and Clay is an arts and crafts center for younger children. Adjacent is Adventure Beach, an area for all the family; it includes swimming pools, a water slide and game areas outdoors.

In terms of sheer size, this ship dwarfs all other ships in the cruise industry (except *Queen Mary 2*), but in terms of personal service, the reverse tends to be the case, unless you happen to reside in one of the top suites. Royal Caribbean International does, however, try hard to provide a good standard of programmed service from its hotel service staff.

Remember that, if you meet someone somewhere and want to meet them again, you'll need to make an appointment – for this really is a large, Las Vegas-style American floating resort-city for the lively of heart and fleet of foot. The best advice I can give you is to arrange to meet somewhere along the Royal Promenade.

ACCOMMODATION. There is an extensive range of 22 cabin categories in four major groupings: Premium ocean-view suites and cabins, Promenade-view (interior-view) cabins, Ocean-view cabins, and Interior (no view) cabins. Many cabins are of a similar size – good for incentives groups and other large groups, and 300 have interconnecting doors – good for families.

A total of 138 interior (no view) cabins have bay windows that look into a horizontal atrium – first used to good effect aboard the Baltic passenger ferries *Silja Serenade* (1990) and *Silja Symphony* (1991) with interior cabins that look into a central shopping plaza. Regardless of what cabin grade you choose, however, all except for the Royal Suite and Owner's Suite feature twin beds that convert to a queen-sized unit, television, radio and telephone, personal safe, vanity unit, mini-bar (called an Automatic Refreshment Center) hairdryer and private bathroom.

The largest cabins include luxuriously appointed penthouse suites (whose occupants, sadly, must share the rest of the ship with everyone else, except for their own exclusive, and private, concierge club). The grandest is the Royal Suite; positioned on the port side of the ship, it measures 1,146 sq. ft (106.5 sq. meters). It features a king-sized bed in a separate, large bedroom, a living room with an additional queen-sized sofa bed, baby grand piano (no pianist is included, however), refrigerator/wet bar, dining table, entertainment center, and large bathroom.

Slightly smaller, but still highly desirable are 10 Owner's Suites (all located in the center of the ship, on both port and starboard sides, each measuring 468 sq. ft/43 sq. meters) and four Royal Family suites (each 574 sq. ft/53 sq. meters), all of which have similar facilities. However, the four Royal Family suites, which have two bedrooms (including one with third/fourth upper Pullman berths) are at the stern of the ship and have magnificent views over the ship's wake (and seagulls).

No matter what grade of cabin you choose, all cabins feature twin beds that convert to a queen-sized bed, a private bathroom with shower enclosure (towels are 100% cotton), as well as interactive, closed circuit and satellite television, and pay-per-view movies. Cabins with "private balconies" are not so private, as the partitions are only partial, not full. The balcony decking is made of Bolidt – a sort of rubberized sand – and not wood, while the balcony rail is of wood. If you have a cabin with an interconnecting door to another cabin, be aware that you'll probably be able to hear everything your next-door neighbors say and do. Bathroom toilets are explosively noisy – like a barking dog. Cabin bath towels are small and skimpy. Although the menus and food variety offered have been upgraded since the introduction, remember that you get what you pay for.

CUISINE/DINING. The main dining room (total capacity 1,919) is massive, and is set on three levels, all of which are named after composers (Mozart, Strauss, Vivaldi). A dramatic staircase connects all three levels, and huge, fat support pillars obstruct the sight lines. All three levels feature exactly the same menus and food. There are also two small private wings for private groups: La Cetra and La Notte, each seating 58 persons. The dining room is totally non-smoking, there are two seatings, and tables are for four, six, eight, 10 or 12. The place settings, china and cutlery are of good quality.

Alternative Dining Options: These are for casual and informal meals at all hours and include:
● Cafe Promenade: for continental breakfast, all-day pizzas, pastries, desserts and specialty coffees (sadly provided in paper cups).
● Windjammer Cafe: for casual buffet-style breakfast, lunch and light dinner (except the last night of the cruise).
● Island Grill: (this is actually a section inside the Windjammer Cafe), for casual dinner (no reservations necessary) featuring a grill and open kitchen.
● Portofino: this is the ship's "upscale" (non-smoking) Euro-Italian restaurant, open for dinner only. Reservations are required, and a $6 gratuity per person is charged). The food and its presentation are better than the food in the dining room, although the restaurant is not large enough for all passengers to try even once during a cruise. Choices include: antipasti, soup, salad, pasta, main dish, dessert, cheese and coffee.
● Johnny Rockets, a retro 1950s all-day, all-night diner-style eatery that features hamburgers, malt shakes (at extra cost), and jukebox hits, with both indoor and outdoor seating seating (all indoor tables feature a mini-jukebox; dimes are provided for you to make your selection of vintage records), and all-singing, all-dancing waitresses that'll knock your socks off, if you can stand the volume.
● Sprinkles: for round-the-clock ice cream and yoghurt.

ENTERTAINMENT. The 1,350-seat Lyric Showlounge is really a stunning room that could well be the equal of many such rooms on land. It is located at the forward end of the ship and spans the height of five decks (with only a few slim pillars and almost no disruption of sight lines from almost any seat in the house). The room features a hydraulic orchestra pit and huge stage areas, together with sonic-boom loud sound, and some superb lighting equipment.

In addition to production shows, the ship features a whole array of cabaret acts. Although many of these acts are not what you would call headliners (the strongest cabaret acts are featured in the main showlounge, while lesser acts are presented in the Imperial Lounge, which is also the venue for late-night adults-only comedy), they regularly travel the cruise ship circuit.

The entertainment throughout is really upbeat. There is even background music in all corridors and elevators, and constant music outdoors on the pool deck. If you want a quiet relaxing holiday, this is not the right ship for you.

There is also a television studio (in case you thought you'd need one aboard a cruise ship), located adjacent to rooms that could be used, for example, for trade show exhibit space (good for conventions at sea).

SPA/FITNESS. The ShipShape health spa is large, and measures 15,000 sq. ft (1,400 sq. meters). It includes a large aerobics room, fitness center (with the usual stairmasters, treadmills, stationary bikes, weight machines and free weights), treatment rooms, men's and women's sauna/ steam rooms, while another 10,000 sq. ft (930 sq. meters) is devoted to a Solarium (with magrodome sliding glass roof) for relaxation after you've exercised.

For the more sporting, there is activity galore – including a rock-climbing wall that's 32.8 ft high (10 meters), with five separate climbing tracks. It is located outdoors at the aft end of the funnel. You'll get a great "buzz" being 200 ft (60 meters) above the ocean while the ship is moving. Other sports facilities include a roller-blading track, a dive-and-snorkel shop, a full-size basketball court and 9-hole, par 26 golf course.

● **For more extensive general information about a Royal Caribbean cruise experience, see pages 128–131.**

Aegean I
★★

Mid-Size Ship: . . . . .11,563 tons	Passenger Decks: 8	Cabins (for one person): 0
Lifestyle: . . . . .Standard	Total Crew: 200	Cabins (with private balcony): 8
Cruise Line: . . . . .Golden Star Cruises	Passengers	Cabins (wheelchair accessible): 0
Former Names: . . . . .Aegean Dolphin,	(lower beds/all berths): 560/682	Cabin Current: . . . . .220 volts
Dolphin, Alkyon, Narcis	Passenger Space Ratio	Elevators: 2
Builder: . . . .Santierul N. Galatz (Romania)	(lower beds/all berths): 20.6/16.8	Casino (gaming tables): . . . . .Yes
Original Cost: .n/a	Crew/Passenger Ratio	Slot Machines: . . . . .Yes
Entered Service: 1974/May 2002	(lower beds/all berths): 2.8/3.4	Swimming Pools (outdoors): 1
Registry: .Greece	Navigation Officers: . . . . .Greek	Swimming Pools (indoors): 0
Length (ft/m): 460.9/140.5	Cabins (total): 280	Whirlpools: 0
Beam (ft/m): 67.2/20.5	Size Range (sq ft/m): 134.5–290.6/	Self-Service Launderette: . . . . .No
Draft (ft/m): 20.3/6.2	12.5–27.0	Dedicated Cinema/Seats: Yes/172
Propulsion/Propellers: . . . . .diesel	Cabins (outside view): 198	Library: . . . . .Yes
(10,296kW)/2	Cabins (interior/no view): 82	Classification Society: . . .Lloyd's Register

OVERALL SCORE: 820 (OUT OF A POSSIBLE 2,000 POINTS)

OVERVIEW: Golden Star Cruises had a slight name change in 2002, from Golden Sun Cruises (the company then had three ships, namely, *Aegean I, Aegean Spirit* and *Arcadia*, and three separate owners each put one ship into the combined company. The profile of this ship looks reasonably smart – in some ways almost contemporary – although the stern is very square and angular, the result of an extensive $26 million conversion, which involved a "chop and stretch" operation between 1986 and 1988.

The open deck space can be said to be moderately good, but it is certainly not enough when the ship is full, and that means it could be difficult to find good sunbathing space. Also, the number of deck lounge chairs is very limited.

Inside, the public rooms are quite tastefully decorated in soft, mostly pastel colors, although there is much use of mirrored surfaces. There is a reasonable showlounge, laid out in a single-level amphitheater-style, although 10 pillars obstruct the sight lines from many seats.

The Belvedere Lounge, which is set high atop the ship and forward, features a smart piano bar and good ocean views through large windows. A dialysis station is a useful addition to medical facilities.

In general, the service, from a mainly Greek hotel staff could be said to be selectively friendly (when they want to be), although there is certainly little finesse. Many members of the ship's crew, including officers, can be seen smoking in public areas (this would be totally against the regulations of almost all non-Greek cruise companies, or any company that is serious about the hospitality industry).

This ship really caters best primarily to European passengers who don't expect much in the way of food and ser-

BERLITZ'S RATINGS		
	Possible	Achieved
Ship	500	175
Accommodation	200	93
Food	400	169
Service	400	196
Entertainment	100	35
Cruise	400	152

vice and just want to take a 3- or 4-day cruise to get around some of the islands in the Aegean Sea, the ship performing more as a water-taxi with full board included. The ship is often placed under charter to various operators, and cruises are sold by a number of different organizations in many countries. Thus, *Aegean I* will provide you with a basic cruise experience in moderately comfortable but very densely populated surroundings, but at a reasonable price – therefore you should not expect the spit and polish that other ships might provide in the same price range. The onboard currency is the euro.

Note that although at first glance the ship appears to have a good range of nicely decorated public rooms, on closer inspection some of the materials used in their construction are held together by the "patch and fix" method of outfitting and refurbishment, which is definitely below internationally accepted standards. The decor is now dated and unkempt in places. There are too many unnecessary announcements (often made in several languages, depending on the passenger mix and cruise).

The teakwood decking is not in good condition. The gangway is narrow and steep in some ports. There are no cushioned pads for the deck lounge chairs (lying on a towel on plastic ribbing is no fun for more than a few minutes). The poor attitude and hospitality from most officers and crew is unacceptable, and officers should learn to turn their two-way radios down. This ship would be unlikely to pass even the basic USPH hygiene and sanitation requirements.

SUITABLE FOR: *Aegean I* best suits couples and single travelers who want a first cruise experience in an unpretentious ship with modest food and service, at a very low cost, but without the frills and finesse that newer ships offer.

ACCOMMODATION. This ship has nine different cabin price grades. Most of the cabins have an outside-view, and most are of the same size and configuration, although the largest cabins can be found on Sun Deck. All cabins feature a small refrigerator and telephone. They are reasonably spacious considering the size of the ship, and they are quite pleasantly decorated, although closet, drawer and luggage storage space for two is limited (it certainly is not enough for a long cruise), but adequate for one; the walls and ceilings are very plain (perhaps more artwork would help). Tthe cabin soundproofing is extremely poor, and you can hear almost everything that's happening in the adjacent cabin(s).

The bathrooms are partly tiled, although they are small and basic, and only just adequate, but there really is little space for personal toiletry items. Bathrobes are typically only provided for occupants of accommodation designated as suites (although this also depends on anyone who may charter and operate the vessel). All toilets are of the non-vacuum type and are quiet, although the toilet seats are extremely high, at 20 inches (52 cm).

There are two suites on Sun Deck – the largest accommodation aboard this ship. Although the lounge area is not even curtained off from the sleeping area, it is quite large. The bathroom has a full-size bathtub, but the "lip" (step) into the bathroom is unnecessarily high (11 inches/28 cm).

CUISINE/DINING. The dining room, located on one of the lowest passenger decks, features restful colors, and has mostly large tables (there are no tables for two). It is a no-smoking room, there are two seatings, and the ceilings are plain. There is a decent amount of space around each table, allowing waiters the room to provide acceptable service, although this tends to be quite hurried at times.

A mixture of Continental and Greek cuisine is featured, although there is only a limited selection of breads, cheeses and fruits, all of which tend to be very standard, and meats, fish and poultry items that are not of high quality.

For casual meals, small (limited choice) self-serve breakfast and lunch buffets are available on the Lido Deck aft, where a popular outdoor gyro and salad bar is available, although the standards of food handling and hygiene leave much to be desired.

ENTERTAINMENT. The showlounge is a single-level room, with a bar at one end, and seating that is mainly in tub-style chairs. The sightlines to the "stage" are poor from many seats. The occasional cabaret act is presented, although these are of the end-of-pier, low-budget variety that have to try to appeal to a multi-lingual passenger carry.

SPA/FITNESS. The facilities are minimal and cramped.

AIDAaura
★★★★

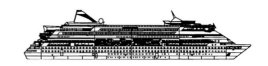

Mid-size Ship: . . . . .42,280 tons	Total Crew: 418	Cabins (with private balcony): 60
Lifestyle: . . . . .Standard	Passengers	Cabins (wheelchair accessible): 4
Cruise Line: . . . . . .Aida Cruises (Seetours)	(lower beds/all berths): 1,266/1,582	Cabin Current: . . . . .220 volts
Former Names: . . . . .None	Passenger Space Ratio	Elevators: 6
Builder: . . . . .Aker MTW (Germany)	(lower beds/all berths): 33.4/26.7	Casino (gaming tables): . . . . .No
Original Cost: . . . .$350 million	Crew/Passenger Ratio	Slot Machines: .No
Entered Service: . . . . .April 2003	(lower beds/all berths): 3.0/3.7	Swimming Pools (outdoors): 2
Registry: . . . . .Great Britain	Navigation Officers: . . . . .German	Swimming Pools (indoors): 0
Length (ft/m): 665.3/202.8	Cabins (total): .633	Whirlpools: 5
Beam (ft/m): 92.2/28.1	Size Range (sq ft/m): 145.3–344.4/	Self-Service Launderette: . . . . .Yes
Draft (ft/m): 20.3/6.2	13.5–32.0	Dedicated Cinema/Seats: . . . . .No
Propulsion/Propellers: . . . . .diesel-electric	Cabins (outside view): 422	Library: . . . . .Yes
(27,150kW)/2	Cabins (interior/no view): 211	Classification Society: Germanischer Lloyd
Passenger Decks: 10	Cabins (for one person): 0	

OVERALL SCORE: 1,528 (OUT OF A POSSIBLE 2,000 POINTS)

OVERVIEW. This is a "Club Ship" (sister to *AIDAvita* and slightly larger sister to *AIDAcara*) and offers a sea-going version of Germany's popular Robinson Clubs. The ship has a contemporary profile, is well proportioned, and has a swept-back funnel and wedge-shaped stern. Its bows feature the red lips, as well as the blue eyes, of Aïda (from Verdi's opera, written to commemorate the opening of the Suez Canal in 1871). Aida Cruises is part of Seetours, which is part of P&O Princess Cruises, which is part of the giant Carnival Corporation.

There is a good amount of open deck and sunbathing space, including some rather nice, quiet space above the navigation bridge. There is an egg-shaped swimming pool, set in a "beach-like" environment with splash and play areas (larger and better than aboard *AIDAcara)*.

This fun ship includes a whole army of "animateurs" (like the *gentils ordinaires* of Club Med, but better) who lead a variety of activities by day (they also act as escorts for shore excursions), and as entertainers by night, alongside the professional entertainers. They (along with other staff) also interact with passengers throughout the ship, and can drink with them at the bars – something not permitted aboard most cruise ships, although this does tend to make them very casual and, at times, sloppy.

Inside, there is no wasted space, and the public rooms are open and flow into each other instead of being contained spaces. The "you are here" (deck plan) signs are excellent. The decor is really bright, upbeat and very trendy, and will appeal particularly to young (and young at heart) passengers, and to those who may not have considered cruising before.

BERLITZ'S RATINGS

	Possible	Achieved
Ship	500	414
Accommodation	200	148
Food	400	296
Service	400	289
Entertainment	100	71
Cruise	400	310

There is a wide array of intimate public rooms and spaces, with four decks of public rooms and facilities above the accommodation decks. The principal rooms include the Aida Bar, the main (but unofficial) social gathering place, with its star-shaped bar (whose combined length makes it perhaps the longest at sea, at 184.7 ft (56.3 meters), Hemingway Lounge (a cognac/cigar lounge), Anytime Lounge/Bar (the ship's disco/late-night spot, with wood-edged bar, granite dance floor, pounding music, and five video games tables set inside a "tunnel" that acts as an entrance). There are two "internet-connect" locations.

This certainly is a family-friendly ship. Children are split into two age groups – Seepferdchen (4–7 years) and Sharks (8–13 years) – and each group has its own dedicated play areas and fun facilities. There is a diverse selection of children's and youth programs in a holiday camp atmosphere. Children can also make their own menus for the week (together with the chef), and visit the galley to make cookies and other items – a novel idea that more ships could adopt.

In summer, *AIDAaura* sails in the Mediterranean, and in the winter, in the Caribbean. Alternating 7-night itineraries can be combined for a 14-day cruise. In addition, packages created by tour operators such as Seetours can add land stays for an even longer cruise and resort holiday experience.

The upbeat crew contains about 20 nationalities. This is a young, vibrant, and fun ship, with plenty of passenger participation. The brochure accurately describes the casual and active lifestyle (few passengers appear to be over 40).

All port taxes and gratuities are included, and, with extremely attractive rates, it is better value than almost any land-based vacation. The euro is the on-board currency.

Note that standing in line for embarkation, disembarkation, shore tenders and for self-serve buffet meals is an inevitable aspect of cruising aboard all large ships.

SUITABLE FOR: *AIDAAura* is best suited to young German-speaking couples, single travelers, and families with children seeking good value for money in a fun environment for a first cruise. The dress code is simple: "very casual" (no dinner jackets or ties) at all times.

ACCOMMODATION. There are seven grades: Suite (344.4 sq. ft/32 sq. meters, including balcony); A-outside-view (188.3 sq. ft/17.5 sq. meters) with balcony; A-outside-view (182.9 sq. ft/17 sq. meters) without balcony; B-outside-view (145.3 sq. ft/13.5 sq. meters); C-interior (no view: 156.0 sq. ft/14.5 sq. meters). All suites and cabins are designed for two persons; however, a total of 94 cabins (grades B and C) also have two extra beds/berths for children, and some cabins have interconnecting doors (useful for families).

The decor is bright, splashy, youthful, and slightly whimsical. All cabins are accented with multi-patterned fabrics, wood-trimmed cabinetry (with nicely rounded edges) and rattan furniture. The twin beds have duvets, and a colorful fabric canopy from headboard to ceiling. Windows have full pull-down blackout blinds. Some cabins in the center of the ship have views obstructed by lifeboats. All cabin bathrooms are compact, but well designed, feature showers, and wall-mounted soap/shampoo dispensers, but you should bring your own conditioner, hand lotion, and other personal toiletry items. Cotton bathrobes are provided. Although the bathrooms do not have a hairdryer, one is located in the vanity unit in the cabin.

Two large suites are located at the front of the ship, each with a private balcony. These offer much more space, including more drawer and storage space, better quality furniture and furnishings, as one would expect, a larger lounge area and a slightly larger bathroom with a bathtub.

CUISINE/DINING. There are two large self-serve buffet restaurants: "Calypso" and "Market", with a wide range of food (more than 1,200 items) available almost 24 hours a day. In addition, there is an la carte option, the "Maritime Restaurant", with waiter and sommelier service. The larger of the two self-serve buffet-style restaurants is the Calypso, one deck above the Market Restaurant. Aft of the funnel, the Calypso Terraces provide a casual dining alternative, complete with a large bar – and seating outdoors (as well as seating under a sailcloth canopied cover).

The standard of food at the self-serve buffet islands is good to very good, with creative presentation and good table-clearing service. The food islands and active stations cut down on the waiting time for food, as is common aboard most other cruise ships of a similar size. There is always a fine selection of breads, cheeses, cold cuts, fruits and make-your-own teas (with a choice of more than 30 types of loose-leaf regular and herbal teas), and coffee.

At peak times, the buffet restaurants may remind you of roadside cafes (albeit elegant ones), with all their attendant noise, but you can sit where you want, when you want, and with whom you want, so dining becomes a socially interactive occasion. Because of the large buffet rooms and self-serve dining concept, the crew to passenger ratio looks poor; but this is because there are no waiters as such (except in the à la carte restaurant), only staff for clearing tables.

The "Maritime Restaurant" (à la carte), with mostly high-back seats, has an intimate atmosphere. It is open for dinner only, and has a set five- or six-course menu (plus daily specials), changed every two or three days. There is no extra charge, except for special à la carte menu items (such as sevruga caviar, smoked salmon, châteaubriand, rib-eye steak), and for wines. Reservations for each evening are made at the reception desk the same morning.

ENTERTAINMENT. The Theater, the main venue for all shows and most cabaret, is two decks high. It has a raised stage, and amphitheater-style bench seating on both main and balcony levels. The benches have back rests, and are quite comfortable, and sight lines are good from most seats, with the exception of port and starboard balcony sections, where sight lines are interrupted by thick safety railings.

The shows are rather amateurish – although they are upbeat, fun, and entertaining (performed to recorded music). The whole entertainment experience is lively and fun – in fact, it's a little like going to the circus. There is a live band in the Aida Bar (which has a large dance floor), and an entertaining pianist in the Night Fly Bar.

SPA/FITNESS. The fitness and sports programming is among the most extensive in the cruise industry. An excellent wellness center, Body and Soul, is located forward on Deck 11. It measures 11,840 sq. ft (1,100 sq. meters), and contains two saunas (one dry, one wet, both with seats for more than 20 persons, and glass walls that look onto the deck), massage and other treatment rooms, and a large lounging area. There are also showers, and two whole "ice walls" to use when you come out of the saunas (simply lean into the ice wall for maximum effect). Forward and outside the wellness center, is an FKK (FreiKoerperKultur) nude sunbathing deck, on two levels. A beauty and hair salon is located just behind the balcony level of the showlounge.

Many types of massage and body pampering treatments are offered. Examples of prices: Swedish Massage, €69 for 50 minutes; Shiatsu Massage, €79 for 50 minutes; Hot Stone Massage, €119 for 90 minutes.

"Hit Bikes" (mountain bikes with tough front and rear suspension units) are provided for conducted biking excursions in each port of call, the concession of Austrian downhill champion skier Erwin Resch. There's a basketball/volleyball court and golf putting course. You can book biking, diving, and golfing excursions.

AIDA Blu
★★★ +

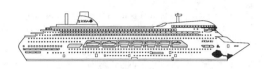

Large (Resort) Ship: ....70,285 tons	Total Crew: 677	Cabins (with private balcony): 192
Lifestyle: ....Standard	Passengers	Cabins (wheelchair accessible): 10
Cruise Line: ...A' Rosa Cruises (Seetours)	(lower beds/all berths): 1,664/1,910	Cabin Current: ....110 and 220 volts
Former Names: ....*Crown Princess*	Passenger Space Ratio	Elevators: 9
Builder: ....Fincantieri Navali (Italy)	(lower beds/all berths): 44.0/36.7	Casino (gaming tables): ....Yes
Original Cost: ....$276.8 million	Crew/Passenger Ratio	Slot Machines: ....Yes
Entered Service: ...July 1990/June 2002	(lower beds/all berths): 2.3/2.7	Swimming Pools (outdoors): 2
Registry: ....Great Britain	Navigation Officers: ....European	Swimming Pools (indoors): 0
Length (ft/m): 804.0/245.08	Cabins (total): 832	Whirlpools: 4
Beam (ft/m): 105.8/32.25	Size Range (sq ft/m): 188.3–538.2/	Self-Service Launderette: ....Yes
Draft (ft/m): 26.9/8.21	17.5–50.0	Dedicated Cinema/Seats: ....No
Propulsion/Propellers: .....diesel-electric	Cabins (outside view): 628	Library: ....Yes
(24,000kW)/2	Cabins (interior/no view): 197	Classification Society: ....RINA
Passenger Decks: 11	Cabins (for one person): 0	

OVERALL SCORE: 1,338 (OUT OF A POSSIBLE 2,000 POINTS)

OVERVIEW. For many years this ship was operated by Princess Cruises as *Crown Princess*. Originally ordered by Sitmar Cruises, the ship debuted in 1990 (although Princess Cruises purchased Sitmar Cruises in 1988). The ship was moved to the A'Rosa brand – marketed by Germany's Seetours – and began operations in 2002 under the ship's former name, the catchy but not so easy to pronounce *A'Rosa Blu*, operating cruises specifically for the German-speaking family market. In April 2004, the ship underwent a refit, its name was change to *AIDA Blu* and it was moved to the Aida Cruises brand.

Aida Cruises is part of Seetours, which is part of P&O Princess Cruises, which is itself now part of Carnival Corporation, the giant of the cruise industry.

The first thing you'll notice is the ship's catchy exterior markings on its bows – a pair of bright red lips holding – you guessed it – a huge, red rose. Perhaps the ship's more ideal name would have been *AIDA Red* instead of *AIDA Blu* (blue roses are, after all, extremely hard to find).

The ship has an interesting, jumbo-airplane look to it when viewed from the front, with a dolphin-like upper structure made of lightweight aluminum alloy to keep the weight down in line with stability requirements (it was designed by the renowned Italian architect Renzo Piano), and a large swept-back funnel (also made from aluminum alloy) placed aft. The new funnel design covers the original one, which looked more like a stark-upright garbage can.

The area that received most attention in the refurbishment was concentrated in what was formerly an observation dome/casino; set high atop the ship in the "dolphin head". The casino was downsized and relocated to a lower deck

BERLITZ'S RATINGS		
	Possible	Achieved
Ship	500	294
Accommodation	200	148
Food	400	270
Service	400	278
Entertainment	100	72
Cruise	400	276

(few passengers from the German-speaking countries like to gamble). The space has been turned into an extensive, two-deck spa/wellness center *(see below).*

The refit/refurbishment was aimed at providing the kinds of facilities that are in line with the tastes of young, active German-speaking families with children, and single travelers. The interior layout is rather disjointed, however, and does take a little getting used to. Some innovative and elegant styling of the period is mixed with traditional features and a reasonably spacious interior layout. An understated decor of soft pastel shades is highlighted by some very colorful artwork.

The atrium lobby is three decks high and is quite elegant, with a grand staircase and a fountain sculpture as its focal point, and provides a good setting for stand-up cocktail parties. Facilities include a library, an internet cafe, a business center, a bike station (mountain bikes are available for rent), and seven bars.

Cruises are designated not in 7-day Caribbean or Mediterranean terms, but by colorful descriptions such as BLU Cotton, BLU Coconut, BLU Mambo, BLU Salsa, BLU Viking, and so on (at least it's original, if a little confusing). At the end of the day, this ship should provide you with a pleasant cruise experience in surroundings that are at once elegant and comfortable, and the young, vibrant staff will make you feel welcome. However, it seems to be neither cruise ship nor Clubship, but something in between – caught in the twighlight zone that needs to identify itself.

Standing in line for embarkation, disembarkation, shore tenders and for the self-serve buffet meals in the Markt Restaurant is an inevitable aspect of cruising aboard this large ship. The vessel is a bit user-unfriendly in places:

for example, you have to carry a charge card *and* a cabin key, there is no decent forward observation viewpoint outdoors. There is no outdoors wrap-around promenade deck (the only walking space being along the port and starboard sides of the ship); in fact, there is very little contact with the outdoors at all, and the sunbathing space is also extremely limited when the ship is full. However, with destination-intensive itineraries, this may not pose so much of a problem, as most first-time passengers will want to be off exploring the ports of call.

Other niggly items include the fact that there are many support pillars throughout the public rooms that obstruct the sightlines and impede passenger flow.

SUITABLE FOR: *AIDA Blu* is best suited to young German-speaking couples, single travelers, and families with children seeking a good value for money first cruise in a casual, large ship setting, with appealing itineraries and destinations, and a range of fun-filled activities.

ACCOMMODATION. There are 10 price categories, including suites and junior suites (both with private balconies), outside view cabins and interior (no view) cabins, and special cabins for the disabled. Generally speaking, accommodation on the higher decks will cost more (location is everything). Occupants of accommodation designated as suites (there are 14 of them) and junior suites (there are 36) also have a private lounge in which to play.

In general, the cabins are well designed and have large bathrooms as well as good soundproofing. Walk-in closets, refrigerator, personal safe, color TV set and an interactive video system are provided in all cabins, as are chocolates on your pillow each night. Twin beds convert to queen-size beds in standard cabins. Bathrobes and personal toiletry amenities are provided. The outside-view cabins for the disabled have views that are obstructed by lifeboats, as do some other cabins on the same deck (Deck 8). Some cabins can accommodate a third and fourth person.

Suites/Junior Suites: The most expensive suites (there are 14) have a large private balcony, and are quite well laid out to a practical design that positions most things in just about the right place. The bedroom is separated from the living room by a heavy wooden door, and there are TVs in both rooms. The closet and drawer space is very generous, even for two back-to-back cruises.

CUISINE/DINING. There are several choices, from self-serve restaurants to full-service dining spots and casual eateries, so you'll need to plan your eating habits carefully. Some items are provided at extra cost.

Cleverly, Seetours has divided what was formerly the ship's principal restaurant into two separate dining spots: Markt (Market) Restaurant, and Bella Donna Restaurant (both restaurants have smoking and non-smoking sections). The Bella Donna Restaurant (this would not be my ideal

name for a restaurant, given that belladonna is a poisonous plant of the deadly nightshade family) is a full-service restaurant with traditional service; tables are for two or four persons, and à la carte items (some are at extra cost). The Markt (Market) Restaurant is a self-serve buffet-style eatery (table wine is provided), and is similar in style to the buffet restaurants aboard *AIDAaura*, *AIDAcara* and *AIDAvita*. There are few tables for two (most are for four, six or eight) however; the most desirable tables (seating six persons) are those that overlook the stern.

The wine list is average but adequate, with a heavy emphasis on Austrian and German wines. Note that 15% is added to all beverage bills, including wines.

Fine food lovers will probably head for Rossini, an elegant, 68-seat Italian restaurant, which features candlelit dining with excellent food (including regional specialties) and personal service. A cover charge of €18 per person applies, and reservations are necessary.

Other alternative dining spots include the Buena Vista Restaurant (featuring Mexican and South American cuisine), and a self-serve lido buffet called the California Grill (open 24 hours a day for hamburgers, hot dogs, steaks, pizza, and salad items). There's also an Asia Bistro (with wok preparation, and themed evening buffets such as Indonesian, Thai, and Vietnamese cuisines), as well as the Dolce Vita Eiscafe. Additionally, a sushi bar (all items are at extra cost) is part of the middle level of the three-deck-high lobby, located quite conveniently adjacent to the shops; the sushi is of the basic (pretend) commercial type – there's no Japanese sushi specialist here.

For sweet snacks during the day, try the Confiserie Leysieffer (pâtisserie), located in the ship's spacious lobby area between the reception desk and the internet center.

ENTERTAINMENT. The Theatre is the venue for the ship's main entertainment events. It spans two decks, with seating on both main and balcony levels (several support pillars obstruct sightlines from a number of seats). There is plenty of colorful entertainment, including a song and dance troupe, and cabaret acts.

SPA/FITNESS. The Spa is a very extensive wellness center that spans two decks, and measures almost 14,000 sq. ft (1,300 sq. meters); a staircase connects the two levels. Located at the top of the ship at the forward stairway, it occupies the space in the "dolphin head" section of the ship (the casino under the ship's former operators). Walking the treadmills or exercycling and facing out to sea feels like you're doing so in the upper deck of a Boeing 747, with its curved surfaces. Exercise classes include aerobics, tai chi, and kick-boxing. Some are free; others incur a charge. Body pampering treatments include various types of massage such as hot-stone massage (€89) and shiatsu massage (€57). There are other Asiatic touch treatments, plus a Turkish steam bath (Hammam). A manicure costs €23.

AIDAcara
★★★★

Mid-size Ship: . . . . .38,600 tons	Passenger Decks: 9	Cabins (for one person): 0
Lifestyle: . . . . .Standard	Total Crew: 370	Cabins (with private balcony): 4
Cruise Line: . . . . . .Aida Cruises (Seetours)	Passengers	Cabins (wheelchair accessible): 4
Former Names: . . . . .Aida	(lower beds/all berths): 1,186/1,230	Cabin Current: . . . . .110 and 220 volts
Builder: . . . . .Kvaerner Masa-Yards	Passenger Space Ratio	Elevators: 5
(Finland)	(lower beds/all berths): 32.5/31.3	Casino (gaming tables): . . . . .No
Original Cost: . . . . .DM300 million	Crew/Passenger Ratio	Slot Machines: .No
Entered Service: . . . . .June 1996	(lower beds/all berths): 3.2/3.3	Swimming Pools (outdoors): 1
Registry: . . . . .Great Britain	Navigation Officers: . . . . .German	Swimming Pools (indoors): 0
Length (ft/m): 634.1/193.3	Cabins (total): 593	Whirlpools: 3
Beam (ft/m): 90.5/27.6	Size Range (sq ft/m): 145.3–376.7/	Self-Service Launderette: . . . . .Yes
Draft (ft/m): 20.3/6.2	13.5–35.0	Dedicated Cinema/Seats: . . . . .No
Propulsion/Propellers: . . . . .diesel	Cabins (outside view): 391	Library: . . . . .Yes
(21,720kw)/2	Cabins (interior/no view): 202	Classification Society: Germanischer Lloyd

OVERALL SCORE: 1,517 (OUT OF A POSSIBLE 2,000 POINTS)

OVERVIEW. The ship (originally the *Aida*, the name was changed in 2001) has a contemporary profile, is well proportioned, and has a swept-back funnel and wedge-shaped stern. There is no mistaking the red lips painted on the bows, as well as the blue eyes of *Aïda* (from Verdi's opera, written to commemorate the opening of the Suez Canal in 1871).

AIDAcara is a "Club Ship," a seagoing version of Germany's popular Robinson Clubs. Aida Cruises is part of Seetours, which is part of P&O Princess Cruises, which is itself part of the giant Carnival Corporation.

This fun ship includes a whole army of "animateurs" (like the *gentils ordinaires* of Club Med, but better) who lead a variety of activities by day (they also act as escorts for shore excursions), and as entertainers by night, acting in the colorful, often funny, shows alongside the professional entertainers. They (and other staff) also interact with passengers throughout the ship, and can drink with them at the bars – something not permitted aboard most cruise ships.

There is a wrap-around promenade deck outdoors, good for strolling, or for sitting in a deck lounge chair and just taking in the sea air. Outside on deck, the swimming pool and surrounding area has several cascading levels at the forward end for deck chairs and sun lounging, plus a basketball court, although the pool itself is small.

Inside, there is no wasted space, and the public rooms are open and flow into each other instead of being contained spaces. The "you are here" (deck plan) signs are excellent, and finding your way round is a simple matter. The decor is upbeat and trendy, and will appeal to younger passengers, particularly those who may not have cruised before. A

BERLITZ'S RATINGS

	Possible	Achieved
Ship	500	412
Accommodation	200	147
Food	400	295
Service	400	287
Entertainment	100	71
Cruise	400	305

large observation lounge is set high atop the ship overlooking the bow. There is a wide array of intimate public rooms and spaces from which to choose.

Central to all social interactions is the Aida Lounge, with novel "lollipop stick" decorations on the bar counter. The bar, 162.4 ft (49.5 meters) long, is one of the longest aboard any cruise ship. The feel is youthful, colorful, unpretentious, casual, relaxed, and sporting. Another popular drinking place is the Lambada Bar, and there's also a late-night discotheque – the Arkona Club.

This is a family-friendly ship, with plenty of activities for younger family members (children are split into two age groups: Seepferdchen, from 4 to 7 years, and Sharks, from 8 to 13 years). Children can make their own menus for the week (together with the chef), and can go into the galley to make cookies and other items – a novel idea that more ships could adopt.

There are two alternating itineraries in the Mediterranean during the summer, and in the winter, two alternating itineraries in the Canary Islands. Alternating 7-night itineraries can be combined for a 14-day cruise. In addition, packages created by tour operators such as Seetours can add land stays for an even longer cruise and resort holiday experience. This presents a good amount of flexibility.

About 20 nationalities are represented among the crew, who are upbeat and cheerful. This is a young, vibrant, and fun ship, with plenty of passenger participation in all kinds of events. The brochure accurately describes the casual, active lifestyle (few passengers appear to be over 40).

All port taxes and gratuities are included, and, with very

reasonable cruise fares, it is almost cheaper than staying home, and better value than almost any land-based vacation. There is a charge for use of the washing machines and the dryers in the self-service launderette. The swimming pool is too small for the number of passengers carried – particularly during the hot winter (Caribbean) season. The euro is the currency used on board.

Standing in line for embarkation, disembarkation, shore tenders and for self-serve buffet meals is an inevitable aspect of cruising aboard all large ships.

SUITABLE FOR: *AIDACara* is best suited to young German-speaking couples, single travelers, and families seeking good value for money in a fun environment. The dress code is simple: "casual" (no dinner jackets or ties) at all times.

ACCOMMODATION. There are five grades: A-outside (182.9 sq. ft/17 sq. meters); B-outside (145.3 sq. ft/13.5 sq. meters); C-Interior (156 sq. ft/14.5 sq. meters); Junior Suite (269.1 sq. ft/25 sq. meters); and Suite (376.7 sq. ft/ 35 sq. meters). The decor is bright, splashy, youthful, and contemporary. All cabins are accented with multi-patterned fabrics, wood-trimmed cabinetry (with nicely rounded edges) and rattan furniture. The twin beds have duvets, and a fabric canopy from headboard to ceiling. Windows have full pull-down blackout blinds.

Grades A, B, and C have just a small amount of drawer space, but as you will not need many clothes, this is not really a drawback. Some cabins in grades A, B and C have one bed and a convertible daytime sofa bed. All cabin bathrooms are compact but well designed, have showers and wall-mounted soap/shampoo dispensers, so there is no wastage of throwaway plastic bottles (environmentally friendly). But you should bring your own conditioner, hand lotion, or any other personal toiletry items. Cotton bathrobes are provided. Although bathrooms do not have a hairdryer, one is located in the vanity unit in the cabin. There is no cabinet for personal toiletry items.

Four Suites have a forward-facing private balcony (all four share the same, ship-wide balcony, as there are no partitions for privacy) and more luxurious furnishings and fittings. Seating in the cabin lounge area is in contemporary rattan chairs. There is a wall unit that houses a television that can be turned for viewing from either lounge or bedroom, and a refrigerator. Suites and Junior Suites have generous closet, drawer and other storage space, a stocked mini-bar, and a VCR. Bathrooms have a full-size bathtub and hairdryer.

The cabins are cleaned and beds are made each morning, but not in the evening. For anyone allergic to natural fibers, down-filled duvets and pillows can be replaced with those made of synthetic materials.

CUISINE/DINING. There are two large self-service buffet restaurants: "Caribbean" and "Market" (open almost 24 hours a day) and Maritime Restaurant, an à la carte restaurant, with waiter and sommelier service. The standard of food offered at the serve-yourself buffet islands is good to very good, with creative presentation and good table-clearing service. There is no standing in long lines, as is common aboard most cruise ships. There is always a fine selection of breads, cheeses, cold cuts, fruits and make-your-own teas (with a choice of more than 30 types of loose-leaf regular and herbal teas, as well as coffee).

At peak times, the buffet restaurants may remind you of roadside cafes (albeit elegant ones), with all their attendant noise, but a good selection of foods is provided (more than 1,200 items). You can sit where you want, when you want, and with whom you want, so dining really becomes a socially interactive occasion. Because of the two large self-serve buffet rooms and dining concept, the crew to passenger ratio looks poor; but this is because there really are no waiters as such (except in the à la carte Maritime Restaurant), only staff for clearing tables.

The Maritime Restaurant, which has 74 mostly high-back seats, has an intimate dining atmosphere. Open for dinner only, it features a set five- or six-course menu that is changed every few days. There is no extra charge, except for additional à la carte menu items (such as sevruga caviar, smoked salmon, chateaubriand, rib-eye steak), and for wines. Reservations are made at the reception desk on the morning of the day you want to eat in the Maritime.

ENTERTAINMENT. The Theater is two decks high. It has a raised stage, and amphitheater-style bench seating on both main and balcony levels. The benches, lacking back rests, can be uncomfortable, but at least your posture will be preserved, as you will need to sit upright to see the shows.

The shows are rather amateurish – not as good as they were when the ship debuted, although they are lively and fun – in fact, it's a little like going to the circus

SPA/FITNESS. The fitness, wellness and sports programming is among the most extensive in the cruise industry. The "Wellness Center" is aft on Deck 10. It measures 11,840 sq. ft (1,100 sq. meters), and contains two saunas (one seats more than 20 persons and has glass ocean-view walls), massage and other treatment rooms, and a large lounging area. Forward and outside the wellness center, is an FKK (FreiKoerperKultur) nude sunbathing deck. In addition, there is a (1,312-ft (400-meter) jogging track.

Many types of massage and body pampering treatments are offered. Examples of prices: Swedish Massage, €69 for 50 minutes; Shiatsu Massage, €79 for 50 minutes; Hot Stone Massage, €119 for 90 minutes; Thalassotherapy Bath with Underwater Massage, €45 for 30 minutes.

As part of the "healthy holiday" programming, "Hit Bikes" (mountain bikes with tough front and rear suspension units) for conducted biking excursions in each port of call are provided (as "beginners" and "advanced" rides), the concept of Austrian Downhill Champion Skier Erwin Resch (operated as a concession)

AIDAvita
★★★★

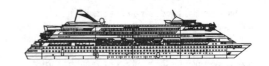

Mid-size Ship: . . . . .42,289 tons	Total Crew: .418	Cabins (with private balcony): 60
Lifestyle: . . . . .Standard	Passengers	Cabins (wheelchair accessible): 4
Cruise Line: . . . . .Aida Cruises	(lower beds/all berths): 1,266/1,582	Cabin Current: . . . . .220 volts
(Seetours)	Passenger Space Ratio	Elevators: 6
Former Names: . . . . .none	(lower beds/all berths): 33.4/26.7	Casino (gaming tables): . . . . .No
Builder: . . . . .Aker MTW (Germany)	Crew/Passenger Ratio	Slot Machines: .No
Original Cost: . . . .$350 million	(lower beds/all berths): 3.0/3.7	Swimming Pools (outdoors): 2
Entered Service: . . . . .Apr 2002	Navigation Officers: . . . . .German	Swimming Pools (indoors): 0
Registry: . . . . .Great Britain	Cabins (total): .633	Whirlpools: 5
Length (ft/m): 666.6/203.2	Size Range (sq ft/m): 145.3–344.4/	Self-Service Launderette: . . . . .Yes
Beam (ft/m): 92.2/28.1	13.5–32.0	Dedicated Cinema/Seats: . . . . .No
Draft (ft/m): 20.7/6.3	Cabins (outside view): 422	Library: . . . . .Yes
Propulsion/Propellers: . . .diesel-electric/2	Cabins (interior/no view): 211	Classification Society: . . . . .Germanischer
Passenger Decks: 10	Cabins (for one person): 0	Lloyd

OVERALL SCORE: 1,528 (OUT OF A POSSIBLE 2,000 POINTS)

OVERVIEW. This is a "Club Ship" (sister to *AIDAaura* and slightly larger sister to *AIDAcara*) and offers a sea-going version of Germany's popular Robinson Clubs. It has a contemporary profile, is well proportioned, and has a swept-back funnel and wedge-shaped stern. Its bows feature the red lips, as well as the blue eyes, of Aïda (from Verdi's opera, written to commemorate the opening of the Suez Canal in 1871). Aida Cruises is part of Seetours, which is part of P&O Princess Cruises, which is itself now part of the giant Carnival Corporation.

There is a good amount of open deck and sunbathing space, including some rather nice, quiet space above the navigation bridge. There is an egg-shaped swimming pool, set in a "beach-like" environment with splash and play areas (these facilities are larger and better than aboard *AIDAcara).

This fun ship includes a whole army of "animateurs" (like the *gentils ordinaires* of Club Med, but better) who lead a variety of activities by day (they also act as escorts for shore excursions), and as entertainers by night, acting in the colorful, often funny, shows alongside the professional entertainers. They (along with other staff) also interact with passengers throughout the ship, and can drink with them at the bars – something not permitted aboard most cruise ships.

Inside, there is no wasted space, and the public rooms are open and flow into each other instead of being contained spaces. The "you are here" (deck plan) signs are excellent, and finding your way round is a simple matter. The decor is really light, upbeat and trendy, and will appeal particularly to younger passengers, and those new to cruising. There is a wide array of intimate public spaces, with four decks of public rooms and facilities located above the accommoda-

BERLITZ'S RATINGS

	Possible	Achieved
Ship	500	414
Accommodation	200	148
Food	400	296
Service	400	289
Entertainment	100	71
Cruise	400	310

tion decks. The principal public rooms and facilities include the Aida Bar, the main (but unofficial) social gathering place, with its star-shaped bar (whose combined length makes it perhaps the longest at sea, at 184.7 ft/56.3 meters), Hemingway Lounge (a cognac/cigar lounge), Anytime Lounge/Bar (the ship's late-night spot). There are also two "internet connect" locations.

This is a family-friendly ship, with plenty of activities for all ages. Children are split into two age groups: Seepferdchen (4–7 years) and Sharks (8–13 years), and each group has its own dedicated play areas and fun facilities. There is a diverse selection of children's and youth programs in a holiday camp atmosphere. Children can also make their own menus for the week (together with the chef), and visit the galley to make cookies and other items – a novel idea that more ships could adopt.

In summer, *AIDAvita* sails itineraries in the Mediterranean, and in winter the Caribbean. Alternating 7-night itineraries can be combined for a 14-day cruise. Packages created by tour operators such as Seetours can add land stays for an even longer cruise and resort holiday experience.

About 20 nationalities are represented among the crew, who are upbeat and cheerful. This is a young, vibrant, and fun ship, with plenty of passenger participation in all kinds of events. The brochure accurately describes the casual, active lifestyle (few passengers appear to be over 40).

All port taxes and gratuities are included, and, with extremely attractive rates, it is better value than most land-based vacations. The euro is the currency used on board.

Standing in line for embarkation, disembarkation, shore tenders and for self-serve buffet meals is an inevitable aspect of cruising aboard all large ships.

SUITABLE FOR: *AIDAVita* is best suited to young German-speaking couples, single travelers, and families with children seeking good value for money in a fun environment for a first cruise. The dress code is simple: "very casual" (no dinner jackets or ties) at all times.

ACCOMMODATION. There are seven grades of accommodation: Suite (344.4 sq. ft/32 sq. meters, including balcony); A-outside-view (188.3 sq. ft/17.5 sq. meters) with balcony; A-outside-view (182.9 sq. ft/17 sq. meters) without balcony: B-outside-view (145.3 sq. ft/13.5 sq. meters); C-interior (no view: 156.0 sq. ft/14.5 sq. meters). All suites and cabins are designed for two persons; however, a total of 94 cabins (grades B and C) also have two extra beds/berths for children, and some cabins have interconnecting doors (useful for families with children).

The decor is bright, splashy, youthful, and slightly whimsical (lemon, avocado green, and blue are the predominant colors). All cabins are accented with multi-patterned fabrics, wood-trimmed cabinetry (with nicely rounded edges) and rattan furniture. The twin beds have duvets, and a colorful fabric canopy from headboard to ceiling. Windows have full pull-down blackout blinds. The views from some cabins in the center of the ship are obstructed by lifeboats. All cabin bathrooms are compact but well designed, have showers and wall-mounted soap/ shampoo dispensers, but you should bring your own conditioner, hand lotion, or other toiletry items. Cotton bathrobes are provided. Although the bathrooms do not have a hairdryer, there's one in the vanity unit in the cabin.

Two large suites, at the front of the ship, have private balconies. These cabins have much more space, including more drawer and storage space, better quality furniture and furnishings, as one would expect, a larger lounge area and a slightly larger bathroom with a bathtub.

CUISINE/DINING. Two large self-serve buffet restaurants, "Calypso" and "Market", have a wide range of food (more than 1,200 items) available almost 24 hours a day. The larger of the two, Calypso, is one deck above the Market Restaurant. Aft of the funnel, the Calypso Terraces provide a casual dining alternative, complete with a large bar – and seating outdoors (as well as seating under a sailcloth canopied cover). There's also an à la carte restaurant, the "Maritime Restaurant", with waiter and sommelier service.

The standard of food at the self-serve buffet islands is good to very good, with creative presentation and good table-clearing service. The food islands and active stations cut down on the waiting time for food, as is common aboard most cruise ships of a similar size. There is always a fine selection of breads, cheeses, cold cuts, fruits and make-your-own teas (with a choice of more than 30 types of loose-leaf regular and herbal teas, as well as coffee).

At peak times, the buffet restaurants may remind you of roadside cafes (albeit elegant ones), with all their attendant noise, but you can sit where you want, when you want, and with whom you want, so dining becomes a socially interactive occasion. Because of the large buffet rooms and self-serve dining concept, the crew to passenger ratio looks poor; but this is because there are no waiters as such (except in the à la carte restaurant), only staff for clearing tables.

The "Maritime Restaurant" (à la carte), with mostly high-back seats, has an intimate atmosphere. Open for dinner only, it has a set five- or six-course menu, changed every two or three days (plus daily specials). There is no extra charge, except for special à la carte menu items (such as sevruga caviar, smoked salmon, chateaubriand, rib-eye steak), and for wines. Reservations for the Maritime are made each morning at the reception desk.

ENTERTAINMENT. The Theater, the main venue for all shows and most cabaret acts, is two decks high. It has a raised stage, and amphitheater-style bench seating on both main and balcony levels. The benches do not have back rests, and can be uncomfortable, but at least your posture will be preserved, as you will need to sit upright to see the shows.

The shows are rather amateurish, although they are fun, and quite entertaining. The whole entertainment experience is lively – it's a little like going to the circus.

SPA/FITNESS. The fitness, wellness and sports programming is among the most extensive in the cruise industry. An excellent wellness center – called Body and Soul – is located forward on Deck 11. It measures approximately 11,840 sq. ft (1,100 sq. meters) and contains two saunas (one dry, one wet, both with seats for more than 20 persons, and glass walls that look onto the deck), several massage and other treatment rooms, and a large lounging area. There are also showers, and two whole "ice walls" to use when you come out of the saunas (simply lean into the ice wall for maximum effect).

Forward and outside the wellness center, is an FKK (FreiKoerperKultur) nude sunbathing deck, on two levels. A beauty and hair salon is located just behind the balcony level of the show lounge.

Many types of massage and body pampering treatments are offered. Examples of prices: Swedish Massage, €69 for 50 minutes; Shiatsu Massage, €79 for 50 minutes; Hot Stone Massage, €119 for 90 minutes; Thalassotherapy Bath with Underwater Massage, €45 for 30 minutes.

As part of the "healthy holiday" programming, "Hit Bikes" (mountain bikes with tough front and rear suspension units) for conducted biking excursions in each port of call are provided (as "beginners" and "advanced" rides), the concept and concession of Austrian downhill champion skier Erwin Resch. Sports facilities include a basketball/volleyball court, golf putting course, and you can book biking, diving, and golfing excursions.

Akademik Sergey Vavilov ★★

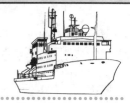

Small Ship:	.................6,231 tons	Total Crew:	45	Cabins (wheelchair accessible):	0
Lifestyle:	....................Standard	Passengers		Cabin Current:	...........110/220 Volts
Cruise Line:	............Poseidon Arctic	(lower beds/all berths):	...........80/80	Elevators:	0
	Expeditions	Passenger Space Ratio		Casino (gaming tables):	.............No
Former Names:	..................none	(lower beds/all berths):	........77.8/77.8	Slot Machines:	......................No
Builder:	.............Hollming (Finland)	Crew/Passenger Ratio		Swimming Pools (outdoors):	1
Original Cost:	......................n/a	(lower beds/all berths):	..........1.7/1.7	Swimming Pools (indoors):	0
Entered Service:	1988	Navigation Officers:	............Russian	Whirlpools:	0
Registry:	.....................Russia	Cabins (total):	40	Self-Service Launderette:	...........No
Length (ft/m):	.............386.4/117.8	Size Range (sq ft/m):	...............n/a	Dedicated Cinema/Seats:	...........No
Beam (ft/m):	.................59.7/18.1	Cabins (outside view):	38	Library:	..........................Yes
Draft (ft/m):	...................19.3/5.9	Cabins (interior/no view):	0	Classification Society:	.........Russian
Propulsion/Propellers:	..........diesel/2	Cabins (for one person):	0		Shipping Register
Passenger Decks:	4	Cabins (with private balcony):	0		

OVERALL SCORE: 942 (OUT OF A POSSIBLE 2,000 POINTS)

OVERVIEW. This vessel was originally specially constructed for the former Soviet Union's polar and oceanographic research program and should not be taken as a cruise ship, although it was converted in the early 1990s to carry passengers, and then refurbished in 1996 and fitted out specifically for expedition cruising. This is the sister ship to *Akademik Ioffe*. Although the ship was, for years, chartered by specialist operators such as Quark Expeditions, it is now operated by Russia's own Poseidon Arctic Expeditions, in conjunction with the owners of the vessel, the P.P. Shirsov Institute of Oceanology.

The vessel has an ice-hardened steel hull, which makes the vessel ideally suited to cruising in both the Arctic and Antarctic regions. There is an open bridge policy, so all passengers have access to the navigation bridge. There are several Zodiac landing craft for close-in shore excursions and nature observation trips. The ship has a seawater swimming pool outdoors, but it is really small – nothing more than a "dip" pool.

Inside, the limited public rooms consist simply of a library and lounge/bar. The dining rooms also serve as a lecture room. This ship does have good medical facilities.

This is expedition style cruising, in a very small ship with limited facilities and the most basic product delivery. But it provides a somewhat primitive, but genuine adventure experience, taking you to places others can only dream about. Bigger ships can't get this close to Antarctica; this little vessel will get you close to the ice. The food is extremely basic, as is the service, as well as the ship's interior decor.

BERLITZ'S RATINGS

	Possible	Achieved
Ship	500	218
Accommodation	200	83
Food	400	194
Service	400	191
Entertainment	N/A	N/A
Cruise	500	256

SUITABLE FOR: *Akademik Sergey Vavilov* is best suited to adventurous, hardy outdoors couples and single travelers who enjoy being with nature and wildlife in one of the most interesting regions on earth, and for whom the ship is secondary – to act purely as a means of transportation and accommodation.

ACCOMMODATION. This is arranged over three decks. Except for a single "suite," quite large for the size of the ship, almost all other cabins are extremely small (dimensionally challenged, you might say), very utilitarian, and clinical, although all have a small desk and a reasonable amount of closet space. There are two-berth cabins with shower and toilet, or there are two-bed cabins on the lowest deck, whose occupants must share an adjacent bathroom and toilet.

CUISINE/DINING. There are two dining rooms (the galley is located between them), and all passengers are accommodated in a single seating. The meals are hearty international fare, with no frills. When under charter to various specialist operators, Western chefs oversee the food operation, which is basic and uninspiring.

ENTERTAINMENT. There is no formal entertainment, although dinner and after-dinner conversation with fellow passengers in the ship's lounge/bar really becomes the entertainment each evening. Otherwise, take a good book.

SPA/FITNESS. These facilities are minimal, due to the fact that this is an expedition cruise vessel.

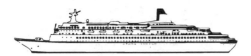

Albatros
★★★ +

Mid-Size Ship:	.28,078 tons	Passenger Decks:	.8	Cabins (for one person):	.0
Lifestyle:	.Standard	Total Crew:	.340	Cabins (with private balcony):	.9
Cruise Line:	.Phoenix Seereisen	Passengers		Cabins (wheelchair accessible):	.0
Former Names:	.Crown, Norwegian	(lower beds/all berths):	.874/1,000	Cabin Current:	.110 and 220 volts
	Star I, Royal Odyssey, Royal Viking Sea	Passenger Space Ratio		Elevators:	.5
Builder:	.Wartsila (Finland)	(lower beds/all berths):	.35.0/24.4	Casino (gaming tables):	.Yes
Original Cost:	.$22.5 million	Crew/Passenger Ratio		Slot Machines:	.Yes
Entered Service:	.Nov 1973/Apr 2004	(lower beds/all berths):	.2.6/2.9	Swimming Pools (outdoors):	.1
Registry:	.The Bahamas	Navigation Officers:	.European	Swimming Pools (indoors):	.0
Length (ft/m):	.674.2/205.50	Cabins (total):	.347	Whirlpools:	.3
Beam (ft/m):	.82.0/25.00	Size Range (sq ft/m):	.123.7– 679.2/	Self-Service Launderette:	.No
Draft (ft/m):	.23.9/7.30		11.8–63.1	Dedicated Cinema/Seats:	.Yes/156
Propulsion/Propellers:	.diesel	Cabins (outside view):	.380	Library:	.Yes
	(13,400 kW)/2	Cabins (interior/no view):	.57	Classification Society:	.Det Norske Veritas

OVERALL SCORE: 1,367 (OUT OF A POSSIBLE 2,000 POINTS)

OVERVIEW. *Albatros* was built for long-distance cruising for the long-defunct Royal Viking Line and is now under long-term charter to Germany's Phoenix Seereisen. It was refurbished in 2004 prior to replacing Phoenix Seereisen's much loved but outdated *Albatros*. There is plenty of open deck and sunbathing space, although the popular aft swimming pool can become crowded.

The ship has a wide array of public rooms, including many lounges and bars, most of which are quite elegant and have high, indented ceilings. The Observation Lounge is a particularly pleasant place. Wide stairways and foyers give a sense of space, even when the ship is full.

Phoenix Seereisen offers extensive destination-intensive itineraries, and friendly staff help with shore excursions and general cruise operations. There is a very informal atmosphere aboard, and a relaxed, casual dress code.

Albatros performs well in most sea conditions, and the onboard product is very good value for money. Where passengers are required to fly to join their cruises, the airline most used by Phoenix Seereisen is LTU. The onboard currency is the euro. A 7% gratuity is added to bar accounts.

SUITABLE FOR: *Albatros* is best suited to older German-speaking adults and families who seek a low-budget value-for-money vacation in fairly contemporary surroundings rather than in a brand new cruise ship.

ACCOMMODATION. There are more than 20 price grades, from expansive suites with private balcony to standard outside-view cabins and small interior (no view) cabins. A Captain's Suite is located at the front, directly under the navigation

BERLITZ'S RATINGS

	Possible	Achieved
Ship	500	367
Accommodation	200	140
Food	400	243
Service	400	265
Entertainment	100	62
Cruise	400	290

bridge, with fine forward-facing views. Nine other Penthouse Suites have a private balcony (with separate bedroom and living area). Most other cabins have an outside view and are quite well appointed, and there is a good amount of storage space; however, some bathrooms in the lower categories have awkward access. All cabins have a TV, bathrobe, and personal safe. Occupants of eight (mostly suite) accommodation grades receive Phoenix VIP service.

CUISINE/DINING. Two dining rooms (Mowe and Pelikan) have high ceilings, and are quite spacious. Dining is in one seating, at assigned tables for two, four, six or eight. Breakfast and luncheon can be taken in the dining room or outdoors in a self-service buffet by the swimming pool. Mid-morning bouillon is a Phoenix seagoing tradition, as is a Captain's Dinner (formal night), and Buffet Magnifique.

The service is friendly and attentive (the mainly Filipino waiters speak a limited amount of German), although there is little finesse in their service style. Table wines are included for lunch and dinner, although the quality is not good. Slightly better quality wines can be purchased.

The food itself best described as "down home" simple. Casual eateries include a pizzeria at the (aft) pool bar.

ENTERTAINMENT. The large Pacific Lounge seats about 500, but thick pillars obstruct some sightlines. The entertainment consists of small-scale production shows presented by a small team of resident singers/dancers, and cabaret acts.

SPA/FITNESS. There's a gymnasium and sauna (but no steam room), body treatment rooms, and a beauty salon.

American Eagle
★★

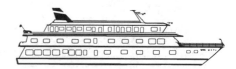

Small Ship: ....1,480 tons	Total Crew: 22	Cabins (with private balcony): 6
Lifestyle: ....Standard	Passengers	Cabins (wheelchair accessible): 2
Cruise Line: ......American Cruise Lines	(lower beds/all berths): 49/49	Cabin Current: ....110 volts
Former Names: ....none	Passenger Space Ratio	Elevators: 1
Builder: ....Chesapeake Shipbuilding	(lower beds/all berths): 30.2/30.2	Casino (gaming tables): ....No
(USA)	Crew/Passenger Ratio	Slot Machines: ....No
Original Cost: ....n/a	(lower beds/all berths): 2.2/2.2	Swimming Pools (outdoors): 0
Entered Service: ....Apr 2000	Navigation Officers: ....American	Swimming Pools (indoors): 0
Registry: ....USA	Cabins (total): 27	Whirlpools: 0
Length (ft/m): 174.0/53.00	Size Range (sq ft/m): 176.0–382.0/	Self-Service Launderette: ....No
Beam (ft/m): 40.5/12.30	16.3–35.4	Dedicated Cinema/Seats: ....No
Draft (ft/m): 6.5/1.98	Cabins (outside view): 27	Library: ....No
Propulsion/Propellers: diesel/2	Cabins (interior/no view): 0	Classification Society: ..American Bureau
Passenger Decks: 4	Cabins (for one person): 5	of Shipping

OVERALL SCORE: 827 (OUT OF A POSSIBLE 2,000 POINTS)

OVERVIEW. American Cruise Lines is the resurrection of a company with the same name that existed between 1974 and 1989. It now features intra-coastal waterway cruising, as well as sailings in New England and the Hudson River Valley. *American Eagle* was built specifically for coastal cruising and cannot venture far into open seas away from the coastline (a sister vessel is planned, with more balcony cabins). The ship's uppermost deck is open (good for scenery observation), and there are tables and chairs, a few deck lounge chairs, and a small putting green.

There are just two public lounges. The larger – the observation lounge – is located forward, with windows on three sides (an open bar is set up each afternoon). This is the main meeting place for passengers. A second, smaller lounge is sandwiched between cabins on the same deck.

The whole point of a cruise aboard this ship is to get close to the inland areas, cities and town of America's intra-coastal waterways and coastline. There's no waiting in line – you can board whenever you want. The ship docks in the center, or within walking distance of most towns on the itineraries. The dress code is "no ties casual".

It really is *extremely* expensive for what you get, compared even to those ships of a similar size and purpose (although this is a new ship and the cabins are of a better size and are slightly better equipped). There is an elevator, but it doesn't go to the uppermost deck (Sun Deck). The limited choice of food is very disappointing.

SUITABLE FOR: *American Eagle* is best suited to couples and single travelers sharing a cabin who are of mature years and want to cruise in an all-American environment aboard

BERLITZ'S RATINGS

	Possible	Achieved
Ship	500	249
Accommodation	200	110
Food	400	196
Service	400	170
Entertainment	100	10
Cruise	400	92

a small ship where the itineraries and destinations are more important than food, service or entertainment.

ACCOMMODATION. There are cabins for couples and singles, six suites, and two wheelchair-accessible cabins. All cabins have twin beds, color TV, a small desk with chair, and clothes hanging space. The six suites also have a VCR and compact disc (audio) player. All cabins have a private bathroom with separate shower enclosure, washbasin and toilet (none of the cabins has a bathtub), as well as windows that open.

CUISINE/DINING. The dining salon has large, panoramic picture windows on three of its sides. It has open seating (no assigned tables). There are no tables for two, and the chairs do not have armrests. The cuisine is very much American fare – good and wholesome, featuring regional cuisines, and presented and served in a basic, unfussy manner. Note that there is little choice of entrées, appetizers, or soups, although it has been improved in the past year. There is no wine list, although basic white and red low-quality American table wines are included in the cruise fare. On the last morning of each cruise, only continental breakfast is available.

ENTERTAINMENT. There is no formal entertainment, although dinner and after-dinner conversation with fellow passengers in the ship's lounge/bar really becomes the entertainment each evening.

SPA/FITNESS. There are no health spa facilities. Also, there are no medical facilities (but then the vessel is always close to land).

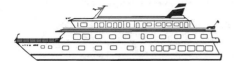

American Glory
★★

Small Ship: ....1,480 tons	Total Crew: 22	Cabins (with private balcony): 14
Lifestyle: ....Standard	Passengers	Cabins (wheelchair accessible): 3
Cruise Line: ......American Cruise Lines	(lower beds/all berths): 49/49	Cabin Current: ....110 volts
Former Names: ....none	Passenger Space Ratio	Elevators: 1
Builder: ....Chesapeake Shipbuilding	(lower beds/all berths): 30.2/30.2	Casino (gaming tables): ....No
(USA)	Crew/Passenger Ratio	Slot Machines: ....No
Original Cost: ....n/a	(lower beds/all berths): 2.2/2.2	Swimming Pools (outdoors): 0
Entered Service: ....July 2002	Navigation Officers: ....American	Swimming Pools (indoors): 0
Registry: ....USA	Cabins (total): 27	Whirlpools: 0
Length (ft/m): 174.0/53.00	Size Range (sq ft/m): 176.0–382.0/	Self-Service Launderette: ....No
Beam (ft/m): 40.5/12.30	16.3–35.4	Dedicated Cinema/Seats: ....No
Draft (ft/m): 6.5/1.98	Cabins (outside view): 27	Library: ....No
Propulsion/Propellers: diesel/2	Cabins (interior/no view): 0	Classification Society: . .American Bureau
Passenger Decks: 4	Cabins (for one person): 5	of Shipping

OVERALL SCORE: 835 (OUT OF A POSSIBLE 2,000 POINTS)

OVERVIEW. American Cruise Lines is the resurrection of a company with the same name that existed between 1974 and 1989. It now features intra-coastal waterway cruising, as well as sailings in New England and the Hudson River Valley. *American Glory* was built specifically for coastal cruising and cannot venture far from the coastline. The ship's uppermost deck is open (good for views), and there are tables and chairs, a few deck lounge chairs, and a small putting green.

There are two public lounges. The main one – the observation lounge – is located forward, with windows on three sides (an open bar is set up each afternoon). A second, smaller lounge is sandwiched between cabins on the same deck.

The point is to get close to the inland areas, cities and town of America's intra-coastal waterways and coastline. There's no waiting in line – you can board whenever you want. The ship docks in the center, or within walking distance of most towns on the itineraries. The dress code is "no ties casual". The score is marginally better than for sister ship *American Eagle* due to some improvements in construction and the addition of more balcony cabins.

It really is *extremely* expensive for what you get, compared even to ships of a similar size and purpose (although this is a new ship and the cabins are of a better size and are slightly better equipped). There is an elevator, but it does not go to the uppermost deck (Sun Deck). The limited choice of food is very disappointing.

SUITABLE FOR: *American Glory* is best suited to couples and single travelers sharing a cabin who are of mature years and want to cruise in an all-American environment aboard

BERLITZ'S RATINGS

	Possible	Achieved
Ship	500	257
Accommodation	200	110
Food	400	196
Service	400	170
Entertainment	100	10
Cruise	400	92

a small ship where the itineraries and destinations are more important than food, service or entertainment.

ACCOMMODATION. There are cabins for couples and singles, seven suites, and five wheelchair-accessible cabins. All cabins have twin beds, color TV, a small desk with chair, and clothes hanging space. The seven most expensive cabins also have a VCR and compact disc (audio) player. All cabins have a private bathroom with separate shower enclosure, washbasin and toilet (none of the cabins has a bathtub), as well as windows that open. Accommodation designated as suites also have a private balcony, although this is very narrow.

CUISINE/DINING. The dining salon, located in the latter third of the vessel, has large, panoramic picture windows on three of its sides. There's open seating (no assigned tables). There are no tables for two, and the chairs do not have armrests The food is very much American fare – good and wholesome, featuring regional cuisines. There is little choice of entrées, appetizers, or soups, although it has been improved in the past year. There is no wine list, although basic white and red low-quality American table wines are included. On the last morning of each cruise, only continental breakfast is available.

ENTERTAINMENT. There is no formal entertainment, although dinner and after-dinner conversation with fellow passengers in the ship's lounge/bar really becomes the entertainment each evening. Otherwise, take a good book.

SPA/FITNESS. There are no health spa facilities, and no medical facilities (the ship is almost always close to land).

American Spirit
NOT YET RATED

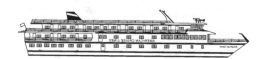

Boutique Ship: . . . . .99 tons
Lifestyle: . . . . .Standard
Cruise Line: . . . . . .American Cruise Lines
Former Names: . . . . .None
Builder: . . . . .Chesapeake Shipyard
(USA)
Original Cost: . . . . .n/a
Entered Service: . . . . .June 2005
Registry: . . . . .USA
Length (ft/m): 220.0/67.0
Beam (ft/m): 46.0/14.0
Draft (ft/m): 8.2/2.5
Propulsion/Propellers: diesel/2
Passenger Decks: 4

Total Crew: 27
Passengers
(lower beds/all berths): 92/92
Passenger Space Ratio
(lower beds/all berths): 1.0/1.0
Crew/Passenger Ratio
(lower beds/all berths): 3.4/3.4
Navigation Officers: . . . . .American
Cabins (total): 51
Size Range (sq ft/m): 204.0-240.0/
18.9-22.2
Cabins (outside view): 51
Cabins (interior/no view): 0
Cabins (for one person): 5

Cabins (with private balcony): 23
Cabins (wheelchair accessible): 1
Cabin Current: . . . . .110 volts
Elevators: 1
Casino (gaming tables): . . . . .No
Slot Machines: . . . . .No
Swimming Pools (outdoors): 0
Swimming Pools (indoors): 0
Whirlpools: 0
Self-Service Launderette: . . . . .No
Dedicated Cinema/Seats: . . . . .No
Library: . . . . .Yes
Classification Society: . .American Bureau
of shipping

OVERALL SCORE: NYR (OUT OF A POSSIBLE 2,000 POINTS)

OVERVIEW. *American Spirit* is the third vessel in the growing fleet of American Cruise Lines (which builds the vessels in its shipyard in Chesapeake, Maryland). It is the resurrection of a company with the same name that existed between 1974 and 1989. The company features intra-coastal waterway cruising, as well as sailings in New England and the Hudson River Valley. *American Spirit* is built specifically for coastal cruising and cannot venture far from the coastline. Its uppermost deck is open (good for views) behind the forward windbreaker, and the expansive open deck sports many deck lounge chairs, and a small putting green.

Inside, the public rooms include an observation lounge, with views forward and to port and starboard side (complimentary cocktails and hors d'oeuvres are offered before dinner); a library/lounge; and a small midships lounge.

Cruises are typically of seven days' duration. There's no waiting in line – you can board whenever you want. The ship docks in the center, or within walking distance of most towns on the itineraries. The dress code is "no ties casual". It really is extremely expensive for what you get (although this is a new ship and the cabins are of a better size and are slightly better equipped than those of smaller half-sisters *American Eagle* and *American Glory*).

SUITABLE FOR: *American Spirit* is best suited to couples and single travelers sharing a cabin who are of mature years and want to cruise in an all-American environment aboard a small ship where the itineraries and destinations are more important than food, service or entertainment.

ACCOMMODATION. There are five cabin price grades (four

BERLITZ'S RATINGS		
	Possible	Achieved
Ship	500	NYR
Accommodation	200	NYR
Food	400	NYR
Service	400	NYR
Entertainment	100	NYR
Cruise	400	NYR

are doubles, one is for singles). All cabins have twin beds, a small desk with chair, color television, and clothes hanging space. The seven most expensive cabins also have a DVD and CD player. All cabins have a private (modular) bathroom with separate shower enclosure, washbasin and toilet (none of the cabins has a bathtub), as well as windows that open, and satellite-feed TV sets. Accommodation designated as suites also have a private balcony, although this is very narrow. Some 23 cabins feature a French balcony (this means you can open the door and get fresh air, but it's too narrow to place chairs on).

CUISINE/DINING. The dining salon, in the latter third of the vessel, has large, panoramic picture windows on three of its sides. There's open seating (no assigned tables) and all passengers dine at a single seating, at large tables, allowing you to get to know your fellow passengers. The food is very much American fare – good and wholesome, featuring regional cuisines. There is a limited choice of entrées, appetizers, and soups. There is no wine list, although basic white and red low-quality American table wines are included. On the last morning of each cruise, only continental breakfast is available.

ENTERTAINMENT. There is no formal entertainment, although dinner and after-dinner conversation with fellow passengers in the ship's lounge/bar really becomes the entertainment each evening. Otherwise, take a good book.

SPA/FITNESS. There is a small fitness room with a few bicycles and other exercise machines.

Amsterdam
★★★★

Large (Resort) Ship:	........61,000 tons	Total Crew:	600	Cabins (wheelchair accessible):	20
Lifestyle:	....................Premium	Passengers		Cabin Current:	........110 and 220 volts
Cruise Line:	.......Holland America Line	(lower beds/all berths):	.....1,380/1,653	Elevators:	12
Former Names:	.................none	Passenger Space Ratio		Casino (gaming tables):	............Yes
Builder:	.............Fincantieri (Italy)	(lower beds/all berths):	........44.2/36.9	Slot Machines:	....................Yes
Original Cost:	............$400 million	Crew/Passenger		Swimming Pools (outdoors):	1
Entered Service:	.............Oct 2000	Ratio (lower beds/all berths):	.....2.3/2.7	Swimming Pools (indoors):	1
Registry:	.............The Netherlands	Navigation Officers:	.............Dutch		(magrodome cover)
Length (ft/m):	............780.8/238.00	Cabins (total):	690	Whirlpools:	2
Beam (ft/m):	..............105.8/32.25	Size Range (sq ft/m):	.....184.0–1,124.8/	Self-Service Launderette:	...........Yes
Draft (ft/m):	................25.5/7.80		17.1–104.5	Dedicated Cinema/Seats:	.......Yes/235
Propulsion/Propellers:	.....diesel-electric	Cabins (outside view):	557	Library:	...........................Yes
	(37,500 kW)/2 azimuthing pods	Cabins (interior/no view):	133	Classification Society:	...Lloyd's Register
	(15.5 MW each)	Cabins (for one person):	0		
Passenger Decks:	12	Cabins (with private balcony):	172		

OVERALL SCORE: 1,542 (OUT OF A POSSIBLE 2,000 POINTS)

OVERVIEW. *Amsterdam* is a close sister ship to *Rotterdam*, and has a nicely raked bow, as well as the familiar interior flow and design style. It was the first ship in the Holland America Line fleet to feature an azimuthing pod propulsion system *(see page 151 for details)*. The pods are powered by a diesel-electric system.

The decor retains much of the traditional ocean liner detailing so loved by frequent Holland America Line passengers, with some use of medium and dark wood panelling. However, some color combinations – particularly for the chairs and soft furnishings – are rather wacky. Much of the artwork reflects Holland America Line's glorious past, as well as items depicting the city of Amsterdam's history.

The interior focal point is a three-deck high atrium, in an oval, instead of circular, shape. A whimsical "Astrolobe" is the featured centerpiece in this atrium. Also clustered in the atrium lobby are the reception desk, shore excursion desk, photo shop and photo gallery.

The ship has three principal passenger stairways – so much better than two from the viewpoint of safety, flow and accessibility. There is a magrodome-covered pool on the Lido Deck between the mast and the twin funnels, watched over by a sculpture of a brown bear catching salmon.

There are children's and teens' play areas (token gestures by a company that traditionally does not cater well to children). Popcorn is available at the Wajang Theater for moviegoers, while adjacent is the popular Java Cafe. The casino, in the middle of a major passenger flow on one of the entertainment decks, has blackjack, roulette, poker and dice tables alongside the requisite rows of slot machines.

BERLITZ'S RATINGS

	Possible	Achieved
Ship	500	430
Accommodation	200	165
Food	400	281
Service	400	272
Entertainment	100	78
Cruise	400	316

Amsterdam is an extremely comfortable ship, with some fine, elegant and luxurious decorative features. However, these are marred by the poor quality of food and service and the lack of understanding of what it takes to make a "luxury" cruise experience, despite what is touted in the company's brochures.

Holland America Line also provides cappuccino and espresso coffees and free ice cream during certain hours of the day aboard its ships, as well as hot hors d'oeuvres in all bars – something other major lines seem to have dropped, or charge extra for.

The onboard currency is the US dollar. Perhaps the ship's best asset is its friendly and personable Filipino and Indonesian crew, although communication can prove frustrating at times.

With one whole deck of suites (and a dedicated, private concierge lounge, with preferential passenger treatment), the company has in effect created a two-class ship. The charge to use the washing machines and dryers in the self-service launderette is petty and irritating, particularly for the occupants of high-priced cabins. Communication (in English) with many of the staff, particularly in the dining room and informal buffet areas, can prove frustrating. The room service menu is limited, and room service is very basic.

SUITABLE FOR: *Amsterdam* is best suited to older adult couples and singles (and their grandchildren), who like to mingle in a large ship, in an unhurried setting with fine quality surroundings, with plenty of eclectic antique artwork, decent (though not gourmet) food and service from a willing Indonesian and Filipino crew that lacks finesse.

ACCOMMODATION. This is spread over five decks (some cabins have full or partially obstructed views), and is in 16 grades: 11 with outside views, and 5 interior grades (no view). There are four penthouse suites, and 50 suites (14 more than aboard sister ship *Rotterdam*). No cabin is more than 130 feet (40 meters) from a stairway, which makes it very easy to find your way from your cabin to the public rooms. Although 81% of cabins have outside views, only 25% of those have balconies.

All of the "standard" interior and outside-view cabins are tastefully furnished, and have twin beds that convert to a queen-sized bed (but the space is a little tight for walking between beds and the vanity unit). There is a decent amount of closet and drawer space, although this will prove tight for longer voyages. The fully tiled bathrooms are disappointingly small (particularly on long cruises), the shower tubs are very small, and the storage for one's personal toiletries is quite basic. There is little detailing to distinguish the bathrooms from those aboard the *Statendam*-class ships. All cabin televisions carry CNN and TNT, as well as movies, and ship information and shopping channels.

There are 50 Verandah Suites and four Penthouse Suites on Navigation Deck. The suites all share a private Concierge Lounge with a concierge to handle such things as special dining arrangements, shore excursions and special requests, although strangely there are no butlers for these suites, as aboard ships with similar facilities. The lounge, with its wood detailing and private library is accessible only by private key-card.

Four Penthouse Suites are extremely civilized. Each has a separate steward's entrance, as well as a separate bedroom with king-sized bed, vanity desk, large walk-in closet with excellent drawer and hanging space, living room, dining room (seating up to eight), wet bar, and pantry. The bathroom is large, and has a big oval Jacuzzi bathtub, separate shower enclosure, two washbasins, separate toilet and bidet. There is also a guest bathroom with toilet and washbasin. There is a good-sized private balcony. Suite occupants get personal stationary, complimentary laundry and ironing, cocktail-hour hors d'oeuvres and other goodies, as well as priority embarkation and disembarkation.

CUISINE/DINING. The La Fontaine Dining Room seats 747, spans two decks, and has a huge stained-glass ceiling measuring almost 1,500 sq. ft (140 sq. meters), with a floral motif and fibre-optic lighting. There are tables for two, four, six or eight (there are few tables for two). Open seating is featured for breakfast and lunch, with a choice of four seatings for dinner – you must pre-select a time and stick with it – at 5.45pm, 6:15pm, 8pm and 8.30pm; there are smoking and no-smoking sections. Rosenthal china and fine cutlery are provided (although there are no fish knives).

Alternative (Reservations Required) Dining Spot
The 88-seat Odyssey Restaurant is available to all passengers on a reservation-only basis (priority reservations are given to those in suite grades). There is no extra charge for dining in the Odyssey Restaurant, which has better food and presentation than in the main dining room (it's open for lunch and dinner). The whimsically surreal artwork features scenic landscapes. The cuisine is decidedly California-Italian in style, with small portions and few vegetables.

Another alternative, the Lido Buffet Restaurant, is open for casual dinners on all except the last night of each cruise, in an open-seating arrangement. Tables are set with crisp linens, flatware and stemware. A set menu is featured, and this includes a choice of four entrées.

For casual breakfasts and lunches, the Lido Buffet Restaurant provides old-style, stand-in-line serve-yourself canteen food – adequate for anyone used to TV dinner food, but most definitely not as lavish as the brochures claim. Although the salad items appear adequate when displayed, they are too cold and quite devoid of taste. The constant supply of iceberg lettuce doesn't seem to go away (but there is little choice of other, more suitable, lettuces and greens).

ENTERTAINMENT. The 577-seat Queen's Lounge is the venue for all production shows, strong cabaret, and other entertainment. It is two decks high (with main and balcony level seating). The stage has hydraulic lifts and three video screens, and closed-loop system for the hearing-impaired.

While Holland America Line is not known for its fine entertainment (the budgets aren't high enough), what the line does offer is a consistently good, tried and tested array of cabaret acts. The production shows, while a good attempt, fall short on storyline, choreography and performance, with colorful costuming and lighting hiding the weak spots.

A number of bands, a string ensemble and solo musicians present live music for dancing and listening in many of the lounges and bars. There's dancing in the Crows Nest (atop the navigation bridge), and serenading string music in the Explorer's Lounge, among other venues.

SPA/FITNESS. The Ocean Spa is located one deck above the navigation bridge at the very forward part of the ship. It includes a gymnasium (with all the latest muscle-pumping exercise machines, including an abundance of treadmills) with forward views over the ship's bows, an aerobics exercise area, large beauty salon with ocean-view windows to the port side, several treatment rooms, and men's and women's saunas, steam rooms and changing areas.

The spa is operated by Steiner, a specialist concession, whose young staff will try to sell you Steiner's own-brand Elemis beauty products. Some fitness classes are free, while some, such as yoga, and kick-boxing, cost $10 per class. Massage facials, pedicures, and beauty salon treatments cost extra (massage, for example, costs about $2 per minute, plus gratuity). Do make appointments early in the cruise as time slots go quickly.

For the sports-minded, two paddle-tennis courts are located at the aft of the Sports Deck.

● **For more extensive general information about a Holland America Line cruise, see pages 118–122.**

Andrea
★★ +

Boutique Ship: . . . . .2,632 tons
Lifestyle: . . . . .Standard
Cruise Line: . . . . .Elegant Cruises & Tours
Former Names: . . . .*Harald Jarl*
Builder: . . . . . .Trondheims Mek (Norway)
Original Cost: . . . . .n/a
Entered Service: 1960/2003
Registry: . . . . .Liberia
Length (ft/m): 286.0/87.4
Beam (ft/m): 43.6/13.2
Draft (ft/m): 15.5/4.7
Propulsion/Propellers: diesel/2
Passenger Decks: 5
Total Crew: 48

Passengers
(lower beds/all berths): 107/110
Passenger Space Ratio
(lower beds/all berths): 24.5/23.9
Crew/Passenger Ratio
(lower beds/all berths): 1.8/1.9
Navigation Officers: . . . . .European
Cabins (total): 57
Size Range (sq ft/m): .66.0-236.8/6.1-22.0
Cabins (outside view): 52
Cabins (interior/no view): 5
Cabins (for one person): 4
Cabins (with private balcony): 0
Cabins (wheelchair accessible): 1

Cabin Current: . . . . .220 volts
Elevators: 1
Casino (gaming tables): 0
Slot Machines: .0
Swimming Pools (outdoors): 0
Swimming Pools (indoors): 0
Whirlpools: 0
Self-Service Launderette: 0
Dedicated Cinema/Seats: 0
Library: . . . . .Yes
Classification Society: . .Croatian Register
of Shipping (CRS)

BERLITZ'S OVERALL SCORE: 1,062 (OUT OF A POSSIBLE 2,000 POINTS)

OVERVIEW. This small ship (formerly operated as one of the Norwegian Coastal Voyages fleet) was extensively refurbished solely for cruise activities in 2003. It has a deep blue hull with white superstructure. During the winter the ship operates cruises in the Antarctic Peninsula (and Amazon regions), and in the summer in the Baltic and Mediterranean regions. The ship, which has a good amount of outdoors space, carries a small fleet of Zodiac inflatable shore boats, but does not have stabilizers.

The interior decor, which is tasteful, follows the 18th-century Gustavian (Swedish) style. There is an observation area (Cormorant Lounge), an aft-facing lounge (Kittiwake Lounge, which incorporates a small library, and two internet-connect computer stations), used also for recaps and lectures. Smoking is permitted only on open decks. Gratuities are suggested at $10–$12 per person, per day, and are divided among all crew members. The onboard currency is the US dollar.

SUITABLE FOR: *Andrea* is best suited to couples and single travelers of mature years who enjoy nature and wildlife at close range, and who would not dream of cruising in the mainstream sense aboard ships with large numbers of people. This is for the hardy, adventurous types who don't need constant entertainment or mind-numbing parlor games.

ACCOMMODATION. There are nine accommodation price

BERLITZ'S RATINGS

	Possible	Achieved
Ship	500	247
Accommodation	200	108
Food	400	219
Service	400	229
Entertainment	N/A	N/A
Cruise	500	259

grades, from two owner's suites to standard (small) interior (no-view) cabins, spread across five decks. Note that passengers occupying cabins on the lowest deck have portholes that are closed during poor weather conditions (example: Drake Passage crossings).

The Owner's Suites are located at the front, directly under the navigation bridge, with forward-facing views.

Most cabins have twin beds (13 cabins have beds connected to make a double bed); most cabins have tiny bathrooms with showers (some suites have a bathtub). All suites/cabins have satellite television and telephone, hairdryer, personal safe (personal amenities include shampoo, conditioner, and body lotion), and underbed space for luggage.

CUISINE/DINING. The Shearwater Restaurant operates one seating, but the chairs do not have armrests. The food is pretty basic, and there are few choices, but it's tasty and well presented. Casual eats can be taken in the aft-facing open-deck Northern Lights Café.

ENTERTAINMENT. There is no formal entertainment, but recaps of the day's experiences and after dinner conversation are all that's needed.

SPA/FITNESS. A small fitness center has only a limited amount of equipment (treadmills, bicycles and free weights), and an adjacent massage therapy room.

Arcadia
NOT YET RATED

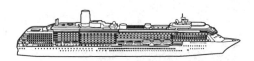

Large (Resort) Ship: ....82,500 tons	Total Crew: 886	Cabins (with private balcony): 677
Lifestyle: ....Standard	Passengers	Cabins (wheelchair accessible): 30
Cruise Line: ....P&O Cruises	(lower beds/all berths): 1,996/2,534	Cabin Current: .... 110/220 volts
Former Names: ....None	Passenger Space Ratio	Elevators: 14
Builder: ....Fincantieri (Italy)	(lower beds/all berths): 43.3/32.5	Casino (gaming tables): ....Yes
Original Cost: ....$400 million	Crew/Passenger Ratio	Slot Machines: ....Yes
Entered Service: ....April 2005	(lower beds/all berths): 2.2/2.8	Swimming Pools (outdoors): 1
Registry: ....Great Britain	Navigation Officers: ....British	Swimming Pools (indoors): 1
Length (ft/m): 951.4/290.0	Cabins (total): 998	Whirlpools: 5
Beam (ft/m): 105.0/32.0	Size Range (sq ft/m): 170.0–516.6/	Self-Service Launderette: ....Yes
Draft (ft/m): 25.5/7.8	15.7–48.0	Dedicated Cinema/Seats: ....No
Propulsion/Propellers: .....diesel-electric	Cabins (outside view): 674	Library: ....Yes
(34,000 kW)/ 2 azimuthing pods	Cabins (interior/no view): 324	Classification Society: ...Lloyds Register
Passenger Decks: 10	Cabins (for one person): 0	

OVERALL SCORE: NYR (OUT OF A POSSIBLE 2,000 POINTS)

OVERVIEW. P&O's new flagship *Arcadia* was originally scheduled to be Cunard Line's *Queen Victoria* (the casual "queen"), for the British cruise market, but was transferred to the P&O Cruises brand (both are owned by the giant Carnival Corporation). The largest cruise ship built specifically for the British cruise market, it can also transit the Panama Canal. The interior layout has been much modified for British tastes. Outdoors facilities include a wrap-around promenade deck (covered in the forward section of the ship), with plenty of deck lounge chairs (and comfortable cushioned pads). The large Lido Deck pool has a moveable glass domed cover – useful in poor weather. Panoramic exterior glass-wall elevators grace the lobby and travel between all 10 passenger decks. Interior decor is "traditionally modern."

Facilities include a forward-facing observation lounge high atop the ship, a florist, and a gift shop arcade. The ship has an Easy Like a Sunday lounge, a sort of all-in one bistro, relaxation room and meeting place, a place to chill out. There's also a Crow's Nest observation lounge and a Monte Carlo casino. Popular drinking places include a traditional English pub, plus a bar overlooking a modest three deck-high atrium lobby.

Arcadia, a child-free ship, blends traditional British cruising with contemporary facilities for adults. Renewal of Vows program costs £250 per couple.

Arcadia is the new generation in contemporary cruise ships, based year-round in Southampton, England. The onboard currency is the UK pound. A daily gratuity is added to your onboard account, while a 15% gratuity is added to all bar and wine accounts.

SUITABLE FOR: *Arcadia* is best suited to couples and sin-

BERLITZ'S RATINGS

	Possible	Achieved
Ship	500	NYR
Accommodation	200	NYR
Food	400	NYR
Service	400	NYR
Entertainment	100	NYR
Cruise	400	NYR

gles that enjoy cruising in a contemporary child-free ship, with entertainment geared specifically for British tastes in a large ship, with an informal setting and plenty of public rooms to play in.

ACCOMMODATION. 86% of cabins have an outside view, while 69% have a private balcony. There are 67 suites and mini-suites.

CUISINE/DINING. The Meridian Restaurant, located aft, is two decks high. There are two seatings, and tables are for two, four, six, or eight. L'Epicure Restaurant, with single seating dining, is for suite passengers, and has better cuisine and service. The Orchid Restaurant (on Deck 11, one of the uppermost decks) has fine panoramic views, and is an alternative, extra charge eatery featuring Asian-fusion cuisine. There's also a casual 24-hour food-court-style eatery.

ENTERTAINMENT. P&O prides itself on its entertainment. The ship has the Stadium Theatre Company, a resident group of actors, singers and dancers who provide theater-style presentations such as mini-versions of well-known musicals, revues and drama. In addition, the ship has a whole array of cabaret acts. Classical concerts are scheduled for many cruises.

Ballroom dance aficionados will be pleased to note that there are several good-sized wooden dance floors aboard this ship, and P&O Cruises normally carries a professional dance couple as hosts and teachers (there is plenty of dancing time included in the entertainment programming).

SPA/FITNESS/RECREATION. The Retreat and Spa has a gymnasium, sauna/steam rooms and a hydrotherapy pool.

Arion
★★

Small Ship: ....5,885 tons	Passenger Decks: 5	Cabins (with private balcony): 0
Lifestyle: ....Standard	Total Crew: 120	Cabins (wheelchair accessible): 0
Cruise Line: ....Classic International Cruises	Passengers (lower beds/all berths): 334/340	Cabin Current: ....220 volts
		Elevators: 1
Former Names: ....Astra I, Istra	Passenger Space Ratio (lower beds/all berths): 17.6/17.3	Casino (gaming tables): ....Yes
Builder: ......Brodgradiliste (Yugoslavia)		Slot Machines: ....Yes
Original Cost: ....n/a	Crew/Passenger Ratio (lower beds/all berths): 2.7/2.8	Swimming Pools (outdoors): 1
Entered Service: 1965/1999		Swimming Pools (indoors): 0
Registry: ....Portugal	Navigation Officers: ....Portuguese	Whirlpools: 0
Length (ft/m): 381.5/116.3	Cabins (total): 169	Self-Service Launderette: ....No
Beam (ft/m): 54.1/16.5	Size Range (sq ft/m): ....n/a	Dedicated Cinema/Seats: ....No
Draft (ft/m): 18.3/5.6	Cabins (outside view): 142	Library: ....Yes
Propulsion/Propellers: ....diesel (11,030kW)/2	Cabins (interior/no view): 27	Classification Society: ....Bureau Veritas & Rinave
	Cabins (for one person): 4	

OVERALL SCORE: 859 (OUT OF A POSSIBLE 2,000 POINTS)

OVERVIEW. *Arion* is a small ship, originally built for weekly service between Venice and Egypt. It underwent a $15 million reconstruction by its new owners, Classic International Cruises (even the navigation bridge was relocated forward) after the company bought the ship at auction in Haifa in 1999, and emerged in its present form in May 2000.

The ship is being operated under charter to various tour operators, and thus attracts an international mix of passengers who like smaller ships with some character.

The ship has some interesting itineraries, at very low prices. It is particularly suited to the "nooks and crannies" style of cruising to some of the more out-of-the-way ports in the Mediterranean. The dress code is extremely casual and there is a relaxed ambiance throughout.

Because this is a small ship, there are few public rooms and facilities, and very little open deck space. The interior passageways are narrow and could be better lit. The public rooms are always busy and it is difficult to avoid smokers. There are no cushioned pads for the deck lounge chairs. The ship is not suitable for disabled passengers.

SUITABLE FOR: *Arion* is best suited to adult couples (typically over 50) looking for a basic cruise holiday, in a traditional ship. This could be good for your first cruise experience, in a setting that provides basic comforts, and at a price that is low, but provides fair value for money.

ACCOMMODATION. There are 12 cabin price grades (though this may depend on tour operators that charter the vessel). Except for the top two grades, the cabins are modest in size and features, and one would not want to spend much time

BERLITZ'S RATINGS

	Possible	Achieved
Ship	500	186
Accommodation	200	82
Food	400	177
Service	400	218
Entertainment	100	37
Cruise	400	159

in them. Cabins 1–8, which have windows, suffer from lifeboat-obstructed views. Cabins on the higher decks have windows, while others have portholes.

Each cabin has a small TV set, personal safe, and hairdryer. There is little closet and storage space (so take the minimal amount of clothing), although each cabin does have a set of bedside drawers. Some cabins have a twin bed arrangement (side by side), while others are "L"-shaped (only a few cabins have a double bed). Some cabins have a third, or third and fourth berth. The bathrooms are tiny and basic, yet adequate.

CUISINE/DINING. The restaurant is warm and mildly attractive, with ocean-view windows on two sides, and standard place settings. There are tables (very close together) for four, six or eight. The chairs do not have armrests. All passengers dine together in one seating.

The menus are limited, although there is a good choice of breads and bread rolls. Dinner menus typically consist of one or two appetizers, two soups, and three entrées. The wine list is quite basic, and the wine glasses are small. The Portuguese waiters are quite friendly and attentive. Casual breakfasts and luncheons can be taken in the Lido Lounge, just forward of the swimming pool and the open deck aft.

ENTERTAINMENT. There is little entertainment, and what is provided is of the cabaret variety. There is a band for dancing, but little else, except for the pianist in the piano bar, which is located just aft of the main lounge.

SPA/FITNESS. None, although there is a small beauty salon. The small swimming pool is really only a "dip" pool.

Astor
★★★★

Mid-Size Ship: . . . . .20,606 tons	Total Crew: 300	Cabin Current: . . . . .220 volts
Lifestyle: . . . . .Standard	Passengers	Elevators: 3
Cruise Line: . . . . .Transocean Tours	(lower beds/all berths): 590/650	Casino (gaming tables): . . . . .Yes
Former Names: . . . . .Fedor Dostoyevskiy,	Passenger Space Ratio	Slot Machines: . . . . .Yes
Astor (II)	(lower beds/all berths): 34.9/31.7	Swimming Pools (outdoors): 1
Builder: . . . . . . .Howaldtswerke Deutsche	Crew/Passenger Ratio	Swimming Pools (indoors): 1
Werft (Germany)	(lower beds/all berths): 1.9/2.1	Whirlpools: 0
Original Cost: . . . .$65 million	Navigation Officers: . . .Russian/Ukrainian	Fitness Center: . . . . .Yes
Entered Service: . . . . . Feb 1987/Apr 1997	Cabins (total): 295	Sauna/Steam Room: . . . . .Yes/No
Registry: . . . . .The Bahamas	Size Range (sq ft/m): 140.0–280.0/	Massage: . . . . .Yes
Length (ft/m): 579.0/176.50	13.0–26.0	Self-Service Launderette: . . . . .No
Beam (ft/m): 74.1/22.61	Cabins (outside view): 199	(ironing room)
Draft (ft/m): 20.0/6.10	Cabins (interior/no view): 96	Dedicated Cinema/Seats: . . . . .No
Propulsion/Propellers: . . . . .diesel	Cabins (for one person): 0	Library: . . . . .Yes
(15,400kW)/2	Cabins (with private balcony): 0	Classification Society: . . . . .Germanischer
Passenger Decks: 7	Cabins (wheelchair accessible): 0	Lloyd

OVERALL SCORE: 1,450 (OUT OF A POSSIBLE 2,000 POINTS)

OVERVIEW. *Astor* was the original name for this ship, the larger of two ships bearing this same name in the 1980s (the other being the present Transocean Tours ship *Arkona*, originally built for the now-defunct Astor Cruises. Its previous owners, the also defunct Aqua-Marin Cruises, again brought back the ship's name to *Astor* from its previous name *Fedor Dostoyevskiy*. In 1996, *Astor* was under charter to Transocean Tours for 10 years.

This is an attractive modern ship with a raked bow, a large square funnel and a nicely balanced contemporary profile. The ship is slightly larger than the first *Astor* (presently renamed *Astoria*), and has been well maintained and refurbished throughout the years. Introduced by Transocean Tours in 1996, this ship was placed under a long-term charter agreement until 2007 (when the ship will be 20 years old) from its present owners, Russia's Sovcomflot. *Astor* and its (slightly smaller) sister ship *Astoria* now operate in tandem – two ships of a similar size and with very similar facilities (even built in the same shipyard, with the same bathroom fittings and washbasins, the same conservative decor and ambiance – operating as one product.

This ship represents a good mix of traditional and contemporary styling, with restful decor that does not jar the senses (though some say it's a little too dark). Built to a high standard in Germany, fine teakwood decking and polished wooden rails are seen outside almost everywhere.

There is an excellent amount of open deck and sunbathing space, as well as cushioned pads for the deck lounge chairs. There is a basketball court for active passengers, as well as a large deck chess game on an aft deck, and the usual shuffleboard courts.

The interior fittings are of extremely fine quality. There is a supremely comfortable and varied array of public rooms and conference facilities, most of which have high ceilings. Apart from a showlounge, public rooms include a Captain's Club lounge, a library and card room, and two large boutiques. A wood-paneled Hansa Tavern (with good German lager on draft) is a fine retreat, and extremely popular as a late-night drinking club.

Transocean Tours has interesting and well-designed destination-intensive worldwide itineraries, and cruises are provided at a very attractive price. The Russian/Ukrainian hotel staff is friendly without being obtrusive, although you may find the occasional one or two crew that appears to have had a hospitality bypass.

This ship, which caters exclusively to German-speaking passengers, provides a certain degree of style, comfort and elegance, and a fine leisurely cruise experience in a relaxed, spacious setting (there is no crowding anywhere) that is less formal than a ship such as *Europa*. In typical German style, a Fruhschoppen with the appropriate music, Bavarian sausages and complimentary beer is presented on the open lido deck once each cruise.

The ship represents a good choice for those people who are looking for a well-packaged cruise in traditional surroundings. Transocean Tours staff can be found aboard every cruise, some of which are designated as special-theme cruises.

BERLITZ'S RATINGS	Possible	Achieved
Ship	500	376
Accommodation	200	145
Food	400	290
Service	400	291
Entertainment	100	62
Cruise	400	286

The currency aboard *Astor* is the euro. Port taxes, insurance and gratuities to staff are all included in the cruise fare. The drinks prices are inexpensive, particularly when compared to land-based prices.

A service provided by ABX Logistics will collect your luggage from your house, and transport it to the ship for you; when you return, the service will collect it from the ship and bring it to your house – all for a nominal fee (this service is only available to/from certain ports).

SUITABLE FOR: *Astor* is best suited to German-speaking couples, and single travelers of mature years who seek a good value for money holiday in a traditional cruise ship setting, with appealing itineraries and destinations, good food and friendly service.

ACCOMMODATION. The accommodation, spanning 18 price categories, is spread over three decks, and comprises 32 suites and 263 outside-view and interior (no view) cabins. No matter what grade of accommodation is chosen, rosewood cabinetry and plain beige walls is the norm – a restful environment. All suites and cabins with outside-view windows have blackout blinds (good for cruises to the land of the midnight sun).

Suites: The suites (279.8 sq.ft/26 sq. meters) are tastefully decorated in pastel colors, and have rosewood cabinetry and accents. Each has a separate bedroom (with brass clock), lounge/living room (another brass clock), with mini-bar/refrigerator. The bathroom has a decent sized cabinet for personal toiletry items, as well as a sit-in bathtub/shower combination, toilet, and a white enamel washbasin. A wide array of bathroom amenities is provided, including built-in hairdryer, soap, shampoo, shower cap, comb, sewing kit, shoe polish, shoehorn, clothes lint collector, nail file, matches, and a basket of fruit, replenished daily.

Outside-view and Interior (No View) Cabins: These cabins (139.9 sq. ft/13 sq. meters) are well appointed and tastefully decorated in fresh pastel colors, and have dark wood accents and cabinetry, making them very restful. There is plenty of closet and drawer space, as well as some under-bed storage space for luggage. The bathrooms are very practical, and each has a decent sized cabinet for personal toiletry items, as well as all the necessary fittings, including a white enamel washbasin.

Outside-view Family (4-Berth) Cabins: These large cabins (258.3 sq.ft/24 sq. meters) have two lower beds, one upper berth and one sofa bed – good for families with children. The tiled bathroom has a shower enclosure, white enamel washbasin and toilet.

No matter what grade of accommodation you choose, all passengers get European duvets, 100 percent cotton towels, cotton bathrobe, soap, shampoo, shower cap, sewing kit and a basket of fruit. The cabin service menu is very limited and could be better, although German-speaking passengers in general seldom use room service for food items. There is an extra charge for sandwiches, and little else is available. However, there is plenty of food elsewhere around the ship. Note that there is an extra charge for freshly-squeezed orange juice, as aboard all ships in the German-speaking market. The bathroom towels are too small.

CUISINE/DINING. The Waldorf Dining Room is reasonably elegant, well laid-out, and operates two seatings. It also has two small wings (good for private parties or groups of up to 30). The service throughout is friendly and unpretentious, and the food quality and presentation has received some attention from the food caterer, although remember that you get what you pay for, and food is not a particularly high priority for Transocean Tours. The menus are reasonably attractive, and both quality and presentation are acceptable standard fare, but nothing special – there's certainly no "wow" factor. In addition to the regular entrées (typically three entrées for dinner), there may also be a pasta dish, and a vegetarian specialty dish. The wine list contains a decent selection of wines from many regions, and all at inexpensive to moderate price levels.

The casual breakfast and lunch buffets (both in the restaurant and another lounge) are reasonably well presented, and constantly refreshed, although they tend to be somewhat repetitive; the choice of foods is limited and there is room for improvement.

ENTERTAINMENT. The Showlounge is a single-level room (14 pillars unfortunately obstruct the sight lines). The stage is also the dance floor, and cannot be raised for shows; entertainment, therefore, is mostly cabaret-style, with singers, magicians, and other visual acts providing the bulk of the shows.

SPA/FITNESS. The Wellness Oasis is located on the lowest passenger deck, and contains a fitness room, sauna (there is no steam room), solarium, indoor swimming pool, beauty salon, treatment rooms and changing areas. Massage, facials, manicures and pedicures are some of the services offered.

Astoria
★★★★

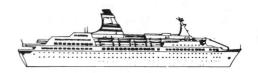

Mid-Size Ship: ....18,591 tons	Passenger Decks: 8	Cabins (for one person): 0
Lifestyle: ....Standard	Total Crew: 243	Cabins (with private balcony): 0
Cruise Line: ....Transocean Tours	Passengers	Cabins (wheelchair accessible): 0
Former Names: ....*Arkona, Astor*	(lower beds/all berths): 500/618	Cabin Current: ....220 volts
Builder: ......Howaldtswerke Deutsche	Passenger Space Ratio	Elevators: 3
Werft (Germany)	(lower beds/all berths): 36.0/30.0	Casino (gaming tables): ....No
Original Cost: ....$55 million	Crew/Passenger Ratio	Slot Machines: ....No
Entered Service: .....Dec 1981/Feb 2002	(lower beds/all berths): 2.1/2.5	Swimming Pools (outdoors): 1
Registry: ....The Bahamas	Navigation Officers: ....European	Swimming Pools (indoors): 1
Length (ft/m): 539.2/164.35	Cabins (total): 259	Whirlpools: 0
Beam (ft/m): 74.1/22.60	Size Range (sq ft/m): 150.0–725.0/	Self-Service Launderette: ....No
Draft (ft/m): 20.0/6.11	13.4–65.3	Dedicated Cinema/Seats: ....No
Propulsion/Propellers: ....diesel	Cabins (outside view): 177	Library: ....Yes
(13,200kW)/2	Cabins (interior/no view): 82	Classification Society: Germanischer Lloyd

OVERALL SCORE: 1,433 (OUT OF A POSSIBLE 2,000 POINTS)

OVERVIEW. *Astoria* is a traditional style of cruise ship (slightly smaller than sister ship *Astor*), originally constructed for the now defunct Astor Cruises. The ship cruised under the Seetours banner from October 1985 and continued until February 2002, when it was transferred to its new operators, Transocean Tours. The ship underwent a very slight name change, to *Astoria*. Some minor modifications took place so that *Astor* and *Astoria* now operate in tandem – two ships of a similar size and with very similar facilities (even built in the same shipyard, with the same bathroom fittings and washbasins), the same conservative decor and ambiance – operating as one product.

Astoria is a well-constructed modern vessel with a well-balanced profile. There is a very good amount of open deck and sunbathing space for its size, with some excellent teak-wood decking and polished railings, and cushioned pads for the deck lounge chairs. For the sports-minded, there is a volleyball court.

Astoria, like its sister ship *Astor*, has beautifully appointed interior fittings and decor, with a great deal of rosewood paneling and wood accents throughout. The ship has been maintained extremely well. Subdued lighting and soothing ambiance, highlighted by fine artwork throughout, make for a pleasant, relaxing cruise experience. There are good meetings facilities, and a well-stocked library. The late-night meeting-place is definitely the excellent pub (with draft German lager) looking aft over the sun deck.

Passengers who use dialysis machines will find that Transocean Tours operates several special cruises, complete with specially trained medical personnel (dialysis equipment is installed aboard *Astoria*).

BERLITZ'S RATINGS

	Possible	Achieved
Ship	500	361
Accommodation	200	144
Food	400	290
Service	400	291
Entertainment	100	61
Cruise	400	286

The ship has good traditional European-style hotel service, with German navigaton and engineering officers and a mostly Ukrainian service staff. The reception desk is open 24 hours daily.

Astoria provides good value for money cruising in comfort, and is best recommended for passengers who appreciate quality, fine surroundings, and excellent destination-intensive itineraries, all packaged neatly in a relaxed, informal ambiance. Many cruises have special themes. Transocean Tours staff is available aboard every cruise; they will go out of their way to make sure that you will have an excellent cruise experience in very comfortable surroundings. The ship has many repeat passengers, who enjoy the extremely friendly, mostly German crew (who provide a fun crew show). The currency aboard *Astoria* is the euro. Port taxes, insurance and gratuities to staff are all included in the cruise fare.

A service by ABX Logistics will collect your luggage from your house, and transport it to the ship for you; when you return, the service will collect it from the ship and take it to your house – all for a nominal fee.

There is no wrap-around promenade deck outdoors. Finally, non-smokers should note that there are many cigarette and cigar smokers, and they are often hard to avoid.

SUITABLE FOR: *Astoria* is best suited to German-speaking couples, and single travelers of mature years who seek a good value for money holiday in a traditional cruise ship setting, with appealing itineraries and destinations, good food and friendly service.

ACCOMMODATION. The accommodation, of which there are

18 price categories, is spread over three decks, and comprises one Senator Suite, 34 suites, and 263 outside-view and interior (no view) cabins. There are no balcony cabins (the ship having been built before they became popular). **Senator Suite:** This Boat Deck suite (725 sq. ft/65.3 sq. meters) is simply lovely, and has just about everything needed for refined, private living aboard this ship. There is a separate bedroom with double bed, living room with sofa, dining table and chairs. The tiled bathroom has a large bathtub, separate shower enclosure, and plenty of storage space for personal toiletry items.

Suites: Suites (269.1 sq. ft/25 sq. meters) have a separate bedroom with double bed, living room with sofa, dining table and chairs. The tiled bathroom has a large bathtub, separate shower enclosure, and plenty of storage space for personal toiletry items.

Outside-view Cabins/Interior (No View) Cabins: The standard cabins (139.9 sq. ft/13 sq. meters) are quite well appointed and decorated, and all feature crisp, clean colors (some might find them plain). The bathrooms are quite compact units, although there is a decent-sized shower enclosure. They are fully tiled, however, and have a decent cabinet for storing personal toiletry items.

No matter what grade of accommodation you choose, all passengers get 100% cotton towels, and bathrobe. The cabin service menu is very limited and could be better, although German-speaking passengers in general seldom use room service for food items. There is an extra charge for sandwiches, and little else is available; however, there is plenty of food elsewhere around the ship. Note that there is an extra charge for fresh-squeezed orange juice, as aboard all ships in the German-speaking market.

CUISINE/DINING. The Astoria Restaurant, located high in the ship, has big, ocean-view picture windows and is reasonably attractive, with dark wood paneling and restful decor; there are two seatings. The food is adequate to very good, though choice is somewhat limited, but the service, by some charming waitresses, does help. Do remember that, when it comes to food and ingredients, you get what you pay for, and food is not a particularly high priority for Transocean Tours. There's certainly no "wow" factor in this food or its presentation. The occasional formal candlelight dinners provide a romantic ambiance. The wine list contains a decent selection of wines from many regions, and all at inexpensive to moderate price levels.

The self-serve buffets (for breakfast and luncheon) are varied, although the presentation could be improved. The cabin service food menu is very limited.

ENTERTAINMENT. The showlounge is a single-level room. However, there are 14 pillars to obstruct the sight lines from some seats. The stage is also the dance floor and cannot be raised for shows. The entertainment, therefore, consist mostly of cabaret-style shows typically with singers, magicians and other visual acts.

SPA/FITNESS. The Wellness Oasis is located on the lowest passenger deck, and contains a fitness room (small gymnasium), sauna (there is no steam room), solarium, indoor swimming pool, treatment rooms and changing areas. Massage, facials, manicures and pedicures are some of the services offered. The beauty salon is located one deck higher. In addition, sophisticated hospital facilities include oxygen multi-step therapy.

Asuka
★★★★ +

Mid-Size Ship: . . . . .28,856 tons	Passenger Decks: 8	Cabins (for one person): 0
Lifestyle: . . . . .Premium	Total Crew: 262	Cabins (with private balcony): 108
Cruise Line: . . . . .NYK Cruises	Passengers	Cabins (wheelchair accessible): 2
Former Names: . . . . .none	(lower beds/all berths): 600/618	Cabin Current: . . . . .110 volts
Builder: . . . . .Mitsubishi Heavy Industries	Passenger Space Ratio	Elevators: 5
(Japan)	(lower beds/all berths): 48.0/46.6	Casino (gaming tables): . . . . .Yes
Original Cost: . . . .$150 million	Crew/Passenger Ratio	Slot Machines: . . . . .Yes
Entered Service: . . . . .Dec 1991	(lower beds/all berths): 2.2/2.3	Swimming Pools (outdoors): 1
Registry: . . . . .Japan	Navigation Officers: . . . . .Japanese	Swimming Pools (indoors): 0
Length (ft/m): 632.5/192.81	Cabins (total): 300	Whirlpools: 3
Beam (ft/m): 81.0/24.70	Size Range (sq ft/m): 182.9–649.0/	Self-Service Launderette: . . . . .Yes
Draft (ft/m): 21.6/6.6	17.0–60.3	Dedicated Cinema/Seats: Yes/97
Propulsion/Propellers: . . . . .diesel	Cabins (outside view): 300	Library: . . . . .Yes
(17,300kW)/2	Cabins (interior/no view): 0	Classification Society: Nippon Kaiji Kyokai

OVERALL SCORE: 1,616 (OUT OF A POSSIBLE 2,000 POINTS)

OVERVIEW. When introduced in 1991, *Asuka* was the first all-new large ship specially designed for the still slow-growing Japanese cruise market, and the largest cruise ship built in Japan for the local market. But it is quickly becoming outdated, although a refurbishment in 2001 refreshed some of the interiors.

The ship has pleasing exterior styling and profile, with a large, rounded, but squat funnel. There is a good amount of open deck space (although Japanese passengers do not use it much, as most are not keen on sunbathing). There is a wide wrap-around teakwood promenade deck outdoors, good for strolling.

The "cake-layer" stacking of the public rooms hampers passenger flow and makes it somewhat disjointed, although the ship's Japanese passengers do like the separation of public rooms. There are many intimate public rooms and plenty of space so that there is never a feeling of crowding.

The interior decor is elegant but understated, with pleasing color combinations, quality fabrics and fine soft furnishings. Fascinating Japanese artwork is featured, including a four-deck-high mural located on the wall of the main foyer staircase by Noriko Tamara, called "Song of the Seasons".

The Mariner's Club, decorated in the style of an English gentleman's club with wood paneled walls, deep leather chairs, and a bar is a popular evening spot. Cellular pay phones are located in one of the deck foyers, good for use when the ship takes short cruises around Japan. There are good facilities for meetings and groups.

As for the dress code, there is a mix of formal and informal nights, while during the day the dress code is very casual. In case you want to do your own laundry, there is a

BERLITZ'S RATINGS		
	Possible	Achieved
Ship	500	400
Accommodation	200	163
Food	400	332
Service	400	328
Entertainment	100	79
Cruise	400	314

self-service launderette, which has 12 washing machines. One nice touch is the fact that streamers are still thrown when the ship is cruising around Japan – a maritime tradition that so many other cruise ships have ceased. Gratuities are neither expected nor allowed. Children under 10 are not generally accepted, except during special summer festival and holiday cruises.

Asuka has, over the years, gathered a loyal following, perhaps because the ship provides an extremely comfortable and serene environment in which to cruise, particularly for its annual around-the-world cruise and the longer cruises in Southeast Asia and South Pacific. Regular passengers enjoy these because many more activities, lecturers and entertainers are planned than on the short cruises typical throughout much of the summer. Now that the ship is more than 10 years old, however, the refurbished areas (new carpeting throughout, expanded Lido Cafe) tend to show up some of the other areas that need attention.

Note that there is no butler service in the Asuka Club suites. The ship is in need of further refurbishment and upgrading in some areas in order to compete effectively in the international marketplace. The green turf on the upper, outermost deck is like a patchwork quilt and makes it look sloppy when compared with other areas. The white caulking of teakwood decking looks dirty and should be replaced by black caulking.

A specialist courier company provides an excellent luggage service and will collect your luggage from your home before the cruise, and deliver it back to your home after the cruise (this service is available only in Japan). The onboard currency is the Japanese yen.

SUITABLE FOR: *Asuka* is best suited to Japanese-speaking couples and single travelers of senior years (children are discouraged as there are no facilities for them) who enjoy highly comfortable surroundings, and good food and service.

ACCOMMODATION. There are seven categories (Suite, and grades A, B, C, D, F and J), although in reality there are just five types of suites and cabins. Three decks (8, 9 and 10) have suites and cabins with a private balcony (note that the floor is laid with green simulated turf, and there is no outside light). No matter what grade you choose, all suites and cabins have ocean views, although some are slightly obstructed by the ship's gangway, when it is in the raised (stowed) position; there are no interior (no view) cabins.

In all grades, the cabinetry featured is cherry wood, with nicely rounded edges. The cabin insulation is excellent. There is a good amount of closet and drawer space, including some lockable drawers and a personal safe. Facilities include a hot water (tea-making) unit (with a selection of Japanese and non-Japanese teas), refrigerator (stocked with beer and cold coffee – the kind you find in street corner vending machines in Japan), 100% cotton bathrobe, yukata (cotton house robe), slippers, and down duvets (instead of sheets/blankets).

All grades have bathrooms with full, deep bathtubs (while the "club" suite bathrooms are of generous proportions, the standard bathrooms are rather small), and all have a tiled floor and bath/shower area. The range of personal toiletry items includes soap, shampoo, rinse, toothbrush /toothpaste, comb, shower cap, razor set, and vanity pack for ladies.

Two suites provide the largest accommodation (one is decorated in blue, the other in salmon); these are larger versions of the "A" grade cabins. Each has a separate bedroom, with walk-in closet that includes a luggage deck, and twin beds that convert to a queen-sized bed), sofa, two chairs and coffee table, large vanity desk, plenty of drawer space, and large color TV set. The marble-clad bathroom is large and has a whirlpool bathtub set alongside large ocean-view windows overlooking the private balcony, and twin washbasins set in a marble surround; a living room, and separate guest bathroom. The private balcony is quite large and has a tall tropical plant set in a glass display enclosure.

"A" grade cabins are excellent living spaces, and feature twice the size and space of the standard cabins in categories "D," "F" and "J". They are very nicely decorated and outfitted, and have twin beds (convertible to a queen-sized bed), sofa, two chairs and coffee table, large vanity desk, plenty of drawer space, and large color television. However, when in its twin bed configuration, the room's *feng shui* is not good, as one of the beds is facing a large mirror at the writing/vanity desk – which is not permissible. Many have a private balcony (with full floor-to-ceiling partition and a green synthetic turf floor, although there is no outside light), with floor-to-ceiling sliding door (the door handles are quite awkward, however). In addition to all the standard cabin amenities, an illuminated walk-in closet (with long hanging rail and plenty of drawer space) is provided. The bathrooms are partly tiled and of generous proportions, and include a glass-fronted (plastic) toiletries cabinet, and two washbasins set in a thick marble surround. During a 1999 dry-dock, four new suites were added to Panorama Deck 10 in what had been an unused space.

The room service menu is small (it is, in effect, rarely used by Japanese passengers), but it does include such things as continental breakfast, and light snacks throughout the day and evening. Sashimi and sushi items are available during the hours when the sushi bar is open (typically 6pm–11pm), at extra cost.

CUISINE/DINING. The Four Seasons dining room is a no-smoking area, and cellular phones are thankfully not permitted (many people take mobile phones with them, particularly on the short cruises that are so popular in Japan). It is laid out in two sections, with ocean-view windows along one side only (in the aft section), and along two sides (forward section only), has a good amount of space around the tables, although there are only a few tables for two. There are two seatings, and both Japanese and Western cuisine is provided daily – traditional Japanese breakfast and luncheon in the restaurant (Western cuisine in the Lido Cafe), and Japanese dinners, with the occasional Western dinner. There is a limited, but very reasonable, selection of second-tier wines.

"Umihiko" is a small alternative dining spot. It is an à la carte sushi bar (with both counter and table seating) that has superb fresh seafood, beautifully prepared and presented (at extra cost), together with a good selection of Japanese sake. It is open for lunch as well as dinner on some short cruises, and for dinner (and occasionally lunch) on longer cruises.

For casual breakfasts and lunches, an informal, improved, upgraded and expanded self-serve Lido Cafe is provided, with indoor-outdoor seating, and a bar. This popular eatery now provides better indoor seating, and an improved layout that is much more user-friendly.

A traditional *washitsu* room (in which the floor is covered in tatami mats, and no shoes are allowed) is provided for special afternoon tea ceremonies, haiku readings and other traditional Japanese ceremonies. The entrance has a small black stone and wood entrance.

ENTERTAINMENT. The Grand Lounge is the venue for most entertainment events, social functions, and lectures. The room spans two decks, with seating on both main and balcony levels. The entertainment is typically an interesting mix of Western acts (including colorful production shows), and traditional Japanese acts (including storytellers).

SPA/FITNESS. There is a decent, spacious true Japanese grand bath facility. It has large ocean-view windows, two baths, one hot tub, a sauna, a proper steam room with wood floor and wood ceiling, several washing stations, showers, and a changing area with vanity counter (grooming aids and hairdryers are supplied). The massage room, however, is located away from the grand bath area and would be better if integrated.

Atalante
★

Mid-Size Ship: ....13,562 tons	Passenger Decks: 7	Cabins (for one person): 2
Lifestyle: ....Standard	Total Crew: 170	Cabins (with private balcony): 0
Cruise Line: ....New Paradise Cruises	Passengers	Cabins (wheelchair accessible): 0
Former Names: ....*Tahitien*	(lower beds/all berths): 518/705	Cabin Current: ....220 volts DC
Builder: .....Direction des Construction	Passenger Space Ratio	Elevators: 0
et Armes Navales (France)	(lower beds/all berths): 26.1/19.2	Casino (gaming tables): ....Yes
Original Cost: ....n/a	Crew/Passenger Ratio	Slot Machines: ....Yes
Entered Service: ...May 1953/Dec 1992	(lower beds/all berths): 3.0/4.1	Swimming Pools (outdoors): 2
Registry: ....Cyprus	Navigation Officers: ......Cypriot/Greek	Swimming Pools (indoors): 0
Length (ft/m): 548.5/167.20	Cabins (total): 260	Whirlpools: 0
Beam (ft/m): 67.9/20.70	Size Range (sq ft/m): 129.1–247.5/	Self-Service Launderette: ....No
Draft (ft/m): 20.7/6.30	12.0–23.0	Dedicated Cinema/Seats: ....No
Propulsion/Propellers: ....diesel	Cabins (outside view): 171	Library: ....No
(7,700kW)/2	Cabins (interior/no view): 89	Classification Society: ....Bureau Veritas

OVERALL SCORE: 645 (OUT OF A POSSIBLE 2,000 POINTS)

OVERVIEW. Now more than 50 years old, *Atalante*, a former passenger-car liner, is well worn. The ship has a small, squat funnel amidships and a really long fore-deck (something not generally found aboard new ships). This is quite a stable ship at sea, however, with a deep draft, and it rides well. There is a generous amount of open deck and sunbathing space, but the outdoor decking is well worn, as are the deck lounge chairs and other deck furniture.

The number of public rooms is very limited, and the lay-out is quite awkward and very disjointed. The main public room is the showlounge, an uncomfortable room that is immersed in high-volume, low-quality shows and cabaret. Recent decor changes are for the better, although much of the interior decor is dated, yet adequate and comfortable for those who do not want the glitz of newer ships. Much emphasis is placed on duty-free shopping.

The ship operates two- and three-night casual cruises from Cyprus to Egypt and Israel. The onboard currency is the Cyprus pound. There will be a wide variety of nation-alities on board, so language skills may be useful.

Ceilings in the public rooms are low. The nightlife is disco-loud, as is the music. There is no finesse, although the staff is reasonably enthusiastic. Many passengers smoke, so it is difficult to get away from the smell of stale smoke everywhere. This ship has passed its "sell-by" date and really should be retired or replaced by newer tonnage.

SUITABLE FOR: *Atalante* is best suited to young passengers on a tight budget wanting to party and travel with just the basic food and service, a casual dress code. They won't

BERLITZ'S RATINGS

	Possible	Achieved
Ship	500	135
Accommodation	200	67
Food	400	135
Service	400	158
Entertainment	100	30
Cruise	400	120

don't mind an old ship with limited facilities and service.

ACCOMMODATION. The cabins, in 10 dif-ferent price grades, are all rather small and Spartan, although most are deco-rated in pastel shades. While many cab-ins have two lower beds, many also have third- and fourth-person upper Pullman berths (good for families with children or friends who don't mind sharing in order to keep the per person price low). There is a limited amount of closet space, but you really do not need much clothing for this casual cruise. Additional cabins installed in a 1993 refit are noisy and rather squeaky, which makes them quite difficult to sleep in. The top-grade cabins also have a refrigerator, and a little more space; otherwise there is little to distinguish them.

CUISINE/DINING. The Venus Dining Room is located low down in the ship and always seems to have a musty odor and aroma of stale food. Self-serve buffets are featured for most meals, and the food really is quite basic – with few choices and poor presentation. Service is provided mainly by Greek waiters, who are friendly but are without finesse, and very little training. A small cafeteria has casual snacks.

ENTERTAINMENT. The Main Lounge is the venue for any entertainment events and social functions. It is a single-level room, but the sightlines are quite poor, obstructed by pillars. The entertainment consists mainly of cabaret-style singers on low pay. In other words, don't expect much.

SPA/FITNESS. No facilities.

Aurora
★★★★

Large (Resort) Ship:	.......76,152 tons	Passengers		Cabins (wheelchair accessible): 22
Lifestyle:	.................Standard	(lower beds/all berths): 1,868/1,975		(8 with private balcony)
Cruise Line:	.............P&O Cruises	Passenger Space Ratio		Cabin Current: ....110 and 220 volts
Former Names:	.................none	(lower beds/all berths): 40.7/38.5		Elevators: 10
Builder:	........Meyer Werft (Germany)	Crew/Passenger Ratio		Casino (gaming tables): ....Yes
Original Cost:	............$375 million	(lower beds/all berths): 2.2/2.4		Slot Machines: ....Yes
Entered Service:	............May 2000	Navigation Officers: ....British		Swimming Pools (outdoors): 3
Registry:	................Great Britain	Cabins (total): 934		(1 with magrodome)
Length (ft/m):	............885.8/270.0	Size Range (sq ft/m): 150.6–953.0/		Swimming Pools (indoors): 0
Beam (ft/m):	...............105.6/32.2		14.0–88.5	Whirlpools: 5
Draft (ft/m):	.................25.9/7.9	Cabins (outside view): 655		Self-Service Launderette: ....Yes
Propulsion/Propellers: .....diesel-electric		Cabins (interior/no view): 279		Dedicated Cinema/Seats: Yes/200
	(40,000kW)/2	Cabins (for one person): 0		Library: ....Yes
Passenger Decks:	10	Cabins (with private balcony): 406		Classification Society: ...Lloyd's Register
Total Crew:	816			

OVERALL SCORE: 1,540 (OUT OF A POSSIBLE 2,000 POINTS)

OVERVIEW. *Aurora* is named after the goddess of the dawn in Greek, Melanesian and Slavonic mythologies. Or perhaps the carnation Dianthus Aurora. Or it could be the famous Northern and Southern Lights, aurora borealis and aurora australis). At any rate, it was built specifically for Britain's growing traditional cruise market.

As ships evolve, slight differences in layout occur, as is the case with *Aurora* compared to earlier close sister *Oriana*. One big difference can be found in the addition of a large, magrodome-covered indoor/outdoor swimming pool (good in all weathers). The stern superstructure is nicely rounded and has several tiers that overlook the aft decks, pool and children's outdoor facilities. There is a good amount of open deck and sunbathing space, an important plus for the outdoors-loving mainly British passengers. There is an extra-wide wrap-around promenade deck outdoors, with plenty of white (plastic) deck lounge chairs (cushioned pads are available).

The ship's interiors are gentle, welcoming and restrained, with good colors and combinations that don't clash. The public rooms and areas have been designed in such a way that each room is individual, and yet there appears to be an open, yet cohesive flow throughout all of the public areas – something difficult to achieve when a number of designers are involved. There is good horizontal passenger flow, and wide passageways help to avoid congestion. Very noticeable are the fine, detailed ceiling treatments.

As it is a ship for all types of people, specific areas have been designed to attract different age groups and lifestyles. The focal point is a four-decks-high atrium lobby and a

BERLITZ'S RATINGS

	Possible	Achieved
Ship	500	422
Accommodation	200	161
Food	400	271
Service	400	307
Entertainment	100	81
Cruise	400	298

dramatic, calming, 35-ft (10.6-meter) high, Lalique-style sculpture (it's actually made of fiberglass) of two mythical figures behind a veil of water. At the top of the atrium is the ship's library.

The carpeting throughout is of an excellent quality, much of it custom designed and made of long-lasting 100% wool. Original artworks by British artists include several tapestries and sculptures. For a weird experience, try standing on the midships staircase and look at the oil on canvas paintings by Nicholas Hely Hutchinson – they are curved – this has a dramatic effect on one's ability not to be seasick while cruising through the Bay of Biscay.

Other features include a virtual reality games room, 12 lounges/bars (among the nicest are Andersons – similar to Anderson's aboard *Oriana*, with a fireplace and mahogany paneling, and the Crow's Nest – complete with a lovely one-sided model of one of P&O's former liners: *Strathnaver* of 1931, scrapped in Hong Kong in 1962. There is also a cinema that doubles as a concert and lecture hall.

There are special facilities and rooms for children and teenagers – even a night nursery (for under-5s, as well as slumber parties for 6–9 year olds), and a whole deck outdoors to play on (swimming pools and whirlpools included just for the youngsters). In addition, 16 cabins have interconnecting doors – good for families with children (or maid). At peak holiday times (summer, Christmas, Easter) there could be 400 or more children on board. However, the ship absorbs them well, and the children's programming helps keep them occupied. Toybox is the playroom for

2–5 year olds, Jack's for the 6–9 year olds, Quarterdeck for 10–13 year olds, and Decibels for 14–17 year olds.

The library has several writing desks, large leather audio listening chairs, a good range of hardback books (and a librarian), and skillfully crafted inlaid wood tables. On the second day of almost any cruise, however, it will have been almost stripped of books by word-hungry passengers. The library also sells some nautical books. An internet center was added in 2002, and is located on the port side of the Crow's Nest observation lounge.

Children and teens have "Club Aurora" programs with their own rooms and their own outdoor pool. Children can be entertained until 10pm, which gives parents time to have dinner and go dancing. All cabins also have a baby-listening device. A night nursery for small children (ages 2–5) is available at no extra charge (6pm–2am). Teenagers have their own hangout, Decibels.

In this ship, P&O Cruises has improved on the facilities of older sister ship *Oriana*, with larger cabins and suites and with more dining options and choice of public areas. *Aurora* provides a decent, standardized cruise experience – good value for the money – for its mainly British passengers (of all dialects) and is ideal for those who don't want to fly to join a cruise, as the ship sails from Southampton. Each year, the *Aurora* undertakes an around-the-world cruise; this is excellent value for money.

However, in the quest for increased onboard revenue (and shareholder value), even birthday cakes now cost extra, as do espressos and cappuccinos (fake ones, made from instant coffee, are available in the dining rooms). Also at extra cost are ice creams, and bottled water (this can add up to a considerable amount on an around-the-world cruise). The onboard currency is the British pound. For gratuities, you should typically allow £3.50 ($5.25) per person, per day.

A fine British brass band send-off accompanies all sailings. Other touches include church bells that sound throughout the ship for the interdenominational Sunday church service. A coach service for passengers embarking or disembarking in Southampton covers much of the UK. Car parking is available (one rate for undercover parking, one rate for an open compound).

The ship's layout is a little disjointed in certain places, and there are several dead-ends and some poor signage. The reception desk's opening hours (7am–8pm) are too short. Shuttle buses, once provided in the various ports, are no longer free when provided (except on the around-the-world cruise). Standing in line for embarkation, disembarkation, shore tenders, and for self-serve buffet meals is an inevitable aspect of cruising aboard all large ships. During the school holidays, there will be many children aboard; this can irritate some older passengers. The cost of sending emails (from the four computers in the library) is high, at £3 ($4.50) for 10 minutes. "Cashless Cruising" doesn't include tips (for an around-the-world cruise, this means carrying more than $750 in cash).

The final word: *Aurora* is the new *Canberra*, and there will typically be lots of smokers aboard..

SUITABLE FOR: *Aurora* is best for adults of all ages (although most cruises attract the over-50s), and families with children of all ages who want a cruise that starts and ends in the UK, aboard a large ship with all the facilities of a small resort, with food and service that are very acceptable, though not as good as aboard some other cruise ships.

ACCOMMODATION. There are five main grades of cabins, in 26 price categories (location and size govern price). Included are 2 two-level penthouses, 10 suites with balconies, 18 mini-suites with balconies, 368 cabins with balconies, 225 standard outside-view cabins, 16 interconnecting family cabins, and 279 interior (no view) cabins.

All grades, from the largest to the smallest, provide the following common features: polished cherry wood laminate cabinetry, full-length mirror, tea and coffee-making facilities, as well as a personal safe, refrigerator, television, individually controlled air conditioning; twin beds that convert to a queen-size double bed, sofa and coffee table. There are four whole decks of cabins with private balconies (this is about 40% of all cabins), and these feature easy-to-open sliding glass floor-to-ceiling doors; the partitions are of the almost full floor-to-ceiling type – so they really are quite private – and cannot be overlooked from above.

Cabin insulation could be much better (particularly poor is the noise created by the magnetic catches in drawers and on the closet doors). Also, the TV sets provide only monaural sound. Although most doorways are 26 inches (66 cm) wide, the measurement of actual access is 2 inches (5 cm) less because of the doorframe; however, some doorways are only 21.5 inches (55 cm) wide.

A good range of Molton Brown products (shampoo, body lotion, shower gel) is provided for all cabins designated as penthouse suites, suites or mini-suites. For all other cabins, only soap is provided, plus a "sport wash" combination soap and shampoo in a dispenser in the shower (so take your favorite shampoo and conditioner), and a small pouch of assorted personal-care items. All grades get thick, 100% cotton bathrobes, and 100% cotton towels. Except for the suites, no cabins have illuminated closets, and cabin ceilings are very plain.

Penthouse Suites: The largest cabins consist of two penthouse suites (named Library Suite and Piano Suite), each 953 sq. ft (88.5 sq. meters). They have forward-facing views, being located directly underneath the navigation bridge (the blinds must be drawn at night so as not to affect navigation). Each is spread over two decks in height, and connected by a beautiful wood curved staircase. One suite has a baby grand piano (which can be played manually or electronically), while the other has a private library. The living area is on the lower deck (Deck 10), and incorporates a dining suite (a first in a P&O ship) and a small private balcony. In the bedroom, upstairs, there is a walk-in closet, while the bathroom is decked out in porcelain and polished granite, with twin basins, bathtub and separate shower enclosure. There is also a small private balcony. **Suites:** The suites (there are 10 of them) measure about 445 sq. ft (41.3 sq. meters). They have a separate bedroom with two lower beds that convert to a queen-sized bed. There is a walk-in dressing area and closet, with plenty of drawer space, a trouser press and ironing board. The lounge has a sofa, armchairs, dining table and chairs, writing desk, television, radio and stereo system. The marble-clad bathroom has a whirlpool bath, shower and toilet. The private balcony has space for two deck lounge chairs, plus two chairs and two tables. Butler service is provided.

Mini-Suites: These measure 325 sq. ft (30.1 sq. meters), and have a separate bedroom area with two lower beds that convert to a queen-sized bed. There's one double and two single closets, a good amount of drawer space, binoculars, a trouser press and ironing board. Each private balcony has a blue plastic deck covering, one deck lounge chair, one chair and table, and exterior light.

Standard Outside-view/Interior (No View) Cabins: Any cabin designated as a double with private balcony measure about 175 sq. ft (16.2 sq. meters). They have two lower beds that convert to a queen-sized bed. The sitting area has a sofa and table. There's also a vanity table/writing desk, and a private balcony with blue plastic deck covering, two chairs (with only a small recline) and a small table. Note that a 110-volt (American) socket is located underneath the vanity desk drawer – in a difficult to access position.

Outside-view or Interior (with no view) Cabins have two lower beds that convert to a queen-sized bed, closet (but few drawers), and are 150 sq. ft (14 sq. meters). The bathroom has a mini-bath/shower and toilet, or shower and toilet.

All bathrooms in all grades (except those designated as suites) are compact, modular units, and have mirror-fronted cabinets, although the lighting is quite soft (not strong enough for the application of make-up), and, in cabins with bathtubs, the retractable clothesline is located too high for most people to reach.

There are 22 wheelchair-accessible cabins, well outfitted for the physically challenged passenger and almost all within easy access to lifts. However, one cabin (D165 on Deck 8) is located between forward and mid-ships stairways, and it is difficult to access the public rooms on Deck 8 without first going to the deck below, due to several steps and tight corners. All other wheelchair-accessible cabins are well positioned, and eight have a private balcony.

CUISINE/DINING. The two main dining rooms (each seats about 525) have tables for 2, 4, 6, 8 and 10, and there are two seatings. Medina, the midships restaurant, has a vaguely Moorish theme, while Alexandria, with windows on three sides, has Egyptian decor. Both are non-smoking, and both have more tables for two than in the equivalent restaurants aboard close sister ship *Oriana*. The china is Wedgwood, the silverware is by Elkington, the food by P&O.

The cuisine is very British – a little adventurous at times, but always with plenty of curry dishes and other standard British items – but with good presentation (better than other ships in the P&O Cruises fleet). You should not expect exquisite dining, though – this is British hotel catering that doesn't pretend to offer caviar and other gourmet foods. But what it does present is attractive and tasty, with some

excellent gravies and sauces to accompany all dining room meals. In keeping with the Britishness of P&O Cruises, the desserts and cakes are always good. The service is provided by a team of friendly stewards from Goa, with which P&O has had a long relationship.

In addition to the two formal dining rooms, there are several other dining options. You can, for example, also have dinner in the 24-hour, 120-seat French bistro-style restaurant, Cafe Bordeaux, for which there is a cover charge (for dinner only). Breakfasts and lunches are also featured here, as are several types of coffees: espresso, cappuccino, latte, ristretto, as well as flavored coffees. So, if you want a croque-monsieur (a toasted ham and Gruyère cheese sandwich) at five in the morning, you can have it.

Casual, self-serve breakfasts and lunches can be taken from the buffet in a dazzlingly colorful eatery named "The Orangery", which has fine ocean views. Other casual dining spots include the Sidewalk Cafe (for fast food items poolside), a French pâtisserie (for pastries and coffee), champagne bar and, in a first for a P&O cruise ship, Raffles coffee and chocolate bar (but without the ceiling fans). All informal dining spots are non-smoking.

ENTERTAINMENT. There is a wide variety of mainly British entertainment, from production shows to top British "name" and lesser name cabaret artists. The Stadium Theater Company is a group of resident actors, singers and dancers. They provide theater-style presentations such as mini versions of well-known musicals, "book" shows, revues, and drama presentations. There is also a program of theme cruises (antiques, art appreciation, classical music, comedy, cricket, gardening, jazz, Scottish dance, etc).

Ballroom dance fans will make use of the four good-sized wooden dance floors. The ship always carries a professional dance couple as hosts and teachers, and plenty of dancing time is included in the programming.

SPA/FITNESS. The Oasis Spa is midships on Lido Deck – almost at the top of the ship, just forward of the Crystal swimming pool. It is moderately large, and facilities include a gymnasium with the latest high-tech muscle-pumping and body toning toning equipment. There is also a sauna and steam room (both unisex, so you'll need a bathing suit). There's a beauty salon, a spiral staircase, and a relaxation area overlooking the forward Riviera swimming pool.

The spa is operated by Harding Brothers, a UK concession that provides the staff and a wide range of beauty and wellness treatments. Examples of treatments include: Body Toning (detox for the body); Seaweed Wrap; Collagen Velvet Facial Mask, and a range of aromatherapy treatments. Book spa treatments as soon after you embark as possible, as time slots fill up quickly aboard large ships such as this. Examples of prices: a full body massage is £60 for 50 minutes; an Indian head massage is £42 for 45 minutes; a holistic facial is £45 for 75 minutes. A manicure is £24 for 45 minutes, while a pedicure is £35 for 45 minutes.

A sports court incorporates a golf practice cage and a golf simulator (for which an extra charge applies).

Ausonia
★★ +

Mid-Size Ship: . . . . .12,609 tons	Passenger Decks: 8	Cabins (with private balcony): 0
Lifestyle: . . . . .Standard	Total Crew: 280	Cabins (wheelchair accessible): 0
Cruise Line: . . . . .Louis Cruise Lines/	Passengers	Cabin Current: . . . . .220 volts
First Choice	(lower beds/all berths): 508/701	Elevators: 1
Former Names: . . . . .none	Passenger Space Ratio	Casino (gaming tables): . . . . .Yes
Builder: . . . .Cantieri Riuniti dell' Adriatico	(lower beds/all berths): 24.8/17.9	Slot Machines: . . . . .Yes
(Italy)	Crew/Passenger Ratio	Swimming Pools (outdoors): 1
Original Cost: . . . . .n/a	(lower beds/all berths): 1.8/2.5	Swimming Pools (indoor): 0
Entered Service: . . . .Sept 1957/May 1998	Navigation Officers: . . . . . . .Greek/Cypriot	Whirlpools: 1
Registry: .Cyprus	Cabins (total): .254	Self-Service Launderette: . . . . .No
Length (ft/m): 522.5/159.26	Size Range (sq ft/m): 69.9–269.1/	Dedicated Cinema/Seats: Yes/125
Beam (ft/m): 69.8/21.29	6.5–25.0	Library: . . . . .Yes
Draft (ft/m): 21.4/6.54	Cabins (outside view): 152	Classification Society: . . .Registro Navale
Propulsion/Propellers: . . . . .steam turbine	Cabins (interior/no view): 102	Italiano (RINA)
(12,799kW)/2	Cabins (for one person): 1	

OVERALL SCORE: 996 (OUT OF A POSSIBLE 2,000 POINTS)

OVERVIEW. This all-white ship has a classic steamship profile, with a large, single funnel placed amidships. There is a decent amount of open deck and sunning space although the swimming pool is tiny (a "dip" pool). The ship was bought by Louis Cruise Lines in 1997, and underwent extensive refurbishing and upgrading in 1998. It has also had much mechanical and galley upgrading.

Most public rooms are on one deck (Corfu Deck), so it's easy to find one's way around. The number of public lounges and rooms is, however, limited. The Majorca Lounge (main showlounge) is pleasantly decorated, although the sight lines to the stage are poor; the seats on the raised sections on the port and starboard sides are slightly better. There is a small nightclub, casino, duty-free shop, an enclosed "winter garden" lounge/reading area on the starboard side, and a cinema.

There are few public rooms. Many passengers are heavy smokers and it is difficult to avoid them. The ship has a narrow gangway, which can be quite steep in some ports. You can book the deck you want your cabin to be on, but cabins are assigned by First Choice Cruises. The onboard currency is the British pound.

SUITABLE FOR: *Ausonia* is best suited to adult couples and singles looking for a basic cruise holiday, in a ship that is more traditional than modern, and doesn't have the latest facilities. This could be good for your first cruise experience, in a setting that is comfortable, not luxurious, and at a price that is low, but provides fair value for money.

ACCOMMODATION. From suites to standard interior and out-

BERLITZ'S RATINGS

	Possible	Achieved
Ship	500	146
Accommodation	200	93
Food	400	260
Service	400	241
Entertainment	100	48
Cruise	400	208

side cabins, all are small and compact, yet reasonably comfortable, in six cabin grades. They have all the basics, including a private bathroom and adequate closet space for frugal packers (drawer space is limited, however).

The uppermost cabin grades have a full-sized bathtub (two suites have whirlpool baths), while all others have showers. There are several family cabins. Some interior and outside standard cabins have upper and lower berths.

CUISINE/DINING. The no-smoking Pharaoh's Dining Room, located high up in the vessel on the same deck as most of the few public rooms aboard this ship, has good ocean views from large picture windows, and has fine china and pleasant table settings. There are tables for four, six or eight, and meals are in two seatings. The international cuisine provides a good mix of Continental fare, with some regional Mediterranean specialties and British favorites. The selection of fruits and cheeses is limited. The basic wine list provides an inexpensive range and a decent choice.

ENTERTAINMENT. The Discovery Showlounge is a single-level room designed for cabaret acts and lectures, not lavish shows. Pillars obstruct sight lines from several seats. The entertainment is low-key, low-budget, and a bit "end-of-pier-ish". Several musical units provide music for dancing and listening.

SPA/FITNESS. There is a small gymnasium, and a sauna. Free fitness classes include stretch 'n' relax, aerobics, and others aimed at a general audience (mostly women).

Black Prince
★★ +

Small Ship:	11,209 tons	Total Crew:	200	Cabins (with private balcony):	0
Lifestyle:	Standard	Passengers		Cabins (wheelchair accessible):	2
Cruise Line:	Fred Olsen Cruise Lines	(lower beds/all berths):	439/472	Cabin Current:	230 volts
Former Names:	none	Passenger Space Ratio		Elevators:	2
Builder:	Fender Werft (Germany)	(lower beds/all berths):	25.3/23.7	Casino (gaming tables):	Yes
Original Cost:	$20 million	Crew/Passenger Ratio		Slot Machines:	No
Entered Service:	1966	(lower beds/all berths):	2.2/2.3	Swimming Pools (outdoors):	1
Registry:	The Bahamas	Navigation Officers:	European	Swimming Pools (indoors):	1
Length (ft/m):	470.4/143.40	Cabins (total):	234	Whirlpools:	2
Beam (ft/m):	66.6/20.30	Size Range (sq ft/m):	80.7–226.0/	Self-Service Launderette:	No
Draft (ft/m):	20.0/6.10		7.5–21.0	Dedicated Cinema/Seats:	No
Propulsion/Propellers:	diesel	Cabins (outside view):	167	Library:	Yes
	(12,310kW)/2	Cabins (interior/no view):	67	Classification Society:	Det Norske
Passenger Decks:	7	Cabins (for one person):	29		Veritas

OVERALL SCORE: 1,093 (OUT OF A POSSIBLE 2,000 POINTS)

OVERVIEW. *Black Prince* is a traditional style of ship (the name is 14th-century, originally referring to the son of Edward III), owned and operated as a family-run business. With its thick hull, it is as solidly built as a battleship. Originally used for winter cruising and summer North Sea crossings, the ship has been well maintained, though it has a rather ungainly profile, and tends to pitch in unkind seas (but probably less so than any new ship would). One nice feature of this old-style ship is that it has many nooks and crannies around its open decks (most of which are either painted steel decks or decks covered with blue "turf"; among them is one forward observation deck that lets you look over the bows and navigation bridge.

There are few public rooms, the principal one being the Neptune Lounge – a two-decks high room (with bars on both levels) that is the ship's main show lounge.. Another room, the Aquitaine Lounge, sits in the front part of the ship, and tends to be the quiet room – good for reading an absorbing book. There is a small, little used casino section located on the starboard side of this lounge. Additionally, a passageway that was formerly part of two restaurants is now a photo gallery and lounge area.

The decor has a very homely, restrained feel and ambiance, with soft lighting and no glitz anywhere. Many of the soft furnishings are hand-tailored on board by Filipino upholsterers. The ship has good wooden stairways throughout, although the steps are a little steep. An ironing room is provided – another useful addition for the ship's mainly British passengers. This is one solidly built ship (they don't make them like this anymore) that plods along at teenage speeds, but will always arrive on time, no mat-

BERLITZ'S RATINGS		
	Possible	Achieved
Ship	500	271
Accommodation	200	109
Food	400	209
Service	400	236
Entertainment	100	51
Cruise	400	217

ter what. Although it was really constructed as a dual purpose cruise-ferry (it used to carry tomatoes from the Canary Islands below decks, and passengers above decks), over the years it has been converted into a handy-sized vessel that will give you a comfortable ride. Actually, coming into (and leaving from) port reminds me of those Holiday Inn beds years ago that vibrated for you when you inserted a quarter (25 cents) into a little box by its side. Still, there are other ships of the same era that do the same thing.

Although the names sound similar, *Black Prince* is not at all like the larger *Black Watch*, which has many more facilities and is altogether a better ship. *Black Prince* does have an unstuffy, unpretentious feel, an almost totally Filipino staff, and is well suited to the informal, older British passenger. However, standards of cleanliness, food and service have been allowed to become sloppy. While there are many repeat passengers who would not dream of trying another ship, some newcomers will feel that this is an old, tired ship that should be heading for retirement – soon, particularly in light of the increased competition from other, newer ships.

The artwork aboard this ship is eclectic, to say the least, totally uncoordinated and not looked after, but there are a few interesting pieces if you seek them out: one, a huge wood carving in the Lido Lounge (it was originally in a house in Oslo), has five bullet holes in it (but to get the full story, you'll need to book a cruise).

So, what are the good points about cruising aboard *Black Prince*? You'll have a good, well-rounded cruise experience, with well organized cruises, interesting itineraries, very few announcements, complimentary shuttle buses in many ports of call (few companies offer this facility today), a reasonably comfortable (but quite basic and dated) ship, a decent standard of food, and with friendly service from (mostly Filipino) crew members who smile and mean well. Cruising aboard *Black Prince* also means that drinks prices are extremely reasonable (well below those of most other ships operating from UK ports) and you won't be fleeced and poked for onboard revenue at every turn. It also means cruising with experienced Norwegian navigation officers and itineraries that are well planned, with long port stays. So, for all I have said about the ship being of the old ilk, cruising aboard it is a comfortable, cosseting experience.

Port taxes are included for UK passengers. For the ship's (mainly) British passengers, the National Express bus operator works in conjunction with Fred Olsen Cruise Lines to provide a dedicated Cruiselink service via London's Victoria Coach Station to the UK departure ports of Dover or Southampton.

The crew is extremely friendly by nature, although the feeling that many passengers have is that the ship now operates more for the crew than for its passengers. Standards of product delivery and professionalism have fallen over the past few years (a stronger onboard middle management with properly recognized training is needed). The onboard currency is the British pound.

It is often hard to get away from smokers, and the service has become overly casual of late. The company lists recommended gratuities of £4 (around $6) per passenger per day, which, to some, seems a lot. The air-conditioning is inconsistent; in particular in many cabins it is not good (the ship was built when forced air circulation was the norm). Handrails throughout the ship are topped with black plastic (reminiscent of old schools and ferries) and would look and feel so much better in wood.

Yet, despite all the negatives, it's the friendly ambiance and caring crew aboard this ship that make passengers want to come back again and again (rather like going back to a favourite B&B).

SUITABLE FOR: *Black Prince* is best suited to the older British passenger (those over 60) who enjoys seeking out the world's duty-free shops, with British-style entertainment and cabaret acts. This ship is for people who like Morris Minor cars, who don't want the latest high-tech plastic laminate cruise ship, and couldn't care less about things like having a telephone in each cabin, or internet connectivity, and for those who really like the intimacy that only small ships can provide.

ACCOMMODATION. There is a wide range of cabin sizes and configurations (the brochure lists 14) to choose from (from dimensionally challenged to quite adequate), and a good percentage of cabins are particularly reserved for single passengers. Do note, however, that many cabins have poor air-conditioning, and hard beds, and some cabins have second-person beds that fold down at night and are used as seating by day. If your accommodation is in the aft third of the ship, you won't need an alarm clock to get you out of

bed in the mornings when the ship is coming into port, because the ship's vibration performs that function for you.

Duvets are provided in all grades of cabin, the bathroom towels are 100% cotton and reasonably sized (not large). A hairdryer is also supplied. A package of Gilchrist & Soames personal toiletry items (bath gel, shampoo/conditioner, sewing kit, shower cap) is provided for all passengers.

The outside-view suites are reasonably decent (particularly comfortable are the Gran Canaria and Lanzarote suites, with their wood-paneled walls) and nicely appointed. Other cabins are small, but reasonably well equipped (except for the lowest grades, which are very small and rather utilitarian), and tastefully decorated, for a smaller ship. There is a charge for some room service items. The upper-grade cabins also have a refrigerator.

CUISINE/DINING. The dining room has two sections, Fleur de Lys and Royal Garter, both non-smoking and with big picture windows along one side. There are two seatings (sometimes, first- and second-seating diners exchange seatings, a pleasant arrangement). The Balblom Restaurant (with wood/glass ceiling and patio-style tables and chairs), is located atop the ship, and provides another choice for dining (reservations required for dinner when featured).

Fred Olsen Cruise Lines has above-average cuisine that is attractively presented, with a good range of fish, seafood, meat and chicken dishes, and vegetarian options. The food is generally of good quality, with a decent selection of main course items to suit most British tastes. Breakfast buffets tend to be repetitive, although they appear to satisfy most.

Communication with the Filipino waiters can prove a little frustrating at times (although it is better now than it has been in the past, and smiles can compensate). There is a very decent range of wines, at moderate prices, but few of the wine stewards have much knowledge of wines.

ENTERTAINMENT. The Neptune Lounge is the name of the ship's showlounge. It has two levels (although sight lines to the stage are quite restricted from many seats due to the configuration of the room).

The entertainment mainly consists of small revue shows by a small team of resident singers/dancers, and cabaret acts of questionable quality (they seem to rotate around many ships of the same style and size in the cruise industry), although, to be fair, passengers who cruise aboard this ship are not really looking for first-rate entertainment, but rather something to fill the time after dinner, which is the main event for most passengers.

SPA/FITNESS. The one facility that is extremely good (for a small ship) is the indoor fitness/leisure center, complete with an indoor swimming pool and health spa area with gymnasium, sauna, and small beauty salon. To get to it, though, you have to negotiate a steep staircase with short steps. The spa is operated by Harding Brothers, a concession. Some fitness classes are free, while some, such as yoga (£5 per class or £15 for four classes), cost extra. Make appointments as early as possible, as time slots go quickly.

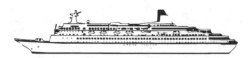

Black Watch
★★★★

Mid-Size Ship: . . . . .28,492 tons	Passenger Decks: 8	Cabins (for one person): 38
Lifestyle: . . . . .Standard	Total Crew: 310	Cabins (with private balcony): 9
Cruise Line: . . . . .Fred Olsen Cruise Lines	Passengers	Cabins (wheelchair accessible): 4
Former Names: . . . .*Star Odyssey,*	(lower beds/all berths): 762/843	Cabin Current: . . . . .110 and 220 volts
Westward, Royal Viking Star	Passenger Space Ratio	Elevators: 4
Builder: . . . . .Wartsila (Finland)	(lower beds/all berths): 37.4/33.7	Casino (gaming tables): . . . . .Yes
Original Cost: . . . .$22.5 million	Crew/Passenger Ratio	Slot Machines: . . . . .Yes
Entered Service: . . . June 1972/Nov 1996	(lower beds/all berths): 2.4/2.7	Swimming Pools (outdoors): 2
Registry: . . . . .The Bahamas	Navigation Officers: . . . . .European	Swimming Pools (indoors): 0
Length (ft/m): 674.1/205.47	Cabins (total): 400	Whirlpools: 3
Beam (ft/m): 82.6/25.20	Size Range (sq ft/m): 135.6–819.1/	Self-Service Launderette: . . . . .Yes
Draft (ft/m): 24.7/7.55	12.6–76.1	Dedicated Cinema/Seats: Yes/156
Propulsion/Propellers: . . . . .diesel	Cabins (outside view): 352	Library: . . . . .Yes
(13,400kW)/2	Cabins (interior/no view): 48	Classification Society: Det Norske Veritas

OVERALL SCORE: 1,429 (OUT OF A POSSIBLE 2,000 POINTS)

OVERVIEW. Acquired by Fred Olsen Cruise Lines in late 1996, this handsome ship, originally built for long-distance cruising for the now-defunct Royal Viking Line (actually it was built for one of the three original shipping partners who formed the line – Bergenske Dampskibsselskab), has a sharply raked bow and a sleek appearance that was "stretched" in 1981 with the addition of a mid section. The ship's name is taken from the famous Scottish Black Watch regiment, although the ship itself is an all-white color. There is an excellent amount of open deck and sunbathing space, and a good health-fitness area high atop the ship, as well as a wide wrap-around teakwood promenade deck (with wind-breaker on the aft part of the deck).

The interior decor is quiet and restful, with wide stairways and foyers, soft lighting and no glitz anywhere, although many passengers find the artwork a little drab (it is, in reality, rather more Scandinavian eclectic than anything). In general, good materials, fabrics (including the use of the Black Watch tartan) and soft furnishings add to a pleasant ambiance and comfortable feeling experienced throughout the public rooms, most of which are quite spacious and have high, indented ceilings.

There is a wide selection of public rooms, most of which (including the main dining room) are located on one deck in a horizontal layout that makes access easy. An observation lounge (called The Observatory) high atop the ship, is decorated in nautical memorabilia, has commanding views and is a popular spot – particularly when the ship leaves ports of call in the evenings (Boddington's and Stella Artois beers are available on draft here, and in all bars throughout the ship). There is a good cinema (few ships today have a

BERLITZ'S RATINGS

	Possible	Achieved
Ship	500	371
Accommodation	200	158
Food	400	268
Service	400	281
Entertainment	100	73
Cruise	400	278

dedicated cinema) with a steeply tiered floor, and a pleasant library (with an adjacent computer/internet access room containing two computer terminals), and a card room.

One of the most popular public spaces is the Braemar Room, a large lounge close to the restaurant. It has a self-help beverage corner for coffees and teas (open 24 hours a day), comfortable chairs, and large ocean-view windows along one side. Afternoon tea is served here. On one wall is an old iron figurehead from a ship called *Braemar Castle* (it's one of several iron figureheads found aboard this ship, from a collection owned by the Olsen family).

Smokers will appreciate a special, small, cigar and pipe smoking room (The Cove), as well as a bar (Pipers Bar) for general smoking (these are the only two locations inside the ship where smoking is permitted).

The casino consists of two blackjack tables and a roulette table, and is presently located in a passageway opposite the Starlite Nightclub; a separate room houses a clutch of rarely used slot machines. A self-serve launderette (very useful on the longer cruises operated by this ship) has four washing machines, five dryers, and a couple of irons in a large user-friendly room.

Black Watch, which was originally constructed for long-distance cruising, has settled in well under the Fred Olsen Cruise Lines brand, and should provide you with a good, well-rounded cruise experience; there is plenty of space per passenger, even when the ship is full. The cruises are well organized, with interesting itineraries, and complimentary shuttle buses in many ports of call.

Black Watch is a very comfortable (not luxurious) ship in

which to cruise, with a good standard of food and service from a friendly, mostly Filipino staff that provides decent (though not faultless) service.

All in all, Fred Olsen Cruise Lines has come a long way from humble beginnings, and now offers extremely good value for money cruises in a relaxed environment that provides passengers with many of the comforts of home. Port taxes are included for UK passengers.

For the ship's mainly British passengers, the National Express bus operator works in conjunction with Fred Olsen Cruise Lines to provide a dedicated Cruiselink service via London's Victoria Coach Station to the UK departure ports of Dover or Southampton. The onboard currency is the British pound.

Although it is being well maintained, do remember that this ship is more than 30 years old, which means that little problems such as gurgling plumbing, creaking joints, and other idiosyncrasies can occur occasionally, and air conditioning may not be all that it should be (this is particularly true in some cabins). The company lists recommended gratuities of £4 ($6) per passenger per day, which, to some, seems a lot. Only a few suites have private balconies.

SUITABLE FOR: *Black Watch* is best suited to the older British passenger who enjoys seeking out the world's duty-free shops, and wants a British cruise environment, in very comfortable surroundings, with British food and entertainment, and more formal attire than is found aboard *Black Prince* and *Braemar*.

ACCOMMODATION. There are 18 price categories of cabins (plus one for the owner's suite, whose price is not listed in the brochure), including four grades of cabin for those traveling solo (these are spread across most of the cabin decks, and not just the lower decks, as some lines do). The wide range of cabins provides something for everyone, from spacious suites with separate bedrooms, to small (interior – no view) cabins. While most cabins are for two persons, some can accommodate a third, fourth, or even a fifth person.

In all grades, duvets are provided, the bathroom towels are 100% cotton and are quite large, and a hairdryer is provided. A package of Gilchrist & Soames personal toiletry items (bath gel, shampoo/conditioner, sewing kit, shower cap) is supplied to all passengers. Occupants of suite grades also get a cotton bathrobe and cold canapes each evening (as well as priority seating in the dining rooms). The room service menu is quite limited and could be improved (although there is an abundance of food available at most times of the day). The suites and cabins on Decks 7, 8, and 9 are quiet units. A number of cabins located in the aft section of Decks 3, 4 and 5 can prove to be uncomfortable, with noise from throbbing engines and generator units a major source (particularly from cabins adjacent to the engine casing).

Outside-view/Inside (No View) Cabins: Spread across Decks 3, 4, 5, 7 and 8, all cabins (approximately 135–200 sq. ft/12.6–18.5 sq. meters) are quite well equipped, and there is plenty of good (illuminated) closet, drawer and storage space (the drawers are metal and tinny, however, and in some closets they consist of wire baskets – like you might find in inexpensive hotels in Europe). No-smoking cabins are available. Some cabin bathrooms have awkward access, and insulation between some of the lower grade cabins could be better. The bathrooms are of a decent size. All have had a facelift, with new toiletries cabinets, washbasin facings, and re-tiled floors. Some cabins have a small bathtub, although many have only a shower enclosure.

Deluxe/Bridge/Junior Suites: These suites 240–260 sq. ft/22.2–24.1 sq. meters), on Decks 7 and 8, have a large sleeping area and lounge area with ocean-view picture windows and refrigerator, plenty of hooks for hanging bathrobes, outerwear and luggage; and a bathroom with bathtub and shower (cabin 8019 is the exception, with a shower instead of a bathtub).

Marquee Suites: These suites (approximately 440 sq. ft/40.8 sq. meters) have a large sleeping area and lounge area with bigger ocean view picture windows and a refrigerator, more hooks for hanging bathrobes, outerwear and luggage; and a bathroom with bathtub and shower.

Premier Suites: Anyone wanting the largest cabins on board (apart from one owner's suite), should consider one of nine suites, each of which is named after a place: Amalfi (9006), Lindos (9002), Nice (9004), each measuring 547.7 sq. ft/50.8 sq. meters; Seville (9001), Singapore (9003), Carmel (9005), Bergen (9007), Waterford (9009), each measuring 341.7 sq ft/31.7 m2; and Windsor (9008), measuring 574.8 sq. ft/53.4 sq. meters. These suites feature a separate bedroom with ample closet and other storage space, a lounge with large windows (with large television and VCR, refrigerator and mini-bar), and bathroom with full-size bathtub and shower, and separate toilet.

Owner's Suite: This measures 819.1 sq. ft/76.1 sq. meters (including the balcony), or 625.4 sq. ft/58.1 sq. meters (excluding the balcony). It consists of a foyer leading into a lounge, with sofa, table and chairs, audio center (television, CD player, video player), refrigerator and mini-bar. A separate bedroom has a double bed, and ample closet and drawer space. A second bedroom has two bunk beds (good for families with children). The bathroom is large and has a full-size bathtub, separate shower enclosure, toilet, and two washbasins. There is a large private balcony with space enough for a table and six chairs, plus more space for a couple of deck lounge chairs. It is located just aft of the navigation bridge on the starboard side of the ship.

CUISINE/DINING. The Glentanar Dining Room has a high ceiling, a white sail-like focal point at its center, and ample space at each table. It is a non-smoking dining room, and the chairs, which have armrests, are quite comfortable. There is also a smaller offshoot of the dining room called the Orchid Room, which can be reserved for a more intimate (and quieter) dining experience (suite occupants get first choice for seats in this room). While breakfast is typically in an open seating arrangement, there are two seatings for lunch and dinner. Two cold food display counters are provided for passengers to help themselves to breakfast and lunch items.

The Garden Cafe (also a non-smoking room) is a small, more casual dining spot with a light, breezy decor that will remind you of a garden conservatory. It sometimes has special themed dinners, such as French, Indian, or Thai. There is a self-help salad bar and hot food display so you can eat with the minimum of fuss from waiters, although they are available for service when you need them. The room is also the location for late-night snacks.

Fred Olsen Cruise Lines has above-average cuisine that is attractively presented, with a good range of fish, seafood, meat and chicken dishes, as well as vegetarian options. The food is generally of good quality, with a decent selection of main course items to suit most British tastes. Breakfast buffets tend to be quite repetitive, although they appear to satisfy most.

Communication with the Filipino waiters can prove a little frustrating at times (although it is better now than it has been in the past, and smiles can compensate to some extent). There is a reasonably decent range of wines, at moderate prices, but few of the wine stewards have much knowledge of wines.

Coffee and tea are available round-the-clock in the Braemar Room, a large lounge that is adjacent to, but aft of, the Glentanar Restaurant.

ENTERTAINMENT. The Neptune Lounge is the ship's show-lounge. It is a large room that seats about 400, although some pillars do obstruct sight lines from several seats.

The entertainment mainly consists of small-scale production shows presented by a small team of resident singers/dancers, and cabaret acts. The production shows try hard, but the standards are quite poor in reality, and the cast self-congratulatory. Apart from the production shows, cabaret acts that typically rotate around many cruise ships of the same standard fill in the time after dinner. To be fair, however, passengers who cruise aboard this ship are not really looking for first-rate entertainment, but rather something to fill the time after dinner, which is the main event for most.

There is plenty of live music for dancing (many of the musicians are Filipino) and listening in several lounges, and good British sing-alongs are a feature on each cruise.

SPA/FITNESS. A decent amount of space is given to providing health and fitness facilities, located at the top of the ship at the front (it is inaccessible for anyone in a wheelchair). There is a combined gymnasium/aerobics room, while a door provides acces to steam rooms, saunas, and changing rooms. Spa Rituals is the name of the treatments provided by Steiner. Here are some examples of prices: Elemis Aromapure facial: £29; Well-being massage (50 minutes): £35; Personal Training Session (60 minutes): £20. Sports facilities include a large paddle tennis court, golf practice nets, shuffleboard, and ring toss.

Note that many of the spa staff are quite young, and they will probably try to sell you Steiner's own-brand Elemis beauty products (spa girls have sales targets). Some fitness classes are free, while some, such as yoga and kick-boxing, cost extra. However, being aboard will give you an opportunity to try some of the more exotic treatments (particularly some of the massages available).

Do make appointments as early as possible, as treatment time slots go quickly, so the day you board is the best time to book your preferred treatments.

WIND SPEEDS

A navigational announcement to passengers is normally made once or twice a day, giving the ship's position, temperature, and weather information.

Various winds affect the world's weather patterns. Such well-known winds as the Bora, Mistral, Northwind, and Sirocco, among others, play an important part in the makeup of weather at and above sea level. Wind velocity is measured on the Beaufort scale, a method that was devised in 1805 by Commodore Francis Beaufort, later Admiral and Knight Commander of the Bath, for measuring the force of wind at sea. Originally, it measured the effect of the wind on a fully rigged man-of-war (which was usually laden with cannon and heavy ammunition). It became the official way of recording wind velocity in 1874, when the International Meteorological Committee adopted it.

Bolero
★★ +

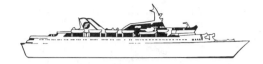

Mid-Size Ship: . . . . .15,781 tons	Total Crew: 330	Cabins (with private balcony): 0
Lifestyle: . . . . .Standard	Passengers	Cabins (wheelchair accessible): 2
Cruise Line: . . . . . . .Spanish Cruise Line	(lower beds/all berths): 802/984	Cabin Current: . . . . .110 and 220 volts
Former Names: . . . . .Starward	Passenger Space Ratio	Elevators: 4
Builder: . . . . .A.G. Weser (Germany)	(lower beds/all berths): 19.6/16.0	Casino (gaming tables): . . . . .Yes
Original Cost: .n/a	Crew/Passenger Ratio	Slot Machines: . . . . .Yes
Entered Service: . . . .Dec 1968/May 2001	(lower beds/all berths): 2.4/2.9	Swimming Pools (outdoors): 2
Registry: . . . . .Panama	Navigation Officers: . . . . .Greek	Swimming Pools (indoors): 0
Length (ft/m): 525.9/160.30	Cabins (total): 401	Whirlpools: 0
Beam (ft/m): 74.9/22.84	Size Range (sq ft/m): 111.9–324.0/	Self-Service Launderette: . . . . .No
Draft (ft/m): 22.5/6.86	10.4–30.1	Dedicated Cinema/Seats: Yes/210
Propulsion/Propellers: . . . . .diesel	Cabins (outside view): 237	Library: . . . . .Yes
(12,950kW)/2	Cabins (interior/no view): 164	Classification Society: . . . . . .Det Norske
Passenger Decks: 7	Cabins (for one person): 0	Veritas

OVERALL SCORE: 988 (OUT OF A POSSIBLE 2,000 POINTS)

OVERVIEW. When it was built in the late 1960s, *Bolero* had a fairly contemporary upper profile with dual swept-back funnels, although now the design looks quite dated. *Bolero* was formerly a Caribbean-based ship owned and operated for many years by Norwegian Cruise Line. The now defunct Festival Cruises acquired the ship in 1995. In May 2001 *Bolero* began operations for Spanish Cruise Line, a joint venture between Spanish tour operator Iberojet and Spanish ferry operator Transmed.

The open deck and sunbathing space is extremely limited (some of the decks are of plain steel, painted blue), and totally cluttered with plenty of plastic deck lounge chairs and sun umbrellas for shade at the aft outdoor decks (but there are no cushioned pads for the deck lounge chairs). Just forward of the twin blue funnels is an enclosed basketball/volleyball court, while aft of the mast is a large solarium-style shielded housing, with multi-level lounge/bar/disco that is adjacent to one of the ship's two swimming pools.

Inside the ship, there is a reasonable choice of public rooms and bars for this size of vessel, and they feature clean, contemporary furnishings and upbeat, cheerful fabric colors and decor. There is a good, steeply tiered dedicated cinema, with good sight lines.

Bolero is acceptable for a first Mediterranean cruise, with a warm, friendly, and lively ambiance. A reasonably attractive ship, it should prove a good choice for first-timers seeking a destination-intensive cruise at a very attractive price, although there is absolutely no finesse anywhere.

Spanish Cruise Line provides a totally Spanish shipboard life and cruise experience in extremely crowded,

BERLITZ'S RATINGS	Possible	Achieved
Ship	500	214
Accommodation	200	96
Food	400	212
Service	400	222
Entertainment	100	48
Cruise	400	196

though moderately comfortable (certainly not elegant or glitzy) surroundings, at a very modest price that translates to very good value for money. The friendly staff try hard to make you feel welcome, like a member of the family. The onboard currency is the euro.

This is a very high-density vessel that really does feel crowded when full (some might call it "ambiance"). It has a less than handsome "duck-tailed" sponson stern (this acts rather like a stabilizer). Smokers are everywhere, and are difficult to avoid (in typical European fashion, ashtrays are simply moved – if used at all – to wherever smokers happen to be sitting. The diesel engines are noisy and tend to "throb" in some parts of the vessel (particularly when the ship is going full speed), including in many cabins on the lower decks. Cabins do not have TV sets. There are simply too many loud, repetitive announcements (all in Spanish).

SUITABLE FOR: *Bolero* is best suited to Spanish-speaking adult couples and single travelers who want to take their first cruise aboard a ship that is unpretentious, with a casual dress code, and food and service that is acceptable but not special, all on a low budget.

ACCOMMODATION. Except for five decent-sized suites, the cabins are very compact units that are moderately comfortable, and are decorated in soft colors, accented by colorful soft furnishings. They are, however, adequate for a one-week cruise, particularly as this company specializes in destination-intensive cruises. While the closet space is limited, there are plenty of drawers, although they are metal and tinny. The bathrooms are small and tight, and the towels are not large, although they are made of 100 percent cotton; the toilets are of the "gentle flush" and not the "barking dog suction" variety as found aboard newer ships. The soundproofing between cabins could be better (each cabin has a notice asking passengers to keep the audio system to a minimum to avoid "cabin rage" complaints from neighbors).

The five suites (all, strangely, with Jamaican names) are of a good size, with a "privacy" curtain between the hallway/closet and the sleeping/lounge area. There is plenty of space to walk in these suites, which feature separate vanity desk, curtained-off closet, plenty of drawer and storage space for luggage, a lounge with a sofa that converts into an additional bed, drinks table and two chairs. The bathroom has a small but deep bathtub with shower.

CUISINE/DINING. The 452-seat Miramar Restaurant is cheerful, even almost charming, with some prime tables overlooking the stern (most are for four, six or eight). There are two seatings (Spanish dining hours are much later than those of most other nationalities – dinner is at 9pm or 10pm). The reasonable buffet-style food selection is totally geared to Spanish tastes. The service is cheerful, friendly, and comes with a smile (remember, this is an inexpensive, informal cruise experience, so you should not expect haute cuisine). The wine list is acceptable, but the wines, for the most part, are very young.

In addition, breakfast and lunch buffets are provided indoors at Las Banderas, a casual self-service café with seating provided outdoors at tables set around the aft swimming pool (but space is tight and there simply isn't enough of it). There is a good selection of bread and rolls, cold cuts of salad and tapas items, which are presented reasonably well, given the space limitations.

ENTERTAINMENT. The 420-seat El Cabaret showlounge is a single-level room that is best suited to cabaret-style entertainment, with the stage and dance floor located as you enter the room at the aft section of the ship. Entertainment, as such, is what would be referred to as of the "low budget, low quality" variety, with individual cabaret acts as well as a clutch of showgirl dancers to open and close shows. There's also the La Bachata discotheque for the late-night loud crowd.

SPA/FITNESS. Spas were not thought about when this ship was built, and so the facilities are really very limited, and they are not adjacent. There is a small fitness room, a beauty salon, and a massage/body treatment room – all in different locations, on two different decks.

Braemar
★★★ +

Mid-Size Ship: . . . . .19,089 tons	Passenger Decks: 7	Cabins (with private balcony): 16
Lifestyle: . . . . .Standard	Total Crew: .320	Cabins (wheelchair accessible): 4
Cruise Line: . . . . .Fred Olsen Cruise Lines	Passengers	Cabin Current: . . . . .110 and 220 volts
Former Names: . . . .*Crown Dynasty,*	(lower beds/all berths): 733/821	Elevators: 5
Norwegian Dynasty, Crown Majesty,	Passenger Space Ratio	Casino (gaming tables): . . . . .Yes
Cunard Dynasty, Crown Dynasty	(lower beds/all berths): 26.1/23.8	Slot Machines: . . . . .Yes
Builder: . .Union Navale de Levante (Spain)	Crew/Passenger Ratio	Swimming Pools (outdoors): 1
Original Cost: . . . .$100 million	(lower beds/all berths): 1.8/2.0	Swimming Pools (indoors): 0
Entered Service: . . . .July 1993/Aug 2001	Navigation Officers: . . . . . . .Scandinavian	Whirlpools: 2
Registry: . . . . .The Bahamas	Cabins (total): 377	Self-Service Launderette: . . . . .No
Length (ft/m): 537.4/163.81	Size Range (sq ft/m): 139.9–349.8/	Dedicated Cinema/Seats: . . . . .No
Beam (ft/m): 73.8/22.50	13.0–32.5	Library: . . . . .No
Draft (ft/m): 17.7/5.40	Cabins (outside view): 251	Classification Society: . . . . . . .Det Norske
Propulsion/Propellers: . . . . .diesel	Cabins (interior/no view): 126	Veritas
(13,200kW)/2	Cabins (for one person): 21	

OVERALL SCORE: 1,325 (OUT OF A POSSIBLE 2,000 POINTS)

OVERVIEW. This ship was purchased by Fred Olsen Cruise Lines in spring 2001 and renamed *Braemar* following the demise of Crown Cruise Line, the ship's previous operator. Following an extensive refurbishment, *Braemar* started operating cruises targeted mostly at British and Scandinavian passengers.

This is quite a handsome-looking mid-sized ship for informal cruising, with attractive exterior styling, and a lot of glass space that provides contact with the outside. It will be a refreshing change for those who do not want to cruise aboard the larger (some say warehouse-size) ships. Surprisingly, however, the ship does roll somewhat, quite probably due to its shallow draft design (meant for warm weather cruise areas).

There is quite a good amount of open deck and sunbathing space for a ship of this size, and this incorporates two outdoors bars (one aft and one midships adjacent to the swimming pool) that feature Boddington's and Stella Artois beers on draught. Four open decks, located aft of the funnel, provide good, quiet, places to sit and read, and teak chairs add a touch of elegance to these decks.

The promenade deck, laid with teakwood decking, is a complete wrap-around deck. Passengers can also go right to the bow of the ship (this provides a photo opportunity for camera users inspired by the vision of Kate Winslet and Leonardo di Caprio spreading their arms on the bow of *Titanic*). Blue plastic mat-style floor covering is used on the deck where the swimming pool is located; it may look a bit tacky, but it works well in the heat of the Caribbean, where the ship was meant to spend most of its time.

Inside, there is a pleasant five-deck-high, glass-walled

BERLITZ'S RATINGS

	Possible	Achieved
Ship	500	364
Accommodation	200	135
Food	400	237
Service	400	255
Entertainment	100	61
Cruise	400	273

atrium, offset to the starboard side. Off-center stairways appear to add a sense of spaciousness to a clever interior design that surrounds passengers with light. The interior decor in public spaces is warm and inviting, with contemporary, but not brash, art-deco color combinations. The artwork is quite colorful and pleasant, in the Nordic manner.

The Neptune Showlounge sits longitudinally along one side of the ship, with amphitheater-style seating in several tiers, but its layout is less than ideal for either shows or cocktail parties. There are smoking and non-smoking sections (most being non-smoking).

In what was once a casino, the Braemar Room is now an open-plan style of lounge, with its own bar, split by a walkway that leads to the showlounge (forward) and the shops (midships). Despite being open, it has cozy seating areas and is very comfortable, with a tartan carpet; one section is for smokers, the other for non-smokers. A model of the first Fred Olsen ship named *Braemar* (4,775 tons) is displayed in the center of the room, as is a large carved wood plaque bearing the name Braemar Castle in Scotland. There is a baby grand piano (typically played during cocktail hours); otherwise this lounge is good for reading as there is no piped music to disturb the gentle, homey feeling.

The (mostly) Filipino staff is friendly and attentive, and the hospitality factor is reasonably good, although the standard of service itself and attention to detail is quite poor when compared with ships that have European staff. This is particularly noticeable in the restaurant and other food service areas. Training to a better standard of food service and product delivery is needed, and this is slowly being achieved. All in all, Fred Olsen Cruise Lines has come a long way from its humble beginnings, and now offers extremely good value for money cruises in a relaxed environment that provides passengers with many of the comforts of home. The dress code is casual (less formal than that found aboard *Black Prince* and *Black Watch*). The onboard currency is the British pound.

Note that the ship has had a number of lives under different operators, and, although Fred Olsen Cruise Lines has spent huge sums of money in interior refinishing, there remain many areas in passenger hallways where you'll find scuffed paneling.

Do expect some crowding for the self-serve buffets, tenders, and the few elevators aboard this ship. British passengers should note that no suites or cabins have bathtubs. Non-smokers should be aware that the typical passenger mix may include many passengers who smoke, and it may be difficult to avoid them, given the space constraints of the ship. There is no self-service launderette (although there is one ironing room). The company charges for shuttle buses in many ports of call.

SUITABLE FOR: *Braemar* is geared specifically toward the middle-aged and older British passenger who wants to cruise in a casual, unstuffy environment, and who appears to enjoy seeking out the world's duty-free shops, in a ship with British food and entertainment.

ACCOMMODATION. There are 16 cabin price categories, and, no matter whether you choose a suite or standard outside-view or interior (no view) cabin, the higher the deck, the higher the price (in real estate terminology, this translates to location, location, location). No matter what price grade you choose, a small television and hairdryer are provided (some are awkward to retract from their wall-mount holders), as are European duvets. The bathroom towels are 100% cotton and are quite large (bathrobes are available upon request in suite-grade cabins). A package of Gilchrist & Soames personal toiletry items (soap, bath gel, sewing kit, shampoo/conditioner, shower cap) is provided for all passengers. Note that there is no separate audio system in the cabin, so the only music you can obtain is from one of the television channels, but you'll have to leave the picture on (suites, however, do have a CD music system).

Standard (Outside-view)/Inside (No View) Cabin Grades: The standard outside-view and interior (no view) cabins, almost all of which are the same size, are really quite small, although they are nicely furnished, and trimmed with blond wood cabinetry. Most of them have broad picture windows (some deluxe cabins on Deck 6 and Deck 7 have lifeboat-obstructed views). They are practical and comfortable, with wood-trimmed accents and multi-colored soft furnishings, but there is very little drawer space, and the closet (hanging) space is extremely limited (the ship having been purpose-built originally only for 7-day cruises). So, as there is little room for luggage, take only the clothing that you think necessary. Each of the outside-view cabins on Deck 4 has a large picture window, while those on the lower

Decks 2 and 3 have a porthole. They are quite well equipped, with a small vanity desk unit, a minimal amount of drawer space, curtained windows, and personal safe (hard to reach as it is positioned close to the floor in many cabins – so you'll have to kneel down for access).

Each cabin has a private bathroom (of the "me first, you next" variety) with a tiled floor, small shower enclosure (with curtain you'll probably need to dance with, particularly if you are of above-average size), toiletries cupboard, washbasin, and low-height toilet (of the barking dog vacuum variety), and some under-basin storage space, and an electrical socket for shavers.

When the ship was bought by Fred Olsen Cruise Lines a number of cabins were changed from double-occupancy units to cabins for the single traveler, as aboard other ships operated by the company – a nice touch for the many singles not wishing to share.

Some cabins do unfortunately suffer from inadequate soundproofing; passengers in cabins on Deck 4 in particular are disturbed by anyone running or jogging on the promenade deck above. Note that cabins on the lowest deck (Deck 2) in the center of the ship are subject to some noise from the adjacent engine room.

Suites: On Deck 7, cabins designated as suites all feature a name as well as a number, as follows: 7001 (Owner's Suite); 7002 (Buenos Aires); 7003 (Cartagena); 7004 (Lima); 7005 (Cartagena); 7006 (New York); 7007 (Washington, D.C.); 7008 (Honolulu); 7009 (La Habana); 7010 (Hamilton); 7011 (Rio de Janeiro); 7012 (Bilboa); 7014 (Willemstad); 7016 (Toronto); 7018 (Santiago); 7031 (San Francisco); 7032 (Mexico City); 7033 (Montevideo); 7034 (Bridgetown). While they are not large, the suites do feature a sleeping area that can be curtained off from the living area. All of the suites are decorated in individual styles befitting their name, and each has its own small CD player/music system.

CUISINE/DINING. The Thistle Restaurant is a pleasing and attractive totally non-smoking restaurant, with large ocean-view windows on three sides; its focal point is a large oil painting on a wall behind the buffet food display counter. However, it is rather tight on space, and the tables are extremely close together, making proper service quite difficult for the waiters. There are tables for two, four, six or eight; the Porsgrund china has the familiar Venus pattern. The ambiance, however, is quite warm, and service is friendly and quite attentive.

There are two seatings for dinner, and an open seating for breakfast and lunch. A varied menu is provided. The salad items are quite poor and very basic, with little variety, although there is a decent choice of dessert items. For breakfast and lunch there are two food display counters so that you can help yourself, but at peak times these create much congestion (the layout is less than ideal).

Casual breakfasts and luncheons can be taken in the self-service buffet that is located in the Palms Cafe, although these tend to be quite repetitive and poorly supervised (dishes not replaced or refreshed properly). Both indoor and outdoor seating is available. Although it is the casual dining spot, tablecloths are provided. The indoor flooring is wood, which makes it rather a noisy room in which to eat, and some tables adjacent to the galley entrance are to be avoided at all costs.

Out on the pool deck, there is a barbecue grill, for casual eating; this is a useful addition, particularly when the ship is in the Caribbean or other warm water areas.

ENTERTAINMENT. The Neptune Lounge is the name of the ship's showlounge (note that there is often congestion between first- and second-seating passengers at the entrance to the showlounge, which is small). The showlounge itself is poorly designed for passenger movement, some 15 pillars obstruct sightlines to the stage, and the banquet and individual tub chair seating arrangement is actually quite poor.

The entertainment mainly consists of small-scale production shows and mini-musicals presented by a small troupe of resident singers/dancers, and cabaret acts. The production shows try hard, but are very amateurish and self-congratulatory, with a (mainly Filipino) cast that wouldn't stand a chance at real auditions. Apart from the production shows, there are cabaret acts (such as singers, magicians, ventriloquists, comedy jugglers, and comedi-

ans), which typically rotate around many cruise ships of the same standard. To be fair, however, passengers who cruise aboard this ship are not really looking for first-rate entertainment, but rather something to fill the time after dinner, which is the main event for most.

SPA/FITNESS. There is a health spa, although it is small, and has limited facilities. It includes a combined gymnasium/aerobics room, and a separate room for women and men, with sauna, steam room and small changing area. Spa Rituals is the name of the treatments provided by Steiner. Here are some examples of prices: Elemis Aromapure facial: £29.00; Well-being massage (50 minutes): £35; Personal Training Session (60 minutes): £20.

Note that many of the spa staff are quite young, and they will probably try to sell you Steiner's own-brand Elemis beauty products (spa girls have sales targets). Some fitness classes are free, while some, such as yoga and kick-boxing, cost extra. However, being aboard will give you an opportunity to try some of the more exotic treatments (particularly some of the massages available).

Do make appointments as early as possible, as treatment time slots go quickly, so the day you board is the best time to book your preferred treatments.

RULES OF THE ROAD

Ships, the largest moving objects made by man, are subject to stringent international regulations. They must keep to the right in shipping lanes, and pass on the right (with certain exceptions). When circumstances raise some doubt, or shipping lanes are crowded, ships use their whistles in the same way an automobile driver uses directional signals to show which way he will turn. When one ship passes another and gives a single blast on its whistle, this means it is turning to starboard (right). Two blasts mean a turn to port (left).

The other ship acknowledges by repeating the same signal. Ships switch on navigational running lights at night — green for starboard, red for port, plus two white lights on the masts, the forward one lower than the aft one.

Flags and pennants form another part of a ship's communication facilities and are displayed for identification purposes. Each time a country is visited, its national flag is shown. While entering and leaving a port, the ship flies a blue-and-white vertically striped flag to request a pilot, while a half-red, half-white flag (divided vertically) indicates that a pilot is on board. Cruise lines also display their own "house" flag from the mast.

A ship's funnel (smokestack) is one other means of identification, each line having its own design and color scheme. The size, height, and number of funnels were all points worth advertising at the turn of the

20th century. Most ocean liners of the time had four funnels and were called "four-stackers."

There are numerous customs at sea, many of them older than any maritime law. Superstition has always been an important element, as in the following example quoted from the British Admiralty Manual of Seamanship: "The custom of breaking a bottle of wine over the stem of a ship when it is being launched originates from the old practice of toasting prosperity to a ship with a silver goblet of wine, which was then cast into the sea in order to prevent a toast of ill intent being drunk from the same cup. This was a practice that proved too expensive, and it was replaced in 1690 by the breaking of a bottle of wine over the stem."

Bremen
★★★★

Small Ship: ....6,752 tons
Lifestyle: ....Premium
Cruise Line: ....Hapag-Lloyd Cruises
Former Names: ....*Frontier Spirit*
Builder: .....Mitsubishi Heavy Industries
(Japan)
Original Cost: ....$42 million
Entered Service: .....Nov 1990/Nov 1993
Registry: ....The Bahamas
Length (ft/m): 365.8/111.51
Beam (ft/m): 55.7/17.00
Draft (ft/m): 15.7/4.80
Propulsion/Propellers: ....diesel
(4,855kW)/2
Passenger Decks: 6

Total Crew: 94
Passengers
(lower beds/all berths): 164/184
Passenger Space Ratio
(lower beds/all berths): 41.1/36.6
Crew/Passenger Ratio
(lower beds/all berths): 1.7/1.9
Navigation Officers: ....European
Cabins (total): 82
Size Range (sq ft/m): 174.3–322.9/
16.2–30.0
Cabins (outside view): 82
Cabins (interior/no view): 0
Cabins (for one person): 0
Cabins (with private balcony): 18

Cabins (wheelchair accessible): 2
Cabin Current: ....110 and 220 volts
Elevators: 2
Casino (gaming tables): ....No
Slot Machines: ....No
Swimming Pools (outdoors): 1
Swimming Pools (indoors): 0
Whirlpools: 0
Self-Service Launderette: ....No
Lecture/Film Room: ......Yes (seats 164)
Library: ....Yes (open 24 hours)
Zodiacs: 12
Helicopter Pad: ....Yes
Classification Society: Germanischer Lloyd

OVERALL SCORE: 1,461 (OUT OF A POSSIBLE 2,000 POINTS)

OVERVIEW. This purpose-built expedition cruise vessel (formerly *Frontier Spirit*, for the now defunct US-based Frontier Cruises) has a handsome, wide, though squat, contemporary profile and decent equipment. Its wide beam provides decent stability and the vessel's long cruising range and ice-hardened hull provides the ship with access to remote destinations. The ship carries the highest ice classification for passenger vessels. In 1993 Hapag-Lloyd spent $2 million to reconfigure the restaurant and make other changes to the ship, and, in another refurbishment in 2000, the hull color was changed from blue to white. This is one of the few ships that will allow you to take a tour of the engine room.

Zero-discharge of waste matter is fiercely practiced; this means that absolutely nothing is discharged into the ocean that does not meet with the international conventions on ocean pollution (MARPOL). Equipment for in-depth marine and shore excursions is provided, including a boot-washing station with three water hoses and boot cleaning brushes.

An open bridge policy applies. There is almost a wrap-around walking deck (you must go up and down the steps at the front of the deck to complete the "wrap"). A large open deck aft of the mast provides a good viewing platform (also useful for sunbathing on warm-weather cruises).

The ship has a good number of public rooms for its size, including a forward-facing observation lounge/lecture room (with portside bar), and a main lounge (the Club) with a high ceiling, bandstand, dance floor and large bar, and an adjacent library with 12 bookcases (most books are in German).

Bremen has superb, well-planned destination-intensive

BERLITZ'S RATINGS		
	Possible	Achieved
Ship	500	349
Accommodation	200	150
Food	400	298
Service	400	311
Entertainment	N/A	N/A
Cruise	500	353

itineraries, with good documentation, port information, and maps. It provides a good degree of comfort (although it is not as luxurious as the slightly larger sister ship *Hanseatic*). There is a reception desk (open 24 hours a day), a fine array of expert lecturers, and a friendly crew.

Bremen is a very comfortable, practical, and unpretentious expedition cruise vessel; perhaps it is arguably a better expedition vessel than *Hanseatic*, and, although not as luxurious in its interiors and appointments, the ship has a very loyal following. Its cruises will provide you with a fine learning and expedition experience, particularly its Antarctic cruises (all shore landings and tours are included, as is seasickness medication). The onboard ambiance is completely casual, comfortable, unstuffy (no tux needed), friendly, and very accommodating. Passengers also appreciate the fact that there is no television (on expedition cruises, although there are videos daily) and no music in hallways or on open decks.

Arctic/Antarctic Cruises: When the ship goes to cold weather or ice areas, red parkas (waterproof outdoor jackets) are supplied, as are waterproof rubber (Wellington) boots. You should, however, take some waterproof trousers and several pairs of thick socks, plus "thermal" underwear. Each of the fleet of 12 Zodiacs (rubber-inflatable landing craft) is named after a place: Amazon, Antarctic, Asmat, Bora Bora, Cape Horn, Deception, Jan Mayen, Luzon, Pitcairn, San Blas, Spitzbergen, and Ushuaia. On Arctic and Antarctic cruises, it is particularly pleasing to go to the bridge wings late at night to stargaze under pollution-free skies (the watch officers will be pleased to show you the night skies).

Special sailings may be under the auspices of various

tour operators, although the ship is operated by Hapag-Lloyd Cruises. Thus, your fellow passengers (I prefer to refer to them as expedition cruise participants) may well be from many different countries. Insurance, port taxes and all staff gratuities are typically included in the cruise fare, and an expedition cruise logbook is provided at the end of each expedition cruise for all participants – a reminder of what's been seen and done during the course of your adventure experience. The onboard currency is the euro.

Note that the ship does not have a "bulbous bow" and so is liable to deep pitching in some sea conditions (it does, however, have stabilizers). The swimming pool is very small, as is the open deck space around it, although there are both shaded and open areas. In-cabin announcements cannot be turned off (on cruises in the Arctic and Antarctic regions, announcements are often made at or before 7am on days when shore landings are permitted). Sadly, the ship was not built with good cabin soundproofing. Bathrooms are subject to gurgling plumbing noises (between the washbasin and shower enclosure) as a result of their design and construction.

SUITABLE FOR: *Bremen* is best suited to travelers (rather than cruise passengers) who would not dream of cruising aboard the large, glitzy cruise ships. This is for anyone who enjoys nature and the natural world, and traveling off the beaten path to sample what the world has to offer in the more remote and unspoiled (a relative term) regions of the world, in moderate comfort, yet venturing on the wild side of cruising. It is for those who do not need entertainment, bingo, horse racing, art auctions, or parlour games.

ACCOMMODATION. There are only four different configurations. All cabins have an outside view (the cabins on the lowest deck have portholes; all others have good-sized picture windows). All cabins are well equipped for the size of the vessel. Each has wood accenting, a color TV (small) for videos, telephone, refrigerator (soft drinks are provided free and replenished daily), vanity desk (with 110v American-style and 220v European-style electrical sockets) and sitting area with small drinks table. Cabins have either twin beds (convertible to a queen-sized bed, but with individual European cotton duvets) or double bed, according to location. There is also a small indented area for outerwear and rubber boots, while a small drawer above the refrigerator unit provides warmth when needed for such things as wet socks and gloves.

Each cabin has a private bathroom (of the "me first, you next" variety) with a tiled floor, shower enclosure (with curtain), toiletries cupboard, washbasin (located quite low) and low-height toilet (vacuum type, with delay), a decent amount of under-basin storage space, and an electrical socket for shavers). Large towels and 100% cotton bathrobes are provided for all passengers, as is a range of personal toiletry items (shampoo, body lotion, shower gel, soap, and shower cap).

Each cabin has a moderate amount of (illuminated)

closet space (large enough for two weeks for two persons, but very tight for more than that cruise length) although the drawer space is limited (suitcases can be stored under the beds). Some Sun Deck and Bridge Deck cabins also have a small balcony (the first expedition cruise vessel to have them) with blue plastic (easily cleanable) decking and wooden handrail, but no exterior light. The balconies, which have two teak chairs and drinks table, are, however, quite small and narrow, with partial partitions and doors that open outwards onto the balcony.

Two Sun Deck suites have a separate lounge area with sofa and coffee table, bedroom (with large wall clock), large walk-in closet, and bathroom with a bathtub and two washbasins.

CUISINE/DINING. The dining room has open seating when operating for mixed German and international passenger cruises, and open seating for breakfast and lunch, and one seating for dinner (with assigned seats) when operated only as German-speaking cruises. It is fairly attractive, with pleasing decor and colors; it also has big picture windows. The dining room has 12 pillars placed in inconvenient positions (the result of old shipbuilding techniques).

The food, made with high-quality ingredients, is extremely good. Although the portions are small, the presentation is appealing to the eye. There is always an excellent choice of freshly made breads and pastries, and a good selection of cheeses and fruits.

Dinner typically includes a choice of two appetizers, two soups, an entremets (in-between course), two entrées (main courses) and two or three desserts, plus a cheese board (note that Europeans typically have cheese before dessert). There is always a vegetarian specialty, as well as a healthy (light) eating option. The service is also good, with smartly dressed bi-lingual (German- and English-speaking) waiters and waitresses.

As an alternative to the dining room, breakfast and luncheon buffets are available in "The Club", or outside on the Lido Deck (weather permitting), where "The Starboard Bar/Grill" provides hamburgers and other grilled food.

ENTERTAINMENT. Although there is a small main lounge, this is used as a gathering place after meals (and before expedition landings ashore). There is no formal entertainment as such, although lectures are the principal feature of any cruise aboard this ship (unless under charter for special theme cruises during the summer), as are after-dinner recaps of the day. Occasionally, the crew may put on a little amateur dramatics event, or a seaman's choir. And at the end of each expedition cruise, the ship's chart is auctioned off one evening to the highest bidder, and any profits are sent to a charity organization.

SPA/FITNESS. There is a small fitness room, and a decent sized sauna, but nothing else. Out on the open deck is a small swimming pool (heated when the ship is sailing in cold weather regions such as the Arctic or Antarctica).

Brilliance of the Seas
★★★★

Large (Resort) Ship: ....90,090 tons	Total Crew: 869	Cabins (with private balcony): 577
Lifestyle: ....Standard	Passengers	Cabins (wheelchair accessible): 24
Cruise Line: Royal Caribbean International	(lower beds/all berths): 2,112/2,500	Cabin Current: ....110/220 volts
Former Names: ....none	Passenger Space Ratio	Elevators: 9
Builder: ....Meyer Werft (Germany)	(lower beds/all berths): 42.6/36.0	Casino (gaming tables): ....Yes
Original Cost: ....$350 million	Crew/Passenger Ratio	Slot Machines: ....Yes
Entered Service: ....July 2002	(lower beds/all berths): 2.5/2.8	Swimming Pools (outdoors): 2
Registry: ....The Bahamas	Navigation Officers: ....Norwegian	Swimming Pools (indoors): 0
Length (ft/m): 961.9/293.2	Cabins (total): 1,056	Whirlpools: 3
Beam (ft/m): 105.6/32.2	Size Range (sq ft/m): 165.8–1,216.3/	Self-Service Launderette: ....No
Draft (ft/m): 27.8/8.5	15.4–113.0	Dedicated Cinema/Seats: Yes/40
Propulsion/Propellers: ......Gas turbine/	Cabins (outside view): 818	Library: ....Yes
2 pods (19.5 MW each)	Cabins (interior/no view): 238	Classification Society: ......Det Norske
Passenger Decks: 12	Cabins (for one person): 0	Veritas

OVERALL SCORE: 1,546 (OUT OF A POSSIBLE 2,000 POINTS)

OVERVIEW. This is a streamlined contemporary ship (built in 66 blocks), and has a two-deck-high wrap-around structure in the forward section of the funnel. Along the ship's port side, a central glass wall protrudes, giving great views (cabins with balconies occupy the space directly opposite on the starboard side). The gently rounded stern has nicely tiered decks, which gives the ship an extremely well-balanced look. As is common aboard all Royal Caribbean International vessels, the navigation bridge is of the fully enclosed type (good for cold-weather areas). One of two swimming pools can be covered by a large glass dome (called a magrodome) for use as an indoor/outdoor pool.

The interior decor is contemporary, yet elegant, bright and cheerful, designed for active, young and trendy types. The artwork is abundant and truly eclectic. A nine-deck high atrium lobby has glass-walled lifts (on the port side) that travel through 12 decks, face the sea and provide a link with nature and the ocean. The Centrum (as the atrium is called) has several public rooms connected to it: the guest relations (the erstwhile purser's office) and shore excursions desks, a Lobby Bar, Champagne Bar, the Library, Royal Caribbean Online, the Concierge Club, and a Crown & Anchor Lounge. A great view can be had of the atrium by looking down through the flat glass dome high above it.

There's also a Champagne Bar, and a large Schooner Bar that houses maritime art in an integral art gallery, not to mention the Casino Royale. There's also a small, deeply tiered, dedicated movie screening room (with space for two wheelchairs), as well as a 194-seat conference center, a business center, and several conference rooms.

A Viking Crown Lounge is set around the ship's funnel.

BERLITZ'S RATINGS

	Possible	Achieved
Ship	500	433
Accommodation	200	163
Food	400	259
Service	400	298
Entertainment	100	81
Cruise	400	312

This functions as an observation lounge during the daytime; in the evening, the space hosts Starquest, a futuristic, high-energy dance club, and Hollywood Odyssey, a more intimate and relaxed entertainment venue for softer mood music and "black-box" theater.

Youth facilities include Adventure Ocean, an "edutainment" area with four separate age-appropriate sections for junior passengers: Aquanaut Center (for ages 3–5); Explorer Center (6–8); Voyager Center (9–12); and the Optix Teen Center (13–17). Adventure Beach includes a splash pool with waterslide; Surfside has computer lab stations with entertaining software; and Ocean Arcade is a video games hangout.

This second of a new generation of RCI ships (more are to follow) has been constructed for longer itineraries, with more space and comfortable public areas, larger cabins and more dining options – for the young, active, and trendy set. A computer business center has 12 IBM computers with high-speed internet access for sending and receiving emails. The onboard currency is the US dollar.

ACCOMMODATION. A wide range of suites and standard outside-view and interior (no view) cabins comes in 10 categories and 19 price groups.

Apart from the six largest suites (called owner's suites), which have king-sized beds, almost all other cabins have twin beds that convert to a queen-sized bed (all sheets are 100% Egyptian cotton, although the blankets are of nylon). All cabins have rich (faux) wood cabinetry, including a vanity desk (with hairdryer), faux wood drawers that close silently (hooray), television, personal safe, and three-sided mirrors. Some cabins have ceiling recessed, pull-down berths for third and fourth persons, although closet and drawer space would be extremely tight for four persons (even if two are children), and some have interconnecting doors. Audio channels are available through the TV set, so if you want to go to sleep with soft music playing you'll need to put a towel over the television screen.

Most bathrooms have tiled accenting and a terrazzo-style tiled floor, and a half-moon shower enclosure (it is rather small, however), 100% Egyptian cotton towels, a small cabinet for personal toiletries and a small shelf. There is little space to stow personal toiletries for two (or more).

The largest cabins consist of a family suite with two bedrooms. One bedroom has twin beds (convertible to queen-sized bed), while a second has two lower beds and two upper Pullman berths, a combination that can sleep up to eight persons (good for large families).

Occupants of cabins designated as suites also get the use of a private Concierge Lounge (where priority dining room reservations, shore excursion bookings and beauty salon/spa appointments can be made).

Many of the "private" balcony cabins are not very private, as they can be overlooked from the port and starboard wings of the Solarium, and from other locations.

CUISINE/DINING. Minstrel, the main dining room, spans two decks (the upper deck level has floor-to-ceiling windows, while the lower deck level has windows). It seats 1,104, and has Middle Ages music as its themed decor. There are tables for two, four, six, eight or 10 in two seatings for dinner. Two small private dining rooms (Zephyr, with 94 seats and Lute, with 30 seats) are located off the main dining room. Smoking is banned in all dining venues.

The cuisine in the main dining room is typical of mass banquet catering that offers standard fare comparable to that found in American family-style restaurants ashore – mostly disappointing and without much taste. However, a decent selection of light meals is provided, and a vegetarian menu is available. Caviar (once a standard menu item) incurs a hefty extra charge. Special orders, tableside carving and flambéed items are not offered. Menus typically include a "Welcome Aboard" Dinner, French Dinner, Italian Dinner, International Dinner, Captain's Gala Dinner.

There are two alternative dining spots: "Portofino", with 112 seats, has Italian-American cuisine (choices include antipasti, soup, salad, pasta, main dish, dessert, cheese and coffee); and "Chops Grille Steakhouse", with 95 seats and an open (show) kitchen, has premium veal chops and steaks (New York Striploin Steak, Filet Mignon, Prime Rib of Beef). Both these spots have food that is of a much higher quality than in the main dining room. There is an additional charge of $20 per person (including gratuities), and reservations are required for both dining spots, which are typically open between 6pm and 11pm. Be prepared to eat a lot of food (perhaps this justifies the cover charge, as these are Texas-sized portions presented on large plates. Menus don't change throughout the cruise. The dress code is smart casual.

Also, casual meals can be taken (for breakfast, lunch and dinner) in the self-serve, buffet-style Windjammer Cafe, which can be accessed directly from the pool deck.

Additionally, the Seaview Cafe is open for lunch and dinner. Choose from the self-serve buffet, or from the menu for fast-food seafood items, hamburgers and hot dogs. The decor, naturally, is marine- and ocean related.

ENTERTAINMENT. The Pacifica Theatre, the main show-lounge, is three decks high, has 874 seats (including 24 stations for wheelchairs), and good sight lines from most seats.

SPA/FITNESS. The ShipShape Spa's health, fitness and spa facilities have themed decor, and include a 10,176 sq.-ft (945 sq.-meter) solarium with whirlpool and counter current swimming under a retractable magrodome roof, a gymnasium (with 44 cardiovascular machines), 50-person aerobics room, sauna and steam rooms, and therapy treatment rooms. All are located on two of the uppermost decks of the ship, forward of the mast.

For the more sporting, youthful passengers, there is activity galore – including a rock-climbing wall that's 30-ft (9 meters) high, with five separate climbing tracks. It is located outdoors at the aft end of the funnel. Other sports facilities include a golf course, jogging track, basketball court, 9-hole miniature golf course (with novel decorative ornaments), and an indoor/outdoor country club with golf simulator. There is also an exterior jogging track.

● **For more extensive general information about a Royal Caribbean cruise experience, see pages 128–131.**

Calypso
★★ +

Small Ship: ....11,162 tons	Total Crew: 220	Cabins (with private balcony): 0
Lifestyle: ....Standard	Passengers	Cabins (wheelchair accessible): 2
Cruise Line: ....Louis Cruise Lines	(lower beds/all berths): 486/596	Cabin Current: ....110 volts
Former Names: ......Regent Jewel, Sun	Passenger Space Ratio	Dining Rooms: 1
Fiesta, Ionian Harmony, Canguro Verde	(lower beds/all berths): 22.9/18.8	Elevators: 2
Builder: ....Fincantieri (Italy)	Crew/Passenger Ratio	Casino (gaming tables): ....Yes
Original Cost: ....n/a	(lower beds/all berths): 2.2/2.7	Slot Machines: ....Yes
Entered Service: 1968/July 2000	Navigation Officers: ....European	Swimming Pools (outdoors): 1
Registry: ....The Bahamas	Cabins (total): 243	Swimming Pools (indoors): 0
Length (ft/m): 444.2/135.4	Size Range (sq ft/m): 135–244/	Whirlpools: 0
Beam (ft/m): 62.9/19.2	12.5–22.6	Self-Service Launderette: ....No
Draft (ft/m): 20.6/6.3	Cabins (outside view): 158	Dedicated Cinema/Seats: ....No
Propulsion/Propellers: diesel (9,000kW)/2	Cabins (interior/no view): 85	Library: ....Yes
Passenger Decks: 8	Cabins (for one person): 0	Classification Society: ...Lloyd's Register

OVERALL SCORE: 1,062 (OUT OF A POSSIBLE 2,000 POINTS)

OVERVIEW. *Calypso*, a former Mediterranean ferry, has been extensively reconstructed and now carries mostly British and Cypriot passengers who seek to travel from Cyprus to the Greek Islands in modest surroundings, at a very low price.

One practical feature is the enclosed wooden promenade deck, good for strolling, or just sitting and reading a book. There are plenty of public rooms, bars and lounges, considering the ship's size. The vessel's fit and finish is disappointingly poor, as is the quality of some of the interior decoration. There's a cozy, unpretentious ambiance, and the dress code is very relaxed, with formal attire definitely not required. The onboard currency is the euro.

This is a high-density ship, which means that it is very crowded when full. Expect some lines to form for shore excursions and buffets. Expect a large number of smokers. There are very steep, narrow stairways on the outer decks.

SUITABLE FOR: *Calypso* is best suited to adult couples seeking a low-priced, but comfortable ship for a first short cruise experience, with unpretentious and unstuffy (non-glitzy) surroundings and acceptable food and service.

ACCOMMODATION. There are four suites, seven semi-deluxe, 147 outside-view cabins and 85 interior (no view) cabins. The price you pay depends on the grade, size and location you choose (cabins on higher decks command higher prices). No matter which cabin you choose, however, all have double or twin beds, television, telephone, personal safe, and bathrooms have a shower enclosure, toilet and washbasin. The cabins have warm pastel decor, although

BERLITZ'S RATINGS

	Possible	Achieved
Ship	500	212
Accommodation	200	97
Food	400	224
Service	400	249
Entertainment	100	55
Cruise	400	225

the artwork is minimal, and the fabrics and other soft furnishings could be of better quality.

Some cabins have a third and fourth upper berth (there is only one personal safe), and drawer and storage space is very limited (in other words, take as little clothing as possible). Those designated as suites also have a refrigerator/minibar. There is a cabin service menu, although it is quite limited.

CUISINE/DINING. The dining room, in the aft section of the ship, is reasonably attractive and decorated, although its layout is somewhat awkward, as it is positioned on two slightly different levels. There are two seatings, and tables are for four, six or eight persons.

The menu choice is quite good (it includes a vegetarian option), and the food has plenty of taste. The service comes with a smile. Breakfast and lunch buffets are quite attractive, with plenty of variety. The wine list is very small, but prices are reasonable (don't expect vintage wines).

ENTERTAINMENT. The showlounge is a single-level room, and several pillars obstruct sightlines from many of the seats. The entertainment is minimal for these short cruises this ship features, and consists mainly of cabaret acts (singers, comedians, magic acts) strung together to make shows that are sometimes overlong.

There are several bands and musical units to provide live music for dancing and listening.

SPA/FITNESS. Apart from a small gymnasium and sauna, there is little else. Massage, however, is available (the massage room is tiny), as are beauty/hair treatments.

Caribbean Princess
★★★★

Large (Resort) Ship: ....116,000 tons	Total Crew: 1,163	Cabins (with private balcony): 881
Lifestyle: ....Standard	Passengers	Cabins (wheelchair accessible): 25
Cruise Line: ....Princess Cruises	(lower beds/all berths): 3,114/3,782	Cabin Voltage: ....110 volts
Former Names: ....None	Passenger Space Ratio	Elevators: 14
Builder: ....Fincantieri (Italy)	(lower beds/all berths): 37.2/30.6	Casino (gaming tables): ....Yes
Original Cost: ....$500 million	Crew/Passenger Ratio	Slot Machines: ....Yes
Entered Service: ....Apr 2004	(lower beds/all berths): 2.6/3.2	Swimming Pools (outdoors): 4
Registry: ....Bermuda	Navigation Officers: .....British/European	Swimming Pools (indoors): 0
Length (ft/m): 951.4/290.0	Cabins (total): 1,557	Whirlpools: 9
Beam (ft/m): 118.1/36.0	Size Range (sq ft/m): 163-1,279/	Self-Service Launderette: ....Yes
Draft (ft/m): 26.2/8.0	15.1-118.8	Dedicated Cinema/Seats: ....No
Propulsion/Propellers: .....diesel-electric	Cabins (outside view): 1,105	Library: ....Yes
(42,000kW)/2	Cabins (interior/no view): 452	Classification Society: ....Lloyds Register
Passenger Decks:.................15	Cabins (for one person): 0	

OVERALL SCORE: 1,547 (OUT OF A POSSIBLE 2,000 POINTS)

OVERVIEW. Designed to be a (somewhat smaller) competitor to Royal Caribbean International's *Voyager*-class ships (but with a similar passenger carry), *Caribbean Princess* has the same profile as half-sisters *Golden Princess, Grand Princess,* and *Star Princess*, but has two jet engine-like pods that sit high up on its funnel structure. This ship accommodates many more passengers than half-sisters due to an additional extra deck (Riviera Deck) full of cabins, and the fact that two of the ship's 17 upper decks are made of aluminum (although lighter than steel, it does tend to "harden" over time).

Although the ship accommodates over 500 more passengers, the outdoor deck space remains the same, as do the number of elevators (so waiting time could well increase during peak usage). The Passenger Space Ratio is also reduced considerably compared to that of its half-sisters. *Caribbean Princess* has been built for year-round service in the Caribbean.

There is a good sheltered teakwood promenade deck, which almost wraps around (three times round is equal to one mile) and a walkway which goes to the (enclosed, protected) bow of the ship. The outdoor pools have various beach-like surroundings, and "Movies Under the Stars" and major sporting events are shown on a 300-sq-ft (28-sq-meter) movie screen located at the pool in front of the large funnel structure (lounge chair reservations must be made through the ship's concierge) in what, aboard *Golden, Grand* and *Star Princess* would be The Conservatory. Movies afloat in the open are a big hit with passengers (they reminds many of drive-in movies, which have mostly disappeared from land-based venues).

BERLITZ'S RATINGS

	Possible	Achieved
Ship	500	433
Accommodation	200	168
Food	400	256
Service	400	293
Entertainment	100	82
Cruise	400	315

Unlike the outside decks, there is plenty of space inside (but there are also plenty of passengers), and a wide array of public rooms to choose from, with many "intimate" (this being a relative word) spaces and places to play. The passenger flow has been well thought-out, and there is little congestion.

Four areas center on swimming pools, one of which is two decks high and can be covered by a magrodome.

High atop the stern of the ship is a ship-wide glass-walled disco pod. It looks like an aerodynamic "spoiler" and is positioned high above the water, with spectacular views from the extreme port and starboard side windows (it would make a great penthouse).

The interior decor is attractive, with lots of earth tones (well suited to both American and European tastes). In fact, this is a culmination of the best of all that Princess Cruises has to offer from its many years of operating what is now a well-tuned, good-quality product.

An extensive collection of artworks has been chosen, and this complements the interior design and colors well. If you see something you like, you will probably be able to purchase it on board – it's almost all for sale.

Caribbean Princess also includes a Wedding Chapel (a live web-cam can relay ceremonies via the internet). The ship's captain can legally marry (American) couples, thanks to the ship's Bermuda registry and a special dispensation (which should be verified when in the planning stage, according to where you reside). But to get married and take your close family members and entourage with you on your honeymoon is going to cost a lot. The "Hearts & Minds" chapel is also useful for "renewal of vows" ceremonies.

For children, there is a two-deck-high playroom, teen

room, and a host of specially trained counselors. Children have their own pools, hot tubs, and open deck area at the stern of the ship, thankfully away from adult areas. There are good netted-in areas; one section has a dip pool, while another has a mini-basketball court.

Gamblers should enjoy what is presently one of the largest casinos at sea (Grand Casino), with more than 260 slot machines, and blackjack, craps and roulette tables, plus newer games such as Let It Ride Bonus, Spanish 21 and Caribbean Draw Progressive. But the highlight could well be the specially linked slot machines that provide a combined payout.

Other features include a decent library/CD-Rom computer room, and a separate card room. Ship lovers should enjoy the wood-paneled Wheelhouse Bar, finely decorated with memorabilia and ship models tracing part of parent company P&O's history (this ship highlights the 1950-built cargo ship *Ganges*. A sports bar, Shooters, has two billiard tables, and several television screens. A high-tech hospital is provided, with SeaMed tele-medicine link-ups to specialists at the Cedars-Sinai Medical Center in Los Angeles, who are available for emergency help.

The ship is a stunning, grand resort playground in which to roam when you are not ashore. Princess Cruises delivers a consistently fine, well-packaged vacation product, always with a good degree of style, at an attractive, highly competitive price. Whether this really can be considered a relaxing holiday is a moot point, but with so many choices and "small" rooms to enjoy, the ship has been extremely well designed, and the odds are that you'll have an enjoyable cruise vacation. If you are not used to large ships, it will take you some time to find your way around this one, despite the company's claim that it offers passengers a "small ship feel, big ship choice."

Caribbean Princess is Princess Cruises' first year-round Caribbean cruise ship, but the company, and competes with Carnival Cruise Lines and Royal Caribbean International in the same segment, the world's most popular but overtonnaged (saturated would be a better description) and discounted cruise region – the Caribbean. However, *Caribbean Princess* is among the very best of them in the region (in the standard market segment).

ACCOMMODATION. There are six principal types of cabins and configurations: (a) grand suite, (b) suite, (c) mini-suite, (d) outside-view double cabins with balcony, (e) outside-view double cabins, and (f) interior (no view) double cabins. These come in 35 different brochure price categories. The choice is quite bewildering for both travel agents and passengers; pricing will depend on two things, size and location. By comparison, the largest suite is slightly smaller, and the smallest interior (no-view) cabin is slightly larger than the equivalent suite/cabins aboard *Golden, Grand* and *Star Princess.*

Cabin bath towels are small, and drawer space is very limited. There are no butlers – even for the top-grade suites (which are not really large in comparison to similar suites aboard some other ships). Cabin attendants have too many cabins to look after (typically 20), which does not translate to fine personal service.

(a) The largest, most lavish suite is the Grand Suite (A750, located at the ship's stern). It has a large bedroom with queen-sized bed, huge walk-in (illuminated) closets, two bathrooms, a lounge (with fireplace and sofa bed) with wet bar and refrigerator, and a large private balcony on the port side (with hot tub that can be accessed from both balcony and bedroom).

(b/c) Suites (with a semi-private balcony) have a separate living room (with sofa bed) and bedroom (with a television in each). The bathroom is quite large and has both a tub and shower stall. The mini-suites also have a private balcony, and a separate living and sleeping area (with a television in each). The differences between the suites and mini-suites are basically in the size and appointments, the suite being more of a square shape while mini-suites are more rectangular, and have few drawers. Both suites and mini-suites have plush bathrobes, and fully tiled bathrooms with ample open shelf storage space. Suite and mini-suite passengers receive greater attention, including priority embarkation and disembarkation privileges. What is not good is that the most expensive accommodation has only semi-private balconies that can be seen from above and so there is little privacy (Suites C401, 402, 404, 406, 408, 410, 412, 401, 405, 411, 415 and 417 on Riviera Deck 14). Also, the suites D105 and D106 (Dolphin Deck 9), which are extremely large, have balconies that are overlooked from above.

(d/e/f). Both interior (no view) and outside-view (the outsides come either with or without private balcony) cabins are of a functional, practical, design, although almost no drawers are provided. They are quite attractive, with warm, pleasing decor and fine soft furnishing fabrics; 80 percent of the outside-view cabins have a private balcony. Interior (no view) cabins measure 163 sq. ft (15.1 sq. meters).

The 28 wheelchair-accessible cabins measure 250–385 sq. ft (23.2–35.7 sq. meters); surprisingly, there is no mirror for dressing, and no full-length hanging space for long dresses (yes, some passengers in wheelchairs do also use mirrors and full-length clothing). Additionally, two family suites consist of two suites with an interconnecting door, plus a large balcony. These can sleep up to 10 (if at least four are children) or up to eight people (if all are adults).

All cabins receive turndown service and chocolates on pillows each night, bathrobes (on request) and toiletry amenity kits (larger, naturally, for suite/mini-suite occupants) that typically include soap, shampoo, conditioner, and hand/body lotion. A hairdryer is provided in all cabins, sensibly located at the vanity desk unit in the living area. All bathrooms have tiled floors, and there is a decent amount of open shelf storage space for personal toiletries, although the plain beige decor is very basic and unappealing.

Most outside-view cabins on Emerald Deck have views obstructed by the lifeboats. There are no cabins for singles. Your name is placed outside your suite or cabin in a documents holder – making it simple for delivery service personnel but also diminishing privacy. There is 24-hour room service (but some items on the room service menu are not available during early morning hours).

Some cabins can accommodate a third and fourth person in upper berths. However, in such cabins, the lower beds cannot then be pushed together to make queen-sized bed.

Almost all balcony suites and cabins can be overlooked both from the navigation bridge wing, as well as from the port and starboard sections of the ship's discotheque – high above the ship at the stern. Cabins with balconies on Dolphin, Caribe and Baja decks can be overlooked by passengers on balconies on the deck above. They are, therefore, not private. However, perhaps the least desirable balcony cabins are eight balcony cabins located forward on Emerald Deck, as the balconies do not extend to the side of the ship and can be passed by walkers and gawkers on the adjacent Upper Promenade walkway (so occupants need to keep their curtains closed most of the time). Also, passengers occupying some the most expensive suites with balconies at the stern of the vessel may experience considerable vibration during certain ship maneuvers. Note that most cabins on Emerald Deck 8 have a lifeboat-obstructed view.

CUISINE/DINING. As befits the size of the ship, there are a variety of dining options. There are three main dining rooms, plus Sterling Steakhouse, Sabatini's Trattoria, Tequila's.

The three principal dining rooms for formal dining are Coral, Island, and Palm. The Palm Dining Room has traditional two seating dining, while "anytime dining" (you choose when and with whom you want to eat) is features in Coral and Island. All are no-smoking and split into multitier sections in a non-symmetrical design that breaks what are quite large spaces into smaller sections for better ambiance. Each dining room has its own galley. While four elevators go to Fiesta Deck, where the Coral and Island restaurants are located, only two go to Plaza Deck 5, where the Palm Restaurant is located (this can cause waiting problems at peak times, particularly for anyone in a wheelchair).

Specially designed dinnerware (by Dudson of England), high-quality linens and silverware, Frette Egyptian cotton table linens, and silverware by Hepp of Germany are used in the main dining rooms. Note that 15% is added to all beverage bills, including wines.

Alternative (Extra Charge) Dining Options: There are three: Sabatini's Trattoria, Tequila's, and Sterling Steakhouse. All are open for lunch and dinner on days at sea. Sabatini's is an Italian eatery, with colorful tiled Mediterranean-style decor; it is named after Trattoria Sabatini, the 200-year old institution in Florence (where there is no cover charge). It has Italian-style pizzas and pastas, with a variety of sauces, as well as Italian-style entrées (including tiger prawns and lobster tail – all provided with flair and entertainment from by the staff of waiters (by reservation only, with a cover charge of $15 per person, for lunch or dinner).

Sterling Steakhouse is located just aft of the upper level of the Princess Theater, adjacent to the Internet Café and

shops, in a somewhat open area, to tempt you as you pass by, with people walking through as you eat – not a particularly comfortable arrangement. The cover charge is $10.

The cuisine in the alternative dining spots is decidedly better than in the three main dining rooms, with better quality ingredients and more attention to presentation and taste.

Casual eateries include a poolside hamburger grill and pizza bar (no additional charge), while extra charges do apply if you order items to eat at either the coffee bar/patisserie, or the caviar/champagne bar. Other casual meals can be taken in the Horizon Court, which is open 24 hours a day. It has large ocean-view on port and starboard sides and direct access to the two principal swimming pools and lido deck. There is no real finesse in presentation, however, as plastic plates are provided.

Ultimate Balcony Dinner/Breakfast: For something different, you could try a private dinner on your balcony, an all-inclusive evening featuring cocktails, fresh flowers, champagne and a deluxe four-course meal including Caribbean lobster tail – all served by a member of the dining staff on your private balcony; of course, it costs extra - $50 per person (or $25 per person for the Ultimate Balcony Breakfast).

ENTERTAINMENT. The Princess Theater (showlounge) is the main entertainment venue; it spans two decks and has comfortable seating on both main and balcony levels. It has $3 million worth of sound and light equipment, plus a 9-piece orchestra, and a scenery loading bay that connects directly from stage to a hull door for direct transfer to the dockside).

A special show called "Caribbean Caliente" (highlighting contemporary and classic artists, ranging from Ricky Martin to Bob Marley) is featured. The ship carries its own resident troupe of 19 singers and dancers, plus and audio-visual support staff.

Club Fusion is a second entertainment lounge (located aft). It features cabaret acts (magicians, comedy jugglers, ventriloquists and others) at night, and lectures, bingo and horse racing during the day. Explorers, a third entertainment lounge, can also host cabaret acts and dance bands. A variety of other lounges and bars have live music, and Princess Cruises employs a number of male dance hosts as partners for women traveling alone.

SPA/FITNESS/RECREATION. The Lotus Spa is located forward on Sun Deck – one of the uppermost decks. Separate facilities for men and women include a sauna, steam room, and changing rooms; common facilities include a relaxation/waiting zone, body-pampering treatment rooms, and a gymnasium with packed with the latest high-tech muscle-pumping, cardio-vascular equipment, and great ocean views. Some fitness classes are free, while some cost extra.

● For more extensive general information on what a Princess Cruises cruise is like, see pages 124–127.

Carnival Conquest
★★★★

Large (Resort) Ship: ....110,329 tons	Passengers	Cabin Current: ....110 volts
Lifestyle: ....Standard	(lower beds/all berths): 2,974/3,700	Elevators: 18
Cruise Line: ......Carnival Cruise Lines	Passenger Space Ratio	Casino (gaming tables): ....Yes
Former Names: ....none	(lower beds/all berths): 36.9/29.7	Slot Machines: ....Yes
Builder: ....Fincantieri (Italy)	Crew/Passenger Ratio	Swimming Pools (outdoors): 3
Original Cost: ....$500 million	(lower beds/all berths): 2.5/3.1	(+1 with magrodome)
Entered Service: ....Dec 2002	Navigation Officers: ....Italian	Swimming Pools (indoors): 0
Registry: ....Panama	Cabins (total): 1,487	Whirlpools: 7
Length (ft/m): 951.4/290.0	Size Range (sq ft/m): 179.7–482.2/	Fitness Center: ....Yes
Beam (ft/m): 116.4/35.5	16.7–44.8	Sauna/Steam Room: ....Yes/Yes
Draft (ft/m): 27.0/8.2	Cabins (outside view): 917	Massage: ....Yes
Propulsion/Propellers: .....diesel-electric	Cabins (interior/no view): 570	Self-Service Launderette: ....Yes
(63,400kW)/2	Cabins (for one person): 0	Dedicated Cinema/Seats: ....No
Passenger Decks: 13	Cabins (with private balcony): 574	Library: ....Yes
Total Crew: 1,160	Cabins (wheelchair accessible): 25	Classification Society: ...Lloyd's Register

OVERALL SCORE: 1,457 (OUT OF A POSSIBLE 2,000 POINTS)

OVERVIEW. *Carnival Conquest* is the 19th new-build for this very successful cruise line. It is presently the largest ship in the Carnival Cruise Lines fleet, and has the same well-balanced profile as the earlier ships of a similar, but slightly smaller type: *Carnival Destiny, Carnival Triumph* and *Carnival Victory*. The ship, whose bows are extremely short, has the distinctive, large, swept-back wing-tipped funnel that is the trademark of Carnival Cruise Lines, in the company colors of red, white and blue. However, due to its size, the ship is unable to transit the Panama Canal, and is thus dedicated to itineraries in the Caribbean.

This is quite a stunning ship, built to impress at every turn. Amidships on the open deck is a long water slide (200 ft/60 meters in length), as well as tiered sunbathing decks positioned between two swimming pools and several hot tubs. As aboard all Carnival ships, there is a "topless" sunbathing area set around the funnel base, which can't be seen from the pool deck below.

The layout of the ship is quite logical, so finding your way around is not difficult. The decor is all about the world's great Impressionist painters, such as Degas, Monet and Van Gogh. You'll also find large Murano glass flowers on antiqued brass stems in several public areas. It is very imaginative, and a fantasy land for the senses (though it isn't as glitzy as the *Fantasy*-class ships).

As for public areas, there are three decks full of lounges, 10 bars and lots of rooms to play in. There are two atriums: the largest, the Atelier Atrium (in the forward third of the ship) goes through nine decks, while the aft atrium goes through three decks. The ship has a doublewide indoor

BERLITZ'S RATINGS		
	Possible	Achieved
Ship	500	430
Accommodation	200	165
Food	400	221
Service	400	269
Entertainment	100	85
Cruise	400	287

promenade, nine-deck-high, and a glass-domed rotunda atrium lobby.

For those who like to gamble, the Tahiti casino is certainly large and action-packed; there are also more than 320 slot machines. There are several other nightspots for just about every musical taste (except for opera, ballet and classical music lovers).

Children are provided with good facilities, including their own two-level Children's Club (with an outdoor pool), and are well cared for with "Camp Carnival", the line's extensive children's program.

It is difficult to escape from noise and loud music (it's even played in cabin hallways and lifts), not to mention smokers, and masses of people walking around in unsuitable clothing, clutching plastic sport drinks bottles, at any time of the day or night. You have to carry a credit card to operate the personal safes, which is inconvenient.

The many pillars in the dining room make it difficult for proper food service by the waiters. The public toilets are spartan and could do with some cheering up.

ACCOMMODATION. There are 20 cabin price categories, in 7 different grades: suites with private balcony; deluxe outside-view cabin with private balcony; outside-view cabin with private balcony; outside-view cabin with window; cabin with a porthole instead of a window; interior (no-view) cabin; interior (no-view cabin) with upper and lower berths. The price you pay will depend on the grade, location and size you choose. There are five decks of cabins with private balcony – more than any other Carnival ship to date – over 150 more than *Carnival Destiny, Carnival Triumph* or *Carnival Victory*, for example. Many of the private balconies are not so private, and can be overlooked from various public locations.

There are even "fitness" cabins aboard this ship – in a block of 18 cabins located directly around and behind the SpaCarnival; so, fitness devotees can get out of bed and go straight to the treadmill without having to go through any of the public rooms first.

The standard cabins are of good size and come equipped with all the basics, although the furniture is rather angular, with no rounded edges. Three decks of cabins (eight on each deck, each with private balcony) overlook the stern. Most cabins with twin beds can be converted to a queen-size bed format. A gift basket is provided in all grades of cabins; it includes aloe soap, shampoo, conditioner, deodorant, breath mints, candy, and pain relief tablets (albeit all in sample sizes).

Note: If you book one of the suites (Category 11 or 12 in the Carnival Cruise Lines brochure) you automatically qualify for "Skipper's Club" priority check-in at any US homeland port – useful for getting ahead of the crowd.

CUISINE/DINING. There are two principal dining rooms: the Renoir Restaurant, with 744 seats, and the larger Monet Restaurant, with 1,044 seats. Both are two decks high, and both have a balcony level for diners (the balcony level in the Monet Restaurant is larger). Two additional wings in the Renoir Restaurant, named Cassat and Pissaro, provide room to accommodate large groups in a private dining arrangement. Dining is in four seatings, for greater flexibility: 6pm, 6.45pm, 8pm and 8.45pm (these times are approximate but equal two sittings per restaurant). Although the menu choice looks good, the actual cuisine delivered is typically adequate, but quite unmemorable.

The Cezanne Restaurant is the ship's casual self-serve international food court-style lido deck eatery, which has a capacity of over 1,200. Its decor reflects the style of a 19th-century French cafe. It has two main serving lines; it is adjacent to the aft pool and can be covered by a magrodome glass cover in inclement weather. Included in this eating

mall are Paul's Deli, PC's Wok (Chinese cuisine, with wok preparation), a 24-hour pizzeria, and a patisserie (there's an extra charge for yummy pastries, however), as well as a grill for fast foods such as hamburgers and hot dogs. Each night, the Cezanne Restaurant is turned into the "Seaview Bistro", and provides a casual (dress down) alternative to eating in the main dining rooms, serving pasta, steaks, salads and desserts (typically between 6pm and 9pm). And, if you are still hungry, there's always a midnight buffet around the corner.

Alternative (Reservations-Only, Extra Cost) Dining: The Point is the name of the reservations-only, extra cost, alternative dining spot. The decor includes wall murals in the style of Seurat's famous Le Cirque (The Circus). Fine table settings, china and silverware are featured, as well as leather-bound menus.

ENTERTAINMENT. The Toulouse-Lautrec Showlounge is a multi-deck showroom seating 1,400, and serves as the main entertainment venue. It has a revolving stage, hydraulic orchestra pit, superb sound, and seating on three levels (the upper levels being tiered through two decks). There is a proscenium over the stage that acts as a scenery loft.

SPA/FITNESS. SpaCarnival is a large health, fitness and spa complex that spans two decks (the walls display hand-painted reproductions of the artist's poster work). It is located directly above the navigation bridge in the forward part of the ship (and is accessed from the forward stairway).

Facilities on the lower level include a solarium, eight treatment rooms, lecture rooms, sauna and steam rooms for men and women, and a beauty parlor. The upper level consists of a large gymnasium with floor-to-ceiling windows on three sides, including forward-facing ocean views, and an aerobics room with instructor-led classes (some at extra cost).

● **For more extensive general information on what a Carnival cruise is like, see pages 107–111.**

Carnival Destiny
★★★★

Large (Resort) Ship: ....101,353 tons	Total Crew: 1,000	Cabins (with private balcony): 418
Lifestyle: ....Standard	Passengers	Cabins (wheelchair accessible): 25
Cruise Line: ......Carnival Cruise Lines	(lower beds/all berths): 2,642/3,400	Cabin Current: ....110 volts
Former Names: ....none	Passenger Space Ratio	Elevators: 18
Builder: ....Fincantieri (Italy)	(lower beds/all berths): 38.3/29.8	Casino (gaming tables): ....Yes
Original Cost: ....$400 million	Crew/Passenger Ratio	Slot Machines: ....Yes
Entered Service: ....Nov 1996	(lower beds/all berths): 2.6/3.4	Swimming Pools (outdoors): 3
Registry: ....The Bahamas	Navigation Officers: ....Italian	(+1 with magrodome)
Length (ft/m): 892.3/272.0	Cabins (total): 1,321	Swimming Pools (indoors): 0
Beam (ft/m): 116.0/35.3	Size Range (sq ft/m): 179.7–482.2/	Whirlpools: 7
Draft (ft/m): 27.0/8.2	16.7–44.8	Self-Service Launderette: ....Yes
Propulsion/Propellers: .....diesel-electric	Cabins (outside view): 806	Dedicated Cinema/Seats: ....No
(63,400kW)/2	Cabins (interior/no view): 515	Library: ....Yes
Passenger Decks: 12	Cabins (for one person): 0	Classification Society: ...Lloyd's Register

OVERALL SCORE: 1,455 (OUT OF A POSSIBLE 2,000 POINTS)

OVERVIEW. *Carnival Destiny* is the 11th new ship for this very successful cruise line. However, because of its size, the ship is unable to transit the Panama Canal, and is thus dedicated to itineraries in the Caribbean. The ship, whose bows are extremely short, has the distinctive, large, swept-back wing-tipped funnel that is the trademark of Carnival Cruise Lines, in the company colors of red, white and blue.

This is quite a stunning ship, built to impress at every turn, with the most balanced profile of all the ships in the Carnival fleet. Amidships on the open deck is a very long water slide (200 ft/60 meters in length), as well as tiered sunbathing decks positioned between two swimming pools and several hot tubs. As aboard all Carnival ships, there is a "topless" sunbathing area set around the funnel base, which can't be seen from the pool deck below.

Inside, Joe Farcus, the designer who creates all the interiors for the ships of Carnival Cruise Lines, has done a fine job. The decor is a fantasyland for the senses (though nowhere near as glitzy as the *Fantasy*-class ships). The layout is logical, so finding your way around is easy. As for public areas, there are three decks full of lounges, 10 bars and lots of rooms to play in. The ship has a double-wide indoor promenade, nine decks high, and a glass-domed rotunda atrium lobby. For those who like to gamble, the Millionaire's Club Casino is certainly large and action-packed; there are also more than 320 slot machines.

An additional feature that this ship has which the *Fantasy*-class ships do not have is the Flagship Bar, located in the Rotunda (atrium), which faces forward to glass-walled lifts. Another feature is the All Star Bar – a sports bar with tables that include sporting memorabilia.

BERLITZ'S RATINGS

	Possible	Achieved
Ship	500	430
Accommodation	200	165
Food	400	219
Service	400	269
Entertainment	100	85
Cruise	400	287

Youngsters are provided with good facilities, including their own two-level Children's Club (including an outdoor pool), and are well cared for with "Camp Carnival", the line's extensive children's program.

From the viewpoint of safety, passengers can embark directly into the lifeboats from their secured position without having to wait for them to be lowered, thus saving time in the event of a real emergency.

The terraced pool deck is really cluttered, and there are no cushioned pads for the deck chairs. Getting away from people and noise is difficult. The Photo Gallery, adjacent to the atrium/purser's office, becomes extremely congested when photos are on display.

There is no escape from repetitious announcements (for activities that bring revenue, such as art auctions, bingo, and horse racing) that intrude constantly into your cruise. There is also much hustling for drinks, although accomplished with a knowing smile.

ACCOMMODATION. There are 18 price grades. The price you pay depends on grade, size and location. Over half of all cabins have an ocean-view, and at 225 sq. ft./21 sq. meters they are the largest in the standard market. The cabins are spread over four decks and have private balconies (with glass rather than steel balustrades, for better, unobstructed ocean views), extending over the ship's side. The balconies have bright fluorescent lighting.

The standard cabins are of good size and come equipped with all the basics, although the furniture is rather angular, with no rounded edges. Three decks of cabins (eight on each deck, each with private balcony) overlook the stern (with three days at sea on each of two alternating itineraries, vibration is kept to a minimum).

There are eight penthouse suites, and each has a large private balcony. Although they are quite lavish in their appointments, at only 483 sq. ft (44.8 sq. meters), they are really quite modest when compared to the best suites even in many smaller ships. There are also 40 other suites, each of which has a decent sized bathroom, and a good amount of lounge space, although they are nothing special.

In those cabins with balconies (more cabins have balconies aboard this ship than those that do not), the partition between each balcony is open at top and bottom, so you can hear noise from neighbors (or smell their cigarettes). It is disappointing to see three categories of cabins (both outside and interior) with upper and lower bunk beds (lower beds are far more preferable, but this is how the ship accommodates an extra 600 people over and above the lower bed capacity).

The cabins have soft color schemes and soft furnishings in more attractive fabrics than some other ships in the fleet. Interactive "Fun Vision" technology lets you choose movies on demand (for a fee). The bathrooms, which have good-sized showers, have good storage space in the toiletries cabinet. A gift basket is provided in all grades; it includes aloe soap, shampoo, conditioner, deodorant, breath mints, candy, and pain relief tablets (albeit all in sample sizes).

If you book one of the suites (Category 11 or 12 in the Carnival Cruise Lines brochure) you automatically qualify for "Skipper's Club" priority check-in at any US homeland port – useful for getting ahead of the crowd.

CUISINE/DINING. The ship has two dining rooms: the Galaxy, forward, with windows on two sides, has 706 seats; and the Universe, aft, with windows on three sides, has 1,090 seats). Both are non-smoking. Each spans two decks (a first for any Carnival ship), and incorporate a dozen pyramid-shaped domes and chandeliers, and a soft, mellow peachy color scheme.

The Universe dining room has a two-deck-high wall of glass overlooking the stern. There are tables for four, six and eight (and even a few tables for two that the line tries to keep for honeymooners). Dining is in four seatings, for greater flexibility: 6pm, 6.45pm, 8pm and 8.45pm (these times are approximate but equal two seatings per restaurant). Although the menu choices look good, the actual cuisine delivered is adequate, but quite unmemorable.

Casual eaters will find a serve-yourself Lido Buffet –

open for breakfast and lunch, while for dinner this turns into the Seaview Bistro for use as an alternative eatery – for those that do not want to dress to go to the formal dining rooms (between 6pm and 9pm). These include specialty stations where you can order omelets, eggs, fajitas, Chicken Caesar salad, pasta and stir-fry items. Iif you are still hungry, there's always a midnight buffet around the corner.

The dining room entrances have comfortable drinking areas for pre-dinner cocktails. There are also many options for casual dining, particularly during the daytime. The Sun and Sea Restaurant is two decks high; it is the ship's informal international food court-style eatery, which is adjacent to the aft pool and can be covered by a magrodome glass cover in inclement weather. Included in this eating mall are a Trattoria (for Italian cuisine, with made-to-order pasta dishes), Happy Valley (Chinese cuisine, with wok preparation), a 24-hour pizzeria, and a patisserie (extra charge for pastries), as well as a grill (for fast foods such as hamburgers and hot dogs).

At night, the area becomes the "Seaview Bistro" (it typically operates 6pm–9pm), providing a casual (dress down) alternative to eating in the main dining rooms. It serves pasta, steaks, salads and desserts. The good thing is that, if you really want to eat 24 hours a day, you can do it aboard this ship, which has something for (almost) everyone.

ENTERTAINMENT. The three-level (non-smoking) Palladium showlounge, the setting for all production shows and large-scale cabaret acts, is quite stunning, and has a revolving stage, hydraulic orchestra pit, superb sound, and seating on three levels (the upper levels being tiered through two decks). There is a proscenium over the stage that acts as a scenery loft.

SPA/FITNESS. SpaCarnival spans two decks (with a total area of 13,700 sq. ft/1,272 sq. meters), and is located directly above the navigation bridge in the forward part of the ship (its accessed from the forward stairway). Facilities on the lower level include a solarium, eight treatment rooms, lecture rooms, sauna and steam rooms for men and women, and a beauty parlor; the upper level consists of a large gymnasium with floor-to-ceiling windows on three sides, including forward-facing ocean views, and an aerobics room with instructor-led classes (some at extra cost).

● **For more extensive general information on what a Carnival cruise is like, see pages 107–111.**

Carnival Glory
★★★★

Large (Resort) Ship: ......110,000 tons	Total Crew: 1,160	Cabins (with private balcony): 574
Lifestyle: ....Standard	Passengers	Cabins (wheelchair accessible): 25
Cruise Line: ......Carnival Cruise Lines	(lower beds/all berths): 2,974/3,700	Cabin Current: ....110 volts
Former Names: ....none	Passenger Space Ratio	Elevators: 18
Builder: ....Fincantieri (Italy)	(lower beds/all berths): 36.9/29.7	Casino (gaming tables): ....Yes
Original Cost: ....$500 million	Crew/Passenger Ratio	Slot Machines: ....Yes
Entered Service: ....July 2003	(lower beds/all berths): 2.5/3.1	Swimming Pools (outdoors): 3
Registry: ....Panama	Navigation Officers: ....Italian	(+1 with magrodome)
Length (ft/m): 951.4/290.0	Cabins (total): 1,487	Swimming Pools (indoors): 0
Beam (ft/m): 116.4/35.5	Size Range (sq ft/m): 179.7–482.2/	Whirlpools: 7
Draft (ft/m): 27.0/8.2	16.7–44.8	Self-Service Launderette: ....Yes
Propulsion/Propellers: .....diesel-electric	Cabins (outside view): 917	Dedicated Cinema/Seats: ....No
(63,400kW)/2	Cabins (interior/no view): 570	Library: ....Yes
Passenger Decks: 13	Cabins (for one person): 0	Classification Society: ...Lloyd's Register

OVERALL SCORE: 1,457 (OUT OF A POSSIBLE 2,000 POINTS)

OVERVIEW. *Carnival Glory* is the 20th new ship for this very successful cruise line. It is, together with sister ship *Carnival Conquest*, the largest ship in the Carnival Cruise Lines fleet, and has the same generally well-balanced profile as the earlier ships of a similar type: *Carnival Destiny, Carnival Triumph* and *Carnival Victory*. The ship is unable to transit the Panama Canal, due to its size. With extremely short bows, it has the distinctive, large, swept-back wing-tipped funnel that is the trademark of Carnival Cruise Lines, in the company colors of red, white and blue.

The ship's interior decor is truly a fantasyland of colors (the central design theme), and every hue of the rainbow (and a few more) is represented in the public rooms and hallways throughout this ship. Also, the layout is logical, so finding your way around is easy. Most public rooms are located off the Kaleidoscope Boulevard, or main interior promenade (great for strolling and people-watching).

As for public areas, there are three decks full of lounges, 10 bars and lots of rooms to play in. There are two atriums: the largest, called The Colors Lobby, in the forward third of the ship (check out the interpretative paintings of U.S. flags at the Color Bar) goes through nine decks – the colors on the towering atrium wall really are kaleidoscopic – while the aft atrium goes through three decks.

There are nightspots for just about every musical taste (except for opera, ballet and classical music lovers), and for those who like to gamble, the Camel Club Casino, with its Egyptian motif, is certainly large and action-packed; there are also more than 320 slot machines.

Youngsters are provided with good facilities, including their own two-level Children's Club (including an outdoor

BERLITZ'S RATINGS

	Possible	Achieved
Ship	500	430
Accommodation	200	165
Food	400	221
Service	400	269
Entertainment	100	85
Cruise	400	287

pool), and are well cared for with "Camp Carnival", the line's extensive children's program. Note that soft-drinks packages can be purchased for children (and adults).

Many pillars obstruct passengers flow. Those in the dining room, for example, make it difficult for the waiters to serve food properly. The public toilets are spartan and could do with some cheering up.

ACCOMMODATION. There are 20 cabin price categories, in 7 different grades: suites with private balcony; deluxe outside-view cabins with private balcony; outside-view cabins with private balcony; outside-view cabins with window; cabins with a porthole instead of a window; interior (no-view) cabins; and interior (no-view cabins) with upper and lower berths. There are five decks of cabins with private balcony – like sister ship *Carnival Conquest*. The price will depend on the grade, location and size you choose.

The standard cabins are of good size and come equipped with all the basics, although the furniture is rather square and angular, with no rounded edges. Three decks of cabins (eight on each deck, each with private balcony) overlook the stern. Most cabins with twin beds can be converted to a queen-size bed format.

If you book one of the suites (Category 11 or 12 in the Carnival Cruise Lines brochure) you automatically qualify for "Skipper's Club" priority check-in at any US homeland port – useful for getting ahead of the crowd.

There are even "fitness" cabins – in a block of 18 cabins located directly around and behind the SpaCarnival; so, fitness devotees can get out of bed and go straight to the treadmill without having to go through any of the public rooms.

A gift basket is provided in all grades of cabins; it includes aloe soap, shampoo, conditioner, deodorant, breath mints, candy, and pain relief tablets (albeit all in sample sizes).

CUISINE/DINING. There are two principal dining rooms (Golden and Platinum). Both are two decks high, and both have a balcony level for diners (the balcony level in the aft dining room is larger than the other). The decor is interesting and includes wall coverings featuring a pattern of Japanese bonsai trees. Two additional wings provide room to accommodate large groups in a private dining arrangement.

Dining is in four seatings, for greater flexibility: 6pm, 6.45pm, 8pm and 8.45pm (these times are approximate but equal two seatings per restaurant). Although the menu choice looks good, the actual cuisine delivered is typically adequate, and quite unmemorable.

There is also a casual self-serve international food court-style lido deck eatery, the two-level Red Sail Restaurant. It has two main serving lines; it is adjacent to the aft pool and can be covered by a magrodome glass cover in inclement weather. Included in this eating mall are Paul's Deli, PC's Wok (Chinese cuisine, with wok preparation), a 24-hour pizzeria, and a patisserie (there's an extra charge for yummy pastries, however), as well as a grill for fast foods such as hamburgers and hot dogs. Each night, the Cezanne Restaurant is turned into the "Seaview Bistro", and provides a casual (dress down) alternative to eating in the main dining rooms, serving pasta, steaks, salads and desserts (typically between 6pm and 9pm).

Alternative (Reservations-Only, Extra Cost) Dining: There is one reservations-only, extra cost, alternative dining spot, the Emerald Room. Fine table settings, china and silverware are featured, as well as leather-bound menus, cobalt-blue walls and lighting fixtures resembling giant emeralds.

ENTERTAINMENT. The Amber Palace Showlounge (named after Russia's great Amber Room, a gift by Frederick the Great in 1715) is a multi-deck showroom seating up to 1,400, and serves as the principal entertainment venue for large-scale entertainment, including Las-Vegas-style production shows and major cabaret acts. It has a revolving stage, hydraulic orchestra pit, superb sound, and seating on three levels (the upper levels being tiered through two decks). There is a proscenium over the stage that acts as a scenery loft.

For those who enjoy the body-throbbing sensations of loud music, the White Heat Dance Club is the ship's discotheque, with its "Liberace-like" tall candelabra, and a video wall with projections live from the dance floor. Jazz lovers should enjoy the Bar Blue, while those whoe enjoy the sounds of the piano can do so in the Cinn-A-Bar, with its curved aluminum walls.

SPA/FITNESS. SpaCaarnival spans two decks (with a total area of approximately 13,300 sq. ft/1,235 sq. meters), and is located directly above the navigation bridge in the forward part of the ship (it is accessed from the forward stairway). The decor is Polynesian in style, a theme that incorporates lush foliage, teak flooring, and a waterfall.

Facilities on the lower level include a solarium, eight treatment rooms, lecture rooms, sauna and steam rooms for men and women, and a beauty parlor; the upper level consists of a large gymnasium with floor-to-ceiling windows on three sides, including forward-facing ocean views, and an aerobics room with instructor-led classes (some at extra cost).

● **For more extensive general information on what a Carnival cruise is like, see pages 107–111.**

PLIMSOLL MARK

The safety of ships at sea and all those aboard owes much to the 19th-century social reformer Samuel Plimsoll, a member of the British Parliament concerned about the frequent loss of ships due to overloading. In those days, some shipowners would load their vessels down to the gunwales to squeeze every ounce of revenue out of them. They gambled on good weather, good fortune, and good seamanship to bring them safely into port. Consequently, many ships went to the bottom of the sea – the result of their buoyancy being seriously impaired by overloading.

Plimsoll helped to enact legislation that came to be known as the Merchant Shipping Act of 1875. This required shipowners to mark their vessels with a circular disc 12 inches (30 cm) long bisected by a line 18 inches (46 cm) long, as a measure of their maximum draft; that is, the depth to which a ship's hull could be safely immersed at sea.

The Merchant Shipping Act of 1890 went even further, and required the Plimsoll mark (or line) to be positioned on the sides of vessels in accordance with tables drawn up by competent authorities.

The Plimsoll mark is now found on the ships of every nation. The Plimsoll mark indicates three different depths: the depth to which a vessel can be loaded in fresh water, which is less buoyant than salt water; the depth in summer, when seas are generally calmer; and the depth in winter, when seas are much rougher.

Carnival Legend
★★★★

Large (Resort) Ship: .... 85,920 tons	Passengers	Elevators: 15
Lifestyle: .... Standard	(lower beds/all berths): 2,124/2,680	Casino (gaming tables): .... Yes
Cruise Line: ...... Carnival Cruise Lines	Passenger Space Ratio	Slot Machines: .... Yes
Former Names: .... none	(lower beds/all berths): 40.4/32.0	Swimming Pools (outdoors): .... 2+1
Builder: .... Kvaerner Masa-Yards	Crew/Passenger Ratio	children's pool
Original Cost: .... $375 million	(lower beds/all berths): 2.2/2.6	Swimming Pools (indoors): 1
Entered Service: .... Aug 2002	Navigation Officers: .... Italian	(indoor/outdoor)
Registry: .... Panama	Cabins (total): 1,062	Whirlpools: 5
Length (ft/m): 959.6/292.5	Size Range (sq ft/m): 185.0–490.0/	Fitness Center: .... Yes
Beam (ft/m): 105.6/32.2	17.1–45.5	Sauna/Steam Room: .... Yes/Yes
Draft (ft/m): 25.5/7.8	Cabins (outside view): 849	Massage: .... Yes
Propulsion/Propellers: ..... diesel-electric	Cabins (interior/no view): 213	Self-Service Launderette: .... Yes
(62,370 kW)/2 azimuthing pods	Cabins (for one person): 0	Dedicated Cinema/Seats: .... No
(17.6 MW each)	Cabins (with private balcony): 750	Library: .... Yes
Passenger Decks: 12	Cabins (wheelchair accessible): 16	Classification Society: ... Registro Navale
Total Crew: 1,030	Cabin Current: .... 110 volts	Italiano (RINA)

OVERALL SCORE: 1,474 (OUT OF A POSSIBLE 2,000 POINTS)

OVERVIEW. *Carnival Legend* (sister ship to *Carnival Miracle, Carnival Pride* and *Carnival Spirit*) is the 18th new ship for this very successful cruise line. Its launch made headlines in 2002 when actress Dame Judi Dench, the celebrity chosen to break the traditional bottle of champagne on its hull, had difficulty doing so; a final hefty heave smashed the bottle, drenching Dame Judi with champagne. The ship, whose bows are extremely short, has the distinctive, large, swept-back wing-tipped funnel that is the Carnival's trademar, in the company colors of red, white and blue.

This ship is longer than the company's larger quintet (*Carnival Conquest, Carnival Destiny, Carnival Glory, Carnival Triumph,* and *Carnival Victory*), and only a hair's breadth shorter than Cunard Line's *Queen Elizabeth 2* (which the Carnival Corporation, Carnival Cruise Lines' parent company, owns). The immense lobby spans eight decks. The atrium lobby presents a stunning wall decoration that is best seen from any of the multiple viewing balconies on each deck above the main lobby floor level. Take a drink from the lobby bar and look upwards – the surroundings are simply stunning, with a mural of the Colossus of Rhodes.

The interior decor is dedicated to the world's great legends, from wonders of the ancient world and heroes of antiquity to 20th-century jazz masters and great athletes – an eclectic mix that somehow works well. There are two entertainment/public room decks, the upper with an exterior promenade deck – something new for this fun cruise line.

Without doubt, the most dramatic room aboard this ship is the Follies Showlounge. Spanning three decks in the for-

BERLITZ'S RATINGS

	Possible	Achieved
Ship	500	435
Accommodation	200	154
Food	400	234
Service	400	270
Entertainment	100	86
Cruise	400	295

ward section of the ship, it recalls the movie palaces of the 1920s. Spiral stairways at the back of the lounge connect all three levels. Stage shows are best seen from the upper three levels, from where the sight lines are reasonably good. Directly underneath is the Firebird Lounge, which has a bar in its starboard aft section.

A small wedding chapel is forward of the uppermost level of the two main entertainment decks, adjacent to the library and internet center. Other facilities include a winding shopping street with several boutique stores, photo gallery, video games room, an observation balcony in the center of the vessel (at the top of the multi-deck atrium), and the large Club Merlin Casino, with its castle-like atmosphere (damsels, knights and wizards are painted on the walls).

In the medical department, Tele-Radiology is installed. This system enables shipboard physicians to digitally transmit X-rays and other patient information to shore-side facilities – useful for peace of mind for passengers and crew.

The information desk in the lobby is quite small, and can become congested. It is hard to escape from noise and loud music (it's even played in cabin hallways and lifts), not to mention smokers, and masses of people walking around in unsuitable clothing, clutching plastic sport drinks bottles, at any time of the day or night. Many private balconies are not so private, and can be overlooked from public locations.

Many pillars obstruct passenger flow. Those in the dining room, for example, make it difficult for proper food service by the waiters. Books and computers are cohabitants in the ship's library/internet center, but anyone wanting a book has to lean over others who may be using a computer – a very awkward arrangement. Public toilets are spartan and could do with cheering up.

ACCOMMODATION. There are 20 cabin categories, priced by grade, location and size. The range of cabins includes suites (with private balcony), outside-view cabins with private balcony, 68 ocean view cabins with French doors (pseudo balconies that have doors which open, but no balcony to step out onto), and a healthy proportion of standard outside-view to interior (no view) cabins.

All cabins have spy-hole doors, and have twin beds that can be converted into a queen-sized bed, individually controlled air-conditioning, television, and telephone. A number of cabins on the lowest deck have views that are obstructed by lifeboats. Some cabins can accommodate a third and fourth person, but have little closet space, and there's only one personal safe. There is no separate radio in each cabin – instead, audio channels are provided on the in-cabin TV system, but you can't turn the picture off. A gift basket of (sample sized) personal amenities is provided in all grades.

If you book one of the suites (Category 11 or 12 in the Carnival Cruise Lines brochure), you automatically qualify for "Skipper's Club" priority check-in at any US homeland port – useful for getting ahead of the crowd.

Among the most desirable suites and cabins are those on five of the aft-facing decks; these have private balconies overlooking the stern and ship's wash. You might think that these units would suffer from vibration, but they don't – a bonus provided by the pod propulsion system *(see page 151).*

For the ultimate in extra space, it would be worth your while trying one of the large deluxe balcony suites on Deck 6, with its own private teakwood balcony. These tend to be quiet suites, with a large lounge and sleeping areas, a good-sized bathroom with twin washbasins, toilet and bidet, and whirlpool bathtub. They have twin beds that convert to a queen-sized bed, three (illuminated) closets, and a huge amount of drawer space. The balcony has an outside light, and a wide teakwood deck with smoked glass and wood railing (you could easily seat 10 people here).

Even the largest suites, however, are quite small compared with suites aboard other ships of a similar size – for example, Celebrity Cruises' *Constellation, Infinity, Millennium,* and *Summit,* where penthouse suites measure up to 2,530 sq. ft (235 sq. meters). Carnival Cruise Lines has fallen behind in the move to larger living spaces, and, with this ship, lost an opportunity to provide more space. But Carnival's philosophy has always been to get its passengers out into public areas to socialize and spend money.

CUISINE/DINING. This ship has a single, large, two-decks-high, 1,300-seat main dining room, Truffles Restaurant, with seating on both upper and main levels. Its huge ceiling has large murals of a china pattern made famous by Royal Copenhagen, and wall-mounted glass display cases contain fine china. The galley is located underneath the restaurant, with waiter access by escalators. There are tables for two, four, six or eight, and small rooms on both upper

and lower levels can be closed off for groups of up to 60. Dining is in two seatings (main and late) for lunch and dinner, while breakfast is in an open-seating arrangement.

For casual eaters, while there is no lido cafe, the Unicorn Cafe is an extensive eatery that forms the aft third of Deck 9 (part of it also wraps around the upper section of the huge atrium). Murals of unicorns are everywhere. The cafe includes a central area with small buffet counters (deli sandwich corner, Asian corner, rotisserie, and International counter); there are salad counters, a dessert counter, and a 24-hour Pizzeria counter, all of which form a large eatery with both indoor and outdoor seating. Movement around the buffet area is slow, and you have to stand in line for everything. Each night, the Unicorn Cafe becomes Seaview Bistro, for casual, serve-yourself dinners (typically open 6pm–9.30pm).
Alternative (Reservations-Only, Extra Cost) Dining: The Golden Fleece Supper Club is a more upscale dining spot atop the ship, with just 156 seats and a show kitchen. It is located on two of the uppermost decks of the ship, above the Unicorn, in the lower, forward section of the funnel housing, with great views over the multi-deck atrium. The decor is set around the Greek legend of Jason and the Argonauts. The bar is the setting for a large sculpture of the Golden Fleece. Fine table settings, china and silverware are featured, as well as leather-bound menus.

ENTERTAINMENT. The Follies Showlounge is the ship's principal venue for large-scale production shows and cabaret shows. Stage shows are best seen from the upper three levels. Directly underneath the showlounge is the Firebird Lounge, which has a bar in its starboard aft section.

Almost every lounge/bar, including Billie's Bar (a piano lounge), and Satchmo's Club (a nightclub with bar and dance floor) has live music in the evening. Finally, for the very lively, there's the disco; and there's always karaoke as well as a Passenger Talent Show during each cruise.

SPA/FITNESS. SpaCarnival spans two decks, is located directly above the navigation bridge in the forward part of the ship and has 13,700 sq. ft (1,272 sq. meters) of space. Facilities on the lower level include a solarium, eight treatment rooms, lecture rooms, sauna and steam rooms for men and women, and a beauty parlor; the upper level consists of a large gymnasium with floor-to-ceiling windows on three sides, including forward-facing ocean views, and an aerobics room with instructor-led classes.

There are two centrally located swimming pools outdoors, and one can be used in inclement weather due to its retractable glass dome. There are two whirlpool tubs, adjacent to the swimming pools. A winding water slide that spans two decks in height is located at an aft, upper deck. Another smaller pool is available for children. An outdoor jogging track is located around the ship's mast and the forward third of the ship; it doesn't go around the whole ship, but it's long enough for some serious walking.

● **For more extensive general information on what a Carnival cruise is like, see pages 107–111.**

Carnival Liberty
NOT YET RATED

Large (Resort) Ship: ....110,000 tons	Total Crew: 1,160	Cabins (with private balcony): 574
Lifestyle: ....Standard	Passengers	Cabins (wheelchair accessible): 25
Cruise Line: ....Carnival Cruise Lines	(lower beds/all berths): 2,974/3,700	Cabin Current: ....110 volts
Former Names: ....None	Passenger Space Ratio	Elevators: 18
Builder: ....Fincantieri (Italy)	(lower beds/all berths): 36.9/29.7	Casino (gaming tables): ....Yes
Original Cost: ....$500 million	Crew/Passenger Ratio	Slot Machines: ....Yes
Entered Service: ....July 2005	(lower beds/all berths): 2.5/3.1	Swimming Pools (outdoors): 3
Registry: ....Panama	Navigation Officers: ....Italian	(+1 with magrodome)
Length (ft/m): 951.4/290.0	Cabins (total): 1,487	Swimming Pools (indoors): 0
Beam (ft/m): 116.4/35.5	Size Range (sq ft/m): 179.7–482.2/	Whirlpools: 7
Draft (ft/m): 27.0/8.2	16.7–44.8	Self-Service Launderette: ....Yes
Propulsion/Propellers: .....diesel-electric	Cabins (outside view): 917	Dedicated Cinema/Seats: ....No
(63,400kW)/2	Cabins (interior/no view): 570	Library: ....Yes
Passenger Decks: 13	Cabins (for one person): 0	Classification Society: ...Lloyd's Register

OVERALL SCORE: NYR (OUT OF A POSSIBLE 2,000 POINTS)

OVERVIEW. *Carnival Liberty* is the 23rd new ship for this incredibly successful cruise line. It shares the same generally well-balanced profile as *Carnival Destiny, Carnival Glory, Carnival Triumph, Carnival Valor* and *Carnival Victory*. The ship is unable to transit the Panama Canal, due to its size (so it's called a non-Panamax ship). With extremely short bows, it has the distinctive, large, swept-back wing-tipped funnel that is the trademark of Carnival Cruise Lines, in the company colors of red, white and blue.

The ship's interior decor is truly a fantasyland of colors, and every hue of the rainbow (and a few more) is represented in the public rooms and hallways. The layout is logical, so finding your way around is easy. Most public rooms are located off a main boulevard, or main interior promenade (great for strolling and people watching from the Jardin Café or Promenade Bar). Good hangouts and drinking places include The Stage (live music/karaoke lounge), the Flower Bar (main lobby), Gloves Bar (sports Bar), Paparazzi (wine bar), and The Cabinet.

As for public areas, there are three decks full of lounges, 10 bars and lots of rooms to play in. There are two atriums: the largest, in the forward third of the ship goes through nine decks, while the aft atrium spans three decks.

There are nightspots for just about every musical taste (except for opera, ballet and classical music lovers), and for those who like to gamble, the Czar's Palace Casino, with its Russian motifs and theme, is certainly large and action-packed; there are more than 320 slot machines.

Youngsters are provided with good facilities, including their own two-level Children's Club (including an outdoor pool), and are well cared for with "Camp Carnival", the

BERLITZ'S RATINGS

	Possible	Achieved
Ship	500	NYR
Accommodation	200	NYR
Food	400	NYR
Service	400	NYR
Entertainment	100	NYR
Cruise	400	NYR

line's extensive children's program. Soft-drinks packages can be purchased for children (and adults).

Many pillars obstruct passenger flow (those in the two main restaurants, for example, make it difficult for the waiters to serve food properly). The public toilets are spartan and could do with some cheering up.

ACCOMMODATION. There are 20 cabin price categories, in 7 different grades: suites with private balcony; deluxe outside-view cabins with private balcony; outside-view cabins with private balcony; outside-view cabins with window; cabins with a porthole instead of a window; interior (no-view) cabins; and interior (no-view) cabins with upper and lower berths. There are five decks of cabins with private balconies. The price will depend on the grade, location and size you choose.

The standard cabins are of good size and come equipped with all the basics, although the furniture is rather square and angular, with no rounded edges. Three decks of cabins (eight on each deck, each with private balcony) overlook the stern. Most cabins with twin beds can be converted to a queen-size bed format.

Book one of the suites (Category 11 or 12 in the Carnival Cruise Lines brochure) and you qualify for "Skipper's Club" priority check-in at any US homeland port – useful for getting ahead of the crowd.

There are even "fitness" cabins aboard this ship – in a block of 18 cabins located directly around and behind SpaCarnival; so, fitness devotees can get out of bed and go straight to the treadmill without having to go through any of the public rooms first.

A gift basket is provided in all grades of cabins; it

includes aloe soap, shampoo, conditioner, deodorant, breath mints, candy, and pain relief tablets (albeit all in sample sizes).

CUISINE/DINING. There are two principal dining rooms (Golden Olympian Restaurant, forward, seating 744: and Silver Olympian Restaurant, aft, seating 1,122). Both are two decks high, and both include a balcony level for diners (the balcony level in the aft dining room is larger than the other). Two additional wings (the Persian Room and Satin Room) have room to accommodate large groups in a private dining arrangement. Dining is in four seatings, for greater flexibility: 6pm, 6.45pm, 8pm and 8.45pm (these times are approximate, but equal two seatings per restaurant). Although the menu choice looks good, the actual cuisine delivered is typically adequate, and quite unmemorable.

There is also a casual self-serve international food court-style lido deck eatery, the two-level Emile's. It has two main serving lines; it is adjacent to the aft pool and can be covered by a magrodome glass cover in inclement weather. Included in this eating mall are a deli, Chinese cuisine eatery, with wok preparation, a 24-hour pizzeria, and a patisserie (there's an extra charge for yummy pastries, however), as well as a grill for fast foods such as hamburgers and hot dogs. Each night, Emilie's morphs into the "Seaview Bistro", and provides a casual (dress down) alternative to eating in the main dining rooms, serving pasta, steaks, salads and desserts (typically 6pm–9pm).

Alternative (Reservations-Only, Extra Cost) Dining: There is one reservations-only, extra cost, alternative dining spot, Harry's. Fine table settings, china and silverware are featured, as well as leather-bound menus, cobalt-blue walls and lighting fixtures resembling giant emeralds.

ENTERTAINMENT. The Venetian Palace Showlounge is a multi-deck showroom seating up to 1,400, and serves as the principal entertainment venue for large-scale entertainment, including Las-Vegas-style production shows and major cabaret acts. It has a revolving stage, hydraulic orchestra pit, superb sound, and seating on three levels (the upper levels being tiered through two decks). There is a proscenium over the stage that acts as a scenery loft.

The Victoria Lounge, located aft, seats 425 and typically features live music and late-night cabaret acts, including adult comedy.

Body-throbbing loud music sensations can be found in the Tattooed Lady Dance Club is the ship's discotheque; it includes a video wall with projections live from the dance floor. Piano bar lovers should enjoy the 100-seat Piano Man piano bar.

SPA/FITNESS. SpaCarnival spans two decks (with a total area of approximately 13,300 sq. ft/1,235 sq. meters), and is located directly above the navigation bridge in the forward part of the ship (it is accessed from the forward stairway). The decor is Polynesian in style, a theme that incorporates lush foliage, teak flooring, and a waterfall.

Facilities on the lower level include a solarium, eight treatment rooms, lecture rooms, sauna and steam rooms for men and women, and a beauty parlor; the upper level consists of a large gymnasium with floor-to-ceiling windows on three sides, including forward-facing ocean views, and an aerobics room with instructor-led classes (some cost extra).

● For more extensive general information on what a Carnival cruise is like, see pages 107–111.

Carnival Miracle
★★★★

Large (Resort) Ship: . . . . .85,920 tons	Total Crew: 961	Cabins (wheelchair accessible): 16
Lifestyle: . . . . .Standard	Passengers	Cabin Current: . . . . .110 volts
Cruise Line: . . . . . . .Carnival Cruise Lines	(lower beds/all berths): 2,124/2,680	Elevators: 15
Former Names: . . . . .none	Passenger Space Ratio	Casino (gaming tables): . . . . .Yes
Builder: . . . . .Kvaerner Masa-Yards	(lower beds/all berths): 40.4/32.0	Slot Machines: . . . . .Yes
Original Cost: . . . .$375 million	Crew/Passenger Ratio	Swimming Pools (outdoors): . . . . .2+1
Entered Service: . . . . .April 2004	(lower beds/all berths): 2.2/2.7	children's pool
Registry: . . . . .Panama	Navigation Officers: . . . . .Italian	Swimming Pools (indoors): 1
Length (ft/m): 959.6/292.5	Cabins (total): 1,062	(indoor/outdoor)
Beam (ft/m): 105.6/32.2	Size Range (sq ft/m): 185.0–490.0/	Whirlpools: 5
Draft (ft/m): 25.5/7.8	17.1–45.5	Self-Service Launderette: . . . . .Yes
Propulsion/Propellers: . . . . .diesel-electric	Cabins (outside view): 849	Dedicated Cinema/Seats: . . . . .No
(62,370 kW)/2 azimuthing pods	Cabins (interior/no view): 213	Library: . . . . .Yes
(17.6 MW each)	Cabins (for one person): 0	Classification Society: . . .Registro Navale
Passenger Decks: 13	Cabins (with private balcony): 750	Italiano (RINA)

OVERALL SCORE: 1,474 (OUT OF A POSSIBLE 2,000 POINTS)

OVERVIEW. *Carnival Miracle* (sister to *Carnival Legend, Carnival Pride* and *Carnival Spirit*) is the 21st new ship for this very successful cruise line. Built from more than 100 blocks (each weighing up to 450 tons), the ship, whose bows are extremely short, has the distinctive, large, swept-back wing-tipped funnel that is the trademark of Carnival Cruise Lines, in the company colors of red, white and blue. The ship is longer than the company's larger quin-tet (*Carnival Conquest, Carnival Destiny, Carnival Glory, Carnival Triumph,* and *Carnival Victory*), and only a hair's breadth shorter than Cunard Line's *Queen Elizabeth 2* (which the Carnival Corporation, Carnival Cruise Lines' parent company, owns).

The interior decor is very artistic (and overwhelmingly colorful – there are no restful colors), with "fictional icons" as the design theme, with such luminaries as the Phantom of the Opera, Sherlock Holmes, Philip Marlowe, and Captain Ahab among the many art images (bronze statues of Orpheis, Sirenes, and Ulysses adorn the swimming pools).

The dramatic atrium lobby space spans eight decks and presents a stunning wall decoration best seen from any of the multiple viewing balconies on each deck above the main lobby floor level. Take a drink from the lobby bar and look upwards – the surroundings are simply stunning, with a mural of the Colossus of Rhodes (one of the seven wonders of the world). The interior decor is dedicated to the world's great legends, from wonders of the ancient world and heroes of antiquity to 20th-century jazz masters and great athletes – an eclectic mix of "entertainment architecture" that somehow works well.

BERLITZ'S RATINGS		
	Possible	Achieved
Ship	500	435
Accommodation	200	154
Food	400	234
Service	400	270
Entertainment	100	86
Cruise	400	295

There are two whole entertainment/public room decks, the upper of which also has an exterior promenade deck – something new for this fun cruise line. A small wedding chapel is forward of the uppermost level of the two main entertainment decks, adjacent to the library and internet center. Other facilities include a winding shopping street with several boutique stores (including those selling the usual Carnival logo items), photo gallery, video games room, an observation balcony in the center of the vessel (at the top of the multi-deck atrium), and a large Club Merlin Casino, with its castle-like atmosphere (damsels, knights and wizards are painted on the walls).

In the medical department, Tele-Radiology is installed. This system enables shipboard physicians to digitally transmit X-rays and other patient information to shore-side facil!ities – useful for peace of mind for passengers and crew.

The information desk in the lobby is really quite small, and can become quite congested. It is difficult to escape from noise and loud music (it's even played in cabin hallways and lifts), not to mention smokers, and masses of people walking around in unsuitable clothing, clutching plastic sport drinks bottles, at any time of the day or night. Many of the private balconies aren't so private, and can be overlooked from public locations. A stream of flyers advertises daily art auctions and other promotions, while "artworks" for auction are strewn throughout the ship.

Many pillars obstruct passengers flow. Those in the dining room, for example, make it hard for proper food service by the waiters. Books and computers are cohabitants in the ship's library/internet center, but anyone wanting a book has to lean over others who may be using a computer – a very awkward arrangement. Public toilets are spartan and could do with cheering up.

ACCOMMODATION. There are 20 cabin categories, priced according to grade, location and size. The range of cabins includes suites (with private balcony), outside-view cabins with private balcony, 68 ocean view cabins with French doors (pseudo balconies that have doors which open, but no balcony to step out onto), and a healthy proportion of standard outside-view to interior (no view) cabins. All cabins have original motifs of nature, plant life and lake views.

All cabins have spy-hole doors, and twin beds that can be converted into a queen-sized bed, individually controlled air-conditioning, TV, and telephone. Some cabins on the lowest deck have views obstructed by lifeboats. Some cabins that can accommodate a third and fourth person have very little closet space, and there's only one personal safe. There is no separate radio in each cabin – instead, audio channels are provided on the in-cabin television system (however, you can't turn the picture off). A gift basket of (sample sized) personal amenities is provided in all grades.

If you book one of the suites (Category 11 or 12 in the Carnival Cruise Lines brochure), you automatically qualify for "Skipper's Club" priority check-in at any US homeland port – useful for getting ahead of the crowd.

Among the most desirable suites and cabins are those on five of the aft-facing decks; these have private balconies overlooking the stern and ship's wash. You might think that these units would suffer from vibration, but they don't – a bonus provided by the pod propulsion system *(see page 151).*

For the ultimate in extra space, it would be worth your while trying one of the large deluxe balcony suites on Deck 6, with its own private teakwood balcony. These tend to be quiet suites, with a large lounge and sleeping areas, a good-sized bathroom with twin (his 'n' hers) washbasins, toilet and bidet, and whirlpool bathtub. These suites have twin beds that convert to a queen-sized bed, three (illuminated) closets, and a huge amount of drawer space. The balcony has an outside light, and a wide teakwood deck with smoked glass and wood railing (you could easily seat 10 people with comfort and still have space left over).

Even the largest suites are quite small, however, compared with suites aboard other ships of a similar size – for example, Celebrity Cruises' *Constellation, Infinity, Millennium,* and *Summit,* where penthouse suites measure up to 2,530 sq. ft (235 sq. meters). Carnival Cruise Lines has fallen behind in the move to larger living spaces, and, with this ship, lost an opportunity to provide more space for those seeking it.

CUISINE/DINING. This ship has a single, large, two-decks-high, 1,300-seat main dining room called the Bacchus Restaurant, with seating on both upper and main levels. Its huge ceiling has large murals of a china pattern made famous by Royal Copenhagen, and wall-mounted glass display cases feature fine china. There are tables for two, four,

six or eight, and small rooms on both upper and lower levels can be closed off for groups of up to 60. Dining is in two seatings (main and late) for lunch and dinner, while breakfast is in an open-seating arrangement.

For casual eaters, while there is no lido cafe, Horatio's Cafe is an extensive eatery that forms the aft third of Deck 9 (part of it also wraps around the upper section of the huge atrium). Murals of unicorns are everywhere. The cafe includes a central area with small buffet counters (deli sandwich corner, Asian corner, rotisserie, and International counter); there are salad counters, a dessert counter, and a 24-hour Pizzeria counter, all of which form a large eatery with both indoor and outdoor seating. Movement around the buffet area is slow, and you have to stand in line for everything. At night, the cafe becomes Seaview Bistro, for casual, serve-yourself dinners (typically open 6pm–9.30pm).

Alternative (Reservations-Only, Extra Cost) Dining: Nick and Nora's Supper Club is a more upscale dining spot, with just 156 seats and a show kitchen. It is located on two of the uppermost decks of the ship, above the Unicorn Grille, in the lower, forward section of the funnel housing, with great views over the multi-deck atrium. The decor is set around the Greek legend of Jason and the Argonauts. Fine table settings, china and silverware are featured, as well as leather-bound menus.

ENTERTAINMENT. The Mad Hatter's Ball Showlounge is the ship's principal venue for large-scale production shows and other evening cabaret shows. Stage shows are best seen from the upper three levels, from where the sight lines are reasonable. Directly underneath the showlounge is the Phantom Lounge, which has a bar in its starboard aft section. Stage smoke appears to be in constant use during the production shows, and volumes are of the ear-splitting type.

SPA/FITNESS. SpaCarnival spans two decks, is located directly above the navigation bridge in the forward part of the ship, and has 13,700 sq. ft (1,272 sq. meters) of space. Facilities on the lower level include a solarium, eight treatment rooms, lecture rooms, sauna and steam rooms for men and women, and a beauty parlor; the upper level consists of a large gymnasium with floor-to-ceiling windows on three sides, including forward-facing ocean views, and an aerobics room with instructor-led classes.

There are two centrally located swimming pools outdoors, and one of the pools can be used in inclement weather due to its retractable glass dome. There are two whirlpool tubs, located adjacent to the swimming pools. A winding water slide that spans two decks in height is located at an aft, upper deck. Another smaller pool is available for children. There is an additional whirlpool tub outdoors. A jogging track is located around the mast and the forward third of the ship. Although it doesn't go around the whole ship, it's long enough for some serious walking.

● **For more extensive general information on what a Carnival cruise is like, see pages 107–111.**

Carnival Pride
★★★★

Large (Resort) Ship: ....85,920 tons	Total Crew: 1,029	Cabins (wheelchair accessible): 16
Lifestyle: ....Standard	Passengers	Cabin Current: ....110 volts
Cruise Line: ....Carnival Cruise Lines	(lower beds/all berths): 2,124/2,680	Elevators: 15
Former Names: ....none	Passenger Space Ratio	Casino (gaming tables): ....Yes
Builder: ....Kvaerner Masa-Yards	(lower beds/all berths): 40.4/32.0	Slot Machines: ....Yes
Original Cost: ....$375 million	Crew/Passenger Ratio	Swimming Pools (outdoors): ....2+1
Entered Service: ....Jan 2002	(lower beds/all berths): 2.2/2.6	children's pool
Registry: ....Panama	Navigation Officers: ....Italian	Swimming Pools (indoors): 1
Length (ft/m): 959.6/292.5	Cabins (total): 1,062	(indoor/outdoor)
Beam (ft/m): 105.6/32.2	Size Range (sq ft/m): 185.0–490.0/	Whirlpools: 5
Draft (ft/m): 25.5/7.8	17.1–45.5	Self-Service Launderette: ....Yes
Propulsion/Propellers: .....diesel-electric	Cabins (outside view): 849	Dedicated Cinema/Seats: ....No
(62,370 kW)/2 azimuthing pods	Cabins (interior/no view): 213	Library: ....Yes
(17.6 MW each)	Cabins (for one person): 0	Classification Society: ...Registro Navale
Passenger Decks:................12	Cabins (with private balcony): 750	Italiano (RINA)

OVERALL SCORE: 1,474 (OUT OF A POSSIBLE 2,000 POINTS)

OVERVIEW. *Carnival Pride* (sister to *Carnival Legend, Carnival Miracle* and *Carnival Spirit,* all of which can transit the Panama Canal) is the 17th new ship for this very successful cruise line. The ship, whose bows are extremely short, has the distinctive, large, swept-back wing-tipped funnel that is the trademark of Carnival Cruise Lines, in the company colors of red, white and blue. The ship is longer than the company's larger quintet (*Carnival Conquest, Carnival Destiny, Carnival Glory, Carnival Triumph,* and *Carnival Victory,* all of which measure over 100,000 tons), and only a hair's breadth shorter than Cunard Line's *Queen Elizabeth 2* (which the Carnival Corporation, Carnival Cruise Lines' parent company, owns).

The lobby is immense, spanning eight decks, and the decor includes lots of larger than life women's breasts, bums, and nude men – all reproductions from the Renaissance period. The atrium lobby has a stunning 37-ft high (11-meter) reproduction of Raphael's Nymph Galatea that is best seen from any of the multiple viewing balconies on each deck above the main lobby floor level. There's no question about it – the surroundings are quite stunning.

The decor is extremely artistic (eclectic, in fact), with art being the theme throughout the ship – even elevator doors and interiors display reproductions (blown-up, overgrainy photographic copies) of some of the great Renaissance masters such as Gauguin, Matisse and Vignali.

There are two whole entertainment/public room decks, the upper of which also has an exterior promenade deck – something new for this cruise line. Although it doesn't go around the whole ship, it's long enough to do some serious

BERLITZ'S RATINGS		
	Possible	Achieved
Ship	500	435
Accommodation	200	154
Food	400	234
Service	400	270
Entertainment	100	86
Cruise	400	295

walking on. There is also a jogging track outdoors, located around the ship's mast and the forward third of the ship.

A small wedding chapel is forward of the uppermost level of the two main entertainment decks, adjacent to the library and internet center. Other facilities include a winding shopping street with boutique sections for brands such as Fendi, Fossil, Tommy Hilfiger, plus Carnival logo items. There's a photo gallery, video games room, an observation balcony in the center of the vessel (at the top of the multi-deck atrium), and a large casino, with gaming tables, slot machines, bar and entertainment.

The information desk in the lobby is quite small, and can become congested. You need a credit card to operate the personal safe, an inconvenience. You'll endure a stream of flyers advertising daily promotions, while "artworks" for auction are strewn throughout the ship. Many pillars obstruct passenger flow. Those in the dining room, for example, make it difficult for proper food service by the waiters.

Books and computers are cohabitants in the library/internet center, but to get a book you have to lean over those using a computer – an awkward arrangement. Public toilets are spartan and could do with some cheering up.

ACCOMMODATION. There are 20 cabin price categories, in 6 different grades, with the price depending on grade, location and size. The range of cabins includes suites (with private balcony), outside-view cabins with private balcony (many are not really private, and can be overlooked from above), 68 ocean view cabins with French doors (pseudo-balconies that have doors which open, but no balcony to step out onto

– although you do get fresh air), and a healthy proportion of standard outside-view to interior (no view) cabins. While the smallest cabin measures a very decent 185 sq. ft (17.1 sq. meters), the largest suite measures only 490 sq. ft (45.5 sq. meters) – small when compared with many other ships of a similar size, although still a healthy chunk of living space.

While the bathrooms are quite compact, they do include a shower enclosure, several shelves, a shaving mirror, and 100% cotton towels. A gift basket of (sample sized) personal amenities is provided in all grades; it includes aloe soap, shampoo and conditioner sachets, deodorant, breath mints, candy, and pain relief tablets.

All cabins have spy-hole doors, and have twin beds that can be converted into a queen-sized bed, individually controlled air-conditioning, TV set, telephone, hairdryer (in the vanity desk), and neat, yellow glass bedside lights that might remind you of Tin Man in *The Wizard of Oz*. Some cabins on the lowest cabin deck (Main Deck) have views obstructed by lifeboats. Some cabins that can accommodate a third and fourth person have very little closet space, and there's only one personal safe. There is no separate radio in each cabin – instead, audio channels are provided on the in-cabin television system (however, you can't turn the picture off).

Among the most desirable suites and cabins are those on five of the aft-facing decks; these have private balconies with views over the stern and ship's wash. You might think that these units would suffer from vibration, but they don't, thanks to the two-pod propulsion system *(see page 151)*.

For the ultimate in extra space, try one of the large deluxe balcony suites on Deck 6 with a large private teakwood balcony. These tend to be quiet suites, with a large lounge and sleeping areas, large bathroom with twin (his 'n' hers) washbasins, toilet and bidet, and whirlpool bathtub. These suites have twin beds that convert to a queen-sized bed, three (illuminated) closets, and a huge amount of drawer space. The balcony has an outside light, and wide teak deck with smoked glass and wood railing (you could seat 10 people with comfort and still have space left over).

To keep things in perspective, note that even the largest suites are small compared with suites aboard other ships of a similar size – for example, Celebrity Cruises' *Constellation, Infinity, Millennium,* and *Summit,* where penthouse suites measure up to 2,530 sq. ft (235 sq. meters). Carnival Cruise Lines has fallen behind in the move to larger living spaces. However, Carnival's philosophy has always been to get its passengers out into public areas to socialize, and spend money (this is, after all, a holiday). If you book one of the suites (Category 11 or 12 in the Carnival Cruise Lines brochure) you automatically qualify for "Skipper's Club" priority check-in at any US homeland port – useful for getting ahead of the crowd.

CUISINE/DINING. This ship has a single, large, two-decks-high, 1,300-seat main dining room called the Normandie Restaurant, with seating on both upper and main levels. The decor is designed to give the impression that you are dining in the grand style of the famous French liner *Normandie,* although ship buffs would probably be critical of the results. The galley is located underneath the restaurant, with waiter access by escalators. There are tables are for two, four, six or eight, and small rooms on both upper and lower levels can be closed off for groups of up to 60. Dining is in two seatings, main and late, for lunch and dinner, while breakfast is in an open seating arrangement.

For casual meals, there is the extensive Mermaid's Grille is the equivalent of a lido cafe – which is an eatery that forms the aft third of Deck 9 (part of it also wraps around the upper section of the huge atrium). It includes a central area with small buffet counters (deli sandwich corner, Asian corner, rotisserie, and International counter) in an eclectic mix; there are salad counters, a dessert counter, and a 24-hour Pizzeria counter, all of which form a large eatery with both indoor and outdoor seating. There is plenty of variety, although it's uninspiring. Movement around the buffet area is very slow. Each night, Mermaid's Grille changes its name to Seaview Bistro, for casual, serve-yourself dinners in a dress-down setting (typically open 6pm–9.30pm).

Alternative (Reservations-Only, Extra Cost) Dining: David's Supper Club is a more upscale dining spot located on two of the uppermost decks, under a huge glass dome, with seating for approximately 150. It has a show kitchen where chefs can be seen preparing their masterpieces. It is directly above Mermaid's Grille (the self-serve buffet area), in the lower, forward section of the funnel housing, with superb views over the multi-deck atrium, as well as to the sea. The decor includes a 12-ft (3.7-meter) replica of Michaelangelo's *David.* Fine table settings, china and silverware are featured, as are well as leather-bound menus.

ENTERTAINMENT. The 1,170-seat Taj Mahal Showlounge (the venue for large-scale production shows and major cabaret acts) is a dramatic room that spans three decks in the forward section. Spiral stairways at the back of the lounge connect all three levels. Stage shows are best seen from the upper three levels. Directly underneath the showlounge is Butterflies, a large lounge with its own bar.

SPA/FITNESS. SpaCarnival is quite large, spans two decks, is located directly above the navigation bridge in the forward part of the ship and has 13,700 sq. ft (1,272 sq. meters) of space. Facilities on the lower level include a solarium, eight treatment rooms, lecture rooms, sauna and steam rooms for men and women, and a beauty parlor; the upper level consists of a large gymnasium with floor-to-ceiling windows on three sides, including forward-facing ocean views, and an aerobics room with instructor-led classes.

One of the two centrally located outdoor swimming pools can be used in inclement weather due to its retractable glass dome. There are two whirlpool tubs, located adjacent to the swimming pools. A winding water slide that spans two decks in height is located at an aft, upper deck. Another smaller pool is available for children. There is also an additional whirlpool tub outdoors.

● **For more extensive general information on what a Carnival cruise is like, see pages 107–111.**

Carnival Spirit
★★★★

Large (Resort) Ship:	.......85,920 tons	Total Crew:	930	Cabins (wheelchair accessible):	16
Lifestyle:	..................Standard	Passengers		Cabin Current:	..............110 volts
Cruise Line:	......Carnival Cruise Lines	(lower beds/all berths):	.....2,124/2,680	Elevators:	12
Former Names:	...................none	Passenger Space Ratio		Casino (gaming tables):	.............Yes
Builder:	.........Kvaerner Masa-Yards	(lower beds/all berths):	........40.4/32.0	Slot Machines:	...................Yes
Original Cost:	............$375 million	Crew/Passenger Ratio		Swimming Pools (outdoors):	........2+1
Entered Service:	............Apr 2001	(lower beds/all berths):	.........2.2/2.6	children's pool
Registry:	...................Panama	Navigation Officers:	............Italian	Swimming Pools (indoors):	1
Length (ft/m):	............959.6/292.5	Cabins (total):	1,062	(indoor/outdoor)
Beam (ft/m):	..............105.6/32.2	Size Range (sq ft/m):	......185.0–490.0/	Whirlpools:	5
Draft (ft/m):	.................25.5/7.8		17.1–45.5	Self-Service Launderette:	...........Yes
Propulsion/Propellers:	.....diesel-electric	Cabins (outside view):	849	Dedicated Cinema/Seats:	..........No
(62,370 kW)/2 azimuthing pods	Cabins (interior/no view):	213	Library:	........................Yes
(17.6 MW each)	Cabins (for one person):	0	Classification Society:	...Registro Navale
Passenger Decks:	12	Cabins (with private balcony):	750	Italiano (RINA)

OVERALL SCORE: 1,474 (OUT OF A POSSIBLE 2,000 POINTS)

OVERVIEW. *Carnival Spirit* is the 16th new ship for this very successful cruise line. It has Carnival's trademark large wing-tipped funnel in the Miami-based company's red, white and blue colors. It is just a hair's breath shorter than Cunard Line's *Queen Elizabeth 2* (which Carnival Corporation, the parent company of Carnival Cruise Lines, owns). The design makes the ship look much sleeker than any other in the Carnival Cruise Lines fleet (except for its sister ships), a process of continuing ship design and evolvement. Sister ships in the same class and internal layout and design are *Carnival Legend, Carnival Miracle* and *Carnival Pride*, and all can transit the Panama Canal.

There are two centrally located swimming pools outdoors, and one can be used in inclement weather due to its retractable magrodome (glass dome) cover. Two whirlpool tubs, located adjacent to the swimming pools, are abridged by a bar. Another smaller pool is available for children; it incorporates a winding water slide that spans two decks in height. There is also a whirlpool tub outdoors.

The interior design theme is a tribute to the world's great architecture, from art nouveau to postmodern. The immense lobby space spans eight decks. The atrium lobby, with its two grand stairways, presents a stunning wall decoration best seen from any of the multiple viewing balconies on each deck above the main lobby floor level.

There are two entertainment/public room decks, the upper of which also has an exterior promenade deck – something new for this fun cruise line. Although it doesn't go around the whole ship, it's long enough for some serious walking. There is also a jogging track outdoors, around the

BERLITZ'S RATINGS

	Possible	Achieved
Ship	500	435
Accommodation	200	154
Food	400	234
Service	400	270
Entertainment	100	86
Cruise	400	295

ship's mast and the forward third of the ship.

There is a winding shopping street with several boutique stores (selling all the usual Carnival logo items). A small wedding chapel is located forward of the uppermost level of the two main entertainment decks, adjacent to the combined library and internet center. Other facilities include a photo gallery, video games room, an observation balcony in the center of the vessel (at the top of the multi-deck atrium), a large casino, and a piano lounge/bar. The casino is large (one has to walk through it to get from the restaurant to the showlounge on one of the entertainments decks), and it has all the gaming paraphernalia and array of slot machines you can imagine.

There is a "tele-radiology" system that enables shipboard physicians to digitally transmit X-rays and other patient information to shore-side facilities – useful for peace of mind for passengers and crew.

The information desk in the lobby is quite small, and can become quite congested. It is difficult to escape from smokers, noise and loud music (it's even played in cabin hallways and elevators). Many private balconies are not so private, being overlooked from various public locations. You'll need to carry a credit card to operate the personal safe in your suite or cabin – an inconvenience. You'll endure a stream of flyers advertising various products.

Books and computers are cohabitants in the ship's library/internet center, but anyone wanting a book has to lean over others who may be using a computer – a very awkward arrangement. Public toilets are spartan and could do with some cheering up.

ACCOMMODATION. There are 20 cabin categories, priced according to grade, location and size. The range of cabins includes suites (with private balcony), outside-view cabins with private balcony, 68 ocean view cabins with French doors (pseudo balconies that have doors which open, but no balcony to step out onto), and a healthy proportion of standard outside-view to interior (no view) cabins. While the smallest cabin measures a very decent 185 sq. ft (17.1 sq. meters), the largest suite measures only 490 sq. ft (45.5 sq. meters) – small compared with many similar ships.

The bathrooms are quite compact, but include a circular shower enclosure, several shelves, a shaving mirror, and 100% cotton towels. A gift basket of (sample sized) personal amenities is provided in all grades; it includes aloe soap, shampoo, conditioner, deodorant, breath mints, candy, and pain relief tablets.

Regardless of the grade of cabin chosen, all cabins have spy-hole doors, and have twin beds that can be converted into a queen-sized bed, individually controlled air-conditioning, television, and telephone. A number of cabins on the lowest cabin deck have views obstructed by lifeboats. Some cabins that can accommodate a third and fourth person have very little closet space, and there's only one personal safe. There is no separate radio in each cabin – instead, audio channels are provided on the in-cabin television system (however, you can't turn the picture off).

If you book one of the suites (Category 11 or 12 in the Carnival Cruise Lines brochure), you automatically qualify for "Skipper's Club" priority check-in at any US homeland port – useful for getting ahead of the crowd.

Among the most desirable suites and cabins are those on five of the aft-facing decks; these have private balconies overlooking the stern and ship's wash. You might think that these units would suffer from vibration, but they don't – a bonus provided by the pod propulsion system (*see page 151*).

For the ultimate in extra space, try one of the large deluxe balcony suites on Deck 6 with large private teak balcony. These tend to be quiet, with a large lounge and sleeping areas, a large bathroom with twin (his 'n' hers) washbasins, toilet and bidet, and whirlpool bathtub. These suites have twin beds that convert to a queen-sized bed, three (illuminated) closets, and a huge amount of drawer space. The balcony has an outside light, and a wide teak deck with smoked glass and wood railing (you could seat 10 people with comfort and still have space left over).

To keep things in perspective, note that even the largest suites are small compared with suites aboard other ships of a similar size – for example, Celebrity Cruises' *Constellation*, *Infinity*, *Millennium*, and *Summit*, where penthouse suites measure up to 2,530 sq. ft (235 sq. meters). Carnival Cruise Lines has fallen behind in the move to larger living spaces, and, with this ship, lost an opportunity to provide more space for those seeking it.

CUISINE/DINING. This ship has a single, large, two-decks-high, 1,300-seat main dining room called the Empire Restaurant, with seating on both upper and main levels. The decor is heavily "Napoleonic" (early 19th-century

French) style. The galley is located underneath the restaurant, with waiter access by escalators. There are tables for two, four, six or eight, and small rooms on both upper and lower levels can be closed off for groups of up to 60. Dining is in two seatings, main and late, for lunch and dinner, while breakfast is in an open seating arrangement.

For casual eaters, while there is no lido cafe, there is the extensive La Playa Grille, which forms the aft third of Deck 9 (part of it also wraps around the upper section of the huge atrium). It includes a central area with small buffet counters (deli sandwich corner, Asian corner, rotisserie, and International counter); there are salad counters, a dessert counter, and a 24-hour Pizzeria counter, all forming a large eatery with both indoor and outdoor seating. Movement around the buffet area is very slow, with frequent lines. Each night, La Playa Grille becomes Seaview Bistro, for casual, serve-yourself dinners (typically open 6pm–9.30pm).

There is an outdoor self-serve buffet (adjacent to the fantail pool), which serves fast-food items such as hamburgers and hot dogs, chicken and fries, as well as two smaller buffets adjacent to the midships pool area. If you want to eat 24 hours a day, you can do it aboard this ship, which has something for (almost) everyone.

Alternative (Reservations-Only, Extra Cost) Dining: The Nouveau Supper Club is a more upscale dining spot located on two of the uppermost decks of the ship under a huge glass dome, with seating for approximately 150. It has a open-view kitchen where chefs can be seen preparing their masterpieces. It is located directly above La Playa Grille Mermaid's Grille, in the lower, forward section of the funnel housing, with some superb views over the multi-deck atrium, as well as to the sea. Fine table settings, china and silverware are used, as well as leather-bound menus. The decor has a floral pattern and there is a stained-glass balcony on the upper level. There is also a stage and dance floor.

ENTERTAINMENT. The 1,170-seat Pharaoh's Palace Showlounge is a dramatic room which spans three decks in the forward section of the ship. Spiral stairways at the back of the lounge connect all levels. Stage shows are best seen from the upper three levels, from where the sight lines are reasonably good. Directly underneath the showlounge is the Versailles Lounge (in the highy decorative manner of 18th-century France), a large lounge with its own bar.

SPA/FITNESS. A large Nautica health spa, spanning two decks, is located directly above the navigation bridge in the forward part of the ship and has 13,700 sq. ft (1,272 sq. meters) of space. Facilities on the lower level include a solarium, eight treatment rooms, lecture rooms, sauna and steam rooms for men and women, and a beauty parlor; the upper level consists of a large gymnasium with floor-to-ceiling windows on three sides, including forward-facing ocean views, and an aerobics room with instructor-led classes (some at extra cost).

● **For more extensive general information on what a Carnival cruise is like, see pages 107–111.**

Carnival Triumph
★★★★

Large (Resort) Ship: ......101,509 tons	Total Crew: 1,100	Cabins (wheelchair accessible): 25
Lifestyle: ....Standard	Passengers	Cabin Current: ....110 volts
Cruise Line: ......Carnival Cruise Lines	(lower beds/all berths): 2,758/3,473	Elevators: 18
Former Names: ....none	Passenger Space Ratio	Casino (gaming tables): ....Yes
Builder: ....Fincantieri (Italy)	(lower beds/all berths): 36.8/29.2	Slot Machines: ....Yes
Original Cost: ....$420 million	Crew/Passenger Ratio	Swimming Pools (outdoors): 3
Entered Service: ....Oct 1999	(lower beds/all berths): 2.3/3.0	(+1 with magrodome)
Registry: ....The Bahamas	Navigation Officers: ....Italian	Swimming Pools (indoors): 0
Length (ft/m): 893.0/272.2	Cabins (total): 1,379	Whirlpools: 7
Beam (ft/m): 116.0/35.3	Size Range (sq ft/m): 179.7–482.2/	Self-Service Launderette: ....Yes
Draft (ft/m): 27.0/8.2	16.7–44.8	Dedicated Cinema/Seats: ....No
Propulsion/Propellers: .....diesel-electric	Cabins (outside view): 853	Library: ....Yes
(34,000 kW)/2 azimuthing pods	Cabins (interior/no view): 526	Classification Society: ...Lloyd's Register
(17.6 MW each)	Cabins (for one person): 0	
Passenger Decks: 13	Cabins (with private balcony): 508	

OVERALL SCORE: 1,455 (OUT OF A POSSIBLE 2,000 POINTS)

OVERVIEW. *Carnival Triumph* is the 14th new ship for this very successful cruise line. It is unable to transit the Panama Canal due to its size. The ship, whose bows are extremely short, has the distinctive, large, swept-back wing-tipped funnel that is the trademark of Carnival Cruise Lines, in the company colors of red, white and blue.

This is quite a stunning ship, built to impress at every turn, and has the most balanced profile of all the ships in the Carnival Cruise Lines fleet. Amidships on the open deck is the longest water slide at sea (200ft /60 meters in length, it travels from just aft of the ship's mast), as well as tiered sunbathing decks positioned between two small swimming pools and several hot tubs. As aboard all Carnival ships, there is a "topless" sunbathing area set around the base of the funnel (it can't be seen from the pool deck below). The Lido Deck space is more expansive than aboard earlier sister ship *Carnival Destiny* (the swim-up bar has been eliminated), and the pool is larger, as it is aboard sister *Carnival Victory*.

The ship is a fantasy land for the senses (though nowhere near as glitzy as the "Fantasy"-class ships). The layout is logical, so finding your way around is fairly simple. There are three decks full of lounges, 10 bars and lots of rooms to play in. Like her smaller (though still large) predecessors, this ship has a doublewide indoor promenade, and a deck-high, glass-domed rotunda atrium lobby. For those that like to gamble, the Club Monaco is certainly a large (and noisy) casino. There are more than 320 slot machines.

An additional feature that this ship has which the Fantasy-class ships do not have is the Flagship bar, located in

BERLITZ'S RATINGS	Possible	Achieved
Ship	500	430
Accommodation	200	165
Food	400	219
Service	400	269
Entertainment	100	85
Cruise	400	287

the Rotunda (atrium), which faces forward to the glass-walled lifts. A sports bar (Olympic Bar) has tables that feature sports memorabilia.

Children are provided with good facilities, including their own two-level Children's Club (including an outdoor pool), and are well cared for with "Camp Carnival", the line's extensive children's program.

From the viewpoint of safety, passengers can embark directly into the lifeboats from their secured position without having to wait for them to be lowered, thus saving time in the event of a real emergency. Well done.

The terraced pool deck is really cluttered, and there are no cushioned pads for the deck chairs. Although the outdoor deck space has been improved, there is still much crowding when the ship is full and at sea. Getting away from people and noise is difficult. The Photo Gallery becomes extremely congested when photos are on display.

ACCOMMODATION. There are 20 categories, the price depending on grade, location and size. Over half of all cabins are of the outside view type (and at 225 sq. ft./21 sq. meters they are among the largest in the mainstream cruise market). They are spread over four decks and have private balconies (with glass rather than steel balustrades, for unobstructed ocean views) extending from the ship's side. The balconies have bright fluorescent lighting.

The standard cabins are of good size and come equipped with all the basics, although the furniture is rather angular, with no rounded edges. Three decks of cabins (eight cabins on each deck, each with private balcony) overlook the stern.

There are eight penthouse suites, and each has a large private balcony. Although they are quite lavish in their appointments, at only 483 sq. ft (44.8 sq. meters), they are really quite small when compared to the best suites even in many smaller ships. There are also 40 other suites, each of which has a decent sized bathroom, and a good amount of lounge space, although they are nothing special.

In the cabins with balconies (more cabins have balconies aboard this ship than those that do not), the partition between each balcony is open at top and bottom, so you may well hear noise from neighbors (or smell their cigarettes. It is disappointing to see three categories of cabins (both outside and interior) with upper and lower bunk beds (lower beds are far more preferable, but this is how the ship accommodates an extra 600 people over and above the lower bed capacity).

The cabins feature soft color schemes and soft furnishings in more attractive fabrics than other ships in the fleet. Interactive "Fun Vision" technology lets you choose movies on demand (and for a fee). The bathrooms, which have good-sized showers, feature good storage space in the toiletries cabinet. A gift basket is provided in all grades; it includes aloe soap, shampoo, conditioner, deodorant, breath mints, candy, and pain relief tablets (albeit all in sample sizes).

If you book one of the suites (Category 11 or 12 in the Carnival Cruise Lines brochure) you automatically qualify for "Skipper's Club" priority check-in at any US homeland port – useful for getting ahead of the crowd.

CUISINE/DINING. The ship's two dining rooms (the London, forward, with windows on two sides, has 706 seats; the Paris, aft, with windows on three sides, has 1,090 seats), and both are non-smoking. Each dining room spans two decks, and incorporates a dozen domes and chandeliers. The Paris dining room has a two-deck-high wall of glass overlooking the stern. There are tables for four, six and eight (and even a few tables for two that the line tries to keep for honeymooners). Dining is in four seatings, for greater flexibility: 6pm, 6.45pm, 8pm and 8.45pm (times are approximate but equal two seatings per restaurant). Although the menu choice looks good, the cuisine delivered is adequate, but quite unmemorable.

The ship also has a serve-yourself casual Lido Buffet – for breakfast and lunch, while for dinner this turns into the Sea View Bistro for use as a casual alternative eatery – for those that do not want to dress to go to the formal dining rooms. The buffet and bistro include speciality stations where you can order omelets, eggs, fajitas, Chicken Caesar salad, and pasta and stir-fry items. And, if you're still hungry, there's a midnight buffet around the corner.

The dining room entrances have comfortable drinking areas for pre-dinner cocktails. There are also many options for casual dining, particularly during the day.

The South Beach Club (a lido cafe) is the ship's informal international self-serve buffet-style eatery, with seating on two levels. Included in this eatery are the New York Deli (typically open 11am–11pm), and the Hong Kong Noodle Company (for Chinese cuisine, with wok preparation), and a 24-hour pizzeria (this ship typically serves an average of more than 800 pizzas every day).

There is a grill for fast foods (such as chicken, hamburgers and hot dogs), and a salad bar – all part of the poolside South Beach Club. In addition, there is a self-serve ice cream and frozen yogurt station (no extra charge).

At night, the South Beach Club is turned into the "Seaview Bistro" (typically in operation between 6pm and 9pm) and provides a casual (dress down) alternative to eating in the main dining rooms, serving pasta, steaks, salads and desserts. The good thing is that, if you want to eat 24 hours a day, you can do it aboard this ship, which has something for (almost) everyone.

ENTERTAINMENT. The three-level (non-smoking) Rome Showlounge is quite a stunning room, and has a revolving stage, hydraulic orchestra pit, superb sound, and seating on three levels (the upper levels being tiered through two decks). There is also a proscenium over the stage that acts as a scenery loft.

SPA/FITNESS. SpaCarnival spans two decks (with a total area of 13,700 sq. ft/1,272 sq. meters), and is located directly above the navigation bridge in the forward part of the ship (its is accessed from the forward stairway). Facilities on the lower level include a solarium, eight treatment rooms, lecture rooms, sauna and steam rooms for men and women, and a beauty parlor; the upper level consists of a large gymnasium with floor-to-ceiling windows on three sides, including forward-facing ocean views, and an aerobics room with instructor-led classes (some at extra cost).

● **For more extensive general information on what a Carnival cruise is like, see pages 107–111.**

Carnival Valor
NOT YET RATED

Large (Resort) Ship: ....110,000 tons	Total Crew: 1,160	Cabins (with private balcony): 574
Lifestyle: ....Standard	Passengers	Cabins (wheelchair accessible): 25
Cruise Line: ....Carnival Cruise Lines	(lower beds/all berths): 2,974/3,700	Cabin Current: ....110 volts
Former Names: ....None	Passenger Space Ratio	Elevators: 18
Builder: ....Fincantieri (Italy)	(lower beds/all berths): 36.9/29.7	Casino (gaming tables): ....Yes
Original Cost: ....$500 million	Crew/Passenger Ratio	Slot Machines: ....Yes
Entered Service: ....December 2004	(lower beds/all berths): 2.5/3.1	Swimming Pools (outdoors): 3
Registry: ....Panama	Navigation Officers: ....Italian	(+1 with magrodome)
Length (ft/m): 951.4/290.0	Cabins (total): 1,487	Swimming Pools (indoors): 0
Beam (ft/m): 116.4/35.5	Size Range (sq ft/m): 179.7–482.2/	Whirlpools: 7
Draft (ft/m): 27.0/8.2	16.7–44.8	Self-Service Launderette: ....Yes
Propulsion/Propellers: .....diesel-electric	Cabins (outside view): 917	Dedicated Cinema/Seats: ....No
(63,400kW)/2	Cabins (interior/no view): 570	Library: ....Yes
Passenger Decks: 13	Cabins (for one person): 0	Classification Society: ...Lloyd's Register

OVERALL SCORE: NYR (OUT OF A POSSIBLE 2,000 POINTS)

OVERVIEW. *Carnival Valor* is the 22nd new ship for this very successful cruise line. It shares the same generally well-balanced profile as *Carnival Conquest, Carnival Destiny, Carnival Glory, Carnival Liberty, Carnival Triumph* and *Carnival Victory.* The ship is unable to transit the Panama Canal, due to its size. With extremely short bows, it has the distinctive, large, swept-back wing-tipped funnel that is the trademark of Carnival Cruise Lines, in the company colors of red, white and blue.

The ship's interior decor is truly a fantasyland of colors; just about every hue of the rainbow (and a few more) is represented in the public rooms and hallways throughout this ship. The layout is logical, so finding your way around is easy. Most public rooms are located off a main boulevard, or main interior promenade (great for strolling and people watching, particularly from the Dream Bar or Java Cafe).

There are three decks full of lounges, 10 bars and lots of rooms to play in. There are two atriums: the largest, located in the forward third of the ship goes through nine decks, while the aft atrium spans three decks.

Good hangouts and drinking places include Paris Hot (live music/karaoke lounge), the American Bar (main lobby), Bronx Bar (sports Bar), Jeanne's (wine bar), and Heroe's Club lounge. There are nightspots for just about every musical taste (except for opera, ballet and classical music lovers). For gamblers, the Shogun Club casino, with its Japanese motif and theme, is certainly large and action-packed; there are also more than 320 slot machines.

Youngsters are provided with good facilities, including their own two-level Children's Club (which has an outdoor pool), and are well cared for with "Camp Carnival", the

BERLITZ'S RATINGS

	Possible	Achieved
Ship	500	NYR
Accommodation	200	NYR
Food	400	NYR
Service	400	NYR
Entertainment	100	NYR
Cruise	400	NYR

line's extensive children's program. Note that soft-drinks packages can be purchased for children (and adults).

Many pillars obstruct passengers flow. Those in the dining room, for example, make it difficult for the waiters to serve food properly. The public toilets are spartan and could do with some cheering up.

ACCOMMODATION. There are 20 cabin price categories, in 7 different grades: suites with private balcony; deluxe outside-view cabins with private balcony; outside-view cabins with private balcony; outside-view cabins with window; cabins with a porthole instead of a window; interior (no-view) cabins; and interior (no-view cabins) with upper and lower berths. There are five decks of cabins with private balconies. Standard cabins are of good size and come equipped with all the basics, although the furniture is rather square and angular, with no rounded edges. Three decks of cabins (eight on each deck, each with private balcony) overlook the stern. Most cabins with twin beds can be converted to a queen-size bed format.

Book one of the suites (Category 11 or 12 in the Carnival Cruise Lines brochure) and you'll get "Skipper's Club" priority check-in at any US homeland port – useful for getting ahead of the crowd.

There are even "fitness" cabins aboard this ship – in a block of 18 cabins located directly around and behind SpaCarnival; so fitness devotees can get out of bed and go straight to the treadmill without having to go through any of the public rooms first.

A gift basket is provided in all grades of cabins; it includes aloe soap, shampoo, conditioner, deodorant, breath mints, candy, and pain relief tablets (all in sample sizes).

CUISINE/DINING. There are two principal dining rooms (Lincoln Restaurant, forward, seating 744: and Washington Restaurant, aft, seating 1,122). Both are two decks high and have a balcony level for diners (the balcony level in the aft dining room is larger than the other). The decor is interesting and includes wall coverings featuring a pattern of Japanese bonsai trees. Two additional wings (the Betsy Ross Room and the John Paul Jones Room) provide room to accommodate large groups in a private dining arrangement. Dining is in four seatings, for greater flexibility: 6pm, 6.45pm, 8pm and 8.45pm (these times are approximate, but equal two seatings per restaurant). Although the menu choice looks good, the actual cuisine delivered is typically adequate, and quite unmemorable.

There is also a casual self-serve international food court-style lido deck eatery, the two-level Rosie's Restaurant. It has two main serving lines; it is adjacent to the aft pool and can be covered by a magrodome glass cover in inclement weather. Included in this eating mall are a deli, a Chinese eatery, with wok preparation, a 24-hour pizzeria, and a patisserie (there's an extra charge for yummy pastries, however). There's also a grill for fast foods such as hamburgers and hot dogs. Each night, Rosie's Restaurant morphs into the "Seaview Bistro", and provides a casual (dress down) alternative to eating in the main dining rooms, serving pasta, steaks, salads and desserts (typically between 6pm and 9pm).

Alternative (Reservations-Only, Extra Cost) Dining: There is one reservations-only, extra-cost dining spot, the Emerald Room. It has fine table settings, china and silverware, as well as leather-bound menus, cobalt-blue walls and lighting fixtures resembling giant emeralds.

ENTERTAINMENT. The Ivanhow Theater is a multi-deck showroom seating up to 1,400, and serves as the principal entertainment venue for large-scale entertainment, including Las-Vegas-style production shows and major cabaret acts. It has a revolving stage, hydraulic orchestra pit, superb sound, and seating on three levels (the upper levels being tiered through two decks). There is a proscenium over the stage that acts as a scenery loft.

The Eagles lounge, located aft, seats 425 and typically features live music and late-night cabaret acts including adult comedy.

Body-throbbing loud music sensations can be found in the One Small Step Dance Club is the ship's discotheque; it includes a video wall with projections live from the dance floor. Piano bar lovers should enjoy the 100-seat Lindy Hop piano bar.

SPA/FITNESS. SpaCarnival spans two decks (with a total area of approximately 13,300 sq. ft/1,235 sq. meters), and is located directly above the navigation bridge in the forward part of the ship (it is accessed from the forward stairway). The decor is Polynesian in style, a theme that incorporates lush foliage, teak flooring, and a waterfall. Facilities on the lower level include a solarium, eight treatment rooms, lecture rooms, sauna and steam rooms for men and women, and a beauty parlor; the upper level consists of a large gymnasium with floor-to-ceiling windows on three sides, including forward-facing ocean views, and an aerobics room with instructor-led classes (some at extra cost).

● **For more extensive general information on what a Carnival cruise is like, see pages 107–111.**

Carnival Victory
★★★★

Large (Resort) Ship: ....101,509 tons	Passenger Decks: 13	Cabins (with private balcony): 508
Lifestyle: ....Standard	Total Crew: 1,100	Cabins (wheelchair accessible): 25
Cruise Line: ......Carnival Cruise Lines	Passengers	Cabin Current: ....110 volts
Former Names: ....none	(lower beds/all berths): 2,758/3,473	Elevators: 18
Builder: ....Fincantieri (Italy)	Passenger Space Ratio	Casino (gaming tables): ....Yes
Original Cost: ....$410 million	(lower beds/all berths): 36.8/29.2	Slot Machines: ....Yes
Entered Service: ....Aug 2000	Crew/Passenger Ratio	Swimming Pools (outdoors): 3
Registry: ....Panama	(lower beds/all berths): 2.3/3.0	(+1 with magrodome)
Length (ft/m): 893.0/272.2	Navigation Officers: ....Italian	Swimming Pools (indoors): 0
Beam (ft/m): 116.0/35.3	Cabins (total): 1,379	Whirlpools: 7
Draft (ft/m): 27.0/8.2	Size Range (sq ft/m): 179.7–482.2/	Self-Service Launderette: ....Yes
Propulsion/Propellers: .....diesel-electric	16.7–44.8	Dedicated Cinema/Seats: ....No
(34,000 kW)/2 azimuthing pods	Cabins (outside view): 853	Library: ....Yes
(17.6 MW each)	Cabins (interior/no view): 526	Classification Society: ...Lloyd's Register
	Cabins (for one person): 0	

OVERALL SCORE: 1,455 (OUT OF A POSSIBLE 2,000 POINTS)

OVERVIEW. *Carnival Victory* is the 15th new ship for this very successful cruise line. It is unable to transit the Panama Canal due to its size. The ship, whose bows are extremely short, has the distinctive, large, swept-back wing-tipped funnel that is the trademark of Carnival Cruise Lines, in the company colors of red, white and blue.

This is quite a stunning ship, built to impress at every turn, has the most balanced profile of all the ships in the Carnival Cruise Lines fleet. Amidships on the open deck is the longest water slide at sea (200 ft /60 meters in length, it travels from just aft of the ship's mast), as well as tiered sunbathing decks positioned between two small swimming pools and several hot tubs. As aboard all Carnival ships, there is a "topless" sunbathing area set around the base of the funnel (it cannot be seen from the pool deck below). The Lido Deck space is more expansive than aboard the earlier sister ship *Carnival Destiny* (the swim-up bar has been eliminated), and the pool is larger, as aboard sister ship *Carnival Triumph*.

IThe ship's decor is actually quite tasteful – the theme being a tribute to the oceans of the world (although nowhere near as glitzy as the "Fantasy"-class ships). Seahorses (no, you can't race them), corals and shells are prominent throughout the design. The layout is logical, so finding your way around is a fairly simple matter.

There are three decks full of lounges, 10 bars and lots of rooms to play in (their names all relating to oceans or seas). Like its smaller (though still large) predecessors, this ship has a doublewide indoor promenade, nine-deck-high, with statues of Neptune at either end, and a glass-domed rotunda

BERLITZ'S RATINGS

	Possible	Achieved
Ship	500	430
Accommodation	200	165
Food	400	219
Service	400	269
Entertainment	100	85
Cruise	400	287

atrium lobby. For those who like to gamble, the South China Sea Club is certainly a large (and noisy) casino, with more than 320 slot machines.

An additional feature that the Fantasy-class ships do not have is the square-shaped Capitol bar, located in the Rotunda (atrium), which faces forward to the glass-walled lifts and sits under the 10-deck-high atrium dome. A sports bar (Aegean Bar) has tables that feature sports memorabilia.

Children are provided with good facilities, including their own two-level Children's Club (including an outdoor pool), and are well cared for with "Camp Carnival", the line's extensive children's program.

From the viewpoint of safety, passengers can embark directly into the lifeboats from their secured position without having to wait for them to be lowered, thus saving time in the event of a real emergency. Well done.

Note that the terraced pool deck is really cluttered, and there are no cushioned pads for the deck chairs. Although the outdoor deck space has been improved, there is still much crowding when the ship is full and at sea. Getting away from people and noise is extremely difficult. The Photo Gallery becomes extremely congested when photos are on display.

ACCOMMODATION. There are 20 price categories (the price you pay will depend on the grade, location and size you choose). Over half of all cabins are outside (and at 225 sq. ft./21 sq. meters they are among the largest in the standard market). They are spread over four decks and have private balconies (with glass rather than steel balustrades, for unobstructed ocean views) extending from the ship's side. The balconies have bright fluorescent lighting.

The standard cabins are of good size and have all the basics, although the furniture is angular, with no rounded edges. Three decks of cabins (eight on each deck, each with private balcony) overlook the stern (with three days at sea on each of two alternating itineraries, vibration is kept to a minimum).

There are eight penthouse suites, and each has a large private balcony. Although they are quite lavish in their appointments, at only 483 sq. ft (44.8 sq. meters), they are really quite small when compared to the best suites even in many smaller ships. There are also 40 other suites, each of which has a decent sized bathroom, and a good amount of lounge space, although they are nothing special.

In cabins with balconies (more cabins have balconies aboard this ship than those that do not), the partition between each balcony is open at top and bottom, so you may well hear noise from neighbors or smell their cigarettes. It is disappointing to see three categories of cabins (both outside and interior) with upper and lower bunk beds (lower beds are far more preferable, but this is how the ship accommodates an extra 600 over and above the lower bed capacity).

The cabins have soft color schemes and more soft furnishings in more attractive fabrics than other ships in the fleet. Interactive "Fun Vision" technology lets you choose movies on demand (and for a fee). The bathrooms, which have good-sized showers, feature good storage space in the toiletries cabinet. A gift basket is provided in all grades; it includes aloe soap, shampoo, conditioner, deodorant, breath mints, candy, and pain relief tablets (albeit all in sample sizes).

If you book one of the suites (Category 11 or 12 in the Carnival Cruise Lines brochure) you automatically qualify for "Skipper's Club" priority check-in at any US homeland port – useful for getting ahead of the crowd.

CUISINE/DINING. The ship's two main dining rooms (the Atlantic, forward, with windows on two sides, has 706 seats; the Pacific, aft, with windows on three sides, has 1,090 seats), and both are non-smoking. Each dining room spans two decks, and incorporate a dozen domes and chandeliers. The Pacific dining room has a two-deck-high wall of glass overlooking the stern. There are tables for four, six and eight (and even a few tables for two that the line tries to keep for honeymooners). Dining is in four seatings, for

greater flexibility: 6pm, 6.45pm, 8pm and 8.45pm (these times are approximate but equal two seatings per restaurant). Note that this gives you very little time to "dine" – although it should give you some idea of what to expect from your dining experience. Although the menu choice looks good, the actual cuisine delivered is adequate, but quite unmemorable.

The dining room entrances have comfortable drinking areas for pre-dinner cocktails. There are also many options for casual dining, particularly during the day.

The Mediterranean Restaurant, the ship's informal international self-serve buffet-style eatery, has seating on two levels. Included in this eatery are the East River Deli (a New York-style deli, open 11am–11pm), the Yangtse Wok (for Chinese cuisine, with wok preparation), and a 24-hour pizzeria (this ship typically serves an average of more than 800 pizzas every day). At night, the Mediterranean Restaurant is turned into the "Seaview Bistro" and provides a casual (dress down) alternative to eating in the main dining rooms, serving pasta, steaks, salads and desserts. If you want to eat 24 hours a day, you can do it aboard this ship, which has something for (almost) everyone.

There is also the Mississippi Barbecue for fast grilled foods (such as chicken, hamburgers and hot dogs), and a salad bar. In addition, there is a self-serve ice cream and frozen yogurt station (at no extra charge).

ENTERTAINMENT. The three-level (non-smoking) Caribbean Showlounge is stunning, and has a revolving stage, hydraulic orchestra pit, superb sound, and seating on three levels (the upper levels being tiered through two decks). There is a proscenium over the stage that acts as a scenery loft.

SPA/FITNESS. SpaCarnival spans two decks (with a total area of 13,700 sq. ft/1,272 sq. meters), and is located directly above the navigation bridge in the forward part of the ship (its is accessed from the forward stairway). Facilities on the lower level include a solarium, eight treatment rooms, lecture rooms, sauna and steam rooms for men and women, and a beauty parlor; the upper level consists of a large gymnasium with floor-to-ceiling windows on three sides, including forward-facing ocean views, and an aerobics room with instructor-led classes (some at extra cost).

● For more extensive general information on what a Carnival cruise is like, see pages 107–111.

Celebration
★★★ +

Large (Resort) Ship:	.......47,262 tons	Passenger Decks:	10

Large (Resort) Ship: ....47,262 tons
Lifestyle: ....Standard
Cruise Line: ....Carnival Cruise Lines
Former Names: ....none
Builder: ....Kockums (Sweden)
Original Cost: ....$130 million
Entered Service: ....Mar 1987
Registry: ....Panama
Length (ft/m): 732.6/223.30
Beam (ft/m): 92.5/28.20
Draft (ft/m): 25.5/7.80
Propulsion/Propellers: ....diesel
(23,520kW)/2

Passenger Decks: 10
Total Crew: 670
Passengers
(lower beds/all berths): 1,486/1,896
Passenger Space Ratio
(lower beds/all berths): 31.8/24.9
Crew/Passenger Ratio
(lower beds/all berths): 2.2/2.8
Navigation Officers: ....Italian
Cabins (total): 743
Size Range (sq ft/m): 184.0/17.1
Cabins (outside view): 453
Cabins (interior/no view): 290
Cabins (for one person): 0

Cabins (with private balcony): 10
Cabins (wheelchair accessible): 14
Cabin Current: ....110 volts
Elevators: 8
Casino (gaming tables): ....Yes
Slot Machines: ....Yes
Swimming Pools (outdoors): 3
Swimming Pools (indoors): 0
Whirlpools: 2
Self-Service Launderette: ....Yes
Dedicated Cinema/Seats: ....No
Library: ....Yes
Classification Society: ...Lloyd's Register

OVERALL SCORE: 1,252 (OUT OF A POSSIBLE 2,000 POINTS)

OVERVIEW. When introduced, this was the fourth new ship for this very successful cruise line. Its exterior is rather angular, but typical of the space-conscious designs introduced in the early 1980s, particularly by Carnival Cruise Lines, in an effort to maximize interior (revenue-generating) space.

The ship, whose bows are extremely short, has the distinctive, large, swept-back wing-tipped funnel that is Carnival's trademark, in the company colors of red, white and blue. The swimming pools are smaller than one would expect, but the open deck space is good, provided the ship is not full – when, as with most ships, the deck always seems crowded.

Inside, this ship has double-width indoor promenades and a very good selection of public rooms. The flamboyant interior decor in public rooms is stimulating instead of relaxing, as is the colorful artwork. The interior decor theme is that of New Orleans throughout the public rooms, except for some nautical themes in the Wheelhouse Bar/Grill. There is a large, very active, and noisy casino.

The party atmosphere is good for anyone looking for a stimulating cruise experience. As is the case aboard all Carnival ships, there is a very wide range of entertainment and passenger participation activities from which to choose.

This ship is a floating playground for young, active adults who enjoy constant stimulation, close contact with lots and lots of others, as well as the three Gs – glitz, glamour and gambling. It is a live board game with every move executed in typically grand, colorful, fun-filled Carnival Cruise Lines style. This ship should prove a good choice for families with children (there are so many places for kids to explore). There are entertaining shows on stage – good for

BERLITZ'S RATINGS		
	Possible	Achieved
Ship	500	331
Accommodation	200	131
Food	400	221
Service	400	258
Entertainment	100	71
Cruise	400	240

the whole family.

This ship is fine if you are taking your first cruise, as long as you like lots of people, noise and lively action. Having fun is the sine qua non of a Carnival cruise. Gratuities are added to your onboard account at $9.75 per person, per day (the amount charged when this book was completed); you can have this amount adjusted, although you'll have to visit the information desk to do so. The onboard currency is the US dollar.

There is absolutely no escape from repetitive announcements (particularly for activities that bring revenue, such as art auctions, bingo, or horse racing. There's a great deal of hustling for drinks, although it is sometimes done with a knowing smile. There really is nowhere to go for privacy, peace and quiet, but then you should choose another ship for that. Standing in line for embarkation, disembarkation, shore tenders and for self-serve buffet meals is an inevitable aspect of cruising aboard all large ships.

SUITABLE FOR: *Celebration* is best suited to young-minded couples and singles of all ages, families with toddlers, tots, children, and teenagers (anyone under 21 must be accompanied by a parent, relative or guardian) who like to mingle in a large ship setting with plenty of life and entertainment for everyone, with food that emphasizes quantity rather than quality, all delivered with friendly service that lacks polish, but delivers a fun vacation.

ACCOMMODATION. *Celebration* has a range of suites, outside-view cabins and interior (no view) cabins. The price you pay depends on grade, location and size. The cabins are quite standard and mostly identical in terms of layout and decor (which means they are good for large groups who generally like to have identical cabins for their participants), are of fairly generous proportions, except for the interior (no view) cabins, which are quite small. They are reasonably comfortable and well equipped, but nothing special. A gift basket is provided in all grades; it includes aloe soap, shampoo, conditioner, deodorant, breath mints, candy, and pain relief tablets (all in sample sizes).

The best living spaces on board are in 10 suites, each of which has more space, its own private balcony, a larger bathroom and more closet, drawer and storage space. Note that if you book one of the suites (Category 11 or 12 in the Carnival Cruise Lines brochure) you automatically qualify for "Skipper's Club" priority check-in at any US homeland port – useful for getting ahead of the crowd.

CUISINE/DINING. There are two dining rooms (Horizon and Vista). They are quite cramped when full, and extremely noisy (both are non-smoking), and they have low ceilings in the raised sections of their centers. There are tables for four, six or eight (there are no tables for two). The decor is bright and extremely colorful, to say the least. Dining is in four seatings, for greater flexibility: 6pm, 6.45pm, 8pm and 8.45pm (times are approximate).

Carnival works hard to improve the cuisine, but few find the meals memorable (you get what you pay for). While menu items sound appetizing, their presentation and taste may prove disappointing. Meats are of a decent quality; fish and seafood is not. Presentation is simple, and few garnishes are used. Many meat and fowl dishes are disguised with gravies and sauces. The selection of fresh green vegetables, breads, rolls, cheeses and fruits is limited, and there is too much use of canned fruit and jellied desserts. However, do remember that this is banquet catering, with all its attendant standardization and production cooking (it is, therefore, difficult to obtain anything remotely unusual or off-menu).

Although there is a decent wine list, there are no wine waiters and so the regular waiters are expected to serve both food and wine. The service is highly programmed, although the waiters are willing and reasonably friendly. However, the waiters do sing and dance, and there are constant waiter parades; the dining room is show business – all done in the name of gratuities at the end of your cruise.

Casual meals can be taken as self-serve buffets in the Wheelhouse Bar & Grill, although the meals provided are very basic, and quite disappointing, with much repetition (particularly for breakfast) and little variety. At night, the "Seaview Bistro", as the Lido Cafe is known, provides a casual (dress down) alternative to eating in the main dining rooms, serving pasta, steaks, salads and desserts (it typically is in operation from 6pm to 9pm).

ENTERTAINMENT. The Astoria Showlounge is the principal venue for large-scale production shows and major cabaret acts (although several pillars obstruct the views from some seats). During a typical 7-day cruise, there will be two, large-scale, trend-setting production shows, with a cast of two lead singers and a clutch of dancers, backed by a 10-piece live orchestra. These have been the mainstay of Carnival's "we've got the fun" entertainment theme for years. They are of the ritzy-glitzy, razzle-dazzle, Las Vegas-style revues that have little or no story line or flow (there's lots of running around on stage and stepping in place, but very little dancing). However, the skimpy costumes are very colorful, as is the lighting (with extensive use of "color mover" lights). Stage smoke appears to be in constant use during the production shows, and volumes are of the ear-splitting type.

With all the audio-visual support staff, dressers, and stage managers, the personnel count comes to almost 40. Make no mistake about it, the shows are lavish, and loud. Other specialty acts take center stage on nights when there is no production show, and late-night adults-only comedy (typically with very blue material) is also standard aboard the ships of Carnival Cruise Lines. Carnival rotates entertainers aboard its ships, so passengers see different acts each night.

Almost every lounge/bar has live bands and musical units, so there is always plenty of live music happening (mostly in the evenings).

SPA/FITNESS. SpaCarnival is located on the ship's uppermost deck (Verandah Deck), just aft of the mast, and accessed by the center stairway and lifts. It has a gymnasium (with some high-tech muscle-pumping cardiovascular machines) and views over the ship's only swimming pool, men's and women's changing rooms and saunas. The beauty salon is located in another spot, on Admiral Deck, just aft of the Astoria Showlounge.

The spa is operated by Steiner, a specialist concession, whose young staff will try to sell you Steiner's own-brand Elemis beauty products (spa girls have sales targets). Some fitness classes are free, while some, such as yoga and kickboxing, cost $10 per class. However, being aboard will give you an opportunity to try some of the more exotic treatments (particularly some of the massages available). Massage (including exotic massages such as Aroma Stone massage, Chakra Balancing massage and other well-being massages), facials, pedicures, and beauty salon treatments are at extra cost (massage, for example, costs about $2 per minute, plus gratuity). Do make appointments as early as possible as time slots can go quickly.

● **For more extensive general information on what a Carnival cruise is like, see pages 107–111.**

Celebrity Xpedition
NOT YET RATED

Boutique Ship:	2,329 tons	Passengers		Cabin Voltage:	220
Lifestyle:	Premium	(lower beds/all berths):	92/94	Elevators:	0
Cruise Line:	Celebrity Cruises	Passenger Space Ratio		Casino (gaming tables):	No
Former Names:	Sun Bay	(lower beds/all berths):	25.3/24.7	Slot Machines:	No
Builder:	Cassens-Werft (Germany)	Crew/Passenger Ratio		Swimming Pools (outdoors):	No
Original Cost:	DM 35 million	(lower beds/all berths):	1.4/1.4	Swimming Pools (indoors):	No
Entered Service:	June 2001/June 2004	Navigation Officers:	European	Whirlpools:	1
Registry:	The Bahamas	Cabins (total):	47	Fitness Center:	Yes
Length (ft/m):	290.3/88.5	Size Range (sq ft/m):	156.0–460.0/	Sauna/Steam Room:	Yes/No
Beam (ft/m):	45.9/14.0		14.5–42.7	Massage:	Yes
Draft (ft/m):	11.4/3.5	Cabins (outside view):	47	Self-Service Launderette:	No
Propulsion/Propellers:	diesel	Cabins (interior/no view):	0	Dedicated Cinema/Seats:	No
	(3,000kW)/2	Cabins (for one person):	0	Library:	Yes
Passenger Decks:	4	Cabins (with private balcony):	9	Classification Society:	Lloyds Register
Total Crew:	64	Cabins (wheelchair accessible):	0		

OVERALL SCORE: NYR (OUT OF A POSSIBLE 2,000 POINTS)

OVERVIEW. This is the first specialist boutique ship for Celebrity Cruises. It's like a small private club, positioned specifically for Galápagos cruises, and is very different from the rest of the fleet of biggies. The brochure rates may or may not include the Galápagos Islands visitor tax (about $100), which must typically be paid in cash at Guayaquil or Quito airports or in the islands.

There is a surprisingly good amount of open deck space – far better, in proportion, than many ships far larger, and much of it with teakwood decking (as well as teak deck lounge chairs and patio furniture). Although there is no swimming pool (the ship's too small for one), there is a whirlpool tub on the uppermost open deck. Stabilizers were fitted during a 2004 refit.

All accommodation is located in the forward half, with public rooms located in the aft half. The ambience is unpretentious and unhurried, but subtly elegant. Except for the dining room (which can double as a conference room), there is only one public room: the main lounge, complete with bar, dance floor and bandstand.

SUITABLE FOR: *Celebrity Xpedition* is best suited to mature adults who want an intimate and casual cruise experience without the crowds, and would enjoy learning about the nature and wildlife of the Galápagos Islands.

ACCOMMODATION. There are four price categories in two cabin types: 9 Suites, measuring 247 sq. ft (23 sq. meters); 34 Comfort Cabins, 172 sq. ft (16 sq. meters); and 3 Comfort cabins, 156 sq. ft (14.5 sq. meters).

BERLITZ'S RATINGS

	Possible	Achieved
Ship	500	NYR
Accommodation	200	NYR
Food	400	NYR
Service	400	NYR
Entertainment	100	NYR
Cruise	400	NYR

All suites and cabins have twin beds (four comfort cabins have a double bed), TV, sofa, drinks table, vanity desk with hairdryer, mini-bar/ refrigerator, and personal safe, while bathrooms all have a good-sized shower enclosure (no suites/cabins have bathtubs) with soap/shampoo dispenser, black granite washbasin, white marble-clad walls, and 100% cotton bathrobes and towels.

The largest accommodation is in nine suites, each with a private balcony. One suite is located forward, with forward-facing views, and has a sloping ceiling with much character. The balconies have partitions that are almost private, and a teakwood deck. Two of the suites can be joined together through an interconnecting wall. One bedroom has two pull-down Murphy beds, so that it can be used as a lounge in the daytime.

CUISINE/DINING. The Darwin Dining Room is an intimate room that accommodates all passengers in one seating and operates on an open-seating basis. Nicely decorated, it has ocean-view windows along one side. A self-serve buffet offers salads, cold cuts and cheeses. House wines and beer are included in the fare; a few better wines can be bought.

The casual, self-serve Seagull Buffet is just behind the main lounge on the open deck, with teak tables and chairs.

ENTERTAINMENT. Dinner and after-dinner conversation with fellow passengers is the main entertainment each evening.

SPA/FITNESS. There is a small fitness room, and adjacent unisex sauna located inside on the uppermost deck, while a small beauty salon is located on the lowest deck.

Century
★★★★ +

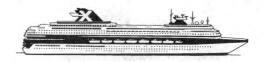

Large (Resort) Ship: ....70,606 tons	Total Crew: 858	Cabins (with private balcony): 61
Lifestyle: ....Premium	Passengers	Cabins (wheelchair accessible): 8
Cruise Line: ....Celebrity Cruises	(lower beds/all berths): 1,750/2,150	Cabin Current: ....110 and 220 volts
Former Names: ....none	Passenger Space Ratio	Elevators: 9
Builder: ....Meyer Werft (Germany)	(lower beds/all berths): 40.3/32.8	Casino (gaming tables): ....Yes
Original Cost: ....$320 million	Crew/Passenger Ratio	Slot Machines: ....Yes
Entered Service: ....Dec 1995	(lower beds/all berths): 2.0/2.5	Swimming Pools (outdoors): 2
Registry: ....The Bahamas	Navigation Officers: ....Greek	Swimming Pools (indoors): ...1 hydropool
Length (ft/m): 807.1/246.0	Cabins (total): 875	Whirlpools: 4
Beam (ft/m): 105.6/32.2	Size Range (sq ft/m): 168.9–1,514.5/	Self-Service Launderette: ....No
Draft (ft/m): 24.6/7.5	15.7–140.7	Dedicated Cinema/Seats: Yes/190
Propulsion/Propellers: ....diesel	Cabins (outside view): 569	Library: ....Yes
(29,250kW)/2	Cabins (interior/no view): 306	Classification Society: ...Lloyd's Register
Passenger Decks: 10	Cabins (for one person): 0	

OVERALL SCORE: 1,663 (OUT OF A POSSIBLE 2,000 POINTS)

OVERVIEW. This ship, which looks externally like a larger version of the company's smaller, popular *Horizon/Zenith*, is quite well balanced despite its squared-off stern. It has the distinctive Celebrity Cruises' "X" funnel ("X" being the Greek letter "C" which stands for Chandris, the former owning company, before Royal Caribbean purchased it). With a high passenger space ratio for such a large ship, there is no real sense of crowding, and the passenger flow is very good. A high crew/passenger ratio provides a sound basis for good passenger service.

BERLITZ'S RATINGS		
	Possible	Achieved
Ship	500	444
Accommodation	200	177
Food	400	315
Service	400	319
Entertainment	100	78
Cruise	400	330

The interior decor is elegant and understated. Technical and engineering excellence prevails, and there is perhaps too much fire and safety equipment. This is a contemporary ship, with fine public rooms, and an array of Sony television and video screens in many of them. The medical facilities are also excellent.

There is a three-quarter, two-level teak wood promenade deck, and a wrap-around jogging track atop the ship. One wall of the three-deck-high main foyer (atrium) has nine large television screens providing constantly changing scenery. The atrium is not glitzy, but its decor somehow doesn't closely match the rest of the ship. There are 4.5 acres (1.8 hectares) of open deck space, together with a fine array of other public rooms and enhanced passenger facilities.

Wide passageways provide plenty of indoor space for strolling, so there's no feeling of being crowded. In fact, the ship absorbs passengers really well. A small, dedicated cinema also doubles as a conference and meeting center with all the latest audio-visual technology.

Cigar smokers will love Michael's Club – a cigar and cognac room of fine taste; a lovely triangular-shaped room, it has become a favorite watering hole for those who smoke, with large comfortable chairs and the feel of a real gentlemen's club. Features include a cigar humidor, and a choice of almost 20 different cigars. Those who like gambling will find that the ship's large casino is tightly packed with slot machines and gaming tables, and even has a satellite-linked ATM machine.

Outstanding are the 500 pieces of art that adorn the ship – a $3.8 million art collection that includes many Warhol favorites and some fascinating contemporary sculptures (look for the colored violins on Deck Seven). The "Century Collection" includes a comprehensive survey of the most important artists and the major developments in art since the 1960s, and embraces Abstract Expressionism, Pop, Conceptualism, Minimalism and Neo-Expressionism.

Overall, *Century* is a fine vessel for a big-ship cruise vacation, but some wear and tear and sloppy maintenance show in some areas, although general cleanliness is excellent. There are few annoying announcements. A 15% gratuity is automatically added to all bar and wine accounts. The onboard currency is the US dollar.

After Celebrity Cruises was bought by Royal Caribbean International, standards aboard all the ships in the fleet dropped as cuts were made by its new parent. However, new management was brought in to bring Celebrity Cruises back to the premium product that was envisioned when the company first started.

Although this is a beautiful ship, the shore excursion operation, embarkation and disembarkation remain weak links in the Celebrity Cruises operation, and the cruise staff is unpolished and has little finesse. Standing in line for embarkation, disembarkation, shore tenders and for self-serve buffet meals is an inevitable aspect of cruising aboard all large ships. The room service menu is poor, and room service food items are below the standard of food featured in the dining room. The interactive TV system is frustrating to use, and the larger suites have three remotes for TV/audio equipment (one would be better).

SUITABLE FOR: *Century* is best suited to well traveled couples and singles of age 40 and above (it is not particularly recommended for children and teenagers) seeking a large ship with a sophisticated environment, good itineraries, fine food and good European-style service from a well trained crew that cares and delivers an onboard product that is well above average.

ACCOMMODATION. There are 12 different grades of accommodation. The price you pay depends on the grade, size and location you choose. The wide variety of cabin types includes 18 family cabins, each with two lower beds, two foldaway beds and one upper berth..

All cabins have wood cabinetry and accenting, hairdryers in the bathrooms, 100 % cotton towels, and interactive television and entertainment systems (you can shop, book shore excursions or play casino games interactively in English, German, French, Italian or Spanish). However, the standard 24-hour cabin menu is disappointing, and very limited. There are no cabins for single occupancy.

All cabins feature a personal safe, mini-bar/refrigerator (there is a charge if you use anything, of course) and are nicely equipped and decorated, with warm wood-finish furniture, and none of the boxy feel of cabins in many ships, due to the angled placement of vanity and audio-video consoles. In addition, all suites on Deck 10 (and the Sky Deck suites on Deck 12) feature butler service and in-cabin dining facilities. Suites that have private balconies also have floor-to-ceiling windows and sliding doors to balconies (a few have outward opening doors).

For the ultimate in living spaces aboard this ship, choose one of two beautifully decorated Presidential Suites, each 1,173 sq. ft (109 sq. meters). These are located amidships in the most desirable position (each can be combined with the adjacent mini-suite via an inter-connecting door, to provide a living space of 1,515 sq. ft (140.7 sq. meters). Each suite has a marble-floored foyer, a living room with mahogany wood floor and hand-woven rug. Other features include a separate dining area with six-seat dining table; butler's pantry with wet bar; a wine bar with private label stock, refrigerator and microwave. There is a large private balcony with dining table for two, chaise lounge chairs with cushioned pads, hot tub and dimmer-controlled lighting; master bedroom with king-sized bed, dressed with fine fabrics and draperies, Egyptian cotton bed linen, and walk-in closet with abundant storage space. The all-marble bathroom has a jet-spray shower and whirlpool bath.

All cabins designated as suites feature European duvets instead of sheets/blankets, fresh flowers, VCR, use of the AquaSpa without charge, and butler service. Electrically operated blinds and other goodies are also standard in some suites.

CUISINE/DINING. A grand staircase connects the upper and lower levels of the splendid two-level Grand Dining Room. Huge windows overlook the stern (electrically operated blinds picture different backdrops). Each of the two levels has a separate finishing galley. There are two seatings for dinner (open seating for breakfast and lunch), at tables for two, four, six, eight or 10. The dining room is a no-smoking area. The design of the two galleys is excellent, and is such that food that should be hot does arrive hot at the table. Three different decorative panels, changed according to theme nights, adorn the huge aft windows. The dining room chairs, which are heavy, should, but do not, have armrests.

All meals, including full dinners, can be served, course-by-course, in all suites and cabins, no matter what grade you choose. For those who can't live without them, freshly baked pizzas (boxed) can be delivered, in an insulated pouch, to your cabin.

Celebrity Cruises has established an enviable reputation for fine dining aboard its ships, and this tradition is being continued. Michel Roux designs the line's menus and exerts tight personal control over their correct cooking and delivery to assure consistency of product. All meals are made from scratch, with nothing pre-cooked or pre-packaged ashore. However, the food served as room-service items is decidedly below the standard of food featured in the dining room.

There is also a large indoor/outdoor Lido Cafe (called "Islands") with four separate self-service buffet lines, as well as two-grill serving stations located adjacent to the swimming pools outdoors.

The Cova Cafe di Milano is a signature item aboard all the ships of Celebrity Cruises, and a seagoing version of the real Cafe di Milano originally opened in 1817 next to La Scala Opera House in Milan. The cafe is placed in a prominent position, on the second level of the atrium lobby, and several display cases show off the extensive range of Cova coffee, chocolates and alcoholic digestives; this is the place to see and be seen. It is a delightful setting (and meeting place) for those who appreciate fine Italian coffees (for espresso, espresso macchiato, cappuccino, latte), pastries and superb cakes in an elegant, refined setting.

ENTERTAINMENT. There is a good two-level, 1,000-seat showlounge/theater with side balconies. It has a large stage, a split orchestra pit (hydraulic), and the latest in high-tech lighting and sound equipment. Unfortunately, the production shows are not nearly as lavish. In fact, compared to some of the other major cruise lines, the shows are a let-down, and not in keeping with the elegant nature of the interior decor. Bar service, supplied continuously during shows, can prove irritating.

While there are some good cabaret acts, they are the same ones seen aboard many ships of the major cruise lines.

In other words, it is disappointing to note that there is absolutely nothing to distinguish Celebrity Crusies in the entertainment department. The ship does have a number of bands, although there is very little music for social dancing, other than disco and pop music.

SPA/FITNESS. The AquaSpa has 9,040 sq. ft (840 sq. meters) of space dedicated to well-being and body treatments, all set in a calming environment, complete with shoji screens and a Japanese-inspired rock garden. It includes a large fitness/exercise area, complete with all the latest high-tech muscle machines and video cycles, thalassotherapy pool, and seven treatment rooms. The spa has some of the more unusual wellness treatments (including a Rasul room – for Mediterranean mud and gentle steam bathing).

The spa is operated by Steiner, a specialist concession,

whose young staff will try to sell you Steiner's own-brand Elemis beauty products (spa girls have sales targets). Some fitness classes are free, while some, such as yoga and kick-boxing, cost $10 per class. However, being aboard will give you an opportunity to try some of the more exotic treatments (particularly some of the massages available). Massage (including Aroma Stone massage, Chakra Balancing massage and other well-being massages), facials, pedicures, and beauty salon treatments are at extra cost. Examples of treatment costs: massage, at $109 (50 minutes), facial, at $109, seaweed wrap (75 minutes) $190, all plus a "gratuity" of 10 percent. Personal training sessions in the gymnasium cost $83 for one hour.

Do make appointments as early as possible – aboard a ship so large, time slots go quickly, so the day you board is the best time to book your preferred treatments.

SHIP TALK

Abeam: off the side of the ship, at a right angle to its length.
Aft: near, toward, or in the rear of the ship.
Ahead: something that is ahead of the ship's bow.
Alleyway: a passageway or corridor.
Alongside: said of a ship when it is beside a pier or another vessel.
Amidships: in or toward the middle of the ship; the longitudinal center portion of the ship.
Anchor Ball: black ball hoisted above the bow to show that the vessel is anchored.
Astern: is the opposite of Ahead (i.e., meaning something behind the ship).
Backwash: motion in the water caused by the propeller(s) moving in a reverse (astern) direction.
Bar: sandbar, usually caused by tidal or current conditions near the shore.
Beam: width of the ship between its two sides at the widest point.
Bearing: compass direction,

expressed in degrees, from the ship to a particular objective or destination.
Below: anything beneath the main deck.
Berth: dock, pier, or quay. Also means bed on board ship.
Bilge: lowermost spaces of the infrastructure of a ship.
Boat Stations: allotted space for each person during lifeboat drill or any other emergency when lifeboats are lowered.
Bow: the forward most part of the vessel.
Bridge: navigational and command control center.
Bulkhead: upright partition (wall) dividing the ship into compartments.
Bunkers: the space where fuel is stored; "bunkering" means taking on fuel.
Cable Length: a measured length equaling 100 fathoms or 600 feet.
Chart: a nautical map used for navigating.
Colors: refers to the national flag or emblem flown by the ship.
Companionway: interior stairway.

Course: direction in which the ship is headed, in degrees.
Davit: a device for raising and lowering lifeboats.
Deadlight: a ventilated porthole cover to prevent light from entering.
Disembark (also debark): to leave a ship.
Dock: berth, pier, or quay.
Draft (or draught): measurement in feet from the ship's waterline to the lowest point of its keel.
Embark: to join a ship.
Fantail: the rear or overhang of the ship.
Fathom: distance equal to 6 ft.
Flagstaff: a pole at the stern of a ship where the flag of its country of registry is flown.
Free Port: port or place free of customs duty and regulations.
Funnel: chimney from which the ship's combustion gases are propelled into the atmosphere.
Galley: the ship's kitchen.
Gangway: the stairway or ramp that provides the link between ship and shore.
● *More Ship Talk, page 254.*

Clipper Adventurer
★★★

Boutique Ship: . . . . .5,750 tons	Total Crew: 84	Cabins (with private balcony): 0
Lifestyle: . . . . .Standard	Passengers	Cabins (wheelchair accessible): 0
Cruise Line: . . . . .Clipper Cruise Line	(lower beds/all berths): 122/122	Cabin Current: . . . . .220 volts
Former Names: . . . .*Alla Tarasova*	Passenger Space Ratio	Elevators: 0
Builder: . . . . .Brodgradiliste Uljanik	(lower beds/all berths): 47.1/47.1	Casino (gaming tables): . . . . .No
(Yugoslavia)	Crew/Passenger Ratio	Slot Machines: .No
Original Cost: .n/a	(lower beds/all berths): 1.4/1.4	Swimming Pools (outdoors): . . . . .No
Entered Service: 1976/Apr 1998	Navigation Officers: . . . . .European	Swimming Pools (indoors): . . . . .No
Registry: . . . . .The Bahamas	Cabins (total): .61	Whirlpools: . . . . .No
Length (ft/m): 328.1/100.01	Size Range (sq ft/m): 119.0–211.0/	Self-Service Launderette: . . . . .No
Beam (ft/m): 53.2/16.24	11.0–19.6	Dedicated Cinema/Seats: . . . . .No
Draft (ft/m): 15.2/4.65	Cabins (outside view): 61	Library: . . . . .Yes
Propulsion/Propellers: diesel (3,884kW)/2	Cabins (interior/no view): 0	Classification Society: . .Russian Shipping
Passenger Decks: 5	Cabins (for one person): 0	Register

OVERALL SCORE: 1,175 (OUT OF A POSSIBLE 2,000 POINTS)

OVERVIEW. *Clipper Adventurer* is a small ship – originally one of eight built for the Murmansk Shipping Company. It has an ice-strengthened (A-1 ice classification), and a royal blue hull and white funnel, bow-thruster and stabilizers. But, even with an ice classification, it got stuck in an ice field in the Bellingshausen Sea in 2000. Fortunately, the Argentine Navy icebreaker *Almirante Irizar* freed it. The ship isn't new, but it had a $15 million refit/conversion in 1997–98, and meets international safety codes and requirements. It specializes in operating close-in expedition-style cruising. There are 10 Zodiac rubber inflatable landing craft for in-depth excursions, and a covered promenade deck.

This cozy ship caters to travelers rather than mere passengers. The dress code is casual during the day, although at night many passengers wear jacket and tie. For trekking ashore, take long-sleeved garments. The public spaces are a little limited, with just one main lounge and bar. There is a small but decent library, with high wingback chairs.

There is no observation lounge with forward-facing views, although there is an outdoor observation area directly below the bridge. Clipper Cruise Line provides its own cruise staff, and experienced historians and naturalist lecturers accompany all cruise expeditions. Smoking is permitted, but only on the outside decks. Travel insurance is included in the cruise fare. The onboard currency is the US dollar.

The passageways are narrow (it is difficult to pass housekeeping carts), and the stairs are steep on the outer decks.

SUITABLE FOR: *Clipper Adventurer* is best suited to couples and single travelers who enjoy nature and wildlife up

BERLITZ'S RATINGS

	Possible	Achieved
Ship	500	292
Accommodation	200	120
Food	400	247
Service	400	242
Entertainment	100	40
Cruise	400	234

close and personal, and who would not dream of cruising in the mainstream sense aboard ships with large numbers of people. This is for hardy, adventurous types who don't need vacuous entertainment or mindless parlor games.

ACCOMMODATION. All cabins (there are seven grades, including a dedicated price for single cabin occupancy) have outside views and twin lower beds, with private bathroom with shower, and toilet. The bathrooms are really tiny, although they are tiled, and have all the basics. Several double-occupancy cabins can be booked by single travelers (but special rates apply).

All cabins have a lockable drawer for valuables, telephone, and individual temperature control. Some have picture windows, while others have portholes. Two larger cabins (called suites in the brochure, which they really are not) are quite well equipped for the size of the vessel.

CUISINE/DINING. The dining room, with deep ocean-view windows, seats all passengers at a single seating. The food is a combination of American and Continental cuisine, prepared freshly by chefs trained at some of America's finest culinary institutions. There are limited menu choices, but the food is wholesome, and simply and attractively presented, but certainly not gourmet. Casual, self-service breakfast and luncheon buffets are taken in the main lounge, as are cocktail-hour hors d'oeuvres and other snacks.

ENTERTAINMENT. Dinner and after-dinner conversation in the ship's lounge/bar is the main entertainment.

SPA/FITNESS. There is a small sauna.

Clipper Odyssey
★★★★

Boutique Ship: ....5,218 tons	Total Crew: 52	Cabins (with private balcony): 8
Lifestyle: ....Standard	Passengers	Cabins (wheelchair accessible): 1
Cruise Line: ....Clipper Cruise Line	(lower beds/all berths): 128/128	Cabin Current: ....115 volts
Former Names: ....Oceanic Odyssey,	Passenger Space Ratio	Elevators: 1
Oceanic Grace	(lower beds/all berths): 43.4/43.4	Casino (gaming tables): ....No
Builder: ......NKK Tsu Shipyard (Japan)	Crew/Passenger Ratio	Slot Machines: ....No
Original Cost: ....$40 million	(lower beds/all berths): 2.4/2.4	Swimming Pools (outdoors): 1
Entered Service: .....Apr 1989/Nov 1999	Navigation Officers: ....European	Swimming Pools (indoors): 0
Registry: ....The Bahamas	Cabins (total): 64	Whirlpools: 1
Length (ft/m): 337.5/102.9	Size Range (sq ft/m): 182.9–258.3/	Self-Service Launderette: ....No
Beam (ft/m): 50.5/15.4	17.0–24.0	Dedicated Cinema/Seats: ....No
Draft (ft/m): 14.1/4.3	Cabins (outside view): 64	Library: ....Yes
Propulsion/Propellers: diesel (5,192kW)/2	Cabins (interior/no view): 0	Classification Society: ....Nippon Kaiji
Passenger Decks: 5	Cabins (for one person): 0	Kyokai

OVERALL SCORE: 1,451 (OUT OF A POSSIBLE 2,000 POINTS)

OVERVIEW. *Clipper Odyssey* has a somewhat square, angular, but contemporary profile, with twin outboard funnels. The ship, designed in Holland and built in Japan, was an attempt to copy the original *Sea Goddess* small ship/ ultra-yacht concept specifically for the Japanese market. Operated by Japan's Showa Line, the ship was not particularly successful for the often choppy seas around Japan. After 10 years, the company withdrew from passenger cruises, and Clipper Cruise Line bought the ship as an ideal addition to its small ship fleet.

Considering the size of this ship, there are expansive areas outdoors, excellent for sunbathing or for viewing wildlife. The small swimming pool is just a "dip" pool, however. There is a wide teakwood outdoor jogging track. A decompression chamber for divers, originally included, is no longer used due to insurance requirements. But free snorkeling equipment is available, as is a small fleet of Zodiacs (inflatable landing craft for "soft" expedition use).

Inside, nothing jars the senses, as the interior design concept successfully balances East–West color combinations with some Indonesian accents. The ambiance is warm and intimate, and is for those who seek a small ship where entertainment and loud music isn't a priority. *Clipper Odyssey* will provide a pleasing antidote to cruising aboard the large ships. The onboard currency is the US dollar.

There are lots of pillars in almost all public areas, which do tend to spoil the decor and sightlines.

SUITABLE FOR: *Clipper Odyssey* is best suited to couples and single travelers who enjoy nature and wildlife up close and personal, and who would not dream of cruising in the

BERLITZ'S RATINGS

	Possible	Achieved
Ship	500	418
Accommodation	200	162
Food	400	271
Service	400	244
Entertainment	100	71
Cruise	400	285

mainstream sense aboard ships with large numbers of people. This is for hardy, adventurous types who don't need entertainment or parlor games.

ACCOMMODATION. There are six cabin categories. The ship has all-outside cabins that are quite tastefully furnished and feature blond wood cabinetry, twin- or queen-sized beds, living area with sofa, personal safe, mini-bar/refrigerator, TV set and VCR, and three-sided mirror. All bathrooms have a deep, half-sized tub. Some cabins have private balconies; but these are very small, with awkward door handles. The bathroom toilet seats are extremely high. There is one suite, which is actually the size of two cabins. It provides more room, of course, with a lounge area, and more storage space.

CUISINE/DINING. The dining room has large ocean view picture windows. It is quite warm and inviting, and all passengers eat in a single seating. The cuisine includes fresh foods from local ports, in a mix of regional and some Western cuisine, with open seating. A young, friendly American staff provides the service.

ENTERTAINMENT. There is no formal entertainment, although dinner and after-dinner conversation with fellow passengers in the ship's lounge/bar really becomes the entertainment each evening. Otherwise, it might be a good idea to bring a good book or two.

SPA/FITNESS. There is a tiny beauty salon, and an adjacent massage/body treatment room, while a small fitness room is located on a different deck.

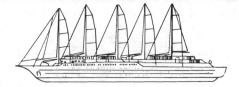

Club Med 2
★★★★

Small Ship: . . . . .14,983 tons	Sail Area (sq ft/m2): 26,910/2,500	Cabins (outside view): 197	
Lifestyle: . . . . .Premium	Main Propulsion: . . . . . .a) engines/b) sails	Cabins (interior/no view): 0	
Cruise Line: . . . . .Club Med Cruises	Propulsion/Propellers: diesel (9,120kW)/2	Cabins (for one person): 0	
Former Names: . . . . .none	Passenger Decks: 8	Cabins (with private balcony): 0	
Builder: . . . .Ateliers et Chantiers du Havre	Total Crew: 200	Cabins (wheelchair accessible): 0	
(France)	Passengers	Cabin Current: . . . . .110 and 220 volts	
Original Cost: . . . .$125 million	(lower beds/all berths): 394/409	Elevators: 2	
Entered Service: . . . . Dec 1992	Passenger Space Ratio	Casino (gaming tables): . . . . .No	
Registry: . . . . .Wallis & Fortuna	(lower beds/all berths): 38.0/36.6	Slot Machines: . . . . .No	
Length (ft/m): 613.8/187.10	Crew/Passenger Ratio	Swimming Pools (outdoors): 2	
Beam (ft/m): 65.6/20.00	(lower beds/all berths): 1.9/2.0	Whirlpools: 0	
Draft (ft/m): 16.4/5.00	Navigation Officers: . . . . .French	Self-Service Launderette: . . . . .No	
Type of Vessel: . . . . .high-tech sail-cruiser	Cabins (total): 197	Library: . . . . .Yes	
No. of Masts: . . . . .5 (164 ft high)	Size Range (sq ft/m): 193.8–322.0/	Classification Society: . . . .Bureau Veritas	
7 computer-controlled sails	18.0–30.0		

OVERALL SCORE: 1,532 (OUT OF A POSSIBLE 2,000 POINTS)

OVERVIEW. *Club Med 2* is one of a pair of the world's largest high-tech sail-cruisers ever built (the other is *Wind Surf*, operated by Windstar Cruises), part-cruise ship, part-yacht. Five huge masts rise 221 ft (67.5 meters) above sea level; they carry seven triangular, self-furling Dacron sails with a total surface area of 26,881 sq. ft (2,497 sq. meters). No human hands touch the sails, as everything is controlled by computer from the bridge. The system computer also keeps the ship on an even keel (via the movement of a hydraulic ballast system, so there is no heeling (rolling) over 6 degrees. When the ship is not using the sails, four diesel-electric motors propel it at up to 12 knots.

There are extensive water sports facilities (all except scuba gear included in the cruise fare) and an aft marina platform. The equipment includes 12 windsurfers, 3 sailboats, 2 water ski boats, several kayaks, 20 single scuba tanks, snorkels, and 4 motorized water sport boats. There are two (saltwater) swimming pools (really dip pools); one is located amidships on the uppermost deck of the ship, while the other is located aft, together with two hot tubs, and an adjacent bar. There is an open bridge policy.

Inside, other facilities include a main lounge, meeting room and a golf simulator (extra charge) as well as a fitness and beauty center, and piano bar. The onboard activities come under the direction of a large team of young, energetic GOs *(gentils ordinaires)*. No gratuities are expected or accepted. The onboard currency is the euro or US dollar.

SUITABLE FOR: *Club Med 2* is best suited to youthful couples and singles who want contemporary facilities and some

BERLITZ'S RATINGS

	Possible	Achieved
Ship	500	402
Accommodation	200	164
Food	400	293
Service	400	292
Entertainment	100	76
Cruise	400	305

watersports in a very relaxed but quite chic and trendy setting that is different to "normal" cruise ships, with good food and service, but with little or no entertainment.

ACCOMMODATION. There are five suites and 192 standard cabins (all the same size). All cabins are nicely equipped and very comfortable, and have an inviting decor that includes much blond wood cabinetry. They all feature a mini-bar/refrigerator, 24-hour room service (but you pay for food), a personal safe, color television, plenty of storage space, bathrobes, and a hairdryer. There are six, four-person cabins, and some 35 doubles are fitted with an extra Pullman berth – good for young families but cramped.

CUISINE/DINING. The two main rooms have tables for one, two or more. There is open seating, so you can sit with whom you wish. The Odyssey Restaurant has a delightful open terrace for informal meals. Complimentary wines and beers are available with lunch and dinner (there is also an à la carte wine list, at a price). Afternoon tea is a delight. The cuisine provides French, continental and Japanese specialties, and the creativity and presentation are good.

ENTERTAINMENT. This is limited to occasional cabaret acts. There is live music for dancing and listening each evening

SPA/FITNESS. The Health Spa has a unisex sauna, beauty salon, and treatment rooms for massage, facials and body wraps; there is also a decent fitness room, and a beauty salon. The spa facilities are split on three separate decks.

C. Columbus
★★★ +

Small Ship: ....14,903 tons	Total Crew: 170	Cabins (with private balcony): 2
Lifestyle: ....Standard	Passengers	Cabins (wheelchair accessible): 0
Cruise Line: ....Hapag-Lloyd Cruises	(lower beds/all berths): 410/423	Cabin Current: ....110 volts
Former Names: ....none	Passenger Space Ratio	Elevators: 3
Builder: ....MTW Schiffswerft (Germany)	(lower beds/all berths): 36.3/35.2	Casino (gaming tables): ....No
Original Cost: ....$69 million	Crew/Passenger Ratio	Slot Machines: ....No
Entered Service: ....July 1997	(lower beds/all berths): 2.4/2.4	Swimming Pools (outdoors): 1
Registry: ....The Bahamas	Navigation Officers: ....German	Swimming Pools (indoors): 0
Length (ft/m): 472.8/144.13	Cabins (total): 205	Whirlpools: 0
Beam (ft/m): 70.5/21.50	Size Range (sq ft/m): 139.9–339.0/	Self-Service Launderette: ....No
Draft (ft/m): 16.8/5.15	13.0–31.5	Dedicated Cinema/Seats: ....No
Propulsion/Propellers: ....diesel	Cabins (outside view): 158	Library: ....Yes
(10,560kW)/2	Cabins (interior/no view): 47	Classification Society: .....Germanischer
Passenger Decks: 6	Cabins (for one person): 0	Lloyd

BERLITZ'S OVERALL SCORE: 1,383 (OUT OF A POSSIBLE 2,000 POINTS)

OVERVIEW. *C. Columbus* has a smart contemporary profile, with a single, large funnel (painted in Hapag-Lloyd's orange/blue colors). Hapag-Lloyd Cruises has chartered the ship from the German company Conti Reederei, the owner, until 2007.

The ship also has an ice-hardened hull, which is useful for cold-weather cruise areas. In addition, the bridge "wings" can be folded inwards (as can the overhang lights) flush with the ship's side so that the vessel can enter the locks in the US/Canada Great Lakes region, including the St. Lawrence Seaway and Welland Canal, for which the ship was specifically built.

The ship has a good passenger space ratio. Each deck has a distinctly different color scheme and carpeting, making it easy to find one's way around. There is a reasonable range of public rooms to choose from, most of which are located in a "cake-layer" vertical stacking aft of the accommodation. Although the ceilings in the public rooms are plain and unimaginative (except for the Palm Garden), the decor is really bright and upbeat, and very different to all other ships in the Hapag-Lloyd fleet. The most popular room is arguably the delightful multi-function Palm Garden, which is also the ship's forward-facing observation lounge.

The fit and finish of the ship's interiors can best be described as a little utilitarian (the mottled gray walls are somewhat cold, but a contrast to the splashes of color found in carpeting and other decorative touches). The artwork chosen is, for the most part, minimal and uncoordinated, yet it all works together to provide cheerful surroundings. Ship buffs will be pleased to find some superb original photographs from the Hapag-Lloyd archives adorning the stairways.

BERLITZ'S RATINGS

	Possible	Achieved
Ship	500	347
Accommodation	200	146
Food	400	269
Service	400	292
Entertainment	100	61
Cruise	400	268

You should know that the level of "luxury" is well below that of Hapag-Lloyd's *Europa*, and the experience on this very informal ship is completely different (so, of course, is the cruise price). The onboard currency is the euro. Gratuities are extra and are recommended at €5–€6 per person per day.

First-time cruise passengers in particular will find this a fresh, comfortable, casual and unpretentious ship for a cruise vacation. You don't need to buy a new wardrobe, and you can leave your tuxedo at home; for this ship you need only informal and casual clothes.

Well-planned itineraries and destination-intensive cruises are featured. Of particular note are the Great Lakes cruises, which are only possible because of the pencil-slim design of *C. Columbus* (previously, the last ocean-going cruise vessel to operate Great Lakes cruises was *World Discoverer* in 1974).

Note that the swimming pool is small (more like a "dip" pool), as is the open deck space. The standard cabins are also very small. There is no wrap-around promenade deck outdoors. The layout and sight lines (including several pillars) in the showlounge are poor.

SUITABLE FOR: *C. Columbus* is best suited to youthful-minded German-speaking couples and single travelers who are seeking good value for money on a first cruise, aboard a ship with contemporary, comfortable (but not pretentious or luxurious) surroundings, and good itineraries, at a very modest price.

ACCOMMODATION. The standard cabins are really small, and many of them are interior. All but 10 cabins have lower berths, but the 16 price grades established really are a lot for this size of ship. Except for two forward-facing suites, there are no balcony cabins.

The cabin decor is bright and upbeat, and a good amount of closet and shelf space is provided. The bathrooms are fully tiled and have large shower stalls (none have bathtubs). All cabins feature a mini-bar/refrigerator (all items are at extra cost, as in hotels ashore), personal safe, and hairdryer (bathrobes are available on request, incurring a small surcharge).

There are eight suites (each is at least double the size of a standard cabin), and each has a curtained partition between its lounge and sleeping areas, with a wall unit that houses a television that can be turned 360 degrees for viewing from either the lounge or bedroom. Two of the suites located at the bow each have a narrow private veranda (with two teak lounge chairs and coffee table), bedroom (with large wall clock) and lounge area separated by a curtain, two televisions, and an excellent amount of closet, drawer and shelf space. The cabinetry, with its walnut-finish and birds-eye pattern, makes these suites feel warm and luxurious. All the suites have a small room service menu. The bathrooms have a large shower (it is big enough for two), hairdryer, and under-sink storage space. There is 24-hour room service. Only a limited room service menu is available for all cabins.

CUISINE/DINING. There is one large main dining room, located at the stern, with large ocean-view windows on three sides, and seats all passengers in a single seating, with assigned tables. There are just two tables for two), but other tables can accommodate up to 16 – good for family reunions. The cuisine, which is presented in an unstuffy way, is fairly good, although the menu selection is quite limited (there are just two or three entrée options for dinner). There is an excellent selection of fresh-baked breads and rolls every day.

Breakfast and lunch can be taken in the bright, but casual, setting of the Palm Garden, which is also the ship's very comfortable observation lounge. Light dinners also can be taken in the Palm Garden, where a small dance floor adds another dimension.

ENTERTAINMENT. The Columbus Lounge is a single level, H-shaped room that is quite large, with banquette and individual seating in tub chairs, and a bar is situated on the port side in the aft corner of the room. Because the apron stage is in the center of the room, the sightlines from many seats are not that good. Entertainment consists mainly of cabaret acts typical of the cruise ship circuit. Plenty of live music, for dancing, is also provided.

SPA/FITNESS. A fitness room is located forward on the uppermost deck of the ship. A sauna is located on the lowest passenger deck, next to the beauty salon, and massage/facial treatments are available.

KNOTS AND LOGS

A knot is a unit of speed measuring one nautical mile. (A nautical mile is equal to one-60th of a degree of the earth's circumference and measures exactly 6,080.2 ft (1,852 km). It is about 800 ft (243 meters) longer than a land mile. Thus, when a ship is traveling at a speed of 20 knots (note: this is never referred to as 20 knots per hour), it is traveling at 20 nautical miles per hour (1 knot equals 1.151 land miles).

This unit of measurement has its origin in the days prior to the advent of modern aids, when sailors used a log and a length of rope to measure the distance that their boat had covered, as well as the speed at which it was advancing. In 1574, a tract by William Bourne, entitled A Regiment for the Sea, records the method by which this was done. The log was weighted down at one end while the other end was affixed to a rope. The weighted end, when thrown over the stern, had the effect of making the log stand upright, thus being visible. Sailors believed that the log remained stationary at the spot where it had been cast into the water, while the rope unraveled. By measuring the length of rope used, they could ascertain how far the ship had traveled, and were thus able to calculate its speed.

Sailors first tied knots at regular intervals, eventually fixed at 47 ft 3 inches (14.4 meters) along a rope, then counted how many knots had passed through their hands in a specified time (later established as 28 seconds), and measured by the amount of sand that had run out of an hourglass. They then used simple multiplication to calculate the number of knots their ship was traveling at over the period of an hour.

The data gathered in this way were put into a record, called a logbook. Today, a logbook is used to record the day-to-day details of the life of a ship and its crew as well as other pertinent information.

Constellation
★★★★ +

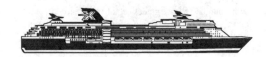

Large (Resort) Ship: ....90,228 tons	Total Crew: 999	Cabins (wheelchair accessible): 26
Lifestyle: ....Premium	Passengers	(17 with private balcony)
Cruise Line: ....Celebrity Cruises	(lower beds/all berths): 1,950/2,450	Cabin Current: ....110 and 220 volts
Former Names: ....none	Passenger Space Ratio	Elevators: 10
Builder: ....Chantiers de l'Atlantique	(lower beds/all berths): 46.2/36.8	Casino (gaming tables): ....Yes
(France)	Crew/Passenger Ratio	Slot Machines: ....Yes
Original Cost: ....$350 million	(lower beds/all berths): 1.9/2.4	Swimming Pools (outdoors): 2
Entered Service: ....May 2002	Navigation Officers: ....Greek	Swimming Pools (indoors): 1
Registry: ....The Bahamas	Cabins (total): 975	(with magrodome)
Length (ft/m): 964.5/294.0	Size Range (sq ft/m): 165.1–2,530.0/	Whirlpools: 4
Beam (ft/m): 105.6/32.2	15.34–235.0	Self-Service Launderette: ....No
Draft (ft/m): 26.2/8.0	Cabins (outside view): 780	Dedicated Cinema/Seats: Yes/368
Propulsion/Propellers: .....gas turbine/2	Cabins (interior/no view): 195	Library: ....Yes
azimuthing pods (39,000kW)	Cabins (for one person): 0	Classification Society: ...Lloyd's Register
Passenger Decks: 11	Cabins (with private balcony): 590	

BERLITZ'S OVERALL SCORE: 1,697 (OUT OF A POSSIBLE 2,000 POINTS)

OVERVIEW. *Constellation* is a sister ship to *Infinity, Millennium,* and *Summit* (the *Millennium*-class ships). Jon Bannenberg, the famous mega-yacht designer, dreamed up the exterior featuring a royal blue and white hull, and racy lines in red, blue and gold – although it has turned out to look quite ungainly. This is the fourth Celebrity Cruises ship to be fitted with the "pod" propulsion system *(see page 17)* coupled with a quiet, smokeless, energy-efficient gas turbine powerplant (two GE gas turbines provide engine power while a single GE steam turbine drives the electricity generators).

On one side of Sky Deck, there is a huge bronze sculpture of a gorilla holding a fish under its arm; created by Angus Fairhurst, it is titled "A couple of differences between thinking and feeling."

One delightful feature is a large conservatory located in a glasshouse and spreading across a whole foyer. It includes a botanical environment with flowers, plants, tress, mini-gardens and fountains, all designed by the award-winning floral designer Emilio Robba of Paris. It is directly in front of the main funnel and a section of it has glass walls overlooking the ship's side.

Inside, the ship has a similar standard of decor and materials, and public rooms that have made the existing ships in the fleet so user-friendly. Although the main part of the atrium lobby is three decks high, glass-walled lifts on the port side travel through 11 decks.

Facilities include a combination Cinema/Conference Center, an expansive shopping arcade with 14,447 sq. ft (1,300 sq. meters) of retail store space (with trendy brand name labels such as Fendi, Fossil, Hugo Boss, and Versace),

BERLITZ'S RATINGS

	Possible	Achieved
Ship	500	454
Accommodation	200	180
Food	400	327
Service	400	330
Entertainment	100	78
Cruise	400	328

a lavish four-decks-high showlounge with the latest in staging and lighting equipment, a two-level library (one level for English-language books; a second for books in other languages and reference material), card room, music listening room, and an observation lounge/discotheque with outstanding views. Michael's Club (originally a cigar smoker's haven), is now a piano lounge/bar. An internet cafe has almost 20 computers with custom-made wood-surround flat-screen monitors and internet access.

The artwork throughout the ship (particularly the sculptures) is eclectic, provocative, thoughtful, and intelligent, and at almost every turn another piece appears to break the monotony associated with large ships.

Gaming sports include the ship's overly large Fortunes Casino, with blackjack, roulette, and slot machines, and lots of bright lights and action. Families with children will appreciate the Fun Factory (for children) and The Tower (for teenagers). Children's counselors and youth activities staff provide a wide range of supervized activities.

After the downturn in business following 2001's terrorist attacks on the US, new management was brought in to restore Celebrity Cruises to the premium product envisioned when the company first started, and the improvements introduced in 2003 have restored the art of hospitality and provide a taste of luxury for all. For example, on days at sea (in warm weather areas) if you are sunbathing on deck, someone will bring you a cold towel, and a sorbet, ice water and iced tea. Little touches like this differentiate Celebrity Cruises from other major cruise lines.

A cruise aboard a large ship such as this provides a wide

range of choices and possibilities. If you travel in one of the suites, the benefits include the highest level of personal service, while cruising in non-suite accommodation is almost like in any large ship. One thing really is certain: cruising in a hassle-free environment such as this is hard to beat no matter how much or how little you pay. The onboard currency is the US dollar. A 15% gratuity is added to all bar and wine accounts.

Note that there is, sadly, no wrap-around wooden promenade deck outdoors. Standing in line for embarkation, disembarkation, shore tenders and for self-serve buffet meals is an inevitable aspect of cruising aboard all large ships (however, more flexible embarkation hours do help to spread the flow), but the worst time is when large numbers of passengers return from shore excursions and have to wait to go through a security check; the result being long lines outside the ship. The ship's two seating dining and two shows detract from an otherwise excellent product, and this ship (together with sister ships *Infinity*, *Millennium* and *Summit*) can be said to provide the very best of the ships in the Premium segment of the marketplace, providing a taste of luxury for those who book in the largest suites.

ACCOMMODATION. There are 20 different grades from which to choose, depending on your preference for the grade, size and location of your living space. Almost half of the ship's cabins feature a "private" balcony; approximately 80 percent are outside-view suites and cabins, and 20 percent are interior (no view) cabins. The cabins are extremely comfortable throughout this ship, regardless of which cabin grade you choose. Suites, naturally, have more space, butler service (whether you want it or not), more and better amenities and more personal service than if you choose any of the standard cabin grades. There are several categories of suites, but those at the stern of the ship are in a prime location and have huge balconies that are really private and not overlooked from above.

Regardless of the grade you choose, all suites and cabins have wood cabinetry and accenting, interactive television and entertainment systems (you can go shopping, book shore excursions, play casino games interactively, and even watch soft porn movies). The bathrooms have hairdryers and 100 % cotton towels.

Penthouse Suites: Two Penthouse Suites (on Penthouse Deck) are the largest cabins aboard this ship. Each occupies one half of the beam (width) of the ship, overlooking the ship's stern. Each measures a huge 2,530 sq. ft (235 sq. meters), consisting of 1,431.6 sq. ft (133 sq. meters) of living space, plus a huge wrap-around terrace measuring 1,098 sq. ft (102 sq. meters) with 180-degree views. This terrace includes a wet bar, hot tub and whirlpool tub – but much of it can be overlooked by passengers on other decks above. Features include a marble foyer, a separate living room (complete with ebony baby grand piano – bring your own pianist if you don't play yourself – and a formal dining room. The master bedroom has a large walk-in closet, personal exercise equipment, dressing room with vanity desk, exercise equipment, marble-clad master bathroom with

twin washbasins, deep whirlpool bathtub, separate shower, toilet and bidet areas, flat-screen televisions (one in the bedroom and one in the lounge), and electronically controlled drapes. Butler service is standard, and a butler's pantry, with separate entry door, has a full-size refrigerator, temperature-controlled wine cabinet, microwave oven and good-sized food preparation and storage areas. For even more space, an interconnecting door can be opened into the adjacent suite (ideal for multi-generation families).

Royal Suites: Eight Royal Suites, each measuring 733 sq ft (68 sq. meters), are located towards the aft of the ship (four each on the port and starboard sides). Each has a separate living room with dining and lounge areas (with refrigerator, mini-bar and Bang & Olufson CD sound system), and a separate bedroom. There are two entertainment centers with DVD players, and two flat-screen televisions (one in the living area, one in the bedroom), and a large walk-in closet with vanity desk. The marble-clad bathroom has a whirlpool bathtub with integral shower, and there is also a separate shower enclosure, two washbasins and toilet. The teakwood decked balcony is extensive (large enough for on-deck massage) and also has a whirlpool hot tub.

Celebrity Suites: Eight Celebrity Suites, each 467 sq. ft (44 sq. meters), have floor-to-ceiling windows, a separate living room with dining and lounge areas, two entertainment centers with flat-screen televisions (one in the living room, one in the bedroom), and a walk-in closet with vanity desk. The marble-clad bathroom has a whirlpool bathtub with integral shower (a window with movable blind lets you look out of the bathroom through the lounge to the large ocean-view windows). Interconnecting doors allow two suites to be used as a family unit (as there is no balcony, these suites are ideal for families with small children). These suites overhang the starboard side of the ship (they are located opposite a group of glass-walled lifts), and provide stunning ocean views from the glass-walled sitting/dining area, which extends out from the ship's side. A personal computer with wood-surround screen allows direct internet connectivity. Butler service is standard.

Sky Suites: There are 30 Sky Suites, each 308 sq. ft (28.6 sq. meters), including the private balcony (note that some balconies may be larger than others, depending on the location). Although these are designated as suites, they are really just larger cabins that feature a marble-clad bathroom with bathtub/shower combination. The suites also have a VCR player in addition to a TV set, and have a larger lounge area (than standard cabins) and sleeping area. Butler service is standard.

Butler Service: Butler service (in all cabins designated as suites) includes full breakfast, in-suite lunch and dinner service (as required), afternoon tea service, evening hors d'oeuvres, complimentary espresso and cappuccino, daily news delivery, shoeshine service, and other personal touches.

Suite occupants in Penthouse, Royal, Celebrity and Sky suites also get welcome champagne; a full personal computer in each suite, including a printer and internet access (on request in the Sky Suites); choice of films from a video library; personalized stationery; tote bag; priority dining room seating preferences; private portrait sitting, bathrobe; and in-suite massage service.

Standard Outside-View/Interior (No View) Cabins: All other outside-view and interior (no view) cabins have a lounge area with sofa or convertible sofa bed, sleeping area with twin beds that can convert to a double bed, a good amount of closet and drawer space, personal safe, mini-bar/refrigerator (extra cost), interactive television, and private bathroom. The cabins are nicely decorated with warm wood-finish furniture, and there is none of the boxy feel of cabins in so many ships, due to the angled placement of vanity and audio-video consoles. Even the smallest cabin has a good-sized bathroom and shower enclosure.

Wheelchair-Accessible Suites/Cabins: Wheelchair accessibility is provided in six Sky Suites, three premium outside-view, eight deluxe ocean-view, four standard ocean-view and five interior (no view) cabins measuring 347–362 sq. ft (32.2–33.6 sq. meters). They are located in the most practical parts of the ship and close to lifts for good accessibility – all have doorways and bathroom doorways, and showers are wheelchair-accessible. Some cabins have extra berths for third or third and fourth occupants (note, however, that there is only one safe for personal belongings, which must be shared).

CUISINE/DINING. The 1,198-seat San Marco Restaurant is the ship's formal dining room. It is two decks high, has a grand staircase connecting the two levels (on the upper level of which is a musicians' gallery), and a huge glass wall overlooking the sea at the stern of the ship (electrically operated blinds provide several different backdrops). There are two seatings for dinner (with open seating for breakfast and lunch), at tables for two, four, six, eight or 10. The dining room, like all large dining halls, can be extremely noisy. The menu variety is good, the food is tasty, and it is very attractively presented and served in a well orchestrated operation that displays fine European traditions and training. Full service in-cabin dining is also available for all meals (including dinner).

For casual eating, the Seaside Cafe & Grill is a self-serve buffet area, with six principal serving lines, and around 750 seats; there is also a grill and pizza bar. Each evening, casual alternative dining takes place here (reservations are needed, although there's no additional charge), with tablecloths on tables and a modicum of service.

Alternative (Reservations-Only, Extra Cost) Dining: The Ocean Liners Restaurant is the ship's alternative dining salon; it is adjacent to the conference center. The decor includes some lacquered paneling from the famed 1920s French ocean liner Ile de France. Fine tableside prepara-

tion is the feature of this alternative dining room, whose classic French cuisine and service is outstanding (it is masterminded by Michel Roux, owner of a three-star Michelin restaurant in England). Menu items have been culled from galleys of the ocean liners of yesteryear. This is haute cuisine at the height of professionalism, for this is, indeed, a room for a full savoring, and not merely for dinner, featuring the French culinary arts of découpage and flambé. However, with just 115 seats, not all passengers are able to experience it even once during a one-week cruise (reservations are necessary, and a cover charge of $25 per person applies). There's a dine-in wine cellar (with more than 200 labels from around the world) and a demonstration galley.

Cova Café di Milano: The Cova Café di Milano is a signature item aboard all the ships of Celebrity Cruises, and a seagoing version of the original 1756 Café di Milano, located next to La Scala Opera House in Milan. The café is in a prominent position, on the third level of the atrium lobby. It is a delightful meeting place, and the place to see and be seen, for those who appreciate fine Italian coffees (for espresso, espresso macchiato, cappuccino, latte), pastries and superb cakes in an elegant, refined setting. The breakfast pastries are really superb (the favourite seems to be Pane con Cioccolata – chocolate pastry).

ENTERTAINMENT. The 900-seat Celebrity Theatre is the three-deck-high venue for the ship's production shows and major cabaret acts. It is located in the forward part of the ship, with seating on the main level and two balcony levels. The large stage is equipped with a full fly loft behind its traditional proscenium.

SPA/FITNESS. Wellness facilities include a large AquaSpa measuring 24,219 sq. ft (2,250 sq. meters). It has a large thalassotherapy pool under a huge solarium dome, complete with health bar for light breakfast and lunch items and fresh squeezed fruit and vegetable juices. There are 16 treatment rooms, plus eight treatment rooms with showers and one treatment room specifically designed for wheelchair passengers, an aerobics room, gymnasium (complete with over 40 exercise machines), large male and female saunas (with a large ocean-view porthole window), a unisex thermal suite (containing several steam and shower mist rooms with different fragrances such as chamomile, eucalyptus and mint, and a glacial ice fountain), and beauty salon.

Sports facilities include a full-size basketball court, compact football, paddle tennis and volleyball, golf simulator, shuffleboard (on two different decks) and a jogging track.

● **For more extensive general information on what a Celebrity cruise is like, see pages 111–115.**

Coral Princess
★★★★

Large (Resort) Ship: . . . . .91,627 tons	Passengers	Cabins (wheelchair accessible): 20
Lifestyle: . . . . .Standard	(lower beds/all berths): 1,974/2,590	Cabin Current: . . . . .110 volts
Cruise Line: . . . . .Princess Cruises	Passenger Space Ratio	Elevators: 12
Former Names: . . . . .none	(lower beds/all berths): 46.4/35.3	Casino (gaming tables): . . . . .Yes
Builder: Chantiers de l'Atlantique (France)	Crew/Passenger Ratio	Slot Machines: . . . . .Yes
Original Cost: . . . .$360 million	(lower beds/all berths): 2.1/2.8	Swimming Pools (outdoors): 2
Entered Service: . . . . .Dec 2002	Navigation Officers: . . . . .British	(+ 1 splash pool)
Registry: . . . . .Bermuda	Cabins (total): 987	Swimming Pools (indoors): 0
Length (ft/m): 964.5/294.0	Size Range (sq ft/m): 156–470.0/	Whirlpools: 5
Beam (ft/m): 105.6/32.2	14.4–43.6	Self-Service Launderette: . . . . .Yes
Draft (ft/m): 26/7.9	Cabins (outside view): 879	Dedicated Cinema/Seats: . . . . .No
Propulsion/Propellers: . . . . .gas turbine/2	Cabins (interior/no view): 108	Library: . . . . .Yes
Passenger Decks: 11	Cabins (for one person): 0	Classification Society: . . .Lloyd's Register
Total Crew: 900	Cabins (with private balcony): 727	

OVERALL SCORE: 1,544 (OUT OF A POSSIBLE 2,000 POINTS)

OVERVIEW. *Coral Princess* has an instantly recognizable funnel due to two jet engine-like pods that sit high up on its structure but really are mainly for decoration. Four diesel engines provide the generating power. Electrical power is provided by a combination of four diesel and one gas turbine (CODAG) unit; the diesel engines are located in the engine room, while the gas turbine unit is located in the ship's funnel housing. The ship also has three bow thrusters and three stern thrusters.

The ship's interior layout is similar to that of the *Grand Princess*-class ships (but with two decks full of public rooms, lounges and bars instead of just one), and sensibly has three major stair towers for passengers (good from the safety and evacuation viewpoint), with plenty of lifts for easy access. For a large ship, the layout is quite user-friendly, and less disjointed than many ships of a similar size and, because of its slim beam, the ship is able to transit the Panama Canal, thus providing greater flexibility in deployment than the *Grand Princess*-class ships.

New facilities not before incorporated into a Princess Cruises ship include a flower shop (where you can order flowers and Godiva chocolates for cabin delivery – good for a birthday or anniversary), cigar lounge (Churchill Lounge), and martini bar (Crooners). Also different is a casino with a London theme.

What is very civilized is the fact that sunbathers who use the "quiet" deck forward of the mast have their own splash pool, so they won't have to go down two decks to get to the two main pools. Strollers will like the ship's full wrap-around exterior promenade deck.

Surfers can find an AOL Internet Cafe conveniently

BERLITZ'S RATINGS

	Possible	Achieved
Ship	500	436
Accommodation	200	154
Food	400	261
Service	400	294
Entertainment	100	85
Cruise	400	314

located on the top level of the four-deck-high lobby. The dreaded "fine arts" get their own room, so that paintings to be sold during the art auctions are not spread all over the ship. Adjacent is the Wedding Chapel (a live web-cam can relay ceremonies via the internet). The ship's captain can legally marry (American) couples, due to the ship's registry and a special dispensation (this should, however, be verified when in the planning stage, and may depend on where you live). Princess Cruises offers three wedding packages – Pearl, Emerald, Diamond; the fee includes registration and official marriage certificate. The Wedding Chapel can also host "renewal of vows" ceremonies (there is a fee).

ACCOMMODATION. There are 33 price categories, in six types: 16 Suites with balcony (470 sq. ft/43.6 sq. meters); 184 Mini-Suites with balcony (285–302 sq. ft/26.4–28.0 sq. meters); 8 Mini-Suites without balcony (300 sq. ft/27.8 sq. meters; 527 Outside-View Cabins with balcony (217–232 sq. ft/ 20.1–21.5 sq. meters); 144 Standard Outside-view Cabins (162 sq. ft/15 sq. meters); Interior (no view) Cabins (156 sq. ft/144.5 sq. meters). There are also 20 wheelchair-accessible cabins (217–374 sq. ft/20.1–34.7 sq. meters). Note that all measurements are approximate. Almost all of the outside-view cabins have a private balcony. Some cabins can accommodate a third, or third and fourth person (good for families with children). Some cabins on Emerald Deck (Deck 8) have a view obstructed by lifeboats.

Suites: There are just 16 suites and, although none are really that large (when compared to such ships as *Norwegian Dawn* and *Norwegian Star*, where the largest suites measure a whopping 5,350 sq. ft/497 sq. meters, for example), each has a private balcony. All are named after islands (mostly coral-based islands in the Indian Ocean and Pacific Ocean). All suites are located on either Deck 9 or Deck 10. In a departure from many ships, *Coral Princess* does not have any suites or cabins with a view of the ship's stern. There are also four Premium Suites, located sensibly in the center of the ship, adjacent to a bank of six lifts. Six other suites (called Verandah Suites) are located further aft.

All Accommodation: All suites and cabins are equipped with a refrigerator, personal safe, television (with audio channels), hairdryer, satellite-dial telephone, and twin beds that convert to a queen-sized bed (there are a few exceptions). All accommodation has a bathroom with shower enclosure and toilet. Accommodation designated as suites and mini-suites (there are seven price categories) has a bathtub and separate shower enclosure, and two televisions.

All passengers receive turndown service and chocolates on pillows each night, bathrobes (on request) and toiletry amenity kits (larger, naturally, for suite/mini-suite occupants). There are no cabins for singles. Princess Cruises typically includes CNN, CNBC, ESPN and TNT on the in-cabin color television system (when available). There are no butlers – even for the top-grade suites. Cabin attendants have too many cabins to look after (typically 20), which does not translate to fine personal service.

CUISINE/DINING. The two main dining rooms, Bordeaux and Provence, are located in the forward section of the ship on the two lowest passenger decks, with the galley all the way forward so it doesn't intersect public spaces. Both are almost identical in design and layout (the ceilings are quite low and make the rooms appear more cramped than they are), and have plenty of intimate alcoves and cozy dining spots, with tables for two, four, six, or eight. There are two seatings for dinner, while breakfast and lunch are on an open-seating basis; you may have to stand in line at peak times, just as in almost any large restaurant ashore. Both dining rooms are non-smoking.

Horizon Court is the ship's casual 24-hour eatery, and is located in the forward section of Lido Deck, with superb ocean views. Several self-serve counters provide an array of food for breakfast and lunch buffets, and offer bistro-style casual dinners in the evening.

Alternative (Extra Charge) Eateries: There are two "alternative" dining rooms (Sabatini's and the Bayou Cafe), both enclosed (i.e. not open areas which passengers can walk through, as in some Princess Cruises ships). Both cost extra, and you must make a reservation.

Sabatini's is an Italian eatery, with colorful tiled Mediterranean-style decor; it is named after Trattoria Sabatini, the 200-year old institution in Florence (where there is no cover charge). It has Italian-style pizzas and pastas, with a variety of sauces, as well as Italian-style entrées (including tiger prawns and lobster tail – all provided with flair and entertainment by the waiters). The food is both creative and tasty (with seriously sized portions). Sabatini's is by reservation only, and there is a cover charge of $15 per person, for lunch or dinner (on sea days only).

The Bayou Cafe is open for lunch and dinner, and has a cover charge of $10 per person (including a free Hurricane cocktail), and evokes the charm of New Orleans' French Quarter, complete with wrought-iron decoration. The Bayou Cafe has Creole food (with platters such as Peel 'n' Eat Shrimp Piquante, Sausage Grillades, Oysters Sieur de Bienville and N'Awlins Crawfish "Mud Bug" Bisque delivered to the table when you arrive). Popular entrées include Seafood Gumbo, and Chorizo Jambalaya with fresh seafood and traditional dried spice mixes, as well as Cajun Grill items such as Smothered Alligator Ribs, Flambeaux Grilled Jumbo Prawns, Corn Meal Fried Catfish, Blackened Chicken Brochette, and Red Pepper Butter Broiled Lobster; desserts include sweet potato pie and banana whiskey pound cake. The room sports a small stage, with baby grand piano, and live jazz is also part of the dining scenario.

Other outlets include La Pâtisserie, in the ship's reception lobby coffee, cakes and pastries spot; a good place for informal meetings; there's also a Pizzeria, hamburger grill, and an ice cream bar (extra charge for the ice cream). Meanwhile, puffers and sippers should enjoy Churchill's, a neat cigar and cognac lounge, cleverly sited near a little hideaway bar called the Rat Pack Bar.

ENTERTAINMENT. The Princess Theatre is two decks high, and, unusually, there is much more seating in the upper level than on the main floor below. There are typically two production shows on a 7-day cruise, and three on a 10-day cruise. These are colorful, glamorous shows with well designed costumes and good lighting.

A second entertainment lounge (Universe Lounge) is designed more for cabaret-style features. It also has two levels (a first for a Princess Cruises ship), and three separate stages – so nonstop entertainment can be provided without constant set-ups. Some 50 of the room's seats are equipped with a built-in laptop computer. The room is also used for cooking demonstrations (it has a full kitchen set), and other life-enrichment participation activities. There is a good mix of music in the various bars and lounges.

For self-improvement, Princess Cruises' new "Scholar-Ship@Sea" program offers about 20 courses per cruise (six on any given day at sea). Although all introductory classes are free, if you want to continue any chosen subject in a smaller setting, charges apply. There are four core subjects: Culinary Arts, Visual/Creative Arts, Photography, and Computer Technology. There is a full culinary demonstration kitchen and a pottery studio complete with kiln.

SPA/FITNESS. The Lotus Spa is located aft on one of the ship's uppermost decks. It contains men's and women's saunas, steam rooms, changing rooms, relaxation area, beauty salon, aerobics exercise room and gymnasium with ocean-views packed with the latest high-tech muscle-pumping, cardio-vascular equipment. There are several large rooms for individual treatments.

● **For more extensive general information about a Princess Cruises cruise experience, see pages 124–127.**

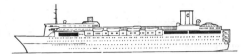

Costa Allegra
★★★

Mid-Size Ship: ....28,430 tons	Total Crew: 400	Cabins (with private balcony): 10
Lifestyle: ....Standard	Passengers	Cabins (wheelchair accessible): 8 (interior)
Cruise Line: Costa Crociere (Costa Cruises)	(lower beds/all berths): 820/1,072	Cabin Current: ....110 and 220 volts
Former Names: ....Annie Johnson	Passenger Space Ratio	Elevators: 4
Builder: ....Mariotti Shipyards (Italy)	(lower beds/all berths): 34.7/26.5	Casino (gaming tables): .... Yes
Original Cost: ....$175 million	Crew/Passenger Ratio	Slot Machines: ....Yes
Entered Service: ....Dec 1992	(lower beds/all berths): 2.0/2.6	Swimming Pools (outdoors): 1
Registry: ....Italy	Navigation Officers: ....Italian	Swimming Pools (indoors): 0
Length (ft/m): 616.1/187.8	Cabins (total): 410	Whirlpools: 2
Beam (ft/m): 83.9/25.6	Size Range (sq ft/m): 105.4–575.8/	Self-Service Launderette: ....No
Draft (ft/m): 23.9/7.3	9.8–53.5	Dedicated Cinema/Seats: ....No
Propulsion/Propellers: ....diesel	Cabins (outside view): 218	Library: ....Yes
(19,200kW)/2	Cabins (interior/no view): 192	Classification Society: ...Registro Navale
Passenger Decks: 8	Cabins (for one person): 0	Italiano (RINA)

OVERALL SCORE: 1,206 (OUT OF A POSSIBLE 2,000 POINTS)

OVERVIEW. *Costa Allegra* originally began life as a container ship built for Sweden's Johnson Line. However, the ship underwent a skillful transformation into contemporary cruise ship, which resulted in a jazzy, rather angular-looking ship with a low-slung appearance (fine when it debuted, but now looking rather outdated). There are three bolt-upright yellow funnels that have become a signature item for almost all Costa Cruises' ships. Slightly longer and larger than its sister ship *Costa Marina* (after the addition of a 44ft/13.4-meter section), this vessel has a much better standard of interior fit and finish, and more outdoors space than its sister ship. It has an interesting glass-enclosed stern.

There is a high glass-to-steel ratio for the size of the ship, with numerous glass domes and walls admitting light, as well as Murano glass light fixtures in some places. There is a good amount of outdoor deck and sunbathing space, although there is no observation lounge with forward-facing views over the ship's bows. Cushioned pads are provided for the deck lounge chairs outdoors.

The decks are named after famous painters. This ship has surprisingly nice interior decor, with cool, restful colors and soft furnishings, as well as domed ceilings and an extensive use of glass.

Costa Allegra will provide a decent first cruise experience for young adults who enjoy European-style service and a real upbeat, almost elegant atmosphere with an Italian accent and lots of noise. However, few of the officers and crew are actually Italian, as one might expect. The onboard currency is the euro.

There are few public restrooms. The children's room is

BERLITZ'S RATINGS

	Possible	Achieved
Ship	500	307
Accommodation	200	130
Food	400	218
Service	400	249
Entertainment	100	62
Cruise	400	240

really far too small, and the ship is simply not equipped to handle large numbers of children (particularly during peak holidays). The many loud and extended announcements (in several languages) quickly become tiresome. The opening hours for the small library are minimal. Tipping envelopes state the amount you are expected to give.

ACCOMMODATION. There are 12 categories (the price will depend on grade, location and size). The standard cabins are quite light and airy, with splashes of fabric colors, and wood accenting, and are laid out in a practical manner. However, they are small, and there is little closet and drawer space, so take only casual clothing. There are many small interior (no view) cabins, and all cabins suffer from poor soundproofing. Many cabins also have pull-down (Pullman-style) berths for a third or fourth occupant. The bathrooms are compact, although they do have good shower enclosures, with sliding circular door instead of the usual limp curtain. The cabin service menu is extremely limited.

On Rousseau Deck there are three forward-facing suites (the largest accommodation on board), each of which has a living room, dinette and wet bar. A further 10 slightly smaller mini-suites feature a small, very narrow balcony, but it is really not private, as it can be seen from the walking track on the deck above.

CUISINE/DINING. The Montmartre Restaurant has 370 seats, and operates in two seatings. It is fairly spacious and has expansive glass windows that look out over the stern, while the port side and starboard side have large portholes. It is a very noisy room, with tables for four, six, eight or 10 (there are no tables for two). Note that the time for dinner is later when the ship operates in Europe. Romantic candlelight dining is typically part of a formal night. The Yacht Club is the informal dining spot, with two small centrally located buffet lines. As far as breakfast and lunch buffets are concerned, Costa Cruises comes way down the list; the self-service buffets are rather plain, repetitive and unimaginative, and fresh (ripe) fruit and cheese selections are quite poor. For ice-cream lovers, a gelati cart provides welcome relief at least once each day.

Excellent cappuccino and espresso coffees are always available in various bars around the ship, served in the right sized china cups.

ENTERTAINMENT. The Folies Berg res Showroom is a single level room. The sight lines are adequate, but could be better (14 pillars obstruct sight lines from several seats). Because it is only a single-level room, its poor ceiling height precludes jugglers and the like from working, and limits what can be achieved. In other words, don't expect much. The room is quite adequate, however, as a cabaret lounge.

For live dance music and listening music, head to the Flamenco Ballroom, located at the aft end of the ship. In addition, the Crystal Club Discotheque, one deck above the Flamenco Ballroom, is the place for the young at heart, late of night, and hard of hearing.

SPA/FITNESS. The Caracalla Spa facilities are not large, but they include a solarium, eight treatment rooms, sauna and steam rooms for men and women, beauty salon and gymnasium with floor-to-ceiling windows on three sides. There is also a jogging track outdoors.

The spa is operated by Steiner, a specialist concession, whose young staff will try to sell you Steiner's own-brand Elemis beauty products (spa girls have sales targets). Some fitness classes are free, while some, such as yoga, and kick-boxing, cost $10 per class. However, being aboard will give you an opportunity to try some of the more exotic treatments (particularly some of the massages available). Massage (including exotic massages such as Aroma Stone massage, Chakra Balancing massage and other well-being massages), facials, pedicures, and beauty salon treatments are at extra cost (massage, for example, costs about $2 per minute, plus gratuity). Do make appointments early as time slots can go quickly aboard the ship.

● **For more extensive general information on what a Costa Cruises cruise is like, see pages 115–118.**

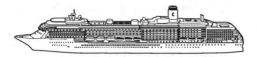

Costa Atlantica
★★★★

Large (Resort) Ship: ....85,700 tons	Passenger Decks: 12	Cabins (with private balcony): 742
Lifestyle: ....Standard	Total Crew: 920	Cabins (wheelchair accessible): 8
Cruise Line: ....Costa Crociere	Passengers	Cabin Current: ....110 volts
(Costa Cruises)	(lower beds/all berths): 2,112/2,680	Elevators: 12
Former Names: ....none	Passenger Space Ratio	Casino (gaming tables): ....Yes
Builder: ....Kverner Masa-Yards (Finland)	(lower beds/all berths): 40.5/31.9	Slot Machines: ....Yes
Original Cost: ....$335 million	Crew/Passenger Ratio	Swimming Pools (outdoors): 2
Entered Service: ....July 2000	(lower beds/all berths): 2.3/2.9	(+1 indoor/outdoor)
Registry: ....Italy	Navigation Officers: ....Italian	Swimming Pools (indoors): ....No
Length (ft/m): 959.6/292.5	Cabins (total): 1,056	Whirlpools: ....Yes
Beam (ft/m): 105.6/32.2	Size Range (sq ft/m): 161.4–387.5/	Self-Service Launderette: ....No
Draft (ft/m): 25.5/7.8	15.0–36.0	Dedicated Cinema/Seats: ....No
Propulsion/Propellers: .....diesel-electric	Cabins (outside view): 843	Library: ....Yes
(34,000 kW)/2 azimuthing pods	Cabins (interior/no view): 213	Classification Society: ...Registro Navale
(17.6 MW each)	Cabins (for one person): 0	Italiano (RINA)

OVERALL SCORE: 1,438 (OUT OF A POSSIBLE 2,000 POINTS)

OVERVIEW. *Costa Atlantica* has basically the same exterior design and internal layout as that of parent company Carnival Cruise Lines' *Carnival Legend, Miracle, Pride* and *Spirit*. There are two centrally located swimming pools outdoors, one of which can be used in poor weather due to its retractable magrodome cover. A bar abridges two adjacent whirlpool tubs. There's a smaller pool for children, and a winding water slide that spans two decks in height (it starts on a platform bridge between the two aft funnels). There is an additional whirlpool tub outdoors.

Inside, the layout is somewhat of an extension of that found in previous newbuilds for Costa Cruises – particularly that of *Costa Victoria*. As you might expect, the deck names are inspired by Federico Fellini movies (Roma Deck, Le Notte di Cabiria, La Voce della Luna, La Strada, La Luci del Varieta). There's even a deck named after a Fellini TV movie, Ginger and Fred. The interior design is, however, bold and brash – a mix of classical Italy and contemporary features. Good points include the fact that the interior design allows good passenger flow from one public space to another, and there are several floor spaces for dancing, and a range of bars and lounges for socializing.

You'll be struck by the immense size of the lobby space spanning eight decks. Take a drink from the lobby bar and look upwards – the surroundings are stunning. A small chapel is located forward of the uppermost level.

Other facilities include a winding shopping street with boutique stores (Fendi, Gianni Versace, Paul & Shark Yachting – as well as a shop dedicated to selling Caffe Flo-

BERLITZ'S RATINGS

	Possible	Achieved
Ship	500	427
Accommodation	200	152
Food	400	240
Service	400	273
Entertainment	100	64
Cruise	400	282

rian products), photo gallery, video games room, an observation balcony, a casino and library (with internet access).

Costa Cruises has updated its image, and is retraining its staff. With the debut of *Costa Atlantica* came many new, better, uniforms for many departments, as well as more choice in a ship that is designed to wow the hip and trendy as well as pay homage to many of Italy's great art and past masters.

Food and service levels have been raised to a better standard than that found aboard most other Costa Cruises ships to date. All printed materials (room service folio, menus, etc.) are in six languages (Italian, English, French, German, Portuguese, Spanish). The onboard currency is the US dollar or euro, depending on the region of operation.

Some tables in the Tiziano Dining Room have a less than comfortable view of the harsh lighting of the escalators between the galley and the two decks of the dining room.

Too many pillars obstruct passenger flow and sight lines throughout the ship. The many pillars in the dining room make it difficult for waiters to provide proper food service. The fit and finish of some interior decoration is quite poor. The hospitality levels and service are inconsistent, and below the standard of several other "major" cruise lines.

SUITABLE FOR: *Costa Atlantica* is best suited to young (and young at heart) couples and singles (plus families with children) that enjoy big city life, piazzas and outdoor cafes, constant activity accompanied by lots of noise (some call it ambiance), late nights, entertainment that is consistently loud, and an international mix of fellow passengers.

ACCOMMODATION. There are 14 categories. There is a healthy (78 percent) proportion of outside-view to interior (no view) cabins. All cabins have twin beds that convert into a queen-sized bed, individually controlled air-conditioning, television, and telephone. Many cabins have views obstructed by lifeboats on Deck 4 (Roma Deck), the lowest of the accommodation decks, as well as some cabins on Deck 5. Some cabins have pull-down (Pullman-style) berths that are fully hidden in the ceiling when not in use. There is too much use of fluorescent lighting in the suites and cabins, and the soundproofing could be much better. Some bathroom fixtures – bath and shower taps in particular – are frustrating to use until you get the hang of them.

Some of the most desirable suites and cabins are those with private balconies on five aft-facing decks (Decks 4, 5, 6, 7, and 8) with views overlooking the stern and ship's wash. The other cabins with private balconies will find the balconies not so private – the partition between one balcony and the next is not a full partition – so you might be able to hear your neighbors.

However, these balcony occupants all have good views through glass and wood-topped railings, and the deck is made of teak. The cabins are well laid out, typically with twin beds that convert to a queen-sized bed, vanity desk (with built-in hairdryer), large TV set, personal safe, and one closet that has moveable shelves – providing more space for luggage storage. However, the lighting is fluorescent, and much too harsh. The bathroom is a simple, modular unit that has shower enclosures with soap dispenser.

The largest suites are designated Penthouse Suites, although they are really quite small when compared with suites aboard other ships of a similar size. However, they do at least offer more space to move around in, and a slightly larger, better bathroom.

CUISINE/DINING. The large Tiziano Dining Room is located in the aft section of the ship on two levels, with a spiral stairway between them. There are two seatings, with tables for two, four, six or eight. Dinner on European cruises is typically scheduled at 7pm and 9pm to accommodate the later eating habits of Europeans. Themed evenings are a part of the Costa Cruises tradition, and three different window blinds help create a different feel. However, the artwork is placed at table height, so the room seems more closed-in than it should.

Alternative Dining: A reservations-only alternative for dinner, Ristorante Club Atlantica, with menus by Gualtiero Marchesi, is available six nights a week. There is a cover/service charge of $18.75 per person (passengers occupying suite-grade accommodation get a free pass for one evening). The food is decidedly better than in the main dining room, although it's nothing special.

Undoubtedly the place that most people will want to see and be seen is in the informal Caffe Florian – a replica of the famous indoor/outdoor cafe that opened in 1720 in St. Mark's Square, Venice. There are four separate salons (Sala delle Stagioni, Sala del Senato, Sala Liberty, and Sala degli Uomini Illustri), and the same fascinating mosaic, marble and wood floors, opulent ceiling art, and special lampshades. Even the espresso/cappuccino machine is a duplicate of that found in the real thing. The only problem is that the chairs are much too small.

Casual breakfast and luncheon self-serve buffet-style meals can be taken in the Botticelli Buffet Restaurant, adjacent to the swimming pools, with seating both indoors and outdoors. A grill (for hamburgers and hot dogs) and a pasta bar are conveniently adjacent to the second pool, while indoors is the Napoli Pizzeria.Excellent cappuccino and espresso coffees are always available in various bars around the ship, served in the right-sized china cups.

ENTERTAINMENT. A three-deck-high showlounge (the Caruso Theater) is an imposing room, with just over 1,000 seats. Spiral stairways at the back of the lounge connect all levels. Stage shows are best seen from the upper three levels, from where the sight lines are reasonably good. Directly underneath the showlounge is the Coral Lounge, a large lounge complete with its own bar. An onboard resident troupe of singers and dancers provides the cast members for colorful, high-energy production shows. However, the production shows are loud and quite poor. For nights when there are no production shows, the showlounge presents cabaret acts such as singers, comedy jugglers, magicians, ventriloquists, and so on. These are generally ho-hum, however.

A number of bands and small musical units provide a variety of live music in many of the ship's lounges and bars, and there is a discotheque.

SPA/FITNESS. The Ischia Spa is quite expansive, spanning two decks. Facilities include a solarium, eight treatment rooms, lecture rooms, sauna and steam rooms for men and women, a beauty parlor. A large gymnasium has floor-to-ceiling windows on three sides, including forward-facing ocean views, and an aerobics room with instructor-led classes. There is also a jogging track outdoors.

The spa is operated by Steiner, a specialist concession, whose young staff will try to sell you Steiner's own-brand Elemis beauty products. Some fitness classes are free, while some, such as yoga, and kick-boxing, cost $10 per class.

Massage (including exotic massages such as Aroma Stone massage, Chakra Balancing massage and other well-being massages), facials, pedicures, and beauty salon treatments are at extra cost (massage, for example, costs about $2 per minute, plus gratuity). Do make appointments as early as possible since time slots go quickly.

● **For more extensive general information on what a Costa Cruises cruise is like, see pages 115–118.**

Costa Classica
★★★ +

Mid-Size Ship: . . . . .52,950 tons	Total Crew: 650	Cabins (wheelchair accessible): 6	
Lifestyle: . . . . .Standard	Passengers	(interior)	
Cruise Line: . . . . .Costa Crociere	(lower beds/all berths): 1,308/1,766	Cabin Current: . . . . .110 and 220 volts	
(Costa Cruises)	Passenger Space Ratio	Elevators: 8	
Former Names: . . . . .none	(lower beds/all berths): 40.4/29.9	Casino (gaming tables): . . . . .Yes	
Builder: . . . . .Fincantieri (Italy)	Crew/Passenger Ratio	Slot Machines: . . . . .Yes	
Original Cost: . . . .$287 million	(lower beds/all berths): 2.0/2.7	Swimming Pools (outdoors): 2	
Entered Service: . . . . .Jan 1992	Navigation Officers: . . . . .Italian	Swimming Pools (indoors): 0	
Registry: . . . . .Italy	Cabins (total): 654	Whirlpools: 4	
Length (ft/m): 718.5/220.61	Size Range (sq ft/m): 185.1–430.5/	Self-Service Launderette: . . . . .No	
Beam (ft/m): 98.4/30.80	17.2–40.0	Dedicated Cinema/Seats: . . . . .No	
Draft (ft/m): 25.0/7.60	Cabins (outside view): 438	Library: . . . . .Yes	
Propulsion/Propellers: . . . . .diesel	Cabins (interior/no view): 216	Classification Society: . . .Registro Navale	
(22,800kW)/2	Cabins (for one person): 0	Italiano (RINA)	
Passenger Decks: 10	Cabins (with private balcony): 10		

OVERALL SCORE: 1,368 (OUT OF A POSSIBLE 2,000 POINTS)

OVERVIEW. *Costa Classica* is an all-white ship (now over 10 years old) with a straight slab-sided unflattering profile, which is topped by Costa Cruises' unmistakable trademark trio of tall yellow funnels. This was the ship that brought Costa into the mainstream of cruising, Italian-style, and was part of a multi-million plan to modernize the Costa Cruises (Costa Crociere) fleet.

Inside, the ship has contemporary, innovative Italian design and styling that is best described as befitting European tastes. The design incorporates much use of circles (large portholes instead of windows can be found in cabins on lower decks, and in the dining room, self-serve buffet area, coffee bar, and discotheque, for example). There is an excellent range of public rooms, lounges and bars. A number of specially designed business and meeting facilities can be found; the rooms provide multi-flexible configurations.

Some fascinating artwork includes six hermaphrodite statues in one lounge. There is a fine, if unconventional multi-tiered amphitheater-style showlounge, but the seats are bolt upright and downright uncomfortable for more than a few minutes. The multi-level atrium is stark, angular, and cold. The marble-covered staircases look pleasant, but are uncarpeted and a little dangerous if water or drinks are spilled on them when the ship is moving).

Perhaps the interior is best described as an innovative design project that almost works. A forward observation lounge/nightclub sits atop ship like a lump of cheese, and, unfortunately, fails to work well as a nightclub. Internet access is available from one of several computer terminals in the Internet Cafe.

BERLITZ'S RATINGS

	Possible	Achieved
Ship	500	388
Accommodation	200	154
Food	400	218
Service	400	282
Entertainment	100	64
Cruise	400	262

In November 2002 the ship was scheduled to enter dry-dock for a $10 million "chop-and-stretch" operation to increase its tonnage to 78,000, its length to 870.7 ft (265.4 meters), and its passenger capacity to 2,516. However, this was shelved due to a dispute over the quality of workmanship that was produced by British shipyard Cammell Laird.

There is no wrap-around promenade deck outdoors. The ship's rather slow service speed (19.5 knots) means that itineraries have to be carefully chosen, as the ship cannot compete with the newer ships with faster service speeds.

The air-conditioning system in the Tivoli Dining Room is noisy. There are too many loud, repetitious and irritating announcements. Shore excursions are very expensive. Tipping envelopes provided in your cabin state the amount you are expected to give. The onboard currency is the euro.

SUITABLE FOR: *Costa Classica* is best suited to young (and young at heart) couples and singles (plus families with children) that enjoy big city life, piazzas and outdoor cafes, constant activity accompanied by lots of noise (some call it ambiance), late nights, and entertainment that is consistently loud, and an international mix of fellow passengers.

ACCOMMODATION. There are 11 categories, the price depending on grade, size and location). These include 10 suites, while other cabins are fairly standard in size, shape, and facilities, a higher price being asked for cabins on the highest decks. All suites and cabins have twin lower beds, color television, and telephone.

Suites: The 10 suites, located in the center of Portofino Deck, each have a private rounded balcony, marble-clad bathrooms with Jacuzzi bathtub, and separate shower enclosure. There is plenty of space in the living and sleeping areas, and for the storage of luggage, as these really are very spacious suites.

Standard Outside-View/Interior (No View) Cabins: In general, the cabins are of a fairly generous size, and are laid out in a practical manner. They have cherry wood veneered cabinetry and accenting, and include a vanity desk unit with a large mirror. There are useful (unusual, for a cruise ship) sliding doors to the bathroom and closets, and the good cabin soundproofing is much appreciated. The soft furnishings are of good quality, but the room service menu is disappointing. The suites have more space (although they are not large by any means), and hand-woven bedspreads.

Some cabins have one or two extra pull-down (Pullman-style) berths – useful for families with small children.

CUISINE/DINING. The Tivoli Dining Room has a lovely indented clean white ceiling, although it is extremely noisy (there are two seatings, with dinner typically at 7pm and 9pm to accommodate the later eating habits of Europeans), and there are a good number of tables for two, as well as tables for four, six or eight. Changeable wall panels help create a European Renaissance atmosphere, albeit at the expense of blocking off windows (but during dinner, it's dark outside anyway – unless you are in the far North). Romantic candlelight dining is provided on formal nights.

For casual outdoor eating, the Alfresco Cafe, with its teak deck and traditional canvas sailcloth awning, is moderately good, depending on what you expect. Unfortunately, breakfast and luncheon buffets are repetitious, quite poor and uncreative; there is little variety, and long lines are typical. The selection of bread rolls, fruits and cheeses is disappointing.

Excellent cappuccino and espresso coffees are always available in various bars around the ship, served in the right-sized china cups.

ENTERTAINMENT. The Colosseo Theater, the ship's main showlounge, has an interesting amphitheatre-like design. However, the seats are bolt upright, and quite uncomfortable for any length of time. The Galileo discotheque, located atop the ship, for the young at heart, late of night, and hard of hearing.

SPA/FITNESS. The Caracalla Spa, located on one of the ship's uppermost decks, contains a gymnasium (with good forward-facing views over the ship's bows) with some high-tech muscle-pump machines, an aerobics exercise area, two hot tubs, Roman bath, health bar, sauna and steam rooms, and beauty salon.

The spa is operated by Steiner, a specialist concession, whose young staff will try to sell you Steiner's own-brand Elemis beauty products (spa girls have sales targets). Some fitness classes are free, while some, such as yoga and kick-boxing, cost $10 per class. However, being aboard will give you an opportunity to try some of the more exotic treatments (particularly some of the massages available). Massage (including exotic massages such as Aroma Stone massage, Chakra Balancing massage and other well-being massages), facials, pedicures, and beauty salon treatments are at extra cost (massage, for example, costs about $2 per minute, plus gratuity). Do make appointments as early as possible as time slots can go quickly.

● **For more extensive general information on what a Costa Cruises cruise is like, see pages 115–118.**

THE BRIDGE

A ship's navigation bridge is manned at all times, both at sea and in port. Besides the captain, who is master of the vessel, other senior officers take "watch" turns for four- or eight-hour periods. In addition, junior officers are continually honing their skills as experienced navigators, waiting for the day when they will be promoted to master.

The captain is always in command at times of high risk, such as when the ship is entering or leaving a port, when the density of traffic is particularly high, or when visibility is severely restricted by poor weather.

Navigation has come a long way since the days of the ancient mariners, who used only the sun and the stars to calculate their course across the oceans. The space-age development of sophisticated navigation devices (using satellites) has enabled us to eliminate the guesswork of early navigation (the first global mobile satellite system came into being in 1979).

A ship's navigator today uses a variety of sophisticated instruments to pinpoint the ship's position at any time and establish its course.

Costa Europa
★★★ +

Large (Resort) Ship: ....53,872 tons	Total Crew: 650	Cabins (with private balcony): 0
Lifestyle: ....Standard	Passengers	Cabins (wheelchair accessible): 4
Cruise Line: ....Costa Crociere	(lower beds/all berths): 1,494/1,744	Cabin Current: ....110/220 volts
(Costa Cruises)	Passenger Space Ratio	Elevators: 7
Former Names: ....*Westerdam, Homeric*	(lower beds/all berths): 36.0/30.8	Casino (gaming tables): ....Yes
Builder: ....Meyer Werft (Germany)	Crew/Passenger Ratio	Slot Machines: ....Yes
Original Cost: ....$150 million	(lower beds/all berths): 2.4/2.6	Swimming Pools (outdoors): 2
Entered Service: .....May 1986/Apr 2002	Navigation Officers: ....Italian	(1 with magrodome)
Registry: ....Italy	Cabins (total): 747	Swimming Pools (indoors): 0
Length (ft/m): 797.9/243.23	Size Range (sq ft/m): 129.1–425.1/	Whirlpools: 2
Beam (ft/m): 95.1/29.00	12.0–39.5	Self-Service Launderette: ....Yes (5)
Draft (ft/m): 23.6/7.20	Cabins (outside view): 495	Dedicated Cinema/Seats: Yes/237
Propulsion/Propellers: diesel (23,830kW)/2	Cabins (interior/no view): 252	Library: ....Yes
Passenger Decks:.................9	Cabins (for one person): 18	Classification Society: ...Lloyd's Register

OVERALL SCORE: 1,394 (OUT OF A POSSIBLE 2,000 POINTS)

OVERVIEW. *Costa Europa* was originally a Home Lines cruise ship (*Homeric*) that underwent an $84 million "chop and stretch" operation in 1990 after being purchased by the previous owner, Holland America Line. You don't even have to look closely to tell where the mid-section was inserted, because the windows are larger than the fore and aft sections. The ship was moved to Costa Cruises (a cruise line wholly owned by Carnival Corporation) in 2002.

When Costa Cruises took over the ship, no structural changes were made, although some of the soft furnishings were changed and the decor was made brighter and more European in style, although, after a £5 million refit, surprisingly few changes are really noticeable. The funnel, however, looks surprisingly good in Costa Cruises' trademark yellow.

The ship has good teak outside decks and a wrap-around promenade deck with real wooden deck lounge chairs. There is also a good amount of open deck space for sunbathing. There is a magrodome-covered swimming pool deck, but unfortunately it is simply too small for the number of passengers carried.

The ship has elegant, functional, and restful interior decor. The public rooms are decorated in pastel tones, although some decor looks dated. The ship absorbs passengers well, and has good passenger flow, but the layout is a little awkward to learn at first.

Most of the public entertainment rooms are located on one deck, which makes access a simple matter. An addition, made when Costa Cruises took over the ship, is the Medusa Ballroom, with stage and proper hardwood dance floor. Also added were more children's facilities, for the

BERLITZ'S RATINGS

	Possible	Achieved
Ship	500	350
Accommodation	200	142
Food	400	271
Service	400	285
Entertainment	100	71
Cruise	400	275

increase in families that now choose this ship. There are several bars and lounges to choose from, some small and intimate, others larger and noisier. However, there are, fortunately, lots of nooks and crannies to play in – much nicer than the warehouse-style public rooms of the latest, larger, ships.

Costa Europa is a well-run, modern ship (comfortable, but certainly not luxurious) that provides a satisfactory cruise experience, particularly for families with children. There are few Italians among the crew, however (except in key positions), as many are from the Philippines.

Communication with staff is not easy; room service is particularly poor. There are no cabins with private balconies. There are too many loud, repetitious and irritating announcements. Shore excursions are very expensive. There is some noticeable vibration in some areas. Tipping envelopes provided in your cabin state the amount you are expected to give.

SUITABLE FOR: *Costa Europa* is best suited to young (and young at heart) couples and singles (plus families with children) who enjoy big city life, piazzas and outdoor cafes, constant activity accompanied by lots of noise (some call it ambiance), late nights, entertainment that is consistently loud, and an international mix of fellow passengers.

ACCOMMODATION. There are 13 cabin price categories; these include suites, mini-suites, outside-view cabins, and inside (no view) cabins (the price will depend on the grade, size and location you choose).

Except for the suite category cabins (there are five suites, each with king-sized beds, separate lounge area and bathroom with full size bathtub), almost all other cabins are of a similar size. In general, they are generously proportioned units that are well appointed and equipped with almost everything you need. Features include ample closet, drawer and storage space, hairdryer, and good-sized bathrooms (the towels are quite small, however). Unfortunately, there are far too many interior (no view) cabins (over 50 percent of all cabins), and the cabin soundproofing is rather poor – so you really can hear your neighbors brushing their hair. All cabin televisions receive European news channels.

Note that most cabins have twin beds, although there are a number that have the old-style upper and lower berths, so do make sure you request (and get) the kind of cabin with the sleeping arrangements you want when you book. Some of the larger cabins also have a sofa that turns into a bed – good for families with small children. There are four cabins for the disabled, suitably located, on higher decks, close to lifts.

CUISINE/DINING. The Orion Restaurant is a traditional dining room that has a raised central, cupola-style dome, and port and starboard side portholes are highlighted at night by pleasing lighting. There are two seatings for all meals; note that on European cruises, dinner is typically at 7pm and 9pm to accommodate the later eating habits of Europeans. Also, do take note that dining room tables are extremely close together, and, except for the center section, the ceiling is quite low (being only one deck high), and so the noise level is extremely high. The service is reasonable, but communication can prove frustrating sometimes, and smiles from the waiters and assistants can only do so much.

The cuisine is Continental in nature, but, although there is plenty of food, its quality and presentation often proves disappointing. While the quality of meats is adequate, it could be better, and is often disguised with gravies and rich sauces. Fish and seafood tend to be lacking in taste and are typically overcooked, and green vegetables are hard to come by. However, good pasta dishes are served each day (the pasta is made fresh on board daily), although quantity, not quality, is what appears from the galley. Breads and rolls are typically good, but desserts tend to be past their sell-by date.

The Andromeda Restaurant and Sirens Restaurant (both located in the aft section of the ship) provide breakfast and lunch in self-serve buffet style, but lines and a crowded environment are noisy and not really enjoyable.

Excellent cappuccino and espresso coffees are always available in various bars around the ship, served in the right-sized china cups.

ENTERTAINMENT. Entertainment facilities include the Atlantic Theater, the ship's two-decks-high showlounge, with seating on both main and balcony levels. However, several pillars obstruct sightlines from a number of seats.

An onboard resident troupe of singers and dancers provides the cast members for colorful, high-energy production shows. However, these are quite poor compared to many of the shows aboard similar sized ships, and there seems to be little consistency when it comes to entertainment strategy. Stage smoke is used a lot during the production shows, and the volume is ear-splitting. For nights when production shows are not featured, the showlounge presents cabaret acts such as singers, comedy jugglers, magicians, ventriloquists, and so on. These are generally ho-hum, however, and are more based on price rather than coherent themes.

A number of bands and small musical units provide live music in many of the ship's lounges and bars – so there is always plenty of music to dance to or listen to, from light classical to jazz to pop, dance and rap. In addition, there is a discotheque for the young at heart and hard of hearing.

SPA/FITNESS. The Nereidi Fitness Center (located on an upper deck, aft of the ship's mast) includes a gymnasium, saunas and massage rooms, although there is no steam room. The facility is rally small, considering the number of passengers carried – although, to be fair, such facilities were not very popular when the ship was built.

The spa is operated by Steiner, a specialist concession, whose young staff will try to sell you Steiner's own-brand Elemis beauty products (spa girls have sales targets). Some fitness classes are free, while some, such as yoga and kickboxing, cost $10 per class.

However, being aboard will give you an opportunity to try some of the more exotic treatments (particularly some of the massages available). Massage (including Aroma Stone massage, Chakra Balancing massage and other well-being massages), facials, pedicures, and beauty salon treatments cost extra (massage, for example, costs about $2 per minute, plus gratuity). Do make appointments as early as possible – aboard a ship so large, time slots go quickly, so the day you board is the best time to book your treatments.

● For more extensive general information on what a Costa Cruises cruise is like, see pages 115–118.

Costa Fortuna
★★★★

Large (Resort) Ship: ....105,000 tons	Passenger Decks: 13	Cabins (for one person): 0
Lifestyle: ....Standard	Total Crew: 1,068	Cabins (with private balcony): 522
Cruise Line: Costa Crociere (Costa Cruises)	Passengers	Cabins (wheelchair accessible): 8
Former Names: ....none	(lower beds/all berths): 2,716/3,470	Cabin Current: ....220 volts
Builder: .....Cantieri Sestri Navale (Italy)	Passenger Space Ratio	Elevators: 14
Original Cost: ....$381 million	(lower beds/all berths): 38.6/30.2	Casino (gaming tables): ....Yes
Entered Service: ....November 2003	Crew/Passenger Ratio	Slot Machines: ....Yes
Registry: ....Italy	(lower beds/all berths): 2.5/3.2	Swimming Pools (outdoors): 3
Length (ft/m): 892.3/272.0	Navigation Officers: ....Italian	Swimming Pools (indoors): 0
Beam (ft/m): 124.6/38.0	Cabins (total): 1,358	Whirlpools: 5
Draft (ft/m): 27.2/8.3	Size Range (sq ft/m): 179.7–482.2/	Self-Service Launderette: ....No
Propulsion/Propellers: ...diesel-electric	16.7–44.8	Dedicated Cinema/Seats: ....No
34,000kW/2 azimuthing pods	Cabins (outside view): 857	Library: ....Yes
(17.6 MW each)	Cabins (interior/no view): 501	Classification Society: ....RINA

OVERALL SCORE: 1,432 (OUT OF A POSSIBLE 2,000 POINTS)

OVERVIEW. *Costa Fortuna* (sister ship *Costa Magica* made its debut in late 2004) is the largest ship size in the Costa Cruises fleet (and the largest in Italian history). Its design is based on the platform of *Carnival Triumph* and, although the bow is extremely short, the ship presents a well balanced profile. The name Fortuna is an interesting one: in Greek mythology, Fortuna is the daughter of Poseidon (it's also the name of the Temple Fortuna, located along one of the conserved streets of Pompeii).

The aft decks are tiered, with cut off quarters that make the ship look less square than it otherwise would. There are three pools, one of which can be covered by a sliding glass dome (magrodome) in case of inclement weather, while one pool has a long water slide. There is not a lot of open deck space for the number of passengers carried, so deck lounge chairs tend to be crammed together (there are no cushioned pads).

Costa Fortuna is built to impress at every turn, and the ship absorbs passengers quite well, with a good passenger space ratio. The interior decor focuses on the Italian passenger ships of yesteryear, so much of the finishing detail replicates the Art Deco interiors fitted aboard ocean liners such as the *Conte de Savoia*, *Michaelangelo*, *Neptunia*, *Rafaello*, *Rex*, etc., although in the kind of contemporary colors not associated with such ships (their interiors were rather subdued). Deck names are those of major cities in Europe and South America (examples: Barcelona, Buenos Aires, Caracas, Lisbon, Genoa, Miami). Passenger flow is generally good, with few congestion points.

There are three decks full of lounges and there are 11 bars plus lots of rooms to play in. This ship has a nine-deck-

BERLITZ'S RATINGS

	Possible	Achieved
Ship	500	427
Accommodation	200	146
Food	400	240
Service	400	273
Entertainment	100	64
Cruise	400	282

high, glass-domed rotunda atrium lobby (it houses the Costa Bar on the lower level, and a fine collection of 26 replicas of Costa ships of yesteryear)). For those who like to gamble, the Neptunia 1932 Casino is the place to go. There's also a chapel – standard aboard all Costa ships – and a small library that could be laid out better, an internet center, card room, art gallery, and video game room.

There are few Italians among the crew, however (except in key positions), as many are from the Philippines. The greater percentage of passengers are Italian, so the ship is lively, but quite noisy, with lots of children running around (particularly during school holiday periods).

ACCOMMODATION. There are 15 grades, from 2-bed interior cabins to grand suites with private balcony, although in reality there are only three different sizes: Suites with balcony, 2- or 4-bed outside view cabins (some 335 of which have portholes rather than windows), and 2- or 4-bed interior (no-view) cabins. In an example of good design, no cabins have lifeboat obstructed views – something not easy with large ships such as this. The largest accommodation can be found in 8 Grand Suites, located in the center of the ship on one of the higher decks. They have a queen-sized bed; bathrooms have a bathtub and two washbasins.

CUISINE/DINING. The two dining rooms, the Michaelangelo 1965 Restaurant (aft), whose ceiling features frescoes by the Great Masters, and the Rafaello 1965 Restaurant (midships), are both two decks high and have two seatings. Dinner on European cruises is typically scheduled at 7pm and 9pm. There is a wine list, although there are no wine waiters and almost all wines (the majority of which are Italian) are young.

Alternative (Reservations Required Dining Option: The Conte Grande 1927 Club is an upscale dining spot with seating for around 150 under a huge glass dome (if the lights were turned out, you might be able to see the stars). In its show kitchen, chefs can be seen preparing their masterpieces. Fine table settings, china, silverware and leather-bound menus are used. Reservations are required and there is a cover charge of $18.75 per person (for service and tip)..

The Christoforo Columbus 1954 Buffet Restaurant is a self-serve eatery for breakfast, lunch, afternoon pizzas, and beverages at any time. Excellent cappuccino and espresso coffees are always available in various bars.

ENTERTAINMENT. The Rex 1932 Theater spans three decks in the forwardmost section of the ship. It is the setting for all production shows and large-scale cabaret acts, is quite stunning, and has a revolving stage, hydraulic orchestra pit, superb sound, and seating on three levels (the upper levels being tiered through two decks).

SPA/FITNESS. Facilities in the two-decks-high Saturnia 1927 Spa include a solarium, eight treatment rooms, sauna and steam rooms for men and women, and a beauty parlor. A large gymnasium has floor-to-ceiling windows on three sides, including forward-facing ocean views, and an aerobics room with instructor-led classes (some, such as yoga and kick-boxing, cost extra). If you want to be near the spa, note that there are 18 two-bed cabins (with ocean view windows) located adjacent (aft) of the spa.

● **For more extensive general information on what a Costa Cruises cruise is like, see pages 115–118.**

SHIP TALK

Gross Tons (gt): not the weight of a ship but the total volume measurement of all permanently enclosed spaces above and below decks, with certain exceptions, such as the bridge, radio room, galleys, washing facilities, and other specified areas. It is the basis for harbor dues. International regulations introduced in 1982 required shipowners to re-measure the grt (formerly gross register tons) of their vessels (1 grt = 100 cubic ft of enclosed space/2.8 cubic meters). This unit of measure was invented in England centuries ago for taxation purposes, when wine shipped from France was stored in standard-size casks, called tonneaux. Thus a ship carrying 20 casks measured 20 tons, and taxes were applied accordingly. Gross tonnage measurements may or may not include balconies.

Helm: the apparatus for steering a ship.

House Flag: the flag denoting the company to which a ship belongs.

Hull: the frame and body of the ship exclusive of masts or superstructure.

Leeward: the side of a ship that is sheltered from the wind.

Luff: the side of a ship facing the wind

Manifest: a list of the ship's passengers, crew, and cargo.

Nautical Mile: one-sixtieth of a degree of the circumference of the Earth.

Pilot: a person licensed to navigate ships into or out of a harbor or through difficult waters, and to advise the captain on handling the ship during these procedures.

Pitch: the rise and fall of a ship's bow that may occur when the ship is under way.

Port: the left side of a ship when facing forward.

Quay: berth, dock, or pier.

Rudder: a finlike device astern and below the waterline, for steering the vessel.

Screw: a ship's propeller.

Stabilizer: a gyroscopically operated retractable "fin" extending from either or both sides of the ship below the waterline to provide a more stable ride.

Starboard: the right side of the ship when facing forward.

Stern: the aftmost part of the ship that is opposite the bow.

Tender: a smaller vessel, often a lifeboat, used to transport passengers between ship and shore when the vessel is at anchor.

Wake: the track of agitated water left behind a ship when in motion.

Waterline: the line along the side of a ship's hull corresponding to the water surface.

Windward: the side of a ship facing the direction in which the wind blows.

Yaw: the erratic deviation from the ship's set course, usually caused by a heavy sea.

● *More Ship Talk, page 234.*

Costa Magica
NOT YET RATED

Large (Resort) Ship: ......105,000 tons
Lifestyle: ....Standard
Cruise Line: Costa Crociere (Costa Cruises)
Former Names: ....None
Builder: ....Fincantieri (Italy)
Original Cost: ....$418.5 million
Entered Service: ....November 2004
Registry: ....Italy
Length (ft/m): 893.3/272.3
Beam (ft/m): 124.6/38
Draft (ft/m): 27.2/8.3
Propulsion/Propellers: ....diesel-electric
34,000kW/2
azimuthing pods (17.6 MW each)

Passenger Decks: 13
Total Crew: 1,068
Passengers
(lower beds/all berths): 2,718/3,788
Passenger Space Ratio
(lower beds/all berths): 38.6/27.7
Crew/Passenger Ratio
(lower beds/all berths): 2.5/3.2
Navigation Officers: ....Italian
Cabins (total): 1,359
Size Range (sq ft/m): 179.7/482.2
Cabins (outside view): 857
Cabins (interior/no view): 501
Cabins (for one person): 0

Cabins (with private balcony): 522
Cabins (wheelchair accessible): 8
Cabin Current: ....220 volts
Elevators: 14
Casino (gaming tables): ....Yes
Slot Machines: ....Yes
Swimming Pools (outdoors): 3
Swimming Pools (indoors): 0
Whirlpools: 5
Self-Service Launderette: ....No
Dedicated Cinema/Seats: ....No
Library: ....Yes
Classification Society: ....RINA

OVERALL SCORE: NYR (OUT OF A POSSIBLE 2,000 POINTS)

OVERVIEW. Although the bow is extremely short, the ship actually presents a nicely balanced profile for a large vessel. The aft decks are tiered, with cutoff quarters that make the ship look less square than it otherwise would. There is not a lot of open deck space for the number of passengers carried, so deck lounge chairs tend to be crammed together. *Costa Magica* is built to impress at every turn, and the ship absorbs passengers quite well, with a good passenger space ratio. Passenger flow is generally good.

There are three decks full of lounges, 11 bars overall, and lots of rooms to play in. This ship has a nine-deck high, glass-domed rotunda atrium lobby (it houses the Costa Bar on the lower level). For those who like to gamble, the Casino is the place to go. There's also a chapel. There are few Italians among the crew, however (except in key positions), as many are from the Philippines. Most passengers are Italian, so the ship is lively (noisy), with lots of children running around (particularly during school holidays).

ACCOMMODATION. There are 15 grades, from two bed interior cabins to grand suites with private balcony. No cabins have lifeboat obstructed views. The largest accommodation can be found in 8 Grand Suites, located in the center of the ship on one of the higher decks. They have a queen-sized bed; bathrooms feature a bathtub and two washbasins.

CUISINE/DINING. The two dining rooms, Costa Smeralda Restaurant (aft) and the Portofino Restaurant (midships), are both two decks high, and both have two seatings. Dinner on European cruises is typically scheduled at 7pm and 9pm. Almost all the wines available are young.

BERLITZ'S RATINGS

	Possible	Achieved
Ship	500	NYR
Accommodation	200	NYR
Food	400	NYR
Service	400	NYR
Entertainment	100	NYR
Cruise	400	NYR

Alternative (Reservations Required) Dining Option: The Vincenza Tavernetta Club is an upscale dining spot with seating for around 150 under a huge glass dome. In its show kitchen, chefs can be seen preparing their masterpieces. Fine table settings, china, silverware and leather-bound menus are used. There is a cover charge of $18.75 per person (for service and tip).

The Bellagio Buffet Restaurant is a self-serve eatery for breakfast, lunch, afternoon pizzas, and beverages at any time. Excellent cappuccino and espresso coffees are available in various bars.

ENTERTAINMENT. The Urbino Theater spans three decks in the forwardmost section of the ship. It is the setting for all production shows and large-scale cabaret acts, is quite stunning, and has a revolving stage, hydraulic orchestra pit, superb sound, and seating on three levels (the upper levels being tiered through two decks).

SPA/FITNESS. Facilities in the two-decks high Saturnia Spa (it spans almost 14,000 sq. ft/1,300 sq. meters) include a solarium, eight treatment rooms, sauna and steam rooms for men and women, and a beauty parlor. A large gymnasium has floor-to-ceiling windows on three sides, including forward-facing ocean views, and an aerobics room with instructor-led classes (some, such as yoga, kick-boxing, cost extra). If you want to be near the spa, note that there are 18 two-bed cabins (with ocean view windows) located adjacent (aft) of the spa.

● **For more extensive general information on what a Costa Cruises cruise is like, see pages 115–118.**

Costa Marina
★★★

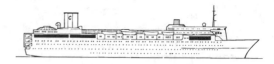

Mid-Size Ship: . . . . .25,441 tons
Lifestyle: . . . . .Standard
Cruise Line: . . . . .Costa Crociere
(Costa Cruises)
Former Names: . . . .*Axel Johnson*
Builder: . . . . . . .Mariotti Shipyards (Italy)
Original Cost: . . . .$130 million
Entered Service: . . . . .July 1990
Registry: . . . . .Italy
Length (ft/m): 571.8/174.25
Beam (ft/m): 84.6/25.75
Draft (ft/m): 26.1/8.20
Propulsion/Propellers: diesel (19,152kW)/2
Passenger Decks: 8

Total Crew: 400
Passengers
(lower beds/all berths): 772/1,005
Passenger Space Ratio
(lower beds/all berths): 32.9/25.3
Crew/Passenger Ratio
(lower beds/all berths): 1.9/2.5
Navigation Officers: . . . . .Italian
Cabins (total): 386
Size Range (sq ft/m): 104.4–264.8/
9.7–24.6
Cabins (outside view): 183
Cabins (interior/no view): 205
Cabins (for one person): 0

Cabins (with private balcony): 8
Cabins (wheelchair accessible): 0
Cabin Current: . . . . .110 and 220 volts
Elevators: 8
Casino (gaming tables): . . . . .Yes
Slot Machines: . . . . .Yes
Swimming Pools (outdoors): 1
Swimming Pools (indoors): 0
Whirlpools: 3
Self-Service Launderette: . . . . .No
Dedicated Cinema/Seats: . . . . .No
Library: . . . . .Yes
Classification Society: . . .Registro Navale
Italiano (RINA)

OVERALL SCORE: 1,224 (OUT OF A POSSIBLE 2,000 POINTS)

OVERVIEW. *Costa Marina* is an interesting, though very angular-looking, mid-sized ship, the first of two such ships converted from container carriers to passenger cruise ships (its almost identically designed, though slightly longer sister ship is *Costa Allegra*). There is a high glass-to-steel ratio, with numerous glass domes and walls. The vessel has a contemporary, cutaway stern that is virtually replaced by a glass wall (in fact, the dining room windows), and a stark upright cluster of three yellow funnels. However, today the design seems dated.

Most of the public rooms are above the accommodation decks and include several bars and lounges. This is very much an Italian ship that will provide a good first cruise experience for young European passengers. There is generally good passenger flow throughout its public room spaces, although congestion occurs when first seating passengers move from the dining room to the showlounge and other public rooms, and when second-seating passengers move from the public rooms to the dining room.

In 2002, *Costa Marina* became a ship dedicated to the German-speaking market. The ship underwent a considerable amount of interior redecoration and emerged as an Italian ship for German-speaking passengers ("La Deutsche Vita"). The onboard currency is the euro.

The fit and finish of this vessel, when it debuted as a cruise ship, were well below standard. There is a very limited amount of open deck and sunbathing space. Note that there is no observation lounge with forward-facing views. The swimming pool is really very small, and should only be considered a "dip" pool. There are simply too many interior (no view) cabins. The library is really poor. Tipping

BERLITZ'S RATINGS		
	Possible	Achieved
Ship	500	312
Accommodation	200	130
Food	400	218
Service	400	249
Entertainment	100	62
Cruise	400	253

envelopes provided in your cabin state the amount you are expected to give.

SUITABLE FOR: *Costa Marina* is best suited to young (and young at heart) German-speaking couples and singles (plus families with children) that enjoy European city life, piazzas and outdoor cafes, plenty of activities, and entertainment that is consistently loud.

ACCOMMODATION. There are 12 categories (the price will depend on the grade, size and location you choose). Both the outside view and interior (no view) cabins are quite comfortable, but have very plain, almost clinical, decor and no warmth. Bathrooms are functional, but there is little space for personal toiletry items. The illuminated cabin numbers outside each cabin are novel. The room service menu is poor.

CUISINE/DINING. The 452-seat Cristal Restaurant is fairly spacious and has expansive glass windows overlooking the stern, while port and starboard sides feature large portholes. There are two seatings but few tables for two, most of the tables being for four, six or eight. Romantic candlelight dining is typically featured on a formal night.

The cuisine is Continental in nature (with some German regional specialties featured), and, although there is plenty of food, its presentation and quality can, at times, be disappointing. The quality of meats is good (particularly the dark meats that many German-speaking passengers enjoy), although it is often disguised with gravies and rich sauces. Fish and seafood tend to be lacking in taste and are typically overcooked, and green vegetables are hard to come by. However, good pasta dishes are served each day (the pasta is made fresh on board daily), although quantity, not quality, is what appears from the galley. While the breads and rolls are typically good, the desserts are not.

The service is basically sound, although you will probably note that there are few Italian waiters, as one might expect given the vessel's ownership. There is a wine list, although there are no wine waiters (the table waiters are expected to serve both food and wine, which does not work well), and almost all wines are young – very young.

Excellent cappuccino and espresso coffees are always available in various bars around the ship, served in the right sized (proper) china cups.

ENTERTAINMENT. The Tropicana Showroom is a single level room; however, 14 pillars obstruct the sight lines from many seats. The room's poor ceiling height precludes jugglers and the like from working, and limits what can be achieved. In other words, don't expect much. The room is quite adequate, however, as a cabaret lounge.

SPA/FITNESS. The spa/fitness facilities are not large, but they include a solarium, several treatment rooms, sauna and steam rooms for men and women, beauty salon and gymnasium with floor-to-ceiling windows on three sides. There is also a jogging track outdoors.

● **For more extensive general information on what a Costa Cruises cruise is like, see pages 115–118.**

STEERING

Two different methods can be used to steer a ship: **Electrohydraulic steering** uses automatic (telemotor-type) transmission from the wheel itself to the steering gear aft. This is generally used when traffic is heavy, during maneuvers into and out of ports, or when there is poor visibility. **Automatic steering** (gyropilot) is used only in the open sea. This system does not require anyone at the wheel because it is controlled by computer. However, aboard all ships, a quartermaster is always at the wheel, for extra safety, and just in case a need should arise to switch from one steering system to another.

Satellite Navigator
Using this latest high-tech piece of equipment, ship's officers can read, on a small television screen, the ship's position in the open ocean anywhere in the world, any time, and in any weather with pinpoint accuracy.

Satellite navigation systems use the information transmitted by a constellation of orbiting satellites. Each is in a normal circular polar orbit at an altitude of 450 to 700 nautical miles, and orbits the Earth in about 108 minutes.

Data from each gives the current orbital position every two minutes. Apart from telling the ship where it is, it continuously provides the distance from any given point, calculates the drift caused by currents and so on, and tells the ship when the next satellite will pass.

The basis of the satellite navigation is the US Navy Satellite System (NNSS). This first became operational in January 1964 as the precision guidance system for the Polaris submarine fleet and was made available for commercial use in 1967.

The latest (and more accurate) system is the GPS (Global Positioning System), which is now fitted to an increasing number of ships. This uses 24 satellites (18 of which are on-line at any given time) that provide accuracy in estimating a ship's position to plus or minus 6 ft. Another variation is the NACOS (Navigational Command System), which collects information from a variety of sources: satellites, radar, gyroscopic compass, speed log, and surface navigational systems as well as engines, thrusters, rudders, and human input. It then displays relevant computations and information on one screen, controlled by a single keyboard.

Costa Mediterranea
★★★★

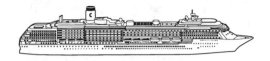

Large (Resort) Ship: . . . . .85,700 tons	Passenger Decks: 11	Cabins (with private balcony): 742
Lifestyle: . . . . .Standard	Total Crew: 920	Cabins (wheelchair accessible): 8
Cruise Line: . . . . .Costa Crociere	Passengers	Cabin Current: . . . . .110 volts
(Costa Cruises)	(lower beds/all berths): 2,112/2,680	Elevators: 12
Former Names: . . . . .none	Passenger Space Ratio	Casino (gaming tables): . . . . .Yes
Builder: . . .Kvaerner Masa-Yards (Finland)	(lower beds/all berths): 40.5/31.9	Slot Machines: . . . . .Yes
Original Cost: . . . .$335 million	Crew/Passenger Ratio	Swimming Pools (outdoors): 2
Entered Service: . . . . .May 2003	(lower beds/all berths): 2.2/2.9	(+1 indoor/outdoor)
Registry: . . . . .Italy	Navigation Officers: . . . . .Italian	Swimming Pools (indoors): . . . . .No
Length (ft/m): 959.6/292.5	Cabins (total): 1,056	Whirlpools: . . . . .Yes
Beam (ft/m): 105.6/32.2	Size Range (sq ft/m): 161.4–387.5/	Self-Service Launderette: . . . . .No
Draft (ft/m): 25.5/7.8	15.0–36.0	Dedicated Cinema/Seats: . . . . .No
Propulsion/Propellers: . . . . .diesel-electric	Cabins (outside view): 843	Library: . . . . .Yes
(34,000 kW)/2 azimuthing pods	Cabins (interior/no view): 213	Classification Society: . . .Registro Navale
(17.6 MW each)	Cabins (for one person): 0	Italiano (RINA)

OVERALL SCORE: 1,438 (OUT OF A POSSIBLE 2,000 POINTS)

OVERVIEW. The first thing that regular passengers will notice is the length of this ship, which gives it an attractive sleekness. There are two centrally located swimming pools outdoors, one of which can be used in poor weather due to its retractable glass dome (magrodome) cover. A bar abridges two adjacent whirlpool tubs. Another smaller pool is for children; there is also a winding water slide that spans two decks in height (it starts on a platform bridge located between the two aft funnels). There is also an additional whirlpool tub outdoors.

Inside, the layout is just the same as in sister ship *Costa Atlantica*. The interior design is, however, bold and brash – a mix of classical Italy and contemporary features. There is good passenger flow from one public space to another, several floor spaces for dancing, and a range of bars and lounges for socializing. The dramatic eight-deck atrium lobby, with two grand stairways, presents a stunning wall decoration consisting of two huge paintings and 25-piece wall sculpture by Gigi Rigamonte (called *Danza*) that is best seen from any of the multiple viewing balconies on each deck above the main lobby-floor level (the squid-shaped wall lighting sconces are neat, too). But pillars throughout the ship obstruct passenger flow and pillars in the dining room provide an obstacle course for waiters.

The decor is said to be inspired by many Italian palaces (some known, many not) and by a profound live for art and architecture. It is extremely upbeat, bright, glitzy, and in-your-face wherever you go (I was amused by one of three larger than life digital faces of Dionisio in the Dionisio Lounge, with a door handle that sticks out of his mouth

BERLITZ'S RATINGS

	Possible	Achieved
Ship	500	427
Accommodation	200	152
Food	400	240
Service	400	273
Entertainment	100	64
Cruise	400	282

in a style that recalls Monty Python.

A small chapel is located forward of the uppermost level. Other facilities include a winding shopping street with boutique stores (typically including Fendi, Fossil, Paul & Shark Yachting), a photo gallery, video games room, observation balcony, a large Grand Canal Casino, and a library (with internet access but very few books). Food and service levels have been raised to a better standard than that found aboard most other Costa Cruises ships to date. But do expect irritating announcements (particularly for activities that bring in revenue, such as art auctions, bingo, horse racing), and much hustling for drinks. All printed materials (room service folio, menus, etc.) are in six languages (Italian, English, French, German, Portuguese, Spanish). The onboard currency is the euro or US dollar, depending on region of operation.

SUITABLE FOR: The vessel is best suited to young (and young at heart) couples and singles (plus families with children) that enjoy big city life, piazzas and outdoor cafes, constant activity accompanied by lots of noise, late nights, loud entertainment, and an international mix of passengers.

ACCOMMODATION. There are 14 price grades. There is a healthy (78 percent) proportion of outside-view to interior (no view) cabins. All of the cabins have twin beds that can be converted into a queen-sized bed, individually controlled air-conditioning, television, and telephone. Some many cabins have their views obstructed by lifeboats – on Deck 4 (Roma Deck), the lowest of the accommodation decks, as well as some cabins on Deck 5. Some cabins have pull-down Pullman berths that are fully hidden in the ceiling when not in use. There is too much use of fluorescent lighting in the suites and cabins, and the soundproofing could be much better. Some bathroom fixtures – bath and shower taps in particular – are frustrating to use until you get the hang of them.

Some of the most desirable suites and cabins are those with private balconies on the five aft-facing decks (Decks 4, 5, 6, 7, and 8) with views overlooking the stern and ship's wash. The other cabins with private balconies will find the balconies not so private – the partition between one balcony and the next is not a full partition, so you will be able to hear your neighbors (or smell their smoke).

However, these balcony occupants all have good views through glass and wood-topped railings, and the deck is made of teak. The cabins are well laid out, typically with twin beds that convert to a queen-sized bed, vanity desk (with built-in hairdryer), large television, personal safe, and one closet that has moveable shelves – thus providing more space for luggage storage. However, note that the lighting is fluorescent, and much too harsh (the bedside control is for a master switch only – other individual lights cannot be controlled). The bathroom is a simple, modular unit that has shower enclosures with soap dispenser; there is a good amount of stowage space for personal toiletry items.

The largest suites are those designated as Penthouse Suites, although they are really quite small when compared with suites aboard other ships of a similar size. However, they do at least offer more space to move around in, and a slightly larger, better bathroom.

CUISINE/DINING. The Ristorante degli Argentiere, the ship's main dining room, is extremely large and is located at the aft section of the ship on two levels with a spiral stairway between them. There are two seatings, with tables for two, four, six or eight. Dinner on European cruises is typically scheduled at 7pm and 9pm. Some tables in the dining room have a less than comfortable view of the harsh lighting of the escalators between the galley and the two decks of the dining room.

Alternative (Reservations-Only, Extra Cost) Dining: The Medusa Supper Club (with menu by Zeffirino – a famous restaurant in Genoa) is a more upscale dining spot located on two of the uppermost decks of the ship under a huge glass dome, with seating for approximately 150. It has an open kitchen where chefs can be seen preparing their masterpieces. Fine table settings, china and silverware are featured, as are leather-bound menus. Reservations are required and there is a cover charge of $18.75 per person (for service and tip). But you may think it's worth it in order to have dinner in a setting that is quieter and more refined than the main dining room.

The Perla del Lago Buffet is an extensive eatery that forms the aft third of Deck 9 (part of it also wraps around the upper section of the huge atrium). It includes a central area with several small buffet counters; there are salad counters, a dessert counter, and a 24-hour Posillipo Pizzeria counter, all forming a large eatery with indoor and outdoor seating. Movement around the buffet area is very slow, and requires you to stand in line for everything. Venture outdoors and you'll find a grill (for hamburgers and hot dogs) and a pasta bar, both conveniently located adjacent to the second of two swimming pools on the lido deck.

Other Venues: The place that most people will want to see and be seen is at the casual Oriental Cafe; there are four separate salons, which provide intimate spaces for drinks, conversation, and people-watching. Excellent cappuccino and espresso coffees are always available in various bars around the ship, served in the right-sized china cups.

ENTERTAINMENT. The Osiris Theater is the principal venue for all production shows and major cabaret acts. It spans three decks, and seating on all three levels. Sightlines to the stage are better from the second and third levels. Spiral stairways at the back of the lounge connect all three levels.

SPA/FITNESS. The expansive Ischia Spa spans two decks, is located directly above the navigation bridge in the forward part of the ship (accessed by the forward stairway elevators) and has approximately 13,700 sq. ft (1,272 sq. meters) of space. Facilities on the lower level include a solarium, eight treatment rooms, lecture rooms, sauna and steam rooms for men and women, a beauty parlor; the upper level consists of a large gymnasium with floor-to-ceiling windows on three sides, including forward-facing ocean views, and an aerobics room with instructor-led classes (the aerobics room and gymnasium together measure almost 6,000 sq. ft (557 sq. meters). There is also a jogging track outdoors, around the ship's mast and the forward third of the ship, as well as a multi-purpose court for basketball, volleyball and deck tennis.

● **For more extensive general information on what a Costa Cruises cruise is like, see pages 115–118.**

Costa Romantica
★★★ +

Mid-Size Ship:	.53,049 tons	Total Crew:	.610
Lifestyle:	.Standard	Passengers	
Cruise Line:	.Costa Crociere	(lower beds/all berths):	.1,356/1,779
	(Costa Cruises)	Passenger Space Ratio	
Former Names:	.none	(lower beds/all berths):	.39.1/29.8
Builder:	.Fincantieri (Italy)	Crew/Passenger Ratio	
Original Cost:	.$325 million	(lower beds/all berths):	.2.2/2.9
Entered Service:	.Nov 1993	Navigation Officers:	.Italian
Registry:	.Italy	Cabins (total):	.678
Length (ft/m):	.718.5/220.61	Size Range (sq ft/m):	.185.1–430.5/
Beam (ft/m):	.98.4/30.89		17.2–40.0
Draft (ft/m):	.25.0/7.60	Cabins (outside view):	.462
Propulsion/Propellers: diesel (22,800kW)/2		Cabins (interior/no view):	.216
Passenger Decks:	.10	Cabins (for one person):	.0

Cabins (with private balcony):	.10
Cabins (wheelchair accessible): 6 (interior)	
Cabin Current:	.110 volts
Elevators:	.8
Casino (gaming tables):	.Yes
Slot Machines:	.Yes
Swimming Pools (outdoors):	.2
Swimming Pools (indoors):	.0
Whirlpools:	.4
Self-Service Launderette:	.No
Dedicated Cinema/Seats:	.No
Library:	.Yes
Classification Society:	.Registro Navale Italiano (RINA)

OVERALL SCORE: 1,369 (OUT OF A POSSIBLE 2,000 POINTS)

OVERVIEW. *Costa Romantica* is a bold, contemporary ship with an upright yellow funnel cluster of three typical of Italian styling today. Sadly, there is no wrap-around promenade deck outdoors, and so contact with the sea is minimal, although there is some good open space on several of the upper decks. Being Italian, the ship is chic and very tasteful, and will appeal to the sophisticated. The layout and flow are somewhat disjointed, however. The ship has a good number of business and conference facilities, with several flexible meeting rooms. The multi-level atrium is open and spacious, and has a revolving mobile sculpture. There is a small chapel and an Internet Cafe.

BERLITZ'S RATINGS

	Possible	Achieved
Ship	500	389
Accommodation	200	154
Food	400	218
Service	400	282
Entertainment	100	64
Cruise	400	262

ACCOMMODATION. There are 11 price categories. These include 16 suites, 10 of which have a private semi-circular balcony, while six suites command views over the ship's bows. The other cabins are fairly standard in size, shape, and facilities; the ones on the highest decks cost more.

Suites/Mini-Suites: The 16 suites (with floor-to-ceiling windows) and 18 mini-suites are quite pleasant (except for the rounded balconies of the 10 suites on Madrid Deck, where a solid steel half-wall blocks the view). A sliding door separates the bedroom from the living room, and bathrooms are of a decent size. Cherry wood walls and cabinetry help make these suites warm and attractive.

The six suites at the forward section of Monte Carlo Deck are the largest, and have huge glass windows with commanding forward views, although they do not have balconies.

Standard Outside-View/Interior (No View) Cabins: All other cabins are of a moderately generous size, and all have

nicely finished cherry wood cabinetry and walls. However, the cabin bathrooms and shower enclosures are quite small. There are a good number of triple and quad cabins, ideal for families with children. The company's in-cabin food service menu is extremely basic.

CUISINE/DINING. The 728-seat Botticelli Restaurant is of a superior design. There are several tables for two, four, six or eight. There are two seatings (dinner on European cruises is typically at 7pm and 9pm), and there are both smoking and non-smoking sections. Romantic candlelight dining is typically featured on a formal night.

For informal dining, the buffet layout is far too small, and buffets are very much standard fare, with the exception of some good commercial pasta dishes. One would expect Italian waiters, but, sadly, this is not the case now, with most of the waiters coming from countries other than Italy

ENTERTAINMENT. The L'Opera Theater, the main show-lounge, is an interesting amphitheater-like design that spans two decks, with seating on both main and balcony levels. However, the seats are bolt upright, and quite uncomfortable and 10 large pillars obstruct many sightlines.

SPA/FITNESS. The Caracalla Spa, on one of the uppermost decks forward, contains a gymnasium with some high-tech muscle-pump machines, an aerobics exercise area, two hot tubs, Roman bath, health bar, sauna and steam rooms, and beauty salon.

● **For more extensive general information on what a Costa Cruises cruise is like, see pages 115–118.**

Costa Tropicale
★★★

Mid-Size Ship: . . . . .35,190 tons	Total Crew: 550	Cabins (with private balcony): 12
Lifestyle: . . . . .Standard	Passengers	Cabins (wheelchair accessible): 11
Cruise Line: . . . . .Costa Crociere	(lower beds/all berths): 1,022/1,412	Cabin Current: . . . . .110 volts
(Costa Cruises)	Passenger Space Ratio	Elevators: 8
Former Names: . . . . .Tropicale	(lower beds/all berths): 34.4/24.9	Casino (gaming tables): . . . . .Yes
Builder: . . . . . . .Aalborg Vaerft (Denmark)	Crew/Passenger Ratio	Slot Machines: . . . . .Yes
Original Cost: . . . .$100 million	(lower beds/all berths): 1.8/2.5	Swimming Pools (outdoors): 3
Entered Service: . . . .Jan 1982/June 2001	Navigation Officers: . . . . .Italian	Swimming Pools (indoors): 0
Registry: . . . . .Italy	Cabins (total): 511	Whirlpools: 0
Length (ft/m): 671.7/204.76	Size Range (sq ft/m): 180.0–398.2/	Self-Service Launderette: . . . . .Yes
Beam (ft/m): 86.7/26.45	16.7–37.0	Dedicated Cinema/Seats: . . . . .No
Draft (ft/m): 23.3/7.11	Cabins (outside view): 324	Library: . . . . .Yes
Propulsion/Propellers: diesel (19,566kW)/2	Cabins (interior/no view): 187	Classification Society: . . .Registro Navale
Passenger Decks: 10	Cabins (for one person): 0	Italiano (RINA)

OVERALL SCORE: 1,237 (OUT OF A POSSIBLE 2,000 POINTS)

OVERVIEW. *Costa Tropicale* was the first new ship ordered by the former owner, Carnival Cruise Lines (parent company of Costa Cruises), and its exterior design led the way for that company's clutch of new buildings during the following years. The ship was acquired by Costa Cruises in January 2001 and given a $24 million refit and refurbishment, including a new yellow funnel. The ship has a fairly distinctive, though somewhat squared-off look.

The interior design is reasonably well laid out, and passenger flow is generally good. The public rooms are decorated in European colors, designed to make everyone feel alive and lively. There is an Internet Cafe. Costa Cruises goes out of its way to entertain young cruisers as well as their parents, particularly during school holiday periods.

Costa Tropicale now looks spiffy and more contemporary under the Costa Cruises banner, although it is one of the smallest ships in the fleet. This is not a luxury cruise product, nor does it pretend to be. But you and your family will probably have fun; there are plenty of opportunities for gaming and partying.

ACCOMMODATION. There are 10 categories. Most of the "standard" interior (no view) and outside-view cabins are all of the usual cookie-cutter variety (although they are of quite a decent size), with an imaginative European-style decor, and just enough closet and drawer space for a week's cruise. The bathrooms are quite plain, but adequate. A number of cabins have third and fourth person upper berths added – these are good for families with children.

The best accommodation can be found in 12 "suites" – each with a small (narrow) semi-private balcony. Naturally,

BERLITZ'S RATINGS		
	Possible	Achieved
Ship	500	312
Accommodation	200	121
Food	400	217
Service	400	268
Entertainment	100	72
Cruise	400	247

there is more space, with the living and sleeping areas divided. The bathroom is marginally larger, too. However, all of these suites have their views substantially blocked by the positioning of the lifeboats. The cabin soundproofing could be better. The room service menu is quite basic, but there's plenty of food elsewhere aboard this ship.

CUISINE/DINING. The Corallo Restaurant is located on the ship's lowest deck. It is colorful, very cheerful, brightly lit, but noisy and extremely cramped, which makes correct service quite difficult. There are tables for four, six or eight (there are no tables for two), and dining is in two seatings (dinner on European cruises is typically at 7pm and 9pm).

The Lido Cafe has self-service buffets, which are very basic and unimaginative, as is the selection of breads, rolls, fruit and cheeses. At night, the Lido Cafe becomes a bistro and provides a casual (dress-down) alternative to eating in the main dining room. Excellent cappuccino and espresso coffees are always available in various bars around the ship, served in the right sized china cups.

ENTERTAINMENT. The Tropicana Showroom is a single-level room that has bright, cheerful decor, although sightlines to the stage are obstructed from several seats.

SPA/FITNESS. The Olympia Spa is small, and is located just behind the ship's mast. It contains a gymnasium, sauna and changing rooms for men and women.

● **For more extensive general information on what a Costa Cruises cruise is like, see pages 115–118.**

Costa Victoria
★★★★

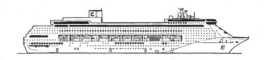

Large (Resort) Ship: . . . . .75,200 tons	Total Crew: 800	Cabins (with private balcony): 246
Lifestyle: . . . . .Standard	Passengers	Cabins (wheelchair accessible): 6
Cruise Line: . . . . .Costa Crociere	(lower beds/all berths): 1,928/2,464	Cabin Current: . . . . .110 and 220 volts
(Costa Cruises)	Passenger Space Ratio	Elevators: 12
Former Names: . . . . .none	(lower beds/all berths): 39.0/30.5	Casino (gaming tables): . . . . .Yes
Builder: . . . . . . .Bremer Vulkan (Germany)	Crew/Passenger Ratio	Slot Machines: . . . . .Yes
Original Cost: . . . .$388 million	(lower beds/all berths): 2.4/3.0	Swimming Pools (outdoors): 2
Entered Service: . . . . .July 1996	Navigation Officers: . . . . .Italian	Swimming Pools (indoors): 1
Registry: . . . . .Italy	Cabins (total): .964	Whirlpools: 4
Length (ft/m): 823.0/251.00	Size Range (sq ft/m): 120.0–430.5/	Self-Service Launderette: . . . . .Yes
Beam (ft/m): 105.5/32.25	11.1–40.0	Dedicated Cinema/Seats: . . . . .No
Draft (ft/m): 25.6/7.8	Cabins (outside view): 573	Library: . . . . .Yes
Propulsion/Propellers: diesel (30,000kW)/2	Cabins (interior/no view): 391	Classification Society: . . .Registro Navale
Passenger Decks: 10	Cabins (for one person): 0	Italiano (RINA)

OVERALL SCORE: 1,406 (OUT OF A POSSIBLE 2,000 POINTS)

OVERVIEW. *Costa Victoria*'s exterior profile is similar to that of an enlarged version of the popular and very successful *Costa Classica* and *Costa Romantica*, with huge upright yellow funnels that are instantly recognizable. A sister ship, *Costa Olympia*, was scheduled for delivery in 1998, but was not completed due to the bankruptcy of the shipyard. Having replaced almost all its older tonnage in the past few years, Costa Cruises now has a good contemporary fleet, operating in the Caribbean, Mediterranean and in South America. This ship has a fully enclosed bridge. There is an outdoor wrap-around promenade deck (but it is full of deck lounge chairs) as well as a wraparound jogging track.

Inside the ship is a lovely four-deck-high forward-facing observation lounge (Concorde Plaza) with a "beam-me-up" glass elevator; in the center is a cone-shaped waterfall (huge video screens flank the walls), while "pod" balconies overlook the room's center. It is a stunning space, and has its own bar. Sadly, thick floor-to-ceiling pillars obstruct sightlines from most seats.

The seven-deck-high "planetarium" atrium (a novel, but somewhat impractical design) has four glass lifts that travel up to a clear crystal dome (you can see the weather through it). The uppermost level of the atrium is the deck where two outside swimming pools are located, together with four blocks of showers, and an ice cream bar and grill.

There is a large forward shopping area, adjacent to the atrium. Ship lovers should look in the Tavernetta Lounge (aft) for 10 paintings of past and present Costa Cruises ships. There is also a small chapel.

Unusual for a new ship (and welcomed by European pas-

BERLITZ'S RATINGS

	Possible	Achieved
Ship	500	418
Accommodation	200	158
Food	400	220
Service	400	273
Entertainment	100	73
Cruise	400	264

sengers) is a pleasant (but small) indoor swimming pool and a sauna (it is tiny, and there are no adjacent changing or locker facilities, which makes it very user-unfriendly). Also adjacent is a steam room, and gymnasium (limited assortment of equipment), as well as a covered walking/jogging track. There is also a tennis court. Sunbathers on the forwardmost section of the outdoor deck close to the mast have their own showers (excellent) and no music (good).

Where this ship differs from most large ships is in its distinct European interior decor, with decidedly Italian styling. The ship is contemporary without being glitzy – and bold without being brash. When inside, there is absolutely no feeling that this is a ship. Internet access is available from one of several computer terminals in the Teens Center. The telephone numbering system is impossible to remember (examples: 05313 for the information desk or 06718 to book a massage).

The onboard currency is the euro or US dollar, depending on the region of operation. Tipping envelopes provided in your cabin state the amount you are expected to give.

ACCOMMODATION. There are 13 price categories (the price will depend on the grade, size and location you choose).

There are six large Panorama suites (each has third/fourth Pullman berths in a separate, tiny, train-like compartment) and 14 mini-suites (the six suites feature Laura Ashley-style fabrics), all with butler service; 65 percent of all other cabins have outside views, but they are small (for two). While the suites are not large, all other cabins are of rather mean dimensions. Some (only 16) of the interior (no view) cabins accommodate four people, while all other cabins are for two or three. In 2004, the ship benefitted from the addition of balconies to 246 cabins.

All cabins have wood cabinetry. There is a decent amount of closet and drawer space for two for a one-week cruise, excellent air-conditioning, mini-bar/refrigerator, and electric blackout window blind (no curtains). The ocean-view cabins have large picture windows. The cabin bathrooms are small but well appointed, and (sensibly) have a sliding door. There are six cabins for the disabled (each has two bathrooms); all are well located, and adjacent to elevators in the center of the ship.

The location of the personal safe could be better. The cabin service menu is limited, but there is plenty of food elsewhere aboard this ship.

CUISINE/DINING. This ship has two main dining rooms: the 594-seat Minuetto Restaurant, and the 506-seat Fantasia Restaurant, both of which are separated by the main galley. There are two seatings (dinner on European cruises is typically at 7pm and 9pm to accommodate the later eating habits of Europeans), and smoking and no-smoking sections in both restaurants. They are expansive (there are a few tables for two, most being for four, six or eight) and feature marble and pine walls. Romantic candlelight dining is typically featured on a formal night. The cuisine is good basic fare, and the presentation is adequate, but nothing special. Somewhat lacking is the use of garnishes to dress the plates. As you would expect on an Italian ship, there is always plenty of pasta (freshly made on board daily).

Alternative (reservations-only) dining: Ristorante Magnifico by Zeffirino, is available six nights each week, with a service charge of $18.75 per person (passengers occupying suites will get a free pass for one evening).

The ship also has casual breakfast and lunch buffets with indoor/outdoor seating (under a canvas sailcloth canopy for the outdoor section), although the buffet displays are very disappointing. There is also a pizzeria, open in the afternoon and evening and popular with fast-food devotees who are used to frozen/re-heated commercial pizzas.

Excellent cappuccino and espresso coffees are always available in various bars around the ship, served in the right-sized china cups.

ENTERTAINMENT. The Festival Showlounge, located aft above one of the two dining rooms, spans two decks, and has seating on both main and balcony levels. It is the venue for all major entertainment events such as production shows, major cabaret, as well as social functions.

SPA/FITNESS. The spa/fitness area, on a lower deck, is much too small for the size of the ship, and very poorly designed; it is therefore always congested, noisy, not at all relaxing. It has a beauty salon, indoor swimming pool, treatment rooms, sauna and steam room, but cramped changing areas with no locker facilities.

● **For more extensive general information on what a Costa Cruises cruise is like, see pages 115–118.**

Crystal Harmony
★★★★+

Mid-Size Ship: . . . . .49,400 tons	Total Crew: .545	Cabins (with private balcony): 260
Lifestyle: . . . . .Luxury/Premium	Passengers	Cabins (wheelchair accessible): 4
Cruise Line: . . . . .Crystal Cruises	(lower beds/all berths): 960/1,010	Cabin Current: . . . . .115 and 220 volts
Former Names: . . . . .none	Passenger Space Ratio	Elevators: 8
Builder: . . . . .Mitsubishi Heavy Industries	(lower beds/all berths): 51.4/48.9	Casino (gaming tables): . . . . .Yes
(Japan)	Crew/Passenger Ratio	Slot Machines: . . . . .Yes
Original Cost: . . . .$240 million	(lower beds/all berths): 1.7/1.8	Swimming Pools (outdoors): 2
Entered Service: . . . . .July 1990	Navigation Officers: . . . . . . .Scandinavian/	(1 with magrodome)
Registry: . . . . .The Bahamas	Japanese	Swimming Pools (indoors): 0
Length (ft/m): 790.5/240.96	Cabins (total): 480	Whirlpools: 2
Beam (ft/m): 97.1/29.60	Size Range (sq ft/m): 182.9–947.2/	Self-Service Launderette: . . . . .Yes
Draft (ft/m): 24.6/7.50	17.0–88.0	Dedicated Cinema/Seats: Yes/270
Propulsion/Propellers: . . . . .diesel-electric	Cabins (outside view): 461	Library: . . . . .Yes
(32,800kW)/2	Cabins (interior/no view): 19	Classification Society: . . .Lloyd's Register/
Passenger Decks: 8	Cabins (for one person): 0	Nippon Kaiji Kyokai

OVERALL SCORE: 1,666 (OUT OF A POSSIBLE 2,000 POINTS)

OVERVIEW. *Crystal Harmony* is a handsome, contemporary ship with raked clipper bow and well-balanced, sleek flowing lines. There is almost no sense of crowding anywhere aboard this ship, a superb example of comfort by design. There is a wrap-around teakwood deck for walking, and an abundance of open deck and sunbathing space.

Inside, the layout is similar to that of larger (and newer) sister ships *Crystal Serenity* and *Crystal Symphony*, with a design that shows that form follows function superbly well, combining the best of large ship facilities with the intimacy of rooms found aboard most small ships. There is a wide assortment of public entertainment lounges and small intimate rooms (except for a nightclub/lounge that is simply too large for the number of late-night passengers frequenting it), and passenger flow is excellent. Fine-quality fabrics and soft furnishings, china, flatware and silver are used throughout.

Outstanding are the Vista (observation) Lounge and the supremely tranquil, elegant Palm Court, one of the nicest rooms afloat, as well as the always popular Avenue Saloon (piano bar/lounge). A Connoisseur Club (cigar and cognac lounge with a private club atmosphere) was added (adjacent to the Avenue Saloon) in a 2002 refit.

A Business Center has laptop computers, printers, satellite faxes, and phones, and there is a very good book and video library. The theater is a dedicated room that has high-definition video projection and headsets for the hearing-impaired. There is a self-service launderette on each deck, particularly useful for long voyages.

This ship has a very friendly, well-trained, highly pro-

BERLITZ'S RATINGS

	Possible	Achieved
Ship	500	412
Accommodation	200	157
Food	400	336
Service	400	341
Entertainment	100	83
Cruise	400	337

fessional staff and excellent teamwork (with one of the lowest turnovers of staff in the industry) that is under the direction of a solid, all-European middle management. It is the superb extra attention to detail that makes a cruise aboard this ship so worthwhile, such as almost no announcements, and no background music anywhere. The company pays attention to its fine base of repeat passengers (particularly those in Deck 10 accommodation), and constantly makes subtle changes to fine-tune its product.

This ship has just about everything for the discerning, seasoned traveller who wants and is prepared to pay for fine style, space, and the comfort and the facilities of a large vessel capable of longer voyages. *Crystal Harmony* is a fine example of the style in contemporary grand hotels afloat and provides abundant choices and flexibility, and an excellent guest lecture programme. The passenger mix is approximately 85% North American (typically half of these will be from California) and 15% other nationalities.

Following a 1977 refit, some of the public rooms were expanded (most notably the casino) and refurbished. Although now 15 years old (and showing signs of wear in both accommodation and public areas), the ship is being well maintained, and should continue to give pleasure to passengers. A Computer Learning Center was also added, complete with more than 20 desktop and laptop computers. Private lessons are available (although they are expensive).

The final words: this is announcement-free cruising in a well-tuned, very professionally run, service-oriented, ship, approximately the equivalent of a Four Seasons hotel. However, note that the score has gone downwards a little recently, the result of the age of the ship and its facilities (particularly the many small cabins), in comparison to newer ships available in the discounted marketplace, and the fact that this is still a two-seating ship, which makes it too highly structured in terms of timing than it really should be. All bottled water and (non-alcoholic) soft drinks are included in the cost of your cruise (this feature was introduced with the debut of *Crystal Serenity*, but has now been applied fleet-wide). The onboard currency is the US dollar and gratuities are at your discretion (15% is added to bar accounts, however).

Your evenings will be necessarily time-structured due to the fact that there are two seatings for dinner (unless you eat in one of the alternative dining spots), and two shows (the showlounge cannot seat all passengers at once). This detracts from the otherwise luxurious setting of the ship and the fine professionalism of its staff. Many passengers feel that gratuities should really be included on a ship that is rated this highly (they can, however, be pre-paid). The ship's greatest asset, however, is its well-trained staff and excellent food.

SUITABLE FOR: *Crystal Harmony* is best suited to sophisticated travellers (typically over 50) that seek contemporary ship surroundings, with fine-quality fittings and furnishings, a wide range of public rooms and facilities, and excellent food and service from a well trained staff that enjoys providing the art of hospitality.

ACCOMMODATION. There are 10 categories of suites and cabins, including four Crystal Penthouses with private balcony; 26 Penthouse Suites with balcony; 32 Penthouses with balcony; 198 Cabins with balcony; 241 Cabins without balcony. Regardless of the category you select, duvets and down pillows are provided, as are lots of other niceties, together with a data socket for connecting a personal laptop computer. All accommodation includes a refrigerator and mini-bar, television, satellite-linked telephone, and hairdryer. A full range of Aveda personal toiletries is provided, as is a plush cotton bathrobe, and plenty of cotton towels, the largest of which measures a generous 70 by 34 inches (180 by 85cm). The in-cabin television programming is excellent, and close-captioned videos are provided for the hearing-impaired.

Deck 10 Penthouses: The four delightful Crystal penthouses measure 948–982 sq. ft (88–91.2 sq. meters) and have a huge private balcony and lounge with audio-visual entertainment center, separate master bedroom with king-sized bed and electric curtains, large walk-in closets, and stunning ocean-view bathrooms that come with jet bathtub, bidet, two washbasins, and plenty of storage space for one's personal toiletry items. These really are among the best in fine, private, pampered living spaces at sea, and come with all the best priority perks, including butler service, free laundry service, a wide variety of alcoholic beverages and other goodies – in fact, almost anything you require.

Other Deck 10 Suites: All the other suites on this deck are worth the asking price, have plenty of space (all have a private balcony, with outside light), including a separate lounge with large couch, coffee table and chairs, large television/VCR, and a separate sleeping area that can be curtained off (thick drapes mean you can sleep totally in the dark). The bathrooms are quite large, and extremely well appointed. Any of the suites on this deck are equipped with everything necessary for refined, private living at sea.

Butlers provide the best in personal service in all the top category suites on this deck (with a total of 132 beds), where all room service food arrives correctly on large silver trays. Afternoon tea trolley service and evening hors d'oeuvres are standard fare in the "butler service" suites.

Deck 9/8/7/5 Cabins: Many of the cabins feature a private balcony (in fact, 50 percent of all cabins have private balconies, with outside lights), and are extremely comfortable, although a little tight for space. They are very compact units, with one-way traffic past the bed, but there is a reasonable amount of drawer and storage space (the drawers are small, however) although the closet hanging space is somewhat limited for long voyages. Some cabins in grades G and I have lifeboat-obstructed views. All cabins have a color television, VCR, mini-refrigerator, personal safe, small couch and coffee table, and excellent soundproofing. The bathrooms, although well appointed, are of the "you first, me next" variety (and size), but they do come with generously sized personal toiletry items and amenities.

CUISINE/DINING. There are several dining choices aboard this pleasant ship. The dining room (totally non-smoking) is moderately elegant, with plenty of space around each table, well-placed waiter service stations and a good number of tables for two, as well as tables for four, six or eight. It is noisy at times (particularly in the raised, center section), making it difficult to carry on a conversation.

Sadly, dinner in the main dining room is in two seatings and fixed table assignments. Clearly, the early seating is simply too rushed for many, although with other alternative restaurants, off-menu choices, a hand-picked European staff and excellent service, dining can still be a memorable affair. The advantage of fixed table assignments is that your waiters get to know your personal preferences, likes and dislikes (unlike dining rooms with open seating, where you may be seated with different people each evening, and your waiter changes constantly). Each evening at dinner, a wandering trio serenades passengers at their tables, but this is tacky and not representative of fine dining.

The food is very attractively presented on large plates, and well served (using both plate service as well as silver service in the best European traditions). It is of a very high standard with fine quality (high cost) ingredients. European dishes are predominantly featured (but in an American style). The menus are extremely varied, and feature a fine selection of meat, fish and vegetarian dishes. Special (off-menu) orders are available, as are caviar and other culinary niceties – the caviar is sevruga (malossol) and not beluga (this is hard to find today, and incredibly expensive). Kosher meals are also available (frozen when brought on board; Kosher pots, pans and utensils are all sterilized in salt water, and all plates used during service are hand-washed separately.

Overall, the food is really good for the size of ship, and, with the choice of the two alternative dining spots, receives high praise. Sadly, dinner in the main dining room is in two seatings, the company having used the space that could have provided a second main dining room, for public areas. While the early seating is simply too rushed for many, with two alternative restaurants, off-menu choices, a hand-picked European staff and excellent service, dining is often memorable. Fresh pasta and dessert flambeau specialties are made at the table each day by accommodating headwaiters.

The wine list is superb, with an outstanding collection of across-the-board wines, including a mouthwatering connoisseur selection.

Afternoon tea (and coffee) in the Palm Court is good. The choice of sandwiches, cakes and pastries is also good. Needless to say, service is generally excellent.

The two alternative dining spots are Prego (features fine pasta dishes and other Italian-inspired specialties), and Kyoto, featuring pseudo-Japanese and other southeast Asian specialties (there is no extra charge, other than a recommended $6 waiter gratuity per meal that would be better to include in the cruise fare). The two non-smoking restaurants are intimate, have great views and feature fine food. There should be separate entrance (at present a single entrance serves both).

Additionally, The Bistro (located on the upper level of the two-deck-high lobby) is a casual spot for coffees and pastries, served in the style and atmosphere of a European street cafe. The Bistro has unusual, Crystal Cruises-logo china that can be purchased in one of the ship's boutiques.

For casual meals, the Lido Cafe has an extensive self-serve buffet area, located high up in the ship, and with great views from its large picture windows. For casual poolside lunches, there is also the Trident Grill, as well as an ice cream/frozen yoghurt counter (all at no extra charge).

Several special themed luncheon buffets, with appropriate decor and service staff dressed accordingly, are provided at the Trident indoor/outdoor pool area. These include the popular Asian Buffet and Follow the Sun (Mediterranean) buffet.

ENTERTAINMENT. The Galaxy Showlounge is a large room, but on one level (with a tiered floor). The sightlines are good from most seats, although there are a few pillars that obstruct the view from some seats. Both banquette and individual seating is provided.

The shows are elegant, with excellent costuming and scenery, but they are now seriously dated, too long, and Crystal Cruises' many repeat passengers know them all. In addition, many nights feature cabaret acts that are of a good caliber, and constantly changing. The bands and musical units are also, for the most part, of a high caliber, and there is plenty of music for social dancing. The ship also provides male hosts (called Ambassador Hosts) for the many single women who enjoy traveling with Crystal Cruises.

SPA/FITNESS. In a 2002 refit, the Crystal Spa & Fitness Center was greatly expanded. Facilities include one room dedicated to yoga and pilates classes (no extra charge), an aerobics/exercise room, plus separate sauna, steam rooms, and changing rooms for both men and women. There are seven treatment rooms (including one for couples, and one room featuring a "dry float bed") for various types of massage, facials, and other treatments, as well as a separate beauty salon, and a private relaxation area on a canopied outdoors sundeck. Treatments are provided under the aegis of Steiner Platinum Service (Steiner is the concession).

Some staff will try to sell you Steiner's own-brand Elemis beauty products (spa girls have sales targets). Being aboard this ship will give you an opportunity to try some of the more exotic treatments (particularly some of the massages available). Massage (including Aroma Stone massage, Chakra Balancing massage and other well-being massages), facials, pedicures, and beauty salon treatments are at extra cost. Examples: Swedish Massage ($109 for 50 minutes); Deep Tissue Massage ($116 for 50 minutes); Yin Yang Facial ($109 for 50 minutes).

There are also some excellent multi-therapy packages that provide you with hours of pampering. Some examples: Ceremony of Precious Metal (exotic lime and ginger salt glow, aroma spa ocean wrap, well-being massage) lasting 3 hours 30 minutes, for $323; Ceremony of Water (aroma stone therapy, Japanese silk booster facial, Japanese eye zone therapy) lasting 3 hours 30 minutes, for $365; Ceremony of Earth (frangipani body nourish ritual, absolute spa ritual, frangipani hair and scalp conditioning with style dry, exotic hand ritual with paraffin wax, sole delight foot treatment with paraffin wax) lasting 6 hours and 30 minutes, for $561. A simple hair cut (for men) costs $25, while it is $57 for women with short hair for a shampoo, cut and blow-dry. Do make appointments as early as possible – aboard a ship of this size, time slots go quickly, so the day you board is the best time to book your desired treatments.

The ship also has an excellent amount of open deck and sunbathing space, and sports facilities that include a full-size paddle tennis court, electronic golf simulator, and golf driving range. One of two outdoor swimming pools has a magrodome (retractable glass dome) cover, while the one that is in the open is one of the longest aboard any ship today.

Crystal Serenity
★★★★★

Mid-Size Ship: . . . . .68,870 tons	Total Crew: 650	Cabins (with private balcony): 466
Lifestyle: . . . . .Luxury/Premium	Passengers	Cabins (wheelchair accessible): 8
Cruise Line: . . . . .Crystal Cruises	(lower beds/all berths): 1,100/1,100	Cabin Current: . . . . .110/220 volts
Former Names: . . . . .none	Passenger Space Ratio	Elevators: 8
Builder: Chantiers de l'Atlantique (France)	(lower beds/all berths): 62.6/62.6	Casino (gaming tables): . . . . .Yes
Original Cost: . . . .$350 million	Crew/Passenger Ratio	Slot Machines: .Yes
Entered Service: . . . . .June 2003	(lower beds/all berths): 1.7/1.7	Swimming Pools (outdoors): 1
Registry: . . . . .The Bahamas	Navigation Officers: . . . . . . .Scandinavian	Swimming Pools (indoors): 1
Length (ft/m): 820.2/250.0	Cabins (total): 550	(indoor/outdoor)
Beam (ft/m): 111.5/34.0	Size Range (sq ft/m): 226–1,345.5/	Whirlpools: 2
Draft (ft/m): 24.9/7.6	21–125	Self-Service Launderette: . . . . .Yes
Propulsion/Propellers: . . . . .2 pods/	Cabins (outside view): 550	Dedicated Cinema/Seats: Yes/202
diesel power	Cabins (interior/no view): 0	Library: . . . . .Yes
Passenger Decks: 9	Cabins (for one person): 0	Classification Society: . . .Lloyd's Register

OVERALL SCORE: 1,702 (OUT OF A POSSIBLE 2,000 POINTS)

OVERVIEW. *Crystal Serenity* is the latest (slightly larger but still mid-size) close sister ship to the elegant, and successful *Crystal Harmony* and *Crystal Symphony*. This new ship carries forward the same look, and profile. *Crystal Serenity* is a contemporary ship with a nicely raked clipper bow and well-balanced lines. While some might not like the "apartment block" look of the ship's exterior, it is the contemporary, "in" look, with balconies having become important standard features aboard almost all new cruise ships built today.

BERLITZ'S RATINGS

	Possible	Achieved
Ship	500	431
Accommodation	200	165
Food	400	341
Service	400	339
Entertainment	100	84
Cruise	400	342

The latest in podded propulsion is provided *(see page 17 for details)*. Electrical power is provided by the latest generation of environmentally friendly diesel engines.

This ship has an excellent amount of open deck, sunbathing space, and sports facilities. The aft of two outdoor swimming pools can be covered by a magrodome (retractable glass dome) in poor weather. There is no sense of crowding in this superb example of comfort by design, high-quality construction and engineering. There is also a wide wrap-around teakwood deck for walking, pleasingly uncluttered by deck lounge chairs.

With the exception of a gray, clinical photo gallery passageway, the decor in most areas is warm, inviting and contemporary. There is much use of rich wood paneling and detailing. The main lobby houses the reception desk (staffed 24 hours a day), concierge and shore excursion desks, and a lounge/bar (Crystal Cove) with baby grand piano. However, there are no passenger cabins forward of the lobby (they have instead become accommodation for officers and staff, a more sensible arrangement since this area really is considered to be "back of house").

Some of the most elegant public rooms include Palm Court (evoking images of Colonial-style grand hotel lounges); the Avenue Saloon (a favorite watering hole of the late-night crowd and a throwback to the gentlemen's clubs of yesteryear); the Connoisseur Club (for cigar and cognac enthusiasts); and the Stardust Club (cabaret entertainment lounge). Other new additions include a dedicated room for viewing art for auction, computer-learning center (24 terminals), an internet center, and Vintage Room (private dining room where 12 invited diners can enjoy exclusive vintage wines from around the world in special wine-tasting dinners).

The Caesar's Palace At Sea casino has been centrally located, with no outside views to distract passengers who are intent on gaming. Instead, the location is adjacent to lifeboats on both sides (in this arrangement, the lifeboats do not obstruct either cabins or public rooms).

This ship has just about everything for the discerning, seasoned traveler who is prepared to pay for fine style, abundant space and the comfort and the facilities of a large vessel, including an excellent program of guest lecturers. The one thing that lets the product down is the fact that the dining room operation is in two seatings (however, many older passengers do want to eat early, while the line's younger passengers prefer to dine later, so there is some balance).

Your evenings will be necessarily rather structured due to the fact that there are two seatings for dinner (unless you eat in one of the alternative dining spots), and two shows (the showlounge cannot seat all passengers at once). This detracts from the otherwise luxurious setting of the ship and the fine professionalism of its staff. Many passengers feel that gratuities should really be included on a ship that is rated this highly (they can, however, be pre-paid).

The ship achieves a high rating because of its fine facilities, service and crew. It is the extra attention to detail that makes a cruise with this ship so special. The passenger mix is usually 85% North American (half from California) and 15% other nationalities. The ship should provide you with announcement-free cruising in a well-tuned, very professionally run, service-oriented ship, roughly the equivalent of a Four Seasons or Ritz Carlton hotel. All bottled water and (non-alcoholic) soft drinks are included in the price. The onboard currency is the US dollar, and gratuities are at your discretion (15% is added to bar accounts, however).

SUITABLE FOR: *Crystal Serenity* is best suited to sophisticated travelers (typically over 50) who seek contemporary ship surroundings, with fine quality fittings and furnishings, a wide range of public rooms and facilities, and excellent food and service from a well trained staff.

ACCOMMODATION. This consists of: four Crystal Penthouses with balcony; 32 Penthouse Suites with Balcony; 66 Penthouses with balcony; 78 superior outside-view cabins with balcony; 286 outside-view cabins with balcony; 84 outside-view cabins without balcony but with large picture windows. Two whole decks of accommodation are designated as suites (Deck 11, and Deck 10), while all other accommodation is located on Decks 9, 8 and 7.

Duvets and down pillows are provided, as are lots of other niceties, together with a data socket for connecting a laptop computer. All accommodation has a refrigerator and mini-bar, television, satellite-linked telephone, and hairdryer. There's a full range of Aveda personal toiletry amenities, and a plush, full-length cotton bathrobe, and plenty of cotton towels (the largest of which measures a generous 70 by 34 inches/180 by 85cm). The in-cabin TV programming is excellent (although why it starts at Channel 53, and not Channel 1, is unclear), and close-captioned videos are provided for the hearing-impaired. The air-conditioning in bathrooms and walk-in closets is extremely loud. In suites/cabins with "private" balcony, the balcony partition is of the partial, not full, type, and so noisy neighbors (particularly if using mobile phones in ports of call) can prove intrusive. The balcony decking is teak, however.

Butlers provide excellent service in all the top category suites on Decks 10 and 11, where room service food arrives on silver trays. Afternoon tea trolley service and evening hors d'oeuvres are standard fare in "butler service" suites.
Crystal Penthouses (with balcony): There are four Crystal Penthouses with private balcony (1,345 sq. ft/125 sq. meters). These are ideally located in the center of the ship on Penthouse Deck 11, each with outstanding views and large private balconies with outside lighting (they are a slightly different shape to those of the other ships in the fleet). There is a lounge with audio-visual entertainment center, separate master bedroom with king-sized bed and electric curtains, large walk-in closets, and large vanity desk.

The marble-clad bathrooms have ocean views; they are stunning and come with a whirlpool bathtub with integral shower, two washbasins, separate large shower enclosure, bidet and toilet, and plenty of storage space for toiletries.
Penthouse Suites (with balcony): There are 32 of these (538 sq. ft/50 sq. meters), all on Penthouse Deck 11. Each has a separate bedroom, walk-in closet and en-suite bathroom with full-size bathtub with integral shower, two washbasins, separate shower enclosure, bidet, toilet, and ample space for toiletries. The lounge has a large couch, coffee table and several armchairs, and there is a dining table and four chairs.
Penthouse Deck Cabin (with balcony): These are 66 of these, located on Penthouse Decks 10 and 11. They measure 403.6 sq. ft/37.5 sq. meters. All come with a private balcony, although eight that are located at the aft of Deck 11 have larger balconies. These units are really large cabins that have a sleeping area that can be curtained off from the lounge area, with its large, long vanity desk. The bathroom is large, and has a full-size bathtub (with integral shower), separate shower enclosure, and a bidet and toilet.
Superior Deluxe Outside-View Cabins (with balcony): This really is a standard outside-view cabin that is larger than any standard cabin aboard most other ships, and measures 269 sq. ft (25 sq. meters). The 78 cabins are longer than cabins that don't have a private balcony. They have a sleeping area with clothes closets, small couch, and drinks table, vanity desk with hairdryer. The bathroom has a bathtub with integral shower, two washbasins, and toilet. Large patio doors open onto a private balcony.
Deluxe Outside-View Cabins (with balcony): This is really a standard outside-view cabin that is larger than any standard cabin aboard most other ships, and measures 269 sq. ft (25 sq. meters). The 286 cabins, about the same size and shape as the "Deluxe" version but on a "superior" deck (Penthouse Deck 10), are longer than cabins that don't have a private balcony. They have a sleeping area with clothes closets, small couch, and drinks table, vanity desk with hairdryer. The bathroom has a tub with integral shower, two basins, and toilet. Patio doors open to a private balcony.
Deluxe Outside-View Cabins (no balcony): This is really a standard outside-view cabin (located on Deck 7, with the wrap-around promenade deck outside each cabin) that is larger than any standard cabin aboard most ships. The 84 cabins measure 226 sq. ft (21 sq. meters), and have a large window, sleeping area with clothes closets, small sofa and drinks table, vanity desk with hairdryer. The small bathroom has a bathtub with integral shower, two washbasins, and toilet.
Wheelchair Accessible Accommodation: This includes two penthouse grades, two cabins with balconies, and four cabins with large picture windows.

CUISINE/DINING. There is one main dining room (the Crystal Dining Room), two alternative dining rooms (reservations are required), and a sushi bar. The Crystal Dining Room is quite elegant, with a crisp, clean "California Modern" style that includes plenty of space around each table. It is well laid-out, and has a raised, circular central section, although it is noisy at times, and not conducive to a fine dining experience. There are tables for two (many positioned adjacent to large windows), four, six or eight. All restaurants are non-smoking areas. At dinner, a wandering trio serenades passengers at their tables, but this is tacky and not representative of fine dining.

The food is very attractively presented on large plates, and well served (using both plate service and silver service). It is of a very high standard with fine quality (high cost) ingredients. European dishes are predominantly featured (but in an American style). The menus are extremely varied, and feature a fine selection of meat, fish and vegetarian dishes. Special (off-menu) orders are available, as are caviar and other culinary niceties. Kosher meals are also available (frozen when brought on board); Kosher pots, pans and utensils are sterilized in salt water, and all plates used during service are hand-washed separately.

Overall, the food is really good for the size of ship, and, with the choice of the two alternative dining spots, receives high praise. Sadly, dinner in the main dining room is in two seatings amd fixed-table assignments, the company having used the space that could have provided a second main dining room, for public areas. While the early seating is simply too rushed for many, with two alternative restaurants, off-menu choices, a hand-picked European staff and excellent service, dining is often memorable. Fresh pasta and dessert flambeau specialties are made at the table each day by accommodating headwaiters.

Alternative Dining Spots (reservations required, no extra charge): There are two alternative restaurants (one Italian, the other Asian). Both are aft on Deck 7, and both have excellent views from large picture windows. Prego is for Italian food, Italian wines, and service with a flair. Silk Road has Asian-California "fusion" food. Although there is no extra charge, a "gratuity" is added to your account.

There is a separate sushi bar, with items selected by superb Los-Angeles-based Japanese super-chef Nobu Matsuhisa, and skillfully prepared on board by a Nobu-trained chef; the high-cost ingredients are flown regularly to the ship. The alternative dining spots provide an excellent standard of culinary fare – with food cooked to order at no extra charge (although many Crystal regulars feel the recommended $6 waiter gratuity per meal should be included in the cruise fare). To eat in one of Nobu's restaurants ashore costs a considerable amount; aboard the ship, not only is the food free, it is outstanding.

The Bistro: Located on the upper level of the two-deck-high lobby, this is a casual spot for coffees and pastries, served in the style and atmosphere of a European street cafe. The Bistro has unusual Crystal Cruises-logo china that can be bought in one of the ship's boutiques.

Casual Eateries: For casual meals, the Lido Cafe has an extensive self-serve buffet area. It's high up in the ship, with great views from its large picture windows. For casual poolside lunches, there is also the Trident Grill, as well as an ice cream/frozen yoghurt counter (no extra charge). Special themed luncheon buffets, with appropriate decor and

service staff dressed accordingly, are provided at the Trident indoor/outdoor pool area. These include the popular Asian Buffet and Follow the Sun (Mediterranean) buffet.

ENTERTAINMENT. The Galaxy Lounge is the ship's principal showlounge. It is quite a large room with a high ceiling, but on one level (with a nicely sloping floor) for good visibility. Indeed, the sightlines are good from almost all seats. Both banquette and individual seating is provided. The stage, lighting, and sound equipment are all excellent.

The shows are elegant, with excellent costuming (though not much in the way of scenery), but some are seriously dated, too long, and Crystal Cruises' many repeat passengers know them all. In addition, many nights feature cabaret acts and classical artistes that are of a good caliber, and constantly changing. The bands and musical units are also, for the most part, of a high caliber, and there is plenty of music for social dancing. The ship also provides gentlemen hosts (called Ambassador Hosts) for the many single ladies that enjoy traveling with Crystal Cruises.

SPA/FITNESS. The Crystal Spa is located aft on Lido Deck 12, one of the ship's uppermost decks. Facilities include men's and women's changing rooms with sauna (which has a large porthole-shaped window) and steam rooms, gymnasium with high-tech muscle-pumping equipment, an aerobics exercise area, and reception/relaxation area.

Treatments are provided under the aegis of Steiner Platinum Service (Steiner being the concession). Facilities include one room dedicated to yoga and pilates classes (no extra charge), an aerobics/exercise room, plus separate sauna, steam rooms, and changing rooms for both men and women. There are seven treatment rooms (including one for couples, and one with a "dry float bed") for massage, facials, and other treatments, and a separate beauty salon.

Some staff will try to sell you Steiner's own-brand Elemis beauty products). Massage (including exotic massages such as Aroma Stone massage, Chakra Balancing massage and other well-being massages), facials, pedicures, and beauty salon treatments cost extra. Examples: Swedish Massage ($109 for 50 minutes); Deep Tissue Massage ($116 for 50 minutes). There are also some excellent multi-therapy packages that provide you with hours of pampering. Example: Ceremony of Precious Metal (exotic lime and ginger salt glow, aroma spa ocean wrap, well-being massage) lasting 3 hours 30 minutes, for $323. A simple hair cut (for men) costs $25, while it is $57 for women with short hair for a shampoo, cut and blow-dry.

The ship has excellent open deck and sunbathing space, and sports facilities that include two full-size paddle tennis courts, electronic golf simulator, and golf driving range. One of two outdoor swimming pools has a magrodome (retractable glass dome) cover, while the one that is in the open is one of the longest aboard any ship today. Anyone trying to sunbathe quietly on the deck under and close to the paddle tennis courts will hear the noise of play (bat against ball) when the court is in use.

Crystal Symphony
★★★★★

Mid-Size Ship: . . . . .51,044 tons	Total Crew: 545	Cabins (with private balcony): 276
Lifestyle: . . . . .Luxury/Premium	Passengers	Cabins (wheelchair accessible): 7
Cruise Line: . . . . .Crystal Cruises	(lower beds/all berths): 960/1,010	Cabin Current: . . . . .110 and 220 volts
Former Names: . . . . .none	Passenger Space Ratio	Elevators: 8
Builder: . . . . .Masa-Yards (Finland)	(lower beds/all berths): 53.1/50.5	Casino (gaming tables): . . . . .Yes
Original Cost: . . . .$300 million	Crew/Passenger Ratio	Slot Machines: . . . . .Yes
Entered Service: . . . . .Mar 1995	(lower beds/all berths): 1.7/1.8	Swimming Pools (outdoors): 2
Registry: . . . . .The Bahamas	Navigation Officers: . . . . . . .Scandinavian	(1 with magrodome)
Length (ft/m): 777.8/237.10	Cabins (total): 480	Swimming Pools (indoors): 0
Beam (ft/m): 98.0/30.20	Size Range (sq ft/m): 201.2–981.7/	Whirlpools: 2
Draft (ft/m): 24.9/7.60	18.7–91.2	Self-Service Launderette: . . . . .Yes
Propulsion/Propellers: . . . . .diesel-electric	Cabins (outside view): 480	Dedicated Cinema/Seats: Yes/143
(33,880kW)/2	Cabins (interior/no view): 0	Library: . . . . .Yes
Passenger Decks: 8	Cabins (for one person): 0	Classification Society: . . .Lloyd's Register

---

OVERALL SCORE: 1,701 (OUT OF A POSSIBLE 2,000 POINTS)

OVERVIEW. *Crystal Symphony* is a contemporary ship with a nicely raked clipper bow and well-balanced lines. While some might not like the "apartment block" look of its exterior, it is the contemporary, "in" look, balconies having become standard aboard almost all new cruise ships. This ship has an excellent amount of open deck, sunbathing space, and sports facilities. The aft of two outdoor swimming pools can be covered by a magrodome in inclement weather. There is no sense of crowding anywhere – a superb example of comfort by design, high-quality construction and more up-to-date engineering technology (and better built and finished than *Crystal Harmony*). There is a wide wrap-around teakwood deck for walking, uncluttered by lounge chairs.

Inside, the layout is similar to that of *Crystal Harmony* and *Crystal Serenity*, with a design that shows that form follows function superbly well, combining the best of large ship facilities with the intimacy of rooms found aboard most small ships. The interior decor is restful, with color combinations that don't jar the senses. It has a good mixture of public entertainment lounges and small intimate rooms. Outstanding is the Palm Court, an observation lounge with forward-facing views over the ship's bows – it is tranquil, and one of the nicest rooms afloat (it is larger than aboard the sister ship).

There is an excellent book, video and CD-ROM library (combined with a Business Center). The theater (smaller than aboard sister ship *Crystal Harmony*) has high-definition video projection and headsets for the hearing-impaired. Useful self-service launderettes are provided on each deck. Fine-quality fabrics and soft furnishings, china, flatware and silver are used. Excellent in-cabin television programming

BERLITZ'S RATINGS

	Possible	Achieved
Ship	500	430
Accommodation	200	163
Food	400	340
Service	400	342
Entertainment	100	84
Cruise	400	342

(including CNN) is transmitted, as well as close-captioned videos for the use of the hearing-impaired.

In 1999, a "Connoisseurs Club" was added, adjacent to the Avenue Saloon. Features in this intimate room include fine premium brands of liquor and cigars for those who can appreciate (and pay for) such things. Also added was a Computer Learning Center, with more than 20 computer stations. Private lessons are available (although they are expensive).

This ship has just about everything for the discerning, seasoned traveler who wants and is prepared to pay good money for fine style, abundant space and the comfort and the facilities of a large vessel capable of extended voyages, including an excellent program of guest lecturers.

The one thing that lets the product down is the fact that the dining room operation is in two seatings (however, having said that, there are many older passengers who want to eat early, while the line's younger passengers prefer to dine later, so there is some semblance of balance).

Crystal Cruises takes care of its ships, and its staff, and it is the staff that make the cruise experience special. They are a well-trained group that stress hospitality at all times. The ship achieves a high rating because of its fine facilities, service and crew. It is the extra attention to detail that really counts. The passenger mix is approximately 85 percent North American (typically half will be from California) and 15% other nationalities.

This is announcement-free cruising in a well-tuned, very professionally run, service oriented, ship, the approximate equivalent of a Four Seasons hotel. However, note that the score has gone downwards a little recently, the result of the fact that, in comparison to other ships available in the discounted marketplace, this is still a two-seating ship, which makes it more highly structured in terms of timing than it really should be. All bottled water and (non-alcoholic) soft drinks are included in the cost of your cruise (this feature was introduced with the debut of *Crystal Serenity*, but has now been applied fleet-wide). The onboard currency is the US dollar, and gratuities are at your discretion (15% is added to bar accounts, however).

Your evenings will be necessarily rather structured due to the fact that there are two seatings for dinner (unless you eat in one of the alternative dining spots), and two shows (the showlounge cannot seat all passengers at once). This detracts from the otherwise luxurious setting of the ship and the fine professionalism of its staff. Many passengers feel that gratuities should really be included on a ship that is rated this highly (they can, however, be pre-paid).

Plastic patio furniture on suite and cabin balconies would be better replaced with the more elegant teak variety, to go with the teak decking.

SUITABLE FOR: *Crystal Symphony* is best suited to discerning adult travelers (typically over 50) that seek contemporary ship surroundings, with fine-quality fittings and furnishings, a wide range of public rooms and facilities, and excellent food and service from a well trained staff.

ACCOMMODATION. There are eight categories, with the most expensive suites located on the highest accommodation deck (Deck 10). There are two Crystal Penthouses with private balcony; 18 Penthouse Suites with private balcony; 44 Penthouse Cabins with balcony; 214 Cabins with balcony; 202 Cabins without balcony. Some cabins (grades G and I), have obstructed views. Except for the suites on Deck 10, most other cabin bathrooms are very compact units.

Regardless of the accommodation category you select, duvets and down pillows are provided, as are lots of other niceties, together with a data socket for connecting a personal laptop computer. All accommodation has a refrigerator and mini-bar, television, satellite-linked telephone, and hairdryer. A full range of Aveda personal toiletry amenities is provided, as is a plush cotton bathrobe, and plenty of cotton towels (the largest of which measures a generous 70 by 34 inches(180 by 85cm). The in-cabin television programming is excellent, and close-captioned videos are provided for the hearing-impaired.

Deck 10 Penthouses: Two delightful Crystal Penthouses measure 982 sq. ft (91 sq. meters) and have a huge private balcony (with outside light) and lounge with audio-visual entertainment center, separate master bedroom with king-sized bed and electric curtains, large walk-in closets, and stunning ocean-view marble bathrooms with a whirlpool bathtub, bidet, two washbasins, and plenty of storage space for one's personal toiletry items. These really are among the best in fine, private, pampered living spaces at sea, and come with all the best priority perks, including laundry service.

Other Deck 10 Suites: All of the other suites on this deck have plenty of space (all feature a private balcony, with outside light), including a lounge with large sofa, coffee

table and chairs, a sleeping area and walk-in closet. Rich wood cabinetry provides much of the warmth of the decor. The bathrooms are quite large, and are extremely well appointed, with full-sized bathtub and separate shower enclosure, two washbasins, bidet and toilet. In fact, any of the suites on this deck are equipped with everything necessary for refined, private living at sea.

Five butlers provide the best in personal service in all the top category suites on Deck 10 (with a total of 132 beds), where all room service food arrives on silver trays. Afternoon tea trolley service and evening hors d'oeuvres are standard fare in the "butler service" suites.

Decks 5/6/7/8/9: More than 50 percent of all cabins have private balconies. All are well equipped, and extremely comfortable, with excellent sound insulation. The balcony partitions, however, do not go from floor to ceiling, so you can hear your neighbours. Even in the lowest category of standard cabins, there is plenty of drawer space, but the closet hanging space may prove somewhat limited for long voyages. There are generously sized personal bathroom amenities, duvets and down pillows. European stewardesses provide excellent service and attention.

CUISINE/DINING. The Crystal Dining Room (totally non-smoking) is quite an elegant room, with crisp design, plenty of space around each table, and well-placed waiter service stations. It is well laid out, and has a raised, circular central section, although it is somewhat noisy at times, and not conducive to a fine dining experience. There are tables for two (many of them positioned adjacent to large windows), four, six or eight. Each evening at dinner, a wandering trio serenades passengers at their tables, but this is tacky and not representative of fine dining.

The food is very attractively presented on large plates, and well served (using both plate service as well as silver service in the best European traditions). It is of a very high standard with fine quality (high cost) ingredients. European dishes are predominantly featured (but in an American style). The menus are extremely varied, and feature a fine selection of meat, fish and vegetarian dishes. Special (off-menu) orders are available, as are caviar and other culinary niceties. Kosher meals are also available (frozen when brought on board). Kosher pots, pans and utensils are sterilized in salt water, and all plates used during service are hand-washed separately.

Overall, the food is really good for the size of ship, and, with the choice of the two alternative dining spots, receives high praise. Sadly, dinner in the main dining room is in two seatings (with fixed table assignments), the company having used the space that could have provided a second main dining room, for public areas. While the early seating is simply too rushed for many, with two alternative restaurants, off-menu choices, a hand-picked European staff and excellent service, dining is often memorable. The advantage of fixed table assignments is that your waiters get to know your personal preferences, likes and dislikes (unlike dining rooms with open seating, where you may be seated with different people each evening, and your waiter changes constantly).

Fresh pasta and dessert flambeau specialties are made at the table each day by accommodating headwaiters.

The wine list is excellent (though pricey), with an outstanding collection of across-the-board wines, including a mouthwatering connoisseur selection.

Afternoon tea in the Palm Court is a civilized daily event. The Lido provides breakfast and luncheon buffets that are fairly standard fare.

Alternative Dining Spots (reservations required, no extra charge): Two alternative dining spots are the 75-seat Prego (featuring fine Italian cuisine, and specializing in good Italian wines), and the revamped 100-seat Jade Garden (featuring five contemporary Chinese/French fusion dishes in association with Wolfgang Puck's Chinois on Main restaurant in Santa Monica). These rooms are appreciably larger than those aboard *Crystal Harmony*, and set on a lower deck (Deck 6); each restaurant has a separate entrance and themed decor. Both provide an excellent standard of culinary fare, with food cooked to order at no extra charge (although many feel that the recommended $6 waiter gratuity per meal should be included in the cruise fare).

The Bistro (on the upper level of the two-deck-high lobby) is a casual spot for coffees and pastries, served in the style and atmosphere of a European street cafe. The Bistro has unusual, Crystal Cruises-logo china that can also be purchased in one of the ship's boutiques.

For casual meals, the Lido Cafe has an extensive self-serve buffet area, located high up in the ship, and with great views from its large picture windows. For casual poolside lunches, there is also the Trident Grill, as well as an ice cream/frozen yoghurt counter (all at no extra charge). Several special themed luncheon buffets, with appropriate decor and service staff dressed accordingly, are provided at the Trident indoor/outdoor pool area. These include the popular Asian Buffet and Follow the Sun (Mediterranean) buffet.

ENTERTAINMENT. The Galaxy Lounge is the ship's principal showlounge. It is quite a large room with a high ceiling, but on one level (with a tiered floor) for good visibility. The sightlines are good from most seats, although there are a few pillars that obstruct sight lines from some seats. Both banquette and individual seating is provided. The stage, lighting, and sound equipment are all excellent.

The shows are elegant, with excellent costuming and scenery, but they are now seriously dated, too long, and Crystal Cruises' many repeat passengers know them all. In addition, many nights feature cabaret acts that are of a good caliber, and constantly changing. The bands and musical units are also, for the most part, of a high caliber, and there is plenty of music for social dancing. The ship also provides male hosts (called Ambassador Hosts) for the many single women who enjoy traveling with Crystal Cruises.

SPA/FITNESS. In 2000 an expanded range of Spa facilities and treatments was introduced, under the aegis of Steiner Platinum Service (Steiner being the concession). Facilities include one room dedicated to yoga and pilates classes (no extra charge), an aerobics/exercise room, plus separate sauna, steam rooms, and changing rooms for both men and women. There are seven treatment rooms (including one for couples, and one room featuring a "dry float bed") for various types of massage, facials, and other treatments, as well as a separate beauty salon.

Some staff will try to sell you Steiner's own-brand Elemis beauty products (spa girls have sales targets). Being aboard this ship will give you an opportunity to try some of the more exotic treatments (particularly some of the massages available). Massage (including exotic massages such as Aroma Stone massage, Chakra Balancing massage and other well-being massages), facials, pedicures, and beauty salon treatments are at extra cost. Examples: Swedish Massage ($109 for 50 minutes); Deep Tissue Massage ($116 for 50 minutes); Yin Yang Facial ($109 for 50 minutes).

There are also some excellent multi-therapy packages that provide you with hours of pampering. Some examples: Ceremony of Precious Metal (exotic lime and ginger salt glow, aroma spa ocean wrap, well-being massage) lasting 3 hours 30 minutes, for $323; Ceremony of Water (aroma stone therapy, Japanese silk booster facial, Japanese eye zone therapy) lasting 3 hours 30 minutes, for $365; Ceremony of Earth (frangipani body nourish ritual, absolute spa ritual, frangipani hair and scalp conditioning with style dry, exotic hand ritual with paraffin wax, sole delight foot treatment with paraffin wax) lasting 6 hours and 30 minutes, for $561. A simple hair cut (for men) costs $25, while it is $57 for women with short hair for a shampoo, cut and blow-dry.

Do make appointments as early as possible as time slots go quickly, so the day you board is the best time to book your desired treatments.

The ship also has excellent open deck and sunbathing space, and sports facilities that include a full-sized paddle tennis court, electronic golf simulator, and golf driving range. One of two outdoor swimming pools has a magrodome (retractable glass dome) cover, while the one that is in the open is one of the longest aboard any ship today.

Dawn Princess
★★★★

Large (Resort) Ship:	.......77,499 tons	Total Crew:	900
Lifestyle:	..................Standard	Passengers	
Cruise Line:	..........Princess Cruises	(lower beds/all berths):	.....1,950/2,250
Former Names:	.................none	Passenger Space Ratio	
Builder:	.............Fincantieri (Italy)	(lower beds/all berths):	.......39.7/34.4
Original Cost:	.............$300 million	Crew/Passenger Ratio	
Entered Service:	............May 1997	(lower beds/all berths):	.........2.1/2.5
Registry:	................Great Britain	Navigation Officers:	......British/Italian
Length (ft/m):	............857.2/261.3	Cabins (total):	975
Beam (ft/m):	..............105.6/32.2	Size Range (sq ft/m):	......135.0–635.0/
Draft (ft/m):	.................26.5/8.1		12.5–59.0
Propulsion/Propellers:	.....diesel-electric	Cabins (outside view):	603
	(46,080kW)/2	Cabins (interior/no view):	372
Passenger Decks:	10	Cabins (for one person):	0

Cabins (with private balcony):	446
Cabins (wheelchair accessible):	19
Cabin Current:	........110 and 220 volts
Elevators:	11
Casino (gaming tables):	............Yes
Slot Machines:	....................Yes
Swimming Pools (outdoors):	4
Swimming Pools (indoors):	0
Whirlpools:	5
Self-Service Launderette:	..........Yes
Dedicated Cinema/Seats:	...........No
Library:	...........................Yes
Classification Society:	...Registro Navale
	Italiano (RINA)

OVERALL SCORE: 1,539 (OUT OF A POSSIBLE 2,000 POINTS)

OVERVIEW. *Dawn Princess* is an all-white ship with a decent contemporary profile, well balanced by a large funnel that contains a deck tennis/basketball/volleyball court in its sheltered aft base. There is a wide, teakwood wrap-around promenade deck outdoors, some real teak steamer-style deck chairs (complete with royal blue cushioned pads), and 93,000 sq. ft (8,640 sq. meters) of space outdoors. A great amount of glass area on the upper decks provides plenty of light and connection with the outside world.

The ship absorbs passengers well, and has an almost intimate feel to it. The interiors are very pretty and warm, with attractive colors and welcoming decor that includes some very attractive wall murals and other artwork. The signage throughout the ship could be better, however. There are a number of dead ends in the interior layout, so it's not as user-friendly as a ship this size could be. The cabin numbering system is extremely illogical, with numbers going through several hundred series on the same deck.

There is a wide range of public rooms, with several intimate rooms and spaces so that you don't get the feel of being overwhelmed by large spaces. The interior focal point is a huge four-deck-high atrium lobby with winding, double stairways, and two panoramic glass-walled elevators.

There are two showlounges, one at each end of the ship; one is a superb 550-seat, theater-style showlounge (movies are also shown here) and the other is a 480-seat cabaret-style lounge, complete with bar.

The library, a very warm room, has six large butter-colored leather chairs for listening to compact audio discs, with ocean-view windows. There is a conference center for up to 300, as well as a business center with computers, copy

BERLITZ'S RATINGS

	Possible	Achieved
Ship	500	428
Accommodation	200	162
Food	400	266
Service	400	291
Entertainment	100	86
Cruise	400	306

and fax machines. The collection of artwork is good, particularly on the stairways, and helps make the ship feel smaller than it is, although in places it doesn't always seem coordinated. The casino, while large, is not really in the main passenger flow and so it does not generate the "walk-through" factor found aboard so many ships.

The most traditional room is the Wheelhouse Lounge/Bar, which is decorated in the style of a late 19th-century gentleman's club, with wood paneling and comfortable seating. The focal point is a large ship model from the P&O collection archives: aboard *Dawn Princess* it is *Kenya*.

One nice feature is the captain's cocktail party – it is typically held in the four-deck-high main atrium – so you can come and go as you please, and there's no standing in line to have your photograph taken with the captain if you don't want to. However, note that cruising aboard large ships such as this one has become increasingly an onboard revenue-based product. The in-your-face art auctions are simply overbearing, and the paintings, lithographs and faux, framed pictures that are strewn throughout the ship (and clash irritatingly with the ship's interior decor) are an annoying intrusion into what should be a holiday, not a cruise inside a floating "art" emporium. There are no cushioned pads for the deck lounge chairs on the open lido decks.

The swimming pools are quite small for so many passengers, and the pool deck is cluttered with white, plastic deck lounge chairs, without cushioned pads. Waiting for tenders in anchor ports can prove irritating, but typical of large ship operations. Charging for use of the machines and washing powder in the self-service launderette is trifling.

As is the case aboard most large ships today, if you live

in the top suites, you will be well attended; if you do not, you will merely be one of a large number of passengers.

ACCOMMODATION. The brochure shows that there are 28 different cabin grades: 20 outside-view and 8 interior (no view) cabins. Although the standard outside-view and interior (no view) cabins are a little small, they are well designed and functional in layout, and have earth tone colors accentuated by splashes of color from the bedspreads. Proportionately, there are quite a lot of interior (no view) cabins. Many of the outside-view cabins have private balconies, and all seem to be quite well soundproofed, although the balcony partition is not the floor-to-ceiling type, so you can hear your neighbors clearly (or smell their smoke). Note that the balconies are very narrow, only just large enough for two small chairs, and there is no dedicated lighting.

A reasonable amount of closet and abundant drawer and other storage space is provided in all cabins – adequate for a 7-night cruise, as are a television and refrigerator. Each night a chocolate will appear on your pillow. The cabin bathrooms are practical, and come complete with most of the things needed, although they really are tight spaces, and are best described as one person at-a-time units. They do, however, have a decent shower enclosure, a small amount of shelving for your personal toiletries, real glasses, a hairdryer and a bathrobe.

The largest accommodation is in six suites, two on each of three decks located at the stern of the ship, with large private balcony (536–754 sq.ft/49.8–21.3 sq.meters, including balcony). These are well laid out, and have large bathrooms with two sinks, a Jacuzzi bathtub, and a separate shower enclosure. The bedroom has generous amounts of wood accenting and detailing, indented ceilings, and television sets in both bedroom and lounge areas. The suites also have a dining room table and four chairs.

The 32 mini-suites (374–536 sq.ft/34.7–49.7 sq.meters) typically have two lower beds that convert into a queen-sized bed. There is a separate bedroom/sleeping area with vanity desk, and a lounge with sofa and coffee table, indented ceilings with generous amounts of wood accenting and detailing, walk-in closet, and larger bathroom with Jacuzzi bathtub and separate shower enclosure.

There are 19 wheelchair-accessible cabins, which measure 213–305 sq. meters/19.7–28.2 sq.ft and are a mix of 7 outside view and 12 interior (no view) cabins.

Princess Cruises has CNN, CNBC, ESPN and TNT on the in-cabin color television system (when available, depending on cruise area).

CUISINE/DINING. There are two main dining rooms of asymmetrical design (each seats about 500), Florentine and Venetian (both non-smoking, as are all dining rooms aboard the ships of Princess Cruises), located adjacent to the two lower levels of the four-deck high atrium lobby. Each has its own galley and each is split into multi-tier sections, which help create a feeling of intimacy, although there is a lot of noise from the waiter stations, which are adjacent to

many tables. Breakfast and lunch are provided in an open seating arrangement, while dinner is in two seatings.

On any given 7-day cruise, a typical menu cycle will include a Sailaway Dinner, Captain's Welcome Dinner, Chef's Dinner, Italian Dinner, French Dinner, Captain's Gala Dinner, and Landfall Dinner. The wine list is reasonable, but not good, and the company has, sadly, seen fit to eliminate all wine waiters. Note that 15% is added to all beverage bills, including wines.

For some really good meat, however, consider the Sterling Steakhouse; it's for those who want to taste four different cuts of Angus beef from the popular "Sterling Silver" brand of USDA prime meats – Filet Mignon, New York Strip, Porterhouse, and Rib-Eye – all presented on a silver tray.

There is also a barbecue chicken option, plus the usual baked potato or French fries as accompaniments. This is available as an alternative to the dining rooms, between 6.30pm and 9.30pm only, at an additional charge of $8 per person. However, it is not, as you might expect, a separate, intimate dining room, but is located in a section of the Horizon Buffet, with its own portable bar and some decorative touches to set it apart (from the regular Horizon Buffet).

The Horizon Buffet is open 24 hours a day, and, at night, has an informal dinner setting with sit-down waiter service; a small bistro menu is also available. The buffet displays are, for the most part, quite repetitious, but better than they have been in the past few years (there is no real finesse in presentation, however, as plastic plates are provided, instead of trays). The cabin service menu is very limited, and presentation of the food items featured is poor.

There is also a patisserie (for cappuccino/espresso coffees and pastries), a wine/caviar bar, and a pizzeria (with cobblestone floors and wrought-iron decorative features), and excellent pizzas (there are six to choose from).

ENTERTAINMENT. There are two showlounges (both theatre and cabaret style). The main one, Princess Theater, has a sloping floor, with aisle-style seating (as found in shoreside movie theaters) that is well tiered, and with good sight lines to the raised stage from most of the 500 seats.

The second showlounge (Vista Lounge), located at the aft end of the ship, has cabaret entertainment, and also acts as a lecture and presentation room. Princess Cruises has a good stable of regular cabaret acts to draw from, so there should be something for almost all tastes.

SPA/FITNESS. A glass-walled health spa complex is located high atop the ship and includes a gymnasium with the latest high-tech machines. One swimming pool is "suspended" aft between two decks (there are two other pools, although they are not large for the size of the ship).

Sports facilities are located in an open-air sports deck positioned inside the ship's funnel and adaptable for basketball, volleyball, badminton or paddle tennis. Joggers can exercise on the wrap-around open Promenade Deck.

● **For more extensive general information about the Princess Cruises experience, see pages 124–127.**

Delphin Renaissance
NOT YET RATED

Mid-Size Ship: . . . . .30,277 tons	Total Crew: 300	Cabins (with private balcony): 232
Lifestyle: . . . . .Standard	Passengers	Cabins (wheelchair accessible): 4
Cruise Line: . . . . .Delphin Seereisen	(lower beds/all berths): 698/777	Cabin Current: . . . . .110 and 220 volts
Former Names: . . . . .R Seven	Passenger Space Ratio	Elevators: 4
Builder: . .Chantiers de l'Atlantique (France)	(lower beds/all berths): 43.3/38.9	Casino (gaming tables): . . . . .No
Original Cost: . . . .$150 million	Crew/Passenger Ratio	Slot Machines: .No
Entered Service: . . . . . . .Oct 2000/July 2003	(lower beds/all berths): 1.8/2.5	Swimming Pools (outdoors): 1
Registry: . . . . .Marshall Islands	Navigation Officers: . . . . .European	Swimming Pools (indoors): 0
Length (ft/m): 593.7/181.0	Cabins (total): .349	Whirlpools: 2
Beam (ft/m): 83.5/25.5	Size Range (sq ft/m): 145.3–968.7/	(+ 1 thalassaotherapy)
Draft (ft/m): 19.5/6.0	13.5–90.0	Self-Service Launderette: . . . . .Yes
Propulsion/Propellers: . . . . .diesel	Cabins (outside view): 326	Dedicated Cinema/Seats: . . . . .No
(18,600 kW)/2	Cabins (interior/no view): 23	Library: . . . . .Yes
Passenger Decks: 9	Cabins (for one person): 0	Classification Society: . . . . . .Bureau Veritas

OVERALL SCORE: NYR (OUT OF A POSSIBLE 2,000 POINTS)

OVERVIEW. *Delphin Renaissance* was previously one of a series of eight almost identical ships in the now defunct Renaissance Cruises fleet. (When it was in operation, between 1998 and 2001, Renaissance Cruises was the cruise industry's only totally non-smoking cruise line). Delphin Seereisen (which acquired the ship on a 14-year lease/purchase arrangement) now operates it. *Delphin Renaissance* is larger than *Delphin* (now on charter to another company) and loses some of the ambiance for which the smaller ship was known, but the facilities and dining options are far better, and it can cruise faster than *Delphin*, allowing the company to offer even busier itineraries.

The exterior design manages to balance the ship's high sides by combining a deep blue hull with the white superstructure and large, square blue funnel. An outdoors lido deck has a swimming pool, and good sunbathing space, while one of the aft decks features a thalassaotherapy pool. A jogging track circles the swimming pool deck (but one deck above it). The exterior decks are covered with Bolidt – a rubber and grit-like surface (teak, although very expensive, would be much better, and more in keeping with the decor of the ship). The uppermost outdoors deck includes a golf driving net and shuffleboard court.

The interior decor is quite elegant, and is a throwback to the ocean liner decor of the 1920s and '30s. This includes detailed ceiling cornices, both real and faux wrought-iron staircase railings, leather paneled walls, *trompe l'oeil* ceilings, rich carpeting in hallways with an Oriental rug-look center section, and other interesting (and expensive-looking, but faux) decorative touches. The overall ambiance is that of an old-world country club. The staircase in the main,

BERLITZ'S RATINGS

	Possible	Achieved
Ship	500	NYR
Accommodation	200	NYR
Food	400	NYR
Service	400	NYR
Entertainment	100	NYR
Cruise	400	NYR

two-deck-high foyer will remind you of something similar in a blockbuster hit about a certain ship in which movie stars Kate Winslet and Leonardo di Caprio met. Delphin Seereisen's regular passengers must be pleased with the taste with which its interiors have been designed and executed, and with the variety of public rooms featured.

The public rooms are basically spread over three decks. Some changes were made when Delphin Seereisen took over the ship: the casino, for example, was dispensed with and replaced by a lounge/bar combination (with a fireplace), while a sports bar/observation lounge was converted into a restful panoramic observation lounge with fine views from its floor-to-ceiling windows. The room has a long bar which faces forward (the barmen actually have the best view), and very comfortable seating.

There are several other bars and lounges. The Library is a really grand, restful room (perhaps the nicest of all the public rooms), and is designed in the Regency period style. It has a fireplace, a high, indented, *trompe l'oeil* ceiling, and a good selection of books, plus some very comfortable wingback chairs with footstools, and sofas you could sleep on. An internet cafe with eight computer terminals is located within the card room. The ship also has a dialysis center for nine passengers (special dialysis cruises only).

Delphin Seereisen provides a seamless cruise and tour package, geared specifically to German-speaking passengers, at a price that's very hard to beat considering the destination-rich itineraries, together with pre- and post-cruise land stays at good-quality hotels, all transfers, and the lecturers that accompany every cruise. You should experience a fine, hassle-free cruise vacation package aboard this ship.

There may not be marble bathroom fittings and other niceties, but the value for money is excellent.

There are well planned, in-depth itineraries and shore excursions (most included in the cruise fare) accompanied by some fine lecturers. All gratuities and shore excursions (usually carried out with almost military precision) are included. This ship cannot be recommended for children. Note that when this edition was completed the names of some of the public rooms and restaurants had not been finalized. The onboard currency is the euro.

There is no wrap-around promenade deck outdoors (there is, however, a small jogging track around the perimeter of the swimming pool, and port and starboard side open decks for short strolls), and no wooden decks outdoors (instead, they are covered by Bollidt, a sand-colored rubberized material). The stairways, although carpeted, sound quite tinny.

SUITABLE FOR: *Delphin Renaissance* is best suited to adult couples and single travelers of a mature age who seek to cruise to interesting destinations in comfortable, fairly sophisticated surroundings, and who do not need the entertainment and mindless organized parlor games found aboard the large contemporary cruise ships, but would rather have intellectual conversation with fellow passengers, and life enrichment lectures on the subject matter dictated by the ship's itineraries.

ACCOMMODATION. There are five basic cabin size categories, the price depending on the category and location. In order of size, they are: Owner's Suites (6), Master Suites (4), Deluxe with balcony, Superior Plus with balcony, Superior with balcony, and Standard Outside View/Standard Interior (No View) Cabins. Some cabins have interconnecting doors (good for families with children), while 18 cabins on Deck 6 have lifeboat obstructed views. No matter what grade of accommodation you choose, a range of personal toiletry items is supplied to all; these include soap, shampoo, body lotion, shower cap, and shoeshine mitt. All accommodation grades also have a color TV set and satellite-linked telephone.

Standard Outside-View and Interior (no view) Cabins: All of the standard interior (no view) and outside-view cabins (the lowest four grades) are extremely compact units, and very tight for two persons (particularly for cruises longer than five days). They have twin beds (or queen-size bed), with good under-bed storage areas, personal safe, vanity desk with large mirror, and a good amount of closet and drawer space (in rich, dark woods).

Cabins with Private Balcony: Cabins with private balconies (about two-thirds of all cabins) have partial, and not full, balcony partitions, sliding glass doors, and, due to good design and layout, only 14 cabins on Deck 6 have lifeboat-obstructed views. The bathrooms, which have tiled floors and plain walls, are compact, standard units, and include a shower stall with a strong, removable hand-held

shower unit, hairdryer, 100% cotton towels, toiletries storage shelves and retractable clothesline.

Owner's Suites/Master Suites: The six Owner's Suites and four Master Suites provide the most spacious accommodation. These are fine, large living spaces located in the forward-most and aft-most sections of the accommodation decks (particularly nice are those that overlook the stern, on Deck 6, 7 and 8). They have more extensive private balconies that really are private and cannot be overlooked by anyone from the decks above. There is an entrance foyer, living room, bedroom (the bed faces the sea, which can be seen through the floor-to-ceiling windows and sliding glass door), CD player (with selection of audio discs), bathroom with Jacuzzi bathtub, and a small guest bathroom.

CUISINE/DINING. There is one main dining room and one alternative restaurant.

The Seven Seas Restaurant has a raised central section, and seats all passengers in one seating. There are large ocean-view windows on three sides, several prime tables overlooking the stern. music. The menu changes daily for lunch and dinner, and male passengers are asked to wear jacket and tie.

Alternative dining: The Portofino Restaurant has ocean-view windows along two sides, and the cuisine has food from Italy and the Mediterranean region. Tables are for four or six (with a few tables for two).

The Lido Cafe has both indoor and outdoor seating, and is the ship's casual dining spot, in a self-serve buffet style. It is open for breakfast, lunch and casual dinners. In addition, there is a Poolside Grill and Bar for fast-food items.

ENTERTAINMENT. The Lounge, located forward on Deck 5, is the venue for all main entertainment events, and some social functions. While this is not the ideal ship for large-scale production shows, in the evenings, the entertainment consists of a mix of classical concerts, revues, as well as comedy and drama presentations. The entertainment has a cultural tone to it, and is a far cry from the razzle-dazzle productions aboard the large cruise ships of the world. Additionally, local entertainers are brought on board in various destinations, providing a taste of the traditions in countries being visited.

SPA/FITNESS. The health/fitness spa has a gymnasium with some of the latest muscle toning equipment, a thalassotherapy pool, and several treatment rooms. Out on deck, there is a small swimming pool, two hot tubs, and a jogging track.

The spa facility is staffed and operated by Steiner Leisure, a concession that provides the staff and a wide range of beauty and wellness treatments. Examples of treatments include massage (€43 for 50 minutes); foot massage (€12 for 15 minutes); facial (€40 for 55 minutes); manicure (€15) and pedicure (€19). If you want to book spa treatments, it is wise to do so as soon after you embark as possible, as time slots do tend to fill up quickly.

Deutschland
NOT YET RATED

Mid-Size Ship:	.22,400 tons	Passenger Decks:	.7
Lifestyle:	.Premium	Total Crew:	.270
Cruise Line:	.Peter Deilmann Reederei	Passengers	
Former Names:	.None	(lower beds/all berths):	.548/560
Builder:	.Howaldswerke Deutsche	Passenger Space Ratio	
	Werft	(lower beds/all berths):	.40.8/40.0
Original Cost:	.DM 212 million	Crew/Passenger Ratio	
Entered Service:	.May 1998	(lower beds/all berths):	.2.0/2.0
Registry:	.Germany	Navigation Officers:	.European
Length (ft/m):	.574.1/175.0	Cabins (total):	.292
Beam (ft/m):	.75.4/23.0	Size Range (sq ft/m):	.161.4–365.9/
Draft (ft/m):	.19.0/5.8		15.0–34.0
Propulsion/Propellers:	.diesel	Cabins (outside view):	.218
	(12,300 kW)/2	Cabins (interior/no view):	.74

Cabins (for one person):	.36
Cabins (with private balcony):	.2
Cabins (wheelchair accessible):	.1
Cabin Current:	.230 volts
Elevators:	.3
Casino (gaming tables):	.No
Slot Machines:	.No
Swimming Pools (outdoors):	.1
Swimming Pools (indoors):	.1
Whirlpools:	.0
Self-Service Launderette:	.No
Dedicated Cinema/Seats:	.Yes/83
Library:	.Yes
Classification Society: Norddeuscher-Lloyd	

OVERALL SCORE: NYR (OUT OF A POSSIBLE 2,000 POINTS)

OVERVIEW. *Deutschland* is an important vessel for the German-speaking passenger seeking a traditional ship. It has an angular, low-in-the-water profile that is not particularly handsome, and a large, single, squat, traditional funnel. The ship, built in sections by four shipyards, was assembled in Kiel, Germany.

There is no wrap-around promenade deck outdoors as such (it's full of chairs around the central section where a swimming pool is located), but you can walk along some of the open space (although there are windbreakers to negotiate). There are also port and starboard mid-ship walking decks under the inboard lifeboats. There is, in fact, a decent amount of open deck and sunbathing space for a ship of this size, including three aft decks for open-air lovers, and real teakwood deck chairs, with thick royal blue cushioned pads.

The Lido Deck has sides covered by canvas shading and white support pillars – like the ones you would find on seaside piers in England – as a setting for the outdoor swimming pool. The Lido Deck is a self-contained deck that has not only the pool, but also the casual Lido Buffet restaurant and Lido Terrasse Cafe. One could spend all day outdoors on this deck without having to dress to go indoors to eat. There is also a small waterfall aft of the pool.

The ship is laid out in a classic symmetrical pattern, and the interior decor has been successfully designed to recreate and reproduce the atmosphere of the ocean liners of the 1920s. The ship is beautifully decorated throughout (some might say overly decorated), with rich, dark woods and intricate brass and wrought-iron staircases that remind one of what were once called "gentlemen's clubs." There is so much detail in the decoration work, and especially in

BERLITZ'S RATINGS

	Possible	Achieved
Ship	500	NYR
Accommodation	200	NYR
Food	400	NYR
Service	400	NYR
Entertainment	100	NYR
Cruise	400	NYR

the ornate ceilings, and cleaning it all is rather labor-intensive. There are quite a number of real statues, which don't seem to fit well aboard a cruise ship.

There's a good range of public rooms and spaces, although these have been possible only by making the cabins smaller than one would expect of a ship of this size. The ship has an interesting, eclectic decor from different periods, as well as a wide assortment of cabin sizes, configurations and grades. The passenger mix is also somewhat varied.

There are two favorite drinking places: Zum Alten Fritz (Old Fritz) Bar, with dark wood interiors and Belle Epoque ambiance; and the Lili Marleen Salon (adjacent to the Berlin Restaurant), with mahogany channeled ceiling. Another nice public room is the Lido Terrace, which would have made a superb observation lounge had the designers extended it to the forward extremes of the deck. It is reminiscent of the winter gardens aboard the early transatlantic liners, and a delightful place to read or take afternoon tea.

Owner Peter Deilmann's personal touch in the heavily detailed interiors is evident everywhere. *Deutschland* is registered under the German flag, but is actually placed under a second German register, which allows for the employment of many non-German staff. Thus, you will find Filipinos and other nationalities in the hotel service areas (the friendliness of the staff is good). The currency aboard is the euro, and the ship operates cashless cruising – charges must be settled on the last day of the cruise, when all purchases must, inconveniently, be made in cash. Gratuities are recommended at $13 per person, per day (cabin steward $5; dining room steward $5; bus boy $3).

Although the ship absorbs passengers well, the space

ratio is not particularly good. While the onboard product is satisfactory, the hotel, food and catering side of the operation could be better. While the interiors are very attractive, the vessel does not come close to ships such as *Europa*, *Silver Shadow*, and *Silver Whisper*, with their much larger suites/cabins, open-seating dining (except *Europa*, which has open seating for breakfast and lunch, and assigned tables for dinner) and their abundance of cabins with private balconies. All public rooms in *Deutschland* have smoking and non-smoking sections.

Only two cabins, designated as suites, have private balconies; most other cabins are very small when compared to other ships in the luxury and premium sectors of the international market. International passengers should note that the entertainment is almost totally in German; in fact, the whole ship is geared almost exclusively to German tastes.

SUITABLE FOR: *Deutschland* is best suited to German-speaking couples, and single travelers of mature years who seek a good value for money holiday in a very traditional cruise ship setting, with appealing itineraries and destinations, good food and friendly service. It could also appeal to English-speaking travelers used to being in European surroundings with a heavy German-speaking influence, and who can do without entertainment, onboard activities or shore excursions in English. I cannot recommend the ship for children, due to the lack of facilities for them.

ACCOMMODATION. According to the brochure, there are 10 categories (the higher the deck, the higher the cost). There are 18 outside view suites, 189 outside view doubles, 17 outside view single cabins; 12 interior (no view) doubles, 50 interior (no view) single cabins.

While many cabins are disappointingly small, all are furnished in fancy bird's-eye maple, and all the ceilings are fine, one-piece units, unlike the metal strip ceilings of most contemporary cruise vessels, and come with molded coving and ornamentation. The closet and drawer space is quite generous, and the attention to detail is very good. All beds have duvets and pillows. All cabins have a TV set, direct-dial satellite telephone, mini-bar/refrigerator, and real cabin keys (not plastic cards) are provided for all passengers.

The bathrooms are also generously appointed and have a pink marble sink, gold anodized fittings, gilt-edged mirrors, hairdryer, and ample space for one's personal toiletry items. There is an electrical power outlet for shavers, with both 110 and 230 volts. Bathrobes are provided for all passengers.

Accommodations designated as suites (of which there are two grades) are reasonably large, with a living area that contains a large couch, coffee table and two chairs, and the bathroom has full-size bathtubs, while all other cabins have showers. Only the Executive Suites and Owner's Suites are (sensibly) located in the center of the ship, and each has a small private balcony. There is one wheelchair-accessible cabin (8042) available for disabled passengers.

CUISINE/DINING. The main restaurant (Berlin), with 300 seats (and two seatings), is a very pleasant room, and all the chairs have armrests, although space for serving at window-side tables is limited, and the hard backs of the chairs are not really very comfortable.

There are tables for two, four, six or eight, and two seatings for dinner. Two cold buffet bars for cold cuts of meat, cheese and salad items (either your waiter can obtain the food for you or you can choose it yourself) are featured for breakfast and lunch. Overall, the cuisine is quite creative (with lots of courses, with small portions of nouvelle cuisine), with a wide variety of choice and good taste, although it is not really memorable (the desserts, however, are extremely good). The place settings are extensive.

The Restaurant Vierjahreszeiten (Four Seasons), with 104 seats, is an intimate dining room (principally for suite occupants and for à la carte dining, for which a reservation is necessary). There is much detailing and ornamentation in the decor, and the ornate ceiling lamps and indented ceiling coving create an elegant ambiance that is relatively intimate. There are tables for two, four or six. There is also a small private dining room (the Chancellor Room) with a large oval table which seats 10–12 (ideal for those special occasions and celebrations).

The wine list is extensive and includes a great variety of wines from Germany and Austria, although the selection of wines from other countries is very limited. Eating in this restaurant takes considerably longer than in the Berlin Restaurant, and is best for those seeking an evening of fine dining and conversation.

The Lido Restaurant, with 152 seats, is the ship's casual dining venue. It has large ocean-view windows on two sides and a centrally located, multi-section self-serve buffet station. Additionally, there is a Lido Terrasse, at the stern, with windows on three sides. It is set on two slightly different levels, houses the ship's library, and has statuary and a relaxing, garden conservatory-like setting. This room also has a bar, plus elegant tea (and coffee) service.

ENTERTAINMENT. The Kaisersaal (Emperor's Saloon) is the ship's showlounge. It is a galleried period room with red velveteen chairs but is more like a ballroom than showlounge. It is reminiscent of a small opera house, and has a beautiful, huge central chandelier. However, sight lines are obstructed from some seats (on both upper and lower seating levels) by many large marble-effect pillars. The entertainment is geared to German tastes, and is mostly in German.

SPA/FITNESS. The main spa area is on Deck 3, and this includes a small indoor swimming pool (with a statue of a female diver at one end), sauna, solarium, thalassotherapy baths, and massage/body therapy rooms; there is also a dialysis station. On Deck 6 is a fitness/sport center (with only a few exercise machines), and another sauna. A beauty salon is in yet another location, on Deck 7.

Diamond Princess
★★★★

Large (Resort) Ship: ....115,875 tons
Lifestyle: ....Standard
Cruise Line: ....Princess Cruises
Former Names: ....none
Builder: .....Mitsubishi Heavy Industries
(Japan)
Original Cost: ....$400 million
Entered Service: ....February 2004
Registry: ....Bermuda
Length (ft/m): 951.4/290.00
Beam (ft/m): 123.0/37.50
Draft (ft/m): 26.4/8.05
Propulsion/Propellers: ....gas turbine (25
MW)/2 azimuthing pods (21,000 kW each)

Passenger Decks: 13
Total Crew: 1,238
Passengers
(lower beds/all berths): 2,674/3,100
Passenger Space Ratio
(lower beds/all berths): 43.3/37.3
Crew/Passenger Ratio
(lower beds/all berths): 2.1/2.5
Navigation Officers: ......British/Italian
Cabins (total): 1,337
Size Range (sq ft/m): 168–1,329.3/
15.6–123.5
Cabins (outside view): 1,000
Cabins (interior/no view): 337
Cabins (for one person): 0

Cabins (with private balcony): 750
Cabins (wheelchair accessible): 28
(18 outside/10 interior)
Cabin Current: ....110 volts
Elevators: 14
Casino (gaming tables): ....Yes
Slot Machines: ....Yes
Swimming Pools (outdoors): 4
Swimming Pools (indoors): 0
Whirlpools: 9
Self-Service Launderette: ....Yes
Dedicated Cinema/Seats: ....No
Library: ....Yes
Classification Society: ....Lloyds Register

OVERALL SCORE: 1,548 (OUT OF A POSSIBLE 2,000 POINTS)

OVERVIEW. *Diamond Princess* has an instantly recognizable funnel due to two jet engine-like pods that sit high up on its structure but really are mainly for decoration. This is the first ship to be constructed by a Japanese shipyard for Princess Cruises (sister ship: *Sapphire Princess*). The ship is similar in size and internal layout to *Golden Princess, Grand Princess* and *Star Princess* (although of a slightly greater beam). Unlike its half-sister ships, however, all of which had a "spoiler" (containing a discotheque) located aft of the funnel, this has thankfully been removed from both *Diamond Princess* and *Sapphire Princess*, and has been replaced by a more sensible (and less weighty) aft-facing nightclub/discotheque structure (Skywalkers Nightclub) set around the base of the adjoining the funnel structure. The view from the nightclub overlooks aft-facing cascading decks and children's pool.

In December 2002, while the ship was under construction in the shipyard, a fire broke out on Deck 5. This lasted for 20 hours and burned some (548,980 sq ft (51,000 sq. meters) from Deck through Deck 13. The ship's hull was switched with that of identical sister *Sapphire Princess*, which was also under construction in the same yard at the same time. Consequently, the ship's debut was delayed from July 2003 to February 2004.

Diamond Princess is the first of the "Grand Class" ships to have a "pod" propulsion system installed *(for details, see page 17)*. Electrical power is provided by a combination of four diesel and one gas turbine (CODAG) unit; the diesel engines are located in the engine room, while the gas turbine unit is located in the ship's funnel housing, on each

BERLITZ'S RATINGS	Possible	Achieved
Ship	500	435
Accommodation	200	168
Food	400	256
Service	400	293
Entertainment	100	82
Cruise	400	314

side of which is a cosmetic pod that resembles a jet aircraft engine. Four areas focus on swimming pools, one of which is two decks high and is covered by a retractable glass dome, itself an extension of the funnel housing.

Unlike the outside decks, there is plenty of space inside the ship (but there are also plenty of passengers), and a wide array of public rooms, with many "intimate" (this being a relative word) spaces and places to play and enjoy. The passenger flow has been well thought out, and works with little congestion. The decor is attractive, with lots of earth tones. An extensive collection of art works has been chosen, and this complements the interior design and colors well.

Like half-sisters *Golden Princess, Grand Princess* and *Star Princess*, this ship also has a Wedding Chapel (a live web-cam can relay ceremonies via the internet). The ship's captain can legally marry (American) couples, due to the ship's Bermuda registry and a special dispensation (which should be verified when in the planning stage, according to where you reside). Princess Cruises offers three wedding packages – Pearl, Emerald, Diamond; the fee includes registration and official marriage certificate. The "Hearts & Minds" chapel is useful for "renewal of vows" ceremonies.

Gaming lovers should enjoy what is one of the largest casinos at sea (Grand Casino), with more than 260 slot machines; there are blackjack, craps and roulette tables, plus newer games such as Let It Ride Bonus, Spanish 21 and Caribbean Draw Progressive. But the highlight could well be the specially linked slot machines that provide a combined payout.

Other features include a library/CD-Rom computer

room, and a separate card room. Ship lovers should enjoy the wood-paneled Wheelhouse Bar, finely decorated with memorabilia and ship models tracing part of parent company P&O's history. Aft of the International Dining Room is the Wake View Bar, with a spiral stairway that leads down to a great viewing spot for those who want to watch the ship's wake (like the one aboard the rivercruise stern paddle-wheeler *American Queen*); it is reached from the back of Club Fusion, on Promenade Deck. A high-tech hospital is provided, with live SeaMed tele-medicine link-ups with specialists at the Cedars-Sinai Medical Center in Los Angeles available for emergency help.

For youngsters and teenagers there is a two-deck-high playroom, teen room, and a host of specially trained counselors. Children have their own pools, hot tubs, and open deck area at the stern of the ship (away from adult areas).

If you are not used to large ships, it will take you some time to find your way around this one, despite the company's claim that this vessel offers passengers a "small ship feel, big ship choice." The cabin bath towels are small, and drawer space is limited. There are no butlers – even for the top grade suites (which are not really large in comparison to similar suites aboard some other ships). Cabin attendants have too many cabins to look after (typically 20), which does not translate to fine personal service. You'll have to live with the many extra charge items (such as for ice cream, and freshly squeezed orange juice) and activities (such as yoga, group exercise bicycling and kick boxing classes at $10 per session, not to mention $4 per hour for group babysitting services – at the time this book was completed). There's also a charge for using the washers and dryers in the self-service launderettes.

ACCOMMODATION. All passengers receive turndown service and chocolates on pillows each night, as well as bathrobes (on request) and toiletry amenity kits (larger for suite/mini-suite occupants). A hairdryer is provided in all cabins, sensibly located at the vanity desk unit in the living area. All bathrooms are tiled and have a decent amount of open shelf storage space for personal toiletries. Princess Cruises has BBC World, CNN, CNBC, ESPN and TNT on the in-cabin color TV system (when available, depending on cruise area).

The majority of the outside cabins on Emerald Deck have views obstructed by the lifeboats. Sadly, there are no cabins for singles. Your name is typically placed outside your suite or cabin – making it simple for delivery service personnel but also limiting your privacy. There is 24-hour room service (but some items on the room service menu are not available during early morning hours). Most balcony suites and cabins can be overlooked both from the navigation bridge wing. Cabins with balconies on Baja, Caribe, and Dolphin decks are also overlooked by passengers on balconies on the deck above.

CUISINE/DINING. All dining rooms are located on one of two decks. There are five principal dining rooms with themed decor and cuisine – smaller than the three dining rooms on the similarly sized *Golden Princess*, *Grand Princess* and

Star Princess because two dining rooms have been halved to become four; they are Sterling Steakhouse (for steak and grilled meats), Vivaldi (Italian fare), Santa Fe (southwestern USA cuisine), Pacific Moon (Asian cuisine) and International (the largest, located aft, with two seatings and "traditional" cuisine). These offer a mix of two seatings (with seating assigned according to the location of your cabin) or "anytime dining" (where you choose when and with whom you want to eat). All dining rooms are non-smoking and are split into sections in a non-symmetrical design that breaks what are quite large spaces into many smaller sections, for better ambience and less noise pollution.

Specially designed dinnerware and good quality linens and silverware are featured: Dudson of England (dinnerware), Frette Egyptian cotton table linens, and silverware by Hepp of Germany.

Alternative dining options: Trattoria Sabatini is an informal eatery (reservations required; cover charge $20 per person). It features an eight-course meal, including Italian-style pizzas and pastas, with a variety of sauces, as well as Italian-style entrées (including tiger prawns and lobster tail – all provided with flair and entertainment by the waiters (by reservation only; the cover charge is $20 per person). The cuisine in this eatery is potentially better than in all the other dining rooms, with better quality ingredients and more attention to presentation, taste and delivery.

A poolside hamburger grill and pizza bar (no additional charge) are additional dining spots for casual bites, while extra charges will apply if you order items to eat at either the coffee bar/patisserie, or the caviar/champagne bar.

Other casual meals can be taken in the Horizon Court, open 24 hours a day, with large ocean-view on port and starboard sides and direct access to the two main swimming pools and lido deck (there is no finesse in presentation, however, and plastic plates, not trays, are provided).

ENTERTAINMENT. The Princess Theatre (showlounge) spans two decks and has comfortable seating on both main and balcony levels. It has $3 million in sound and light equipment, plus a 9-piece orchestra.

A second large entertainment lounge, Club Fusion, features cabaret acts at night, and lectures, bingo and horse racing during the day. A third entertainment lounge can also host cabaret acts and dance bands. Many other lounges and bars have live music, and a number of male dance hosts act as partners for women traveling alone.

SPA/FITNESS. The Lotus Spa complex, which has Japanese-style decor, surrounds one of the swimming pools (you can have a massage or other spa treatment in an ocean-view treatment room). Lotus Spa treatments include Chakra hot stone massage, Asian Lotus ritual (featuring massage with reflexology, reiki and shiatsu massage), deep-tissue sports therapy massage, lime and ginger salt glow, wild strawberry back cleanse, and seaweed mud wraps.

● **For more extensive general information about the Princess Cruises experience is like, see pages 124–127.**

Discovery
NOT YET RATED

Mid-Size Ship: . . . . .21,186 tons	Total Crew: 350	Cabins (with private balcony): 0
Lifestyle: . . . . .Standard	Passengers	Cabins (wheelchair accessible): 2
Cruise Line: . . . . .Discovery World Cruises	(lower beds/all berths): 610/717	Cabin Current: . . . . .110 and 220 volts
Former Names: .Platinum, Hyundai Pungak,	Passenger Space Ratio	Elevators: 4
Island Princess, Island Venture	(lower beds/all berths): 34.7/29.5	Casino (gaming tables): . . . . .Yes
Builder: Rheinstahl Nordseewerke (Germany)	Crew/Passenger Ratio	Slot Machines: . . . . .Yes
Original Cost: . . . .$25 million	(lower beds/all berths): 1.7/2.0	Swimming Pools (outdoors): 2
Entered Service: . . . . . .Feb 1972/May 2003	Navigation Officers: . . . . .Greek	Swimming Pools (indoors): 0
Registry: . . . . .The Bahamas	Cabins (total): .305	Whirlpools: 0
Length (ft/m): 553.6/168.74	Size Range (sq ft/m):	Self-Service Launderette: . . . . .No
Beam (ft/m): 105.7/32.22	125.9 – 441.3/11.7 – 41.0	Dedicated Cinema/Seats: Yes/170
Draft (ft/m): 80.8/24.64	Cabins (outside view): 238	Library: . . . . .Yes
Propulsion/Propellers: diesel (13,400 kW)/2	Cabins (interior/no view): 67	Classification Society: . . .Lloyd's Register
Passenger Decks: 8	Family Cabins: .2	

OVERALL SCORE: NYR (OUT OF A POSSIBLE 2,000 POINTS)

OVERVIEW. *Discovery*, formerly operated from 1972 to 1999 by Princess Cruises, has a very attractive traditional ship profile and well balanced, somewhat rounded exterior styling. As the former *Island Princess*, it was, together with sister ship *Pacific Princess*, one of the pair of original "Love Boats" in the American television series *The Love Boat*. Hyundai Asan Cruises acquired the ship in 1999, and operated it for cruises from South Korea to North Korea. In 2001, entrepreneur and ship lover Gerry Herrod, who formerly founded the now defunct Ocean Cruise Lines (and Orient Lines, presently owned by Star Cruises/Norwegian Cruise Line) bought the ship. He then spent $10 million refurbishing and updating it for its present cruising role under the brand name of Discovery World Cruises (principally for the American market from December to April, when the ship operates in US dollars) and under charter to Voyages of Discovery (principally for the UK market from May to December, when the ship operates in British pounds). For the winter season, the ship carries five Zodiac inflatable shore landing craft.

One of the ship's two outdoor swimming pools has a glass dome (magrodome) cover, which can be used in inclement weather conditions. There is no wrap-around promenade deck outdoors, however.

Inside, the public areas are quite spacious considering the size of the ship, and there are numerous public rooms (some with high ceilings), with reasonably wide passageways. These include a lobby with mezzanine level and curved staircase (several shops and offices are on the upper level), and the Discovery Lounge, located aft, has a two-deck high glass wall overlooking the aft deck. There's an

BERLITZ'S RATINGS		
	Possible	Achieved
Ship	500	NYR
Accommodation	200	NYR
Food	400	NYR
Service	400	NYR
Entertainment	100	NYR
Cruise	400	NYR

internet center, equipped with six computer stations, and a library with 5,000 books provided by the Marine Society. Tasteful decor is featured throughout, with pastel colors and fine artwork that is pleasing to the eye, if a little bland. The forward observation lounge also acts as an indoor buffet dining area.

The ship, which has been well maintained, and is quite elegant, with comfortable surroundings for the older passenger who wants plenty of space and does not want to be part of larger, more impersonal ships. *Discovery* competes directly with *Marco Polo* (Orient Lines), which is an older ship with the same type of passengers and following that *Discovery* seeks to attract, in this limited, but growing, marketplace. After a messy start-up as *Discovery*, the ship has now settled down. Concessions run the dining, spa/beauty services, and shops. All gratuities are included.

SUITABLE FOR: *Discovery* is best suited to couples and single travelers of mature years who enjoy being transported to interesting destinations in the comfort of a ship that is now considered to be traditional in style, unpretentious and with a casual dress code, and without the trappings of much entertainment or organized parlor games.

ACCOMMODATION. There are as many as 15 price categories (rather a lot for a mid-sized ship). The price you will pay will depend on the grade, location and size of the cabin.

There are five suites; these are of quite a decent size, and well designed, with plenty of space to move around in. Two of the suites are located forward, just under the navigation bridge, and command good views.

Most other cabins have ample room, are quite well appointed, and there is plenty of closet and drawer space. All cabins have a color television. The top category cabins (on Bridge Deck and Promenade Deck) have a full bathtub, while all others have a shower enclosure. None of the suites or cabins has a private balcony (the ship was built before private balconies came into vogue).

No matter what category of suites or cabin you choose, there is a television, telephone, personal safe and hairdryer in each. Some cabins have interconnecting doors, and some can accommodate a third/fourth person.

CUISINE/DINING. The Seven Continents Dining Room is a reasonably comfortable room, and is operated in two seatings. The cuisine (upgraded from previous Voyages of Discovery ships) is quite acceptable fare, but certainly not adventurous or memorable; ingredients are of questionable quality and the presentation and service are quite poor. The wine list is adequate, and prices are reasonable, although the selection is small and consists mostly of younger wines. Casual breakfasts and lunches can be taken in the Yacht Club (an observation lounge), with fine ocean views on three sides or outdoors on the Lido Deck, adjacent to the swimming pool.

Alternative (Reservations Only) Dining Option: Alternative dinners can also be taken in the Yacht Club (there is no cover charge). You can also opt for Continental Breakfast to be served in your cabin if you wish. All dining areas are non-smoking.

ENTERTAINMENT. The "theater-in-the-round" Carousel Showlounge has banquette-style seating in several tiers, set around a "thrust" stage. The entertainment is low-key, which means only the occasional cabaret act is featured. There is live music throughout the ship for dancing.

SPA/FITNESS. The Spa Atlantis is positioned aft on two of the uppermost decks (a stairway connects the two). A beauty salon is on the upper deck, while a gymnasium (with aft-facing ocean-view windows), three treatment rooms, and male and female saunas are on the lower level. It is operated by the UK-based spa/fitness concession, Harding Brothers (featured products: Guinot and Thalgo).

Sample prices include: full body massage, €45 (50 minutes); back, neck and shoulder massage, €30 (30 minutes); reflexology, €25; Indian head massage, €35; course of four yoga classes, €15; Pilates class, €5 (30 minutes); personal training session, €39 (75 minutes); hairdressing services include a shampoo, cut and finish, €15; wet cut, €8; manicure, €25 (45 minutes); pedicure, €20.0.

Disney Magic
★★★★

Large (Resort) Ship:	.83,338 tons	Passengers	
Lifestyle:	.Standard	(lower beds/all berths):	.1,750/3,325
Cruise Line:	.Disney Cruise Line	Passenger Space Ratio	
Former Names:	.none	(lower beds/all berths):	.47.6/25.0
Builder:	.Fincantieri (Italy)	Crew/Passenger Ratio	
Original Cost:	.$350 million	(lower beds/all berths):	.1.8/3.5
Entered Service:	.July 1998	Navigation Officers:	.European/
Registry:	.The Bahamas		Scandinavian
Length (ft/m):	.964.5/294.00	Cabins (total):	.875
Beam (ft/m):	.105.7/32.22	Size Range (sq ft/m):	.180.8–968.7/
Draft (ft/m):	.26.2/8.0		16.8–90.0
Propulsion/Propellers:	.diesel-electric	Cabins (outside view):	.720
	(38,000kW)/2	Cabins (interior/no view):	.155
Passenger Decks:	.11	Family Cabins:	.80
Total Crew:	.945	Cabins (with private balcony):	.388

Cabins (wheelchair accessible):	.12
Cabin Current:	.110 volts
Elevators:	.12
Casino (gaming tables):	.No
Slot Machines:	.No
Swimming Pools (outdoors):	.3
Swimming Pools (indoors):	.0
Whirlpools:	.6
Fitness Center:	.Yes
Sauna/Steam Room:	.Yes/Yes
Massage:	.Yes
Self-Service Launderette:	.Yes (3)
Dedicated Cinema/Seats:	.Yes/270
Library:	.No
Classification Society:	.Lloyd's Register

OVERALL SCORE: 1,526 (OUT OF A POSSIBLE 2,000 POINTS)

OVERVIEW. Zip-a-Dee-Do-Dah, Zip-a-Dee-Day! *Disney Magic*'s profile has managed to combine streamlining with tradition and nostalgia, and has two large red and black funnels designed to remind you of the ocean liners of the past. *Disney Magic* is the first cruise ship built with two funnels since the 1950s. However, one of the funnels is a dummy, and contains a variety of public spaces, including a neat ESPN sports bar and a broadcast center. The ship was actually constructed in two halves, which were then joined together in the shipyard in Venice, Italy. The ship's whistle even plays "When You Wish Upon a Star" (or a sort of sickly version of it). The bow has handsome gold scrollwork that more typically seen adorning the tall ships of yesteryear. There is a wrap-around promenade deck outdoors for strolling.

Disney Cruise Line has not added ostentatious decoration to the exterior. However, Mickey Mouse's ears are painted on the funnels; there is also a special 85-ft (26-meter) long paint stripe that cleverly incorporates Disney characters into the whimsical yellow paintwork along each side of the hull at the bow. Cute. The exterior colors are also those of Mickey himself. Also of note is a 15-ft (4.5-meter) long Goofy hanging upside down in a bosun's chair, painting the stern of the vessel.

On deck, a sports deck has a paddle tennis court, table tennis, basketball court, shuffleboard, and golf driving range. An ESPN Skybox Bar has 12 TV sets of differing sizes for live (by satellite) sports events and noisy conversation (cigar smokers welcome). There are three outdoor pools: one pool for adults only (in theory), one for chil-

BERLITZ'S RATINGS

	Possible	Achieved
Ship	500	437
Accommodation	200	170
Food	400	207
Service	400	297
Entertainment	100	90
Cruise	400	325

dren, and one for families (guess which one has Mickey's ears painted into the bottom?). However, there's music everywhere (four different types), and it's impossible to find a quiet spot (in fact, you can sit in many places a get two types of music blaring at you at the same time). The children's pool has a long yellow water slide (available at specified times), held up by the giant hand of Mickey Mouse, although the pool itself really is too small considering the number of small children typically carried.

Inside, the ship is quite stunning, although poorly finished in several places. The Art Deco theme of the old ocean liners has been tastefully carried out (check out the stainless steel/pewter Disney detailing on the handrails and balustrades in the three-deck-high lobby). Most public rooms have high ceilings. The decor is reminiscent of New York's Radio City Music Hall. Much of the interior detailing is whimsical – pure Disney. The lobby provides a real photo opportunity, with a 6-ft (1.8-meter) high bronze statue of Mickey in the role of a ship's helmsman (there is probably some pixie dust around somewhere, too). Mickey is also visible in many other areas, albeit subtly (for Disney). If you can't sleep, try counting the number of times Mickey's logo appears – it's an impossible task.

There are two large shops and an abundance of Disney-theme clothing, soft toys, collectibles and specialty items. Other facilities include a superb, 1,040-seat Walt Disney Theater (spread over four decks but without a balcony), piano bar, adults-only nightclub/disco, family lounge, and a dedicated cinema (where classic Disney films are shown, as well as first-run movies).

The children's entertainment areas measure 13,000 sq. ft (1,200 sq. meters); more than 30 children's counselors run the extensive programmes. There is also a separate teen club and video game arcade. A child drop-off service is available in the evenings, and private babysitting services are available ($11 per hour), as are character "tuck-ins" for children, and character breakfasts and lunches. Strollers are available, at no charge, and parents can be provided with beepers, so that they can also enjoy their time alone, away from their offspring for much of the day.

Other notable Disney exclusives include the game show "Who Wants to be a Mouseketeer?" The prizes include free cruises and onboard credits of up to $1,000 and Tea with Wendy Darling (from Disney's version of *Peter Pan*).

Apart from the ports of call, the highlight for most is a day spent on Disney's private island, Castaway Cay. It is an outstanding private island (perhaps the benchmark for all private islands for families with children), with its own pier so that the ship can dock alongside – a cruise industry first. There is a post office with its own special Bahamas/Disney stamp, and a whole host of dedicated, well thought-out attractions and amenities for all ages (including a large adults-only beach, complete with massage cabanas).

Disney characters are aboard for all cruises and lots of photo opportunities; they come out to play mainly when children's activities are scheduled. All the artwork in public areas comes from Disney films or animation features, with many original drawings dating from the early 1930s.

Disney Magic has year-round 7-day cruises to the Eastern Caribbean (and Castaway Cay in the Bahamas) – more relaxing than the 3- or 4-day version featured by sister ship *Disney Wonder* – and passengers will find more activities, more lecturers and additional shows that make it all worthwhile. It's all tied up in one encapsulated, well-controlled, seamless, and crime-free environment that promises escape and adventure. American Express cardholders get special treatment and extra goodies.

At Port Canaveral, a special terminal has been constructed; it's a copy of the original Ocean Terminal used by the transatlantic liners *Queen Elizabeth* and *Queen Mary* in Southampton, England. Transfers between Walt Disney World resorts in Orlando and the ship are included. Special buses feature vintage 1930s/1940s style interior decor (30 sets of Mickey's face and ears can be found in the blue fabric of each seat). Five of the 45 custom-made buses are outfitted to carry wheelchair passengers.

Embarkation and disembarkation is an entertainment event rather than the hassle-laden affair that it has become for many cruise lines with large ships (if all the buses do not arrive together).

Disney Magic is really a floating theme park – a seagoing Never-Never Land. You should be aware, however, that this is a highly programmed, strictly timed and regimented onboard experience, with tickets, lines and reservations necessary for almost everything. Since its introduction, the product has improved almost to the point that Disney now understands that cruise ships are different to operate than its theme parks. Parents can relax knowing that security

is very good, and all registered children must wear an ID bracelet (showing name, cabin number and muster station number), and parents are given pagers for emergencies.

Take mainly casual clothing (casual with a capital "C"), although there are two formal nights on the 7-day cruise, and wish upon a star – that's really all you'll need to do to enjoy yourself aboard this stunning ship. The onboard currency is the US dollar. Members of Disney's Holiday Club can exchange points for cruises.

Note that there is no observation lounge with forward-facing views over the ship's bows. There is no dance floor with live orchestra for adults (other than "Rockin Bar D" in Beat Street for throbbing disco/country-style music). The lifts are very small, and so is the gymnasium (for such a large ship). It is expensive (but then so is a week at any Disney resort), gratuities are extra, and 15% is added to all bar/beverage/wine and spa accounts. Don't even think about it if you are not a Disney fan, or if you don't like kids, or lining up and registering for things. Service with only a moderate sprinkling of hospitality.

Standing in line for embarkation, disembarkation, shore tenders and for self-serve buffet meals is an inevitable aspect of cruising aboard all large ships. Lines at various outlets can prove irritating (some creative Disney Imagineering is needed, including a large sprinkling of pixie dust), as can trying to get through to Guest Services by telephone. The food product and delivery has improved, but falls short of less expensive cruise products. There is no proper library – something many regular cruise passengers miss.

In 2005 the ship will operate a series of 12 seven-day cruises from Los Angeles, starting May 28, to tie in with the 50th anniversary of Disneyland.

SUITABLE FOR: *Disney Magic* is ideally suited to families with children (or grandchildren), although couples and singles are also welcome (there are few activities for couples during the daytime, but plenty of entertainment at night). Whether cruising with 1,000 (or more) kids aboard will make for a relaxing holiday for those without kids will depend on how much noise they can absorb. You will, however, need to be a real Disney fan, as *everything* revolves around Disney and the family theme; this means that everything is based on entertainment and good times, while food takes a back step into the world of "theme park" cuisine. For children of all ages, there's simply nothing better than *Disney Magic* or *Disney Wonder*.

ACCOMMODATION. There are 12 price grades for accommodation (price will depend on grade, size and location you choose). Spread over six decks, all suites/cabins have been designed for practicality and have space-efficient layouts. Most cabins have common features such as a neat vertical steamer trunk for clothes storage, illuminated closets, a hairdryer located at a vanity desk (or in the bathroom), and bathrobes for all passengers. Many cabins have third- and fourth pull-down berths that rise and are totally hidden in the ceiling when not in use, but the standard interior and outside cabins, while acceptable for two, are extremely tight with three or four. The decor is practical, creative, and colorful, with lots of neat styling touches. Cabins with refrigerators can have them stocked with one of several packages (at extra cost).

The bathrooms, although compact (due to the fact that the toilet is separate), are really functional units, designed with split-use facilities so that more than one person can use them at the same time (good for families). Many have bathtubs (really shower tubs).

Accommodation designated as suites offers much more space, and extra goodies such as VCRs, CD players, large screen TVs, and extra beds (useful for larger families). Some of the suites are beneath the pool deck, teen lounge, or informal cafe, so there could be noise as the ceiling insulation is poor (but the cabin to cabin insulation is good).

Wheelchair-bound passengers have a variety of cabin sizes and configurations, including suites with a private balcony (unfortunately you cannot get a wheelchair through the balcony's sliding door) and extra-large bathrooms with excellent roll-in showers, and good closet and drawer space (almost all the vessel is accessible). For the sight-impaired, cabin numbers and elevator buttons are braille-encoded.

A 24-hour room service is available (suite occupants also get concierge service); but the room service menu and cabin breakfast menu are limited. There is a 15% service charge for all beverage deliveries (including tea and coffee).

CUISINE/DINING. There are three main dining rooms (all non-smoking), each with over 400 seats, two seatings, and unique themes. Lumiere's has Beauty and the Beast; Parrot Cay has a tacky, pseudo-Caribbean theme; Animator's Palate (the most visual of the three) has food and electronic art that makes the evening decor change from black and white to full-color. You will eat in all three dining rooms in rotation (twice per 7-day cruise), and move with your assigned waiter and assistant waiter to each dining room in turn, thus providing a different dining experience (each has a different decor, different menus). As you will have the same waiter in each of the three restaurants, any gratuities go only to "your" waiter. Parrot Cay and Lumiere's have open seating for breakfast and lunch (the lunch menu is pitiful). The noise level in all three dining rooms is extremely high. If the formal nights happen to fall on the evening you are due to eat in Parrot Cay, formal wear and the decor of Parrot Cay Restaurant do not go together at all.

In addition, Palo is an elegant 140-seat reservations-only alternative restaurant (with a $5 cover/gratuity charge) featuring Italian cuisine. It has a 270° view, and is for adults only (no "Munchkins" allowed); the à la carte cuisine is cooked to order, and the wine list is good (although prices are high). Make your reservations as soon as you board or miss out on the only decent food aboard this ship. Afternoon High Tea is also presented here, on days at sea.

For casual eating, Topsider's is an indoor/outdoor cafe featuring low-quality self-serve breakfast and lunch buffets with very poor choice and presentation, and a buffet dinner for children (consisting mostly of fried foods). There is also an ice cream and frozen yogurt bar (Scoops) that opens infrequently; other fast food outlets include Pluto's (for hamburgers, hot dogs), Pinocchio's, which is open throughout the day but not in the evening (for basic pizza and sandwiches). On one night of the cruise, there is also an outdoor self-serve "Tropicalifragilisticexpialidocious" buffet.

Overall, the food has improved since the ship was first introduced (it needed to, it was of a very low quality), and is now more attractively presented, although there are still so few green vegetables. Vegetarians and those seeking light cuisine will be totally underwhelmed. Guest chefs from Walt Disney World Resort prepare signature dishes each cruise, and also host cooking demonstrations.

ENTERTAINMENT. The entertainment and activities programming for families and children are extremely good. There are four large-scale stage shows (in the stunning 977-seat showlounge) featuring original Disney musicals; *Disney Dreams, Hercules – The Muse-ical, The Golden Mickeys* and *Morty the Magnificent.* Sadly, they are performed without a hint of a live orchestra, although the lighting, staging and technical effects are excellent. There is also a Disney-themed Trivia Game Show.

For grown-ups, there is "Route 66" – an adult entertainment area that includes a wacky Hollywood-style street, complete with three entertainment rooms. "Cadillac" is a jazz piano lounge, with private headphones for listening to music of all types when no live music is scheduled; "Wavebands" (for ear-splitting rock 'n' roll and country music); and "Barrel of Laughs" (for improvisational comedy involving the audience). During the day, creative enrichment programs have been added.

SPA/FITNESS. Fancy a little pampering? The Vista Spa is a fitness/wellbeing complex that measures 8,500 sq. ft/790 sq. meters. The fitness/workout room (with high-tech Cybex muscle-toning equipment) has ocean-view windows that overlook the navigation bridge on the deck below. There are 11 rooms for spa/beauty treatments (however, note that the pounding from the basketball court located directly above makes relaxing spa treatments almost impossible).

Thermal bath rooms feature a "tropical rain shower", sauna, mild steam room, aromatic steam room and a fog shower. Aromatic scents such as eucalyptus, lime, peppermint, rose and sage can be infused into the mild steam room, while camomile is used in the aromatic steam room.

Massage (including exotic massages such as Aroma Stone massage and other well-being massages, as well as underwater massage in a hydrotherapy bath), aromatherapy facials, pedicures, and beauty salon treatments are at extra cost (massage, for example, costs about $2 per minute, plus gratuity). For something different, try the Rasul mud and steam room (it's an absolute delight for couples). Do make appointments as early as possible – aboard a ship so large, treatment time slots go quickly, so the day you board is the best time to book your treatments.

For something extra special, consider booking a massage at Castaway Cay – in a private beach hut on the beach that is open to the sea. It's magical.

Disney Wonder
★★★★

Large (Resort) Ship:	.85,000 tons	Total Crew:	.945
Lifestyle:	.Standard	Passengers	
Cruise Line:	.Disney Cruise Line	(lower beds/all berths):	.1,750/3,325
Former Names:	.none	Passenger Space Ratio	
Builder:	.Fincantieri (Italy)	(lower beds/all berths):	.48.5/25.5
Original Cost:	.$350 million	Crew/Passenger Ratio	
Entered Service:	.Aug 1999	(lower beds/all berths):	.1.8/3.5
Registry:	.The Bahamas	Navigation Officers:	European/Norwegian
Length (ft/m):	.964.5/294.00	Cabins (total):	.875
Beam (ft/m):	.105.7/32.22	Size Range (sq ft/m):	.180.8–968.7/
Draft (ft/m):	.26.2/8.0		16.8–90.0
Propulsion/Propellers:	.diesel-electric	Cabins (outside view):	.720
	(38,000kW)/2	Cabins (interior/no view):	.155
Passenger Decks:	.11	Family Cabins:	.80

Cabins (with private balcony):	.388
Cabins (wheelchair accessible):	.12
Cabin Current:	.110 volts
Elevators:	.12
Casino (gaming tables):	.No
Slot Machines:	.0
Swimming Pools (outdoors):	.3
Swimming Pools (indoors):	.0
Whirlpools:	.6
Self-Service Launderette:	.Yes (3)
Dedicated Cinema/Seats:	.Yes/270
Library:	.Yes
Classification Society:	.Lloyd's Register

OVERALL SCORE: 1,526 (OUT OF A POSSIBLE 2,000 POINTS)

OVERVIEW. Zip-a-Dee-Do-Dah, Zip-a-Dee-Day! *Disney Wonder*'s profile has managed to combine streamlining with tradition and nostalgia, and has two large red and black funnels designed to remind you of the ocean liners of the past. *Disney Wonder* is only the second cruise ship built with two funnels since the 1950s (the first was *Disney Magic*). However, one of the funnels is a dummy, and contains a variety of public spaces, including a neat ESPN sports bar and a broadcast center. The ship was actually constructed in two halves, which were then joined together in the shipyard in Venice, Italy. The ship's whistle even plays "When You Wish Upon a Star" (or a sort of sickly version of it). The bow has handsome gold scrollwork that more typically seen adorning the tall ships of yesteryear. There is a wraparound promenade deck outdoors for strolling.

Disney Cruise Line has not added ostentatious decoration to the ship's exterior. However, Mickey Mouse's ears are painted on the funnels; there is also a special 85-ft (26-meter) long paint stripe that cleverly incorporates Disney characters into the whimsical yellow paintwork along each side of the hull at the bow. Cute. The ship's exterior colors are also those of Mickey himself. Also of note is a whimsical, 15-ft (4.5-meter) tall Donald Duck and Huey hanging upside down in a bosun's chair, painting the stern.

On deck, a sports deck has a paddle tennis court, table tennis, basketball court, shuffleboard, and golf driving range. An ESPN Skybox Bar has 12 TV sets of differing sizes for live (by satellite) sports events and noisy conversation (cigar smokers welcome). There are three outdoor pools: one pool for adults only (in theory), one for children, and one for families (guess which one has Mickey's

BERLITZ'S RATINGS

	Possible	Achieved
Ship	500	437
Accommodation	200	170
Food	400	207
Service	400	297
Entertainment	100	90
Cruise	400	325

ears painted into the bottom?). However, there's music everywhere (four different types), and it's impossible to find a quiet spot (in fact, you can sit in many places a get two types of music blaring at you at the same time). The children's pool has a long yellow water slide (available at specified times), held up by the giant hand of Mickey Mouse, although the pool itself really is too small considering the number of small children typically carried.

Inside, the ship is quite stunning, although poorly finished in several places. The Art Deco theme of the old ocean liners has been tastefully carried out (check out the stainless steel/pewter Disney detailing on the handrails and balustrades in the three-deck-high lobby). Most public rooms have high ceilings. The decor is reminiscent of New York's Radio City Music Hall. Much of the interior detailing is whimsical – pure Disney. The lobby provides a photo opportunity that should not be missed: a 6-ft (1.8-meter) bronze statue of "The Little Mermaid." Mickey himself is visible in many areas, albeit subtly (for Disney). If you can't sleep, try counting the number of times Mickey's logo appears – it's an impossible task.

There are two large shops and an abundance of Disney-theme clothing, soft toys, collectibles and specialty items. There's a superb 1,040-seat Walt Disney Theater (spread over four decks but without a balcony), piano bar, adults-only nightclub/disco, family lounge, and a cinema (where classic Disney films are shown, as well as first-run movies).

The children's entertainment areas measure 13,000 sq. ft (1,200 sq. meters); more than 30 children's counselors run the extensive programmes. There is also a separate teen club and video game arcade. A child drop-off service is available in the evenings, and private babysitting services are available ($11 per hour), as are character "tuck-ins" for children, and character breakfasts and lunches. Free strollers are available, and parents can be provided with beepers, so that they can also enjoy their time alone, away from their offspring for much of the day.

Although Nassau is decidedly unappealing and not tourist-friendly, the highlight of the itinerary is Disney's private island, Castaway Cay. It is an outstanding private island (perhaps the benchmark for all private islands), with its own pier so that the ship can dock alongside – a cruise industry first. The post office has its own special Bahamas/Disney stamp, and a whole host of dedicated, well thought out attractions and amenities for all ages (including a large adults-only beach, complete with massage cabanas). Watersports equipment (floats, paddleboats, kayaks, hobie cats, aqua fins, aqua trikes, and snorkels) can be rented.

Disney characters are aboard for all cruises and lots of photo opportunities; they come out to play mainly when children's activities are scheduled. All the artwork in public areas comes from Disney films or animation features, with many original drawings dating from the early 1930s.

Disney Wonder has year-round 3- and 4-day cruises to The Bahamas – part of a 7-night vacation package that includes a 3- or 4-day stay at a Walt Disney World resort hotel in Orlando; the cruise then forms the second half of the vacation. It's all tied up in one encapsulated, well-controlled, seamless, and crime-free environment that promises escape and adventure. You can also book just the cruise without the resort stay. American Express cardholders get special treatment and extra goodies. Members of Disney's Vacation Club can exchange points for cruises.

At Port Canaveral, a special terminal has been constructed; it's a copy of the original Ocean Terminal used by the transatlantic liners *Queen Elizabeth* and *Queen Mary* in Southampton, England. Transfers between Walt Disney World resorts in Orlando and the ship are included. Special buses feature vintage 1930s/1940s style interior decor (30 sets of Mickey's face and ears can be found in the blue fabric of each seat). Five of the 45 custom-made buses are outfitted to carry wheelchair passengers. Embarkation and disembarkation is an entertainment event rather than the hassle-laden affair that it has become for many cruise lines with large ships (if all the buses do not arrive together).

Disney Wonder (and sister ship *Disney Magic*) are the cruise industry's floating theme parks – sea-going Never-Never Lands that are rated on their own, in common with all other ships. The rating does not include any additional 3- or 4-day stay at a Disney World resort, which forms part of the total Disney Cruise Line vacation (although it is now possible to book just the cruise). Be aware, however, that this is a highly programmed, strictly timed and regimented onboard experience, with tickets, lines and reservations necessary for almost everything. Since its introduction, the product has improved almost to the point that Disney now understands that cruise ships are different to operate than its theme parks. Parents can relax knowing that security is very good, and all registered children must wear an ID

bracelet (showing name, cabin number and muster station number), and parents are given pagers for emergencies.

Take mainly casual clothing (casual with a capital "C"), although there are two formal nights on the 7-day cruise, and wish upon a star – that's really all you'll need to do to enjoy yourself aboard this stunning ship. The onboard currency is the US dollar. Members of Disney's Holiday Club can exchange points for cruises.

There is no observation lounge with forward-facing views over the ship's bows. There is no dance floor with live orchestra for adults (other than "Rockin Bar D" in Beat Street for throbbing disco/country-style music). The elevators are very small, and so is the gymnasium (for such a large ship). It is expensive (but then so is a week at any Disney resort), gratuities are extra, and 15% is added to all bar/beverage/wine and spa accounts. Don't even think about it if you are not a Disney fan, or if you don't like kids, or lining up and registering for things. Service with only a moderate sprinkling of hospitality.

Standing in line for embarkation, disembarkation, shore tenders and for self-serve buffet meals is an inevitable aspect of cruising aboard all large ships. Lines at various outlets can prove irritating (some creative Disney Imagineering is needed, including a large sprinkling of pixie dust), as can trying to get through to Guest Services by telephone. The food product and delivery has improved, but falls short of less expensive cruise products. There is no proper library – something many regular cruise passengers miss.

SUITABLE FOR: *Disney Wonder* is ideally suited to families with children (or grandchildren), although couples and singles are also welcome (there are few activities for couples during the daytime, but plenty of entertainment at night). Whether cruising with 1,000 (or more) kids aboard will make for a relaxing holiday for those without kids will depend on how much noise they can absorb. You will, however, need to be a real Disney fan, as *everything* revolves around Disney and the family theme; this means that everything is based on entertainment and good times, while food takes a back step into the world of "theme park" cuisine. For children of all ages, there's simply nothing better than *Disney Magic* or *Disney Wonder*.

ACCOMMODATION. There are 12 price grades for accommodation (price will depend on grade, size and location you choose). Spread over six decks, all suites/cabins have been designed for practicality and have space-efficient layouts. Most cabins have common features such as a neat vertical steamer trunk for clothes storage, illuminated closets, a hairdryer located at a vanity desk (or in the bathroom), and bathrobes for all passengers. Many cabins have third- and fourth pull-down berths that rise and are totally hidden in the ceiling when not in use, but the standard interior and outside cabins, while acceptable for two, are extremely tight with three or four. The decor is practical, creative, and colorful, with lots of neat styling touches. Cabins with refrigerators can have them stocked with one of several packages (at extra cost).

The bathrooms, although compact (due to the fact that the toilet is separate from the rest of the bathroom), are really functional units, designed with split-use facilities so that more than one person can use them at the same time – good for families. Many have bathtubs (really shower tubs).

Accommodation designated as suites offers much more space, and extra goodies such as VCRs, CD players, large screen TVs, and extra beds (useful for larger families). But some suites are beneath the pool deck, teen lounge, or informal cafe, so there could be lots of noise as the ceiling insulation is poor (but the cabin to cabin insulation is good).

Wheelchair-bound passengers have a variety of cabin sizes and configurations, including suites with a private balcony (unfortunately you cannot get a wheelchair through the balcony's sliding door) and extra-large bathrooms with excellent roll-in showers, and good closet and drawer space (almost all the vessel is accessible). For the sight-impaired, cabin numbers and elevator buttons are braille-encoded.

A 24-hour room service is available (suite occupants also get concierge service); but the room service menu and cabin breakfast menus are limited. There is a 15% service charge for all beverage deliveries (including tea and coffee).

CUISINE/DINING. There are three main dining rooms (all non-smoking), each with over 400 seats, two seatings, and unique themes. Lumiere's has Beauty and the Beast; Parrot Cay has a tacky, pseudo-Caribbean theme; Animator's Palate (the most visual of the three) has food and electronic art that makes the evening decor change from black and white to full-color. You will eat in all three dining rooms in rotation (twice per 7-day cruise), and move with your assigned waiter and assistant waiter to each dining room in turn, thus providing a different dining experience (each has a different decor, different menus). As you will have the same waiter in each of the three restaurants, any gratuities go only to "your" waiter. Parrot Cay and Lumiere's have open seating for breakfast and lunch (the lunch menu is pitiful). The noise level in all three dining rooms is extremely high. If the formal nights happen to fall on the evening you are due to eat in Parrot Cay, formal wear and the decor of Parrot Cay Restaurant do not go together at all.

In addition, Palo is an elegant 140-seat reservations-only alternative restaurant (with a $5 cover/gratuity charge) serving Italian cuisine. It has a 270° view, and is for adults only (no "Munchkins" allowed); the à la carte cuisine is cooked to order, and the wine list is good (although prices are high). Make your reservations as soon as you board or miss out on the only decent food aboard this ship. Afternoon High Tea is also presented here, on days at sea.

For casual eating, Topsider's is an indoor/outdoor cafe featuring low-quality self-serve breakfast and lunch buffets with very poor choice and presentation, and a buffet dinner for children (consisting mostly of fried foods). There is also an ice cream and frozen yogurt bar (Scoops) that opens infrequently; other fast food outlets include Pluto's (for hamburgers, hot dogs), Pinocchio's, which is open throughout the day but not in the evening (for basic pizza and sandwiches). On one night of the cruise, there is also an outdoor self-serve "Tropicalifragilisticexpialidocious" buffet.

Overall, the food has improved since the ship was first introduced (it needed to, it was of a very low quality), and is now more attractively presented, although there are still so few green vegetables. Vegetarians and those seeking light cuisine will be totally underwhelmed. Guest chefs from Walt Disney World Resort prepare signature dishes each cruise, and also host cooking demonstrations.

ENTERTAINMENT. The entertainment and activities programming for families and children are extremely good. There are four large-scale stage shows (in the stunning 977-seat showlounge) featuring original Disney musicals. Sadly, they are performed without a hint of a live orchestra, although the lighting, staging and technical effects are excellent. There is also a Disney-themed Trivia Game Show.

For grown-ups, there is "Route 66" – an adult entertainment area that includes a wacky Hollywood-style street, complete with three entertainment rooms. "Cadillac" is a jazz piano lounge, with private headphones for listening to music of all types when no live music is scheduled; "Wavebands" (for ear-splitting rock 'n' roll and country music); and "Barrel of Laughs" (for improvisational comedy involving the audience). During the day, creative enrichment programs have been added.

SPA/FITNESS. Fancy a little pampering? The Vista Spa is a fitness/wellbeing complex that measures 8,500 sq. ft/790 sq. meters. The fitness/workout room (with high-tech Cybex muscle-toning equipment) has ocean-view windows that overlook the navigation bridge on the deck below. There are 11 rooms for spa/beauty treatments (however, note that the pounding from the basketball court located directly above makes relaxing spa treatments almost impossible).

Thermal bath rooms have a "tropical rain shower", sauna, mild steam room, aromatic steam room and a fog shower. Aromatic scents such as eucalyptus, lime, peppermint, rose and sage can be infused into the mild steam room, while camomile is used in the aromatic steam room.

Massage (including exotic massages such as Aroma Stone massage and other well-being massages, as well as underwater massage in a hydrotherapy bath), aromatherapy facials, pedicures, and beauty salon treatments are at extra cost (massage, for example, costs about $2 per minute, plus gratuity). For something different, try the Rasul mud and steam room (it's an absolute delight for couples). Do make appointments as early as possible – aboard a ship so large, treatment time slots go quickly, so the day you board is the best time to book your treatments.

For something extra special, consider booking a massage at Castaway Cay – in a private beach hut on the beach that is open to the sea. It's magical.

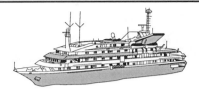

easyCruise I
NOT YET RATED

Boutique Ship: . . . . .3,990 tons	Passenger Decks: 5	Cabins (with private balcony): 4
Lifestyle: . . . . .Below Standard	Total Crew:	Cabins (wheelchair accessible): 0
Cruise Line: . . . . .easyCruise	Passengers	Cabin Current: . . . . .110 volts
Former Names: . . . .*Neptune Two*,	(lower beds/all berths): 180/180	Elevators: 1
Renaissance Two	Passenger Space Ratio	Casino: . . . . .Yes
Builder: . . . .Cantieri Navale Ferrari (Italy)	(lower beds/all berths): 22.1/22.1	Slot Machines: . . . . .Yes
Original Cost: . . . .$20 million	Crew/Passenger Ratio	Swimming Pools (outdoors): 1
Entered Service: . . . .April 1990/May 2005	(lower beds/all berths): 180/180	Swimming Pools (indoors): 0
Registry: . . . .???	Navigation Officers: . . . . .European	Whirlpools: 1
Length (ft/m): 289.6/88.30	Cabins (total): 50	Self-Service Launderette: . . . . .No
Beam (ft/m): 50.1/15.30	Size Range (sq ft/m): 90/8.3	Dedicated Cinema/Seats: . . . . .No
Draft (ft/m): 11.9/3.65	Cabins (outside view): 50	Library: . . . . .No
Propulsion/Propellers: . . . . .diesel	Cabins (interior/no view): . . . . .,. 0	Classification Society: . . . . .Registro
(3,514kW)/2 (CP)	Cabins (for one person): 0	Navale Italiano

OVERALL SCORE: NYR (OUT OF A POSSIBLE 2,000 POINTS)

OVERVIEW. Camping at sea is what easyCruise is all about (although this may change as the product comes into being). The no-frills ship delivers exactly that – a no-frills, no-facilities, no service, no space, no-nothing cruise that cannot be considered a cruise at all. It is an anti-cruise – a no-vacation vacation for backpackers and others without shoes, clothes or social manners. Technical and operated personnel are provided by V-Ships.

Originally one of a fleet of four small, identical and intimate cruise vessels (with mega-yacht looks and styling), out of a fleet of eight ships for the now-defunct Renaissance Cruises, the ship was purchased in 2003 by Stelios Haji-Iannou, founder of the no-frills airline easyJet. Refitted in Singapore, it now carries almost double its original passenger load of 100, and sports a bright orange hull with "easyCruise.com" splashed along it. The open deck and sunning space was always very cramped when the ship carried 100 passengers; now that it carries more, it could well be easyAwful.

Its claim to fame is its pricing of £29 per person, per day. But what do you get for that? Not much, except passage, a bed, and bathroom cubicle. Want food? Pay extra! Want your bed changed? Pay extra! Want a captain? Pay extra! So the £29 base fare plus, plus, plus, all adds up to more than the per-day cost of a *real* cruise. Cruising unbundled? Oh dear! You can get on in any port on the itinerary, which means that there will be little ambiance, and no cohesive cruise experience at all. In other words, it is a ferry with several destinations – somewhat like the Norwegian Coastal Voyages journey.

The decor is upbeat, trendy, and minimalist, in a manner

BERLITZ'S RATINGS

	Possible	Achieved
Ship	500	NYR
Accommodation	200	NYR
Food	400	NYR
Service	400	NYR
Entertainment	100	NYR
Cruise	400	NYR

that is new and now, but cannot be recommended for traditional cruisegoers. Out has gone all the polished rosewood paneling and good looks of the original interiors, and in has come the contemporary, plastic look of Ikea's cheapest bed-sit-look furniture and fittings.

easyCruise provides destination-intensive budget travel, but, quite honestly, the ship, when full, will be extremely cramped, with a poor Passenger Space Ratio. Forget reality cruising, easyCruise has the potential to be "Cruising – get me out of here!" and not particularly beneficial either to the cruise industry or the cruisegoer. It's a waste of what was formerly a nice ship.

ACCOMMODATION. The minimalist cabins (designed in the modular fashion of easyHotel's rooms at its 14 Lexham Gardens, London W8 property, which opened in 2004) have a double bed, but little else. They are tiny, so don't bring clothes or a suitcase – there's no storage space. The modular, plastic bathrooms have only the most basic facilities (shower, wash basin, toilet). easyHousekeeping services (cabin cleaning) are at extra cost.

CUISINE/DINING. The dining room, which has open seating, is small and elegant. It is on lowest deck and has portholes and not windows (a construction regulations requirement). Sit where you like, when you like. Food costs extra.

ENTERTAINMENT. What entertainment?

SPA/FITNESS. There are no facilities, but carrying your own bags should keep you fit. Easy!

Ecstasy
★★★ +

Large (Resort) Ship: . . . . .70,367 tons	Total Crew: 920	Cabins (with private balcony): 54
Lifestyle: . . . . .Standard	Passengers	Cabins (wheelchair accessible): 22
Cruise Line: . . . . . .Carnival Cruise Lines	(lower beds/all berths): 2,052/2,594	Cabin Current: . . . . .110 volts
Former Names: . . . . .none	Passenger Space Ratio	Elevators: 14
Builder: . . .Kvaerner Masa-Yards (Finland)	(lower beds/all berths): 34.2/27.1	Casino (gaming tables): . . . . .Yes
Original Cost: . . . .$275 million	Crew/Passenger Ratio	Slot Machines: . . . . .Yes
Entered Service: . . . . .June 1991	(lower beds/all berths): 2.2/2.8	Swimming Pools (outdoors): 3
Registry: .Panama	Navigation Officers: . . . . .Italian	Swimming Pools (indoors): 0
Length (ft/m): 855.8/260.6	Cabins (total): 1,026	Whirlpools: 6
Beam (ft/m): 103.0/31.4	Size Range (sq ft/m): 173.2–409.7/	Self-Service Launderette: . . . . .Yes
Draft (ft/m): 25.9/7.9	16.0–38.0	Dedicated Cinema/Seats: . . . . .No
Propulsion/Propellers: . . . . .diesel-electric	Cabins (outside view): 618	Library: . . . . .Yes
(42,240kW)/2	Cabins (interior/no view): 408	Classification Society: . . .Lloyd's Register
Passenger Decks: 10	Cabins (for one person): 0	

OVERALL SCORE: 1,385 (OUT OF A POSSIBLE 2,000 POINTS)

OVERVIEW. This the second in the *Fantasy*-class of eight almost identical ships for Carnival Cruise Lines, and the sixth new ship for this very successful cruise line. Almost vibration-free service is provided by the diesel electric propulsion system. It has proven to be a successful design for this company that targets the standard (mainstream) market, particularly first-time passengers.

The ship, whose bows are extremely short, has the distinctive, large, swept-back wing-tipped funnel that is the trademark of Carnival Cruise Lines, in the company colors of red, white and blue. The ship has expansive open deck areas (sadly, there is no wrap-around open promenade deck), but they quickly become inadequate when it is full and everyone wants to be out on deck (the aft decks tend to be less noisy, whereas all the activities are focused around the main swimming pool and hot tubs). There is also a "banked" jogging track outdoors on the deck above a large, glass-enclosed enclosed health spa that is always busy. A well-defined "topless" sunbathing area can be found around the funnel base on Verandah Deck.

The passenger flow is good, and the interior design is clever, functional, and extremely colorful – "entertainment architecture." The neon lighting in the interior decor takes a little getting used to, as the color combinations are quite vivid. A dramatic six-deck-high atrium (whose balconied shape may remind you of a great opera house), with cool marble and hot neon, is topped by a large colored glass dome, and has a spectacular artistic centerpiece, a 10-ton sculpture. Leading off from an indoor double-width promenade there are public entertainment lounges, bars and clubs galore, with something for everyone – there's even a

BERLITZ'S RATINGS

	Possible	Achieved
Ship	500	395
Accommodation	200	151
Food	400	221
Service	400	270
Entertainment	100	81
Cruise	400	267

vintage Rolls-Royce car located on the promenade. The library has delightful decor, but few books. The Chinatown Lounge has Oriental decor, hanging lanterns and smoking dragon.

SUITABLE FOR: *Ecstasy* is best suited to first-time young (and young at heart) couples, singles, children and teenagers (anyone under 21 must be accompanied by a parent, relative or guardian) that enjoy big city nightlife, who want contemporary, upbeat surroundings, and the latest in facilities, plenty of entertainment lounges and bars and high-tech sophistication, and food that is acceptable but nothing more (unless you are prepared to pay extra for dining in the "alternative" restaurant), all delivered with friendly service that lacks polish.

ACCOMMODATION. There are 13 grades, the price depending on the grade, size and location. The standard outside-view and interior (no view) cabins have decor that is rather plain and non-memorable. They are marginally comfortable, yet spacious enough and practical (most are of the same size and appointments), with good storage space and practical, well-designed no-nonsense bathrooms. Anyone booking one of the outside suites will find more space, whirlpool bathtubs, and some fascinating, rather eclectic decor and furniture. These are mildly attractive, but nothing special, and they are much smaller than those aboard the ships of a similar size of several competing companies.

A gift basket is provided in all grades; it includes aloe soap, shampoo, conditioner, deodorant, breath mints, candy, and pain relief tablets (albeit all in sample sizes).

If you book accommodation in one of the suites (Category 11 or 12 in the Carnival Cruise Lines brochure) you qualify for "Skipper's Club" priority check-in at any US homeland port – useful for getting ahead of the crowd.

CUISINE/DINING. There are two dining rooms (Wind Star and Wind Song, with the galley between them). They have attractive decor and colors, but they are large, crowded and very noisy (some would call it ambiance). The food is adequate. Dining in each restaurant is now in four seatings, for greater flexibility: 6pm, 6.45pm, 8pm and 8.45pm (times are approximate). Carnival meals stress quantity, not quality, although the company constantly works hard to improve the cuisine.

While the menu items sound good, their presentation and taste leave much to be desired. While meats are of a high quality, fish and seafood is not. Presentation is simple, and few garnishes are used. Many meat and fowl dishes are disguised with gravies and sauces. The selection of fresh green vegetables, breads, rolls, cheeses and fruits is limited, and there is too much use of canned fruit and jellied desserts. However, do remember that this is banquet catering, with all its attendant standardization and production cooking (it is, therefore, difficult to obtain anything unusual or off-menu). The selection of breads, rolls, cheeses and fruits is limited (there is too much use of canned fruit).

Although there is a decent wine list, there are no wine waiters (the waiters are expected to serve both food and wine, which does not work well). The service is highly programmed, although the waiters are willing and reasonably friendly. However, they do sing and dance, and there are constant waiter parades; the dining room is show business – all done in the name of gratuities at the end of your cruise.

The Lido Cafe provides the usual casual serve-yourself buffet foods, although it's completely unmemorable. At night, the "Seaview Bistro", as the Lido Cafe becomes known, provides a casual (dress down) alternative to eating in the main dining rooms, serving pasta, steaks, salads and desserts (it typically is in operation between 6pm and 9pm).

ENTERTAINMENT. The Blue Sapphire Showlounge is the principal venue for large-scale production shows and major cabaret acts (although 20 pillars obstruct the views from several seats). With all the audio-visual support staff, dressers, and stage managers, the personnel count comes to just over 40.

SPA/FITNESS. SpaCarnival is a large health, fitness and spa complex located on the uppermost interior deck, forward of the ship's mast, and accessed from the forward stairway. It consists of a gymnasium with oceanview windows that look out over the ship's bow (it has a large array of the latest in muscle-pumping electronic machines), an aerobics exercise room, men's and women's changing rooms, sauna and steam rooms, and beauty salon.

The spa is operated by Steiner, a specialist concession, whose staff will try to sell you Steiner's own-brand Elemis beauty products (spa girls have sales targets). Some fitness classes are free, while some, such as yoga, and kick-boxing, cost $10 per class. However, being aboard will give you an opportunity to try some of the more exotic treatments (particularly some of the massages available).

● **For more extensive general information on what a Carnival cruise is like, see pages 107–111.**

MAY THE FORCE BE WITH YOU

You might be confused by the numbering system for wind velocity. There are 12 velocities, known as "force" on the Beaufort scale. They are as follows:

Force	Speed (mph)	Description/Ocean Surface	Force	Speed (mph)	Description/Ocean Surface
0	0–1	Calm; glassy (like a mirror)	7	32–38	Moderate gale; streaky white foam
1	1–3	Light wind; rippled surface	8	39–46	Fresh gale; moderately high waves
2	4–7	Light breeze; small wavelets	9	47–54	Strong gale; high waves
3	8–12	Gentle breeze; large wavelets, scattered whitecaps	10	55–63	Whole gale; very high waves, curling crests
4	13–18	Moderate breeze; small waves, frequent whitecaps	11	64–73	Violent storm; extremely high waves, froth and foam, poor visibility
5	19–24	Fresh breeze; moderate waves, numerous whitecaps	12	73+	Hurricane; huge waves, thundering white spray, visibility nil
6	25–31	Strong breeze; large waves, white foam crests			

Elation
★★★ +

Large (Resort) Ship: . . . . .70,367 tons	Passenger Decks: 10	Cabins (for one person): 0
Lifestyle: . . . . .Standard	Total Crew: 920	Cabins (with private balcony): 54
Cruise Line: . . . . . .Carnival Cruise Lines	Passengers	Cabins (wheelchair accessible): 22
Former Names: . . . . .none	(lower beds/all berths): 2,052/2,594	Cabin Current: . . . . .110 volts
Builder: . . .Kvaerner Masa-Yards (Finland)	Passenger Space Ratio	Elevators: 14
Original Cost: . . . .$300 million	(lower beds/all berths): 34.2/27.1	Casino (gaming tables): . . . . .Yes
Entered Service: . . . . .Mar 1998	Crew/Passenger Ratio	Slot Machines: . . . . .Yes
Registry: . . . . .Panama	(lower beds/all berths): 2.2/2.8	Swimming Pools (outdoors): 3
Length (ft/m): 855.0/260.6	Navigation Officers: . . . . .Italian	Swimming Pools (indoors): 0
Beam (ft/m): 103.3/31.5	Cabins (total): 1,026	Whirlpools: 6
Draft (ft/m): 25.9/7.9	Size Range (sq ft/m): 173.2–409.7/	Self-Service Launderette: . . . . .Yes
Propulsion/Propellers: . . . . .diesel-electric	16.0–38.0	Dedicated Cinema/Seats: . . . . .No
42,842 kW)/2 azimuthing pods	Cabins (outside view): 618	Library: . . . . .Yes
(14 MW each)	Cabins (interior/no view): 408	Classification Society: . . .Lloyd's Register

OVERALL SCORE: 1,387 (OUT OF A POSSIBLE 2,000 POINTS)

OVERVIEW. Although externally angular and not particularly handsome, *Elation* is the seventh in a series of eight ships of the same series and identical internal configuration (others in the series being *Ecstasy, Fantasy, Fascination, Imagination, Inspiration, Paradise* and *Sensation*), but actually the 12th new ship ordered by Carnival Cruise Lines. It has proven to be a successful design for this company that targets the standard (mainstream) market, and particularly the first-time passenger.

The ship, whose bows are extremely short, has the distinctive, large, swept-back wing-tipped funnel that is the trademark of Carnival Cruise Lines, in the company colors of red, white and blue. The ship has expansive open deck areas (sadly, there is no wrap-around open promenade deck), but they quickly become inadequate when it is full and everyone wants to be out on deck (the aft decks tend to be less noisy, whereas all the activities are focused around the main swimming pool and hot tubs). There is also a "banked" jogging track outdoors on the deck above a large, glass-enclosed enclosed health spa that is always busy. A well-defined "topless" sunbathing area can be found around the funnel base on Verandah Deck.

The ship has a bold, forthright, angular appearance that is typical of today's space-creative designs. *Elation* is rather special in modern-day cruise ship terms, as it was the first ship in the cruise industry to be fitted with a "pod" propulsion system *(see page 151)*.

Briefly, the ship is powered through the water by a "pod" propulsion system (this replaces the traditional propeller shaft and rudder combination that is normally fitted aboard most cruise ships), which gives the ship more maneuvra-

BERLITZ'S RATINGS

	Possible	Achieved
Ship	500	395
Accommodation	200	151
Food	400	223
Service	400	270
Entertainment	100	81
Cruise	400	267

bility, while reducing machinery space requirements, as well as vibration at the stern, and the need for stern thrusters. The pods themselves (each weighs 170 tons without its mounting) look rather like huge outboard motors that are capable of 360° rotation. When going ahead the pods face with the propeller forward; to go astern the poods can be rotated through 180°, or simply by reversing the thrust when the propeller is in the forward position.

Inside, the general passenger flow is good, and the interior design is clever, functional, and extremely colorful. The neon lighting in the interior decor takes a little getting used to at first, as the color combinations are quite vivid. The theme of the decor is mythical muses, and composers and their compositions (many of the public rooms have musical names), and the colors, while bright, are less so than aboard previous ships in this series.

As in its sister ships, there is a dramatic six-deck-high atrium (whose balconied shape may remind you of some of the world's great opera houses), appropriately dressed to impress, topped by a large glass dome, and featuring a fascinating, entertaining artistic centerpiece. There are expansive open-deck areas and a large, glass-enclosed enclosed health spa that is always busy.

The splashy, showy, public rooms and interior design are pure Las Vegas, and ideal for those who love colors and neon lights. There are public entertainment lounges, bars and clubs galore, with something for everyone, including a children's playroom, larger than aboard the previous ships in this series. Some busy colors and design themes abound in the handsome public rooms – these are connected by wide indoor boulevards and beg your attention and indulgence. There is also a good art collection, much of it bright and vocal. The library is a fine room, as aboard most Carnival ships (but there are few books). One neat feature (not found aboard previous ships in this series) is an atrium bar, complete with live classical music.

This ship is not for those who want a quiet, relaxing cruise experience. There are simply too many annoying announcements, and a great deal of hustling for drinks. Shore excursions are booked via the in-cabin "Fun Vision" television system, so obtaining advice and suggestions is not easy. In fact, getting anyone to answer your questions can prove utterly frustrating.

ACCOMMODATION. There are 13 grades of accommodation. The price will depend on the grade, size and location you choose. The standard outside-view and interior (no view) cabins have decor that is rather plain and unmemorable. They are marginally comfortable, yet spacious enough and practical (most are of the same size and appointments), with good storage space and practical, well-designed no-nonsense bathrooms.

Anyone booking one of the outside suites will find more space, whirlpool bathtubs, and some fascinating, rather eclectic decor and furniture. These are mildly attractive, but nothing special, and they are much smaller than those aboard similarly sized ships of several competitors.

A gift basket is now provided in all grades of accommodation; it includes aloe soap, shampoo, conditioner, deodorant, breath mints, candy, and pain relief tablets (albeit all in sample sizes).

If you book accommodation in one of the suites (Category 11 or 12 in the Carnival Cruise Lines brochure) you qualify for "Skipper's Club" priority check-in at any US homeland port – useful for getting ahead of the crowd.

CUISINE/DINING. There are two dining rooms (Imagination and Inspiration, with the galley between them). They have attractive decor and colors, but they are large, crowded and very noisy (some call it ambiance). The food is adequate, but no more. Dining in each restaurant is now in four seatings, for greater flexibility: 6pm, 6.45pm, 8pm and 8.45pm (times are approximate).

For casual meals, there's The Lido, which, aboard this ship, has some improvements and additions worthy of note, such as: orange juice machine, where you put in oranges and out comes fresh juice (better than the concentrate stuff supplied in the dining room). There's also a sushi bar. Things are looking up, which means more choices.

At night, the "Seaview Bistro", as the Lido Cafe becomes known provides a casual (dress down) alternative to eating in the main dining rooms, serving pasta, steaks, salads and desserts (it typically operates 6pm–9pm).

ENTERTAINMENT. The Mikado Showlounge seats 1,010 and is the principal venue for large-scale production shows and major cabaret acts (although 20 pillars obstruct the views from several seats). Almost every lounge and bar has live music.

SPA/FITNESS. SpaCarnival is a large health, fitness and spa complex that is located on the uppermost interior deck, forward of the ship's mast, and accessed from the forward stairway. It consists of a gymnasium with oceanview windows that look out over the ship's bow (it has a large array of the latest in muscle-pumping electronic machines), an aerobics exercise room, men's and women's changing rooms, sauna and steam rooms, and beauty salon. A common complaint from passengers is that the area is that there are not enough staff to keep the area clean and tidy, and used towels are often strewn around the changing rooms (particularly on the men's side).

● **For more extensive general information on what a Carnival cruise is like, see pages 107–111.**

Empress of the Seas
★★★ +

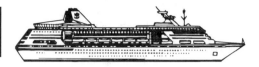

Large (Resort) Ship: . . . . .48,563 tons	Passenger Decks: 9	Cabins (with private balcony): 69
Lifestyle: . . . . .Standard	Total Crew: 685	Cabins (wheelchair accessible): 4
Cruise Line: . . . . .Royal Caribbean	Passengers	Cabin Current: . . . . .110 volts
International	(lower beds/all berths): 1,600/2,020	Elevators: 7
Former Names: . . . . .Nordic Empress	Passenger Space Ratio	Casino (gaming tables): . . . . .Yes
Builder: . . . . . . .Chantiers de l'Atlantique	(lower beds/all berths): 30.2/24.0	Slot Machines: . . . . .Yes – 220
(France)	Crew/Passenger Ratio	Swimming Pools (outdoors): 1
Original Cost: . . . .$170 million	(lower beds/all berths): 2.3/2.9	(+1 wading pool)
Entered Service: . . . . .June 1990	Navigation Officers: . . . . . . .Scandinavian	Swimming Pools (indoors): 0
Registry: . . . . .Liberia	Cabins (total): 800	Whirlpools: 4
Length (ft/m): 692.2/211.00	Size Range (sq ft/m): 117.0–818.0/	Self-Service Launderette: . . . . .No
Beam (ft/m): 100.7/30.70	10.8–76.0	Dedicated Cinema/Seats: . . . . .No
Draft (ft/m): 24.9/7.60	Cabins (outside view): 471	Library: . . . . .No
Propulsion/Propellers: . . . . .diesel	Cabins (interior/no view): 329	Classification Society: . . . . . .Det Norske
(16,200 kW)/2	Cabins (for one person): 0	Veritas

OVERALL SCORE: 1,313 (OUT OF A POSSIBLE 2,000 POINTS)

OVERVIEW. This contemporary ship (now 15 years old and the smallest in the fleet) has a short bow and squared-off stern, and yet it manages to look reasonably well balanced. *Empress of the Seas* was (as the former *Nordic Empress*) was designed specifically for the short-cruise market, for which the ship is quite well suited. It was designed for Admiral Cruises, which Royal Caribbean Cruise Line (as it was then called) purchased; the original name of the ship was to have been *Future Seas*, although this name was not finally adopted. The ship went through an extensive refurbishment in 2003 just before the name change to bring it into line with other ships in the RCI fleet – all of which have "*of the Seas*" as part of their name.

There is a polished wrap-around wood promenade deck outdoors, and a dramatic use of glass-enclosed viewing spaces that provide good contact from the upper, open decks to the sea. Although the outdoor pool is decent enough (good at night for evenings under the stars), the two swimming pools provided are very small. In other words, there's not a lot of open deck space, and deck lounge chairs are crammed together with little room to maneuver around them on sunny days at sea.

A nine-deck-high atrium is the focal point of the interior design, which tends to have many Scandinavian influences. Lots of crystal and brass have been used to good effect to reflect light. Indeed, the clever use of lighting effects provides illuminating interiors that make you feel warm. Passenger flow is generally good, although, because two seatings and two show times are operated, some congestion is inevitable adjacent to the entrance foyer at show time. A

BERLITZ'S RATINGS

	Possible	Achieved
Ship	500	350
Accommodation	200	126
Food	400	236
Service	400	270
Entertainment	100	71
Cruise	400	260

small library was added a few years ago – a needed facility that was not included when the ship was built.

A three-level casino has a sailcloth ceiling, but it is a noisy room (ambiance?). The Viking Crown Lounge, aft of the funnel, is a two-level nightclub-disco for the late-night set.

Empress of the Seas is a fairly smart contemporary ship with a high passenger density, and you won't be bored – there is an adequate array of activities for all ages. In the final analysis, you will probably be overwhelmed by the public spaces, and underwhelmed by the size of the cabins. However, this is basically a well-run, fine-tuned, highly structured cruise product geared particularly to those seeking an action-packed cruise vacation at a moderately good price, with lots of fellow passengers to keep you company. The onboard currency is the US dollar.

Overpriced drinks are aggressively pushed as soon as passengers board the ship, and constant, loud announcements are irritating. The two swimming pools are very small considering the number of passengers carried. Standing in line for embarkation, disembarkation, shore tenders and for self-serve buffet meals is an inevitable aspect of cruising aboard all large ships.

ACCOMMODATION. There are 15 different price categories. The largest accommodation can be found in the Royal Suite, which is located just under the navigation bridge on the port side. This has a queen-sized bed, walk-in closet, separate living area with bar, refrigerator and entertainment center; the bathroom has a whirlpool tub, and vanity dressing area. There is a private balcony.

Nine cabins have private balconies that overlook the ship's stern (these consist of two owner's suites and seven "superior" ocean-view cabins). The other cabins with private balconies also have a decent amount of living space, and a small sofa, coffee table and chair, and vanity desk.

Almost all the other cabins are dimensionally challenged, although reasonably comfortable. All grades of accommodation have twin beds that can convert to a queen-size configuration. The bathrooms (all refurbished in 2004) are nicely laid-out, and have a decent amount of space for personal toiletry items.

CUISINE/DINING. The Hollywood musical-themed Carmen Dining Room is non-smoking. It is two decks high, with both a main and balcony level, as well as large windows that overlook the stern of the ship, but it really is a noisy room. There are two seatings. The dining operation is well orchestrated, with emphasis on highly programmed (insensitive), extremely hurried service that many find intrusive.

The cuisine is typical of mass banquet catering that offers standard fare comparable to that found in American family-style restaurants ashore. While the menu descriptions provide a tempting read, the food, when it arrives, has little taste (many items are pre-prepared ashore to keep costs down). However, a decent selection of light meals is provided, and a vegetarian menu is available. The selection of breads, rolls, fruit and cheese could be better. Caviar (once a standard menu item) now incurs a hefty extra charge. Special orders, tableside carving and flambeau items are not offered. The menus typically include a Welcome Aboard Dinner, French Dinner, Italian Dinner, International Dinner, and Captain's Gala Dinner.

Alternative Dining Option: Portofino was added in a 2004 refurbishment. The restaurant offers Italian-style cuisine (reservations are required, and there's a cover charge of $20 per person). However, it's worth it, as the food is so much better than in the dining room (although the portions are really large), and the intimacy of the room makes it a nice, romantic place (it has a good number of tables for two).

Casual Dining Option: For casual breakfasts and lunches, the Windjammer Cafe, with its two buffet display lines, provides an alternative to the dining room, although there are often lines at peak times, and the selection is at best very average. There are no "active stations" – where items such as omelets could be made to order.

ENTERTAINMENT. The two-level Strike Up the Band show lounge has poor sight lines in the upper lateral balconies. It has a main floor level as well as a balcony level. However, the sightlines from the balcony are almost useless as they are ruined by railings. Strong cabaret acts are also featured in the main showlounge.

The entertainment throughout is upbeat (in fact, it is difficult to get away from music and noise), but is typical of the kind of resort hotel found ashore in Las Vegas. There is even background music in all corridors and lifts, and constant music outdoors on the pool deck. If you want a quiet relaxing holiday, choose another ship.

SPA/FITNESS. The ShipShape Fitness Center is a two-decks high facility, and contains a gymnasium (with some good muscle-pump equipment), men's and ladies saunas and changing areas, and massage treatment rooms. The beauty salon is located on the port side of Showtime Deck 6, and has ocean view windows.

● **For more extensive general information on what a Royal Caribbean International cruise is like, see pages 128–131.**

Enchantment of the Seas ★★★★

Large (Resort) Ship: . . . . .74,137 tons	Total Crew: 760	Cabins (with private balcony): 212
Lifestyle: . . . . .Standard	Passengers	Cabins (wheelchair accessible): 14
Cruise Line: . . . . .Royal Caribbean	(lower beds/all berths): 1,950/2,446	Cabin Current: . . . . .110 and 220 volts
International	Passenger Space Ratio	Elevators: 9
Former Names: . . . . .none	(lower beds/all berths): 38.0/30.3	Casino (gaming tables): . . . . .Yes
Builder: . . .Kvaerner Masa-Yards (Finland)	Crew/Passenger Ratio	Slot Machines: . . . . .Yes
Original Cost: . . . .$300 million	(lower beds/all berths): 2.4/3.2	Swimming Pools (outdoors): 1
Entered Service: . . . . .July 1997	Navigation Officers: . . . . .Norwegian/	Swimming Pools (indoors): 1
Registry: . . . . .The Bahamas	International	(indoor/outdoor w/sliding glass roof)
Length (ft/m): 915.6/279.1	Cabins (total): 975	Whirlpools: 6
Beam (ft/m): 105.6/32.2	Size Range (sq ft/m): 158.2–1,267.0/	Self-Service Launderette: . . . . .No
Draft (ft/m): 25.5/7.6	14.7–117.7	Dedicated Cinema/Seats: . . . . .No
Propulsion/Propellers: . . . . .diesel-electric	Cabins (outside view): 576	Library: . . . . .Yes
(50,400kW)/2	Cabins (interior/no view): 399	Classification Society: . . . . . . .Det Norske
Passenger Decks: 11	Cabins (for one person): 0	Veritas

OVERALL SCORE: 1,521 (OUT OF A POSSIBLE 2,000 POINTS)

OVERVIEW. This is one of a pair of ships for this popular cruise line (sister to *Grandeur of the Seas*). It has a long profile, with a single funnel located well aft (almost a throwback to designs used during the 1950s). The stern is nicely rounded (rather like the older *Sovereign of the Seas*-class ships), and a Viking Crown Lounge is set amidships. This, together with the forward mast, provides three distinct focal points in its exterior profile. There is a wrap-around promenade deck outdoors (but no cushioned pads for the tacky home patio-style plastic deck lounge chairs).

A large Viking Crown Lounge (a trademark of all Royal Caribbean International ships) sits between funnel and mast at the top of the atrium lobby, and overlooks the forward section of the swimming pool deck, as aboard *Legend of the Seas* and *Splendour of the Seas*, with access provided from stairway off the central atrium.

The principal interior focal point is a seven-deck-high Centrum (atrium lobby), which provides a good meeting point (the Purser's Desk and Shore Excursion Desk are located on one of the lower levels). Many public entertainment rooms and facilities are located off the atrium.

This ship has good passenger flow inside. There is a good, varied collection of artworks (including several sculptures), principally by British artists, with classical music, ballet and theater themes. The casino is large and glitzy, and has a fascinating, theatrical glass-covered, but under-floor exhibit. The children's and teens' facilities are good, much expanded from previous ships in the fleet.

A delightful champagne terrace bar sits forward of the lower level of the two-deck-high dining room. There is a

BERLITZ'S RATINGS

	Possible	Achieved
Ship	500	430
Accommodation	200	166
Food	400	248
Service	400	302
Entertainment	100	81
Cruise	400	294

good use of tropical plants throughout the public rooms, which helps to counteract the rather plain and clinical pastel wall colors, while huge murals of opera scenes adorn several stairways.

Enchantment of the Seas has quite attractive interiors, and will provide a good cruise vacation, particularly for first-time passengers seeking comfortable surroundings similar to those in a Hyatt Hotel, with fabrics and soft furnishings that blend together to provide a contemporary resort environment. This company provides a well organized, but rather homogenous cruise experience, with the same old passenger participation activities and events that have been provided for more than 25 years. The onboard currency is the US dollar.

Between mid-May and early July, 2005, *Enchantment of the Seas* will undergo a "chop-and-stretch" operation that will add a 72.8-ft (22.2-meter) mid-section, increasing the ship's overall length to 990.1 ft (301.8 meters). Its tonnage will increase to 80,700 tons. The upgrade will add another 151 passenger cabins, and a complete make-over of public rooms will be undertaken at the same time.

ACCOMMODATION. There are 16 price grades (the price depending on the grade, size and location, with location and grade perhaps more important, since so many of the cabins are of the same, or a very similar size).

There are five grades of suites: Royal Suite (1), Owner's Suite (5), Royal Family Suite (4), Grand Suite (12), and Superior Suite (44, including two superior suites for the disabled). All are well appointed and have pleasing decor (best described as Scandinavian Moderne), with good wood and color accenting (the largest has a baby grand piano). **Royal Suite.** The largest accommodation can be found in the Royal Suite, located directly aft of the ship's navigation bridge on the starboard side. It has a separate bedroom with kind-size bed, walk-in closet and vanity dressing area, living room with queen-sized sofa bed, baby grand piano, refrigerator and wet bar, dining table, entertainment center, and large private balcony. The bathroom has a whirlpool tub, separate shower enclosure, two washbasins, and toilet.

Owner's Suite. The five owner's suites are at the forward end of the ship, just behind the navigation bridge (close to the Royal Suite). They have a queen-sized bed, separate living area with queen-size sofa bed, vanity dressing area, refrigerator and wet bar. The bathroom has a full-size tub, separate shower enclosure, toilet and two washbasins.

Royal Family Suite. These have two bedrooms with twin beds that convert to queen-size beds, living area with double sofa bed and Pullman bed, refrigerator, two bathrooms (one with tub), and private balcony. This suite can accommodate eight, and might suit families.

Grand Suite. Features include twin beds that can be convert to a queen-size bed, vanity dressing area, lounge area with sofa bed, refrigerator, and a bathroom with bathtub. There's also a private balcony.

Superior Suite. Features include twin beds that can be convert to a queen-size bed, vanity dressing area, lounge area with sofa bed, refrigerator, and a bathroom with tub. Private balcony. Note that although this is called a suite, it really is little more than a larger standard cabin with balcony.

Other Grades. All standard cabins have twin beds that convert to a queen-size bed, ample closet space for a one-week cruise, and a good amount of drawer space, although under-bed storage space is not good for large suitcases. The bathrooms have nine mirrors. Plastic buckets are provided for champagne/wine and are really tacky.

All grades of suite/cabin are provided with a hairdryer. The room service menu has only the most basic selection.

CUISINE/DINING. The 1,195-seat, no-smoking My Fair Lady Dining Room spreads over two decks, connected by a grand, sweeping staircase. There are two seatings for dinner. Casual, self-serve breakfasts and luncheons can be taken in the 790-seat informal Windjammer Cafe. It has a great expanse of ocean-view glass windows, and the decor is bright and cheerful. An intimate Champagne/Caviar Bar terrace is forward of the lower level of the two-deck-high dining room and just off the atrium for those who might like to taste something a little bit out of the ordinary, in a setting that is both bright and contemporary.

ENTERTAINMENT. The Orpheum Theater, the ship's the principal showlounge, is a grand room located at the forward part of the ship, and has 875 seats. This is where the big production shows and major cabaret acts are staged.

A second showlounge, the 575-seat Carousel Lounge, is located aft, and is for smaller shows and adult cabarets, including late-night adult (blue) comedy. A variety of other lounges and bars feature almost constant live music; there's no real quiet (no music) bar to have a drink in.

There is even background music in all corridors and elevators, and constant music outdoors on the pool deck. If you want a quiet relaxing holiday, choose another ship.

SPA/FITNESS. The ShipShape Spa is aft of the funnel and spans two decks. Facilities include a gymnasium (with all the latest machines), aerobics exercise room, sauna and steam rooms, a beauty salon, and several treatment rooms.

● **For more extensive general information about the Royal Caribbean cruise experience, see pages 128–131.**

Endeavour
★★★

Boutique Ship: ....3,132 tons	Passenger Decks: 6	Cabins (with private balcony): 0
Lifestyle: ....Standard	Total Crew: 64	Cabins (wheelchair accessible): 0
Cruise Line: ....Lindblad Expeditions	Passengers	Cabin Current: ....110 and 220 volts
Former Names: ....*Caledonian Star,*	(lower beds/all berths): 113/124	Elevators: 0
North Star, Lindmar, Marburg	Passenger Space Ratio	Casino (gaming tables): ....No
Builder: .......A.G. Weser Seebeckwerft	(lower beds/all berths): 27.7/25.2	Slot Machines: ....No
(Germany)	Crew/Passenger Ratio	Swimming Pools (outdoors): 1
Original Cost: ....n/a	(lower beds/all berths): 1.7/1.9	Whirlpools: 0
Entered Service: 1966/1984	Navigation Officers: ......Scandinavian	Self-Service Launderette: ....No
Registry: ....The Bahamas	Cabins (total): 62	Lecture/Film Room: ....Yes
Length (Ft/m): 292.6/89.20	Size Range (sq ft/m): 191.6–269.1/	Library: ....Yes
Beam (ft/m): 45.9/14.00	17.8–25.0	Zodiacs: 10
Draft (f//m): 20.3/6.20	Cabins (outside view): 62	Helicopter Pad: ....No
Propulsion/Propellers: ....diesel	Cabins (interior/no view): 0	Classification Society: ......Det Norske
(3,236kW)/1	Cabins (for one person): 11	Veritas

OVERALL SCORE: 1,242 (OUT OF A POSSIBLE 2,000 POINTS)

OVERVIEW. *Endeavour* was built as a stern factory trawler for North Sea service, before being converted into a passenger ship. Today, it is a reasonably handsome ship that is extremely tidy and has been well cared for as an expedition cruise vessel operating soft expedition cruises. There is an open bridge policy for all passengers. The vessel carries Zodiac landing craft for in-depth excursions, and there is an enclosed shore tender. An aft stairway (it is steep) leads down to the landing craft platform. The ship has a warm, intimate ambiance, and a casual dress code.

For such a small ship, there is a decent enough range of public rooms and facilities that includes a reasonably equipped lecture lounge/bar/library, where videos are stocked for in-cabin use. An excellent set of lecturers accompany each cruise make this a real life-enrichment experience for a clientele wanting to travel and learn, while enveloped in comfortable, unpretentious surroundings.

This likeable, homey little ship runs well-tuned destination-intensive, soft expedition-style cruises, at a very reasonable price. It attracts loyal repeat passengers who don't want to sail aboard ships that look like apartment blocks. The itineraries include Antarctica, where this ship started operating in 1998. The onboard currency is the US dollar.

The interior stairways are a little steep, as is the exterior stairway to the Zodiac embarkation points. Noise from the diesel engines can be irksome, particularly on the lower decks. Communication with staff can also prove frustrating.

SUITABLE FOR: *Endeavour* and its type of soft adventure/exploration cruising are best suited to adventur-

BERLITZ'S RATINGS

	Possible	Achieved
Ship	500	267
Accommodation	200	116
Food	400	257
Service	400	282
Entertainment	N/A	N/A
Cruise	500	320

ous, hardy types who enjoy being with nature and wildlife in some of the most interesting (sometimes inhospitable) places on earth, but cosseted aboard a small, modestly comfortable ship.

ACCOMMODATION. There are five categories of cabins: 1 suite category and 4 non-suite categories. The all-outside-view cabins (all above the waterline) are very compact, but reasonably comfortable, and they are decorated in warm, muted tones. All cabins have a mini-bar/refrigerator, VCR, a decent amount of closet and drawer space (but tight for long voyages), and a clock. The bathrooms are tight, with little space for the storage of personal toiletries.

Four "suites" are basically double the size of a standard cabin, and have a wood partition separating the bedroom and lounge area. The bathroom is still small, however.

CUISINE/DINING. The dining room is small and charming, but the low-back chairs are not very comfortable. Open seating is operated in this non-smoking room. The cuisine is European in style with reasonably high quality, fresh ingredients, but not a lot of menu choice. Salad items, in particular, are rather scarce on variety, as are international cheeses. Service is attentive and friendly.

ENTERTAINMENT. The main lounge is the venue for lectures, slide shows and occasional film presentations. There are no shows (none are needed), and no facilities for them.

SPA/FITNESS. There is a small fitness room (about three people and it is full) and tiny sauna.

Europa
★ ★ ★ ★ ★ +

Small Ship: . . . . .28,437 tons	Total Crew: 264	Cabins (wheelchair accessible): 2
Lifestyle: . . . . .Utterly Exclusive	Passengers	Cabin Current: . . . . .110 and 220 volts
Cruise Line: . . . . . . .Hapag-Lloyd Cruises	(lower beds/all berths): 408/450	Elevators: 4
Former Names: . . . . .none	Passenger Space Ratio	Casino (gaming tables): . . . . .No
Builder: . . .Kvaerner Masa-Yards (Finland)	(lower beds/all berths): 69.6/63.1	Slot Machines: .No
Original Cost: . . . . .DM260 million	Crew/Passenger Ratio	Swimming Pools (outdoors): 1
Entered Service: . . . . .Sept 1999	(lower beds/all berths): 1.5/1.7	Swimming Pools (indoors): 1
Registry: . . . . .The Bahamas	Navigation Officers: . . . . .German	(indoor/outdoor with magrodome)
Length (ft/m): 651.5/198.6	Cabins (total): 204	Whirlpools: 1
Beam (ft/m): 78.7/24.0	Size Range (sq ft/m): 355.2–914.9/	Self-Service Launderette: . . . . .Yes (2)
Draft (ft/m): 20.0/6.1	33.0–85.0	Dedicated Cinema/Seats: Yes/60
Propulsion/Propellers: . . . . .diesel-electric	Cabins (outside view): 204	Library: . . . . .Yes
(21,600 kW)/2 azimuthing pods	Cabins (interior/no view): 0	Classification Society: . . . . .Germanischer
(13.3 MW each)	Cabins (for one person): 0	Lloyd
Passenger Decks: 7	Cabins (with private balcony): 168	

OVERALL SCORE: 1,858 (OUT OF A POSSIBLE 2,000 POINTS)

OVERVIEW. *Europa* has a sleek appearance that should please the most critical of passengers, with its sweeping lines, graceful profile, and Hapag-Lloyd's orange/blue funnel. Look down from the aft Lido Deck fantail and you will see the nicely curved lines of a graceful stern – unlike the box-like rears of so many of contemporary ships.

Europa is the first Hapag-Lloyd ship to have the "pod" propulsion system, designed to improve efficiency and handling, by pulling, rather than pushing, the ship through the water, while virtually eliminating vibration *(for further details, see page 151)*.

This is a very stable ship in the open sea, and there is absolutely no vibration or noise. It carries 12 Zodiac landing craft for use during close-up shore excursions. Port and starboard boot-washing/changing rooms are also provided. There is a jogging track for the sporting, as well as an FKK (FreiKörperKultur) deck for those who enjoy nude sunbathing, and a wrap-around teakwood promenade deck outdoors. The deck lounge chairs are aluminum with teak armrests, and have thick cushioned pads (the ship's name is embroidered on them).

There is one swimming pool, in a long, rectangular in shape (it was modified from its original "bottle"-shaped design in December 2000), and, while not the widest, it is longer than the pools aboard most other cruise ships today; it measures 56.7 by 16.8 ft (17.3 by 5.15 meters).

With this ship, Hapag-Lloyd has been able to reach and maintain the high standards that the ship's passengers expect and demand. The ship's principal measurements (length and beam) are very close to that of the former

BERLITZ'S RATINGS

	Possible	Achieved
Ship	500	479
Accommodation	200	189
Food	400	371
Service	400	359
Entertainment	100	90
Cruise	400	370

Europa, and yet the ship carries about 200 fewer passengers. So the space per passenger is high, there is never a hint of a line anywhere, and both restaurant and show lounge seat a full complement of passengers. *Europa* is one of the world's most spacious purpose-built cruise ships – an exquisite retreat. Step aboard this ship and you'll be shown a world of relaxed, contemporary cruising that is intensely welcoming.

Europa is beautifully appointed, in the contemporary style so popularly described as "minimalism" in the hotel industry. Only the finest quality soft furnishings have been chosen for the ship's interiors, subtly blending traditional with modern designs and materials. Most public rooms and hallways have extremely high ceilings, providing an enhanced sense of space and grandeur. The colors used in the ship's interior decor are light and contemporary.

Public rooms include the Club Belvedere (the venue for afternoon tea and intimate music recitals), the Europa Lounge (the main showlounge), which has a U-shaped seating configuration and a proper stage, although there are several pillars. In addition, there is a Clipper Lounge/Bar (with high ceilings), an Atrium Piano Bar (set opposite the reception and shore excursion desks), with Steinway baby grand piano. When the ship first debuted there was a casino, although this proved to be so little used that Hapag-Lloyd Cruises turned it into a multi-functional space for small cocktail parties, and meetings.

There is also a fine sidewalk Havana Bar cigar lounge set off to one side of a winding indoor promenade. This is equipped with three large glass-fronted, fully temperature-controlled and conditioned humidor cabinets, and carries an extensive range of cigars from Cuba and other countries. Cigars stocked include a range (from 102mm to 232mm) of the following well-known makes: Avo Uvezian, Cohiba, Cohiba Linea 1492, Davidoff, Griffin's, Montechristo, Partagas, Romeo y Julia, and Sancho Pansa. Cigar types include Giant, Double Corona, Panetela (short, regular and long), Churchill, Lonsdale, Torpedo, Toro, Corona, Robusto, Petit Corona and Chico. The bar also serves a fine range of armagnacs, calvados and cognacs, all poured tableside, as well as Cuban beer. Embedded in a wall adjacent to the bar is a digital MP3 jukebox, with a push-button selection of 15,000 songs and instrumental music of every description, so you can choose what you want to hear.

Other features include a business center, an electronic golf simulator room (there are also golf driving ranges, a deck tennis court, and shuffleboard court), and dedicated rooms for hobbies (arts and crafts), and for children. A fully stocked library (open 24 hours) has internet access via two computers with flat-screen monitors, and per-minute billing to your onboard account. There's also a small cinema/meeting/function room. In 2004, a new indoor/outdoor bar (Zanzibar) was added above the Lido Café (with great aft-facing views), destined to become the "in" place for the trendy late-night set. Just forward of Zanzibar is a new, much larger electronic golf simulator.

An experienced concierge is available to all passengers, for any special or private arrangements both aboard and ashore. A very friendly but discreet crew and unobtrusive service of the highest standards are hallmarks of the cruise experience aboard this ship. There is a seven-deck-high central atrium, together with two glass-walled elevators (operated by "piccolos" on embarkation day), and a lobby on the lower level that has a Steinway grand piano and lobby bar, reception desk, concierge desk, shore excursion desk and a future cruise sales desk.

Wheelchair passengers should note that a special ramp is provided from the swimming pool/outdoors deck down to where the lifeboats are located. When the ship was delivered there were several small lips at door thresholds (particularly at fire zone doors) throughout the ship. Some of these have been ramped or replaced with airtight-sealing rubber strips, so that wheelchair access is now good everywhere. When this latest evaluation and rating were completed, only one toilet in the public areas (outdoors on Lido Deck 8) was wheelchair-accessible, although others may be modified in the future.

This ship will appeal to all those who desire to be aboard what is arguably the most luxurious and finest of all the latest (small) cruise ships. For the German-speaking market, nothing else comes close (the crew also speaks English for the few British and American passengers). Combined with a mostly young, enthusiastic and well-trained crew, whose aim is to serve and please passengers in the most sumptuous but unobtrusive manner, the tradition of luxury cruising in a contemporary setting is taken to its highest expression. Although a children's playroom is provided, *Europa* really is a ship for adults to cruise in a quiet, refined setting that mixes formality and informality well.

The reason that *Europa* scores so highly can be found in the little details that most other cruise lines have long left behind in the age of discounts, the extras and the meticulous attention to personal comfort and service (there is no charge for in-suite movies on demand, for example, whereas Silversea Cruises charges extra). If you are relaxing at the swimming pool in a hot climate, the deck steward will set your deck lounge chair and cover the mattress pad with a towel, serve you drinks, give you a cold towel, and spray you with Evian water to keep you cool while you take the sun. Naturally, only real glasses are used at the swimming pool and on the open decks – no plastic glasses would ever be considered. When drinks are served, they are placed on cotton doilies (not paper or cork – a luxurious touch not found aboard any other cruise ship). Flowers, pot pourri and cloth towels (paper towels are not permissible at this rating level) are provided in all public restrooms. Indeed, fresh flowers are everywhere. Each passenger has his or her own e-mail address (all e-mails are free). The in-suite infotainment system is simply the best (it's now also available aboard *Hanseatic* and *Queen Mary 2*).

Details, details, details – that's what *Europa* cruising is all about, and what the ship's many repeat passengers expect. The prices for drinks and wines are also very reasonable (they are not included for the simple reason that ships that include drinks typically have a much more restricted selection, including young table wines that may not be to all tastes); also, the ship provides many social functions and parties where drinks *are* provided free.

Excellent port information is provided (both in written form and via the TV infotainment system). All port taxes and gratuities are included, although further tipping is not prohibited. The currency on board is the euro. A souvenir logbook of every cruise is provided for each passenger at the end of each cruise.

When taking all things into account – the unhurried lifestyle of single seating dining, plenty of suites with private balconies, a fine array of classical music artists and lecturers, absolutely no vibration anywhere, and the outstanding cuisine and friendly, very attentive personal service from a staff dedicated to working aboard the world's finest cruise ship – it all adds up to the very best luxurious cruise ship and cruise experience available today (unless you have your own private motor yacht). While most cruise lines have been engaged in dressing down, Hapag-Lloyd has done the opposite: in 2003, hotel service staff donned stunning new uniforms for formal nights, consisting of tails and trousers.

Having said all that, there *are* ships with more grandiose penthouse suites, larger balconies, show lounges, health spas and other appointments – but aboard *Europa*, everything is in scale, and in relation to the requirements of its passengers. At present, while there are plenty of imitators, there are no equals. There are really few weak points, although perhaps an indoor swimming pool might be welcome. The balcony partitions are part-partitions, but would be more private if they were of the full (floor-to-ceiling) type – although this rarely presents a problem for passengers.

Some German-speaking passengers might be inclined to compare *Europa* (Hapag-Lloyd Cruises) with *Deutschland* (Peter Deilmann Cruises). However, some comparisons may be in order: *Europa* has 168 balcony suites, *Deutschland* has just two. *Europa*'s suites measure 355–915 sq. ft (33–85 sq. meters); those aboard *Deutschland* measure approximately 161–366 sq. ft (15–34 sq. meters). *Europa*'s decor is light and contemporary, and the ship has an open feeling, with high ceilings; *Deutschland*'s decor is dark and heavy (albeit in a beautiful, well-stated 1920s style). Food, creativity, variety and presentation, and service aboard *Europa* are far superior to *Deutschland*. Vibration is non-existent aboard *Europa*, while it is noticeable aboard *Deutschland*, according to many passengers.

SUITABLE FOR: *Europa* is best suited to well-traveled, discerning passengers who simply want the best at sea in an uncluttered, utterly refined setting, with superb food, creature comforts, and a caring, very professional and pampering staff that has been well trained, and enjoys practising the fine art of hospitality in a chic, trendy setting.

ACCOMMODATION. This is provided in four configurations and 12 price categories. It consists of all-outside-view suites: 2 Penthouse Grand Suites (Hapag, and Lloyd) and 10 Penthouse Deluxe Suites (Bach, Beethoven, Brahms, Handel, Lehar, Haydn, Mozart, Schubert, Strauss, Wagner), 156 suites with private balcony, and 36 standard suites. There are two suites (with private balcony) for the disabled and 8 suites with interconnecting doors (good for families). Almost all suites have a private balcony (with wide teakwood deck, and lighting), and come complete with see-through glass topped by a teakwood rail. However, 12 suites that overlook the stern are among the most sought-after accommodation (six on each of two decks, each suite having private balconies with canvas "ceilings" for shade and privacy).

General Information: Each suite has a wood floor entryway, and each has a sleeping area with twin beds that can convert to a queen-sized bed, and two bedside tables with lamps and two drawers. There is a separate lounge area (with curtain divider) and bird's-eye maple wood cabinetry and accenting (with rounded edges). Facilities include a refrigerator/mini-bar (beer and soft drinks are supplied at no extra charge), a writing/vanity desk and couch with large table in a separate lounge area. An illuminated walk-in closet provides ample hanging rail space, six drawers, personal safe (this can be opened with a credit card), umbrella, shoehorn, and clothes brush. European duvets are provided, and, in another cruise industry first, so is a full-color daily newspaper: *Die Welt* (*Welt am Sonntag* on Sundays), or any one of about 10 different newspapers from a passenger's home region. Almost all suites have totally unobstructed views and excellent soundproofing between the suites, as well as above and below. All passengers receive a strong tote bag in one of two colors (cognac or blue).

In what was a cruise industry first, a superb integrated color TV/computer monitor and "CIN" (Cruise Infotain-

ment System) – 24 hours per day video and audio on-demand – is provided free, so you choose when you want to watch any one of up to 100 movies, or when you want to listen to a specific compact audio disc (there are more than 300 to choose from). The infotainment system is provided by a full-sized computer located in a cabinet that also houses a refrigerator and the TV set, with a full keyboard that is located in a drawer in the adjacent vanity unit.

Restaurant seating plans, menus, ship's position and chart, deck plan, shore excursion video clips, plus other informational video clips and items are featured. The keyboard also allows you to access email sent to you aboard ship and to write your own emails. Your own private email address is provided with your tickets and other documentation (there is no charge for incoming or outgoing emails, only for attachments, and for internet access). A modem (data) socket is also provided should you decide to bring your own laptop computer (the ship can also provide a laptop for your use). Online connectivity is 24 hours a day, anywhere in the world.

All suites have a 100% air-circulation system, 24-hour room service, illuminated walk-in closets and a generous amount of hanging and storage space. Western European butlers and cabin stewardesses are employed (butlers for the 12 premium suites on Deck 10, cabin stewardesses for all other suites).

The white/gray/sea green marble-tiled bathrooms are very well designed, have light decor, and include two good size cabinets for personal toiletries. All bathrooms have a full tub (plus an integral shower and a retractable clothesline) and separate glass-fronted shower enclosure. Thick, 100% cotton bathrobes are provided, as are slippers and an array of personal toiletry amenities.

Penthouses (Deck 10): There are two Penthouse Grand suites, and 10 Penthouse Deluxe suites. These have a teakwood entrance hall, spacious living room with full-size dining table and four chairs, fully stocked drinks cabinet with refrigerator butler service, complimentary bar set-up (replenished with whatever you need), laundry and ironing service included, priority spa reservations, caviar daily before dinner, hand-made chocolates, canapés, petit-fours and other niceties at no extra charge. For the ultimate in exclusivity, the two Penthouse Grand suites also have larger bathrooms (each with its own sauna), and extensive forward views from their prime, supremely quiet location one deck above the navigation bridge, a very large wrap-around private balcony, and large flat-screen televisions.

Suites for the Disabled (Deck 7): These spacious suites have one electronically operated bed with hydraulic elevator plus one regular bed, while a non-walk-in closet with drawers replaces the walk-in closet in all other suites. The bathroom has a roll-in shower area. All fittings are at the correct height, and there are several grab handles, plus an emergency call-for-help button. Wheelchair-accessible public toilets are provided on the main restaurant/entertainment deck.

CUISINE/DINING. The Europa Restaurant is a beautiful dining room that is two decks high, and can accommodate all passengers in one seating, with tables assigned for dinner only (breakfast and lunch are open seating). Passengers thus keep their favorite waiter throughout each cruise (for dinner). There are two sections, forward and aft, the aft section being slightly raised (gently sloping carpeted wheelchair ramping is provided). In common with most German ships, both smoking and non-smoking sections are provided. There are tables for two (quite a few), four, six or eight. For superb service, a *chef de rang* and an assistant waiter are provided, so that the *chef de rang* is always at the station, with the assistant waiter acting as runner. Just two words can be used to describe the cuisine: simply superb. Plated presentation of food is provided for entrées with silver service for additional vegetables, as well as tableside flambeaux. The size of portions is sensible, and never overwhelming. On days at sea, in addition to the regular, extensive breakfast, a Gourmet Breakfast menu includes such things as beef tartar and other specialties rarely found aboard cruise ships today.

Table settings include Dibbern china, 150-gram weight Robbe & Berking silverware and Riedel wine glasses (these are delicate and have to be hand-washed). The cuisine is very international, but includes German favorites as well as regional dishes from around the world. The quality of food is extremely high. Although top-grade caviar is found on dinner menus at least once each week, it is always available on request (at extra cost). An extensive wine list is provided, and includes a good selection of vintage French wines, as well as a well-balanced selection of Austrian, German and Swiss wines.

Alternative dining options: There are two intimate alternative dining spots: the Oriental Restaurant, for Euro-Asian cuisine that is both extremely creative and beautifully presented, and Venezia, for Italian cuisine (and a wide variety of olive oils and grappa). Both are adjacent to and forward of the main restaurant, and provide the setting for a truly intimate dining experience, in nicely appointed surroundings. These are available by reservation, and there is no extra charge. The Oriental Restaurant has custom-made Bauscher china, while in Venezia Rosenthal china is used.

For more casual dining, there is a Lido Cafe for serve-yourself breakfasts, luncheons and dinners, with both indoor and outdoor seating and adjacent indoor/outdoor bar. New, colorful Dibbern china (in three patterns) was added in 2003. Themed evening dining is also featured here, with full waiter service. There is a wide variety of food, and many special lunch buffets have a number of popular themes and regional specialties.

Europa is famous for its German sausages, available in the Clipper Bar, and at a special Bavarian Fruschoppen.

Late each night, "light bites", beautifully presented on silver trays, are taken around the various bars and lounges.

Finally, afternoon tea is a sheer delight, with a selection of about 30 teas to choose from (plus several types of coffee and impeccably made liqueur coffees – heated in a hand-turned glass enclosure), and a superb selection of cakes (made fresh every day) that even the most critical could not fail to be impressed with.

ENTERTAINMENT. The Europa Lounge, the ship's principal showlounge, has a sloping floor, providing good sightlines from almost every seat. The ship excels in its fine, intellectual entertainment program (it is tailored more to the theme of the cruise), which includes a constant supply of high-quality classical and contemporary musical artistes, a variety of cabaret acts, as well as a programme of expert lecturers, poetry readers, and so on, together with an occasional colorful production show, and local shows brought on board in various ports.

The smaller, more intimate Clipper Lounge provides a setting for late-night cabaret (vocalists, magicians, ballroom dance specialists, comedians, and others). The ship carries a main showband, plus a number of small musical units to provide live music for listening or dancing. Classical concerts and recitals are regularly provided in the Belvedere Lounge.

SPA/FITNESS. The Futuresse Health Spa has a wide range of beauty services and treatments, including hot stone massage, and an array of other rejuvenating treatments (including full-day spa packages. Fribad Cosmetics, which produces the exclusive Futuresse brand, operates the spa, and provides the superb, well-trained staff in a joint venture with the hotel operations division. Facilities include a steam room and sauna (co-ed), two shower enclosures and two foot-washing stations, relaxation room, and two changing/dressing rooms. There is also a separate gymnasium and a beauty salon. A special Japanese Spa is featured (treatment in this room includes a cream body massage, gentle steam room and a two-tatami mat relaxation area), which is booked individually for a special 90-minute treatment.

Other treatment samples and prices: Asian style spa special (hot aroma body wrap with head, shiatsu and food reflex massages) (€90 for 60 minutes); Pacific style spa special – Lomi Lomi massage with warm aroma oils and body pack (€90 for 60 minutes); Classic Massage (€40 for 30 minutes); Shiatsu Massage (€60 for 30 minutes); Ocean Spa Facial (€110 for 90 minutes); Goddess of the Sea total indulgence program (€290 for three hours of pampering including a Lomi Lomi massage, body pack, and facial).

Explorer II
★★★ +

Small Ship: ....12,500 tons	Total Crew: 157	Cabins (with private balcony): 12
Lifestyle: ....Premium	Passengers	Cabins (wheelchair accessible): 4
Cruise Line: ....Abercrombie & Kent	(lower beds/all berths): 352/474	Cabin Current: ....220 volts
Former Names: ....Minerva, Okean	Passenger Space Ratio	Elevators: 2
Builder: ....Mariotti (Italy)	(lower beds/all berths): 35.5/26.3	Casino (gaming tables): ....No
Original Cost: ....n/a	Crew/Passenger Ratio	Slot Machines: ....No
Entered Service: ....Apr 1996/Dec 2003	(lower beds/all berths): 2.1/3.0	Swimming Pools (outdoors): 1
Registry: ....The Bahamas	Navigation Officers: ....European	Whirlpools: 0
Length (ft/m): 436.3/133.0	Cabins (total): 178	Self-Service Launderette: ....Yes
Beam (ft/m): 65.6/20.0	Size Range (sq ft/m): 139.9–360.6/	Dedicated cinema/Seats: Yes/96
Draft (ft/m): 19.6/6.0	13.0–33.5	Library: ....Yes
Propulsion/Propellers: ....2 x diesels	Cabins (outside view): 126	Classification Society: .... Registro Navale
(3,480 kW)/2	Cabins (interior/no view): 52	Italiano (RINA)
Passenger Decks: 6	Cabins (for one person): 4	

OVERALL SCORE: 1,357 (OUT OF A POSSIBLE 2,000 POINTS)

OVERVIEW. Originally intended to be a spy ship (called *Okean*) for the Soviet navy, the 1989-built hull was constructed at Nikolajev on the River Ingul in Ukraine. The hull originally had a stern ramp for launching submersibles for submarine tracking. The ship was then purchased by the Monaco-based V-Ships (the present owners), who towed it to Italy, where it was converted into a ship tailored to the requirements of Swan Hellenic Cruises as the ship's charterer and operator (originally until 2011, although *Minerva* was handed back to V-Ships in 2003). The ship, which has an ice-strengthened hull, operates under charter as *Explorer II* for Abercrombie & Kent from December to April. Unfortunately, the shape of its hull is such that the ship does not handle unkind seas well, and is less than ideal for operating in what can be tough Antarctic conditions. In other words, this is not an ideal ship for expedition cruising. During the summer, the ship operates under charter to Phoenix Seereisen as the *Alexander von Humboldt*.

Explorer II has a squat, squarely balanced profile, with a single, central funnel, and a stern that is slightly rounded. The navigation bridge, however, always looks as if it should have been located one deck higher than it is. There is ample open and shaded deck space for this size of ship (particularly in the aft section), and there is also a teak wrap-around promenade deck. The uppermost passenger deck is Astro-turf (useless in Antarctica). A fleet of rubber inflatable Zodiacs is carried for in-depth excursions ashore, ideal for those inhospitable locations without landing piers or formal docking arrangements (such as in Antarctica). Parkas and backpacks are provided for all passengers. An open bridge policy is a popular feature, so you can visit the navigation

BERLITZ'S RATINGS

	Possible	Achieved
Ship	500	351
Accommodation	200	125
Food	400	268
Service	400	280
Entertainment	100	60
Cruise	400	273

officers at any time for a glimpse into the nautical operations on board.

There is a decent selection of public rooms that includes a large, well-stocked library, with classical decor and motifs. In general, the decor throughout the ship is best described as softly contemporary, homely, restrained and not in the slightest bit glitzy, for passengers with good taste (although cushions would be a nice addition to the many sofas). Lectures and briefings are taken in the Auditorium, the ship's main lounge. Cigar smokers should appreciate the special smoking room and humidor service (although the decor is plain), and high back leather chairs that provide a sense of well-being and privacy.

The ship has fine wool carpets throughout, with an Oriental motif running through the passageways and public rooms. Perhaps the most used public room in the ship is the library, with its fine range of reference books (many of university-standard). Passengers often take delight in a multitude of puzzles and games, and jigsaw puzzles. The reception desk is staffed 24 hours a day. The one disappointment is in the plain white ceilings in most of the public rooms.

A cruise aboard *Explorer II* really is cruising for intelligent passengers who yearn to learn more about life and wildlife, albeit in a fairly refined and comfortable setting, with intelligent conversation playing a major part of any Abercrombie & Kent cruise. The company has well planned, in-depth itineraries and shore excursions, accompanied by some fine expedition leaders and lecturers. All gratuities and shore excursions are included, as are all bar drinks and house wines, although port charges are extra. The onboard currency is the US dollar. However, the ship is not really ideal for expedition cruises, as there is no proper boot washing/storage station, and other items associated with proper expedition cruising are missing.

SUITABLE FOR: *Explorer II* is best suited to couples and single travelers of a mature age who seek to cruise to interesting destinations in comfortable, but not sophisticated surroundings, and who do not need the entertainment and mindless organized parlor games found aboard large contemporary cruise ships, but would rather have intellectual conversation with fellow passengers, and life enrichment lectures on the subject matter dictated, by the ship's itineraries. Note that this ship is not recommended for children.

ACCOMMODATION. There are five different grades of cabins, in 8 different price categories: Owner's Suite, Suite, Deluxe, Superior, and Standard. The price will depend on the grade and location rather than any great difference in the size of the accommodation (most of the standard cabins really are quite small, particularly when compared to the "standard" cabin size on the latest ships today). There are very few cabins with private balcony.

Owner's Suites: There are two owner's suites, 360 sq. ft (33.5 sq. meters) in size, on Bridge Deck. Facilities include a queen-sized bed, an extra-large double closet and ample drawer space; separate lounge area with sofa, table and chair, and vanity table/writing desk, television and VCR, refrigerator, hairdryer and binoculars; floor to ceiling patio doors leading to private balcony; bathroom with bath/shower combination and toilet.

Suites: There are 10 suites, (290 sq. ft/27 sq. meters) located on Bridge Deck. Facilities include twin beds or queen-sized bed, two double closets and ample drawer space; separate lounge area with sofa, table and chair, and vanity table/writing desk, television and VCR, refrigerator, hairdryer and binoculars; floor to ceiling patio doors leading to private balcony; bathroom with tub/shower and toilet.

Deluxe: These are 226 sq. ft (21 sq. meters) in size. Facilities include twin beds or queen-sized bed, two double closets and ample drawer space; separate lounge area with sofa, table and chair, and vanity table/writing desk, television and VCR, refrigerator, hairdryer and binoculars; large picture window; bathroom with bath/shower and toilet.

Superior: These are 162 sq. ft (15 sq. meters) in size. Facilities include twin beds or queen-sized bed, two double closets and ample drawer space; separate lounge area with sofa, table and chair, and vanity table/writing desk, television and VCR, refrigerator, hairdryer and binoculars; large picture window; bathroom with bath/shower and toilet.

Standard Outside-View or Interior (No View) Cabins: These standard cabins are dimensionally challenged (140 sq. ft/13 sq. meters) when compared to the size of standard cabins aboard today's newest ships, which is approximately 182 sq. ft (17 sq. meters). The facilities include twin beds or queen-sized bed, two double closets and ample drawer space; separate lounge area with sofa, table and chair, and vanity table/writing desk, television and VCR, refrigerator, hairdryer and binoculars; large picture window (outside-view cabins only; or porthole, depending on deck and price category you choose); bathroom with shower enclosure (small) and toilet.

The cabin bathrooms (there is a raised "lip" to step over) are totally white, and have very small showers (except for the suites, which have bathtubs and green/black marble floors), although plumbing fixtures were poorly installed. All cabin electrical sockets are of the standard British square, three-pin type. All grades have a pair of binoculars, hairdryer, 100% cotton bathrobe, TV with music channels, and a direct-dial satellite-linked telephone. However, there is little space for hanging outerwear parkas and other gear for expedition cruises. Some cabins on B Deck are subject to noise and vibration from the ship's engines/generators.

CUISINE/DINING. The Dining Room has open seating dining (this means that you can dine with whomever you wish) in both the main restaurant and an informal indoor/outdoor cafe. The menus are quite simple, but the food is attractively presented and has good taste. A staff that is a mix of East European and Filipinos provides the dining room service.

Coffees and teas are available 24 hours a day from a beverage station in the self-serve Bridge Cafe, which also serves casual breakfasts, luncheons, and dinners in an open seating arrangement (the menu choice is simpler than in the dining room).

ENTERTAINMENT. Although there is a main lounge, this is used principally for lectures. There are no shows or cabaret acts, and none is really needed aboard this kind of ship. However, occasionally, concerts performed by a visiting classical music ensemble provide some cultural entertainment in the evenings. The ship has a small band and solo pianists to provide live music for dancing and listening.

SPA/FITNESS. There is a small gymnasium on Funnel Deck (with side-facing views), while a beauty salon is located near the restaurant. Massages and aromatherapy facials, manicures, pedicures and hair beautifying treatments are available, and there is also a small sauna and adjacent shower, but no changing facilities.

Explorer of the Seas
★★★★

Large (Resort) Ship: ....137,308 tons	Total Crew: 1,181	Cabins (with private balcony): 757
Lifestyle: ....Standard	Passengers	Cabins (wheelchair accessible): 26
Cruise Line: Royal Caribbean International	(lower beds/all berths): 3,114/3,840	Cabin Current: ....110 volts
Former Names: ....none	Passenger Space Ratio	Elevators: ....14 (6 glass-enclosed)
Builder: ...Kvaerner Masa-Yards (Finland)	(lower beds/all berths): 44.0/35.7	Casino (gaming tables): ....Yes
Original Cost: ....$500 million	Crew/Passenger Ratio	Slot Machines: ....Yes
Entered Service: ....Oct 2000	(lower beds/all berths): 2.6/3.2	Swimming Pools (outdoors): 3
Registry: ....The Bahamas	Navigation Officers: ......Scandinavian	Swimming Pools (indoors): 0
Length (ft/m): 1,020.6/311.1	Cabins (total): 1,557	Whirlpools: 6
Beam (ft/m): 155.5/47.4	Size Range (sq ft/m): 151.0–1,358.0/	Self-Service Launderette: ....No
Draft (ft/m): 28.8/8.8	14.0–126.1	Dedicated Cinema/Seats: ....No
Propulsion/Propellers: ....diesel-electric	Cabins (outside view): 939	Library: ....Yes
(75,600kW)/3 azimuthing pods	Cabins (interior/no view): 618	Classification Society: ......Det Norske
Passenger Decks: 14	Cabins (for one person): 0	Veritas

OVERALL SCORE: 1,537 (OUT OF A POSSIBLE 2,000 POINTS)

OVERVIEW. This is a large, stunning, floating leisure resort (sister to *Adventure of the Seas*, *Mariner of the Seas*, *Navigator of the Seas* and *Voyager of the Seas*, which debuted between 1999 and 2003). The exterior design is not unlike an enlarged version of the company's Vision-class ships. The *Voyager*-class ships are, at present, the largest cruise vessels in the world in terms of tonnage measurement (except for Cunard Line's *Queen Mary 2*).

The ship's propulsion is derived from three pod units, powered by electric motors (two azimuthing, and one fixed at the centerline) in the latest configuration of high-tech propulsion systems *(for details, see page 151)*.

With its large proportions, the ship provides more facilities and options, and caters to more passengers than any other Royal Caribbean International ship has in the past, and yet it has a healthy amount of space per passenger. It is simply too large to go through the Panama Canal, thus limiting itineraries almost exclusively to the Caribbean (where few islands can accept it), or for use as a floating resort. Spend the first few hours exploring the many facilities and public spaces and it will be time well spent.

Although *Explorer of the Seas* is a large ship, the cabin hallways are warm and attractive, with artwork cabinets and wavy lines to lead you along and break up the monotony. There are plenty of colorful, even whimsical, decorative touches to prevent the environment being too clinical.

Embarkation and disembarkation take place through two stations/access points, designed to minimize the inevitable lines (that's over 1,500 people for each access point). Once inside the ship, you'll need good walking shoes, particularly to go from one end to the other – it really is a long way.

BERLITZ'S RATINGS

	Possible	Achieved
Ship	500	431
Accommodation	200	160
Food	400	252
Service	400	294
Entertainment	100	83
Cruise	400	317

The four-decks-high Royal Promenade, which is 394 ft (120 meters) long, is the main interior focal point (it's a good place to hang out, to meet someone, or to arrange to meet someone). The length of two football fields (American football, that is), it has two internal lobbies (atria) that rise to as many as 11 decks high. Restaurants, shops and entertainment locations front this winding street and interior "with-view" cabins look into it from above.

The Guest Reception and Shore Excursion counters are located at the aft end of the promenade, as is an ATM machine. Things to watch for: look up to see the large moving, asteroid-like sculpture (constantly growing and contracting), parades and street entertainers.

Arched across the promenade is a captain's balcony. Meanwhile, in the center of the promenade is a stairway that connects you to the deck below, where you'll find Schooner Bar (a piano lounge that is a feature of all RCI ships) and the colorful Casino Royale. This is naturally large and full of flashing lights and noises. Casino gaming includes blackjack, Caribbean stud poker, roulette, and craps, as well as 300 slot machines.

Aft of the casino is the Aquarium Bar, while close by are some neat displays of oceanographic interest. Royal Caribbean International has teamed up with the University of Miami's Rosenstiel School of Marine and Atmospheric Science to study the ocean and the atmosphere. To this end, a small onboard laboratory is part of the project.

There is a regulation-size ice-skating rink (Studio B), featuring real, not fake, ice, with stadium-style seating for up to 900, and the latest in broadcast facilities. Ice Follies shows are also presented here. Slim pillars obstruct clear-view arena stage sightlines, however. If ice-skating in the Caribbean doesn't appeal, perhaps you'd like the stunning two-deck library (open 24 hours a day). A grand $12 million has been spent on permanent artwork.

Drinking places include a neat Aquarium Bar, which comes complete with 50 tons of glass and water in four large aquariums (whose combined value is more than $1 million). Other drinking places include the small and intimate Champagne Bar, Crown & Anchor Pub, a Sidewalk Cafe (for continental breakfast, all-day pizzas, specialty coffees and desserts), Sprinkles (for round-the-clock ice cream and yoghurt), and Weekend Warrior (a sports bar), and a Connoisseur Club (for cigars and cognacs). Lovers of jazz might appreciate Dizzy's, an intimate room for cool music within the Viking Crown Lounge, or the Schooner Bar piano lounge. Golfers might enjoy the 19th Hole, a golf bar, as they play the Explorer Links.

There are also several shops on the Royal Promenade – jewelry shop, gift shop, liquor shop and a logo souvenir shop. At times, street entertainers appear, and parades happen, while at other (carefully orchestrated) times it's difficult to walk through the area as it is filled to the brim with shopping items – like a cheap bazaar.

A large TV studio is adjacent to rooms that can be used for trade show exhibit space, with conference center that seats 400 and a multi-media screening room that seats 60. Lovers could tie the knot in a wedding chapel in the sky, the Skylight Chapel (it's located on the upper level of the Viking Crown Lounge, and even has wheelchair access via an electric stairlift). Meanwhile, outdoors, the pool and open deck areas provide a resort-like environment.

Families with children are also well catered to, as facilities for children and teenagers are quite extensive. "Aquanauts" is for 3–5 year olds; "Explorers" (6–8); "Voyagers" (9–12). Optix is a dedicated area for teenagers, including a daytime club (with computers), soda bar, disco with disc jockey and dance floor. Challenger's Arcade has the latest video games. Paint and Clay is an arts and crafts center for younger children. Adjacent to these indoor areas is Adventure Beach, an area for all the family to enjoy: it includes swimming pools, a water slide and game areas outdoors.

In terms of sheer size, this ship dwarfs most other ships in the cruise industry, but in terms of personal service, the reverse is the case, unless you have one of the top suites. Royal Caribbean International does try hard to provide a good standard of programmed service from its hotel staff. But this is impersonal city life at sea, and a superb, well-designed alternative to a land-based resort, which is what the company wanted to build. Perhaps if you dare to go outside, you might even be able to see the sea. Remember to take lots of extra pennies – you'll need them to pay for all the additional-cost items.

If you meet someone somewhere, and want to see them again, it's best to arrange to meet somewhere along the Royal Promenade.

The cabin bath towels are small and skimpy. There are very few quiet places to sit and read – almost everywhere there is intrusive background music. If you have a cabin with a door that interconnecting door to another cabin, be aware that you'll be able to hear everything your next-door neighbours say and do. Bathroom toilets are explosively noisy.

ACCOMMODATION. There is an extensive range of 22 cabin categories, in four major groupings: Premium ocean-view suites and cabins, Promenade-view (interior-view) cabins, Ocean-view cabins, and Interior (no view) cabins. Many cabins are of a similar size – good for incentives and large groups, and 300 have interconnecting doors – good for families. Prices depend on grade, size and location.

A total of 138 interior (no view) cabins have bay windows that look into a horizontal atrium, with interior cabins that look into a central shopping plaza. However, all cabins except for the Royal Suite and Owner's Suite have twin beds that convert to a queen-sized unit, television, radio and telephone, personal safe, vanity unit, mini-bar, hairdryer and private bathroom.

The largest accommodation includes luxurious penthouse suites (whose occupants, sadly, must share the rest of the ship with everyone else, except for their own exclusive, and private, concierge club). The grandest is the Royal Suite, positioned on the port side of the ship, and measures 1,146 sq. ft (106.5 sq. meters). It has a king-sized bed in a separate, large bedroom, a living room with an additional queen-sized sofa bed, baby grand piano, refrigerator/wet bar, dining table, entertainment center, and large bathroom.

The slightly smaller, but still highly desirable Owner's Suites (there are 10, all in the center of the ship, on both port and starboard sides, each measuring 468 sq. ft (43 sq. meters)) and four Royal Family suites (each measures 574 sq. ft (53 sq. meters), all of which feature similar items. However, the four Royal Family suites, which have two bedrooms (including one with third/ fourth upper Pullman berths) are located at the stern of the ship and have magnificent views over the ship's wake (and seagulls).

All cabins have a private bathroom with shower enclosure (towels are 100% cotton), plus interactive television and pay-per-view movies. Cabins with "private balconies" are not so private, as the partitions are only partial, leaving you exposed to your neighbor's smoke or conversation. The balcony decking is made of Bolidt – a sort of rubberized sand – and not wood, while the balcony rail is of wood.

CUISINE/DINING. The large main dining room is set on three levels, named after explorers (Christopher Columbus, Da Gama and Magellan). A dramatic staircase connects all three levels, and huge, fat support pillars obstruct the sight lines. All three feature exactly the same menus and food. The dining room is totally non-smoking, there are two seatings, and tables are for four, six, eight 10 or 12.

Alternative Dining Options: Alternative dining options for casual and informal meals at all hours (according to company releases) include:

● Cafe Promenade, for continental breakfast, all-day pizzas and speciality coffees (provided in paper cups).

● Windjammer Cafe, for casual buffet-style breakfast, lunch and light dinner (except on a cruise's last night).

● Island Grill (actually a section inside the Windjammer Cafe), for casual dinner (no reservations needed), with a grill and open kitchen.

● Portofino: the ship's "upscale" (non-smoking) Italian restaurant, open for dinner only. Reservations are required, and there's a $6 gratuity per person. The food and its presentation are better than the food in the dining room, although the restaurant is not large enough for all passengers to try even once during a cruise. Choices include antipasti, soup, salad, pasta, main dish, dessert, cheese and coffee. The menu does not change throughout the cruise.

● Johnny Rockets, a retro 1950s all-day, all-night diner-style eatery, has hamburgers, malt shakes (at extra cost), and jukebox hits, with both indoor and outdoor seating (all indoor tables feature a mini-jukebox; dimes are provided for you to make your selection of vintage records), and all-singing, all-dancing waitresses.

● Sprinkles, for round-the-clock ice cream and yogurt, pastries and coffee.

ENTERTAINMENT. The 1,350-seat Palace Showlounge is a stunning room that could well be the equal of many such rooms on land. It is located at the forward end of the ship and spans the height of five decks (with only a few slim pillars and almost no disruption of sight lines from almost any seat in the house). The room has a hydraulic orchestra pit and huge stage areas, together with sonic-boom loud sound, and some superb lighting equipment.

The ship also has an array of cabaret acts. Although many are not what you would call headliners (the strongest cabaret acts are featured in the main showlounge, while others are presented in the Maharaja's Lounge, also the site for late-night adults-only comedy), they regularly travel the cruise ship circuit.

SPA/FITNESS. The ShipShape health spa is large, and measures 15,000 sq. ft (1,400 sq. meters). Iit includes a large aerobics room, fitness center (with the usual stairmasters, treadmills, stationary bikes, weight machines and free weights), treatment rooms, men's and women's sauna/steam rooms, while another 10,000 sq. ft (930 sq. meters) is devoted to a Solarium (with magrodome sliding glass roof) for relaxation after you've exercised too much.

There is a rock-climbing wall that's 32.8 ft high (10 meters), with five separate climbing tracks. It is located outdoors at the aft end of the funnel.

Other sports facilities include a roller-blading track, a dive-and-snorkel shop, a full-size basketball court and 9-hole, par 26 golf course.

● **For more extensive general information about the Royal Caribbean cruise experience, see pages 128–131.**

Fantasy
★★★ +

Large (Resort) Ship: ....70,367 tons	Total Crew: 920	Cabins (with private balcony): 54
Lifestyle: ....Standard	Passengers	Cabins (wheelchair accessible): 22
Cruise Line: ......Carnival Cruise Lines	(lower beds/all berths): 2,056/2,634	Cabin Current: ....110 volts
Former Names: ....none	Passenger Space Ratio	Elevators: 14
Builder: ...Kvaerner Masa-Yards (Finland)	(lower beds/all berths): 34.4/26.7	Casino (gaming tables): ....Yes
Original Cost: ....$225 million	Crew/Passenger Ratio	Slot Machines: ....Yes
Entered Service: ....Mar 1990	(lower beds/all berths): 2.2/2.8	Swimming Pools (outdoors): 3
Registry: ....Panama	Navigation Officers: ....Italian	Swimming Pools (indoors): 0
Length (ft/m): 855.8/263.6	Cabins (total): 1,028	Whirlpools: 6
Beam (ft/m): 103.0/31.4	Size Range (sq ft/m): 173.2–409.7/	Self-Service Launderette: ....Yes
Draft (ft/m): 25.9/7.9	16.0–38.0	Dedicated Cinema/Seats: ....No
Propulsion/Propellers: .....diesel-electric	Cabins (outside view): 620	Library: ....Yes
(42,240kW)/2	Cabins (interior/no view): 408	Classification Society: ...Lloyd's Register
Passenger Decks: 10	Cabins (for one person): 0	

OVERALL SCORE: 1,385 (OUT OF A POSSIBLE 2,000 POINTS)

OVERVIEW. Although externally angular and not handsome, *Fantasy* was the first of eight almost identical, very successful ships built for Carnival Cruise Lines, and the company's fifth new ship (others in the series are *Ecstasy, Elation, Fascination, Imagination, Inspiration, Paradise* and *Sensation*). Almost vibration-free service is provided by the diesel electric propulsion system. It has proven to be a successful design for this company that targets the standard (mainstream) market, particularly first-time passengers.

The ship, whose bows are extremely short, has the distinctive, large, swept-back wing-tipped funnel that is the trademark of Carnival Cruise Lines, in the company colors of red, white and blue. The ship has expansive open deck areas (sadly, there is no wrap-around open promenade deck), but they quickly become inadequate when it is full and everyone wants to be out on deck (the aft decks tend to be less noisy, whereas all the activities are focused around the main swimming pool and hot tubs).

There is also a "banked" jogging track outdoors on the deck above a large, glass-enclosed enclosed health spa that is always busy. A well-defined "topless" sunbathing area can be found around the funnel base on Verandah Deck.

Inside, the general passenger flow is good, and the interior design is clever, functional, and extremely colorful. The neon lighting in the interior decor takes a little getting used to at first, as the color combinations are vivid (think total sensory stimulation). The theme of the interior decor is mythical muses, and composers and their compositions (many of the public rooms have musical names), and the colors, while bright, are less so than aboard some other ships in this series. There are public entertainment lounges, bars

BERLITZ'S RATINGS

	Possible	Achieved
Ship	500	395
Accommodation	200	151
Food	400	221
Service	400	270
Entertainment	100	81
Cruise	400	267

and clubs galore, with something for everyone (except quiet space). The public rooms, connected by a wide indoor boulevard called "Via Marina" – with decor inspired by the ancient Roman city of Pompeii, beat a colorful mix of classic and contemporary design elements that beg your indulgence.

As in its sister ships, there is a dramatic six-deck-high atrium (whose balconied shape may remind you of some of the world's great opera houses), appropriately dressed to impress, topped by a large glass dome, and featuring a fascinating, entertaining artistic centerpiece. There are expansive open-deck areas and a large, glass-enclosed enclosed health spa that is always busy. The large casino has almost non-stop action, as one would expect aboard any Carnival Cruise Lines ship. There is a fine-looking library and reading room, but few books.

What should be of great interest to families, however, is a special partnership with Universal Studios' travel company, which packages a cruise together with a land stay and choice of three different theme parks: Universal Studios, Wet 'n' Wild and Sea World. The pricing is competitive with that of the Disney land-cruise product.

Aboard the ship, kids will, I am sure, enjoy "Children's World", a 2,500 sq. ft (230 sq. meter) play-area with games and fun stuff for kids of all ages, including Apple computers loaded with educational software, and an arts and crafts area with spin and sand art machines.

The cuisine is just so-so, but the real fun begins at sundown when Carnival really excels in sound, lights, razzle-dazzle shows and late-night sounds. From the futuristic Electricity Disco to the ancient Cleopatra's Bar, this ship will entertain you well.

ACCOMMODATION. There are 13 grades of accommodation. The price you pay will depend on the grade, size and location you choose. The standard outside-view and interior (no view) cabins have decor that is rather plain and unmemorable. They are marginally comfortable, yet spacious enough and practical (most are of the same size and appointments), with good storage space and practical, well-designed no-nonsense bathrooms.

Anyone booking one of the outside suites will find more space, whirlpool bathtubs, and some fascinating, rather eclectic decor and furniture. These are mildly attractive, but nothing special, and they are much smaller than those aboard the ships of a similar size of several competing companies. A gift basket is provided in all grades of accommodation; it includes aloe soap, shampoo, conditioner, deodorant, breath mints, candy, and pain relief tablets (albeit all in sample sizes).

If you book accommodation in a suites (Category 11 or 12 in the Carnival Cruise Lines brochure) you automatically qualify for "Skipper's Club" priority check-in at any US homeland port – useful for getting ahead of the crowd.

CUISINE/DINING. There are two large dining rooms (Celebration, located midships, and Jubilee, located aft, with the galley between them). Both have ocean-view windows; both are non-smoking, and noisy, but the decor is attractive, although it is rather vivid. Dining in each restaurant is now in four seatings, for greater flexibility: 6pm, 6.45pm, 8pm and 8.45pm (these times are approximate).

At night, the "Seaview Bistro", as the Windows on the Sea is known in the evenings, provides a casual (dress down) alternative to eating in the main dining rooms, serving pasta, steaks, salads and desserts (it typically is in operation between 6pm and 9pm).

In addition, there is a patisserie (Piazza Cafe) that offers specialty coffees and sweets (at an extra charge).

ENTERTAINMENT. The Universe Showlounge is the principal venue for large-scale production shows and major cabaret acts (although 20 pillars obstruct the views from several seats). In a typical 3- or 4-day cruise, there will be one or two, large-scale, trend-setting production shows, with a cast of two lead singers and a clutch of dancers, backed by a 10-piece live orchestra.

SPA/FITNESS. The Nautica Spa is a large health, fitness and spa complex that is located on the uppermost interior deck, forward of the ship's mast, and accessed from the forward stairway. It consists of a gymnasium with ocean-view windows that look out over the ship's bow (it has a large array of the latest in muscle-pumping electronic machines), an aerobics exercise room, men's and women's changing rooms, sauna and steam rooms, and beauty salon.

A common complaint from passengers is that the area is that there are not enough staff to keep the area clean and tidy, and used towels are often strewn around the changing rooms (particularly on the men's side).

● **For more extensive general information on what a Carnival cruise is like, see pages 107–111.**

Fascination
★★★ +

Large (Resort) Ship: ....70,367 tons	Total Crew: 920	Cabins (with private balcony): 54
Lifestyle: ....Standard	Passengers	Cabins (wheelchair accessible): 22
Cruise Line: ....Carnival Cruise Lines	(lower beds/all berths): 2,056/2,634	Cabin Current: ....110 volts
Former Names: ....none	Passenger Space Ratio	Elevators: 14
Builder: ...Kvaerner Masa-Yards (Finland)	(lower beds/all berths): 34.4/26.7	Casino (gaming tables): ....Yes
Original Cost: ....$315 million	Crew/Passenger Ratio	Slot Machines: ....Yes
Entered Service: ....July 1994	(lower beds/all berths): 2.2/2.8	Swimming Pools (outdoors): 3
Registry: ....The Bahamas	Navigation Officers: ....Italian	Swimming Pools (indoors): 0
Length (ft/m): 855.0/260.60	Cabins (total): 1,028	Whirlpools: 6
Beam (ft/m): 103.0/31.40	Size Range (sq ft/m): 173.2–409.7/	Self-Service Launderette: ....Yes
Draft (ft/m): 25.7/7.86	16.0–38.0	Dedicated Cinema/Seats: ....No
Propulsion/Propellers: .....diesel-electric	Cabins (outside view): 620	Library: ....Yes
(42,240kW)/2	Cabins (interior/no view): 408	Classification Society: ...Lloyd's Register
Passenger Decks: 10	Cabins (for one person): 0	

OVERALL SCORE: 1,385 (OUT OF A POSSIBLE 2,000 POINTS)

OVERVIEW. Although externally angular and not handsome, *Fascination* is the fourth in a series of eight almost identical, very successful ships built for Carnival Cruise Lines, and the company's eighth new ship (others in the series are *Ecstasy, Elation, Fantasy, Imagination, Inspiration, Paradise* and *Sensation*). Almost vibration-free service is provided by the diesel electric propulsion system. It has proven to be a successful design for this company that targets the standard (mainstream) market, and particularly the first-time passenger.

The ship, whose bows are extremely short, has the distinctive, large, swept-back wing-tipped funnel that is the trademark of Carnival Cruise Lines, in the company colors of red, white and blue. The ship has expansive open deck areas, but they quickly become inadequate when it is full and everyone wants to be out on deck (the aft decks tend to be less noisy, whereas all the activities are focused around the main swimming pool and hot tubs). There is also a "banked" jogging track outdoors on the deck above a large, glass-enclosed enclosed health spa. A well-defined "topless" sunbathing area can be found around the funnel base on Verandah Deck.

Inside, the general passenger flow is good, and the interior design is clever, functional, and extremely colorful. The neon lighting in the interior decor takes a little getting used to at first, as the color combinations are quite vivid (think total sensory stimulation). The theme of the interior decor is mythical muses, and composers and their compositions (many of the public rooms have musical names), and the colors, while bright, are less so than aboard some other ships in this series. There are public entertainment

BERLITZ'S RATINGS

	Possible	Achieved
Ship	500	395
Accommodation	200	151
Food	400	221
Service	400	270
Entertainment	100	81
Cruise	400	267

lounges, bars and clubs galore, with something for everyone (except quiet space). The public rooms, connected by a wide indoor boulevard, beat a colorful mix of classic and contemporary design elements that beg your indulgence. As in its sister ships, there is a dramatic six-deck-high atrium (whose balconied shape may remind you of some of the world's great opera houses), appropriately dressed to impress, topped by a large glass dome, and featuring a fascinating, entertaining artistic centerpiece. There are expansive open-deck areas and a large, glass-enclosed enclosed health spa that is always busy. The large casino has almost non-stop action, as one would expect aboard any Carnival Cruise Lines ship. There is a fine-looking library and reading room, but few books.

This is another ship that reflects the fine creative interior design work of Joe Farcus. It has a somewhat ungainly external profile, but the interior spaces have been well utilized. A dramatic atrium lobby spans six decks, and features cool marble and hot neon topped by a large glass dome and a spectacular artistic centerpiece called "Nucleus" which illustrates the kleig lights of a Hollywood premiere, according to Farcus.

The ship offers public entertainment lounges, bars and clubs galore, with something for everyone. The principal public rooms are connected by a double-width indoor promenade. The interior decor aboard all Carnival ships is themed; this one sports a sophisticated Hollywood motif that begs your indulgence.

Excellent photo opportunities exist with some 24 superb life-like figures from the movies. Look for Marilyn Monroe and James Dean outside the casino at Stars Bar, while

Humphrey Bogart and Ingrid Bergman are seated at the piano at Bogart's Cafe; Sophia Loren and Paul Newman are close by, and Vivien Leigh and Clark Gable can be found in Tara's Library. Meanwhile, John Wayne is for some reason at the entrance to the Passage to India Lounge, while Edward G. Robinson is inside. Outside the Diamonds Are Forever discotheque are Elizabeth Taylor and Elvis Presley. Lena Horne and Sydney Poitier can be found outside the Beverly Hills Bar, while Katherine Hepburn and Spencer Tracy are inside. Just in case you want to gamble, you'll find Lucille Ball outside the casino. Incidentally, all the slot machines aboard all Carnival ships are linked into a big prize, called, naturally, Megacash.

There's a dramatic, well-segmented three-deck-high glass-enclosed health spa and gymnasium with the latest muscle-pump equipment. There's also a large shop, but it's stuffed to the gills with low-quality merchandise.

ACCOMMODATION. There are 13 price grades. The price you pay will depend on the grade, size and location you choose. The standard outside-view and interior (no view) cabins have decor that is rather plain and unmemorable. They are marginally comfortable, yet spacious enough and practical (most are of the same size and appointments), with good storage space and practical, well-designed no-nonsense bathrooms.

Those booking one of the outside suites will find more space, whirlpool bathtubs, and some fascinating, rather eclectic decor and furniture. These are mildly attractive, but nothing special, and are much smaller than those aboard the ships of a similar size of several competing companies.

A gift basket is provided in all grades; it includes aloe soap, shampoo, conditioner, deodorant, breath mints, candy, and pain relief tablets (albeit all in sample sizes).

If you book accommodation in one of the suites (Category 11 or 12 in the Carnival Cruise Lines brochure) you qualify for "Skipper's Club" priority check-in at any US homeland port – useful for getting ahead of the crowd.

CUISINE/DINING. There are two large, noisy dining rooms (Sensation, located midships, and Imagination, located aft, with the galley between them). Both are non-smoking, and with Carnival's typically usual efficient, fast but assertive service. The buffets are rather run-of-the-mill, with little creativity, and only basic supermarket foods. Dining is now in four seatings, for greater flexibility: 6pm, 6.45pm, 8pm and 8.45pm (times are approximate).

At night, the "Seaview Bistro", as the Lido Cafe becomes known, provides a casual (dress down) alternative to eating in the main dining rooms, serving pasta, steaks, salads and desserts (it typically is in operation between 6pm and 9pm).

ENTERTAINMENT. The Palace Showlounge is the principal venue for large-scale production shows and major cabaret acts (although 20 pillars obstruct the views from several seats). In a typical 3- or 4-day cruise, there will be one or two, large-scale, trend-setting production shows, with a cast of two lead singers and a clutch of dancers, backed by a 10-piece live orchestra.

SPA/FITNESS. SpaCarnival is a large health, fitness and spa complex that is located on the uppermost interior deck, forward of the ship's mast, and accessed from the forward stairway. It consists of a gymnasium with ocean-view windows that look out over the ship's bow (it has a large array of the latest in muscle-pumping electronic machines), an aerobics exercise room, men's and women's changing rooms, sauna and steam rooms, and beauty salon.

A common complaint from passengers is that the area is that there are not enough staff to keep the area clean and tidy, and used towels are often strewn around the changing rooms (particularly on the men's side).

● **For more extensive general information on what a Carnival cruise is like, see pages 107–111.**

Flying Cloud
★★

Boutique Ship: ....400 tons	Main Propulsion: ....sail power	Cabins (outside view): 18
Lifestyle: ....Standard	Propulsion/Propellers: diesel/1	Cabins (interior/no view): 15
Cruise Line: Windjammer Barefoot Cruises	Passenger Decks: 3	Cabins (for one person): 0
Former Names: ......*Oisseau des Isles*	Total Crew: 28	Cabins (with private balcony): 0
Builder: .....Ancione Chantiers Dibignon	Passengers	Cabins (wheelchair accessible): 0
(France)	(lower beds/all berths): 66/66	Cabin Current: ....110 volts
Entered Service: 1935/1968	Passenger Space Ratio	Elevators: 0
Registry: ....Equatorial Guinea	(lower beds/all berths): 5.8/5.8	Casino (gaming tables): ....No
Length (ft/m): 208.0/63.3	Crew/Passenger Ratio	Slot Machines: ....No
Beam (ft/m): 32.0/9.7	(lower beds/all berths): 2.3/2.3	Swimming Pools (outdoors): 0
Draft (ft/m): 16.0/4.8	Navigation Officers: ....International	Whirlpools: 0
Type of Vessel: ....barkentine	Cabins (total): 33	Self-Service Launderette: ....No
No. of Masts: 3	Size Range (sq ft/m): 60.2–148.0/	Library: ....Yes
Sail Area (sq ft/m2): 10,500.5/975.5	5.6–13.7	Classification Society: ....none

OVERALL SCORE: 902 (OUT OF A POSSIBLE 2,000 POINTS)

OVERVIEW. *Flying Cloud* was built in 1935 for the French Navy and originally was operated as a cadet sail-training vessel. Its interior decor includes such things as stained-glass windows, a spiral staircase, and lots of lovely wood, having been refurbished when Windjammer Barefoot Cruises bought the ship in 1968.

Aboard one of the Windjammer Barefoot Cruises' fleet you can let the crew do all the work, or you can lend a hand at the helm yourself, if you feel so inclined. One neat thing to do is just to sit or lie in the nets at the bows of the vessel, without a care in the world.

The mood is free and easy, the ships are equipped very simply; only the most casual clothes are required (T-shirts and shorts), and shoes are optional, although you will need them if you go off in one of the ports. Quite possibly the most useful item will be your bathing suit – better take more than one. Smoking is allowed only on the open decks.

Jammin' aboard a Windjammer (first-time passengers are called "crewmates" while repeat passengers are called "jammers") is no-frills cruising. Indeed, it could be called an "anti-cruise". There is a no-nonsense, friendly environment, for the young at heart and those who don't feel the need for lots of programmed activities. It's all about going to sea and the romance of being at sea under sail.

Although the itineraries (well, islands) are provided in the brochure, the captain actually has the freedom to decide which islands to go to in any given area, depending on sea and weather conditions. *Flying Cloud* has year-round cruises in the British and US Virgin Islands. Brochure rates might seem inexpensive, but you'll need to add on the air-

BERLITZ'S RATINGS

	Possible	Achieved
Ship	500	219
Accommodation	200	79
Food	400	166
Service	400	188
Entertainment	N/A	N/A
Cruise	500	250

fare in order to get the true cost. Tips to the crew are suggested, at $50 per week.

This tall ship complies with all international safety regulations, with the exception of the 1966 fire safety standards. It sails from Tortola (British Virgin Islands). The onboard currency is the US dollar.

Other ships of the fleet featured in this book are *Legacy, Mandalay, Polynesia,* and *Yankee Clipper*.

SUITABLE FOR: *Flying Cloud* is best suited to young, carefree singles that enjoy beaches, scuba diving and snorkeling, and are happy with just the basic necessities, all in an ultra-casual setting with no pretension whatsoever.

ACCOMMODATION. There are four grades. All are dimensionally challenged, particularly when compared to standard cruise ships, but this is a casual cruise experience and you will need so few clothes anyway. All are equipped with upper and lower berths, and most are quite narrow.

CUISINE/DINING. There is one dining room, and meals are all casual in style and service. Breakfast is served on board, as is dinner, while lunch could be either on board or at a beach, picnic-style.

ENTERTAINMENT. Entertainment in the evenings consists of – you and the crew. You can put on a toga, take or create a pirate outfit and join in the fun.

SPA/FITNESS. No facilities provided aboard this tall ship. Recreation consists of the deck, you, the sun, and the sea.

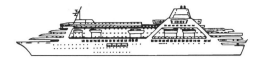

Fuji Maru
★★★ +

Small Ship: . . . . .23,340 tons	Total Crew: 190	Cabins (with private balcony): 0
Lifestyle: . . . . .Standard	Passengers	Cabins (wheelchair accessible): 2
Cruise Line: . . .Mitsui OSK Passenger Line	(lower beds/all berths): 328/603	Cabin Current: . . . . .100 volts
Former Names: . . . . .none	Passenger Space Ratio	Elevators: 5
Builder: . . . . .Mitsubishi (Japan)	(lower beds/all berths): 71.1/38.7	Casino (gaming tables): . . . . .Yes
Original Cost: . . . .$63.5 million	Crew/Passenger Ratio	(no cash can be won, only gifts)
Entered Service: . . . . Apr 1989	(lower beds/all berths): 1.7/3.1	Slot Machines: .No
Registry: .Japan	Navigation Officers: . . . . .Japanese	Swimming Pools (outdoors): 1
Length (ft/m): 547.9/167.00	Cabins (total): .164	Swimming Pools (indoors): 0
Beam (ft/m): 78.7/24.00	Size Range (sq ft/m): 182.9–376.7/	Whirlpools: . . . . .0 (4 Japanese Baths)
Draft (ft/m): 21.4/6.55	17.0–35.0	Self-Service Launderette: . . . . .Yes
Propulsion/Propellers: . . . . .diesel	Cabins (outside view): 164	Dedicated Cinema/Seats: Yes/142
(15,740kW)/2	Cabins (interior/no view): 0	Library: . . . . .Yes
Passenger Decks: 8	Cabins (for one person): 0	Classification Society: Nippon Kaiji Kyokai

OVERALL SCORE: 1,346 (OUT OF A POSSIBLE 2,000 POINTS)

OVERVIEW. When *Fuji Maru* was completed in 1989, it was Japan's largest cruise ship. It has a well thought-out, and flexible, design for multifunctional uses, but its main use is for incentives, conventions, as a seminar and training ship, and only occasionally for individual passengers. The utilitarian outdoor decks are little used. The interiors are plain and a little clinical, although there is some good artwork throughout to brighten things up. There are extensive lecture and conference facilities. The largest lecture hall is two decks high, seats 600, and converts into a sports stadium or exhibition hall for industrial product introductions. The lobby is quite elegant and open and is part of a two-level atrium.

The ship has a classic, wood-paneled library. Other features include Japanese grand baths and a traditional Washitsu tatami mat room, and lecture room. A Hanaguruma owner's room is reasonably elegant for small formal functions. The Sakura Salon is soothing, with a blend of Western and traditional Japanese design. The media and TV systems include much high-tech equipment.

There are many more modern ships in the international marketplace (also serving Japanese passengers), with better facilities, more dining choices, and a less utilitarian ambience, and so the score for this ship has been lowered slightly.

A specialist courier company will collect your luggage from your home before the cruise, and deliver it back after the cruise (this service available only in Japan). The onboard currency is the Japanese yen. As in any ship for Japanese passengers, tipping is not allowed.

There is a complete waste of open deck space, and maintenance of it is poor. The deck furniture is plastic. The lighting is too bright, which also increases the noise level.

BERLITZ'S RATINGS

	Possible	Achieved
Ship	500	317
Accommodation	200	135
Food	400	282
Service	400	284
Entertainment	100	65
Cruise	400	263

SUITABLE FOR: Japanese-speaking couples and single travelers looking for modestly comfortable surroundings, decent food and service, all at low cost.

ACCOMMODATION. There are seven price grades. There are two suites that are quite lovely, with separate bedroom and living room. The deluxe cabins are also of a good standard, and come with a vanity/writing desk, mini-bar/refrigerator, and full-sized, deep bathtub. Almost all the other (standard) cabins are furnished very simply, but they are good for seminar and school cruises, with many accommodating three or four persons. The cabin insulation is reasonable, but could be better. The bathrooms are small and utilitarian. The folded blankets, a MOPAS (Mitsui OSK Passenger Line) tradition, are lovely.

CUISINE/DINING. The single, large dining room is quite attractive and has a high ceiling, but rather bright lighting. Both Japanese and Western cuisines are featured for all meals, in a single seating. The food itself is good, with simple, but colorful, presentation, and a good variety.

ENTERTAINMENT. The Pacific Lounge is the venue for entertainment events, social functions, and social dancing. It is a two deck high room, with seating on both main and balcony levels. On most cruises, special featured entertainers are brought on board from ashore.

SPA/FITNESS. There is no spa, but there are two Japanese Grand Baths (men's and women's) with ocean-view windows. These include washing stations and two small communal baths. There is a sauna, and massage is available.

Funchal
★★ +

Small Ship . . . . .9,563 tons	Total Crew: 155	Cabins (with private balcony): 0
Lifestyle: . . . . .Standard	Passengers	Cabins (wheelchair accessible): 0
Cruise Line: Classic International Cruises	(lower beds/all berths): 430/524	Cabin Current: . . . . .220 volts
Former Names: . . . . .none	Passenger Space Ratio	Elevators: 3
Builder: . . .Helsingor Skibsvog (Denmark)	(lower beds/all berths): 22.218.2	Casino (gaming tables): . . . . .Yes
Original Cost: .n/a	Crew/Passenger Ratio	Slot Machines: . . . . .Yes
Entered Service: . . . . .Oct 1961/May 1986	(lower beds/all berths): 2.7/3.3	Swimming Pools (outdoors): 1
Registry: . . . . .Portugal	Navigation Officers: . . .Greek/Portuguese	Swimming Pools (indoors): 0
Length (ft/m): 503.6/153.51	Cabins (total): 222	Whirlpools: 0
Beam (ft/m): 62.5/19.08	Size Range (sq ft/m): 102.2–252.9/	Self-Service Launderette: . . . . .No
Draft (ft/m): 20.3/6.20	9.5–23.5	Dedicated Cinema/Seats: . . . . .No
Propulsion/Propellers: . . . . .diesel	Cabins (outside view): 151	Library: . . . . .Yes
(7,356kW)/2	Cabins (interior/no view): 71	Classification Society: . . . . .Rinave
Passenger Decks: 6	Cabins (for one person): 14	Portuguesa

OVERALL SCORE: 1,089 (OUT OF A POSSIBLE 2,000 POINTS)

OVERVIEW. *Funchal* has a classic 1960s small ship profile with well balanced, rounded lines, and pleasing real wooden decks, including one outdoor deck with two sheltered promenades, although they do not completely encircle the ship. Originally, the ship was built as a dual-purpose mail and passenger ship, but was rebuilt as a one-class cruise ship in 1972–73 and has since undergone regular refurbishments. Its interior has lots of fine woodwork and heavy-duty fittings. One deck houses all the main public rooms, the most appealing of which is the Porto Bar, reminiscent of a classy 19th-century drinking club. A highly polished wooden spiral stairway is a beautiful, classic piece of decoration not found today's ships.

The mostly Portuguese staff are friendly and quite attentive. This ship is popular with Europeans and Scandinavians during the summer and Brazilians during the winter. It provides destination-intensive cruises in a pleasant, old-world atmosphere.

Funchal is like an old, well-worn shoe – comfortable, but in need of a little spit and polish, and so it hovers just a tad under the three-star level (a two-and-a-half star vessel with a three-star heart). The ship and overall product is actually quite good if you enjoy small, vintage vessels with all their accompanying eccentricities. While the ship cannot be compared to the latest brand new, larger ships, *Funchal* has a delightful character and charm. The feeling of camaraderie and friendliness from the loyal crew (many of whom have been aboard the ship for many years) offsets some of the hardware negatives. The ship often operates under charter to various tour packagers and operators. The onboard currency is the euro.

BERLITZ'S RATINGS

	Possible	Achieved
Ship	500	225
Accommodation	200	101
Food	400	242
Service	400	250
Entertainment	100	58
Cruise	400	213

Much of the ship's exterior paintwork is sloppy. The showlounge is extremely poor. A lack of proper maintenance in its early life is evident.

SUITABLE FOR: *Funchal* is best suited to couples and single travelers seeking a first cruise aboard a small ship of vintage character and charm, with few facilities, but at a low price.

ACCOMMODATION. The cabins are extremely compact but tasteful, and come in both twin and double-bedded configurations. Each now has a private bathroom, and there is just enough closet and drawer space providing you don't pack too many clothes. All bathrooms are typically provided with soap, shampoo, shower cap, shoeshine and sewing kits, and bathrobe.

CUISINE/DINING. There are two tastefully decorated dining rooms, Lisboa and the smaller Coimbra (which doubles as a video screening room after dinner). Both have ocean-view picture windows on port and starboard sides. There is just one seating, and tables are for four, six or eight (there are no tables for two). The food is European in style (and includes plenty of fresh fish) and is surprisingly good. The wine list includes Portuguese wines at modest prices.

ENTERTAINMENT. The Main Lounge is the showlounge, an H-shaped room that extends to the sides of the ship. The room has a flat floor, and the sight lines to the stage are poor from some seats. As this is a small and older vessel, entertainment is a low priority (and has a low budget).

SPA/FITNESS. There is a small sauna and beauty salon.

Galapagos Explorer II
★★★ +

Boutique Ship: .... 3,990 tons	Total Crew: .... .72	Cabins (with private balcony): 4
Lifestyle: .... Standard	Passengers	Cabins (wheelchair accessible): 0
Cruise Line: .... Kleintours	(lower beds/all berths): 100/111	Cabin Current: .... 110 volts
Former Names: ...... Renaissance Three	Passenger Space Ratio	Elevators: 1
Builder: .... Cantieri Navale Ferrari (Italy)	(lower beds/all berths): 39.9/35.9	Casino (gaming tables): .... Yes
Original Cost: .... $20 million	Crew/Passenger Ratio	Slot Machines: .... Yes
Entered Service: ..... Aug 1990/Jan 1998	(lower beds/all berths): 1.3/1.5	Swimming Pools (outdoors): 1
Registry: .... Liberia	Navigation Officers: .... International	Swimming Pools (indoors): 0
Length (ft/m): 289.6/88.30	Cabins (total): .... .50	Whirlpools: 1
Beam (ft/m): 50.1/15.30	Size Range (sq ft/m): 231.4–282.0/	Self-Service Launderette: .... No
Draft (ft/m): 11.9/3.65	21.5–26.2	Dedicated Cinema/Seats: .... No
Propulsion/Propellers: .... diesel	Cabins (outside view): .... .50	Library: .... No
(3,514kW)/2	Cabins (interior/no view): 0	Classification Society: ... Registro Navale
Passenger Decks: 5	Cabins (for one person): 0	Italiano (RINA)

OVERALL SCORE: 1,365 (OUT OF A POSSIBLE 2,000 POINTS)

OVERVIEW. This is quite a comfortable and inviting ship (built as one of a series of eight similar small ships for the now defunct Renaissance Cruises). While it is in good condition, the maintenance could be better. Its looks are quite contemporary in the style of a mega-yacht, with handsome styling. There is a wooden promenade deck outdoors. The limited number of public rooms have smart and restful, non-glitzy decor. The main lounge doubles as a lecture room, but perhaps it is the piano bar that provides the best place to relax after dinner in the evening.

This ship provides a destination-intensive, refined, quiet and relaxed cruise for those who don't like crowds or dressing up. Naturalist guides trained at the Darwin Station lead the shore excursions (included in the fare). If you are going on a Galápagos cruise, it is important to take along passport, short and long-sleeve cotton shirts, good walking shoes, windbreaker, mosquito repellent, sunglasses with retaining strap, and personal medication. You will need to fly from Quito to San Cristobal (via Guayaquil) to join your cruise.

Galapagos Explorer II operates three-, four-, and seven night Galápagos cruises year-round from San Cristobal. Liquor, beer, cocktails, bottled water and soft drinks are included in the fare, but wine and champagne are not. Also included are guided visits to the islands. The brochure rates may or may not include the Galápagos Islands visitor tax (about $100), which must be paid in cash at Guayaquil or Quito airports or in the islands. Shore visits take place in "pangas" (local lingo for "dinghies").

Gratuities for shipboard staff are excessive, at a recommended $80 per person, per seven-night cruise. The onboard currency is the US dollar or Ecuadorian sucre.

BERLITZ'S RATINGS

	Possible	Achieved
Ship	500	361
Accommodation	200	156
Food	400	244
Service	400	287
Entertainment	N/A	N/A
Cruise	500	317

The tiny "dip" pool is not a swimming pool. The open deck and sunbathing space is cramped. Plastic wood is used everywhere (but it looks good). While the service is without finesse, the crew is willing. The small library is attractive, but the book selection is poor. The ship does not sail well in inclement weather.

SUITABLE FOR: The ship is good for couples and single travelers who want to cruise around the primitive Galápagos Islands, but want to do so in comfortable, stylish surroundings.

ACCOMMODATION. This is located forward, with public rooms aft. Pleasant, all-outside cabins have a large picture window and combine gorgeous, highly polished imitation rosewood paneling with lots of mirrors, hand-crafted Italian furniture, and wet bar. All cabins have a queen-sized bed, a sitting area, a mini-bar/refrigerator, TV set, VCR and hairdryer. The small bathrooms have showers with a fold-down seat, real teakwood floors and marble vanities.

CUISINE/DINING. The small, elegant dining room has open seating. There are tables for two, four, six, and even eight. The meals are self-service buffet-style cold foods for breakfast and lunch (sometimes lunch will be on deck), with local delicacies. There is limited choice.

ENTERTAINMENT. Dinner and after-dinner conversation with fellow passengers forms the entertainment each evening.

SPA/FITNESS. There is a sauna. Water sports facilities include an aft platform, sailfish, snorkel gear, and Zodiacs.

Galaxy
★★★★ +

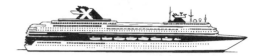

Large (Resort) Ship:	77,713 tons	Total Crew:	909	Cabins (with private balcony): 220

Large (Resort) Ship: ....77,713 tons
Lifestyle: ....Premium
Cruise Line: ....Celebrity Cruises
Former Names: ....none
Builder: ....Meyer Werft (Germany)
Original Cost: ....$320 million
Entered Service: ....Dec 1996
Registry: ....The Bahamas
Length (ft/m): 865.8/263.9
Beam (ft/m): 105.6/32.20
Draft (ft/m): 25.2/7.70
Propulsion/Propellers: ....diesel
(31,500kW)/2
Passenger Decks: 10

Total Crew: 909
Passengers
(lower beds/all berths): 1,870/2,681
Passenger Space Ratio
(lower beds/all berths): 41.5/28.9
Crew/Passenger Ratio
(lower beds/all berths): 2.0/2.9
Navigation Officers: ....Greek
Cabins (total): 935
Size Range (sq ft/m): 1,219.0/
15.7–113.2
Cabins (outside view): 639
Cabins (interior/no view): 296
Cabins (for one person): 0

Cabins (with private balcony): 220
Cabins (wheelchair accessible): 8
Cabin Current: ....110 and 220 volts
Elevators: 10
Casino (gaming tables): ....Yes
Slot Machines: ....Yes
Swimming Pools (outdoors): 2
Swimming Pools (indoors): 1
indoor/outdoor (magrodome)
Whirlpools: 4
Self-Service Launderette: ....No
Dedicated Cinema/Seats: Yes/200
Library: ....Yes
Classification Society: ...Lloyd's Register

OVERALL SCORE: 1,663 (OUT OF A POSSIBLE 2,000 POINTS)

OVERVIEW. Slightly longer than sister ship *Century* (by 45.9 ft/14 meters), *Galaxy*'s extra length provides room for a third swimming pool, which is covered by a retractable glass magrodome. Although there are more than 4.5 acres (1.8 hectares) of space on the open decks, it does seem a little small and crowded when the ship is full. Inside, there are two foyers (atriums); one is a four-deck-high main foyer, and the second is a three-deck-high atrium. There is a 1,000-seat showlounge with large side balconies and good sight lines from just about every seat. There is also a small, dedicated cinema, which doubles as a conference and meeting center with all the latest audio-visual technology, including simultaneous translation in three languages and headsets for the hearing-impaired.

The ship has a superb, somewhat whimsical collection of artwork, which casts an eclectic look at life in some of its many forms. The collection is the result of the personal work of Christina Chandris. The company's "zero announcement" policy is much appreciated by its passengers.

Apart from the "front of house" aspects of this ship, it is the "back of house" facilities, the design and flow of the main galley (23,700 sq. ft/2,200 sq. meters), where the ship really shines. The consideration for safety is second to none. This ship also has excellent tender loading platforms.

"Stratosphere," the large combination observation lounge (with forward-facing as well as wrap-around views) and discotheque, provides what is probably the best viewing room when the ship operates Alaska cruises.

For a big-ship cruise experience, this one has just about all you need to have an enjoyable and rewarding cruise experience. *Galaxy* delivers a fine product that is worth

BERLITZ'S RATINGS

	Possible	Achieved
Ship	500	444
Accommodation	200	177
Food	400	315
Service	400	319
Entertainment	100	78
Cruise	400	330

much more than the cruise fare charged when compared to several other large-ship cruise lines. A 15% gratuity is added to bar and wine accounts. The onboard currency is the US dollar.

After Celebrity Cruises was bought by Royal Caribbean International, standards aboard ships in the Celebrity fleet went down as the new owner made cuts. However, new management is bringing Celebrity Cruises back to the premium product that was envisioned when the company first started.

Although this is a beautiful ship, the shore excursion operation, embarkation and disembarkation remain weak links in the Celebrity Cruises operation, and the cruise staff has little finesse. Standing in line for embarkation, disembarkation, shore tenders and for self-serve buffet meals is an inevitable aspect of cruising aboard all large ships.

The room service menu is quite poor, and room service items are below the standard of food served in the dining room. The interactive television system can prove frustrating to use, and the larger suites have several remotes for television/audio equipment (one would be better). The one area of congestion is the Photo Gallery, when passenger flow at peak evening times is impeded. The officers have become more aloof lately, with far less contact with passengers than in the company's early days.

SUITABLE FOR: *Galaxy* is best suited to well traveled couples and singles of 40 and above (not particularly recommended for children and teenagers). They will be seeking a large ship with a sophisticated environment, good itineraries, fine food and good European-style service from a well trained crew that delivers a product that's well above average.

ACCOMMODATION. There are 15 category/price grades, depending on your preference for the size and location of your living space, but the accommodation is extremely comfortable throughout. Occupants of all accommodation designated as suites get gold cards to open their doors (and priority service throughout the ship, free cappuccino/espresso coffees when served by a butler, welcome champagne, flowers, VCR, and use of the AquaSpa thalasso-therapy pool). Occupants of standard (interior no view and outside-view) cabins have white cards. Suites with private balconies have floor-to-ceiling windows and sliding doors to balconies (a few suites have outward opening doors).

All suites and cabins have interactive television for booking shore excursions, ordering room service, playing electronic casino games and buying goods from the ship's boutiques (available in English, French, German, Italian and Spanish). So you don't have to leave your quarters if you don't wish to, especially if you dislike the ports of call.

Most of the suites with private balconies have floor-to-ceiling windows and sliding doors to balconies (a few have outward opening doors). All accommodation designated as suites has duvets on the beds instead of sheets/blankets. In-suite massage service is available (with the right balcony, such as those in the Sky Suites, this is an excellent service). **Penthouse Suites:** These two suites, located amidships, are the largest. Each is 1,173 sq. ft (108.9 sq. meters), and comes with its own butler's pantry. There is an inter-connecting door so that it can link to the suite next door to become an impressive 1,515-sq. ft (141-sq. meter) apartment.

Most of the Deck 10 suites and cabins are of generous proportions, are beautifully equipped, and have balconies with full floor-to-ceiling partitions, as well as VCRs. The Sky Deck suites are also excellent, and have huge balconies (sadly, the partitions are not quite of the floor-to-ceiling type, so you can hear your neighbors). Also included are wall clock, large floor-to-ceiling mirrors, marble-topped vanity/writing desk, excellent closet and drawer space, and even dimmer-controlled ceiling lights. **Standard Outside-view/Interior (No View) Cabins:** All of the standard interior and outside cabins are of a good size and come nicely furnished with twin beds that convert to a queen-sized unit. The bathrooms are spacious and well equipped (with generous-size showers, hairdryers, and space for personal toiletry items). Baby-monitoring telephones are in all cabins. There are no cabins for singles.

CUISINE/DINING. The Orion Restaurant is a huge two-level dining hall. It is reminiscent of the dining halls aboard the ocean liners of the 1930s, with a grand staircase that flows between both levels and perimeter alcoves that provide more intimate dining spaces. Each level of the dining room has its own separate galley, and the noise level in the two sections is quite acceptable (more noise is noticeable on the larger, lower level, however). There are two seatings for dinner (open seating for breakfast and lunch), at tables for two, four, six, eight or 10, and the dining room is a no-smoking area. The cuisine is based on menus created by

top chef Michel Roux. The food has lots of taste (in particular, the sauces accompanying many of the main dishes); it also has fine color balance, and is nicely presented.

Just outside the lower-level entrance to the dining room, a champagne and caviar bar has ossetra and sevruga caviar – well presented with all the trimmings, and, of course, champagne and vodka to go with it.

For informal breakfasts and lunches, there is a two-level Oasis (lido) Cafe with several serving lines (it has a warm wood-accented decor), and eight bay windows provide some really prime seating spots. There are also two poolside grills – one located adjacent to the midships pools, the other wedged into the aft pool.

Tastings is a coffee lounge and bar for specialty coffees and pastries. For passengers in the two Presidential and 48 other suites, in-cabin dining is an option. However, the food served as room-service items is decidedly below the standard of food featured in the dining room.

ENTERTAINMENT. The 927-seat Celebrity Theater is the ship's principal showlounge. It spans two decks, with seating on both main and cantilevered balcony levels (with excellent sight lines from all seats). A revolving stage, "hard" curtain and large fly tower are featured.

Unfortunately, the production shows are not nearly as lavish as the showlounge they play in. In fact, compared to some of the other major cruise lines, the shows are a let-down, and not in keeping with the elegant nature of the interior decor. Most consist mainly of running, jumping, smoke, colored laser lighting, very loud music and click tracks, and little story line intelligence. Bar service, supplied continuously during shows, can prove irritating.

While there are some good cabaret acts, they are the same ones seen aboard many ships of the major cruise lines. The ship has a number of bands, although there is little music for social dancing, other than disco and pop music.

SPA/FITNESS. The AquaSpa, containing 9,040 sq. ft (840 sq. meters) of space, includes a large fitness/exercise area, complete with all the latest high-tech muscle machines and video cycles, thalassotherapy pool, and seven treatment rooms. The spa has some of the more unusual wellness treatments (including a steamy Rasul room – for Mediterranean mud and gentle steam bathing).

The spa is operated by Steiner, a specialist concession, whose staff will try to sell you Steiner's own-brand Elemis beauty products. Personal training sessions in the gymnasium cost $83 for one hour. Some fitness classes are free, while some, such as yoga and kick-boxing, cost $10 per class. Massage (including exotic massages such as Aroma Stone massage, Chakra Balancing massage and other well-being massages), facials, pedicures, and beauty salon treatments cost extra. Examples of treatment costs: massage $109 for 50 minutes, facial $109, seaweed wrap $190 for 75 minutes – all plus a "gratuity" of 10 percent.

Make appointments as early as possible – aboard a ship so large, time slots go quickly.

Golden Princess
★★★★

Large (Resort) Ship: . . . . . . .108,865 tons	Passengers	Cabins (wheelchair accessible): 28
Lifestyle: . . . . .Standard	(lower beds/all berths): 2,600/3,100	(18 outside/10 interior)
Cruise Line: . . . . .Princess Cruises	Passenger Space Ratio	Cabin Current: . . . . .110 and 220 volts
Former Names: . . . . .none	(lower beds/all berths): 41.8/35.1	Elevators: 14
Builder: . . . . .Fincantieri (Italy)	Crew/Passenger Ratio	Casino (gaming tables): . . . . .Yes
Original Cost: . . . .$450 million	(lower beds/all berths): 2.3/2.8	Slot Machines: . . . . .Yes
Entered Service: . . . . .May 2001	Navigation Officers: . . . . . .British/Italian	Swimming Pools (outdoors): 4
Registry: . . . . .Bermuda	Cabins (total): 1,300	Swimming Pools (indoors): 0
Length (ft/m): 951.4/290.0	Size Range (sq ft/m): 161.4–764.2/	Whirlpools: 9
Beam (ft/m): 118.1/36.0	15.0–71.0	Self-Service Launderette: . . . . .Yes
Draft (ft/m): 26.2/8.0	Cabins (outside view): 928	Dedicated Cinema/Seats: . . . . .No
Propulsion/Propellers: . . . . .diesel-electric	Cabins (interior/no view): 372	Library: . . . . .Yes
(42,000kW)/2	Cabins (for one person): 0	Classification Society: . . .Registro Navale
Passenger Decks: 13	Cabins (with private balcony): 710	Italiano (RINA)
Total Crew: 1,100		

OVERALL SCORE: 1,545 (OUT OF A POSSIBLE 2,000 POINTS)

OVERVIEW. *Golden Princess* (sister to *Grand Princess* and *Star Princess*) presents a bold, forthright profile, with a racy "spoiler" effect at the stern that I do not consider handsome (this acts as an observation lounge with aft-facing views by day, and a noisy discotheque by night). The ship has a flared snub-nosed bow and a galleon-like transom stern. At 118 ft/36 meters (but more than 43 ft/13 meters wider than the canal, including the navigation bridge wings) *Golden Princess* is too wide to transit the Panama Canal, with many balcony cabins overhanging the ship's hull.

There is a good sheltered teakwood promenade deck, which almost wraps around (three times round is equal to one mile) and a walkway that goes right to the (enclosed, protected) bow of the ship. The outdoor pools have various beach-like surroundings. One lap pool has a pumped "current" to swim against.

Unlike the outside decks, there is plenty of space inside the ship (but also plenty of passengers), and a wide array of public rooms, with many "intimate" (this being a relative word) spaces and places to play. The passenger flow has been well thought-out, and works with little congestion, except at the photo gallery on Promenade Deck (Deck 7), where there is congestion at peak times when passengers try to go through the gallery to get to the Vista Lounge. The decor is very attractive and warm, with lots of earth tones. In fact, this ship is the culmination of the best of all that Princess Cruises has to offer from its many years of operating what is now a well-tuned, good quality product.

Four areas center on swimming pools, one of which is two decks high and is covered by a magrodome, itself an

BERLITZ'S RATINGS

	Possible	Achieved
Ship	500	432
Accommodation	200	168
Food	400	256
Service	400	293
Entertainment	100	82
Cruise	400	314

extension of the funnel housing. High atop the stern of the ship is a ship-wide glass-walled disco pod. It looks like an aerodynamic "spoiler" and is positioned high above the water, with spectacular views from the extreme port and starboard side windows.

There is an extensive collection of art works, which complement the elegant, non-glitzy interior design and colors. If you see something you like, you'll probably be able to buy it.

This ship also has a Wedding Chapel (a live web-cam can relay ceremonies via the internet). The ship's captain can legally marry (American) couples, due to the ship's Bermuda registry and a special dispensation (this should, however, be verified when in the planning stage, and may vary according to where you reside). Princess Cruises offers three wedding packages: Pearl, Emerald, Diamond – the fee includes registration and official marriage certificate. However, to get married and take your close family members and entourage with you on your honeymoon is going to cost a lot. The "Hearts & Minds" chapel can also be used for "renewal of vows" ceremonies.

Teenagers (and others) might like the array of video games (50 cents to $3 per game), while photo enthusiasts should find "FX" (the digital photo shop) of interest – you can have your photo morphed into almost any setting. For youngsters there is a two-deck-high playroom and teen room located in the forward section of the ship (although the video games room is located at the opposite end of the ship), and a host of trained counselors.

Gamblers should enjoy the large casino, with more than 260 slot machines. There are blackjack, craps and roulette tables, plus games such as Let It Ride Bonus, Spanish 21 and Caribbean Draw Progressive.

Ship lovers should enjoy the wood-paneled Wheelhouse Bar, finely decorated with memorabilia and ship models tracing part of parent company P&O's history. There is an Internet Cafe, with a couple of dozen AOL-linked computer terminals ($7.50 per 15 minutes when this book was completed); but it should be called an Internet Center, as there is no cafe – not even any coffee.

Princess Cays – Princess Cruises' own "private island" in the Caribbean – is "yours" (along with other passengers, of course) for a day on Caribbean itineraries; however, you will need to take a shore tender to get to and from it, and this can take some time. A high-tech hospital is provided, with live SeaMed tele-medicine link-up to specialists at the Cedars-Sinai Medical Center in Los Angeles available for emergency help (hardly useful for international passengers who don't reside in the USA).

The automated telephone system is frustrating to use, and luggage delivery is inefficient. Lines form for many things, but particularly for the purser's desk, and for open-seating breakfast and lunch in the three main dining rooms.

You'll have to live with the many extra charge items (such as for ice cream, and freshly squeezed orange juice) and activities (such as yoga, group exercise bicycling and kick boxing classes at $10 per session, not to mention $4 per hour for group babysitting services). There is a charge for using the washers and dryers in the self-service launderettes (coins are needed).

Whether all this really can be considered a relaxing holiday is a moot point, but with many choices and "small" rooms to enjoy, the ship has been extremely well designed, and the odds are that you'll have a fine time, in a controlled, well packaged way.

ACCOMMODATION. There are six principal types of cabins and configurations: (a) grand suite, (b) suite, (c) mini-suite, (d) outside double with balcony, (e) outside double, and (f) interior (no view) double. There are, however, 35 different brochure price categories, making the choice bewildering for both travel agents and passengers. The price depends on grade, size and location. Many cabins have additional upper berths (there are 609), good for those with children.

(**a**) The largest, most lavish suite is the Grand Suite (B748, which is at the ship's stern – a different position to the two Grand Suites aboard sister ship *Grand Princess*). Although large for Princess Cruises, it does not compare with much larger suites (three times the size, in fact) aboard such ships as *Constellation, Infinity, Millennium, Norwegian Dawn, Norwegian Star, Summit*. It has a large bedroom with a queen-sized bed, huge walk-in (illuminated) closets, a large bathroom with full-size tub and separate shower enclosure, toilet, and washbasin, and a hot tub (accessed from the bedroom), a lounge (with sofa bed, dining table and chairs, wet bar and refrigerator, a guest bathroom (with toilet and washbasin), and a large private balcony.

(**b/c**) Suites (with a semi-private balcony) have a separate living room (with sofa bed) and bedroom (with a TV set in

each). The bathroom is quite large and has both a tub and shower stall. The mini-suites also have a semi-private balcony, and a separate living and sleeping area (with a television in each). The bathroom is also quite spacious, with both a bathtub and shower stall. The differences between the suites and mini-suites are basically in the size and appointments, the suite being more of a square shape while mini-suites are more rectangular, and have few drawers. Plush bathrobes and fully tiled bathrooms with ample open shelf storage space are provided. Passengers occupying the best suites receive greater attention, including priority embarkation and disembarkation privileges. What is not good is that some of the most expensive accommodation has only semi-private balconies that can be seen from above, so there is no privacy whatsoever (Suites C401, 402, 409, 410, 414, 415, 420, 421, 422, 423, 424 and 425 on Caribe Deck in particular). Also, the suites D105 and D106 (Dolphin Deck), which are extremely large, have balconies that can be seen from above.

(**d/e/f**) The standard interior and outside-view (the outsides come either with or without private balcony) cabins are of a functional, practical, design, although almost no drawers are provided. They are very attractive, with warm, pleasing decor and fine soft furnishing fabrics.

Additionally, two family suites consist of two suites with an interconnecting door, plus a large balcony. These can sleep up to 10 (if at least four are children), or up to eight people (if all are adults).

All passengers receive turndown service and chocolates on pillows each night, bathrobes (on request) and toiletry amenity kits (larger, naturally, for suite/mini-suite occupants) that typically include soap, shampoo, conditioner, and hand/body lotion. A hairdryer is provided in all cabins. All bathrooms are tiled and have a decent amount of open shelf storage space for personal toiletries. Princess Cruises receives BBC World, CNN, CNBC, ESPN and TNT on the in-cabin color television system (when available, depending on cruise area).

Most outside cabins on Emerald Deck have views obstructed by lifeboats. Your name is placed outside your suite or cabin – making it simple for delivery service personnel but also making it intrusive with regard to your privacy. Some cabins can accommodate a third and fourth person in upper berths. However, in such cabins, the lower beds cannot then be pushed together to make queen-sized bed. There are no cabins for singles.

Almost all balcony suites and cabins can be overlooked both from the navigation bridge wing, as well as from the port and starboard sections of the ship's discotheque – located high above the ship at the stern. Cabins with balconies on Dolphin, Caribe and Baja decks are also overlooked by passengers on balconies on the deck above; they are, therefore, not at all private. However, perhaps the least desirable balcony cabins are the eight located forward on Emerald Deck, as the balconies do not extend to the side of the ship and can be passed by walkers and gawkers on the adjacent Upper Promenade walkway (so occupants need to keep their curtains closed most of the time). Also, passengers occupying some the most expensive suites with balconies at the stern of the vessel may experience considerable vibration during certain ship maneuvers.

Cabin bath towels are too small, and drawer space is limited. There are no butlers – even for the top-grade suites. Cabin attendants have too many cabins to look after (typically 20), which cannot translate to fine personal service.

CUISINE/DINING. There are a number of "Personal Choice" dining options. For formal meals there are three principal dining rooms (Bernini, Canaletto, and Donatello). There are two seatings in one restaurant, while "anytime dining" (where you choose when and with whom you want to eat) is typically featured in the other two. All three are non-smoking and split into multi-tier sections in a non-symmetrical design that breaks what are quite large spaces into many smaller sections, for better ambience. Each dining room has its own galley. While four elevators go to Fiesta Deck where the Canaletto and Donatello restaurants are located, only two go to Plaza Deck 5 where the Bernini Restaurant is located (this can cause long wait problems at peak times, particularly for anyone in a wheelchair). Note that 15% is added to beverage bills, including wines.

Alternative (Extra Charge) Dining: There are two alternative informal dining areas: Sabatini's Trattoria and Desert Rose. Both serve lunch and dinner. Sabatini's is an Italian eatery, with colorful tiled Mediterranean-style decor; it is named after Trattoria Sabatini, the 200-year-old institution in Florence. It has Italian-style pizzas and pastas, with a variety of sauces, as well as Italian-style entrées (including tiger prawns and lobster tail). Sabatini's is by reservation only, and there is a cover charge of $15 per person, for lunch or dinner (on sea days only).

Desert Rose has "southwestern American food"; by reservation only, with a cover charge of $8 per person, for lunch or dinner on sea days only. However, do note that Desert Rose is spread over the whole beam (width) of the ship, and two walkways intersect it, which means that it's a very open area, with people walking through it as you eat. The cuisine in both of these spots is decidedly better than in the three main dining rooms.

A poolside hamburger grill and pizza bar (no additional charge) are additional dining spots for casual bites, while extra charges will apply if you order items to eat at either the coffee bar/patisserie, or the caviar/champagne bar.

Other casual meals can be taken in the Horizon Court – open 24 hours a day, with large ocean-view on port and starboard sides and direct access to the two principal swimming pools and lido deck. Plastic plates are used.

ENTERTAINMENT. The Princess Theatre (showlounge) spans two decks and has comfortable seating on both main and balcony levels. It has a 9-piece orchestra, and a scenery loading bay that connects directly from stage to a hull door for direct transfer to the dockside). Princess Cruises prides itself on its glamorous all-American production shows (there are typically two or three shows each 7-day cruise).

The Vista Lounge is a second entertainment lounge. It has cabaret acts at night, and lectures, bingo and horse racing during the day. Explorers, a third entertainment lounge, can host cabaret acts and dance bands. Many other lounges and bars have live music, and there are male dance hosts as partners for women traveling alone.

SPA/FITNESS. The Lotus Spa is a large complex that surrounds one of the swimming pools at the forward end of the ship. It comprises a large gymnasium with all the usual equipment, an aerobics room, sauna and steam rooms, beauty salon, treatment rooms, and a relaxation area.

● **For more extensive general information about the Princess Cruises experience, see pages 124–127.**

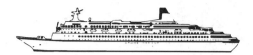

Grand Latino
★★★ +

Mid-Size Ship: ....28,388 tons	Propulsion/Propellers: ....diesel	Cabins (with private balcony): 10
Lifestyle: ....Standard	(13,400kW)/2 (CP)	Cabins (wheelchair accessible): 0
Cruise Line: ....Viajes Iberojet	Passenger Decks: 8	Cabin Current: ....110 and 220 volts
Former Names: ....*SuperStar Capricorn,*	Total Crew: 380	Cabin TV: ....Yes
Hyundai Keumgang, SuperStar Capricorn,	Passengers	Elevators: 5
Golden Princess, Sunward, Birka Queen,	(lower beds/all berths): 902/1,200	Casino (gaming tables): ....Yes
Royal Viking Sky	Passenger Space Ratio	Slot Machines: ....Yes
Builder: ....Wartsila (Finland)	(lower beds/all berths): 31.4/23.6	Swimming Pools (outdoors): 2
Original Cost: ....$22.5 million	Navigation Officers: ....European	Swimming Pools (indoors): 1
Entered Service: ....June 1973/	Cabins (total): 451	Whirlpools: 1
May 2004	Size Range (sq ft/m): 135.6–579.1/	Self-Service Launderette: ....Yes
Registry: ....Panama	12.6–53.8	Movie Theater/Seats: ....No
Length (ft/m): 674.1/205.47	Cabins (outside view): 405	Library: ....Yes
Beam (ft/m): 82.6/25.20	Cabins (interior/no view): 46	Classification Society: ....Det Norske
Draft (ft/m): 24.7/7.55	Cabins (single occupancy): 0	Veritas

OVERALL SCORE: 1,343 (OUT OF A POSSIBLE 2,000 POINTS)

OVERVIEW. This vessel's outer styling is quite handsome for an early 1970s-built vessel, a benefit from its original life as a ship for the now-defunct Royal Viking Line, and afterwards for Star Cruises. *Grand Latino,* now operated by the Spanish tour operator Viajes Iberojet, which spent €10 million refurbishing it, has an extensive program aimed at families with children. The single funnel bears the company's starfish logo, and balances the shapely profile of this attractive (though dated) ship.

The ship benefits from an extensive amount of open deck and sunbathing space; in fact, there is plenty of space everywhere and little sense of crowding (unless every bed/berth is filled). There is a good wrap-around promenade deck outdoors. Inside, the decor in public rooms is quite contemporary, with splashes of bright colors and high ceilings. There are lots of (small) public rooms to play in, unlike the newer, and larger, ships built today. The casino action is, to say the least, very lively. Gratuities and insurance are not included. The onboard currency is the euro.

SUITABLE FOR. *Grand Latino* is best suited to couples, singles, and families with children of all ages looking for a ship with some sense of space, decent facilities dedicated to Spanish-speaking passengers, at a very reasonable price.

ACCOMMODATION. There is something for every taste and wallet, from spacious family suites to small interior (no view) cabins. While most cabins are for two persons, some can accommodate a third, fourth, or even a fifth person.
Suites: These have a separate bedroom with ample closet

BERLITZ'S RATINGS

	Possible	Achieved
Ship	500	344
Accommodation	200	148
Food	400	265
Service	400	264
Entertainment	100	60
Cruise	400	262

and other storage space, lounge with large windows (with large TV/VCR, refrigerator and mini-bar), and a bathroom that has a full-size bathtub and shower, and a separate toilet. There is also a private outdoor balcony.
Standard Outside-View/Interior (No View) Cabins: The cabins are quite well equipped, and there is plenty of good (illuminated) closet, drawer and storage space, but the insulation between some of the lower grade cabins could be better. The bathrooms are of a decent size, but access is awkward in some of them. Some cabins have a small bathtub, although many have only a shower enclosure.

A number of cabins in the aft section of the three lowest passenger accommodation decks can be uncomfortable, with throbbing engines and generator units a major source of noise (particularly cabins adjacent to the engine casing).

CUISINE/DINING. The main dining room is quite spacious and has a high ceiling; it is generally quiet, and provides a reasonably elegant setting for cuisine that is totally geared to the Spanish-speaking family cruise market. There are two seatings.

ENTERTAINMENT. The main show lounge features shows that are totally geared to the Spanish family cruise passengers carried. Amateurish revues and low-budget cabaret acts provide a mix that appeals to the audience

SPA/FITNESS. A gymnasium has high-tech muscle-toning equipment and several treadmills. There is a sauna and steam room, changing rooms, and a beauty salon.

Grand Princess
★★★★

Large (Resort) Ship: ....108,806 tons	Passengers	Cabins (wheelchair accessible): 28
Lifestyle: ....Standard	(lower beds/all berths): 2,600/3,100	(18 outside/10 interior)
Cruise Line: ....Princess Cruises	Passenger Space Ratio	Cabin Current: ....110 and 220 volts
Former Names: ....none	(lower beds/all berths): 41.8/35.0	Elevators: 14
Builder: ....Fincantieri (Italy)	Crew/Passenger Ratio	Casino (gaming tables): ....Yes
Original Cost: ....$450 million	(lower beds/all berths): 2.3/2.8	Slot Machines: ....Yes
Entered Service: ....May 1998	Navigation Officers: ......British/Italian	Swimming Pools (outdoors): 4
Registry: ....Bermuda	Cabins (total): 1,300	Swimming Pools (indoors): 0
Length (ft/m): 951.4/290.0	Size Range (sq ft/m): 161.4–764.2/	Whirlpools: 9
Beam (ft/m): 118.1/36.0	15.0–71.0	Self-Service Launderette: ....Yes
Draft (ft/m): 26.2/8.0	Cabins (outside view): 928	Dedicated Cinema/Seats: ....No
Propulsion/Propellers: .....diesel-electric	Cabins (interior/no view): 372	Library: ....Yes
(42,000kW)/2	Cabins (for one person): 0	Classification Society: ...Registro Navale
Passenger Decks: 13	Cabins (with private balcony): 710	Italiano (RINA)
Total Crew: 1,100		

OVERALL SCORE: 1,545 (OUT OF A POSSIBLE 2,000 POINTS)

OVERVIEW. *Grand Princess* (sister to *Golden Princess* and *Star Princess*) presents a bold, forthright profile, with a racy "spoiler" effect at the stern that many do not consider handsome (this acts as an observation lounge with aft-facing views by day, and a stunning discotheque by night). The ship has a flared snub-nosed bow and a galleon-like transom stern. At 118 ft/36 meters (but more than 43 ft/13 meters wider than the canal, including the navigation bridge wings) *Grand Princess* is too wide to transit the Panama Canal, with many balcony cabins overhanging the ship's hull.

BERLITZ'S RATINGS		
	Possible	Achieved
Ship	500	432
Accommodation	200	168
Food	400	256
Service	400	293
Entertainment	100	82
Cruise	400	314

There is a good sheltered teakwood promenade deck, which almost wraps around (three times round is equal to one mile) and a walkway that goes right to the (enclosed, protected) bow of the ship. The outdoor pools have various beach-like surroundings. One lap pool has a pumped "current" to swim against.

Unlike the outside decks, there is plenty of space inside the ship (but also plenty of passengers), and a wide array of public rooms, with many "intimate" (this being a relative word) spaces and places to play. The passenger flow has been well thought-out, and works with little congestion, except at the photo gallery on Promenade Deck (Deck 7), where there is congestion at peak times when passengers try to go through the gallery to get to the Vista Lounge. The decor is very attractive and warm, with lots of earth tones. In fact, this ship is the culmination of the best of all that Princess Cruises has to offer from its many years of operating what is now a well-tuned, good-quality product.

Four areas center on swimming pools, one of which is two decks high and is covered by a magrodome, itself an extension of the funnel housing. High atop the stern of the ship is a ship-wide glass-walled disco pod. It looks like an aerodynamic spoiler and is positioned some 150 ft (45 meters) above the waterline, with spectacular views from the extreme port and starboard side windows (you can look along the ship's side and onto lots of "private" balconies).

There's an extensive collection of art works, which complements the interior design and colors well. If you see something you like, you'll probably be able to buy it on board.

This ship also has a Wedding Chapel (a live web-cam can relay ceremonies via the internet). The ship's captain can legally marry (American) couples, due to the ship's Bermuda registry and a special dispensation (this should, however, be verified when in the planning stage, and may vary according to where you reside). Princess Cruises offers three wedding packages: Pearl, Emerald, Diamond – the fee includes registration and official marriage certificate. However, to get married and take your close family members and entourage with you on your honeymoon is going to cost a lot. The "Hearts & Minds" chapel can also be used for "renewal of vows" ceremonies.

Another neat feature is the motion-based "virtual reality" room with its enclosed motion-based rides, and a "blue screen" studio, where passengers can star in their own videos. There is an excellent library/CD-Rom computer room, and a separate card room. Youngsters have a two-deck-high playroom, teen's room, and specially trained counselors.

Gamblers should enjoy what is one of the largest casinos

at sea, with more than 260 slot machines (all with dolphin-shaped handles); there are blackjack, craps and roulette tables, plus games such as Let It Ride Bonus, Spanish 21 and Caribbean Draw Progressive. A highlight is Neptune's Lair, a multimedia gaming extravaganza.

Ship lovers should enjoy the wood-paneled Wheelhouse Bar, finely decorated with memorabilia and ship models tracing part of parent company P&O's history.

Princess Cays – Princess Cruises' own "private island" in the Caribbean – is "yours" (along with a couple of thousand other passengers) for a day; however, you will need to take a shore tender to get to and from it, and this can take some time. A high-tech hospital is provided with live SeaMed tele-medicine link-ups with specialists at the Cedars-Sinai Medical Center in Los Angeles available for emergency help (hardly useful for international passengers that do not reside in the USA).

This ship is full of revenue centers, designed to help you part with more money. The dress code has been simplified – reduced to formal or smart casual. Gratuities are automatically added to your account, at $10 per person, per day (gratuities for children are charged at the same rate). If you want to pay less, you'll have to line up at the reception desk to have these charges adjusted. The onboard currency is the US dollar.

Whether this really can be considered a relaxing holiday is a moot point, but with so many choices and "small" rooms to enjoy, the ship has been extremely well designed; the odds are that you'll have a fine time, in a controlled, well-packaged way. If you are not used to large ships, it will probably take you some time to find your way around (take good walking shoes), despite the company's claim that this vessel offers a "small ship feel, big ship choice".

The automated telephone system frustrates many passengers, and luggage delivery needs to be more efficient.

ACCOMMODATION. There are six types of cabins and configurations: (a) grand suite, (b) suite, (c) mini-suite, (d) outside double with balcony, (e) outside double, and (f) interior (no view) double. There are, however, 35 different brochure price categories; the choice is bewildering for both travel agents and passengers. Price depends on grade, size and location. Many cabins have additional upper berths (there are 609 of them), good for families with children.

(a) The plushest suite is the Grand Suite, which has a hot tub accessible from both the private balcony and from the bedroom, two bedrooms, lounge, two bathrooms, a huge walk-in closet, and plenty of drawer and storage space.

(b/c) Suites (with a semi-private balcony) have a separate living room (with sofa bed) and bedroom (with a TV set in each). The bathroom is quite large and has both a bathtub and shower stall. The mini-suites also have a private balcony, and feature a separate living and sleeping area (with a television in each). The differences between the suites and mini-suites are basically in the size and appointments, the suite being more of a square shape while mini-suites are more rectangular, and have few drawers. Both suites and mini-suites feature really plush bathrobes, fully tiled

bathrooms with ample open shelf storage space. Suite and mini-suite passengers receive priority attention, including speedy embarkation and disembarkation privileges. What is really unacceptable is that the most expensive accommodation aboard this ship has only semi-private balconies that can be seen from above and so there is absolutely no privacy whatsoever (Suites C401, 402, 409, 410, 414, 415, 420, 421/422, 423, 424 and 425 on Caribe Deck). Also, the suites D105 and D106 (Dolphin Deck) are extremely large, but their balconies can be seen from above.

(d/e/f) Both interior and outside-view (the outsides come either with or without private balcony) cabins are functional and practical, although almost no drawers are provided. They are attractive, with warm, pleasing decor and fine soft furnishing fabrics; 80% of the outside cabins have a private balcony. The tiled bathrooms have a good amount of open shelf storage space for personal toiletries.

There are also two family suites. These consist of two suites with an interconnecting door, plus a large balcony, and can sleep up to 10 (if at least four are children), or up to eight people (if all are adults).

Most outside cabins on Emerald Deck have views obstructed by lifeboats. Sadly, there are no cabins for singles. Your name is placed outside your suite or cabin – making it simple for delivery service personnel but compromising privacy. Some cabins can accommodate a third and fourth person in upper berths – but in such cabins, the lower beds cannot then be pushed together to make queen-sized bed.

Almost all balcony suites and cabins can be overlooked both from the navigation bridge wing, as well as from the port and starboard sections of the ship's discotheque – located high above the ship at the stern. Perhaps the least desirable balcony cabins are the eight located forward on Emerald Deck, as the balconies do not extend to the side of the ship and can be passed by walkers and gawkers on the adjacent Upper Promenade walkway (so occupants need to keep their curtains closed most of the time). Also, passengers occupying some the most expensive suites with balconies at the stern of the vessel may experience considerable vibration during certain ship maneuvers.

The cabin bath towels are small, and drawer space is very limited. There are no butlers – even for the top grade suites. Cabin attendants have too many cabins to look after (typically 20), which cannot translate to fine personal service.

CUISINE/DINING. There is a variety of "Personal Choice" dining options. For formal meals, there are three principal dining rooms, Botticelli, with 504 seats, Da Vinci (486), and Michelangelo (486). There are two seatings in one restaurant, while the other two have "anytime dining" (where you choose when and with whom you want to eat). All three are non-smoking and split into multi-tier sections in a non-symmetrical design that breaks what are quite large spaces into many smaller sections, for better ambiance. Each dining room has its own galley. While four elevators go to Fiesta Deck where the Botticelli and Da Vinci restaurants are located, only two go to Plaza Deck 5 where the Michaelangelo Restaurant is located (this can cause long waits at peak times, particularly for anyone in a wheelchair).

Alternative (Extra Charge) Dining: There are two alternative informal dining areas: Sabatini's Trattoria and Painted Desert. Both are open for lunch and dinner. Sabatini's is an Italian eatery, with colorful tiled Mediterranean-style decor; it is named after Trattoria Sabatini, the 200-year old institution in Florence. It has Italian-style pizzas and pastas, with a variety of sauces, as well as Italian-style entrées (including tiger prawns and lobster tail). Sabatini's is by reservation only, and there is a cover charge of $15 per person, for lunch or dinner (on sea days only). Painted Desert has "southwestern American food"; by reservation only, with a cover charge of $8 per person, for lunch or dinner on sea days only. However, do note that Painted Desert is spread over the whole beam (width) of the ship, and two walkways intersect it, which means that it's a very open area, with people walking through it as you eat. The cuisine in both of these spots is decidedly better than in the three main dining rooms.

The poolside hamburger grill and pizza bar (no additional charge) are additional dining spots for casual bites, while extra charges will apply if you order items to eat at either the coffee bar/patisserie, or the caviar/champagne bar.

Other casual meals can be taken in the Horizon Court – open 24 hours a day, with large ocean-view on port and starboard sides and direct access to the two principal swimming pools and lido deck. Plastic plates are used.

ENTERTAINMENT. The Princess Theater (showlounge) spans two decks and has comfortable seating on both main and balcony levels. It has a 9-piece orchestra, and a scenery loading bay that connects directly from stage to a hull door for direct transfer to the dockside.

The Vista Lounge is a second entertainment lounge. It has cabaret acts at night, and lectures, bingo and horse racing during the day. Explorers, a third entertainment lounge, can also host cabaret acts and dance bands. Many lounges and bars have live music, and a number of gentlemen dance hosts act as partners for women traveling alone.

SPA/FITNESS. The Lotus Spa is a large complex that surrounds one of the swimming pools at the forward end of the ship. It comprises a large gymnasium with all the usual equipment, an aerobics room, sauna and steam rooms, beauty salon, a number of ocean-view treatment rooms, and a relaxation area.

● **For more extensive general information about the Princess Cruises experience, see pages 124–127.**

Grand Voyager
NOT YET RATED

Mid-Size Ship: . . . . .24,391 tons	Passenger Decks: 8	Cabins (for one person): 0
Lifestyle: . . . . .Standard	Total Crew: 360	Cabins (with private balcony): 12
Cruise Line: . . . . .Viajes Iberojet	Passengers	Cabins (wheelchair accessible): 4
Former Names: . . . . .Olympia Voyager,	(lower beds/all berths): 840/920	Cabin Current: . . . . .110 and 230 volts
Olympic Voyager	Passenger Space Ratio	Elevators: 4
Builder: . . . . . . .Blohm & Voss (Germany)	(lower beds/all berths): 29.0/26.5	Casino (gaming tables): . . . . .Yes
Original Cost: . . . .$150.8 million	Crew/Passenger Ratio	Slot Machines: . . . . .Yes
Entered Service: . . .July 2000 /June 2004	(lower beds/all berths): 2.3/2.5	Swimming Pools (outdoors): 1
Registry: . . . . .The Bahamas	Navigation Officers: . . . . .European	Swimming Pools (indoors): 0
Length (ft/m): 590.5/180.0	Cabins (total): 420	Whirlpools: 0
Beam (ft/m): 83.6/25.5	Size Range (sq ft/m): 140.0–375.0/	Self-Service Launderette: . . . . .No
Draft (ft/m): 23.2/7.1	13.0–34.8	Dedicated Cinema/Seats: . . . . .No
Propulsion/Propellers: . . . . .diesel	Cabins (outside view): 294	Library: . . . . .Yes
(37,800 kW)/2	Cabins (interior/no view): 126	Classification Society: Germanischer Lloyd

OVERALL SCORE: NYR (OUT OF A POSSIBLE 2,000 POINTS)

OVERVIEW. *Grand Voyager* (original name *Olympic Voyager*) was the first new ship ordered by Royal Olympia Cruises. However, the ship's high building cost was a problem, and it was put up for auction in March 2003. Having been bought by Horizon Navigation, it was placed under charter to Viajes Iberojet and dedicated to the Spanish-speaking market.

The exterior hull design (called a "fast monohull") is similar to that of naval frigates, with a slender fore-body, and two engine rooms (forward and midships) that can provide a 28-knot speed (and even some additional power in reserve). The ship is well suited to destination-intensive (port-hopping) itineraries, allowing passengers more time in each port (or more ports per cruise). Its funnel is of a streamlined, swept-back design.

There is a reasonable amount of open deck space (provided the ship isn't full), although there are not many deck lounge chairs. All exterior railings are made – unusually – of stainless steel (topped with thick, beautifully polished wood). The seawater swimming pool is located aft, and is quite small (most passengers will be enjoying the destinations served by this cruise line); adjacent are two shower enclosures.

The interior design combines contemporary touches with restrained decor, intended to remind one of the Mediterranean region the ship is designed for, with warm colors and an abundance of wood and opaque glass paneling. Perhaps the most striking, yet subtle, features in terms of design and decoration can be found in the artwork. Of particular note are two flowing poems etched in backlit opaque glass panels on the stairways (these poems are from Greece and

BERLITZ'S RATINGS

	Possible	Achieved
Ship	500	NYR
Accommodation	200	NYR
Food	400	NYR
Service	400	NYR
Entertainment	100	NYR
Cruise	400	NYR

Cyprus). However, to read the poems, you'll need to walk down the complete set of stairways. One poem, from 1911 (Ithaca) by the Greek poet Constantinos Petrou Kavafis, complements the other poem, Let's Say, by Cypriot poet Yannis Papadopoulos.

Most public rooms are located on one principal deck in a horizontal-flow layout that makes it easy to quickly find your way around, with a slightly winding open passageway that links several leisure lounges in one neat "street scene." There's a smoking room, adjacent to the main show lounge (Sala de Fiestas), for cigar and cognac devotees (with a black fireplace from the 1890s). In the popular Piano Bar, three ship models are cleverly displayed behind large glass wall panels. There's also a nightclub, a small library and a card room. Additionally, a casino (with its own bar) has table games, as well as slot machines.

There is no full wrap-around promenade deck, although you can walk around parts of the vessel outdoors. There is considerable vibration when the ship is underway at high speed, and when maneuvering at slow speeds. There are no dedicated facilities or rooms for the large numbers of children or teens that are typically carried during the July/August summer holidays. None of the public toilets is accessible by wheelchair. There are not enough deck lounge chairs considering the number of passengers carried, and not enough open deck space.

While service isn't perfect, it comes with a smile. The onboard currency is the euro.

SUITABLE FOR: *Grand Voyager* is best suited to Spanish-speaking couples and single travelers who want to see as much as possible (in terms of destinations), in contemporary, comfortable, but not luxurious surroundings, and with food and service that are acceptable, but nothing special, all at a very modest cruise fare.

ACCOMMODATION. The 11 price grades consist of 12 Sky Suites, 16 Bay Window Suites, 20 Junior Suites, 292 cabins (double occupancy), 72 cabins (two lower beds, one upper berth), 4 four-person cabins (two lower beds, two upper berths) and 4 wheelchair accessible cabins (with spacious bathrooms and roll-in showers). The price will depend on grade, location and size.

Standard Cabins: The standard interior (no view) and outside-view cabins are quite compact, but practically laid-out, and the decor includes warm blond wood cabinetry, accents and facings, and pleasing soft furnishings. The bathrooms are small, but have a decent-sized shower enclosure, and good storage facilities for personal toiletry items. All cabins include TV set, hairdryer, mini-bar/refrigerator and personal safe. You should note that only one personal safe is provided in each cabin, although there could be as many as four persons sharing a cabin.

Junior Suites: The accommodations designated as Junior Suites simply have a little more room than the standard interior (no view) and outside-view cabins. The bathrooms are small, but have a decent-sized shower enclosure, and good storage facilities for personal toiletries.

Bay Window Suites: There are 16 bay window cabins in the forward section of the ship; each features a large window that extends over the side of the ship, and a lounge area and sleeping area.

Sky Suites: The largest accommodation can be found in 12 Sky Suites located high atop the ship and in the forward-most section. They have large private balconies (some are more like large terraces), floor-to-ceiling windows, limited butler service, and 24-hour dining service.

Some suites have walk-in closets, while others have closets facing the entranceway, but all have an abundance of drawer and hanging space, and a chrome pullout shoe rack and tie rack. The bathroom has a combination tub/shower (although the bathtub is extremely small and is really only for sitting in) and retractable clothesline. All suites have wood paneled walls with vanity desk, mini-bar/refrigerator, sofa, drinks table (this is fixed and cannot be raised for dining), and sleeping area partly separated from the lounge area by a wood/glass divider. Four of the suites have large structures above their balconies that are the port side and starboard side gangway lowering mechanisms; they are

noisy in ports of call and anchor ports, and thus the balconies cannot be considered very private.

Also, when the ship is traveling at speed, considerable wind sweeps across the balconies, and renders them almost useless. The balconies, however, do have (expensive) stainless steel railings (instead of glass) topped with a thick wooden rail. Outside-view and interior (no-view) cabins located aft on Deck 3 (Neptune Deck: Numbers 3120–3138 and 3121– 3151) are subject to a substantial amount of throbbing noise from the diesel engines, and should be avoided (unless you like throbbing engine noise, that is).

CUISINE/DINING. The 470-seat Selenes Restaurant is located aft (one deck below the main "street" of public rooms and thus out of the main flow), and has picture windows on three sides. It has a semi-circular walkway, with minimalist decor, as its entrance.

The decor in the dining room itself is warm and welcoming, and quite tasteful, finished in what is best described as a "Greek Moderne" style; the chairs, however, do not have armrests. There are two seatings, and there are tables for two, four, six or eight. A few tables close to the entrance to the galley's escalators suffer from the service area, and, because of the single deck ceiling height and open waiter stations, the noise level can be considerable at times (depending on the nationalities of your fellow passengers).

For casual breakfast and lunch self-service buffets, the Garden Bufet is a pleasant but basic room, with large picture windows and an open feel. It has seating for 210 indoors and about 200 outdoors (where smokers congregate), and a bar outdoors is covered with a sailcloth-style cover. The two self-service buffet lines are small, and have a user-unfriendly layout that invites congestion – a victim of poor design. Additional munching outlets include a pizza serving area/salad bar, and an ice cream bar.

ENTERTAINMENT. The Main Lounge is the venue for entertainment events. It is a single-level room with 420 seats although there are many pillars to obstruct the sight lines from many of those seats (about 40 per cent are almost useless). Entertainment is limited aboard this ship, whose show lounge is best for cabaret-style shows. There's a disco.

SPA/FITNESS. One of the nicest and most useful facilities aboard this ship can be found in the Spa. It includes a large fitness room, several massage/treatment rooms, sauna, steam room, and rest/changing area.

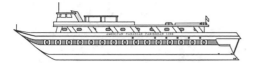

Grande Caribe
★★ +

Boutique Ship: . . . . .99 tons	Total Crew: 17	Cabins (with private balcony): 0
Lifestyle: . . . . .Standard	Passengers	Cabins (wheelchair accessible): 0
Cruise Line: . . . . .American Canadian	(lower beds/all berths): 100/100	Cabin Current: . . . . .110 volts
Caribbean Line	Passenger Space Ratio	Elevators: 0
Former Names: . . . . .none	(lower beds/all berths): 0.99/0.99	Casino (gaming tables): . . . . .No
Builder: . . . . .Blount Industries (USA)	Crew/Passenger Ratio	Slot Machines: . . . . .No
Original Cost: . . . .$8 million	(lower beds/all berths): 5.8/5.8	Swimming Pools (outdoors): 0
Entered Service: . . . . .June 1997	Navigation Officers: . . . . .American	Swimming Pools (indoors): 0
Registry: . . . . .USA	Cabins (total): .50	Whirlpools: 0
Length (ft/m): 183.0/55.7	Size Range (sq ft/m): 72.0–96.0/	Self-Service Launderette: . . . . .No
Beam (ft/m): 40.0/12.1	6.6–8.9	Dedicated Cinema/Seats: . . . . .No
Draft (ft/m): 6.5/1.9	Cabins (outside view): 41	Library: . . . . .Yes
Propulsion/Propellers: diesel (1,044kW)/2	Cabins (interior/no view): 9	Classification Society: . .American Bureau
Passenger Decks: 3	Cabins (for one person): 0	of Shipping

OVERALL SCORE: 963 (OUT OF A POSSIBLE 2,000 POINTS)

OVERVIEW. *Grande Caribe* is the largest and the most contemporary of the Blount-built vessels. During passenger emergency drill, passengers are taught how to use fire extinguishers – a useful piece of training.

This vessel's shallow draft enables it to cruise into off-the-beaten-path destinations well out of reach of larger ships, and also has a retractable navigation bridge – practical for those low bridges along inland waterways. *Grande Caribe*, together with sister vessel *Grande Mariner* (but not *Niagara Prince*), has stabilizers. An underwater video camera allows passengers, while seated in (dry) comfort in the lounge, to view on large-screen TV monitors what a scuba diver might see underneath the ship. Underwater lights, which attract fish and other marine life, are also fitted.

The style is casual (no jackets or ties) by day and night. There are two 24-passenger launches (one of which is a glass-bottomed boat), and some snorkeling equipment.

There is one lounge/bar, located on a different deck to the dining room. Water sports facilities include a glass-bottom boat, and sunfish sailboat.

This vessel will be good for anyone who does not want crowds, or entertainment of any kind, or a high standard of service. An electric chair-lift is provided at all stairways for those who do not walk well. All gratuities given by passengers are pooled and shared by all the staff (although you should note that the suggested daily rate is very high). The onboard currency is the US dollar.

SUITABLE FOR: *Grande Caribe* is best suited to couples and single travelers who enjoy nature and wildlife up close and personal, and who would not dream of cruising in the main-

BERLITZ'S RATINGS

	Possible	Achieved
Ship	500	212
Accommodation	200	77
Food	400	205
Service	400	220
Entertainment	N/A	N/A
Cruise	500	249

stream sense aboard ships with large numbers of people. This is for outdoors types who don't need entertainment or mindless parlor games, but do want an all-American cruise experience, albeit at a high price.

ACCOMMODATION. The cabins are all extremely small, relatively utilitarian units, with very little closet space (but just enough drawers) and very small bathrooms. The twin beds convert to queen-sized beds (there is good storage space under the beds). There is no room service menu, and only soap is supplied (bring your own shampoo and other toiletries). Each cabin has its own air conditioner, so passengers do not have to share air with the rest of the ship (and other passengers). Refreshingly, there are no cabin keys.

CUISINE/DINING. The dining room seats all passengers in one open seating, so you dine with whomever you wish, making new friends and enjoying different conversation each day (it is also good for small groups). The tables convert to card tables for use between meals. Passengers are welcome to bring their own alcohol, as the company does not sell it aboard ship. Effervescent, young American waitresses provide the service, although there is no finesse.

ENTERTAINMENT. There is no formal entertainment, although dinner and after-dinner conversation with fellow passengers in the ship's lounge/bar really becomes the entertainment each evening. So, if you don't want to talk to your fellow passengers, take a good book.

SPA/FITNESS. No facilities.

Grande Mariner
★★ +

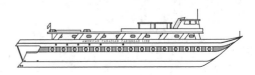

Boutique Ship: ....99 tons	Passenger Decks: 3	Cabins (with private balcony): 0
Lifestyle: ....Standard	Total Crew: 17	Cabins (wheelchair accessible): 0
Cruise Line: ....American Canadian	Passengers	Cabin Current: ....110 volts
Caribbean Line	(lower beds/all berths): 100/100	Elevators: 0
Former Names: ....none	Passenger Space Ratio	Casino (gaming tables): ....No
Builder: ....Blount Industries (USA)	(lower beds/all berths): 0.99/0.99	Slot Machines: ....No
Original Cost: ....$8 million	Crew/Passenger Ratio	Swimming Pools (outdoors): 0
Entered Service: ....June 1998	(lower beds/all berths): 5.8/5.8	Swimming Pools (indoors): 0
Registry: ....USA	Navigation Officers: ....American	Whirlpools: 0
Length (ft/m): 183.0/55.7	Cabins (total): 50	Self-Service Launderette: ....No
Beam (ft/m): 40.0/12.1	Size Range (sq ft/m): ..72.0–96.0/6.6–8.9	Dedicated Cinema/Seats: ....No
Draft (ft/m): 6.5/1.9	Cabins (outside view): 41	Library: ....Yes
Propulsion/Propellers: ....diesel	Cabins (interior/no view): 9	Classification Society: ..American Bureau
(1,044kW)/2	Cabins (for one person): 0	of Shipping

OVERALL SCORE: 963 (OUT OF A POSSIBLE 2,000 POINTS)

OVERVIEW. *Grande Mariner* is another example of a Blount-built vessel. During passenger emergency drill, passengers are taught how to use fire extinguishers – useful training.

This vessel has a shallow draft, which enables it to cruise into off-the-beaten-path destinations well out of reach of larger ships, and also has a retractable navigation bridge – practical for those low bridges along the inland waterways. *Grande Mariner*, together with sister vessel *Grande Caribe* (but not *Niagara Prince*), has stabilizers. An underwater video camera allows passengers, while seated in (dry) comfort in the lounge, to view on large-screen TV monitors what a scuba diver might see underneath the ship. Underwater lights, which attract fish and other marine life, are also fitted.

The style is unpretentious and extremely casual (definitely no jackets or ties) both day and night. There are two 24-passenger launches (one of which is a glass bottom boat), and some snorkeling equipment.

There is one lounge/bar, located on a different deck to the dining room – a departure for ACCL from the company's former vessels. An electric chair-lift is provided at all stairways for those who do not walk well. Water sports facilities include a glass-bottom boat, and sunfish sailboat.

All gratuities are pooled and shared by the staff (although the suggested daily rate is very high for the product delivered). The onboard currency is the US dollar.

SUITABLE FOR: *Grande Mariner* is best suited to couples and single travelers who enjoy nature and wildlife up close and personal and would not dream of cruising in the mainstream sense aboard ships with large numbers of people.

BERLITZ'S RATINGS

	Possible	Achieved
Ship	500	212
Accommodation	200	77
Food	400	205
Service	400	220
Entertainment	N/A	N/A
Cruise	500	249

This is for outdoors types who don't need entertainment or mindless parlor games, but do want an all-American cruise experience, albeit at a high price.

ACCOMMODATION. The cabins are all extremely small, relatively utilitarian units, with very little closet space (but just enough drawers) and very small bathrooms. There are 50 cabins, each with twin beds that convert to queen-sized beds (there is good storage space under the beds). There is no room service menu, and only soap is supplied (bring your own shampoo and other toiletries). Each cabin has its own air conditioner, so passengers do not have to share air with the rest of the ship (and other passengers). Refreshingly, there are no cabin keys.

CUISINE/DINING. The dining room seats all passengers in a single, open seating, so you dine with whomever you wish. The advantage of this is that you can make new friends and enjoy different conversation each day (it is also good for small groups). The dining tables convert to card tables for use between meals. Passengers are welcome to bring their own alcohol, as the company does not sell it aboard ship. Effervescent, young American waitresses provide the service, although there is no finesse.

ENTERTAINMENT. There is no formal entertainment, although dinner and after-dinner conversation with fellow passengers in the ship's lounge/bar really provides the entertainment each evening. So, if you don't want to talk to your fellow passengers, take a good book.

SPA/FITNESS. No spa facilities.

Grandeur of the Seas
★★★★

Large (Resort) Ship:	.......74,137 tons	Total Crew:	760	Cabins (with private balcony):	212
Lifestyle:	.................Standard	Passengers		Cabins (wheelchair accessible):	14
Cruise Line:	Royal Caribbean International	(lower beds/all berths):	.....1,950/2,446	Cabin Current:	........110 and 220 volts
Former Names:	................none	Passenger Space Ratio		Elevators:	9
Builder:	...Kvaerner Masa-Yards (Finland)	(lower beds/all berths):	........38.0/30.3	Casino (gaming tables):	...........Yes
Original Cost:	............$300 million	Crew/Passenger Ratio		Slot Machines:	...................Yes
Entered Service:	............Dec 1996	(lower beds/all berths):	.........2.5/3.2	Swimming Pools (outdoors):	1
Registry:	...............The Bahamas	Navigation Officers:	.......International	Swimming Pools (indoors):	1
Length (ft/m):	............916.0/279.6	Cabins (total):	975	(indoor/outdoor w/sliding glass roof)
Beam (ft/m):	..............105.6/32.2	Size Range (sq ft/m):	.....158.2–1,267.0/	Whirlpools:	6
Draft (ft/m):	.................25.5/7.6		14.7–117.7	Self-Service Launderette:	..........No
Propulsion/Propellers:	.....diesel-electric	Cabins (outside view):	576	Dedicated Cinema/Seats:	..........No
	(50,400kW)/2	Cabins (interior/no view):	399	Library:	........................Yes
Passenger Decks:	11	Cabins (for one person):	0	Classification Society: Det Norske Veritas

OVERALL SCORE: 1,521 (OUT OF A POSSIBLE 2,000 POINTS)

OVERVIEW. This is one of a pair of ships for this popular cruise line (sister to *Enchantment of the Seas*). The vessel has an attractive contemporary profile, with a single funnel located well aft (almost a throwback to some ship designs used in the 1950s), and has a nicely rounded stern (rather like the older *Sovereign of the Seas*-class ships), and a Viking Crown Lounge is set amidships. This, together with the forward mast, provides three distinct focal points in its exterior profile. There is a wrap-around promenade deck outdoors (there are no cushioned pads for the tacky home patio-style plastic deck lounge chairs, however).

A large Viking Crown Lounge (a trademark of all Royal Caribbean International ships) sits between funnel and mast at the top of the atrium lobby, and overlooks the forward section of the swimming pool deck, with access provided from stairway off the central atrium.

The principal interior focal point is a seven-deck-high Centrum (atrium lobby), which provides a good meeting point (the Purser's Desk and Shore Excursion Desk are located on one of the lower levels). Many public entertainment rooms and facilities can be located off the atrium.

This ship has good interior passenger flow. There is a good, varied collection of artworks (including several sculptures), principally by British artists, with classical music, ballet and theater themes. The casino is large and glitzy, and has a fascinating, somewhat theatrical glass-covered, but under-floor exhibit. The children's and teens' facilities are good, much expanded from previous ships in the fleet.

A delightful champagne terrace bar sits forward of the lower level of the two-deck-high dining room. There is a good use of tropical plants throughout the public rooms,

BERLITZ'S RATINGS

	Possible	Achieved
Ship	500	430
Accommodation	200	166
Food	400	248
Service	400	302
Entertainment	100	81
Cruise	400	294

which helps counteract the rather plain and clinical pastel wall colors, while huge murals of opera scenes adorn several stairways. There are good children's and teens' facilities – larger than those of previous ships in the fleet. The onboard currency is the US dollar.

ACCOMMODATION. There are 16 price grades (the price depending on grade, size and location, with location and grade perhaps more important, since so many of the cabins are of the same, or a very similar size).

There are five grades of suites: Royal Suite (1), Owner's Suite (5), Royal Family Suite (4), Grand Suite (12), and Superior Suite (44, including two superior suites for the disabled). All are well appointed and have pleasing decor (best described as Scandinavian Moderne), with good wood and color accenting (the largest has a baby grand piano).
Royal Suite. The largest accommodation can be found in the Royal Suite, located directly aft of the ship's navigation bridge on the starboard side. It has a separate bedroom with king-sized bed, walk-in closet and vanity dressing area, living room with queen-sized sofa bed, baby grand piano, refrigerator and wet bar, dining table, entertainment center, and large private balcony. The bathroom has a whirlpool tub, separate shower enclosure, two washbasins, and toilet.
Owner's Suite. The five owner's suites are at the forward end of the ship, just behind the navigation bridge (close to the Royal Suite). They have a queen-sized bed, separate living area with queen-sized sofa bed, vanity dressing area, refrigerator and wet bar. The bathroom has a full-size bathtub, separate shower enclosure, toilet and two washbasins.
Royal Family Suite. Features include two bedrooms with twin beds that convert to queen-sized beds, living area

with double sofa bed and Pullman bed, refrigerator, two bathrooms (one with bathtub), and private balcony. This suite can accommodate eight, and might be suitable for families.

Grand Suite. Twin beds convert to a queen-sized bed. Vanity dressing area, lounge area with sofa bed, refrigerator, and a bathroom with bathtub, plus a private balcony.

Superior Suite. Twin beds that convert to a queen-sized bed. Vanity dressing area, lounge area with sofa bed, refrigerator, plus private balcony, and a bathroom with bathtub. Although this is called a suite, it really is little more than a larger standard cabin with balcony.

Other Grades. All standard cabins have twin beds that convert to a queen-sized bed, ample closet space for a one-week cruise, and a good amount of drawer space, although under-bed storage space is not good for large suitcases. The bathrooms have nine mirrors. Plastic buckets are provided for champagne/wine and are really tacky.

All grades of suite/cabin include a hairdryer. The room service menu is minimal, with only the most basic selection.

CUISINE/DINING. The 1,195-seat (non-smoking) Great Gatsby Dining Room is a large dining hall that is spread over two decks, with both levels connected by a grand, sweeping staircase. There are two seatings.

The cavernous, 790-seat informal Windjammer Cafe is the ship's casual eatery. It has a great expanse of ocean-view glass windows, and is where breakfast and lunch buffets are available as an alternative to the dining room.

An intimate terrace Champagne Bar is located forward of the lower level of the two-deck-high dining room and just off the atrium for those who might like to taste something a little out of the ordinary, in a setting that is bright and contemporary.

ENTERTAINMENT. The Palladium Theater is the ship's principal showlounge. It is located at the forward part of the ship (accessed by the forward stairway/lift bank), and is used for big production shows. It has excellent sightlines from 98 percent of the 875 seats. Another showlounge, the 575-seat South Pacific Lounge, is used for smaller shows and cabaret acts, including late-night adult (blue) comedy.

SPA/FITNESS. The ShipShape Spa is located aft of the funnel and spans two decks. Facilities include a gymnasium (with all the latest muscle-pumping exercise machines), aerobics exercise room, sauna and steam rooms, a beauty salon, and a clutch of treatment rooms.

For the sporting, there is activity galore – including a rock-climbing wall, with several separate climbing tracks. It is located outdoors at the aft end of the funnel.

● **For more extensive general information about the Royal Caribbean experience, see pages 128–131.**

Hanseatic
★★★★★

Boutique Ship: ....8,378 tons	Total Crew: 122	Cabins (with private balcony): 0
Lifestyle: ....Luxury	Passengers	Cabins (wheelchair accessible): 2
Cruise Line: ....Hapag-Lloyd Cruises	(lower beds/all berths): 184/194	Cabin Current: ....220 volts
Former Names: ......*Society Adventurer*	Passenger Space Ratio	Elevators: 2
Builder: ....Rauma Yards (Finland)	(lower beds/all berths): 45.5/43.1	Swimming Pools (outdoors): 1
Original Cost: ....$68 million	Crew/Passenger Ratio	Whirlpools: 1
Entered Service: ....Mar 1993	(lower beds/all berths): 1.5/1.5	Self-Service Launderette: ....No
Registry: ....The Bahamas	Navigation Officers: ....German	Lecture/Film Room: ......Yes (seats 160)
Length (ft/m): 402.9/122.80	Cabins (total): 92	Library: ....Yes
Beam (ft/m): 59.1/18.00	Size Range (sq ft/m): 231.4–470.3/	Zodiacs: 14
Draft (ft/m): 15.5/4.71	21.5–43.7	Helicopter Pad: ....Yes
Propulsion/Propellers: ....diesel	Cabins (outside view): 92	Classification Society: ......Det Norske
(5,880kW)/2	Cabins (interior/no view): 0	Veritas
Passenger Decks: 7	Cabins (for one person): 0	

OVERALL SCORE: 1,740 (OUT OF A POSSIBLE 2,000 POINTS)

OVERVIEW. Originally ordered for Society Cruises as *Society Adventurer* (although it never actually sailed under that name, because the company declared itself bankrupt and didn't take possession of the ship), *Hanseatic* was well designed and constructed specifically to provide worldwide expedition-style cruises in contemporary, but quite luxurious, surroundings. The ship is extremely environmentally friendly and has the latest "zero-discharge", non-polluting waste disposal system including a pollution-filtered incinerator, full biological sewage treatment plant, and a large storage capacity. This is one of only very few ships that will allow you to sign up for a tour of the engine room.

This is an outstanding ship for the best in destination-intensive exploration voyages, and is under long-term charter to Hapag-Lloyd Cruises. It has a fully enclosed bridge (which you can visit) and an ice-hardened hull with the highest passenger vessel ice classification. The ship also has the very latest in high-tech navigation equipment.

A fleet of 14 Zodiac inflatable craft, each named after a famous explorer, is used for in-depth shore landings. These craft provide the ship with tremendous flexibility in itineraries, and provide excellent possibilities for up-close wildlife viewing in natural habitats, with small numbers of passengers. Rubber boots, parkas, a boot-washing and storage room are provided for passengers, particularly useful for Arctic and Antarctic cruises.

Inside, the ship is equipped with fine quality luxury fittings and soft furnishings. There is a choice of several public rooms, all of them well-furnished and decorated, and all of them have high ceilings, which help to provide an impression of space; the result is that the ship feels much

BERLITZ'S RATINGS

	Possible	Achieved
Ship	500	434
Accommodation	200	172
Food	400	345
Service	400	343
Entertainment	N/A	N/A
Cruise	500	446

larger than its actual size. The library/observation lounge provides a good selection of hardback books and videos in both the English and German languages.

Hanseatic provides destination-intensive, nature and life-enrichment cruises and expeditions in elegant, but unstuffy surroundings, to some of the world's most fascinating destinations, at a suitably handsome price. The passenger maximum is generally kept to about 150, which means plenty of comfort, no lines, and lots of space.

The ship is at its best when operating in Arctic and Antarctic regions (however, infirm passengers would be well advised to be wary of the difficult conditions for shore landings in these areas). Safety is paramount, particularly in the Antarctic and, in this regard, the ship excels with professionalism, pride and skilled seamanship. It always operates in two languages, English and German (many staff speak several languages) and caters well to both sets of passengers. All port taxes, insurance, gratuities, Zodiac trips and most shore excursions (except when the ship operates in Europe) are included. A relaxed ambience prevails on board. The onboard currency is the euro.

Hapag-Lloyd Cruises specializes in providing outstanding, well-planned itineraries. Where this ship really scores, however, is in its Antarctic sailings, where the experience of the captain, the cruise director and the crew really shine. The lectures, briefings, and the amount of information provided about the itinerary and ports of call are outstanding. Well-qualified lecturers and naturalists accompany each cruise, and a discreet crew and unobtrusive service are hallmarks of the cruise experience. Insurance, port taxes and all staff gratuities are typically included in the fare, and an expedition cruise logbook is provided at the end of each cruise for all passengers – a superb reminder of what's been seen and done during the course of your cruise.

Note that there are few negative things about this ship. It is principally marketed to German-speaking and English-speaking passengers, so other nationalities may find it hard to integrate. There are no Marine quality telescopes mounted outdoors; these would be a useful addition.

SUITABLE FOR: *Hanseatic* is best suited to well-traveled couples and single travelers who are adventurous and enjoy learning about nature and the natural sciences, geography, history, gardening, art, architecture, and want to be aboard a very small ship with almost no entertainment or mindless parlor games. This ship is ideal for those who would never wish to set foot aboard one of the big "floating resort" ships which go on highly programmed cruises, and for those who want to experience destinations that are probably out of the ordinary (such as Antarctica) in style and a high degree of comfort.

ACCOMMODATION. There are no bad cabins aboard this ship, and accommodation is priced in seven grades. The price will depend on the grade, size and location you choose. The all-outside cabins, located in the forward section of the ship, are large and very well equipped, and include a separate lounge area next to a large picture window (which has a pull-down blackout blind as well as curtains) and refrigerator. All furniture is in warm woods such as beech, and everything has rounded edges. Wood trim accents the ceiling perimeter, and acts as a divider between bed and lounge areas. Each cabin has a mini-bar, television, VCR, two locking drawers, and plenty of closet and drawer space, as well as two separate cupboards and hooks for all-weather outerwear. There really should be (but there isn't, at present) a privacy curtain between the cabin door and the sleeping area of the cabin (passengers can be seen from the hallway as soon as the cabin door is opened).

In 2003 a complete, high-tech in-cabin infotainment system was added to all suites/cabins (similar to the one aboard *Europa* and *Queen Mary 2*), which provides a large selection of on-demand videos (at no charge) and audio tracks.

All cabin bathrooms have a large bathtub, two toiletries cabinets, wall-mounted hairdryer, and bathrobe. There are only two types of cabins; 34 have double beds, others have twin beds. Towels, bed linens and pillowcases are 100% cotton. Individual cotton-filled duvet covers are provided.

The suites and cabins on Bridge Deck have impeccable butler service and full in-cabin dining privileges, as well as personalized stationery, larger flat-screen televisions and DVD player. Soft drinks are supplied in the cabin refrigerator, and replenished daily, at no charge (all liquor is at extra cost, however).

CUISINE/DINING. The dining room is elegant, warm and welcoming, and has large picture windows on two sides as well as aft, and table settings are graced with fine Rosenthal china and silverware. There is one seating for dinner, and open seating for breakfast and lunch. The cuisine and service are absolutely first-rate, but are more informal than, for example, aboard the larger *Europa* (which is at or close to the same price level). Top-quality ingredients are always used, and most items are purchased fresh when available. The meals are very creative and nicely presented, and each is appealing to the eye as well as to the palate. There is always an excellent selection of breads, cheeses, desserts and pastry items. Note that when operating in the Arctic or Antarctic, table set-ups are often minimal, due to the possible movement of the ship (stabilizers cannot be used in much of the Antarctic region), so cutlery is provided and changed for each course.

In 1996, the ship added an alternative dining room. The Columbus Lounge, which is an informal, open seating, self-serve (or waiter service) buffet-style eatery by day, changes into a second dining room night, with regional theme dinners and barbeques. Reservations are required (you make them in the morning of the day you want to dine there), but there is no extra charge, and there is no tipping at any time. Also, on each cruise a full Viennese teatime is featured, as well as a daily teatime.

ENTERTAINMENT. There is no showlounge as such, although there is a lecture room. Entertainment is certainly not a priority aboard this ship, but the itinerary and destinations are the main show. There is no formal entertainment (except on some cruises in the summer, when, typically, a little classical music ensemble may be carried), nor does the ship normally carry a band. Lectures, by some of the foremost authorities and experts in various fields associated with expeditions and nature are a principal attraction of any cruise aboard this ship (unless under charter for special theme cruises during the summer), as are after-dinner recaps of the day.

Occasionally, the ship's crew may put on a little amateur dramatics event, or a seamen's choral presentation. And on one evening at the end of each expedition cruise, the ship's chart is auctioned off to the highest bidder, with any profits being sent to a charity organisation.

SPA/FITNESS. The spa facilities, expanded in 2004, include a decently-sized gymnasium (with up-to-date cardiovascular and muscle-toning equipment, treadmills and exercycles), a sauna, and massage facilities, all located forward on the Sun Deck in an area that also includes a solarium and hot tub. Nothing more is really needed on this kind of expedition-style cruising as most of each day is taken up with being ashore, and evenings mainly consist of dinner and daily recaps.

Hebridean Princess
★★★★★

Boutique Ship: . . . . .2,112 tons	Total Crew: 37	Cabins (with private balcony): 4
Lifestyle: .Luxury	Passengers	Cabins (wheelchair accessible): 0
Cruise Line: . . . .Hebridean Island Cruises	(lower beds/all berths): 49/49	Cabin Current: . . . . .240 volts
Former Names: . . . . .Columba	Passenger Space Ratio	Elevators: 0
Builder: . . . . .Hall Russell (Scotland)	(lower beds/all berths): 43.1/43.1	Casino (gaming tables): . . . . .No
Original Cost: .n/a	Crew/Passenger Ratio	Slot Machines: .No
Entered Service: 1964/Apr 1989	(lower beds/all berths): 1.3/1.3	Swimming Pools (outdoors): 0
Registry: . . . . .Great Britain	Navigation Officers: . . . . .British	Swimming Pools (indoors): 0
Length (ft/m): 235.0/71.6	Cabins (total): .30	Whirlpools: 0
Beam (ft/m): 46.0/14.0	Size Range (sq ft/m): 144.0–340.0/	Self-Service Launderette: . . . . .No
Draft (ft/m): 10.0/3.0	13.4–31.6	Dedicated Cinema/Seats: . . . . .No
Propulsion/Propellers: . . . . .diesel	Cabins (outside view): 24	Library: . . . . .Yes
(1,790kW)/2	Cabins (interior/no view): 6	Classification Society: . . .Lloyd's Register
Passenger Decks: 5	Cabins (for one person): 11	

OVERALL SCORE: 1,701 (OUT OF A POSSIBLE 2,000 POINTS)

OVERVIEW. Small can be beautiful. *Hebridean Princess*, originally one of three Scottish ferries built for for David MacBayne Ltd – although actually owned by the British government – was skillfully converted into a gem of a cruise ship in order to operate island-hopping itineraries in Scotland, together with the occasional jaunt to Ireland and Norway. It was renamed in 1989 by the Duchess of York. There is an outdoors deck for occasional sunbathing and al fresco meals, as well as a bar (occasionally, formal cocktail parties are held here when the weather conditions are right). There is no wrap-around deck, although inside the ship there is a mini-gym for those seeking to pedal or row themselves to the next destination. The ship carries a Zodiac inflatable runabout, as well as a rowing boat (for passenger use).

Use of the ship's small boats, speedboat, bicycles, and fishing gear are included in the price, as are entrance fees to gardens, castles, other attractions, and the occasional coach tour (depending on the itinerary). The destination-intensive cruises have very creative itineraries and there really is plenty to do, despite the lack of big-ship features. Specialist guides, who give nightly talks about the destinations to be visited and some fascinating history and the local folklore, accompany all cruises.

The principal inside room is the Tiree Lounge, which has a real brick-walled fireplace, as well as a very cozy bar with a wide variety of whiskeys (the selection of single malts is excellent) and cognacs for connoisseurs.

This utterly charming little ship has a warm, totally cosseted, traditional country house ambiance and stately home service that is unobtrusive but always at hand when you need it. Inspector Hercule Poirot would be very much at

BERLITZ'S RATINGS

	Possible	Achieved
Ship	500	425
Accommodation	200	177
Food	400	350
Service	400	341
Entertainment	N/A	N/A
Cruise	500	408

home here. Who needs megaships when you can take a retro-cruise aboard this absolute gem of a ship? Direct bookings are accepted.

What is so appreciated by passengers is the fact that the ship does not have photographers or some of the trappings found aboard larger ships. Passengers also love the fact that there is no bingo, horse racing, art auctions, or mindless parlor games. The onboard currency is the British pound.

Hebridean Princess has an all-UK crew who are discreet and provide unobtrusive service, and remains one of the world's best-kept travel secrets. A polished gem, it is especially popular with single passengers, and more than 50 percent of her passengers are repeaters (children under the age of nine are not accepted). If you cruise from Oban, you will be met at Glasgow station (or airport) and taken to/from the ship by private motor coach. All gratuities and soft drinks are included in the fare (the company requests that no additional gratuities be given).

Hebridean Island Cruises has a slightly larger sister ship, acquired in 2001 (*Hebridean Spirit*), which offers the same style and comfort, but has more international itineraries.

Although this vessel is strong, it does have structural limitations and noisy engines that cause some vibration (however, the engines do not run at night and the ship anchors before bedtime, providing soul-renewing tranquility). Alcoholic drinks are not included in the fare, although soft drinks are. It is often cold and very wet in the Scottish islands, so take plenty of warm clothing for layering.

SUITABLE FOR: *Hebridean Princess* is best suited to adult couples and single travelers of mature years who enjoy learning about nature and the natural sciences, geography, history, gardening, art, architecture, and want to be aboard a very small ship with almost no entertainment or mindless parlor games. This is ideal for those who would abhor big ship cruising.

ACCOMMODATION. The price will depend on the grade, size and location you choose. All cabins have different color schemes and names (there are no numbers, and, refreshingly, no door keys, although the cabins can be locked from the inside). All are individually designed (no two cabins are identical) and created, with delightfully eclectic chintz curtains and sweeping drapes over the beds. They really are quite delightful and come in a wide range of configurations (some with single, some with double, some with twin beds), including four that have a private balcony (a delightfully private and self-indulgent plus).

All except two cabins have a private bathroom with bath or shower; all have a refrigerator, ironing board with iron, trouser press, and tea/coffee making set. All towels and bathrobe are 100% cotton, as is the bed linen. Molton Brown personal toiletry items are provided.

All cabins come with Victorian-style bathroom fittings (some are even gold-plated), and some have brass cabin portholes that actually open. Three of the newest cabins added are outfitted in Scottish Baronial style. Some cabins also have a VCR.

CUISINE/DINING. There is a non-smoking dining room with ocean-view windows, and tables that are laid with crisp white linen, and sometimes with lace overlays. Villeroy & Boch china is used. There is a single seating, at assigned tables. Some chairs have armrests while some do not. The cuisine is extremely creative, and at times outstanding – and about the same quality and presentation as *SeaDream I* and *SeaDream II*. Fresh ingredients are purchased locally – a welcome change from the mass catering of most ships. Although there are no flambeau items (the galley has electric, not gas, cookers), what is created is beautifully presented and of the highest standard. The desserts are definitely worth saving space for.

The breakfast menu is standard each day, although you can always ask for any favorites you may have, and each day a speciality item is featured. Try the "porridge and a wee dram" – it's lovely on a cold morning, and it sets you up for the whole day. Although there is waiter service for most things, there is also a good buffet table display for breakfast and luncheon. This little ship has a very decent wine list and extremely moderate prices (an additional connoisseur's list is available for those seeking fine vintage wines). Many wonderful whiskeys and vintage cognacs are also available. Highly personal and attentive service from an attentive British/Scottish crew completes the picture.

ENTERTAINMENT. The Tiree Lounge is the equivalent of a main lounge aboard this very small ship. Dinner is *the* entertainment of the evening. Occasionally, there might be after-dinner drinks, piano or harp music in the Tiree Lounge, but little else (passengers neither expect nor need it).

SPA/FITNESS. There is no spa, as the ship is too small. The only concessions to fitness are a couple of exercycles.

Hebridean Spirit
★★★★★

Boutique Ship:	4,200 tons	Total Crew:	72

Boutique Ship: . . . . .4,200 tons
Lifestyle: .Luxury
Cruise Line: . . . .Hebridean Island Cruises
Former Names: . . . . *Sun Viva II,*
 MegaStar Capricorn, Renaissance Six
Builder: . . . .Nuovi Cantieri Apuania (Italy)
Entered Service: . . . .Mar 1991/July 2001
Registry: . . . . .Great Britain
Length (ft/m): 297.2/90.60
Beam (ft/m): 50.1/15.30
Draft (ft/m): 13.7/4.20
Propulsion/Propellers: . . . . .diesel
 (5,000kW)/2
Passenger Decks: 5

Total Crew: 72
Passengers
(lower beds/all berths): 81/97
Passenger Space Ratio
(lower beds/all berths): 51.8/43.2
Crew/Passenger Ratio
(lower beds/all berths): 1.1/1.3
Navigation Officers: . . . . .British
Cabins (total): 49
Size Range (sq ft/m): 215.0–365.9/
 20.0–34.0
Cabins (outside view): 49
Cabins (interior/no view): 0
Cabins (for one person): 18

Cabins (with private balcony): 8
Cabins (wheelchair accessible): 0
Cabin Current: . . . . .110/220 volts
Dining Rooms: .1
Elevators: 1
Casino (gaming tables): . . . . .No
Slot Machines: . . . . .No
Swimming Pools (outdoors): 1
Swimming Pools (indoors): 0
Whirlpools: 0
Self-Service Launderette: . . . . .No
Dedicated Cinema/Seats: . . . . .No
Library: . . . . .Yes
Classification Society: . . . .Lloyds Register

OVERALL SCORE: 1,707 (OUT OF A POSSIBLE 2,000 POINTS)

OVERVIEW. *Hebridean Spirit* has a contemporary look, although there is also a traditional single funnel. The navigation bridge is a well-rounded half-moon design. It was one of four identical vessels originally built for Renaissance Cruises, and acquired by Hebridean Island Cruises in November 2000. After being chartered to Star Cruises until March 2001, the ship underwent an extensive redesign and refurbishment program. Its exterior design has been altered somewhat with the addition of an enclosed lounge deck forward of the single funnel, which has been made to look similar to that of smaller (and quite different) and much older sister ship *Hebridean Princess.* An open bridge policy means that passengers can go to the bridge at any time (except during maneuvers or in inclement weather conditions), and may also visit the engine room.

There is one wrap-around teakwood promenade deck outdoors, and a very reasonable amount of open deck and sunbathing space. All of the deck furniture – the tables and chairs – are made of teak and the deck lounge chairs have thick cushioned pads. All exterior handrails are of beautifully polished wood. There is also a teakwood water sports platform at the stern of the ship, where two fine, water-jet driven shore tenders (Ardbeg and Talisker) are located (these have high central rails inside for passengers to hold when standing up). The ship also carries a number of lightweight bicycles (helmets are also provided, and required), for those who like to be independent explorers in ports of call.

Inside the ship, you will find elegant interior design and the touches reminiscent of a small, lavish country house hotel (most of its original furnishings and fittings were removed in a multi-million pound refurbishment

BERLITZ'S RATINGS

	Possible	Achieved
Ship	500	432
Accommodation	200	177
Food	400	350
Service	400	341
Entertainment	N/A	N/A
Cruise	500	407

program when the ship was delivered to Hebridean Island Cruises in 2001). The Skye Lounge is the ship's main lounge, and it has the unmistakable feel of a traditional drawing room; it includes a large, white, Bath stone fireplace with an imitation log fire (safety regulations prohibit a real one). This is the focal point for all social activities and cocktail parties, although it does look a little large considering the size of the room.

Smokers can enjoy their very own (small) Lookout Room, adjacent to the Panorama Lounge (where you'll find internet-connect computer stations), located forward of the funnel, atop the ship. A humidor is provided. There is also a good travel library/reading room.

About a half-dozen bicycles are kept on board for passengers who want to explore independently, otherwise, shore excursions are typically included, and well arranged. Destination lecturers are provided during the cruise.

The ship's itineraries take participants mostly to quiet, off-the-beaten-track ports not often visited by larger cruise ships. So, what is so good about a cruise aboard this ship? It's the faultless, friendly but unobtrusive service, and the attention to detail so lacking in most large ships today. This utterly charming little vessel has a warm, totally cosseted, traditional country house ambience that is unobtrusive but always at hand when you need it. Inspector Hercule Poirot would be very much at home here, as it is rather like a small, exclusive club. The fact that the ship does not have photographers and some of the trappings found aboard larger ships does not matter one bit.

Although the dress code is casual and comfortable, most passengers dress well for dinner; there are typically two formal evenings each cruise when passengers do enjoy dressing in evening dress.

Mid-morning bouillon, afternoon tea with homemade cakes and biscuits (cookies) are a lovely fact of lifestyle aboard this floating country house hotel.

All in all, a cruise aboard *Hebridean Spirit* should prove to be ideal for those who don't like large cruise ships. The service is friendly but unobtrusive; the atmosphere is quiet and sophisticated, and the ship is well run by a crew who are proud to provide the kind of personal service expected by passengers who are intellectual and well-traveled. In fact, a discreet crew and unobtrusive service are hallmarks of the cruise experience aboard this ship.

Hebridean Island Cruises also operates a much smaller, even more intimate sister ship, mainly in the western islands off the coast of Scotland, *Hebridean Princess*. The company's brochure uses only real passengers in its photographs. Children under nine are not accepted on board (the ship really is too small to provide children's facilities).

The onboard currency is the British pound. All gratuities and all soft drinks are included in the fare (the company requests that no additional gratuities be given).

Several pillars (needed for structural support) provide obstructions in some public rooms and hallways. The interior decor consists of plastic woods instead of real woods (it looks almost too perfect in places), although it does work in providing a warm, welcoming ambiance.

SUITABLE FOR: *Hebridean Spirit* is best suited to couples and singles who enjoy learning about nature and the natural sciences, geography, history, gardening, art, architecture, and want to be aboard a very small ship with little or no entertainment. This is ideal for those who would abhor big ship cruising.

ACCOMMODATION. There are five grades of double or twin-bedded cabins, and four grades of cabins for single travellers. The price you pay will depend on the grade, size and location you choose. The cabins (named after glens, isles, castles, and clans) are quite spacious units, measuring between 215 and 365 sq. ft (20–34 sq. meters), including bathrooms and balconies.

This is quite generous for a small ship such as this one. All are decorated in a similar fashion to those aboard *Hebridean Princess*. All have outside views, and most feature wallpapered walls, lighted walk-in closets (one of the two large suites and 24 other cabins only), full-length mirror, dressing table with three-sided vanity mirrors, personalized stationery, tea/coffee-making equipment, combination large-screen color television and DVD player, refrigerator/mini-bar (always stocked with fresh milk and mineral water), direct-dial satellite telephone, personal safe, ironing board, and electric trouser press. The two suites and 14 other cabins have an additional sofa bed.

Naturally, all towels and thick, plush bathrobe are 100% cotton, as is the bed linen, which has traditional sheets and blankets (not duvets), and thick, patterned bedspread. There

are no music channels, and there is no switch to turn announcements off in your cabin.

The bathrooms are of a reasonably decent size, and all are marble clad; they have tiled floors, marble vanities, and shower enclosures (except for "Suite", "Glen" and "Isle" grade cabins, which have a bathtub/shower combination). An abundance of popular Molton Brown personal toiletry items is provided. Note that there is a small step between bedroom and bathroom.

The two largest suites (Saint Columba and Saint Oran) and all balcony cabins feature a combination color television and integral DVD player.

CUISINE/DINING. The Argyll Restaurant is a non-smoking dining room with ocean-view portholes, and operates with table assignments for dinner, in a single seating, and an open seating arrangement for breakfast and lunch. It is a very elegant and pleasant room, with wood paneling, fine furnishings, subtle lighting, and plenty of space around each table. A mix of chairs with and without armrests is provided. There are many tables for two, although there are also tables for four, six, and eight. Tables are always laid with crisp white linen, and ship's officers eat with passengers each night. Villeroy & Boch patterned china is used. Dinner is typically at 7.30 pm. The cuisine is extremely creative – at times outstanding – and about the same quality and presentation (although not quite the variety) as can be found aboard *SeaDream I* and *SeaDream II*.

Fresh ingredients are often purchased locally when possible – a welcome change from the mass catering of most ships. The desserts are worth saving space for. Note that Hebridean Island Cruises operates within European Community regulations concerning genetically modified foods, which are not used aboard *Hebridean Spirit*.

Breakfasts and lunches can also be taken outdoors at the alfresco Mizzen Deck Brasserie, particularly when the ship is operating in warm weather areas. Morning coffee and afternoon tea can be taken in the lounge areas or (weather permitting) on the open decks.

ENTERTAINMENT. The Skye Lounge is the equivalent of a main lounge aboard this small ship. Passengers really like the fact that there is no formal entertainment (the ship does not carry a band), game shows, bingo, horse racing, art auctions, or mindless parlor games – just good company and easy conversation, and very soft, gentle music in the lounges at certain times.

SPA/FITNESS. The Asian-style spa is located at the aft end of Promenade Deck, and is a haven of tranquility and peace. It contains a hairdressing salon, gymnasium, steam room and a relaxation room. It is operated by hand-picked staff from Mandara Spa (a concession that is owned by Steiner Leisure) that are more mature than those found aboard the large cruise ships. Several types of massage are offered, as well as aromatherapy facials, pedicures, manicures, and hairdressing services.

Holiday
★★★ +

Large (Resort) Ship: ....46,052 tons	Total Crew: 660	Cabins (with private balcony): 10
Lifestyle: ....Standard	Passengers	Cabins (wheelchair accessible): 15
Cruise Line: ......Carnival Cruise Lines	(lower beds/all berths): 1,452/1,800	Cabin Current: ....110 volts
Former Names: ....none	Passenger Space Ratio	Elevators: 8
Builder: ......Aalborg Vaerft (Denmark)	(lower beds/all berths): 31.7/25.5	Casino (gaming tables): ....Yes
Original Cost: ....$170 million	Crew/Passenger Ratio	Slot Machines: ....Yes
Entered Service: ....July 1985	(lower beds/all berths): 2.2/2.7	Swimming Pools (outdoors): 3
Registry: ....The Bahamas	Navigation Officers: ....Italian	Swimming Pools (indoors): 0
Length (ft/m): 726.9/221.57	Cabins (total): 726	Whirlpools: 2
Beam (ft/m): 92.4/28.17	Size Range (sq ft/m): 189.2–420.0/	Self-Service Launderette: ....Yes
Draft (ft/m): 25.5/7.77	17.0–39.0	Dedicated Cinema/Seats: ....No
Propulsion/Propellers: ....diesel	Cabins (outside view): 447	Library: ....Yes
(22,360kW)/2	Cabins (interior/no view): 279	Classification Society: ...Lloyd's Register
Passenger Decks: 9	Cabins (for one person): 0	

OVERALL SCORE: 1,252 (OUT OF A POSSIBLE 2,000 POINTS)

OVERVIEW. *Holiday,* the second new ship ordered by Carnival Cruise Lines, is a bold, high-sided, all-white contemporary ship with short, rakish bow and stubby stern typical of so many recently built vessels. The ship, whose bows are extremely short, has the distinctive, large, swept-back wing-tipped funnel that is the trademark of Carnival Cruise Lines, in the company colors of red, white and blue.

BERLITZ'S RATINGS

	Possible	Achieved
Ship	500	331
Accommodation	200	131
Food	400	221
Service	400	258
Entertainment	100	71
Cruise	400	240

Inside, the passenger flow is quite good. There are numerous public rooms on two entertainment decks to choose from and play in, and these flow from a double-width indoor promenade. A real red-and-cream bus is located right in the middle of one of the two promenades, and this is used as a snack Cafe.

The bright (very bright) interior decor has a distinct Broadway theme. The Carnegie Library (which has very few books) is the only public room that is not bright. The casino is good, and there is around-the-clock action. There is plenty of dazzle and sizzle entertainment, while "Camp Carnival" takes care of the junior cruisers (facilities include virtual-reality machines).

This ship, now around 20 years old, is ideal for a first cruise experience in glitzy, very lively surroundings, and for the active set who enjoy constant stimulation, loud music, and a fun-filled atmosphere, at an attractive price. The line does not provide finesse, nor does it claim to. But, forget fashion – having fun is the *sine qua non* of a Carnival cruise. There is no doubt that Carnival does a great job of providing a fun venue, but many passengers say that once is enough, and afterwards you will want to move to a more upscale experience.

Gratuities are automatically added to your onboard account at $9.75 per person, per day; you can have this amount adjusted, although you'll have to visit the information desk to do so. The onboard currency is the US dollar.

A cruise aboard this ship can be noisy and not relaxing at all (although it is good if you enjoy big-city nightlife), with little chance to escape from announcements that intrude (particularly those that bring revenue, such as art auctions, bingo, horse racing), and much hustling for drinks (although this is often done with a knowing smile from the bar waiters, working for gratuities).

SUITABLE FOR: *Holiday* is best suited to first-time young (and young at heart) couples, single passengers, tots, children and teenagers (anyone under 21 must be accompanied by a parent, relative or guardian). They should enjoy big city nightlife, be looking for contemporary, upbeat surroundings, and the latest in facilities, plenty of entertainment lounges and bars and high-tech sophistication. This should come in one neat, highly programmed, well-packaged cruise holiday, with plenty of music, constant activity, and fairly brash entertainment including adult late-night smutty comedy, and food that is acceptable but nothing more (unless you are prepared to pay extra for dining in the "alternative" restaurant), all delivered with friendly service that lacks polish.

ACCOMMODATION. There are 11 differerent grades. The price will depend on the grade, size and location you choose. Carnival Cruise Lines has always tried to provide an adequate amount of space in passenger cabins, and the cabins aboard *Holiday* are no exception. They are quite functional and provide all the basics; bathrooms are practical units, with decent-sized shower stalls.

A gift basket is provided in all grades of accommodation; it includes aloe soap, shampoo, conditioner, deodorant, breath mints, candy, and pain relief tablets (in sample sizes).

If you book accommodation in one of the suites (Category 11 or 12 in the Carnival Cruise Lines brochure) you qualify for "Skipper's Club" priority check-in at any US homeland port – useful for getting ahead of the crowd.

CUISINE/DINING. There are two dining rooms (Four Winds, and Seven Seas); both are large and have low ceilings, making the raised center sections seem crowded (intimate?) and noisy because they are always full. Dining in each restaurant is now in four seatings, for greater flexibility: 6pm, 6.45pm, 8pm and 8.45pm (times are approximate). Carnival meals stress quantity, not quality, although the company constantly works hard to improve the cuisine. However, food is still not the company's strongest points (you get what you pay for, remember).

While the menu items sound good, their presentation and taste may prove disappointing. Meats are of a high quality, but fish and seafood are not. Presentation is simple, and few garnishes are used. Many meat and fowl dishes are disguised with gravies and sauces. The selection of fresh green vegetables, breads, rolls, cheeses and fruits is limited, and there is too much canned fruits and jellied desserts. However, do remember that this is banquet catering, with all its attendant standardization and production cooking (it is, therefore, difficult to ask for anything remotely unusual or off-menu).

Although there is a decent wine list, there are no wine waiters. The service is highly programmed, although the waiters are willing and reasonably friendly. However, the waiters do sing and dance, and there are constant waiter parades; the dining room is show business – all done in the name of eventual gratuities.

The Lido Cafe self-serve buffets are very basic, as is the selection of breads, rolls, fruit and cheeses. At night, the "Seaview Bistro", as the Lido Cafe becomes known, provides a casual (dress down) alternative to eating in the main dining rooms, serving pasta, steaks, salads and desserts (it typically is in operation between 6pm and 9pm).

ENTERTAINMENT. The American Showlounge is the principal venue for large-scale production shows and major cabaret acts (although some pillars obstruct the views from several seats). In a typical 4- or 5-day cruise, there will be one or two, large-scale, trend-setting production shows, with a cast of two lead singers and a clutch of dancers, backed by a live orchestra. These have been the mainstay of Carnival's "we've got the fun" entertainment theme for years. They are of the razzle-dazzle, Las Vegas-style revues that have little or no story line or flow (there's lots of running around on stage and stepping in place, but very little dancing). However, the skimpy costumes are very colorful, as is the lighting (with extensive use of "color mover" lights). Stage smoke appears to be in constant use during the production shows, and volumes are ear-splitting.

With all the audio-visual support staff, dressers, and stage managers, the personnel count comes to almost 40. Other speciality acts take center stage on nights when there is no production show, and late-night adults-only comedy (typically with very blue material and language) is also standard aboard the ships of Carnival Cruise Lines. Carnival rotates entertainers aboard its ships, so passengers see different acts each night.

Almost every lounge/bar has live bands and musical units, so there is always plenty of live music happening (mostly in the evenings).

SPA/FITNESS. SpaCarnival is located on the ship's uppermost deck (Verandah Deck), just aft of the mast, and is accessed by the center stairway and lifts. It has a gymnasium (with some high-tech muscle-pumping cardio-vascular machines) with views over the ship's only swimming pool, men's and women's changing rooms and saunas. The beauty salon is located in another spot, on America Deck, just aft of the Americana Showlounge.

The spa is operated by Steiner, a specialist concession, whose staff will try to sell you Steiner's own-brand Elemis beauty products (spa girls have sales targets). Some fitness classes are free, while some, such as yoga, and kickboxing, cost $10 per class. However, being aboard will give you an opportunity to try some of the more exotic treatments (particularly some of the massages available).

Massage (including exotic massages such as Aroma Stone massage, Chakra Balancing massage and other well-being massages), facials, pedicures, and beauty salon treatments are at extra cost (massage, for example, costs about $2 per minute, plus gratuity).

Do make appointments as early as possible – aboard a ship so large, time slots go quickly.

● **For more extensive general information on what a Carnival cruise is like, see pages 107–111.**

Holiday Dream
★★★ +

Mid-Size Ship: . . . . .37,301 tons	Total Crew: 560	Cabins (wheelchair accessible): 1
Lifestyle: . . . . .Standard	Passengers	Cabin Current: . . . . .110 and 220 volts
Cruise Line: . . . . .Pullmantur Cruises	(lower beds/all berths): 752/1,158	Elevators: 4
Former Names: . . . .*SuperStar Aries,*	Passenger Space Ratio	Casino (gaming tables): . . . . .Yes
SuperStar Europe, Europa	(lower beds/all berths): 49.6/32.2	Slot Machines: . . . . .Yes
Builder: . . . . . . .Bremer Vulkan (Germany)	Crew/Passenger Ratio	Swimming Pools (outdoors): 2
Original Cost: . . . .$120 million	(lower beds/all berths): 1.3/2.0	(1 magrodome)
Entered Service: . . . Jan 1982/June 2004	Navigation Officers: . . . . .European	Swimming Pools (indoors): . . . .
Registry: . . . . .Bahamas	Cabins (total): 376	1 (fresh water)
Length (ft/m): 654.9/199.63	Size Range (sq ft/m): 135.6–683.5/	Whirlpools: 0
Beam (ft/m): 93.8/28.60	12.6–63.5	Self-Service Launderette: . . . . .Yes
Draft (ft/m): 27.6/8.42	Cabins (outside view): 282	Dedicated Cinema/Seats: Yes/238
Propulsion/Propellers: . . . . .diesel	Cabins (interior/no view): 94	Library: . . . . .Yes
(21,270 kW)/2	Cabins (for one person): 0	Classification Society: . . . .Holiday Dream
Passenger Decks: 10	Cabins (with private balcony): 6	

OVERALL SCORE: 1,400 (OUT OF A POSSIBLE 2,000 POINTS)

OVERVIEW. Originally constructed for Hapag-Lloyd Cruises, this was the flagship of the German cruise industry for many years before the company ordered a replacement that came into service in 1999. Star Cruises bought the ship in April 1998 and leased it back to Hapag-Lloyd until 1999, when it went into dry-dock for a $15 million refit and renovation. In 2002 *SuperStar Aries* was moved into Southeast Asia for cruises to Thailand and China. In 2004 it was sold to the Spain-based tour operator Pullmantur Cruises, and underwent some changes to public rooms and dining facilities to accommodate the growing Spanish-speaking market.

The ship has a sponson stern – a kind of "skirt" added in order to comply with stability regulations, although it still maintains its moderately handsome, balanced profile. There is an excellent amount of outdoor deck and sunbathing space, and the ship has both outdoor and outdoor/indoor pools (the latter can be covered by a glass dome). While there is no wrap-around outdoors promenade deck, there are half-length teak port and starboard promenades).

The ship was constructed with a wide range of good-sized public rooms, most with high ceilings that promote a great sense of spaciousness. Restful colors were applied in many public rooms and cabins, and subtle, hidden lighting was used throughout, particularly on the stairways. The public rooms are located aft in a cake-layer stacking, with accommodation located forward, thus separating noisy areas from quieter ones.

Pullmantur Cruises has made changes to some public rooms and open areas, and has added splashes of bright colors, motifs, and new signage. Under the its brand, the hospitality and the range and variety of food have been altered to cater to its Spanish-speaking family clientele. The ship provides a very informal, relaxed setting, with an extremely casual dress code. This ship is the most upscale in the growing Pullmantur Cruises fleet. You will typically find a lot of smokers aboard. The onboard currency is the euro.

BERLITZ'S RATINGS

	Possible	Achieved
Ship	500	382
Accommodation	200	143
Food	400	258
Service	400	288
Entertainment	100	62
Cruise	400	267

SUITABLE FOR: *Holiday Dream* is best suited to young (and young at heart) Spanish-speaking couples, singles, and families with children of all ages who want a first cruise experience in a traditional (not new) ship, with plenty of public rooms and a lively atmosphere, food that is quantity rather than quality, at low cost.

ACCOMMODATION. There is a wide range of suites and cabins, reflecting Pullmantur Cruises' pricing and grading system. All of the original cabins are quite spacious. All have illuminated closets, dark wood cabinetry with rounded edges, several full-length mirrors, color TV and VCR, mini-bar/refrigerator, and personal safe, hairdryer, excellent cabin insulation. There is a small room service menu (for such things as omelets, fried noodles, chicken wings, etc.), and all items cost extra. Most cabins can accommodate one or two additional persons, which mean the ship's original spacious feel has been greatly eroded in order to cater more to families with children.

Most bathrooms have deep tubs (cabins without bathtub have a large shower enclosure), a three-head shower unit, two deep sinks (not all cabins), large toiletries cabinet and handsome personal toiletries. The bath towels, although made of 100% cotton, are a little small.

The largest living spaces are six suites that were added during a 1999 refit. However, because of their location (they were created from what were formerly officers' cabins) they have lifeboat-obstructed views. Six other suites had private balconies added (Beethoven, Handel, Haydn, Mozart, Schubert, Wagner); all have generous living spaces. There is a separate bedroom (with either queen-sized or twin beds), illuminated closets, and vanity desk. The lounge includes a wet bar with refrigerator and glass cabinets and large audio-visual center complete with large-screen TV/VCR and CD player. The marble-clad bathroom has a large shower enclosure, with retractable clothesline.

CUISINE/DINING. The Grand Restaurant is large, with ocean-view windows on two sides, and a good amount of space around each table. There are two seatings for meals. There is also a large, extremely varied self-serve cold table for all meals, with colorful displays of a wide variety of foods. All meals are included in the price. The cuisine is adequate, no more, and dining room service is of a very basic standard – there is absolutely no finesse. Although food is plentiful, there is a limited selection of breads, cheeses and fruits. The wine list is reasonably decent (with many Spanish wines included), and prices are reasonable. Dinner is typically at 8pm and 10.15pm.

For casual meals, self-serve breakfasts, luncheons and supper buffets are provided at the Clipper Buffet, an outdoor area near one of the swimming pools.

ENTERTAINMENT. The Europa Lounge is the venue for entertainment events. The sight lines in the show lounge are quite poor from many of the seats (the room was originally built more for use as a single-level concert salon than a room for shows). However, there really is little entertainment other than live music for social dancing (which is very popular in Southeast Asia), and the occasional cabaret act (vocalists, magicians, comedians).

The shows consist of a troupe of showgirl dancers, whose routines are reminiscent of high-school shows. Cabaret acts are the main feature; these include singers, magicians, and comedians, among others, and very much geared to the family audience that this ship carries for much of the time. There is also plenty of live music for listening or dancing to in various bars and lounges, and there is the inevitable discotheque.

SPA/FITNESS. The spa is really an indoor wellness center. Indeed, the indoor swimming pool aboard this ship is larger than most outdoor pools aboard new, much larger ships. Adjacent facilities include a hot tub, sauna, fitness/exercise centre, a reflexology center, coin-operated solarium, hydrotherapy bath, spa bar, and beauty salon.

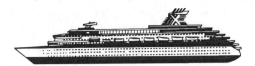

Horizon
★★★★

Large (Resort) Ship: ....46,811 tons	Total Crew: 642	Cabins (with private balcony): 0
Lifestyle: ....Premium	Passengers	Cabins (wheelchair accessible): 4
Cruise Line: ....Celebrity Cruises	(lower beds/all berths): 1,354/1,660	Cabin Current: ....110 volts
Former Names: ....none	Passenger Space Ratio	Elevators: 7
Builder: ....Meyer Werft (Germany)	(lower beds/all berths): 34.5/28.1	Casino (gaming tables): ....Yes
Original Cost: ....$185 million	Crew/Passenger Ratio	Slot Machines: ....Yes
Entered Service: ....May 1990	(lower beds/all berths): 2.1/2.5	Swimming Pools (outdoors): 2
Registry: ....The Bahamas	Navigation Officers: ....Greek	Swimming Pools (indoors): 0
Length (ft/m): 681.1/207.6	Cabins (total): 677	Whirlpools: 0
Beam (ft/m): 95.1/29.0	Size Range (sq ft/m): 172.0–340.0/	Self-Service Launderette: ....No
Draft (ft/m): 23.6/7.2	17.0–31.0	Dedicated Cinema/Seats: ....No
Propulsion/Propellers: ....diesel	Cabins (outside view): 529	Library: ....Yes
(19,960kW)/2	Cabins (interior/no view): 148	Classification Society: ...Lloyd's Register
Passenger Decks: 9	Cabins (for one person): 0	

OVERALL SCORE: 1,536 (OUT OF A POSSIBLE 2,000 POINTS)

OVERVIEW. *Horizon* is a handsome, contemporary ship (it was the first brand-new ship ordered by Celebrity Cruises), with any sharp angles softened by clever exterior styling (blue striping along the ship's hull break up the monotonous all-white exterior of so many of today's ships). There is a good amount of open deck space, and cushioned pads are provided for poolside deck lounge chairs.

BERLITZ'S RATINGS

	Possible	Achieved
Ship	500	397
Accommodation	200	157
Food	400	298
Service	400	317
Entertainment	100	68
Cruise	400	299

Inside, the public rooms are spacious, have high ceilings, and provide very good passenger flow throughout. Elegant furnishings and appointments are the norm, with fine quality fabrics used throughout. Soothing pastel colors are relaxing, but not boring. The wood-paneled casino has a stately look (outside is a satellite-linked BankAtlantic ATM machine, with a $5 access charge).

The two-level showlounge has excellent sight lines from most seats, including the balcony level. There is nothing brash or glitzy about this ship anywhere, although the decor is a little plain and clinical in places. The two-deck-high lobby has a peachy Miami Beach art-deco hotel look. A self-service launderette would have proven useful for longer cruises. Much appreciated by many passengers is the "zero announcement" policy.

An extensive refurbishment in 1998 saw the addition (on Deck 8) of a grand "Michael's Club" cigar-smoking lounge in what was formerly the underused discotheque (it includes a bar, fireplace, extremely comfortable chairs and leather sofas). A new library was added, complete with audio CD listening seats, card room and small business area with two computers/printers for passenger use. Also added, on Deck 7, was a small, delightful art deco-style martini bar (with 26 martinis to choose from). A room dedicated to the display

of artwork (for art auctions) was added. The health spa has also been expanded. This now includes a rasul treatment room, relocated beauty salon, enlarged fitness/exercise areas and five massage and other treatment rooms. A Cova Cafe has replaced what was formerly the Plaza Bar (Cova was the name of the Milan-based coffee house that also makes exclusive chocolates and liqueurs – the original Cova Cafe, located near the La Scala Opera House, opened in 1756). Celebrity Cruises has an exclusive agreement with Pasticceria Confetteria Cova).

Horizon delivers a well-defined North American cruise experience at a very modest price. A 15% gratuity is automatically added to all bar and wine accounts. The onboard currency is the US dollar.

It can be difficult to reach Cabin Service or the Guest Relations Desk by phone (to order breakfast, for example) at peak times, although this is not uncommon aboard large ships. The room service menu is limited, although there is always a good choice of food available at the informal cafe.

Doors to public restrooms and the outdoor decks are heavy (the public restrooms themselves are plain and could do with some warmer decor). Cushioned pads for deck lounge chairs on any other deck except the pool deck are hard to find. Some of the passenger participation activities are quite amateurish.

As we went to press, *Horizon* was expected to undergo a major refit/reconstruction program that will move the navigation bridge forward so that additional cabins can be added. Plans include the addition of balconies to cabins on Bermuda Deck (9), while the spa/fitness area will be expanded, the America's Cup (observation) lounge will be expanded forwards; a new "alternative" restaurant will be added, and public rooms and foyers will be completely redecorated. All cabins will be refurbished (new furniture will be introduced), and bathrooms will be renewed. Until this has been completed (and the ship re-inspected and evaluated), the present scores and rating remain in place.

SUITABLE FOR: *Horizon* is best suited to well-traveled couples and singles of 40 and above (not particularly recommended for children and teenagers) seeking a large ship with a sophisticated environment, good itineraries, fine food and good European-style service from a well-trained crew that cares and delivers an onboard product that is well above average.

ACCOMMODATION. There are 12 grades, including outside-view suites and cabins, and interior (no view) cabins, but even the smallest cabin is considerably larger than most of the standard outside and interior (no view) cabins aboard the ships of sister company Royal Caribbean International. The price you pay will depend on the grade, size and location you choose. Note that no cabins have private balconies (they were not yet in vogue when this ship was constructed). Most outside cabins on Bermuda Deck have lifeboat-obstructed views.

Standard Cabins: All standard outside-view and interior (no view) cabins have good quality fittings with lots of wood accenting, are tastefully decorated and of an above-average size, with an excellent amount of closet and drawer space, and reasonable insulation between cabins. All have twin beds that convert to a queen-sized bed, and a good amount of closet and drawer space. The cabin soundproofing is fair to very good, depending on the location. All accommodation has interactive Celebrity Television, including pay-per-view movies.

The bathrooms have a generous shower area, and a small range of toiletries is provided (typically soap, shampoo/conditioner, body lotion, and shower cap), although bathroom towels are a little small, as is storage space for personal toiletry items. The lowest-grade outside-view cabins have a porthole, but all others have picture windows.

Presidential Suites: The largest accommodation can be found in two Presidential Suites on Atlantic Deck (Deck 10). These have butler service, and have a separate bedroom (with European duvets instead of sheets and blankets) and lounge with dining table, CD player and VCR player in addition to the large TV set. The bathroom is larger and comes with a whirlpool bathtub with integral shower.

Another 18 suites (also on Atlantic Deck) are very tastefully furnished, although they are really just larger cabins and should not be called suites. They are not as large as the suites aboard the company's larger vessels, *Century, Constellation Galaxy, Infinity, Mercury, Millennium,* and *Summit* (but then this ship is also smaller). They do have a generous amount of drawer and other storage space, however, and a sleeping area (with European duvets on the beds instead of sheets and blankets) plus a lounge area. They also have good bathrooms. Butler service is standard.

CUISINE/DINING. Celebrity Cruises has achieved an enviable reputation for providing outstanding quality food, fine presentation and service. The Starlight Restaurant, which also has two "wings" (good for small groups); it is set on a single level with a raised central section, is large, yet feels almost intimate. There are two seatings for dinner (open seating for breakfast and lunch), at tables for two, four, six, eight or 10, and the dining room is a no-smoking area. The chairs do not have armrests, due to space limitations. There are separate menus for vegetarians and children. The wine list is quite extensive, and the prices quite reasonable.

A casual Coral Seas Cafe has decent self-serve buffets for breakfast (including an omelet station) and lunch (including a pasta station and vegetarian salad bar); waiters take your trays of food and escort you to tables. At night, the casual Cafe changes into an alternative dining venue for those who want good food, but in a more casual setting than the main restaurant, with items such as grilled salmon, steaks, and rotisserie chicken, as well as specialities that change frequently (ideal for families with children).

Additionally, an outdoor grill serves fast-food items such as hamburgers and hot dogs. Caviar, at extra cost, is available in the America's Cup Club. For those who can't live without them, freshly baked pizzas (in a box) can be delivered, in an insulated pouch, to your cabin.

ENTERTAINMENT. The two-level Palladium Showlounge/theater with side balconies is a good showlounge. It has a large stage (for this size of ship) and decent lighting and sound equipment. Unfortunately, the production shows are not nearly as lavish. In fact, compared to some of the other major cruise lines, they are a real letdown, and not in keeping with the elegant nature of the interior decor. Bar service, supplied continuously during shows, can prove irritating.

While there are some decent cabaret acts, they are the same ones seen aboard many ships of the major cruise lines. In other words, it is disappointing to note that there is absolutely nothing to distinguish Celebrity Cruises in the entertainment department. The ship does have a number of bands, although there is very little music for social dancing, other than disco and pop music.

SPA/FITNESS. The AquaSpa health and fitness center is located aft of the funnel on Sun Deck. It has a gymnasium with ocean view windows and the latest in high-tech muscle-pump equipment, an exercise area, several therapy treatment rooms, and men's/women's sauna. Note that there is a charge for using the AquaSpa/ sauna/steam room complex unless you are purchasing a spa treatment.

The spa is operated by Steiner, a specialist concession. Some fitness classes are free, while some, such as yoga, and kickboxing, cost $10 per class. Massage, facials, pedicures, and beauty salon treatments cost extra. Examples of treatment costs: well-being massage, $99 (50 minutes); hot stone massage, $158 (90 minutes); facial, $99; seaweed wrap (75 minutes) $171. Personal training sessions in the gymnasium also cost extra. Do make appointments as early as possible as time slots go quickly.

Imagination
★★★ +

Large (Resort) Ship: ....70,367 tons	Total Crew: 920	Cabins (with private balcony): 54
Lifestyle: ....Standard	Passengers	Cabins (wheelchair accessible): 22
Cruise Line: ......Carnival Cruise Lines	(lower beds/all berths): 2,056/2,634	Cabin Current: ....110 volts
Former Names: ....none	Passenger Space Ratio	Elevators: 14
Builder: ...Kvaerner Masa-Yards (Finland)	(lower beds/all berths): 34.4/26.7	Casino (gaming tables): ....Yes
Original Cost: ....$330 million	Crew/Passenger Ratio	Slot Machines: ....Yes
Entered Service: ....July 1995	(lower beds/all berths): 2.2/2.8	Swimming Pools (outdoors): 3
Registry: ....The Bahamas	Navigation Officers: ....Italian	Swimming Pools (indoors): 0
Length (ft/m): 855.0/260.6	Cabins (total): 1,028	Whirlpools: 6
Beam (ft/m): 103.0/31.4	Size Range (sq ft/m): 173.2–409.7/	Self-Service Launderette: ....Yes
Draft (ft/m): 25.9/7.9	16.0–38.0	Dedicated Cinema/Seats: ....No
Propulsion/Propellers: ....diesel-electric	Cabins (outside view): 620	Library: ....Yes
(42,240 kW)/2	Cabins (interior/no view): 408	Classification Society: ...Lloyd's Register
Passenger Decks: 10	Cabins (for one person): 0	

OVERALL SCORE: 1,385 (OUT OF A POSSIBLE 2,000 POINTS)

OVERVIEW. *Imagination* has a forthright, angular appearance typical of today's space-creative designs. This is the fifth in a series of eight identically sized Carnival ships, but actually the ninth new ship for the company (others in the same series are *Ecstasy, Elation, Fantasy, Fascination, Inspiration, Paradise,* and *Sensenation*). Almost vibration-free service is provided by the diesel electric propulsion system. It has proven to be a successful design for this company that targets the standard (mainstream) market, and particularly the first-time passenger.

BERLITZ'S RATINGS

	Possible	Achieved
Ship	500	395
Accommodation	200	151
Food	400	221
Service	400	270
Entertainment	100	81
Cruise	400	267

The ship has expansive open deck areas (sadly, there is no wrap-around open promenade deck), but they quickly become inadequate when it is full and everyone wants to be out on deck (the aft decks tend to be less noisy, whereas all the activities are focused on the main swimming pool and hot tubs). There is a "banked" jogging track outdoors on the deck above a large, glass-enclosed health spa that is always busy. There is a well-defined "topless" sunbathing area around the funnel base on Verandah Deck.

Inside, the ship reflects the talents of interior designer Joe Farcus, whose philosophy is that the cruise ship environment should provide fantasy and an escape from routine with "entertainment architecture." The general passenger flow is good, and the interior design is clever, functional, and extremely colorful. The neon lighting takes a little getting used to at first, as the color combinations are quite vivid (think total sensory stimulation).

The theme of the interior decor is musical muses and classical mythology. The ethereal decor can be found throughout the public rooms, and composers and their compositions (many of the public rooms have musical names),

and the colors, while bright, are less so than aboard some other ships in this series. There is also a $1 million art collection, with many items in public areas featuring some timeless mosaics. There are public entertainment lounges, bars and clubs galore, with something for everyone (except quiet space).

The public rooms, which are connected by a wide indoor boulevard, beat a colorful mix of classic and contemporary design elements that beg your indulgence. As in its sister ships, there is a dramatic six-deck-high atrium (whose balconied shape may remind you of some of the world's great opera houses), appropriately dressed to impress, topped by a large glass dome, and featuring a fascinating, entertaining artistic centerpiece. The large casino has almost non-stop action, as one would expect aboard any Carnival Cruise Lines ship. There is a fine-looking library and reading room, but few books.

Ship buffs will enjoy six Stephen Card paintings of clipper ships, in the Grand Bar. The Victorian-style library is a curious room, with intentionally mismatched furnishings (it reminds one of *Alice in Wonderland*), fine oriental rugs, and even a few books. An ATM machine is located outside the large casino, and all the slot machines aboard all Carnival ships are linked into a Megacash give-away.

ACCOMMODATION. There are 13 grades, prices depending on grade, size and location. The standard outside-view and interior (no view) cabins have decor that is rather plain. They are marginally comfortable, yet spacious enough and practical (most are of the same size and appointments), with good storage space and practical, well-designed no-nonsense bathrooms.

Anyone booking one of the outside suites will find more space, whirlpool bathtubs, and some fascinating, rather eclectic decor and furniture. These are mildly attractive, but nothing special, and they are much smaller than those aboard the ships of a similar size of several competing companies.

A gift basket is provided in all grades of accommodation; it includes aloe soap, shampoo, conditioner, deodorant, breath mints, candy, and pain relief tablets.

If you book accommodation in one of the suites (Category 11 or 12 in the Carnival Cruise Lines brochure) you qualify for "Skipper's Club" priority check-in at any US homeland port – useful for getting ahead of the crowd.

CUISINE/DINING. There are two large, colorful, noisy dining rooms (Pride, located midships, and Spirit, located aft, with the galley between the two). Both are non-smoking. Shorts are permitted in the dining room for one dinner each cruise. Dining in each restaurant is now in four seatings, for greater flexibility: 6pm, 6.45pm, 8pm and 8.45pm (times are approximate) – this should give you some idea what to expect from your dining experience.

The Lido Cafe self-serve buffets are very basic, as is the selection of breads, rolls, fruit and cheeses. At night, the "Seaview Bistro", as the Lido Cafe becomes known, provides a casual (dress down) alternative to eating in the main dining rooms, serving pasta, steaks, salads and desserts (it typically is in operation between 6pm and 9pm). There's also a Pizzeria (this one is open 24 hours a day and typically serves over 500 every single day).

ENTERTAINMENT. The Dynasty Showlounge is the principal venue for large-scale production shows and major cabaret acts (although 20 pillars obstruct the views from several seats).

SPA/FITNESS. The Nautica Spa is a large health, fitness and spa complex consisting of a gymnasium with ocean-view windows, an aerobics exercise room, men's and women's changing rooms, sauna and steam rooms, and beauty salon. A common complaint from passengers is that there are not enough staff to keep the area clean and tidy, and used towels are often strewn around the changing rooms (particularly on the men's side).

● **For more extensive general information on what a Carnival cruise is like, see pages 107–111.**

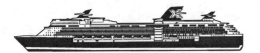

Infinity
★★★★ +

Large (Resort) Ship: ....90,228 tons	Total Crew: 999	Cabins (wheelchair accessible): 26
Lifestyle: ....Premium	Passengers	(17 with private balcony)
Cruise Line: ....Celebrity Cruises	(lower beds/all berths): 1,950/2,450	Cabin Current: ....110 and 220 volts
Former Names: ....none	Passenger Space Ratio	Elevators: 10
Builder: ....Chantiers de l'Atlantique	(lower beds/all berths): 46.2/36.8	Casino (gaming tables): ....Yes
(France)	Crew/Passenger Ratio	Slot Machines: ....Yes
Original Cost: ....$350 million	(lower beds/all berths): 1.9/2.4	Swimming Pools (outdoors): 2
Entered Service: ....Mar 2001	Navigation Officers: ....Greek	Swimming Pools (indoors): 1
Registry: ....The Bahamas	Cabins (total): 975	(with magrodome)
Length (ft/m): 964.5/294.0	Size Range (sq ft/m): 165.1–2,530.0/	Whirlpools: 4
Beam (ft/m): 105.6/32.2	15.34–235.0	Self-Service Launderette: ....No
Draft (ft/m): 26.2/8.0	Cabins (outside view): 780	Dedicated Cinema/Seats: Yes/368
Propulsion/Propellers: .....gas turbine/2	Cabins (interior/no view): 195	Library: ....Yes
azimuthing pods (39,000 kW)	Cabins (for one person): 0	Classification Society: ...Lloyd's Register
Passenger Decks: 11	Cabins (with private balcony): 590	

OVERALL SCORE: 1,697 (OUT OF A POSSIBLE 2,000 POINTS)

OVERVIEW. *Infinity* is a sister ship to *Constellation, Millennium* and *Summit.* Jon Bannenberg (famous for his mega-yacht designs) designed the exterior that features a royal blue and white hull, and racy lines in red, blue and gold. This is the second Celebrity Cruises ship to be fitted with a "pod" propulsion system *(see page 151)* coupled with a quiet, smokeless, energy-efficient gas turbine powerplant (two GE gas turbines provide engine power while a single GE steam turbine drives the electricity generators).

One neat feature is a conservatory that includes seating, set in a botanical environment of flowers, plants, trees, mini-gardens and fountains, designed by the award-winning floral designer Emilio Robba of Paris. It is located directly in front of the main funnel and has glass walls that overlook the ship's side. It has fresh flowers for any occasion, and a selection of Emilio Robba glass and flower creations, as well as pot pourri and other flora and fauna items.

Inside, the ship features the same high-class decor and materials, and public rooms that have made the existing ships in the fleet so popular and user-friendly. But in a first for Celebrity Cruises, the atrium spans 11 decks. It is capped with a glass dome, and four glass elevators travel through the port side of the atrium.

Facilities include a combination Cinema and Conference Center, an expansive shopping arcade with a 14,447 sq.-ft (1,300 sq.-meter) retail store space (including H. Stern, Donna Karan, Fossil, and the exclusive Michel Roux culinary store), a lavish four-decks-high showlounge with the latest in staging and lighting equipment, two-level library (one level for English-language books; a second level for

BERLITZ'S RATINGS

	Possible	Achieved
Ship	500	454
Accommodation	200	180
Food	400	327
Service	400	330
Entertainment	100	78
Cruise	400	328

books in other languages); card room; compact disc listening room; art auction center (with seating that look rather more like a small chapel); Cosmos, a combination observation lounge/discotheque; an Internet Center with 18 computer stations. Michael's Club (originally a cigar smoker's haven), is now a piano lounge/bar.

Gaming sports include the ship's overly large Fortunes Casino, with blackjack, roulette, and slot machines, and lots of bright lights and action. Families with children will like the Fun Factory (for young children) and The Tower (for teenagers). Children's counselors and youth activities staff provide a wide range of supervised activities.

New management was brought in during the past couple of years to restore Celebrity Cruises to the premium product envisioned when the company first started, and the improvements introduced in 2003 have restored the art of hospitality and provide a taste of luxury for all. For example, on days at sea (in warm weather areas) if you are sunbathing on deck, someone will bring you a cold towel, and a sorbet, ice water and iced tea. Little touches like this differentiate Celebrity Cruises from other major cruise lines.

A cruise aboard a large ship such as this provides a wide range of choices and possibilities. If you travel in one of the suites, the benefits provide you with the highest level of personal service, while cruising in non-suite accommodation is almost like in any large ship – you'll be one of a number, with little access to the niceties and benefits of "upper class" cruising. It all depends how much you are willing to pay. The onboard currency is the US dollar. A 15% gratuity is added to bar and wine accounts. The ship's two-seating dining and two shows sadly detract from an otherwise excellent product.

There is, sadly, no wrap-around wooden promenade deck outdoors. There are cushioned pads for poolside deck lounge chairs only, but not for chairs on other outside decks. Trying to reach Cabin Service or the Guest Relations Desk to answer the phone (to order breakfast, for example, if you don't want to do so via the interactive television) is a matter of luck, timing and patience.

ACCOMMODATION. There are 20 different price grades. Almost half of the ship's accommodation features a "private" balcony; approximately 80% are outside-view suites and cabins, and 20 percent are interior (no view) cabins. The accommodation is extremely comfortable throughout this ship. Suites, naturally, have more space, butler service (whether you want it or not), more and better amenities and more personal service than any of the standard cabin grades. There are several categories of suites, but those at the stern of the ship are in a prime location and have huge balconies that are very private and not overlooked from above.

All suites and cabins have wood cabinetry and accenting, interactive television and entertainment systems (you can go shopping, book shore excursions, play casino games, interactively, and even watch soft porn movies). Bathrooms have hairdryers, and 100% cotton towels.

Penthouse Suites: Two Penthouse Suites (on Penthouse Deck) are the largest accommodation aboard. Each occupies one half of the beam (width) of the ship, overlooking the ship's stern. Each measures a huge 2,530 sq. ft (235 sq. meters): 1,431.6 sq. ft (133 sq. meters) of living space, plus a huge wrap-around balcony measuring 1,098 sq. ft (102 sq, meters) with 180° views, which occupies one half of the beam (width) of the ship, overlooking the stern (it includes a wet bar, hot tub and whirlpool tub); however, much of this terrace can be overlooked from other decks above.

Features include a marble foyer, a separate living room (complete with ebony baby grand piano – bring your own pianist if you don't play yourself) and a formal dining room. The master bedroom has a large walk-in closet; personal exercise equipment; dressing room with vanity desk; exercise equipment; marble-clad master bathroom with twin washbasins; deep whirlpool bathtub; separate shower; toilet and bidet areas; flat-screen televisions (one in the bedroom and one in the lounge); and electronically controlled drapes. Butler service is standard, and a butler's pantry, with separate entry door, features a full-size refrigerator, temperature-controlled wine cabinet, microwave oven and good-sized food preparation and storage areas. For even more space, an interconnecting door can be opened into the adjacent suite.

Royal Suites: Eight Royal Suites, each measuring 733 sq. ft (68 sq. meters), are located towards the aft of the ship (four each on the port and starboard sides). Each features a separate living room with dining and lounge areas (with refrigerator, mini-bar and a Bang & Olufsen CD sound system), and a separate bedroom. There are two entertainment centers with DVD players, and two flat-screen televisions (one in the living area, one in the bedroom), and a large walk-in closet with vanity desk. The marble-clad bathroom has a

whirlpool bathtub with integral shower, and there is also a separate shower enclosure, two washbasins and toilet. The teakwood decked balcony is extensive (large enough for on-deck massage) and also features a whirlpool hot tub.

Celebrity Suites: Eight Celebrity Suites, each measuring 467 sq. ft (44 sq. meters), have floor-to-ceiling windows, a separate living room with dining and lounge areas, two entertainment centers with flat-screen televisions (one in the living room, one in the bedroom), and a walk-in closet with vanity desk. The marble-clad bathroom has a whirlpool bathtub with integral shower (a window with movable shade lets you look out of the bathroom through the lounge to the large ocean-view windows). Interconnecting doors allow two suites to be used as a family unit (as there is no balcony, these suites are ideal for families with small children). These suites overhang the starboard side of the ship (they are located opposite a group of glass-walled elevators), and provide stunning ocean views from the glass-walled sitting/dining area, which extends out from the ship's side. A personal computer with wood-surround screen allows direct internet connectivity. Butler service is standard.

Sky Suites: There are 30 Sky Suites, each measuring 308 sq. ft (28.6 sq. meters), including the private balcony (some balconies may be larger than others, depending on the location). Although these are designated as suites, they are really just larger cabins that feature a marble-clad bathroom with bathtub/shower combination. The suites also have a VCR player in addition to a television, and have a larger lounge area and sleeping area than standard cabins. Butler service is standard.

Butler Service: Butler service (in all accommodation designated as suites) includes full breakfast, in-suite lunch and dinner service (as required), afternoon tea service, evening hors d'oeuvres, complimentary espresso and cappuccino, daily news delivery, and shoeshine service.

Suite occupants in Penthouse, Royal, Celebrity and Sky suites also get welcome champagne; a full personal computer in each suite, including a printer and internet access (on request in the Sky Suites); choice of films from a video library; personalized stationery; tote bag; priority dining room seating preferences; private portrait sitting; bathrobe; and in-suite massage service.

Concierge Class: In 2003, Celebrity Cruises added a third service "class" to some of the accommodation grades aboard this ship. Positioned between the top grade suite grades and standard cabin grades, Concierge Class adds value to these "middle-class" cabins.

Enhanced facilities include priority embarkation, disembarkation, tender tickets, alternative dining and spa reservations. Here's what you get in the Concierge Class cabins that others don't (except for the suites): European duvet; double bed overlay (no more falling "between the cracks" for couples); choice of four pillows (goose down pillow, isotonic pillow, body pillow, conformance pillow); eight-vial flower vase on vanity desk; throw pillows on sofa; fruit basket; binoculars; golf umbrella; leather telephone notepad; larger beach towels; hand-held hairdryer. The balcony gets better furniture. In the bathrooms: plusher Frette bathrobes; larger towels in sea green and pink (alternating days); flower in silver vase. It all adds up to excellent value for money.

Standard Outside-View/Interior (No View) Cabins: All other outside-view and interior (no view) cabins feature a lounge area with sofa or convertible sofa bed, sleeping area with twin beds that can convert to a double bed, a good amount of closet and drawer space, personal safe, mini-bar/refrigerator (extra cost), interactive television, and private bathroom. The cabins are nicely decorated with warm wood-finish furniture, and there is none of the boxy feel of cabins in so many ships, due to the angled placement of vanity and audio-video consoles. Even the smallest cabin has a good-sized bathroom and shower enclosure.

Wheelchair-Accessible Accommodation: Wheelchair-accessible accommodation is available in six Sky Suites, three premium outside-view, eight deluxe ocean-view, four standard ocean-view and five interior (no view) cabins measure 347 sq. ft to 362 sq. ft (32.2–33.6 sq. meters) and are located in the most practical parts of the ship and close to elevators for good accessibility (all doorways and bathroom doorways and showers are wheelchair-accessible). Some cabins have extra berths for third or third and fourth occupants (note, however, that there is only one safe for personal belongings, which must be shared).

CUISINE/DINING. The Thellis Restaurant is the ship's 1,170-seat formal dining room. It is two decks high, has a grand staircase connecting the two levels, a huge glass wall overlooking the sea at the stern of the ship (electrically operated shades provide several different backdrops), and a musician's gallery on the upper level (typically for a string quartet/quintet). There are two seatings for dinner (open seating for breakfast and lunch), at tables for two, four, six, eight or 10. The dining room is a totally no-smoking area, and, you should note, that, like all large dining halls, it can prove to be extremely noisy. The menu variety is good, the food has taste, and it is very attractively presented and served in a well orchestrated operation that displays fine European traditions and training. Full service in-cabin dining is also available for all meals (including dinner).

Besides this principal restaurant, there are several other dining options, particularly for those seeking more casual dining, or for an extra-special (extra cost) meal in a more intimate (and quiet) setting. Full service in-cabin dining is also available for all meals (including dinner).

For casual eating, the Las Olas Café and Grill is a self-serve buffet area, with six principal serving lines, and seating for 754; there is also a grill and pizza bar. For champagne and caviar lovers, not to mention martinis, Carlisle's is the place to see and be seen.

Alternative (Reservations-Only, Extra Cost) Dining Option: The United States Restaurant is the ship's alternative dining salon, located adjacent to the main lobby. Actual glass panelling from the former United States Lines liner *United States* is featured (in 1952, the *United States* gained renown for the fastest transatlantic crossing by a passenger ship, and took the famed "Blue Riband" from the Cunard liner *Queen Mary*). The United States Restaurant is not nearly as luxurious as the alternative dining salons aboard sister ships *Constellation*, *Millennium* or *Summit*.

A team of 10 chefs prepares the cuisine exclusively for this restaurant. Fine tableside preparation is the attraction of this alternative dining room, whose classic French cuisine (but including some menu items from the *United States*) and service are outstanding (masterminded by Michel Roux, owner of a three-star Michelin restaurant near Windsor in England). This is haute cuisine at the height of professionalism, for this is, indeed, a room for a full degustation, and not merely a dinner. However, with just 134 seats, not all passengers will be able to experience it even once during a one-week cruise (reservations are necessary, and a cover charge of $25 per person applies). A dine-in wine cellar is also a feature, as is a demonstration galley.

Additionally, a Cova Café di Milano (with 92 seats) is a signature item aboard all the ships of Celebrity Cruises, and a seagoing version of the real Café di Milano that was originally located next to La Scala Opera House in Milan. It is located in a prominent position, on the second level of the atrium lobby, and several display cases show off the extensive range of Cova coffee, chocolates and alcoholic digestives; this is the place to see and be seen. The Cova Café is for anyone who appreciates fine Italian coffees (for espresso, espresso macchiato, cappuccino, and latte), pastries and superb cakes in an elegant, refined setting. The breakfast pastries are really superb (the favorite seems to be Italy's pane con cioccolata – chocolate pastry).

ENTERTAINMENT. The 900-seat Celebrity Theater is the three-deck-high venue for production shows and major cabaret acts. It is located in the forward part of the ship, with seating on main, and two balcony levels. The large stage has a full fly loft behind its traditional proscenium.

SPA/FITNESS. There is a large AquaSpa measuring 24,219 sq. ft (2,250 sq. meters). It features a large thalassotherapy pool under a huge solarium dome, complete with health bar for light breakfast and lunch items and fresh squeezed fruit and vegetable juices. Spa facilities include 16 treatment rooms, plus eight treatment rooms with showers and one treatment room specifically designed for wheelchair passengers, aerobics room, gymnasium (complete with over 40 exercise machines), large men's and women's saunas (with large ocean-view porthole window), a unisex thermal suite (containing several steam and shower mist rooms with different fragrances such as chamomile, eucalyptus and mint, and a glacial ice fountain), and beauty salon. The spa is operated by Steiner, a specialist concession. Sports facilities include a full-size basketball court, compact football, paddle tennis and volleyball, golf simulator, shuffleboard (on two different decks) and a jogging track.

● **For more extensive general information on what a Celebrity cruise is like, see pages 111–115.**

Insignia
★★★★ +

Mid-Size Ship: ....30,277 tons	Passengers	Cabin Voltage: ....110 and 220
Lifestyle: ....Premium	(lower beds/all berths): 684/824	Elevators: 4
Cruise Line: ....Oceania Cruises	Passenger Space Ratio	Casino (gaming tables): ....Yes
Former Names: R1	(lower beds/all berths): 44.2/36.7	Slot Machines: ....Yes
Builder: ....Chantiers de l'Atlantique	Crew/Passenger Ratio	Swimming Pools (outdoors): 1
Original Cost: ....$150 million	(lower beds/all berths): 1.7/2.1	Swimming Pools (indoors): 0
Entered Service: .....July 1998/Apr 2004	Navigation Officers: ....European	Whirlpools: ......2 (+ 1 thalassotherapy)
Registry: ....Marshall Islands	Cabins (total): 342	Fitness Centre: ....Yes
Length (ft/m): 593.7/181.0	Size Range (sq ft/m): .....145.3 – 968.7/	Sauna/Steam Room: ....No/Yes
Beam (ft/m): 83.5/25.5	13.5 – 90.0	Massage: ....Yes
Draft (ft/m): 19.5/6.0	Cabins (outside view): 317	Self-Service Launderette: ....Yes
Propulsion/Propellers: ....diesel	Cabins (interior/no view): 25	Dedicated Cinema/Seats: ....No
(18,600 kW)/2	Cabins (for one person): 0	Library: ....Yes
Passenger Decks: 9	Cabins (with private balcony): 232	Classification Society: ....Bureau Veritas
Total Crew: 386	Cabins (wheelchair accessible): 0	

OVERALL SCORE: 1,553 (OUT OF A POSSIBLE 2,000 POINTS)

OVERVIEW. *Insignia* (sister to *Regatta*) was one of a series of almost identical ships originally built for the now-defunct Renaissance Cruises. The ship's present owners (Cruiseinvest) have chartered the ship to new company Oceania Cruises. The exterior design manages to balance the ship's high sides by painting the whole ship white (it previously had a dark blue hull), with a large, square white funnel. The addition of teak overlaid decking and teak lounge chairs has greatly improved what was a bland pool deck outdoors.

The interior decor is quite stunning, a throwback to ship decor of the ocean liners of the 1920s and '30s, with dark woods and warm colors, all carried out in fine taste (but a bit faux in places). This includes detailed ceiling cornices, both real and faux wrought-iron staircase railings, leather-paneled walls, trompe l'oeil ceilings, rich carpeting in hallways with an Oriental rug-look center section, and many other interesting (and expensive-looking) decorative touches. It feels like an old-world country club.

The public rooms are spread over three decks. The reception hall (lobby) features a staircase with intricate wrought-iron railings. A large observation lounge, the Horizon Bar, is located high atop ship. This has a long bar with forward views (for the barmen, that is).

There are plenty of bars – including one in each of the restaurant entrances. Perhaps the nicest is the casino bar/lounge, a beautiful room which is reminiscent of London's grand hotels and includes a martini bar. It has an inviting marble fireplace, comfortable sofas and individual chairs.

The Library is a grand Regency-style room, with a fire-

BERLITZ'S RATINGS

	Possible	Achieved
Ship	500	415
Accommodation	200	155
Food	400	304
Service	400	295
Entertainment	100	76
Cruise	400	308

place, a high, indented, trompe l'oeil ceiling, and excellent selection of books, plus very comfortable wingback chairs with footstools, and sofas you could sleep on. Oceania@Sea is the ship's internet connect center.

There may not be marble bathroom fittings, or caviar and other expensive niceties, but the value for money is extremely good. The dress code is "smart casual." The onboard currency is the US dollar. Gratuities are added at $10.50 per person, per day (accommodation designated as suites have an extra $3 per person charge for the butler). A 15% gratuity is added to bar and spa accounts.

There is no wrap-around promenade deck outdoors (there is, however, a small jogging track around the perimeter of the swimming pool, and port and starboard side decks). Stairways, though carpeted, are tinny. The staircase in the main, two-deck-high foyer will remind you of something similar in the 1998 blockbuster movie *Titanic*.

Oceania Cruises is a young company with a refreshing vision and desire to provide an extremely high level of food and service in an informal setting that is at once elegant yet comfortable, and that is exactly what it has achieved in a short space of time.

SUITABLE FOR: *Insignia* is best suited to couples who like good food and style, but want informality with no formal nights on board, and interesting itineraries, all at a very reasonable price well below what the luxury ships charge.

ACCOMMODATION. There are six cabin categories, and 10 price grades (3 suite price grades; 5 outside-view cabin grades; 2 interior (no view) cabin grades. All of the standard interior (no view) and outside-view cabins (the lowest four grades) are extremely compact units, and extremely tight for two persons (particularly for cruises longer than five days). They have twin beds (or queen-sized bed), with good under-bed storage areas, personal safe, vanity desk with large mirror, good closet and drawer space (in rich, dark woods), 100% cotton bathrobe and towels, slippers, clothes brush and shoe horn. Color TVs carry a major news channel (where obtainable), plus a sports channel and round-the-clock movie channels.

Certain cabin categories (about 100 of them) qualify as "Concierge Level" accommodation, and occupants get extra goodies such as enhanced bathroom amenities, complimentary shoeshine, tote bag, cashmere throw blanket, bottle of champagne on arrival, hand-held hairdryer, priority restaurant reservations, priority embarkation and dedicated check-in desk,

Owner's Suites. The six Owner's Suites, measuring 962 sq.ft/89.3 sq.meters, provide the most spacious accommodation. They are fine, large living spaces located aft overlooking the stern on Decks 6, 7, and 8 (they are, however, subject to more movement and some vibration). They have extensive teak-floor private balconies that really are private and cannot be overlooked from the decks above. Each has an entrance foyer, living room, separate bedroom (the bed faces the sea, which can be seen through the floor-to-ceiling windows and sliding glass door), CD player (with selection of audio discs), fully tiled bathroom with Jacuzzi bathtub, and a small guest bathroom.

Vista Suites. There are four, each around 785.7 sq.ft/73 sq.meters, and located forward on Decks 5 and 6. They have extensive teak-floor private balconies that cannot be overlooked from the decks above. Each has an entrance foyer, living room, separate bedroom (the bed faces the sea, which can be seen through the floor-to-ceiling windows and sliding glass door), CD player (with selection of audio discs), and fully tiled bathroom with Jacuzzi bathtub.

Penthouse Suites. There are 52 of these (actually, they are not suites at all, but large cabins as the bedrooms aren't separate from the living areas). They do, however, measure around 322.9 sq.ft (30 sq. meters), and have a good-sized teak-floor balcony with sliding glass door (but with partial, and not full, balcony partitions) and teak deck furniture. The lounge area has a proper dining table and there is ample clothes storage space. The bathroom has a tub, shower enclosure, washbasin and toilet.

Cabins with Balcony. Cabins with private balconies (around 216 sq.ft/20 sq. meters), comprise about 66% of all cabins. They have partial, not full, balcony partitions, sliding glass doors, and only 14 cabins on Deck 6 have lifeboat-obstructed views. The living area has a refrigerated mini-bar, lounge area with breakfast table, and a balcony with teak floor, two teak chairs and a drinks table. The bathrooms, with tiled floors and plain walls, are compact, standard units, and include a shower stall with a strong, removable hand-held shower unit, hairdryer, toiletries storage shelves and retractable clothesline.

Outside View and Interior (No View) Cabins. These measure around 160–165 sq.ft (14.8–15.3 sq.meters), and have twin beds (convertible to a queen-sized bed), vanity desk, small sofa and coffee table, and bathroom with a shower enclosure with a strong, removable hand-held shower unit, hairdryer, toiletries storage shelves, retractable clothesline, washbasin, and toilet. Although they are not large, they are quite comfortable, with decent storage space.

CUISINE/DINING. Flexibility and choice are what the dining facilities aboard the Oceania ships are all about. There are four different restaurants:
● The **Grand Dining Room** has around 340 seats, and a raised central section, but the problem is the noise level: it's atrocious when the dining room is full – the effect of the low ceiling height. Being located at the ship's stern, there are large ocean-view windows on three sides (prime tables overlook the stern). The chairs are comfortable and have armrests. The menus change daily for lunch and dinner.
● The **Toscana Italian Restaurant** has 96 seats, windows along two sides, and a set menu (plus daily chef's specials).
● The cozy **Polo Grill** has 98 seats, windows along two sides and a set menu including prime steaks and seafood.
● The **Terrace Cafe** has seats for 154 indoors – not enough during cruises to cold-weather areas – and 186 outdoors. It is open for breakfast, lunch and casual dinners, when it has tapas (Tapas on the Terrace) and other Mediterranean food. As the ship's self-serve buffet restaurant, it incorporates a small pizzeria and grill. There are basic salads, a meat carving station, and a reasonable selection of cheeses.

All restaurants have open-seating dining, so you can dine when you want, with whom you wish. Reservations are needed in Toscana Restaurant and Polo Grill (but there's no extra charge), where there are mostly tables for four or six; there are few tables for two. There is a Poolside Grill Bar. All cappuccino and espresso coffees cost extra.

The food and service staff is provided by Apollo, a respected maritime catering company that has an interest in Oceania Cruises. The consultant chef is Jacques Pepin (well-known as a TV chef in America). Oceania Cruises' brochure reference to "cuisine so extraordinary it's unrivalled at sea" is hogwash – it's good, but not that good.

ENTERTAINMENT. The Regatta Lounge has entertainment, lectures and some social events. There is little entertainment due to the intensive nature of the itineraries. However, there is live music in several bars and lounges.

SPA/FITNESS/RECREATION. A lido deck has a swimming pool, and good sunbathing space, plus a thalassotherapy tub. A jogging track circles the swimming pool deck (but one deck above.) The uppermost outdoors deck includes a golf driving net and shuffleboard court. The Oceania Spa consists of a beauty salon, three treatment rooms, men's and women's changing rooms, and steam room (there is no sauna). Harding Brothers operates the spa and beauty salon, and provides the staff. Note that 15% is added to your spa account, whether you like it or not.

Inspiration
★★★ +

Large (Resort) Ship: ....70,367 tons	Total Crew: 920	Cabins (with private balcony): 54
Lifestyle: ....Standard	Passengers	Cabins (wheelchair accessible): 22
Cruise Line: ......Carnival Cruise Lines	(lower beds/all berths): 2,056/2,634	Cabin Current: ....110 volts
Former Names: ....none	Passenger Space Ratio	Elevators: 14
Builder: ...Kvaerner Masa-Yards (Finland)	(lower beds/all berths): 34.4/26.7	Casino (gaming tables): ....Yes
Original Cost: ....$270 million	Crew/Passenger Ratio	Slot Machines: ....Yes
Entered Service: ....Apr 1996	(lower beds/all berths): 2.2/2.8	Swimming Pools (outdoors): 3
Registry: ....The Bahamas	Navigation Officers: ....Italian	Swimming Pools (indoors): 0
Length (ft/m): 855.0/260.6	Cabins (total): 1,028	Whirlpools: 6
Beam (ft/m): 103.0/31.4	Size Range (sq ft/m): 173.2–409.7/	Self-Service Launderette: ....Yes
Draft (ft/m): 25.9/7.9	16.0–38.0	Dedicated Cinema/Seats: ....No
Propulsion/Propellers: .....diesel-electric	Cabins (outside view): 620	Library: ....Yes
(42,240 kW)/2	Cabins (interior/no view): 408	Classification Society: ...Lloyd's Register
Passenger Decks:.................10	Cabins (for one person): 0	

OVERALL SCORE: 1,385 (OUT OF A POSSIBLE 2,000 POINTS)

OVERVIEW. *Inspiration* is the 10th new ship for this very successful cruise line (others in the same series include *Ecstasy, Elation, Fantasy, Fascination, Imagination, Paradise,* and *Sensation*). The vessel, whose bows are extremely short, has the distinctive, large, swept-back wing-tipped funnel that is the trademark of Carnival Cruise Lines, in the company colors of red, white and blue. Almost vibration-free service is provided by the diesel electric propulsion system. It has proven to be a successful design for this company that targets the standard (mainstream) market, and particularly the first-time passenger.

The ship, whose bows are extremely short, has the distinctive, large, swept-back wing-tipped funnel that is the trademark of Carnival Cruise Lines, in the company colors of red, white and blue. The ship has expansive open deck areas (sadly, there is no wrap-around open promenade deck), but they quickly become inadequate when it is full and everyone wants to be out on deck (the aft decks tend to be less noisy, whereas all the activities are focused on the main swimming pool and hot tubs). There is also a "banked" jogging track outdoors on the deck above a large, glass-enclosed health spa. A well-defined "topless" sunbathing area can be found around the funnel base on Verandah Deck.

Inside, the ship reflects the talents of interior designer Joe Farcus, whose philosophy is that the cruise ship environment should provide fantasy and an escape from routine with "entertainment architecture." The general passenger flow is good, and the interior design is clever, functional, and extremely colorful. The neon lighting takes a little getting used to at first, as the color combinations are quite vivid

BERLITZ'S RATINGS

	Possible	Achieved
Ship	500	395
Accommodation	200	151
Food	400	221
Service	400	270
Entertainment	100	81
Cruise	400	267

(think total sensory stimulation). There is also a $1 million art collection. Particularly fascinating is an avant-garde rendition of the famed Mona Lisa, in Pablo's Lounge. The decor itself is themed after the arts (in an art nouveau style) and literature. There are public entertainment lounges, bars and clubs galore, with something for everyone (except quiet space).

The public rooms, which are connected by a wide indoor boulevard, beat a colorful mix of classic and contemporary design elements that beg your indulgence. As in its sister ships, there is a dramatic six-deck-high atrium (whose balconied shape may remind you of some of the world's great opera houses), appropriately dressed to impress, topped by a large glass dome, and featuring a fascinating, entertaining artistic centerpiece. The atrium has scrolled shapes resembling the necks and heads of violins, and a marble staircase. The large casino has almost non-stop action. There is a fine-looking library and reading room, but few books.

The Shakespeare Library is a fine, stately room (25 of his quotations adorn the oak veneer. Another dazzling room is the Rock and Roll Discotheque, with its guitar-shaped dance floor and video dance club and dozens of video monitors around the room. The ship also has a lavish, multi-tiered showlounge (although some 20 pillars cause some seats to have obstructed sight lines) and high-energy razzle-dazzle shows. The casino is large, but always humming with hopeful action.

ACCOMMODATION. There are 13 grades. The price you pay will depend on the grade, size and location you choose. The standard outside-view and interior (no view) cabins have decor that is rather plain and unmemorable. They are marginally comfortable, yet spacious enough and practical (most are of the same size and appointments), with good storage space and practical, well-designed no-nonsense bathrooms. Anyone booking one of the outside suites will find more space, whirlpool bathtubs, and some fascinating, rather eclectic decor and furniture. These are mildly attractive, but nothing special, and they are much smaller than those aboard the ships of a similar size of several competing companies. A gift basket is provided in all grades of accommodation; it includes aloe soap, shampoo, conditioner, deodorant, breath mints, candy, and pain relief tablets (albeit all in sample sizes).

If you book accommodation in one of the suites (Category 11 or 12 in the Carnival Cruise Lines brochure) you qualify for "Skipper's Club" priority check-in at any US homeland port – useful for getting ahead of the crowd.

CUISINE/DINING. There are two large, rather noisy – or perhaps one should say "lively" – dining rooms (Mardi Gras, located midships, and Carnival, located aft, with the galley between them), both of which are non-smoking. The service is attentive, but far too fast and assertive, and lacks any kind of finesse. Dining in each restaurant is now in four seatings, for greater flexibility: 6pm, 6.45pm, 8pm and 8.45pm (these times are approximate).

Carnival meals stress quantity, not quality, although the company constantly works hard to improve the cuisine. However, food and its taste are still not the company's strongest points (you get what you pay for, remember).

Casual meals can be taken at informal food outlets such as the Brasserie Bar and Grill, which also includes a Pizzeria (open 24 hours a day – it typically serves over 500 every single day). At night, the "Seaview Bistro", as the Lido Café becomes known, provides a casual (dress down) alternative to eating in the main dining rooms, serving pasta, steaks, salads and desserts (it typically is in operation from 6pm to 9pm).

ENTERTAINMENT. The Paris Showlounge is the principal venue for large-scale production shows and major cabaret acts (although 20 pillars obstruct views from some seats).

SPA/FITNESS. The Nautica Spa is a large health, fitness and spa complex on the uppermost interior deck, forward of the ship's mast, and accessed from the forward stairway. It consists of a gymnasium with oceanview windows that look out over the ship's bow (it features a large array of the latest in muscle-pumping electronic machines), an aerobics exercise room, men's and women's changing rooms, sauna and steam rooms, and beauty salon.

A common complaint to me from passengers is that cleanliness and tidiness leave much to be desired (used towels are often left strewn around the changing rooms, particularly on the men's side).

● **For more extensive general information on what a Carnival cruise is like, see pages 107–111.**

Island Escape
★★★ +

Large (Resort) Ship:	.40,132 tons	Total Crew:	.540	Cabins (with private balcony):	.5
Lifestyle:	.Standard	Passengers		Cabins (wheelchair accessible):	.3
Cruise Line:	.Island Cruises	(lower beds/all berths):	.1,504/1,710	Cabin Current:	.110 volts
Former Names:	.Viking Serenade,	Passenger Space Ratio		Elevators:	.5
	Stardancer, Scandinavia	(lower beds/all berths):	.26.6/23.4	Casino (gaming tables):	.Yes
Builder:	.Dubigeon-Normandie (France)	Crew/Passenger Ratio		Slot Machines:	.Yes
Original Cost:	.$100 million	(lower beds/all berths):	.2.7/3.1	Swimming Pools (outdoors):	.1
Entered Service:	.Oct 1982/Mar 2002	Navigation Officers:	.International		(magrodome)
Registry:	.Bahamas	Cabins (total):	.757	Swimming Pools (indoors):	.0
Length (ft/m):	.623.0/189.89	Size Range (sq ft/m):	.143.1–398.2/	Whirlpools:	.0
Beam (ft/m):	.88.6/27.01		13.3–37.0	Self-Service Launderette:	.No
Draft (ft/m):	.23.6/7.20	Cabins (outside view):	.462	Dedicated Cinema/Seats:	.No
Propulsion/Propellers: diesel (19,800 kW)/2		Cabins (interior/no view):	.295	Library:	.Yes
Passenger Decks:	.10	Cabins (for one person):	.0	Classification Society: Det Norske Veritas

OVERALL SCORE: 1,258 (OUT OF A POSSIBLE 2,000 POINTS)

OVERVIEW. This ship, once a Baltic passenger-car ferry, has been extensively reconstructed to operate as a cruise ship. It has only a token bow, a fairly decent amount of open deck and sunbathing space, and a pool (more a "dip" pool) with a sliding glass dome (called a magrodome) that can be used in case of inclement weather. The ship suffers from having an extremely boxy, angular shape, and sports a "sponson" skirt that goes around the stern at the waterline (this is required for stability reasons). *Island Escape* underwent a $75 million reconstruction in 1991, when Royal Caribbean International (then Royal Caribbean Cruise Line) took over the ship.

In 2001 it transferred to Island Cruises, a new joint venture between the UK's First Choice Holidays and Royal Caribbean International, and began cruising in 2002 as *Island Escape*. Inside, the accommodation is mostly located forward, while the public rooms are mostly located in the aft third of the ship. There is a decent enough array of public rooms and facilities, including six bars and a lounge/ discotheque that is cantilevered around the funnel with excellent ocean views). The decor features tasteful colors and furnishings of decent quality, but some have seen better days. Other facilities include a cyber center (for internet connection and email), and a coffee/pastry shop with three internet computer stations. The ceilings in many public areas and accommodation hallways are quite low (a legacy of the ship's original role as a cruise-ferry).

The ship, now more than 20 years old, has a dual existence: in summer it operates specifically for the British family market, providing one-week cruises. In other words, this is cruising in utterly casual, comfortable, unpretentious

BERLITZ'S RATINGS

	Possible	Achieved
Ship	500	307
Accommodation	200	117
Food	400	231
Service	400	269
Entertainment	100	62
Cruise	400	272

surroundings that are quite upbeat, with a "totally relaxed" ambience that appeals to the young at heart. Children should have a good time ("Palmy" is a children's character they can have fun with, and eat with), and there are plenty of planned, well-supervised activities.

Vacations can be extended with a "cruise-and-stay" package, with special pricing to make your extended break more affordable. If you book two cruises back-to-back, however, some of the entertainment may be repeated for the second week.

Island Cruises provides scheduled or charter air service (through its own Air 2000 fleet – but do expect cramped "knees-up" seats) to get you to and from the ship (from the UK). Island Cruises' airport transfer and baggage handling/delivery operation makes for a hassle-free start to your cruise vacation. Gratuities are included. The onboard currency is the British pound.

The ship spends winters in Brazil (operating short cruises for the young, mainly Brazilian market), when the locals arise late, dance and gyrate (and smoke) until dawn (the onboard currency being the Brazilian real). Some onboard concessions and entertainment change for the winter season.

Background music is played almost everywhere inside the ship (and on deck around the pool), making it difficult to find quiet spots to relax, chill out and simply read a book. Passenger participation events tend to be quite amateurish (although this opinion depends on what you compare them to). Smokers are everywhere.

Standing in line for embarkation, disembarkation, shore tenders and for self-serve buffet meals can be an inevitable aspect of cruising aboard all ships carrying more than 1,000 passengers.

SUITABLE FOR: *Island Escape* is best suited to young (and young-minded) couples and singles of all ages, families with children and teenagers, who like to mingle in a fairly large ship setting with plenty of life and entertainment for everyone, with food that is quantity rather than quality, delivered with friendly service that lacks polish, but the price is right – particularly for a first cruise.

ACCOMMODATION. There are just six categories, so choosing the right one for you shouldn't be difficult. The price will depend on grade, size and location. The cabins, however, are quite small, with little closet space, so take as few clothes as possible. They are moderately appointed with soft furnishings that are very cheerful, with upbeat colors.

Almost all cabins have twin beds that can be pushed together to form a queen-sized bed (some cabins have an L-shaped arrangement, with immovable beds). No matter what grade of accommodation you choose, all feature a television, telephone, and three-channel radio, dressing table and mirror. There are many interior (no view) cabins, and drawers and other storage space is extremely limited. If you'd like to have more space, it's best to go for one of the suite categories.

The cabin bathrooms are extremely small, so you can expect to dance with the shower curtain, particularly if you have a larger than average sized body (only some of the accommodation designated as suites have a bathtub). Eleven outside-view cabins have even numbers, and all interior (no view) cabins have odd numbers. Also, if you are cruising with young children, there's almost no space for baby strollers. If, after looking at the deck plans, you want to book a specific cabin number, it currently costs £20 per cabin extra. Some cabins have extra Pullman upper berths (good for families with young children). An in-cabin room service menu is available, but all items cost extra.

Island Suite: The "Island Suite", towards the aft of the ship on the port side, provides the largest accommodation. Although it doesn't have a balcony, it's relatively spacious. A bathtub and shower are provided in the bathroom, and there's a walk-in closet, and mini-bar/refrigerator.

Club Suites: Five other cabins (with balconies) are designated as suites. These are at the stern and have great views over the wash created by the ship's propellers, although they may be subject to a little vibration now and then. A bathtub and shower are provided in the marble-clad bathroom, and there's a walk-in closet in the sleeping area, and mini-bar/refrigerator and entertainment center in the living room. Additionally, another two suites (without balcony or bathtub) are located in the forward third of the ship one deck lower than the aft-facing suites, but with the same facilities.

CUISINE/DINING. The Island Restaurant, the ship's main dining room, has ocean-view windows on two sides, and upbeat decor (there are tables for two, four, six or eight). It is open for breakfast, lunch and dinner; you can serve yourself from the buffets, or be served by a waiter. It's a very casual open-seating arrangement, and so waiters do not get to know your preferences. Although there is much repetition of salad items (for lunch), there are plenty of main dish and dessert choices. The menus contain a wide variety of foods, most of which is well presented and has taste.

Oasis, a smaller (more intimate and exclusive, and quieter) restaurant, is located one deck below the Island Restaurant. This à la carte (extra cost) dining spot is open only for dinner, with full waiter service for all courses. Reservations are required; the ship's officers eat here, and you are welcome to join them, or invite them to your table. The wine list is quite typical of a high street eatery, with European prices that provide quite good value for money.

There are tables for two or four. The ceilings are low in both restaurants, which results in a feeling of being crowded, and adds to the noise level.

For breakfast, lunch and dinner (in fact, 24 hours a day), there is another place to go – the Beachcomber Cafe. This is even more casual, and is ideal for grabbing a bite to eat while "taking the sun" on the open decks. Again, it's a self-serve buffet, with food constantly being refreshed. Tea and coffee are provided at a beverage station, with plastic cups and mugs. Additionally, there's the Café Brazil for pastries, extremely sinful cakes and pastries, and a range of espresso/cappuccino coffees, all at extra cost.

ENTERTAINMENT. The Ocean Theater is a single level showlounge, with banquette and individual seating surrounding a "thrust" stage. Although it is a comfortable room, several pillars obstruct sight lines from some seats.

A resident troupe of young, enthusiastic singer/dancers provide the low-budget revue-style "shows" that are, at best, slightly amateurish, with weak click tracks but lots of colour. In addition, visiting cabaret acts (typically strong singers, magicians, comedians and others) are presented, both in their own shows and as the middle of a "pie" that includes the ship's resident troupe.

There is a main ship's band and several small musical units and pianists to provide live music for dancing and listening in the bars and lounges. In addition, a throbbing discotheque is provided for those who enjoy such things.

SPA/FITNESS. The Ship Shape Hair and Beauty Spa is surprisingly good for the size of the ship. There are treatment rooms for massage, separate saunas and changing rooms for men and women, and a large beauty salon. The gymnasium itself is quite large and contains lots of muscle-pumping, body toning equipment. It is located just aft of the main swimming pool on the port side of the ship, and contains some high-energy muscle-pumping equipment.

The spa staff are provided by Harding Brothers (a concession), and treatments offered include massages, aromatherapy facials, manicures, pedicures, and hair beautifying treatments. Examples: Massage, £45 (50 minutes); Back, Neck and Shoulders Massage, £30 (20 minutes); Marine Algae Body Wrap, £40; Hydrodermie Facial, £45 (75 minutes). Do book appointments for beauty/body treatments early, as time slots go quickly.

Island Princess
★★★★

Large (Resort) Ship:	.......91,627 tons	Passengers		Cabins (wheelchair accessible):	20
Lifestyle:	.................Standard	(lower beds/all berths):	.....1,974/2,590	Cabin Current:	..............110 volts
Cruise Line:	..........Princess Cruises	Passenger Space Ratio		Elevators:	12
Former Names:	...................none	(lower beds/all berths):	........46.4/35.3	Casino (gaming tables):	............Yes
Builder: Chantiers de l'Atlantique (France)		Crew/Passenger Ratio		Slot Machines:	...................Yes
Original Cost:	............$360 million	(lower beds/all berths):	..........2.1/2.8	Swimming Pools (outdoors):	2
Entered Service:	...........June 2003	Navigation Officers:	............British		(+ 1 splash pool)
Registry:	.................Bermuda	Cabins (total):	987	Swimming Pools (indoors):	0
Length (ft/m):	............964.5/294.0	Size Range (sq ft/m):	........156–470.0/	Whirlpools:	5
Beam (ft/m):	.............105.6/32.2		14.4–43.6	Self-Service Launderette:	...........Yes
Draft (ft/m):	...................26/7.9	Cabins (outside view):	879	Dedicated Cinema/Seats:	..........No
Propulsion/Propellers:	.....gas turbine/2	Cabins (interior/no view):	108	Library:	........................Yes
Passenger Decks:	11	Cabins (for one person):	0	Classification Society:	...Lloyd's Register
Total Crew:	900	Cabins (with private balcony):	727		

BERLITZ'S OVERALL SCORE: 1,544 (OUT OF A POSSIBLE 2,000 POINTS)

OVERVIEW. *Island Princess* (sister ship to *Coral Princess*) has an instantly recognizable funnel due to two jet engine-like pods that sit high up on its structure. Four diesel engines provide the generating power. Electrical power is provided by a combination of four diesel and one gas turbine (CODAG) unit; the diesel engines are located in the engine room, while the gas turbine unit is located in the ship's funnel housing. The ship also has three bow thrusters and three stern thrusters.

The ship's interior layout is similar to that of the *Grand Princess*-class ships (but with two decks full of public rooms, lounges and bars instead of just one), and sensibly features three major stair towers for passengers (good from the safety and evacuation viewpoint), with plenty of elevators for easy access. For a large ship, the layout is quite user-friendly, and less disjointed than many ships of a similar size. Because of its slim beam, the ship is able to transit the Panama Canal, thus providing greater flexibility in deployment than the *Grand Princess*-class ships.

New facilities for a Princess Cruises ship include a flower shop (where you can order flowers and Godiva chocolates for cabin delivery – good for a birthday or anniversary), cigar lounge (Churchill Lounge), martini bar (Crooners). Also different is a casino with a London theme.

What is very civilized is the fact that sunbathers who use the "quiet" deck forward of the mast have their own splash pool, so they won't have to go down two decks to get to the two main pools. Strollers will like the ship's full wrap-around exterior promenade deck.

Surfers can find an AOL Internet Cafe conveniently located on the top level of the four-deck-high lobby.

BERLITZ'S RATINGS

	Possible	Achieved
Ship	500	436
Accommodation	200	154
Food	400	261
Service	400	294
Entertainment	100	85
Cruise	400	314

Meanwhile, it's good to see that the dreaded "fine arts" get their own room, so that paintings to be sold during the art auctions are not spread all over the ship. Adjacent is the Wedding Chapel (a live web-cam can relay ceremonies via the internet). The ship's captain can legally marry (American) couples, due to the ship's registry and a special dispensation (this should, however, be verified when in the planning stage, and may depend on where you live). Princess Cruises offers three wedding packages – Pearl, Emerald, Diamond; the fee includes registration and official marriage certificate. The Wedding Chapel can host "renewal of vows" ceremonies (there is a charge for these).

ACCOMMODATION. There are 33 price categories, in six types: 16 Suites with balcony (470 sq. ft/43.6 sq. meters); 184 Mini-Suites with balcony (285–302 sq. ft/26.4–28.0 sq. meters); 8 Mini-Suites without balcony (300 sq. ft/27.8 sq. meters; 527 Outside-View Cabins with balcony (217–232 sq. ft/ 20.1–21.5 sq. meters); 144 Standard Outside-view Cabins (162 sq. ft/15 sq. meters); Interior (no view) Cabins (156 sq. ft/144.5 sq. meters). There are also 20 wheelchair-accessible cabins (217–374 sq. ft/20.1–34.7 sq. meters). The price you pay will depend on grade, size and location. Note that all measurements are approximate. Almost all of the outside-view cabins have a private balcony. Some cabins can accommodate a third, or third and fourth person (good for families with children). Some cabins on Emerald Deck (Deck 8) have a view obstructed by lifeboats.

Suites: There are just 16 suites and, although none are really that large (compared to such ships as *Norwegian Dawn* and *Norwegian Star*, where the largest measure a whopping 5,350 sq. ft/497 sq. meters, for example), each has a private balcony. All are named after islands (mostly coral-based islands in the Indian Ocean and Pacific Ocean). All suites are located on either Deck 9 or Deck 10. In a departure from many ships, *Coral Princess* does not have any suites or cabins with a view of the ship's stern. There are also four Premium Suites, located sensibly in the center of the ship, adjacent to a bank of six lifts. Six other suites (called Verandah Suites) are located further aft.

All Accommodation: Suites and cabins have a refrigerator, personal safe, television (with audio channels), hairdryer, satellite-dial telephone, and twin beds that convert to a queen-sized bed (there are a few exceptions). All accommodation has a bathroom with shower enclosure and toilet. Accommodation designated as suites and mini-suites (there are seven price categories) have a bathtub and separate shower enclosure, and two TV sets.

All passengers receive turndown service and chocolates on pillows each night, bathrobes (on request) and toiletry kits. Most "outside-view" cabins on Emerald Deck have views obstructed by the lifeboats. There are no cabins for singles. Princess Cruises typically includes CNN, CNBC, ESPN and TNT on the in-cabin color television system (when available). There are no butlers – even for the top-grade suites. Cabin attendants have too many cabins to look after (typically 20), which does not translate to fine personal service.

CUISINE/DINING. There are two main dining rooms, named Bordeaux and Provence; they are located in the forward section of the ship on the two lowest passenger decks, with the galley all the way forward so it doesn't intersect public spaces (an example of good design). Both are almost identical in design and layout (the ceilings are quite low and make the rooms appear more cramped than they are), and have plenty of intimate alcoves and cozy dining spots, with tables for two, four, six, or eight. There are two seatings for dinner, while breakfast and lunch are on an open seating basis; you may have to stand in line at peak times. Both dining rooms are non-smoking.

Horizon Court is the ship's casual 24-hour eatery, and is located in the forward section of Lido Deck, with superb ocean views. Several self-serve counters provide an array of food for breakfast and lunch buffets, while each evening, bistro-style casual dinners are available.

Alternative (Extra Charge) Eateries: There are two "alternative" dining rooms, Sabatini's and the Bayou Cafe, both enclosed. They incur an extra charge, and you must make a reservation. Sabatini's is an Italian eatery, with colorful tiled Mediterranean-style decor; it has Italian-style pizzas and pastas, with a variety of sauces, as well as Italian-style entrées (including tiger prawns and lobster tail), all provided with flair and entertainment by the waiters. The food that is both creative and tasty (with seriously sized portions). There is a cover charge of $15 per person, for lunch or dinner (on sea days only).

The Bayou Cafe is open for lunch and dinner, and has a cover charge of $10 per person (including a free Hurricane cocktail), and evokes the charm of New Orleans' French Quarter, complete with wrought-iron decoration. The Bayou Cafe features Creole food (with platters such as Peel 'n' Eat Shrimp Piquante, Sausage Grillades, Oysters Sieur de Bienville and N'Awlins Crawfish "Mud Bug" Bisque delivered to the table when you arrive). Popular entrées include Seafood Gumbo, and Chorizo Jambalaya with fresh seafood and traditional dried spice mixes, as well as Cajun Grill items such as Smothered Alligator Ribs, Flambeaux Grilled Jumbo Prawns, Corn Meal Fried Catfish, Blackened Chicken Brochette, and Red Pepper Butter Broiled Lobster; desserts include sweet potato pie and banana whiskey pound cake. The room has a small stage, with baby grand piano, and live jazz is also part of the dining scenario.

Other outlets include La Pâtisserie, in the ship's reception lobby, a coffee, cakes and pastries spot and good for informal meetings. There's also a Pizzeria, hamburger grill, and an ice cream bar (extra charge for the ice cream). Meanwhile, puffers and sippers should enjoy Churchill's, a neat cigar and cognac lounge, cleverly sited near a neat little hideaway bar called the Rat Pack Bar.

ENTERTAINMENT. The Princess Theatre is two decks high, and, unusually, there is much more seating in the upper level than on the main floor below. A second entertainment lounge (Universe Lounge) is designed more for cabaret-style features. It also has two levels, and three separate stages – so non-stop entertainment can be provided without constant set-ups. Some 50 of the room's seats are equipped with a built-in laptop computer. The room is also used for cooking demonstrations (it has a full kitchen set), and other life enrichment participation activities.

Princess Cruises always provides plenty of live music in bars and lounges, with a wide mix of light classical, jazz, and dance music, from solo entertaining pianists to showbands, and volume is normally kept to an acceptable level.

Feel in need of education? Now you can learn aboard ship, with "ScholarShip@Sea," a new Princess Cruises program, which debuted aboard this vessel. It includes about 20 courses per cruise (six on any given day at sea). Although all introductory classes are free, if you want to continue any chosen subject in a smaller setting, there are fees. There are four core subjects: Culinary Arts, Visual/Creative Arts, Photography, and Computer Technology. A full culinary demonstration kitchen set has been built into the Universe Lounge (this can also play host to wine tasting), and a pottery studio complete with kiln has been built into the ship as part of the facilities.

SPA/FITNESS. The Lotus Spa is located aft on one of the ship's uppermost decks. It contains men's and women's saunas, steam rooms, changing rooms, relaxation area, beauty salon, aerobics exercise room and gymnasium with aft-facing ocean-views packed with the latest high-tech muscle-pumping, cardio-vascular equipment. There are several large rooms for individual treatments.

● **For more extensive general information about the Princess Cruises experience, see pages 124–127.**

Island Sky
NOT YET RATED

Boutique Ship: . . . . .4,280 tons	Passenger Decks: 5	Cabins (for one person): 0
Lifestyle: . . . . .Standard	Total Crew: 66	Cabins (with private balcony): 4
Cruise Line: . . . . .Mauritius Island Cruises	Passengers	Cabins (wheelchair accessible): 0
Former Names: . . . . .*Regina Renaissance,*	(lower beds/all berths): 112/122	Cabin Voltage: .110
Renaissance VII	Passenger Space Ratio	Lifts: 1
Builder: . . . . . . .Nuovi Cantieri Appaunia	(lower beds/all berths): 38.2/38.2	Casino (gaming tables): . . . . .Yes
(Italy)	Crew/Passenger Ratio	Slot Machines: . . . . .Yes
Original Cost: . . . .$25 milltion	(lower beds/all berths): 1.7/1.8	Swimming Pools (outdoors): 1
Entered Service: . . .Dec 1991/May 2004	Navigation Officers: . . . . .Norwegian/	Swimming Pools (indoors): 0
Registry: . . . . .Mauritius	European	Whirlpools: 1
Length (ft/m): 297.2/90.6	Cabins (total): 61	Self-Service Launderette: . . . . .No
Beam (ft/m): 50.1/15.3	Size Range (sq ft/m): . . . . .234.6 – 353.0/	Dedicated Cinema/Seats: . . . . .No
Draft (ft/m): 12.9/2.95	21.8 – 32.8	Library: . . . . .Yes
Propulsion/Propellers: . . . . .diesel	Cabins (outside view): 61	Classification Society: . . . . . .Det Norske
(5000kW)/2	Cabins (interior/no view): 0	Veritas

OVERALL SCORE: NYR (OUT OF A POSSIBLE 2,000 POINTS)

OVERVIEW. *Island Sky* has contemporary mega-yacht looks and handsome styling, with twin flared funnels give this ship a smart profile, and a "ducktail" (sponson) stern provides good stability and seagoing comfort. This ship was originally built as one of a series of eight similar ships for the now-defunct Renaissance Cruises. The ship is owned by an Oslo-based company, and operated by Mauritius Island Cruises year-round in an attractive destination-specific region renowned for wildlife. There is one teak wrap-around promenade deck outdoors, and a reasonable amount of open deck and sunbathing space.

Island Sky was upgraded in 2004 before entering service for Mauritius Island Cruises (although it was chartered by Noble Caledonia for summer 2004).

A "baby island" tender hangs off the aft deck and acts as ship-to-shore transportation. Some equipment for watersports is carried, and active types can enjoy wind surfing, scuba diving and snorkeling, deep sea fishing, mountain biking, golfing, and hiking.

Inside, you will find an elegant interior design, with polished wood-finish paneling throughout. There is also a very small book and video library.

This vessel is very comfortable and totally inviting, and features warm-weather cruising in an area devoid of large cruise ships (the South Indian Ocean). The itinerary includes two uninhabited islands in the Cargados group. Although this intimate ship is not up to the standard of a Seabourn or Silversea vessel, it will provide a good cruise experience at a moderate cost. Gratuities are appreciated but not required. The onboard currency is the Mauritius rupee.

BERLITZ'S RATINGS

	Possible	Achieved
Ship	500	NYR
Accommodation	200	NYR
Food	400	NYR
Service	400	NYR
Entertainment	100	NYR
Cruise	400	NYR

SUITABLE FOR: Young, active types who like watersports facilities and a relaxed lifestyle combined with good food and service, and an itinerary that says "get away from it all, but in comfort."

ACCOMMODATION. The spacious cabins (four were added in the 2003 refit) combine highly polished imitation rosewood paneling with lots of mirrors and hand-crafted Italian furniture, lighted walk-in closets, three-sided vanity mirrors (in fact there are a lot of mirrored surfaces in the decor), and just about everything you need, including a TV set and VCR, and a refrigerator).

The bathrooms are extremely compact units; they have real teakwood floors and marble vanities, and shower enclosures (none have bathtubs, not even the owner's suite).

CRUISE/DINING. The dining room operates with an open seating for all meals. It is small but quite smart, with tables for two, four, six, and eight. You simply sit where you like, with whom you like, and at what time you like. The meals are self-service, buffet-style cold foods for breakfast and lunch, with hot foods chosen from a table menu and served properly. The dining room operation works well. The food quality, choice, and presentation are all very decent.

ENTERTAINMENT. There is no formal entertainment in the main lounge, the venue for all social activities (six pillars obstruct the sightlines to the small stage area anyway).

SPA/FITNESS/RECREATION. Water sports facilities include an aft platform, sailfish, snorkel equipment, and zodiacs.

Island Sun
NOT YET RATED

Boutique Ship: . . . . .4,280 tons	Passenger Decks: 5	Cabins (for one person): 0
Lifestyle: . . . . .Standard	Total Crew: 66	Cabins (with private balcony): 4
Cruise Line: . . . . .Mauritius Island Cruises	Passengers	Cabins (wheelchair accessible): 0
Former Names: . . . . .*Regina Renaissance,*	(lower beds/all berths): 112/122	Cabin Voltage: .110
Renaissance VIII	Passenger Space Ratio	Lifts: 1
Builder: . . . . . . .Nuovi Cantieri Appaunia	(lower beds/all berths): 38.2/38.2	Casino (gaming tables): . . . . .Yes
(Italy)	Crew/Passenger Ratio	Slot Machines: . . . . .Yes
Original Cost: . . . .$25 milltion	(lower beds/all berths): 1.7/1.8	Swimming Pools (outdoors): 1
Entered Service: . . . .Dec 1991/May 2004	Navigation Officers: . . . . .Norwegian/	Swimming Pools (indoors): 0
Registry: . . . . .Mauritius	European	Whirlpools: 1
Length (ft/m): 297.2/90.6	Cabins (total): 61	Self-Service Launderette: . . . . .No
Beam (ft/m): 50.1/15.3	Size Range (sq ft/m): . . . . .234.6 – 353.0/	Dedicated Cinema/Seats: . . . . .No
Draft (ft/m): 12.9/2.95	21.8 – 32.8	Library: . . . . .Yes
Propulsion/Propellers: . . . . .diesel	Cabins (outside view): 61	Classification Society: . . . . . . .Det Norske
(5000kW)/2	Cabins (interior/no view): 0	Veritas

OVERALL SCORE: NYR (OUT OF A POSSIBLE 2,000 POINTS)

OVERVIEW. *Island Sun* has contemporary mega-yacht looks and handsome styling, with twin flared funnels give this ship a smart profile, and a "duck-tail" (sponson) stern provides good stability and seagoing comfort. This ship was originally built as one of a series of eight similar ships for the now-defunct Renaissance Cruises. The ship is owned by an Oslo-based company, and operated by Mauritius Island Cruises year-round in an attractive destination-specific region renowned for wildlife. There is one teak wrap-around promenade deck outdoors, and a reasonable amount of open deck and sunbathing space.

Island Sun was upgraded in 2004 before entering service for Mauritius Island Cruises (although it was chartered by Noble Caledonia for summer 2004).

A "baby island" tender hangs off the aft deck and acts as ship-to-shore transportation. Some equipment for watersports is carried, and active types can enjoy wind surfing, scuba diving and snorkeling, deep sea fishing, mountain biking, golfing, and hiking.

Inside, you will find an elegant interior design, with polished wood-finish paneling throughout. There is also a very small book and video library.

This vessel is very comfortable and totally inviting, and features warm-weather cruising in an area devoid of large cruise ships (the South Indian Ocean). The itinerary includes two uninhabited islands in the Cargados group. Although this intimate ship is not up to the standard of a Seabourn or Silversea vessel, it will provide a good cruise experience at a moderate cost. Gratuities are appreciated but not required. The onboard currency is the Mauritius rupee.

BERLITZ'S RATINGS

	Possible	Achieved
Ship	500	NYR
Accommodation	200	NYR
Food	400	NYR
Service	400	NYR
Entertainment	100	NYR
Cruise	400	NYR

SUITABLE FOR: Young, active types who like watersports facilities and a relaxed lifestyle combined with good food and service, and an itinerary that says "get away from it all, but in comfort."

ACCOMMODATION. The spacious cabins (four were added in the 2003 refit) combine highly polished imitation rosewood paneling with lots of mirrors and hand-crafted Italian furniture, lighted walk-in closets, three-sided vanity mirrors (in fact there are a lot of mirrored surfaces in the decor), and just about everything you need, including a TV set and VCR, and a refrigerator).

The bathrooms are extremely compact units; they have real teakwood floors and marble vanities, and shower enclosures (none have bathtubs, not even the owner's suite).

CRUISE/DINING. The dining room operates with an open seating for all meals. It is small but quite smart, with tables for two, four, six, and eight. You simply sit where you like, with whom you like, and at what time you like. The meals are self-service, buffet-style cold foods for breakfast and lunch, with hot foods chosen from a table menu and served properly. The dining room operation works well. The food quality, choice, and presentation are all very decent.

ENTERTAINMENT. There is no formal entertainment in the main lounge, the venue for all social activities (six pillars obstruct the sightlines to the small stage area anyway).

SPA/FITNESS/RECREATION. Water sports facilities include an aft platform, sailfish, snorkel equipment, and zodiacs.

Jewel of the Seas
★★★★

Large (Resort) Ship: ....90,090 tons	Total Crew: 858	Cabins (wheelchair accessible): 14
Lifestyle: ....Standard	Passengers	(8 with private balcony)
Cruise Line: ....Royal Caribbean	(lower beds/all berths): 2,110/2,500	Cabin Voltage: 110
International	Passenger Space Ratio	Elevators: 9
Former Names: ....None	(lower beds/all berths): 42.9/36.0	Casino (gaming tables): ....Yes
Builder: ....Meyer Werft (Germany)	Crew/Passenger Ratio	Slot Machines: ....Yes
Original Cost: ....$350 million	(lower beds/all berths): 2.4/2.9	Swimming Pools (outdoors): 2
Entered Service: ....June 2004	Navigation Officers: ....Norwegian	Swimming Pools (indoors): 0
Registry: ....The Bahamas	Cabins (total): 1,055	Whirlpools: 3
Length (ft/m): 961.9/293.2	Size Range (sq ft/m): 165.8–1,216.3/	Self-Service Launderette: ....No
Beam (ft/m): 105.6/32.2	15.4–113.0	Dedicated Cinema/Seats: Yes/40
Draft (ft/m): 27.8/8.5	Cabins (outside view): 817	Library: ....Yes
Propulsion/Propellers: .....Gas turbine/2	Cabins (interior/no view): 238	Classification Society: .... Det Norske
azimuthing pods (20 MW each)	Cabins (for one person): 0	Veritas
Passenger Decks: 12	Cabins (with private balcony): 577	

OVERALL SCORE: 1,546 (OUT OF A POSSIBLE 2,000 POINTS)

OVERVIEW. *Jewel of the Seas* is the fourth Royal Caribbean International ship to use gas and steam turbine power (sister ships: *Brilliance of the Seas, Radiance of the Seas* and *Serenade of the Seas*) instead of the conventional diesel or diesel-electric combination. Pod propulsion power (*see page 151 for description*) is also provided. As is common aboard almost all new cruise ships today, the navigation bridge is of the fully enclosed type. In the very front of the ship is a helipad, which also acts as a viewing platform for passengers.

Jewel of the Seas is a streamlined, contemporary ship, and has a two-deck-high wrap-around structure in the forward section of the funnel. Along the starboard side, a central glass wall protrudes, giving great views (cabins with balconies occupy the space directly opposite on the port side). The gently rounded stern has nicely tiered decks, which gives the ship an extremely well-balanced look.

Inside, the decor is contemporary, yet elegant, bright and cheerful, designed for young, active, hip types. The artwork is quite eclectic (so there should be something for all tastes), and provides a spectrum and a half of color works.

The ship's interior focal point is a nine-deck high atrium lobby that has glass-walled elevators (on the port side of the ship only) that travel through 12 decks, face the sea and provide a link with nature and the ocean. The Centrum (as the atrium is called) has several public rooms connected to it: the guest relations and shore excursions desks, a Lobby Bar, Champagne Bar, the Library, Royal Caribbean Online (an internet-connect center), the Concierge Club, and a Crown & Anchor Lounge. A great view can be had of the

BERLITZ'S RATINGS

	Possible	Achieved
Ship	500	433
Accommodation	200	163
Food	400	259
Service	400	298
Entertainment	100	81
Cruise	400	312

atrium by looking down through the flat glass dome high above it.

Other facilities include a delightful but very small library, a Champagne Bar, and a large Schooner Bar that houses maritime art in an integral art gallery. Gambling devotees should enjoy the rather large, noisy and colorful Casino Royale. There's also a small dedicated screening room for movies (with space for two wheelchairs), as well as a 194-seat conference center, and a business center.

This ship also contains a Viking Crown Lounge (a Royal Caribbean International trademark), a large structure set around the base of the ship's funnel. It functions as an observation lounge during the daytime (with views forward over the swimming pool). In the evening, the space becomes a futuristic, high-energy dance club, as well as a more intimate and relaxed entertainment venue for softer mood music and "black box" theater.

Royal Caribbean Online is a dedicated computer center that has 12 PCs with high-speed internet access for sending and receiving email, located in a semi-private setting.

Youth facilities include Adventure Ocean, an "edu-tainment" area with four separate age-appropriate sections for junior passengers: Aquanaut Center (for ages 3–5); Explorer Center (6–8); Voyager Center (9–12); and the Optix Teen Center (13–17). There is also Adventure Beach, which includes a splash pool complete with waterslide; Surfside, with computer lab stations with entertaining software; and Ocean Arcade, a video games hangout.

The onboard product delivery is more casual and unstructured than RCI has previously been delivering.

Jewel of the Seas offers more space and more comfortable public areas (and several more intimate spaces), slightly larger cabins and more dining options than most of the larger ships in the RCI fleet.

While the ship is quite delightful in many ways, however, the onboard operation is less spectacular, and suffers from a lack of service staff. There are no cushioned pads for the deck lounge chairs, and the deck towels provided are quite thin and small. Spa treatments are extravagantly expensive (as they are aboard most ships today, in line with land-based spa prices in the U.S.). It is virtually impossible to escape background music anywhere.

The onboard currency is the US dollar, and 15 percent is added to all bar and spa bills.

SUITABLE FOR: *Jewel of the Seas* is best suited to young-minded adult couples and singles of all ages, families with toddlers, tots, children, and teenagers who like to mingle in a large ship setting with plenty of life and high-energy entertainment for everyone, with food that is acceptable quantity rather than quality (unless you are prepared to pay extra for dining in the "alternative" restaurant), all delivered with friendly service that lacks polish.

ACCOMMODATION. There is a wide range of suites and standard outside-view and interior (no view) cabins to suit different tastes, requirements, and depth of wallet, in 10 different categories and 19 different price groups.

Apart from the largest suites (six owner's suites), which have king-sized beds, almost all other cabins have twin beds that convert to a queen-sized bed (all sheets are of 100% Egyptian cotton, although blankets are of nylon). All cabins have rich (but faux) wood cabinetry, including a vanity desk (with hairdryer), faux wood drawers that close silently (hooray), TV set, personal safe, and three-sided mirrors. Some cabins have ceiling-recessed, pull-down berths for third and fourth persons, although closet and drawer space would be extremely tight for four (even if two are children), and some have interconnecting doors (so families with children can cruise together, in adjacent cabins. Note that audio channels are available through the TV set, so you can't switch off its picture while listening. Data ports are provided in all cabins. Many of the "private" balcony cabins are not very private, as they can be overlooked by anyone standing in the port and starboard wings of the Solarium, and from other locations.

Most cabin bathrooms have tiled accenting and a terrazzo-style tiled floor, and a shower enclosure in a half-moon shape (it is rather small, however, considering the size of some passengers), 100 % Egyptian cotton towels, a small cabinet for personal toiletries and a small shelf. There is little space to stow toiletries for two (or more).

The largest accommodation consists of a family suite with two bedrooms. One bedroom has twin beds (convertible to queen-sized bed), while a second has two lower beds and two upper Pullman berths, a combination that can sleep up to eight persons (this would be suitable for large families). Occupants of accommodation designated as suites also get the use of a private Concierge Lounge (where priority dining room reservations, shore excursion bookings and beauty salon/spa appointments can be made).

CUISINE/DINING. Reflections, the principal dining room, spans two decks; the upper deck level has floor-to-ceiling windows, while the lower deck level has picture windows. It is a fine, but inevitably noisy dining hall, and eight huge, thick pillars obstruct the sightlines. Reflections seats 1,104, and its decor has a cascading water theme. There are tables for two, four, six, eight or 10 in two seatings. Two small private dining rooms (Illusions and Mirage) are located off the main dining room. No smoking is permitted in dining venues. There is an adequate wine list, with moderate prices. **Alternative Restaurants:** Portofino, with 112 seats, offers Italian cuisine, and Chops Grille Steakhouse, with 95 seats and an open "show" kitchen, serves premium meats in the form of chops and steaks. Both have food that is of a much higher quality than in the main dining room and are typically open 6pm–11pm. There is an additional charge of $20 per person (including gratuities), and reservations are required. The dress code is smart casual.

Casual Eateries: Casual meals (for breakfast, lunch and dinner) can be taken in the self-serve, buffet-style Windjammer Cafe, which can be accessed directly from the pool deck. It has about 400 seats, and islands dedicated to specific foods, and indoors and outdoors seating. Additionally, there is the Seaview Cafe, open for lunch and dinner. Choose from the self-serve buffet, or from the menu for casual, fast-food seafood items including fish sandwiches, popcorn shrimp, fish 'n' chips, as well as non-seafood items such as hamburgers and hot dogs.

ENTERTAINMENT. Entertainment facilities include the three-level Coral Reef Theater, with 874 seats (including 24 wheelchair stations) and good sightlines from most seats due to steep tiers. A second entertainment venue is the Safari Club, which hosts cabaret shows, late-night adult (blue) comedy, and dancing to live music.

The entertainment throughout this ship is upbeat (in fact, it is virtually impossible to get away from music and noise), but is typical of the kind of resort hotel found in Las Vegas.

SPA/FITNESS. The ShipShape health, fitness and spa facilities have themed decor, and include a 10,176 sq.-ft (945 sq.-meter) solarium with whirlpool and counter current swimming under a retractable magrodome roof, a gymnasium (with 44 cardiovascular machines), 50-person aerobics room, sauna and steam rooms, and therapy treatment rooms.

For the more sporting, there is activity galore – including a rock-climbing wall that's 30 ft (9 meters) high, with five separate climbing tracks. It's free, and all safety gear is included, but you'll need to sign up.

Other sports facilities include a 9-hole miniature golf course, and an indoor/outdoor country club with golf simulator, a jogging track, and basketball court. Want to play pool? You can, thanks to two special tables whose technology adjusts automatically to the movement of the ship.

Kapitan Dranitsyn
★★★

Boutique Ship: . . . . .12,288 tons	Passenger Decks: 4	Cabins (with private balcony): 0
Lifestyle: . . . . .Standard	Total Crew: 90	Cabins (wheelchair accessible) 0
Cruise Line: . . . . . . .Murmansk Shipping/	Passengers	Cabin Current: . . . . .220 volts
Quark Expeditions	(lower beds/all berths): 106/113	Elevators: 0
Former Names: . . . . .none	Passenger Space Ratio	Casino (gaming tables): . . . . .No
Builder: . . . . .Wartsila (Finland)	(lower beds/all berths): 115.9/108.7	Slot Machines: .No
Original Cost: .n/a	Crew/Passenger Ratio	Swimming Pools (outdoors): 0
Entered Service: . . . . .Dec 1980	(lower beds/all berths): 1.1/1.2	Swimming Pools (indoors): 1
Registry: . . . . .Russia	Navigation Officers: . . . . .Russian	Whirlpools: 0
Length (ft/m): 434.6/132.49	Cabins (total): .53	Lecture/Film Room: . . . . .No
Beam (ft/m): 86.9/26.50	Size Range (sq ft/m): 150.6–269.0/	Library: . . . . .Yes
Draft (ft/m): 27.8/8.50	14.0–25.0	Zodiacs: 4
Propulsion/Propellers: . . . . .diesel-electric	Cabins (outside view): 53	Helicopter Pad: . . . . .Yes (1 helicopter)
(18,270 kW)/3	Cabins (interior/no view): 0	Classification Society: . . . . .RS
	Cabins (for one person): 0	

OVERALL SCORE: 1,164 (OUT OF A POSSIBLE 2,000 POINTS)

OVERVIEW. *Kapitan Dranitsyn* is a real, working icebreaker, one of a fleet of 10 built in Finland to exacting Russian specifications for the challenging seas and conditions in the Arctic. Converted to passenger use in 1994 (and since upgraded), it has an incredibly thick hull, forthright profile, and a bow like an inverted whale head. An open bridge policy allows passengers to visit the bridge at almost any time. Strong diesel-electric engines (delivering 24,000 horsepower) allow it to plow through ice several feet thick. There is plenty of open deck and observation space, and a heated (but very small) indoor swimming pool.

There is always a team of excellent naturalists and lecturers aboard. A helicopter is usually (but not always) carried and can be used by all passengers for sightseeing forays, as is a fleet of Zodiac rubber landing craft for in-your-face shore landings and wildlife spotting. Light but warm parkas are provided for passengers.

Kapitan Dranitsyn is particularly good for tough expedition cruising, and will provide thoroughly practical surroundings, a friendly, experienced and dedicated group of crew members, and excellent value for the money. An expedition cruise logbook is typically provided at the end of each cruise for all passengers – a superb keepsake.

The ship offers only basic cruise amenities and very spartan, no-frills decor. Also, be prepared for some tremendous roaring noise when the ship breaks through pack ice.

SUITABLE FOR: This type of cruising suits adventurous, hardy outdoors types of mature years who enjoy being with nature in some of the earth's most inhospitable places.

BERLITZ'S RATINGS

	Possible	Achieved
Ship	500	267
Accommodation	200	113
Food	400	237
Service	400	224
Entertainment	N/A	N/A
Cruise	500	311

ACCOMMODATION. The cabins, in four price categories, are spread over four decks in an accommodation block, and all have private facilities and plenty of storage space. Although nothing special, the cabins are quite comfortable, with two lower beds (typically one is a fixed bed, the other being a convertible sofa bed, either in a twin or an L-shaped format), large closets, storage for outerwear and boots, and portholes that actually open. The bathrooms are practical units, although storage space for personal toiletries is tight. Four of the accommodation units are designated as "suites" that have more room, including a larger bathroom.

CUISINE/DINING. The one dining room is plain and unpretentious, yet quite comfortable. It is non-smoking; there is a single seating, with assigned tables, formally laid with white tablecloths and full place settings. The food is hearty fare, with generous portions (and an emphasis on fish and potatoes). Fruits, vegetables and international cheeses tend to be in limited supply. Quark Expeditions has its own catering team and so European chefs oversee the cuisine and its presentation, and only the best ingredients are provided. The wine list is pretty basic.

ENTERTAINMENT. Dinner is the main event of the evening, followed by discussion of what lies ahead for the next day. You might actually do a shore landing at night.

SPA/FITNESS. There is a gymnasium with some basic equipment, a small (heated) indoor swimming pool (really a "dip" pool), and a sauna.

Kapitan Khlebnikov
★★★

Boutique Ship: . . . . .12,288 tons
Lifestyle: . . . . .Standard
Cruise Line: . . . . . . .Murmansk Shipping/
Quark Expeditions
Former Names: . . . . .none
Builder: . . . . .Wartsila (Finland)
Original Cost: . . . . .n/a
Entered Service: 1981
Registry: . . . . .Russia
Length (ft/m): 434.6/132.49
Beam (ft/m): 87.7/26.75
Draft (ft/m): 27.8/8.50
Propulsion/Propellers: . . . . .diesel-electric
(18,270 kW)/3
Passenger Decks: 4

Total Crew: 60
Passengers
(lower beds/all berths): 108/114
Passenger Space Ratio
(lower beds/all berths): 113.7/107.7
Crew/Passenger Ratio
(lower beds/all berths): 1.8/1.9
Navigation Officers: . . . . .Russian
Cabins (total): 54
Size Range (sq ft/m): 150.6–269/
14.0–25.0
Cabins (outside view): 54
Cabins (interior/no view): 0
Cabins (for one person): 0
Cabins (with private balcony): 0

Cabins (wheelchair accessible): 0
Cabin Current: . . . . .220 volts
Elevators: 1
Casino (gaming tables): . . . . .No
Slot Machines: . . . . .No
Swimming Pools (outdoors): 0
Swimming Pools (indoors): 1
Whirlpools: 0
Lecture/Film Room: . . . . .No
Library: . . . . .Yes
Zodiacs: 4
Helicopter Pad: . . . . . . .Yes (1 helicopter)
Classification Society: . .Russian Shipping
Register

OVERALL SCORE: 1,164 (OUT OF A POSSIBLE 2,000 POINTS)

OVERVIEW. *Kapitan Khlebnikov* is a real, working icebreaker, one of a fleet of 10 built in Finland to exacting Russian specifications for the challenging seas and conditions in the Arctic. Converted to exclusive passenger use in 1994 (and since upgraded), it has an incredibly thick hull, forthright profile, a bow like an inverted whale head, and a huge amount technical equipment. In 1997, *Kapitan Khlebnikov* became the first vessel ever to circumnavigate Antarctica with passengers. An open bridge policy allows passengers to visit the bridge at almost any time. Strong diesel-electric engines (delivering 24,000 horsepower) allow it to plow through ice several feet thick. There is plenty of open deck and observation space, and a heated (but very small) indoor swimming pool.

There is always a team of excellent naturalists and lecturers aboard. A helicopter, when carried, can be used for sightseeing forays, as is a fleet of Zodiac rubber landing craft for in-your-face shore landings and wildlife spotting.

Kapitan Khlebnikov is particularly good for tough expedition cruising, and will provide thoroughly practical surroundings, a friendly, experienced and dedicated group of crew members, and excellent value for the money. An expedition cruise logbook is typically provided at the end of each cruise for all passengers – a superb keepsake.

The ship offers only basic cruise amenities and very spartan, no-frills decor. Also, be prepared for some tremendous roaring noise when the ship breaks through pack ice.

SUITABLE FOR: This type of cruising suits adventurous, hardy outdoors types of mature years who enjoy being with

BERLITZ'S RATINGS		
	Possible	Achieved
Ship	500	267
Accommodation	200	113
Food	400	237
Service	400	224
Entertainment	N/A	N/A
Cruise	500	311

nature in some of the earth's most inhospitable places.

ACCOMMODATION. The cabins, in four price categories, are spread over four decks in an accommodation block, and all have private facilities and plenty of storage space. Although nothing special, the cabins are quite comfortable, with two lower beds (typically one is a fixed bed, the other being a convertible sofa bed, either in a twin or an L-shaped format), large closets, storage for outerwear and boots, and portholes that actually open. The bathrooms are practical units, although storage space for personal toiletries is tight. Four of the accommodation units are designated as "suites" that have more room, including a larger bathroom.

CUISINE/DINING. The one dining room is plain and unpretentious, yet quite comfortable. It is non-smoking; there is a single seating, with assigned tables. The food is hearty fare, with generous portions (and an emphasis on fish and potatoes). Fruits, vegetables and international cheeses tend to be in limited supply. Quark Expeditions has its own catering team and only the best ingredients are provided. The wine list is pretty basic.

ENTERTAINMENT. Dinner is the main event of the evening, followed by discussion of what lies ahead for the next day. You might actually do a shore landing at night.

SPA/FITNESS. There is a gymnasium with some basic equipment, a small (heated) indoor swimming pool (really a "dip" pool), and a sauna.

Kristina Regina
★★ +

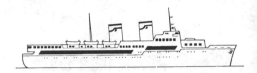

Boutique Ship: . . . . .4,295 tons	Total Crew: 55	Cabins (with private balcony): 0
Lifestyle: . . . . .Standard	Passengers	Cabins (wheelchair accessible): 0
Cruise Line: . . . . .Kristina Cruises	(lower beds/all berths): 186/245	Cabin Current: . . . . .220 volts
Former Names: . . . . .Borea, Bore	Passenger Space Ratio	Elevators: 0
Builder: . .Oskarshamn Shipyard (Sweden)	(lower beds/all berths): 14.8/11.6	Casino (gaming tables): . . . . .No
Original Cost: .n/a	Crew/Passenger Ratio	Slot Machines: . . . . .No
Entered Service: 1960/1987	(lower beds/all berths): 5.2/6.7	Swimming Pools (outdoors): 0
Registry: . . . . .Finland	Navigation Officers: . . . . .Finnish	Swimming Pools (indoors): 0
Length (ft/m): 327.5/99.83	Cabins (total): 119	Whirlpools: 0
Beam (ft/m): 50.0/15.25	Size Range (sq ft/m): 64.5–150.6/	Self-Service Launderette: . . . . .No
Draft (ft/m): 18.0/5.50	6.0–14.0	Dedicated Cinema/Seats: . . . . .No
Propulsion/Propellers: . . . . .diesel	Cabins (outside view): 98	Library: . . . . .Yes
(3,233 kW)/2	Cabins (interior/no view): 21	Classification Society: . . .Lloyd's Register
Passenger Decks: 6	Cabins (for one person): 30	

OVERALL SCORE: 1,052 (OUT OF A POSSIBLE 2,000 POINTS)

OVERVIEW. *Kristina Regina,* a lovely family-owned old-world ship, originally a coastal ferry, was converted for close-in northern European coastal and archipelago cruises, and was extensively refurbished in 2000. It originally had steam turbines powerplant, but this was converted to diesel in 1987. This is one of the few ships left today that has two funnels, and is owned by a single family, many of whose members work aboard the ship. Passengers can visit the navigation bridge at any time (conditions permitting).

Exterior features include a wrap-around wooden promenade deck outdoors. There are few public rooms (there are, however, two small conference rooms), but the ship does have some beautiful hardwoods throughout its interiors, plus lots of brass accents. The Scandinavian artwork is also fascinating. The ship has a good-sized auditorium that doubles as a cinema and lecture hall, built into what was formerly a car deck. During the 2000 refit and refurbishment, a small gymnasium was installed.

Unusually, the fare includes only breakfast. However, meal packages (for lunch and dinner) can be purchased for the principal restaurant. The onboard currencies are the US dollar and the euro. Non-alcoholic drinks are free; alcoholic drinks are expensive. The ship's itineraries take it to the Baltic States and Russia, into White Sea ports, and to many ports in Europe and the Mediterranean.

SUITABLE FOR: *Kristina Regina* is best suited to couples and solo travellers who would not dream of stepping foot aboard a regular (large) cruise ship, but want a highly personalized vacation aboard a very traditional ship that is reminiscent of how ship travel used to be.

BERLITZ'S RATINGS

	Possible	Achieved
Ship	500	233
Accommodation	200	110
Food	400	238
Service	400	233
Entertainment	100	42
Cruise	400	196

ACCOMMODATION. There is a wide assortment of cabin sizes and configurations, from "suites" to cabins that are small (compartments, really). Some cabins have a queen-sized bed; others have two lower beds, or a single bed. All grades have a shower and toilet, radio, telephone (for internal calls only), but not much else, and they are really tiny, as are the bathrooms. As the cabins have very little storage space, you should take only what's really necessary. There are also five allergy-free cabins, as well as several cabins with interconnecting doors – good for families with children.

CUISINE/DINING. The principal dining room, Restaurant Regina, is quite charming and features Continental (European) cuisine, with much emphasis on fresh fish, seafood, and fresh berries (in season). The breads and cheeses are also good. There is single seating at assigned tables, and fine, hearty, and friendly service comes with a smile.

A second dining spot, the Kotka Restaurant, has an à la carte menu (everything is cooked to order), although all items are at extra cost. Additionally, continental breakfast and light snack foods can be found in the cafe.

ENTERTAINMENT. There is no formal entertainment, although dinner and after-dinner conversation with fellow passengers in the ship's lounge/bar really becomes the entertainment each evening.

SPA/FITNESS. There are none, except, of course, for a sauna (this *is* a Finnish cruise company, after all) and a small fitness room.

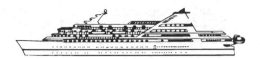

Le Diamant
★★★★

Boutique Ship: ....8,282 tons	Passenger Decks: 6	Cabins (for one person): 0
Lifestyle: ....Premium	Total Crew: 140	Cabins (with private balcony): 10
Cruise Line: ....Diamant Cruises	Passengers	Cabins (wheelchair accessible): 0
Former Names: ....Song of Flower,	(lower beds/all berths): 198/198	Cabin Current: ....220 volts
Explorer Starship	Passenger Space Ratio	Elevators: 2
Builder: ....KMV (Norway)	(lower beds/all berths): 41.8/41.8	Casino (gaming tables): ....Yes
Original Cost: ....n/a	Crew/Passenger Ratio	Slot Machines: ....Yes
Entered Service: 1986/May 2004	(lower beds/all berths): 1.4/1.4	Swimming Pools (outdoors): 1
Registry: ....Wallis and Fortuna	Navigation Officers: ....European	Swimming Pools (indoors): 0
Length (ft/m): 407.4/124.2	Cabins (total): 99	Whirlpools: 1
Beam (ft/m): 52.4/16.0	Size Range (sq ft/m): 183.0-398.0/	Self-Service Launderette: ....No
Draft (ft/m): 16.0/4.9	17.0-37.0	Dedicated Cinema/Seats: ....No
Propulsion/Propellers: ....diesel	Cabins (outside view): 99	Library: ....Yes
(5,500kW)/2 (CP)	Cabins (interior/no view): 0	Classification Society: ....Bureau Veritas

OVERALL SCORE: 1,544 (OUT OF A POSSIBLE 2,000 POINTS)

OVERVIEW. *Le Diamant* is a charming boutique-sized cruise ship (originally built as the ro-ro vessel *Begonia* in 1974 and fully converted for cruising in 1986). Operated for many years by Radisson Seven Seas Cruises, the ship was sold to the French company, Compagnie des Isles du Ponant/Tapis Rouges, a joint venture. The ship has rather tall, twin funnels (with a platform between them) that give a somewhat squat profile. If only the foredeck and bow could be a little longer, it would provide a more sleek appearance! The ship has been well maintained and cared for and is very clean throughout, although its interiors are now looking quite tired. There is a good amount of sheltered open deck and sunbathing space. Water sports facilities include snorkel equipment.

The interior decor is warm, with pastel colors, accented by splashes of color are used throughout the public rooms, passageways, and stairways. Good quality soft furnishings and fabrics are provided, and make the ship feel chic and comfortable, though not luxurious.

The ship has a warm and caring crew that really tries hard to make you feel at home and comfortable and at home during your cruise vacation. Totally understated elegance and a warm, informal lifestyle are the hallmarks of a cruise aboard this nice ship. *Le Diamant* should provide you with a pleasing, destination-intensive, yet relaxing cruise experience, delivered with a decent amount of style and panache.

SUITABLE FOR: *Le Diamant* is best suited to young-minded French-speaking couples and singles who want contemporary and sophisticated facilities in a very relaxed but chic,

BERLITZ'S RATINGS

	Possible	Achieved
Ship	500	375
Accommodation	200	139
Food	400	326
Service	400	332
Entertainment	100	70
Cruise	400	302

yacht-like small ship setting that is different to "normal" cruise ships, with very good food and decent service.

ACCOMMODATION. There are 10 elegant suites; 10 cabins are strictly non-smoking. All others are well equipped, complete with bathrobes and slippers, refrigerator, and VCR. All come with excellent closet and drawer space. Many have bathtubs, but they are tiny (shower tubs would be a better description). Disabled passengers should choose a cabin with a shower instead of a bath. There are no in-cabin dining facilities for dinner. When compared with the Seabourn and Silversea ships, the cabins are somewhat lacking and plain.

CUISINE/DINING. The dining room is really most charming and has warm colors, a welcoming ambience, and one seating, with no assigned tables(tables are for two, four or six. Dining is in open seating. Free wines accompany lunch and dinner. The cuisine is, naturally, classic French, with small portions that are attractively presented. The personal service is excellent, from the warm, highly personable and attentive staff.

ENTERTAINMENT. The well-tiered show lounge is a good, comfortable room, and there are good sight lines from almost all the banquette-style seating.

SPA/FITNESS. The health spa facility is very compact and short on space, but is reasonably adequate, and includes a beauty salon and sauna.

Le Levant
★★★★ +

Boutique Ship: . . . . .3,504 tons	Passenger Decks: 5	Cabins (with private balcony): 0
Lifestyle: . . . . .Premium	Total Crew: 50	Cabins (wheelchair accessible): 0
Cruise Line: . . . . .Ponant Cruises/	Passengers	Cabin Current: . . . . .110 and 220 volts
Classical Cruises	(lower beds/all berths): 90/90	Elevators: 1
Former Names: . . . . .none	Passenger Space Ratio	Casino (gaming tables): . . . . .No
Builder: . . . . .Leroux & Lotz (France)	(lower beds/all berths): 38.9/38.9	Slot Machines: .No
Original Cost: . . . .$35 million	Crew/Passenger Ratio	Swimming Pools (outdoors): 1
Entered Service: . . . . .Jan 1999	(lower beds/all berths): 1.8/1.8	Swimming Pools (indoors): 0
Registry: . . . . .Wallis and Fortuna	Navigation Officers: . . . . .French	Whirlpools: 0
Length (ft/m): 328.0/100.00	Cabins (total): .45	Self-Service Launderette: . . . . .No
Beam (ft/m): 45.9/14.00	Size Range (sq ft/m): 199.1/18.5	Dedicated Cinema/Seats: . . . . .No
Draft (ft/m): 11.4/3.50	Cabins (outside view): 45	Library: . . . . .Yes
Propulsion/Propellers: . . . . .diesel	Cabins (interior/no view): 0	Classification Society: . . . .Bureau Veritas
(3,000 kW)/2	Cabins (for one person): 0	

OVERALL SCORE: 1,609 (OUT OF A POSSIBLE 2,000 POINTS)

OVERVIEW. *Le Levant* is a high-class vessel that has the looks of a streamlined private mega-yacht. It has two slim funnels that extend over port and starboard sides to carry any soot away from the vessel. It was built in a specialist yacht-building yard in St Malo, France. There is an "open bridge" policy, so passengers may visit the bridge at any time (except when the ship is maneuvering in difficult conditions).

A stern "marina" platform is used for scuba diving, snorkeling or swimming. Two special landing craft are carried for shore visits, hidden in the stern, as well as six inflatable Zodiacs runabouts for landings in "soft" expedition areas such as the Amazon.

Inside, the vessel features contemporary, clean and uncluttered decor, and all the facilities of a private yacht. The public rooms are elegant and refined, with much use of wood trim and accenting. Particularly pleasing is the wood-paneled library. There is one grand salon, which accommodates all passengers, and is used by day as a lecture room, and by night as the main lounge/bar. A resident scuba dive master is aboard for all Caribbean sailings. Each cruise has life-enrichment lecturers aboard, as well as tour leaders.

This ship is often under charter to the New York-based Classical Cruises, which operates it in some offbeat destinations and cruise regions. In summer it may be in the Great Lakes, sailing between Toronto and Chicago (its pencil-slim beam allows it to navigate the locks). During the fall the ship heads to Canada/New England, and in the winter to the Caribbean and South America.

This is all-inclusive cruising, with all port charges, gratuities, and shore excursions included in the fare. The crew is almost entirely French. The onboard currency is the euro.

BERLITZ'S RATINGS

	Possible	Achieved
Ship	500	424
Accommodation	200	173
Food	400	312
Service	400	319
Entertainment	N/A	N/A
Cruise	500	381

SUITABLE FOR: *Le Levant* is best suited to young-minded couples and singles who want contemporary and sophisticated facilities in a very relaxed but chic, yacht-like small ship setting that is different to "normal" cruise ships, with very good food and decent service.

ACCOMMODATION. There are 45 ocean-view cabins (the brochure incorrectly calls them "suites") and all are midships and forward, in five price categories (a lot for such a small ship). Each cabin has a large ocean-view window, inlaid wood furniture and accenting, designer fabrics, two beds that will convert to a queen-sized bed, a television, VCR, refrigerator, personal safe, and personal amenity kits in the marble-appointed bathrooms, all of which feature a shower with a (circular) door (much better than a shower curtain); there are no bathtubs.

CUISINE/DINING. The Lafayette is a wood-panelled room that is warm and welcoming, with round and oval tables. The informal Veranda Restaurant has a panoramic view overlooking the stern (with both indoor and outdoor seating). Dining is in open seating. Free wines accompany lunch and dinner. The cuisine is, naturally, classic French.

ENTERTAINMENT. The Grand Salon, the main lounge, accommodates all passengers. It is the only room where smoking is allowed, and there are built-in video screens for showing movies. The only other entertainment is a singer/pianist (the room has a small dance floor in its center).

SPA/FITNESS. There is a small fitness room, and a steam room (there is no sauna) and shower.

Le Ponant
★★★★

Boutique Ship: . . . . .1,489 tons	Main Propulsion: . . . . . .a) engine/b) sails	Cabins (outside view): 32
Lifestyle: . . . . .Premium	Propulsion/Propellers: . . . . .diesel/	Cabins (interior/no view): 0
Cruise Line: . . . . .Ponant Cruises	sail power/1	Cabins (for one person): 0
Former Names: . . . . .none	Passenger Decks: 3	Cabins (with private balcony): 0
Builder: . . . . .SFCN (France)	Total Crew: 30	Cabins (wheelchair accessible): 0
Original Cost: . . . . .n/a	Passengers	Cabin Current: . . . . .220 volts
Entered Service: 1991	(lower beds/all berths): 64/67	Elevators: . . . . .No
Registry: . . . . .France	Passenger Space Ratio	Casino (gaming tables): . . . . .No
Length (ft/m): 288.7/88.00	(lower beds/all berths): 23.2/22.2	Slot Machines: . . . . .No
Beam (ft/m): 39.3/12.00	Crew/Passenger Ratio	Swimming Pools (outdoors): 0
Draft (ft/m): 13.1/4.00	(lower beds/all berths): 2.1/2.2	Whirlpools: 0
Type of Vessel: . . . . .high tech sail-cruiser	Navigation Officers: . . . . .French	Self-Service Launderette: . . . . .No
No. of Masts: .3	Cabins (total): 32	Library: . . . . .Yes
Sail Area (sq ft/m2): 16,150/1,500	Size Range (sq ft/m): 139.9/13.0	Classification Society: . . .Lloyd's Register

OVERALL SCORE: 1,540 (OUT OF A POSSIBLE 2,000 POINTS)

OVERVIEW. Ultra sleek, and very efficiently designed, this contemporary sail-cruise ship has three masts that rise 54.7 ft (16.7 meters) above the water line, and features electronic winches that assist in the furling and unfurling of the sails. The total sail area measures approximately 1,500 sq. meters/16,140 sq. ft. This captivating ship has plenty of room on its open decks for sunbathing (although they have padded cushions, somehow the off-white plastic deck lounge chairs are not at all elegant – teak would be so much more in keeping with the otherwise ultra-yacht look of the ship, although there probably is no room for them).

The very elegant, no-glitz interior design is clean, stylish, functional and ultra-high-tech. Three public lounges have pastel decor, soft colors and great European flair.

One price fits all. The ship is marketed mainly to young, sophisticated French-speaking passengers who love yachting and the sea. This is *très* French, and *très* chic and venturing off the beaten path is what cruising aboard *Le Ponant* is all about. The company also has a stunning mega-yacht cruise vessel, *Le Levant*. Gratuities are not "required", but they are expected. The onboard currency is the euro.

SUITABLE FOR: *Le Ponant* is best suited to young-minded couples and singles who want contemporary, sophisticated facilities in a very relaxed but chic setting that is different to "normal" cruise ships, with good food and service, no entertainment, and plenty of time for quiet relaxation.

ACCOMMODATION. There are 5 cabins on Antigua Deck (the open deck) and 27 cabins on Marie Galante Deck (the lowest deck). Crisp, clean blond woods and pristine white cabins have twin beds that convert to a double. There's a mini-bar, personal safe, and a private bathroom. All cabins have portholes, crisp artwork, and a refrigerator. There is limited storage space, however, and few drawers (they are also very small). The cabin bathrooms are quite small, but efficiently designed.

CUISINE/DINING. The lovely Karukera dining room has an open seating policy), so you can sit where you wish and dine with anyone you want. There is fresh fish daily (when available), and dinner is always treated as a true *affaire gastonomique*. The chef goes out to buy fresh local food items, including fresh fish, produce and fruits.

Free wines are included for lunch and dinner, and the cuisine is, naturally, classic French. Being French, the selection of cheeses and bread (and breakfast croissants) are good. Free cappuccinos and espresso are available.

For casual breakfasts and luncheons, there is also the charming outdoor café under a canvas sailcloth awning.

ENTERTAINMENT. There is no professional entertainment as such (although occasionally the crew may put on a little soirée). Dinner is the main event each evening, and, being a French product, dinner can provide several hours' worth of entertainment in itself.

SPA/FITNESS. There is no spa, fitness room, sauna, or steam room aboard *Le Ponant*. However, for recreation, there are water sports facilities, and these include an aft marina platform (from which you can swim), windsurfers, water-ski boat, scuba and snorkel equipment (scuba diving is an extra cost item, per dive).

BERLITZ'S RATINGS

	Possible	Achieved
Ship	500	399
Accommodation	200	166
Food	400	310
Service	400	319
Entertainment	N/A	N/A
Cruise	500	346

Legacy
★★ +

Boutique Ship: . . . . .1,740 tons	Sail Area (sq ft/m2): 19,900/1,848.7	Cabins (outside view): 46
Lifestyle: . . . . .Standard	Main Propulsion: . . . . .sail power	Cabins (interior/no view): 15
Cruise Line: . . . . . . .Windjammer Barefoot	Propulsion/Propellers: diesel/1	Cabins (for one person): 0
Cruises	Passenger Decks: 4	Cabins (with private balcony): 0
Former Names: . . . .*France II*	Total Crew: 43	Cabins (wheelchair accessible): 0
Builder: . . .Forges et al Mediterraneee du	Passengers	Cabin Current: . . . . .110 volts
Havre (France)	(lower beds/all berths): 122/122	Elevators: 0
Original Cost: . . . . .n/a	Passenger Space Ratio	Casino (gaming tables): . . . . .No
Entered Service: 1959/1997	(lower beds/all berths): 14.2/14.2	Slot Machines: . . . . .No
Registry: . . . . .Equatorial Guinea	Crew/Passenger Ratio	Swimming Pools (outdoors): 0
Length (ft/m): 294.0/89.6	(lower beds/all berths): 2.8/2.8	Whirlpools: 0
Beam (ft/m): 40.0/12.1	Navigation Officers: . . . . . . .International	Self-Service Launderette: . . . . .No
Draft (ft/m): 23.0/7.0	Cabins (total): 61	Library: . . . . .Yes
Type of Vessel: . . . . .barkentine	Size Range (sq ft/m): 75.0–159.0/	Classification Society: . .American Bureau
No. of Masts: .4	6.9–14.7	of Shipping

OVERALL SCORE: 998 (OUT OF A POSSIBLE 2,000 POINTS)

OVERVIEW. When built, this barquentine with four masts was a meteorological research and exploration vessel for the French Government. It was converted into a traditional tall ship by Windjammer Barefoot Cruises in 1998–9. Aboard a Windjammer vessel, you can let the crew do all the work, or you can lend a hand at the helm yourself. A neat thing to do is just to sit or lie in the nets at the bows of the vessel, feeling carefree.

Only the most casual clothes are required (T-shirts and shorts), and shoes are optional, although you may need them if you go off in one of the ports. The most used item may be your bathing suit – better take more than one. Smoking is allowed only on the open decks.

Jammin' aboard a Windjammer (first-time passengers are called "crewmates" while repeat passengers are called "jammers") is no-frills cruising (it could be called an "anti-cruise") in a no-nonsense, friendly environment, for those who don't need programmed activities.

It's all about going to sea and the romance of being at sea under sail. This ship can anchor in neat little Caribbean hideaways that larger cruise ships can't get near. *Legacy* features year-round cruises in the British and US Virgin Islands. Brochure rates might seem inexpensive, but you'll need to add on the airfare.

Legacy operates Caribbean cruises (from Fajardo, Puerto Rico). Other tall ships in the fleet include *Flying Cloud, Mandalay, Polynesia,* and *Yankee Clipper.* The onboard currency is the US dollar. This is an extremely casual vessel. There is very little room per passenger. Everything is

BERLITZ'S RATINGS

	Possible	Achieved
Ship	500	251
Accommodation	200	94
Food	400	188
Service	400	178
Entertainment	N/A	N/A
Cruise	500	287

basic, basic, basic. Tips to the crew are suggested – at $50 per week.

SUITABLE FOR: *Legacy* is best suited to young couples and singles who enjoy beaches, scuba diving and snorkeling, and are happy with just the basic necessities, all in an ultra-casual setting of sails, sea and sun, with no pretension.

ACCOMMODATION. There are eight grades (Burke's Berth, Admiral De-Luxe, Admiral Suite, Commodore Double, Commodore Triple, Ensign Cabin, Standard Cabin and Standard Single). Except for the top three grades, all other cabins are very small, however, particularly when compared to regular cruise ships. Remember, however, that this is a very casual cruise experience, so you won't need a lot of clothes anyway. All cabins are equipped with upper and lower berths, mostly quite narrow.

CUISINE/DINING. There is one dining room, and the meals are all very simple in style and service, with little choice and only the most basic presentation. Breakfast is served on board, as is dinner, while lunch could be either on board or at a beach, picnic-style. Wine is included for dinner.

ENTERTAINMENT. Entertainment in the evenings consists of just you and the crew. You can put on a toga, take or create a pirate outfit and join in the fun. This is cruising free 'n' easy style.

SPA/FITNESS. No facilities are provided.

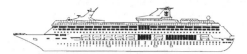

Legend of the Seas
★★★★

Large (Resort) Ship: ....69,130 tons	Total Crew: 720	Cabins (with private balcony): 231
Lifestyle: ....Standard	Passengers	Cabins (wheelchair accessible): 17
Cruise Line: Royal Caribbean International	(lower beds/all berths): 1,800/2,076	Cabin Current: ....110 and 220 volts
Former Names: ....none	Passenger Space Ratio	Elevators: 11
Builder: Chantiers de l'Atlantique (France)	(lower beds/all berths): 38.3/33.2	Casino (gaming tables): ....Yes
Original Cost: ....$325 million	Crew/Passenger Ratio	Slot Machines: ....Yes
Entered Service: ....May 1995	(lower beds/all berths): 2.5/2.8	Swimming Pools (outdoors): 2
Registry: ....The Bahamas	Navigation Officers: ....Norwegian	(1 with sliding roof)
Length (ft/m): 867.0/264.2	Cabins (total): 900	Swimming Pools (indoors): 0
Beam (ft/m): 105.0/32.0	Size Range (sq ft/m): 137.7–1,147.4/	Whirlpools: 4
Draft (ft/m): 23.9/7.3	12.8–106.6	Self-Service Launderette: ....No
Propulsion/Propellers: ....diesel	Cabins (outside view): 575	Dedicated Cinema/Seats: ....No
(40,200 kW)/2	Cabins (interior/no view): 325	Library: ....Yes
Passenger Decks: 11	Cabins (for one person): 0	Classification Society: Det Norske Veritas

OVERALL SCORE: 1,511 (OUT OF A POSSIBLE 2,000 POINTS)

OVERVIEW. This vessel (sister to *Splendour of the Seas*) has a contemporary profile and a nicely tiered stern. The pool deck amidships overhangs the hull to provide an extremely wide deck, while still allowing the ship to navigate the Panama Canal. With engines placed midships, there is little noise and no noticeable vibration, and the ship has an operating speed of up to 24 knots.

The interior decor is colorful, but too glitzy for European tastes. The outside light is brought inside in many places, with over 2 acres (8,000 sq. meters) of glass providing contact with sea and air. There's an innovative single-level sliding glass roof (not a magrodome) over the more formal setting of one of two swimming pools, providing a multi-activity, all-weather indoor-outdoor area, called the Solarium. The glass roof provides shelter for the Roman-style pool and the health and fitness facilities (which are good) and slides aft to cover the miniature golf course when required (both cannot be covered at the same time, however).

Golfers might enjoy the 18-hole, 6,000-sq. ft (560 sq.-meter) miniature golf course. It has the topography of a real course, complete with trees, foliage, grass, bridges, water hazards, and lighting for play at night. The holes themselves are 155-230 sq. ft (14.3–21.3 sq. meters).

Inside, two full entertainment decks are sandwiched between five decks full of cabins, so there are plenty of public rooms to lounge and drink in. A multi-tiered seven-deck-high atrium lobby, complete with a huge stainless steel sculpture, connects with the impressive Viking Crown Lounge via glass-walled lifts. The casino is really expansive, overly glitzy and absolutely packed. The library, outside of which is a bust of Shakespeare, is a fine facility, and has

BERLITZ'S RATINGS

	Possible	Achieved
Ship	500	426
Accommodation	200	163
Food	400	248
Service	400	302
Entertainment	100	78
Cruise	400	294

more than 2,000 books.

There is, sadly, no separate cinema. The casino could be somewhat disorienting, with its mirrored walls and lights flashing everywhere, although it is no different to those found in Las Vegas gaming halls.

ACCOMMODATION. There are 17 different grades – rather too many – but no cabins for singles. Royal Caribbean International has designed a ship with much larger standard cabins than in any of the company's previous vessels (except *Splendour of the Seas*). Some cabins on Deck 8 also have a larger door for wheelchair access in addition to the 17 cabins for the physically disabled, and the ship is very accessible, with ample ramped areas and sloping decks. All cabins have a sitting area and beds that convert to double configuration, and there is ample closet and drawer space. There is not much space around the bed, though, and the showers could have been better designed. Those cabins with balconies have glass railings rather than steel/wood to provide less intrusive sightlines.

The largest accommodation is the Royal Suite, which is beautifully designed, finely decorated, and features a baby grand piano, whirlpool bathtub, and other fine amenities. Several quiet sitting areas are located adjacent to the best cabins amidships.

CUISINE/DINING. The Romeo and Juliet Dining Room has dramatic two-deck-high glass side walls, so many passengers both upstairs and downstairs can see both the ocean and each other in reflection (it would, perhaps, have been even better located at the stern), but it is quite noisy when full (call it atmosphere). The two seatings are non-smoking.

A cavernous indoor-outdoor Windjammer Café, located towards the bow and above the bridge, has good views on three sides from large ocean-view windows. A good-sized snack area provides even more informal eating options.

ENTERTAINMENT. The "That's Entertainment" Theatre seats 802 and is a single-level showlounge with tiered seating levels. Sight lines are generally good from almost all seats.

Strong cabaret acts are also featured in the main showlounge. A second entertainment lounge, the Anchors Aweigh Lounge, is where cabaret acts, including late-night adult (blue) comedy are featured. Other lounges and bars have live music for listening and dancing.

The entertainment throughout is upbeat (in fact, it is difficult to get away from music and noise), but is typical of the kind of resort hotel found ashore in Las Vegas. There is even background music in all corridors and elevators, and constant music outdoors on the pool deck. If you want a quiet relaxing holiday, you should choose another ship.

SPA/FITNESS. The ShipShape Fitness Center has a gymnasium (it is located on the port side of the ship, aft of the funnel), and has a small selection of high-tech muscle-pumping equipment. There is also an aerobics studio (classes are offered in a variety of keep fit regimes), a beauty salon, and a sauna, as well as treatment rooms for such pampering things as massages, facials, etc. While the facilities are quite small when compared with those aboard the company's newer ships, they are adequate for the short cruises that this ship operates. For more sporting passengers, there is activity galore – including a rock-climbing wall, with several separate climbing tracks. It is located outdoors at the aft end of the funnel.

● **For more extensive general information about the Royal Caribbean experience, see pages 128–131.**

Maasdam
★★★★

Large (Resort) Ship: ....55,451 tons	Total Crew: 557	Cabins (with private balcony): 150
Lifestyle: ....Premium	Passengers	Cabins (wheelchair accessible): 6
Cruise Line: ......Holland America Line	(lower beds/all berths): 1,266/1,627	Cabin Current: ....110 and 220 volts
Former Names: ....none	Passenger Space Ratio	Elevators: 12
Builder: ....Fincantieri (Italy)	(lower beds/all berths): 43.8/34.0	Casino (gaming tables): ....Yes
Original Cost: ....$215 million	Crew/Passenger Ratio	Slot Machines: ....Yes
Entered Service: ....Dec 1993	(lower beds/all berths): 2.2/2.9	Swimming Pools (outdoors): 1
Registry: ....The Netherlands	Navigation Officers: ....Dutch	Swimming Pools (indoors): 1
Length (ft/m): 719.3/219.30	Cabins (total): 632	(magrodome)
Beam (ft/m): 101.0/30.80	Size Range (sq ft/m): 186.2–1,124.8/	Whirlpools: 2
Draft (ft/m): 24.6/7.50	17.3–104.5	Self-Service Launderette:...........Yes
Propulsion/Propellers: .....diesel-electric	Cabins (outside view): 502	Dedicated Cinema/Seats: Yes/249
(34,560 kW)/2	Cabins (interior/no view): 131	Library: ....Yes
Passenger Decks:.................10	Cabins (for one person): 0	Classification Society: ...Lloyd's Register

OVERALL SCORE: 1,533 (OUT OF A POSSIBLE 2,000 POINTS)

OVERVIEW. *Maasdam* is one of a series of four almost identical ships in the same series – the others are *Statendam*, *Ryndam* and *Veendam*. Although the exterior styling is rather angular (some would say boxy – the funnel certainly is), it is softened and balanced somewhat by the fact that the hull is painted black. There is a full wrap-around teak promenade deck outdoors – excellent for strolling, and, thankfully, no sign of synthetic turf anywhere. The deck lounge chairs on the exterior promenade deck are wood, and have comfortable cushioned pads, while those at the swimming pool on Lido Deck are of white plastic. Holland America Line keeps its ships clean and tidy, and there is good passenger flow throughout the public areas.

In the interiors of this "S"-class ship, an asymmetrical layout helps to reduce bottlenecks and congestion. Most of the public rooms are concentrated on two decks, Promenade Deck, and Upper Promenade Deck, which creates a spacious feel to the ship's interiors. In general, a restrained approach to interior styling is taken, using a mixture of contemporary materials combined with traditional woods and ceramics. There is, fortunately, little "glitz" anywhere.

What is noticeable is the array of artworks throughout the ship (costing about $2 million), assembled and nicely displayed to represent the fine Dutch heritage of Holland America Line and to present a balance between standard itineraries and onboard creature comforts. Several oil paintings of former Holland America Line ships by Stephen Card (an ex-captain) adorn stairway landings. Also noticeable are the fine flower arrangements throughout the public areas and foyers – used to good effect to brighten up what to some is dull decor.

BERLITZ'S RATINGS

	Possible	Achieved
Ship	500	418
Accommodation	200	162
Food	400	267
Service	400	299
Entertainment	100	77
Cruise	400	310

Atop the ship, with forward facing views that wrap around the sides, is the Crow's Nest Lounge. By day it makes a fine observation lounge, with large ocean-view windows, while by night it turns into a nightclub with extremely variable lighting.

The atrium foyer is three decks high, although its light-catching green glass sculpted centerpiece (*Totem* by Luciano Vistosi, composed of almost 2,000 pieces of glass) makes it look a little crowded, and leaves little room in front of the purser's office (called the Front Office). A hydraulic magrodome (glass) roof covers the reasonably-sized swimming pool/whirlpools and central Lido area (whose focal point is a large dolphin sculpture) so that this can be used in either fine or inclement weather.

Maasdam, a well-built ship, has fairly decent interior decor. Holland America Line is constantly fine-tuning its performance and its regular passengers (almost all of whom are North American – there are few international passengers) find the company's ships comfortable and well-run. The company continues its strong maritime traditions, although the food and service components still let the rest of the cruise experience down. Perhaps the ship's best asset is its friendly and personable Filipino and Indonesian crew, although communication can prove frustrating and service is inconsistent. The onboard currency is the US dollar.

This ship has a large, relaxing library (Leyden Library); there's also a cardroom, an Explorer's Lounge (good for relaxing in, for afternoon tea, and after-dinner coffee), a Crows Nest (the ship's observation lounge that doubles as a late-night spot and discotheque), an intimate Piano Bar, and, of course, a casino.

Holland America Line's many repeat passengers always seem to enjoy the fact that social dancing is always on the menu. In the final analysis, however, the score for this ship ends up just a disappointing tad under what it could be if the food and food service staff were more memorable (more professional training might help).

An escalator travels between two of the lower decks (one of which was originally planned to be the embarkation point), but it is almost pointless. The charge to use the washing machines and dryers in the self-service launderette is petty, particularly for suite occupants, as they pay high prices for their cruises. The men's urinals in public restrooms are unusually high.

ACCOMMODATION. The accommodation ranges from small interior (no view) cabins to a large penthouse suite, in 17 price categories. The price you pay will depend on the grade, size and location you choose. All cabin televisions receive CNN and TNT.

The interior (no view) and outside (with a view) standard cabins feature twin beds that convert to a queen-size bed, and there is a separate living space with sofa and coffee table. However, although the drawer space is generally good, the closet space is actually very tight, particularly for long cruises (although more than adequate for a 7-night cruise). Bathrobes are also provided for all suites/cabins, as are hairdryers, and a small range of personal toiletries (soap, conditioning shampoo, body lotion, shower cap, vanity kit). The bathrooms are quite well laid out, but the bathtubs are small units better described as shower tubs.

On Navigation Deck, 28 suites have accommodation for up to four. These suites also have in-suite dining as an alternative to the dining room, for private, reclusive meals. These are very spacious, tastefully decorated and well laid-out suites, and have a separate, good-sized living room, bedroom with two lower beds (convertible to a king-size bed), dressing room, plenty of closet and drawer space (walk-in closet), marble bathroom with Jacuzzi tub and separate toilet/washroom with bidet.

The largest accommodation of all is a penthouse suite. There is only one, located on the starboard side of Navigation Deck at the forward staircase. It has a king-sized bed (television and video player) and vanity desk; large walk-in closet with superb drawer space, oversize whirlpool bath (it could seat four) and separate shower enclosure, separate washroom with toilet, bidet and washbasin; living room with writing desk, large television and full set of audio equipment; dressing room, large private balcony (with teak lounge chairs and drinks tables, dining table and four chairs), pantry (with large refrigerator, toaster unit, and full coffee/tea making facilities and food preparation area, and a separate entrance from the hallway), mini-bar/refrigerator, a guest toilet and floor-to-ceiling windows. Note that there is no bell push.

CUISINE/DINING. The Rotterdam Dining Room, which has both smoking and no-smoking sections, spans two decks. It is located at the stern of the ship, is quite dramatic, and has a grand staircase (although few seem to use it), panoramic views on three sides, and a music balcony. It has open seating for breakfast and lunch, and four seatings for dinner (you must pre-select a time and stick with it) at 5.45pm, 6.15pm, 8pm and 8.30pm (tables for two, four, six or eight are available). The waiter stations in the dining room are very noisy for anyone seated adjacent to them.

Alternative dining option: Added in 2003, the Pinnacle Grill is located just forward of the balcony level of the main dining room on the starboard side. The 66-seat dining spot features Pacific Northwest cuisine (Dungeness crab, Alaska salmon, halibut and other regional specialties). The new venue (reservations are necessary, and a cover/service charge of $20 applies) was created out of the former private dining wing of the main dining room, plus a slice of the Explorer's Lounge. A Bvlgari show plate, Rosenthal china, Reidel wine glasses, and Frette table linen are used. The Pinnacle Grill is a much better dining experience than the main dining room and worth it for that special celebration.

For more casual evening eating, the Lido Buffet is open for casual dinners on all except the last night of each cruise, in an open-seating arrangement. Tables are set with crisp linens, flatware and stemware. A set menu is featured, and this includes a choice of four entreés.

The dual-line, self-serve Lido Buffet (one side is for smokers, the other side for non-smokers) is also the place for casual breakfasts and lunches. Again there is much use of canned fruits (good for older passengers with few teeth) and packeted items, although there are several commercial low-calorie salad dressings. The beverage station also lets it down, for it is no better than those found in family outlets ashore in the United States. In addition, a poolside grill provides basic American hamburgers and hot dogs.

Passengers will need to eat in the Lido Cafe on any days when the dining room is closed for lunch (this is typically once or twice per cruise, depending on the itinerary).

ENTERTAINMENT. The Rembrandt Showlounge, located at the forward part of the ship, spans two decks, with banquette seating on both main and upper levels. It is basically a well-designed room, but the ceiling is low and the sight lines from the balcony level are quite poor.

SPA/FITNESS. The Ocean Spa is located one deck below the navigation bridge at the very forward part of the ship. It includes a gymnasium (with all the latest muscle-pumping exercise machines, including an abundance of treadmills) with ocean views, an aerobics exercise area, large beauty salon with ocean-view windows to the port side, several treatment rooms, and men's and women's sauna, steam room and changing areas.

● **For more extensive general information on what a Holland America Line cruise is like, see pages 118–222.**

Majesty of the Seas
★★★ +

Large (Resort) Ship: ....73,941 tons	Passenger Decks: 14	Cabins (for one person): 0
Lifestyle: ....Standard	Total Crew: 827	Cabins (with private balcony): 62
Cruise Line: ....Royal Caribbean	Passengers	Cabins (wheelchair accessible): 4
International	(lower beds/all berths): 2,350/2,744	Cabin Current: ....110 volts
Former Names: ....none	Passenger Space Ratio	Elevators: 11
Builder: ....Chantiers de l'Atlantique	(lower beds/all berths): 31.4/26.9	Casino (gaming tables): ....Yes
Original Cost: ....$300 million	Crew/Passenger Ratio	Slot Machines: ....Yes
Entered Service: ....Apr 1992	(lower beds/all berths): 2.8/3.3	Swimming Pools (outdoors): 2
Registry: ....The Bahamas	Navigation Officers: ....Norwegian	Swimming Pools (indoors): 0
Length (ft/m): 879.9/268.2	Cabins (total): 1,175	Whirlpools: 2
Beam (ft/m): 105.9/32.3	Size Range (sq ft/m): 118.4–670.0/	Self-Service Launderette: ....No
Draft (ft/m): 24.9/7.6	11.0–62.2	Dedicated Cinema/Seats: Yes/200
Propulsion/Propellers: ....diesel	Cabins (outside view): 732	Library: ....Yes
(21,844 kW)/2	Cabins (interior/no view): 443	Classification Society: Det Norske Veritas

OVERALL SCORE: 1,394 (OUT OF A POSSIBLE 2,000 POINTS)

OVERVIEW. When first introduced, this ship (together with its two sisters, *Monarch of the Seas* and *Sovereign of the Seas*) was an innovative vessel. Royal Caribbean International's trademark Viking Crown lounge and bar surrounds the funnel and provides a stunning view. The open deck space is very cramped when full, as aboard any large ship, although there seems to be plenty of it. There is a basketball court.

The interior layout is a little awkward, as it is designed in a vertical stack, with most of the public rooms located aft, and the accommodation located forward (this ensures quiet areas) There is, however, an impressive array of spacious and elegant public rooms, although the decor calls to mind the IKEA school of interior design. A stunning five-deck-high Centrum lobby has cascading stairways and two glass-walled lifts.

There is a decent two-level showlounge and a decent array of shops, albeit with lots of tacky merchandise. Casino gamers will find blackjack, craps, Caribbean stud poker and roulette tables, plus an array of slot machines in Casino Royale. Among the public rooms, the library is a nice feature for quite relaxation, and there is a decent selection of books. The entertainment program is quite sound, and there is a decent range of children's/teens' programs and cheerful youth counselors.

This floating resort provides a well tuned, yet impersonal, short cruise experience for a lot of passengers. The dress code is very casual. In the final analysis, you will probably be overwhelmed by the public spaces, and under whelmed by the size of the cabins. Because the public rooms are mostly located aft (accommodation is located in the forward section of the ship), there is often a long wait for elevators, particularly at peak times (after dinner, shows, and talks). The ship was extensively refurbished in 2003.

BERLITZ'S RATINGS	Possible	Achieved
Ship	500	381
Accommodation	200	141
Food	400	245
Service	400	286
Entertainment	100	75
Cruise	400	266

ACCOMMODATION. There are 17 price categories. The price will depend on the grade, size and location you choose.

Suites: Thirteen suites on Bridge Deck are reasonably large and nicely furnished (the largest is the Royal Suite), with separate living and sleeping spaces. They provide more space, with better service and more perks than standard-grade accommodation.

Standard Cabins: The standard outside-view and interior (no view) cabins are very small, however, although an arched window treatment and colorful soft furnishings do give the illusion of more space. Almost all cabins have twin beds that can be converted to a queen-sized or double bed configuration, together with moveable bedside tables. All of the standard cabins have very little closet and drawer space (you will need some luggage engineering to stow your cases). You should, therefore, think of packing only minimal clothing, which is all you really need for a short cruise.

All cabins have a private bathroom, with shower enclosure, toilet and washbasin.

CUISINE/DINING. The two large dining rooms, named Maytime and Mikado (both non-smoking) have Hollywood musical themes. The Maytime Dining Room is located on the lowest level of the atrium lobby, while the Mikado Dining Room is located one deck higher. There are tables for four, six or eight, but no tables for two, and there are two seatings. The dining operation is well orchestrated, with emphasis on highly programmed (insensitive), extremely hurried service that many find intrusive.

For casual breakfasts and lunches, the Windjammer Cafe is the place to go, although there are often lines at peak times, and the selection is very average.

ENTERTAINMENT. A Chorus Line is the ship's principal show lounge; it has both main and balcony levels, with banquette seating. On the stage is a video wall with 50 screens – good for visual presentations.

Royal Caribbean's large-scale production shows are extremely colorful spectaculars that will remind you of Las Vegas casino hotel shows, with their high-energy hype, presentation and glitz. They are fast-moving, razzle-dazzle shows that rely a lot on lighting and special effects, but have little or no storyline, often poor linkage between themes and scenes, and choreography that is more stepping in place rather than dancing. Strong cabaret acts are also featured in the main showlounge.

A smaller entertainment lounge, the Paint Your Wagon Lounge, is where cabaret acts, including late-night adult (blue) comedy are featured, as well as music for dancing.

The entertainment throughout is upbeat (in fact, it is difficult to get away from music and noise), but is typical of the kind of resort hotel found ashore in Las Vegas. There is even background music in all corridors and lifts, and constant music outdoors on the pool deck.

SPA/FITNESS. The ShipShape Fitness Center has a gymnasium with aft-facing views (it is located at the aft of the ship), and a selection of high-tech muscle-pumping equipment. There is also an aerobics studio, and classes are offered in a variety of keep fit regimes. There is also a beauty salon, and a sauna, as well as treatment rooms for such pampering things as massages, facials, etc. While the facilities are not as extensive as those aboard the company's newer ships, they are adequate for the short cruises that this ship operates.

For the more sporting, there is activity galore – including a rock-climbing wall, with several separate climbing tracks. It is located outdoors at the aft end of the funnel.

● **For more extensive general information about the Royal Caribbean cruise experience, see pages 128–131.**

FUN FACTS

● Cruise ship design is interesting. The beauty of design lies in curves, not in straight lines. Today's large resort ships, designed merely for cruising in warm weather regions and not for voyaging across the North Atlantic (heaven forbid, the delivery voyage was enough), are made of straight lines. They are boxy and cold in appearance, although they provide much more usable space inside the ship (some call it warehouse cruising). Take a look at *Saga Rose* (the former *Sagafjord*) and you won't find a straight line anywhere. Then take a look at *Imagination* and compare the two.

● Beatrice Muller, in her early 80s, makes her permanent home at sea. She lives year-round aboard Cunard Line's *Queen Elizabeth 2*, paying a set amount to reside in Cabin 4068. She prefers being aboard the ship rather than sit around in a retirement home in Britain's damp cli-

mate, and proves that the world is her oyster. She loves it because she doesn't have to deal with the daily drudgery of shopping, doesn't need a car, or pay electric, gas or telephone bills. She communicates with her family by using the computer center's email service.

● Cruise lines and charity go hand in hand. Cunard donated 1,500 pieces of classic furniture from the 1994 refit of *QE2* to the Salvation Army for its adult rehabilitation program. Crew aboard the same ship donate money to buy guide dogs for the blind, or an ambulance for St. John's Ambulance Brigade in the UK. Princess Cruises made a "sizeable" contribution to UNICEF following the death of Audrey Hepburn in 1993 (she named the company's *Star Princess*, now operating as *Adonia* for P&O Cruises). Passengers of Hapag-Lloyd's *Europa* have donated more than 1 million euros to children's homes in Vietnam.

Both Holland America Line and Princess Cruises have contributed heavily to the Raptor Center in Juneau, Alaska.

● Someone forgot to "score" the champagne bottle when Dame Judi Dench named Carnival Legend in Harwich, England, on August 21, 2002. On the first two tries, the bottle didn't break. Then Dame Judi took the bottle in her own hands and smashed it against the side of the ship. It broke, and the foam and champagne went all over her. She was dubbed Dame Judi Drench.

● In the mid-1960s there were 12 "bell boys" ("piccolos" in hotels-peak) aboard the Cunard Line's RMS *Queen Elizabeth* and *Queen Mary*. They manned the elevators and opened the doors to the various restaurants. Each day, before they were allowed to work, they all lined up and their fingernails were inspected. Those were the days.

Mandalay
★★

Boutique Ship: ....420 tons	Sail Area (sq ft/m2): 12,002.1/1,115.0	Cabins (outside view): 30
Lifestyle: ....Standard	Main Propulsion: ....sail power	Cabins (interior/no view): 6
Cruise Line: ....Windjammer Barefoot	Propulsion/Propellers: diesel/1	Cabins (for one person): 0
Cruises	Passenger Decks: 3	Cabins (with private balcony): 2
Former Names: ....*Vema, Hussar*	Total Crew: 28	Cabins (wheelchair accessible): 0
Builder: ....Cox & Stevens (UK)	Passengers	Cabin Current: ....110 volts
Original Cost: ....n/a	(lower beds/all berths): 72/72	Elevators: 0
Entered Service: 1923/1982	Passenger Space Ratio	Casino (gaming tables): ....No
Registry: ....Equitorial Guinea	(lower beds/all berths): 5.8/5.8	Slot Machines: ....No
Length (ft/m): 236.0/71.9	Crew/Passenger Ratio	Swimming Pools (outdoors): 0
Beam (ft/m): 33.0/10.0	(lower beds/all berths): 2.5/2.5	Whirlpools: 0
Draft (ft/m): 15.0/4.5	Navigation Officers: ....International	Self-Service Launderette: ....No
Type of Vessel: ....barkentine	Cabins (total): 36	Library: ....Yes
No. of Masts: 3	Size Range (sq ft/m): 65.0–100.1/6.0–9.3	Classification Society: ....none

OVERALL SCORE: 902 (OUT OF A POSSIBLE 2,000 POINTS)

OVERVIEW. *Mandalay* was built for the American financier E.F. Hutton; it was then sold to shipping magnate George Vettelman. Windjammer Barefoot Cruises acquired it in 1982. Aboard a Windjammer ship, you can let the crew do all the work, or you can lend a hand at the helm yourself. One neat thing to do is just to sit or lie in the nets at the bows of the vessel, feeling carefree.

The mood is free and easy, the ships are equipped very simply, and only the most casual clothes are required (T-shirts and shorts), and shoes are optional, although you may need them if you go off in one of the ports. Quite possibly the most used item will be your bathing suit – so you should take more than one. Smoking is allowed only on the open decks.

Jammin' aboard a Windjammer (first-time passengers are called "crewmates" while repeat passengers are called "jammers") is no-frills cruising in a no-nonsense, friendly environment, for the young at heart and those who don't need programmed activities. It's all about going to sea and enjoying the romance of being at sea under sail.

Anyone who enjoys beaches, scuba diving and snorkeling around the Caribbean, and anyone seeking sun, sea, and sand will be best suited to a Windjammer Barefoot Cruises cruise, as well as lovers of old sailing ships.

This ship can anchor in neat little Caribbean hideaways that larger (regular) cruise ships can't get near. Although itineraries (well, islands) are provided in the brochure, the captain actually decides which islands to go to in any given area, depending on the sea and weather conditions. *Mandalay* operates year-round cruises in the Caribbean, and sails from Antigua and Grenada. Although at first glance the brochure rates might seem inexpensive, you'll need to add

BERLITZ'S RATINGS

	Possible	Achieved
Ship	500	219
Accommodation	200	79
Food	400	166
Service	400	188
Entertainment	N/A	N/A
Cruise	500	250

on the airfare in order to get the true cost. Other tall ships in the fleet include *Flying Cloud, Legacy, Polynesia,* and *Yankee Clipper.* The onboard currency is the US dollar.

There really is very little space per passenger. Tips to the crew are suggested – at $50 per week.

SUITABLE FOR: *Mandalay* is best suited to young, carefree singles that enjoy beaches, scuba diving and snorkeling, and are happy with just the basic necessities, all in an ultra-casual setting of sails, sea and sun, with no pretension.

ACCOMMODATION. There are four grades (Admiral's Suite, Deck Cabin, Captain's Cabin and Standard Cabin). The cabins are small (designed more for packages than people), however, particularly when compared to regular cruise ships. But this is a very casual cruise experience and you will need few clothes anyway. All cabins have upper and lower berths, and most of them are quite narrow.

CUISINE/DINING. There is one dining room, and meals are all very simple in style and service, with little choice and only the most basic presentation. Breakfast is served on board, as is dinner, while lunch could be either on board or at a beach, picnic-style. Wine is included for dinner.

ENTERTAINMENT. Entertainment in the evenings consists of just passengers and crew. You can put on a toga, take or create a pirate outfit and join in the fun. This is cruising free 'n' easy style.

SPA/FITNESS. There are no facilities.

Marco Polo
★★★

Mid-Size Ship: . . . . .22,080 tons	Total Crew: 356	Cabins (with private balcony): 0
Lifestyle: . . . . .Standard	Passengers	Cabins (wheelchair accessible): 2
Cruise Line: . . . . .Orient Lines	(lower beds/all berths): 848/915	Cabin Current: . . . . . . .110 and 220 volts
Former Names: . . . . . .*Aleksandr Pushkin*	Passenger Space Ratio	Elevators: 4
Builder: . . . . . .VEB Mathias Thesen Werft	(lower beds/all berths): 26.0/24.1	Casino (gaming tables): . . . . .Yes
(Germany)	Crew/Passenger Ratio	Slot Machines: . . . . .Yes
Original Cost: .n/a	(lower beds/all berths): 2.3/2.5	Swimming Pools (outdoors): 1
Entered Service: . . . .Apr 1966/Nov 1993	Navigation Officers: . . . . . .Scandinavian	Swimming Pools (indoors): 0
Registry: . . . . .The Bahamas	Cabins (total): .425	Whirlpools: 3
Length (ft/m): 578.4/176.28	Size Range (sq ft/m): 93.0–484.0/8.6–44.9	Self-Service Launderette: . . . . .No
Beam (ft/m): 77.4/23.60	Cabins (outside view): 292	Dedicated Cinema/Seats: . . . . .No
Draft (ft/m): 26.8/8.17	Cabins (interior/no view): 133	Library: . . . . .Yes
Propulsion/Propellers: .diesel(14,444 kW)/2	Cabins (for one person): . . .(many doubles	Classification Society: . . . .Bureau Veritas
Passenger Decks: 8	sold for single occupancy)	

OVERALL SCORE: 1,232 (OUT OF A POSSIBLE 2,000 POINTS)

OVERVIEW. This ship was built as one of five almost identical sister ships for the Russian/Ukrainian fleet (it was originally constructed to re-open the Leningrad to Montreal transatlantic route in 1966, after a long absence since 1949). The ship has a fine, traditional "real-ship" profile, an extremely strong ice-strengthened hull and huge storage spaces for long voyages. After being completely refitted (from the hull and engines up) and refurbished, the ship now features well-designed destination-intensive cruises, at realistic prices.

Orient Lines, and its single ship *Marco Polo* was bought by Norwegian Cruise Line in 1998 (and then by Star Cruises in 2000), but continues to operate under the Orient Lines brand name. A second ship (*Crown Odyssey*) was added to the fleet in 2000, but in 2003 it was transferred to the NCL fleet.

Marco Polo is fitted with the latest navigational aids and biological waste treatment center, and carries 10 Zodiac landing craft for in-depth shore trips in eco-sensitive areas.

This is a comfortable vessel throughout and, because it has a deep draft, rides well in unkind sea conditions. There are two large, forward-facing open-deck viewing areas. There is also a helicopter-landing pad atop the ship. The wood decked aft swimming pool/lido deck area is kept in good condition. Joggers and walkers can circle around the ship – not on the promenade deck, but one deck above, although this goes past vast air intakes that are noisy, and the walkway is very narrow.

As soon as you walk aboard, you feel a warm, welcoming, homely ambiance that is instantly comforting. There is a wide range of public rooms, most of which are arranged

BERLITZ'S RATINGS

	Possible	Achieved
Ship	500	312
Accommodation	200	127
Food	400	234
Service	400	256
Entertainment	100	58
Cruise	400	245

on one horizontal deck. A sense of spaciousness pervades, as most have high ceilings. The interior decor is very tasteful, with careful use of mirrored surfaces, as well as colors that do not clash and are relaxing but not boring; the subdued lighting helps maintain an air of calmness and relaxation.

Although this ship is more than 35 years old, it is in remarkably fine shape – a tribute to the management and crew. Indeed, it's in better shape than many ships only 10 years old, and its interiors are constantly being refurbished and refreshed.

All in all, *Marco Polo* has well-planned destination-intensive cruises, and offers really good value for money in very comfortable, elegant but unpretentious surroundings, while a friendly and accommodating Filipino crew helps to make a cruise a pleasant, no-hassle experience. Despite the fact that the ship is beautifully maintained, the slightly lower score than it was given in last year's edition reflects changing times (there's a lot of new tonnage around), less crew training in service areas, and other items.

There is no observation lounge with forward-facing views over the ship's bows. There is a little too much use of plastic and Styrofoam cups when glass would be much better for presentation. There are many "lips" or raised thresholds, so you need to be on your guard when walking through the ship, and particularly when walking up or down the exterior stairways. This could prove difficult for wheelchair passengers. Many of the Filipino crew speak Tagalog in public areas (they should be speaking in English). Drinks prices are high.

SUITABLE FOR: *Marco Polo* is best suited to couples and single travelers of mature years who enjoy being transported to interesting destinations in the comfort of a ship that is traditional in style, unpretentious yet pleasing, and without the trappings of much entertainment or organized parlor games.

ACCOMMODATION. The cabins, which come in 13 different price grades (depending on location and size), are a profusion of different sizes and configurations. The price you pay will depend on the grade, size and location you choose. All are pleasingly decorated, and feature rich wood cabinetry, wood and mirror-fronted closets, adequate drawer and storage space, television, thin cotton bathrobe, and hairdryer (in the bathroom) and non-vacuum (non-noisy) toilets. Carpets curtains and bedspreads are all nicely color coordinated. Weak points include extremely poor sound insulation between cabins (you can probably hear you neighbours brushing their hair), and the fact that the bathrooms are small, with little storage space for toiletries (particularly during long cruises).

The largest accommodation is found in two deluxe suites and two junior suites. The deluxe suites (Dynasty and Mandarin), have a queen-sized bed, separate living room, and marble bathroom with bathtub/shower, walk-in closet, refrigerator, television and VCR. The Junior Suites feature two lower beds, lounge area, and marble bathroom with bathtub/shower, walk-in closet, and refrigerator.

Also very comfortable are the Superior Deluxe oceanview cabins that have two lower beds (some can be converted to a queen-sized bed), marble bathroom with bathtub/shower, and refrigerator.

Some cabins on Upper Deck and Sky Deck have lifeboat-obstructed views. Since many passengers are of senior years, there should be 24-hour room service – but there isn't. It would be advisable to avoid cabins 310/312 as these are located close to the engine room doorway and the noise level is considerable.

CUISINE/DINING. The Seven Seas Restaurant is nicely decorated in soft pastel colors, practical in design, and functions well, but it has a low ceiling, is noisy, and the tables are very close together. There are two seatings. There are tables for two to 10, and fine place settings and china. The food itself is of a good standard, with good presentation. The wine list is quite extensive, and the prices are very reasonable, although most wines are young.

Raffles is the place to head for informal self-serve breakfasts and lunches (there is seating inside as well as outdoors around the ship's swimming pool). On some evenings during each cruise it also becomes an alternative dining spot, for about 75 people. Reservations are required, but there is no extra charge. A 15% gratuity is added to all bar and wine accounts. The onboard currency is the US dollar.

ENTERTAINMENT. The Ambassador Lounge is the principal venue for shows and cabaret acts. It is a single-level room with banquette seating and reasonably decent sightlines, although there are several pillars to obstruct the view from several seats. Orient Lines' entertainment is low-key and low-budget, and consists of a few cabaret acts (singers, magicians, ventriloquists, comedians and others) who regularly perform on the cruise ship circuit.

Several bands and musical units provide live music for social dancing and listening in several of the ship's bars and cocktail lounges.

SPA/FITNESS. This is an older ship that was built when spa and wellbeing facilities were not really thought about. A Health Spa was added in a later refit. It is located aft on Upper Deck, and contains a small gymnasium (it's not large, but there are a few treadmills, exercycles, and some muscle-toning equipment), a beauty salon, a sauna, changing facilities, and treatment rooms (for massages, facials, and other body pampering treatments).

The spa is operated by Mandara Spa (originally a Balinese spa, but now owned by Steiner Leisure), and treatments have a Far Eastern flavor (Indonesian facials, coconut body polish, aromatherapy massages).

Mariner of the Seas
★★★★

Large (Resort) Ship: ....137,276 tons	Total Crew: 1,185	Cabins (with private balcony): 765
Lifestyle: ....Standard	Passengers	Cabins (wheelchair accessible): 26
Cruise Line: Royal Caribbean International	(lower beds/all berths): 3,114/3,840	Cabin Current: ....110 volts
Former Names: ....none	Passenger Space Ratio	Elevators: ....14 (6 glass-enclosed)
Builder: ...Kvaerner Masa-Yards (Finland)	(lower beds/all berths): 44.0/35.7	Casino (gaming tables): ....Yes
Original Cost: ....$500 million	Crew/Passenger Ratio	Slot Machines: ....Yes
Entered Service: ....Spring 2004	(lower beds/all berths): 2.6/3.2	Swimming Pools (outdoors): 3
Registry: ....The Bahamas	Navigation Officers: ......Scandinavian	Swimming Pools (indoors): 0
Length (ft/m): 1,020.6/311.1	Cabins (total): 1,557	Whirlpools: 6
Beam (ft/m): 155.5/47.4	Size Range (sq ft/m): 151.0–1,358.0/	Self-Service Launderette: ....No
Draft (ft/m): 28.8/8.8	14.0–126.1	Dedicated Cinema/Seats: ....No
Propulsion/Propellers: .....diesel-electric	Cabins (outside view): 939	Library: ....Yes
(75,600kW)/3 azimuthing pods	Cabins (interior/no view): 618	Classification Society: ....Det Norske
Passenger Decks: 14	Cabins (for one person): 0	Veritas

BERLITZ'S OVERALL SCORE: 1,537 (OUT OF A POSSIBLE 2,000 POINTS)

OVERVIEW. *Mariner of the Seas* is a stunning, large, floating leisure resort, sister to *Adventure of the Seas, Explorer of the Seas, Navigator of the Seas* and *Voyager of the Seas*, which debuted between 1999 and 2003, respectively. The exterior design is not unlike an enlarged version of the company's Vision-class ships. The *Voyager*-class ships are, at present, the largest cruise vessels in the world in terms of tonnage measurement except for Cunard Line's *Queen Mary 2.*

The ship's propulsion is derived from three pod units, powered by electric motors (two azimuthing, and one fixed at the centerline) instead of conventional rudders and propellers, in the latest configuration of high-tech propulsion systems.

With large proportions, the ship provides more facilities and options, and caters to more passengers than any other Royal Caribbean International ship has in the past, and yet the ship manages to have a healthy passenger space ratio (the amount of space per passenger). Being a "non-Panamax" ship, it is simply too large to go through the Panama Canal, thus limiting its itineraries almost exclusively to the Caribbean (where only a few islands can accept it), or for use as a floating island resort. Spend the first few hours exploring all the many facilities and public spaces aboard this vessel and it will be time well spent.

Although *Mariner of the Seas* really is a large ship, the cabin hallways are warm and attractive, with artwork cabinets and wavy lines to lead you along and break up the monotony. In fact, there are plenty of colorful, even whimsical, decorative touches to help you avoid what would be a very clinical environment.

BERLITZ'S RATINGS

	Possible	Achieved
Ship	500	431
Accommodation	200	160
Food	400	252
Service	400	294
Entertainment	100	83
Cruise	400	317

Embarkation and disembarkation take place through two stations/access points, designed to minimize lines (that's more than 1,500 people for each access point). Once inside the ship, you'll need good walking shoes, particularly when you need to go from one end to the other – it really is quite a long way.

The four-decks-high Royal Promenade, which is 393.7 ft (120 meters) long, is the main interior focal point (it's a good place to hang out, to meet someone, or to arrange to meet someone). The length of two football fields (American football, that is), it has two internal lobbies (atria) that rise to as many as 11 decks high. Restaurants, shops and entertainment locations front this winding street and interior "with-view" cabins look into it from above. It is designed loosely in the image of London's fashionable Burlington Arcade – although there's not a real brick in sight, and I wonder if the designers have ever visited the real thing. It is, however, an imaginative piece of design work, and most passengers (particularly those who enjoy shopping malls) enjoy it immensely.

The super-atrium houses a "traditional" pub (the Wig & Gavel), with draft beer and plenty of "street-front" seating (North American passengers always seem to sit down, while British passengers prefer to stand at the bar). There is also a Champagne Bar, a Sidewalk Cafe (for continental breakfast, all-day pizzas, specialty coffees and desserts), Sprinkles (for round-the-clock ice cream and yoghurt), and a sports bar. There are also several shops – jewelry shop, gift shop, logo souvenir shop, and a Tommy Hilfiger signature store. Altogether, the Royal promenade is a nice place to see and be seen, and it sees action throughout the day and night. Comedy art has its place here, too, for example in the *trompe l'oeil* painter climbing up the walls. The Guest Reception and Shore Excursion counters are located at the aft end of the promenade, as is an ATM machine. Things to watch for: look up to see the large moving, asteroid-like sculpture (constantly growing and contracting). At times, street entertainers appear, and parades happen, while at other (carefully orchestrated) times it's difficult to walk through the area as it is filled to the brim with shopping items – like a cheap bazaar.

Arched across the promenade is a captain's balcony. Meanwhile, in the center of the promenade is a stairway that connects you to the deck below, where you'll find the Schooner Bar (a piano lounge that is a feature of all RCI ships) and the colorful Casino Royale. This is naturally large and full of flashing lights and noises. Gaming includes blackjack, Caribbean stud poker, roulette, and craps, as well as 300 slot machines. Aft of the casino is Bolero's Bar.

There's also a regulation-size ice-skating rink (Studio B), featuring real, not fake, ice, with "bleacher" seating for up to 900, and the latest in broadcast facilities. Ice Follies shows are presented here. Slim pillars obstruct clear-view arena stage sight lines, however. If ice-skating in the Caribbean doesn't appeal, you may enjoy the stunning two-deck library (open 24 hours a day). A grand $12 million was spent on permanent artwork. Drinking places include a neat Aquarium Bar, complete with 50 tons of glass and water in four large aquariums (whose combined value is over $1 million).

Drinking places include the small and intimate Champagne Bar, and a Connoisseur Club – for cigars and cognacs. Lovers of jazz might appreciate Ellington's, an intimate room for cool music atop the ship in the Viking Crown Lounge, or the Schooner Bar piano lounge. Golfers might enjoy the golf bar, as they play the Mariner Dunes.

There is a large television studio, adjacent to rooms that can be used for trade show exhibit space, with conference center that seats 400 and a multi-media screening room that seats 60. Lovers could tie the knot in a wedding chapel in the sky, the Skylight Chapel (it's located on the upper level of the Viking Crown Lounge, and even has wheelchair access via an electric stairway lift). Outdoors, the pool and open deck areas provide a resort-like environment.

Families with children are also well catered to, as facilities for children and teenagers are quite extensive. "Aquanauts" is for 3–5 year-olds; "Explorers" is for 6–8 year-olds; "Voyagers" is for 9–12 year-olds. Optix is a dedicated area for teenagers, including a daytime club (with several computers), soda bar, and dance floor. "Challenger's Arcade" features an array of the latest video games. Paint and Clay is an arts and crafts center for younger children. Adjacent is Adventure Beach, an area for all the family; it includes swimming pools, a water slide and game areas outdoors.

In terms of sheer size, this ship dwarfs almost all other ships in the cruise industry, but in terms of personal service, the reverse tends to be the case, unless you happen to reside in one of the top suites. Royal Caribbean International does, however, try hard to provide a good standard of programmed service from its hotel service staff. Remember

to take lots of extra pennies – you'll need them to pay for all the additional-cost items.

ACCOMMODATION. There is an extensive range of 22 cabin categories in four major groupings: Premium ocean-view suites and cabins, Promenade-view (interior-view) cabins, Ocean-view cabins, and Interior (no view) cabins. Many cabins are of a similar size – good for incentives and large groups, and 300 have interconnecting doors – good for families. If you do have a cabin with an interconnecting door to another cabin, be aware that you'll probably be able to hear everything your next-door neighbors say and do. Bathroom toilets are explosively noisy – like a barking dog.

A total of 138 interior (no view) cabins have bay windows that look into a horizontal atrium – first used to good effect aboard the Baltic passenger ferries *Silja Serenade* (1990) and *Silja Symphony* (1991) with interior cabins that look into a central shopping plaza. Regardless of what cabin grade you choose, however, all except for the Royal Suite and Owner's Suite have twin beds that convert to a queen-sized unit, television, radio and telephone, personal safe, vanity unit, mini-bar (called an Automatic Refreshment Center) hairdryer and private bathroom.

The largest cabins includes luxuriously appointed penthouse suites (whose occupants, sadly, must share the rest of the ship with everyone else, except for their own exclusive, and private, concierge club). The grandest is the Royal Suite, which is positioned on the port side of the ship, and measures 106.5 sq. meters/ 1,146 sq. ft). It features a king-sized bed in a separate, large bedroom, a living room with an additional queen-sized sofa bed, baby grand piano (no pianist is included, however), refrigerator/wet bar, dining table, entertainment center, and large bathroom.

Slightly smaller, but still highly desirable are the Owner's Suites (there are 10, all located in the center of the ship, on both port and starboard sides, each measuring 43 sq. meters/ 468 sq. ft) and four Royal Family suites (each 53 sq. meters/574 sq. ft), all of which feature similar items. However, the four Royal Family suites, which have two bedrooms (including one with third/fourth upper Pullman berths) are at the stern of the ship and have magnificent views over the ship's wake (and seagulls).

All cabins feature twin beds that convert to a queen-sized bed, a private bathroom with shower enclosure (towels are 100% cotton), as well as interactive, closed-circuit and satellite television, and pay-per-view movies. Cabins with "private balconies" are not so private, as the partitions are only partial, not full. The balcony decking is made of Bolidt – a sort of rubberized sand – and not wood, while the balcony rail is of wood.

CUISINE/DINING. The main dining room has a total seating capacity of 1,919); it is massive, and is set on three levels. A dramatic staircase connects all three levels, and huge, fat support pillars obstruct the sight lines. All three levels (Rhapsody in Blue, Top Hat and Tails, and Sound of Music) have exactly the same menus and food. There are also two small private wings for private groups, each seating 58 persons. The dining room is totally non-smoking, there are two seatings, and tables are for four, six, eight 10 or 12. The place settings, china and cutlery are of good quality. **Alternative Dining Options:** These are for casual and informal meals at all hours and include:

● **Cafe Promenade:** for continental breakfast, all-day pizzas, pastries, desserts and specialty coffees (sadly provided in paper cups).

● **Windjammer Cafe:** for casual buffet-style breakfast, lunch and light dinner (except the last night of the cruise).

● **Island Grill:** (this is actually a section inside the Windjammer Cafe), for casual dinner (no reservations necessary) featuring a grill and open kitchen.

● **Portofino:** this is the ship's "upscale" (non-smoking) Euro-Italian restaurant, open for dinner only. Reservations are required, and a $6 gratuity per person is charged. The food and its presentation are better than the food in the dining room, although the restaurant is not large enough for all passengers to try even once during a cruise. Choices include antipasti, soup, salad, pasta, main dish, dessert, cheese and coffee. The menu does not change throughout the cruise.

● **Johnny Rockets**, a retro 1950s all-day, all-night diner-style eatery that features hamburgers, malt shakes (at extra cost), and jukebox hits, with both indoor and outdoor seating (all indoor tables feature a mini-jukebox; dimes are provided for you to make your selection of vintage records), and all-singing, all-dancing waitresses who'll knock your socks off, if you can stand the volume.

● **Sprinkles:** for round-the-clock ice cream and yoghurt.

ENTERTAINMENT. The 1,350-seat Savoy showlounge is a stunning room that could well be the equal of many such rooms on land. It is located at the forward end of the ship and spans the height of five decks (with only a few slim pillars and almost no disruption of sight lines from almost any seat in the house). The room features a hydraulic

orchestra pit and huge stage areas, together with sonic-boom loud sound, and some superb lighting equipment.

In addition, the ship has a whole array of cabaret acts. Although many of the cabaret acts are not what you would call headliners (the strongest cabaret acts are featured in the main showlounge, while lesser acts are presented in the Lotus Lounge, which is also the venue for late-night adults-only comedy), they regularly travel the cruise ship circuit.

The entertainment throughout is really upbeat, but is typical of the kind of resort hotel found ashore in Las Vegas. There is even background music in all corridors and lifts, and constant music outdoors on the pool deck. If you want a quiet relaxing holiday, this isn't the right ship for you.

There is also a television studio (in case you thought you'd need one aboard a cruise ship), located adjacent to rooms that could be used, for example, for trade show exhibit space (good for conventions at sea).

SPA/FITNESS. The ShipShape health and fitness spa is large, and measures 15,000 sq. ft (1,400 sq. meters). It includes a large aerobics room, fitness center (with the usual stairmasters, treadmills, stationary bikes, weight machines and free weights), treatment rooms, men's and women's sauna/ steam rooms, while another 10,000 sq. ft (930 sq. meters) is devoted to a Solarium (with magro-dome sliding glass roof) for relaxation after you've exercised too much.

For the more sporting, there is activity galore – including a rock-climbing wall that's 32.8 ft high (10 meters), with five separate climbing tracks. It is located outdoors at the aft end of the funnel. You'll get a great "buzz" being 200 ft (60 meters) above the ocean while the ship is moving. Other sports facilities include a roller-blading track, a dive-and-snorkel shop.

● **For more extensive general information about the Royal Caribbean experience, see pages 128–131.**

Maxim Gorkiy
★★★ +

Mid-Size Ship: . . . . .24,981 tons	Passenger Decks: 10	Cabins (for one person): 2
Lifestyle: . . . . .Standard	Total Crew: 340	Cabins (with private balcony): 0
Cruise Line: . . . . .Phoenix Seereisen	Passengers	Cabins (wheelchair accessible): 0
Former Names: . . . . .*Hanseatic, Hamburg*	(lower beds/all berths): 650/88	Cabin Current: . . . . .220 volts
Builder: . .Howaldtswerke Deutsche Werft	Passenger Space Ratio	Elevators: 4
(Germany)	(lower beds/all berths): 38.4/31.7	Casino (gaming tables): . . . . .No
Original Cost: . . . .£5.6 million	Crew/Passenger Ratio	Slot Machines: .No
Entered Service: . . . . .Mar 1969/Jan 1974	(lower beds/all berths): 1.9/2.3	Swimming Pools (outdoors): 1
Registry: . . . . .The Bahamas	Navigation Officers: . . .Russian/Ukrainian	Swimming Pools (indoors): 1
Length (ft/m): 638.8/194.72	Cabins (total): 326	Whirlpools: 0
Beam (ft/m): 87.3/26.62	Size Range (sq ft/m): 145.3–296.0/	Self-Service Launderette: . . . . .Yes
Draft (ft/m): 27.0/8.25	13.5–27.0	Dedicated Cinema/Seats: Yes/290
Propulsion/Propellers: . . . . .steam turbine	Cabins (outside view): 210	Library: . . . . .Yes
(16,900 kW)/2	Cabins (interior/no view): 116	Classification Society: Det Norske Veritas

OVERALL SCORE: 1,342 (OUT OF A POSSIBLE 2,000 POINTS)

OVERVIEW. *Maxim Gorkiy* is an all-white ship originally built as *Hamburg* for the transatlantic service of the now defunct Deutsche Atlantik Linie (German Atlantic Line). The vessel has long, pleasing lines and outer styling, and is easily identified by its platform-topped funnel, which was designed to disperse smoke away from the aft, tiered, open decks.

In 1974 the ship was sold to the Black Sea Shipping Company and renamed *Maxim Gorkiy*. It was modernized in 1988, but on June 20, 1989 the ship gained notoriety when it rammed the cruise ship *Vasco da Gama* (now scrapped) in the ice near Spitzbergen. Later in 1989, *Maxim Gorkiy* hit the headlines when it played host to an international summit in Malta between America's then president, George Bush Sr., and Russia's leader, Mikhail Gorbachev.

Since December 1992 it has operated under a long-term charter arrangement (until 2008) to Phoenix Seereisen from its present owners, Russia's Sovcomflot.

The ship has been generally well-maintained throughout its life. There is a generous amount of open deck and sunbathing space, and the deck lounge chairs have cushioned pads. Open-deck sports include a large basketball court aft of the funnel.

Inside, there are some handsome, well-designed, though now slightly dated, public rooms (virtually all of the public rooms have been retained since the ship first debuted in 1969); the passenger flow is good, with few congested areas. A generous amount of wood paneling was used in the construction, and most of it still looks good, although some refinishing is needed in some areas. The decor is dark and somewhat dull, although it is quite relaxing and

BERLITZ'S RATINGS

	Possible	Achieved
Ship	500	327
Accommodation	200	132
Food	400	273
Service	400	285
Entertainment	100	60
Cruise	400	265

soporific. The showlounge, an important room, is decent enough, although it simply doesn't have enough seating; the stage and lighting facilities could also be improved. There are two relaxing winter gardens with large ocean-view windows. An added bonus is an indoor swimming pool – good for those times when the outdoor pool can't be used because of inclement weather.

Maxim Gorkiy will provide a very good general cruise experience in comfortable, quite elegant, but very traditional surroundings, at a modest price, although you should remember that this is an older ship that does not have the latest in facilities. This ship is particularly targeted to German-speaking passengers who appreciate good value and well-planned, destination-intensive itineraries. The mostly Russian and Ukrainian service staff provides friendly, attentive service. Port taxes, insurance and gratuities are included.

Phoenix Seereisen has, over the years, attained almost a cult status among its passengers, in that the company provides a consistently fine, very popular product for those wanting a casual cruise experience and lifestyle among friendly passengers. Where passengers are required to fly to join their cruises, the airline most used by Phoenix Seereisen is LTU. The currency on board is the euro.

SUITABLE FOR: *Maxim Gorkiy* is best suited to the German-speaking traveler who is seeking good value for money in a ship with very traditional, quite comfortable (but not pretentious or luxurious) surroundings, at a low price.

ACCOMMODATION. The brochure shows outside-view and interior (no view) cabins in 18 grades. Most cabins are actually quite spacious, and many of them have wood paneling, accenting and trim, while the decor is comfortable and quite restful. The bathrooms are quite large and have full-sized bathtubs in all except 20 cabins. There is a decent amount of space for the storage of one's personal toiletry items.

Cabins designated as deluxe are of a good size, come fully equipped with almost everything one would need, and have huge picture windows (most others have portholes). The in-cabin television system has both German and Russian satellite TV programming.

Anyone booking a suite or one of the top five grades receives Phoenix VIP service, which includes flowers for the cabin, a separate check-in desk and priority disembarkation.

CUISINE/DINING. There are three restaurants (all have one seating, with assigned tables, so you have the same waiter throughout your cruise). All three are located low down in the ship, but they are cheerfully decorated. Draft lager is always available, and the wine list has many wines from different regions of Germany, Switzerland and Austria, as well as a modest selection from France and other countries.

Moderately decent food is served, and wine at lunch and dinner is included in the cruise fare. Generally, though, more choice, and better presentation would be welcome.

The service is quite attentive and courteous from the well-meaning staff, although it is somewhat hurried despite there being only one seating for all meals. Cushions would be a welcome addition to some of the banquette seating.

ENTERTAINMENT. The showlounge is not a showlounge as such, but a room for "cabaret" acts. The sightlines to the stage are obstructed from many seats by 10 thick pillars. The entertainment is really of the low-cost "end-of-pier" type – the sort that you would have seen in the 1960s, but the lack of facilities prohibit anything more lavish.

SPA/FITNESS. The spa facilities are located on the lowest passenger deck of the ship (named Sauna Deck). It contains the indoor swimming/aquacise pool, sauna, medicinal bath, massage room, and changing area. The lighting is subdued, and this helps create a calming atmosphere. There is also a fitness room, but it is located in a different position, near the funnel on Lido Deck; it is very small.

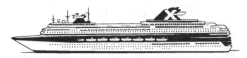

Mercury
★ ★ ★ ★ +

Large (Resort) Ship: ....77,713 tons	Total Crew: 909	Cabins (with private balcony): 220
Lifestyle: ....Premium	Passengers	Cabins (wheelchair accessible): 8
Cruise Line: ....Celebrity Cruises	(lower beds/all berths): 1,870/2,681	Cabin Current: ....110 and 220 volts
Former Names: ....none	Passenger Space Ratio	Elevators: 10
Builder: ....Meyer Werft (Germany)	(lower beds/all berths): 41.5/28.9	Casino (gaming tables): ....Yes
Original Cost: ....$320 million	Crew/Passenger Ratio	Slot Machines: ....Yes
Entered Service: ....Nov 1997	(lower beds/all berths): 2.0/2.9	Swimming Pools (outdoors): 2
Registry: ....The Bahamas	Navigation Officers: ....Greek	Swimming Pools (indoors): 1
Length (ft/m): 865.8/263.90	Cabins (total): 935	indoor/outdoor (magrodome)
Beam (ft/m): 105.6/32.20	Size Range (sq ft/m): 171.0–1,219.0/	Whirlpools: 4
Draft (ft/m): 25.2/7.70	15.8–113.2	Self-Service Launderette: ....No
Propulsion/Propellers: ....diesel	Cabins (outside view): 639	Dedicated Cinema/Seats: Yes/183
(31,500 kW)/2	Cabins (interior/no view): 296	Library: ....Yes
Passenger Decks: 10	Cabins (for one person): 0	Classification Society: ...Lloyd's Register

OVERALL SCORE: 1,663 (OUT OF A POSSIBLE 2,000 POINTS)

OVERVIEW. *Mercury* is a stunning ship, inside and outside. Looking externally like a larger version of the company's smaller, popular *Horizon/ Zenith*, it is quite well-balanced despite its squared-off stern. It has the distinctive Celebrity Cruises' "X" funnel ("X" being the Greek letter "C" which stands for Chandris, the former owning company, before Royal Caribbean bought it). With a high passenger space ratio for such a large ship, there is no real sense of crowding, and the passenger flow is very good.

Facilities include a three-deck-high main foyer with marble floored lobby and waterfall; more than 190,000 sq. ft (18,000 sq. meters) of open deck space (poolside lounge chairs have cushioned pads, those on other decks do not); a magrodome-covered indoor-outdoor pool; AquaSpa thalassotherapy pool (with several "active" water jet stations), and assorted treatment rooms including a "rasul" mud treatment room.

Other facilities include "Michael's Club", a cigar/cognac room on Promenade Deck that overlooks the atrium, a small but luxurious cinema, a large casino (this is extremely glitzy, with confusing and congested layout). The children's facilities are good. As well as the "Fun Factory," there's an outdoor play area and a paddling pool.

The interior decor is elegant and understated. It includes plenty of wood (or wood-look) paneling and accenting throughout, and many refinements have been made during the three-ship "Century Series" that Celebrity Cruises has introduced in the past few years. The ship also houses a $3.5 million living art collection with true, museum-quality pieces. The health and fitness facilities are among the nicest aboard any ship, and have been well thought-out and

BERLITZ'S RATINGS

	Possible	Achieved
Ship	500	444
Accommodation	200	177
Food	400	315
Service	400	319
Entertainment	100	78
Cruise	400	330

designed for quiet, efficient operation, with everything in just the right place.

This ship will provide you with a finely packaged cruise holiday in elegant surroundings. It is efficiently run. There are more crew members per passenger than would be found aboard other ships of the same size in the premium category, and hence service in general is very good indeed. Note that a 15% gratuity is added to all bar and wine accounts.

After Celebrity Cruises was purchased by Royal Caribbean International, the standard of product delivery aboard all the ships in the Celebrity Cruises fleet went down as cuts were made by the new owner. However, new management has been brought in to put things right, and I (and many passengers) look forward to experiencing the improvements. The onboard currency is the US dollar.

Trying to reach Cabin Service or the Guest Relations Desk to answer the phone (to order breakfast, for example, if you don't want to do so via the interactive television) is a matter of luck, timing and patience (a sad reminder of the automated age, and lack of personal contact). The library is disappointingly small, and poorly located away from the main flow of passengers. There is a charge for using the Aquaspa/ sauna/steam room complex. The room-service menu is poor, and food items are below the standards of food featured in the dining room. Standing in line for embarkation, disembarkation, shore tenders and for self-serve buffet meals is an inevitable aspect of cruising aboard all large ships.

While under the direction of its former owner, John Chandris, Celebrity Cruises managed to create a superb quality cruise holiday product virtually unbeatable at the prices charged in the Alaska and Caribbean markets, representing outstanding value for money. However, given the subtle changes that have occurred since Celebrity Cruises was integrated into the Royal Caribbean Cruises family in 1997, it has become evident that some slippage of product delivery standards and staff have occurred, and the latest score reflects these changes. Passenger participation activities are amateurish and should be upgraded. The officers have become more aloof lately, with far less contact with passengers than when the company first commenced operations.

SUITABLE FOR: *Mercury* is best suited to well-traveled couples and singles of 40 and above (not particularly recommended for children and teenagers) seeking a large ship with a sophisticated environment, good itineraries, fine food and good European-style service from a well-trained crew that cares and delivers an onboard product that is well above average.

ACCOMMODATION. There are 13 different grades. The price you pay will depend on the grade, size and location. The accommodation is extremely comfortable, regardless of which cabin grade you choose. Naturally, if you select a suite, you will find more space, butler service (whether you want it or not), more and better amenities and more personal service than if you choose any of the standard cabin grades.

Occupants of all accommodation designated as suites get gold cards to open their doors (and priority service throughout the ship, free cappuccino/espresso coffees when served by a butler, welcome champagne, flowers, VCR, and use of the AquaSpa thalassotherapy pool). All occupants of standard (interior no view and outside-view) cabins have white cards. Suites that have private balconies also have floor-to-ceiling windows and sliding doors to balconies (a few suites have outward opening doors).

Two Presidential Suites are located amidships. These provide spectacular living spaces, perhaps even better than those in *Century* and *Galaxy*, depending on your personal taste. There is a separate bedroom (with high-tech Sony multimedia entertainment center), large lounge (complete with dining table), huge walk-in closet with mountains of drawers, and king-sized marble-tiled bathroom with every appointment necessary.

There is in-suite dining for the two Presidential and 12 Century Suites, as well as for the 24 Sky Suites (1202, 1203, 1236 and 1237 have enormous fully private balconies, while the others are only semi-private). All suites feature full butler service, personalized stationery, and business cards. If you choose one of the forward-most Sky Deck suites, however, be warned that you may well be subject to constant music and noise from the pool deck (one deck below) between 8am and 6pm (not good if you want to relax). The closet and drawer space provided in these suites is superb. In the bathrooms of the Sky Suites, the shaving mirror is positioned too high, and in the bedroom, the TV set cannot be viewed from the bed. Push-button bell and privacy curtains should be provided, but are not. In-

suite massage is available (this really is pleasant when provided on the balcony of the Sky Suites).

The standard (interior and outside) cabins are quite spacious and nicely decorated with cheerful fabrics, and marble-topped vanity unit. The bathrooms are generous with space, tiled from floor to ceiling, and the power showers are extremely practical units.

All cabins have interactive TV for booking shore excursions, ordering cabin service items and purchasing goods from the ship's boutiques, so you don't have to leave your quarters, especially if you dislike the ports of call. The system works in English, French, German, Italian and Spanish. There are five channels of music – all available from the TV set (therefore you cannot have music without having a picture). All cabins are also equipped with a "baby monitoring telephone system" which allows you to telephone your cabin whilst you are elsewhere, and have a two-way intercom to "listen in". Automatic "wake-up" calls can also be dialed in. All accommodation designated as suites has duvets on the beds instead of sheets and blankets.

CUISINE/DINING. The two-level formal Manhattan Restaurant, located at the ship's stern, is quite grand and elegant (each level has its own full galley); a grand staircase connects the two levels. Large picture windows provide sea views on three sides; at night, large shades (with scenes of Manhattan, the name of the dining room) roll down electronically to cover the stern-facing windows. There are two seatings for dinner (open seating for breakfast and lunch), at tables for two, four, six, eight or 10, and the dining room is a totally no-smoking area.

Three-Michelin-starred chef Michel Roux directs the same excellent cuisine that has made Celebrity Cruises the shining star of the contemporary cruise industry. The menus are creative and the food is very attractively presented. There is also an excellent wine list, and real wine waiters (unlike so many other large cruise companies), although prices are high (particularly for good champagne) and the wine vintages are quite young.

There are also several informal dining spots as an alternative to the main dining room: a Lido Cafe, with four main serving lines; a poolside grill, and another indoor/outdoor grill located behind the aft swimming pool. The Lido Cafe has fine wood paneling and is much more elegant than the informal dining areas found aboard most ships, and has some seating in bay window areas with great ocean views.

In the center of the ship is Tastings, a delightful coffee/tea lounge; in one corner is a presentation of goodies made by COVA, the Milanese chocolatier – an exclusive to Celebrity Cruises (the original Cova Cafe di Milano is adjacent to the La Scala Opera House in Milan). This is the place to see and be seen. It is a delightful setting (as well as a good meeting place) for those who appreciate fine Italian coffees (espresso, espresso macchiato, cappuccino, and latte), pastries, and superb cakes.

Finally, for those who cannot live without them, freshly baked pizzas can be ordered and delivered to your cabin inside an insulated pouch.

ENTERTAINMENT. As aboard its identical sister *Galaxy*, there is a 1,000-seat showlounge, with side balconies, and no pillars to obstruct views (there are three high-tech "dazzle and sizzle" production shows per 7-night cruise.

Unfortunately, the production shows are not nearly as lavish as the showlounge they play in. In fact, compared to some of the other major cruise lines, the shows are a letdown, and not in keeping with the elegant nature of the interior decor. Most consist mainly of running, jumping, smoke, colored laser lighting, very loud music and click tracks, and very little storyline. Bar service, supplied continuously during shows, can prove irritating to some people.

While there are some good cabaret acts, they are the same ones seen aboard many ships of the major cruise lines. In other words, it is disappointing to note that there is absolutely nothing to distinguish Celebrity Cruises in the entertainment department. The ship does have a number of bands, although there is very little music for social dancing, other than disco and pop music.

SPA/FITNESS. The AquaSpa contains 9,040 sq. ft (840 sq. meters) of space dedicated to well-being and body treatments, and includes a large fitness/exercise area, complete with all the latest high-tech muscle machines and video cycles, thalassotherapy pool, and seven treatment rooms. The spa features some of the more unusual wellness treatments (including a steamy rasul room – for Mediterranean mud and gentle steam bathing).

The spa is operated by Steiner, a specialist concession, whose enthusiastic staff will try to and sell you Steiner's own-brand Elemis beauty products (spa girls have sales targets). Personal training sessions in the gymnasium cost $83 for one hour. Some fitness classes are free, while some, such as yoga, and kickboxing, cost $10 per class. However, being aboard will give you an opportunity to try some of the more exotic treatments (particularly some of the massages available). Massage (including exotic massages such as Aroma Stone massage, Chakra Balancing massage and other well-being massages), facials, pedicures, and beauty salon treatments are at extra cost.

Examples of treatment costs: massage at $109 (50 minutes), facial at $109, seaweed wrap (75 minutes) $190 – all plus a gratuity of 10 percent. Do make appointments as early as possible – aboard large ships, time slots go quickly, so the day you board is the best time to book treatments.

DID YOU KNOW...

● that when sailing from England to the Caribbean in "the old days" a rule of thumb was to sail south until the butter melts, then proceed west?

● that the word "buccaneer" comes from the French word *boucanier*, which means: "to cure meat on a bucan (barbeque)?" Since pirates often used this method of cooking, they became known as buccaneers. The word buccaneer, strictly speaking, was used to denote pirates in the Caribbean.

● that in 1992 Carnival Cruise Lines used its original ship *Mardi Gras* as an accommodation ship? It was for senior executives and staff who were made homeless when Hurricane Andrew hit Miami in August that year.

Millennium
★★★★ +

Large (Resort) Ship: . . . . . . .90,228 tons	Total Crew: 999	Cabins (wheelchair accessible): 26
Lifestyle: . . . . .Premium	Passengers	(17 with private balcony)
Cruise Line: . . . . .Celebrity Cruises	(lower beds/all berths): 1,950/2,450	Cabin Current: . . . . .110 and 220 volts
Former Names: . . . . .none	Passenger Space Ratio	Elevators: 10
Builder: . . . . . . .Chantiers de l'Atlantique	(lower beds/all berths): 46.2/36.8	Casino (gaming tables): . . . . .Yes
(France)	Crew/Passenger Ratio	Slot Machines: . . . . .Yes
Original Cost: . . . .$350 million	(lower beds/all berths): 1.9/2.4	Swimming Pools (outdoors): 2
Entered Service: . . . . .June 2000	Navigation Officers: . . . . .Greek	Swimming Pools (indoors): 1
Registry: . . . . .The Bahamas	Cabins (total): 975	(with magrodome)
Length (ft/m): 964.5/294.0	Size Range (sq ft/m): 170.0–2,350.0/	Whirlpools: 4
Beam (ft/m): 105.6/32.2	15.7–235.0	Self-Service Launderette: . . . . .No
Draft (ft/m): 26.2/8.0	Cabins (outside view): 780	Dedicated Cinema/Seats: Yes/368
Propulsion/Propellers: . . . . .gas turbine/2	Cabins (interior/no view): 195	Library: . . . . .Yes
azimuthing pods (39,000 kW)	Cabins (for one person): 0	Classification Society: . . .Lloyd's Register
Passenger Decks: 11	Cabins (with private balcony): 590	

OVERALL SCORE: 1,697 (OUT OF A POSSIBLE 2,000 POINTS)

OVERVIEW. *Millennium*, whose sister ships are *Constellation, Infinity* and *Summit*, is a slightly enlarged and elongated version of the company's successful trio, *Century, Galaxy* and *Mercury*, and was built in the same dock where the famous former ocean liner *France* was built. Jon Bannenberg (famous as a mega-yacht designer) designed the exterior that has a royal blue and white hull.

This was the first Celebrity Cruises ship to be fitted with a "pod" propulsion system coupled with a gas turbine powerplant. Indeed, this is the first cruise ship in the world to be powered by quiet, smokeless, energy-efficient gas turbines (two GE gas turbines provide engine power while a single GE steam turbine drives the electricity generators). The ship was dogged by technical problems in its early days.

One delightful feature is a large conservatory located in a glasshouse environment and spreading across a whole foyer. It includes a botanical environment with flowers, plants, tress, mini-gardens and fountains, all designed by the award-winning floral designer Emilio Robba of Paris. It is directly in front of the main funnel and a section of it has glass walls overlooking the ship's side. It has fresh flowers for any occasion, and a selection of Emilio Robba glass and flower creations, as well as pot pourri and other flora and fauna items. Facilities outdoors include two outdoor pools, one indoor/outdoor pool, and six whirlpools.

Inside, the ship has an understated elegance, with the same high-class decor and materials (including lots of wood, glass and marble) and public rooms that have made the existing ships in the fleet so popular and user-friendly.

BERLITZ'S RATINGS

	Possible	Achieved
Ship	500	454
Accommodation	200	180
Food	400	327
Service	400	330
Entertainment	100	78
Cruise	400	328

The atrium (with separately enclosed room for shore excursions) is four decks high and houses the reception desk, tour operator's desk, and bank. Four dramatic glass-walled elevators travel through the ship's exterior (port) side, connecting the atrium with another seven decks, thus traveling through 11 passenger decks, including the tender stations – a nice ride.

Other facilities include a combination cinema/conference center, an expansive shopping arcade, with more than 14,450 sq. ft (1,300 sq. meters) of retail store space (including some trendy brand names: H. Stern, Donna Karan, Fossil), a lavish four-decks-high showlounge with the latest in staging and lighting equipment, two-level library (one level for English-language books; a second level for books in other languages); card room; compact disc listening room; art auction center (with seating that look rather more like a small chapel); Cosmos, a combination observation lounge/discotheque; an Internet Center with 19 computer stations (with custom-made wood-surround flat screens).

Gaming sports include the ship's overly large Fortunes Casino, with blackjack, roulette, and slot machines, and lots of bright lights and action. Michael's Club, originally a cigar smoker's haven, is now a piano lounge/bar.

Families cruising with children will appreciate the Fun Factory (for children) and The Tower (for teenagers). Children's counselors and youth activities staff are on hand to provide a wide range of supervised activities.

Millennium delivers a well-defined North American cruise experience at a very modest price. The "zero announcement policy" means there is little intrusion. My advice is to book a suite-category cabin for all the extra benefits it brings – it really is worth it. The ship's two seating dining and two shows sadly detract from an otherwise excellent product, and this ship (together with sister ships *Constellation*, *Infinity* and *Summit*) can be said to provide the very best of the ships in the Premium segment of the marketplace, providing a taste of luxury for those who book in the largest suites.

There is, sadly, no wrap-around wooden promenade deck outdoors. There are cushioned pads for poolside deck lounge chairs only, but not for chairs on other outside decks. Passenger participation activities are amateurish and should be upgraded. Although the officers have become more aloof lately, with far less contact with passengers than when the company first started, new management has done much to restore the art of hospitality. One thing is certain: cruising in a hassle-free, crime-free environment such as this is hard to beat, no matter how much or how little you pay.

ACCOMMODATION. There are 20 different grades, depending on your preference for the size and location of your living space. Almost half of the ship's accommodation has a "private" balcony; around 80 percent are outside-view suites and cabins, and 20 percent are interior (no view) cabins. The accommodation is extremely comfortable throughout this ship. Suites, naturally, have more space, butler service (whether you want it or not), more and better amenities and more personal service than if you choose any of the standard cabin grades. There are several categories of suites, but those at the stern of the ship are in a prime location and have huge balconies that are really private and not overlooked from above.

All suites and cabins have wood cabinetry and accenting, interactive television and entertainment systems (you can go shopping, book shore excursions, play casino games, interactively, and even watch soft porn movies). Bathrooms have hairdryers, and 100% cotton towels.

Penthouse Suites: Two Penthouse Suites (on Penthouse Deck) are the largest accommodation aboard. Each occupies one half of the beam (width) of the ship, overlooking the ship's stern. Each measures a huge 2,530 sq. ft. (235 sq. meters): 1,432 sq. ft. (133 sq. meters) of living space, plus a huge wrap-around balcony measuring 1,098 sq. ft. (102 sq. meters) with 180° views, which occupies one half of the beam (width) of the ship, overlooking the ship's stern (it includes a wet bar, hot tub and whirlpool tub); however, note that much of this terrace can be overlooked by passengers on other decks above.

Features include a marble foyer, a separate living room (complete with ebony baby grand piano – bring your own pianist if you don't play yourself) and a formal dining room. The master bedroom has a large walk-in closet; personal exercise equipment; dressing room with vanity desk, exercise equipment; marble-clad master bathroom with twin washbasins; deep whirlpool bathtub; separate shower; toilet and bidet areas; flat-screen televisions (one in the bedroom and one in the lounge) and electronically controlled drapes. Butler service is standard, and a but-

ler's pantry, with separate entry door, has a full-size refrigerator, temperature-controlled wine cabinet, microwave oven and good-sized food preparation and storage areas. For even more space, an interconnecting door can be opened into the adjacent suite (ideal for multi-generation families).

Royal Suites: Eight Royal Suites, each measuring 733 sq. ft (68 sq. meters), are located towards the aft of the ship (four each on the port and starboard sides). The decor in each is different, and is in the style of a country (Africa, China, Mexico, France, India, Italy, Morocco and Portugal). Each features a separate living room with dining and lounge areas (with refrigerator, mini-bar and Bang & Olufsen CD sound system), and a separate bedroom. There are two entertainment centers with DVD players, and two flat-screen televisions (one in the living area, one in the bedroom), and a large walk-in closet with vanity desk. The marble-clad bathroom has a whirlpool bathtub with integral shower, and there is also a separate shower enclosure, two washbasins and toilet. The teakwood decked balcony is extensive (large enough for on-deck massage) and also has a whirlpool hot tub.

Celebrity Suites: Eight Celebrity Suites, each 467 sq ft (44 sq. meters), feature floor-to-ceiling windows, a separate living room with dining and lounge areas, two entertainment centers with flat-screen televisions (one in the living room, one in the bedroom), and a walk-in closet with vanity desk. The marble-clad bathroom features a whirlpool tub with integral shower (a window with movable shade lets you look out of the bathroom through the lounge to the large ocean-view windows). Interconnecting doors allow two suites to be used as a family unit (as there is no balcony, these suites are ideal for families with small children). These suites overhang the starboard side of the ship (they are located opposite a group of glass-walled lifts), and provide stunning ocean views from the glass-walled sitting/dining area, which extends out from the ship's side. A personal computer with wood-surround screen allows direct internet connectivity. Butler service is standard.

Sky Suites: There are 30 Sky Suites, each 308 sq ft (28.6 sq. meters), including the private balcony (note that some balconies may be larger than others, depending on the location). Although these are designated as suites, they are really just larger cabins that feature a marble-clad bathroom with bathtub/shower combination. The suites also have a VCR player in addition to a television, and have a larger lounge area (than standard cabins) and sleeping area. Butler service is standard.

Butler Service: Butler service (in all accommodation designated as suites) includes full breakfast, in-suite lunch and dinner service (as required), afternoon tea service, evening hors d'oeuvres, free espresso and cappuccino, daily news delivery, shoeshine service, and other personal touches. Suite occupants in Penthouse, Royal, Celebrity and Sky suites also get welcome champagne; a full personal computer in each suite, including a printer and internet access (on request in the Sky Suites); choice of films from a video library; personalized stationery; tote bag; priority dining room seating preferences; private portrait sitting, and bathrobe; and in-suite massage service.

Concierge Class: In 2003, Celebrity Cruises added a third service "class" to some of the accommodation grades aboard this ship. Positioned between the top grade suite grades and standard cabin grades, Concierge Class offers added value to purchasers of these "middle-class" cabins.

Enhanced facilities include priority embarkation, disembarkation, tender tickets, alternative dining and spa reservations. Here's what you get in the Concierge Class cabins that others don't (except for the suites): European duvet; double bed overlay (no more falling "between the cracks" for couples); choice of four pillows (goose down pillow, isotonic pillow, body pillow, conformance pillow); eight-vial flower vase on vanity desk; throw pillows on sofa; fruit basket; binoculars; golf umbrella; leather telephone notepad; larger beach towels; hand-held hairdryer. The balcony gets better furniture. In the bathrooms: plusher Frette bathrobes; larger towels in sea green and pink (alternating days); flower in silver vase. It all adds up to excellent value for money.

Standard Outside-View/Interior (No View) Cabins: All other outside-view and interior (no view) cabins (those not designated as suites) feature a lounge area with sofa or convertible sofa bed, sleeping area with twin beds that can convert to a double bed, a good amount of closet and drawer space, personal safe, mini-bar/refrigerator (all items are at extra cost), interactive television, and private bathroom. The cabins are nicely decorated with warm wood-finish furniture, and there is none of the boxy feel of cabins in so many ships, due to the angled placement of vanity and audio-video consoles. Even the smallest interior (no view) cabin has a good-sized bathroom and shower enclosure.

Wheelchair-Accessible Accommodation: This is available in six Sky Suites, three premium outside-view cabins, eight deluxe ocean-view cabins, four standard ocean-view and five interior (no view) cabins measure 347 sq. ft to 362 sq. ft (32.2 to 33.6 sq. meters) and are located in the most practical parts of the ship and close to lifts for good accessibility (all have doorways and bathroom doorways and showers that are wheelchair-accessible.

CUISINE/DINING. The Metropolitan Dining Room, which seats 1,224 passengers, is the ship's principal dining hall. It is two decks high, has a grand staircase connecting the two levels, a huge glass wall overlooking the sea at the stern of the ship (electrically operated blinds provide several different backdrops), and a musician's gallery on the upper level (typically for a string quartet or quintet). There are two seatings for dinner (open seating for breakfast and lunch), at tables for two, four, six, eight or 10. The dining room is a totally non-smoking area, and, you should note, that, like all large dining halls, it can prove to be extremely noisy. The menu variety is good, the food has taste, and it is very attractively presented and served in a well orchestrated operation that displays fine European traditions and training. Full service in-cabin dining is also available for all meals (including dinner).

For casual meals, the self-serve buffet-style Ocean Cafe is an extensive area that features six principal serving lines, and can seat 754. At the after end of the Ocean Buffet, a separate pasta bar, sushi counter, grill/rotisserie and pizza servery provide freshly created items. Note that all pizzas are made aboard from pizza dough and do not come ready made for reheating, as with many cruise lines. On selected evenings, alternative dinners can be taken here (reservations are necessary); . There is also an outdoors grill, for hamburgers and hot dogs, roast chicken and other fast food items, adjacent to the swimming pool.

For champagne and caviar lovers, the Platinum Club has a platinum and silver *belle-époque* decor reminiscent of a 1930s gentleman's club. It has a diamond-pane reflective mirror wall. It includes a Champagne Bar and a Martini Bar, each with a cut-crystal chandelier.

Cova Cafe di Milano: This is a signature item aboard all the ships of Celebrity Cruises, and is a seagoing version of the original Cafe di Milano that was located next to La Scala Opera House in Milan. The ship's cafe is in a prominent position, on the second level of the atrium lobby, and several display cases show off the extensive range of Cova coffee, chocolates and alcoholic digestives; this is the place to see and be seen. It is a delightful setting (and meeting place) for anyone who appreciates fine Italian coffees (espresso, espresso macchiato, cappuccino, and latte), pastries and superb cakes. The breakfast pastries are really superb (the favorite seems to be the Italian pane con cioccolata – chocolate pastry).

Alternative (Reservations-Only, Extra Cost) Dining: Celebrity Cruises created its first true alternative restaurant (actually a more accurate description would be dining salon) aboard this ship. The Olympic Restaurant is named after White Star Line's transatlantic ocean liner of the same name, *Olympic* (sister ship to the ill-fated *Titanic*). It is adjacent to the atrium lobby, and has a dining lounge that is rather like an ante-room that contains figured French walnut wood paneling from the à la carte dining room of the 1911 ship, which was decorated in Louis XVI splendor, complete with ornate gold accenting. Ship buffs should be delighted with this rare find. The paneling was found in a house in the north of England, and bought at auction in 1999 (actually the entire house had to be purchased in order to get at the paneling).

A team of 10 chefs prepares the cuisine exclusively for this restaurant. Superb tableside preparation is the feature of this alternative dining room, whose classic French cuisine and service are absolutely outstanding and at the height of professionalism, for this is, indeed, a room for a full dégustation, and not merely a dinner. Throughout each dinner, a piano and violin duo plays music appropriate to the period, in costumes that have been reproduced from the designs used by the musicians aboard the trio of sister ships *Britannic, Olympic* and *Titanic*.

A wine cellar, in which it is possible to dine, is also a feature, as is a demonstration galley. The wine list is extremely extensive (with more than 400 labels represented). But the real treat for rare wine lovers is an additional list of rare vintage wines, including (when I was last aboard) a magnum of 1949 Château Petrus (at $12,400), a 1907 Heidsieck Monopole Champagne (a mere $7,000 and brought to the surface from a sunken German ship), and a Château Lafite-Rothschild Pouillac from 1890 (a snip at $2,160).

To undertake dinner in this exquisite setting – it's rather like dining in a living museum – takes a minimum of three hours of culinary excellence and faultless service, and is, without any shadow of doubt, among the very finest dining experiences at sea today. Superb tableside preparation is the feature of this alternative dining room, whose classic French cuisine and service are absolutely outstanding (masterminded by Michel Roux, owner of a three-star Michelin restaurant near Windsor in England).

This is haute cuisine at the height of professionalism. However, with just 134 seats, not all passengers will be able to experience it even once during a one-week cruise (reservations are necessary, and a cover charge of $25 per person applies). A dine-in wine cellar is also provided, as is a demonstration galley, and tableside preparation is a feature of this alternative dining spot.

ENTERTAINMENT. The 900-seat Celebrity Theater is the three-deck-high venue for the ship's production shows and major cabaret acts. It is located in the forward part of the ship, with seating on main, and two balcony levels. The large stage is equipped with a full fly loft behind its traditional proscenium.

SPA/FITNESS. Wellness facilities include a large AquaSpa measuring 24,219 sq. ft (2,250 sq. meters). It features a large thalassotherapy pool under a huge solarium dome, complete with health bar for light breakfast and lunch items and fresh squeezed fruit and vegetable juices. There are 16 treatment rooms, plus eight treatment rooms with showers and one treatment room specifically designed for wheelchair passengers, aerobics room, gymnasium (complete with over 40 exercise machines), large men's and women's saunas (with large ocean-view porthole window), a unisex thermal suite (containing several steam and shower mist rooms with different fragrances such as camomile, eucalyptus and mint, and a glacial ice fountain), and beauty salon.

Sports facilities include a full-size basketball court, compact football, paddle tennis and volleyball, golf simulator, shuffleboard (on two different decks) and a jogging track. A 70-person capacity sports bar called Extreme (a first for a Celebrity Cruises' ship, although it just doesn't, somehow, belong) is located directly in front of the main funnel and has glass walls that overlook the ship's side.

● **For more extensive general information on what a Celebrity cruise is like, see pages 111–115.**

Minerva II
★★★★

Mid-Size Ship: . . . . .30,277 tons	Total Crew: 300	Cabins (with private balcony): 258
Lifestyle: . . . . .Premium	Passengers	Cabins (wheelchair accessible): 4
Cruise Line: . . . . . .Swan Hellenic Cruises	(lower beds/all berths): 710/838	Cabin Current: . . . . .110 and 220 volts
Former Names: . . . . .R Eight	Passenger Space Ratio	Elevators: 4
Builder: Chantiers de l'Atlantique (France)	(lower beds/all berths): 42.6/36.1	Casino (gaming tables): . . . . .No
Original Cost: . . . .$150 million	Crew/Passenger Ratio	Slot Machines: .No
Entered Service: . . . . .Feb 2001/Apr 2003	(lower beds/all berths): 1.8/2.2	Swimming Pools (outdoors): 1
Registry: . . . . .Marshall Islands	Navigation Officers: . . . . .European	Swimming Pools (indoors): 0
Length (ft/m): 592.0/180.45	Cabins (total): 355	Whirlpools: 2
Beam (ft/m): 83.5/25.46	Size Range (sq ft/m): 145.3–968.7/	(+ 1 thalassaotherapy)
Draft (ft/m): 19.5/6.0	13.5–90.0	Self-Service Launderette: . . . . .Yes
Propulsion/Propellers: . . . . .diesel	Cabins (outside view): 332	Dedicated Cinema/Seats: . . . . .No
(18,600 kW)/2	Cabins (interior/no view): 23	Library: . . . . .Yes
Passenger Decks: 9	Cabins (for one person): 0	Classification Society: . . . .Bureau Veritas

OVERALL SCORE: 1,498 (OUT OF A POSSIBLE 2,000 POINTS)

OVERVIEW. *Minerva II* was previously the final one in a series of eight almost identical ships in the now defunct Renaissance Cruises fleet (at the time, the cruise industry's only totally non-smoking cruise line). Swan Hellenic Cruises now operates this ship under charter for a period of seven years (it is much larger than *Minerva*, and loses some of the ambiance for which previous Swan Hellenic ships were known). The ship's square, royal blue funnel sports a white swan, the company's logo, and balances the royal blue hull, white superstructure, and high sides. *Minerva II* can cruise at faster speeds than the previous *Minerva*, thus allowing the company to offer even better itineraries that cover more ground (well, water, actually).

An outside lido deck has a swimming pool and good sunbathing space, while one of the aft decks has a thalassaotherapy pool. A jogging track circles the swimming pool deck (but one deck above). The uppermost outdoors deck includes a golf driving net and shuffleboard court.

The interior decor is quite elegant, and is a throwback to ship decor of the ocean liners of the 1920s and '30s. This includes detailed ceiling cornices, both real and faux wrought iron staircase railings, leather paneled walls, *trompe l'oeil* ceilings, rich carpeting in hallways with an Oriental rug-look center section, and many other interesting (and expensive-looking) decorative touches. The overall feel is of an old-world country club. The staircase in the main, two-deck-high foyer will remind you of something similar in a blockbuster hit about a certain ship on which movie stars Kate Winslet and Leonardo di Caprio met. Swanners (regular Swan Hellenic Cruises passengers) will surely be pleased with the taste with which its interiors have been designed and executed.

BERLITZ'S RATINGS

	Possible	Achieved
Ship	500	408
Accommodation	200	155
Food	400	273
Service	400	287
Entertainment	100	72
Cruise	400	303

The public rooms are basically spread over three decks. The reception hall (lobby) has a staircase with intricate, real wrought-iron railings (but painted on plasti-glass panels on the stairways on other decks). A large observation lounge, the Orpheus Room, is located high atop the ship, with great views from its floor-to-ceiling windows. The room has a long bar which faces forward (the barmen actually have the best view) and very comfortable seating. There is also a small bandstand and wooden dance floor, while the aft section on the port side has six internet-connect computer terminals (although there's little privacy).

Other public rooms: The Lounge is used principally for lectures and evening theatrical and musical performances. The delightful wood-paneled Wheeler Bar (it used to be a casino) has a fireplace, a long bar, and a large half-model of S.S. *Caledonia*, a former P&O ship.

The vessel has several bars – including one in each of the restaurant entrances. The Library is a beautiful, grand, restful room (perhaps the nicest public room), designed in Regency style. It features a fireplace, a high, indented, *trompe l'oeil* ceiling, and an excellent collection of about 4,000 books, plus some very comfortable wingback chairs with footstools, and sofas you could sleep on.

Swan Hellenic Cruises provides a seamless cruise and tour program, geared specifically to British and North American passengers, at a price that's very hard to beat considering the destination-rich itineraries, pre- and post-cruise land stays at high-quality hotels, all transfers, and the expert lecturers that accompany every cruise. You should experience a fine, hassle-free cruise holiday aboard this ship. There may not be marble bathroom fittings, or caviar and other (more expensive) niceties, but the value for money is excellent. The onboard currency is the British pound.

There is no wrap-around promenade deck outdoors, but there is a small jogging track around the perimeter of the swimming pool, and open decks on the port and starboard sides. There areno wooden decks outdoors (they are covered by Bollidt, a sand-colored rubberized material). There is no sauna. The stairways, although carpeted, sound tinny.

SUITABLE FOR: *Minerva II* is best suited to couples and single travelers of a mature age and an academic interest who seek to cruise to destinations of mainly historical importance in comfortable, but not sophisticated surroundings. They do not need the entertainment and mindless organized parlor games found aboard the large contemporary cruise ships, but would rather have conversation with fellow passengers, and life enrichment lectures on the topics covered by the ship's itineraries. *Minerva II* is not recommended for children.

ACCOMMODATION. There are six basic cabin size categories, but 20 price categories (14 for double occupancy and 6 for single occupancy). The cabin size categories include: Owner's Suites (6), Master Suites (4), Deluxe with balcony, Superior Plus with balcony, Superior with balcony, and Standard Outside View/Standard Interior (No View) Cabins. The price you pay will depend on the grade, size and allocation you choose. Some cabins have interconnecting doors (good for families with children), while 18 cabins on Deck 6 have lifeboat obstructed views. All suites/cabins have tea/coffee making facilities (however, the milk supplied is powdered, not fresh). One thing really spoils the many balcony cabins is the patio-style white plastic furniture – it would be more in keeping with the "country house" style of the Swan Hellenic product if this were changed to teak).

Standard Outside-View and Interior (no view) Cabins: All the standard interior (no view) and outside-view cabins (the lowest four grades) are extremely compact units, and tight for two persons (particularly for cruises longer than five days). They have twin beds (or queen-sized bed), with good under-bed storage areas, personal safe, vanity desk with large mirror, good closet and drawer space (in rich, dark woods), and bathrobe. Color TV sets carry a major news channel (where obtainable), plus sport and movies.

Cabins with Private Balcony: Cabins with private balconies (about 66 percent of all cabins) have partial, and not full, balcony partitions, sliding glass doors, and, due to good design and layout, only 14 cabins on Deck 6 have lifeboat-obstructed views. The bathrooms, which have tiled floors and plain walls, are compact, standard units, and include a shower stall with a strong, removable hand-held shower unit, hairdryer, 100% cotton towels, toiletries storage shelves and retractable clothesline. Personal toiletry items include soap, shampoo, body lotion, shower cap, and shoeshine mitt.

Owner's Suites/Master Suites: The six Owner's Suites and four Master Suites provide the most spacious accommodation (in my view, well worth the extra cost). These are fine, large living spaces located in the forward-most and aft-most sections of the accommodation decks (particularly nice are those that overlook the stern, on Deck 6, 7 and 8). They have more extensive private balconies that really are private and cannot be overlooked by anyone on the decks above. There is an entrance foyer, living room, bedroom (the bed faces the sea, which can be seen through the floor-to-ceiling windows and sliding glass door), CD player (with selection of audio discs), bathroom with Jacuzzi bathtub, and a small guest bathroom.

CUISINE/DINING. There are four restaurants:

The Dining Room (the most formal) has 338 seats, a raised central section, and is located in the aft section of the ship. It has large ocean-view windows on three sides, several prime tables overlooking the stern, and a small bandstand for occasional live dinner music. The menu changes daily for lunch and dinner, and male passengers are asked to wear jacket and tie for dinner. However, the noise level in this main dining room can be high, due to its single-deck-height ceiling.

The Swan Restaurant has ocean-view windows along two sides, and the cuisine has a Mediterranean emphasis.

The Grill is the place for steak and other plain but tasty dishes, with ocean-view windows along two sides and a set menu (plus daily chef's specials).

The Bridge Cafe has both indoor and outdoor seating, and is the ship's casual dining spot, in a self-serve buffet style. It is open for breakfast, lunch and casual dinners (the dinner menu is the same as that in the formal Dining Room). The oversized cutlery is rather cumbersome, however.

All restaurants have open-seating dining, although reservations are usually necessary in the Swan Restaurant and The Grill, where there are mostly tables for four or six – there are few tables for two). In addition, there is a Poolside Grill and Bar for casual fast food.

ENTERTAINMENT. The Lounge, forward on Deck 5, is the venue for all main entertainment events, and some social functions. The entertainment consists mainly of classical concerts, choral music, light opera, jazz, as well as comedy and drama presentations. London's Guildhall School of Music and Drama is involved in supplying artists. Local entertainers are brought on board in various destinations.

The ship has an excellent lecture programme, featuring renowned authorities on subjects such as archeology, genealogy, anthropology, zoology, wildlife and nature.

SPA/FITNESS. The health/fitness spa has a gymnasium with some of the latest muscle toning equipment, a thalassotherapy pool, a steam room (no sauna), and several treatment rooms, and beauty salon. Out on deck, there is a small swimming pool, two hot tubs, and a jogging track.

The spa is operated by Harding Brothers, a UK concession that provides beauty and wellness treatments. Examples include: Body Toning (detox for the body); Body Bien Etre (body scrub and massage); Seaweed Wrap; Collagen Velvet Facial Mask, and aromatherapy treatments.

Mona Lisa
★★★

Mid-Size Ship: . . . . .28,891 tons	Passenger Decks: 8	Cabins (for one person): 14
Lifestyle: . . . . .Standard	Total Crew: 417	Cabins (with private balcony): 0
Cruise Line: . . . . .Holiday Cruises	Passengers	Cabins (wheelchair accessible): 10
Former Names: . . .Victoria, Sea Princess,	(lower beds/all berths): 744/778	Cabin Current: . . . . .220 volts
Kungsholm	Passenger Space Ratio	Elevators: 4
Builder: . . . . .John Brown & Co. (UK)	(lower beds/all berths): 38.8/37.0	Casino (gaming tables): . . . . .Yes
Original Cost: . . . .$22 million	Crew/Passenger Ratio	Slot Machines: . . . . .Yes
Entered Service: . . . . .Apr 1966/Dec 2002	(lower beds/all berths): 1.7/1.8	Swimming Pools (outdoors): 2
Registry: . . . . .Great Britain	Navigation Officers: . . . . .European	Swimming Pools (indoors): 1
Length (ft/m): 660.2/201.23	Cabins (total): .379	Whirlpools: 1
Beam (ft/m): 87.1/26.57	Size Range (sq ft/m): 137.7–466.0/	Self-Service Launderette: . . . . .Yes
Draft (ft/m): 28.0/8.56	12.8–43.3	Dedicated Cinema/Seats: Yes/289
Propulsion/Propellers: . . . . .diesel	Cabins (outside view): 291	Library: . . . . .Yes
(18,800 kW)/2	Cabins (interior/no view): 88	Classification Society: . . .Lloyd's Register

OVERALL SCORE: 1,218 (OUT OF A POSSIBLE 2,000 POINTS)

OVERVIEW. *Mona Lisa* is a solidly built ex-ocean liner with flowing, rounded lines, a well-balanced profile, and a mid-ship sag (a "sheer") that makes it look like a traditional ship. It has been nicely refurbished over the years, quite well maintained, and arguably improved since it was operated by P&O Cruises (1979–2002). The funnel has a replica of Leonardo da Vinci's painting of Mona Lisa. The ship – still charming, but well worn and decidedly out-of-date – is under long-term charter to Holiday Kreutzfahrten, of Germany, until 2007, being promoted as a classic cruise liner.

Mona Lisa's open deck and sunbathing space is good. Some real teak steamer-style deck lounge chairs add a sense of the past, and cushioned pads make it a pleasure to simply sit outside and read a book; other deck chairs are made of aluminium. Inside, spacious public rooms are trimmed with fine woods and have good furnishings and fabrics, and rich carpeting. A much appreciated feature is an indoor (sea-water) swimming pool. There is a decent variety of entertainment spaces, bars and lounges.

Port taxes and insurance are included for all passengers, as are all gratuities. The onboard currency is the euro.

SUITABLE FOR: *Mona Lisa* best suits German-speaking couples and single travelers seeking good value for money for a first cruise aboard a ship with very traditional, quite comfortable (but not pretentious or luxurious) surroundings.

ACCOMMODATION. The wide range of cabins includes six suites. These are in 17 grades, including two suite grades, and two grades of cabins with single beds. Most cabins have a decent amount of space, and many have fine pol-

BERLITZ'S RATINGS

	Possible	Achieved
Ship	500	297
Accommodation	200	123
Food	400	237
Service	400	250
Entertainment	100	62
Cruise	400	249

ished real wood-paneled walls. Most have excellent closet and drawer space, and fine wood-paneled walls. The bathrooms are of a generous size; the fixtures solid, and most cabins have ample storage space for personal toiletries. Some have upper and lower berths. The bathroom towels are small, however.

CUISINE/DINING. The elegant and tiered European-style Coral Restaurant is in the center of the ship on one of the lower decks. There are tables for two, four, six and eight, and the dining room is operated in two seatings. The cuisine is tailored for German tastes, with breakfast and lunch buffets featuring a good selection of cold cuts of meat, and a good array of breads (including dark breads) and cheeses. The wine list provides a good selection of German wines.

There is also Toscana, an à la carte restaurant set along the starboard side of Lido Deck. Reservations are required for this intimate dining spot. For casual eating, the outdoor Lido Buffet has more temperature-controlled display space and better serving lines. Plastic chairs prevail.

ENTERTAINMENT. The International Music Salon, a single level room, is designed for cabaret-style shows. Entertainment consists of a number of variety acts (typically singers, magicians, and others), plus the ship's own troupe of showgirl dancers. A professional dance couple is usually on hand to provide a cabaret act as well as teach dance classes and give private lessons.

SPA/FITNESS. The Fitness Center has an indoor swimming/exercise pool, saunas and changing rooms, and two massage/body treatment rooms.

Monarch of the Seas
★★★ +

Large (Resort) Ship: . . . . .73,941 tons	Passenger Decks: 11	Cabins (for one person): 0
Lifestyle: . . . . .Standard	Total Crew: 858	Cabins (with private balcony): 62
Cruise Line: . . . . .Royal Caribbean	Passengers	Cabins (wheelchair accessible): 4
International	(lower beds/all berths): 2,354/2,744	Cabin Current: . . . . .110 volts
Former Names: . . . . .none	Passenger Space Ratio	Elevators: 11
Builder: . . . . .Chantiers de l'Atlantique	(lower beds/all berths): 31.0/26.9	Casino (gaming tables): . . . . .Yes
Original Cost: . . . .$300 million	Crew/Passenger Ratio	Slot Machines: . . . . .Yes
Entered Service: . . . . .Nov 1991	(lower beds/all berths): 2.8/3.3	Swimming Pools (outdoors): 2
Registry: . . . . .The Bahamas	Navigation Officers: . . . . .Norwegian	Swimming Pools (indoors): 0
Length (ft/m): 879.9/268.2	Cabins (total): 1,177	Whirlpools: 2
Beam (ft/m): 105.9/32.3	Size Range (sq ft/m): 118.4–670.0/	Self-Service Launderette: . . . . .No
Draft (ft/m): 24.9/7.6	11.0–62.2	Dedicated Cinema/Seats: Yes-2/146 each
Propulsion/Propellers: . . . . .diesel	Cabins (outside view): 732	Library: . . . . .Yes
(21,844 kW)/2	Cabins (interior/no view): 445	Classification Society: Det Norske Veritas

OVERALL SCORE: 1,394 (OUT OF A POSSIBLE 2,000 POINTS)

OVERVIEW. The ship is almost identical in size and appearance to sister ship *Majesty of the Seas* and *Sovereign of the Seas* but with an improved internal layout, better public room features, passenger flow and signage. Royal Caribbean International's trademark Viking Crown lounge and bar surrounds the funnel and provides a stunning view. The open deck space is very cramped when full, as aboard any large ship, although there seems to be plenty of it. There is a basketball court for sports lovers.

Following a grounding just before Christmas 1998, the ship underwent the replacement of 460 tons of bottom shell plating. At the same time, a new facility for toddlers was created. The children's and teens' programs are good, overseen by enthusiastic youth counselors, and there is a busy but sound activities program for adults.

The interior layout is a little awkward, as it is designed in a vertical stack, with most public rooms located aft, and the accommodation forward. There is, however, an impressive array of spacious and elegant public rooms, although the decor definitely brings to mind the IKEA school of interior design. A stunning five-deck-high Centrum lobby has cascading stairways and two glass-walled elevators.

There is a decent two-level showlounge and decent shops, albeit with lots of tacky merchandise. Casino gamers will find blackjack, craps, Caribbean stud poker and roulette tables, plus an array of slot machines.

This floating resort provides a well-tuned, yet very impersonal, short cruise experience for a lot of passengers. The dress code is very casual. There are many public rooms and spaces to play in, including a five-deck-high atrium, which really is the interior focal point of the ship, and has

BERLITZ'S RATINGS

	Possible	Achieved
Ship	500	381
Accommodation	200	141
Food	400	245
Service	400	286
Entertainment	100	75
Cruise	400	266

glass lifts. Among the public rooms, the library offers space for relaxation and has a decent selection of books.

The ship provides a wide range of facilities with consistently sound, but highly programmed service from a reasonably attentive, though rather insensitive, young staff. In the final analysis, you will probably be overwhelmed by the public spaces, and underwhelmed by the size of the cabins. The ship underwent an extensive internal refurbishment in 2003 and looks fresher (better) for it.

ACCOMMODATION. There are 17 categories. The price you pay will depend on the grade, size and location you choose. Note that there are no cabins with private balconies.

Suites: Thirteen suites on Bridge Deck are reasonably large and nicely furnished (the largest is the Royal Suite), with separate living and sleeping spaces. They provide more space, with better service and more perks than standard-grade accommodation.

Standard Cabins: The standard outside-view and interior (no view) cabins are very small, although an arched window treatment and colorful soft furnishings do give the illusion of more space.

Almost all cabins have twin beds that can be converted to a queen-sized or double bed configuration, together with moveable bedside tables. All of the standard cabins have very little closet and drawer space (you will need some luggage engineering to stow your cases). You should, therefore, think of packing only minimal clothing, which is all you really need for a short cruise. All cabins have a private bathroom, with shower enclosure, toilet and washbasin.

CUISINE/DINING. The two large dining rooms (both are non-smoking) have Hollywood musical themes (Brigadoon and Flower Drum Song). There are tables for four, six or eight, but no tables for two, and there are two seatings. The dining operation is well-orchestrated, with emphasis on highly programmed service.

The cuisine is typical of mass banquet catering that offers standard fare comparable to that found in American family-style restaurants ashore. While menu descriptions are tempting, the actual food may be somewhat disappointing and unmemorable (many items are pre-prepared ashore to keep costs down).

However, a decent selection of light meals is provided, and a vegetarian menu is available. The selection of breads, rolls, fruit and cheese is quite poor, however, and could do with improvement. Caviar (once a standard menu item) now incurs a hefty extra charge. Menus typically include a Welcome Aboard Dinner, French Dinner, Italian Dinner, International Dinner, and Captain's Gala Dinner.

The wine list is not extensive, but the prices are moderate. The waiters, many from Caribbean countries, are perhaps overly friendly for some tastes – particularly on the last night of the cruise, when tips are expected.

For casual breakfasts and lunches, the Windjammer Cafe is the place to go, although there are often long lines at peak times, and the selection is very average.

ENTERTAINMENT. The Sound of Music is the name of the principal showlounge; it has both main and balcony levels, with banquette seating. On the stage is a video wall with 50 screens – good for visual presentations.

A smaller entertainment lounge, the April in Paris Lounge, is where cabaret acts, including late-night adult (blue) comedy are featured, as well as music for dancing.

The entertainment throughout is upbeat (in fact, it is difficult to get away from music and noise). There is even background music in all corridors and elevators, and constant music outdoors on the pool deck. If you want a quiet relaxing holiday, choose another ship.

SPA/FITNESS. The ShipShape Fitness Center has a gymnasium with aft-facing views (it is located at the aft of the ship) and a selection of high-tech muscle-pumping equipment. There is also an aerobics studio, and classes are offered in a variety of keep fit regimes. There is also a beauty salon, and a sauna, as well as treatment rooms for pampering massages, facials, etc. While the facilities are not as extensive as those aboard the company's newer ships, they are adequate for the short cruises that this ship operates.

For the more sporting, there is activity galore – including a rock-climbing wall, with several separate climbing tracks. It is located outdoors at the aft end of the funnel.

● **For more extensive general information about the Royal Caribbean experience, see pages 128–131.**

QUOTABLE QUOTES

These are some of the questions I have been asked by passengers cruising for the first time:

"Does the crew sleep on board?"

"How far above sea level are we?"

"Is the island surrounded by water?"

"Are all Caribbean islands the same size?"

"How does the captain know which port to go to?"

"Can we get off in the Panama Canal?"

"Does the ship generate its own electricity?"

"Does this elevator go up as well as down?"

"Will this elevator take me to my cabin?"

"Why is the sauna so hot?"

"What time's the midnight buffet?"

"Are there two seatings at the midnight buffet?"

"Do we have to stay up until midnight to change our clocks?"

"Does the chef cook himself?"

"What happens to the ice sculptures after they melt?"

"How many fjords to the dollar?"

"What time's the 2 o'clock tour?"

"Where's the bus for the walking tour?"

"Can you see the Equator from the deck?"

Monet
★★ +

Boutique Ship: . . . . .1,480 tons	Total Crew: 27	Cabins (with private balcony): 0
Lifestyle: . . . . .Standard	Passengers	Cabins (wheelchair accessible): 0
Cruise Line: . . . . .Elegant Cruises & Tours	(lower beds/all berths): 56/61	Cabin Current: . . . . .220 volts
Former Names: . .*Stella Dalmatiae, Yushar*	Passenger Space Ratio	Elevators: 0
Builder: . .Brodoremont Shipyard (Croatia)	(lower beds/all berths): 26.4/24.2	Casino (gaming tables): . . . . .No
Original Cost: .n/a	Crew/Passenger Ratio	Slot Machines: . . . . .No
Entered Service: 1970/2001	(lower beds/all berths): 2.0/2.2	Swimming Pools (outdoors): 1
Registry: . . . . .St Vincent	Navigation Officers: . . . . .Croatian	Swimming Pools (indoors): 0
Length (ft/m): 223.4/68.1	Cabins (total): .30	Whirlpools: 2
Beam (ft/m): 33.1/10.1	Size Range (sq ft/m): 92.0–151.0/	Self-Service Launderette: . . . . .No
Draft (ft/m): 11.5/3.5	8.5/14.0	Dedicated Cinema/Seats: . . . . .No
Propulsion/Propellers: . . . . .diesel	Cabins (outside view): 30	Library: . . . . .Yes
(1,000kW)/1 (CP)	Cabins (interior/no view): 0	Classification Society: . .Croatian Register
Passenger Decks: 4	Cabins (for one person): 4	of Shipping

OVERALL SCORE: 1,097 (OUT OF A POSSIBLE 2,000 POINTS)

OVERVIEW. *Monet*, named after the immortal French Impressionist Claude Monet (1840–1926), is a little gem of a ship that inhabits the small ports of the Adriatic Sea. It is a cute, all-white boutique ship (a tad smaller than the somewhat similar size and profile of Hebridean Princess), and is good for up-close, in-depth coastal cruising. Originally built at the Dimitov shipyard in Bulgaria, the vessel went through an extensive refit in 1997 in Croatia, with a new superstructure built onto an existing hull. The ship is operated by New York-based Elegant Cruises & Tours (fellow passengers will typically be American and British). *Monet* has smart hardwood teak decks, with hardwood tables and chairs on the open Sun Deck aft. Formerly operated by the now-defunct Swiss company Leisure Cruises, *Monet* specializes in cruises around the Dalmatian islands and coastal ports of the Adriatic.

The ship's interior decor is quite charming, with warm colors used throughout the limited public spaces, which are highlighted by the brass and chrome on its stairways. There is just one (small) main lounge (with photographs of Claude Monet), a restaurant, and a small boutique, so the ambiance is intimate and extremely cozy. The dress code is totally relaxed, and informality rules. The staff is from Croatia, and they provide warm, friendly, well-meaning, but unsophisticated service.

This is a pleasant little ship for those who do not like lines, hubbub, or crowds, or for anyone wanting to escape from the rest of the world. Note, however, that there is no elevator, so you will need to be able to walk up and down steps well (the same is true of some of the ports of call). Typically, 7-day Adriatic Coastal cruises are the staple diet

BERLITZ'S RATINGS

	Possible	Achieved
Ship	500	231
Accommodation	200	120
Food	400	256
Service	400	277
Entertainment	100	30
Cruise	400	183

of this ship, although occasional longer cruises are occasionally featured. Shore excursions, gratuities, and port charges are extra (shore excursions may be included on special, longer itineraries). There are no medical facilities, and there is no doctor on board. The ship is often chartered by various groups, organizations and tour operators, which can prove frustrating when you are trying to book as an individual.

SUITABLE FOR: Adult couples and single travelers of mature years who prefer a go-slow lifestyle, and who wouldn't be interested in venturing aboard those big ships with hordes of passengers. This is for passengers who seek in-depth coastal cruising along the shores of the Adriatic, with a chance to learn about the region's history and architecture.

ACCOMMODATION: There are five price grades for the all-outside view cabins, and the price you pay depends on the size, grade and location you choose. The cabins are located on three of the ship's four passenger decks, with a central passageway separating port and starboard cabins.

All cabins have hardwood cabinetry and soft furnishings of a decent quality, color television and video player, multiple music channels, telephone, hairdryer, and vanity desk with lighted mirror. Closet space is tight, so take only what is absolutely necessary. All (except for four single occupancy cabins) have lower beds, in either a twin-bed or double-bed arrangement (two of the cabins can accommodate three persons) and all have a tiny (wet shower) bathroom with hand-held shower (there's little space for personal toiletries). The washbasins are positioned extremely low. There is no room service menu.

There are also two Master Cabins, with forward-facing views, and more space than any other cabin (although the bathrooms do not have bathtubs).

CUISINE/DINING: The Nymphea Restaurant, which is located just forward of the reception desk, has large square ocean-view picture windows, and an indented central ceiling section. It is intimate and quite charming, with decor and colors that are light and contemporary. Single seating, leisurely dining is featured (for dinner) at tables for two, four or six (the dining rooms chairs all have armrests), while breakfasts and lunches are self-service.

The cuisine, which is reasonably varied, encompasses regional specialties, and wine, beer and soft drinks are typically included for lunch and dinner, but espresso and cappuccino coffees (from the bar) cost extra.

ENTERTAINMENT: The Giverny Bar/Piano Bar, the gathering place for after-dinner conversation, has a cozy wood-topped bar, and also has a musical unit that provides music for listening and dancing.

SPA/FITNESS: The ship really is too small to have any spa facilities, although there are two hot tubs on outside decks.

HOW SYSTEMS WORK

Radar
Radar is one of the most important discoveries ever made for the development of navigational aids, providing a picture of all solid objects in a range selected by the navigator, which is from a half-mile (800 meters) to a 72-mile (116-km) radius. Its greatest asset is as an aid to collision avoidance with other ships, although it is of value in finding a position at a distance when navigational marks or charted coastlines are within its range.

Engine Telegraph
These automatic signaling devices are used to communicate orders between the bridge and the engine room. There may be three, one on the bridge and one on each bridgewing.

Bow Thruster
This small two-way handle is used to control the bow thrusters, powerful engines in the bow that push the ship away from the dockside without tugs. Some new ships may also have thrusters positioned at the stern.

Rudder Angle Indicator
This device is normally positioned in front of, and above, the quartermaster. It provides both the commanding officer and the quartermaster with a constant readout of the degrees of rudder angle, either to port (left) or starboard (right).

VHF Radio
This is a radio receiver and transmitter, operating on VHF (Very High Frequency) with a "line-of-sight" range. It is used for communicating with other ships, pilots, port authorities, and so on.

Radio Direction Finder
This operates on radio waves, enabling its operator to take bearings of shore radio stations. By crossing two or more bearings, you find the ship's position.

Depth Indicator
This equipment (which is an echo-sounder) provides a ship with a constant digital monitor readout, together with a printed chart.

Course Recorder
This records and prints all courses followed by the ship at all times.

Clearview Screen
This device makes simple but effective use of centrifugal force, where instead of an automobile-type windshield wiper, a ship has circular screens that rotate at high speed to clear rain or sea spray away, providing those on the bridge with the best possible view in even the worst weather.

Engine Speed Indicators
These provide a reading of the number of revolutions per minute being generated by the engines. Each engine has a separate indicator, giving the speed in forward or reverse.

Facsimile Recorder
This special radio device is designed to receive meteorological and oceanographic maps, satellite pictures, and other pertinent weather information transmitted by maritime broadcast stations throughout the world.

MSC Armonia
★★★★

Large (Resort) Ship: ....58,600 tons	Passenger Decks: 10	Cabins (for one person): 0
Lifestyle: ....Standard	Total Crew: 710	Cabins (with private balcony): 132
Cruise Line: ....MSC Italian Cruises	Passengers	Cabins (wheelchair accessible): 2
Former Names: ....*European Vision*	(lower beds/all berths): 1,566/2,223	Cabin Current: ....110 and 220 volts
Builder: ....Chantiers de l'Atlantique	Passenger Space Ratio	Elevators: 9
(France)	(lower beds/all berths): 37.4/27.6	Casino (gaming tables): ....Yes
Original Cost: ....$245 million	Crew/Passenger Ratio	Slot Machines: ....Yes
Entered Service: ...June 2001/May 2004	(lower beds/all berths): 2.2/3.1	Swimming Pools (outdoors): 2
Registry:........................Italy	Navigation Officers: ....European	Swimming Pools (indoors): 0
Length (ft/m): 823.4/251.0	Cabins (total): 783	Whirlpools: ....1 (thalassotherapy)
Beam (ft/m): 94.4/28.8	Size Range (sq ft/m): 139.9–236.8/	Self-Service Launderette: ....No
Draft (ft/m): 22.4/6.85	13.0–22.0	Dedicated Cinema/Seats: ....No
Propulsion/Propellers: .....diesel-electric	Cabins (outside view): 511	Library: ....Yes
(31,680kW)/2 pods	Cabins (interior/no view): 272	Classification Society: ....RINA

OVERALL SCORE: 1,449 (OUT OF A POSSIBLE 2,000 POINTS)

OVERVIEW. Built originally for the now defunct Festival Cruises (known as First European Cruises in the USA) the ship was a cousin to Festival's first new ship *Mistral*, but with an additional deck that allowed for the addition of more suites with private balconies in what is really a premium real estate area. The additional deck also provided a better balance to the ship's overall profile. A 115-ft (35-meter) mid-section was added to increase the ship's length and provide more cabins and public rooms.

The ship is fitted with a high-tech azimuthing "pod" propulsion system *(see page 151 for a definition)*. As *European Vision*, the ship began its working life auspiciously, having been selected to be a floating hotel to accommodate the leaders and staff of the G8 summit in 2001. In 2004, Festival Cruises ceased operations (the result of heavy discounts and competition in the marketplace which sadly resulted in many crew members losing their jobs). The ship was bought by MSC Italian Cruises for €215 million and renamed *MSC Armonia*.

The exterior deck space is barely adequate for the number of passengers carried, no more. The lido deck surrounding the outdoor swimming pool also has whirlpool tubs and a large bandstand is set in raised canvas-covered pods (all deck lounge chairs have cushioned pads).

Inside, the layout and passenger flow is good, as are the "you are here" deck signs. The decks are named after European cities – e.g. Oxford Deck (with British public room names), Venice Deck (with Italian public room names), and Biarritz Deck (with French public room names). The decor is "European Moderne" – whatever that means – but it does include crisp, clean lines, minimalism in furniture designs

BERLITZ'S RATINGS		
	Possible	Achieved
Ship	500	397
Accommodation	200	155
Food	400	258
Service	400	301
Entertainment	100	54
Cruise	400	284

(including some chairs that look interesting but are totally impractical). However, the interior colors chosen are extremely good; nothing jars the senses, but rather calms them, unlike many ships today.

Facilities include Amadeus, the ship's nightclub, and La Gondola Theater, for production shows and cabaret, plays and other theatrical presentations. There's a cigar smoking room (called Ambassador), which has all the hallmarks of a gentleman's club; as well as Vivaldi, a piano lounge. The Goethe Library/Card Room has real writing desks (something many ships seem to omit). There is an extensive internet cafe, as well an English pub called the White Lion. Gamblers will find solace in the Lido Casino, with blackjack, poker and roulette games, plus an array of slot machines.

The onboard currency is the euro. Gratuities are recommended at $8.50 per person, per day. Additionally, 15% is added to all bar bills and heath spa treatments.

Standing in line for embarkation, disembarkation, shore tenders and for self-serve buffet meals is an inevitable aspect of cruising aboard all large ships. Heavy smokers are everywhere, and are virtually impossible to avoid (in typical European fashion, ashtrays are simply moved – if used at all – to wherever smokers happen to be sitting or standing). Announcements are in several languages.

The constant push for onboard revenue is irritating. The staff is more focused on Italian passengers than those who speak any other European language. If you are considering two back-to-back 7-day cruises, note that some ports may be duplicated, and menus and entertainment are based on a 7-day cycle, so there is much product repetition (including the cruise director's jokes). Regular passenger complaints include poor ports of call information.

The wheelchair-bound should note that there is no access to the uppermost forward and aft decks, although access throughout most of the interior of the ship is very good. The passenger hallways are a little narrow on some accommodation decks to pass when housekeeping carts are in place, however.

The company keeps prices low by providing air transportation that may be at inconvenient times, or that involves long journeys by bus. In other words, be prepared for a little discomfort in getting to and from your cruise in exchange for low cruise rates.

SUITABLE FOR: *MSC Armonia* is best suited to adult couples and singles (plus families with children) who enjoy big city life, piazzas and outdoor cafes, constant activity accompanied by lots of noise (some call it ambiance), late nights, entertainment that is loud and of questionable quality, and food that is quantity rather than quality. It is for those who are comfortable hearing several (European) languages everywhere around them.

ACCOMMODATION. There are 11 categories, the price depending on grade, size and location. These include 132 suites with private balcony (the partitions are only of the partial and not the full type), outside-view cabins and interior (no view) cabins.

Suite grade accommodation (they are not true suites, as there is no separate bedroom and lounge) also has more room, a larger lounge area, walk-in closet, wall-to-wall vanity counter, a bathroom with combination tub and shower, toilet, and private balcony (with light). Bathrobes are provided. In general, the "suites" are well laid out and nicely furnished. However, except for the very highest category, the suite bathrooms are very plain, with white plastic washbasins and white walls, and mirrors that steam up.

Even the smallest interior (no- view) cabins are quite spacious, with plenty of space between the two lower beds. All grades of accommodation have sheets and blankets as bed linen (no duvets), and are equipped with a TV set, hairdryer, mini-bar/refrigerator, personal safe (cleverly positioned behind a vanity desk mirror), bathroom with shower and toilet, and 100% cotton towels. However, the standard grade cabins are quite small when compared to many other ships, at a modest 140 sq. ft (13 sq. meters).

CUISINE/DINING. The four dining spots are no-smoking. The principal dining room, the 610-seat Marco Polo

Restaurant, typically has two seatings for dinner, and open seating for breakfast and lunch. However, for breakfast and lunch, you may well be seated with others with whom you may not be able to communicate very satisfactorily, given the mixture of languages on board.

In general, the cuisine is acceptable, if unmemorable. The menus are varied and the presentation is generally sound, and should prove a highlight for most passengers. The wine list has a wide variety of wines at fairly reasonable prices, although most of the wines are very young.

La Pergola, the most formal restaurant, has stylish Italian cuisine. It is assigned to all passengers occupying accommodation designated as suites, although other passengers can dine in it too, on a reservations-only basis.

Chez Claude, on the starboard side aft, adjacent to the ship's funnel, is a grill area for fast-food items. La Brasserie is a casual, self-serve buffet eatery, open 24 hours a day. The selections are very standardized (minimal). Cafe San Marco, on the upper, second level of the main lobby, is available for coffee and pastry items.

ENTERTAINMENT. La Gondola Theater is two decks high, and is the main venue for production shows, cabaret acts, plays and other theatrical presentations. It is a well designed room (except for the fact that no space was allocated for a live showband), with good sight lines from most seats, and four entrances that allow easy access (and exit).

Entertainment is weak, although it could improve somewhat as more ships are brought into service by MSC Italian Cruises. Other shows consist of unknown cabaret acts (typically singers, magicians, mime artistes, comedy jugglers, and others) doing the cruise ship circuit. The ship carries a number of bands and small musical units that provide live music for dancing or listening.

SPA/FITNESS. The Atlantica Spa has numerous body-pampering treatments, a gymnasium with ocean views, and an array of high-tech, muscle-toning and strengthening equipment. There's also a thermal suite (with different kinds of steam rooms combined with aromatherapy infusions such as chamomile and eucalyptus) and a rasul chamber (a combination of two or three different kinds of special application mud, and gentle steam shower).

The spa, operated by a European concession under the name of Espace Elegance, offers a wide range of well-being treatments.

For the sports-minded, there's a simulated climbing wall outdoors, while other sports and fitness facilities include volleyball/basketball court, and mini-golf.

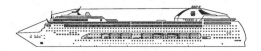

MSC Lirica
★★★★

Large (Resort) Ship: ....58,600 tons	Passenger Decks: 10	Cabins (with private balcony): 132
Lifestyle: ....Standard	Total Crew: 701	Cabins (wheelchair accessible): 4
Cruise Line: ....MSC Italian Cruises	Passengers	Cabin Current: ....110/220 volts
Former Names: ....none	(lower beds/all berths): 1,560/2,065	Elevators: 9
Builder: ....Chantiers de l'Atlantique	Passenger Space Ratio	Casino (gaming tables): ....Yes
(France)	(lower beds/all berths): 37.5/28.3	Slot Machines: ....Yes
Original Cost: ....$266 million	Crew/Passenger Ratio	Swimming Pools (outdoors): 2
Entered Service: ....Mar 2003	(lower beds/all berths): 2.2/2.9	Swimming Pools (indoors): 0
Registry:.......................Italy	Navigation Officers: ....Italian	Whirlpools: 2
Length (ft/m): 830.7/253.25	Cabins (total): 780	Self-Service Launderette: ....No
Beam (ft/m): 94.4/28.8	Size Range (sq ft/m): ....n/a	Dedicated Cinema/Seats: ....No
Draft (ft/m): 22.4/6.85	Cabins (outside view): 504	Library: ....Yes
Propulsion/Propellers: ....diesel	Cabins (interior/no view): 276	Classification Society: ....Bureau Veritas
(31,680kW)/2 pods	Cabins (for one person): 0	

OVERALL SCORE: 1,451 (OUT OF A POSSIBLE 2,000 POINTS)

OVERVIEW. Very similar in size and structure to the (now defunct) Festival Cruises' sister ships *European Dream* and *European Vision*, but arguably with a more attractive exterior profile, *MSC Lirica* (sister to *MSC Opera*) is the first of a pair of newbuilds for Mediterranean Shipping Cruises (MSC), Italy's largest privately owned cruise line (its former name was Star Lauro Cruises). The white funnel is quite sleek, with a swept-back design that closely resembles that of the Princess Cruises ships, and carries the MSC logo. From a technical viewpoint, the ship is fitted with an azimuthing pod propulsion system *(see page 151)*.

Inside, the layout and passenger flow is quite good with the exception of a couple of points of congestion (typically when the first seating comes out of the dining room and passengers on second seating are waiting to go in. The decor has many Italian influences, and this includes clean lines, minimalism in furniture design, and an eclectic collection of colors and soft furnishings that somehow work well together, and without any hint of garishness.

Real wood and marble have been used extensively in the interiors, and the high quality reflects the commitment that MSC has in the vessel's future. The "fit and finish" of the interior decor, and most carpeting, is very good throughout.

Facilities include the ship's main showlounge, a nightclub/discotheque, several lounges and bars, an internet center (Cyber Cafe, with 10 terminals), a virtual reality center, a shopping gallery named Rodeo Drive (with shops that have an integrated bar and entertainment area so that shopping becomes a city-like environment where you can shop, drink, and be entertained all in one convenient area), and a

BERLITZ'S RATINGS

	Possible	Achieved
Ship	500	407
Accommodation	200	156
Food	400	243
Service	400	304
Entertainment	100	55
Cruise	400	286

children's club. Gamblers may find solace in the Las Vegas Casino, with blackjack, poker and roulette games, together with an array of slot machines. There is also a card room, but the integral library is small and disappointing, and there are no hardback books.

The ship is designed to accommodate families with children, who have their own play center, youth counselors, and programming.

MSC Lirica features Mediterranean cruises during the summer and Caribbean cruises during the winter. The onboard currency is the euro (summer) and US$ (winter). Note that gratuities are extra, and bar service incurs a charge of 10%.

Anyone who is wheelchair-bound should note that there is no access to the uppermost forward and aft decks, although access throughout most of the interior of the ship is very good (there are also several wheelchair-accessible public restrooms). The passenger hallways are a little narrow on some decks for you to pass when housekeeping carts are in place, however.

Some things that passengers find irritating: the ship's photographers always seem to be in your face; the telephone numbering system to reach such places as the information bureau (2224) and hospital (2360) are not easy to remember (single digit numbers would be more user-friendly). Note that standing in line for embarkation, disembarkation, shore tenders and for self-serve buffet meals is an inevitable aspect of cruising aboard all large ships. Heavy smokers are everywhere, and are virtually impossible to avoid (in typical European fashion, ashtrays are simply moved – if used at all – to wherever smokers happen to be sitting).

SUITABLE FOR: *MSC Lirica* is best suited to young adult couples, singles, and families with tots, children and teens who enjoy big ship surroundings, a big city life, with all its attendant noise (some call it ambience), and passengers of different nationalities and languages (mostly European).

ACCOMMODATION. There are 11 different price levels for accommodation, depending on the grade and location you choose: one suite category, five outside-view cabin grades, and five interior (no view) cabin grades. Included are 132 "suites" with private balcony (note that the partitions between each balcony are of the partial and not the full wall type), outside-view cabins and interior (no view) cabins.

No matter what grade of cabin you choose, all have a mini-bar and personal safe, satellite-linked television, several audio channels, and 24-hour room service (note that while tea and coffee are complimentary, snacks for room service carry a delivery charge of €2.50 each time).

Accommodation designated as Suites (they are not true suites, as there is no separate bedroom and lounge – in other words, it is not a "suite" of rooms) also has more room, a larger lounge area, walk-in closet, wall-to-wall vanity counter, a bathroom with combination bathtub and shower, toilet, and semi-private balcony with light (the partitions are of the partial, not full, type). The bathrobes are 100% cotton. However, except for the very highest category, the suite bathrooms are very plain, with white plastic wash-basins and white walls, and mirrors that steam up.

According to the rules of feng shui, it is bad luck to place any mirror in such a position that it can be seen by anyone lying in bed (there are two floor-to-ceiling mirrors opposite the bed).

Some cabins on Scarlatti Deck have views obstructed by lifeboats, while those on Deck 10 aft (10105–10159) can be subject to late-night noise from the discotheque on the deck above.

CUISINE/DINING. There are two dining rooms (La Bussola Restaurant, and the smaller, slightly more intimate L'Ippocampo Restaurant, located one deck above), both of which have large ocean-view picture windows at the aft end of the ship. There are two seatings for meals, in keeping with all other ships in the MSC fleet, and tables are for two, four, six or eight.

La Pergola is the most formal restaurant, offering stylish Italian cuisine. It is assigned to all passengers occupying accommodation designated as suites, although other passengers can dine in it too, on a reservations-only basis. As you might expect, the food and service are superior to that in the main dining room.

Casual, self-serve buffets (for breakfast and lunch) can be taken in Le Bistrot Cafeteria (there are serving lines on both port and starboard sides). For fast foods, there is also a grill and a pizzeria (both are located outside, adjacent to the swimming pool and ship's funnel).

The Coffee Corner, located on the upper, second level of the main lobby, is the place for coffees and pastry items – as well for people-watching throughout the day. Although there are windows, the view is not of the ocean, but of the stowed gangways and associated equipment.

ENTERTAINMENT. The Broadway Theater is the ship's main showlounge, located in the forward section of the ship. It has tiered seating set in a sloping floor, and sightlines are good from most seats. The room can also serve as a venue for large social functions. There is no separate bandstand, and the shows work with recorded music; hence there is little consistency in orchestration and sound balance.

High-quality entertainment has not, to date, been part of MSC's mindset. Hence, production shows and variety acts tend to be adequate at best. The Lirica Lounge (located one deck above the showlounge) is the place for social dancing, with live music provided by a band. Meanwhile, for the young and lively set, there is The Blue Club (the ship's throbbing, ear-melting discotheque).

SPA/FITNESS. The Lirica Health Center is located one deck above the navigation bridge at the forward end of the ship. The complex features a beauty salon, several treatment rooms offering massage and other body-pampering treatments, as well as a gymnasium with ocean views and an array of high-tech, muscle-toning and strengthening equipment. There's also a thermal suite, containing different kinds of steam rooms combined with aromatherapy infusions, at €12 per session, or six sessions for €60.

The health center is run as a concession by the Italian company Blue Ocean, with European hairstylists and Balinese massage and body treatment staff. Examples of treatment prices: full body massage, shiatsu massage, both at €90 for 50 minutes; cranial massage, €20 for 20 minutes; facial, €65; shampoo and finish, €32. Gratuities are not included, and are not charged to your account.

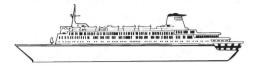

MSC Melody
★★★ +

Mid-Size Ship: . . . . .36,500 tons	Total Crew: .535	Cabins (with private balcony): 0
Lifestyle: . . . . .Standard	Passengers	Cabins (wheelchair accessible): . . . . . .Yes
Cruise Line: . . . . .MSC Italian Cruises	(lower beds/all berths): 1,098/1,600	Cabin Current: . . . . .110 volts
Former Names: .Star/ShipAtlantic, Atlantic	Passenger Space Ratio	Elevators: 4
Builder: . . . . .C.N.I.M. (France)	(lower beds/all berths): 33.2/22.8	Casino (gaming tables): . . . . .Yes
Original Cost: . . . .$100 million	Crew/Passenger Ratio	Slot Machines: . . . . .Yes
Entered Service: . . . .Apr 1982/June 1997	(lower beds/all berths): 2.0/2.9	Swimming Pools (outdoors): 1
Registry: . . . . .Panama	Navigation Officers: . . . . .Italian	Swimming Pools (indoors): 1
Length (ft/m): 671.9/204.8	Cabins (total): 549	Whirlpools: 3
Beam (ft/m): 89.7/27.4	Size Range (sq ft/m): 137.0–427.0/	Self-Service Launderette: . . . . .No
Draft (ft/m): 25.5/7.8	12.7–39.5	Dedicated Cinema/Seats: Yes/227
Propulsion/Propellers: . . . . .diesel	Cabins (outside view): 392	Library: . . . . .Yes (2 book racks)
(22,070 kW)/2	Cabins (interior/no view): 157	Classification Society: .American Bureau
Passenger Decks:. 9	Cabins (for one person): 0	of Shipping

BERLITZ'S OVERALL SCORE: 1,252 (OUT OF A POSSIBLE 2,000 POINTS)

OVERVIEW. The ship has a short, stubby, foreshortened bow and squat funnel, and an all-white hull and superstructure, although it cannot be considered at all handsome. There is a good amount of outdoor deck space, but noise levels can be high when the ship is full (particularly in summer).

The interior is quite spacious, with plenty of public rooms to play in, most of which have high ceilings. The decor is somber in places, and the lighting is quite subdued. There is a generous amount of stainless steel and teakwood trim. A large observation lounge (with good views from large picture windows) is rather wasted as an informal eating area.

There is a good indoor-outdoor pool area (this can be covered by a magrodome in bad weather). There is a fairly good children's program during peak periods, and several children's (and teens') counselors. Typically about 60% of passengers will be Italian. Expect lots of extra charges. The onboard currency is the euro (although during the winter the ship typtically sails in South American waters, when the onboard currency may change).

The almost constant loud announcements are intrusive. There is no wrap-around promenade deck outdoors, and cushioned pads are not provided for the deck lounge chairs. The ship has only four elevators – not nearly enough. Standing in line for embarkation, disembarkation, and buffet meals is inevitable aboard large ships.

SUITABLE FOR: Melody is best suited to young couples, singles, and families with children and teens who enjoy big ship surroundings, a big city life, with all its attendant noise, and passengers of different nationalities and languages.

BERLITZ'S RATINGS

	Possible	Achieved
Ship	500	349
Accommodation	200	148
Food	400	215
Service	400	241
Entertainment	100	58
Cruise	400	241

ACCOMMODATION. There are 12 categories and price grades. Six suites have plenty of space for families of four, and have a decent walk-in closet. The bathroom is large and has a full-size bathtub, oversize basin (large enough to bathe twins in), and an uncomfortable square toilet. Other outside-view and interior (no view) cabins are of a good size, and have ample closet and drawer space. Many cabins have upper berths – good for families, although with four persons there is very little space for anything else, such as luggage. The cabin soundproofing is extremely poor, and the room service menu is quite basic. The bathrooms are of a decent size, and quite practical in their facilities.

CUISINE/DINING. The Galaxy Restaurant, on a lower deck (Restaurant Deck), is large and quite attractive, but the tables are very close together. Also, the chairs do not have armrests, and the noise level is extremely high. There are two seatings, and the cuisine is Italian. The food quality generally is adequate for the price, but doesn't live up to menu descriptions. There is a limited wine list.

ENTERTAINMENT. The Club Universe is just forward of midships on Lounge Deck. Although the ceiling is high, it is a single-level room with banquette seating. The ship has a showband and several small musical units to provide live music for dancing or listening in various lounges and bars.

SPA/FITNESS. The SeaSport Health and Fitness Center has a gymnasium (with treadmills, exercycles, and muscle-pumping, body toning equipment), beauty salon, and massage room. The facility is not very large, so book early.

MSC Monterey
★★ +

Mid-Size Ship: . . . . .20,040 tons	Total Crew: 280	Cabins (with private balcony): 0
Lifestyle: . . . . .Standard	Passengers	Cabins (wheelchair accessible): 0
Cruise Line: . . . . .MSC Italian Cruises	(lower beds/all berths): 588/638	Cabin Current: . . . . .110 volts
Former Names: . . . . . .Free State Mariner	Passenger Space Ratio	Elevators: 2
Builder: . . . .Bethlehem Steel Corp. (USA)	(lower beds/all berths): 34.0/31.4	Casino (gaming tables): . . . . .Yes
Original Cost: . . . . .n/a	Crew/Passenger Ratio	Slot Machines: . . . . .Yes
Entered Service: . . . . .Dec 1952/Aug 1988	(lower beds/all berths): 2.0/2.2	Swimming Pools (outdoors): 1
Registry: . . . . .Panama	Navigation Officers: . . . . .Italian	Swimming Pools (indoors): 0
Length (ft/m): 563.6/171.8	Cabins (total): 294	Whirlpools: 2
Beam (ft/m): 80.3/24.5	Size Range (sq ft/m): 64.5–344.4/	Self-Service Launderette: . . . . .No
Draft (ft/m): 29.3/9.0	6.5–32.0	Dedicated Cinema/Seats: Yes/107
Propulsion/Propellers: . . . . .steam turbine	Cabins (outside view): 167	Library: . . . . .Yes
(14,400 kW)/1	Cabins (interior/no view): 127	Classification Society: .American Bureau
Passenger Decks: 4	Cabins (for one person): 0	of Shipping

BERLITZ'S OVERALL SCORE: 984 (OUT OF A POSSIBLE 2,000 POINTS)

OVERVIEW. *MSC Monterey*, originally built for the United States Maritime Commission as a C-4 cargo vessel (together with sister ship *Mariposa*), has a traditional, but now dated 1950s ocean liner profile. Since then the ship has had a long life and several owners. In 1956 it was sold to the Matson Navigation Company of San Francisco, and rebuilt as a passenger ship, for voyages to Australia and New Zealand.

With a strong hull, this is a very solid, stable ship at sea. It has an almost vertical bow and an overhanging aircraft-carrier-like stern that is not at all handsome when viewed from ashore, although it does provide a good amount of open deck space around the white-tiled swimming pool and Jacuzzis. There are partly enclosed port and starboard walking promenades, although they do not wrap around the vessel.

The ship was refurbished in a moderate art deco style, and a new sports deck was added several years ago. There is a reasonable amount of sheltered and open deck space, and some forward open observation deck space atop some suites that were added in the late 1980s when it was owned and operated by the now defunct Aloha Pacific Cruises.

Inside, there are a reasonable number of public rooms for the size of the ship. All have high ceilings, although there is little elegance. There is too much cold steel and not enough warmth in the interior decoration, although this was rectified to some extent some time ago when decor changes were made. Rising through three decks is a large, slim totem pole, a carry-over from the ship's brief period with Aloha Pacific Cruises.

This ship will cruise you in reasonable style and surroundings, with mainly European, and particularly Italian

BERLITZ'S RATINGS

	Possible	Achieved
Ship	500	228
Accommodation	200	95
Food	400	190
Service	400	224
Entertainment	100	48
Cruise	400	199

speaking passengers (about 60%). Port taxes are included. A 10% gratuity is added to all bar purchases. The onboard currency is the euro.

There is no observation lounge with forward-facing views over the ship's bows. There are far too many loud, repetitive and unnecessary announcements – often in up to five languages. There is a charge for the sauna, which is located inside the beauty salon and operated by the concession.

SUITABLE FOR: *MSC Monterey* is best suited to mature adult couples, single travelers, and families with tots, children and teens who enjoy traditional ship surroundings, and city life, with all its attendant noise, and passengers of different nationalities and languages (mostly European), and food that is the opposite of gourmet.

ACCOMMODATION. There is a wide choice of cabin sizes and configurations in 14 price grades, but note that there are many interior (no view) cabins (if this is your first cruise, I recommend that you consider booking a cabin with an outside view). The price you pay depends of the grade, size and location you choose.

Only the top three categories have full bathtubs, while all other cabins have shower enclosures. The suites are extremely spacious; other outside-view and interior (no view) cabins are very quite roomy and well-appointed, but most have tinny metal drawers (a carry-over from the ship's former years with the long defunct Matson Line).

The cabins located forward on Boat Deck have lifeboat-obstructed views, but other cabins on this deck are quite large; all have a window, plenty of closet and drawer space, together with a vanity desk, coffee table, sofa and chair. Bathrobes are provided for all passengers. Note that all drawers are steel, and can be noisy.

CUISINE/DINING. The two-level dining room (simply called The Restaurant, it has just under 300 seats) is set low down, and is charmingly decorated in soft earth tones, so the ambience is quite cozy, although it is noisy when full. There are two seatings.

The ship has continental (European) cuisine, with some decent pasta dishes and sauces. There is only the most basic selection of breads, cheeses and fruits, however. The service is friendly and attentive, in typical Italian style, but rather hurried.

For self-serve breakfasts and luncheons, there is a small, casual cafe, called Café de Paris, which has good views overlooking the aft pool deck and stern of the ship. The cabin Service breakfast menu is limited (continental breakfast items only).

ENTERTAINMENT. The Seven Pearls Lounge is the venue for most entertainment events and social functions. It is really more of a ballroom, and was not designed for big variety shows (there are almost no backstage facilities or dressing rooms, for example). Thus, entertainment typically consists of cabaret acts such as vocalists, magicians, musical specialty acts and others, geared mostly to the mainly Italian passengers. MSC Italian Cruises pays little attention to entertainment, most of which is low-key and low-budget. There is live music for dancing and listening in several locations. Occasionally, special theme cruises such as jazz or light classical music are featured.

SPA/FITNESS. The Palestra health/fitness center is located at the forward part of the ship on Aloha Deck (the lowest deck with passenger access). It is a small gymnasium, with only the most basic exercise equipment. A beauty salon and adjacent massage room are located on Aloha Deck close to the reception desk. Treatments available include massage, facial, manicure, pedicure, depilation (face, legs, bikini-line), and the usual hairdressing (shampoo, cut, blow dry, conditioning, coloring).

Volleyball, paddle tennis, and outdoor table tennis can be played on Sport Deck (aft of the navigation bridge).

WHO'S WHO IN ON-BOARD ENTERTAINMENT

Although production companies differ in their approach, the following gives some idea of the various people involved behind the scenes.

Executive Producer

Transfers the show's concept from design to reality. First, the brief from the cruise line's director of entertainment might be for a new production show (the average being two major shows per seven-day cruise). After deciding on an initial concept, they then call in the choreographer, vocal coach, and musical arranger.

Choreographer

Responsible for auditioning the dancers and for creating, selecting, and teaching the routines.

Musical Director

Coordinates all musical scores and arrangements; trains the singers in voice and microphone techniques, projection, accenting, phrasing, memory, and general presentation; and oversees session singers and musicians for the recording sessions.

Musical Arranger

After the music has been selected, the musical arrangements must be made. Just one song can cost more than $2,000 for a single arrangement for a 12-piece orchestra.

Costume Designer

Provides creative original designs for a minimum of seven costume changes in one show lasting 45 minutes. The costumes must also be practical, as they will be used repeatedly.

Costume Maker

Buys all materials, and must be able to produce all required costumes in time for a show.

Graphic Designer

Provides all the set designs, whether they are physical one- two- or three-dimensional sets for the stage, or photographic images created on slide film, video, laser disk, or other electronic media.

Lighting Designer

Creates the lighting patterns and effects for a production show. Sequences and action on stage must be carefully lit to the best advantage. The completed lighting plot is computerized.

Bands/Musicians

Before the big production shows and artists can be booked, bands and musicians must be hired, often for long contracts. Naturally, live musicians are favored for a ship's show band, as they are excellent music readers (necessary for all visiting cabaret artists and for big production shows). Big bands are often placed in some of the larger ships for special sailings, or for world cruises, on which ballroom dancing plays a large part. Most musicians work to contracts of about six months.

MSC Opera
★★★★

Large (Resort) Ship:	.58,600 tons	Passenger Decks:	.10	Cabins (with private balcony):	.200
Lifestyle:	Standard	Total Crew:	.701	Cabins (wheelchair accessible):	.4
Cruise Line:	MSC Italian Cruises	Passengers		Cabin Voltage:	.110 and 220
Former Names:	None	(lower beds/all berths):	.1,756/2,200	Elevators:	.9
Builder:	Chantiers de l'Atlantique	Passenger Space Ratio		Casino (gaming tables):	No
	(France)	(lower beds/all berths):	.33.3/26.6	Slot Machines:	No
Original Cost:	.$266 million	Crew/Passenger Ratio		Swimming Pools (outdoors):	.2
Entered Service:	Mar 2004	(lower beds/all berths):	.2.5/3.1	Swimming Pools (indoors):	.0
Registry:	Italy	Navigation Officers:	Italian	Whirlpools:	.2
Length (ft/m):	.830.7/253.25	Cabins (total):	.878	Self-Service Launderette:	No
Beam (ft/m):	.94.4/28.8	Size Range (sq ft/m):	n/a	Dedicated Cinema/Seats:	No
Draft (ft/m):	.22.4/6.85	Cabins (outside view):	.504	Library:	Yes
Propulsion/Propellers:	diesel	Cabins (interior/no view):	.276	Classification Society:	.Bureau Veritas
	(31,680kW)/2 pods	Cabins (for one person):	.0		

OVERALL SCORE: 1,452 (OUT OF A POSSIBLE 2,000 POINTS)

OVERVIEW. *MSC Opera* is the second of a pair of newbuilds for MSC Italian Cruises (the first being *MSC Lirica*), Italy's largest privately owned cruise line (formerly Star Lauro Cruises). The white funnel is quite sleek, with a swept-back design that closely resembles that of the Princess Cruises ships, and carries the MSC logo in gold lettering. The ship is similar in size and structure to *MSC Lirica,* there are many modifications (mostly in technical spaces), and improvements in the layout of public rooms; there are also more cabins with private balcony. All decks are named after operas.

From a technical viewpoint, the ship is fitted with an azimuthing pod propulsion system *(see page 151 for an explanation)*, instead of conventional rudders and propellers.

The interior layout and passenger flow is quite good with the exception of a couple of points of congestion, typically when the first seating exits the dining room and passengers on second seating are waiting to enter. The decor has many Italian influences, including clean lines, minimalism in furniture design, and a collection of colors, soft furnishings and fabrics that work well together, and without any hint of garishness. Real wood and marble have been used extensively in the interiors, and the high quality reflects the commitment that MSC Italian Cruises has in the vessel's future. The "fit and finish" of the interior decor, and most carpeting, is very good.

Facilities include the ship's main show lounge, a nightclub/discotheque, several lounges and bars, an internet center with 10 terminals, a virtual reality center, a children's club, a shopping gallery named Via Conditti (with shops that have an integrated bar and entertainment area so that shopping becomes a city-like environment where you can

BERLITZ'S RATINGS

	Possible	Achieved
Ship	500	408
Accommodation	200	156
Food	400	243
Service	400	304
Entertainment	100	55
Cruise	400	286

shop, drink, and be entertained all in one convenient area). Gamblers will find pleasure in the Monte Carlo Casino, with blackjack, poker and roulette games, together with an array of slot machines. There is also a card room, but the integral library is small and disappointing, and there are no hardback books. Possible drinking places include the Sotto Vento Pub (under the show lounge), or the La Cabala lounge.

The ship is designed to accommodate families with children, who have their own play center, youth counselors, and programming.

MSC Opera features Mediterranean cruises during the summer and Caribbean cruises during the winter. The onboard currency is the euro (summer) and US$ (winter). Note that gratuities are extra, and bar service incurs a charge of 10 percent.

Anyone who is wheelchair-bound should note that there is no access to the uppermost forward and aft decks, although access throughout most of the interior of the ship is very good (there are also several wheelchair-accessible public restrooms). The passenger hallways are a little narrow on some decks for you to pass when housekeeping carts are in place, however.

Minor niggles include the ship's photographers who always seem to be in your face; constant music in every lounge; and the fact that standing in line for embarkation, disembarkation, shore tenders and for self-serve buffet meals is an inevitable aspect of cruising aboard all large ships. Smokers are everywhere, and are virtually impossible to avoid (in typical European fashion, ashtrays are simply moved – if used at all – to wherever smokers happen to be sitting). Sadly, there is no forward observation lounge.

SUITABLE FOR: *MSC Opera* is best suited to young adult couples, singles, and families with tots, children and teens who enjoy big ship surroundings, a big city life, with all its attendant noise (some call it ambience), and passengers of different nationalities and languages (mostly European).

ACCOMMODATION. There are 11 price levels, depending on grade and location: one suite category, five outside-view cabin grades, and five interior (no view) cabin grades. Included are 172 "suites" with private balcony (note that the partitions between each balcony are of the partial and not the full wall type), outside-view cabins and interior (no view) cabins. The cabin numbering system has even numbered cabins on the starboard side, and odd numbered cabins on the port side – contrary to nautical convention.

All cabins have a mini-bar and personal safe, satellite TV, several audio channels, and 24-hour room service (note that while tea and coffee are complimentary, snacks for room service carry a delivery charge of €2.50 each time).

Accommodation designated as Suites (they are not true suites, as there is no separate bedroom and lounge) also has more room, a larger lounge area, walk-in closet, wall-to-wall vanity counter, a bathroom with combination tub and shower, toilet, and semi-private balcony with light (the partitions are of the partial, not full, type). 100 percent cotton bathrobes are provided. However, except for the very highest category, the suite bathrooms are very plain, with white plastic washbasins and white walls, and mirrors that steam up.

Note that some cabins on Othello Deck and Rigoletto Deck have views obstructed by lifeboats, while those on Turandot Deck aft (10105–10159) are subject to late-night noise from the Byblos discotheque on the deck above. Also, cabins on the uppermost accommodation deck are subject to deck chairs and tables being dragged across the deck when it is set up or cleaned early in the morning.

CUISINE/DINING. There is one principal dining room (La Bitta Restaurant), with large ocean view picture windows in the aft third of the ship. There are two seatings for meals, in keeping with other ships in the MSC fleet, and tables are for two, four, six or eight.

L'Approdo Restaurant is assigned to all passengers occupying accommodation designated as suites, although other passengers can dine in it too, on a reservations-only basis. As you might expect, the food and service are superior to that in the main dining room.

Casual, self-serve buffets (for breakfast and lunch) can be taken in Le Vele Cafeteria (there are poorly laid out serving lines on both port and starboard sides), although the food is really quite basic; or at the La Pergola fast food eatery, where the featured cuisine is, you guessed it, Italian, with grill and pizzeria (both located outside, adjacent to the swimming pool and ship's funnel). Meanwhile, coffee/tea and pastries can be taken in the Aroma Café set around the upper level of the two-deck-high atrium lobby, but annoying music videos are constantly played on the television sets in the forward sections.

ENTERTAINMENT. The 713-seat Theatre dell Opera is the ship's main show lounge, located in the forward section of the ship. It has tiered seating set in a sloping floor, and sightlines are good from most seats. The room can also serve as a venue for large social functions. There is no separate bandstand, and the shows work with recorded music; hence there is little consistency in orchestration and sound balance.

High-quality entertainment has not, to date, been a priority for MSC Italian Cruises. Hence, production shows and variety acts tend to be amateurish at best (when compared to some other major cruise lines).

The Opera Lounge (it is located one deck above the show lounge) is the lounge for social dancing, with live music provided by a band. Meanwhile, for the young and lively set, there is the Byblos Discotheque (the ship's throbbing, ear-melting discotheque).

SPA/FITNESS. The Opera Health Center is located one deck above the navigation bridge at the forward end of the ship. The complex features a beauty salon, several treatment rooms offering massage and other body-pampering treatments, as well as a gymnasium with ocean views and an array of high-tech, muscle-toning and strengthening equipment. There's also a thermal suite, containing different kinds of steam rooms combined with aromatherapy infusions, at €12 per session, or six sessions for €60.

The health center is run as a concession by the Italian company Blue Ocean, with European hairstylists and Balinese massage and body treatment staff. Examples of treatment prices: Balinese massage, €93 (45 minutes); shiatsu massage, €90 (45 minutes); hot stone therapy, €100 (45 minutes); facial, €65; pedicure, €40. Gratuities are not included, and are not charged to your account.

MSC Rhapsody
★★★

Mid-Size Ship: . . . . .17,495 tons	Passenger Decks: 8	Cabins (for one person): 0
Lifestyle: . . . . .Standard	Total Crew: 350	Cabins (with private balcony): 0
Cruise Line: . . . . .MSC Italian Cruises	Passengers	Cabins (wheelchair accessible): 0
Former Names: . . . . . . .Cunard Princess,	(lower beds/all berths): 788/959	Cabin Current: . . . . .220 volts
Cunard Conquest	Passenger Space Ratio	Elevators: 2
Builder: . . .Burmeister & Wein (Denmark)	(lower beds/all berths): 22.2/18.1	Casino (gaming tables): . . . . .Yes
Original Cost: . . . .£12 million	Crew/Passenger Ratio	Slot Machines: . . . . .Yes
Entered Service: . . . . .Mar 1977/May1995	(lower beds/all berths): 2.2/2.7	Swimming Pools (outdoors): 1
Registry: . . . . .Panama	Navigation Officers: . . . . .Italian	Swimming Pools (indoors): 0
Length (ft/m): 541.0/164.9	Cabins (total): 394	Whirlpools: 2
Beam (ft/m): 76.1/23.2	Size Range (sq ft/m): 87.1–264.8/	Self-Service Launderette: . . . . .No
Draft (ft/m): 19.0/5.8	8.1–24.6	Dedicated Cinema/Seats: Yes/135
Propulsion/Propellers: . . . . .diesel	Cabins (outside view): 267	Library: . . . . .Yes
(15,670 kW)/2	Cabins (interior/no view): 127	Classification Society: . . .Lloyd's Register

---

BERLITZ'S OVERALL SCORE: 1,177 (OUT OF A POSSIBLE 2,000 POINTS)

OVERVIEW. *MSC Rhapsody* is almost identical to its sister, *Ocean Countess* (originally *Cunard Countess*), with the same contemporary profile and good looks. The ship was originally completed for Cunard Line as an informal Caribbean cruise vessel named *Cunard Princess*, although the original name (which was not used) was to have been *Cunard Conquest*. However, the ship was actually ordered for a US airline, Overseas National Airways, which went bankrupt, after which Cunard took over the contract. The ship was acquired in 1995 by StarLauro Cruises, which in turn was renamed Mediterranean Shipping Cruises (and, subsequently, MSC Italian Cruises), as a replacement for its *Achille Lauro*, which caught fire and sank off the coast of East Africa in 1995.

There is a good amount of open deck space for sun-worshippers. There is a good selection of public rooms with attractive decor, in light, bright colors, including an observation lounge above the bridge, overlooking the bow.

The ship has an excellent indoor-outdoor entertainment nightclub and bar, which incorporates the occasional use of an aft open deck area. The show lounge, a one-deck high room with raised seating on its port and starboard sides, has eight pillars that obstruct sightlines (the ceiling height is also very low).

This ship will provide a very comfortable first cruise experience, featuring destination-intensive itineraries, in a pleasing, casual, but very high-density environment.

This ship is now marketed mostly to Europeans and to Italian passengers in particular (who form about 60% of the passengers. While it still looks sharp following an extensive refit and refurbishment in 1997, the standard of

BERLITZ'S RATINGS		
	Possible	Achieved
Ship	500	315
Accommodation	200	112
Food	400	216
Service	400	238
Entertainment	100	62
Cruise	400	234

food and service offered are disappointingly commonplace. There is no outdoor wrap-around promenade deck outdoors. The cabins really are very small. The onboard currency is the euro.

SUITABLE FOR: *MSC Rhapsody* is best suited to young couples, singles, and families with tots, children and teens on their first cruise. The ship is for those who would not enjoy large or palatial ships, but do enjoy being among fellow passengers of different nationalities and languages.

ACCOMMODATION. There are 11 grades, the price depending on grade, size and location.
Deluxe/Standard Outside View/Interior No View Cabins. The cabins are mostly of a standard (very compact) size, and come in light colors and plain, but pleasant decor that is adequate for short cruises. They are best described as space-efficient units with metal fixtures and poor insulation – you can talk to your neighbors without having to use the telephone. All standard cabins have two lower beds (some are in a twin shape, while others are in an L-shape; they are fixed and cannot be moved together). Many cabins also have a third upper berth. The cabins on the lowest deck suffer from vibration and the odor of diesel fuel, and have portholes (as do cabins on the deck above), while all other cabins on the upper decks have windows. The cabin bathrooms are small modular units, good for one, but quite impossible for two to be together in (they contain a shower enclosure, toilet and washbasin, but little storage space for personal toiletries).
Suites. The largest accommodation is found in the "suites"

(in two price grades). These all have a double bed, a good amount of closet space, lounge area with sofa or chairs, television, and a larger bathroom with bathtub and shower, toilet and washbasin. If you are seeking more space, these are the rooms to go for.

CUISINE/DINING. The Meridian Restaurant is located in the middle of the ship. It has sea views from large picture windows, but is fairly noisy because of its open design. There are two seatings. The standard "banquet" food is reasonable and tailored mainly to Italian passengers, with typical Italian dishes including plenty of pasta (but sadly no tableside cooking). The service is bubbly, cheerful, attentive, and comes with a smile, but it lacks finesse. There is a limited selection of breads and fruits. The cabin service menu is very limited.

Additionally, a casual self-serve open-air area is available for breakfast, lunches and (sometimes, depending on the itinerary) buffet dinners.

ENTERTAINMENT. The Pisto da Ballo Lounge is the ship's main lounge, and is the principal venue for entertainment events and social functions. It is a single-level, rectangular-shaped room with a black granite dance floor, designed for cabaret acts, and not production-style shows. Although the sides of the room are raised, several pillars obstruct the sightlines.

The ship has a main showband, together with small musical units and solo pianists to provide live music for dancing and listening, in the various lounges and bars.

SPA/FITNESS. There is a small gymnasium located on one side of the funnel housing, on the pool deck, while a jogging track is provided on the deck above (difficult to use because it is narrow and passengers place their deck chairs there for sunbathing); massage facilities and changing area are provided on the opposite side to the gymnasium.

A beauty salon is located indoors on another deck, adjacent to the reception desk and shops. Body pampering treatments include various massages, facials, body wraps, manicures, pedicures, and hairdressing services.

LATITUDE AND LONGITUDE

Latitude signifies the distance north or south of the equator, while **longitude** signifies distance east or west of the 0 degree at Greenwich Observatory in London ("where time begins"). Both are recorded in degrees, minutes, and seconds. At the equator, one minute of longitude is equal to one nautical mile, but as the meridians converge after leaving the equator and meeting at the poles, the size of a degree becomes smaller. It was in 1714 that an Act of Parliament established a Board of Commissioners for the Discovery of Longitude at Sea. A prize of £20,000, then a huge sum, was set. The English clockmaker John Harrison (1693–1776) won it for his highly accurate chronometer. Indeed, none other than Captain Cook used a Harrison-designed chronometer on one of his voyages to the Pacific in 1775.

MSC Sinfonia
★★★★

Large (Resort) Ship:	58,600 tons	Total Crew:	710	Cabins (with private balcony):	132
Lifestyle:	Standard	Passengers		Cabins (wheelchair accessible):	2
Cruise Line:	MSC Italian Cruises	(lower beds/all berths):	1,566/2,223	Cabin Current:	110 and 220 volts
Former Names:	European Stars	Passenger Space Ratio		Elevators:	9
Builder: Chantiers de l'Atlantique (France)		(lower beds/all berths):	37.4/27.6	Casino (gaming tables):	Yes
Original Cost:	$245 million	Crew/Passenger Ratio		Slot Machines:	Yes
Entered Service:	Apr 2002/Mar 2005	(lower beds/all berths):	2.2/3.1	Swimming Pools (outdoors):	1
Registry:	Italy	Navigation Officers:	European	Swimming Pools (indoors):	0
Length (ft/m):	823.4/251.0	Cabins (total):	783	Whirlpools:	1 (thalassotherapy)
Beam (ft/m):	94.4/28.8	Size Range (sq ft/m):	139.9–236.8/	Self-Service Launderette:	No
Draft (ft/m):	22.4/6.85		13.0–22.0	Dedicated Cinema/Seats:	No
Propulsion/Propellers:	diesel	Cabins (outside view):	511	Library:	Yes
	(31,680 kW)/2 pods	Cabins (interior/no view):	272	Classification Society:	Bureau Veritas
Passenger Decks:	10	Cabins (for one person):	0		

BERLITZ'S OVERALL SCORE: 1,436 (OUT OF A POSSIBLE 2,000 POINTS)

OVERVIEW.. *MSC Sinfonia* was originally built and operated by the now-defunct Festival Cruises. Like sister ship *MSC Armonia*, it was built on the platform of the *Mistral*, with an 114.8-ft long (35-meter) mid-section added to increase the ship's length and provide more space per passenger than *Mistral*. *MSC Sinfonia* has an azimuthing pod propulsion system, instead of conventional rudders and propellers, in the latest configuration of high-tech propulsion systems *(for explanation, see page 151)*. The lido deck surrounding the outdoor swimming pool also has whirlpool tubs and a large bandstand is set in raised canvas-covered pods.

The interior layout and passenger flow is good, as are the "you are here" deck signs. The decor is decidedly "European Moderne" and includes clean lines, minimalism in furniture designs (including some chairs that look interesting but are totally impractical unless you are prepared to face reconstructive surgery).

Facilities include Amadeus, the ship's show lounge, and La Gondola Theater, for plays and other theatrical presentations. There's a cigar smoking room (Ambassador), with the hallmarks of a gentleman's club of former times, as well as a piano bar. The Goethe Library/Card Room has real writing desks (something many ships seem to omit), and this ship has an internet cafe, as well an English pub called the White Lion. Those who enjoy gambling may find excitement in the Lido Casino, with blackjack, poker and roulette games, plus the usual one-armed slot machines. The onboard currency is the euro.

Standing in line for embarkation, disembarkation, shore tenders and for self-serve buffet meals is an inevitable aspect of cruising aboard all large ships. The

BERLITZ'S RATINGS

	Possible	Achieved
Ship	500	396
Accommodation	200	155
Food	400	254
Service	400	295
Entertainment	100	54
Cruise	400	282

heavy smokers are virtually impossible to avoid (in typical European fashion, ashtrays are simply moved – if used at all – to wherever smokers happen to be sitting). All announcements are in several languages, although these are thankfully fewer than in the past. The entertainment is of a low standard, with intrusive animateurs that mean well, but who perform as one would expect to find in a holiday camp – with enthusiasm but little else.

The cruise line keeps prices low by providing air transportation that may be at inconvenient times, or transportation involving long journeys by bus. In other words, be prepared for a little discomfort in getting to and from your cruise in exchange for low cruise rates. The constant push for onboard revenue is also very irritating – you have to pay extra even for a visit to the ship's navigation bridge. The staff is much more focused on Italian passengers than those who speak any other European language (including English).

If you are considering doing two back-to-back 7-day cruises, note that some ports may be duplicated, and all menus and entertainment are based on a 7-day cycle, so there is much product repetition (including the cruise director's jokes). Regular passenger complaints include poor ports of call information and rudeness of shore excursion staff.

SUITABLE FOR: *MSC Sinfonia* is best suited to young adult couples, singles, and families with tots, children and teens who enjoy big ship surroundings, a big city life, with all its attendant noise (some call it ambience), and passengers of different nationalities and languages (mostly European).

ACCOMMODATION. There are 11 price categories, the price

depending on the grade, size and location. These include 132 suites with private balcony (note that the partitions are only of the partial and not the full type), outside-view cabins and interior (no view) cabins.

Suite grade accommodation has more room, a larger lounge area, walk-in closet, wall-to-wall vanity counter, a bathroom with combination tub and shower, toilet, and private balcony (with light). But they are not true suites, as there is no separate bedroom and lounge – in other words, these are not "suites" of rooms. Bathrobes are provided.

In general, the "suites" are well laid out and nicely furnished. However, except for the very highest category, the suite bathrooms are very plain, with white plastic washbasins and white walls, and mirrors that steam up. According to the rules of feng shui, however, it is bad luck to place any mirror in such a position that it can be seen by anyone lying in bed.

Even the smallest interior cabins are sensibly spacious, with plenty of space between lower beds. All grades of accommodation have sheets and blankets as bed linen (no duvets), and are equipped with a TV set, hairdryer, minibar/refrigerator, personal safe (cleverly positioned behind a vanity desk mirror), bathroom with shower and toilet, and 100% cotton towels (except for hand towels, which, when I last sailed, were 86% cotton and 14% polyester). However, the standard grade cabins are quite small when compared to many other new ships, at a modest 140 sq. ft (13 sq. meters).

CUISINE/DINING. The four dining spots are all non-smoking areas. The principal dining room, the 610-seat Marco Polo Restaurant, has two seatings. The cuisine is reasonably sound, and, with varied menus and good presentation, should prove a highlight for most passengers. The wine list has a wide variety of wines at fairly reasonable prices, although almost all are very young.

La Pergola, the most formal restaurant, has stylish Italian cuisine. This is the restaurant assigned to all passengers occupying accommodation designated as suites, and other passengers can dine in it too, although reservations must be made. Chez Claude, on the starboard side aft, and adjacent to the ship's funnel, is a grill area for fast food. La Brasserie is the ship's casual, self-serve buffet eatery, open 24 hours a day. The selections are very standardized, however, and could be better.

Meanwhile, coffee/tea and pastries can be taken in the café, set around the upper level of the two-deck high atrium lobby. It's a good location for people-watching, but annoying music videos are constantly played on the televisions in the forward sections.

ENTERTAINMENT. The Gondola Theater is two decks high, and is the main show lounge, for production shows, cabaret acts, plays and other theatrical presentations. It is a well designed room (except for the fact that no space was allocated for a live showband), with good sightlines from most seats, and four entrances that allow easy access.

Entertainment is a weak area for MSC Italian Cruises, although this could improve as more ships are brought into service and more money is assigned to this important aspect of the company's cruise product. Other shows consist of unknown cabaret acts (typically singers, magicians, mime artistes, comedy jugglers, and others) doing the cruise ship circuit. The principal difficulty aboard this ship is that the ship operates year-round in five or six languages, making any entertainment (other than visual acts such as mime, magic or juggling) virtually impossible.

The ship carries a number of bands and small musical units that provide live music for dancing or listening in various lounges and bars throughout the ship.

SPA/FITNESS. The Atlantica Spa, one deck above the navigation bridge at the forward end of the ship, has numerous body-pampering treatments, as well as a gymnasium with ocean views and an array of high-tech, muscle-toning and strengthening equipment. There's also a thermal suite (this contains different kinds of steam rooms combined with aromatherapy infusions such as camomile and eucalyptus) and a rasul chamber (a combination of two or three different kinds of special application mud, and gentle steam shower – highly recommended for couples).

The spa is run as a concession by the Italian company Blue Ocean, with European hairstylists and Balinese massage and body treatment staff. Examples of treatment prices: Balinese massage, €93 (45 minutes); shiatsu massage, €90 (45 minutes); hot stone therapy, €100 (45 minutes); facial, €65; pedicure, €40. Gratuities are not included, and are not charged to your account.

For the sports-minded, there is a simulated climbing wall outdoors, while other sports and fitness facilities include volleyball/basketball court, and mini-golf.

Nantucket Clipper
★★ +

Boutique Ship: ....1,471 tons	Total Crew: 32	Cabins (with private balcony): 0	
Lifestyle: ....Standard	Passengers	Cabins (wheelchair accessible): 0	
Cruise Line: ....Clipper Cruise Line	(lower beds/all berths): 102/102	Cabin Current: ....110 volts	
Former Names: ....none	Passenger Space Ratio	Elevators: 0	
Builder: ....Jeffboat (USA)	(lower beds/all berths): 14.4/14.4	Casino (gaming tables): ....No	
Original Cost: ....$9 million	Crew/Passenger Ratio	Slot Machines: ....No	
Entered Service: ....Dec 1984	(lower beds/all berths): 3.1/3.1	Swimming Pools (outdoors): 0	
Registry: ....USA	Navigation Officers: ....American	Swimming Pools (indoors): 0	
Length (ft/m): 207.0/63.00	Cabins (total): 51	Whirlpools: 0	
Beam (ft/m): 37.0/11.20	Size Range (sq ft/m): 120.5–137.7/	Self-Service Launderette: ....No	
Draft (ft/m): 8.0/2.40	11.2–12.8	Dedicated Cinema/Seats: ....No	
Propulsion/Propellers: ....diesel	Cabins (outside view): 51	Library: ....Yes	
(700 kW)/2	Cabins (interior/no view): 0	Classification Society: ..American Bureau	
Passenger Decks: 4	Cabins (for one person): 0	of Shipping	

OVERALL SCORE: 982 (OUT OF A POSSIBLE 2,000 POINTS)

OVERVIEW. This small, shallow draft, American-registered ship was built for coastal and inland cruises and is very maneuverable. It has been quite well maintained, although it is now showing signs of aging, and some serious attention is needed. There is a wrap-around teakwood walking deck outdoors. The extremely high-density ship has only two public rooms – the dining room, and an observation lounge. Passengers can visit the bridge at any time. This ship is not recommended for night owls. Although passengers are typically over 60, there is no elevator.

The service is provided by young, friendly all-American college-age types. This is most definitely an "Americana" experience for those seeking particularly to learn more about the coastal ports around the USA. The ship has a casual, unstructured lifestyle, rather like a small (but certainly not luxurious) country club afloat. This should not be compared with big-ship ocean cruising. Thankfully, there are no mindless activities or corny parlor games.

Specialist lecturers are part of every cruise. These highlight the learning experience that is an essential part of cruising with Clipper Cruise Lines. As the ship is often in coastal destinations, a few bicycles would be a welcome addition for many passengers. There is a no-smoking policy for all interior areas. The onboard currency is the US dollar.

This really is a high-density ship, with only two public rooms: a dining room and a lounge. The engine noise level is high when the ship is underway. The per diem price is steep for what you get, and the air fare is extra.

SUITABLE FOR: *Nantucket Clipper* is best suited to couples and single travelers who enjoy nature and wildlife up close

BERLITZ'S RATINGS

	Possible	Achieved
Ship	500	206
Accommodation	200	78
Food	400	220
Service	400	233
Entertainment	N/A	N/A
Cruise	500	245

and personal, and who would not dream of cruising in the mainstream sense, aboard ships with large numbers of people. This is for outdoors types who don't need entertainment or mindless parlor games, but do want an all-American cruise experience.

ACCOMMODATION. There are four grades of all-outside cabins. All are extremely small and equipped in a very basic manner (think mobile home rather than cruise ships or hotels). They are fairly tastefully furnished, with wood-accented trim and good sound insulation. The The windows are fixed and cannot be opened. Honeymooners and lovers should note that beds are of the twin variety, and are bolted to the deck and wall. Bathrooms are cramped and the shower head is fixed, but, thoughtfully, a night-light is provided. There's little space for personal toiletries. No cabins have personal balconies.

CUISINE/DINING. The dining room is warm and inviting, and has large picture windows. There is one seating, and you can sit with whomever you wish. There are no tables for two. The ship has simple and plain American cuisine that is quite tasty, although the menu choice is limited and the portions are small. The chefs are tained by the Culinary Institute of America, and all ingredients are fresh. The chocolate chip cookies are popular and are served at various times, typically in the lounge.

ENTERTAINMENT. The main entertainment is dinner and after-dinner conversation with fellow passengers.

SPA/FITNESS. No facilities aboard this very small vessel.

Navigator of the Seas
★★★★

Large (Resort) Ship: ....137,276 tons	Passenger Decks: 14	Cabins (for one person): 0
Lifestyle: ....Standard	Total Crew: 1,185	Cabins (with private balcony): 765
Cruise Line: ....Royal Caribbean	Passengers	Cabins (wheelchair accessible): 26
International	(lower beds/all berths): 3,114/3,840	Cabin Current: ....110 volts
Former Names: ....none	Passenger Space Ratio	Elevators: ....14 (6 glass-enclosed)
Builder: ...Kvaerner Masa-Yards (Finland)	(lower beds/all berths): 44.0/35.7	Casino (gaming tables): ....Yes
Original Cost: ....$500 million	Crew/Passenger Ratio	Slot Machines: ....Yes
Entered Service: ....Spring 2003	(lower beds/all berths): 2.6/3.2	Swimming Pools (outdoors): 3
Registry: ....The Bahamas	Navigation Officers: ......Scandinavian	Swimming Pools (indoors): 0
Length (ft/m): 1,020.6/311.1	Cabins (total): 1,557	Whirlpools: 6
Beam (ft/m): 155.5/47.4	Size Range (sq ft/m): 151.0–1,358.0/	Self-Service Launderette: ....No
Draft (ft/m): 28.8/8.8	14.0–126.1	Dedicated Cinema/Seats: ....No
Propulsion/Propellers: .....diesel-electric	Cabins (outside view): 939	Library: ....Yes
(75,600 kW)/3 azimuthing pods	Cabins (interior/no view): 618	Classification Society: Det Norske Veritas

OVERALL SCORE: 1,537 (OUT OF A POSSIBLE 2,000 POINTS)

OVERVIEW. *Navigator of the Seas* is a stunning, large, floating leisure resort (sister to *Adventure of the Seas, Explorer of the Seas*, and *Voyager of the Seas*), although the visual effect of glass on the balcony cabins is more appealing. The *Voyager*-class ships are, at present, the largest cruise vessels in the world in terms of tonnage (except for *Queen Mary 2*).

The ship's propulsion is derived from three pod units, powered by electric motors (two azimuthing, and one fixed at the centerline) instead of conventional rudders and propellers, in the latest configuration of high-tech propulsion systems. With its large proportions, the ship provides more facilities and options, and caters to more passengers than any other Royal Caribbean International ship has in the past, and yet the ship manages to have a healthy passenger space ratio (the amount of space per passenger).

Being a "non-Panamax" ship, it is simply too large to go through the Panama Canal, thus limiting its itineraries almost exclusively to the Caribbean (where few islands can accept it), or for use as a floating island resort. Spend the first few hours exploring all the many facilities and public spaces aboard this vessel and it will be time well spent.

Although *Navigator of the Seas* really is a large ship, the cabin hallways are warm and attractive, with artwork cabinets and wavy lines to lead you along and break up the monotony. In fact, there are plenty of colorful, even whimsical, decorative touches to help you avoid what would otherwise be a very clinical environment.

Embarkation and disembarkation take place through two stations/access points, designed to minimize the inevitable lines at the start and end of the cruise (that's more than

BERLITZ'S RATINGS

	Possible	Achieved
Ship	500	431
Accommodation	200	160
Food	400	252
Service	400	294
Entertainment	100	83
Cruise	400	317

1,500 people for each access point). Once inside the ship, you'll need good walking shoes, particularly when you need to go from one end to the other – it really is quite a long way.

The four-decks-high Royal Promenade, which is 394 ft (120 meters) long, is the main interior focal point of the ship (it's also a good place to hang out, or to meet someone). The length of two football fields (American football, that is), it has two internal lobbies (atria) that rise to as many as 11 decks high. Restaurants, shops and entertainment locations front this winding street and interior "with-view" cabins look into it from above. It is designed loosely in the image of London's fashionable Burlington Arcade – although there's not a real brick in sight. It is, however, an imaginative piece of design work, and most passengers (particularly those who like shopping malls) enjoy it immensely.

The super-atrium houses a "traditional" English-style pub (Two Poets Pub), with draft beer and plenty of "street-front" seating (it's funny, but North American passengers sit down, while British passengers prefer to stand at the bar). There is also a Champagne Bar, a Sidewalk Cafe (for continental breakfast, all-day pizzas, specialty coffees and desserts), Sprinkles (for round-the-clock ice cream and yoghurt). There are also several shops – for jewelry, gifts, liquor and logo souvenirs. Altogether, the Royal promenade is a nice place to see and be seen, and there is action throughout the day and night. The Guest Reception and Shore Excursion counters are located at the aft end of the promenade, as is an ATM, while opposite is the cozy Champagne Bar. Watch for the parades and street entertainers.

Arched across the promenade is a Captain's Balcony.

Meanwhile, in the center of the promenade is a stairway that connects you to the deck below, where you'll find the Schooner Bar (a piano lounge that is a feature found aboard all RCI ships) and the colorful Casino Royale. This is naturally large and full of flashing lights and noises. Gaming includes blackjack, Caribbean stud poker, roulette, and craps, as well as 300 slot machines.

There is also a regulation-size ice-skating rink (Studio B), featuring real, not fake, ice, with "bleacher" seating for up to 900, and the latest in broadcast facilities. Ice Follies shows are also presented here. A number of slim pillars obstruct clear-view arena stage sight lines, however. If ice-skating in the Caribbean doesn't appeal, perhaps you'd like the stunning two-deck library (it's the first aboard any ship, and it is open 24 hours a day). A grand amount of money was spent on permanent artwork.

Drinking places include a neat Aquarium Bar, which comes complete with 50 tons of glass and water in four large aquariums (whose combined value is over $1 million). Other drinking places include the aforementioned Champagne Bar, the Crown & Anchor Pub, and a Connoisseur Club – for cigars and cognacs.

Lovers of jazz might appreciate the Cosmopolitan Club, an intimate room for cool music atop the ship within the Viking Crown Lounge, or the Schooner Bar piano lounge. Golfers might enjoy the 19th Hole, a golf bar, as they play the Navigator Links.

There is a large TV studio, adjacent to rooms that can be used for trade show exhibit space, with conference center that seats 400 and a multi-media screening room that seats 60. Lovers could tie the knot in a wedding chapel in the sky, the Skylight Chapel (it's located on the upper level of the Viking Crown Lounge, and even has wheelchair access via an electric stairway lift). Meanwhile, outdoors, the pool and open deck areas provide a resort-like environment.

Families with children are also well catered to, as facilities for children and teenagers are extensive (they are much larger than aboard sister ships *Adventure of the Seas, Explorer of the Seas and Voyager of the Seas*). An area called Adventure Ocean is split into age-related areas: "Aquanauts" is for 3–5 year-olds; "Explorers" is for 6–8 year-olds; "Voyagers" is for 9–12 year-olds. The Living Room and Fuel are dedicated areas for teenagers, that include a daytime club (with several computers), soda bar, and disco; there's also an array of the latest video games. Paint and Clay is an arts and crafts center for younger children. Adjacent to these indoor areas is Adventure Beach, an area for all the family; this includes swimming pools, a water slide and game areas outdoors.

In terms of sheer size, this ship dwarfs all others in the cruise industry, but in terms of personal service, the reverse is the case, unless you happen to reside in one of the top suites. Royal Caribbean International does, however, try hard to provide a good standard of programmed service from its hotel staff. This is impersonal city life at sea, millennium-style, and a superb, well-designed alternative to a land-based resort, which is what the company wanted to build. Welcome to the escapist world of highly programmed

resort living aboard ship. Remember to take plenty of extra funds – you'll need them to pay for all the additional-cost items. The onboard currency is the US dollar.

The ship is large, so remember that if you meet someone somewhere, and want to meet them again you'll need to make an appointment – for this really is a large, Las Vegas-style floating resort-city for the lively of heart and fleet of foot. The best advice I can give you is to arrange to meet somewhere along the Royal Promenade.

SUITABLE FOR: *Navigator of the Seas* is best suited to young-minded adults and couples of all ages, families with toddlers, tots, children, and teenagers who like to mingle in a large ship setting with plenty of life and entertainment for everyone, with food that focuses on quantity rather than quality (unless you are prepared to pay extra for dining in the "alternative" restaurant), all delivered with friendly service that lacks polish.

ACCOMMODATION. There is an extensive range of 22 cabin categories, in four major groupings: Premium ocean-view suites and cabins, Promenade-view (interior-view) cabins, Ocean-view cabins, and Interior (no view) cabins. Note that many cabins are of a similar size (good for incentives and large groups), and 300 have interconnecting doors (good for families). Suites and cabins with private balcony have Bolidt floors (a substance that looks like rubberized sand) instead of wood. If you have a cabin with an inter-connecting door to another cabin, you should be aware that noise can filter through from the adjoining room. Also, the bathroom toilets are quite noisy. The price you pay will depend on the grade, size and location you choose.

A total of 138 interior (no view) cabins have bay windows that look into a horizontal atrium – first used to good effect aboard the Baltic passenger ferries *Silja Serenade* (1990) and *Silja Symphony* (1991) with interior cabins that look into a central shopping plaza. These cabins measure 157 sq. ft (15 sq. meters). Regardless of which cabin grade you choose, all except for the Royal Suite and Owner's Suite have twin beds that convert to a queen-sized unit, a TV set, radio and telephone, personal safe, vanity unit, mini-bar (called an Automatic Refreshment Center) hairdryer and private bathroom.

The largest accommodation includes luxuriously appointed penthouse suites (whose occupants, sadly, must share the rest of the ship with everyone else, except for their own exclusive, and private, concierge club). The grandest is the Royal Suite, which is positioned on the port side of the ship, and measures 1,146 sq. ft/106.5 sq. meters). It has a king-sized bed in a separate, large bedroom, a living room with an additional queen-sized sofa bed, baby grand piano (no pianist is included, however), refrigerator/wet bar, dining table, entertainment center, and large bathroom.

The slightly smaller, but still highly desirable, Owner's Suites (there are 10 of these, all located in the center of the ship, on both port and starboard sides, each measuring 468 sq. ft/43 sq. meters) and four Royal Family suites (each 574 sq. ft/53 sq. meters), all featuring similar items. However, the four Royal Family suites, which have two bedrooms (including one with third/fourth upper Pullman berths) are at the stern of the ship and have magnificent views over the ship's wake (and seagulls).

All cabins have a private bathroom with shower enclosure (towels are 100% cotton), as well as interactive, closed circuit and satellite television, and pay-per-view movies. Cabins with "private balconies" are not so private, as the partitions are only partial, not full. The balcony decking is made of Bolidt and not wood, while the balcony rail is of wood.

CUISINE/DINING. The main dining room, with a capacity of almost 2,000, is large and noisy. It is set on three levels, with a dramatic staircase connecting all three levels. All three have exactly the same menus and food. There are also two small private wings for private groups, each seating about 58 persons. The dining room is totally non-smoking, there are two seatings, and tables are for four, six, eight 10 or 12. The china and cutlery are good-quality.

Alternative (Extra Cost) Dining

Alternative dining options for casual and informal meals at all hours (according to company releases) include:

● **Cafe Promenade:** for continental breakfast, all-day pizzas and specialty coffees (provided in paper cups).

● **Windjammer Cafe:** for casual buffet-style breakfast, lunch and light dinner (except for the cruise's last night).

● **Chops Grille** (a steakhouse that is actually a little section inside the Windjammer Cafe): for casual dinner (no reservations necessary) featuring a grill and open kitchen. A cover charge of $20 per person applies. Meats and steaks featured include Veal Chop, New York Striploin Steak, Filet Mignon, and Prime Rib of Beef.

● **Portofino:** this is the ship's "upscale" (non-smoking) Euro-Italian restaurant, open for dinner only. Reservations are required (a $20 cover charge/gratuity of $20 per person applies). The food and its presentation are better than the food in the dining room, although the restaurant is not large enough for all passengers to try even once during a cruise. Choices include: antipasti, soup, salad, pasta, main dish, dessert, cheese and coffee.

● **Johnny Rockets:** a retro 1950s all-day, all-night American diner-style eatery that features hamburgers, malt shakes (at extra cost), and jukebox hits, with both indoor and outdoor seating (all indoor tables have a mini-jukebox; dimes are provided for you to make your selection of vintage records), and all-singing, all-dancing waitresses that'll knock your socks off, if you can stand the volume.

● **Sprinkles:** for round-the-clock ice cream and yoghurt (in the Royal Promenade).

ENTERTAINMENT. The 1,350-seat Metropolis Showlounge is a really stunning room that could well be the equal of many such rooms on land. It is located at the forward end of the ship and spans the height of five decks (with only a few slim pillars and almost no disruption of sight lines from almost any seat in the house). The room features a hydraulic orchestra pit and huge stage areas, together with sonic-boom loud sound, and some superb lighting equipment.

In addition, the ship has a whole array of cabaret acts. Although many of these are not what you would call headliners (the strongest cabaret acts are featured in the main showlounge, while others are presented in the Ixtapa Lounge, which is also the venue for late-night adults-only comedy), they regularly travel the cruise ship circuit.

There is also a television studio, located adjacent to rooms that could be used, for example, for trade show exhibition space (good for conventions at sea).

SPA/FITNESS. The ShipShape Spa is large, and measures 15,000 sq. ft (1,400 sq. meters). It includes a large aerobics exercise room, fitness center (with the usual stairmasters, treadmills, stationary bikes, weight machines and free weights), treatment rooms, men's and women's sauna/steam rooms, while another 10,000 sq. ft (930 sq. meters) is devoted to a Solarium (with magrodome sliding glass roof) for relaxation after you've exercised too much.

For the more sporting, there is activity galore – including a rock-climbing wall that's 32.8 ft high (10 meters), with five separate climbing tracks. It is located outdoors at the aft end of the funnel. You'll get a great "buzz" being 200 ft (60 meters) above the ocean while the ship is moving.

Other sports facilities include a roller-blading track, a dive-and-snorkel shop, a full-size basketball court and 9-hole, par 26 golf course.

● **For more extensive general information about the Royal Caribbean experience, see pages 128–131.**

New Flamenco
★★ +

Mid-Size Ship: . . . . .17,042 tons	Propulsion/Propellers: . . . . .diesel	Cabins (for one person): 4
Lifestyle: . . . . .Standard	(13,450kW)/2	Cabins (with private balcony): 0
Cruise Line: . . . . .Travelplan Cruises	Passenger Decks: 7	Cabins (wheelchair accessible): 2
Former Names: . . . . .Flamenco,	Total Crew: 350	Cabin Current: . . . . .110 and 220 volts
Southern Cross, Star/Ship Majestic,	Passengers	Elevators: 4
Sun Princess, Spirit of London	(lower beds/all berths): 798/987	Casino (gaming tables): . . . . .Yes
Builder: . . . . . .Cantieri Navale Del Tirreno	Passenger Space Ratio	Slot Machines: . . . . .Yes
& Riuniti (Italy)	(lower beds/all berths): 21.3/17.2	Swimming Pools (outdoors): 1
Original Cost: .n/a	Crew/Passenger Ratio	(+children's wading pool)
Entered Service: . . . . . . .Nov 1972/2004	(lower beds/all berths): 2.2/2.8	Swimming Pools (indoors): 0
Registry: . . . . .The Bahamas	Navigation Officers: . . . . .Greek	Whirlpools: 0
Length (ft/m): 535.7/163.30	Cabins (total): 401	Self-Service Launderette: . . . . .No
Beam (ft/m): 73.4/22.40	Size Range (sq ft/m): 96.8–236.8/9.0–22.0	Dedicated Cinema/Seats: Yes/186
Draft (ft/m): 22.4/6.85	Cabins (outside view): 272	Library: . . . . .Yes
	Cabins (interior/no view): 129	Classification Society: . . .Lloyd's Register

OVERALL SCORE: 1,026 (OUT OF A POSSIBLE 2,000 POINTS)

OVERVIEW. *New Flamenco* has a moderately pleasing but now dated 1970s profile, with a rakish superstructure, an all-white hull, and a single large blue funnel. It underwent a $9 million refurbishment in 1997, after being acquired by the now-defunct Festival Cruises, and it is now under charter to Spanish tour operator Travelplan (a member of Spain's Globalia group).

The ship has a reasonable open deck and sunbathing space, although it is tight when full. Inside, the public rooms are quite comfortable, with attractive decor and soft furnishings. Particularly nice is the Piano Bar/Casino lounge area, with its warm wood room dividers and long bar. But this is not a new ship, and cannot compare with the latest vessels. Where it does score highly is in the friendliness of the crew, which is very international.

There is no wrap-around promenade deck outdoors, although you can walk around the front sections of one of the open decks. There are too many loud announcements (all in Spanish). Many passengers and crew are heavy smokers. *New Flamenco* provides good value for money, and a comfortable cruise experience in relaxed surroundings. The onboard currency is the euro. Globalia's airline, Air Europe, provides air transportation for *New Flamenco* passengers.

SUITABLE FOR: *New Flamenco* is best suited to youthful Spanish-speaking couples and single travelers who want to take their first, inexpensive cruise aboard a ship that is unpretentious in style and has acceptable food and service.

ACCOMMODATION. Suites described in the brochure as

BERLITZ'S RATINGS

	Possible	Achieved
Ship	500	210
Accommodation	200	108
Food	400	227
Service	400	228
Entertainment	100	46
Cruise	400	207

deluxe are reasonably spacious, with separate sleeping and living areas. All other interior and outside-view cabins are on the small side, but quite well equipped. However, the cabin walls are really thin. There is little drawer space. Bathrooms are compact but adequate.

CUISINE/DINING. The restaurant, an airy room, has two seatings. However, it can be extremely noisy as the tables are very close together. The quality of food and its presentation are adequate (considering the low cruise price). There is a limited choice of breads, rolls, cheeses and fruits. There is also much use of canned fruits for desserts. Vegetarian selections are not good.

Informal self-service buffets for breakfast and lunch are attractive, but repetitious, and are presented in the Cafe.

ENTERTAINMENT. The Universe Lounge is a single-level room, with several pillars and an H-shape that means obstructed sightlines. The stage lighting is very poor, as is the sound quality in the room. The revue-style shows are of the decidedly low-budget variety, although the resident troupe of dancers and singers tries hard. Other shows consist of unknown cabaret acts doing the cruise ship circuit (the principal difficulty aboard this ship is that the ship operates in five or six languages, which favors blandly visual acts such as mime, magic or juggling.

SPA/FITNESS. There is a small gymnasium, massage room and beauty salon, in one area on the port side of Lounge Deck, just forward of the ship's casino – not an ideal location. Services and treatments are very basic.

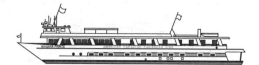

Niagara Prince
★★ +

Boutique Ship:	.99 tons	Passenger Decks:	.3	Cabins (with private balcony):	.0
Lifestyle:	Standard	Total Crew:	17	Cabins (wheelchair accessible):	.0
Cruise Line:	American Canadian	Passengers		Cabin Current:	110 volts
	Caribbean Line	(lower beds/all berths):	.84/94	Elevators:	.0
Former Names:	none	Passenger Space Ratio		Casino (gaming tables):	No
Builder:	Blount Industries (USA)	(lower beds/all berths):	1.1/1.0	Slot Machines:	No
Original Cost:	$7.5 million	Crew/Passenger Ratio		Swimming Pools (outdoors):	.0
Entered Service:	Nov 1994	(lower beds/all berths):	4.9/5.5	Swimming Pools (indoors):	.0
Registry:	USA	Navigation Officers:	American	Whirlpools:	.0
Length (ft/m):	177.0/53.9	Cabins (total):	48	Self-Service Launderette:	No
Beam (ft/m):	40.0/12.1	Size Range (sq ft/m):	72.0–96.0/6.6–8.9	Dedicated Cinema/Seats:	No
Draft (ft/m):	6.7/2.0	Cabins (outside view):	40	Library:	Yes
Propulsion/Propellers:	diesel	Cabins (interior/no view):	2	Classification Society:	American Bureau
	(1044 kW)/2	Cabins (for one person):	6		of Shipping

OVERALL SCORE: 964 (OUT OF A POSSIBLE 2,000 POINTS)

OVERVIEW. The vessel is equipped with a unique, retractable wheelhouse for passage under low bridges on island waterway itineraries, and there is also a small platform for those who want to swim off the stern. There is also a glass-bottom boat, and a sunfish sailboat.

An underwater video camera allows passengers to see what a scuba diver might see underneath the ship, while seated in (dry) comfort in the lounge, on large-screen TV monitors. Underwater lights, which attract fish and other marine life, are also fitted.

Cruising aboard this ship is for those who do not want or need pampering, much service, entertainment, or the facilities provided aboard regular cruise ships. This vessel is enjoyed by a high percentage of repeat passengers, who seek a simple, unpretentious lifestyle. Take only casual clothing and the odd sweater or jacket.

Although there is no elevator, there is an electric chairlift at all stairways for those who need a little help. All gratuities are pooled by the entire complement of staff. The onboard currency is the US dollar.

This ship has small, utilitarian cabins. No alcoholic beverages are available. There's no laundry aboard, so bed linen, towels and other items are taken ashore for cleaning.

SUITABLE FOR: *Niagara Prince* is best suited to couples and single travelers who enjoy nature and wildlife up close and personal, and who would not dream of taking a cruise in the mainstream sense aboard ships with large numbers of people. This is for outdoors types who don't need entertainment or corny parlor games, but are looking for an all-

BERLITZ'S RATINGS

	Possible	Achieved
Ship	500	213
Accommodation	200	77
Food	400	205
Service	400	220
Entertainment	N/A	N/A
Cruise	500	249

American cruise experience, albeit at a high price.

ACCOMMODATION. The cabins are small (designed for packages rather than people), basic, and very plain. Only a metal cabinet is provided for hanging your clothes, and there are a few small metal drawers. No smoking is allowed in any cabin. The air conditioning consists of re-circulated air. Beds in 75 percent of the cabins can be made up as two singles or a queen-sized bed (10 cabins have a third berth). The bathrooms are the size of a telephone kiosk (tiny), and very frustrating.

CUISINE/DINING. The dining room is operated in one open seating (no assigned tables), with tables for four, six, eight, or ten. Meals are served "family-style." The cuisine features good, wholesome American fare, with fresh-baked breads, muffins, and regional dishes. There are, perhaps, too many high-cholesterol, fatty foods for the older passengers carried. A "bring your own bottle" policy exists for those who want wine with dinner, or any alcoholic beverages (mixers are, however, available).

ENTERTAINMENT. There is no formal entertainment, although dinner and after-dinner conversation with fellow passengers in the ship's lounge/bar really becomes the entertainment each evening. So, if you don't want to talk to your fellow passengers, take a good book.

SPA/FITNESS. There are no such facilities aboard this very small vessel.

Nippon Maru
★★★ +

Small Ship: . . . . .21,903 tons	Total Crew: 160	Cabins (wheelchair accessible): 2
Lifestyle: . . . . .Standard	Passengers	Cabin Current: . . . . .100 volts
Cruise Line: . . .Mitsui OSK Passenger Line	(lower beds/all berths): 408/607	Elevators: 5
Former Names: . . . . .none	Passenger Space Ratio	Casino (gaming tables): . . . . .Yes
Builder: . . . .Mitsubishi Heavy Industries	(lower beds/all berths): 53.6/36.0	(no cash can be won, only gifts)
(Japan)	Crew/Passenger Ratio	Slot Machines: . . . . .No
Original Cost: . . . .$59.4 million	(lower beds/all berths): 2.5/3.7	Swimming Pools (outdoors): 1
Entered Service: . . . . .Sept 1990	Navigation Officers: . . . . .Japanese	Swimming Pools (indoors): 0
Registry: .Japan	Cabins (total): 204	Whirlpools: . . . . .4 (Japanese baths)
Length (ft/m): 546.7/166.65	Size Range (sq ft/m): 150.6–430.5/	Self-Service Launderette: . . . . .Yes
Beam (ft/m): 78.7/24.00	14.0–40.0	Dedicated Cinema/Seats: Yes/135
Draft (ft/m): 21.4/6.55	Cabins (outside view): 189	Library: . . . . .Yes
Propulsion/Propellers: . . . . .diesel	Cabins (interior/no view): 15	Classification Society: . . . . . .Nippon Kaiji
(15,740 kW)/2	Cabins (for one person): 0	Kyokai
Passenger Decks: 7	Cabins (with private balcony): 0	

OVERALL SCORE: 1,391 (OUT OF A POSSIBLE 2,000 POINTS)

OVERVIEW. *Nippon Maru* has a single, large, orange, swept-back funnel aft of amidships, with an exterior styling that is very traditional. There is a decent amount of open outdoors space, and the teakwood decking outdoors is good.

The focal point of the interiors is an atrium lobby that spans six decks. The public rooms have very high ceilings, giving a sense of spaciousness, and are well-designed, with high-quality furnishings and soothing color combinations. Public rooms include a main lounge, main hall/lecture room, piano lounge, cinema/lecture room, and a washitsu tatami room. Organized children's activities are provided only on leisure cruises.

A specialist courier company provides an excellent luggage service and will collect your luggage from your home before the cruise, and deliver it back to your home after the cruise (this service is available only in Japan). The onboard currency is the Japanese yen.

The white cheap plastic deck furniture is difficult to keep clean and looks really shoddy. The seats in the theater are very plain and utilitarian. Hospitality towards passengers could be improved (particularly by the officers).

SUITABLE FOR: *Nippon Maru* is best suited to Japanese-speaking couples and single travelers who want modestly comfortable surroundings, and who enjoy decent food and service, all at a low cost. There is no tipping.

ACCOMMODATION. Most cabins are located forward, with public rooms positioned aft. The suites are quite large (larger than aboard half-sister ship *Fuji Maru*), and have a

BERLITZ'S RATINGS

	Possible	Achieved
Ship	500	349
Accommodation	200	135
Food	400	287
Service	400	289
Entertainment	100	62
Cruise	400	269

separate bedroom and living room with a solid wall divider (except for the doorway, where there is a curtain but no door). A large sofa, four chairs, and coffee table occupy one section of the lounge; there is also a vanity/writing desk. The bedroom has a good amount of closet and drawer space and two beds. The bathroom is very small. Slippers and bathrobes are provided.

The deluxe cabins are nicely decorated, and the living area has a table and two chairs, and two beds (they cannot be pushed together). The standard cabins are utilitarian and clinical (adequate for convention and seminar cruise passengers). Many of these have a third (or third and fourth) pull-down upper Pullman berth. The lighting is minimal and utilitarian.

CUISINE/DINING. The dining room, which seats around 320, is pleasing but basic. It features both traditional Japanese cuisine and some Western dishes. There is one seating dining for leisure cruises, and two seatings for when the ship is under charter. Food presentation is decent, but plain.

ENTERTAINMENT. The Main Hall has a theater-style stage, wooden dance floor, and seating in individual chairs on both the lower (main) level and the upper (balcony) level of this two-deck high room. Social dancing is on the agenda each evening. On most cruises, special featured entertainers are brought on board from ashore..

SPA/FITNESS. There is a traditional Japanese Grand Bath (one for women, one for men), with washing stations, a sauna, and beauty salon. Massages and facials are available.

Norwegian Crown
★★★★

Mid-size Ship: . . . . .32,242 tons	Total Crew: 550	Cabins (with private balcony): 24
Lifestyle: . . . . .Standard	Passengers	Cabins (wheelchair accessible): 4
Cruise Line: . . . . .Norwegian Cruise Lines	(lower beds/all berths): . . . . ".1,104/1,247	Cabin Current: . . . . .110 AC
Former Names: . . . . .Crown Odyssey,	Passenger Space Ratio	Elevators: 4
Norwegian Crown	(lower beds/all berths): 431.0/27.4	Casino (gaming tables): . . . . .Yes
Builder: . . . . .Meyer Werft (Germany)	Crew/Passenger Ratio	Slot Machines: . . . . .Yes
Original Cost: . . . .$178 million	(lower beds/all berths): 2.0/2.2	Swimming Pools (outdoors): 1
Entered Service: . . . .Jun 1998, Sept 2003	Navigation Officers: .European/Norwegian	Swimming Pools (indoors): 1
Registry: . . . . .Bahamas	Cabins (total): .552	Whirlpools: 4
Length (ft/m): 615.9/187.75	Size Range (sq ft/m): 153.9–613.5/	Self-Service Launderette: . . . . .No
Beam (ft/m): 92.5/28.2	14.3–57.0	Dedicated Cinema/Seats: . . . . .No
Draft (ft/m): 23.8/7.26	Cabins (outside view): 418	Library: . . . . .Yes
Propulsion/Propellers: diesel (21,330kW)/2	Cabins (interior/no view): 134	Classification Society: . . . .Bureau Veritas
Passenger Decks: 10	Cabins (for one person): 0	

OVERALL SCORE: 1,445 (OUT OF A POSSIBLE 2,000 POINTS)

OVERVIEW. *Norwegian Crown* is a well-designed and built ship, originally constructed for the now defunct Royal Cruise Line. Norwegian Cruise Line operated the ship for several years, before it was transferred to Orient Lines in 2000, and then back to Norwegian Cruise Line in September 2003. The vessel has a relatively handsome exterior profile, and is now an all-white ship again (the royal blue hull having been painted white).

One nice feature is a full, wrap-around teak promenade deck outdoors, although it does become quite narrow at the fore part of the vessel; a jogging track is also to be found on the uppermost deck outdoors. There is one swimming pool outdoors on an aft lido deck.

Inside, there is generally a good passenger flow, ample space and fine-quality interiors. Generous amounts of warm woods and marble have been used in the decor, although there are many mirrored surfaces. A refurbishment in March 2003 changed some public rooms for the ship's role change from an Orient Lines ship to a Norwegian Cruise Line ship incorporating "Freestyle Dining".

The ship has a spacious layout and a good array of public rooms, including a lobby that is two decks high; a large, gold sculpture of the world (by Pomodoro) is located on the lower level, adjacent to the semi-circular staircase that connects the two levels. On the upper level there are boutiques, a piano lounge with bar, and a casino.

At the top of the ship is an observation lounge (called Top of the Crown) with panoramic views, which, in the evenings, becomes a nightclub. Other facilities include a library, an Internet Center (with four computer terminals), a cinema, and a palm court area. There is a center for chil-

BERLITZ'S RATINGS

	Possible	Achieved
Ship	500	401
Accommodation	200	156
Food	400	264
Service	400	274
Entertainment	100	66
Cruise	400	284

dren. Teens have their own separate hangout, with dance floor and high-tech sound and light system, and juice bar. A video arcade separates the teens from the children's center.

Norwegian Crown should be a good choice for passengers wanting destination-intensive cruising in a ship that has some semblance of European quality, style, and charm, for what is really a very moderate cruise price offering value for money. A friendly and accommodating multinational crew helps make a cruise aboard the ship a pleasant, no-hassle experience.

Some of the paneling in passageways is scuffed (due, in part, to its light color), and lets down an otherwise pleasant, but undistinguished ship. While staff hospitality is generally good, there is little polish or finesse to service. Congestion occurs between first- and second-seating passengers on days when the captain's cocktail parties are held in the showlounge, and a line forms outside.

SUITABLE FOR: *Norwegian Crown* is best suited to first-time young (and young at heart) couples and single passengers (preferably without children, who be better suited to the larger, newer ships in the fleet) that enjoy fairly modern, upbeat surroundings, several entertainment lounges and bars – all in one neat, highly programmed, well packaged cruise vacation. There's plenty of activities and entertainment, and food that is acceptable but nothing more, all delivered by a smiling, friendly service staff that lacks polish but is willing.

ACCOMMODATION. There are 18 price categories; typically the higher the deck, the more expensive will be your accommodation. Most cabins are of the same size and layout, have blond wood cabinetry, an abundance of mirrors, and closet and drawer space, and are very well equipped. Although almost all cabins show some signs of wear and tear, ongoing refurbishment keeps them looking good. All have a color TV, a hairdryer, thin 100% cotton bathrobe, music console (and a button that can be used to turn announcements on or off), personal safe, and private bathroom with shower (many upper-grade cabins have a good-sized bathtub). All towels are 100% cotton, although they could be larger; soap, shampoo, body lotion, shower cap and sewing kit are the amenities provided. The cabin sound-proofing is generally good.

Some cabins have interconnecting doors, so that they can connect to make a two-room suite. You should note that almost all cabins on Deck 8 have lifeboat-obstructed views. Ice machines can be found in all passageways along the accommodation decks.

The largest accommodation is in the 16 suites on Penthouse Deck 10. Each is decorated in a different style, in accordance with the name of the suite (from fore to aft they are: Edinburgh, Inverness, Balmoral, Sandringham, Shalimar, Taj Mahal, Mykonos, Portofino, Bel Air, Hollywood, Bali, Tahiti, Imperial, Shangri-La, Dynasty, Mandarin). They are quite spacious units, and provide a sleeping area and separate living room (including some nicely finished wood cabinetry and a huge amount of drawer space), together with a large, white marble-clad bathroom with a full-sized tub and integral shower), and a semi-private balcony (the balcony can be overlooked from the open deck above). Passengers occupying these suites have the use of a concierge, who will arrange private parties, obtain theater tickets, and provide assistance for private shore excursions.

The next most spacious accommodation can be found in cabins with bay windows. These include a separate sleeping area with twin beds, a huge amount of drawer space in a large vanity/writing desk, and a lounge typically with two sofas, tub chairs and heavy glass table, refrigerator and TV set. Electrically operated window blinds, together with the curtains that front them provide good blackouts for the bay windows. The white marble-clad bathroom is also large and features a full-sized bathtub with integral shower.

There are four wheelchair-accessible cabins; these provide plenty of space to maneuver, and all four include a bathroom with roll-in shower. But wheelchair accessibility in some ports on the many itineraries operated by this ship (particularly in Europe) may prove quite frustrating and wheelchair-accessible transportation will be very limited.

CUISINE/DINING. With "Freestyle Dining", you can choose which restaurant you would like to eat in, at what time, and with whom. While this is fine in theory, in practice it means that you have to make reservations (including the time that you want to eat), so "freestyle dining" means programmed dining. All restaurants and eateries are non-smoking.

The Seven Seas Dining Room, with picture windows on both port and starboard sides, is large. It is also, unfortunately, quite noisy (particularly for tables adjacent to the open waiter stations). It has a stained-glass ceiling, and comfortable seating at tables for two, four, six or eight (although the chairs do not have armrests), and two seatings.

The cuisine, while it is not gourmet either in quality or presentation, is adequate. It is unfussy, yet there is plenty of taste. What is noticeable is the extensive use of fresh vegetables (whenever obtainable). However, the food quality and presentation is best described as inconsistent.

As for service, the waiters are generally good, and provide friendly service that is reasonably attentive, although there is a distinct lack of polish and consistency. There is a decent, well-priced wine list, although the wines are almost all extremely young; the waiters have little knowledge of wines, or how to pour them (note that a 15% gratuity is automatically added to all wine and drinks bills).

The 70-seat Le Bistro is an alternative NCL signature venue for informal dinners (reservations only, and a cover charge of $15 per person). The intimate room has wood banquette seating, and the decor colors are coral, green and gold. In addition, casual luncheons can be taken in the 40-seat Pasta Cafe, on an open deck aft, adjacent to a sunbathing and whirlpool area, and an open-air bar. This is also used for dining outdoors on selected nights. An Asian-themed eatery, Chopsticks, was added when the ship changed from Orient Lines to NCL.

ENTERTAINMENT. The Stardust Showlounge is the venue for all entertainment shows, cabaret acts, lectures, and some social functions. It is a single level room with sight lines that are generally good, but could be better.

Revue-style production shows (the ship has a resident troupe of singer/dancers) and cabaret acts are the featured entertainment, although the quality of the shows is so-so. Cabaret acts (typically singers, magicians, ventriloquists, comedy jugglers, and comedians) are featured as individual acts or as part of the revue shows.

There are a number of small bands and musical units to provide live music for dancing. The piano bar in the Monte Carlo Court is a favorite hangout and drinking place.

SPA/FITNESS. There is a decent indoor spa, pool, gymnasium, and nine beauty treatment rooms, with services provided by Mandara Spa (a Steiner concession).

● **For more extensive general information on what an NCL cruise is like, see page 122–124.**

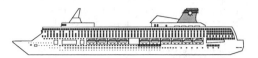

Norwegian Dawn
★★★★

Large (Resort) Ship: ....91,740 tons	Passenger Decks:.................11	Cabins (for one person):..............0
Lifestyle: ....Standard	Total Crew: 1,318	Cabins (with private balcony): 511
Cruise Line: .....Norwegian Cruise Lines	Passengers	Cabins (wheelchair accessible): 20
Former Names: ....none	(lower beds/all berths): 2,244/4,080	Cabin Current: ....110 AC
Gross Tonnage: 91,000	Passenger Space Ratio	Elevators: 12
Builder: ....Meyer Werft (Germany)	(lower beds/all berths):........40.8/22.4	Casino (gaming tables): ....Yes
Original Cost: ....$400 million	Crew/Passenger Ratio	Slot Machines: ....Yes
Entered Service: ....Oct 2002	(lower beds/all berths):.........1.7/3.0	Swimming Pools (outdoors): 2
Registry: ....Bahamas	Navigation Officers: ....Scandinavian	Swimming Pools (indoors): 1
Length (ft/m): 964.9/294.13	Cabins (total): 1,122	Whirlpools: ...4 (+ 1 children's whirlpool)
Beam (ft/m): 105.6/32.2	Size Range (sq ft/m): 142.0–5,350.0/	Self-Service Launderette: ....No
Draft (ft/m): 26.9/8.2	13.2–497.0	Dedicated Cinema/Seats: ....No
Propulsion/Propellers: ...diesel-electric/2	Cabins (outside view): 787	Library: ....Yes
pods (19.5MW each)	Cabins (interior/no view): 335	Classification Society: Det Norske Veritas

OVERALL SCORE: 1,524 (OUT OF A POSSIBLE 2,000 POINTS)

OVERVIEW. *Norwegian Dawn* (sister to *Norwegian Star*, which debuted in 2001) was constructed in 64 sections, ("blocks"). It is a state-of-the-art vessel for Norwegian Cruise Line, and features a "pod" propulsion system *(see page 151 for a detailed explanation).*

The hull displays interesting logos on top of its white paint, depicting the ship's itineraries: the port side features the cruise itinerary from New York to the Bahamas and Florida, while the starboard side features the winter itinerary from Miami to the Caribbean. Dolphins, the Statue of Liberty, and representations of the four original paintings displayed on board (the Impressionists Matisse, Renoir, Van Gogh, and the pop artist Andy Warhol). It is a colorful concept, and makes the ship easy to spot in a sea of similar-sized ships in port.

Facilities include a large Dawn Club Casino gaming area, an Internet Cafe (with 24 computer stations and internet connection), a 1,150-seat showlounge with main floor and balcony level, a 3,000-book library, a card room, a writing and study room, a business center, conference and meeting rooms, and a retail shopping complex measuring 20,000 sq. ft (1,800 sq. meters).

As in sister ship *Norwegian Star*, a good deal of space is devoted to children's facilities (the T-Rex Kids' Center and Teen Club) – all tucked well away from adult recreation areas, at the aft end of the ship. Children of all ages will get to play in a superb wet 'n' wild space-themed water park (complete with large pool, water slide, and paddle pool). There's a room full of cots for toddlers to use for sleepovers, and even the toilets are at a special low height. Teens, too, are well catered for, and get their own cinema (with

BERLITZ'S RATINGS		
	Possible	Achieved
Ship	500	422
Accommodation	200	156
Food	400	293
Service	400	284
Entertainment	100	66
Cruise	400	303

DVD movies), discotheque with dance floor, and their own whirlpool (hot) tub.

With so many dining choices (some of which cost extra), your final cruise and dining experience will be determined by how much you are prepared to spend. To make the most of your cruise holiday, you will need to plan where you want to eat well in advance, and make the necessary reservations, or you may be disappointed.

More choices, including more dining options, add up to a very attractive holiday package, particularly suitable for families with children, in a very contemporary floating leisure center that really does provide ample facilities for you to have an enjoyable time. The dress code is casual – very casual (no jacket and tie needed, although you are welcome to dress formally if you so wish). There is no suggested dress code on the daily programme.

While the initial cruise fare seems very reasonable, the extra costs and charges soon mount up if you want to sample more than the basics. Although service levels and finesse are sometimes inconsistent, the level of hospitality is very good – made so much better and brighter by the addition of a great number of Asian female staff rather than the surly and inconsistent (Caribbean Basin) staff still found aboard some NCL ships.

Despite the company's name (Norwegian Cruise Line), there's almost nothing Norwegian about this product, except for some senior officers. The staff, incidentally, includes many Southeast Asians who already have service experience aboard parent company Star Cruises' big ships.

Cruising aboard large ships such as this has become increasingly an onboard revenue-based product. The ship is full of revenue centers designed to help you part with even more money than what is paid for in the price of your cruise ticket. You can expect to be subjected to a stream of flyers advertising daily art auctions, "designer" watches, "inch of gold/silver" and other promotions.

Gratuities for staff (cabin attendants, dining room waiters, etc.) are automatically added to your onboard account at $10 per person, per day (you can, however, reduce or otherwise amend these if necessary before you disembark, but in May 2005 the gratuity becomes a non-adjustable "service charge"). In addition, a 15% gratuity is added to all bar and spa treatment accounts. The onboard currency is the US dollar.

Although the suites and junior suites are quite spacious, the standard interior (no view) and outside-view cabins are very small when compared to those of other major cruise lines such as Carnival or Celebrity, particularly when occupied by three or four persons (the bathrooms, however, are of quite a decent size, and have large shower enclosures). Music played in some areas bleeds through into others; for example, Latin music played in Salsas (on the second level of the lobby) is heard throughout the lobby and the internet cafe (on the third level of the lobby) and is most disconcerting. Communication (particularly between some of the Asian staff and passengers) is weak. Standing in line for embarkation, disembarkation, shore tenders and for self-serve buffet meals is an inevitable aspect of cruising aboard all large ships – even those designated as "Freestyle".

ACCOMMODATION. There are 29 price/grades (the price will depend on the grade, location and size). Regardless of the accommodation you choose, all cabins have tea and coffee making sets (note that only "coffee creamer" is provided, so tea drinkers who want fresh milk need to arrange this with their steward, or call room service), rich cherry wood cabinetry, bathroom with sliding door and separate toilet, shower enclosure and washbasin compartments, and European duvets. The private balconies of the top suites have teak decks, while most other cabins with balconies feature a "Bolidt" (rubberized sand-like) deck, and smoked glass/wood rail panels that provide good sightlines. Audio channels can be found on the in-cabin television system, but you cannot turn off the picture.

Garden Villas. The largest living spaces are two huge Garden Villas (Vista and Horizon), high atop the ship in a pod located forward of the ship's funnel, and overlooking the main swimming pool and recreation deck. These villas have huge glass walls and landscaped private roof gardens for outdoor dining (with whirlpool tubs, naturally), and huge private sunbathing areas completely shielded from anyone. Each has three bedrooms and bathrooms, and a large living room overlooking the lido/pool deck. These units have their own private elevator access and private stairway. Each is 5,350 sq ft. (497 sq meters, including the private Italian outdoor garden), and can be combined to create a huge, 10,700 sq.-ft (994-sq.-meter) "house". Butler service is provided.
Owner's Suites. Four Owner's Suites (each measures 750 sq.ft./69.6 sq. meters) are located in the very front of the ship. Two of these are nestled under the enclosed nav-

igation bridge wings on Deck 11 (the other two are located in the equivalent space on the deck below). They have an entrance (with wooden door front), large lounge/dining room, and separate bedroom (with king-sized bed beneath a mirrored ceiling, and television with integral DVD player. The bathroom (almost as large as a standard cabin) has a full-sized tub with shower and TV; separate shower enclosure, separate toilet, and a dressing area with his-and-hers walk-in closets. There are forward facing (open) and side facing (enclosed) private balconies. Butler service is provided. If you don't need the entertaining space of the Garden Villas, these owner's suites are delightful living spaces. However, they do suffer occasionally from noise generated in Spinnaker's (a nightclub/disco on the deck above. Each Owner's Suite can also be interconnected to a Penthouse Suite and balcony cabin (very useful for large families when parents want their privacy).
Penthouse Suites. There are 30 Penthouse Suites; each measures 366 sq.ft./34 sq. meters. Features include a bedroom with queen sized bed, walk-in closet, living room with dining table, and bathroom with separate shower enclosure and bathtub. Penthouse Suites on Deck 11 can be interconnected to children's cabin with double sofa bed and a pull-down Pullman-style) bed with separate bathroom and shower enclosure. These suites also have a private balcony, and butler service.
Romance Suites. There are four Romance Suites, each measuring 288 sq.ft./26.7 sq. meters. They include a separate bedroom with queen-sized bed, a sitting area with double sofa bed, and living and dining areas. The bathroom has a full-sized tub and shower. These suites also have a private balcony.
Mini Suites. There are 107 mini suites (measuring 229 sq. ft/21.2 sq. meters), each with two lower beds that convert into a queen-sized bed, and a sitting area with double sofa bed. The bathroom has a full-sized tub and shower. Floor-to-ceiling windows open onto a private balcony.

All suites are lavishly furnished (most in rich cherry wood), although closet space in some of the smaller units is tight. Some suites have extras like a trouser press, and a full range of toiletries by L'Occidentale. Suites also get butlers, who can serve all meals en-suite from the menus of a number of restaurants.

Although they are nicely furnished and quite well equipped, the standard outside-view and interior (no view) cabins are quite small, particularly when occupied by three or four persons. Some cabins have interconnecting doors (good for families with children). Many cabins have third- and fourth-person pull-down berths or trundle beds.

A small room service menu is available (all items are at extra cost, and a 15% service charge and a gratuity are added to your account). Bottled water is placed in each cabin (but a charge will be made to your account if you open the bottle).

CUISINE/DINING. With "Freestyle Dining", you can choose which restaurant to eat in, at what time, and with whom (there are no assigned dining rooms, tables or seats). While this is fine in theory, in practice it means that you have to make reservations (including the time that you want to eat), so "freestyle dining" actually turns out to be programmed dining. All restaurants and eateries are non-smoking.

Although there are three principal dining rooms, there are also a number of other themed eating establishments, giving a wide range of choice – though some cost extra, and require advance reservations (particularly for dinner). There are two entire decks of restaurants to choose from, involving 10 different restaurants and eateries. Note that NCLs dress code states that: "jeans, T-shirts, tank tops and bare feet are not permitted in restaurants."

● **Venetian:** the first main dining room (seats 472) offers traditional six-course dining (open 5.30pm–midnight). The dining room is located aft, and has good views over the ship's stern (at least in the daytime), although the sightlines from some seats are obstructed by 14 pillars. The room has a baby grand piano in the center of the forward part of the room. If you want a quieter table, I recommend being seated in one of two wings in the forward section (near the entrance/steps).

● **Aqua:** the second main dining room (seats 344) offers traditional six-courses (open 5.30pm–midnight).

● **Impressions:** the third main dining room (seats 236) offers lighter cuisine (open 5.30pm to midnight). The waiter stations are too close to the tables and are very noisy.

● **Bamboo (a Taste of Asia):** a Japanese/Thai/Chinese restaurant, with 140 seats, features a sit-up conveyor-belt style sushi/sashimi bar, sake bar, show galley, and separate room with a teppanyaki grill. In the evenings, music from Gatsby's lounge/bar (on the deck below) completely fill the restaurant (through an open lobby-like well), and a quiet meal is almost impossible. All items are at extra cost (there is an "all you can eat" sushi charge of $10).

● **Le Bistro:** a French restaurant with 72 seats, featuring Le Bistro nouvelle cuisine (the decor includes four Impressionist paintings on loan from the private collection of the chairman of Star Cruises, parent company of NCL), although they don't really match the room's decor. A cover charge of $12.50 applies (there's also a line for you to add an *extra* gratuity – very cheeky).

● **Blue Lagoon:** a food court-style eatery; 68 seats; serving hamburgers, fish & chips, pot pies and wok fast dishes.

● **Garden Cafe:** an indoor/outdoor self-serve buffet eatery (seats 490). It includes "action stations" featuring made-to-order omelets, waffles, fruit, soups, ethnic specialities and pasta dishes.

● **Salsa:** a Spanish tapas eatery and bar (seats 112) with a selection of hot and cold tapas dishes and authentic entertainment, located on the second level of the atrium lobby.

● **La Trattoria;** located inside the indoor/outdoor buffet (seats 162), this eatery serves pasta, pizza and other popular Italian fare.

● **Cagney's Steak House:** arranged atop the ship (seats 112), incorporates a show kitchen, and serves US prime steaks and seafood. Be prepared for large portions, and a cover charge of $17.50.

Other eating/drinking spots include the Pearly Kings (an English pub for draft beer and perhaps a game of darts); Havanas, a cigar and cognac lounge; Java, an atrium lobby Cafe and bar (hot and frozen coffees, teas and pastries); a Beer Garden (grilled foods); a Gelato Bar (ice cream); and a Gym and Spa Bar (health food snacks and drinks).

ENTERTAINMENT. The Stardust Theatre seats 1,037, and is the venue for colorful Las-Vegas-style production shows and major cabaret acts. It is designed in the style of an opera house, spans three decks, and has a steeply tiered main floor and port and starboard balconies.

There are three production shows in a typical 7-day cruise (all ably performed by the Jean Ann Ryan Company): Bollywood, Music of the Night, and South Beach Rave. These are all very colorful, high-energy, razzle-dazzle shows (with much use of pyrotechnics, laser and color-mover lighting), with so much happening on stage that by the end of the evening, if you are a typical passenger, you will be tired and unable to remember much about the shows, which are, however, very entertaining.

The ship carries a number of bands and solo entertaining musicians, which provide live music for listening and dancing in several of the lounges and bars. Throughout the ship, loud Latin music prevails. In Spinnakers Lounge (the ship's nightclub), a Pachanga Party is featured each cruise (a Miami South Beach rave).

SPA/FITNESS. Wellness devotees should enjoy the two-deck-high El Dorado health spa complex (operated by the Hawaii-based Mandara Spa, owned by Steiner), located at the stern of the ship (with large ocean-view windows on three sides). There are many facilities and services (almost all at extra charge), including Thai massage (in the spa, outdoors on deck, in your cabin or on your private balcony).

In addition, there is an indoor lap pool (measuring 37 ft/11.2 meters); hydrotherapy pool, two sit-in deep tubs, aromatherapy and wellness centers, and mud treatment room treatment rooms (there are 15 treatment rooms in all, including one specifically designed for couples).

The fitness and exercise rooms are located not within the spa, but at the top of the glass-domed atrium lobby (they feature the latest Cybex muscle-pumping equipment). Included is a room for exercycle classes. Some classes, such Pathway to Yoga, Body Cycling Class and Body Beat Class (cardio kick-boxing), cost extra.

Recreational sports facilities include a jogging track, golf driving range, basketball and volleyball courts, as well as four levels of sunbathing decks.

● **For more extensive general information on what an NCL cruise is like, see pages 122–124.**

Norwegian Dream
★★★ +

Large (Resort) Ship: . . . . .50,760 tons	Total Crew: 700	Cabins (wheelchair accessible): 6
Lifestyle: . . . . .Standard	Passengers	(+ 30 for hearing-impaired)
Cruise Line: . . . . . .Norwegian Cruise Line	(lower beds/all berths): 1,750/2,156	Cabin Current: . . . . .110 volts
Former Names: . . . . .Dreamward	Passenger Space Ratio	Elevators: 11
Builder: . . . . . . .Chantiers de l'Atlantique	(lower beds/all berths): 29.0/23.5	Casino (gaming tables): . . . . .Yes
(France)	Crew/Passenger Ratio	Slot Machines: . . . . .Yes
Original Cost: . . . .$240 million	(lower beds/all berths): 2.5/3.1	Swimming Pools (outdoors): 2
Entered Service: . . . . .Dec 1992	Navigation Officers: . . . . .Norwegian	Swimming Pools (indoors): 0
Registry: . . . . .The Bahamas	Cabins (total): 875	Whirlpools: 4
Length (ft/m): 754.0/229.80	Size Range (sq ft/m): 139.9–336.0/	Self-Service Launderette: . . . . .No
Beam (ft/m): 93.5/28.50	13.0–31.2	Dedicated Cinema/Seats: . . . . .No
Draft (ft/m): 22.3/6.80	Cabins (outside view): 695	Library: . . . . .Yes
Propulsion/Propellers: . . . . .diesel	Cabins (interior/no view): 180	Classification Society: . . . . . . .Det Norske
(18,480 kW)/2	Cabins (for one person): 0	Veritas
Passenger Decks: 10	Cabins (with private balcony): 48	

OVERALL SCORE: 1,381 (OUT OF A POSSIBLE 2,000 POINTS)

OVERVIEW. Built before its sister ship, *Norwegian Wind*, this vessel has a fairly handsome profile (despite its large, square funnel) that was better balanced before it underwent a "chop and stretch" operation in spring 1998. A completely new mid-section was added, and the funnel was adapted so that it could be "folded" over to allow the ship to pass under the low bridges on Germany's Kiel Canal. Following the "stretch" its exterior shape is not as handsome. Included in the 131-ft (40-meter) mid-section were 251 new passenger cabins and 50 crew cabins, together with several new or enlarged public rooms (although there simply are not enough) and a 60-seat conference center.

Some innovative features were incorporated in the original design, and these have been enhanced. The passenger flow is generally good – indeed, the ship absorbs people well except at peak traffic periods around meal times.

The lifeboats are inboard. There is a blue rubber-covered wrap-around promenade deck outdoors. The tiered pool deck is neat, as are the multi-deck aft sun terraces and all the fore and aft connecting exterior stairways.

The overall exterior design emphasizes a clever and extensive use of large windows that create a sense of open spaces, although the interior design provides many smaller public rooms rather than the large hangers found aboard so many other ships. However, there is no big atrium lobby, as one might expect. The pastel interior colors used are quite soothing, and it is considered by many to be a pretty ship inside. The entrance lobby is not at all attractive, and feels rather confined for a vessel of this size.

This ship has been highly successful for Norwegian

BERLITZ'S RATINGS

	Possible	Achieved
Ship	500	377
Accommodation	200	145
Food	400	237
Service	400	282
Entertainment	100	73
Cruise	400	267

Cruise Line's younger, active sports-minded passengers (when the ship operates Caribbean itineraries), and provides a good alternative to the larger ships and their larger passenger numbers, although there are still plenty of people around.

The ship is full of revenue centers, designed to part you from your money. You will be subjected to a stream of flyers advertising daily art auctions, "designer" watches and other promotions, while "artworks" for auction are strewn throughout the ship.

Gratuities for staff (cabin attendants, dining room waiters, etc) are automatically added to your onboard account at $10 per person, per day (you can, however, reduce or otherwise amend these if necessary before you disembark, but in May 2005 the gratuity becomes a non-adjustable "service charge"). In addition, a 15% gratuity is added to all bar and spa treatment accounts. The onboard currency is the US dollar.

The room service menu is limited and could be improved. The ship's layout is quite disjointed in places, and outdoor stairways are numerous and confusing. When the ship was "stretched" this reduced the amount of outdoor space per passenger, and this is now reflected in increased densify around the pools. Standing in line for embarkation, disembarkation, shore tenders and for self-serve buffet meals is an inevitable aspect of cruising aboard all large ships.

ACCOMMODATION. There are 15 grades of cabins (the price you pay will depend on the grade, size and location you choose). Most cabins have outside views, wood-trimmed cabinetry and warm decor, with multi-colored soft furnishings. But there is almost no drawer space (the closets have open shelves, however), so take minimal clothing. All cabins have a sitting area, but this takes away any free space, making movement pretty tight. The bathrooms are small but practical, although there is little space for storage of personal toiletries. Bottled water is placed in each cabin (but you pay for it once you open the bottle).

There are 18 suites (12 with a private entrance and a small, private balcony), each with separate living room and bedroom, fine quality cabinetry, and lots of closet and drawer space. Occupants of suites get "concierge" service, which provides extra personal attention. In addition, 16 suites and 70 cabins have inter-connecting doors – good for families cruising together, or perhaps for those who want separate "his and hers" living spaces. There are several cabins specially equipped for the hearing-impaired. All cabins on the port side of the ship are designated non-smoking

CUISINE/DINING. The two main full-service dining rooms are: The Terraces (arguably the nicer, with windows that look out over the ship's tiered aft decks), and the Four Seasons (with approximately 450 seats), located amidships. All are non-smoking and have the same menu and food, in an open seating, come when you want (and with whom) arrangement (NCL terms it "Freestyle Dining").

The Four Seasons is the largest, and has some prime tables at ocean-view window seats in a section that extends from the ship's port and starboard sides in half-moon shapes (nice for lunch, but it's either dark or the curtains are drawn for dinner). However, this ship was not built with this kind of "free for all" dining arrangements in mind, and so the flow, timing, and success of this concept aboard this ship quite simply doesn't work well. Note that jeans, T-shirts, tank tops and bare feet are not permitted in restaurants.

In addition to the two principal dining rooms, there are a number of other themed eating establishments, giving a wide range of choice – although it would be wise to plan in advance, particularly for dinner. Italian fare is served in the Trattoria (formerly the Sun Terraces), which overlooks the aft swimming pool. There is also The Bistro, which features informal evening dining at no extra charge in more intimate surroundings. A 200-seat Sports Bar (typically open between 6am and 1am) features breakfast, luncheon, dinner, and snacks throughout the day. There's also a poolside pizzeria, and a small coffee lounge.

While "Freestyle" dining works best aboard the newer, larger ships in the fleet, aboard *Norwegian Dream* and sister *Norwegian Wind* it simply creates food outlets instead of restaurants, and causes confusion. Although the various menus make meals sound appetizing, the food provided is unmemorable fare that lacks taste and presentation quality, and is often overcooked.

There is a decent selection of breads, rolls, and fruits, although the selection of cheeses is poor. The wine list is quite decent and well put together, with moderate prices, although you won't find any good vintage wines (and the wine glasses are small). There are many types of beer (including some on draught in the popular Sports Bar & Grill). The cutlery is very ordinary (there are no fish knives). There is no formal afternoon tea, although you can make your own from various beverage stations.

You can eat breakfast or lunch in any dining room when it's "open seating". A lavish "chocoholics" buffet is featured once each cruise – this is a firm favorite.

ENTERTAINMENT. The Stardust Lounge is the ship's venue for production shows and major cabaret acts. It is two decks high (but the banquette and individual tub chair seating is only on the main level) and is located not in the forward part of the ship as is normal, but in the center.

Two or three production shows are presented in a typical 7-day cruise (all ably performed by the Jean Ann Ryan Company). These are all very colorful, high-energy, high-volume razzle-dazzle shows (with much use of pyrotechnics, laser and color-mover lighting). There's so much happening that, by the end of the evening, if you are a typical passenger, you'll be tired and won't remember much about the shows, which are, however, very entertaining.

The ship carries a number of bands and solo entertaining musicians. These provide live music for listening and dancing in several of the ship's lounges and bars.

SPA/FITNESS. Spa/fitness facilities are located in the forward section of Sports Deck 12 (just aft of an observation lounge), and include a gymnasium with high-tech muscle-toning equipment, a beauty salon, several massage and associated treatment rooms, and men's and women's saunas and changing rooms.

Mandara Spa (headquartered in Honolulu, but owned by Steiner Leisure) is the operator of the spa/fitness center, and provides all staff and treatments as the concession. Note that many of the staff is quite young, and will try to sell you Steiner's own-brand Elemis beauty products.

● **For more extensive general information on what an NCL cruise is like, see pages 122–124.**

Norwegian Majesty
★★★ +

Large (Resort) Ship:	.......40,876 tons	Passenger Decks: 9	Cabins (for one person): 0
Lifestyle:	.................Standard	Total Crew: 620	Cabins (with private balcony): 0
Cruise Line:	......Norwegian Cruise Line	Passengers	Cabins (wheelchair accessible): 7
Former Names:	.........*Royal Majesty*	(lower beds/all berths): 1,460/1,790	Cabin Current: ....110 and 220 volts
Builder:	.........Kvaerner Masa-Yards	Passenger Space Ratio	Elevators: 6
	X(Finland)	(lower beds/all berths): 27.9/22.8	Casino (gaming tables): ....Yes
Original Cost:	.............$229 million	Crew/Passenger Ratio	Slot Machines: ....Yes
Entered Service:	....Sept 1992/Nov 1997	(lower beds/all berths): 2.0/2.5	Swimming Pools (outdoors): 2
Registry:	...............The Bahamas	Navigation Officers: ....Norwegian	Swimming Pools (indoors): 0
Length (ft/m):	...........680.0/207.20	Cabins (total): 730	Whirlpools: 3
Beam (ft/m):	..............90.5/27.60	Size Range (sq ft/m): 118.4–374.5/	Self-Service Launderette: ....No
Draft (ft/m):	................20.3/6.20	11.0–34.8	Dedicated Cinema/Seats: ....No
Propulsion/Propellers:	..........diesel	Cabins (outside view): 481	Library: ....Yes
	(21,120 kW)/2	Cabins (interior/no view): 249	Classification Society: ...Lloyd's Register

OVERALL SCORE: 1,386 (OUT OF A POSSIBLE 2,000 POINTS)

OVERVIEW. This smart, stylish, contemporary cruise ship, originally built for the now defunct Majesty Cruise Line, now has an improved profile and is generally a well-designed vessel (its original lines were those of a Baltic ferry, albeit with a rounded bow, and not at all handsome). The ship underwent a $53.3 million, 110-ft (34-meter) "chop and stretch" and refurbishment operation in 1999, which added more cabins, new public rooms, much more open deck space and two new elevators, while all other existing public spaces were refreshed. For a real "wind-in-the-hair" experience, passengers can actually stand at the very bow of this ship (weather permitting) because all the mooring ropes and winches are on the deck below.

The open deck and sunbathing space has been improved (there are now two swimming pools, plus a splash pool for children). The ship's exterior profile is sleeker and more aerodynamic. Cutting the ship in half, however, required ingenuity, for, unlike *Norwegian Dream* and *Norwegian Wind*, it was never designed for such a splicing operation.

Inside, it is quite a pretty ship, and is tastefully appointed, with lots of wood paneling and chrome/copper accents, reasonably discreet lighting, soothing colors, no glitz and almost no neon lighting. Wide passageways provide a feeling of inner spaciousness. The ship has a nice touch of elegance, and open walking areas provide a fine feel to it. The circular lobby is bright and classical in appearance.

There are several public rooms, bars and lounges in which to play. The Royal Observatory observation lounge has fine views, but is sometimes used as a karaoke lounge. The showlounge, while comfortable, is poorly designed, with 14 pillars obstructing the sightlines. Families with

BERLITZ'S RATINGS

	Possible	Achieved
Ship	500	395
Accommodation	200	156
Food	400	246
Service	400	255
Entertainment	100	69
Cruise	400	265

children will find "Kids' Corner" a useful place to deposit young ones for a full programme of activities.

Norwegian Majesty should provide you with a comfortable cruise experience in warm, fairly elegant surroundings, with generally good food (and plenty of it), and a modicum of hospitality from a reasonably friendly crew, although the service has little finesse. The ship is full of revenue centers, however, which are designed to help part you from your money. You can expect to be subjected to a stream of flyers advertising daily art auctions, "designer" watches and other promotions, while "artworks" for auction are strewn throughout the ship.

Gratuities for staff (cabin attendants, dining room waiters, etc.) are automatically added to your onboard account at $10 per person, per day (you can, however, reduce or otherwise amend these if necessary before you disembark, but in May 2005 the gratuity becomes a non-adjustable "service charge"). In addition, a 15% gratuity is added to all bar and spa treatment accounts. The onboard currency is the US dollar.

There are no cushioned pads for the plastic deck chairs. The buffet area is simply too small for the extra number of passengers carried (while the ship was expanded, the buffet and seating areas were not). While adequate for 3- and 4-day cruises, the ship is only moderately comfortable for 7-day cruises. Standing in line for embarkation, disembarkation, shore tenders and for self-serve buffets is inevitable aboard all large ships.

ACCOMMODATION. There are 22 different price grades – a bewildering choice, and too many for a ship of this size.

The price you pay will depend on the grade, size and location you choose. The suites have concierge service and extra goodies such as late afternoon snacks and hors d'oeuvre items. Although they cannot be considered large, they are quite well equipped, and come with VCRs as well as televisions. Bottled water is placed in each cabin (but a charge will be made if you open the bottle).

Almost all other outside-view and interior (no view) cabins are on the small side, but quite comfortable. The closets are really small, so suitcases have to be stored under the bed to keep them out of the way (this is also the best place for shoes). The bathrooms are a little tight, although there is a generous amount of room in the shower enclosures. A number of cabins are designated for non-smokers. Many cabins on Norway and Viking Decks have obstructed views; so check the deck plans carefully.

CUISINE/DINING. With what NCL calls "Freestyle Dining", you choose which restaurant you wish to eat in, at what time, and with whom (there are no assigned dining rooms, tables or seats). All restaurants and eateries are non-smoking. NCL's dress code states that: "jeans, T-shirts, tank tops and bare feet are not permitted in restaurants."

Although there are two principal dining rooms, there are also a number of other themed eating establishments, giving a wide range of choice – although it would be wise to plan in advance, particularly for dinner.

The main dining rooms are Seven Seas, with 636 seats, and the more intimate Four Seasons (added when the ship was "stretched" in 1999), with 266 seats. However, they are quite noisy and the tables are close together, which means that correct service is difficult. The food, menu, creativity and service are basically quite sound, with a good selection of breads and bread rolls, but the choice of cheeses and fruits is limited (almost all cheeses are American). Some dinners are "themed" – a popular feature.

There is also a 56-seat Le Bistro Restaurant, which serves Italian- and Continental-style cuisine for alternative dinners in an intimate environment (no reservations needed).

For casual, self-serve meals, the Cafe Royale is a small buffet dining spot with 112 seats (not nearly enough for the number of passengers now carried). It is open for breakfast, lunch and snacks. An outdoor grill (oddly named the Piazza San Marco) serves fast food items, including pizza (this can also be delivered to your cabin). A small coffee bar/lounge in an open passageway (street cafe) serves a variety of coffees, coffee-flavored drinks, "flaming" specialty drinks, and teas.

Overall, the food is best described as adequate, but lacks taste and presentation, although the menus make the dishes sound good. The wine list is quite decent and well arranged, together with moderate prices, although you won't find any good vintage wines (and the wine glasses are small). The cutlery is very ordinary (there are no fish knives). There is no formal afternoon tea, although you can make your own from various beverage stations. The service is adequate at best, which proves that good staff members that can communicate well (and know about food) are difficult to find. The breakfast and lunch buffets tend to have unimaginative presentation (more variety and better ingredients needed).

A lavish "chocoholics" buffet is featured once each cruise – this is a firm favorite among Norwegian Cruise Line's passengers.

ENTERTAINMENT. The Palace Showlounge is the room for production shows and major cabaret acts. It is located aft on Majesty Deck and is shaped like an amphitheater, with banquette and individual tub chairs.

Two or three production shows are presented in a typical 7-day cruise (all ably performed by the Jean Ann Ryan Company). These are all very colorful, high-energy, high-volume razzle-dazzle shows (with much use of pyrotechnics, laser and color-mover lighting). There's so much happening that by the end of the evening, if you are a typical passenger, you'll be tired and won't remember much about the shows, which are, however, very entertaining.

The ship carries a number of bands and solo entertaining musicians. These provide live music for listening and dancing in several of the ship's lounges and bars.

SPA/FITNESS. Bodywaves, the spa/fitness center, is located adjacent to the disco at the aft of Promenade Deck, and contains a small gymnasium with muscle-toning equipment, an aerobics exercise area, men's and women's saunas and changing rooms (these are extremely cramped), and Vanity Fair beauty salon.

Mandara Spa (headquartered in Honolulu, but owned by Steiner Leisure) is the operator of the spa/fitness center, and provides all staff and treatments as the concession.

● **For more extensive general information on what an NCL cruise is like, see pages 122–124.**

Norwegian Sea
★★★ +

Large (Resort) Ship: . . . . .42,276 tons	Total Crew: 680	Cabins (with private balcony): 0
Lifestyle: . . . . .Standard	Passengers	Cabins (wheelchair accessible): 4
Cruise Line: . . . . . .Norwegian Cruise Line	(lower beds/all berths): 1,510/1,798	Cabin Current: . . . . .110 volts
Former Names: . . . . .Seaward	Passenger Space Ratio	Elevators: 6
Builder: . . . . .Wartsila (Finland)	(lower beds/all berths): 28.0/23.5	Casino (gaming tables): . . . . .Yes
Original Cost: . . . .$120 million	Crew/Passenger Ratio	Slot Machines: . . . . .Yes
Entered Service: . . . . .June 1988	(lower beds/all berths): 2.3/2.8	Swimming Pools (outdoors): 2
Registry: . . . . .The Bahamas	Navigation Officers: . . . . .Norwegian	Swimming Pools (indoors): 0
Length (ft/m): 708.6/216.0	Cabins (total): 755	Whirlpools: 2
Beam (ft/m): 95.1/29.0	Size Range (sq ft/m): 109.7–269.1/	Self-Service Launderette: . . . . .No
Draft (ft/m): 22.9/7.0	10.2–25.0	Dedicated Cinema/Seats: . . . . .No
Propulsion/Propellers: . . . . .diesel	Cabins (outside view): 512	Library: . . . . .No
(21,120 kW)/2	Cabins (interior/no view): 243	Classification Society: . . . . . . .Det Norske
Passenger Decks: 9	Cabins (for one person): 0	Veritas

OVERALL SCORE: 1,366 (OUT OF A POSSIBLE 2,000 POINTS)

OVERVIEW. *Norwegian Sea* is an angular yet reasonably attractive vessel that has a contemporary European cruise-ferry profile with a sharply raked bow and sleek mast and funnel added. There is a full wrap-around promenade deck outdoors (although it is a plain steel deck, painted nautical blue).

This ship is quite well designed, with generally sound passenger flow and no major areas of congestion, and an abundance of public rooms and open interior spaces, many with high ceilings. The interior decor is designed to remind you of sea and sky by stressing coral, blue and mauve colors. Although the hallways and stairways are plain, two glass-walled stairways provide good connection with sea and sky.

The Crystal Court lobby is two decks high and is pleasing without being overwhelming, although at times it appears quite cluttered. It has a tube-shaped crystal and water sculpture and seatback-less seating around its perimeter.

There is a large nightclub (again there are several pillars obstructing sightlines), and a disco (accurately called "Boomers"). For those seeking a more intimate lounge, the mahogany-panelled Oscar's Lounge is the place to go.

This ship will provide a cruise in good taste for first-time cruise passengers who want to have fun in comfortable surroundings, at a sensible, competitive price. If you like sports bars, country and western music, hoedowns and amateurish participation games, this ship will prove a lot of fun.

Gratuities for staff are added to your onboard account at $10 per person, per day (you can reduce or otherwise amend these if necessary before you disembark, but the gratuity is to become a non-adjustable "service charge"). A 15% gratuity is added to all bar and spa treatment accounts.

BERLITZ'S RATINGS

	Possible	Achieved
Ship	500	357
Accommodation	200	148
Food	400	237
Service	400	278
Entertainment	100	74
Cruise	400	272

The onboard currency is the US dollar.

The open decks are cluttered and largely unclean. The hustling for passengers to attend art auctions is very aggressive and annoying, as is the constant bombardment for revenue activities and the daily junk mail that arrives at one's cabin door. Badly dented and scuffed panels in the accommodation hallways are unattractive. The steps on the stairways are quite tinny. There is no library. The constant background music in the hallways is irritating. There is too much use of synthetic turf on the upper outdoors decks (this gets very soggy when wet). There are no cushioned pads for the deck lounge chairs. The cruise staff is very young and rather amateurish. Standing in line for embarkation, disembarkation, shore tenders and for self-serve buffet meals is an inevitable aspect of cruising aboard all large ships.

REDEPLOYMENT. *Norwegian Sea* will be withdrawn from the NCL fleet in spring 2005, and will be redeployed to the Star Cruises fleet in southeast Asia.

ACCOMMODATION. There are 16 cabin price categories. The price you pay will depend on the grade, to location and size you choose. This ship was built before balcony cabins came into vogue – so there are none.

The cabins are of average size for a standard cruise ship (which translates to "a bit cramped for two") although they are quite tastefully appointed and comfortable, with warm, pastel colors, bright soft furnishings and a touch of art deco styling; however, the walls and ceilings are plain and simple. Audio channels are available via the TV set, although the picture cannot be turned off. The bathrooms are efficient units that are quite well designed, although they are basic; hairdryers (they are weak) are included in all bathrooms. Bottled water is placed in each cabin (but a charge will be made to your account if you open the bottle).

If you book a suite or one of two upper-grade cabins, you'll get a little more space, a lounge area with table and sofa that converts into another bed (good for families), European duvets, and a refrigerator (top three categories only). The bathrooms also have a bathtub, shower and retractable clothesline.

CUISINE/DINING. With NCLs "Freestyle Dining", you can choose which restaurant you would like to eat in, at what time, and with whom (there are no assigned dining rooms, tables or seats). All restaurants and eateries are non-smoking. NCL's dress code states that: "jeans, T-shirts, tank tops and bare feet are not permitted in restaurants."

Although there are two principal dining rooms, there are also a number of other themed eating establishments, giving a wide range of choice – but note that it would be wise to plan in advance, particularly for dinner.

The two main dining rooms are Four Seasons, with 372 seats, and Seven Seas, with 476 seats. They are both comfortable, and have pastel decor. The cuisine, for a mass-market ship, ranges from adequate to reasonably good. Vegetables (few green ones are used) tend to be over-cooked. Fish and poultry items are good. Meat is disappointing. The emphasis is on Tex-Mex cuisine, with a wide choice of hot and spicy courses.

There are several alternative dining spots. For casual breakfast and lunch, there's the Big Apple Cafe (436 seats), which has indoor and outdoor seating. There's also the intimate 82-seat Le Bistro, open for informal dinners; and Gatsby's is a popular wine bar that has a good wine and champagne list. Le Bistro and Gatsby's are both located high in the ship and have large ocean-view picture windows.

Overall, the food provided is best described as adequate, but lacks taste and adequate presentation, although the menus make the dishes sound good. There's a reasonably decent selection of breads, rolls, cheeses and fruits, however. The wine list is quite decent and well arranged, together with moderate prices, although you won't find any good vintage wines (and the wine glasses are small). The cutlery is very ordinary (there are no fish knives). There is no formal afternoon tea, although you can make your own

from various beverage stations. The service is adequate at best, which proves that good staff members that can communicate well (and know about food) are difficult to find. Note that the breakfast and lunch buffets tend to have unimaginative presentation (more variety and better ingredients needed).

A lavish "chocoholics" buffet is featured once each cruise – this is a firm favorite among Norwegian Cruise Line's passengers.

ENTERTAINMENT. The 770-seat Cabaret Lounge is the venue for production shows and major cabaret acts, although 12 thick pillars obstruct the sightlines from many seats.

Two or three production shows are presented in a typical 7-day cruise (all ably performed by the Jean Ann Ryan Company). These are all very colorful, high-energy, razzle-dazzle shows (with much use of pyrotechnics, laser and color-mover lighting). There's so much happening on stage that by the end of the evening, if you are a typical passenger, you will be tired and unable to remember much about the shows, which are, however, very entertaining.

The ship carries a number of bands and solo entertaining musicians, which provide live music for listening and dancing in several of the ship's lounges and bars.

SPA/FITNESS. There's a good gymnasium/fitness center, located around the mast and accessible only from the outside deck (not good when it rains).

Mandara Spa (headquartered in Honolulu, but owned by Steiner Leisure) is the operator of the spa/fitness center, and provides all staff and treatments as the concession. Many of the staff is quite young, and will try to sell you Steiner's own-brand Elemis beauty products (spa girls have sales targets). Some fitness classes are free, while some, such as yoga and kick-boxing, cost $10 per class. However, being aboard will give you an opportunity to try some of the more exotic treatments (particularly some of the massages available). Massage (including Aroma Stone massage, Chakra Balancing massage and other well-being massages), facials, pedicures, and beauty salon treatments cost extra (massage, for example, costs about $2 per minute, plus gratuity).

Do make appointments as early as possible – time slots go quickly, so the day you board is the best time to book your desired treatments.

Norwegian Spirit
★★★★

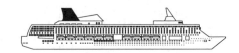

Large (Resort) Ship: . . . . .75,338 tons	Total Crew: .1,300	Cabins (with private balcony): 374
Lifestyle: . . . . .Standard	Passengers	Cabins (wheelchair accessible): 4
Cruise Line: . . . . . .Norwegian Cruise Line	(lower beds/all berths): 1,966/2,475	Cabin Current: . . . . .240 volts
Former Names: . . . .*SuperStar Leo*	Passenger Space Ratio	Elevators: 9
Builder: . . . . .Meyer Werft (Germany)	(lower beds/all berths): 38.1/30.4	Casino (gaming tables): . . . . .Yes
Original Cost: . . . .$350 million	Crew/Passenger Ratio	Slot Machines: . . . . .Yes
Entered Service: . . . . .Oct 1998/May 2004	(lower beds/all berths): 1.5/2.1	Swimming Pools (outdoors): 2
Registry: . . . . .Panama	Navigation Officers: . . . . . .Scandinavian	Swimming Pools (indoors): 0
Length (ft/m): 879.2/268.0	Cabins (total): 983	Whirlpools: 4
Beam (ft/m): 105.6/32.2	Size Range (sq ft/m): 150.6–638.3/	Self-Service Launderette: . . . . .No
Draft (ft/m): 25.9/7.9	14.0–59.3	Dedicated Cinema/Seats: . . . . .No
Propulsion/Propellers: . . . . .2 diesels	Cabins (outside view): 609	Library: . . . . .Yes
(50,400kW)/2	Cabins (interior/no view): 379	Classification Society: . . . . . . .Det Norske
Passenger Decks: 10	Cabins (for one person): 0	Veritas

OVERALL SCORE: 1,497 (OUT OF A POSSIBLE 2,000 POINTS)

OVERVIEW. *Norwegian Spirit* (ex-*Super-Star Leo*), was the first brand new ship ordered by parent company Star Cruises specifically for the Southeast Asia market. It was moved to NCL in 2004 in a fleet redeployment. There is a full wrap-around promenade deck outdoors, good for strolling, and lots of outdoor space, including a whole area devoted to children's outdoor activities and pool.

Inside, there are two indoor boulevards, and a stunning, six-deck-high central atrium lobby, with three glass-walled lifts and ample space to peruse the shops and cafes that line its inner sanctum. The lobby itself is modeled after the lobby of the Hyatt Hotel in Hong Kong, with little clutter from the usual run of desks found aboard other cruise ships.

The interior design theme revolves around art, architecture, history and literature. The ship has a mix of both eastern and western design and decor details. Three stairways are each carpeted in a different color, which helps new cruise passengers find their way around easily.

A 450-seat room atop the ship functions as an observation lounge during the day and a nightclub at night, with live music. From it, a spiral stairway takes you down to a navigation bridge viewing area, where you can see the captain and bridge officers at work.

There is a business center (complete with conference center – good for small groups) and writing room, and a smoking room, for those who enjoy cigars and cognac. A shopping concourse is set around the second level of the lobby.

Want the casino? The casino complex is at the forward end of the atrium boulevard on Deck 7 (not between showlounge and restaurant as in most western ships). This includes a large general purpose, brightly lit casino,

BERLITZ'S RATINGS

	Possible	Achieved
Ship	500	421
Accommodation	200	154
Food	400	286
Service	400	278
Entertainment	100	61
Cruise	400	297

Maharajah's, with gaming tables and slot machines.

Families with children should note that teens have their own huge video arcade, while younger children get to play in a wet 'n' wild aft pool (complete with pirate ship and caves) and two whirlpool tubs. Plus there's all the fun and facilities of Charlie's childcare center, which includes a painting room, computer learning center, and small cinema. Even the toilets are at a special low height, and there's a room full of cots for toddlers. Over 15,000 sq. ft (1,400 sq. meters) is devoted to children's facilities – all tucked well away from adult recreation areas.

The dress code is extremely casual (no jacket and tie needed). Watch out for the extra costs and charges to mount up if you order more than the basics. With many dining choices (some of which cost extra) to accommodate different tastes and styles, your cruise and dining experience will largely depend on how much you are prepared to spend. Gratuities for staff (non-adjustable from May 2005) are added to your onboard account, and 15 percent is added to all bar, wine and spa accounts. The onboard currency is the U.S. dollar.

Because this is quite a stunning ship and offers a wide choice of dining venues, keeping consistency of product delivery will depend on the quality of the service and supervisory staff. There are many extra-cost items (in addition to the à la carte/extra charge dining spots), and there is constant intrusion into your cruise experience with announcements for things such as art auctions, bingo and horse racing. Note that standing in line for embarkation, disembarkation, shore tenders and for self-serve buffet meals is an inevitable aspect of cruising aboard all large ships.

ACCOMMODATION. Three whole decks of cabins have private balconies, while two-thirds of all cabins have an outside view. Both the standard outside-view and interior (no view) cabins really are very small (particularly given that all cabins have extra berths for a third/fourth person), although the bathrooms have a good-sized shower enclosure. So, take only the smallest amount of clothing you can get away with. All cabins have a personal safe, 100% cotton towels and 100% cotton duvets or sheets. Note that, in cabins with balconies, the balconies are extremely narrow, and the cabins themselves are very small (the ship was originally constructed for 3- and 4-day cruises).

Choose one of the six largest Executive Suites (named Hong Kong, Malaysia, Shanghai, Singapore, Thailand and Tokyo) and you'll have an excellent amount of private living space, with separate lounge, and bedroom. Each has a large en-suite bathroom that is part of the bedroom and opens onto it. It has a gorgeous mosaic tiled floor, kidney bean-shaped whirlpool bathtub, two sinks, separate shower enclosure (with floor-to-ceiling ocean-view window) and separate toilet (with glass door). There are TV sets in the lounge, bedroom and bathroom. The Singapore and Hong Kong suites and the Malaysia and Thai suites can be combined to form a double suite (good for families with children). Butler service and concierge come with the territory.

Choose one of the 12 Zodiac suites (each is named after a sign of the Zodiac) and you will get the second largest accommodation aboard the ship. Each suite has a separate lounge, bedroom, and bathroom, and an interconnecting door to an ocean-view cabin with private balcony (good for families). All cabinetry features richly lacquered woods, large (stocked) wet bar with refrigerator, dining table (with a top that flips over to reveal a card table) and four chairs, sofa and drinks table, and trouser press. The bedrooms are small, but have a queen-sized bed; there is a decent amount of drawer space, although the closet space is rather tight (it contains two personal safes). The large en-suite bathrooms are similarly designed to those in the Executive Suites.

A small room service menu is available (all items are at extra cost, and both a 15% service charge as well as a gratuity are added to your account). Butler service and concierge come with the territory.

CUISINE/DINING. There is certainly plenty of choice when it comes to formal dining and casual eateries. There are, in all, eight places to eat (all are non-smoking), of which two are at extra charge. You will, therefore, need to plan where you want to eat well in advance, or you may be disappointed. **Windows Restaurant:** The equivalent of a main dining room, this seats 632 in two seatings, is two decks high at the aft-most section, and has huge cathedral-style windows set in three sections overlooking the ship's stern and wake. Waiter stations are tucked neatly away in side wings, which help to keep down noise levels.

Garden Room Restaurant: This has 268 seats.
Raffles Terrace Cafe: a large self-serve buffet restaurant with indoor/outdoor seating for 400 and pseudo-Raffles Hotel-like decor, with rattan chairs, overhead fans, etc.
Taipan: a Chinese Restaurant, with traditional Hong Kong-themed decor and items such as dim sum made from fresh, not frozen, ingredients (cover charge applicable, reservations necessary).
Shogun Asian Restaurant: a Japanese restaurant and sushi bar, for sashimi, sushi, and tempura. A section can be closed off to make the Samurai Room, with 22 seats, while a traditional Tatami Room has seats for eight. There's also a teppanyaki grill, with 10 seats, where the chef cooks in front of you.
Maxim's: a small à la carte restaurant with ocean-view windows; fine cuisine in the classic French style (cover charge applicable, reservations necessary).
Blue Lagoon Café: a small, casual street cafe with about 24 seats, featuring noodle dishes, fried rice and other Southeast Asian cuisine (adjacent is a street bar called The Bund).
The Café: a casual pâtisserie serving several types of coffees, teas, cakes and pastries (at extra cost), in the atrium lobby.

ENTERTAINMENT. The Moulin Rouge Showlounge, with 973 seats, is the main venue. It is two decks high, with a main and balcony levels. The room has almost no support columns to obstruct the sightlines, and a revolving stage for Broadway-style reviews and other production shows (typically to recorded music), although there's little space for an orchestra. The show lounge is also used as a large-screen cinema, and has excellent surround sound.

SPA/FITNESS. The Roman Spa and Fitness Center is located on one of the uppermost decks, just forward of the Tivoli Pool. It has a gymnasium full of high-tech muscle-toning equipment, and aerobics exercise room, hair and beauty salon, and saunas, steam rooms, and changing rooms for men and women, as well as several treatment rooms, and aqua-swim pools that provide counter-flow jets (swimming against the current). The spa facility is operated by the Hawaii-based Mandara Spa, owned by Steiner Leisure.

The fitness and exercise rooms are located not within the spa, but at the top of the glass-domed atrium lobby (they feature the latest Cybex muscle-pumping equipment). Included is a room for exercycle classes. Sports facilities include a jogging track, golf driving range, basketball and tennis courts, and there are four levels of sunbathing decks.

Norwegian Star
★★★★

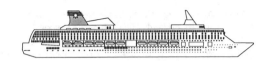

Large (Resort) Ship:	.......91,740 tons	Total Crew:	1,100
Lifestyle:	..................Standard	Passengers	
Cruise Line:	......Norwegian Cruise Line	(lower beds/all berths):	.....2,244/4,080
Former Names:	....................none	Passenger Space Ratio	
Builder:	........Meyer Werft (Germany)	(lower beds/all berths):	........40.8/22.4
Original Cost:	.............$400 million	Crew/Passenger Ratio	
Entered Service:	.............Dec 2001	(lower beds/all berths):	..........2.0/3.7
Registry:	....................Panama	Navigation Officers:	.......Scandinavian
Length (ft/m):	...........964.9/294.13	Cabins (total):	1,122
Beam (ft/m):	..............105.6/32.2	Size Range (sq ft/m):	.....142.0–5,350.0/
Draft (ft/m):	..................26.9/8.2		13.2–497.0
Propulsion/Propellers:	...diesel-electric/2	Cabins (outside view):	787
	azimuthing pods (19.5 MW each)	Cabins (interior/no view):	363
Passenger Decks:	12	Cabins (for one person):	0

Cabins (with private balcony):	509
Cabins (wheelchair accessible):	20
Cabin Current:	.................110 AC
Elevators:	12
Casino (gaming tables):	...........Yes
Slot Machines:	....................Yes
Swimming Pools (outdoors):	2
Swimming Pools (indoors):	1
Whirlpools:	...4 (+ 1 children's whirlpool)
Self-Service Launderette:	...........No
Dedicated Cinema/Seats:	......Yes/151
Library:	..........................Yes
Classification Society:	Det Norske Veritas

OVERALL SCORE: 1,522 (OUT OF A POSSIBLE 2,000 POINTS)

OVERVIEW. *Norwegian Star* is a state-of-the-art vessel for Norwegian Cruise Line – the first of a pair of sister ships, the second being *Norwegian Dawn*, which debuted in 2002. It has a "pod" propulsion system *(see page 151 for explanation)*. A large structure located forward of the funnel houses a children's center, and, one deck above, the two outstanding "villa" suites described in the accommodation section above. The ship's hull is adorned with a decal consisting of a burst of colorful stars and streamers.

There are plenty of deck lounge chairs (in fact, the number is greater than the number of passengers carried). Water slides are included for the adult swimming pools (children have their own pools at the ship's stern – out of sight of the adult areas).

Inside the ship, you'll be met by a truly eclectic mix of bright colors and decor that you probably wouldn't have in your home (unless you were color-blind) – and yet somehow it works extremely well in this large ship setting that is meant to attract young, active types.

Facilities include an Internet Cafe (with 17 computer stations), a 1,150-seat showlounge with main floor and two balcony levels, 3,000-book library, card room, writing and study room, business center, karaoke lounge, conference and meeting rooms and associated facilities, and a retail shopping complex of 20,000 sq. ft (1,800 sq. meters). In 2004, a 929-sq. meter (10,000-sq. ft) casino was added.

Children of all ages will get to play in a superb wet 'n' wild space-themed water park (complete with large pool, water slide, and paddle pool). They also get their own dedicated cinema (DVD movies are featured all day long), a jungle gym, painting area, and computer center. Even the

BERLITZ'S RATINGS

	Possible	Achieved
Ship	500	421
Accommodation	200	156
Food	400	293
Service	400	284
Entertainment	100	66
Cruise	400	302

toilets are at a special low height. Teens, too, are well catered for, and get their own cinema (with DVD movies), discotheque with dance floor, and whirlpool (hot) tub.

With so many dining choices (some costing extra) to accommodate the tastes of an eclectic mix of nationalities, the amount you are prepared to spend will determine what your final cruise and dining experience will be like. To make the most of your vacation, you will need to plan where you want to eat well in advance, and make the necessary reservations, or you may be disappointed. More choices, including more dining options, add up to a very attractive package, particularly suitable for families with children, in a very contemporary floating leisure center that really does provide ample facilities for enjoyment, as well as provide you with the opportunity to immerse yourself in all things Hawaiian. The dress code is very casual (no jacket and tie needed, although you are welcome to dress formally if you wish).

While the initial cruise fare seems very reasonable, the extra costs and charges soon mount up if you want more than the basics. Although service levels and finesse are sometimes inconsistent (this was especially true when the ship was first went into service), the level of hospitality is very good – made so much better and brighter by the addition of a great number of Asian female staff rather than the surly and inconsistent Caribbean staff still found on some of the smaller NCL ships.

Despite the company's name (Norwegian Cruise Line), there's almost nothing Norwegian about this product, except for some of the ship's senior officers. The staff, incidentally, includes many Southeast Asians who have service experience aboard parent company Star Cruises' big ships.

Gratuities for staff (cabin attendants, dining room waiters, etc) are added to your onboard account at $10 per person, per day (you can reduce or otherwise amend these if necessary before you disembark, but in May 2005 the gratuity becomes a non-adjustable "service charge"). In addition, a 15% gratuity is added to all bar and spa treatment accounts. The onboard currency is the US dollar.

There is not really that much time spent in ports in the Hawaiian Islands (the only full day is on the island of Oahu). Although the suites and junior suites are quite spacious, the standard interior (no view) and outside-view cabins are very small when compared to those of other major cruise lines such as Carnival or Celebrity, particularly when occupied by three or four persons (the bathrooms, however, are of quite a decent size, and have large shower enclosures). The hustling for passengers to attend art auctions is both aggressive and annoying. Standing in line for embarkation, disembarkation, shore tenders and for self-serve buffet meals is an inevitable aspect of cruising aboard all large ships – even those designated as "Freestyle".

Reaching room service tends to be an exercise in frustration. Communication (particularly between the many new Asian staff and passengers) remains weak. Mindless "art auctions" are a real turn-off on a Hawaiian cruise.

ACCOMMODATION. With 29 price grades, this is a mix that includes something for everyone. There are 36 suites (including two of the largest aboard any cruise ship); 372 "balcony-class" standard cabins with private balconies, 415 outside-view cabins (no balcony); 363 interior (no view) cabins; 36 suites with balconies, and 20 wheelchair-accessible cabins. Suites and cabins with private balconies have easy-to-use sliding glass doors.

Regardless of the accommodation (and thus the price you pay for your cruise), all have a powerful hairdryer (located in the cabin itself, and not, thankfully, in the bathroom), and a tea and coffee making sets, rich cherry wood cabinetry, and a bathroom with a sliding door and a separate toilet, shower enclosure and washbasin compartments. There is plenty of wood accenting in all accommodation, including wood frames surrounding balcony doors – a nice touch that will be subliminally appreciated by passengers.

The largest accommodation is in two huge Garden Villas (Vista and Horizon), located high atop the ship in a pod that is located forward of the ship's funnel, and overlooks the main swimming pool. These villas have huge glass walls and landscaped private roof gardens (one has a Japanese-style garden, the other a Thai-style garden) for outdoor dining (with whirlpool tubs, naturally), and huge private sunbathing areas that are completely shielded from anyone; the garden itself extends to 1,720 sq. ft (160 sq. meters). Each suite has three bedrooms (one with a sliding glass door that leads to the garden) and bathrooms (one bathroom has a large corner tub, and two washbasins set in front of large glass walls that overlook the side of the ship as well as the swimming pool, although most of the view is of the over-large waterslide), and a large living room (with Yamaha baby grand piano) with glass dining table and eight chairs, overlooking the lido/pool deck. These units have their own private elevator and private stairway, and can be combined to create a large, 10,700 sq.-ft (994 sq.-meter) "house" (the garden is included in the measurements)

There are many suites (the smallest measures 290 sq. ft/27 sq. meters) in several different configurations. Some overlook the stern, while others are in the forward part of the ship. All are lavishly furnished, although closet space in some of the smaller units is tight.

Although they are nicely furnished and quite well equipped, the standard outside-view and interior (no view) cabins are quite small, particularly when occupied by three or four persons. Some cabins have interconnecting doors (good for families with children), and many cabins have third- and fourth-person pull-down berths or trundle beds.

A small room service menu is available (all items are at extra cost, and a 15% service charge and a gratuity are automatically added to your account). Bottled water is placed in each cabin, but a charge will be made to your account if you open the bottle.

CUISINE/DINING. NCL features "Freestyle Dining", so you can choose which restaurant to eat in, at what time, and with whom. You can eat in a different restaurant every night – just like going out on the town ashore – or you can eat in the same restaurant every day, even having the same waiter, as in traditional cruising. Freestyle Dining also appears to work far better for individuals rather than large groups. All restaurants and eateries are non-smoking. The dress code states that: "jeans, T-shirts, tank tops and bare feet are not permitted in restaurants", although this is not followed in practice, particularly when families with young children are aboard at peak holiday times. On Formal Nights, many passengers want to eat in the two large main dining rooms, and this can create a logjam.

Although there are two main dining rooms (come when you want), there are several other themed eating establishments, giving a wide range of choice. It would be wise to plan in advance, particularly for dinner. In fact, there are two entire decks of dining establishments to choose from, involving 10 different restaurants and eateries, and 11 different menus nightly.

● **Versailles**, the ornate 375-seat first main dining room, is decorated in brilliant red and gold. This offers the traditional six-course dining experience (open 5.30pm–midnight). This is located aft and has excellent views through windows that span two decks.

● **Aqua:** a contemporary-styled 374-seat second main dining room, offering lighter cuisine (open 5.30pm–midnight), and an open galley where you can view the preparation of pastries and dessert items.

● **Soho:** Pacific Rim cuisine is where East meets West (California and Asian cuisine) in culinary terms. Has a live lobster tank (the first aboard a ship outside Southeast Asia). A main dining area that can seat 132, plus private dining rooms (each seats 10). A collection of pop art (including Andy Warhol prints) adorns the walls.

● **Ginza:** a Japanese restaurant, with 193 seats, a sit-up sushi bar, tempura bar, show galley, and separate "teppan-yaki grill" room.

● **Le Bistro:** a French restaurant, with 66 seats, serving nouvelle cuisine and six courses.

● **Blue Lagoon:** a funky food court-style eatery with 88 seats (both indoors and outdoors on the Promenade Deck), with hamburgers, fish and chips, potpies and fast (wok stir-fried) dishes.

● **Market Cafe:** a large indoor/outdoor self-serve buffet eatery, with almost 400 ft (120 meters) of buffet counter space. "Action Stations" has made-to-order omelets, waffles, fruit, soups, ethnic specialities and pasta dishes.

● **La Trattoria,** an Italian (evening only) dining spot located within the indoor/outdoor buffet area, has pasta, pizza and other popular Italian fare.

● **Steakhouse:** this serves prime USDA beef steaks and lamb chops.

● **Endless Summer:** a Hawaiian themed restaurant – arranged around the second level of the central atrium and incorporating a performance stage and a large movie screen.

Other eating/drinking spots include the Red Lion (an English pub for draft beer and perhaps a game of darts); Havana Club, a cigar and cognac lounge; Java Cafe, an atrium lobby Cafe and bar (for hot and frozen coffees, teas and pastries); a Beer Garden (for grilled foods); a Spinkles (an ice cream bar); a Gym and Spa Bar (for health food snacks and drinks); and Gatsby's wine bar (at the entrance to Soho).

Overall, the food provided is adequate, but lacks taste and presentation quality, although the menus make the dishes sound good. There's a reasonably decent selection of breads, rolls, cheeses and fruits. The wine list is quite decent and well arranged, together with moderate prices, although you won't find any good vintage wines (and the wine glasses are small). The cutlery is very ordinary (there are no fish knives). There is no formal afternoon tea, although you can make your own from various beverage stations. Overall service is just so-so. Breakfast and lunch buffets tend to have unimaginative presentation (more variety and better ingredients would be useful).

A lavish "chocoholics" buffet is available once each cruise – a firm favorite among regular passengers.

ENTERTAINMENT. The Stardust Theatre seats 1,037, and is the venue for colorful Las-Vegas-style production shows and major cabaret acts. It is designed in the style of an opera house, spans three decks, and has a steeply tiered main floor and port and starboard balconies.

Two or three production shows are presented in a typical 7-day cruise (all ably performed by the Jean Ann Ryan Company). These are all very colorful, high-energy, high-volume razzle-dazzle shows (with much use of pyrotechnics, laser and color-mover lighting). There's so much happening that by the end of the evening, if you are a typical passenger, you'll be tired and won't remember a great deal about the shows – which are, however, very entertaining.

The ship has a number of bands and solo entertaining musicians, which provide live music for listening and dancing in several of the ship's lounges and bars.

SPA/FITNESS. Wellness devotees should enjoy the two-deck-high Barong health spa complex (operated by the Hawaii-based Mandara Spa, owned by Steiner), located at the stern of the ship (with large ocean-view windows on three sides). There are many facilities and services to pamper you (almost all at extra charge), including Thai massage (in the spa, outdoors on deck, in your cabin or on your private balcony). In addition, there is an indoor lap pool (measuring 37 ft/11.2 meters), hydrotherapy pool, aromatherapy and wellness centers, and mud treatment room treatment rooms (there are 15 treatment rooms in all, including one specifically designed for couples).

Mandara Spa (headquartered in Honolulu, but owned by Steiner Leisure) is the operator of the spa/fitness center, and provides all staff and treatments as the concession.

The fitness and exercise rooms are not within the spa, but at the top of the atrium lobby, and have the latest Cybex muscle-pumping equipment. Included is a room for exercycle classes. Recreational sports facilities include a jogging track, golf driving range, basketball and volleyball courts, as well as four levels of sunbathing decks.

● **For more extensive general information on what an NCL cruise is like, see pages 122–124.**

Norwegian Sun
★★★★

Large (Resort) Ship: ....78,309 tons	Total Crew: 980	Cabins (with private balcony): 252
Lifestyle: ....Standard	Passengers	Cabins (wheelchair accessible): 6
Cruise Line: ......Norwegian Cruise Line	(lower beds/all berths): 2,002/2,400	Cabin Current: ....110 volts
Former Names: ....none	Passenger Space Ratio	Elevators: 12
Builder: ....Lloyd Werft (Germany)	(lower beds/all berths):........39.1/32.6	Casino (gaming tables): ....Yes
Original Cost: ....$332 million	Crew/Passenger Ratio	Slot Machines: ....Yes
Entered Service: ....Nov 2001	(lower beds/all berths): 2.0/2.4	Swimming Pools (outdoors): 2
Registry: ....The Bahamas	Navigation Officers: ....Norwegian	Swimming Pools (indoors): 0
Length (ft/m): 853.0/260.00	Cabins (total): 1,001	Whirlpools: 4
Beam (ft/m): 105.8/32.25	Size Range (sq ft/m): 120.5–488.6/	Self-Service Launderette: ....No
Draft (ft/m): 26.2/8.00	11.2–45.4	Dedicated Cinema/Seats: ....No
Propulsion/Propellers: .....diesel-electric	Cabins (outside view): 675	Library: ....Yes
(50,000 kW)/2	Cabins (interior/no view): 326	Classification Society: .....Germanischer
Passenger Decks:.................12	Cabins (for one person): 0	Lloyd

OVERALL SCORE: 1,517 (OUT OF A POSSIBLE 2,000 POINTS)

OVERVIEW. *Norwegian Sun* is a close sister ship to *Norwegian Sky* (now renamed *Pride of Aloha*) but with improved outfitting and finishing detail, with one additional deck of balcony cabins, and crew cabins have been added to accommodate an extra 200 crew. The amount of outdoor space is quite good, especially the ultra-wide pool deck, with its two swimming pools and four Jacuzzi tubs, and plenty of deck lounge chairs, albeit arranged in rows, camp-style.

A separate cabaret venue, Dazzles Lounge, has an extremely long bar. Other features include a large casino (this will operate 24 hours a day, with special facilities and rooms for high-rollers and "club" members), a shopping arcade, children's playroom (there is also a splash pool in a prime open deck area), and a video arcade.

Other facilities include a small conference room, library and beauty salon, a lounge for smoking cigars and drinking cognac, and an internet cafe, located on the Promenade Deck within the ship's atrium lobby, with 20 computer stations. Numerous shops showcase a wide range of goods, from inexpensive to very expensive.

Young passengers will find an array of facilities, which include a children's playroom called Kid's Corner (for "junior sailors" ages 3–5; (First Mates (ages 6–9); Navigators (ages 10–12); and Teens (ages 13–17).

With this ship, Norwegian Cruise Line has made an effort to provide more and better public rooms and more entertainment facilities than aboard its smaller ships. There are certainly plenty of options for eating. But the ship is full of revenue centers, designed to help you part from your money. You can expect to be subjected to a stream of flyers advertising daily art auctions, "designer" watches, and

BERLITZ'S RATINGS

	Possible	Achieved
Ship	500	410
Accommodation	200	152
Food	400	289
Service	400	284
Entertainment	100	78
Cruise	400	304

other promotions, while "artworks" for auction are strewn throughout the ship.

Gratuities for staff (cabin attendants, dining room waiters, etc) are added to your onboard account at $10 per person, per day (you can, however, reduce or otherwise amend these before you disembark, but in May 2005 the gratuity becomes a non-adjustable "service charge"). In addition, a 15% gratuity is added to bar and spa accounts. The onboard currency is the US dollar.

The standard interior (no view) and outside-view cabins are very small when compared to those of other major cruise lines. The food in the large dining rooms is a weak point. There are many plastic plates, Styrofoam and plastic cups and plastic stirrers in use in the casual eateries.

ACCOMMODATION. There are 30 different categories, including 6 grades of suites, 15 grades of outside-view cabins and nine grades of interior (no view) cabins, so choosing the right accommodation requires some thought.

All of the standard outside-view and interior (no view) cabins have common facilities, such as: two lower beds that can convert to a queen-sized bed, a small lounge area with sofa and table, and a decent amount of closet and drawer space, although the cabins themselves are disappointingly small. Over 200 outside-view cabins have a private balcony. Each cabin has a small vanity/ writing desk, color TV set, personal safe, refrigerator, climate control, and laptop computer connection socket. Bottled water is placed in each cabin (but a charge will be made to your account if you open the bottle).

There are two Honeymoon/Anniversary Suites, located at the front of the ship, with forward facing and side views.

Each suite has a separate lounge and bedroom. The lounge has a large dining table and chairs, two sofas, large television, DVD/CD player, coffee table, queen-sized pull-down Murphy's bed, guest closet, writing desk, wet bar with two bar stools, refrigerator and sink, several cupboards for glasses, and several drawers and other cupboards for storage. The sleeping area has twin beds that convert to a queen-sized bed, and walk-in closet with a good amount of hanging space. The tiled bathroom, although not large, has a full-size whirlpool tub and shower, retractable clothesline, deep washbasin, and personal toiletries cabinets.

The largest accommodation is in two Owner's Suites – each with a hot tub, large teak table, two chairs and two deck lounge chairs outside on a huge, private, forward-facing teak floor balcony just under the ship's navigation bridge, with large floor-to-ceiling windows. Each suite has a separate lounge and bedroom. The lounge has a large dining table and chairs, two sofas, large TV set, DVD/CD player, coffee table, queen-sized pull-down Murphy's bed, guest closet, writing desk, wet bar with two bar stools, refrigerator and sink, several cupboards for glasses, and several drawers and other cupboards for storage. The bedroom, with sliding wood half-doors that look into the lounge, has a queen-sized bed (with European duvet) under a leaf-glass chandelier, vanity desk, TV set, walk-in closet with plenty of hanging rail space, several open shelves and large personal safe. The tiled bathroom, although not large, has a full-size tub with retractable clothesline above, separate shower enclosure with glass doors, deep washbasin, and personal toiletries cabinets.

There are also a number of other suites – each with a private teakwood balcony; these suites face aft in a secluded position and overlook the ship's wash. They have some of the same facilities as found in the owner's suites, except for the outdoor hot tub, and the fact that there is less space. All cabins have tea/coffee making sets, personal safe, satellite-linked telephone, and private bathroom with bath or shower.

CUISINE/DINING. NCL has "Freestyle Dining", so you can choose which restaurant you would like to eat in, at what time, and with whom. Although there are two large dining rooms, there are also a number of other themed eating establishments, giving a wide range of choice – although it would be wise to plan in advance, particularly for dinner. All restaurants and eateries are non-smoking, and some incur an extra charge. The dress code states that: "jeans, T-shirts, tank tops and bare feet are not permitted in restaurants."

The two main dining rooms – the 564-seat Four Seasons Dining Room, and the 604-seat Seven Seas Dining Room, have tables for four, six or eight (there are no tables for two). Sandwiched between the two (rather like a train carriage) is a third, 84-seat Italian Restaurant, Il Adagio, available as an à la carte dining option (for which there is an extra charge), with window-side tables for two or four persons. Reservations are necessary.

There are also several other dining options, most located on one of the upper-most decks of the ship, with great views from large picture windows. These include:

● **Le Bistro:** a 90-seat alternative dining spot for some fine French-style meals, including tableside cooking. Reservations are necessary for dinner.
● **Las Ramblas:** a Spanish/Mexican style eatery serving tapas (light snack items).
● **Ginza:** a Japanese Restaurant, with a sushi bar and a teppanyaki grill (show cooking in a U-shaped setting where you sit around the chef). Reservations are needed for dinner.
● **East Meets West:** a Pacific Rim Fusion Restaurant, featuring a la carte California/Hawaii/Asian cuisine. Reservations are necessary for dinner.
● **Pacific Heights:** a Healthy Living Restaurant (with 80 seats), featuring spa cuisine and Cooking Light menus. Reservations are necessary for dinner.
● **Garden Cafe:** a 24-hour restaurant indoor/outdoor self-serve buffet-style eatery with fast foods and salads.

Although the menus make meals sound appetizing, overall the food is rather unmemorable, lacking taste and mostly overcooked. However, the presentation is generally quite good. There is a reasonable selection of breads, rolls, and pastry items, but the selection of cheeses is very poor.

The wine list is well balanced, and there is also a connoisseur list of premium wines, although the vintages tend to be young. There are many types of beer (including some on draught in the popular Sports Bar & Grill).

There is no formal afternoon tea, although you can make your own at beverage stations (but only the most basic ingredients are provided – it's difficult to get fresh milk, for example, as non-dairy "creamers" are typically supplied). The service is, on the whole, adequate, nothing more.

A lavish "chocoholics" buffet is featured once each cruise – a firm favorite among NCL passengers.

ENTERTAINMENT. The Stardust Theater is a two-level show lounge with more than 1,000 seats and a large proscenium stage. However, the sightlines are obstructed in a number of seats by several slim pillars. Two or three production shows are presented in a typical 7-day cruise (all ably performed by the Jean Ann Ryan Company). These are all very colorful, high-energy, high-volume razzle-dazzle shows (with much use of pyrotechnics, laser and color-mover lighting). The ship carries a number of bands and solo entertaining musicians. These provide live music for listening and dancing in several of the lounges and bars.

SPA/FITNESS. Bodywaves, at the top of the atrium, is a large health/fitness spa (including an aerobics room and separate gymnasium), several treatment rooms, and men's and women's saunas/steam rooms and changing rooms.

There is a wrap-around indoor-outdoor jogging track. a large basketball/volleyball court, baseball-batting cage, golf-driving range, platform tennis, shuffleboard and table tennis facilities, and sports bar with 24-hour live satellite TV coverage of sports events and major games.

● **For more extensive general information on what an NCL cruise is like, see pages 122–124.**

Norwegian Wind
★★★ +

Large (Resort) Ship: ....50,760 tons	Total Crew: 700	Cabins (wheelchair accessible): 6
Lifestyle: ....Standard	Passengers	(+ 30 for hearing impaired)
Cruise Line: ......Norwegian Cruise Line	(lower beds/all berths): 1,750/2,156	Cabin Current: ....110 volts
Former Names: ....*Windward*	Passenger Space Ratio	Elevators: 10
Builder: ....Chantiers de l'Atlantique	(lower beds/all berths): 29.0/23.5	Casino (gaming tables): ....Yes
(France)	Crew/Passenger Ratio	Slot Machines: ....Yes
Original Cost: ....$240 million	(lower beds/all berths): 2.5/3.1	Swimming Pools (outdoors): 2
Entered Service: ....June 1993	Navigation Officers: ....Norwegian	Swimming Pools (indoors): 0
Registry: ....The Bahamas	Cabins (total): 875	Whirlpools: 2
Length (ft/m): 754.0/229.8	Size Range (sq ft/m): 139.9–349.8/	Self-Service Launderette: ....No
Beam (ft/m): 93.5/28.5	13.0–32.5	Dedicated Cinema/Seats: ....No
Draft (ft/m): 22.3/6.8	Cabins (outside view): 696	Library: ....Yes
Propulsion/Propellers: ....diesel	Cabins (interior/no view): 179	Classification Society: ......Det Norske
(18,480 kW)/2	Cabins (for one person): 0	Veritas
Passenger Decks:.................10	Cabins (with private balcony): 48	

OVERALL SCORE: 1,381 (OUT OF A POSSIBLE 2,000 POINTS)

OVERVIEW. *Norwegian Wind* is the sister ship to *Norwegian Dream*, and, as such, has a moderately handsome profile (despite a large, square blue funnel), that was actually rather better balanced before the ship underwent a "chop and stretch" operation in 1998. A completely new mid-section was added, and the funnel was adapted so that it could be "folded" over to allow the ship to transit the Kiel Canal in Germany. Included in the 130-ft (40-meter) section were 251 new passenger cabins and 50 crew cabins, together with several new or enlarged public rooms (although there simply are not enough) and a 60-seat conference center.

Some innovative features were incorporated in the original design, and these have been enhanced. The passenger flow is generally good – indeed, the ship seems to absorb passengers quite well for much of the time, except at peak traffic times between dinner seatings. There is a blue rubber-covered wrap-around promenade deck outdoors. The tiered pool deck is neat, as are the multi-deck aft sun terraces and all her fore and aft connecting exterior stairways.

The overall exterior design emphasizes a clever and extensive use of large windows that create a sense of open spaces, although the interior design provides many smaller public rooms rather than the large hangers found aboard so many other ships. However, there is no big atrium lobby, as one might expect. The pastel interior colors used are quite soothing, and is considered by many to be a pretty ship inside. The entrance lobby is not at all attractive, and feels rather confined for a ship of this size.

This ship has been highly successful for Norwegian Cruise Line's younger, active sports-minded passengers, and

BERLITZ'S RATINGS

	Possible	Achieved
Ship	500	377
Accommodation	200	145
Food	400	237
Service	400	282
Entertainment	100	73
Cruise	400	267

is a good alternative to the bigger ships and their larger passenger numbers, although there are still plenty of other passengers to keep you company. The dress code is casual, and there are no formal nights when you have to dress up.

Gratuities for staff (cabin attendants, dining room waiters, etc) are automatically added to your onboard account at $10 per person, per day (you can, however, reduce or otherwise amend these if necessary before you disembark, but in May 2005 the gratuity becomes a non-adjustable "service charge"). In addition, a 15% gratuity is added to all bar and spa treatment accounts. The onboard currency is the US dollar.

The hustling for passengers to attend art auctions is very aggressive and annoying, as is the constant bombardment for revenue activities and the daily junk mail that arrives at one's cabin door. The room service menu is still poor and could be improved. The outdoor stairways are numerous and confusing. The carpeted steel interior stairwell steps are quite tinny. When the ship was "stretched" it reduced the amount of outdoor space per passenger, and this is reflected in increased density around the pools. There simply are not enough public rooms to absorb the increase in passengers well. Standing in line for embarkation, disembarkation, shore tenders and for self-serve buffet meals is an inevitable aspect of cruising aboard all large ships.

ACCOMMODATION. There are 15 grades of cabins (the price you pay will depend on the grade, location and size you choose). The majority of cabins have outside views and feature wood-trimmed cabinetry and warm decor, with multi-colored soft furnishings, but there is almost no drawer space (the closets have open shelves, however), so take minimal clothing. All cabins have a sitting area, but this takes away any free space, making movement pretty tight. The bathrooms are small but practical, although there is little space for storage of personal toiletry items.

There are 18 suites (12 of which have a private entrance and a small, private balcony), each with separate living room and bedroom, fine quality cabinetry, and lots of closet and drawer space. Occupants of suites receive "concierge" service, which provides extra personal attention. In addition, 16 suites and 70 cabins have inter-connecting doors – good for families cruising together, or perhaps for those that want separate "his and hers" living spaces. Several cabins are specially equipped for the hearing-impaired. All cabins on the port side of the ship are designated non-smoking. Bottled water is placed in each cabin (but a charge will be made to your account if you open the bottle).

CUISINE/DINING. The two main full-service dining rooms are: The Terraces (arguably the nicer, with windows that look out over the ship's tiered aft decks), and the Four Seasons (with approximately 450 seats), located amidships. Both are non-smoking and serve the same food, in an open-seating arrangement ("Freestyle Dining"). The Four Seasons is the larger, and has some prime tables at ocean-view window seats in a section that extends from the ship's port and starboard sides in half-moon shapes (nice for lunch, but it's either dark or the curtains are drawn for dinner). However, this ship was not built with these kinds of "free for all" dining arrangements in mind. Consequently, the flow, timing, and concept aboard this ship are simply not successful. The dress code states that: "jeans, T-shirts, tank tops and bare feet are not permitted in restaurants."

There are a number of other themed eating establishments, giving a wide range of choice – although it would be wise to plan in advance, particularly for dinner. Italian fare is served in the Trattoria (formerly the Sun Terraces), which overlooks the aft swimming pool. There is also The Bistro, which features informal evening dining at no extra charge in more intimate surroundings. A 200-seat Sports Bar (typically open between 6am and 1am) has breakfast, luncheon, dinner, and snacks throughout the day. There's also a poolside pizzeria, and a small coffee lounge.

There is a reasonably decent selection of breads, rolls, and fruits, although the selection of cheeses is poor. The cutlery is very ordinary (there are no fish knives). There is no formal afternoon tea, although you can make your own from various beverage stations. The service is adequate at best. The breakfast and lunch buffets have unimaginative presentation (more variety and better ingredients needed).

The wine list is quite decent and well put together, with moderate prices, although you won't find any good vintage wines. There are many types of beer (including some on draught in the popular Sports Bar & Grill).

A lavish "chocoholics" buffet is featured once each cruise – established as a firm favorite among Norwegian Cruise Line's passengers.

ENTERTAINMENT. The Stardust Lounge is the ship's venue for production shows and major cabaret acts. It is two decks high (but the banquette and individual tub chair seating is only on the main level) and is located not in the forward part of the ship as is normal, but in the center.

Two or three production shows are presented in a typical 7-day cruise (all ably performed by the Jean Ann Ryan Company). These are very colorful, high-energy, high-volume razzle-dazzle shows (with much use of pyrotechnics, laser and color-mover lighting). There's so much happening that by the end of the evening, if you are a typical passenger, you'll be tired and won't remember much about the shows, which are, however, very entertaining.

The ship has a number of bands and solo entertaining musicians, which provide live music for listening and dancing in several of the ship's lounges and bars.

SPA/FITNESS. Spa/fitness facilities are located in the forward section of Sports Deck 12 (just aft of an observation lounge), and contains a gymnasium with high-tech muscle-toning equipment, beauty salon, several massage and associated treatment rooms, and men's and women's saunas and changing rooms.

Mandara Spa (headquartered in Honolulu, but owned by Steiner Leisure) is the operator of the spa/fitness center, and provides all staff and treatments as the concession.

● **For more extensive general information on what an NCL cruise is like, see pages 122–124.**

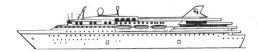

Ocean Majesty
★★ +

Mid-Size Ship: . . . . .10,417 tons	Propulsion/Propellers: . . . . .diesel	Cabins (for one person): 11
Lifestyle: . . . . .Standard	(12,200 kW)/2	Cabins (with private balcony): 8
Cruise Line: . . . . . . .Majestic International	Passenger Decks: 8	Cabins (wheelchair accessible): 2
Cruises/Page & Moy	Total Crew: 235	Cabin Current: . . . . .110 and 220 volts
Former Names: . . . . . . .Homeric, Olympic,	Passengers	Elevators: 3
Ocean Majesty, Kypros Star,	(lower beds/all berths): 535/621	Casino (gaming tables): . . . . .Yes
Sol Christina, Juan March	Passenger Space Ratio	Slot Machines: . . . . .Yes
Builder: . .Union Navale de Levante (Spain)	(lower beds/all berths): 19.4/16.7	Swimming Pools (outdoors): 1
Original Cost: . . . .$65 million	Crew/Passenger Ratio	Swimming Pools (indoors): 0
Entered Service: 1966/Apr 1994	(lower beds/all berths): 2.2/2.6	Whirlpools: 1
Registry: .Greece	Navigation Officers: . . . . .Greek	Self-Service Launderette: . . . . .No
Length (ft/m): 443.8/135.30	Cabins (total): 273	Dedicated Cinema/Seats: . . . . .No
Beam (ft/m): 62.9/19.20	Size Range (sq ft/m): .96.8–182.9/9.0–17.0	Library: . . . . .Yes
Draft (ft/m): 19.5/5.95	Cabins (outside view): 186	Classification Society: . .American Bureau
	Cabins (interior/no view): 87	of Shipping

OVERALL SCORE: 1,054 (OUT OF A POSSIBLE 2,000 POINTS)

OVERVIEW. This ship has a pleasing, balanced, almost handsome profile, with an aft funnel. Its name, *Ocean Majesty*, however, is decidedly ill-suited to such a small ship. There is a good amount of open deck space for the size of the vessel, but the plastic deck furniture looks tacky (thin blue cushioned pads are provided). There are several good public rooms, bars and lounges. The decor includes highly polished mirrored surfaces, but passageways are narrow and public rooms are only one deck high, which makes the ship feel cramped and inadequate.

The ship's size means that it can get into many ports in the Aegean and Mediterranean that larger ships cannot. It is often chartered to various tour operators and packagers, which means the standards of product delivery can vary. In summer, it is under charter to Page & Moy for cruises to Northern Europe and the Baltic (when food and its presentation improve marginally). The onboard currency is the British pound. This is a high-density vessel, so do expect lines to form for shore excursions and buffets.

SUITABLE FOR: *Ocean Majesty* is best suited to adult couples and single mature travelers, who want a basic cruise in unpretentious yet comfortable surroundings, for a first cruise, and at a low price that offers good value for money.

ACCOMMODATION. There are 13 cabin price grades – too many for a ship of this size. Most cabins are very small and barely functional, with a reasonable amount of closet and drawer space for short cruises only (as long as you don't plan on taking many clothes). The ceilings are very

BERLITZ'S RATINGS

	Possible	Achieved
Ship	500	266
Accommodation	200	85
Food	400	219
Service	400	233
Entertainment	100	46
Cruise	400	205

plain, and the soundproofing could be better. All cabins have twin lower beds or double beds. Some also have one or two additional upper (Pullman) berths, but to accommodate three or four persons, you'd all need to be contortionists. The tiled bathrooms (all have a shower; none have a bathtub) are bright and functional, with good lighting, but do lack space for storage of toiletries.

The largest cabins are on two of the uppermost decks (Coral and Aquamarine Decks). Although there are two wheelchair-accessible cabins, wheelchair access throughout much of this small ship is quite awkward.

CUISINE/DINING. The Restaurant has two seatings. There are few tables for two; most are for eight. The cuisine is continental, with Greek specialities and signature dishes. There is a small selection of breads, fruits and cheeses, and the buffets are generally simple and unimaginative.

ENTERTAINMENT. The Starlight Showlounge was intended for cabaret acts and mini-revues, although some sightlines are obstructed. Audio-visual facilities are minimal.

The cabaret acts featured here are the kind that you would see aboard other cruise ships (vocalists, magicians, puppeteers, comedians and others), and are a limited in scope because of the size of the room and ship. A ship's band and small musical units provide live music for dancing and listening in the various lounges.

SPA/FITNESS. There is a tiny gym (no windows, and so no natural light), and a cramped, badly lit beauty salon.

Ocean Monarch
★★★

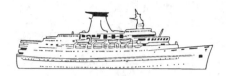

Mid-Size Ship: . . . . .17,074 tons	Passenger Decks: 7	Cabins (for one person): 0
Lifestyle: . . . . .Standard	Total Crew: 240	Cabins (with private balcony): 6
Cruise Line: . . . . . . .Majestic International	Passengers	Cabins (wheelchair accessible): 0
Cruises/Page & Moy	(lower beds/all berths): 560/670	Cabin Voltage: 220
Former Names: . . . Switzerland, Daphne,	Passenger Space Ratio	Elevators: 2
Akrotiri Express, Port Sydney	(lower beds/all berths): 30.4/25.4	Casino (gaming tables): . . . . .Yes
Builder: . . . . .Swan, Hunter (UK)	Crew/Passenger Ratio	Slot Machines: . . . . .Yes
Original Cost: .n/a	(lower beds/all berths): 2.3/2.7	Swimming Pools (outdoors): 1
Entered Service: . . . . . . .Mar 1955/2003	Navigation Officers: . . . . .European	Swimming Pools (indoors): 0
Registry: . . . . .Madeira	Cabins (total): 280	Whirlpools: 2
Length (ft/m): 532.7/162.39	Size Range (sq ft/m): 200.0–270.0/	Self-Service Launderette: . . . . .No
Beam (ft/m): 70.0/21.34	18.5–25.0	Dedicated Cinema/Seats: . . . . .No
Draft (ft/m): 41.9/12.80	Cabins (outside view): 215	Library: . . . . .Yes
Propulsion/Propellers: diesel (9,850 kW)/2	Cabins (interior/no view): 65	Classification Society: . . . . .Lloyd Register

OVERALL SCORE: 1,103 (OUT OF A POSSIBLE 2,000 POINTS)

OVERVIEW. *Ocean Monarch* is a solidly built ship (sister to Classic International Cruises' *Princess Danae*). It was built half a century ago as a cargo-passenger liner, in 1972 it was converted to become a full-time cruise ship and now, several owners later, it is operated by the Athens-based Majestic International Cruises. It was refurbished in 2002 and provides a moderately comfortable cruise experience. The ship has a pleasing, traditional, shipboard ambience, and the interior decor and furnishings combine a mixture of the classic and contemporary, conservative, clean and tidy. There are a limited number of spacious public rooms (there is, sadly, no forward observation lounge), although there is a decent amount of outdoors space for sunbathing.

SUITABLE FOR: *Ocean Monarch* is best suited to adult couples and single traveler of mature years who seek to cruise aboard a traditional style of ship that is of a handy size, with moderate facilities that are unpretentious yet quite comfortable, and at a modest cruise price.

ACCOMMODATION. No matter what price grade or configuration you choose, all suites/cabins have a bathroom either with a full-size bathtub/shower combination or shower only, personal safe, multi-channel audio, television, and satellite-linked telephone. All cabins have good solid fittings, heavy-duty doors and plain decor. There really is plenty of closet and drawer space, but cabin insulation is poor.
Suites: The largest accommodation can be found in six suites. Each has a separate bedroom, with double bed, wood accented cabinetry. The living room features a sofa, large glass-topped coffee table, writing desk, television, radio

BERLITZ'S RATINGS		
	Possible	Achieved
Ship	500	285
Accommodation	200	106
Food	400	216
Service	400	238
Entertainment	100	48
Cruise	400	210

channels, and personal safe. The bathroom features a full-size bathtub/shower, washbasin and toilet. Each suite has a private balcony.
Standard Exterior View or Interior (no view) Cabins: Some grades have double beds, while others have an L-shaped two lower bed configuration.

CUISINE/DINING. The Restaurant has large picture windows, and an uncluttered seating arrangement, with several tables for two located by large picture windows (other tables are for four, six or eight). Breakfast, lunch, and dinner are served in a single seating. One wall has a large, contemporary mural, while the ceiling features circles set inside squares. Casual self-serve buffet lunches can also be taken in the Neptune Bar, with its views aft over the ship's swimming pool and hot tubs.

ENTERTAINMENT. The Admiral's Showlounge is a room meant for cabaret acts. There is a wooden dance floor, and a marginally raised "stage", but in no way should it be termed a show lounge – it's just a lounge with a small stage. There are several slim pillars, and seating is in tub chairs. As it is a single-level room, sightlines from other than the seats close to the stage are pretty poor. However, entertainment is a low-key affair aboard this ship, and this is in accordance with the price you pay. The room is better as a lecture room, and for dancing.

SPA/FITNESS. There is a decent-sized health spa, built in what was formerly a cinema. It houses a gymnasium, with a reasonable array of muscle toning equipment, changing area, sauna, and several massage/treatment rooms.

Ocean Village
★★★ +

Large (Resort) Ship: . . . . .63,524 tons	Passenger Decks: 12	Cabins (for one person): 0
Lifestyle: . . . . .Standard	Total Crew: 514	Cabins (with private balcony): 64
Cruise Line: . . . . .Ocean Village	Passengers	Cabins (wheelchair accessible): 8
Former Names: . . .*Arcadia, Star Princess,*	(lower beds/all berths): 1,624/1,692	Cabin Current: . . . . .220 volts
FairMajesty	Passenger Space Ratio	Elevators: 9
Builder: Chantiers de L'Atlantique (France)	(lower beds/all berths): 39.1/37.5	Casino (gaming tables): . . . . .Yes
Original Cost: . . . .$200 million	Crew/Passenger Ratio	Slot Machines: . . . . .Yes
Entered Service: . . . . Mar 1987/May 2003	(lower beds/all berths): 3.1/3.2	Swimming Pools (outdoors): 3
Registry: . . . . .Great Britain	Navigation Officers: . . . . .British	Swimming Pools (indoors): 0
Length (ft/m): 810.3/247.00	Cabins (total): 812	Whirlpools: 4
Beam (ft/m): 105.6/32.20	Size Range (sq ft/m): 148.0–538.2/	Self-Service Launderette: . . . . .Yes
Draft (ft/m): 26.9/8.20	13.7–50.0	Dedicated Cinema/Seats: Yes/205
Propulsion/Propellers: . . . . .diesel-electric	Cabins (outside view): 622	Library: . . . . .No
(39,000kW)/2	Cabins (interior/no view): 190	Classification Society: . . .Lloyd's Register

BERLITZ'S OVERALL SCORE: 1,351 (OUT OF A POSSIBLE 2,000 POINTS)

OVERVIEW. *Ocean Village* was originally designed and built for Sitmar Cruises, a company that was absorbed into Princess Cruises in 1988 before the ship was completed. The ship was extensively refurbished in 1997 at the Harland & Wolff shipyard in Belfast, and reconfigured specifically for British cruise passengers.

After a refurbishment intended to brighten the interior passageways, public rooms and dining spots, *Arcadia* morphed into *Ocean Village* in April 2003, and is now a trendy, upbeat ship designed for younger couples and families who want to take a cruise, but don't want the sedentary "eat when we tell you to and relax" image typical of traditional cruise ships.

In the 2003 refit, several new cabins were added, although the overall number of crew was reduced (not so many are needed for this more casual style of cruising, particularly in the food service areas; the casino was also relocated (it displaced the library), while the former casino has been turned into a new internet center/bar called Connexions.

Ocean Village is quite a well proportioned ship, with a good amount of open deck space. On the open leisure deck are two swimming pools (one has sloping steps, while the other has vertical steps; one has a sit-in bar), while the aft pool will probably be used by families with children. Four hot tubs sit on a raised platform, and two shower cubicles stand adjacent to a poolside bar.

The ship's interiors are upbeat and trendy in a high-street sort of fashion (with decor by the designers who did such a good job with the ships of Seetours' Aida Cruises), but also include a few items that have a link with the past, such as the art deco touches of stainless steel balustrades and

BERLITZ'S RATINGS

	Possible	Achieved
Ship	500	356
Accommodation	200	138
Food	400	238
Service	400	273
Entertainment	100	72
Cruise	400	274

the rather soulless stainless steel elevators. There aren't a lot of public rooms to play in, although one nice feature is the fact that the public rooms do have ceilings that are higher than average for contemporary cruise ships.

The focal point of the interior is a three-deck-high foyer, highlighted by a large blue and yellow painted (it's actually stainless steel underneath) kinetic sculpture (it resembles a Swiss Army knife, with blades that move slowly) that brings one's attention to the multi-deck horseshoe-shaped staircase.

There is a domed observation lounge (called the Bayside Club, it sits atop the ship, forward of the mast). Although it is a little out of the traffic flow, it is a restful spot for cocktails; at night it turns into a night-spot/discotheque that includes not only a sunken dance floor but also exercise bicycles and step machines – a strange combination (so you can dance, drink, *and* fall off your bike!). There is an internet cafe, with five computer terminals (but no privacy screens); the cost is £7.50 for 15 minutes.

For retail therapy, there are several shops (one of which carries chocolates) clustered around the second and third levels of the three-deck high atrium lobby, plus a dedicated cinema. Other facilities include a casino (aft of the upper level of the two-deck high showlounge), The Oval lounge/bar, Connexions Bar, and the Blue Bar (a more traditional drinking lounge).

Families should enjoy the children's facilities, which are quite extensive. There is a children's indoor play area (Base Camp) located at the aft (blunt) end of the ship, while the exterior aft decks have an outdoor paddling pool and games areas. There's also a Night Nursery for sleepovers (operates

6pm–2am, but there is a per child charge after midnight). Teenagers are catered to with their own area, The Hideout. Babies under 6 months old are not accepted as passengers. Although supplies of disposable nappies, baby wipes and sterilizing fluids are available on board, Ocean Village recommends that you bring your own supplies and top up on board (where such things are necessarily more expensive).

Ocean Village began fly-cruise operations in May 2003, with the ship based on Palma de Majorca. Special fly-cruise packages have been created (for British passengers) from five UK airports (Birmingham, Edinburgh, London Gatwick, London Stansted, and Manchester). You can take a 7-day or 14-day cruise (there are two different itineraries, Palaces and Paella, and Pizzas and Pasta, which alternate each week) and add on a one-week or two-week stay at a choice of Majorcan family resort hotels, one of which is exclusive to Ocean Village.

As part of the "fusion cruise-stay" vacation, a variety of active sports is available. These include mountain biking, abseiling, jet skiing, jeep safaris, quad biking, parasailing, helicopter flight-seeing, and snorkeling (all are at extra cost). The ship carries a "fleet" of mountain bikes. Both active and passive cruising, therefore, are on offer.

In marketing terms, this ship and casual dress-down product is designed to compete head to head with Island Cruises, Sun Cruises and Thomson Cruises, with the same kind of itineraries and cost structure, to appeal specifically to the British market. *Ocean Village*, however, is the superior ship in terms of hardware. Gratuities to staff are included in the cruise/holiday price, but you'll need to budget spending money for all the little things that cost extra on board. The Cruise Comment Card is interesting, with sections for you to tick Fab, Good, OK, or Yuk!

Sadly, there is no full wrap-around promenade deck outdoors (open port and starboard walking areas stretch only partly along the sides). The elevators have a "London Underground" voice that says "mind the doors". There is no library. Standing in line for embarkation, disembarkation, shore tenders and for self-serve buffet meals tends to happen with ships of this size. Smokers are everywhere.

SUITABLE FOR: *Ocean Village* is best suited to young couples and singles of all ages, families with children and teenagers, who like to mingle in a large ship setting with plenty of life, music and entertainment for everyone, with food that is quantity rather than quality, delivered with friendly service that lacks polish, at an attractive price.

ACCOMMODATION. There are four basic types, in 14 different price grades (the price you pay will depend on the grade, location and size you choose). These include two grades of suites (refurbished in 2003): 36 suites with private balcony and bathtub, plus separate shower enclosure, 2 suites with shower, but no balcony. There are also 28 suites with private balcony, and shower. All other accommodation consists of standard outside-view and interior (no view) grade cabins. Many passengers like to fall asleep with soft music playing however, because music is only available

through the TV set, you can't obtain any of the music channels without having a TV picture on. When the ship was converted from *Arcadia* into *Ocean Village*, the accommodation was left untouched. While the cabins are of modestly generous proportions, the bathroom fittings (washbasin, shower) are dated and should have been changed. Accommodation designated as suites did receive a facelift.

Standard Outside-view/Interior (No View) Cabins: All are equipped with twin beds that can (in most cases) be placed together to form a queen-sized bed. All have a good amount of storage space, including wooden drawer units, plus some under-bed space for luggage, and a walk-in (open) closet. A direct dial telephone is provided. However, the sound insulation between cabins is quite poor (TV sound late at night can be particularly irritating, as can loud children, or fellow passengers banging drawers). A number of cabins also have third- and fourth-person berths – good for families with children, but the drawer and storage space becomes tight, and there is only one personal safe.

The bathrooms are of a modular design, and are of quite a decent size, with good shower enclosures, and a retractable clothesline. None have tubs, except in one of the grades designated as suites, as the ship was originally built for American passengers (who prefer showers to baths). Soap is provided, and a soap/ shampoo dispenser is fitted into the shower enclosure (although there is no conditioner). **Suites:** For more living space, choose one of the suite grades. Some have a small private balcony with part partition. Suite occupants also get a 100% cotton bathrobe. **Other Cabins:** Lighting is very subdued, and the fittings are now quite dated (the bathroom cabinets are noisy and the washbasin is small). However, coffee and tea making facilities are provided in all cabins – a very useful item, particularly as tea/coffee costs extra in all bars.

CUISINE/DINING. The idea of Ocean Village (the company) is that the whole cruise experience should be casual, with none of the stuffiness normally associated with traditional dining. So, the dining concept is simple: meals are taken in a self-serve buffet style setting, so you can dress as casually as you like.

To this end there are several dining spots, including two large self-serve buffet restaurants (Plantation, and Waterfront), a bistro, La Luna pizzeria on deck for lunch or dinner (there is a cover charge of £5 a person at night, when reservations are necessary). All dining spots are non-smoking.

Plantation and The Waterfront both have large ocean-view windows and self-serve buffet display counters. There are plenty of tables, most of which are for four, six or eight persons, and all cutlery is supplied in a help-yourself rack (so waiters and waitresses don't have to set tables). Plantation is open 24 hours a day, while The Waterfront has set opening hours, detailed in the daily program. At night, Plantation has Asian and Oriental themed buffets, with such main courses as Pork Vindaloo, Beef Biriyani, Lamb Rogan Josh, and Salmon Tikka.

If you do want to have a little more attention, better food, and more flair in presentation, try The Bistro (located in one corner of the Waterfront Restaurant). This dining spot features Mediterranean cuisine created by celebrity chef James Martin, who joins the occasional cruise; there's a cover charge of £8.50, and reservations are needed.

There are six main courses on The Bistro menu, including two vegetarian. Examples: Honey duck confit with creamy mash and deep fried seaweed; Herb crusted rack of lamb with courgettes, fava beans, pancetta and mint; Pan-fried fillet of beef with stilton rarebit and savoy cabbage; Roast cod wrapped in fennel and Parma ham with cannelloni and spinach; Pumpkin and sage gnocchi with parmesan; Mozzarella, aubergine and polenta stack with a roasted plum tomato compote.

There is a reasonably decent selection of wines, although they are all quite young.

In general, the food is typical of what you would find in a couples-only or family-style holiday village (modern British with a Mediterranean touch), with plenty of choices for families with children. It is straightforward, unfussy and unpretentious, with little use of garnishes. Vegetarian dishes are incorporated into the menu each day.

The service is warm and lighthearted, although communication in English with waiters, waitresses and bar staff (most are from Goa, in India) can be a little frustrating. You'll be able to have the "Great British Breakfast" as well as light, healthy fare.

Bar drinks are reasonably priced (there is a good range of standard brands, as well as a selection of 12 beers), and, with 35ml measures, are 40 percent larger than comparable measures on land in the UK. However, an espresso/cappuccino costs £1.15 a time, and if you want bar snacks such as peanuts or crisps, you have to pay extra.

ENTERTAINMENT. The Marquee Showlounge is the venue for all of the principal entertainment events. It is a horse-shoe-shaped room, with main and balcony levels (connected by two spiral staircases), and there are adequate sightlines from most of the banquette-style seating, although the sightlines from the front row seats on the upper level are obstructed by the required balcony railing.

There is a wide variety of mainly British entertainment, from production shows (accompanied by a live showband and "click" track) to cabaret-style acts that may or may not be well-known British "names" (and lesser artists). And don't be surprised if the occasional "street performer" jumps out to present an impromptu rendering in various locations.

There is plenty of live music throughout the many lounges and bars (in fact there is no bar without music, so sitting down for a quiet drink and chat is not possible).

SPA/FITNESS. There is a beauty salon, gymnasium (the Bayside Club), and wellness centre (called the Karma Spa), including a sauna/steam room complex, although it is located on the lowest passenger deck.

The spa is operated by Harding Brothers, a UK concession that provides the staff and a wide range of beauty and wellness treatments. Examples of treatments include: Full Body Massage, at £45 (1 hour); Indian Head Massage, at £35; Hot/cold stone Massage, at £55; Thalgo Collagen Facial, at £50. A shampoo, cut, and blow-dry costs £28; a manicure is £15, a permanent wave £58.

If you want to book spa treatments (massage, facial, hairdressing), it is wise to do so as soon after you embark as possible, as time slots do fill up quickly aboard large ships such as this. Some exercise classes are free, but most incur a charge (examples: Yoga at £15 for four classes, Pilates £5 per class, Fit Ball £5 per class, Personal Training £39).

QUOTABLE QUOTES

These are some of the questions I have been asked by first-time cruise passengers:

"How many knots does the ship go to the gallon?"

"How does the captain know which port to go to?"

"Does the island float?"

"Do you send the laundry ashore?"

"Do these stairs go up as well as down?"

"Why is it that my 3-year old can wear shorts to dinner but I can't?"

"Do we have to eat dinner at both seatings?"

"I know that ships often serve smoked salmon, but I am a non-smoker"

"Can the iced tea be served hot?"

"Can you please change this spoon for a fork? I've already got five spoons"

"Why can't the late-night show be in the morning?"

"Do we have to leave the ship to go on tour?"

Overheard in Livorno: "Can we book a tour to Pizza from here?"

Overheard aboard an Alaska cruise: "Does the helicopter tour leave from the upper deck?"

Overheard on an around-the-world cruise: "Why did we stop so often?"

Oceana
★★★★

Large (Resort) Ship: ....77,499 tons	Total Crew: 850	Cabins (with private balcony): 410
Lifestyle: ....Standard	Passengers	Cabins (wheelchair accessible): 19
Cruise Line: ....P&O Cruises	(lower beds/all berths): 1,950/2,272	Cabin Current: ....110 and 220 volts
Former Names: ....*Ocean Princess*	Passenger Space Ratio	Elevators: 11
Builder: ....Fincantieri (Italy)	(lower beds/all berths): 39.7/34.1	Casino (gaming tables): ....Yes
Original Cost: ....$300 million	Crew/Passenger Ratio	Slot Machines: ....Yes
Entered Service: .....Feb 2000/Nov 2002	(lower beds/all berths): 2.2/2.5	Swimming Pools (outdoors): 4
Registry: ....Great Britain	Navigation Officers: ....British	Swimming Pools (indoors): 0
Length (ft/m): 857.2/261.30	Cabins (total): 975	Whirlpools: 5
Beam (ft/m): 105.6/32.20	Size Range (sq ft/m): 158.2–610.3/	Self-Service Launderette: ....Yes
Draft (ft/m): 25.9/7.9	14.7–56.7	Dedicated Cinema/Seats: ....No
Propulsion/Propellers: .....diesel-electric	Cabins (outside view): 603	Library: ....Yes
(28,000 kW)/2	Cabins (interior/no view): 372	Classification Society: ....Lloyds Register
Passenger Decks: 10	Cabins (for one person): 0	

OVERALL SCORE: 1,519 (OUT OF A POSSIBLE 2,000 POINTS)

OVERVIEW. The all-white *Oceana* has a pleasing profile for a large ship, and is well balanced by its large funnel, which contains a deck tennis/basketball/ volleyball court in its sheltered aft base. There is a wide, teakwood wraparound promenade deck outdoors, real teak steamer-style deck chairs (complete with royal blue cushioned pads), and 93,000 sq. ft (8,600 sq. meters) of space outdoors. A great amount of glass area on the upper decks provides plenty of light and connection with the outside world. The ship underwent a few changes to make it more user-friendly for British (rather than American) passengers.

The ship, while large, absorbs passengers well, and has an almost intimate feel, which is what the interior designers intended. Its interiors are very pretty and warm, with attractive colors and welcoming decor that includes some very attractive wall murals and other artwork.

There is a wide range of public rooms, with several intimate rooms and spaces, so that you don't feel overwhelmed by large spaces. The interior focal point is a large four-deck-high atrium lobby with winding, double stairways and two panoramic glass-walled lifts.

The main public entertainment rooms are located under three decks of passenger cabins. There is plenty of space throughout the public areas, and the traffic flow is quite good. The library is a warm room and has six large buttery leather chairs for listening to compact audio discs, with ocean-view windows. There is a conference center for up to 300, as well as a business center, with computers, photocopiers and fax machines.

The collection of artwork is quite good, particularly on the stairways, and helps make the ship feel smaller than it is,

BERLITZ'S RATINGS

	Possible	Achieved
Ship	500	424
Accommodation	200	159
Food	400	262
Service	400	290
Entertainment	100	81
Cruise	400	303

and is more coordinated than before (when the ship was operated by Princess Cruises). The Monte Carlo Club Casino, while large, is not really in the main passenger flow and so it does not generate the "walk-through" factor found aboard so many ships. Without question, the most traditional room aboard is the Yacht and Compass Bar, decorated in the style of a turn-of-the-century gentleman's club, with wood paneling and comfortable seating.

Ballroom dance fans will be pleased to note that there are several good-sized wooden dance floors. The ship always carries a professional dance couple as hosts and teachers, and there is plenty of dancing time included in the entertainment programming.

Children have their own Treasure Chest (for ages 2–5), The Hideout (6–9 year-olds), and for older children (aged 10–13) there is The Buzz Zone. P&O Cruises provides an abundance of staff to look after the children, as well as many activities to keep them out of adult areas. A night nursery is available from 6pm to 2am (there is a per child charge after midnight). While many children don't like organized clubs, they will probably find they make new friends quickly during a cruise.

As is the case aboard most large ships, if you live in the best accommodation (a suite), you will be well attended; if you do not, you will merely be one of a very large number of passengers aboard a ship that caters to families with children (lots of them in peak vacation periods). One nice feature is the captain's cocktail party – it is held in the four-deck-high main atrium so you can come and go as you please, with no standing in line to have your photograph taken with the captain if you don't want to.

This ship is all about British-ness and will be comfortingly familiar for families with children who want to go abroad but take their British traditions and food with them. Most cabin stewards and dining room personnel are from India, and provide service with a well-balanced smile and a warmth that many other nationals find hard to equal.

However, note that in the quest for increased onboard revenue (and shareholder value), even birthday cakes are an extra-cost item, as are espressos and cappuccinos (fake ones, made from instant coffee, are available in the dining rooms). Also at extra cost are ice cream, and bottled water (these can add up to a considerable amount on an around-the-world cruise, for example). You can expect to be subjected to a stream of flyers advertising daily art auctions, "designer" watches and other promotions. For gratuities (which are optional), you should typically allow £3.50 (about $5.50) per person, per day. The onboard currency is the British pound.

A fine British brass band send-off accompanies all sailings from Southampton. Other touches include church bells that sound throughout the ship for the interdenominational Sunday church service. A coach service for any passengers embarking or disembarking in Southampton covers much of the UK. Car parking is also available (there is one rate for undercover parking, one rate for parking in an open compound).

There are a number of dead ends in the interior layout, so it's not as user-friendly as it should be. Standing in line for disembarkation, shore tenders and for self-serve buffet meals is an inevitable aspect of cruising aboard all large ships. You may be subjected to announcements for revenue-producing activities such as art auctions, bingo, horse racing that intrude constantly into your cruise.

The swimming pools are actually rather small and will be crowded when the ship is full; also the pool deck is cluttered with white, plastic deck lounge chairs, which don't have cushioned pads (the rule about not leaving deck lounge chairs unattended for more than half an hour is flouted by most British passengers, who are keen to keep their favored position).

SUITABLE FOR: *Oceana* is best suited to adults of all ages (couples and single travelers, young and not so young), and families with children of all ages. The ship is particularly suitable as an excellent value for money cruise for first-time tabloid-reading passengers.

ACCOMMODATION. There are 19 different cabin grades, designated as: suites (with private balcony), mini-suites (with private balcony), outside-view twin-bedded cabin with balcony, outside-view twin bedded cabin, and interior (no view) twin-bedded cabins. The price you pay will depend on the grade, location and size you choose. Although the standard outside-view and interior (no view) cabins are a little small, they are well designed and functional in layout, and have earth tone colors accentuated by splashes of color from the bedspreads. Proportionately, there are quite a lot of interior (no view) cabins.

The cabin numbering system is illogical, with numbers going through several hundred series on the same deck. The walls of the passenger accommodation decks are very plain (some artwork would be an improvement).

Many of the outside-view cabins have private balconies, and all seem to be quite well soundproofed, although the balcony partition is not of the floor to ceiling type, so you can hear your neighbors clearly (or smell their smoke). The balconies are very narrow, and only just large enough for two small chairs, and there is no dedicated outdoor balcony lighting. Many cabins have third- and fourth-person upper bunk beds – these are good for families with children. Tea/coffee making facilities are provided in all cabins – a comforting addition.

There is a reasonable amount of closet and abundant drawer and other storage space in all cabins; although this is adequate for a 7-night cruise, it could prove to be quite tight for longer. Also provided are a color television, and refrigerator, and each night a chocolate will appear on your pillow. The cabin bathrooms are practical units, and come complete with all the details one needs, although again, they really are tight spaces, best described as one person at-a-time units. Fortunately, they have a shower enclosure of a decent size, a small amount of shelving for your personal toiletries, real glasses, and a hairdryer.

Suites: The largest accommodation is in six suites, two on each of three decks at the aft of the ship (with a private balcony giving great views over the stern). Each of these suites, named Oronsay, Orcades, Orion, Orissa, Orsova, Orontes (all P&O ships of yesteryear), has a large private balcony. They are well laid out, and have large, marble-clad bathrooms with two washbasins, a Jacuzzi bathtub, and a separate shower enclosure. The bedroom has generous amounts of wood accenting and detailing, indented ceilings, and TV sets in both bedroom and lounge areas, which also have a dining room table and four chairs.

Mini-Suites: Mini-suites typically have two lower beds that convert to a queen-sized bed. There is a separate bedroom/sleeping area with vanity desk, and a lounge with sofa and coffee table, indented ceilings with generous amounts of wood accenting and detailing, walk-in closet, and a larger, marble-clad bathroom with Jacuzzi bathtub and separate shower enclosure. There is a private balcony.

Standard Outside-view/Interior (No View) Cabins: A reasonable amount of closet and abundant drawer and other storage space is provided in all cabins (adequate for 7 nights but a little tight for longer cruises), as are a TV set and refrigerator. Each night a chocolate will appear on your pillow. The cabin bathrooms are practical, and come with all the details one needs, although they really are tight spaces, best as one-person at-a-time units. They do, however, have a decent shower enclosure, a small amount of shelving for personal toiletries, real glasses, and a hairdryer.

You can receive BBC World channel on the in-cabin color television system (when available, depending on cruise area), as well as movies (there is no dedicated theater aboard this ship).

CUISINE/DINING. There are two principal asymmetrically designed dining rooms, Adriatic and Ligurian (each seats about 500), located adjacent to the two lower levels of the four-deck high atrium lobby. Both dining rooms are non-smoking, as are the dining rooms aboard all ships of P & O Cruises, and which one you are assigned to will depend on the location of your accommodation. Each has its own galley and each is split into multi-tier sections, which help create a feeling of intimacy, although there is a lot of noise from the waiter stations adjacent to many tables. Breakfast and lunch are provided in an open-seating arrangement, while dinner is in two seatings.

The cuisine is decidedly British – a little adventurous at times, but always with plenty of curry dishes and other standard British items. The presentation is good, though – better than other ships in the P&O Cruises fleet. Don't expect exquisite dining – this is British hotel catering that doesn't pretend to offer caviar and other gourmet foods. But what it does present is attractive and tasty, with some excellent gravies and sauces to accompany meals. In keeping with the Britishness of P&O Cruises, the desserts are always good. A statement in the onboard cruise folder states that P&O Cruises does not knowingly purchase genetically modified foods (though it makes no mention of all those commercial American cereals). The service is provided by a team of friendly stewards – most from Goa, with which P&O has had a long relationship. The wine list is quite reasonable. A 15% is added to all beverage bills, including wines.

The Plaza self-serve buffet is open 24 hours a day, and is located above the navigation bridge, with some commanding views. At night, this large room (there are two food lines – one each on both port and starboard sides) is transformed into an informal dinner setting with sit-down waiter service.

Outdoors on deck, with a sheltered view over the Riviera Pool, the Riviera Grill has fast-food items for those who don't want to change from their sunbathing attire.

For informal eats, there is also Cafe Jardin, for pizzas and light snacks; it is on the uppermost level of the four-deck high atrium lobby. In addition, there is a patisserie (for cappuccino/espresso coffees and pastries), a wine/caviar bar (Magnums). The cabin service menu is very limited, and presentation of the food items is poor.

ENTERTAINMENT. There are two showlounges (Footlights Theatre, and Starlights), one at each end of the ship. The Footlights, located at the forward end of the ship, is a superb 550-seat, theater-style showlounge, for production shows and theater events (movies can also be shown here), while Starlights is a 480-seat cabaret-style lounge with bar.

P&O Cruises places a big emphasis on a decent quality of entertainment. To this end, the ship has a group of actors, singers and dancers resident aboard *Oceana*. They provide theater-style presentations such as mini versions of well-known musicals, "book" shows, revues, and drama presentations. In addition, the ship features a whole array of cabaret acts. Although many of the cabaret acts are not what you would call headliners, they do regularly travel the cruise ship circuit. Classical concerts are scheduled for many of the cruises throughout the year.

Ballroom dance aficionados will be pleased to note that there are several good-sized wooden dance floors aboard this ship, and P&O Cruises carries a professional dance couple as hosts and teachers (there is plenty of dancing time included in the entertainment programming).

SPA/FITNESS. The Ocean Spa has facilities that are contained in a glass-walled complex located on one of the highest decks at the aft part of the ship. It includes a gymnasium, with all the associated high-tech muscle-pumping equipment, a combination aerobics/exercise class room, sauna, steam room, and several treatment rooms. If you want to book spa treatments (massage, facial, hair beautification), it is wise to do so as soon after you embark as possible, as time slots do fill up quickly aboard large ships such as this. The spa is operated by Harding Brothers, a UK concession that provides the staff and range of beauty and wellness treatments. Examples of treatments include: Body Toning (detox for the body); Body Bien Etre (body scrub and massage); Seaweed Wrap; Collagen Velvet Facial Mask.

One swimming pool is "suspended" aft between two decks and forms part of the spa complex (two other pools are located in the center of the ship), although they are not large for the size of the vessel. Sports facilities are located in an open-air sports deck positioned inside the ship's funnel structure and can be adapted to basketball, volleyball, badminton or paddle tennis. Joggers can exercise on the wrap-around open Promenade Deck. There's an electronic golf simulator (no need to bring your own clubs).

Oceanic
★★ +

Mid-Size Ship: . . . . .38,772 tons	Total Crew: 565	Cabins (wheelchair accessible): 1
Lifestyle: . . . . .Standard	Passengers	Cabin Current: . . . . .110 volts
Cruise Line: . . . . .Pullmantur Cruises	(lower beds/all berths): 1,124/1,800	Elevators: 5
Former Names: . . .Big Red Boat I, Oceanic	Passenger Space Ratio	Casino (gaming tables): . . . . .Yes
Builder: . . . .Cantieri Riuniti dell' Adriatico	(basis 2): 34.7/21.54	Slot Machines: . . . . .Yes
(Italy)	Passenger Space Ratio	Swimming Pools (outdoors): 2
Original Cost: . . . .$40 million	(all berths): 21.5/3.1	Swimming Pools (inside): 0
Entered Service: . . . . .Apr 1965/May 2001	Navigation Officers: . . . . .Spanish	Whirlpools: 3
Registry: .Spain	Cabins (total): 562	Fitness Center: . . . . .Yes
Length (ft/m): 782.1/238.40	Size Range (sq ft/m): 139.9–454.2/	Sauna/Steam Room: . . . . .No/No
Beam (ft/m): 96.5/29.44	13.0–42.2	Massage: . . . . .Yes
Draft (ft/m): 28.2/8.60	Cabins (outside view): 252	Self-Service Launderette: . . . . .No
Propulsion/Propellers: . . . . .steam turbine	Cabins (interior/no view): 310	Cinema/Seats: . . . . .No
(45,100 kW)/2	Cabins (for one person): 0	Library: . . . . .Yes
Passenger Decks: 10	Cabins (with private balcony): 21	Classification Society: . . . .Bureau Veritas

OVERALL SCORE: 1,093 (OUT OF A POSSIBLE 2,000 POINTS)

OVERVIEW. Built with a strong, riveted hull, originally as an ocean liner for Home Lines, *Oceanic* (the ship's first name), underwent a successful conversion to provide cheap and cheerful family cruises following its purchase by Premier Cruise Lines in 1985. When Premier went into bankruptcy in 2000, the ship was purchased at auction, and is now owned and operated by Spain-based tour operator Pullmantur Cruises, which has kept the ship's exterior in good shape.

There is a reasonable amount of open teakwood-covered deck space for sunbathing, but it becomes cramped and noisy when the ship is full, and there are no cushioned pads for the white plastic deck lounge chairs (except on the deck lounge chairs located along the inside promenade deck). The twin swimming pools atop the ship have a sliding magrodome roof that can be used in inclement weather.

The ship's interiors and public rooms have changed little since the ship was operated by Premier Cruise Lines, and some artwork (particularly on the stairways) exist from its original operator, Home Lines.

The interiors have upbeat decor, and cheerful soft furnishing fabrics. One neat feature is the enclosed promenades (popular on the old ocean liners crossing the North Atlantic in all weather conditions) for strolling around the ship, or for just sitting; however, table tennis tables do restrict the flow around this promenade deck. During a refurbishment in May 2000, a new kids' room and teen room were built, and an Internet Cafe was installed. Framed photographs and paintings, which are for sale, are placed on the walls of the main lounge deck.

BERLITZ'S RATINGS

	Possible	Achieved
Ship	500	263
Accommodation	200	124
Food	400	222
Service	400	220
Entertainment	100	56
Cruise	400	208

One interesting feature of the former ocean liner can be found on the aft of Lounge Deck, which has a bar outdoors (with San Miguel beer on draft), and a small enclosure with original brass emergency steering equipment, made by Hastie of Greenock, Scotland, together with the ship's wheel.

Although the ship got off to a chaotic start under new operators Pullmantur Cruises (a low-cost tour operator), it has now settled down and will provide a family with children with a busy, fun-filled cruise aboard a classic ship setting. But it certainly does remind me of a summer camp at sea, particularly when school vacations mean lots (and I mean lots) of children have the run of the ship, the complaints of many passengers who have cruised aboard other cruise ships. The onboard currency is the euro.

There are many, many interior (no view) cabins. There are lines everywhere and much congestion at the self-service buffets for breakfast and lunch. The noise pollution is high throughout the ship, with constant repetitive announcements, and music throughout all hallways and on open decks. The interiors need more attention to detail, and cleanliness could be better. Many public rooms have numerous support pillars to obstruct sight lines. Smokers are everywhere – there is no escape.

SUITABLE FOR: *Oceanic* is best suited to young (and young at heart) Spanish-speaking couples, singles, and families with children of all ages who want a first cruise experience in a traditional (not new) ship, with plenty of public rooms and a lively atmosphere, food that is quantity rather than quality, at low cost.

ACCOMMODATION. *Oceanic* has a wide range of suites and standard outside-view and interior (no view) cabins, in different 12 price categories (seven for outside-view suites, junior suites and cabins, and five for interior cabins without a view). There are far more interior (no view) cabins than outside-view cabins. There are eight deluxe suites, each with a private balcony; 65 suites (13 with a private balcony), the rest being a mixture of inside (no view) and outside (sea-view) cabins. Many of the suites have their views obstructed by lifeboats.

The ceiling height is good, which helps give an impression of space. All cabins have heavy-duty furniture and are quite well equipped, although many are now in need of refurbishment. Many cabins have double beds. All cabins have a television, telephone, and climate control.

CUISINE/DINING. The Seven Continents Restaurant, which operates in two seatings, is large and cheerful, but it is extremely noisy when full (some might call it ambiance). The tables (for between two and eight persons) are very close together, and chairs do not have armrests (there is simply not enough room for them). All meals are included in the price. The cuisine is adequate, no more, and dining room service is of only a very basic standard – there is absolutely no finesse in service, although the staff are warm and friendly. The food is plentiful and tastes good, but there is a limited selection of breads, cheeses and fruits. Vegetarian selections are always available. The wine list is reasonably decent (with many Spanish wines included), and the prices are reasonable.

ENTERTAINMENT. The Salon Broadway is at the forward end of the ship on the main entertainment/public room deck, called Lounge Deck. Unfortunately, the thrust stage and dance floor are located as you enter the room, rather than be located where they should be, at the opposite end. The shows consist of a troupe of showgirl dancers, whose routines are mediocre – like high-school shows. Cabaret acts are the main feature; these include singers, magicians, and comedians, among others, and very much geared to the family audience that this ship carries for much of the time.

There is also plenty of live music for listening or dancing to in various bars and lounges, and there is the inevitable discotheque, located directly above a clutch of cabins aft on Continental Deck below.

SPA/FITNESS. Although there is no spa as such, there is a fitness room (with some antiquated equipment). There is also a beauty salon, and massage is also available (but the facilities are quite primitive).

SAFETY MEASURES

Fire Control
If anyone sounds the fire alarm, an alarm is automatically set off on the bridge. A red panel light will be illuminated on a large plan, indicating the section of the ship that has to be checked so that the crew can take immediate action.

Ships are sectioned into several zones, each of which can be tightly closed off. In addition, almost all ships have a water-fed sprinkler system that can be activated at the touch of a button, or automatically activated when sprinkler vials are broken by fire-generated heat. New electronic fire detection systems are being installed aboard ships in order to increase safety further.

Emergency Ventilation Control
This automatic fire damper system also has a manual switch that is activated to stop or control the flow of air to all areas of the ship, in this way reducing the fanning effect on flame and smoke via air-conditioning and fan systems.

Watertight Doors Control
Watertight doors throughout the ship can be closed off, in order to contain the movement of water flooding the ship. A master switch activates all the doors in a matter of seconds. All watertight doors can be operated electrically and manually, which means that nobody can be trapped in a watertight compartment.

Stabilizers Control
The ship's two stabilizing fins can be extended, housed, or controlled. They normally operate automatically under the command of a gyroscope located in the engine control room.

Odysseus
★★ +

Small Ship: . . . . .9,821 tons	Passenger Decks: 7	Cabins (for one person): 0
Lifestyle: . . . . .Standard	Total Crew: 194	Cabins (with private balcony): 0
Cruise Line: . . . . . .Royal Olympia Cruises	Passengers	Cabins (wheelchair accessible): 0
Former Names: . . . . . .Aquamarine, Marco	(lower beds/all berths): 452/484	Cabin Current: . . . . .110 volts
Polo, Princesa Isabel	Passenger Space Ratio	Elevators: 1
Builder: . . . . .Astilleros Espanoles (Spain)	(lower beds/all berths): 21.7/20.2	Casino (gaming tables): . . . . .Yes
Original Cost: .n/a	Crew/Passenger Ratio	Slot Machines: . . . . .Yes
Entered Service: 1962/2000	(lower beds/all berths): 2.3/2.4	Swimming Pools (outdoors): 1
Registry: .Greece	Navigation Officers: . . . . .Greek	Swimming Pools (indoors): 0
Length (ft/m): 483.1/147.30	Cabins (total): 226	Whirlpools: 4
Beam (ft/m): 61.2/18.67	Size Range (sq ft/m): 102.2–279.8/	Self-Service Launderette: . . . . .No
Draft (ft/m): 24.1/7.35	9.5–26.0	Dedicated Cinema/Seats: . . . . .No
Propulsion/Propellers: . . . . .diesel	Cabins (outside view): 183	Library: . . . . .Yes
(6,766 kW)/2	Cabins (interior/no view): 43	Classification Society: . . .Lloyd's Register

OVERALL SCORE: 1,042 (OUT OF A POSSIBLE 2,000 POINTS)

OVERVIEW. This moderately attractive traditional style of ship has a balanced, somewhat low profile, with a royal blue, riveted hull and white superstructure. It was acquired and completely reconstructed by Epirotiki Cruise Line (now part of Royal Olympia Cruises) in 1987. There is ample open deck and sunbathing space. There are twin teakwood-decked sheltered promenade walking areas.

There is a reasonable range of public rooms for the size of the vessel. Almost all have dated Mediterranean decor, however, which is quite plain, with rather bland colors that need a few extra splashes to brighten up the interiors, and there is very little artwork. Almost all of the public rooms are located on one principal deck, so finding them is easy. The showlounge, located forward, is quite poor, as four large pillars obstruct sight lines from many seats. A small nightclub/disco is popular with the late-night set.

This ship is really ideal for those who want to see many of the ports and islands in the Aegean and Mediterranean, and is small enough to get into some of the destinations that larger ships can't.

Apart from Royal Olympia Cruises' own, well-organized, destination-intensive cruises, the cruises are often sold by many different cruise-tour operators in various countries. This means that passengers are likely to consist of a wide mix of nationalities, and daily programmes and announcements, therefore, could well be in several languages.

Under Greek Seaman's Union rules, all gratuities (suggested in the brochure at $9 per person per day) are pooled among the crew (you give them to the chief steward). The exception to this is when the ship is operating under char-

BERLITZ'S RATINGS		
	Possible	Achieved
Ship	500	260
Accommodation	200	112
Food	400	206
Service	400	221
Entertainment	100	46
Cruise	400	197

ter and the charterer/operator includes gratuities in the fare. The onboard currency is the euro.

Note that there is no wrap-around outdoor promenade deck. Some of the interior stairways are very steep and have very short steps. There are only two bars. The company provides little port information for passengers wishing to go ashore individually, but heavily sells its own shore excursion programmes. The staff hospitality factor is adequate; more training is needed. In fact, there is little consistency across the company's ships with regard to standards of food, service and hospitality.

SUITABLE FOR: *Odysseus* is best suited to adult couples and single travelers seeking to travel at low cost to a variety of destinations in a short cruise time, with minimal fuss and pretension, and standard small traditional ship surroundings that are quite basic, and nothing more.

ACCOMMODATION. There are eight price grades. The price you pay will depend on the grade, location and size you choose. The attractive, fairly roomy, mostly outside-view cabins have either sofa beds which convert from a sofa during the day into and a bed by night or twin beds (few cabins have genuine double beds). There is a reasonable amount of closet and drawer space, and tasteful gray wood cabinetry that, in most cabins, includes a writing/vanity desk. Some cabins have third/fourth upper Pullman berths.

The cabin bathrooms, however, are really quite small, (particularly the shower enclosures) and very basic, with little storage space, and harsh fluorescent lighting. Personal amenities provided include soap, shampoo/bath foam, perfumed hand lotion, shower cap, and sewing kit. The towels are 100% cotton. Note that some cabins in the center of the ship on Poseidon Deck and Venus Deck may be subject to throbbing diesel generator noise, while all cabins on Hera Deck have views obstructed by the ship's lifeboats.

There is a 24-hour room service menu, but any in-cabin food/beverage service tends to be basic, without the finesse found aboard more expensive vessels.

The largest accommodation comprises four suites (two are located at the front of the ship, and two are located amidships, on Apollo Deck). Each has a separate lounge and two double bedrooms, plenty of closet, drawer and other storage space, and a relatively large bathroom.

CUISINE/DINING. The small dining room seats 208. It is basic in terms of furnishings and setting, and tends to be extremely noisy, due to the low ceiling height and the location of waiter stations. Because it is small, there are two seatings (both non-smoking). The chairs do not have armrests and are quite small, and low. You should note that dining room seating and table assignments are typically provided by the restaurant manager (maître d') upon embarkation (this may or may not be so when the ship is under charter and an open seating is operated).

The cuisine is predominantly Continental, with many regional (Greek) specialities (there is much use of oil and salt). The presentation is spotty and inconsistent. Spa and vegetarian dishes are also available on lunch and dinner menus. However, the food has very little taste. There is a limited (repetitious) choice of bread rolls, fruits and cheeses.

The "old-world" service from the Greek dining room stewards adds to the experience, although it is not nearly as good as it was in former years, and is far too hurried.

An informal eatery is available poolside for casual buffet-style breakfasts and lunches, although the selection is quite limited. Seating is at plastic deck chairs, which, without cushions, are uncomfortable. Only the most basic of beverage stations is provided, with plastic cups.

ENTERTAINMENT. The Main Lounge is the venue for all entertainment events and social functions such as the captain's cocktail party. The single-level room was not designed for large-scale revue-style shows, but is really more for cabaret acts. It has individual tub chair seating clustered around drinks tables. The sightlines are not good from any but the first few rows of seats closest to the stage.

Entertainment has never been a strong point for Royal Olympia Cruises, and there is no cohesive plan for it, other than filling in blank evening spots with whatever cabaret acts are available at low cost (you can expect to find singers, magicians, and other visual acts that can appeal to a range of nationalities). Hence, any shows do tend to be much of an afterthought.

There is a ship's band and a couple of small musical units to provide live music for dancing or listening.

SPA/FITNESS. On the uppermost deck there is a small fitness room with a modicum of exercise equipment, sauna, massage room, changing area, and beauty salon. All the facilities are very small (this is, after all, a small ship).

QUOTABLE QUOTES

Overheard in Alaska: "Are the glaciers always here?"

Overheard in the cigar smoking room: "I'm looking for a no-smoking seat"

Overheard in the dining room in the Caribbean: "Is all the salmon smoked? I am a non-smoker" "Waiter, this vichyssoise is cold." "Was the fish caught this morning by the crew?"

Overheard on an Antarctic cruise: "Where is the good shopping in Antarctica?"

Overheard on a cruise taking in the British Isles: "Windsor Castle is terrific. But why did they build it so close to the airport?"

Overheard on a Greek islands cruise: "Why did the Greeks build so many ruins?"

Overheard in the dining room: *Passenger:* "Waiter: What is caviar?" *Waiter:* "Fish eggs, sir." *Passenger:* "In that case, I'll have two, over-easy!"

Overheard on a QE2 round-Japan cruise, in Kagoshima, with Mount Suribaya in the background: "Can you tell me what time the volcano will erupt? I want to be sure to take a photograph."

Oosterdam
★ ★ ★ ★

Large (Resort) Ship: . . . . . . .81,769 tons	Total Crew: 842	Cabins (wheelchair accessible): 28
Lifestyle: . . . . .Premium	Passengers	Cabin Current: . . . . .110 volts
Cruise Line: . . . . . . .Holland America Line	(lower beds/all berths): 1,848/2,272	Elevators: 14
Former Names: . . . . .none	Passenger Space Ratio	Casino (gaming tables): . . . . .Yes
Builder: . . . . .Fincantieri (Italy)	(lower beds/all berths): 44.2/35.9	Slot Machines: . . . . .Yes
Original Cost: . . . .$400 million	Crew/Passenger Ratio	Swimming Pools (outdoors): 2
Entered Service: . . . . .August 2003	(lower beds/all berths): 2.1/2.6	+1 children's pool
Registry: . . . . .The Netherlands	Navigation Officers: . . . . .European	Swimming Pools (indoors): 1
Length (ft/m): 959.6/292.50	Cabins (total): 924	(indoor/outdoor)
Beam (ft/m): 105.6/32.25	Size Range (sq ft/m): 185.0–1,318.6/	Whirlpools: 5
Draft (ft/m): 25.5/7.80	17.1–122.5	Self-Service Launderette: . . . . .No
Propulsion/Propellers: . . . . .diesel-electric	Cabins (outside view): 788	Dedicated Cinema/Seats: Yes/170
(34,000 kW)/2 pods	Cabins (interior/no view): 136	Library: . . . . .Yes
(17.6 MW each)	Cabins (for one person): 0	Classification Society: . . .Lloyd's Register
Passenger Decks: 10	Cabins (with private balcony): 810	

OVERALL SCORE: 1,546 (OUT OF A POSSIBLE 2,000 POINTS)

OVERVIEW. *Oosterdam* (sister ships: *Westerdam* and *Zuiderdam*) is one of the latest generation of larger ships for Holland America Line, designed to appeal to younger, more vibrant, multi-generational, family-oriented holidaymakers.

The twin working funnels are the result of the slightly unusual machinery configuration; the ship has, in effect, two engine rooms – one with three diesels, and one with two diesels and a gas turbine). A pod propulsion system is provided *(see page 151 for explanation)*, powered by a diesel-electric system, with a small gas turbine located in the funnel for the reduction of emissions.

There is a complete wrap-around exterior teak promenade deck, and teak "steamer" style deck lounge chairs are provided. Additionally, there is a jogging track outdoors, located around the ship's mast and the forward third of the ship. Exterior glass elevators, mounted midships on both port and starboard sides, provide fine ocean views from any one of 10 decks. There are two centrally located swimming pools outdoors, and one can be used in inclement weather due to its retractable sliding glass roof. Two whirlpool tubs, adjacent to the swimming pools, are abridged by a bar. Another smaller pool is available for children; it incorporates a winding water slide that spans two decks in height. There is an additional whirlpool tub outdoors.

The intimate lobby spans three decks, and is topped by a beautiful, rotating, Waterford crystal globe of the world. Adjacent are interior and glass wall elevators with exterior views. The interior decor, while bright in many areas (to attract a younger clientele), is considerably softer than that aboard sister ship *Zuiderdam*. The ceilings are particularly

BERLITZ'S RATINGS

	Possible	Achieved
Ship	500	430
Accommodation	200	163
Food	400	283
Service	400	280
Entertainment	100	77
Cruise	400	313

noticeable in the public rooms. In keeping with the traditions of Holland America Line, a large collection of artwork is a standard feature. Included are some superb paintings of former Holland America Line ships on the mid-ship stairwells by maritime artist Captain Stephen Card. Also notable are many pieces reflecting the former Dutch East Indies. The cast-aluminum elevator doors are also interesting – the design being inspired by the deco designs from New York's Chrysler Building.

There are two whole entertainment/public room decks. Without doubt, the most dramatic room aboard this ship is the showlounge, spanning four decks in the forward section of the ship. Other facilities include a winding shopping street with several boutique stores and logo shops, an internet center, library, card room, an art gallery, photo gallery, and several small meetings rooms. The casino is large (one has to walk through it to get from the restaurant to the showlounge on one of the entertainments decks), and is equipped with all the gaming paraphernalia and slot machines you can think of. Sports enthusiasts can enjoy a basketball court, volleyball court, golf simulator, For families with children, Club HAL's KidZone provides a whole area dedicated to children's facilities and extensive programming for different age groups (5–17), with one counselor for every 30 children. The company provides free coffee at the Java Bar, and free ice cream at certain hours, as well as hot hors d'oeuvres in all bars.

This formula may not work well for those loyal repeat passengers used to the line's smaller ships. However, *Oosterdam* does offer a range of public rooms with a reasonably intimate atmosphere and the overall feel of the ship is quite homely and comforting. Perhaps the ship's best asset is its friendly and personable Filipino and Indonesian crew, although communication (in English) can be frustrating.

The information desk in the lobby is small and somewhat removed from the main passenger flow on the two decks above it. Many pillars obstruct the passenger flow and lines of sight throughout the ship. There are no self-service launderettes (something families with children might miss – although special laundry packages are available).

ACCOMMODATION. There are 24 price categories: 16 outside-view/8 interior (no view). Some cabins on the lowest accommodation deck (Main Deck) have views obstructed by lifeboats. Some cabins that can accommodate a third and fourth person have very little closet space, and only one personal safe. Some cabins have interconnecting doors – good for families with children. Occupants of suites also get exclusive use of the Neptune Lounge and concierge service, priority embarkation and disembarkation, and other benefits. In many of the suites/cabins with private balconies the balconies are not so private, and can be overlooked from various public locations.

Penthouse Verandah Suites: Two suites offer the largest accommodation (1,126 sq. ft/104.6 sq. meters). These have a separate bedroom with a king-sized bed; there's also a walk-in closet, dressing room, living room, dining room, butler's pantry, mini-bar and refrigerator, and private balcony (verandah). The main bathroom has a large whirlpool bathtub, two washbasins, toilet, and plenty of storage space for personal toiletry items. Personalized stationery and free dry cleaning are included, as are hot hors d'oeuvres and other goodies daily.

DeLuxe Verandah Suites: Next in size are 60 of these suites (563 sq. ft/52.3 sq. meters). These have twin beds that convert to a king-sized bed, vanity desk, lounge area, walk-in closet, mini-bar and refrigerator, and bathroom with full-size bathtub, washbasin and toilet. Personalized stationery and complimentary dry cleaning are included, as are hot hors d'oeuvres and other goodies.

Verandah Suites: There are 100 of these Verandah Suites (actually they are cabins, not suites, and measure (284 sq. ft/26.3 sq. meters). Twin beds can convert to a queen-sized bed; there is also a lounge area, mini-bar and refrigerator, while the bathroom has a tub, washbasin and toilet. Floor to ceiling windows open onto a private balcony (verandah).

Outside-view Cabins: Standard outside cabins (197 sq. ft/18.3 sq. meters) have twin beds that can convert to a queen-size bed. There's a small sitting area, while the bathroom has a tub/ shower combination. The interior (no view) cabins are slightly smaller (182.9 sq. ft/ 17 sq. meters).

CUISINE/DINING. The Vista (main) Dining Room is two decks high, with seating (at tables for two, four, six or eight) on both main and balcony levels (the galley is underneath the restaurant, accessed by port and starboard escalators), and is at the stern. It provides a traditional Holland America Line

dining experience, with friendly service from smiling Indonesian and Filipino stewards. There are four seatings for dinner (you must pre-select a time and stick with it), at either 5.45pm, 6.15pm, 8pm or 8.30 pm, at assigned tables, and an open-seating arrangement for breakfast and lunch (you'll be seated by restaurant staff when you enter). The dining room has both smoking and no-smoking sections.

Holland America Line can provide Kosher meals, although these are prepared ashore, frozen, and brought to your table sealed in their original containers.

Alternative Dining Option: The 130-seat Odyssey Restaurant is a slightly more upscale dining spot (with higher quality ingredients, and better presentation than in the larger main dining room). It is on Lower Promenade Deck, and fronts onto the second level of the atrium lobby. Pacific Northwest cuisine is featured (with items such as sesame-crusted halibut with ginger-miso, Peking duck breast with blackberry sauce, and an array of premium quality steaks). Fine table settings, china and silverware are featured, as are leather-bound menus. The wine bar offers mostly American wines. Reservations are required and there is a cover charge of $20 per person for service and gratuity.

Informal Eateries: For casual eating, there is an extensive Lido Cafe, an eatery that wraps around the funnel housing and extends aft; there are also some fine views over the ship's central multi-deck atrium. It includes a pizzeria/Italian specialties counter, a salad bar, Asian stir-fry counter, deli sandwiches, and a separate dessert buffet, although movement around the buffet area can be very slow.

There is an outdoor self-serve buffet (adjacent to the fantail pool), which serves fast-food items such as hamburgers and hot dogs, chicken and fries, as well as two smaller buffets adjacent to the midships swimming pool area, and a Windsurf Cafe in the atrium lobby (open 20 hours a day), for coffee, pastries, snack foods, deli sandwiches and liqueur coffees (evenings only) – all at extra cost.

ENTERTAINMENT. The 867-seat Vista Lounge is the ship's principal venue for Las Vegas-style revues and major cabaret shows. The main floor level has a bar in its starboard aft section. Spiral stairways at the back of the lounge connect all levels. Stage shows are best seen from the upper levels, from where the sightlines are quite good.

SPA/FITNESS. The Greenhouse Spa is a large, two-decks-high health spa, and is located directly above the navigation bridge. Facilities include a solarium, hydrotherapy pool, unisex thermal suite – a unisex area incorporating a Laconium (gentle sauna), Hammam (mild steam), and Camomile Grotto (small aromatic steam room). There is also a beauty parlor, 11 massage/therapy rooms (including one for couples), and a large gymnasium with floor-to-ceiling windows on three sides and forward-facing ocean views, and the latest high-tech muscle-toning equipment.

● **For more extensive general information on what a Holland America Line cruise is like, see pages 118–222.**

Oriana
★★★★

Large (Resort) Ship: ....69,153 tons	Total Crew: 760	Cabins (with private balcony): 118
Lifestyle: ....Standard	Passengers	Cabins (wheelchair accessible): 8
Cruise Line: ....P&O Cruises	(lower beds/all berths): 1,828/1,975	Cabin Current: ....110 and 220 volts
Former Names: ....none	Passenger Space Ratio	Elevators: 10
Builder: ....Meyer Werft (Germany)	(lower beds/all berths): 37.8/35.0	Casino (gaming tables): ....Yes
Original Cost: ....£200 million	Crew/Passenger Ratio	Slot Machines: ....Yes
Entered Service: ....Apr 1995	(lower beds/all berths): 2.4/2.5	Swimming Pools (outdoors): 3
Registry: ....Great Britain	Navigation Officers: ....British	Swimming Pools (indoors): 0
Length (ft/m): 853.0/260.0	Cabins (total): 914	Whirlpools: 5
Beam (ft/m): 105.6/32.2	Size Range (sq ft/m): 150.6–500.5/	Self-Service Launderette: ....Yes
Draft (ft/m): 25.9/7.9	14.0–46.5	Dedicated Cinema/Seats: Yes/189
Propulsion/Propellers: ....diesel	Cabins (outside view): 594	Library: ....Yes
(47,750 kW)/2	Cabins (interior/no view): 320	Classification Society: ...Lloyd's Register
Passenger Decks: 10	Cabins (for one person): 112	

OVERALL SCORE: 1,530 (OUT OF A POSSIBLE 2,000 POINTS)

OVERVIEW. The ship is quite conventional: evolutionary rather than revolutionary, but was the first new ship for P&O Cruises for more than 25 years. This ship takes *Canberra*'s traditional appointments and public rooms and adds more up-to-date touches, together with better facilities and passenger flow, and a feeling of timeless elegance. The ship has a good amount of outdoor space, and enough deck lounge chairs for all passsengers – although I constantly receive written complaints from passengers about others "bagging" the loungers early in the morning (by placing books and towels on them) and not using them; this leads many frustrated passengers to conclude that there should be more deck lounge chairs.

For a little diversion, early references to the name Oriana are contained in 16th-century English romances. Various musical anthologies were composed to celebrate Elizabeth I as Oriana, culminating in a collection of 26 madrigals published by Thomas Morley in 1601 under the title "The Triumphs of Oriana". Although attributed to 23 different composers, each madrigal ends with the words "Long Live Fair Oriana."

Back to the ship: the interiors are gentle, welcoming and restrained. There is a splendid amount of open deck and sunbathing space, an important plus for its outdoors-loving British passengers. It has an extra-wide wrap-around promenade deck outdoors. The stern superstructure is nicely rounded and has several tiers that overlook the aft decks, pool and children's outdoor facilities.

Inside, the well laid-out design provides good horizontal passenger flow, and wide passageways. Very noticeable are the fine, detailed ceiling treatments. As it is a ship for all

BERLITZ'S RATINGS		
	Possible	Achieved
Ship	500	427
Accommodation	200	157
Food	400	260
Service	400	309
Entertainment	100	82
Cruise	400	295

types of people, specific areas have been designed to attract different age groups and lifestyles.

There is a four-deck-high atrium with a soft waterfall. It is elegant but not glitzy, and is topped by a dome of Tiffany glass. The large number of public entertainment rooms provides plenty of choice, with lots of nooks and crannies in which to sit and read.

The L-shaped Anderson's Lounge (named after the founder of the Peninsular Steam Navigation Company in the 1830s) contains an attractive series of 19th-century marine paintings, and is decorated in the manner of a fine British gentleman's club. Although there is no fireplace (there is one in the equivalent room aboard *Aurora*), it is a popular lounge.

Atop the ship and forward is the Crow's Nest, a U-shaped room with two small wings that can be closed off for small groups. There is a long bar, giving the barmen a great view of the bow, while passengers sitting at the bar have a view of a ship model (former P&O ship *Ranpura*) in a glass case. Two small stages are set into the forward port and starboard sections, and there is a wooden dance floor. The lounge has both smoking and non-smoking sections, although smoke lingers everywhere.

The library is a fine room, with a good range of hardback books (and a librarian), inlaid wood tables skillfully crafted by Lord Linley's company, and some comfortable chairs. On the second day of almost any cruise, however, the library will have been almost stripped of books by word-hungry passengers. Adjacent is Thackeray's, the writing room (known as the sleeping room in the afternoons); it is named after the novelist William Makepeace Thackeray, a P&O passenger in 1844. Without a doubt, the most restful room is the Curzon Room, used occasionally for piano recitals.

Lord's Tavern is the most sporting place to pitch a beverage or two, or take part in a singalong (rather like group karaoke). It is decorated with cricket memorabilia.

The carpeting throughout the ship is of an excellent quality, much of it custom designed and made from 100% wool. There are some fine pieces of sculpture that add the feeling of a floating museum, and original artworks by all-British artists that include several tapestries and sculptures.

Children and teens have "Club Oriana", their own rooms (Peter Pan and Decibels), their own daily programming and activities, as well as their own outdoor pool. While many children don't like organized clubs, they will probably find they make new friends quickly during a a cruise. Children can be entertained until 10pm, which gives parents time to have dinner and go dancing. The cabins also have a baby-listening device. A special night nursery for small children (ages 2–5) is available at no extra charge (6pm–2am).

There is a wide variety of mainly British entertainment aboard the ships of P&O Cruises. There is also a program of theme cruises (antiques, art appreciation, classical music, comedy, cricket, gardening, jazz, motoring, popular fiction, Scottish dance, sequence dancing). Check with your travel agent to see what is available for your intended cruise.

Oriana provides a standardized, somewhat bland cruise experience for its mainly British passengers (of all dialects) who do not want to fly to join a cruise ship. However, in the quest for increased onboard revenue, even birthday cakes are an extra cost, as are real espressos and cappuccinos (fake ones, made from instant coffee, are available in the dining rooms). Ice cream and bottled water also cost extra (and can add up to a considerable amount on an around-the-world cruise, for example).

A fine British brass band send-off accompanies all sailings. Other touches include church bells sounded throughout the ship for the interdenominational Sunday church service. The onboard currency is the British pound. For gratuities (optional), you should allow £3 (around US$4.50) per person, per day.

Oriana is all about British-ness and will be comfortingly familiar for families with children who want to go abroad but take their British values and food with them. Most cabin stewards and dining room personnel are from India, and provide service with a well balanced smile and a warmth that many other nationals find hard to equal.

Smokers seem to be everywhere, as is the smell of stale smoke. Shuttle buses, which used to be provided free in some ports, are no longer complimentary (except on the around-the-world cruise). During school holidays, you should be aware that there will be many children aboard; this can be a cause of irritation and frustration to many older passengers. Standing in line for embarkation, disembarkation, shore tenders and for self-serve buffet meals is inevitable aboard all large ships.

SUITABLE FOR: *Oriana* is best to tabloid-reading adults of all ages (although typically, most cruises attract passengers who are over 50), and families with children of all ages

who want a cruise that starts and ends in the UK, aboard a large ship with all the facilities of a small resort, with food and service that are acceptable, though not as good as aboard some other cruise ships.

ACCOMMODATION. There is a wide range of cabin configurations and categories (in 18 grades), including family cabins with extra beds (110 cabins can accommodate up to four persons). The price you pay will depend on the grade, location and size you choose.

The standard interior (no view) cabins and outside-view cabins are well equipped, although disappointingly small. There is much use of rich, warm limed oak or cherry wood in all cabins, which makes even the least expensive four-berth cabin seem inviting. All cabins have a decent amount of closet and drawer space, small refrigerator, television, full-length mirror, and blackout curtains (essential for North Cape cruises). Satellite television provided typically will include BBC World, although reception may not be good in all areas. Cabin soundproofing is quite poor.

A good number of cabins have been provided for passengers traveling singly. Anyone travelling singly who is sharing a cabin should note that only one personal safe is provided in most twin-bedded cabins. Although the cabins for four persons (family cabins) do have four small personal safes, there are no privacy curtains.

The standard cabin bathrooms are very compact units, and have mirror-fronted cabinets, although the lighting is quite soft (not strong enough for the application of make-up). All bathrooms have a wall-mounted hairdryer (it would be better placed at the vanity desk in the living area). A Molton Brown "hair and body sport wash" dispenser is mounted in all bathrooms. Note that it is difficult to use the dispenser while in the bathtub (in those cabins with bathtubs), and neither shampoo nor conditioner is provided.

There are eight suites, each measuring 500 sq. ft (46 sq. meters). All have butler service (there are two butlers). Features include a separate bedroom with two lower beds convertible to a queen-sized bed, walk-in dressing area, two double closets, plenty of drawer space. The lounge area has a sofa, armchairs and table, writing desk, binoculars, umbrella, trouser press, iron and ironing board, two televisions, VCR, personal safe, hairdryer and refrigerator. The bathroom features a whirlpool bath, shower and toilet, and there is also a guest bathroom. The whirlpool bathtubs are reasonable, although they have high sides to step over, and most are of the dimensionally challenged type where you sit in them rather than lie in them. All in all, the suites, and particularly the bathrooms, are very disappointing when compared with similar sized suites in other ships. The private balcony is suitably large enough, and has two deck lounge chairs, tables and chairs.

Other balcony cabins (called outside deluxe) measure 210 sq. ft (19 sq. meters) and, although the balconies are small, they do have good partitions, rubber matting on the deck and a thick wooden railing. Inside, there is a curtain to separate the sleeping and living areas. There is plenty of closet and drawer space. The bathrooms are somewhat disappointing, however, and have a very small, plain sink (one would expect marble or granite units in these grades).

CUISINE/DINING. There are two restaurants, and these are allocated according to the cabin grade and location you choose. The Peninsular Restaurant is located amidships, while the Oriental Restaurant is located aft (the galley is located between the two restaurants). Both are moderately handsome (each has tables for two, four, six or eight). Both have interesting ceilings, chandeliers and decor; the chinaware is Wedgwood, the silverware Elkington. The Oriental Restaurant has windows on three sides, including those overlooking the wash at the stern. There are two seatings in each restaurant, both of which are non-smoking (in fact, all dining spots are non-smoking). For those who are interested, a statement in the cruise folder in your cabin states that P&O Cruises does not knowingly purchase genetically modified foods (what about those American-packaged cereals, then?).

The meals are mostly of the unmemorable "Middle-England" (unpretentious) variety, and the presentation generally lacks creativity (the cuisine does improve on the around-the-world cruise, however). Curries are heavily featured, particularly on luncheon menus. Afternoon tea is disappointing, with a poor selection of teas and sandwiches.

The Conservatory offers self-serve breakfast and luncheon buffets, and 24-hour self-serve beverage stands (although the selection of teas is poor and it's often hard to find teaspoons – only plastic stirrers are provided). The flow is impeded by poor layout design, there's a lack of sauce and condiment stations, and there are too few experienced staff to help at peak usage times. On selected evenings, it becomes a reservation-only alternative restaurant, Le Bistro, with sit-down service, typically featuring French Bistro, Indian or Southeast Asian cuisine – popular with the ship's mainly British clientele.

A former aerobics room (which was not used very much) has been turned into the popular (particularly with children and teenage passengers) Al Fresco Pizzeria. The pizza slices are bread-based and not made from pizza dough.

ENTERTAINMENT. The Theatre Royal, designed by John Wyckham, is the principal venue for production shows, drama presentations, major cabaret acts and other entertainment events. It is a well designed room, located at the forward end of Promenade Deck. It features a sloping floor, and good sightlines from most seats, which, by the way are individually air-conditioned (special places are reserved for anyone in a wheelchair). However, the seats would provide better stage sight lines if they were staggered. There is a wide variety of mainly British entertainment, from production shows to top British "names" and lesser artists.

A second, smaller Pacific Lounge is a multi-function entertainment venue, for cabaret acts (including late-night comedy), and can also be used as a lecture room with audio-visual facilities. However, the room's many pillars obstruct the stage view from a number of seats.

Ballroom dance fans will be pleased to make use of the four good-sized wooden dance floors. The ship always carries a professional dance couple as hosts and teachers, and plenty of dancing time is included in the programming.

SPA/FITNESS. The Oasis Spa is located forward and almost atop the ship. It is quite large, and provides all the latest alternative treatment therapies, and there is a gymnasium with the latest high-tech muscle toning equipment. The unisex sauna is a large facility (most ships have separate saunas for men and women); there is also a steam room.

The spa is operated by Harding Brothers, a UK concession that provides the staff and a wide range of beauty and wellness treatments. Examples of treatments include: Body Toning (detox for the body); Seaweed Wrap; Collagen Velvet Facial Mask, and a range of aromatherapy treatments. Note that if you want to book spa treatments (massage, facial, hairdressing), it is wise to do so as soon after you embark as possible, as time slots do fill up quickly aboard large ships such as this – particularly on the shorter cruises. Examples of prices: a full body massage is £60 for 50 minutes; an Indian head massage is £42 for 45 minutes; a holistic facial is £45 for 75 minutes. A manicure is £24 for 45 minutes, while a pedicure is £35 for 45 minutes.

Orient Venus
★★★ +

Small Ship: ....21,884 tons	Passenger Decks: 6	Cabins (for one person): 0
Lifestyle: ....Standard	Total Crew: 120	Cabins (with private balcony): 2
Cruise Line: ....Venus Cruise	Passengers	Cabins (wheelchair accessible): 0
Former Names: ....none	(lower beds/all berths): 390/606	Cabin Current: ....110 volts
Builder: ....Ishikawajima Heavy	Passenger Space Ratio	Elevators: 3
Industries (Japan)	(lower beds/all berths): 56.1/36.1	Casino (gaming tables): ....No
Original Cost: ....$150 million	Crew/Passenger Ratio	Slot Machines: ....No
Entered Service: ....July 1990	(lower beds/all berths): 3.2/5.0	Swimming Pools (outdoors): 1
Registry: ....Japan	Navigation Officers: ....Japanese	Swimming Pools (indoors): 0
Length (ft/m): 570.8/174.00	Cabins (total): 195	Whirlpools: 0
Beam (ft/m): 78.7/24.00	Size Range (sq ft/m): 182.9–592.0/	Self-Service Launderette: ....Yes
Draft (ft/m): 21.3/6.52	17.0–55.0	Dedicated Cinema/Seats: Yes/606
Propulsion/Propellers: ....diesel	Cabins (outside view): 195	Library: ....Yes
(13,830 kW)/2	Cabins (interior/no view): 0	Classification Society: Nippon Kaiji Kyokai

OVERALL SCORE: 1,361 (OUT OF A POSSIBLE 2,000 POINTS)

OVERVIEW. *Orient Venus* was the first cruise ship built for its owners, Venus Cruise, part of Japan Cruise Line. This is a conventional-shaped ship with a reasonably graceful profile. There is a decent amount of open deck and sunbathing space, which is not often used. There is an expansive amount of open deck space for sunbathing, aft of funnel. Inside, the Night and Day Lounge set at funnel base looks forward over the swimming pool. Windows of the Orient is a small attractive, peaceful forward observation lounge. The conference facilities are excellent, and consist of both main and small conference rooms with 620 movable seats. There is a decent array of public rooms with tasteful, rather plain decor.

This cruise ship, with its western-style decor, will provide its mostly Japanese corporate passengers with extremely comfortable surroundings, and offers a superb cruise and seminar/learning environment and experience. *Orient Venus* was joined by a new, slightly larger sister ship, *Pacific Venus*, in 1998. A specialist courier company provides a luggage service that will collect your luggage from your home before the cruise, and deliver it back to your home after the cruise (this service available only in Japan). The onboard currency is the Japanese yen.

This ship does not really cater well to individual passengers. The decor is rather plain in many public rooms. The crew-to-passenger ratio is quite poor, but typical of seminar-intensive ships.

SUITABLE FOR: *Orient Venus* is best suited to Japanese-speaking couples and single travelers of mature years who enjoy traveling in very comfortable surroundings, and who

BERLITZ'S RATINGS

	Possible	Achieved
Ship	500	338
Accommodation	200	120
Food	400	287
Service	400	283
Entertainment	100	62
Cruise	400	281

enjoy good food and service, all at a moderate cost.

ACCOMMODATION. There are just four cabin grades (royal, deluxe, state and standard). The all-outside standard cabins, many of which have upper berths for third/fourth passengers, have decor that is best described as plain, with a reasonable amount of closet space and little drawer space. The largest suites (there are two) have an expansive lounge area with large, plush armchairs, coffee table, and window-side chairs and drinks table, floor-to-ceiling windows, and a large private balcony. There is a separate sleeping room (curtained off from the living room) with twin- or queen-sized bed, vanity/office desk, and large bathroom. All grades have a tea drinking set (with electric hot water kettle), color television, telephone, and stocked refrigerator.

CUISINE/DINING. The main dining room (single seating with assigned tables) is quite attractive, and there is plenty of space around the dining tables. An alternative Romanesque Grill is unusual, with its classic period Roman decor and a high, elegant ceiling. The ship offers reasonably good, but commercial Japanese cuisine (washoku) exclusively.

ENTERTAINMENT. The horseshoe-shaped Carnival Main Lounge is a single level room, and has good sightlines to the platform stage. On most cruises, special featured entertainers are brought on board from ashore (singers, instrumentalists, storytellers, dance champions, and others).

SPA/FITNESS. There is a Grand Bath each for males and females, and a small gymnasium.

Orion
★★★★ +

Boutique Ship: ....4,050 tons	Total Crew: 65	Cabins (with private balcony): 0
Lifestyle: ....Premium	Passengers	Cabins (wheelchair accessible): 0
Cruise Line: ....Travel Dynamics	(lower beds/all berths): 106/139	Cabin Current: ....110/220 volts
.......................International	Passenger Space Ratio	Elevators: 1
Former Names: ....none	(lower beds/all berths): 38.2/29.1	Casino (gaming tables): ....No
Builder: ......Cassens-Werft (Germany)	Crew/Passenger Ratio	Slot Machines: ....No
Original Cost: ....n/a	(lower beds/all berths): 1.6/2.1	Swimming Pools (outdoors): 0
Entered Service: ....November 2003	Navigation Officers: ....European	Swimming Pools (indoors): 0
Registry: ....The Bahamas	Cabins (total): 53	Whirlpools: 1
Length (ft/m): 337.0/102.7	Size Range (sq ft/m): 175.0–345.0/	Self-Service Launderette: ....No
Beam (ft/m): 46.0/14.00	53.3/105.0	Dedicated Cinema/Seats: ....No
Draft (ft/m): 12.2/3.7	Cabins (outside view): 53	Library: ....Yes
Propulsion/Propellers: diesel/2	Cabins (interior/no view): 0	Classification Society: Germanischer Lloyd
Passenger Decks: 7	Cabins (for one person): 0	

BERLITZ'S OVERALL SCORE: 1,612 (OUT OF A POSSIBLE 2,000 POINTS)

OVERVIEW. This small ship (an enlargement and refinement of two previous cruise ships built at the same shipyard, *Sun Bay* and *Sun Bay II*) is the latest in the quest to build the ideal expedition cruise ship, with all the comforts of home, and then some – as well as specialist equipment for expedition cruising. Although a small ship, *Orion* has stabilizers, as well as bow and stern thrusters for maximum maneuverability. The ship carries a fleet of 10 heavy-duty Zodiac inflatable landing craft and 10 two-seater kayaks for even more personal cruising and discovery. There is also an aft marina platform for swimming off (don't try this in Antarctica!). Travel Dynamics International has a long-term charter of this new expedition vessel.

The interior decor is warm and inviting, and provides a cozy, cosseting atmosphere that is far removed from the majority of (larger) expedition-style cruise ships today. Public rooms include an observation lounge (Galaxy Lounge), which opens onto a wrap-around open promenade deck; it also connects with the Vega Health Spa. Other public rooms include a dedicated Cosmos Lecture Hall (with surround sound system), main lounge, boutique, and an internet-connect computer center. Some rooms are clustered around a glass-walled atrium and the ship's sole elevator. For expedition use, a special "mud room" is provided (complete with boot washing stations), and this is adjacent to a Zodiac/tender loading platform on the port side.

SUITABLE FOR: *Orion* is best suited to mature couples and single travelers who like learning about nature and wildlife up close and personal, who enjoy quietly exploring the world around them, and who would not dream of cruising

BERLITZ'S RATINGS

	Possible	Achieved
Ship	500	422
Accommodation	200	163
Food	400	309
Service	400	300
Entertainment	N/A	N/A
Cruise	400	418

in the mainstream sense aboard ships with large numbers of people and a big city environment around them. This ship is for those in search of life enrichment in high-class surroundings and and the company of very well-educated and well-traveled people.

ACCOMMODATION. There are suites, and cabins. No matter what grade of accommodation you book (the size and location will dictate the price you pay), the facilities are top rate. All suites/cabins feature twin beds that can be converted to a queen-sized bed, a TV set, a DVD/CD player, a mini-refrigerator, ample closet space, and a marble-clad bathroom. All the cabinetry was custom-made, and the bathrooms were fitted individually.

CUISINE/DINING. The Constellation Restaurant has ocean-view picture windows, and serves all passengers in one open seating. The cuisine has become extremely good.

An open deck off the Leda Main Lounge serves as an al fresco dining spot for casual breakfasts and lunches; its name is the Delphinius Outdoor Cafe.

Many of the service staff are bright young people from former Eastern European countries. They communicate well, though their inexperience sometimes shows.

ENTERTAINMENT. There is no formal entertainment, but the lecturers are of the highest academic standards and provide fascinating, in-depth talks on many subjects.

SPA/FITNESS. The Vega Health Spa contains a fitness center, sauna, and private treatment rooms. A beauty salon is located one deck below.

Pacific Princess
★★★★

Mid-Size Ship: . . . . .30,277 tons	Passenger Decks: 9	Cabins (for one person): 0
Lifestyle: . . . . .Standard	Total Crew: 373	Cabins (with private balcony): 232
Cruise Line: . . . . . .P&O Cruises Australia/	Passengers	Cabins (wheelchair accessible): 3
Princess Cruises	(lower beds/all berths): 688/826	Cabin Current: . . . . .110 and 220 volts
Former Names: . . . . .R Three	Passenger Space Ratio	Elevators: 4
Builder: Chantiers de l'Atlantique (France)	(lower beds/all berths): 44.1/36.6	Casino (gaming tables): . . . . .Yes
Original Cost: . . . .$150 million	Crew/Passenger Ratio	Slot Machines: . . . . .Yes
Entered Service: . . . . .Aug 1999/Nov 2002	(lower beds/all berths): 1.8/2.2	Swimming Pools (outdoors): 1
Registry: . . . . .Gibraltar	Navigation Officers: . . . . .European	Swimming Pools (indoors): 0
Length (ft/m): 593.7/181.0	Cabins (total): 344	Whirlpools: . . . . . .2 (+ 1 thalassotherapy)
Beam (ft/m): 83.5/25.5	Size Range (sq ft/m): . . . . .145.3 – 968.7/	Self-Service Launderette: . . . . .Yes
Draft (ft/m): 19.5/6.0	13.5 – 90.0	Dedicated Cinema/Seats: . . . . .No
Propulsion/Propellers: . . . . .diesel-electric	Cabins (outside view): 317	Library: . . . . .Yes
(18,600kW)/2	Cabins (interior/no view): 27	Classification Society: . . . .Bureau Veritas

---

BERLITZ'S OVERALL SCORE: 1,487 (OUT OF A POSSIBLE 2,000 POINTS)

OVERVIEW. *Pacific Princess* was originally one of eight almost identical ships ordered and operated by the now defunct Renaissance Cruises. It now sports an all-white hull (it was formerly a black hull with white superstructure), which makes the ship appear larger. It has a large, square-ish funnel. The vessel cruises for part of the year under the Princess Cruises banner in French Polynesia, and six months under the P&O Cruises brand name in Australia (cruising from Sydney).

A lido deck has a swimming pool, and good sunbathing space, while one of the aft decks has a thalassotherapy pool. A jogging track circles the swimming pool deck (but one deck above). The uppermost outdoors deck includes a golf driving net and shuffleboard court.

The interior decor is quite stunning and elegant, a throwback to ship decor of the ocean liners of the 1920s and '30s, executed in fine taste. This includes detailed ceiling cornices, both real and faux wrought-iron staircase railings, leather- and cherry wood-paneled walls, *trompe l'oeil* ceilings, and rich carpeting in hallways with an Oriental rug-look center section. The overall feel is of an old-world country club. The staircase in the main, two-deck-high foyer recalls the staircase in the 1997 movie *Titanic*.

The public rooms are spread over three decks. The reception hall (lobby) has a staircase with intricate wrought-iron railings. The Nightclub, with forward-facing views, sits high in the ship and has Polynesian-inspired decor and furniture.

There are plenty of bars – including one in the entrance to each restaurant. Perhaps the nicest of all bars and lounges are in the casino bar/lounge that is a beautiful room reminiscent of London's grand hotels and understated gaming

BERLITZ'S RATINGS		
	Possible	Achieved
Ship	500	406
Accommodation	200	155
Food	400	265
Service	400	287
Entertainment	100	72
Cruise	400	302

clubs. It has an inviting marble fireplace (in fact, there are three such fireplaces aboard) and comfortable sofas and individual chairs. There is also a large Card Room, which incorporates an internet center with eight stations.

The Library is a beautiful, grand Regency-style room, with a fireplace, a high, indented, *trompe l'oeil* ceiling, and an excellent selection of books, as well as some very comfortable wing-back chairs with footstools, and sofas you could sleep on (it's the most relaxing room aboard).

Although there may not be marble bathroom fittings, or caviar and other (more expensive) niceties, the value for money is extremely good, and you have the opportunity to cruise in comfort aboard a mid-sized ship with plenty of dining choices. There's very little entertainment, but it is certainly not needed in the cruise areas featured. *Pacific Princess* and its sister ship *Tahitian Princess* are much more about relaxation than the larger ships in the Princess Cruises fleet, and would make good child-free vessels.

In common with all ships in the Princess Cruises fleet, 15% is added to all bar and spa accounts (drink prices are moderate, while beer prices are high), and a standard gratuity (about $10 per person, per day) is automatically added to your onboard account (if you think this is too much and want to reduce the amount, you'll need to go to the reception desk to do so).

There is no wrap-around promenade deck outdoors (there is, however, a small jogging track around the perimeter of the swimming pool, and port and starboard side decks), and no wooden decks outdoors (instead, they are covered by Bollidt, a sand-colored rubberized material). There is no sauna. The room service menu is extremely limited. Stairways, although carpeted, are tinny. In order to keep the prices low, often the air routing to get to/from your ship is not the most direct.

There is a charge (tokens must be obtained from the reception desk) for using the machines in the self-service launderette (a change machine in the launderette itself would be more user-friendly).

ACCOMMODATION. There is a variety of about eight different cabin types to choose from (the price will depend on the grade, location and size you choose).

All of the standard interior (no view) and outside-view cabins are extremely compact units, and extremely tight for two persons (particularly for cruises longer than seven days). Cabins have twin beds (or queen-size bed), with good under-bed storage areas, personal safe, vanity desk with large mirror, good closet and drawer space (in rich, dark woods), and bathrobe. Color TVs carry a major news channel (where obtainable), plus a sports channel and several round-the-clock movie channels. The bathrooms, which have tiled floors and plain walls, are compact, standard units, and include a shower enclosure with a removable, strong handheld shower unit, hairdryer, 100% cotton towels, toiletries storage shelves and a retractable clothesline.

The suites/cabins that have private balconies (66 percent of all suites/cabins, or 73 percent of all outside view suites/cabins) have partial, and not full, balcony partitions, sliding glass doors, and, due to good design and layout, only 14 cabins on Deck 6 have lifeboat-obstructed views. The balcony floor is covered in thick plastic matting (teak would be nicer) and some awful plastic furniture.

Mini-Suites: The 52 accommodation units designated as mini-suites, are in reality simply larger cabins than the standard varieties, as the sleeping and lounge areas are not divided. While not overly large, the bathrooms have a good-sized bathtub and ample space for storing personal toiletry items. The living area has a refrigerated mini-bar, lounge area with breakfast table, and a balcony with two plastic chairs and a table.

Owner's Suites: The 10 Owner's Suites are the most spacious accommodation, and are fine, large living spaces located in the forward-most and aft-most sections of the accommodation decks (particularly nice are those that overlook the stern, on Deck 6, 7 and 8). They have more extensive balconies that really are private and cannot be overlooked by anyone from the decks above. There is an entrance foyer, living room, bedroom (the bed faces the sea, which can be seen through the floor-to-ceiling windows and sliding glass door), CD player, bathroom with Jacuzzi bathtub, as well as a small guest bathroom.

CUISINE/DINING. There are four different dining spots: three restaurants and one casual self-serve buffet:

● **The Club Restaurant** has 338 seats (all chairs have armrests), and includes a large raised central section. There are large ocean-view windows on three sides, and some prime tables that overlook the stern, as well as a small band-stand for occasional live dinner music. However, the noise level can be high, owing to the single-deck-height ceiling.

● **Sabatini's Trattoria** is an Italian restaurant, with 96 seats (all chairs have armrests), windows along two sides, and a set *bellissima* three-hour "degustation" menu. The cover charge is $15 per person.

● **The Sterling Steakhouse** is an "American steak house" (with a good selection of large, prime steaks and other meats). It has 98 comfortable seats (all chairs have armrests), windows along two sides, and a set menu (together with added daily chef's specials). The cover charge is $8 per person.

● **The Lido Cafe** has seating for 154 indoors and 186 outdoors (with white plastic patio furniture). It is open for breakfast, lunch and casual dinners. It is the ship's self-serve buffet restaurant (open 24 hours a day), and has a small pizzeria and grill.

All restaurants have open-seating dining, so you dine when you want, although reservations are necessary for Sabatini's Trattoria and Sterling Steakhouse, where there are mostly tables for four or six (there are few tables for two). In addition, there is a Poolside Grill and Bar for those fast-food items provided for on-deck munching.

ENTERTAINMENT. The 345-seat Cabaret Lounge, located in the forward part of the ship on Deck 5, is the main venue for entertainment events and some social functions. The single-level room has a stage, and circular hardwood dance floor with adjacent banquette and individual tub chair seating, and raised sections on port and starboard sides. It is not a large room, and not really designed for production shows, so cabaret acts and local entertainment form the main focus, with mini-revue style shows with colorful costumes, presented by a troupe of resident singer/dancers in a potted version of what you might experience aboard the large ships of Princess Cruises. Inevitably, art auctions and bingo are pushed almost daily.

The ship carries a band, small musical units, and solo entertaining pianists to provide live music for shows and dancing in the lounges and bars before and after dinner.

SPA/FITNESS. Facilities, which are located in the forward part of the ship on a high deck (Deck 9) consist of a gymnasium (with ocean view windows) with some high-tech muscle-toning equipment and treadmills, steam rooms (no sauna) and changing areas for men and women, and a beauty salon with ocean view windows.

The spa is operated by Steiner, a specialist concession whose retail products will be pushed. Some fitness classes are free (Stepexpress, Power Walk, Total Body Conditioning, Xpress Circuit are examples), while some, such as yoga and kick-boxing, cost $10 per class. Massage (including exotic massages such as Aroma Stone massage, Chakra Balancing massage and other well-being massages), facials, pedicures, and beauty salon treatments are at extra cost (massage, for example, costs about $2 per minute, plus gratuity). Make appointments early as time slots go quickly.

Pacific Sky
★★★ +

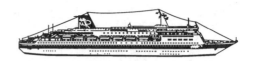

Large (Resort) Ship: ....46,392 tons	Total Crew: 550	Cabins (with private balcony): 10
Lifestyle: ....Standard	Passengers	Cabins (wheelchair accessible): 10
Cruise Line: ......P&O Cruises (Australia)	(lower beds/all berths): 1,200/1,550	Cabin Current: ....110 and 220 volts
Former Names: ....*Sky Princess, Fairsky*	Passenger Space Ratio	Elevators: 6
Builder: .............C.N.I.M. (France)	(lower beds/all berths): 38.6/34.3	Casino (gaming tables): ....Yes
Original Cost: ....$156 million	Crew/Passenger Ratio	Slot Machines: ....Yes
Entered Service: .....Mar 1984/Nov 2000	(lower beds/all berths): 2.1/2.8	Swimming Pools (outdoors): 3
Registry: ....Great Britain	Navigation Officers: ....British	Swimming Pools (indoors): 0
Length (ft/m): 788.6/240.39	Cabins (total): 600	Whirlpools: 1
Beam (ft/m): 91.3/27.84	Size Range (sq ft/m): 168.9–519.9/	Self-Service Launderette: ....Yes
Draft (ft/m): 26.7/8.15	15.7–48.3	Dedicated Cinema/Seats: Yes/283
Propulsion/Propellers: .....steam turbine	Cabins (outside view): 385	Library: ....Yes
(21,700 kW)/2	Cabins (interior/no view): 215	Classification Society: ...Lloyd's Register
Passenger Decks: 11	Cabins (for one person): 0	

OVERALL SCORE: 1,251 (OUT OF A POSSIBLE 2,000 POINTS)

OVERVIEW. *Pacific Sky* is quite a well-designed vessel that has a short, sharply raked bow and a large, swept-back funnel. This was the first cruise ship to have steam turbine machinery since Cunard Line's *Queen Elizabeth 2* debuted in 1969, so there is almost no vibration (it was originally ordered by Sitmar Cruises, which was itself acquired by Princess Cruises in 1988). *Pacific Sky* is a much more contemporary, and spacious ship, with many more facilities than the old but much loved ship it replaced, *Fair Princess*. The outdoors deck and sunbathing space is not really generous, but at least cushioned pads are provided for the deck lounge chairs.

Inside the ship, the layout is quite comfortable and it is easy to find one's way around – good signing also helps. The clean, bland, clinical, yet oddly tasteful minimalist interior decor lacks warmth – some flowers and greenery are needed. There is a decent enough array of public rooms, including some expansive shopping space on Rodeo Drive. There are nine bars/lounges, including a showlounge and Sports Bar, a recently added internet facility, and a 24-hour florist's shop. The Horizon Lounge, set atop the ship, is restful at night. The casino has a split configuration.

Another lounge, the Verandah Lounge, includes a dance floor and live music, while the Starlight Lounge is also for dancing and lively late-night cabaret. The ship has its own dedicated cinema (something that few new ships seem to provide), complete with balcony level.

Families with children are well cared for (parents can enjoy themselves while they leave their children in the capable care of P&O staff). Children also have their own area; it is located aft on Aloha Deck, and has an outdoor splash

BERLITZ'S RATINGS

	Possible	Achieved
Ship	500	336
Accommodation	200	139
Food	400	237
Service	400	230
Entertainment	100	63
Cruise	400	254

pool, and a whole, brightly colored roomful of activities and fun things to play with. A team of children's counselors attends to the children and provides their own daily programming and activities. Children under 18 months old are not accepted as passengers.

This ship provides a reasonably well-balanced, pleasing cruise experience for the mature passenger, with plenty of space and little crowding, although service does suffer from carelessness and lack of training and supervision. British officers and Filipino dining staff help to create a fairly friendly ambiance aboard this ship, which began operations in 2000 when it was renamed *Pacific Sky*, with a home base in Sydney, Australia. The onboard currency is the Australian dollar.

Sadly, there is no wrap-around promenade deck outdoors, although there is a decent enclosed promenade deck. There are simply too many interior (no view) cabins. Public restrooms are often out of order, and cleanliness leaves much to be desired; some of this due to problems with the ship's plumbing. Standing in line for embarkation, disembarkation, shore tenders and for self-serve buffet meals is an inevitable aspect of cruising aboard all large ships, and this one is no exception.

SUITABLE FOR: *Pacific Sky* is best suited to young, and young-at-heart couples and singles for a first cruise Australian style, who want a good basic getaway cruise aboard a ship that offers some good drinking places, lots of noise and good cheer, in fairly comfortable surroundings.

ACCOMMODATION. There are 15 grades (the price you pay will depend on the grade, location and size you choose):

two categories of suites, six outside-view cabin grades and seven interior (no view) cabin grades.

The cabins are, for the most part, fairly spacious, comfortable, and well-appointed, with all the essentials and good-sized rectangular showers. There are, however, too many interior (no view) cabins. The cabin walls and ceilings are plain and unappealing, and need some splashes of color to brighten them.

The largest accommodation can be found in 10 suites on Lido Deck, all of which are named after famous places (Capri, Portofino, Estoril, Monaco, Malaga on the port side, and Antibes, Minorca, St. Tropez, San Remo, Amalfi on the starboard side). These are really fine living spaces, and provide extra comforts such as a mini-bar/refrigerator, walk-in closet, and a larger bathroom (with bathtub and shower), and a private (but narrow) balcony. All have a queen-sized bed, with the exception of Amalfi and Malaga, which have fixed twin beds.

There are 28 mini-suites, all of which have separate sleeping and living areas, with dressing table, sofa, coffee table and chairs, and mini-bar/refrigerator.

Many cabins have one or two additional upper berths, making them extremely cramped when occupied (storage of luggage can be a problem), but they are useful for families with children. All cabins suffer from inadequate soundproofing, but all have a color television, and two lower beds. A room service menu is available 24 hours a day. Cabins at the aft end of Aloha Deck may be subject to noise from the adjacent Children's Playroom.

CUISINE/DINING. There are two dining rooms (Regency and Savoy, with the galley positioned between them), assigned according to the accommodation you choose. Both are non-smoking, brightly lit and have pleasant decor. There are two seatings, and tables are for four, six or eight (there are no tables for two).

The food is largely standard fare and a little repetitive; quality, flair and presentation could be better. Mainly friendly male Filipino waiters provide the dining room service, although it lacks finesse and I receive many complaints from passengers about careless service and tables not being served separately, issues which still need to be addressed.

Dinners are four course events, while lunches consist of three courses. The cuisine is quite adequate, but not by any stretch of the imagination could it be called gourmet. The choice of salad items could be better, and the selection of desserts includes many canned items (cheap and cheerful). A new alternative dining spot, introduced in 2004, is an outdoor steakhouse (reservations are required for dinner and there is a cover charge); it also offers complimentary hamburgers, hot dogs and pasta for lunch.

For casual daytime snacking, there is the Al Fresco self-serve buffet on deck. Also available are New Zealand ice cream, milkshakes and pastries (all at extra cost). Other casual eateries include a Pizzeria, open 24 hours a day. There's also Harry's Cafe de Waves (based on the Sydney icon, and famous for its world renowned "Pie and Peas"), for snacks, including hot dogs. Both the Pizzeria and Harry's Cafe de Waves are extra charge outlets (not included in the cruise price).

ENTERTAINMENT. Production shows and major cabaret acts are presented in the Pacific Sky Showlounge, located at the forward end of Promenade Deck, with easy access from the forward stairway and lifts. Although it is a single level room (most new cruise ships today have at least two levels for their showlounges), decent visibility can be had from most seats, following improvements that were made by the ship's previous owners, Princess Cruises.

SPA/FITNESS. The Spa is located on Sun Deck, and houses an L-shaped gymnasium (with starboard side ocean-view windows), and saunas, massage rooms (there aren't enough of them) and changing rooms for men and women. If you want to book spa treatments (massages, facials, pedicures, hair beautification), it is wise to do so as soon after you embark as possible, as the limited number of time slots do fill up quickly (note that there are few treatments compared to, say the Caribbean ships, because many Australians consider wellbeing treatments rather "namby pamby"). A beauty salon is located in a different area, on Caribe Deck. Outdoors on deck is a jogging track.

Pacific Sun
NOT YET RATED

Mid-Size Ship: . . . . .47,262 tons	Total Crew: 670	Cabins (with private balcony): 10
Lifestyle: . . . . .Standard	Passengers	Cabins (wheelchair accessible): 14
Cruise Line: . . . . . .P&O Cruises (Australia)	(lower beds/all berths): 1,486/1,896	Cabin Current: . . . . .110 volts
Former Names: . . . . .Jubilee	Passenger Space Ratio	Elevators: 8
Builder: . . . . .Kockums (Sweden)	(lower beds/all berths): 31.8/24.9	Casino (gaming tables): . . . . .Yes
Original Cost: . . . .$134 million	Crew/Passenger Ratio	Slot Machines: . . . . .Yes
Entered Service: . . . .July 1986/Oct 2004	(lower beds/all berths): 2.2/2.8	Swimming Pools (outdoors): 3
Registry: . . . . .The Bahamas	Navigation Officers: . . . . .Italian	Swimming Pools (indoors): 0
Length (ft/m): 733.0/223.4	Cabins (total): 743	Whirlpools: 2
Beam (ft/m): 92.5/28.2	Size Range (sq ft/m): 182.9–419.8/	Self-Service Launderette: . . . . .Yes
Draft (ft/m): 24.7/7.5	17.0–39.0	Dedicated Cinema/Seats: . . . . .No
Propulsion/Propellers: . . . . .diesel	Cabins (outside view): 453	Library: . . . . .Yes
(23,520 kW)/2	Cabins (interior/no view): 290	Classification Society: . . .Lloyd's Register
Passenger Decks: 9	Cabins (for one person): 0	

OVERALL SCORE: NYR (OUT OF A POSSIBLE 2,000 POINTS)

OVERVIEW. Formerly *Jubilee*, the third new-build ordered by Carnival Cruise Lines, this ship has a bold, forthright, angular all-white profile, and short bows. In 2004, it was transferred to P&O Cruises (Australia), and was transformed and refurbished to provide passenger facilities for year-round cruises from Australia under its new name, *Pacific Sun*. Fractionally larger and younger than distant sister ship *Pacific Sky*, it has no wrap-around promenade deck outdoors. *Pacific Sun* also has a lower overall per passenger space ratio, but it does have an altogether more youthful, sporty image. There is more sunbathing space outdoors, and one of the swimming pools has a twisting, two-decks high (controlled) water slide that will empty you into it.

Inside the ship, most of the public rooms are arranged on one deck (Atlantic Deck). A double-wide indoor promenade, Park Lane, acts as a boulevard, off which 10 bars and lounges and other public rooms are located. The decor consist of flamboyant, vivid colors in all the public rooms (the rooms themselves were not changed that much during the recent refurbishment) except for the rather more elegant Churchill's Library, a decent place to sit and read, or connect to the internet (watch out for the knights in suits of armor). A large Sporting Club Casino (with gaming tables for blackjack, roulette, pokies, and lots of slot machines) provides almost round-the-clock action.

This ship lays on constant entertainment and activities designed for passenger participation in a party-like setting, and is a floating (Fosters) playground for young, active adults who enjoy constant stimulation, close contact with lots and lots of others, as well as glitz, glamour and gam-

BERLITZ'S RATINGS

	Possible	Achieved
Ship	500	NYR
Accommodation	200	NYR
Food	400	NYR
Service	400	NYR
Entertainment	100	NYR
Cruise	400	NYR

bling. There's plenty for kids to do, too, and facilities (including a children's club and activity center) to cater to up to 300 of them.

Pacific Sun, now more than 10 years old, provides novice Aussie and Kiwi cruisers with a good first-cruise experience in comfortable, but visually busy surroundings. The onboard currency is the Australian dollar. Note that standing in line for embarkation, disembarkation, shore tenders and for self-serve buffet meals is an inevitable aspect of cruising aboard all large ships; this one is no exception. Oh, and it's a pity about those ridiculous art auctions (and the same tacky, useless "art" seen aboard so many other cruise ships, particularly those of P&O/Princess Cruises). But it's all part of "Funship Cruising" in the down-under world.

SUITABLE FOR: *Pacific Sun* is best suited to young, and young-at-heart couples, singles and families with children for a first cruise, Australian style, who want a good basic getaway cruise aboard a ship that offers some good drinking places, lots of noise, good cheer, in fairly upbeat surroundings, all delivered with friendly service that lacks polish.

ACCOMMODATION. There are 13 different price categories for ocean-view and interior (no view) cabins (most of which are of the same approximate size), and two categories for suites. The price you pay depends on the deck and location of the accommodation chosen (typically, the higher the deck, the more you pay).

Especially nice are 10 large suites on Verandah Deck (although there are obstructed views from four of them), each of which has a private balcony. Almost all other cabins are relatively spacious units that are neatly appointed, and have attractive, though rather spartan, decor.

The ocean-view cabins have large picture windows. There are many, many interior (no view) cabins, although they are actually quite spacious, and good for anyone on a low budget (however, if this is your first cruise, try to book one of the ocean-view cabins), with two lower beds, small vanity unit, and a reasonable-sized bathroom. Some cabins have additional upper berths, and even rollaway beds (good for families with small children), although space will be extremely limited unless the kids are very, very small.

CUISINE/DINING. There are two no-smoking dining rooms: Burgundy, located midships, and Bordeaux, located aft, with the galley between them. They are quite cramped when full, and extremely noisy (particularly at those tables adjacent to the large waiter stations), and they have low ceilings in their raised center sections. There are tables for four, six or eight (there are no tables for two), and many banquette seats (individual chairs do not have armrests). Window-side tables are for six (they are typically also the quietest tables). The decor is bright and extremely colorful, and extremely jolly.

The Lido Deck poolside self-serve Outback Bar & Grill offers casual meals. At night, it provides a casual (dress down) alternative to eating in the main dining rooms, serving pasta, steaks, salads and desserts. For casual food there's also a sushi bar and a poolside pizzeria; and New Zealand natural ice cream is served at a counter close by.

ENTERTAINMENT. The Atlantis Showlounge (the principal venue for production shows and major cabaret acts) is two decks high, decorated in high glitz, and has seating on both main and balcony levels. However, pillars obstruct the sight lines on the main level, and railings obstruct sight lines from many seats on the balcony level. In a typical cruise, there will be several production shows, typically with a cast of two lead singers and a clutch of dancers, backed by a live orchestra. The room also doubles as a cinema for big-screen movies.

Almost every lounge/bar has live bands and musical units, so there is always plenty of live music happening (mostly in the evenings).

SPA/FITNESS. The Lotus Spa is on the ship's uppermost deck, just aft of the mast, and accessed by the center stairway and lifts. The facility is small by today's standards, but includes a gymnasium (with some high-tech muscle-pumping cardiovascular machines) with views over one of the ship's swimming pools; there are also changing rooms and saunas for men and women. The beauty salon is located in another spot, just aft of the Showlounge.

If you want to book spa and beauty treatments (massages, facials, pedicures, hair beautification), it is wise to do so as soon after you embark as possible, as the limited number of time slots do fill up quickly (note that there are few treatments compared to, say the Caribbean ships, because many Australians consider wellbeing treatments rather "namby pamby.")

Pacific Venus
★★★★ +

Mid-Size Ship: . . . . .26,518 tons	Passenger Decks: 7	Cabins (with private balcony): 20
Lifestyle: . . . . .Standard	Total Crew: 180	Cabins (wheelchair accessible): 1
Cruise Line: . . . . .Venus Cruise	Passengers	Cabin Current: . . . . .110 volts
Former Names: . . . . .none	(lower beds/all berths): 532/720	Elevators: 4
Builder: . . . . .Ishikawajima Heavy	Passenger Space Ratio	Casino (gaming tables): . . . . .Yes
Industries (Japan)	(lower beds/all berths): 49.8/36.8	Slot Machines: . . . . .No
Original Cost: . . . .$114 million	Crew/Passenger Ratio	Swimming Pools (outdoors): 1
(Yen13 billion)	(lower beds/all berths): 2.9/4.0	(+ 1 for children)
Entered Service: . . . . .Apr 1998	Navigation Officers: . . . . .Japanese	Swimming Pools (indoors): 0
Registry: .Japan	Cabins (total): 266	Whirlpools: 1
Length (ft/m): 601.7/183.4	Size Range (sq ft/m): 164.6–699.6/	Self-Service Launderette: . . . . .Yes (2)
Beam (ft/m): 82.0/25.0	15.3–65.0	Dedicated Cinema/Seats: Yes/94
Draft (ft/m): 21.3/6.5	Cabins (outside view): 250	Library: . . . . .Yes
Propulsion/Propellers: . . . . .diesel	Cabins (interior/no view): 16	Classification Society: . . . . . . .Nippon Kaiji
(13,636 kW)/2	Cabins (for one person): 0	Kyokai

OVERALL SCORE: 1,601 (OUT OF A POSSIBLE 2,000 POINTS)

OVERVIEW. Venus Cruise is part of Japan Cruise Line, which is itself part of SHK Line Group, a joint venture between the Shin Nohonkai, Hankyu and Kanpu ferry companies (operating more than 20 ferries). The company also owns and operates the slightly smaller, older and more basic *Orient Venus*, a ship that was really designed principally for the charter and incentive group market. *Pacific Venus*, which is being operated for individual cruises (no charters) has one more deck than *Orient Venus*, and is slightly longer and beamier.

There is a good amount of open deck space aft of the funnel, good for deck sports, while protected sunbathing space is provided around the small swimming pool (all deck lounge chairs have cushioned pads).

The base of the funnel itself is the site of a day/night lounge, which overlooks the swimming pool (it is slightly reminiscent of Royal Caribbean International's lounges). There is a wrap-around (rubber-coated) promenade deck outdoors. Inside the ship, there is plenty of space per passenger. The decor is clean and fresh, with much use of pastel colors and blond woods, giving the interiors a feeling of warmth.

One deck (Deck 7) has a double-width indoor promenade off which the dining rooms are located. The atrium is three decks high and has a crystal chandelier as its focal point.

There are special rooms for meetings and conference organizers, for times when the ship is chartered. There is a piano salon with colorful low-back chairs, a large main hall (with a finely sculptured high ceiling and 720 moveable seats – production shows are performed here), a 350-seat main lounge for cabaret shows, a small theater, a library

BERLITZ'S RATINGS		
	Possible	Achieved
Ship	500	415
Accommodation	200	150
Food	400	319
Service	400	318
Entertainment	100	78
Cruise	400	321

and card room, a casino, two private karaoke rooms, a Japanese chashitsu room for tea ceremonies (a tatami-matted room), and a beauty salon. There is a 24-hour vending machine corner (juice, beer, camera film and other items), self-service launderette (no charge), and several (credit card/coin) public telephone booths. Overall, this company provides a well-packaged cruise in a ship that presents a very comfortable, serene environment. The dress code is relaxed and no tipping is allowed. The onboard currency is the Japanese yen.

There are few cabins with private balcony. The open walking promenade decks are rubber-coated steel – teak would be more desirable.

SUITABLE FOR: *Pacific Venus* is best suited to Japanese-speaking couples and single travelers of mature years who enjoy traveling in very comfortable surroundings, and who enjoy good food and service, all at a moderate cost.

ACCOMMODATION. There are six different types: royal suites, suites, deluxe cabins, state cabins (in four different price grades), and standard cabins, all located from the uppermost to lowermost decks, respectively.

The four Royal Suites are decorated in two different styles – one contemporary, one more traditional Japanese style. Each has a private balcony, with sliding door (teak table and two chairs), an expansive lounge area with large sofa and plush armchairs, coffee table, window-side chairs and drinks table, floor-to-ceiling windows, and a VCR. There is a separate bedroom, with twin- or queen-sized bed, vanity/writing desk, large walk-in closet with personal safe, and a large bathroom with a tiny Jacuzzi bathtub. The bathroom has ocean-view windows, separate shower and his/hers sinks.

Sixteen suites also have private balconies (with teak table and two chairs), a good-sized living area with vanity/writing desk, dining table, chair and curved sofa, separate sleeping area, and bathroom with deep bathtub slightly larger than the Royal suites, and single large sink. There is ample lighted closet and drawer space (two locking drawers instead of a personal safe), and a VCR.

The 20 Deluxe cabins have large picture windows fronted by a large, curtained arch, sleeping area with twin (or queen) beds, plus a daytime sofa that converts into a third bed.

The 210 state cabins, (172 of which have upper berths for third passengers), have decor that is best described as basic, with a reasonable closet, but little drawer space.

The 16 standard cabins are really plain, but accommodate three persons, although the drawer and storage space is a bit tight.

All cabin grades have a tea drinking set (with electric hot water kettle), color TV, telephone, stocked mini-bar/refrigerator (all items included in the cruise price). Bathrooms have a hairdryer, and lots of Shiseido personal toiletry items (particularly in the suites, which include after-shave, hair liquid, hair tonic, skin lotion, body lotion, shampoo, rinse, razor, toothbrush, toothpaste, sewing kit, shower cap, hairbrush, clothes brush and shoe horn). All room service menu items cost extra (this is typical of all Japanese cruise ships). All passengers receive a yukata (Japanese-style light cotton robe); suite occupants also get a plush bathrobe.

CUISINE/DINING. The Primavera Dining Room (the ship's main dining room) is located aft, with ocean views on three sides. Passengers dine in one seating, and tables are for six, 10 or 12. The food consists of both Japanese and Western items; the menu is varied and the food is attractively presented.

A second, intimate, yet moderately stately 42-seat alternative restaurant, called Grand Siècle, has an à la carte menu, which incurs an extra charge for everything; it is decorated in Regency-style, with much fine wood-paneling and a detailed, indented ceiling.

ENTERTAINMENT. Le Pacific Main Lounge is the venue for all shipboard entertainment (it also functions as a lecture and activities room during the day). It is a single-level room with seating clustered around a "thrust" stage so that entertainers are in the very midst of their audience.

On most cruises, special featured entertainers are brought on board from ashore (singers, instrumentalists, storytellers, dance champions, and others).

SPA/FITNESS. Spa facilities include male and female Grand Baths, which include bathing pool and health/cleansing facilities, ocean-view windows; a gymnasium, also with ocean-view windows; and a sauna. Japanese massage is available, as are hairdressing and barber services in the small salon (located on the lowest passenger-accessible deck of the ship).

Paloma I
★★

Small Ship: ....12,586 tons	Passenger Decks: 6	Cabins (for one person): 0
Lifestyle: ....Standard	Total Crew: 170	Cabins (with private balcony): 0
Cruise Line: D&P Cruises/Hansa Touristik	Passengers	Cabins (wheelchair accessible): 0
Former Names: ....*Paloma, Dimitri*	(lower beds/all berths): 354/400	Cabin Current: ....220 volts
Shostakovich	Passenger Space Ratio	Elevators: 2
Builder: ......Szczesin Stocznia (Poland)	(basis 2/all berths): 35.5/31.4	Casino (gaming tables): ....No
Original Cost: ....n/a	Crew/Passenger Ratio	Slot Machines: ....Yes
Entered Service: 1980	(lower beds/all berths): 2.0/2.3	Swimming Pools (outdoors): 1
Registry: ....The Bahamas	Navigation Officers: ....Ukrainian	Swimming Pools (indoors): 0
Length (ft/m): 449.9/137.15	Cabins (total): 177	Whirlpools: 0
Beam (ft/m): 68.8/21.00	Size Range (sq ft/sq m): 100–320/	Self-Service Launderette: ....No
Draft (ft/m): 19.0/5.8	9.2–29.7	Dedicated Cinema/Seats: ....No
Propulsion/Propellers: ....diesel	Cabins (outside view): 93	Library: ....Yes
(12,806 kW)/2	Cabins (interior/no view): 84	Classification Society: ....KM

OVERALL SCORE: 947 (OUT OF A POSSIBLE 2,000 POINTS)

OVERVIEW. *Paloma I* has a square, very angular profile with a boxy stern (complete with fold-down aft ramp), stubby bow and a fat funnel – otherwise it's moderately handsome! The navigation bridge is of the (almost) fully enclosed type for all-weather operation. There is a small helicopter landing deck.

The ship was originally built in Poland as one of a series of five sister ships (the original names of the five were: *Dimitriy Shostakovich, Konstantin Simonov, Lev Tolstoi, Mikhail Sholokhov,* and *Petr Pervyy*). They were designed for carrying both cars and passengers on line voyages (principally within Europe and Russia) with a large aft ramp for loading cars and stores. The loading ramp is still in use for loading stores, and, when *Paloma I* operates during the summer on European/Mediterranean itineraries, passengers can drive to the port of embarkation and park their cars on board (the ship can carry up to 50 cars).

Inside the ship, the decor is reasonably smart, and consists principally of soft pastel colors, with no glitz in evidence anywhere. Public rooms include a main lounge (low budget, basic evening shows are performed here, although 13 pillars obstruct the sight lines); beer bar, which doubles as a video showing room (but the wooden seats are hard); three bars (one indoors, one by the swimming pool, and one "beer garden").

The ship is comfortable, and the lifestyle is very casual, although you may want to take a jacket and tie/cocktail dress for the one Captain's Dinner evening typical of each cruise. The main thing is that the ship is clean and tidy, and the staff is warm and friendly. Holsten beer (from Hamburg) appears to sponsor the provision

BERLITZ'S RATINGS

	Possible	Achieved
Ship	500	185
Accommodation	200	89
Food	400	215
Service	400	226
Entertainment	100	37
Cruise	400	195

of beer mats, glasses and ashtrays.

Paloma I is owned by an Italian company (Di Maio Cruises), and is presently under charter to Hansa Touristik of Germany, a company well known for providing cruise holidays at very low prices. A cruise aboard *Paloma I* will give you a basic but comfortable cruise experience at very modest rates, but you should not expect too much. The ship simply cannot compete with the much better hardware provided by most other companies operating in the German-speaking market. So book *Paloma I* because you want to go to the destinations and itineraries, which are attractive, and not because of the vessel itself.

While most of the service crew is Ukrainian, there is also a sprinkling of Germans and Austrians in key hotel management positions. Tickets come in a nice pouch that includes pocket guides to the ports of call. The onboard currency is the euro.

Both interior and exterior staircases are quite steep, the ship having been originally constructed as a roll-on, roll-off passenger ferry. There is no observation lounge with forward-facing views over the ship's bows. The amount of open deck and sunning space is limited (particularly if the ship is full) and the small swimming pool is really merely a "dip" pool. The port and starboard open promenade decks are steel, painted blue.

SUITABLE FOR: *Paloma I* is best suited to youthful German-speaking couples and single travelers who are looking for a good value for money first cruise aboard a ship with traditional, modestly comfortable (but not pretentious or luxurious) surroundings, at a low price, with interesting itineraries.

ACCOMMODATION. There are 10 cabin price grades, although there is little difference in the size of most of these price categories, the difference in price being for deck and location. Of these, there are 3 suites, 6 junior suites, the rest of the accommodation being standard exterior view and interior (no view) cabins.

Suites/Junior Suites: The three suites have a completely separate bedroom with plenty of closet space (although there are no drawers, there are a few shelves), and a large bathroom with shower enclosure. The six junior suites have only a larger bathroom, with shower enclosure. The suites and junior suites each have a TV set and a video player.

Standard Exterior View/Interior (no view) Cabins: The standard cabins are very small and somewhat utilitarian in their fittings and furnishings; there is almost no drawer space, and the under-bed storage space for luggage is tight (however, you may need to use your suitcase as storage space, particularly for small items of clothing). Many cabins are fitted with upper Pullman berths, although these are seldom used, except by families with children.

All cabins come with a private bathroom, with shower enclosure, and a small cabinet for personal toiletry items (note that only soap is supplied, so do take your own shampoo, conditioner, hand cream and any other personal toiletries that you might need).

Note that there is no room service menu, nor is it possible to obtain tea/coffee in your cabin.

CUISINE/DINING. The dining room is totally non-smoking, and seats approximately 370 passengers in one seating (a real bonus for leisurely dining). It is quite attractive, and has large picture windows on three sides, although the ceiling is quite low.

There is also a small, additional section that could be used as a private dining room, useful for small groups. Meals are provided by an Italian maritime catering company, which does a fine job (taking into account the low price of a cruise aboard this ship).

High-quality meats and plenty of fresh vegetables is the mainstay of the cuisine. Although fish dishes are disappointing, vegetarian meals are creative. Service is provided by Ukrainian waiters and waitresses. Although they have little finesse and not much knowledge regarding the food, they are attractive, smile, and try hard.

The wine list is also quite basic, with young wines being the mainstay of the list.

ENTERTAINMENT. The showlounge is not strictly a show lounge, and there are very limited facilities. Entertainment is, therefore, very low-key and cabaret style, with individual acts comprising mostly of singers, magicians, and other cabaret acts.

SPA/FITNESS. There is no spa as such, although there is a sauna (a charge applies), with its own changing area.

Paradise
★★★ +

Large (Resort) Ship: ....70,367 tons	Total Crew: 920	Cabins (with private balcony): 26
Lifestyle: ....Standard	Passengers	Cabins (wheelchair accessible): 22
Cruise Line: ......Carnival Cruise Lines	(lower beds/all berths): 2,052/2,594	Cabin Current: ....110 volts
Former Names: ....none	Passenger Space Ratio	Elevators: 14
Builder: ...Kvaerner Masa-Yards (Finland)	(lower beds/all berths): 34.2/26.7	Casino (gaming tables): ....Yes
Original Cost: ....$300 million	Crew/Passenger Ratio	Slot Machines: ....Yes
Entered Service: ....Nov 1998	(lower beds/all berths): 2.2/2.8	Swimming Pools (outdoors): 3
Registry: ....Panama	Navigation Officers: ....Italian	Swimming Pools (indoors): 0
Length (ft/m): 855.0/260.6	Cabins (total): 1,026	Whirlpools: 6
Beam (ft/m): 103.3/31.5	Size Range (sq ft/m): 173.2–409.7/	Self-Service Launderette: ....Yes
Draft (ft/m): 25.9/7.9	16.0–38.0	Dedicated Cinema/Seats: ....No
Propulsion/Propellers: .....diesel-electric	Cabins (outside view): 618	Library: ....Yes
(42,842 kW)/2 azimuthing pods	Cabins (interior/no view): 408	Classification Society: ...Lloyd's Register
Passenger Decks:..................10	Cabins (for one person): 0	

OVERALL SCORE: 1,390 (OUT OF A POSSIBLE 2,000 POINTS)

OVERVIEW. *Paradise* is the eighth (and final) in a series of eight mega-ships of the same series and identical internal configuration (the others are *Ecstasy, Elation, Fantasy, Fascination, Imagination, Inspiration,* and *Sensation*), and the 13th new ship for this cruise line. It has proven to be a successful design for this company that targets the standard (mainstream) market, and particularly the first-time passenger.

The ship, whose bows are extremely short, has the distinctive, large, swept-back wing-tipped funnel that is the trademark of Carnival Cruise Lines, in the company colors of red, white and blue. The ship has expansive open deck areas (sadly, there is no wrap-around open promenade deck), but they quickly become inadequate when it is full and everyone wants to be out on deck (the aft decks tend to be less noisy, whereas all the activities are focused around the main swimming pool and hot tubs). There is also a "banked" jogging track outdoors on the deck above a large, glass-enclosed health spa that is always busy. A well-defined "topless" sunbathing area can be found around the funnel base on Verandah Deck.

The ship has a bold, forthright, angular appearance that is typical of today's space-creative designs. *Paradise* is fitted with a "podded" propulsion system (this replaces the traditional propeller shaft and rudder combination that is normally fitted aboard most cruise ships), which gives the ship more maneuvrability, while reducing machinery space requirements, as well as vibration at the stern, and the need for stern thrusters. The pods themselves (each weighs 170 tons without its mounting) look rather like huge outboard motors that are capable of 360 degree rotation. When going ahead the pods face with the propeller forward; to go astern

BERLITZ'S RATINGS

	Possible	Achieved
Ship	500	395
Accommodation	200	151
Food	400	221
Service	400	270
Entertainment	100	81
Cruise	400	272

the pods can be rotated through 180 degrees, or simply by reversing the thrust when the propeller is in the forward position.

If you remember *Paradise* as a non-smoking ship, forget it: Carnival extinguished the no-smoking policy in 2004, when the ship was redeployed to another home port. Shame!

All of the principal public rooms are set off to one side of a double-width boulevard. The interior decor includes splashy, showy, public rooms and interior colors – pure Las Vegas, ideal for some tastes. Public entertainment lounges, bars and clubs galore offer something for everyone, including a children's playroom that is larger than aboard the other ships in this series of eight. Some busy colors and design themes abound in the handsome public rooms – these are connected by wide indoor boulevards and beg your attention and indulgence. There is also a good art collection, much of it bright and eye-catching. The Blue Riband library is a fine-looking room, as aboard most Carnival ships; although there are few books, there are models of ocean liners.

One neat feature (not found aboard previous ships in this series) is an atrium bar, with live classical music. Facilities include a large shop stuffed to the gills with low-quality merchandise; a large casino with gaming tables for blackjack, craps, roulette, Caribbean stud poker, as well as slot machines (all slot machines aboard all Carnival ships are linked into a big prize, called, naturally, Megacash).

ACCOMMODATION. There are 13 grades, priced according to grade, size and location. The standard outside-view and interior (no view) cabins have decor that is quite plain and unmemorable. They are marginally comfortable, yet spacious enough and practical (most are of the same size and appointments), with good storage space and practical, well-designed no-nonsense bathrooms.

Anyone booking one of the outside suites will find more space, whirlpool bathtubs, and some fascinating, rather eclectic decor and furniture. These are mildly attractive, but nothing special, and they are much smaller than those aboard the ships of a similar size of several competing companies.

A gift basket is provided in all grades; it includes aloe soap, shampoo, conditioner, deodorant, breath mints, candy, and pain relief tablets (albeit in sample sizes).

If you book accommodation in one of the suites (Category 11 or 12 in the Carnival Cruise Lines brochure) you qualify for "Skipper's Club" priority check-in at any US homeland port – useful for getting ahead of the crowd.

CUISINE/DINING. There are two dining rooms (Destiny and Elation), both non-smoking. They have splashy, colorful decor, and are large, crowded and very noisy. While the menu descriptions sound inviting, the food, when it arrives, may prove disappointing. It is adequate, although the company (which provides its own catering) has made improvements. You get what you pay for when it comes to food, and this company pays very little. Dining in each restaurant is now in four seatings, for greater flexibility: 6pm, 6.45pm, 8pm and 8.45pm (times are approximate).

For casual meals, there's the Lido Cafe, which, aboard this ship, has some improvements and additions worthy of note, such as: an orange juice machine, where you put in oranges and out comes fresh juice (better than the concentrate stuff supplied in the dining room). The Pizzeria is open 24 hours a day – and typically serves more than 500 every single day. There's also a sushi bar – things are looking up. At night, the "Seaview Bistro", as the Lido Cafe becomes known, provides a casual (dress down) alternative to eating in the main dining rooms, serving pasta, steaks, salads and desserts (it typically is in operation between 6pm and 9pm).

ENTERTAINMENT. The Normandie Showlounge seats 1,010, and is the principal venue for large-scale production shows

and major cabaret acts (although 20 pillars obstruct the views from several seats).

In a typical 7-day cruise, there will be two, large-scale, trend-setting production shows, with a cast of two lead singers and a clutch of dancers, backed by a 10-piece live orchestra. These have been the mainstay of Carnival's "we've got the fun" entertainment theme for years. They are of the ritzy-glitzy, razzle-dazzle, Las Vegas-style revues that have little or no story line or flow (there's lots of running around on stage and stepping in place, but very little dancing). However, the skimpy costumes are very colorful, as is the lighting. Stage smoke appears to be in constant use during the production shows, and volumes are of the ear-splitting type.

With all the audio-visual support staff, dressers, and stage managers, the personnel count comes to almost 40. Other specialty acts take center stage on nights when there is no production show, and late-night adults-only comedy (typically with very blue material and language) is also standard aboard the ships of Carnival Cruise Lines. Carnival rotates entertainers among its ships, so passengers see different acts each night.

Almost every lounge/bar has live bands and musical units, so there is always plenty of live music happening, (mostly in the evenings).

SPA/FITNESS. SpaCarnival is a large health, fitness and spa complex that is located on the uppermost interior deck, forward of the ship's mast, and is accessed from the forward stairway. It consists of a gymnasium with ocean-view windows that look out over the ship's bow (it features a large array of the latest in muscle-pumping electronic machines), an aerobics exercise room, men's and women's changing rooms, sauna and steam rooms, and beauty salon. A common complaint from passengers is that there are not enough staff to keep the area clean and tidy, and used towels are often strewn around the changing rooms (particularly on the men's side).

● **For more extensive general information on what a Carnival cruise is like, see pages 107–111.**

Paul Gauguin
★★★★ +

Small Ship: ....18,800 tons	Total Crew: 206	Cabins (with private balcony): 80
Lifestyle: ....Luxury/Premium	Passengers	Cabins (wheelchair accessible): 1
Cruise Line: ....Seven Seas Cruises	(lower beds/all berths): 320/320	Cabin Current: ....110 volts
Former Names: ....none	Passenger Space Ratio	Elevators: 4
Builder: Chantiers de l'Atlantique (France)	(lower beds/all berths): 58.7/58.7	Casino (gaming tables): ....Yes
Original Cost: ....$150 million	Crew/Passenger Ratio	Slot Machines: ....Yes
Entered Service: ....Jan 1998	(lower beds/all berths): 1.5/1.5	Swimming Pools (outdoors): 1
Registry: ....Wallis & Fortuna	Navigation Officers: ....European	Swimming Pools (indoors): 0
Length (ft/m): 513.4/156.50	Cabins (total): 160	Whirlpools: 0
Beam (ft/m): 72.1/22.00	Size Range (sq ft/m): 200.0–534.0/	Self-Service Launderette: ....No
Draft (ft/m): 16.8/5.15	18.5–49.6	Dedicated Cinema/Seats: ....No
Propulsion/Propellers: .....diesel-electric	Cabins (outside view): 160	Library: ....Yes
(9,000 kW/2	Cabins (interior/no view): 0	Classification Society: ....Bureau Veritas
Passenger Decks: 7	Cabins (for one person): 0	

OVERALL SCORE: 1,645 (OUT OF A POSSIBLE 2,000 POINTS)

OVERVIEW. Built by a French company, managed, staffed and operated by the US-based (Radisson) Seven Seas Cruises, *Paul Gauguin* is a spacious ship. While it could carry more passengers, it is forbidden to do so by French law operating in the Polynesian islands, it is not permitted to do so. The ship has a look that is quite well balanced, and all in gleaming white, and is topped by a single funnel.

This smart ship also has a retractable aft marina platform, and carries two water skiing boats and two inflatable craft for water sports. Windsurfers, kayaks, plus scuba and snorkeling gear are available for your use (all except scuba gear, are included in the cruise fare).

Inside, there is a pleasant array of public rooms, and both the artwork and the decor have a real French Polynesia look and feel. The interior colors are quite restful, although a trifle bland.

Expert lecturers on Tahiti and Gauguin accompany each cruise, and a Fare (pronounced *foray*) Tahiti Gallery offers books, videos, and other materials on the unique art, history, and culture of the islands. Three original Gauguin sketches are displayed under glass.

Le Casino is where the casino action runs high, the major attraction being the roulette and blackjack gaming tables. The library is pleasant enough, although it really could be larger. This ship presents Seven Seas Cruises with the opportunity to score very high marks with its passengers, as the company is known for its attention to detail and passenger care.

A no-tie policy means that the dress code is very relaxed – every day. The standard itinerary means that the ship docks only in Papeete and shore tenders are used in all

BERLITZ'S RATINGS

	Possible	Achieved
Ship	500	425
Accommodation	200	169
Food	400	326
Service	400	320
Entertainment	100	77
Cruise	400	328

other ports. There is little entertainment, as the ship stays overnight in several ports (so little is needed). The ship's high crew-to-passenger ratio translates to highly personalized service.

The ship has become a firm favorite of travelers to these climes, and the quiet, refined atmosphere on board makes it sort of clubby, with passengers getting to know each other easily. Where the ship really shines is in the provision of a lot of water sports equipment, and its shallow draft allows it to navigate and anchor in lovely little places that larger ships couldn't possibly get to. All in all, it's a delightful cruise and product, and all gratuities to staff are included. The euro is now the currency in Tahiti and its islands, as Tahiti is a French territory.

Although it sounds exotic, the itinerary is only marginally interesting to the well-traveled, the best island experience being in Bora Bora. *Paul Gauguin*'s shallow draft means there could be some movement, as the ship is a little high-sided for its size. A minimum purchase rule in the ship's boutique is irritating (however, this is due to local Government rules); the same is true of the casino (you must pay $10 to play – again, local government rules). The spa is very small, and the fitness room is windowless.

SUITABLE FOR: *Paul Gauguin* is best suited to couples and single travelers (typically over 50) who seek specialized itineraries, good food and service, with almost no entertainment, all wrapped up in a contemporary ship which can best be described as elegant and quiet in its appointments and comfort levels.

ACCOMMODATION. There are eight grades, priced according to grade, location and size. The outside-view cabins, half of which have private balconies, are nicely equipped, although they are strictly rectangular (and none have more interesting shapes). Most have large windows, except those on the lowest accommodation deck, which have portholes. Each has queen- or twin-sized beds (convertible to queen), and wood-accented cabinetry with rounded edges. A mini-bar/refrigerator (stocked with complimentary soft drinks) VCR, personal safe, hairdryer and umbrellas are standard.

The marble-look bathrooms are large and pleasing and have a tub as well as a separate shower enclosure. All passengers are provided with 100% cotton bathrobes, and soft drinks and mineral water are included in the cruise price.

The two largest suites have a private balcony at the front and side of the vessel. Although there is a decent amount of in-cabin space, with a beautiful long vanity unit (and plenty of drawer space), the bathrooms are disappointingly small and plain, and too similar to all other standard cabin bathrooms.

Butler service is provided in all accommodation designated as Owners Suite, Grand Suites, Ocean-view "A" and "B" category suites (this was inaugurated in 2002).

CUISINE/DINING. L'Etoile is the name of the main dining room for lunch and dinner, while La Veranda, an alternative dining spot, is open for breakfast, lunch and dinner. Both dining rooms feature "open seating" which means that passengers can choose when they want to dine and with whom. This provides a good opportunity to meet new people for dinner each evening. The chairs have armrests, making it more comfortable for a leisurely mealtime. La Veranda provides dinner by reservation, with alternating French and Italian menus; the French menus are provided by Jean-Pierre Vigato, a two-star Michelin chef with his own restaurant ("Apicius") in Paris.

The dining operation is well orchestrated, with cuisine and service of a high standard. Complimentary standard table wines are served with dinner (although a connoisseur selection is available, at extra cost, for real wine lovers), and mineral water, fruit juices and soft drinks are complimentary throughout the ship – a nice touch.

An outdoor bistro provides informal cafe fare on deck aft of the pool, while the Connoisseur Club offers a luxurious retreat for cigars, cognacs, and wine tasting.

ENTERTAINMENT. Le Grand Salon is the venue for shows and cabaret acts. It is a single-level room, and seating is in banquette and individual tub chairs. Sightlines are quite good from most seats, although there are some obstructions. Don't expect lavish production shows (there aren't any), as the main entertainment consists of local Polynesian shows brought on board from ashore, plus the odd cabaret act.

SPA/FITNESS. Spa Carita, on Deck 6 in the centre of the ship, is the name of the spa/wellbeing space. It includes a fitness centre with some muscle-pumping and body toning equipment, a steam room, several treatment rooms, changing area (very small), and beauty salon. The Spa/beauty services are provided by Carita of Paris, who also provide the staff. There is no sauna, and use of the steam room incurs an extra charge (it should really be free).

Body pampering treatments include various massages, aromatherapy facials, manicures, pedicures, and hairdressing services.

Polaris
★★ +

Boutique Ship: . . . . .2,214 tons	Total Crew: 44	Cabins (with private balcony): 0
Lifestyle: . . . . .Standard	Passengers	Cabins (wheelchair accessible): 0
Cruise Line: . . . . .Lindblad Expeditions	(lower beds/all berths): 82/84	Cabin Current: . . . . .220 volts
Former Names: *Lindblad Polaris, Oresund*	Passenger Space Ratio	Elevators: 0
Builder: . . . . . . .Aalborg Vaerft (Denmark)	(lower beds/all berths): 27.0/26.3	Casino (gaming tables): . . . . .No
Original Cost: . . . . .n/a	Crew/Passenger Ratio	Slot Machines: . . . . .No
Entered Service: 1960/May 1987	(lower beds/all berths): 1.8/1.8	Swimming Pools (outdoors): 0
Registry: . . . . .Ecuador	Navigation Officers: . . . . .Ecuadorian	Whirlpools: 0
Length (ft/m): 236.6/72.12	Cabins (total): .41	Self-Service Launderette: . . . . .No
Beam (ft/m): 42.7/13.03	Size Range (sq ft/m): 99.0–229.2/	Lecture/Film Room: . . . . .No
Draft (ft/m): 13.7/4.30	9.2–21.3	Library: . . . . .Yes
Propulsion/Propellers: . . . . .diesel	Cabins (outside view): 41	Zodiacs: 8
(2,354 kW)/2	Cabins (interior/no view): 0	Helicopter Pad: . . . . .No
Passenger Decks: 4	Cabins (for one person): 0	Classification Society: . . . .Bureau Veritas

OVERALL SCORE: 1,071 (OUT OF A POSSIBLE 2,000 POINTS)

OVERVIEW. *Polaris* is what is often termed a "soft" expedition cruise vessel. It is of modest proportions, and has a dark blue hull and white superstructure. A "cute" vessel, it has been well maintained and operated, having been skillfully converted from a Scandinavian ferry. It sports a fantail and an aft lounge area outdoors. The ship carries several Zodiac inflatable rubber landing craft, as well as a glass-bottom boat.

Inside, there are few public rooms, although the Scandinavian-style interior furnishings and decor are very tidy and welcoming (if dated), accented by lots of wood trim. Has a friendly, very intimate atmosphere on board, with Filipino service staff. There is a good team of lecturers and nature observers, whose daily recaps are a vital part of the experience. A restful, well-stocked library helps passengers learn more about the region and the natural world.

If you are going on a Galápagos cruise, it is important to take with you: passport, short and long-sleeve cotton shirts, good walking shoes, windbreaker, mosquito repellent (mosquitoes are at their worst between December and July, particularly in Bartolome), sunglasses with retaining strap, and any personal medication. You will need to take a flight from Quito to San Cristobal (via Guayaquil) to join your cruise.

Polaris is a decent enough small vessel, which now operates year-round nature-intensive "soft" expedition cruises around the Galápagos Islands. This is an area to which the ship is well suited (only 90 passengers from any one ship are allowed at any one time in the islands, where tourism is managed well by the local Equadorians). In fact, this ship is among the best suited to this region.

Bottled water is provided at no extra charge. All port

BERLITZ'S RATINGS

	Possible	Achieved
Ship	500	234
Accommodation	200	99
Food	400	219
Service	400	233
Entertainment	N/A	N/A
Cruise	500	286

charges are included in this product, which is marketed by Lindblad Expeditions and Noble Caledonia. The onboard currencies are the US dollar and Ecuadorian sucre.

SUITABLE FOR: *Polaris* and this type of cruising are best suited to adventurous, hardy outdoors types who enjoy being with nature and wildlife in one of the most interesting places on earth.

ACCOMMODATION. There are five price grades. The cabins, all above the waterline (while most have windows, a few have portholes), are fairly roomy and nicely appointed, but there is little drawer space. Some have been refurbished, and have large (lower) beds. Each cabin has either a double bed or two single beds, a small writing desk, and hairdryer. Some of the larger cabins also have a third (upper) berth. The cabin bathrooms are tiny (the towels are small, too).

CUISINE/DINING. The Dining Room has big picture windows and a wrap-around view. Seating is now at individual tables (formerly family style) in a leisurely single seating.

The ship's cuisine is basically sound, with much emphasis on local fish and seafood, and other Ecuadorian regional specialties. Breakfast and lunch are self-serve buffet-style. Although there is a wine list, the selection is very limited.

ENTERTAINMENT. Lectures, briefings and recaps are the main onboard entertainment events, together with dinner and after-dinner conversation.

SPA/FITNESS. There is a small fitness room (large enough for two). Beauty isn't a big concern on such cruises.

Polynesia
★★

Boutique Ship: . . . . .430 tons	Sail Area (sq ft/m2): 18,000/1,672.2	Cabins (outside view): 14
Lifestyle: . . . . .Standard	Main Propulsion: . . . . .sail power	Cabins (interior/no view): 41
Cruise Line: . . . . . . .Windjammer Barefoot	Propulsion/Propellers: diesel/1	Cabins (for one person): 0
Cruises	Passenger Decks: 4	Cabins (with private balcony): 0
Former Names: . . . . .Argus	Total Crew: 45	Cabins (wheelchair accessible): 0
Builder: . . . . .Haan & Oerlemans (Holland)	Passengers	Cabin Current: . . . . .110 volts
Original Cost: . . . . .n/a	(lower beds/all berths): 110/122	Elevators: 0
Entered Service: 1938/1975	Passenger Space Ratio	Casino (gaming tables): . . . . .No
Registry: . . . . .Equatorial Guinea	(lower beds/all berths): 3.9/3.5	Slot Machines: . . . . .No
Length (ft/m): 248.0/75.5	Crew/Passenger Ratio	Swimming Pools (outdoors): 0
Beam (ft/m): 36.0/10.9	(lower beds/all berths): 2.4/2.7	Whirlpools: 0
Draft (ft/m): 18.0/5.4	Navigation Officers: . . . . . . .International	Self-Service Launderette: . . . . .No
Type of Vessel: . . . . .topsail schooner	Cabins (total): 55	Library: . . . . .Yes
No. of Masts: 4	Size Range (sq ft/m): 68.0–104.0/6.3–9.6	Classification Society: . . . . .none

OVERALL SCORE: 902 (OUT OF A POSSIBLE 2,000 POINTS)

OVERVIEW. *Polynesia* was built to be part of the great Portuguese Grand Banks fleet. It was featured in the May 1952 edition of *National Geographic* magazine and in *The Quest of the Schooner Argus* by the late maritime writer, Allen Villers. Windjammer Barefoot Cruises acquired *Polynesia* in 1975.

Aboard one of this company's fleet you can let the crew do all the work, or you can lend a hand at the helm yourself. One neat thing to do is just to sit or lie in the nets at the bows of the vessel, without a care in the world.

The mood is free and easy, the ships are equipped very simply, and only the most casual clothes are required (T-shirts and shorts), and shoes are optional, although you may need them if you go off in one of the ports. Quite possibly the most used item will be your bathing suit – better take more than one! Smoking is allowed only on the open decks.

Jammin' aboard a Windjammer (first-timers are "crew-mates" while repeat passengers are "jammers") is no-frills cruising in a no-nonsense, friendly environment, for the young at heart and those who don't need programmed activities. It's all about the romance of being at sea under sail. You can even lend a hand with the sails. Those who enjoy beaches, scuba diving and snorkeling around the Caribbean will be best suited to a Windjammer Barefoot Cruises cruise. This ship can anchor in neat little sheltered Caribbean hide-aways that larger (regular) cruise ships can't get near.

Although itineraries are provided in the brochure, the captain actually decides which islands to go to in any given area, depending on sea and weather conditions. Polynesia features year-round cruises in the Caribbean. The brochure rates might seem inexpensive, but remember that you will need to add on the air fare. There is very little room per passenger. Everything is basic, basic, basic. Tips to the crew are strongly suggested – at $50 per week.

Other tall ships in the fleet include *Flying Cloud, Legacy, Mandalay*, and *Yankee Clipper*. The onboard currency is the US dollar.

SUITABLE FOR: *Polynesia* is best suited to young, carefree singles that enjoy beaches, scuba diving and snorkeling, and are happy with just the basic necessities, all in an ultra-casual setting of sails, sea and sun, with no pretension whatsoever.

ACCOMMODATION. There are four grades (designated as Admiral Suite, Deck Cabin, Standard Cabin, and Bachelor/ette Cabin). The cabins are very small, however, particularly when compared to regular cruise ships. But remember that this is a very casual cruise experience and you will need so few clothes anyway. All are equipped with upper and lower berths, and most are quite narrow.

CUISINE/DINING. There is one dining room, with views to the outside through real portholes, and meals are all very simple in style and service, with little choice and only the most basic presentation. Breakfast is served on board, as is dinner, while lunch could be either on board or at a beach, picnic-style. Wine is included for dinner.

ENTERTAINMENT. Entertainment in the evenings consists of just you and the crew. You can put on a toga, take or create a pirate outfit and join in the fun.

SPA/FITNESS. There are no facilities.

BERLITZ'S RATINGS

	Possible	Achieved
Ship	500	219
Accommodation	200	79
Food	400	166
Service	400	188
Entertainment	N/A	N/A
Cruise	500	250

Pride of Aloha
★★★ +

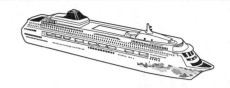

Large (Resort) Ship: . . . . .77,104 tons	Total Crew: 950	Cabins (with private balcony): 252
Lifestyle: . . . . .Standard	Passengers	Cabins (wheelchair accessible): 6
Cruise Line: . . . . .NCL America	(lower beds/all berths): 2,002/2,450	Cabin Current: . . . . .110 volts
Former Names: . . . . .Norwegian Sky	Passenger Space Ratio	Elevators: 12
Builder: . . . . .Lloyd Werft (Germany)	(lower beds/all berths): 38.5/31.4	Casino (gaming tables): . . . . .Yes
Original Cost: . . . .$332 million	Crew/Passenger Ratio	Slot Machines: . . . . .Yes
Entered Service: . . . .Aug 1999/July 2004	(lower beds/all berths): 2.6/3.2	Swimming Pools (outdoors): 2
Registry: . . . . .The Bahamas	Navigation Officers: . . . . .Norwegian	Swimming Pools (indoors): 0
Length (ft/m): 853.0/260.00	Cabins (total): 1,001	Whirlpools: 5
Beam (ft/m): 105.8/32.25	Size Range (sq ft/m): 120.5–488.6/	Self-Service Launderette: . . . . .No
Draft (ft/m): 26.2/8.00	11.2–45.4	Dedicated Cinema/Seats: . . . . .No
Propulsion/Propellers: . . . . .diesel-electric	Cabins (outside view): 574	Library: . . . . .Yes
(50,000 kW)/2	Cabins (interior/no view): 427	Classification Society: . .American Bureau
Passenger Decks: 12	Cabins (for one person): 0	of Shipping/DNV

OVERALL SCORE: 1,387 (OUT OF A POSSIBLE 2,000 POINTS)

OVERVIEW. In 2004 *Norwegian Sky* was "Hawaiianized" and morphed into *Pride of Aloha*. The hull sports flower leis along both sides. The ship operates with 100% American officers and crew (many from Hawaii), and operates Hawaiian island cruises year-round. The outdoor space is quite generous, with an extra wide pool deck (created from port and starboard "overhangs" that resulted from balconies added to cabins on two decks beneath it), with two swimming pools and four whirlpool tubs.

BERLITZ'S RATINGS		
	Possible	Achieved
Ship	500	400
Accommodation	200	149
Food	400	248
Service	400	232
Entertainment	100	79
Cruise	400	279

The interior decor reflects the ship's operating area, with Hawaiian motifs, flowers and fauna, and artwork depicting the heritage and lifestyle of Hawaii and its people (a complete change from the ship's former interior design). The focal point is the ship's eight-deck high atrium lobby, with spiral sculptures and rainbow-colored sails. Public rooms include a shopping arcade, children's playroom (there is also a splash pool in a prime open deck area forward atop ship), internet center (with 14 terminals and coffee available from an adjacent bar), several lounges and bars, small conference room, the Mark Twain library; Captain Cook's for cigars and cognac. Those with a black belt in shopping should know the Black Pearl Gem Shop is a joint venture.

Pride of Aloha is a resort at sea, and caters well to a multi-generational clientele, with lots of choices for dining and entertainment. It provides a fine, comfortable base from which to explore all that the Hawaiian islands have to offer. It's all a bit "twee" but at least it's fresh.

A (non-changeable) *service charge* (this is not a gratuity) for staff is automatically added to your onboard account at $10 per person ($5 for children ages 3–12) per day; this is pooled for all crew and provides payment when they are on

vacation. You will also be expected to also provide gratuities. In addition, a 15% gratuity, plus Hawaii sales tax (this is a US flag ship) is added to all bar and spa treatment accounts. The onboard currency is the US dollar.

The hustling for passengers to attend art auctions is aggressive and annoying, as is the constant bombardment for revenue activities and the daily junk mail that arrives at one's cabin door. There are many announcements – particularly annoying are those that state what is already written in the daily program. There is little connection to the sea from many public rooms. Passenger hallways are quite plain. The all-American crew is fairly friendly and service-oriented, but there is almost a complete lack of finesse and polish – perhaps this will come in time.

SUITABLE FOR: *Pride of Aloha* is best suited as a first-time cruise for adult couples, single passengers, and families with children and teenagers who enjoy big city nightlife, who want contemporary, upbeat, color-rich surroundings, good facilities, plenty of entertainment lounges and bars and high-tech sophistication – all in one neat, well packaged cruise vacation in a Hawaiian setting.

ACCOMMODATION. There are 19 price categories: 13 for outside-view suites and cabins, and six for interior (no view) cabins. All the standard outside-view and interior (no view) cabins have two lower beds that can convert to a queen-sized bed, a small lounge area with sofa and table, and a decent amount of closet space, but very little drawer space, and the cabins themselves are disappointingly small. However, each is decorated in colorful Hawaiian style, with an explosion of floral themes and vibrant colors. More than 200 outside-view cabins have their own private balcony. Each cabin has a small vanity/writing desk, color television (typically CNN, ESPN, and TNT), personal safe, climate control, and a laptop computer connection socket. Audio can be obtained only through the TV set. Bottled water is placed in each cabin (but a charge will be made to your account if you open the bottle).

The largest accommodation is four Owner's Suites. Each has a hot tub, large teak table, two chairs and two deck lounge chairs outside on a huge, very private, forward-facing teakwood floor balcony just under the ship's navigation bridge, with large floor-to-ceiling windows. Each suite has a separate lounge and bedroom. The lounge has a large dining table and four chairs, two two-person sofas, large television, DVD/CD player, coffee table, queen-sized pull-down Murphy's bed, guest closet, writing desk, wet bar with two bar stools, refrigerator and sink, several cupboards for glasses, and several drawers and other cupboards for storage. The bedroom, which has sliding wood half-doors that look into the lounge, has a queen-sized bed (with European duvet) under a leaf-glass chandelier, vanity desk, TV, walk-in closet with plenty of hanging rail space, five open shelves and large personal safe. The white-tiled bathroom, although not large, has a full-sized tub with retractable clothesline above, separate shower enclosure with glass doors, deep washbasin, and toiletries cabinets.

There are 10 Junior Suites, each with a private teak decked balcony; these suites face aft in a secluded position and overlook the ship's wash. They have almost the same facilities as those in the owner's suites, except for the outdoor hot tub, and the fact that there is less space.

CUISINE/DINING. NCL America offers "Freestyle Dining," so you can choose which restaurant you would like to eat in, at what time, and with whom. All restaurants (two main) and four specialty eateries (three have a cover charge of between $12.50 and $17.50 per person) are no-smoking. NCL America's dress code states that "jeans, T-shirts, tank tops and bare feet are not permitted in the ship."

The main dining rooms (Palace Restaurant, with 530 seats, and Crossings Restaurant, with 574 seats and grand yacht decor) have tables for four, six or eight and an open seating arrangement. The cuisine in Palace and Crossings includes regional Hawaiian specialties from seven of the islands' best-known celebrity chefs.

A smaller eatery, the 84-seat Kahili Restaurant, is an à la carte dining option featuring Italian cuisine (it has half-moon alcoves and several tables for two), for which there is an extra charge ($10 per person, including gratuity). The wine list is quite decent and well arranged, with moderate prices, although you won't find many good vintage wines.

The cutlery is very ordinary (and there are no fish knives).

For classic and nouvelle French cuisine, the 90-seat Royal Palm Bistro has an à la carte menu; the decor is inspired by royal and aristocratic gardens.

Other eateries include the Kahili Restaurant, an 84-seat alternative dining spot for some fine meals (including such desserts as flaming cherries jubilee and chocolate fondue), and Pacific Heights, a casual Pacific Rim/Asian Fusion eatery offering Hawaiian cuisine that includes steaks and local fish and seafood items. Both incur a $10 per person cover charge (including gratuity) and reservations are required. Casual meals can be taken in the Hakilau Café and Hakilau Lanai (an outdoor extension of the Hikilau Cafe).

There is also a sports bar and grill (Longboard Bar), featuring a wall of TV screens with live sports action via satellite. Adjacent is The Zone (disco and karaoke room).

ENTERTAINMENT. The 1,000-seat Stardust Theater is the venue for production shows and major cabaret acts, although the sight lines are quite poor. Two or three production shows are presented in a typical 7-day cruise (performed by the Jean Ann Ryan Company). These are all colorful, high-energy, high volume razzle-dazzle shows that are very entertaining, together with one special Hawai'ian production show linking entertainment with education about Hawaii.

Late-night cabaret acts often perform in a separate lounge, the Blue Hawai'i Nightclub. The ship has a number of bands and solo entertaining musicians, which provide live music for listening and dancing in several of the lounges and bars.

SPA/FITNESS. Body Waves is a large health/fitness spa – including an aerobics room and a separate gymnasium, and several treatment rooms. Mandara Spa (headquartered in Honolulu, but owned by Steiner Leisure) is the operator of the spa/fitness center, and provides all staff and treatments as the concession. Hawaii-themed treatments include a Coconut Body Polish made from fresh coconuts. Sample prices: Massage, $99 (50 minutes); Hot Stone Massage $185 (80 minutes); Four Hands Massage $180 (50 minutes), La Theapie Facial $117 (55 minutes).

Sports fans will appreciate the large basketball/volleyball court, baseball-batting cage, golf-driving net, platform tennis, shuffleboard and table tennis facilities, and sports bar (with baseball and surfing themes) with live satellite television coverage of sports events and major games on several TV screens. Joggers will find a wrap-around indoor/outdoor-jogging track.

● **For more extensive general information on what an NCL cruise is like, see pages 122–124.**

Pride of America
NOT YET RATED

Large (Resort) Ship: . . . . .81,000 tons	Total Crew: 1,000	Cabins (wheelchair accessible): 22
Lifestyle: . . . . .Standard	Passengers	Cabin Current: . . . . .110 volts
Cruise Line: . . . . .NCL America	(lower beds/all berths): 2,144/2,440	Elevators: 10
Former Names: . . . . .None	Passenger Space Ratio	Casino (gaming tables): . . . . .Yes
Builder: . . . . . .Ingalls Shipbuilding (USA)/	(lower beds/all berths): 37.7/33.1	Slot Machines: . . . . .Yes
Lloyd Werft (Germany)	Crew/Passenger Ratio	Swimming Pools (outdoors): 2
Original Cost: . . . .$450 million	(lower beds/all berths): 2.1/2.4	Swimming Pools (indoors): 0
Entered Service: . . . . .July 2005	Navigation Officers: . . . . .Norwegian	Whirlpools: . . . . .n/a
Registry: . . . . .USA	Cabins (total): 1,072	Self-Service Launderette: . . . . .No
Length (ft/m): 921.9/281.0	Size Range (sq ft/m): 129.1–1,377.8/	Dedicated Cinema/Seats: . . . . .No
Beam (ft/m): 106.6/32.2	12.0 –128.0	Library: . . . . .Yes
Draft (ft/m): 26.25/8.0	Cabins (outside view): 843	Classification Society: . . . . . . .American
Propulsion/Propellers: . . . .diesel-electric/	Cabins (interior/no view): 229	Bureau of Shipping
2 pods (17MW each)	Cabins (for one person): 0	
Passenger Decks: 15	Cabins (with private balcony): 665	

BERLITZ'S OVERALL SCORE: NYR (OUT OF A POSSIBLE 2,000 POINTS)

OVERVIEW. *Pride of America* is one of four ships planned for the new NCL America division of Norwegian Cruise Line, and sails on seven-day inter-island cruises featuring the four main islands of Hawaii (including two overnight port calls). *Pride of America* was, in fact, originally ordered for the now defunct United States Lines (which itself was part of the defunct American Classic Voyages at the time). But September 11, 2001 put paid to the "Project America" ship – and to the company itself.

Only the hull was nearing completion. Norwegian Cruise Line purchased the hull and towed it to Germany, where the ship was completed and fitted out (a sinking incident delayed its completion). The 85,850 sq.-ft./7,975 sq.-meter open deck space includes a sunning/pool deck inspired by Miami's South Beach (think Ocean Drive/Lincoln Mall) and Art Deco area.

The interior design of the ship was considerably changed by NCL America, and modeled after a "Best of America" theme (all the public rooms are named after famous Americans). Facilities include the Capitol Atrium (a lobby spanning eight decks and said to be inspired by the Capitol Building and White House), a large casino, a conservatory complete with tropical landscaped garden and live exotic birds, Soho Art Gallery (holding art auctions), Washington Library, and Newbury Shopping Center. The Rascal's Kids Center and Kids' Pool is a supervised facility designed around a theme of America's native animals.

There are extensive meeting and conference facilities (US corporations qualify for tax-deductible meetings expenses as the ship sails under the US flag), with six ded-

BERLITZ'S RATINGS

	Possible	Achieved
Ship	500	NYR
Accommodation	200	NYR
Food	400	NYR
Service	400	NYR
Entertainment	100	NYR
Cruise	400	NYR

icated meetings rooms ranging in size from boardrooms for 10 people to an auditorium for up to 250. The ship will have a mainly Hawaiian crew, and you can expect lots of Americana. Few other details were available at press time, although it is expected that the onboard gratuities and cashless cruising operation would be similar to that aboard the ships of Norwegian Cruise Line (parent company of NCL America). A 15% gratuity will be added to bar and spa bills.

SUITABLE FOR: *Pride of America* is best suited to first-time young (and young at heart) couples, single passengers, children and teenagers who enjoy big city nightlife, who want contemporary, upbeat, color-rich surroundings, and the latest in facilities, plenty of entertainment lounges and bars and high-tech sophistication – all in one neat, highly programmed, well packaged cruise vacation, with plenty of music, constant activity and entertainment.

ACCOMMODATION. Of the 950 cabins, 77% have outside views, while 64% of these have private balconies, and there are also a large number of family-friendly interconnecting cabins. Many cabins have third/fourth upper berths, some family-special cabins can accommodate as many as six. Some suites have king-sized beds, while most cabins have twin beds that can be placed together to make a queen-sized bed. A number of cabins are wheelchair-accessible, while some cabins are equipped for the hearing-impaired.

Grand Suite: The largest accommodation is in the Grand Suite, with approximately 1,400 sq. ft./130 sq. meters of living space. The suite is located high atop the ship forward of the sun deck and offers sweeping views from its wrap-around outdoor terrace. It has a large living room with Bang & Olufsen entertainment center (television, DVD/CD player with library), computer internet-connect access, and wet bar, separate dining room with dining table and six chairs (butler included). The master bedroom includes a king-sized bed, large bathroom, with whirlpool tub and separate shower enclosure; dressing area with flat-screen TV, and walk-in closet. At the entrance to the suite is a guest powder room. There is a wrap-around verandah, and facilities include open-air dining and a hot tub), plus a private sunbathing and entertainment area.

Owner's Suite: There are five, each measuring approximately 870 sq.ft./80 sq. meters and named after indigenous flowers in Hawaii (Bird of Paradise, Gardenia, Orchid, Plumeria). Each has a bedroom with king-sized bed, walk-in closet, dressing area, separate living room with Bang & Olufsen entertainment center (television, DVD/CD player with library), and computer internet-connect access. The bathroom has a whirlpool tub and separate shower enclosure. There is also a large private balcony with hot tub, outdoor dining facilities and sun beds.

Deluxe Penthouse Suites: There are six units, each measuring approximately 735 sq.ft./68 sq. meters. They have a separate bedroom with king-size bed and walk-in closet; the bathroom has a whirlpool tub, separate shower enclosure, two washbasins, dressing area; living room with Bang & Olufsen entertainment center, wet bar, and private balcony.

Penthouse Suites: There are 28, each measuring 504–585 sq.ft/47–54.5 sq. meters. These have a separate bedroom with king-size bed and walk-in closet; the bathroom has a whirlpool tub, separate shower enclosure, two washbasins, dressing area; living room with Bang & Olufsen entertainment center, wet bar, and private balcony.

Family Suites: There are eight, each measuring approximately 360 sq.ft./33.5 sq. meters. Each has a main bedroom with two twin beds that can be converted to a queen-sized bed, a living room with double sofa bed and entertainment center, separate den with single sofa bed. Another four family "suites" have an interconnecting door between two cabins (thus there are two bathrooms). These four measure 330–380 sq.ft./30.5–35 sq. meters.

Standard Outside View and Interior (No View) Cabins: Outside view cabins have either a window or porthole, depending on location. All cabins have twin beds that can convert into a queen-sized bed, TV, satellite-dial telephone, and personal safe; the bathrooms have a built-in hairdryer.

CUISINE/DINING. NCL America's ships operate "Freestyle Cruising," which means that there are several restaurants and informal dining spots. You can choose from two main dining rooms, and six other à la carte, informal and casual spots, some of which incur a cover (or portion) charge ($12.50–$17.50 per person). Smoking is banned in all restaurants and food outlets.

Traditional Dining Rooms:
● The 628-seat Skyline Restaurant is the main restaurant, and the decor is inspired by the skyscrapers of the 1930s.

● The 496-seat Liberty Dining Room is the second main restaurant, with two seatings.
Alternative Dining Options:
● The Lone Star Steak House accommodates 106. This is a contemporary steak house with Texan decor (the artwork includes Houston Space Center, Texas Rangers and Dallas Cowboys).
● China Town is a Pacific Rim/Asian Fusion restaurant that has a sushi/sashimi bar and a Teppanyaki grill room with two tables (food is prepared in front of you with a bit of showmanship) that can accommodate up to 32.
● Jefferson's Bistro, which accommodates 104, is the ship's "signature" restaurant, and features an à la carte menu of classic and nouvelle French cuisine. The decor is inspired by that of Thomas Jefferson's home in Monticello (Thomas Jefferson was the US ambassador to France from 1785 to 1789 before becoming America's third president).
● Little Italy is a casual Italian eatery that serves pasta, pizza and other popular light Italian fare. It has 116 seats.
● Cadillac Diner accommodates 106 (70 indoors, 36 outdoors) and is open 24 hours a day. It has Cadillac seats and a video juke box. There's fast food galore, with hamburgers and hot dogs, fish and chips, potpies and wok dishes.
● Aloha Cafe/Kids Cafe is an indoor/outdoor self-serve buffet-style eatery with a Hawaii theme; there are 322 indoor and 310 outdoor seats. A special section for children has counter tops that are just the right height for them, as well as chairs and tables that have been shrunk from adult to a kid-friendly size.

Other indoor eateries and bars include the Napa Wine Bar (wines by the glass), Pink's Champagne and Cigar Bar (inspired by Hawaii's "pink Palace" Hotel on Waikiki Beach), the Gold Rush pub (karaoke is practiced here; there's also a darts board and bar billiards), and the John Adams Coffee Bar; while outdoor eateries and drinking places include the Key West Bar and Grill, and the Waikiki Bar.

ENTERTAINMENT. The Hollywood Theater, the ship's principal showlounge, seats 840. Large-scale production shows will be featured, together with local Hawaiian shows. There is also a 590-seat cabaret lounge, named the Mardi Gras Lounge, which will typically feature cabaret entertainment (including late-night comedy).

SPA/FITNESS. The Santa Fe Spa and Fitness Center is decorated with artifacts from New Mexico and designed to be a tranquil center for mind and body. The spa is staffed and operated by Mandara Spa (originating in Bali, now headquartered in Hawaii, but owned by Steiner Leisure), and includes Ayurvedic-style treatments. While some fitness classes are free, some – such as yoga, and kick-boxing – typically cost $10 per class.

Massage (including exotic massages such as Hot Stone, Lomi Lomi, and other well-being massages), facials, pedicures, and beauty salon treatments cost extra (massage, for example, costs about $2 per minute, plus gratuity). Do make appointments as early as possible – aboard a large ship such as this, the available time slots go quickly.

Princesa Marissa
★★

Small Ship: ....10,487 tons	Total Crew: 185	Cabins (with private balcony): 0
Lifestyle: ....Standard	Passengers	Cabins (wheelchair accessible): 0
Cruise Line: ....Louis Cruise Lines	(lower beds/all berths): 628/839	Cabin Current: ....220 volts
Former Names: ...Princessan, Finnhansa	Passenger Space Ratio	Dining Rooms: 2
Builder: ....Wartsila (Finland)	(lower beds/all berths): 16.6/12.4	Elevators: 1
Original Cost: ....n/a	Crew/Passenger Ratio	Casino (gaming tables): ....Yes
Entered Service: 1966/June 1987	(lower beds/all berths): 3.3/4.5	Slot Machines: ....Yes
Registry: ....Cyprus	Navigation Officers: ......Cypriot/Greek	Swimming Pools (outdoors): 0
Length (ft/m): 440.6/134.30	Cabins (total): 314	Swimming Pools (indoors): 0
Beam (ft/m): 65.2/19.90	Size Range (sq ft/m): 75.3–226.0/	Whirlpools: 0
Draft (ft/m): 18.7/5.70	7.0–21.0	Self-Service Launderette: ....No
Propulsion/Propellers: ....diesel	Cabins (outside view): 148	Movie Theater/Seats: ....No
(10,300 kW)/2 (CP)	Cabins (interior/no view): 166	Library: ....No
Passenger Decks: 9	Cabins (for one person): 0	Classification Society: Det Norske Veritas

OVERALL SCORE: 891 (OUT OF A POSSIBLE 2,000 POINTS)

OVERVIEW. This former ferry has a square stern, twin funnels and a short, stubby bow. There is very little open deck and sunbathing space. The interiors are quite smart and tidy, and the ship has been well maintained. The public room decor is attractive, with warm, fairly bright contemporary colors, well-designed fabrics and soft furnishings. There are some limited facilities for meetings and small conferences.

The ship provides low-fare transportation in unstuffy surroundings and typically operates year-round short cruises to Egypt (principally for residents of Cyprus and for British passengers on vacation there) that include shore excursions. The passenger density is high. Also, the ceilings are low. There are few crew members for so many passengers. Passengers must board through the aft car deck, but that is no real hardship. There is little separation of smokers and non-smokers. The onboard currency is the Cyprus pound.

SUITABLE FOR: Princesa Marissa is best suited to destination-oriented adult couples and single travelers who want to escape on a short cruise, at low cost, but with surprisingly decent food, and minimal facilities.

ACCOMMODATION. There are 10 price grades. Generally, the higher the deck, the more expensive the cabin. A whole section of new cabins was added in 1995. They are of a good size, and have large picture windows; the decor is bright and cheerful, and they also have good, practical bathrooms. Other, more standard cabins are reasonably smart and functional (if small, but typical in a ship that was built as a ferry), although the bathrooms are really small.

BERLITZ'S RATINGS

	Possible	Achieved
Ship	500	193
Accommodation	200	91
Food	400	205
Service	400	204
Entertainment	100	37
Cruise	400	161

All cabins have a double bed or two lower beds (either in a twin, or side by side, arrangement, or in an "L"-shape configuration), and most cabins also have a third or third and fourth upper berth (good for families with children, but extremely cramped for four adults). All cabins have a small clothes closet, and a few drawers. The cabin insulation for all cabins, however, is poor.

The largest accommodation can be found in 2–3 bed suites. These have outside views, two beds plus a third sofa bed, refrigerator, television, and a larger bathroom with whirlpool bathtub and shower, toilet, washbasin, and more storage space for personal toiletry items.

CUISINE/DINING. There are two dining rooms. Both are quite attractive (the forward one is the more intimate), and chairs that are quite comfortable. There are two seatings. There are both à la carte and buffet style meals, and the menu choice includes three entrées. There is also a full vegetarian menu. The selection of breads and ice cream sundaes is good. In fact, the food is perhaps the best part of a cruise aboard this vessel – there is plenty of it. The wine list is adequate, and prices are low, but the wines are all young.

ENTERTAINMENT. The main lounge is the venue for all entertainment events. However, on these short cruises, when time spent in port may extend into the evenings, making dinner timings late, there is little or no entertainment, except for a band that plays for dancing, and the occasional third-rate cabaret act.

SPA/FITNESS. There are no spa or fitness facilities.

Princess Danae
★★★

Mid-Size Ship: . . . . .17,074 tons	(9,850 kW)/2	Cabins (for one person): 0
Lifestyle: . . . . .Standard	Passenger Decks: 7	Cabins (with private balcony): 6
Cruise Line: . . . . .Classic International	Total Crew: 240	Cabins (wheelchair accessible): 0
Cruises	Passengers	Cabin Current: . . . . .220 volts
Former Names: . . . . .Baltica,	(lower beds/all berths): 560/670	Elevators: 2
Starlight Express, Danae,	Passenger Space Ratio	Casino (gaming tables): . . . . .Yes
Therisos Express, Port Melbourne	(lower beds/all berths): 30.4/25.4	Slot Machines: . . . . .Yes
Builder: . . . . .Swan, Hunter (UK)	Crew/Passenger Ratio	Swimming Pools (outdoors): 1
Original Cost: .n/a	(lower beds/all berths): 2.3/2.7	Swimming Pools (indoors): 0
Entered Service: . . . . . . .July 1955/1997	Navigation Officers: . . . . .European	Whirlpools: 2
Registry: . . . . .Portugal	Cabins (total): 280	Self-Service Launderette: . . . . .No
Length (ft/m): 532.7/162.39	Size Range (sq ft/m): 200.0–270.0/	Dedicated Cinema/Seats: Yes/275
Beam (ft/m): 70.0/21.34	18.5–25.0	Library: . . . . .Yes
Draft (ft/m): 41.9/12.80	Cabins (outside view): 215	Classification Society: . .American Bureau
Propulsion/Propellers: . . . . .diesel	Cabins (interior/no view): 65	of Shipping

OVERALL SCORE: 1,101 (OUT OF A POSSIBLE 2,000 POINTS)

OVERVIEW. *Princess Danae* began as a cargo-passenger liner, and was turned into a full-time cruise ship in 1972. Costa Cruises operated it for many years before it was bought by its present Lisbon-based owners, Classic International Cruises. Because *Princess Danae* (sister to *Ocean Monarch)* is well-built with a deep draught, it is stable in bad weather. There is a decent amount of open deck space for sunbathing. Inside, there is a pleasing traditional ambiance, combined with a mixture of both traditional and contemporary features. There are a limited number of public rooms, but their decor is conservative, clean and tidy. A new bar amidships has been added. There is a roomy, traditional cinema.

This ship was refurbished in 1996, but the fit and finish of the areas that were changed was then extremely poor (they have been improved since). It provides a moderately comfortable, cruise experience.

The ship operates Caribbean cruises from Santo Domingo in winter, from Brazil during the summer, and Mediterranean cruises during part of the summer. It is often chartered to tour operators (of various nationalities), and so its character changes, as does the level of food and service. Use the rating only as a guide, as the actual product can be inconsistent. The onboard currency is the US dollar.

There is no observation lounge with forward-facing views over the ship's bows. There is little finesse in the hospitality department, and service is, at best, perfunctory.

SUITABLE FOR: *Princess Danae* is best suited to adult couples and single travelers who want to cruise aboard a traditional (older) ship, with acceptable facilities, food and

BERLITZ'S RATINGS

	Possible	Achieved
Ship	500	288
Accommodation	200	116
Food	400	234
Service	400	223
Entertainment	100	42
Cruise	400	198

service that provide decent value for money without the pretentiousness of better and more upscale ships.

ACCOMMODATION. There are eight price grades. Most cabins are of good size, are quite comfortable, and have rather heavy-duty furniture and fittings with ample closet and drawer space. Cabins on the deck below the discotheque can suffer from thumping noise late at night. The lower-grade cabins are really plain. While 210 cabin bathrooms have a bathtub and shower, 70 have only a shower. The towels are small.

CUISINE/DINING. The Mimosa Restaurant is decorated quite nicely and has a high ceiling. It has open seating, and tables are for four, six or eight (the chairs do not have armrests). The cuisine is Continental/European, with some regional specialties. Typically, a self-serve buffet table is set up in the center of the restaurant for breakfast items, salads and cheeses for lunch, dinner and late-night snacks.

While the quality of meat is not the best, there is a good selection of fish and seafood. The service, by the ship's Portuguese waiters, is fairly attentive, although basic.

ENTERTAINMENT. The Main Lounge is a single-level room with a thrust stage best used for cabaret acts. The stage lighting is minimal, and could be better. The ship carries a main band, and several small musical units, and solo pianists to provide live music for dancing or listening.

SPA/FITNESS. There is a gymnasium and sauna, and a windowless beauty salon.

Prinsendam
★★★★ +

Mid-Size Ship: . . . . .37,845 tons	Passenger Decks: 8	Cabins (for one person): 2
Lifestyle: . . . . .Premium	Total Crew: 460	Cabins (with private balcony): 145
Cruise Line: . . . . . . .Holland America Line	Passengers	Cabins (wheelchair accessible): 4
Former Names: . . . .*Seabourn Sun,*	(lower beds/all berths): 794/840	Cabin Current: . . . . .110 volts
Royal Viking Sun	Passenger Space Ratio	Elevators: 4
Builder: . . . . .Wartsila (Finland)	(lower beds/all berths): 47.6/46.4	Casino (gaming tables): . . . . .Yes
Original Cost: . . . .$125 million	Crew/Passenger Ratio	Slot Machines: . . . . .Yes
Entered Service: . . . .Dec 1988/May 2002	(lower beds/all berths): 1.7/1.8	Swimming Pools (outdoors): 2
Registry: . . . . .The Netherlands	Navigation Officers: . . . . .European	Swimming Pools (indoors): 0
Length (ft/m): 674.2/205.5	Cabins (total): .396	Whirlpools: 2
Beam (ft/m): 91.8/28.0	Size Range (sq ft/m): 137.7–723.3/	Self-Service Launderette: . . . . .Yes
Draft (ft/m): 23.6/7.2	12.8–67.2	Dedicated Cinema/Seats: Yes/101
Propulsion/Propellers: . . . . .diesel	Cabins (outside view): 368	Library: . . . . .Yes
(21,120 kW)/2	Cabins (interior/no view): 25	Classification Society: Det Norske Veritas

---

OVERALL SCORE: 1,691 (OUT OF A POSSIBLE 2,000 POINTS)

OVERVIEW. *Prinsendam* is a contemporary, well-designed ship with sleek, flowing lines, a sharply raked bow, and a well-rounded profile, with lots of floor-to-ceiling glass. Originally ordered and operated by the now defunct Royal Viking Line as *Royal Viking Sun*, it was bought by Seabourn Cruise Line in 1998. Following an extensive refit and refurbishment programme (which didn't go far enough), the ship was renamed *Seabourn Sun* in 1999. In 2002, it was transferred to Holland America Line as *Prinsendam*, and the hull was changed from all-white to a dark blue hull with white superstructure. The shore tenders are thoughtfully air-conditioned and even have radar and a toilet.

Wide teak wood decks provide excellent walking areas including a decent wrap-around promenade deck outdoors. The swimming pool (outdoors on Lido Deck) is not large, but it is quite adequate, while the deck above has a croquet court and golf driving range. The interior layout is very spacious (it is even more ideal when a maximum of 600 passengers are aboard). Impressive public rooms and tasteful decor now reign. Two handrails – one of wood, one of chrome – are provided on all stairways, a thoughtful touch.

The Crow's Nest, the ship's forward observation lounge, is one of the most elegant, but contemporary (at least in decor), lounges at sea. Pebble Beach is the name of the electronic golf simulator room, complete with wet bar, with play possible on 11 virtual courses. The Erasmus Library (formerly the Ibsen Library) is well organized, although it is simply not large enough for long-distance cruising. The former Compass Rose room is now the Explorer's Lounge.

The Oak Room is the ship's cigar/ pipe smoker's lounge; it has a marble fireplace, which sadly cannot be used due to

BERLITZ'S RATINGS

	Possible	Achieved
Ship	500	430
Accommodation	200	174
Food	400	327
Service	400	333
Entertainment	100	85
Cruise	400	345

United States Coast Guard regulations. I have always thought it would make a fine library, although it is also excellent as a cigar smoking room. Adjacent is the popular Java Cafe and Bar.

There is a computer-learning center, with 10 workstations (although there is little privacy when receiving one's emails). A lecture is provided to present subjects of cultural interest, while male "dance hosts" provide partners for women traveling alone.

Whether by intention or not, the ship has a two-class feeling, with passengers in "upstairs" penthouse suites and "A" grade staterooms gravitating to the quieter Stella Polaris lounge (particularly at night), while other passengers (the participants) go to the main entertainment deck.

The ship's wide range of facilities includes a concierge, self-service launderettes (useful on long voyages), an excellent guest lecture program, 24-hour information office, and true 24-hour cabin service, for the discriminating passenger who demands spacious personal surroundings, and good food and service, regardless of price. This ship operates mainly long-distance cruises in great comfort, and free shuttle buses are provided in almost all ports of call.

While *Prinsendam* isn't perfect, the few design flaws (for example: poorly designed bar service counters) are minor points. Even though the hardware is not ideal, the software (personnel and service) is generally sound. It is an extremely comfortable ship – smaller than other Holland America Line ships, and more refined. The elegant decorative features include Dutch artwork and memorabilia.

Added benefits include a fine health spa facility, spacious, wide teakwood decks and teak deck lounge chairs. However, the good points are marred by the bland quality of the dining room food and service, and the lack of understanding of what it takes to make a "luxury" cruise experience, despite what is stated in the company's brochures.

There are only four elevators, so anyone with walking disabilities may have to wait for some time during periods of peak usage (e.g. before meals). The cabin ceilings are plain. This spacious ship shows signs of wear and tear in some areas (particularly in the accommodation passageways), despite recent refurbishments. The library is far too small (particularly for some of the long cruises operated) and difficult to enter for anyone confined to a wheelchair.

SUITABLE FOR: *Prinsendam* is best suited to older adult couples and singles who like to mingle in a mid-size ship operating longer cruises, in an unhurried setting with fine quality surroundings, with some eclectic, antique artwork, good food and service from a smiling Indonesian and Filipino crew who like to serve but who lack finesse.

ACCOMMODATION. There are 15 grades, ranging from Penthouse Verandah Suites to standard interior (no view) cabins. All suites and cabins have undergone some degree of refurbishment since the ship was taken over by Holland America Line in 2002.
Penthouse Verandah Suite: The Penthouse Verandah Suite (723 sq. ft/67 sq. meters), is a most desirable living space, although not as large as other penthouse suites aboard some other ships. It is light and airy, and has two bathrooms, one of which has a large whirlpool bathtub with ocean views, and anodized gold bathroom fittings. The living room contains a large dining table and chairs, and large sofast. There is also a substantial private balcony, and butler service.
Deluxe Verandah Suites: There are 18 of these (8 on Sports Deck/10 on Lido Deck). Located in the forward section of the ship, they have large balconies, two sofas, large bar/entertainment center, (mini-bar/refrigerator, color television, VCR and CD player); bathrooms have separate toilet, sink and toiletries cabinets, connecting sliding door into the bedroom, large mirror, two toiletries cabinets, plenty of storage space, full bathtub, and anodized gold fittings. Each evening the butler brings different goodies – hot and cold hors d'oeuvres and other niceties. Liquor and wines are included in the cruise fare. If you do choose one of these suites, it might be best on the starboard side where they are located in a private hallway, while those on the port side (including the Penthouse Verandah Suite) are positioned along a public hallway. The 10 suites on Lido Deck are positioned along private port and starboard side hallways.

Passengers in Penthouse and Deluxe Verandah Suites are provided with a private concierge lounge, high tea served in the suite each afternoon, hors d'oeuvres before dinner each evening (on request), complimentary laundry pressing and dry cleaning, private cocktail parties with captain, priority disembarkation, and more.
Other Cabin Grades: Most of the other cabins (spread over six other decks) are of generous proportions and have just about everything you would need (including a VCR). Many (about 38 percent) have a small, private balcony. All

cabins have walk-in closets, lockable drawers, full-length mirrors, hairdryers, and ample cotton towels. A few cabins have third berths, while some have interconnecting doors (good for couples who want two bathrooms and more space or for families with children).

In all grades of accommodation, passengers receive a basket of fresh fruit, fluffy cotton bathrobes, evening turndown service, and a Holland America Line signature tote bag. Filipino and Indonesian cabin stewards and stewardesses provide unobtrusive personal service.

Four well-equipped, L-shaped cabins for the disabled are quite well designed, fairly large, and equipped with special wheel-in bathrooms with shower facilities and closets.

CUISINE/DINING. The La Fontaine Dining Room wraps around the aft end of Lower Promenade Deck and has extensive ocean-view windows; there's a second, smaller (quieter) section along the starboard side. There is plenty of space around tables. A good number of window-side tables are for two persons, although there are also tables for four, six or eight. Crystal glasses, and Rosenthal china and fine cutlery are provided. There are four seatings for dinner (you must pre-select a time and stick with it), at either 5.45pm, 6.15pm, 8pm or 8.30pm, at assigned tables, and an open-seating arrangement for breakfast and lunch (you'll be seated by restaurant staff when you enter). The dining room has both smoking and no-smoking sections.
Alternative Dining Option: A small, quiet dining spot is the Odyssey Dining Room, with 48 seats, and wood-paneled decor that increases the feeling of intimacy and privacy. Pacific Northwest cuisine is cuisine is featured (this doesn't seem appropriate when the ship is cruising in northern Europe or the Mediterranean), and seating preference is given to occupants of accommodation designated as suites. Reservations are required, although there is no extra charge. The Odyssey is open for both lunch and dinner.

There is a well-chosen wine list, although there is a great deal of emphasis on California wines, the prices of which are quite high.

There is also the recently enlarged Lido Restaurant, for decent casual dining and self-serve buffet-style meals. This restaurant has both indoor and outdoor seating.

ENTERTAINMENT. The show lounge is an amphitheater-style layout, with a well tiered floor, and both banquette and individual seating. While Holland America Line isn't known for fine entertainment, what it does offer is a consistently good, tried and tested array of cabaret acts.

SPA/FITNESS. The extensive Health Spa includes six treatment rooms (with integral showers), a rasul chamber (for mud and gentle steam heat treatments, combined with gentle steam), a gymnasium with views over the stern, and separate sauna, steam room, and changing rooms for men and women. The spa is operated by Steiner.

● **For more extensive general information on what a Holland America Line cruise is like, see pages 118–222.**

Professor Molchanov
★★

Boutique Ship: . . . . .1,753 tons	Total Crew: 20	Cabins (wheelchair accessible): 0
Lifestyle: . . . . .Standard	Passengers	Cabin Current: . . . . .220 volts
Cruise Line: . . . . . .Oceanwide Expeditions	(lower beds/all berths): 52/52	Elevators: 0
Former Names: . . . . .none	Passenger Space Ratio	Casino (gaming tables): . . . . .No
Builder: . . . . .Wartsila (Finland)	(lower beds/all berths): 33.7/33.7	Slot Machines: .No
Original Cost: . . . . .n/a	Crew/Passenger Ratio	Swimming Pools (outdoors): 0
Entered Service: 1983	(lower beds/all berths): 2.6/2.6	Swimming Pools (indoors): 0
Registry: .Russia	Navigation Officers: . . . . .Russian	Whirlpools: 0
Length (ft/m): 234.9/71.6	Cabins (total): .26	Self-Service Launderette: . . . . .No
Beam (ft/m): 42/12.8	Size Range (sq ft/m): . . . . .n/a	Dedicated Cinema/Seats: . . . . .No
Draft (ft/m): 15.0/4.6	Cabins (outside view): 29	Library: . . . . .Yes
Propulsion/Propellers: . . . . .diesel	Cabins (interior/no view): 0	Classification Society: .Russian Shipping
(2,327 kW)/2	Cabins (for one person): 6	Register
Passenger Decks: 3	Cabins (with private balcony): 0	

OVERALL SCORE: 947 (OUT OF A POSSIBLE 2,000 POINTS)

OVERVIEW. *Professor Molchanov* is an all-white vessel originally specially constructed in Finland for the former Soviet Union's polar and oceanographic research program and should not be taken as a cruise ship, although it was converted in the early 1990s to carry passengers, and then fitted out specifically for expedition cruising when refurbished in 1996. Other ships in the same series are *Akademik Boris Petrov, Akademik Golitsyn, Akademik M.A. Laurentiev, Akademik Nikolaj Strakhov, Livonia, Akademik Shokalskiy, Professor Khromov* and *Professor Multanovskiy*. It has an ice-hardened, steel hull, which is good for cruising in both the Arctic and Antarctic regions, and strong Russian diesel engines.

All passengers have access to the navigation bridge. There are several inflatable Zodiac landing craft for close-in shore excursions and nature observation trips.

Inside, the limited public rooms consist of a library and lounge/bar. The dining rooms also serve as a lecture room. The medical facilities are good.

This is expedition-style cruising, in a very small ship with limited facilities. However, it provides a somewhat primitive, but genuine adventure experience, taking you "up-close and personal" to places others only dream about. The bigger ships cannot get this close to Antarctica or the Arctic, but this little vessel will sail you right to the face of the ice continent.

Quark Expeditions charters this ship for the Antarctic (winter) season, and has its own staff and lecturers on board, as well as oversees the food, to make sure that everything is up to the company's usual high standard.

BERLITZ'S RATINGS

	Possible	Achieved
Ship	500	227
Accommodation	200	87
Food	400	203
Service	400	188
Entertainment	N/A	N/A
Cruise	500	242

SUITABLE FOR: *Professor Molchanov* is best suited to couples and single travelers who enjoy viewing nature and wildlife at close quarters, and who would not dream of cruising in the mainstream sense aboard ships with large numbers of people. This is for hardy, adventurous types who don't feel the need for onboard entertainment.

ACCOMMODATION. There are five grades (the price you pay depends on the grade and location you choose). With the exception of a single "suite," almost all other cabins are very small, Spartan, and rather clinical. There are two-berth cabins with shower and toilet, or there are two-bed cabins on the lowest deck, whose occupants must share a bathroom.

CUISINE/DINING. There are two dining rooms (the galley is located between them), each with a single seating. The meals are hearty international fare, with no frills. When the ship is under charter to Quark Expeditions, Western rather than Russian chefs oversee the food operation, and the quality of meals and variety of food is much better.

ENTERTAINMENT. There is no formal entertainment, although dinner and after-dinner conversation with fellow passengers in the ship's lounge/bar really becomes the entertainment each evening. So, if you don't want to talk to your fellow passengers, take a good book, or go outside, where you'll find nature is nothing less than diverting.

SPA/FITNESS. There are no spa or fitness facilities, although there is a sauna.

Professor Multanovskiy
★★

Boutique Ship: ....1,753 tons	Total Crew: 25	Cabins (wheelchair accessible): 0
Lifestyle: ....Standard	Passengers	Cabin Current: ....220 volts
Cruise Line: ......Oceanwide Expeditions	(lower beds/all berths): 49/49	Elevators: 0
Former Names: ....none	Passenger Space Ratio	Casino (gaming tables): ....No
Builder: ....Wartsila (Finland)	(lower beds/all berths): 35.7/35.7	Slot Machines: ....No
Original Cost: ....n/a	Crew/Passenger Ratio	Swimming Pools (outdoors): 0
Entered Service: 1983	(lower beds/all berths): 1.9/1.9	Swimming Pools (indoors): 0
Registry: ....Russia	Navigation Officers: ....Russian	Whirlpools: 0
Length (ft/m): 234.9/71.6	Cabins (total): 29	Self-Service Launderette: ....No
Beam (ft/m): 42/12.8	Size Range (sq ft/m): ....n/a	Dedicated Cinema/Seats: ....No
Draft (ft/m): 15.0/4.6	Cabins (outside view): 29	Library: ....Yes
Propulsion/Propellers: ....diesel	Cabins (interior/no view): 0	Classification Society: ..Russian Shipping
(2,327 kW)/2	Cabins (for one person): 9	Register
Passenger Decks: 3	Cabins (with private balcony): 0	

OVERALL SCORE: 947 (OUT OF A POSSIBLE 2,000 POINTS)

OVERVIEW. *Professor Multanovskiy,* which has a dark hull and white superstructure, was originally built in Finland for the former Soviet Union's polar and oceanographic research programme and should not be taken as a cruise ship, although it was converted in the early 1990s to carry passengers, and then fitted out specifically for expedition cruising when refurbished in 1996. Other ships in the series are *Akademik Boris Petrov, Akademik Golitsyn, Akademik M.A. Laurentiev, Akademik Nikolaj Strakhov, Akademik Shokalskiy, Livonia, Professor Khromov* and *Professor Molchanov.*

This ship is typically operated under charter to various "expedition" cruise companies. It has an ice-hardened, steel hull, which is good for cruising in both the Arctic and Antarctic, and strong Russian diesel engines. All passengers have access to the navigation bridge. There are several inflatable Zodiac landing craft for close-in shore excursions and nature observation trips. Inside, the limited public rooms consist of a library and lounge/bar. The dining rooms are also used for lectures. Medical facilities are good.

This is expedition-style cruising, in a very small ship with limited facilities. However, it provides a somewhat primitive, but genuine adventure experience, taking you "up-close and personal" to places others only dream about. The bigger ships cannot get this close to Antarctica or the Arctic, but this little vessel will sail you right to the face of the ice continent.

Quark Expeditions charters this ship for the Antarctic (winter) season, and has its own staff and lecturers on board. It also oversees the food, to make sure that everything is up to its usual high (Quark) standard.

BERLITZ'S RATINGS

	Possible	Achieved
Ship	500	227
Accommodation	200	87
Food	400	203
Service	400	188
Entertainment	N/A	N/A
Cruise	500	242

SUITABLE FOR: *Professor Multanovskiy* is best suited to couples and single travelers who enjoy viewing nature and wildlife at close quarters, and who would not dream of cruising in the mainstream sense aboard ships with large numbers of people. This is for hardy, adventurous types who don't feel the need for onboard entertainment.

ACCOMMODATION. There are five grades (the price you pay depends on the grade and location you choose). With the exception of one "suite," almost all other cabins are very small, Spartan, and rather clinical. There are two-berth cabins with shower and toilet, or there are two-bed cabins on the lowest deck, whose occupants must share a bathroom.

CUISINE/DINING. There are two dining rooms (the ship's galley is actually located between them), and all passengers are accommodated in a single seating. The meals are hearty international fare, with no frills. When the ship is under charter to Quark Expeditions, Western rather than Russian chefs oversee the food operation, and the quality of meals and variety of foods is much better.

ENTERTAINMENT. There is no formal entertainment, although dinner and after-dinner conversation with fellow passengers in the ship's lounge/bar really becomes the entertainment each evening. So, if you don't want to talk to your fellow passengers, take a good book, or go outside, where you'll find nature is nothing less than diverting.

SPA/FITNESS. There are no spa or fitness facilities, although there is a sauna.

Queen Elizabeth 2
★★★★+ to ★★★+

Large (Resort) Ship: . . . . .70,327 tons
Lifestyle: . . . . .Luxury/Premium/Standard
Cruise Line: . . . . .Cunard Line
Former Names: . . . . .none
Builder: . . .Upper Clyde Shipbuilders (UK)
Original Cost: . . . . £29 million
Entered Service: . . . . .May 1969
Registry: . . . . .Great Britain
Length (ft/m): 962.93/293.50
Beam (ft/m): 105.1/32.03
Draft (ft/m): 32.4/9.87
Propulsion/Propellers: . . . . .diesel-electric
(99,900 kW)/2
Passenger Decks: 10

Total Crew: .1,015
Passengers
(lower beds/all berths): 1,728/1,906
Passenger Space Ratio
(lower beds/all berths): 39.4/36.8
Crew/Passenger Ratio
(lower beds/all berths): 1.7/1.8
Navigation Officers: . . . . .British
Cabins (total): 950
Size Range (sq ft/m): 107.0–1,184.0/
10.0–110.0
Cabins (outside view): 657
Cabins (interior/no view): 293
Cabins (for one person): 151

Cabins (with private balcony): 32
Cabins (wheelchair accessible): 4
Cabin Current: . . . . .110 and 220 volts
Elevators: 13
Casino (gaming tables): . . . . .Yes
Slot Machines: . . . . .Yes
Swimming Pools (outdoors): 1
Swimming Pools (indoors): 1
(+ AquaSpa pool)
Whirlpools: 4
Self-Service Launderette: . . . . .Yes
Dedicated Cinema/Seats: Yes/530
Library: . . . . .Yes
Classification Society: . . .Lloyd's Register

OVERALL SCORE (OUT OF A POSSIBLE 2,000 POINTS)

GRILL CLASS: 1,687   **CARONIA CLASS: 1,599**   **MAURETANIA CLASS: 1,370**

BERLITZ'S RATINGS		
Grill Class	Possible	Achieved
Ship	500	434
Accommodation	200	169
Food	400	348
Service	400	308
Entertainment	100	82
Cruise	400	346

BERLITZ'S RATINGS		
Caronia Class	Possible	Achieved
Ship	500	415
Accommodation	200	141
Food	400	322
Service	400	312
Entertainment	100	83
Cruise	400	326

BERLITZ'S RATINGS		
Mauretania Class	Possible	Achieved
Ship	500	346
Accommodation	200	99
Food	400	278
Service	400	272
Entertainment	100	82
Cruise	400	293

OVERVIEW. *Queen Elizabeth 2* is really an ocean liner (not a "proper" cruise ship), designed and built for the differing weather and sea conditions of the North Atlantic. The ship has a dark blue hull and single, large funnel, and was introduced in 1969 to make scheduled transatlantic crossings between New York and Southampton. However, when the larger, brand new *Queen Mary 2* entered service in 2004, *Queen Elizabeth 2* became a full-time cruise ship, operating an annual around-the-world cruise (typically from January to April), and a variety of cruises for the rest of the year. The ship could also, conceivably, be brought back into transatlantic service should her consort *Queen Mary 2* ever suffer mechanical troubles.

Queen Elizabeth 2 is a greyhound of the cruise industry – still the fastest cruise ship in the world, as well as the world's most integrated ocean liner. Interestingly, it can go backwards faster than most cruise ships can go forwards, if ever it were necessary to do so (19 knots backwards has been recorded). A good range of joint travel programs and tour configurations is integrated into the ship's marketing. In contrast to so many ships where formal dress has all but disappeared, the dress code is mostly formal – though it is

becoming less so as the company's new American owners market to a more casual population. Male social hosts are provided as dancing partners for women traveling alone – a popular program started by Cunard Line in the 1970s.

Originally constructed with steam turbine propulsion, the ship underwent a $160 million refit in Bremen, Germany, in 1986. The original steam turbines were extracted and exchanged for a diesel-electric propulsion system, resulting in greater speed, better economy and more reliability. A new, fatter funnel was constructed, designed to better keep any soot off the expansive open decks. The ship has a long foredeck (rather like the long snout of a 4.5-liter vintage Bentley), unsurpassed by any other cruise ship. That foredeck makes it look powerful, yet sleek and so graceful – quite unlike today's new block-built ships.

Over the years, QE2 has undergone a number of extensive multi-million dollar interior refurbishments. Fine wood paneling and more traditional furnishings have replaced many of the original laminates that were all the tacky rage in the 1960s. The decor is now more reminiscent of the ocean liners of yesteryear – which is what most passengers expect.

At the end of 1999, the ship had a further $33.1 million

refurbishment (including $19 million on technical items). Bathrooms in all accommodation grades were entirely replaced; all now feature marble fixtures and jazzy art deco-style toiletry cabinets. Several new suites were added. Other facilities include a large library with more than 7,000 books (in about a dozen languages), and an integrated Cunard memorabilia shop. There is also a dedicated florist. The latest enhancements have provided grace, pace and space in what is a ship for all reasons.

Even at a speed of close to 30 knots there is almost no vibration at the stern. There is a wide range of facilities and public rooms with high ceilings.

QE2 is a veritable city at sea, and, as in any conurbation, there are several parts of town. There are three distinct classes: Grill Class, Caronia Class, and Mauretania Class. Grill Class accommodation consists of outstanding penthouse suites (with butler service only in Sun Deck and Sports Deck suites and room service food items provided by Queens Grill chefs, a stocked mini-bar refrigerator, daily fresh fruit and personalized stationery), and large outside-view cabins (with standard cabin service in One Deck and Two Deck cabins that is nothing special).

Dining is in one of three grill rooms: Queens Grill (named after former Cunard transatlantic liners *Queen Elizabeth* and *Queen Mary*), Britannia Grill or Princess Grill, according to the accommodation grade you choose.

Caronia Class accommodation consists of outside-view double cabins, and interior (no-view) and outside-view single cabins, with dining in the beautifully paneled Caronia Restaurant (decorated in an Italian style).

Mauretania Class accommodation features the lowest-priced cabin grades, but dining is in two seatings in the Mauretania Restaurant.

All passengers enjoy the use of all public rooms, except for the Queens Grill Lounge, reserved exclusively for passengers in Grill Class accommodation. QE2 has real wood "steamer" deckchairs (as well it should). Those on Sun Deck (also known as the "helicopter deck" can be reserved (for a small fee). Grill Class is the most desirable and sophisticated way to travel; Caronia Class (formerly known as first class) is good but definitely not what it used to be, while Mauretania Class (formerly known as transatlantic class) provides comfortable travel in a price-sensitive setting.

Gratuities are automatically charged to your onboard account (you will need to visit the information desk to make any changes necessary). In addition, 15% is added to all bar and wine, and health spa/salon bills.

Ship buffs can enjoy the Heritage Trail, a ship-wide display consisting of exhibits of Cunard ocean liner history and ship models, as well as some superb paintings of former Cunard liners, spread around the ship. It includes a stunning 16-ft (5-meter) illuminated model of the company's 1907 *Mauretania* (strangely located outside the Caronia Restaurant, while a model of the former *Caronia* is located in the Mauretania Restaurant). There is a great abundance of memorabilia (some further items are available for sale in the memorabilia bookshop/library).

There is a substantial amount of fine artwork, sculptures and paintings. Two huge, beautiful paintings can be found hanging in the "D" Deck foyer between Boat Deck and Upper Deck. They are the 1948 painting of Queen Elizabeth, the Queen Mother, by Sir Oswald Birley (this used to be aboard RMS *Queen Elizabeth*); and the 1949 painting of Princess Elizabeth and Prince Philip, which used to be aboard RMS *Caronia*.

The ship's wide range of facilities include a Grand Lounge (a dedicated showlounge with thrust stage, three seating tiers and good sound system); Tour and Travel Center (for shore excursions, theater tickets and concierge services); Business Center, Shopping Concourse which has a limited amount of brand-name merchandise at high European prices. The Yacht Club is a nautical, practical and popular aft-facing room that becomes a nightclub (afternoon recorded classical concerts here are a bonus).

The Queens Room is a real ballroom, with a large dance floor, for society dancing to a big band (during the day it is a quiet, stately room with very comfortable lounge chairs), and delightful stand-up cocktail parties. The Midships Lobby, the ship's embarkation point, has a distinctive, ocean liner image, with fine bird's-eye maple woodwork and wrap-around murals of the former and present Cunard Queens. A large computer center (with daily lectures and 22 computer workstations) is popular. There is also a dedicated florist and flower shop, and a large self-service launderette (no charge). The Lido, a large, informal bistro dining spot with 24-hour hot beverage stations, is also a bonus on cruises (all espresso and cappuccino coffees are free). The elegant Chart Room Bar (formerly the Midships Bar) is a charming, quiet drinking spot (it contains a piano from the liner *Queen Mary*).

There is a large cinema/concert hall (with 530 seats), complete with balcony level and 9-ft-long (2.7-meter) Bosendorfer piano. The Golden Lion Pub has Victorian decor and a selection of over 20 beers (both bottled and draught). There is also a superb library – one of the best at sea, with over 7,000 books, in about a dozen languages, and staffed by professional librarians. The Player's Club Casino has fitting art deco and blond wood decor.

QE2 has British officers, with an international hotel staff that is fairly attentive and service-oriented, although many do not speak English well, as is the case aboard so many ships today. There is a decent enough entertainment mix (although it could perhaps be more British in style and more in keeping with the character of the ship), and there is an extensive range of lecture programs. The laundry and dry-cleaning facilities are very good; there are also self-service (no charge) launderettes. There are, as well, English nannies and some facilities for children. This ship offers refined living at sea for those in upper-grade accommodation – otherwise it is just a large ship, albeit with fine facilities.

QE2 has travelled more than 5 million nautical miles (including about 700 visits to New York and about 600 to Southampton), blends high-tech engineering with traditional ocean liner facilities, and has hosted more famous faces than any other ship afloat. It is like a well-worn shoe – comfortable, but a little tired and frayed around the edges in places, which makes it difficult to evaluate. Sadly, there are fewer British crew members serving than passengers expect. As a cruise ship (particularly on short cruises of less than seven days) the ship is a real mismatch, and waiting for tenders (when the ship is at anchor and shore tenders must be used) is a pain. Tender ports should be avoided whenever possible, although the double-deck shore tenders used are very practical units.

If you occupy one of the top-level (Grill Class) suites, with butler service and all the trimmings of finery, your experience should be nothing short of superb, highly civilized quiet living at sea. However, many who occupy lower-grade accommodations (Caronia Class and Mauretania Class) may find that the ship does not quite come up to their high expectations. If you have to count the pennies, taking a longer cruise in lower-grade accommodation may well be preferable to taking a shorter cruise in higher-priced accommodation. Expect some inconsistencies and frustrations, but they will seem insignificant when compared to the splendid experience aboard the world's most legendary ship.

Will *QE2* survive the onslaught of the mega-ships? I believe it will, simply because it isn't one of them, and it does have a lifestyle that somehow will still be in vogue when its rivals have become floating night clubs.

QE2, of course, has now passed its 35th birthday, and it is difficult to compare it with the latest contemporary cruise ships that have more light, multiple balconies and more flexible, high-tech facilities. Although the interior passageways are wide, there is a feeling of being enclosed, and cabins with portholes simply seem dated (however, bear in mind that this is an ocean liner, not a cruise ship).

Sadly, there is no forward observation lounge (there was when the ship was built). Missing are a few grand, flowing staircases, the air of romance, and the high standard of food service personnel of yesteryear's ocean liners.

The shops are, for the most part, tacky, run by a concession more used to high street and mass market trading than Bond Street or Fifth Avenue and are a constant source of complaint from passengers.

The cabins on Five Deck (the lowest of the accommodation decks) are adequate, no more. There are fewer small, intimate hideaway bars than there used to be. As a "classless" cruise ship, the layout is rather disjointed.

The onboard currencies are the British pound and the US dollar. Gratuities are automatically charged to your onboard account (you will need to visit the information desk to make any changes necessary). In addition, 15% is added to all bar and wine, and health spa/salon bills.

SUITABLE FOR: *Queen Elizabeth 2* is best suited to a wide range of seasoned and well-traveled couples and single travelers who enjoy the cosmopolitan setting of a floating international city at sea, with its extensive array of facilities, public rooms, dining rooms, and lecture program. Choose *QE2* if you don't need the glitz and hype of newer larger sister *QM2* and are comfortable with a true classic.

ACCOMMODATION. There is a vast range of grades and cabin configurations, so you should study the brochure and deck plan carefully. The most exclusive (and expensive) accommodation is in the Queen Elizabeth and Queen Mary split-level penthouses on Signal Deck. Next are another 30 suites on Signal Deck and Sun Deck (several on Sun Deck have private balconies, although some have lifeboat-obstructed views) and 10 suites on Boat Deck. Then come the large cabins on Decks 1, 2 and 3, while the smallest outside-view cabins are lower down on Decks 4 and 5 (these have portholes, which tend to make the cabins seem smaller than they are, with little natural light available), and interior (no-view) cabins.

Whichever grade you choose, bathroom cabinets have a lot of storage space – important for anyone choosing this ship for long voyages. Almost all bathrooms were replaced in a 1997 refit, although some that were not replaced are quite tacky in places.

Suites: Many of the suites and cabins on Deck 3, 2, 1, Boat Deck, Sports Deck and Signal Deck have fine wood-paneled walls, generous closet and drawer space, thick, real wood furniture and large, marble bathrooms. From sumptuous, understated two-level suites with private balconies, walk-in closets, stocked refrigerators and mini-bars and bathrooms large enough for four, to modest interior (no-view) cabins that are compact but quite well equipped, you pay for the amount of space and grade you want, and, more important, the location.

The accommodation you choose will determine in which of the ship's five restaurants you will dine. Note that some suites on Sun Deck and Boat Deck have lifeboat-obstructed views (not shown in the brochure), which are the same price as for those without obstructed views – very odd.

Penthouse Suites: The Penthouse Suites (on Signal Deck and Sun Deck) are among the most refined and quiet living spaces at sea. During the ship's 1999 refit, three new suites were added to the list of exclusive living spaces: the Aquitania and Carinthia suites on 2 Deck, and the wheelchair-accessible Caledonia suite on Boat Deck. Occupants of these most exclusive suites have room service food items supplied by chefs from the Queens Grill (during dining hours).

Wheelchair-Accessible Cabins: Four cabins have been created in accordance with the guidelines of the American Disabled Association (ADA). The cabin door is wide enough for a wheelchair (no "lip"); the bathroom door slides open electronically at the touch of a button (located at wheelchair height), and the floor is flat. The full-length bathtub has special assist handles, and the toilet has grab bars. Closets have hanging rails with hydraulically balanced lever to lower them towards the outside of the closet, to the right height. There is an intercom, alarm, and remote controls for lighting, curtains and doors.

These cabins are also good for the hearing-impaired, with three brightly colored lighted signs on the cabin bulkhead, as well as a telephone system for the deaf.

CUISINE/DINING. There are five principal full-service restaurants (all of which include many tables for two, unlike so many ships being introduced today) and two informal dining spots: The Lido (breakfast lunch and dinner) and The Pavilion Grill (for lunchtime fast-food items only). In order of excellence they are: Queens Grill, Britannia Grill and Princess Grill, Caronia Restaurant (very nicely refurbished in 1999, with rich wood paneling, pleasing chandeliers and a quieter, and more elegant decor), and Mauretania Restaurant.

One-seating dining is featured in all except the Mauretania Restaurant, which operates two seatings (note that this is where the student waiters cut their teeth, and food and service are adequate at best). There are both smoking and non-smoking sections in all restaurants. The menus are varied, creative and well balanced, and include spa/light/healthy-eating items.

The Queens Grill has its own separate galley, the best waiters and service, a formal atmosphere for dinner, and memorable food prepared in the best English and French culinary traditions (you can also order from the à la carte menu, as well as "off-menu"). The Britannia Grill, Princess Grill and Mauretania Restaurant share the same galley, but the service and setting in the intimate Britannia Grill and Princess Grill is far superior. The Caronia and Mauretania Restaurants have good, creative and varied menus, with service provided by the least experienced waiters.

Queens Grill: Fine dining (with many items cooked to order) is exemplified in the Queens Grill, the ship's most formal restaurant (it's nicer than that the one aboard *QM2*). This is comparable to a very good shore-side gourmet restaurant, and features tableside carvings, flambeaus and outstanding presentation by dedicated British restaurant managers and head waiters who excel in the art of hospitality. The room, whose decor is classic black and white, features individual chairs (there are, fortunately, no tables with banquette seats) and there are many tables for two or four persons. The cuisine includes many traditional British favorites, together with extensive French dishes as well as regional specialties from around the world. Regular travelers know that special orders are always possible.

Britannia Grill/Princess Grill: Some frequent travelers might, however, prefer the smaller and more intimate Britannia Grill or Princess Grill (this dining spot remains much as it was when the ship debuted more than 30 years ago), which offer almost the same kind of tableside service and fine cuisine. In 2000, the food budget for the ship was cut severely, so you can expect to find some decrease in the quality and variety of foods available. Also, note that the tables in all the Grill Rooms are very close together, more tables having been squeezed in over the years to accommodate the increase in Grill-class capacity. Special orders are, however, always possible.

Caronia Restaurant: This wood-paneled restaurant (formerly the first-class dining room) is large, but extremely comfortable. At the entrance, the three steps leading down into the well of the restaurant were designed so that ladies in gowns could make an elegant entrance that could be seen by most diners. The food, while similar to the grill rooms, is presented with polished service and attentiveness from the international mix of waiters and waitresses.

Mauretania Restaurant: This restaurant, the entrance of which leads off from the lovely Crystal Bar, operates two seatings. Its focal point is a "white horse" sculpture that is bathed in blue light; there is also a mural of Cunard cruising scenes on one wall, as well as a model of the former Cunard world-wide cruising ship *Caronia*. The restaurant has tables for 2, 4, 6, 8 or 10, and many dining alcoves, which help to make it appear smaller than it really is.

The food is quite good, well presented, and comes with service that is reasonably correct, the waiters and waitresses in this restaurant being the new breed (those with the least training). Note that the Mauretania Restaurant may operate as a one-seating dining room when the ship is not full.

The Lido Cafe: Casual dinners can be taken in The Lido, a popular dining spot that is busy all day (casual dress code). It has its own galley, bar and beverage station. The luncheon and midnight buffets provide a good range of foods, although at peak times lines will form.

The Pavilion: For casual fast food, this little hideaway place is located aft, just under the Lido Cafe. Here you can find hamburgers, hot dogs, veggie burgers, and other grilled fast-food items.

ENTERTAINMENT. The Grand Lounge is the principal venue for Broadway-style production shows, major cabaret acts, many social activities, cooking demonstrations, and some lectures. The room is two decks high, with a few seats provided on the upper level, while almost all the seating is on the lower level. It's certainly not a lavish room by today's standards, but it works (much better for cabaret than production shows), and has a "thrust" bandstand. The show lounge is poor when compared with those aboard newer ships; the sight lines and seating could be better, and much of the entertainment is unremarkable. The large-scale production shows featured in this room have been utterly disappointing for the past few years (and not very British), although there is a decent enough selection of cabaret acts.

The Queens Lounge is the venue for ballroom dancing, social activities, classical concerts, big band and jazz concerts, and some cabaret acts. A number of bands, a string ensemble and solo musicians present live music for dancing and listening in many of the ship's lounges and bars.

SPA/FITNESS. The Cunard Royal Spa is operated by Steiner, a specialist concession, whose young staff will try to sell you Steiner's own-brand Elemis beauty products (spa girls have sales targets). Some fitness classes are free, while some, such as yoga and kick-boxing, cost $10 per class. However, being aboard will give you an opportunity to try some of the more indulgent treatments. Massage (including Aroma Stone massage, Chakra Balancing massage and other well-being massages), facials, pedicures, and beauty salon treatments cost extra (massage, for example, costs about $2 per minute, plus gratuity).

Sports facilities include a paddle tennis court, golf driving ranges, basketball, shuffleboard, ring toss and other deck games.

Queen Mary 2
★★★★★ to ★★★★ +

Large Ocean Liner: ....148,528 tons	Total Crew: 1,254	Cabins (wheelchair accessible): 30
Lifestyle: .....Luxury/Premium/Standard	Passengers	Cabin Current: ....110 and 220 volts
Cruise Line: ....Cunard Line	(lower beds/all berths): 2,620/3,090	Elevators: 22
Former Names: ....none	Passenger Space Ratio	Casino (gaming tables): ....Yes
Builder: Chantiers de l'Atlantique (France)	(lower beds/all berths): 56.6/48.0	Slot Machines: ....Yes
Original Cost: ....$800 million	Crew/Passenger Ratio	Swimming Pools (outdoors): 3
Entered Service: ....Jan 2004	(lower beds/all berths): 2.0/2.4	Swimming Pools (indoors): 2
Registry: ....Great Britain	Navigation Officers: ....British	Whirlpools: 8
Length (ft/m): 1,131.9/345.03	Cabins (total): 1,310	Fitness Center: ....Yes
Beam (ft/m): 134.5/41.00	Size Range (sq ft/m): 194.0–2,249.7/	Sauna/Steam Room: ....Yes/Yes
Draft (ft/m): 32.6/9.95	18.0–209	Massage: ....Yes
Propulsion/Propellers: ......gas turbine	Cabins (outside view): 1,017	Self-Service Launderette: ....Yes
(103,000kW) and diesel-electric/4 pods	Cabins (interior/no view): 293	Dedicated Cinema/Seats: ....Yes
(2 azimuthing, 2 fixed/21.5 MW each)	Cabins (for one person): 0	Library: ....Yes
Passenger Decks: 12	Cabins (with private balcony): 953	Classification Society: ...Lloyd's Register

---

OVERALL SCORE: (OUT OF A POSSIBLE 2,000 POINTS): GRILL CLASS 1,754; BRITANNIA CLASS 1,601

OVERVIEW. In January 2004, the cruising world witnessed the birth of a new Queen. RMS *Queen Mary 2* (designated a Royal Mail Ship by the British Post Office – a designation its smaller sister *QE2* does not have) offers the pleasures of crossing the North Atlantic comfortably on a regular schedule, with the latest high-tech facilities and conveniences.

A ship of superlatives, *Queen Mary 2* (nicknamed *Proud Mary 2* by this author) is the largest passenger ship ever built (in terms of gross tonnage, length, and beam, though not passengers carried) and is five times the length of Cunard Line's first ship, *Britannia*. Taller than the Empire State Building, it is the first new ship to be built for Cunard Line since 1969, when *QE2* first sailed from Southampton to New York. *QM2* operates transatlantic crossings for much of the year, but no world cruises (these are left, for the present, to *QE2*).

Queen Mary 2's exterior design bears an uncanny resemblance to that of *QE2*, and for good reason: it was designed by naval architect Stephen Payne, an ocean liner enthusiast. This is a superbly designed ship, able to weather any unkind conditions on the North Atlantic, or anywhere else.

The power and propulsion system comprises an environmentally friendly Rolls-Royce marine gas turbine and diesel-electric power plant developing 157,000 horsepower (117.2 MW) – enough to provide power to the 200,000 inhabitants of its home port, Southampton. The ship is propelled by the world's first four-pod propulsion system, which can power through the waters of the North Atlantic at up to

BERLITZ'S RATINGS		
Grill Class	Possible	Achieved
Ship	**500**	**441**
Accommodation	**200**	**177**
Food	**400**	**351**
Service	**400**	**350**
Entertainment	**100**	**84**
Cruise	**400**	**351**
Britannia Class		
Ship	**500**	**408**
Accommodation	**200**	**157**
Food	**400**	**308**
Service	**400**	**312**
Entertainment	**100**	**84**
Cruise	**400**	**332**

30 knots (the contracted top speed is 29.3 knots, although the ship can easily exceed this). Each pod weighs 250 tons (more than an empty Boeing 747 jumbo jet), and are powered by a diesel-electric system. Indeed, this ship can go backwards faster than many cruise ships can go forwards.

QM2 was built at the Chantiers de l'Atlantique shipyard in France, in a dry dock measuring 1,360 by 207 ft (415 by 63 meters). The first steel was cut on January 16, 2002, while the keel laying took place on July 4, 2002 – 162 years to the day that the first Cunard steamship, *Britannia*, made its first crossing. The huge ship, constructed in 98 blocks, each weighing up to 600 tons, was completed an incredibly short 24 months later (964 days, to be exact).

Externally, the ship looks like a larger sister to the ever-popular *QE2*, although the stern is slightly boxier and more angular, and doesn't have the roundness of *QE2*. Of course, *QM2* has more decks and a lot of balcony cabins, which add to the powerful but bulky look. It also has a moderately long foredeck (an asset on transatlantic crossings), a large, contemporary funnel and beautifully tiered stern. *QM2* is too wide of beam to transit the Panama Canal.

One of the many delightful features is the ship's Tyfon whistle: (there are two: one is new, and the other a copy of the whistle from the original *Queen Mary*, carried to Europe by *QE 2* prior to being fitted to *QM2* in the shipyard). Manufactured by Kockums in Sweden, the replica was inspected, cleaned and converted from steam power to air power. It is 7 ft long and 3 ft high (2.1 meters by 0.9 meters), and weighs 1,400 pounds (635 kg). Both whistles are tuned so that they do not disturb passengers on deck, yet they can be heard 10 miles away.

Almost everything about the new ocean liner is somewhat British in style (but with some American decor input and accents), and even the four tender stations have London names: Belgravia, Chelsea, Kensington and Knightsbridge. There is a wide wrap-around promenade deck outdoors (with the forward section under cover from the weather or wind). Three times around is 6,102 ft (1,860 meters), or 1.1 miles (1.6 km). Inside are several other walking promenades – good if the weather is poor (for instance, it's almost 300 steps, or three minutes, from fore to aft along Deck 9). A full line of teak "steamer" chairs are provided on the open wrap-around promenade deck, and this still leaves plenty of room for walkers to pass (however, plastic deck lounge chairs are provided on some other open decks – particularly those at the aft of the ship). An exterior, winged observation platform, directly under the navigation bridge, offers great sightlines along the length of the ship, as well as forward.

Robert Tillberg Design, a Norwegian company, has produced designs that are, for the most part, stylish and elegant, with towering public spaces, sweeping staircases and grand public rooms that exude a feeling of timelessness. High ceilings (typically two decks of *QM2* are the equivalent of three decks in height of a regular cruise vessel) provide a great sense of space and grandeur. While many ships are designed inward with a central atrium, *QM2* is very different. You enter the public rooms from a central location and will always be looking out, with the sea (which is, after all, the real focal point of an ocean liner) in the background. What's good is the fact that just four staircases traverse all decks (unlike *QE2*, which has 10, having been built as a three-class ship, then changed before introduction to a two-class liner). Deck signage is good, and it's quite easy to find one's way around the ship for the most part, although more fore and aft signs would be useful.

There are a few ostentatious gold pillars and tacky decorative elements (including some awful "bas-reliefs" in the accommodation passageways – criticized as the "Miami Beach" view of what a transatlantic liner looks like). But, for the most part, the ship's interiors are quite stunning, and subtly so. The use of wood laminate paneling may abhor ship buffs (as did the plastic laminates when *QE2* debuted in 1968–69), but is the result of stringent SOLAS regulations.

The spacious atrium lobby, spanning six decks, has an elegant staircase and exclusive works of art. In the main elevator lobby attached to the central atrium, a wall mural of Samuel Cunard welcomes you aboard; it looks like an enlarged photograph, although it is made from almost 700 postage stamp-sized digital images of previous Cunard ships.

Let's take a deck-by-deck preview of the facilities and public rooms featured aboard what is undoubtedly the most superlative ocean liner ever (starting at the lowest deck and working our way upward, forward to aft):
● Deck 2 has Illuminations (with planetarium), and the Royal Court Theatre, the lower level of the six-deck high

atrium lobby, the Purser's Desk, Video Arcade, Empire Casino, Golden Lion Pub, and the lower level of the two-deck high Britannia Restaurant.
● Deck 3 has the upper level of Illuminations and the Royal Court Theatre, the second level of the six-deck high atrium lobby, Mayfair Shops, Sir Samuel's, The Chart Room, Champagne Bar (Veuve Clicquot is the "house" champagne), the upper level of the Britannia Restaurant, the Queens Room, and the G32 Nightclub.
● Decks 4/Deck 5/Deck 6 have accommodation and the third, fourth and fifth levels of the six-deck high atrium lobby; at the aft end of Deck 6 are the facilities for children, including an outdoor pool (Minnows Pool).
● Deck 7 has the Canyon Ranch Spa, the Winter Garden, the sixth and uppermost level of the six-deck high atrium lobby, expansive Kings Court Buffet, Queens Grill Lounge, Queens Grill and Princess Grill dining salons.
● Deck 8 (forward) has the upper level of the Canyon Ranch Spa, and the Library and Bookshop. The center section has accommodation. In the aft section are the alternative restaurant Todd English, Terrace Bar, and swimming pool outdoors.
● Deck 9 (forward) has the Commodore Club, Boardroom and the Cigar Club (Churchills). The rest of the deck has accommodation and a Concierge Club for suite occupants.
● Deck 10 has accommodation only.
● Deck 11 (forward) has an outdoors observation area. The rest of the deck has accommodation. The aft section outdoors has a whirlpool tub and sunbathing deck.
● Deck 12 (forward) has accommodation. The mid-section has an indoor/outdoor pool (with sliding glass roof), and golf areas (Fairways). The aft section has the Boardwalk Cafe, dog kennels, and shuffleboard courts.
● Deck 13 has the Sports Centre, Regatta Bar, a splash pool, and extensive outdoor sunbathing space.

There are 14 lounges, clubs and bars. An observation lounge, the delightful Commodore Club, has commanding views forward over the bows; light jazz is played in this bar, which is connected to the Boardroom, and Cigar Lounge. Other drinking places include a Golden Lion Pub, a wine bar (Sir Samuel's), a nautically-themed cocktail bar (The Chart Room), and Champagne Bar. Bars outdoors include the Regatta Bar and Terrace Bar. The ship's G32 nightclub, which has a main and mezzanine level, is located at the aft end of the ship, away from passenger cabins; it is named after the number designated to the ship by its French builder. The Empire Casino has a bar, as well as the latest high-tech slot machines, and traditional gaming tables.

The Queens Room is a grand ballroom, and, with the largest dance floor at sea, is a stunning, gloriously proportioned room, with a Hollywood-Bowl-style bandstand canopy. It has a dramatic high ceiling, two huge crystal chandeliers, highly comfortable armchairs, and is used for dancing, cocktail parties, and afternoon teas.

Illuminations, the first full-scale planetarium at sea, is a multi-purpose show lounge space that also functions as a 473-seat grand cinema, lecture hall and even a broadcasting studio. As a planetarium, it has tiered seating rows, with 150 very comfortable (reclining) seats and plush fabrics, allowing you to sit in a special area under a dome that forms the setting for the night sky. There are three excellent 20-minute programs, and the space can be used for virtual reality films.

A Maritime Quest Exhibit provides a history of ship-building on Scotland's River Clyde, including John Brown's Shipyard, the yard that built the ocean liners *Queen Elizabeth* and *Queen Mary* in the 1930s. This is beautifully constructed in 50 story boards throughout the ship. Handsets with audio information are available, and some exhibits have touch-screen interactive information.

Just aft of the Canyon Ranch Spa is the colonial-style Winter Garden (reminiscent of London's Kew Gardens), where flowers bloom year-round (which means they are artificial – some are downright tacky). This peaceful garden setting is for relaxation; a string quartet could well be playing for afternoon tea (which is also served in the much larger, and beautifully elegant Queen's Room).

There are five swimming pools, including one that can be enclosed under a retractable sliding glass roof; this is useful in bad weather. A large area (21,100 sq. ft/1,960 sq. meters) of open sunning space includes a sports bar at one end. Sports facilities include electronic golf simulator, putting green, giant chess board and a paddle tennis court.

The ship's Library and Bookshop is located forward; it has a superb range of 8,000 books (in several languages). Full-time librarians are in attendance, and the area includes leather sofas and armchairs, six internet-connect computers, and a large selection of magazines. It is a delightful facility, although the adjacent bookshop is quite small (particularly for transatlantic crossings). A fun statistic: to lock (or unlock) the 160 bookcase doors in the Library takes 25 minutes

ConneXions, a unique education center, includes seven sophisticated classrooms for Cunard Line's College at Sea program. Classes in such things as computer learning, seamanship and navigation, art and wine appreciation, languages and photography are taught. Meanwhile, fast-access internet connectivity and a multitude of computer terminals can be found in the Internet Center (several connection packages are provided: from $13.50 for 50 minutes' use, to $47.95 for 120 minutes, up to $479 for 1,920 minutes); Wi-Fi service (it is excellent) for your own laptop is available round the clock in the Chart Room, Commodore Club, Golden Lion Pub, Grand Lobby, Library, Queens Grill Lounge, Sir Samuels Wine Bar and the Winter Garden.

Children have their own space, with a dedicated play area, the Play Zone. English nannies supervise toddlers, while older children use The Zone. Dogs are provided with 12 kennels and a "dogs-only" exercise run.

SOME COMMENTS: *Queen Mary 2* is, like its smaller sister *QE2*, a floating city, and, like any city, there are several parts of town (some elegant, some not so elegant, some slightly tacky). To the disappointment of many regular transatlantic passengers, there are no single cabins.

QM2, unlike *QE2*, has no dedicated cinema – a shame since the ship is specifically built for the North Atlantic crossings, when a cinema is much appreciated by frequent

passengers (films are, however, shown daily in Illuminations or the Royal Theatre). The grill rooms are too large to be intimate, and are more akin to the kind of grill/steakhouses one finds in large North American cities.

The framed, animated cartoons on display (and for sale) in The Gallery don't quite go with the *QM2*'s ocean liner image; neither do art auctions or the dreaded "inch of gold" bazaar stalls. However, at the end of the day, choose this ship for the wonderfully uplifting experience of crossing the Atlantic by ocean liner (better still, cross both ways, so you won't have to fly back). Gratuities are charged to your onboard account at $13–$15 per person, per day, according to the grade of accommodation chosen. A 15% gratuity is included in all beverage and wine orders. As for extra charges, drinks prices are quite reasonable, but a 10-inch by 8-inch embarkation photo will set you back $27.50.

QM2 passengers are a mixed bunch (most are well dressed, although numerous "tracksuiters'" inhabit the ship, particularly in the Kings Court). Some passengers sail because the ship provides a comfortable manner in which to transit the North Atlantic without having to fly. Some travel because the ship pampers to them. Some travel because of price-sensitive considerations. For whatever reason, the ship has become all things to all people.

A crossing or voyage aboard *QM2* can be considered luxurious only if you travel in Queens Grill accommodation. Otherwise, the experience ranges from "standard" to "premium" in the other accommodation grades (and little different to regular cruise ships in these market segments). While there are a few delightful wooden deck lounge chairs (with green padded cushions), the majority of deck lounge chairs (particularly on the open decks aft) are of plastic.

During the ship first six months in service, concern over flammable materials in suite/cabin bathrooms was quickly rectified by installing smoke alarms – *QM2* now has more smoke alarms than any other cruise ship in the world.

TRANSATLANTIC CROSSINGS: The ship is supremely quiet in operation, with almost no vibration, even when traveling at top speed in poor weather. The large amount of personal luggage allowed is especially useful for anyone relocating, or for extended holidays. When you arrive in New York or Southampton, after six days of not having to lift a finger, it often proves to be a bittersweet anti-climax after the calming effects of *QM2* on one's inner being. I can think of little that is more pleasing to the soul or more civilized than a transatlantic crossing, of being cosseted in the finery of dining in any of the three grill restaurants with their fine cuisine and presentation (Grill Class accommodations only).

As a transatlantic ocean liner, this ship has no equal; it rides extremely well, and displays superb sea-keeping characteristics, with virtually no vibration from its podded propulsion system. If you can afford to travel in Grill Class accommodation, you will be cosseted in high comfort, and experience the very best service available in the grand transatlatic ocean liner traditions of today (including reserved open deck sunning space). If you travel in Britannia Class accommodation, the ship will provide you with a way to cross the North Atlantic, but with dining arrangements that are more akin to many of the large (resort) ships of today (although this equates to a dumbing down of food quality and presentation).

Note that if you travel in accommodation with a balcony and you want sunshine on the crossing from Southampton to New York (westbound), book a suite/cabin on the port side. Eastbound, book on the starboard side. Going westbound, the Statue of Liberty will normally be on the port side, and, on leaving New York, on the starboard side.

Sadly, what lets down the six-day transatlantic crossing experience is the awful passenger terminal in New York – it's an archaic mess totally out of keeping with the grandeur of the ship (the UK's Southampton Queen Elizabeth II passenger terminal is slightly better – but both need some hospitality factor and could be much more user-friendly).

There are certainly a few niggling items that detract from the luxury image the company is trying to portray. Examples include wooden stirrers (instead of real spoons) in the Kings Court (an indication of the "Carnivalization" of Cunard Line – although, to be honest, without the Carnival Corporation, Cunard Line would not have survived in today's harsh economic climate), and the removal of a transatlantic favorite, mid-morning boullion service on deck.

Cunard Line charters the Orient Express Boat Train between London's Waterloo Station and Southampton Docks; the train pulls up right alongside the Ocean Terminal to connect with the ship. This special train consists exclusively of Pullman carriages, richly paneled and fitted with individual deep-upholstery seats. Complimentary hot canapés and champagne are served. Passengers can complete all formalities and ship check-in procedures on the train, and simply walk directly on board QM2 on arrival in Southampton. Baggage loaded onto the train's baggage carriage in Waterloo is delivered directly to your cabin.

THE CRUISE EXPERIENCE: QM2 is a large resort ship (with an elite first-class section), and, where several tender ports are included in itineraries, spending time obtaining tender tickets to go ashore will inevitably detract from the overall experience (although itineraries have been planned to include as many "alongside" ports as possible). However, the passenger flow is generally sound, and the ship absorbs passengers extremely well with no sense of crowding.

COMPARING QM2 AND QE2: Some comparisons are inevitable. QM2 has two classes and only four staircases (QE2 has three classes and 10 staircases). QE2 has many cabins for single occupancy (QM2 has none, and single-occupancy premiums are extremely high). QE2 has a Baggage Master (QM2 does not). QE2's Queens Grill and Princess Grill restaurants are far more intimate, and have better decor than those of QM2. Aboard QM2 there is no private lounge for Princess Grill passengers.

SOME FUN STATISTICS:
● The ship is as long as 41 London double-decker buses laid end to end (or 3½ football fields).

● Propulsion power is equivalent to 1,600 family cars.
● The ship towers 236 ft (72 meters) from the top of the funnel to the base of the keel – taller than the Statue of Liberty, the equivalent of a 23-storey building.
● The ship has 30,000 sq. yards (25,000 sq. meters) of carpet and 1,550 miles (2,500 km) of electric cabling.

SUITABLE FOR: Queen Mary 2 is best suited to a wide range of couples and single travelers who enjoy the cosmopolitan setting of a floating city at sea that has a maritime heritage and background unequaled by any other ship and cruise line today, with its extensive array of facilities, public rooms, and dining rooms.

ACCOMMODATION. QM2 is a two-class ship (Grill Class and Britannia Class), and the restaurant you are assigned to depends on the accommodation grade you choose. There are 10 categories, in 25 price grades. The price you pay will depend on grade, location and size. From standard outside-view cabins to the most opulent suites afloat, there is something for every taste and pocketbook – a choice unrivaled aboard any other cruise vessel. Perhaps the most noticeable difference between this ship and QE2 is the addition of a large number of cabins with private balconies (75 percent of all cabins have them, although they are really of little use when crossing the North Atlantic (when QE2 debuted in 1969, there was not one single balcony cabin). Some 12 cabins look inwards to the atrium lobby, which spans six decks.

All grades have a 20-inch (or larger) color television with concealed interactive keyboard, internet connectivity (via a data port for your laptop). All beds have fluffy European duvets, mini-fridge, personal safe, hand-held hairdryer, and all bathrooms have toiletry amenities supplied by Canyon Ranch (the spa/fitness concession).

Other features include digital video on demand (English-, French- and German-language movies are available), music on demand (with 3,000 titles), audio books on demand, and email and digital photographs preview and purchase (the system can be blocked so that children cannot access it). One channel is devoted to the history of Cunard Line.

The interactive system also lets you make restaurant reservations, order wine, or items from the shops on board, book shore excursions, look at your onboard account, and biuographies of entertainers on board. Portable computers can be connected via a port in the cabin telephone.

A number of cabins can accommodate a third or fourth person, although they are so small as to be useful only for contortionists (they are, however, the most inexpensive way of experiencing this fine ship). Note that you get a different cabin breakfast menu depending on whether you travel in Grill Class or Britannia Class accommodation.

For the largest accommodation in the cruise industry, two combinations offer the equivalent of a large house at sea. At the front of the ship, you can combine the Queen Elizabeth and Queen Mary suites with the Queen Anne and Queen Victoria suites to produce one huge suite measuring

5,016 sq. ft (466 sq. meters). Even this can be eclipsed at the other end of the ship, by joining Grand Duplex apartments at the lower level to the adjacent penthouses to produce an unprecedented 8,288 sq. ft (770 sq. meters).

Balmoral/Sandringham Duplexes (Grade Q1): The largest stand-alone accommodation can be found in the Balmoral and Sandringham Duplexes (2,249 sq. ft/209 sq. meters). These are located aft in prime real estate territory, with superb views along the entire length of the ship. Upstairs is a bedroom with wood-framed king-sized bed, and large (but not so private) balcony; downstairs is a living room with sofa, coffee table, dining table, and writing desk. There are two marble-clad bathrooms with whirlpool bath and separate shower enclosure, toilet and bidet, and two washbasins.

Queen Elizabeth/Queen Mary Suites (Grade Q2): The Queen Elizabeth Suite and Queen Mary Suite (1,194 sq. ft/111 sq. meters) are both located just under the navigation bridge, with good views over the ship's long bows. There are living and dining areas, with a large private balcony (but not as large as the Balmoral/ Sandringham duplex balconies). The master, marble-clad bathroom has a whirlpool bathtub and shower enclosure, and a second bathroom with a shower enclosure (no bathtub). Each suite has the convenience of private elevator access.

Queen Anne/Queen Victoria Suites (Grade Q3): These two suites (796.5 sq. ft/74 sq. meters) have the most commanding views over the ship's long bows. They consist of a bedroom with master, marble-clad bathroom with whirlpool bathtub and separate shower enclosure; separate living/dining area, and a second bathroom with a shower enclosure (no bathtub).

Duplex Apartments: There are three duplex apartments: Buckingham and Windsor (each 1,291 sq. ft/120 sq. meters), and Hollywood (1,566 sq. ft/145 sq. meters). Each has a gymnasium, balcony, butler and concierge service, and superb views over the ship's stern.

Penthouse Suites (Grade Q4): There are six penthouse suites (758 sq. ft/70 sq. meters). These have a living and dining area, large private balcony, bedroom and dressing room with master, marble-clad bathroom with whirlpool bathtub and separate shower enclosure.

Suites (506 sq ft (Grade Q5/Q6): These 82 suites (506 sq. ft/47 sq. meters) have a large private balcony, living area, dressing room, marble-clad bathroom with whirlpool bathtub and separate shower enclosure. Beds can be arranged in a king-size or twin-bed configuration.

Junior Suites (Grade P1/P2): There are 76 Junior Suites (381 sq. ft/35 sq. meters). Each has a lounge area, large private balcony, and marble-clad bathroom with whirlpool bathtub and separate shower enclosure. Beds can be arranged in a king-sized or twin-bed configuration.

Deluxe/Premium Balcony Cabins: These 782 cabins (248 sq. ft/23 sq. meters) include a sitting area with sofa, and bathroom with shower enclosure. Beds can be arranged in a king-sized or twin-bed configuration.

Standard Outside-View/Interior (No View) Cabins: There are 62 outside-view cabins and 281 interior (no view)

cabins measuring 194 sq. ft/18 sq. meters). Beds can be arranged in a king-sized or twin-bed configuration.

Atrium View Cabins: Each of these 12 interior cabins (194 sq. ft/18 sq. meters) has an unusual view – into the six-deck high atrium lobby. Beds can be arranged in a king-sized or twin-bed configuration. An en-suite bathroom has a shower enclosure, washbasin, toilet, and toiletries cabinet.

Wheelchair Accessible Cabins: There are 30 suites and cabins (in various categories) specially designed for wheelchair users. All have pull-down closet hanging rails, above-bed emergency pull-cord, and large, well-equipped bathrooms with roll-in showers and handrails. Facilities for blind passengers include Braille signs and tactile room signs. Eight special wheelchair-accessible elevators are provided to service the dining areas. Additionally, some 36 cabins have been designated to accommodate deaf or hearing-impaired passengers. There are headsets in the Royal Theatre and Planetarium, and close captioned television.

CUISINE/DINING. Naturally, you should expect lavish dining, and accept nothing less. In all there are 14 bars, and 7 galleys serving 10 dining rooms and eateries. All dining rooms and eateries have ocean-view windows. Daniel Boulud is Cunard Line's culinary consultant; his restaurant, Daniel, in New York City commands a waiting list of several months for a table. Fortunately, such is not the case aboard *QM2*.

An outstanding selection of wines and champagnes is available (selections and recommendations were made by Michael Broadbent, one of the world's top wine experts), with per bottle prices varying between $20 and $315 (white wines), $20 and $2,650 (red wines), and $35 and $875 (champagne), all plus a 15% gratuity.

Britannia Restaurant: This main dining room seats 1,347, and spans the full beam of the ship. A lavish room almost three decks high, it has two grand sweeping staircases which enable you to make your entry in style. Above the staircase is a huge light well (reminiscent of the great oceanliners of yesteryear) and large, classic columns, while the centerpiece backdrop to the staircase is a huge tapestry of *QM2* against the New York skyline. Breakfast is in an open-seating arrangement, while dinner is in two seatings, all with crisp linen and fine china, of course. Vegetarian options are provided on all lunch and dinner menus. One downside of open seating for breakfast or lunch is that you will probably have a different waiter each time, who will not know your preferences. Another is that if you are seated on the lower level underneath the balcony formed along the port and starboard sides of the upper level, you'll get the feeling of being enclosed in an inferior space. And that is exactly what it is – an inferior space (better to get a table in the central well or on the upper level).

Queens Grill/Princess Grill: There are two Grill Rooms (Queens Grill and Princess Grill), which I call small dining salons. As in smaller "sister" ship *QE2*, which restaurant you dine in depends on your accommodation grade (and the price paid). Both the 200-seat Queens Grill and 178-seat

Princess Grill are located aft (on a lower deck than aboard *QE2*, which means they are very stable at sea), and have, in theory, fine ocean-view windows (although walkers passing by on the exterior promenade deck can be disturbing in the daytime, so window blinds have to be kept down, which rather negates the outside view). They are quite large and less intimate than those aboard *QE2*, and both feature an ungainly black marble contemporary statue I have named the "Black Widow" – smack in the middle of the busy central walkway (and waiters' service route). Passengers in the most spacious and luxurious suites, therefore, may feel less special, being mixed, as they are, among all others in Grill Class accommodation. Canyon Ranch Spaclub recommendations are provided on all lunch and dinner menus, as are vegetarian options.

The Queens Grill is decorated in gold, and passengers who dine in this exclusive establishment have their own Queens Grill Bar and Terrace. Unfortunately, Cunard chose not to dispense with waiter stations, which can be noisy at times (they also break up sightlines). The chairs are comfortable, and many have armrests (curiously those at tables for two do not – although you could always request them), and the dining table height is just right. An impressive à la carte menu is provided in addition to the regular menu (Queens Grill regulars also know they can order specials at any time). The dining experience in the Queen Grill is, in a word, superb.

Todd English Restaurant: This alternative 216-seat restaurant (reservations are necessary, and cover charges of $20 for lunch and $30 for dinner apply) is named after Todd English, the chef whose restaurant in Boston (Olives) has become one of the best-known in high gastronomic circles in the US. This represents the American television chef's first venture at sea. The restaurant, with its Moorish decor, features his noted Mediterranean cuisine. The room has been designed with intimate detailing and architecture and overlooks the Pool Terrace, allowing for al fresco dining. Food presentation is excellent, although overly fussy at times.

Kings Court: This nondescript, informal eatery has 478 seats and obnoxious daytime lighting, and is reminiscent of such eateries found in land-based shopping malls. It features self-serve breakfast and lunch. At night, decorated screens transform the area into four different restaurants: an Italian Trattoria (La Piazza), Asian cuisine (Lotus), a British eatery (The Carvery) for roast meats, and a Chef's Galley; all have full sit-down tablecloth service. The 36-seat Chef's Galley features a live demonstration of the meal preparation that passengers then enjoy ($30 is charged for accompanying wines); cooking demonstrations can be broadcast via close circuit TV onto a large screen. Colorful "street entertainment" is performed in the Kings Court in the evenings.

Fast Foodies can find comfort foods in the outdoors Boardwalk cafe (weather permitting), while pub lovers can find traditional British pub fare in the Golden Lion pub. If you are shy and retiring and want complete privacy, or if you are recuperating from a busy working life, you can

also order from the restaurant menus and have breakfast, lunch and dinner served in your own suite/cabin.

ENTERTAINMENT. The Royal Court Theatre has tiered seating for 1,094, though some sightlines are less than ideal, and is the main venue for evening entertainment, with lavish West End-style productions as well as featured headline entertainers and cabaret acts such as illusionists, comedians, comedy jugglers, acrobats, vocalists, and others. The Royal Academy of Dramatic Art (RADA) supplies a company of actors/actresses to perform and lead acting workshops in both the Royal Court Theatre and Illuminations (incorporating the Planetarium).

The ship carries a number of high-class bands, small musical units, duos and solo entertainers who provide live music in most of the 14 lounges and bars. Also, under a partnership with Oxford University, the ship's enrichment program features specialist lecturers such as authors, artists, historians, scientists and other celebrated intellectuals.

SPA/FITNESS. Health Spa and Beauty Services are provided in a 20,000 sq. ft (1,850 sq. meters) Canyon Ranch Spa Club arranged on two decks. A wide range of facilities is provided, and wellbeing treatments include many variations on the theme of massage and skin treatments, including Ayurvedic massage, aromatherapy and seaweed treatments, facials and masks, conditioning body scrubs and therapeutic body cocoons. A thalassotherapy pool (with airbed recliner loungers, neck fountains, a deluge waterfall, airtub and body massage jet benches), whirlpool, and thermal suite (with saunas and aromatic steam rooms, and a Rasul treatment chamber) are part of the facilities of the extensive spa; there is a daily charge for using the facilities ($25 on sea days, $19 for port days), although this is waived if you purchase a treatment. In all, there are 24 wellbeing (body and skincare) treatment rooms.

Treatment price examples: Standard Massage $119 for 50 minutes; Hot Stone Massage $189 for 80 minutes; Aromatherapy Massage $129 for 50 minutes, $189 for 80 minutes; Facial $129 for 50 minutes; Aromatherapy Facial $139 for 50 minutes; Qualift Replenishing Facial $199 for 80 minutes; Grape Seed Body Scrub $129 for 50 minutes; Rasul Ceremony $149 per couple/$129 single for 50 minutes; Shampoo/Set/Dry $39-$59 depending on hair length; Manicure $39 for 30 minutes; Pedicure $69-$119 for 60-80 minutes. You could also have a "Euphoria" treatment, which is a bath, facial and scalp massage followed by a body massage, for "just" $239. Prices include a gratuity, whether the treatment is good or not. Treatment prices are for sea days (prices slightly less on port days).

A gymnasium has the latest equipment, as well as free weights. In addition, a beauty salon offers a full menu of services for hair and skin, and Canyon Ranch's own range of natural skincare products (Living Essentials) is available for sale. As there are only six hairdressing chairs, appointments should be booked as early as possible. The spa is staffed by 51 Canyon Ranch employees and operated as a concession.

Radiance of the Seas
★★★★

Large (Resort) Ship: ....90,090 tons	Total Crew: 858	Cabins (wheelchair accessible): 14
Lifestyle: ....Standard	Passengers	(8 with private balcony)
Cruise Line: ....Royal Caribbean	(lower beds/all berths): 2,112/2,500	Cabin Current: ....110/220 volts
International	Passenger Space Ratio	Elevators: 9
Former Names: ....none	(lower beds/all berths): 42.6/36.0	Casino (gaming tables): ....Yes
Builder: ....Meyer Werft (Germany)	Crew/Passenger Ratio	Slot Machines: ....Yes
Original Cost: ....$350 million	(lower beds/all berths): 2.4/2.9	Swimming Pools (outdoors): 2
Entered Service: ....Apr 2001	Navigation Officers: ....Norwegian	Swimming Pools (indoors): 0
Registry: ....The Bahamas	Cabins (total): 1,056	Whirlpools: 3
Length (ft/m): 961.9/293.2	Size Range (sq ft/m): 165.8–1,216.3/	Self-Service Launderette: ....No
Beam (ft/m): 105.6/32.2	15.4–113.0	Dedicated Cinema/Seats: Yes/40
Draft (ft/m): 27.8/8.5	Cabins (outside view): 813	Library: ....Yes
Propulsion/Propellers: .....Gas turbine/2	Cabins (interior/no view): 237	Classification Society: ......Det Norske
azimuthing pods (20 MW each)	Cabins (for one person): 0	Veritas
Passenger Decks: 12	Cabins (with private balcony): 577	

OVERALL SCORE: 1,546 (OUT OF A POSSIBLE 2,000 POINTS)

OVERVIEW. *Radiance of the Seas* was the first Royal Caribbean International ship to use gas and steam turbine power instead of the more conventional diesel or diesel-electric combination (two gas turbines, one steam turbine). Pod propulsion is provided *(see page 17 for detailed explanation).* As aboard all RCI vessels, the navigation bridge is of the fully enclosed type (good for cruising in cold-weather areas such as Alaska). In the very front of the ship is a helipad, which also acts as a viewing platform for passengers.

Radiance of the Seas is a streamlined contemporary ship, and has a two-deck-high wrap-around structure in the forward section of the funnel. Along the ship's starboard side, a central glass wall protrudes, giving great views (cabins with balconies occupy the space directly opposite on the port side). The gently rounded stern has nicely tiered decks. One of two swimming pools can be covered by a large glass dome for use as an indoor/outdoor pool.

Inside, the decor is contemporary, yet elegant, bright and cheerful. A nine-deck high atrium lobby has glass-walled elevators (on the port side of the ship) that travel through 12 decks, face the sea and provide a link with nature and the ocean. The Centrum (as the atrium is called), has several public rooms connected to it: the guest relations (the contemporary term for purser's office) and shore excursions desks, a Lobby Bar, Champagne Bar, the Library, Royal Caribbean Online, the Concierge Club, and a Crown & Anchor Lounge. A great view can be had of the atrium by looking down through the flat glass dome high above it.

Other facilities include a delightful, but very small library. There's also a Champagne Bar, and a large

BERLITZ'S RATINGS

	Possible	Achieved
Ship	500	433
Accommodation	200	163
Food	400	259
Service	400	298
Entertainment	100	81
Cruise	400	312

Schooner Bar that houses maritime art in an integral art gallery. Gamblers should enjoy Casino Royale, with its French Art Nouveau decorative theme and 11 crystal chandeliers. There's also a small dedicated screening room for movies (with space for two wheelchairs), as well as a 194-seat conference center, and a business center.

The Viking Crown Lounge is a large structure set around the base of the ship's funnel. It functions as an observation lounge during the daytime (with views forward over the swimming pool). In the evening, the space features Starquest – a futuristic, high-energy dance club, and Hollywood Odyssey – a more intimate and relaxed entertainment venue for softer mood music and "black box" theater.

For those who wish to go online, Royal Caribbean Online is a dedicated computer center with 12 computers, located in a semi-private setting (in addition, data ports are provided in all cabins). Four more internet-access terminals are located in Books 'n' Coffee, a bookshop with coffee and pastries, located in an extensive area of shops.

Youth facilities include Adventure Ocean, an "edutainment" area with four separate age-appropriate sections for junior passengers: Aquanaut Center (for ages 3–5); Explorer Center (6–8); Voyager Center (9–12); and the Optix Teen Center (13–17). There is also Adventure Beach, which includes a splash pool complete with waterslide; Surfside, with computer lab stations with entertaining software; and Ocean Arcade, a video games hangout.

The artwork aboard this ship is really eclectic (so there should be something for all tastes), and provides a spectrum and a half of color works. It ranges from Jenny M.

Hansen's *A Vulnerable Moment* glass sculpture to David Buckland's "Industrial and Russian Constructionism 1920s" in photographic images on glass and painted canvas, to a huge multi-deck high contemporary bicycle-cum-paddlewheel sculpture design suspended in the atrium.

Radiance of the Seas offers more space and more comfortable public areas (and several more intimate spaces), slightly larger cabins and more dining options – for the younger, active, hip and trendy set – than most RCI ships. The grand amount of glass provides more contact with the ocean around you. In the final analysis, however, while the ship is quite delightful in many ways, the onboard operation is less so, and suffers from a lack of trained service staff.

ACCOMMODATION. There is a wide range of suites and standard outside-view and interior (no view) cabins in 10 different categories and 19 different price groups.

Apart from the largest suites (six owner's suites), which have king-sized beds, almost all other cabins have twin beds that convert to a queen-sized bed (all sheets are of 100% Egyptian cotton, although the blankets are synthetic). All cabins have rich (but faux) wood cabinetry, including a vanity desk (with hairdryer), faux wood drawers that close silently (hooray), television, personal safe, and three-sided mirrors. Some cabins have ceiling recessed, pull-down berths for third and fourth persons, although closet and drawer space would be extremely tight for four persons (even if two of them are children), and some have interconnecting doors (so families with children can cruise together, in separate, but adjacent cabins. Audio channels are available through the TV set, whose picture cannot be turned off while listening to an audio channel.

Most bathrooms have tiled accenting a terrazzo-style tiled floor, and a small shower enclosure in a half-moon shape, 100% Egyptian cotton towels, a small cabinet for personal toiletries and a small shelf. In reality, there is little space to stow personal toiletries for two (or more).

The largest accommodation consists of a family suite with two bedrooms. One bedroom has twin beds (convertible to queen-sized bed), while a second has two lower beds and two upper Pullman berths, a combination that can sleep up to eight persons (this would be suitable for large families).

Occupants of accommodation designated as suites also get the use of a private Concierge Lounge (where priority dining room reservations, shore excursion bookings and beauty salon/spa appointments can be made). Many of the "private" balcony cabins are not very private, as they can be overlooked from various locations.

CUISINE/DINING. Cascades, the main dining room, spans two decks (the upper deck level has floor-to-ceiling windows, while the lower deck level has picture windows), and is a lovely, but noisy, dining hall – reminiscent of those aboard the transatlantic liners in their heyday (however, eight huge, thick pillars do obstruct the sight lines). It seats 1,104, and has cascading water themed decor. There are tables for two, four, six, eight or 10 in two seatings. Two small private dining rooms (Breakers, with 94 seats and Tides, with 30 seats) are located off the main dining room. No smoking is permitted in the dining venues.

Alternative dining options: Portofino, with 112 seats (and a magnificent "cloud" ceiling), has Italian cuisine (choices include: antipasti, soup, salad, pasta, main dish, dessert, cheese and coffee). Chops Grill Steakhouse, with 95 seats and an open (show) kitchen, serves premium meats in the form of veal chops and steaks (New York Striploin Steak, Filet Mignon, and Prime Rib of Beef). The food in these venues is of a much higher quality than in the main dining room, though the menus do not change during the cruise. There is an additional charge of $20 per person (this includes gratuities to staff), and reservations are required for both dining spots, which are generally open 6pm –11pm. The dress code is smart casual.

Casual meals can be taken (for breakfast, lunch and dinner) in the self-serve, buffet-style Windjammer Cafe, accessible directly from the pool deck. It has islands dedicated to specific foods, and indoors and outdoors seating.

Additionally, there is the Seaview Cafe, open for lunch and dinner. The self-serve buffet and the menu feature fast-food seafood items, plus hamburgers and hot dogs.

ENTERTAINMENT. The three-level Aurora Theater has 874 seats (including 24 stations for wheelchairs) and good sight-lines from most seats. The Colony Club hosts casual cabaret shows, including late-night adult (blue) comedy, and provides live music for dancing.

The entertainment throughout is upbeat. There is even background music in all corridors and elevators, and constant music outdoors on the pool deck. If you want a quiet relaxing holiday, choose another ship.

SPA/FITNESS. The ShipShape Spa's health, fitness and spa facilities have themed decor, and include a 10,176 sq.-ft (945 sq.-meter) solarium with whirlpool and counter current swimming under a retractable magrodome roof, a gymnasium (with 44 cardiovascular machines), 50-person aerobics room, sauna and steam rooms, and therapy treatment rooms. All are located on two of the uppermost decks, forward of the mast, with access from the forward stairway.

A climate-controlled 10,176 sq. ft (945 sq. meter) indoor/outdoor Solarium (with sliding glass roof that can be closed in cool or inclement weather) provides facilities for relaxation. It has a fascinating African themed decor, and includes a whirlpool and counter current swimming.

For the more sporting, there is activity galore – including a rock-climbing wall that's 30 ft (9 meters) high, with five separate climbing tracks. It is located outdoors at the aft end of the funnel. There is also an exterior jogging track.

Other sports facilities include a 9-hole miniature golf course (with novel 17th-century decorative ornaments), and an indoor/outdoor country club with golf simulator, a jogging track, and basketball court. Want to play pool? Well, you can, thanks to two specially stabilized tables.

● **For more extensive general information about the Royal Caribbean experience, see pages 128–131.**

Radisson Diamond
★★★★ +

Small Ship: . . . . .20,295 tons	Total Crew: 200	Cabins (for one person): 0
Lifestyle: . . . . .Premium	Passengers	Cabins (with private balcony): 123
Cruise Line: . . . . . . .Seven Seas Cruises	(lower beds/all berths): 354/354	Cabins (wheelchair accessible): 2
Former Names: . . . . .none	Passenger Space Ratio	Cabin Current: . . . . . . .110 and 220 volts
Builder: . . . . .Rauma Yards (Finland)	(lower beds/all berths): 57.3/57.3	Elevators: 3
Original Cost: . . . .$125 million	Crew/Passenger Ratio	Casino (gaming tables): . . . . .Yes
Entered Service: . . . . .May 1992	(lower beds/all berths): 1.7/1.7	Slot Machines: . . . . .Yes
Registry: . . . . .The Bahamas	Navigation Officers: . . . . . . .Scandinavian/	Swimming Pools (outdoors): 1
Length (ft/m): 430.4/131.2	European	Swimming Pools (indoors): 0
Beam (ft/m): 104.9/32.0	Cabins (total): 177	Whirlpools: 1
Draft (ft/m): 26.2/8.0	Size Range (sq ft/m): 220.6–552.0/	Self-Service Launderette: . . . . .No
Propulsion/Propellers: . . . . .diesel	20.5–48.5	Dedicated Cinema/Seats: . . . . .No
(11,340kW)/2 nozzles	Cabins (outside view): 177	Library: . . . . .Yes
Passenger Decks: 6	Cabins (interior/no view): 0	Classification Society: Det Norske Veritas

OVERALL SCORE: 1,591 (OUT OF A POSSIBLE 2,000 POINTS)

OVERVIEW. *Radisson Diamond* features a very innovative design, based on the SWATH (Small Waterplane Area Twin Hull) technology. It is thus very stable when at sea (except in rough seas), with four stabilizing fins (two on the inner side of each pontoon), so that motion is really minimized when compared with conventional (monohull) vessels. The wide beam of this design also provides outstanding passenger space, although the public rooms are stacked vertically and are contained mostly on the inside of the ship's structure, which is like a sea-going version of a Radisson hotel ashore. While the design was novel when first introduced, it has, sensibly, not been repeated in any ship order since (its propulsion system translates to a very slow service speed, making long voyages in open water – such as transatlantic crossings – quite time-consuming).

At the stern of the vessel, there is a retractable, free-floating water sports marina platform, but it is really only useful in dead calm sea conditions. There are jet-skis, and a water-ski boat. There is also a little-used underwater viewing area (it actually consists of just two portholes). There is a good outdoor jogging track, although fitness fanatics will find the gymnasium quite small.

Inside, the central focal point is a five-deck-high atrium, which has glass-enclosed elevators (together with the staircase, however, they take up most of the space). There is a well-stocked library and video center, and a sophisticated business center with facilities that are ideal for small groups and conventions. For groups and meetings, the high-tech audio and video conferencing facilities, and a high-tech security system that uses around 50 cameras to monitor just about everywhere, provide a feeling of security and

BERLITZ'S RATINGS

	Possible	Achieved
Ship	500	392
Accommodation	200	168
Food	400	328
Service	400	328
Entertainment	100	78
Cruise	400	297

exclusivity. The one problem with groups is that public rooms may be reserved for private functions and parties, to the annoyance of regular (non-group) passengers; ask your travel agent to check your sailing.

Other facilities include a casino, with gaming tables on one side of a passageway that connects to the showlounge; it has slot machines on the opposite side to the gaming tables – a sensible arrangement for serious game players who don't want the sound of slot machines to intrude.

This semi-submersible, twin-hulled cruise vessel, which some say looks like a white-caped "Batman" from the stern, certainly has the most unusual and distinctive looks of any cruise ship, although its design has not been as successful as hoped. It should appeal to those seeking a high standard of personalized service in fairly sophisticated and personable, somewhat "hotel-style" surroundings, with mainly unstructured daytime activities, and a dress code that is casual by day and a little more dressy at night. The food and standard of onboard service are good, which helps to make up for the design and structural shortcomings of the vessel. Flowers and greenery help. One nice feature is that all gratuities are included. The onboard currency is the US dollar.

The design means that many public rooms are inside, with little or no connection with the sea. The ship has a maximum speed of 12.5 knots, which makes it fine for leisurely island cruising, but slow going on longer itineraries. The spaciousness of the ship, while providing flexibility of the individual public rooms, actually detracts from the overall flow, and the awkward one-way (contra-flow) interior staircase around the atrium can prove to be quite frustrating. Also awkward is the multilevel entertainment room (showlounge). While the health spa facilities are good, the elevator does not reach the facilities. The meet-and-greet service is inconsistent and remains the subject of passenger complaints.

SUITABLE FOR: *Radisson Diamond* is best suited to sea-soned, well-traveled couples and single travelers (typically over 50) who seek specialized itineraries, good food and service, with only a little entertainment, all wrapped up in an unusual looking ship which can best be described as almost bulldog elegant and quiet in its appointments and comfort levels.

ACCOMMODATION. There are six grades, priced according to grade, size and location. This ship has nicely designed, spacious, and well-equipped all outside-view cabins, most of which have private balconies with outdoor lights (those without balconies have large windows instead). All are furnished in light woods, with marble bathroom vanities and a tiny bathtub. There are bay windows in 47 units.

All cabins are of the same dimensions, with the exception of four Master Suites. Each cabin has an oversized window or floor-to-ceiling balcony windows/door. Each has a spacious sitting area with sofa and chairs, dressing table with hair dryer, mini-bar and refrigerator, telephone, color remote-control television with integral VCR, twin beds that convert to a queen-sized unit, two good, adjustable reading lamps that are bright, a personal safe (somewhat hidden and awkward for older passengers to reach and operate), full-length mirror, and excellent drawer space.

The closet space, however, is really minimal, adequate for short cruises, but tight for two on a 7-night cruise, worse for longer cruises. Each cabin has a mini-bar that is stocked with beer and soft drinks; half-liter bottles of four liquors are provided. Bottled mineral water is provided. The cabin bathrooms have really small tubs (they are really shower tubs).

The four Master Suites (each measuring 522 sq ft/48.4 sq. meters) have a special security entrance, fine wood cabinetry, spacious closets, dressing table with hair dryer, a king-size bed, plush leather furniture, Rousseau-inspired wall murals, mini-bar and refrigerator, telephone, color remote-control television with integral VCR, and a private balcony. The marble-clad bathroom has a full whirlpool bathtub, separate glass-enclosed shower enclosure, and two washbasins. Butler service was introduced in 2002.

Two wheelchair-accessible cabins, formerly located about as far from the elevators as one could get, have sensibly been relocated so that they are adjacent to them. These have wheel-in bathrooms and shower areas, and all fittings are provided at an accessible height.

CUISINE/DINING. The two-deck-high Grand Dining Room is spacious and quite elegant, has a 270° view over the stern, and open seating is featured, so you can dine with whomever you wish, when you wish (within dining room hours, of course). The cuisine quality and food presentation is European in style, and outstanding in quality, choice, and presentation. Health foods and dietary specials are always available. The waitresses (there are no waiters) are charming, and superbly supervised by experienced headwaiters. As far as wines go, although fairly decent whites and reds are included for lunch and dinner, a separate wine list is available for those who appreciate better wines (at extra cost).

"Don Vito" is the name of a 50-seat alternative Italian casual indoor/outdoor dining spot (there is no extra charge). Run like a real restaurant ashore (make your reservations early each day), this informal spot has a fine menu featuring homemade pasta dishes daily, including cream sauces and exotic garnishes. Each day has a different menu, and the food is presented, in small portions, course by course. It is lovingly prepared and exquisite to taste, although somewhat rich. Seating is at sturdy, practical glass-topped wooden tables for two, four, or six. Tableside dessert flambeaus are often featured – oh, and the waiters serenade you.

"The Grill" is the place for casual breakfasts and lunches, with seating in various nooks and crannies. The self-serve buffets are of high quality, with good choice and variety.

You can also be very private if you wish and dine, course by course, in your cabin – or on the balcony (in the right setting, and if weather conditions permit). Dining is definitely the vessel's strong point.

ENTERTAINMENT. The showlounge, designed principally for meetings and conventions, poorly serves acts and passengers alike. Even cabaret acts have a hard time, as they face a blank wall rather than an audience, which are seated, for the most part, at the sides of the stage, but one deck higher. Entertainment is a low priority (many passengers simply prefer to watch a video in their cabins), and consists mostly of a mini-revue show (typically with cast of four singer/dancers), and cabaret acts such as vocalists, magicians, puppeteers, comedians, and others.

SPA/FITNESS. The Diamond Spa is located on the uppermost deck forward and above the navigation bridge, and contains a gymnasium with good ocean views (it has high-tech muscle-building and toning equipment and the ever-popular treadmills and exercycles. There are also saunas, steam rooms, changing areas for men and women, and a few treatment rooms.

The spa is operated by Steiner, a specialist concession. Many of the staff are very young (but enthusiastic), and will try to sell you Steiner's own-brand Elemis beauty products. Some fitness classes are free (Stepexpress, Power Walk, Total Body Conditioning, Xpress Circuit are examples), while some, such as yoga and kick-boxing, cost extra. However, being aboard will give you an opportunity to try some indulgent treatments (particularly some of the massages available). Massage (including Aroma Stone massage, Chakra Balancing massage and other well-being massages), aromatherapy facials, body-wraps, pedicures, manicures, and all beauty salon treatments are at extra cost (massage, for example, costs about $2 per minute, plus gratuity). It's best to make appointments as early as possible as convenient time slots can get booked up quickly.

Outside the spa, a jogging track encircles it.

Regal Empress
★★

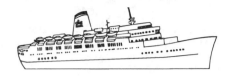

Mid-Size Ship: . . . . .21,909 tons	Total Crew: 396	Cabins (with private balcony): 8
Lifestyle: . . . . .Standard	Passengers	Cabins (wheelchair accessible): 1
Cruise Line: .Imperial Majesty Cruise Line	(lower beds/all berths): 905/1,068	Cabin Current: . . . . .110 and 220 volts
Former Names: . . . . .Caribe I, Olympia	Passenger Space Ratio	Elevators: 3
Builder: . . . . .Alex Stephen & Son (UK)	(lower beds/all berths): 24.2/20.5	Casino (gaming tables): . . . . .Yes
Original Cost: .n/a	Crew/Passenger Ratio	Slot Machines: . . . . .Yes
Entered Service: . . . . .Oct 1953/May 1993	(lower beds/all berths): 2.2/2.6	Swimming Pools (outdoors): 1
Registry: . . . . .The Bahamas	Navigation Officers: . . . . .European	Swimming Pools (indoors): 0
Length (ft/m): 611.8/186.5	Cabins (total): 457	Whirlpools: 2
Beam (ft/m): 79.0/24.1	Size Range (sq ft/m): 104.4–296.0/	Self-Service Launderette: . . . . .No
Draft (ft/m): 28.2/8.6	9.7–27.5	Dedicated Cinema/Seats: Yes/90
Propulsion/Propellers: . . . . .diesel	Cabins (outside view): 230	Library: . . . . .Yes
(10,742kW)/2	Cabins (interior/no view): 227	Classification Society: . . .Lloyd's Register
Passenger Decks: 8	Cabins (for one person): 9	

OVERALL SCORE: 896 (OUT OF A POSSIBLE 2,000 POINTS)

OVERVIEW. *Regal Empress*, now over 50 years old – has a traditional, balanced ocean liner profile, and, for many years, sailed as a two-class transatlantic liner between Greece and the United States. There is a good amount of open deck space for sun worshippers, although this can become very crowded when the ship is full. Traditional liner features include polished teakwood decking and handrails. Although the ship is old, Regal Cruises (the ship's former owners) spent much time and effort to maintain it. In May 2003 the ship was purchased at auction (Regal Cruises ceased operations in 2003 following non-payment of outstanding bills) by the owners of Imperial Majesty Cruise Line, and has provided a replacement for the company's smaller capacity *OceanBreeze*, which was withdrawn from service and scrapped. *Regal Empress* operates short "getaway" cruises. There is an enclosed (air-conditioned) promenade deck, popular with strollers, and for those who like to sit and read.

Because of the age of the ship, you'll find plenty of real woods, heavy brass and art deco detailing throughout many of the public rooms, with fine satin woods and brass featured on the ship's interior staircases. Considering that the ship carries around 1,000 passengers, there really are very few public rooms other than a casino, a single-level show-lounge (with slightly raised port and starboard sections, but poor sight lines from many seats except for the first few rows), a nightclub/disco, and a piano lounge.

There is, however, a fine, old-fashioned library with almost untouched, original wood paneling and wood beam ceiling; the book selection, however, is poor and out of date, and the dog-eared paperbacks just do not look right

BERLITZ'S RATINGS

	Possible	Achieved
Ship	500	209
Accommodation	200	95
Food	400	186
Service	400	201
Entertainment	100	38
Cruise	400	167

(hardback books are better). There is also an internet cafe (it's actually a bar), for those who simply must connect while at sea.

The ship does carry families with children, although the facilities for junior passengers really are minimal as the vessel simply wasn't built to cater to their needs.

Regal Empress provides a basic, no-frills cruise experience at low cost, in reasonably adequate surroundings. Do note that, although it underwent some much-needed refurbishment in 1997, this is a vintage ship, with a very disjointed layout. The onboard currency is the US dollar.

This is a high-density vessel that feels very crowded and makes it difficult to find any quiet places to relax. There are no cushioned pads for the deck lounge chairs outside on the open decks. Expect to be in a line for embarkation, the self-serve buffet meals, and, particularly when disembarking. The ship is extremely cramped, with little space to move around when full. It has an awkward layout, and many passageways do not extend for the length of the ship. Many ceilings in public rooms are low.

SUITABLE FOR: *Regal Empress* is best suited to anyone seeking a party atmosphere in a vintage ship where cheap and cheerful is the motto. The ship is for those on a low budget seeking to cruise in comfortable surroundings, but who do not expect the newest facilities and are comfortable with the fact that the ship is dated but has a lot of character.

ACCOMMODATION. There is.a wide range of cabin sizes and configurations, in 12 suite/cabin price grades. The price you pay will depend on the accommodation grade, size and location you choose. Most cabins are small, yet spacious enough, with a reasonable amount of closet and drawer space, and heavy-duty fittings. However, the decor is generally rather dark and dull. Many cabins have additional upper berths, while some cabins can accommodate five people.

The largest accommodation can be found in four Admiral Suites, which have views over the ship's bows (when you stand up inside them, that is, as the windows are of the half-height, and not the floor-to-ceiling type), and in eight suites with private (covered and enclosed) verandas that were added in 1999, as were TV sets in all cabins (although some are positioned at odd angles, and often do not work).

All other cabins come in an assortment of sizes and configurations (the ship was originally built as a two-class ocean liner), making any kind of uniformity difficult.

CUISINE/DINING. The old-world Caribbean Dining Room is a step back in time to a more gracious era, with its original oil paintings on burnished wood paneling, ornate lighting fixtures and etched glass panels, and original murals depicting New York and Rio. There are two seatings, and the whole dining room is non-smoking. Don't expect a table for two, as most tables are for groups of six or more, with a few tables for four.

The food is plentiful and of a reasonably decent standard considering the price (although there is much use of rice instead of potatoes and other starch-rich alternatives), with the exception of the self-serve buffets, which are really very basic, under-creative, and totally forgettable. Lunches are quite repetitive. While the freshly baked breads (and different flavored butters daily) are good (passengers like the garlic bread, and the donut machine), the selection of real cheeses and fresh fruits is not.

La Trattoria is the place for casual self-serve buffet breakfasts, lunches and dinners. This eatery features Italian and other European-style cuisines.

ENTERTAINMENT. The main lounge is the venue for almost all entertainment events and social functions. It is a single level room designed for cabaret acts and nothing more. The sightlines from a number of seats are obstructed by a number of pillars. Remember that the low price you pay for your cruise will dictate the kind of entertainment you can expect to see (low budget, low on quality, high on volume and color).

SPA/FITNESS. There is a small fitness center, but that's all (on the other hand, for such a short cruise, nothing else is needed, as there is simply no time).

QUOTABLE QUOTES

These are some of the questions I have been asked over the years by passengers taking a cruise for the first time:

"Will we have time to take the shore excursion?"

"If I don't buy a shore excursion, am I allowed off in port?"

"Are the entertainers paid?"

"Why don't we have a Late Night Comedy Spot in the afternoon?"

"Is the mail brought in by plane?"

"Why aren't the dancers fully dressed?"

"How do we know which photos are ours?"

"Will the ship wait for the tour buses to get back?"

"Will I get wet if I go snorkeling?"

"Do the Chinese do the laundry by hand?"

"Does the ship dock in the middle of town?"

"Is the doctor qualified?"

"Who's driving the ship if the captain is at the cocktail party?"

"Does the sun always rise on the left side of the ship?"

"Is trapshooting held outside?"

"I'm married, but can I come to the Singles Party?"

"Should I put my luggage outside the cabin before or after I go to sleep?"

"Does an outside cabin mean it's outside the ship?"

Regal Princess
★★★★

Large (Resort) Ship: . . . . . . .69,845 tons	Total Crew: 696	Cabins (with private balcony): 184
Lifestyle: . . . . .Standard	Passengers	Cabins (wheelchair accessible): 10
Cruise Line: . . . . .Princess Cruises	(lower beds/all berths): 1,590/1,910	Cabin Current: . . . . .110 and 220 volts
Former Names: . . . . .none	Passenger Space Ratio	Elevators: 9
Builder: . . . . .Fincantieri Navali (Italy)	(lower beds/all berths): 43.9/36.5	Casino (gaming tables): . . . . .Yes
Original Cost: . . . .$276.8 million	Crew/Passenger Ratio	Slot Machines: . . . . .Yes
Entered Service: . . . . .Aug 1991	(lower beds/all berths): 2.2/2.7	Swimming Pools (outdoors): 2
Registry: . . . . .Great Britain	Navigation Officers: . . . . .Italian	Swimming Pools (indoors): 0
Length (ft/m): 811.0/247.2	Cabins (total): 795	Whirlpools: 4
Beam (ft/m): 105.6/32.2	Size Range (sq ft/m): 189.4–586.6/	Self-Service Launderette: . . . . .Yes
Draft (ft/m): 25.5/7.8	17.6–54.5	Dedicated Cinema/Seats: Yes/169
Propulsion/Propellers: . . . . .diesel	Cabins (outside view): 624	Library: . . . . .Yes
(24,000kW)/2	Cabins (interior/no view): 171	Classification Society: . . .Registro Navale
Passenger Decks: 11	Cabins (for one person): 0	Italiano (RINA)

OVERALL SCORE: 1,416 (OUT OF A POSSIBLE 2,000 POINTS)

OVERVIEW. *Regal Princess* was the second ship in the 70,000-ton range for Princess Cruises, and as such foreshadowed the even larger ships this successful company went on to build. The ship has an interesting, jumbo-airplane look when viewed from the front, with a dolphin-like upper structure (made of lightweight aluminum alloy), and a large upright "dustbin-like" funnel (also made from aluminum alloy) placed aft.

BERLITZ'S RATINGS	Possible	Achieved
Ship	500	347
Accommodation	200	144
Food	400	260
Service	400	290
Entertainment	100	78
Cruise	400	297

Inside, innovative and elegant styling of the period is mixed with traditional features and a spacious interior layout. The interior spaces are well designed, although the layout itself is somewhat disjointed. An understated decor of soft pastel shades is highlighted by some colorful artwork.

An observation dome, set high atop the ship like the head of a dolphin, has a large casino, numerous rubber trees, a dance floor and live music. The ship has decent health and fitness facilities. A striking, elegant three-deck-high atrium has a grand staircase with fountain sculpture (real, stand-up cocktail parties are held here). Characters Bar, located adjacent to the pizzeria on the open deck forward, has wonderful drink concoctions and some unusual glasses.

This ship provides a very pleasant cruise in elegant and comfortable surroundings, and an attentive staff will make you feel welcome. Princess Cruises provides white-gloved stewards to take you to your cabin when you embark, another nice touch. *Regal Princess* has undergone an extensive refit (remodeled atrium and dining room, new 24-hour Lido restaurant and evening bistro, and children's center).

The open deck space is very limited for the size of the ship and the number of passengers carried and, sadly, there is no forward observation viewpoint outdoors. There is no wrap-around promenade deck outdoors (the only walking space being along the sides of the ship). In fact, there is little contact with the outdoors at all. The sunbathing space is really limited when the ship is full, although as many passengers are often over 50 years old, perhaps this is not quite so crucial. The interior layout is reasonable, but a little disjointed. Galley fumes seem to waft constantly over the aft open decks.

The automated telephone system is frustrating for many passengers, and luggage delivery needs to be more efficient. Lines form for many things, but particularly for the purser's office, and for open-seating breakfast and lunch in the dining room.

ACCOMMODATION. There are 26 different price grades (the price will depend on the location and size you choose). In general, the cabins are well designed and have large bathrooms as well as good soundproofing. Walk-in closets, refrigerator, personal safe, color television and an interactive video system are provided in all cabins, as are chocolates on your pillow each night. Princess Cruises carries BBC World, CNN, CNBC, ESPN and TNT on the in-cabin color television system (when available, depending on cruise area). Twin beds convert to queen-size beds in standard cabins. Bathrobes and personal toiletry amenities are provided. The outside-view cabins for disabled passengers have their views obstructed by lifeboats.

The 14 most expensive suites (each of which has a large private balcony) are very well equipped, with a practical design that positions most things in just the right place. They have the following names (in alphabetical order): Amalfi, Antibes, Cannes, Capri, Corfu, La Palma, Madeira,

Majorca, Malaga, Marbella, Monaco, Portofino, St. Tropez, and Sorrento. The bedroom is separated from the living room by a heavy wooden door, and there are televisions in both rooms. The closet and drawer space is very generous, and there is enough of it even for long cruises.

CUISINE/DINING. The Palm Court Dining Room is a non smoking room (all dining rooms aboard Princess Cruises ships are non-smoking), and is large, although the galley divides it into a U-shape. However, there are no tables for two, although the line's marketing tag line states that this is "The Love Boat" line. Some of the most desirable tables overlook the stern. There are two seatings.

Despite the fact that the portions are generous, the food and its presentation are somewhat disappointing, and tastes bland. The quality of fish is poor (often disguised by crumb or batter coatings), the selection of fresh green vegetables is limited, and few garnishes are used. However, do remember that this is big-ship banquet catering, with all its attendant standardization and production cooking. Meats are of a decent quality, although often disguised by gravy-based sauces. Pasta dishes are large, served by the section head-waiters. If you like desserts, order a sundae at dinner, as most other desserts are just so-so. Remember that ice cream ordered in the dining room is included, but if you order one anywhere else, you'll have to pay for it.

There is an excellent pizzeria, however, for informal meals; this is particularly popular at lunchtime and in the afternoons. Themed late-night buffets are provided, but afternoon teas are poor. For sweet snacks during the day, a Patisserie (items are at extra charge) is located in the spacious lobby.

ENTERTAINMENT. The International Showlounge spans two decks (with seating on both main and balcony levels). It is located at the forward most part of the ship, and accessed by the forward stairway and elevators. The lower level has seating clustered around the stage, which is called a "thrust" stage, like you would find in a true variety theatre ashore.

Princess Cruises always provides plenty of live music for the various bars and lounges, with a wide mix of light classical, jazz, and dance music, from solo entertaining pianists to large show bands, and volume is normally kept to an acceptable level.

SPA/FITNESS. The spa/fitness center is located low down in the ship (accessible by elevator and stairs), and contains a gymnasium, aerobics exercise room, steam room, sauna and changing areas, and Images, the beauty salon.

The spa is operated by Steiner, a specialist concession, whose young staff will try to sell you Steiner's own-brand Elemis beauty products.

● **For more extensive general information about the Princess Cruises experience, see pages 124–127.**

Regatta
★★★★ +

Mid-Size Ship: . . . . .30,277 tons	Total Crew: 386	Cabins (with private balcony): 232
Lifestyle: . . . . .Premium	Passengers	Cabins (wheelchair accessible): 0
Cruise Line: . . . . .Oceania Cruises	(lower beds/all berths): 684/824	Cabin Current: . . . . .110 and 220 volts
Former Names: . . . . .R Two	Passenger Space Ratio	Elevators: 4
Builder: . . . . .Chantiers de l'Atlantique	(lower beds/all berths): 44.2/36.7	Casino (gaming tables): . . . . .Yes
Original Cost: . . . .£150 million	Crew/Passenger Ratio	Slot Machines: . . . . .Yes
Entered Service: Dec1998/Dec 2003	(lower beds/all berths): 1.7/2.1	Swimming Pools (outdoors): 1
Registry: . . . . .Marshall Islands	Navigation Officers: . . . . .European	Swimming Pools (indoors): 0
Length (ft/m): 593.7/181.0	Cabins (total): 342	Whirlpools: . . . . . . .2 (+1 thalassotherapy)
Beam (ft/m): 83.5/25.5	Size Range (sq ft/m):	Self-Service Launderette: . . . . .Yes
Draft (ft/m): 19.5/6.0	. . . . .145.3–968.7/13.5–90.0	Dedicated Cinema/Seats: . . . . .No
Propulsion/Propellers: . . . . .diesel	Cabins (outside view): 317	Library: . . . . .Yes
. . . .(18,600 kW)/2	Cabins (interior/no view): 25	Classification Society: . . . .Bureau Veritas
Passenger Decks: 9	Cabins (for one person): 0	

OVERALL SCORE: 1,553 (OUT OF A POSSIBLE 2,000 POINTS)

OVERVIEW. *Regatta* was formerly one of a series of eight almost identical ships, originally built for the now-defunct Renaissance Cruises, the cruise industry's first totally non-smoking cruise line. The ship's present owners (Cruise-invest) have chartered the ship to new start-up company Oceania Cruises. The exterior design manages to balance the ship's high sides by painting the whole ship white (it previously had a dark blue hull), with a large, square white funnel. The addition of teak overlaid decking and teak lounge chairs have greatly improved what was formerly a bland pool deck outdoors. A sister ship, *Insignia* (formerly Renaissance Cruises' *R2*) joined the Oceania Cruises fleet in July 2004.

The interior decor is stunning and elegant, a throwback to ship decor of the ocean liners of the 1920s and '30s, with dark woods and warm colors, all carried out in fine taste (but a bit *faux* in places). This includes detailed ceiling cornices, both real and *faux* wrought-iron staircase railings, leather-paneled walls, *trompe l'oeil* ceilings, rich carpeting in hallways with an Oriental rug-look center section, and many other interesting (and expensive-looking) decorative touches. It feels like an old-world country club.

The public rooms are spread over three decks. The reception hall (lobby) has a staircase with intricate wrought-iron railings. A large observation lounge, called the Horizon Bar, is located high atop ship.

There are plenty of bars – including one in each of the restaurant entrances. Perhaps the nicest is the casino bar/ lounge, a beautiful room reminiscent of London's grand hotels and includes a martini bar. It has an inviting marble fireplace, comfortable sofas and individual chairs.

The Library is a grand Regency-style room, with a fire-

BERLITZ'S RATINGS		
	Possible	Achieved
Ship	500	415
Accommodation	200	155
Food	400	304
Service	400	295
Entertainment	100	76
Cruise	400	308

place, a high, indented, *trompe l'oeil* ceiling, and excellent selection of books, plus very comfortable wingback chairs with footstools, and sofas you could sleep on. Oceania@Sea is the ship's internet connect center.

The dress code is "smart casual." The onboard currency is the US dollar. Gratuities are added at $10.50 per person, per day (accommodation designated as suites have an extra $3 per person charge for the butler). A 15% gratuity is added to bar and spa accounts.

There is no wrap-around promenade deck outdoors (there is, however, a small jogging track around the perimeter of the swimming pool, and port and starboard side decks). Stairways, though carpeted, are tinny. Oceania Cruises is a young company with a refreshing vision and desire to provide an extremely high level of food and service in an informal setting that is at once elegant yet comfortable, and that is exactly what it has achieved in a short space of time.

SUITABLE FOR: *Regatta* is best suited to couples who like good food and style, but want informality with no formal nights on board, and interesting itineraries, all at a very reasonable price well below what the luxury ships charge.

ACCOMMODATION. There are six cabin categories, and 10 price grades (3 suite price grades; 5 outside-view cabin grades; 2 interior (no view) cabin grades. All of the standard interior (no view) and outside-view cabins (the lowest four grades) are extremely compact units, and extremely tight for two persons (particularly for cruises longer than five days). They have twin beds (or queen-sized bed), with good under-bed storage areas, personal safe, vanity desk with large mirror, good closet and drawer space (in rich, dark woods), 100% cotton bathrobe and towels, slippers, clothes brush and shoe horn. Color TVs carry a major news channel (where obtainable), plus a sports channel and round-the-clock movie channels.

Certain cabin categories (about 100 of them) qualify as "Concierge Level" accommodation, and occupants get extra goodies such as enhanced bathroom amenities, complimentary shoeshine, tote bag, cashmere throw blanket, bottle of champagne on arrival, hand-held hairdryer, priority restaurant reservations, and priority embarkation.

Owner's Suites. The six Owner's Suites, measuring around 962 sq.ft/89.3 sq.meters, provide the most spacious accommodation. They are fine, large living spaces located aft overlooking the stern on Decks 6, 7, and 8 (they are, however, subject to more movement and some vibration). They have extensive teak-floor private balconies that really are private and cannot be overlooked from the decks above. Each has an entrance foyer, living room, separate bedroom (the bed faces the sea, which can be seen through the floor-to-ceiling windows and sliding glass door), CD player (with selection of audio discs), fully tiled bathroom with Jacuzzi bathtub, and a small guest bathroom.

Vista Suites. There are four, each measuring around 785.7 sq.ft/73 sq.meters, and located forward on Decks 5 and 6. They have extensive teak-floor private balconies that cannot be overlooked by anyone from the decks above. Each has an entrance foyer, living room, separate bedroom (the bed faces the sea, which can be seen through the floor-to-ceiling windows and sliding glass door), CD player (with selection of audio discs), and fully tiled bathroom with Jacuzzi bathtub.

Penthouse Suites. There are 52 of these (actually, they are not suites at all, but large cabins as the bedrooms aren't separate from the living areas). They do, however, measure around 322.9 sq.ft (30 sq. meters), and have a good-sized teak-floor balcony with sliding glass door (but with partial, and not full, balcony partitions) and teak deck furniture. The lounge area has a proper dining table and there is ample clothes storage space. The bathroom has a tub, shower enclosure, washbasin and toilet.

Cabins with Balcony. Cabins with private balconies (around 216 sq.ft/20 sq. meters), comprise about 66% of all cabins. They have partial, not full, balcony partitions, sliding glass doors, and only 14 cabins on Deck 6 have lifeboat-obstructed views. The living area has a refrigerated mini-bar, lounge area with breakfast table, and a balcony with teak floor, two teak chairs and a drinks table. The bathrooms, with tiled floors and plain walls, are compact, standard units, and include a shower stall with a strong, removable hand-held shower unit, hairdryer, toiletries storage shelves and retractable clothesline.

Outside View and Interior (No View) Cabins. These measure around 160–165 sq.ft (14.8–15.3 sq.meters), and have twin beds (convertible to a queen-sized bed), vanity desk, small sofa and coffee table, and bathroom with a shower enclosure with a strong, removable hand-held shower unit, hairdryer, toiletries storage shelves, retractable clothes-line, washbasin, and toilet. Although they are not large, they are quite comfortable, with a decent amount of storage space.

CUISINE/DINING. Flexibility and choice are what the dining facilities aboard the Oceania ships are all about. There are four different restaurants:

● The **Grand Dining Room** has around 340 seats, and a raised central section, but the problem is the noise level – because of the low ceiling height, it's atrocious when the dining room is full. Being located at the stern, there are large ocean-view windows on three sides (prime tables overlook the stern). The chairs are comfortable and have armrests. The menus change daily for lunch and dinner.

● The **Toscana Italian Restaurant** has 96 seats, windows along two sides, and a set menu (plus daily chef's specials).

● The cozy **Polo Grill** has 98 seats, windows along two sides and a set menu including prime steaks and seafood.

● The **Terrace Cafe** has seats for 154 indoors – not enough during cruises to cold-weather areas – and 186 outdoors. It is open for breakfast, lunch and casual dinners, when it has tapas (Tapas on the Terrace) and other Mediterranean food. As the ship's self-serve buffet restaurant, it incorporates a small pizzeria and grill. There are basic salads, a meat carving station, and a reasonable selection of cheeses.

All restaurants have open-seating dining, so you can dine when you want, with whom you wish. Reservations are needed in Toscana Restaurant and Polo Grill (but there's no extra charge), where there are mostly tables for four or six; there are few tables for two. There is a Poolside Grill Bar. All cappuccino and espresso coffees cost extra.

The food and service staff is provided by Apollo, a well-known and respected maritime catering company that also has an interest in Oceania Cruises. The consultant chef is Jacques Pepin (well-known as a television chef in America), who oversees the cuisine. Oceania Cruises' brochure claims "Cuisine so extraordinary it's unrivalled at sea" is hogwash – it's good, but not that good..

ENTERTAINMENT. The Regatta Lounge has entertainment, lectures and some social events. There is little entertainment due to the intensive nature of the itineraries. However, there is live music in several bars and lounges.

SPA/FITNESS. A lido deck has a swimming pool, and good sunbathing space, plus a thalassotherapy tub. A jogging track circles the swimming pool deck (but one deck above). The uppermost outdoors deck includes a golf driving net and shuffleboard court. The Oceania Spa consists of a beauty salon, three treatment rooms, men's and women's changing rooms, and steam room (there is no sauna). Harding Brothers operates the spa and beauty salon, and provides the staff. Examples of pricing include: full body massage $99 (50 minutes); foot and ankle massage $39 (20 minutes); body contour wrap, $159 (75 minutes); botanical therapy facial, $99 (75 minutes); personal training session $75 (75 minutes); shampoo, style and dry $29 (short hair); manicure $29; pedicure $39. Note that 15% is added to your spa account, whether you like it or not.

Rhapsody of the Seas
★★★★

Large (Resort) Ship: ....78,491 tons	Total Crew: 765	Cabins (with private balcony): 229
Lifestyle: ....Standard	Passengers	Cabins (wheelchair accessible): 14
Cruise Line: Royal Caribbean International	(lower beds/all berths): 2,000/2,435	Cabin Current: ....110 and 220 volts
Former Names: ....none	Passenger Space Ratio	Elevators: 9
Builder: Chantiers de l'Atlantique (France)	(lower beds/all berths): 39.2/32.2	Casino (gaming tables): ....Yes
Original Cost: ....$275 million	Crew/Passenger Ratio	Slot Machines: ....Yes
Entered Service: ....May 1997	(lower beds/all berths): 2.6/3.1	Swimming Pools (outdoors): 1
Registry: ....The Bahamas	Navigation Officers: ....International	Swimming Pools (indoors): 1
Length (ft/m): 915.3/279.0	Cabins (total): 1,000	(inside/outside)
Beam (ft/m): 105.6/32.2	Size Range (sq ft/m): 135.0–1,270.1/	Whirlpools: 6
Draft (ft/m): 24.9/7.6	12.5–118.0	Self-Service Launderette: ....No
Propulsion/Propellers: .....diesel-electric	Cabins (outside view): 593	Dedicated Cinema/Seats: ....No
(50,400kW)/2	Cabins (interior/no view): 407	Library: ....Yes
Passenger Decks: 11	Cabins (for one person): 0	Classification Society: Det Norske Veritas

OVERALL SCORE: 1,519 (OUT OF A POSSIBLE 2,000 POINTS)

OVERVIEW. This striking all-white ship (sister to *Vision of the Seas*) shares design features that make many (but not all) of the Royal Caribbean International ships identifiable, including a Viking Crown Lounge and a terrific multi-level nightspot (the music can be loud and overbearing, however). The Viking Crown Lounge (which is also the ship's disco) aboard this and sister ship *Vision of the Seas* is positioned just aft of the center of the ship, above the central atrium lobby. The funnel is well aft – a departure from all other RCI ships to date – which position the Viking Crown lounge around the funnel or at its base. The ship's stern is beautifully rounded.

There is a reasonable amount of open-air walking space, although this tends to become cluttered with deck lounge chairs. There's also a wide range of interesting public rooms, lounges and bars, and the interiors have been cleverly designed to avoid congestion and aid passenger flow into revenue areas. Speaking of which, for those who enjoy gambling, the astrologically-themed casino is large and rather glitzy (although not as bold as aboard some of the company's other ships), again typical of most of the new large ships; a couple of pieces of "electrostatic" art in globe form provide fascinating relief.

The atrium lobby is the ship's interior focal point (this is always a good place to arrange to meet anyone), and this one has a large kinetic sculpture, called *Diadem*. It is a multi-material construction that spans six decks, and features an astrological theme, as do many of the decorative elements throughout the ship. The interior decor throughout is imaginative, and provides a connection between sea and stars.

There is, predictably, a large shopping area, although the

BERLITZ'S RATINGS		
	Possible	Achieved
Ship	500	428
Accommodation	200	166
Food	400	248
Service	400	302
Entertainment	100	81
Cruise	400	294

merchandise is consistently tacky. The artwork throughout the ship is really upbeat and colorful, and has a musical theme: classical, jazz, popular and rock 'n' roll. Much improved over previous new ships in the fleet is the theater, with more entrances and fewer bottlenecks; there are still pillars obstructing sightlines from many seats. Also improved are the facilities for children and teens.

Ship enthusiasts will like the chair fabric in the Shall We Dance lounge, with its large aft-facing windows, and the glass case-enclosed mechanical sculptures. What, in particular, makes this ship feel warm and cozy are the use of fine, light wood surfaces throughout its public rooms, as well as the large array of potted plants everywhere.

ACCOMMODATION. There are 18 grades, prices depending on grade, size and location. The standard interior (no view) and exterior view cabins are of an adequate size, and have just enough functional facilities to make them comfortable for a one-week cruise, but longer might prove confining. The decor is bright and cheerful, although the ceilings are plain; the soft furnishings make this home away from home look like the inside of a modern Scandinavian hotel – with minimalist tones, and splashes of color. Twin lower beds convert to queen-sized beds, and there is a reasonable amount of closet and drawer space (there is little room to maneuver between the bed and desk/television unit).

The bathrooms are small but functional, although the shower units themselves are small, and there is no cabinet for one's personal toiletries. The towels should be larger and thicker. In the passageways, upbeat artwork depicts musical themes, from classical to jazz and popular.

Choose a "C" grade suite if you want spacious accommodation that includes a separate (curtained-off) sleeping area, a good-sized outside balcony (with part, not full, partition), lounge with sofa, two chairs and coffee table, three closets, plenty of drawer and storage space, television and VCR. The bathroom is large and has a full-size bathtub, integral shower, and two washbasins/two toiletries cabinets.

For the ultimate accommodation aboard this ship, choose the Royal Suite, which resembles a Palm Beach apartment, and comes complete with a white baby grand (player) piano. It has a separate bedroom with king-size bed, living room with queen-sized sofa bed, refrigerator/mini-bar, dining table, entertainment center, and vanity dressing area. The decor is simple and elegant, with pastel colors, and wood-accented ceiling treatments. Located just under the starboard side navigation bridge wing, it has its own private balcony.

CUISINE/DINING. The two-level Edelweiss Dining Room is attractive and works well, although the noise level can be high. There are two seatings. The quality and serving of meals aboard Royal Caribbean International ships has become quite robotic over the past few years.

The Windjammer Cafe is the casual dining spot for self-serve buffets. The area is well designed, with contemporary decor and colors, but the food is basic fare and disappointing; the four-sided self-service buffet area is small for the number of passengers using it. More money needs to be spent for better ingredients and more variety. Each evening, the room offers an alternative to the more formal dining room. The evening buffets have a different theme, something this company has been doing for more than 25 years – perhaps the time has come for more creativity.

There is a hamburger/hot dog grill counter in the Solarium, but typically you don't get a choice of how well done or not so well done you get your hamburgers – everything appears to be well done. The company has introduced a drinks package (available at all bars, in the form of cards or stickers) that enables you to pre-pay for a selection of standard soft drinks and alcoholic drinks. The packages are not exactly easy to understand.

ENTERTAINMENT. The Broadway Melodies Theater is the ship's principal showlounge. It is a large, but well-designed room with main and balcony levels, and good sight lines from most of the banquette seats.

Other cabaret acts are featured in the Shall We Dance Lounge, located aft, and these include late-night adult (blue) comedy, as well as live music for dancing. A number of other bars and lounges have live music of differing types.

The entertainment throughout is upbeat. There is even background music in all passenger hallways and elevators, and constant music outdoors on the pool deck. If you want a quiet relaxing holiday, choose another ship.

SPA/FITNESS. There are good health spa facilities, set in a spacious environment on one of the uppermost decks. The decor has Egypt as its theme, with pharaohs lining the pool. The spa is operated by Steiner, a specialist concession

For the more sporting, there is activity galore – including a rock-climbing wall, with several separate climbing tracks. It is located outdoors at the aft end of the funnel.

● **For more extensive general information on what a Royal Caribbean cruise is like, see pages 128–131.**

Rotterdam
★★★★

Large (Resort) Ship: ....59,652 tons	Total Crew: 593	Cabins (with private balcony): 160
Lifestyle: ....Premium	Passengers	Cabins (wheelchair accessible): 20
Cruise Line: ......Holland America Line	(lower beds/all berths): 1,320/1,668	Cabin Current: ....110 and 220 volts
Former Names: ....none	Passenger Space Ratio	Elevators: 12
Builder: ....Fincantieri (Italy)	(lower beds/all berths): 45.1/35.7	Casino (gaming tables): ....Yes
Original Cost: ....$250 million	Crew/Passenger Ratio	Slot Machines: ....Yes
Entered Service: ....Dec 1997	(lower beds/all berths): 2.2/2.8	Swimming Pools (outdoors): 1
Registry: ....The Netherlands	Navigation Officers: ....Dutch	Swimming Pools (indoors): 1
Length (ft/m): 777.5/237.00	Cabins (total): 660	(magrodome cover)
Beam (ft/m): 105.8/32.25	Size Range (sq ft/m): 184.0–1,124.8/	Whirlpools: 2
Draft (ft/m): 25.5/7.80	17.1–104.5	Self-Service Launderette: ....Yes
Propulsion/Propellers: .....diesel-electric	Cabins (outside view): 542	Dedicated Cinema/Seats: Yes/235
(37,500kW)/2	Cabins (interior/no view): 118	Library: ....Yes
Passenger Decks: 12	Cabins (for one person): 0	Classification Society: ...Lloyd's Register

OVERALL SCORE: 1,541 (OUT OF A POSSIBLE 2,000 POINTS)

OVERVIEW. This latest *Rotterdam* has been constructed to look like a slightly larger (longer and beamier), but certainly a much sleeker version of the *"S"-class* ships, while retaining the graceful lines of the former *Rotterdam*, including a nicely raked bow and a more rounded exterior, as well as the familiar interior flow and design style. Also retained is the twin-funnel feature well recognized by former Holland America Line passengers, though it has been somewhat more streamlined. This *Rotterdam* (the sixth Holland America Line ship to bear the name) is capable of 25 knots (some call it the *Fastdam*), which is useful for longer itineraries.

Two decks (Promenade Deck and Upper Promenade Deck) house most of the public rooms, and these are sandwiched between several accommodation decks. The layout is quite easy to learn, and the signage is good.

The interior decor is best described as restrained, with much use of wood accenting. As a whole, the decor of this ship is extremely refined, with much of the traditional ocean liner detailing so loved by frequent Holland America Line passengers. The focal interior point is a three-deck high atrium, in an oval, instead of circular, shape. The atrium's focal point is a huge "one-of-a-kind" custom-made clock, which includes an astrolabe, an astrological clock and 14 other clocks in a structure that takes up three decks (the clock's design is based on an antique Flemish original).

One room has a glass ceiling similar to that aboard a former *Statendam*. The Ambassador's Lounge has an interesting brass dance floor, similar to the dance floor that adorned the Ritz-Carlton room aboard the previous *Rotterdam*.

Instead of just two staircases aboard the "S"-class ships,

BERLITZ'S RATINGS

	Possible	Achieved
Ship	500	430
Accommodation	200	165
Food	400	281
Service	400	276
Entertainment	100	77
Cruise	400	312

Rotterdam has three (better from the viewpoint of safety, passenger accessibility and evacuation). There is a magrodome-covered pool on the Lido Deck between the mast and the ship's twin funnels, as aboard the company's "S"-class ships, which have only one large, very square funnel.

The ship has allotted more space to children's and teens' play areas, although these really are token gestures by a company that traditionally does not cater well to children. However, it appears that grandparents take their grandchildren with them (to the delight of parents, who get a well-deserved break). Enhanced children's programming is brought into play according to the number of children carried.

Popcorn is available at the Wajang Theatre for moviegoers, while adjacent is the popular Java Cafe. The casino, which is located in the middle of a major passenger flow, has blackjack, roulette, poker and dice tables alongside the requisite rows of slot machines.

Holland America Line has a long legacy in Dutch maritime history. The artwork aboard this ship (it cost $2 million) consists of a collection of 17th-century Dutch and Japanese artifacts together with contemporary works specially created for the ship, although there seems little linkage between some of the items.

Holland America Line's flagship replaced the former ship of the same name when it was retired in 1997 – just in time for the start of the company's 125th anniversary in 1998. It is a most contemporary ship for Holland America Line, with lighter, brighter decor. It is an extremely comfortable vessel in which to cruise, with some fine, elegant and luxurious decorative features. However, these are marred somewhat by the poor quality of dining room food and service and the lack of understanding of what it takes to make a "luxury" cruise experience, despite what is touted in the company's brochures.

With one whole deck of suites (and a dedicated, private concierge lounge, and preferential passenger treatment), the company has in effect created a two-class ship. The charge to use the washing machines and dryers in the self-service launderette is really petty and irritating, particularly for the occupants of suites, as they pay high prices for their cruises. Room service is poor. Non-smokers should avoid this ship, as smokers seem to be everywhere.

SUITABLE FOR: *Rotterdam* is best suited to older couples and singles (and their grandchildren), who like to mingle in a large ship, in an unhurried setting with fine quality surroundings, with plenty of eclectic antique artwork, decent (though not gourmet) food and service from a smiling Indonesian and Filipino crew.

ACCOMMODATION. There are 17 categories, prices depending on grade, size and location. Accommodation is spread over five decks (some cabins have full or partially obstructed views). Interestingly, no cabin is more than 144 ft (44 meters) from a stairway, which makes it easier to get from cabins to public rooms. All cabin doors have a bird's-eye maple look, and hallways have framed fabric panels to make them less clinical. Cabin televisions carry CNN and TNT.

All standard inside and outside cabins are tastefully furnished, and have twin beds that convert to a queen-sized bed (space is tight for walking between beds and vanity unit). There is a decent amount of closet and drawer space, although this will prove tight for the longer voyages featured. The bathrooms, which are fully tiled, are disappointingly small (particularly for long cruises) and have small shower tubs, utilitarian personal toiletries cupboards, and exposed under-sink plumbing. There is no detailing to distinguish them from bathrooms aboard the "S"-class ships.

There are 36 full verandah suites (Navigation Deck), including four penthouse suites, which share a private Concierge Lounge with a concierge to handle such things as special dining arrangements, shore excursions and special requests – although strangely there are no butlers for these suites, as aboard ships with similar facilities. Each suite has a separate steward's entrance and separate bedroom, dressing and living areas. Suite passengers get personal sta-tionery, complimentary laundry and ironing, cocktail-hour hors d'oeuvres and other goodies, as well as priority embarkation and disembarkation. The concierge lounge, with its latticework teak detailing and private library is accessible only by private key-card.

Disabled passengers have 20 cabins to choose from, including two of the large "penthouse" suites (which include concierge services). However, there are different cabin configurations, and it is wise to check with your booking agent.

CUISINE/DINING. The La Fontaine Dining Room seats 747, and spans two decks. There are tables for four, six or eight, but only nine tables for two. Open seating is featured for breakfast and lunch, with two seatings for dinner (with both smoking and no-smoking sections on both upper and lower levels). Fine Rosenthal china and good cutlery are used (although there are no fish knives).

Alternative (Reservations Required) Dining Option: There is also an 88-seat Odyssey Italian alternative restaurant, decorated in the manner of an opulent 17th-century baroque Italian villa, and available to all passengers. The room, whose basic color is black with gold accenting, is divided into three sections. Cuisines from the Perugia, Tuscany and Umbria regions of Italy are featured, although the portions are very small.

ENTERTAINMENT. The 577-seat Queen's Lounge is the venue for all production shows, strong cabaret, and other entertainment features. It is two decks high (with main and balcony level seating). The decor includes umbrella-shaped gold ceiling lamps of Murano glass, and the stage features hydraulic lifts and three video screens, as well as closed-loop system for the hearing-impaired.

SPA/FITNESS. The Ocean Spa is located one deck above the navigation bridge at the very forward part of the ship. It includes a gymnasium (with all the latest muscle-pumping exercise machines, including an abundance of treadmills) with forward views over the ship's bows, an aerobics exercise area, large beauty salon with ocean-view windows to the port side, several treatment rooms, and men's and women's sauna, steam room and changing areas.

● **For more extensive general information on what a Holland America Line cruise is like, see pages 118–122.**

Royal Clipper
★★★★

Small Ship: ....5,061 tons	Main Propulsion: ....42 sails	Cabins (outside view): 108
Lifestyle: ....Premium	Propulsion/Propellers: diesel (3,700kW)/1	Cabins (interior/no view): 6
Cruise Line: ....Star Clippers	Passenger Decks: 5	Cabins (for one person): 0
Former Names: ....none	Total Crew: 100	Cabins (with private balcony): 14
Builder: ....De Merwede (Holland)	Passengers	Cabins (wheelchair accessible): 0
Original Cost: ....$75 million	(lower beds/all berths): 228/255	Cabin Current: ....110 and 220 volts
Entered Service: ....Oct 2000	Passenger Space Ratio	Elevators: 0
Registry: ....Luxembourg	(lower beds/all berths): 22.1/19.8	Casino (gaming tables): ....No
Length (ft/m): 439.6/134.0	Crew/Passenger Ratio	Slot Machines: ....No
Beam (ft/m): 54.1/16.5	(lower beds/all berths): 2.2/2.5	Swimming Pools (outdoors): 3
Draft (ft/m): 18.5/5.6	Navigation Officers: ....International	Whirlpools: 0
Type of Vessel: sail-cruise (square rigger)	Cabins (total): 114	Self-Service Launderette: ....No
No. of Masts: 5	Size Range (sq ft/m): 100.0–320.0/	Library: ....Yes
Sail Area (sq ft/m2): 56,000/5,204.5	9.3–29.7	Classification Society: ...Lloyd's Register

OVERALL SCORE: 1,540 (OUT OF A POSSIBLE 2,000 POINTS)

OVERVIEW. The culmination of an owner's childhood dream, *Royal Clipper* is truly a stunning sight under sail. Being marketed as the world's largest true fully rigged sailing ship, this is a logical addition to the company's two other, smaller, 4-masted tall ships (*Star Clipper* and *Star Flyer*). *Royal Clipper*'s 5-masted design is based on the only other 5-masted sailing ship to be built, the 1902-built German tall ship *Preussen*, and has approximately the same dimensions, albeit 46 ft (14 meters) shorter (it is much larger than the famous *Cutty Sark*, for example). It is almost 40 ft (12.1 meters) longer than the largest sailing ship presently in commission – the four-mast Russian barkentine *Sedov*. To keep things in perspective, *Royal Clipper* is the same length overall as *Wind Spirit* and *Wind Star* – the computer-controlled cruise-sail vessels of Windstar Cruises.

The construction time for this ship was remarkably short, owing to the fact that its hull had been almost completed (at Gdansk shipyard, Poland) for another owner (the ship was to be named *Gwarek*) but became available to Star Clippers for completion and fitting out. The ship is instantly recognizable due to its geometric blue and white hull markings. Power winches, as well as hand winches, are employed in deck fittings, as well as a mix of horizontal furling for the square sails and hydraulic power assist to roll the square sails along the yardarm. The sail handling system, which was designed by the ship's owner, Mikael Krafft, is such that it can be converted from a full rigger to a schooner in an incredibly short time.

Its masts reach as high as 197 ft (60 meters) above the waterline, and the top 19 ft (5.8 meters) can be hinged over 90° to clear bridges, cable lines and other port-based

BERLITZ'S RATINGS

	Possible	Achieved
Ship	500	406
Accommodation	200	157
Food	400	288
Service	400	296
Entertainment	N/A	N/A
Cruise	500	393

obstacles. Up to 42 sails can be used: 26 square sails (fore upper topgallant, fore lower topgallant, fore upper topsail, fore lower topsail, foresail, main royal, main upper topgallant, main lower topgallant, main upper topsail, main lower topsail, mainsail, middle royal, middle upper topgallant, middle lower topgallant, middle upper topsail, middle lower topsail, middle course, mizzen upper topgallant, mizzen lower topgallant, mizzen upper topsail, mizzen lower topsail, mizzen course, jigger topgallant, jigger upper topsail, jigger lower topsail, crossjack), 11 staysails (main royal staysail, main topgallant staysail, main topmast staysail, middle royal staysail, middle topgallant staysail, middle topmast staysail, mizzen royal staysail, mizzen topgallant staysail, mizzen topmast staysail, jigger topgallant staysail, jigger topmast staysail); 4 jibs (flying jib, outer jib, inner jib, fore topmast staysail) and 1 gaff-rigged spanker, it looks quite magnificent when under full sail – an area of some 54,360 sq. ft (5,050 sq. meters). Also, watching the sailors manipulate ropes, rigging and sails is like watching a ballet – the precision and cohesion of a group of men who make it all look so simple.

As a passenger, you are allowed to climb to special lookout points aloft – maybe even for a glass of champagne. Passengers are also allowed on the bridge at any time (but not in the galley or engine room).

There is a large amount of open deck space and sunning space aboard this ship – something most tall ships lack, although, naturally, this is laid with ropes for the rigging. A marina platform can be lowered at the stern of the vessel, from where you can use the surfboards, sailing dinghies, take a ride on the ship's own banana boat, or go water-skiing or swimming. Snorkeling gear is available free, but there is a charge for scuba diving gear. You will be asked to sign a waiver if you wish to use the water sports equipment.

Inside, a midships atrium three decks high sits under one of the ship's three swimming pools, and sunlight streams down through a piano lounge on the uppermost level inside the ship and down into the dining room, which is on the lower level. A forward observation lounge is a real plus, and this is connected to the piano lounge via a central corridor. An Edwardian library/card room is decorated with a *belle époque* fireplace. A lounge, the Captain Nemo Club, is where passengers can observe fish and sea life when the ship is at anchor, through thick glass portholes (floodlit from underneath at night to attract the fish).

This delightful, quite spectacular tall ship for tourists operates 7-night and 14-day cruises in the Grenadines and Lower Windward Islands of the Caribbean during the winter and 7-night and 14-night cruises in the Mediterranean during the summer. It is good to note that the officers navigate using both traditional (sextant) and contemporary methods (advanced electronic positioning system).

Being a tall ship with true sailing traditions, there is, naturally, a parrot (sometimes kept in a large, gilded cage, but often seen around the ship on someone's shoulder), which is part of the crew (as aboard all Star Clippers' ships). The general ambiance is extremely relaxed, friendly and casual – completely unpretentious. The passenger mix is international (often consisting of a good cross-section of yachting types) and the dress code is casual at all times (shorts and casual tops are the order of the day – yachting wear), with no ties needed at any time.

There is no doubt that *Royal Clipper* is a superb vessel for the actual experience of sailing – a tall ship probably without equal, as much more time is spent actually under sail than aboard almost any other tall ship (including the smaller *Sea Cloud* and *Sea Cloud II*). However, apart from the sailing experience, it is in the cuisine and service that the lack of professionalism and poor standards of delivery shows. Much of this is the result of insufficient training and supervision, which the company is slowly addressing. The result is a score that could be higher if the cuisine and service were better.

The suites and cabins are larger than those aboard the tall ships of the Windjammer Barefoot Cruises fleet, while, in general, smaller than aboard *Sea Cloud* and *Sea Cloud II*. While the food and service are far superior to the Windjammers, both are well below the standard found aboard *Sea Cloud* and *Sea Cloud II*. I do not include the Windstar Cruises ships (*Wind Spirit, Wind Star, Wind Surf*), because they cannot, in any sense of the word, be considered tall ships. *Royal Clipper*, however, is exactly that – a real, working, wind-and-sails-in-your-face tall ship with a highly personable captain and crew that welcome you as if you were part of the team. What also gives the ship a little extra in the scoring department is the fact that many water sports are included in the price of your cruise.

This vessel is not for the physically impaired, or for children. The steps of the internal stairs are steep, as in most

sailing vessels. The tipping system, where all tips are pooled (the suggested amount is $8 per passenger, per day), causes concern for many passengers. The onboard currency is the US dollar.

SUITABLE FOR: *Royal Clipper* is best suited to couples and singles who would probably never even consider a "normal" cruise ship, but who enjoy sailing and the thrill of ocean and wind, but want these things wrapped in a package that includes accommodation, food, like-minded companions, interesting destinations, and don't want the bother of owning or chartering their own yacht.

ACCOMMODATION. There are eight accommodation grades (the price you pay will depend on the grade, size and location you choose): Owner's Suite (2), Deluxe Suite (14), and Categories 1–6. No matter what grade you choose (price will depend on location and size), all have polished wood-trimmed cabinetry and wall-to-wall carpeting, personal safe, full-length mirror, small television with audio channels and 24-hour text-based news, and private bathroom. All feature twin beds (86 of which convert into a queen-sized bed, while 28 are fixed queen-sized beds that cannot be separated), hairdryer and satellite-linked telephone. The six interior (no view) cabins and a handful of other cabins have a permanently fixed double bed.

Most cabins have a privacy curtain, so that you cannot be seen from the hallway when the cabin attendant opens the door (useful if you are not wearing any clothes). In addition, 27 cabins sleep three.

The two owner's suites, located at the very aft of the ship, provide the most lavish accommodation, and have one queen-sized bed and one double bed, a separate living area with semi-circular sofa, large vanity desk, wet bar/refrigerator, marble-clad bathroom with whirlpool bathtub, plus one guest bathroom, and butler service. The two suites have an interconnecting door, so that the combined super-suite can sleep eight persons. However, there is no private balcony.

The 14 "Deck Suites" have interesting names: Ariel, Cutty Sark, Doriana, Eagle Wing, Flying Cloud, France, Golden Gate, Gloria, Great Republic, Passat, Pommern, Preussen, and Thermopylae. However, they are not actually suites, as the sleeping area cannot be separated from the lounge – they are simply larger cabins with a more luxurious interior, more storage space and a larger bathroom. Each has two lower beds convertible to a queen-sized, small lounge area, mini-bar/ refrigerator, writing desk, small private balcony, and marble-clad bathroom with combination whirlpool tub/shower, washbasin and toilet, and butler service. The door to the balcony can be opened so that fresh air floods the room; note that there is a 12-inch (30-cm) threshold to step over.

There are no curtains, only roll-down shades for the windows and balcony door. The balcony itself typically has two white plastic chairs and drinks table; however, teak chairs and table would be more in keeping with the nature of the ship. The 14 balconies are not particularly private, and most have ship's tenders or zodiacs overhanging them, or some rigging obscuring the views.

Two other name cabins (Lord Nelson and Marco Polo – designated as Category 1 cabins) are located aft, but do not have private balconies, although the facilities are similar.

The interior (no view) cabins and the lowest grades of outside-view cabins are extremely small and tight, with very little room to move around the beds. Therefore, take only the minimum amount of clothing and luggage. When in cabins where beds are linked together to form a double bed, you will have to clamber up over the front of the bed, as both sides have built-in storm barriers (this applies in inclement weather conditions only).

There is a small room service menu (all items cost extra).

CUISINE/DINING. The Dining Room is constructed on several connecting levels (getting used to the steps is not easy), and seats all passengers at one seating under a three-deck-high atrium dome. You can sit with whom you wish at tables for four, six, eight or 10. However, it is a noisy dining room, due to the positioning of the many waiter stations, and the waiting staff are poorly trained, making mealtimes less enjoyable than one would wish. Some tables are badly positioned so that correct waiter service is impossible, and much reaching over has to be done in order to serve everyone.

One corner can be closed off for private parties. Breakfasts and lunches are self-serve buffets, while dinner is a sit-down affair with table service, although the ambiance is always friendly and lighthearted. The wine list consists of very young wines, and prices are quite high.

The cuisine is certainly nothing to write home about. Although perfectly acceptable, it certainly cannot be considered in the same class as that found aboard ships such as *Sea Cloud* or *Sea Cloud II*.

ENTERTAINMENT. There are no entertainment shows, nor are any expected by passengers aboard a tall ship such as this, where sailing is the main purpose of a cruise. There is, however, live music, which is provided by a single lounge pianist/singer. Otherwise, dinner is the main evening event, as well as "Captain's Storytime", recaps of the day's interesting events, and conversation with fellow passengers in the lounge or on deck (under the stars) provides engaging entertainment.

During the daytime, when the ship is sailing, passengers can learn about the sails, and the captain or chief officer will give briefings as the sails are being furled and unfurled. The closest this tall ship comes to any kind of "show" is when, one evening towards the end of each cruise, a "sailor's choir", comprised of the ship's crew, presents a nautical performance of sea songs, sea shanties, and other light diversions.

SPA/FITNESS. The Royal Spa is located on the lowest passenger deck and, although not large, incorporates a beauty salon, Moroccan steam room (for which there is a charge), and a small gymnasium with porthole views, several muscle-pump machines body toning equipment, treadmills, rowing machines, and exercycles. Thai massage as well as traditional massage, aromatherapy facials, and other beauty treatments, are available.

Royal Princess
★★★★

Mid-size Ship: ....44,348 tons	Total Crew: 520	Cabins (with private balcony): 152
Lifestyle: ....Standard	Passengers	Cabins (wheelchair accessible): 4
Cruise Line: ....Princess Cruises	(lower beds/all berths): 1,200/1,275	Cabin Current: ....110 and 220 volts
Former Names: ....none	Passenger Space Ratio	Elevators: 6
Builder: ....Wartsila (Finland)	(lower beds/all berths): 36.9/34.7	Casino (gaming tables): ....Yes
Original Cost: ....$165 million	Crew/Passenger Ratio	Slot Machines: ....Yes
Entered Service: ....Nov 1984	(lower beds/all berths): 2.3/2.4	Swimming Pools (outdoors): 2
Registry: ....Great Britain	Navigation Officers: ....·....British	(+2 splash pools)
Length (ft/m): 754.5/230.0	Cabins (total): 600	Swimming Pools (indoors): 0
Beam (ft/m): 95.8/29.2	Size Range (sq ft/m): 186.0–1,126.0/	Whirlpools: 2
Draft (ft/m): 25.5/7.8	17.2–104.5	Self-Service Launderette: ....Yes
Propulsion/Propellers: ....diesel	Cabins (outside view): 600	Dedicated Cinema/Seats: Yes/150
(29,160kW)/2	Cabins (interior/no view): 0	Library: ....Yes
Passenger Decks: 9	Cabins (for one person): 0	Classification Society: ...Lloyd's Register

OVERALL SCORE: 1,496 (OUT OF A POSSIBLE 2,000 POINTS)

OVERVIEW. *Royal Princess* has reasonably contemporary outer styling that could be considered handsome. There is an excellent amount of outdoor deck and sunbathing space, and traditional wraparound teakwood deck. Well-designed, though slightly unconventional interior layout and passenger flow provides passenger cabins located above the public room decks. There are large, beautifully appointed public rooms, spacious passageways and imposing staircases.

BERLITZ'S RATINGS

	Possible	Achieved
Ship	500	396
Accommodation	200	163
Food	400	265
Service	400	289
Entertainment	100	75
Cruise	400	308

It is a contemporary ship, yet not the least bit garish, and the decor reflects the feeling of space, openness and light.

The Horizon Lounge, set around the funnel base, has fine views, and makes for a peaceful environment during the day. When this ship debuted, it was state-of-the-art. It is amazing to see that now it lags behind the latest ships in several ways. *Royal Princess*, one of the smallest ships in the fleet, will still provide you with a good cruise experience in spacious, quite elegant surroundings, at the appropriate price, although attention to the small details of service finesse is often missing.

In May 2005, *Royal Princess* will undergo a transformation, and a name change, to become *Artemis*. The ship will be totally committed to the British child-free cruise market, to which the ageing ship is perhaps more ideally suited.

ACCOMMODATION. The all-outside cabins (152 of which have private balconies) represent just four accommodation types (including suites), although there are 20 price categories. All are quite well thought-out, very comfortable and well appointed. The suites are extremely attractive.

All cabins have a full bathtub and shower, three-sided mirrors, and color TV. Bathrobes are provided for all pas-sengers, as are chocolates on your pillow each night. Prompt, attentive room service is available 24 hours a day. Some cabins on both Baja Deck and Caribe Deck do have views that are obstructed by the lifeboats. The cabin numbering system is extremely illogical.

CUISINE/DINING. The elegant, non-smoking Continental Dining Room is set low down, and is conveniently adjacent to the lobby. There are two seatings for dinner. The service is fairly friendly, and sound.

The in-cabin service menu is really basic. The indoor-outdoor Lido Deck was expanded dramatically in a refit and now has 24-hour food availability for casual dining (though with plastic plates), and better beverage stations.

ENTERTAINMENT. The International Lounge is the venue for production shows, major cabaret acts, other events. It is an amphitheater-shaped room with good sightlines from the majority of seats. Princess Cruises always provides plenty of live music for the various bars and lounges, and volume is normally kept to an acceptable level.

SPA/FITNESS. The Spa is located on one of the uppermost decks, clustered around the base of the funnel housing. It contains a gymnasium with some decent muscle-toning equipment and large picture windows that overlook one of the swimming pools, saunas and changing rooms for men and women, and beauty salon, as well as a display of exercise clothing for sale.

● **For more extensive general information about the Princess Cruises experience, see pages 124–127.**

Royal Star
★★ +

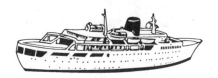

Small Ship: . . . . .5,360 tons	Passenger Decks: 5	Cabins (with private balcony): 1
Lifestyle: . . . . .Standard	Total Crew: 130	Cabins (wheelchair accessible): 0
Cruise Line: . . . . . .African Safari Cruises/	Passengers	Cabin Current: . . . . .110 and 220 volts
Star Line Cruises	(lower beds/all berths): 222/255	Elevators: 1
Former Names: . . . . .Ocean Islander,	Passenger Space Ratio	Casino (gaming tables): . . . . .Yes
San Giorgio, City of Andros	(lower beds/all berths): 24.1/21.0	Slot Machines: . . . . .Yes
Builder: . . . .Cantieri Riuniti dell' Adriatico	Crew/Passenger Ratio	Swimming Pools (outdoors): 1
(Italy)	(lower beds/all berths): 1.7/1.9	Swimming Pools (indoors): 0
Original Cost: . . . . .n/a	Navigation Officers: . . . . .Greek	Whirlpools: 0
Entered Service: 1956/Dec 1990	Cabins (total): 111	Self-Service Launderette: . . . . .No
Registry: . . . . .The Bahamas	Size Range (sq ft/m): 107.0–398.0/	Dedicated Cinema/Seats: . . . . .No
Length (ft/m): 367.4/112.00	10.0–37.0	Library: . . . . .Yes
Beam (ft/m): 51.0/15.55	Cabins (outside view): 97	Classification Society: . .American Bureau
Draft (ft/m): 18.2/5.56	Cabins (interior/no view): 14	of Shipping
Propulsion/Propellers: .diesel (4,817kW)/2	Cabins (for one person): 0	

OVERALL SCORE: 1,069 (OUT OF A POSSIBLE 2,000 POINTS)

OVERVIEW. The African Safari Club, a Swiss hotel and tour operator which manages 13 hotels in Kenya, has been operating this ship for several years (as African Safari Cruises and Star Line Cruises) in conjunction with these land-based safaris. It is a charming, though dated, little vessel, with a well-balanced profile. There is an open-bridge policy while the ship is at sea (weather permitting). The ship has reasonable open deck space for sunbathing (but do remember that, close to the equator, the sun is dangerously strong).

Royal Star, now well over 40 years old, is quite suited to cruising in sheltered areas. Moderately clean and tidy, it has a reasonably warm, friendly, relaxed and personable ambience, although service finesse is lacking. The main reason for taking it is to get to your safari in the lands of the Masai Tribe. So the fact that the ship is old, small, and lacks first-class facilities, food, service and entertainment is not crucial. The official currency on board is the US dollar, and many fellow passengers will be German-speaking.

The African Safari Club has its own A310 aircraft to transport you from Frankfurt (or Basle) to Mombasa. It also has an internal airline (Skytrail) to transport tourists to the high plains, as well as a fleet of four-wheel-drive vehicles. All port taxes, and airport transfers are included in the cruise fare, which also includes a stay at African Safari Club's own Flamingo Beach Hotel (with private beach).

SUITABLE FOR: *Royal Star* is best suited to couples and single travelers of mature years who are seeking a traditional (old) ship and safari park combination holiday that includes air transportation, accommodation, food, and small ship

BERLITZ'S RATINGS

	Possible	Achieved
Ship	500	264
Accommodation	200	108
Food	400	213
Service	400	237
Entertainment	100	46
Cruise	400	201

facilities in one neat package, at a reasonable cost.

ACCOMMODATION. There are eight price grades. Except for one President Suite, with private balcony terrace, the cabins are not large, although they are well furnished and there is reasonable closet and drawer space. The cabin bathrooms are tiny, although accommodation designated as Superior Suites has two bathrooms, with hairdryer. Some cabins have additional third- and fourth-person upper berths. Only about a half dozen cabins have double beds while others have a twin- or L-shaped bed configuration.

CUISINE/DINING. The charming Belvedere Restaurant has large portholes with views of the sea. There are two seatings, and tables are for four, six, or eight. The cuisine is international, although standards are variable. The menu is more like a set table d'hôte menu, with little choice (though some regional dishes are featured). The selection of breads, bread rolls, international cheeses, and fruits is very limited, and the choice of teas is poor. The dining room service is provided by friendly Filipino and Indonesian waiters.

This ship would not meet the minimum standards in cleanliness and hygiene required by the Maritime Evaluations Group (particularly the galley, food preparation, handling and storage areas).

ENTERTAINMENT. Not much, but there is a small dance troupe, and occasional cabaret acts.

SPA/FITNESS. There is a tiny gymnasium and a sauna.

Ryndam
★★★★

Large (Resort) Ship: ....55,451 tons	Total Crew: 557	Cabins (with private balcony): 150
Lifestyle: ....Premium	Passengers	Cabins (wheelchair accessible): 6
Cruise Line: ....Holland America Line	(lower beds/all berths): 1,266/1,627	Cabin Current: ....110 and 220 volts
Former Names: ....none	Passenger Space Ratio	Elevators: 8
Builder: ....Fincantieri (Italy)	(lower beds/all berths): 43.8/34.0	Casino (gaming tables): ....Yes
Original Cost: ....$215 million	Crew/Passenger Ratio	Slot Machines: ....Yes
Entered Service: ....Nov 1994	(lower beds/all berths): 2.2/2.9	Swimming Pools (outdoors): 1
Registry: ....The Netherlands	Navigation Officers: ....British/Dutch	Swimming Pools (indoors): 1
Length (ft/m): 719.3/219.3	Cabins (total): 633	(magrodome)
Beam (ft/m): 101.0/30.8	Size Range (sq ft/m): 186.2–1,124.8/	Whirlpools: 2
Draft (ft/m): 24.6/7.5	17.3–104.5	Self-Service Launderette: ....Yes
Propulsion/Propellers: .....diesel-electric	Cabins (outside view): 502	Dedicated Cinema/Seats: Yes/249
(34,560kW)/2	Cabins (interior/no view): 131	Library: ....Yes
Passenger Decks: 10	Cabins (for one person): 0	Classification Society: ...Lloyd's Register

OVERALL SCORE: 1,533 (OUT OF A POSSIBLE 2,000 POINTS)

OVERVIEW. *Ryndam* is one of a series of four almost identical ships – the others being *Maasdam, Statendam*, and *Veendam.* The exterior styling is rather angular (some would say boxy), although it is softened and balanced by the black hull. There is a full wrap-around teakwood promenade deck outdoors – excellent for strolling, and, thankfully, no sign of synthetic turf. The deck lounge chairs on the exterior promenade deck are wood, and come with comfortable cushioned pads, while those at the swimming pool on Lido Deck are of white plastic. Holland America Line keeps its ships clean and tidy, and there is good passenger flow throughout the public areas.

In the interiors of this "S" -class ship, an asymmetrical layout helps to reduce bottlenecks and congestion. Most of the public rooms are concentrated on two decks, Promenade Deck, and Upper Promenade Deck, which creates a spacious feel. In general, a restrained approach to interior styling is taken, using a mixture of contemporary materials combined with traditional woods and ceramics. There is, fortunately, little "glitz" anywhere.

What is outstanding is the array of artworks throughout the ship (costing about $2 million), assembled and nicely displayed to represent the fine Dutch heritage of Holland America Line. Also noticeable are the fine flower arrangements throughout the public areas and foyers – used to good effect to brighten up what some consider dull decor.

Atop the ship, with forward facing views that wrap around the sides is the Crow's Nest Lounge. By day it makes a fine observation lounge, with large ocean-view windows, while by night it turns into a nightclub with extremely variable lighting. The three-deck high atrium foyer is attractive, although its sculptured centerpiece makes

BERLITZ'S RATINGS

	Possible	Achieved
Ship	500	418
Accommodation	200	162
Food	400	267
Service	400	299
Entertainment	100	77
Cruise	400	310

it look a little crowded, and leaves little room in front of the purser's office. A hydraulic glass roof covers the reasonably sized swimming pool/whirlpools and central Lido area (whose focal point is a large dolphin sculpture) so that this can be used in fine or inclement weather. There is a large and quite lovely and relaxing reference library.

Ryndam is a well-built ship, and has fairly decent interior fit and finish. Holland America Line constantly fine-tunes its performance as a cruise operator and its regular passengers (almost all of whom are North American) find the company's ships very comfortable and well-run, even though the present food and service components let down the rest of the cruise experience.

Perhaps the ship's best asset is its friendly and personable Filipino and Indonesian crew, although communication can prove frustrating at times. The onboard currency is the US dollar.

Holland America Line's many repeat passengers always seem to enjoy the fact that social dancing is on the menu. The company provides complimentary cappuccino and espresso coffees, and free ice cream during certain hours of the day aboard its ships, as well as hot hors d'oeuvres in all bars – something other major lines seem to have dropped, or charge extra for. However, the score for this ship ends up a tad under what it could be if the food and waiting staff were better (more professional training might help). This ship is now deployed year-round in the Caribbean, where its rather dark interior decor contrasts with the strong sunlight.

An escalator travels between two of the lower decks (one of which was originally planned to be the embarkation point), but it is almost pointless. The charge to use the washing machines and dryers in the self-service launderette is petty, particularly for suite occupants, as they pay steep prices for their cruises. The men's urinals in public restrooms are unusually high.

ACCOMMODATION. This ranges from small interior (no view) cabins to a large penthouse suite, in 17 price categories. All cabin televisions carry CNN and TNT.

The interior (no view) and outside (with a view) standard cabins have twin beds that convert to a queen-sized bed, and there is a separate living space with sofa and coffee table. However, although the drawer space is generally good, the closet space is actually very tight, particularly for long cruises (although more than adequate for a 7-night cruise). Bathrobes are also provided for all suites/cabins, as are hairdryers, and a small range of personal amenities. The bathrooms are quite well laid out, but the bathtubs are small units better described as shower tubs. Some cabins have interconnecting doors.

On Navigation Deck, 28 suites have accommodation for up to four. These suites also have in-suite dining as an alternative to the dining room, for private, reclusive meals. These are very spacious, tastefully decorated and well laid-out, and have a separate living room, bedroom with two lower beds (convertible to a king-sized bed), a good sized living area, dressing room, plenty of closet and drawer space, marble bathroom with Jacuzzi tub.

The largest accommodation of all is a penthouse suite. There is only one, located on the starboard side of Navigation Deck at the forward staircase. It has a king-sized bed, a TV set and video player, and a vanity desk, a large walk-in closet with superb drawer space, oversize whirlpool bath (it could seat four) and separate shower enclosure, and a separate washroom with toilet, bidet and washbasin. The living room has a writing desk, a large television and a full set of audio equipment. There's a dressing room, a large private balcony (with teak lounge chairs and drinks tables, dining table and four chairs), a pantry (with large refrigerator, toaster unit, and full coffee/tea making facilities and food prepareation area, and a separate entrance from the hallway), mini-bar/refrigerator, a guest toilet and floor to ceiling windows. Note that there is no bell push.

CUISINE/DINING. The Rotterdam Dining Room spans two decks. It is located at the stern, is quite dramatic, and has two grand staircases to connect the two levels, panoramic views on three sides, and a music balcony. It has open seating for breakfast and lunch, and four seatings for dinner (you must pre-select a time at either 5.45pm, 6.15 pm, 8pm or 8.30 pm). There are tables for two, four, six or eight. The dining room has both smoking and no-smoking sections. The waiter stations in the dining room are very noisy for anyone seated adjacent to them. Fine Rosenthal china and cutlery are used (although there are no fish knives). Live music is provided for dinner each evening; once each cruise, a Dutch Dinner is featured (hats are provided), as is

an Indonesian Lunch. "Lighter option" meals are always available for the health-conscious.

Alternative Dining Option: An intimate restaurant, the Pinnacle Grill, was added in 2002. It is located just forward of the balcony level of the main dining room on the starboard side. The 66-seat dining spot (reservations are necessary, and a cover/service charge of $20 applies) features Pacific Northwest cuisine (fresh Alaskan salmon and halibut, and other regional specialities, plus a selection of premium steaks such as filet mignon from Black Angus beef).. The Pinnacle Grill is a much better dining experience than the main dining room and enhances that special celebration.

For more casual evening eating, the Lido Buffet is open for dinners on all except the last night of each cruise, in an open-seating arrangement. Tables are set with crisp linens, flatware and stemware. The set menu includes a choice of four entrées. The dual-line, self-serve Lido Buffet (one side is for smokers, the other side for non-smokers) is also the place for casual breakfasts and lunches. Again there is much use of canned fruits and packeted items, although there are several commercial low-calorie salad dressings. The choice of cheeses (and accompanying crackers) is very poor. The beverage station is also a let-down, for it is no better than those found in the average family outlet ashore in the United States. In addition, a poolside grill provides basic American hamburgers and hot dogs.

Passengers will need to eat in the Lido Cafe on days when the dining room is closed for lunch (typically once or twice per cruise, depending on the ship's itinerary).

ENTERTAINMENT. The Vermeer Showlounge spans two decks, with banquette seating on both main and upper levels. It is basically a well designed room, but the ceiling is low and the sightlines from the balcony level are poor.

While Holland America Line is not known for its fine entertainment (the budgets aren't high enough), what the line does offer is a consistently good, tried and tested array of cabaret acts that constantly rove the cruise ship circuit. The production shows, however, while a good attempt, fall short on storyline, choreography and performance, with colorful costuming and lighting hiding the weak spots.

A number of bands, a string ensemble and solo musicians present live music in many lounges and bars. There's dancing in the Crow's Nest (by day an observation lounge), and serenading string music in the Explorer's Lounge and dining room.

SPA/FITNESS. The Greenhouse Spa is one deck below the navigation bridge at the very forward part of the ship. It includes a gymnasium with ocean views, an aerobics exercise area, large beauty salon with ocean-view windows to the port side, several treatment rooms, and men's and women's sauna, steam room and changing areas. The spa is operated by Steiner, a specialist concession.

● **For more extensive general information on what a Holland America Line cruise is like, see pages 118–122.**

Saga Rose
★★★★

Mid-Size Ship: . . . . .24,474 tons	Passenger Decks: 7	Cabins (for one person): 60
Lifestyle: . . . . .Premium	Total Crew: 350	Cabins (with private balcony): 26
Cruise Line: . . . . .Saga Cruises	Passengers	Cabins (wheelchair accessible): 8
Former Names: . . . .*Gripsholm, Sagafjord*	(lower beds/all berths): 584/620	Cabin Current: . . . . .110 volts
Builder: . . . . . . .Forges et Chantiers de la	Passenger Space Ratio	Elevators: 4
Mediteranee (France)	(lower beds/all berths): 40.8/39.4	Casino (gaming tables): . . . . .No
Original Cost: . . . .$30 million	Crew/Passenger Ratio	Slot Machines: . . . . .No
Entered Service: . . . . .Oct 1965/May 1997	(lower beds/all berths): 1.6/1.7	Swimming Pools (outdoors): 1
Registry: . . . . .The Bahamas	Navigation Officers: . . . . .British	Swimming Pools (indoors): 1
Length (Ft/m): 619.6/188.88	Cabins (total): 322	Whirlpools: 0
Beam (ft/m): 80.3/24.49	Size Range (sq ft/m): 96.8–468.0/	Self-Service Launderette: . . . . .Yes
Draft (ft/m): 27.0/8.25	9.0–43.5	Dedicated Cinema/Seats: Yes/181
Propulsion/Propellers: . . . . .diesel	Cabins (outside view): 290	Library: . . . . .Yes
(20,150kW)/2	Cabins (interior/no view): 32	Classification Society: Det Norske Veritas

OVERALL SCORE: 1,423 (OUT OF A POSSIBLE 2,000 POINTS)

OVERVIEW. Despite the ship's age, *Saga Rose* is still a finely proportioned, traditional cruise ship, and presents a sweeping profile and line of sheer, with clean, delightfully rounded lines, a royal blue hull and a well-placed buff-colored funnel amidships. This ship has classic liner styling and profile, and really does look like a ship. Like an aging Bentley, it will hopefully not go out of style. In fine maritime tradition, the ship's bell and whistle are sounded at noon each day. There is a wrap-around teakwood promenade deck outdoors, and thick pads for all deck lounge chairs. The ship has expansive open deck and sunbathing areas, and lots of nooks and crannies for privacy.

This classic vessel, built in the mid-1960s for long-distance cruising, provides a traditional cruise experience for discriminating passengers over 50 (note that those younger than 50 are not accepted as passengers). Constructed to a high standard (the French shipyard that built it went bankrupt as a result of the losses incurred), this ship has been quite well maintained and is operated with pride by the present owners, who have spent considerable sums of money in restoring it to fine condition.

The interiors of *Saga Rose* are quite dark (restful) and somber in places (particularly the accommodation hallways). But they are spacious, with high-ceilinged public rooms and tasteful decor (although there are, perhaps, too many low-back chairs). There are fine quality furnishings and fittings, including hardwoods, brass and stainless steel. In fact, it is quite difficult to find any plastic in the interior fittings, except for the laminates used to line the walls of the accommodation areas. The elevator does not go down as far as the indoor pool deck ("C" Deck).

BERLITZ'S RATINGS

	Possible	Achieved
Ship	500	362
Accommodation	200	152
Food	400	280
Service	400	274
Entertainment	100	81
Cruise	400	274

Public room facilities include a real ballroom/main lounge – among the nicest afloat for proper cocktail parties (where you stand and mingle, rather than sit), with furniture that can be moved for almost any configuration, and a large wood dance floor.

Other facilities include an indoor swimming pool (and adjacent fitness center) as well as an outdoor pool, lots of recreational space and delightful little nooks and crannies outdoors. The Britannia Lounge (observation lounge) is a fine room for social activities (or a spot of quiet reading), while the adjacent North Cape Bar provides a good bar and hangout for the cocktail crowd. The ship also has a delightful piano bar/lounge (Shakespeare's), a real, large traditional cinema (good for lectures as well as films), a nightclub, computer-learning center (in what used to be the upper level of the nightclub), and a good library.

Saga Rose fits like an old shoe made from fine materials, and most passengers find it so comfortable that they don't want to discard it. A voyage aboard this ship should prove to be a most pleasurable travel experience.

This is classic cruising for its mainly British passengers (the ship is based at Dover and Southampton), under the banner of Saga Cruises. *Saga Rose* is a gracious old lady, now in her late thirties. Although the ship looks a little tired in places, it continues to offer passengers the chance to cruise in comfortable surroundings of high quality, with roaming worldwide itineraries, and service that is friendly and unobtrusive. Saga Cruises includes many things that other UK-based cruise operators charge extra for. Transfers to the ship, port taxes, insurance and all gratuities are included, shuttle buses are provided in ports of call (where possible), and newspapers are provided in the library in each port of call (subject to availability). If you pay for your onboard expenses with a Saga Visa Card you get a 5% discount. The onboard currency is the UK pound.

SUITABLE FOR: *Saga Rose* is best suited to couples and single travelers over 50 who seek a holiday afloat in a very traditional ship setting that is unpretentious, yet provides a decent standard of accommodation, food and friendly service, as well as interesting itineraries and destinations, with fellow passengers likely to be almost all English.

ACCOMMODATION. There are 22 different grades, the price depending on location, size and grade: 3 designated as suites, 10 outside-view grades and 2 interior (no view) cabins (7 grades are designated for single occupancy, including one with a private balcony). Several cabins have interconnecting doors (useful for couples who, for whatever reason, like to have more space, and a bathroom each), and some have views obstructed by lifeboats.

No matter what grade you choose, all cabins have been refurbished, and have fine quality fittings and appointments, and excellent insulation. There are also many single cabins (useful for passengers who enjoy the privacy of their own space without having to share with someone else). There is a generous amount of drawer, under-bed storage and illuminated closet space, and all cabins have European duvets, and a small personal lockbox. All bathrooms have a combination tub/shower. The service provided by the cabin stewards and stewardesses is good. Soft, 100% cotton bathrobes and towels are provided, as well as several personal toiletry items: shampoo/conditioner, body lotion, bath gel, shower cap and soap.

Those who choose a cabin with a private balcony will find a teak decked balcony, with see-through railings, enough space for two deck lounge chairs and table, and an outside light. The cabin voltage is 110 volts, so do take an adapter if you have a 220-volt electrical appliance (such as a hairdryer). There are few balcony cabins. Access to some of the upper grade cabins is a little disjointed.

CUISINE/DINING. The dining room is superb in the classic sense. It has a central ceiling two decks high (with three beautiful, large crystal chandeliers), with large ocean-view picture windows on the port and starboard sides and a horseshoe-shaped grand staircase at the forward end. There is one-seating dining at assigned tables – this is refreshing,

when so many of today's cruise ships have two seatings – with tables for two (there are lots of these), four, six, eight or 10. The chinaware is Royal Doulton, while the flatware is also of a good quality.

The cuisine is quite creative, with a good variety of menu choices, and good-quality ingredients (diabetic, gluten-free and vegetarian alternatives are always available). The entrées are generally well presented, pastries and dessert items are of a good standard, and there is a reasonable choice of cheeses and fruits. There is a fairly comprehensive wine list, and the prices are very modest. Generally, the service is good, in the style of a grand hotel, from thoughtful and attentive waiters.

For casual meals, the Lido Cafe is available as a serve-yourself venue for breakfast and luncheon, and the outdoors aft of the cafe is expansive and very useful for al fresco dining. Several special theme buffets are provided for each cruise. cruise. While there is some repetition of breakfast items, other meals offer a wide variety of hot and cold food items.

ENTERTAINMENT. The Ballroom is the venue for all production shows, major cabaret acts, social functions, and, yes, dancing. The room was not designed as a showlounge, but as a ballroom, and, as such, it has a large properly sprung hardwood dance floor.

During the past two years, the colorful and intelligent British production shows were very well received by passengers. Since January 2003, however, new shows have been introduced by a different (American) company. String quartets and other classical concerts are much appreciated by passengers (especially delicious are the themed afternoon tea concerts: Chocolate, English, and Viennese).

SPA/FITNESS. The Spa and fitness facilities are located towards the bottom of the ship, on "C" Deck, where there is also an indoor swimming pool (aquacise classes are held here), gymnasium with a good range of muscle-pumping and body toning equipment, treadmills and exercycles; and men's and women's sauna and changing rooms with showers, and treatment rooms. A beauty salon is located in another area, on Main Deck.

The spa treatments and beauty services are staffed and operated by Harding Brothers, a concession whose staff also run the fitness and aerobics classes. Spa treatments offered include several types of massage, aromatherapy facials, seaweed body wraps, and hair beautifying services.

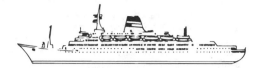

Saga Ruby
NOT YET RATED

Mid-Size Ship: . . . . .24,492 tons	Passenger Decks: 9	Cabins (for one person): 70
Lifestyle: . . . . .Premium	Total Crew: 380	Cabins (with private balcony): 25
Cruise Line: . . . . .Saga Cruises	Passengers	Cabins (wheelchair accessible): 4
Former Names: . . . . . . .Caronia, Vistafjord	(lower beds/all berths): 655/655	Cabin Current: . . . . .110 volts
Builder: . . . . .Swan, Hunter (UK)	Passenger Space Ratio	Elevators: 6
Original Cost: . . . .$35 million	(lower beds/all berths): . . . . . .37.3/37..3	Casino (gaming tables): . . . . .No
Entered Service: . . . . .May 1973/	Crew/Passenger Ratio	Slot Machines: .No
	March 2005	(lower beds/all berths): 1.7/1.7	Swimming Pools (outdoors): 1
Registry: . . . . .Great Britain	Navigation Officers: . . . . .British	Swimming Pools (indoors): 1
Length (ft/m): 626.9/191.09	Cabins (total): 376	Whirlpools: 2
Beam (ft/m): 82.1/25.05	Size Range (sq ft/m): 66.7–871.9/	Self-Service Launderette: . . . . .Yes
Draft (ft/m): 27.0/8.23	6.2–81.0	Dedicated Cinema/Seats: Yes/190
Propulsion/Propellers: . . . . .diesel	Cabins (outside view): 324	Library: . . . . .Yes
(17,900kW)/2	Cabins (interior/no view): 52	Classification Society: . . .Lloyd's Register

---

OVERALL SCORE: NYR (OUT OF A POSSIBLE 2,000 POINTS)

OVERVIEW. *Saga Ruby* has classic liner styling and profile, and really does look like a traditional ship. It is finely proportioned, with delightful, rounded, flowing lines, a sleek profile with a good line of sheer, and a large, buff-colored funnel amidships. The royal blue hull shows off strong, balanced lines, while the profile is further balanced by the buff-colored funnel amidships. The ship was built with excellent quality materials, has been well maintained, is smooth and quiet in operation, and is a stable ship at sea (due to its deep draft). Each day, the ship's bell is sounded at noon in accordance with maritime tradition. As the former *Caronia,* the ship finished its service under Cunard Line, and was taken over by Saga Cruises in 2004. Following an extensive refit in 2004–5, it became *Saga Ruby.*

The open decks and sunbathing space are expansive. There is a teak wrap-around promenade deck outdoors, and deck lounge chairs have cushioned pads (ideal for resting, relaxation, and for reading a good book).

Inside, the spacious and elegant public rooms – mostly located on one deck (Veranda Deck) – have high ceilings and tasteful decor, and wide interior stairwells are subtly illuminated. The Britannia Lounge is at the front of this deck; behind it the Globe Theater, Card Room, Ballroom (show lounge) and the Lido Cafe. There's also a fine library, a computer learning center (The Academy), and separate internet-connect center. Few ships this size can match the relaxing ambience and gracious service from a well-organized, friendly and happy mix of European and Filipino service staff. There are refreshingly few announcements and interruptions.

This ship will provide a refined, user-friendly environ-

BERLITZ'S RATINGS

	Possible	Achieved
Ship	500	NYR
Accommodation	200	NYR
Food	400	NYR
Service	400	NYR
Entertainment	100	NYR
Cruise	400	NYR

ment with a wide range of public rooms for adults (the ship is child-free). Dance hosts are provided for the many single women who travel in the comfortable environment of a cruise ship. Although not shiny and new, the ship has been well cared for, and provides an excellent setting for a pleasant, gracious and civilized travel experience. Saga Cruises includes many things that other UK-based cruise operators charge extra for: transfers to the ship, all gratuities, shuttle buses in ports of call (where possible), and newspapers in the library in each port of call (subject to availability). The onboard currency is the British pound.

SUITABLE FOR: *Saga Ruby* is best suited to couples and single travelers over 50 who seek a holiday afloat in a very traditional ship setting that is unpretentious, yet provides a decent standard of accommodation, food and friendly service, as well as interesting itineraries and destinations, with fellow passengers likely to be almost all English, in a setting that doesn't try to compete with today's warehouse-sized new ships.

ACCOMMODATION. The brochure lists 21 cabin categories (7 of which are for single travelers wanting a cabin for themselves), from duplex penthouse suites with huge private balconies, to small interior (no view) cabins, in a wide range of different configurations.

The grandest living spaces are in two duplex apartments (Saga Suite and Vista Suite). They are superb living spaces and occupy two levels. The lower level has a large bedroom and marble-clad bathroom with Jacuzzi bathtub. The upper level has an expansive living room with floor-to-ceiling windows with unobstructed front and side views, a Bang & Olufsen sound system, treadmill, private bar, and a large bathroom (with Jacuzzi bathtub) and separate private sauna. There is a huge, very private balcony outdoors on deck, complete with a two-person hot tub, a teak deck, and great views. A private internal stairway connects the upper and lower levels.

Most other cabins designated as suites (on Bridge Deck lower level, and Sun Deck) have private balconies, are nicely equipped, and have ample closet and drawer space (some also have a large walk-in closet), vanity desk, large beds, and bookshelves filled with suitable destination books. The marble-clad bathrooms are large and have a full-sized Jacuzzi bathtub, two washbasins, toilet and bidet.

All other cabins are tastefully decorated, and all have a refrigerator, mini-bar, personal safe, European duvets (in two thicknesses), a range of Molton Brown personal toiletries, and thick 100% cotton bathrobes. The wooden cabinetry has nicely rounded edges. Bathrooms have a whisper-quiet (gentle, non-vacuum) toilet.

This ship has an excellent range of cabins for single travelers (unlike almost all new cruise ships). Some Sun Deck and Promenade Deck suites have obstructed views. While the smallest cabins really are quite small, they are well equipped. All suites and cabins have a flat-screen TV and DVD player unit.

CUISINE/DINING. Although it lacks the grandeur, high ceiling or grand stairway of sister ship *Saga Rose*, the Saga Dining Room is elegant, and single-seating dining at assigned tables is featured (this is refreshing, when so many of today's cruise ships have two seatings). There are tables for two, four, six or eight (there are more tables for two than aboard many other cruise ships). Senior officers often host tables for dinner (always on formal nights). Single-waiter service is provided as in the European tradition. Some tables are a little close together, however, making it hard for waiters to serve properly in some areas.

A wide range of menu items is provided (including many British favorites), with a reasonably high standard of quality and variety. A cold table is set for such things as breads and cheeses at lunchtime, and passengers can help themselves or be served. Salad items, many salad dressings, juices, and a selection of international cheeses are always available. Plate service (where vegetables and entrées are set on the main course plate) is provided. Extra vegetables can be obtained on request. This is service in the classic seagoing tradition.

There is always a good selection of cakes and pastry items (and scones, of course) for afternoon tea. Vegetarian items and diabetic desserts are always available and other special dietary items can be provided with sufficient notice. The wine list has a good selection, with prices that reflect excellent value for money. Free cappuccino and espresso coffees are available at any time in the Lido Cafe.

Alternative (Reservations Required) Dining: View is a delightful à la carte restaurant (an alternative no-smoking dining spot located above the nightclub) that is elegant and very intimate, and the cuisine is excellent, from a varied menu. It has the feel of a small, exclusive bistro. Reservations are required, but there is no extra charge.

Casual Eatery: The Lido Café, greatly expanded in the 2004–5 refit, is a well laid out casual dining area with a range of self-service buffets for breakfast, lunch and dinner. While there is some repetition of breakfast items, other meals offer a wide variety of hot and cold food items. A self-serve tea/coffee/beverage station is available 24 hours a day; a machine provides espresso and cappuccino at no extra cost (so many ships now charge extra for these items).

ENTERTAINMENT. The Ballroom is the main venue for entertainment, revue shows, cabaret acts, lectures, and social functions such as the Captain's Cocktail Party. It is among the nicest such rooms afloat for proper cocktail parties (where you stand and mingle, rather than sit), with furniture that can be moved for almost any configuration, and a large real wood dance floor. The port and starboard side seating sections are raised, and sight lines are generally good from most seats. The ship has conservative, reasonably sophisticated, classically oriented entertainment. A resident troupe of singers and dancers presents mini-revue shows.

Most of the other entertainment consists of cabaret acts (such as vocalists, magicians, ventriloquists, comedy jugglers and others), and there is a large floor for social dancing, an important feature for many passengers. A number of bands and musical units provide ample live music for dancing or listening throughout the various lounges and bars. Each evening, the Piccadilly Club, which overlooks the ship's outdoor swimming pool at the aft end of the ship, becomes the late-night spot.

SPA/FITNESS. These facilities are towards the bottom of the ship, on "C" Deck, where there is also an indoor pool, gymnasium, men's and women's sauna and changing rooms with adjacent shower enclosures.

The spa treatments and beauty services are staffed and operated by Harding Brothers, a concession whose staff also run the fitness and aerobics classes. Spa treatments offered include several types of massage, aromatherapy facials, seaweed body wraps, and hair beautifying services.

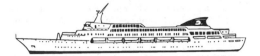

Sapphire
★★ +

Small Ship: ....12,183 tons	Passenger Decks: 8	Cabins (with private balcony): 0
Lifestyle: ....Standard	Total Crew: 250	Cabins (wheelchair accessible): 0
Cruise Line: ....Louis Cruise Lines	Passengers	Cabin Current: ....110 volts
Former Names: ......Princesa Oceanica,	(lower beds/all berths): 576/650	Elevators: 5
Sea Prince V, Sea Prince, Ocean	Passenger Space Ratio	Casino (gaming tables): ....Yes
Princess, Princess Italia, Italia	(lower beds/all berths): 21.1/18.7	Slot Machines: ....Yes
Builder: ...Cantieri Navale Felszegi (Italy)	Crew/Passenger Ratio	Swimming Pools (outdoors): 1
Original Cost: ....n/a	(lower beds/all berths): 2.3/2.6	Swimming Pools (indoors): 0
Entered Service: .....Aug 1967/Apr 1996	Navigation Officers: ....Greek	Whirlpools: 0
Registry: ....Cyprus	Cabins (total): 288	Self-Service Launderette: ....No
Length (ft/m): 491.7/149.8	Size Range (sq ft/m): 75.3–226.0/	Dedicated Cinema/Seats: Yes/170
Beam (ft/m): 70.9/21.5	7.0–21.0	Library: ....Yes
Draft (ft/m): 21.6/6.6	Cabins (outside view): 149	Classification Society: ...Registro Navale
Propulsion/Propellers: ....diesel	Cabins (interior/no view): 139	Italiano (RINA)
(11,050kW)/2	Cabins (for one person): 0	

OVERALL SCORE: 1,036 (OUT OF A POSSIBLE 2,000 POINTS)

OVERVIEW. *Sapphire* has had many previous names and owners, and an interesting life. In 1993, the ship sank in the Amazon River before being bought by its present owners and refitted. It has long, low-slung, handsome lines and a swept-back aft-placed funnel – all of which combine to provide a very attractive profile for this small ship. Louis Cruise Lines purchased the ship in 1995 and, following an extensive refurbishment, placed it into service in 1996. Since it took over the ship, the company has lavished much care and attention in keeping it in good condition.

There is a good amount of open deck and sunbathing space, but the heated swimming pool is very small, and is really only a "dip" pool.

Inside, the contemporary interior decor is fairly smart. There is a mix of attractive colors, together with much use of mirrored surfaces, which help to give the public rooms a feeling of spaciousness and warmth. Most public rooms do have a low ceiling height, however. Harry's Bar is the most popular gathering place, although there are few seats (the gaming tables are adjacent). Other public rooms include the Marco Polo Lounge for evening shows, the Monte Carlo Casino, the Starlight Theater (a cinema with comfortable seating), and a card room and token library.

This ship will take you to some decent destinations (for most of the year it operates 7-day Greek Island and Egypt cruises from Cyprus) in reasonably contemporary surroundings, and in a relaxed, casual, yet comfortable style. The realistic, inexpensive price of this product is a bonus for first-time passengers seeking a cruise aboard a mid-sized ship that is still considered very much a "traditional"

BERLITZ'S RATINGS

	Possible	Achieved
Ship	500	242
Accommodation	200	105
Food	400	204
Service	400	233
Entertainment	100	48
Cruise	400	204

cruise ship rather than one of the floating mega-resorts operated by the major cruise lines. Your fellow travelers are likely to be English-speaking British and Cypriot passengers. Gratuities are added to your onboard account at the rate of £2 per person per day.

The ceilings are quite low throughout the ship, with the exception of a couple of the public rooms. Some cabins are subject to noise from the engines and generators.

SUITABLE FOR: *Sapphire* is best suited to couples and single travelers (not recommended for children) for a first cruise in a comfortable, clubby setting that provides a decent array of public rooms and facilities, and a destination-intensive cruise that provides decent value for money.

ACCOMMODATION. There are five price grades: Premier Outside (the largest), Superior Outside, Standard Outside, Superior Interior (no view), and Standard Interior (no view). The price you pay will depend on the grade, size and location you choose (generally, the higher the deck, the more expensive the accommodation).

The outside-view and interior (no view) cabins are of a reasonable size, and have pleasing, though plain, decor, soft furnishings, and fittings. In almost all cases, the cabin closet and drawer space is very limited. Some cabins (but not many) have a double bed, while most have two beds and many cabins have a third or third and fourth upper berth (good for families with young children).

All cabins have tiled bathrooms, with a shower enclosure, toilet and washbasin, but they are small, and there is little storage space for personal toiletries. There is a 24-hour cabin service menu, although there is only a limited choice of items (and these come at extra cost).

The Premier Outside cabins are the largest, and have two beds, plus a sofa bed, and the bathroom has either a shower or bathtub. Nine out of the 15 Premier Outside grade cabins have a lifeboat-obstructed view (as do two of the Super Outside grade cabins).

CUISINE/DINING. The Four Seasons Restaurant is quite a charming room that has an art deco feel to it, a raised center ceiling, and glass dividers, although the noise level from the waiter stations can be high. There are two seatings. The cuisine is international, but do remember that this is a low-cost cruise, and so you shouldn't expect high-class cuisine. What is provided, however, is surprisingly decent fare that is tasty and well presented. The service from a willing, friendly staff is reasonably attentive. Low-cost vegetarian lunch boxes are available upon request for anyone going ashore on shore excursions. The price of drinks is extremely reasonable, as are wines (but don't expect good vintages, as almost all the wine stock is very young).

For casual breakfasts and luncheons, the Cafe de Paris (located indoors but looking out onto the pool deck) is the place (it also has a bar) to head for (the self-serve breakfast buffets are a little repetitive, however).

ENTERTAINMENT. The Marco Polo Lounge is the venue for all entertainment events and most social functions. It is a single-level room that was designed for cabaret acts rather than "production" shows. The sight lines are fair from the majority of seats, but best from the first few rows closest to the stage. The room also has a hardwood dance floor and social dancing typically takes place after any shows. A resident troupe of dancers provides "openers and closers" for the revue-style shows, where a cabaret act (such as a singer, magician, comedian, or musical specialist) is inserted into the middle "star" spot. This is, however, a small ship operating low-budget cruises, so you should not expect much in the way of quality entertainment.

The ship has a band and a couple of small musical units for live dancing and listening music.

SPA/FITNESS. There are no facilities, with the exception of a small beauty salon, where basic hairdressing and hair beautifying treatments are available.

Sapphire Princess
★★★★

Large (Resort) Ship: . . . . . . .115,875 tons	Passenger Decks: 13	Cabins (with private balcony): 750
Lifestyle: . . . . .Standard	Total Crew: .1,238	Cabins (wheelchair accessible): 28
Cruise Line: . . . . .Princess Cruises	Passengers	(18 outside/10 interior)
Former Names: . . . . .None	(lower beds/all berths): 2,674/3,100	Cabin Current: . . . . .110 volts
Builder: . . . . .Mitsubishi Heavy Industries	Passenger Space Ratio	Elevators: 14
(Japan)	(lower beds/all berths): 43.3/37.3	Casino (gaming tables): . . . . .Yes
Original Cost: . . . .$400 million	Crew/Passenger Ratio	Slot Machines: . . . . .Yes
Entered Service: . . . . .May 2004	(lower beds/all berths): 2.1/2.5	Swimming Pools (outdoors): 4
Registry: . . . . .Bermuda	Navigation Officers: . . . . . .British/Italian	Swimming Pools (indoors): 0
Length (ft/m): 951.4/290.00	Cabins (total): 1,337	Whirlpools: 9
Beam (ft/m): 123.0/37.50	Size Range (sq ft/m): 168–1,329.3/	Self-Service Launderette: . . . . .Yes
Draft (ft/m): 26.4/8.05	15.6–123.5	Dedicated Cinema/Seats: . . . . .No
Propulsion/Propellers: . . . . . .gas turbine	Cabins (outside view): 1,000	Library: . . . . .Yes
(25 MW)/2	Cabins (interior/no view): 337	Classification Society: . . . .Lloyds Register
	Cabins (for one person): 0	

OVERALL SCORE: 1,548 (OUT OF A POSSIBLE 2,000 POINTS)

OVERVIEW. *Sapphire Princess* has an instantly recognizable funnel due to two jet engine-like pods that sit high up on its structure, but really are mainly for decoration. This is the second ship to be constructed by a Japanese shipyard for Princess Cruises (sister ship *Diamond Princess* debuted in 2004). The ship is similar in size and internal layout to *Golden Princess, Grand Princess* and *Star Princess* (although of a slightly greater beam). Unlike its half-sister ships, however, all of which had a "spoiler" (containing a discotheque) located aft of the funnel, this has thankfully been removed from both *Diamond Princess* and *Sapphire Princess*, and has been replaced by a more sensible (and less weighty) aft-facing nightclub/discotheque structure (Skywalkers Nightclub) set around the base of the adjoining the funnel structure. The view from the nightclub overlooks aft-facing cascading decks and children's pool.

In December 2002, while the ship was under construction in the shipyard (as *Diamond Princess*), a fire broke out on Deck 5 and did much damage. The ship's hull was switched with that of identical sister *Sapphire Princess*, which was also under construction in the same yard at the same time.

The actual hull form in *Sapphire Princess* (and sister *Diamond Princess*) is slightly different to that of other "Grand Class" ships, and is slightly wider. Electrical power is provided by a combination of four diesel and one gas turbine (CODAG) unit; the diesel engines are located in the engine room, while the gas turbine unit is located in the ship's funnel housing, on each side of which is a cosmetic pod that resembles a jet aircraft engine. Four areas focus on swim-

BERLITZ'S RATINGS

	Possible	Achieved
Ship	500	435
Accommodation	200	168
Food	400	256
Service	400	293
Entertainment	100	82
Cruise	400	314

ming pools, one of which is two decks high and is covered by a magrodome (retractable glass dome), itself an extension of the funnel housing.

The interiors of the ship are overseen and outfitted by the Okura Group, whose Okura Hotel is one of the best in Tokyo. Fit and finish quality is superior that of the Italian-built *Golden Princess, Grand Princess* and *Star Princess*. Unlike the outside decks, there is plenty of space inside the ship (but there are also plenty of passengers), and a wide array of public rooms to choose from, with many "intimate" (this being a relative word) spaces and places to enjoy. The passenger flow has been well thought out, and works with little congestion. The decor is attractive, with lots of earth tones (well suited to both American and European tastes). In fact, this ship is perhaps the culmination of the best of all that Princess Cruises has to offer from its many years of operating what is now a well-tuned, good-quality product. An extensive collection of art works has been chosen, and this complements the interior design and colors well.

This ship also has a Wedding Chapel. The ship's captain can legally marry (American) couples (a live web-cam can relay ceremonies via the internet), due to the ship's Bermuda registry and a special dispensation (which should be verified when in the planning stage, according to where you reside). Princess Cruises offers three wedding packages – Pearl, Emerald, Diamond. The "Hearts & Minds" chapel is also useful for "renewal of vows" ceremonies.

Gaming lovers should enjoy what is presently one of the largest casinos at sea (Grand Casino), with more than 260 slot machines; there are blackjack, craps and roulette tables, plus newer games such as Let It Ride Bonus, Spanish 21 and Caribbean Draw Progressive. But the highlight could well be the specially linked slot machines that provide a combined payout.

Other features include a library/CD-Rom computer room, and a separate card room. Ship lovers should enjoy the wood-paneled Wheelhouse Bar, finely decorated with memorabilia and ship models tracing part of parent company P&O's history. Aft of the International Dining Room is the Wake View Bar, with a spiral stairway that leads down to a great viewing spot for those who want to watch the ship's wake; it is reached from the back of Club Fusion, on Promenade Deck.

A high-tech hospital is provided, with live SeaMed tele-medicine link-ups with specialists at the Cedars-Sinai Medical Center in Los Angeles available for emergency help.

For youngsters and teenagers there is a two-deck-high playroom, teen room, and a host of specially trained counselors. Children have their own pools, hot tubs, and open deck area at the stern of the ship (away from adult areas). *Sapphire Princess* is a grand playground in which to roam and play when you are not ashore. Princess Cruises delivers a fine, well-packaged holiday product, with some sense of style, at an attractive, highly competitive price, and this ship will appeal to those that really enjoy big city life, with all the trimmings and lots of fellow passengers. The ship is full of revenue centers, however, which are designed to help you part with even more money than you paid for in the price of your cruise ticket (cruise lines have become increasingly shrewd). Expect to be subjected to a stream of flyers advertising daily art auctions, "designer" watches and the like, while "artworks" for auction are strewn throughout the ship.

Whether a cruise aboard this ship really can be considered a relaxing holiday is a moot point, but with so many choices and "small" rooms to enjoy, the ship has been extremely well designed, and the odds are that you'll have a fine cruise holiday, as long as you plan your movements and timing carefully.

The dress code is formal or smart casual (translated by many as jeans and trainers). Gratuities to staff are automatically added to your account, at $10 per person, per day (with gratuities for children charged at the same rate). If you want to pay less, you'll need to go to the reception desk to have these charges adjusted (that could mean lining up with many other passengers wanting to do the same). The onboard currency is the US dollar.

If you are not used to large ships, it will take you some time to find your way around this one, despite the company's claim that this vessel offers passengers a "small ship feel, big ship choice."

Lines tend to form for many things aboard large ships, but particularly so for the purser's (information) office, and for open-seating breakfast and lunch in the four main dining rooms. Long lines for shore excursions and shore tenders are also a fact of life aboard large ships such as this, as is waiting for elevators at peak times, embarkation (an "express check-in" option is available by completing certain documentation 40 days in advance of your cruise) and disembarkation.

You'll have to live with the many extra charge items (such as for ice cream, freshly squeezed orange juice, and activities such as yoga, group exercise bicycling and kick boxing classes (at $10 per session), and $4 per hour for group babysitting services (at the time this book was completed). There's also a charge for using the washers and dryers in the self-service launderettes.

SUITABLE FOR: *Sapphire Princess* is best suited to couples (both young and not so young), families with children and teenagers, and older singles that like to mingle in a large ship setting with pleasing, sophisticated surroundings and lifestyle, reasonably good entertainment and fairly decent food and service, all wrapped up in one package, at an affordable price.

ACCOMMODATION. All passengers receive turndown service and chocolates on pillows each night, bathrobes (on request) and toiletry amenity kits (larger, naturally, for suite/mini-suite occupants) that typically include soap, shampoo, conditioner, and hand/body lotion. A hairdryer is provided in all cabins, sensibly located at the vanity desk unit in the living area. All bathrooms are tiled and have a decent amount of open shelf storage space for toiletries.

You should note that the majority of the outside cabins on Emerald Deck have views obstructed by the lifeboats. Sadly, there are no cabins for singles. Your name is typically placed outside your suite or cabin – making it simple for delivery service personnel but also eroding your privacy. There is 24-hour room service (some items on the room service menu are not, however, available during early morning hours). Most of the balcony suites and cabins can be overlooked both from the navigation bridge wing. Cabins with balconies on Baja, Caribe, and Dolphin decks are also overlooked by passengers on balconies on the deck above; they are, therefore, not at all private. Cabin bath towels are small, and drawer space is limited. There are no butlers – even for the top grade suites (which are not really large in comparison to similar suites aboard some other ships). Cabin attendants have too many cabins to look after (typically 20), which does not translate to fine personal service.

CUISINE/DINING. There are several "personal choice" dining options, but all dining rooms are located on one of two decks in the ship's center. There are five principal dining rooms with themed decor and cuisine – smaller than the three dining rooms in the similarly sized *Golden Princess, Grand Princess* and *Star Princess* (actually two dining rooms were halved in size to become four). They are: Sterling Steakhouse (for steak and grilled meats), Vivaldi (Italian fare), Santa Fe (southwestern USA cuisine) and Pacific Moon (Asian cuisine) and International (the largest, located aft with two seatings and "traditional" cuisine). These offer a mix of two seatings (seating is assigned according to the location of your cabin) or "anytime dining" (where you choose when and with whom you want to eat). All dining rooms are non-smoking and are split into sections in a non-symmetrical design that breaks what are quite large spaces into many smaller sections, for better ambience and less noise pollution. Specially designed dinnerware and good quality linens and silverware are used: Dudson of England (dinnerware), Frette Egyptian cotton table linens, and silverware by Hepp of Germany. Note that 15% is added to all beverage bills, including wines.

Alternative Dining Option: Trattoria Sabatini is an informal eatery (reservations required; cover charge $20 per person). It offers an eight-course meal, including Italian-style pizzas and pastas, with a variety of sauces, as well as Italian-style entrées including tiger prawns and lobster tailThe cuisine in this eatery is potentially better than in all the other dining rooms (better quality ingredients and more attention to presentation and taste, all delivered with more flair).

A poolside hamburger grill and pizza bar (no additional charge) are additional dining spots for casual bites, while extra charges will apply if you order items to eat at either the coffee bar/patisserie, or the caviar/champagne bar. Other casual meals can be taken in the Horizon Court, which is open 24 hours a day, with large ocean-view on port and starboard sides and direct access to the two principal swimming pools and lido deck (there is no finesse in presentation, however, as plastic plates are provided).

ENTERTAINMENT. The Princess Theatre (show lounge) spans two decks and has comfortable seating on both main and balcony levels. It has $3 million in sound and light equipment, plus a 9-piece orchestra, and a scenery loading bay that connects directly from stage to a hull door for direct transfer to the dockside.

For entertainment, Princess Cruises prides itself on its glamorous all-American production shows, and the shows aboard this ship should not disappoint (there are typically two or three shows each 7-day cruise). The ship carries its own resident troupe of singers/dancers and audio-visual support staff.

There is also a second large entertainment lounge, Club Fusion. It features cabaret acts (magicians, comedy jugglers, ventriloquists and others) at night, and lectures, bingo and horse racing during the day. A third entertainment lounge can also host cabaret acts and dance bands. A host of other lounges and bars have live music, and Princess Cruises will have a number of male dance hosts as partners for women traveling alone.

SPA/FITNESS. The Lotus Spa is located forward on Sun Deck – one of the uppermost decks. Separate facilities for men and women include a sauna, steam room, and changing rooms; common facilities include a relaxation/waiting zone, body-pampering treatment rooms, and a gymnasium with packed with the latest high-tech muscle-pumping, cardio-vascular equipment, and great ocean views. Some fitness classes are free, while some incur an extra charge.

The Lotus Spa is operated by Princess Cruises' own in-house department (Princess Cruises was the first of the Big 7 cruise lines to operate its own spa services). You can make online reservations for any spa treatments before your cruise – so you can obtain the time you want, instead of all that frustration often encountered when aboard a ship. The spa features beauty treatment products by the French specialist well-being company Phytomer, and hair products by Carita of Paris.

Seabourn Legend
★★★★★

Boutique Ship: . . . . .9,961 tons	Passenger Decks: 6	Cabins (for one person): 0
Lifestyle: .Luxury	Total Crew: 150	Cabins (with private balcony): 6
Cruise Line: . . . . . . .Seabourn Cruise Line	Passengers	Cabins (wheelchair accessible): 4
Former Names: . . . . .Queen Odyssey,	(lower beds/all berths): 200/200	Cabin Current: . . . . .110 and 220 volts
Royal Viking Queen	Passenger Space Ratio	Elevators: 3
Builder: . . . . . . .Schichau Seebeckwerft	(lower beds/all berths): 49.8/49.8	Casino (gaming tables): . . . . .Yes
(Germany)	Crew/Passenger Ratio	Slot Machines: . . . . .Yes
Original Cost: . . . .$87 million	(lower beds/all berths): 1.3/1.3	Swimming Pools (outdoors): 1
Entered Service: . . . .Mar 1992/July 1996	Navigation Officers: . . . . .Norwegian	Swimming Pools (indoors): 0
Registry: . . . . .Bahamas	Cabins (total): 100	Whirlpools: 3
Length (ft/m): 439.9/134.10	Size Range (sq ft/m): 277.0–575.8/	Self-Service Launderette: . . . . .Yes
Beam (ft/m): 62.9/19.20	25.7–53.5	Dedicated Cinema/Seats: . . . . .No
Draft (ft/m): 16.7/5.10	Cabins (outside view): 100	Library: . . . . .Yes
Propulsion/Propellers: diesel (7,280kW)/2	Cabins (interior/no view): 0	Classification Society: Det Norske Veritas

OVERALL SCORE: 1,786 (OUT OF A POSSIBLE 2,000 POINTS)

OVERVIEW. *Seabourn Legend* is a contemporary ship with a handsome profile, almost identical in looks to *Seabourn Pride* and *Seabourn Spirit*, but younger, and built to a much higher standard, with streamline "decorator" bars (made by Mercedes Benz) located along the side of the upper superstructure and a slightly different swept-over funnel design. The ship has two fine mahogany water taxis for use as shore tenders. There is also an aft water sports platform and marina, which can be used in suitably calm warm-water areas. Water sports facilities include a small, enclosed "dip" pool, sea kayaks, snorkel equipment, windsurfers, water ski boat, and Zodiac inflatable boats. An open-bridge policy exists, so you can visit the ship's navigation bridge at almost any time (except during bad weather or especially tricky maneuvers).

Inside, there is a wide central passageway throughout the accommodation areas. The finest quality interior fixtures, fittings, and fabrics have been combined in its sumptuous public areas to present an outstanding, elegant decor, with warm color combinations (there is no glitz anywhere) and some fine artwork. The dress code, relaxed by day, is more formal at night.

There have been many recent complaints about how the standards aboard the Seabourn ships have gone down, particularly in regard to maintenance (the Seabourn ships are over 10 years old). Food, presentation and service, passengers said, wasn't what it used to be. But the company has turned things around, and I am happy to report that the product delivered is now extremely good, and more consistent (particularly in food and service) than, say, the Silversea Cruises ships, which are larger and carry more people.

BERLITZ'S RATINGS

	Possible	Achieved
Ship	500	461
Accommodation	200	186
Food	400	347
Service	400	353
Entertainment	100	86
Cruise	400	353

Seabourn Legend provides discerning passengers with an outstanding level of personal service and an utterly civilized cruise experience. For a grand, small-ship cruise experience in fine surroundings, with only just over 100 other couples as neighbors, this ship is difficult to beat. All drinks (except premium brands and connoisseur wines) are included, as are gratuities, fine aromatherapy bath selections from Molton Brown and large soaps by Bronnley, Chanel and Hermès, short massages (called "massage moments") on deck, open-seating dining, use of watersports equipment, one free Exclusively Seabourn shore excursion per cruise, and movies under the stars. *Seabourn Legend* can cruise to places where large cruise ships can't, thanks to its ocean-yacht size. DHL provides luggage pick-up and delivery service. Port charges and insurance are not included. The onboard currency is the US dollar.

The three Seabourn ships provide an excellent product, and are superior to other upscale ships such as *Seven Seas Mariner* and *Seven Seas Voyager*, but still not up to the standard of *Europa*'s fine product delivery and hospitality.

The plastic chairs on the open decks really are unacceptable for this type of ship and should be changed to stainless steel or teak. There is no wrap-around promenade deck outdoors. The range of cigars offered is very limited in comparison to ships such as *Europa*. The Club suffers from over-amplified music. Non-American passengers should note that almost all entertainment and activities are geared towards American tastes, despite the increasingly international passenger mix.

SUITABLE FOR: *Seabourn Legend* is best suited to sophisticated, well traveled couples (typically over 50, but possibly younger) who seek a small ship setting (they wouldn't be seen dead aboard today's huge standard resort cruise ships), with excellent food that approaches gourmet standards, and fine European-style service in chic surroundings that border on the elegant and luxurious.

ACCOMMODATION. This is spread over three decks, and there are nine price categories, the price depending on size, grade and location. All suites are comfortably large and very nicely equipped with everything one might need (they are, for example, larger than those aboard the smaller *Sea-Dream I* and *SeaDream II*, but then the ship is also larger, and carries almost twice as many passengers).

All suites have a sleeping area (European duvets are standard, as are Frette linens) and separate lounge area with VCR and television, vanity desk (with hairdyer) and personalized stationery, world atlas, mini-bar and refrigerator (stocked with soft drinks, and two bottles of your favorite liquor when you embark), a large walk-in closet (illuminated automatically when you open the door), electronic personal safe, and wall-mounted clock and barometer. A full passenger list is also provided – a rarity these days – as are a fresh fruit basket (replenished daily) and flowers..

Marble-clad bathrooms have one or two washbasins (depending on the accommodation grade), a decent (but not full-sized) bathtub (four suites have a shower enclosure only – no bathtub), plenty of storage areas, 100% thick cotton towels, plush terrycloth bathrobe, designer soaps and Molton Brown personal amenity items. A selection of five bath preparations by Molton Brown can be ordered from your stewardess, who will prepare your bath for you.

Course-by-course in-cabin dining is available during dinner hours (the cocktail table can be raised to form a dining table); there is 24-hour room service. Also provided are: personalized stationery, and fancy ticket wallet (suitably boxed and nicely packaged before your cruise). Non-smoking cabins are available. Menus for each dinner are delivered to your suite during the day.

In 2001, Seabourn Cruise Line added 36 French balconies to suites on two out of three accommodation decks. These are not balconies in the true sense of the word, but they do have two doors that open wide onto a tiny teakwood balcony that is just 27 cm (about 10.6 inches) wide. The balconies do allow you to have fresh sea air, however, together with some salt spray.

Four Owner's suites (Ibsen/Grieg, each measuring 530 sq. ft/49 sq. meters and Eriksson/Heyerdahl, each 575 sq. ft/53 sq. meters), and two Classic Suites (Queen Maud/Queen Sonja, each 400 sq. ft/37 sq. meters) offer superb, private living spaces. Each has a walk-in closet, second closet, full bathroom plus a guest toilet with washbasin. There is a fully secluded forward- or side-facing balcony, with sun lounge chairs and wooden drinks table (Ibsen/Grieg do not have a balconies). The living area has ample bookshelf space (including a complete edition of *Encyclopaedia Britannica*), large refrigerator/drinks cabinet, television and VCR (plus a second TV set in the bedroom).

All windows, as well as the door to the balcony, have manually operated blackout blinds, and a complete blackout is possible in both bedroom and living room.

CUISINE/DINING. The Restaurant is a part-marble, part-carpeted dining room that has portholes and elegant decor but it is not as warm and intimate as that found aboard the smaller SeaDream ships, with their wood paneling. The silverware (150 gram weight – the best available) is by Robbe & Berking. Open-seating dining means that you can dine when you want, with whom you wish. Course-by-course meals can also be served in your cabin.

Dining is memorable. The menus are nicely balanced, with a wide selection of foods and regional cuisine. Seabourn Cruise Line's fine, creative cuisine is artfully presented, with many items cooked to order. Special orders are available, and caviar is always available on request. Tableside flambeaus are presented, as are flaming desserts cooked at your table. There is always a good selection of exotic fruits and cheeses.

Each day, basic table wine is included for lunch and dinner, but all others (the decent ones) cost extra. The wine list is quite extensive, with prices ranging from moderate to high; many of the wines come from the smaller, more exclusive vineyards. The European dining room staff is hand picked and provides excellent, unhurried service.

In addition, relaxed breakfasts (available until at least 10am – civilized enough for late-risers), lunch buffets and casual candlelight dinners (except on formal nights) can be taken in the popular Veranda Cafe, adjacent to the swimming pool, instead of in the dining room.

ENTERTAINMENT. The King Olaf Lounge is the venue for all entertainment events, including shows, cabaret acts, lectures, and most social functions. It has a sloping floor that provides good sightlines from just about every seat. Because this is a small, upscale ship, the (typically four-person) "production" shows are of limited scope, as dinner is almost always the main event. You can, however, expect to see the occasional cabaret act. Singers also tend to do mini-cabaret performances in The Club (one deck above the showlounge), the gathering place for late-night drinkers.

SPA/FITNESS. A small but well equipped health spa/fitness center, called The Spa at Seabourn, is located just aft of the navigation bridge. The spa complex provides sauna and steam rooms (with separate facilities for men and women) and integral changing room; and a separate exercise room with video tapes for private, individual aerobics workouts; and a beauty salon.

The Spa at Seabourn is staffed and operated by concession Elemis by Steiner. Treatment prices are equal to those in an expensive land-based spa (examples: Elemis Aroma Stone Therapy $178 for 75 minutes). The beauty salon offers hair beautifying treatments and conditioning, while in the gymnasium, personal training sessions, yoga classes, mat Pilates and body composition analysis are available (at extra cost).

Seabourn Pride
★★★★★

Boutique Ship: . . . . .9,975 tons	Total Crew: 150	Cabins (with private balcony): 6
Lifestyle: .Luxury	Passengers	Cabins (wheelchair accessible): 4
Cruise Line: . . . . . .Seabourn Cruise Line	(lower beds/all berths): 200/200	Cabin Current: . . . . .110 and 220 volts
Former Names: . . . . .none	Passenger Space Ratio	Elevators: 3
Builder: . . . . . . .Seebeckwerft (Germany)	(lower beds/all berths): 49.8/49.8	Casino (gaming tables): . . . . .Yes
Original Cost: . . . .$50 million	Crew/Passenger Ratio	Slot Machines: .Yes
Entered Service: . . . . .Dec 1988	(lower beds/all berths): 1.3/1.3	Swimming Pools (outdoors): 1
Registry: . . . . .Bahamas	Navigation Officers: . . . . .Norwegian	(plus 1 aft marina-pool)
Length (ft/m): 439.9/134.10	Cabins (total): .100	Swimming Pools (indoors): 0
Beam (ft/m): 62.9/19.20	Size Range (sq ft/m): 277.0–575.0/	Whirlpools: 3
Draft (ft/m): 16.8/5.15	25.7–53.4	Self-Service Launderette: . . . . .Yes
Propulsion/Propellers: . . . . .diesel	Cabins (outside view): 100	Dedicated Cinema/Seats: . . . . .No
(5,355kW)/2	Cabins (interior/no view): 0	Library: . . . . .Yes
Passenger Decks: 6	Cabins (for one person): 0	Classification Society: Det Norske Veritas

OVERALL SCORE: 1,785 (OUT OF A POSSIBLE 2,000 POINTS)

OVERVIEW. This luxuriously appointed cruise vessel has sleek exterior styling, handsome profile with swept-back, rounded lines, and is an identical sister vessel to *Seabourn Spirit*. It has two fine mahogany water taxis for use as shore tenders. An aft water sports platform and marina can be used in suitably calm warm-water areas. Water sports facilities include a small, enclosed "dip" pool, sea kayaks, snorkel equipment, windsurfers, water ski boat, and Zodiac inflatable boats. An open-bridge policy exists, so you can visit the ship's navigation bridge at almost any time (except during bad weather or especially tricky maneuvers).

There is a wide central passageway throughout the accommodation areas. Inviting, sumptuous public areas have warm colors. Fine quality interior fixtures, fittings, artwork and fabric combine to present an outstanding, elegant decor. For a small ship, there is wide range of public rooms. These include a main lounge (staging small cabaret shows), nightclub (expanded in 1999), an observation lounge with bar, large, deep armchairs, and a cigar smoking area complete with cabinet, cigar humidor and small selection of good cigars. There is a small business center, small meeting room, and a small casino with roulette and blackjack tables, with a few slot machines tucked away.

A small but well-equipped health spa/fitness center has sauna and steam rooms (separate facilities for men and women), and an exercise room, with video tapes for private, individual aerobics workouts, and a beauty salon.

Not for the budget-minded, this ship is for those desiring supremely elegant, stylish, small-ship surroundings, but is perhaps rather small for long voyages in open waters.

During the past two years, there have been many complaints about falling standards aboard the Seabourn ships, particularly with regard to maintenance (they are now over 10 years old), and that food, presentation and service had deteriorated. However, the company has now turned things around, and the product delivered is extremely good.

Seabourn Pride provides discerning passengers with an outstanding level of personal service and an utterly civilized cruise experience. For a grand, small ship cruise experience in fine surroundings, with only just over 100 other couples as neighbors, this ship is difficult to beat. All drinks (except premium brands and connoisseur wines) are included, as are gratuities, fine aromatherapy bath selections from Molton Brown and large soaps by Bronnley, Chanel and Hermès, short massages on deck (called "massage moments"), open-seating dining, use of watersports equipment, one free Exclusively Seabourn shore excursion per cruise, and movies under the stars. *Seabourn Pride* is able to cruise to places where large cruise ships can't, due to its ocean-yacht size. DHL provides luggage pick-up and delivery service. Port charges and insurance are not included. The onboard currency is the US dollar.

In the final analysis, the three Seabourn ships provide an excellent product, and are superior to other upscale ships such as *Seven Seas Mariner* and *Seven Seas Voyager*, but still not up to the standard of *Europa*'s fine product delivery and hospitality.

The deck lounge chairs are plastic (although light and easy to store, they are second-class, and should be made of wood or stainless steel). There is no wrap-around promenade deck outdoors. There are no seat cushions on the wooden chairs at the indoor/outdoor cafe. There is only

BERLITZ'S RATINGS

	Possible	Achieved
Ship	500	460
Accommodation	200	186
Food	400	347
Service	400	353
Entertainment	100	86
Cruise	400	353

one dryer in the self-service launderette. Non-American passengers should note that almost all entertainment and activities are geared towards American tastes, despite the increasingly international passenger mix.

SUITABLE FOR: *Seabourn Pride* is best to sophisticated, well traveled couples (typically over 50, but possible younger) who seek a small ship setting with excellent food that approaches gourmet standards, and fine European-style service in surroundings that can best be described as bordering on the elegant and luxurious.

ACCOMMODATION. This is spread over three decks, and there are nine price categories, the price depending on size, grade and location you choose. The all-outside cabins (called suites in brochure-speak) are comfortably large and beautifully equipped with everything one could reasonably need. Electric blackout blinds are provided for the large windows in addition to curtains. All cabinetry is made of blond woods, with softly rounded edges, and cabin doors are neatly angled away from the passageway.

All the suites have a sleeping area (European duvets are standard, as are Frette linens) and separate lounge area with Bose Wave Radio/CD player, VCR and television, vanity desk (with hairdryer) and personalized stationery, world atlas, mini-bar and refrigerator (stocked with soft drinks, and two bottles of your favorite liquor when you embark), a large walk-in closet (illuminated automatically when you open the door) and wooden hangers, electronic personal safe, umbrella, and wall-mounted clock and barometer. A full passenger list is also provided – a rarity these days – as are a fresh fruit basket (replenished daily) and flowers.

Marble-clad bathrooms have one or two washbasins (depending on the accommodation grade), a decent (but not full-sized) bathtub (four suites have a shower enclosure only – no tub), plenty of storage areas, 100% thick cotton towels, plush terrycloth bathrobe, designer soaps and Molton Brown personal amenity items. A selection of five special bath preparations by Molton Brown can be ordered from your stewardess, who will prepare your bath.

In 2001, Seabourn Cruise Line added 36 French balconies to suites on two out of three accommodation decks. These are not balconies in the true sense of the word, but they do have two doors that open wide, onto a tiny teakwood balcony that is just 27 cm (about 10.6 inches) wide. The balconies allow you to have fresh sea air, however, together with some salt spray.

Course-by-course in-cabin dining is available during dinner hours (the cocktail table can be raised to form a dining table); there is 24-hour room service. Also provided are: personalized stationery, and fancy ticket wallet. Non-smoking cabins are available. Menus for each dinner are delivered to your suite during the day.

Four Owner's suites (King Haakon/King Magnus, each measuring 530 sq. ft/49 sq. meters, and Amundsen/Nansen, each 575 sq. ft/53 sq. meters), and two Classic Suites (King

Harald/King Olav, each 400 sq. ft/ 37 sq. meters) offer superb, private living spaces. Each has a walk-in closet, second closet, full bathroom plus a guest toilet with washbasin. There is a fully secluded forward- or side-facing balcony, with sun lounge chairs and wooden drinks table. The living area has ample bookshelf space (including a complete edition of *Encyclopedia Britannica*), large refrigerator/drinks cabinet, television and VCR (plus a second TV set in the bedroom). All windows, as well as the door to the balcony, have manually operated blackout blinds, and a complete blackout is possible in both bedroom and living room.

CUISINE/DINING. The Restaurant is a part-marble, part-carpeted dining room that has portholes and elegant decor. The silverware (150 gram weight – the best available) is by Robbe & Berking. Open-seating dining means that you can dine when you want, with whom you wish.

The menus are nicely balanced, with a wide selection of foods and regional cuisine. Seabourn Cruise Line's fine, creative cuisine is artfully presented, with many items cooked to order. Special orders are available, and caviar is always available on request. Tableside flambeaus are presented, as are flaming desserts cooked at your table. There is always a good selection of exotic fruits and cheeses.

Each day, basic table wine is included for lunch and dinner, but all others (the decent ones) cost extra. The wine list is quite extensive, with prices ranging from moderate to high; many of the wines come from the smaller, more exclusive vineyards. The hand-picked European dining room staff provides excellent, unhurried service.

In addition, relaxed breakfasts (available until at least 11am) and lunch buffets and casual candlelight dinners (except on formal nights) can be taken in the popular Veranda Cafe adjacent to the swimming pool.

ENTERTAINMENT. The Magellan Lounge is the venue for all entertainment events. It is a room with a sloping floor that provides good sight lines from just about every seat. "Production" shows are of limited scope, as dinner is usually the main event. You can, however, expect to see the occasional cabaret act. Singers also tend to do mini-cabaret performances in The Club (one deck above the showlounge), the gathering place for late-night drinkers.

SPA/FITNESS. A small but well equipped health spa/fitness center, called The Spa at Seabourn, has sauna and steam rooms (with separate facilities for men and women), and a separate exercise room, with video tapes for private, individual aerobics workouts, and a beauty salon.

The spa is staffed and operated by concession Elemis by Steiner. Treatment prices equal those in an expensive land-based spa (examples: Elemis Aroma Stone Therapy $178 for 75 minutes). The beauty salon has hair beautifying treatments and conditioning, while in the gymnasium, personal training sessions, yoga classes, mat Pilates and body composition analysis are available (at extra cost).

Seabourn Spirit
★★★★★

Boutique Ship: . . . . .9,975 tons	Total Crew: 150	Cabins (with private balcony): 6
Lifestyle: .Luxury	Passengers	Cabins (wheelchair accessible): 4
Cruise Line: . . . . . . .Seabourn Cruise Line	(lower beds/all berths): 200/200	Cabin Current: . . . . .110 and 220 volts
Former Names: . . . . .none	Passenger Space Ratio	Elevators: 3
Builder: . . . . . . .Seebeckwerft (Germany)	(lower beds/all berths): 49.8/49.8	Casino (gaming tables): . . . . .Yes
Original Cost: . . . .$50 million	Crew/Passenger Ratio	Slot Machines: . . . . .Yes
Entered Service: . . . . .Nov 1989	(lower beds/all berths): 1.3/1.3	Swimming Pools (outdoors): 1
Registry: . . . . .Bahamas	Navigation Officers: . . . . .Norwegian	(plus aft marina-pool)
Length (ft/m): 439.9/134.10	Cabins (total): 100	Swimming Pools (indoors): 0
Beam (ft/m): 62.9/19.20	Size Range (sq ft/m): 277.0–575.0/	Whirlpools: 3
Draft (ft/m): 16.8/5.15	25.7–53.4	Self-Service Launderette: . . . . .Yes
Propulsion/Propellers: . . . . .diesel	Cabins (outside view): 100	Dedicated Cinema/Seats: . . . . .No
(5,355kW)/2	Cabins (interior/no view): 0	Library: . . . . .Yes
Passenger Decks: 6	Cabins (for one person): 0	Classification Society: Det Norske Veritas

OVERALL SCORE: 1,785 (OUT OF A POSSIBLE 2,000 POINTS)

OVERVIEW. This finely appointed cruise vessel has sleek exterior styling, handsome profile with swept-back, rounded lines, and is an identical sister vessel to *Seabourn Pride*. It has two fine mahogany water taxis for use as shore tenders. An aft water sports platform and marina can be used in suitably calm warm-water areas. Water sports facilities include a small, enclosed "dip" pool, sea kayaks, snorkel equipment, windsurfers, water ski boat, and Zodiac inflatable boats. An open-bridge policy exists, so you can visit the ship's navigation bridge at almost any time (except during bad weather or especially tricky maneuvers).

There is a wide central passageway throughout the accommodation areas. Inviting, sumptuous public areas have warm colors. Fine quality interior fixtures, fittings, fabric and artwork combine to present an outstanding, elegant (but minimalist) decor. For a small ship, there is wide range of public rooms. These include a main lounge (staging small cabaret shows), nightclub (expanded in 1999), an observation lounge with bar, large, deep armchairs, and a cigar smoking area with cabinet, cigar humidor and small selection of good cigars.

There is also a small business center, small meeting room, even a small casino with roulette and blackjack tables, with a few slot machines tucked away.

During the past two years, there have been many complaints about falling standards aboard the Seabourn ships, particularly in regard to maintenance (they are now over 10 years old). Food, presentation and service, passengers said, had deteriorated. However, the company has now turned things around, and the product is extremely good.

Seabourn Spirit provides discerning passengers with an

BERLITZ'S RATINGS

	Possible	Achieved
Ship	500	460
Accommodation	200	186
Food	400	347
Service	400	353
Entertainment	100	86
Cruise	400	353

outstanding level of service and an utterly civilized cruise. For a grand, small ship cruise experience in fine surroundings, with only just over 100 other couples as neighbors, this ship is hard to beat. All drinks (except for premium brands and connoisseur wines) are included, as are gratuities, fine aromatherapy bath selections from Molton Brown and large soaps by Bronnley, Chanel and Hermès, short massages on deck ("massage moments"), open-seating dining, use of watersports equipment, one free Exclusively Seabourn shore excursion per cruise, and movies under the stars. *Seabourn Spirit* is able to cruise to places where large cruise ships can't, due to its ocean-yacht size. Port charges and insurance are not included. The onboard currency is the US dollar.

The three Seabourn ships provide an excellent product, and are superior to other upscale ships such as *Seven Seas Mariner* and *Seven Seas Voyager*, but still not up to the standard of *Europa*'s fine product delivery and hospitality. DHL provides luggage pick-up and delivery service.

The deck lounge chairs are plastic (although light and easy to store, they are second-class, and should be made of wood or stainless steel). There is no wrap-around promenade deck outdoors. There are no seat cushions on the wooden chairs at the indoor/outdoor cafe. There is only one dryer in the self-service launderette. Non-American passengers should note that almost all entertainment and activities are geared towards American tastes, despite the increasingly international passenger mix.

SUITABLE FOR: *Seabourn Spirit* best suits sophisticated couples (mostly over 50, but possibly younger) who seek a small-ship setting with excellent food approaching gourmet standards, and fine European-style service in surroundings best described as bordering on the elegant and luxurious.

ACCOMMODATION. This is spread over three decks, and there are nine price categories, the price depending on size, grade and location you choose. The all-outside cabins (called suites in brochure-speak) are comfortably large and beautifully equipped with everything one could reasonably need. Electric blackout blinds are provided for the large windows in addition to curtains. All cabinetry is made of blond woods, with softly rounded edges, and cabin doors are neatly angled away from the passageway.

The suites are larger than those aboard the smaller *Sea-Dream I* and *SeaDream II*, but then the ship is also larger, and carries almost twice as many passengers. All suites have a sleeping area (European duvets are standard, as are Frette linens) and separate lounge area with Bose Wave Radio/CD player, VCR and television, vanity desk (with hairdryer) and personalized stationery, world atlas, mini-bar and refrigerator (stocked with soft drinks, and two bottles of your favorite liquor when you embark), a large walk-in closet (illuminated automatically when you open the door) and wooden hangers, electronic personal safe, umbrella, and wall-mounted clock and barometer. A full passenger list is also provided – a rarity these days – as are a fresh fruit basket (replenished daily) and flowers.

Marble-clad bathrooms feature one or two washbasins (depending on the accommodation grade), a decent (but not full-sized) bathtub (four suites have a shower enclosure only – no tub), plenty of storage areas, 100% thick cotton towels, plush terrycloth bathrobe, designer soaps and Molton Brown personal amenity items. A selection of five special bath preparations by Molton Brown can be ordered from your stewardess, who will prepare your bath.

Course-by-course in-cabin dining is available during dinner hours (the cocktail table can be raised to form a dining table); there is 24-hour room service. Also provided are: personalized stationery, and fancy ticket wallet (suitably boxed and nicely packaged before your cruise). Non-smoking cabins are available. Menus for each dinner are delivered to your suite during the day.

In 2001, Seabourn Cruise Line added 36 French balconies to suites on two out of three accommodation decks. These are not balconies in the true sense of the word, but they do feature two doors that open wide, onto a tiny teakwood balcony that is just 27 cm (about 10.6 inches) wide. The balconies do allow you to have fresh sea air, however, together with some salt spray.

Four Owner's suites (Bergen/Oslo, each measuring 530 sq. ft/49 sq. meters and Copenhagen/Stockholm, each 575 sq. ft/53 sq. meters), and two Classic Suites (Helsinki/Reykjavik, each 400 sq. ft/37 sq. meters) offer superb, private living spaces. Each has a walk-in closet, second closet, full

bathroom plus a guest toilet with washbasin. There is a fully secluded forward- or side-facing balcony, with sun lounge chairs and wooden drinks table. The living area has ample bookshelf space (including a complete edition of *Encyclopaedia Britannica*), large refrigerator/drinks cabinet, television and VCR (plus a second TV set in the bedroom). All windows, as well as the door to the balcony, have manually operated blackout blinds, and a complete blackout is possible in both bedroom and living room.

CUISINE/DINING. The Restaurant is a part-marble, part-carpeted dining room that has portholes and elegant decor. The silverware (150 gram weight – the best available) is by Robbe & Berking. Open-seating dining means that you can dine when you want, with whom you wish.

The menus are nicely balanced, with a wide selection of foods and regional cuisine. Seabourn Cruise Line's fine, creative cuisine is artfully presented, with many items cooked to order. Special orders are available, and caviar is always available on request. Tableside flambeaus are presented, as are flaming desserts cooked at your table. There is always a good selection of exotic fruits and cheeses.

Basic table wine is included for lunch and dinner, but all others (the decent ones) cost extra. The wine list is quite extensive, with prices ranging from moderate to high; many of the wines come from the smaller, more exclusive vineyards. The hand-picked European dining room staff provides excellent, unhurried service.

In addition, relaxed breakfasts (available until at least 11am), lunch buffets and casual candlelit dinners (except on formal nights) can be taken in the popular Veranda Cafe adjacent to the swimming pool, instead of in the dining room.

ENTERTAINMENT. The Amundsen Lounge is the venue for all entertainment events. It is a room with a sloping floor that provides good sightlines from just about every seat. "Production" shows are of limited scope, as dinner is usually the main event. You can, however, expect to see the occasional cabaret act. Singers also tend to do mini-cabaret performances in The Club (one deck above the show-lounge), the gathering place for late-night drinkers.

SPA/FITNESS. A small but well-equipped health spa/fitness center, called The Spa at Seabourn, has sauna and steam rooms (with separate facilities for men and women), and a separate exercise room, with video tapes for private, individual aerobics workouts, and a beauty salon.

The Spa at Seabourn is staffed and operated by concession Elemis by Steiner. Treatment prices are equal to those in an expensive land-based spa (examples: Elemis Aroma Stone Therapy $178 for 75 minutes). The beauty salon has hair beautifying treatments and conditioning, while in the gymnasium, personal training sessions, yoga classes, mat Pilates and body composition analysis are available (at extra cost).

SeaDream I
★★★★★

Boutique Ship: . . . . .4,253 tons	Total Crew: 89	Cabins (for one person): 0
Lifestyle: . . . . .Utterly Exclusive	Passengers	Cabins (with private balcony): 0
Cruise Line: . . . . . . .Seadream Yacht Club	(lower beds/all berths): 108/108	Cabins (wheelchair accessible): 0
Former Names: . . . . .Seabourn Goddess I,	Passenger Space Ratio	Cabin Current: . . . . .110 and 220 volts
Sea Goddess I	(lower beds/all berths): 39.4/39.4	Elevators: 1
Builder: . . . . .Wartsila (Finland)	Crew/Passenger Ratio	Casino (gaming tables): . . . . .Yes
Entered Service: . . . . .Apr 1984/May 2002	(lower beds/all berths): 1.2/1.2	Slot Machines: . . . . .Yes
Registry: . . . . .The Bahamas	Navigation Officers: . . . . .Norwegian/	Swimming Pools (outdoors): 1
Length (ft/m): 343.8/104.81	Scandinavian	Swimming Pools (indoors): 0
Beam (ft/m): 47.9/14.60	Cabins (total): 54	Whirlpools: 1
Draft (ft/m): 13.6/4.17	Size Range (sq ft/m): 195.0–490.0/	Self-Service Launderette: . . . . .No
Propulsion/Propellers: . . . . .diesel	18.1–45.5	Dedicated Cinema/Seats: . . . . .No
(3,540kW)/2	Cabins (outside view): 54	Library: . . . . .Yes
Passenger Decks: 5	Cabins (interior/no view): 0	Classification Society: . . .Lloyd's Register

OVERALL SCORE: 1,790 (OUT OF A POSSIBLE 2,000 POINTS)

OVERVIEW. This small ship was originally built with money from about 800 investors, and operated under the Norske Cruise banner. It has an ultra-sleek profile, with deep blue hull and white superstructure, and the ambiance of a private club. After the ship was acquired by SeaDream Yacht Club in 2001, it was completely refurbished, with many changes to both public rooms and outdoor areas, and several new features were added to create what is now an extremely contemporary, chic, and desirable vessel.

BERLITZ'S RATINGS		
	Possible	Achieved
Ship	500	441
Accommodation	200	173
Food	400	371
Service	400	370
Entertainment	N/A	N/A
Cruise	500	435

A new "top of the yacht" bar, crafted in warm wood, has been added, as have eight special alcoves equipped with two-person sun loungers with very thick pads (and two equipped for one person); however, there is quite a bit of noise from the adjacent funnel. At the front part of the deck there are more sun loungers and a couple of hammocks, as well as a golf simulator (with a choice of 30 courses). You can sleep under the stars if you wish and cotton sleep suits are provided.

Inside, there is a delightful feeling of unabashed but discreet sophistication. Elegant, chic public rooms have flowers and pot pourri everywhere. The main social gathering places are the lounge, a delightful library/ living room with a selection of 1,200 books, a piano bar, and a casino (two blackjack tables and five slot machines). The library has been enlarged and moved to what was formerly a lounge area, and now provides a very comfortable, warm and cozy setting.

The two SeaDream ships really are the ultimate boutique vessels – like having your own private yacht in which hospitality and anticipation are art forms practiced to a high level. The staff is delightful and accommodating ("no" is not in their vocabulary); if there is anything spe-

cial you want, you have only to ask, and they will be only too happy to oblige. The dress code is resort casual by day (one could almost live in one's bathrobe), informal by night. Oriental rugs are a feature of the lobby. Fine-quality furnishings and fabrics are used throughout, with marble and blond wood accents.

So what type of persons will enjoy the SeaDream Yacht Club experience? Answer: those who enjoy life without dressing up, bingo, discos, or entertainment, and those seeking a totally unstructured lifestyle. It is for experienced, independent travelers who don't like regular cruise ships, large ships, glitzy lounges, a platoon of people and kids running around, or dressing up (no tuxedos or gowns allowed). The *SeaDreams* provide the setting for personal indulgence and refined, unstructured and langorous private living at sea, in a casual setting. One delightful feature of each cruise in warm weather areas is a "caviar in the surf" beach barbecue.

All drinks (with the exception of premium brands and connoisseur wines), sevruga caviar, and gratuities are included, but port charges and insurance are not.

Life could hardly be better at sea – so, as many regular SeaDream Yacht Club passengers say, why bother with ports of call at all? Embarkation never starts before 3pm, in case you are eager to get aboard. These pocket-sized ships would be ideal for charters.

The price of a cruise is just that: the price of a cruise. Air and/or other travel arrangements can be made on your own, or through your own travel agent, or you can use the excellent services of Total Travel Marine (with offices in London and Miami and 24-hour, 365-day service), the agency that specializes in first, business or coach air arrangements as partner to SeaDream Yacht Club. The onboard currency is the US dollar.

These were the first of the mega-yacht-style ships when they were built, and none of the cabins has a private balcony (ships with private balconies made their debut just a couple of years later).

SUITABLE FOR: *SeaDream I* is best suited to sophisticated, independent and well-traveled couples (typically over 40, but possible younger) who seek a small ship setting (they wouldn't be seen dead aboard today's huge standard resort cruise ships), with excellent food that is approaching gourmet standards, and fine European-style service in surroundings that can best be described as bordering on the elegant and luxurious, but trendy.

ACCOMMODATION. There are three types, and five price categories (depending on location, size and grade): Yacht Club (standard) Cabin, Commodore Club Suite, and Owner's Suite.

Yacht Club Cabins: Incorrectly called "suites" in the brochure, the standard cabins are, more correctly, fully equipped "mini-suites" with an outside view through windows or portholes (depending on the deck and price category you choose). Each measures 195 sq. ft (18.1 sq. meters), which is not large by today's cruise ship standards – however, it is large compared to cabins aboard many private motor yachts, and extremely large when compared to ocean-going racing yachts. The sleeping area has twin beds (these can be put together to form a queen-sized configuration); beds are positioned next to the window (or porthole) so that you can entertain in the living area without going past the sleeping area (as you must aboard the slightly larger Seabourn or Silversea ships, for example); a curtain separates the sleeping and lounge areas. All cabinetry and furniture is of thick blond wood, with nicely rounded edges.

A long vanity desk in the sleeping area has a large mirror above it (however, there is no three-sided mirror for women to check the back of their hair) and two small drawers for cosmetic items; there is also a brass clock located on one wall. Note that feng shui advises against placing a mirror opposite your bed, as happens here. In the lounge area, a long desk has six drawers, plus a vertical cupboard unit that houses a sensible safe, refrigerator and drinks cabinet (stocked with your choice of drinks). There is also a 20-inch (51.5-mm) flat-screen television, CD and DVD player, and an MP3 audio player (with a choice of more than 100 selections). The beds have the finest linens, including thick cotton duvets, and non-allergenic pillows (and duvets) are also available. There's little room under the beds for luggage, although this can be taken away and stored for you.

One drawback is the fact that the insulation between cabins is not as good as it could be, although rarely does this present a problem, as most passengers aboard the two SeaDreams are generally extremely quiet, considerate types who are allergic to noise. Incidentally, a sleep suit (pyjama) is supplied in case you want to sleep out on deck under the

stars in one of the on-deck two-person beds – but more of those later.

Since the ship became *SeaDream I*, all bathrooms have been totally refurbished. The old tiling has been discarded and replaced by a new decor that is more hip and trendy, with softer colors and larger (beige) marble tiles. The former (tiny) sit-in bathtubs have been taken out (these will be missed by many regular European passengers) and replaced by a multi-jet power glassed-in shower enclosure. A new washbasin set in a marble-look surround and two glass shelves make up the facilities, while an under-sink cupboard provides further space for larger personal toiletry items. Bulgari personal toiletry amenities are provided. Gorgeously thick, plush, 100% cotton SeaDream-logo bathrobes and towels are also supplied.

However, the bathrooms are small (particularly for those who are of larger than average build), despite their having been completely rebuilt (although the doors still open inward), so space inside really is at a premium. The toilet is located in a rather awkward position, and, unless you close the door, you can see yourself in the mirror facing of the closets, opposite the bathroom door.

Commodore Club Suites: For larger accommodation, choose one of 16 Commodore Club Suites. These consist of two standard cabins with an interconnecting door, thus providing you with a healthy 380 sq. ft (36 sq. meters) of living space. One cabin is made into a lounge and dining room (with table and up to four chairs), while the other becomes your sleeping area. The advantage is that you get two bathrooms (his and hers).

Owner's Suite: For the largest living space aboard this ship, go for the Owner's Suite. This measures a grand 490 sq. ft (45.5 sq. meters). It's the only accommodation with a bathroom that incorporates a real full-sized bathtub; there's also a separate shower enclosure and lots of space for personal toiletries. All passengers receive personalized stationery, a personal email address, a sleep suit, Bulgari personal toiletry amenities, 24-hour room service, and "sweet dreams" chocolates.

CUISINE/DINING. The dining salon is extremely elegant and inviting, and has bird's-eye maple wood paneled walls and wood-accented cafe. It is cozy, yet with plenty of space around each table for fine service, and the ship provides a floating culinary celebration in an open-seating arrangement, so you can dine whenever, and with whomever, you want. A grand piano is located at one end, for quiet dinner music. Course-by-course meals can also be served in your cabin, or out on deck.

Tables can be configured for two, four, six, or eight. They are immaculately laid with settings of real glass base (show) plates, Porsgrund china, pristine white monogrammed table linen, and fresh flowers, while wall sconces house some superb glass ornaments). Candlelit dinners are part of the inviting setting. There is even a box of spare spectacles for menu reading in case you forget your own. You get leather-bound menus, and supremely attentive, close to impeccable personalized European service.

The SeaDream Yacht Club experience really is all about dining. This ship will not disappoint, and culinary excellence prevails. Only the very freshest and finest quality ingredients are used in the best culinary artistry. Fine, unhurried European service is provided.

The ship has exquisite, creative cuisine, and everything is prepared individually to order. Special orders are welcomed, and flaming desserts are showcased at your tableside. You can also dine, course by course in your suite for any meal, at any time (you can also eat à la carte 24 hours a day if you wish). Thankfully, there's never a hint of baked Alaska.

Good-quality table wines are included in the cruise fare for lunch and dinner. Real wine connoisseurs, however, will appreciate the availability of an extra wine list, of special vintages and premier crus (at extra cost). If you want to do something different with a loved one, you can also arrange to dine one evening on the open (but covered) deck, overlooking the swimming pool and stern – it can be a magical and very romantic setting.

A new, informal Topside Restaurant has been created from what used to be the outdoor cafe. Now it has glass sides and a glass roof. Informal dining is the theme here, whether for breakfast, lunch or dinner. Teak tables and chairs add anotherl touch of class. And if you are hungry, no matter at what time of the day or night, you can "raid the pantry" and find something tasty to eat. Additionally, caviar (sevruga malossol) and champagne (Pommery) are always available whenever you want them.

ENTERTAINMENT. There is no evening entertainment as such, other than a duo or solo musician to provide music for listening and dancing in the lounge. Dinner is the main event, and videos are available to take to your cabin.

SPA/FITNESS. The holistic approach to wellbeing plays a big part in relaxation and body pampering aboard *Sea-Dream I*. To this end, a new Asian Spa/Wellness Centre has been created, housed together with a small gymnasium, and beauty salon. There are three massage rooms, a sauna, and steam shower enclosure.

The spa, located in a private area forward on Deck 4, is staffed and operated as a concession by Universal Maritime Services. SeaDream's Signature Massage (a combination of Eastern and Western massage techniques is featured ($150 for 80 minutes). Massage on the beach is featured when the ship operates its famous beach party.

Other types of massages offered include Shiatsu ($110 for 50 minutes), and Swedish Remedial Anti-Stress Massage ($110 for 50 minutes). Body scrubs such as Balinese Salt Glow, Honey Glow Polish, Javanese Lulur, and Papaya Body Polish (all are $190 for 140 minutes of lavish pampering) are also offered.

For the ultimate in "pampership", there's a complete SeaDream Wellness Day (at a cost of $500), or a whole week (a five day programme with treatments of 90 minutes each day, for $700). The spa and wellness centre offerings can also be coordinated with an optional spa cuisine program (at least one of the dishes featured is Oriental, in keeping with the theme of the spa).

Meanwhile, golfers should enjoy the new electronic golf simulator, with a choice of several golf courses to play. For more recreational facilities, note that at the stern is a small, retractable, water sports platform. Equipment carried for sporting types include a water-ski boat, sailboat, two wave runners (jet skis), seven kayaks, wake boards, snorkeling equipment and two Zodiacs. The use of all this equipment is included in the price of your cruise.

The sea conditions have to be just right (minimal swell) for these items to be used, which, on average is once or twice in a 7-night cruise. You may also be allowed to swim off the stern platform if conditions permit. Ten mountain bikes are also carried, so you can pedal away when ashore.

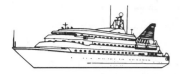

SeaDream II
★★★★★

Boutique Ship:	...........4,333 tons	Total Crew:	89	Cabins (for one person):	0

Boutique Ship: ....4,333 tons
Lifestyle: ....Utterly Exclusive
Cruise Line: ....SeaDream Yacht Club
Former Names: ....Seabourn Goddess II, Sea Goddess II
Builder: ....Wartsila (Finland)
Original Cost: ....$34 million
Entered Service: ....May 1985/Jan 2002
Registry: ....The Bahamas
Length (ft/m): 343.8/104.81
Beam (ft/m): 47.9/14.60
Draft (ft/m): 13.6/4.17
Propulsion/Propellers: diesel (3,540kW)/2
Passenger Decks: 5

Total Crew: 89
Passengers
(lower beds/all berths): 108/108
Passenger Space Ratio
(lower beds/all berths): 39.4/39.4
Crew/Passenger Ratio
(lower beds/all berths): 1.2/1.2
Navigation Officers: ....Norwegian/ Scandinavian
Cabins (total): 58
Size Range (sq ft/m): 195.0–490.0/ 18.1–45.5
Cabins (outside view): 58
Cabins (interior/no view): 0

Cabins (for one person): 0
Cabins (with private balcony): 0
Cabins (wheelchair accessible): 0
Cabin Current: ....110 and 220 volts
Elevators: 1
Casino (gaming tables): ....Yes
Slot Machines: ....Yes
Swimming Pools (outdoors): 1
Swimming Pools (indoors): 0
Whirlpools: 1
Self-Service Launderette: ....No
Dedicated Cinema/Seats: ....No
Library: ....Yes
Classification Society: ...Lloyd's Register

OVERALL SCORE: 1,790 (OUT OF A POSSIBLE 2,000 POINTS)

OVERVIEW. This small ship was originally built with money from about 800 investors, and operated under the Norske Cruise banner. It has an ultra-sleek profile, with deep blue hull and white superstructure, and the ambience of a private club. When it was acquired by SeaDream Yacht Club in 2001, the ship was completely refurbished, with many changes to both public rooms and outdoor areas, and several new features were added to create what is now an extremely contemporary, chic, and desirable ship.

A new "top of the yacht" bar, crafted in warm wood, has been added, as have eight special alcoves equipped with two-person sun loungers with very thick cushioned pads (and two equipped for one person): however there is quite a bit of noise from the adjacent funnel. At the front part of the deck there are more sun loungers and a couple of hammocks, as well as a golf simulator (with a choice of 30 courses). You can sleep under the stars if you wish, and cotton sleep suits are provided.

Inside, there is a delightful feeling of unabashed but discreet sophistication. Elegant, chic public rooms have flowers and pot pourri everywhere. The main social gathering places are the lounge, a delightful library/ living room with a selection of 1,200 books, a piano bar, and a casino (two blackjack tables and five slot machines). The library has been enlarged and moved to what was formerly a lounge area, and now provides a very comfortable, warm and cozy setting (good for afternoon tea or coffee).

The two SeaDream Yacht Club ships really are the ultimate boutique vessels – like having your own private yacht in which hospitality and anticipation are art forms practiced to a high level. The staff is delightful and accommo-

BERLITZ'S RATINGS

	Possible	Achieved
Ship	500	441
Accommodation	200	173
Food	400	371
Service	400	370
Entertainment	N/A	N/A
Cruise	500	435

dating ("no" is not in their vocabulary); if there is anything special you want, you have only to ask, and staff are only too happy to oblige. The dress code is resort casual by day (one could almost live in one's bathrobe), informal (yacht casual) by night (many passengers do like to dress for dinner in the formal dining room). Oriental rugs are a feature of the lobby. Fine-quality furnishings and fabrics are used throughout, with marble and blond wood accents.

Among the ship's toys are several Segway Human Transporters (two-wheel personal riding machines, for which there is a charge), as well as mountain bikes for use in ports of call (no charge).

So what type of persons will enjoy the SeaDream Yacht Club experience? Answer: those who enjoy life without dressing up, bingo, discos, or entertainment, and those seeking a totally unstructured lifestyle, with the attraction of watersports at no extra charge. It is for experienced, independent travelers who don't like regular cruise ships, large ships, glitzy lounges, a platoon of people and kids running around, or dressing up (no tuxedos or gowns allowed, and no tie required). The SeaDreams provide the setting for personal indulgence and refined, unstructured and langorous private living at sea, in a casual setting. One delightful event during each cruise in warm weather areas is a "caviar in the surf" beach barbeque.

All drinks (except for premium brands and connoisseur wines), sevruga caviar and gratuities are included, while port charges and insurance are not included. Life could hardly be better at sea – so, as many regular SeaDream Yacht Club passengers say: why bother with ports of call at all? Embarkation never starts before 3pm, in case you are eager to get aboard. These pocket-sized ships would be ideal for charters.

The price of a cruise is just that: the price of a cruise. Air and/or other travel arrangements can be made on your own, or through your own travel agent, or you can use the excellent services of Total Travel Marine (with offices in London and Miami and 24-hour, 365-day service), the agency that specializes in first, business or coach air arrangements as partner to SeaDream Yacht Club. The onboard currency is the US dollar.

The SeaDream ships were the first of the mega-yacht-style ships when they were built, but none of the cabins has a private balcony (ships with private balconies made their debut just a couple of years later).

SUITABLE FOR: *SeaDream II* is best suited to sophisticated, independent and well-traveled couples (typically over 40, but possibly younger) who seek a small ship setting (they wouldn't be seen dead aboard today's huge standard resort cruise ships), with excellent food approaching gourmet standards, and fine European-style service in surroundings that can best be described as bordering on the elegant and luxurious, but trendy. The ship provides a fine setting for those wanting to de-stress without having to work at it. Not really suitable for children.

ACCOMMODATION. There are three types, and five price categories (price will depend on grade, location and size chosen): Yacht Club (standard) Cabin, Commodore Club Suite, and Owner's Suite.

Yacht Club Cabins: Incorrectly called "suites" in the brochure, the standard cabins are, more correctly, fully equipped "mini-suites" with an outside view through windows or portholes (depending on the deck and price category). Each measures 195 sq. ft (18.1 sq. meters), which is not large by today's cruise ship standards – however, it is large compared to cabins aboard many private motor yachts, and extremely large when compared to ocean-going racing yachts. The sleeping area has twin beds (these can be put together to form a queen-sized configuration; beds are positioned next to the window (or porthole) so that you can entertain in the living area without going past the sleeping area (as you must aboard the slightly larger Seabourn or Silversea ships, for example); a curtain separates the sleeping and lounge areas. All cabinetry and furniture is of thick blond wood, with nicely rounded edges.

A long vanity desk in the sleeping area has a large mirror above it (however, there is no three-sided mirror for women to check the back of their hair) and two small drawers for cosmetic items; there is also a brass clock located on one wall. According to the principles of feng shui, placing a mirror opposite your bed is frowned upon. In the lounge area, a long desk has six drawers, plus a vertical cupboard unit that houses a sensible safe, refrigerator and drinks cabinet (stocked with your choice of drinks). There is also a 20-inch (51.5-mm) flat-screen television, CD and DVD player, and an MP3 audio player (with a choice of over 100 selections). The beds have the finest linens, including thick cotton duvets, and non-allergenic pillows (and duvets) are also available. There's little room under the beds for luggage, although this can be taken away and stored for you.

One drawback is the fact that the insulation between cabins is not as good as it could be, although rarely does this present a problem, as most passengers aboard the two Sea-Dreams are generally extremely quiet, considerate types who are allergic to noise. Incidentally, a sleep suit is supplied in case you want to sleep out on deck under the stars in one of the on-deck two-person beds – but more of those later.

Since the ship became *SeaDream II*, all bathrooms have been totally refurbished. The old tiling has been discarded and replaced by a new decor that is more hip and trendy, with softer colors and larger (beige) marble tiles. The former (tiny) sit-in bathtubs have been taken out (these will be missed by many regular European passengers) and replaced by a multi-jet power glassed-in shower enclosure. A new washbasin set in a marble-look surround and two glass shelves make up the facilities, while an under-sink cupboard provides further space for larger personal toiletry items. Bulgari personal toiletry amenities are provided. Gorgeously thick, plush, 100% cotton SeaDream-logo bathrobes and towels are also supplied.

However, the bathrooms are small (particularly for those who are of larger than average build), despite their having been completely rebuilt (although the doors still open inward), so space inside really is at a premium. The toilet is located in a rather awkward position, and, unless you close the door, you can see yourself in the mirror facing of the closets, opposite the bathroom door.

Commodore Club Suites: For larger accommodation, choose one of 16 Commodore Club Suites. These consist of two standard cabins with an interconnecting door, thus providing you with a healthy 380 sq. ft (36 sq. meters) of living space. One cabin is made into a lounge and dining room (with table and up to four chairs), while the other becomes your sleeping area. The advantage is that you get two bathrooms (his and hers).

Owner's Suite: For the largest living space aboard this ship, go for the Owner's Suite. This measures a grand 490 sq. ft (45.5 sq. meters). It's the only accommodation with a bathroom that incorporates a real full-sized bathtub; there's also a separate shower enclosure and lots of storage space for toiletries.

All passengers receive personalized stationery, personal email address, sleep suit, Bulgari personal toiletry amenities, 24-hour room service, and "sweet dreams" chocolates.

CUISINE/DINING. The dining salon is extremely elegant and inviting, and has bird's-eye maple wood-panelled walls and wood-accented decor. It is cozy, yet with plenty of space around each table for fine service, and the ship provides a floating culinary celebration in an open-seating arrangement, so you can dine whenever, and with whomever you want. Course-by-course meals can also be served in your cabin, or out on deck.

Tables can be configured for two, four, six, or eight. They are immaculately laid with settings of real glass base (show) plates, Porsgrund china, pristine white mono-grammed table linen, and fresh flowers, while wall sconces house some superb glass ornaments). Candlelit dinners are part of the inviting setting. There is even a box of spare spectacles for menu reading in case you forget your own. You get leather-bound menus, and supremely attentive, close to impeccable personalized European service.

The SeaDream Yacht Club experience really is all about dining. This ship will not disappoint, and culinary excellence prevails. Only the very freshest and finest quality ingredients are used in the best culinary artistry. Fine, unhurried European service is provided.

The ship has exquisite, creative cuisine, and everything is prepared individually to order. Special orders are welcomed, and flaming desserts are showcased at your tableside. You can also dine, course by course in your suite for any meal, at any time (you can also eat a la carte 24 hours a day if you wish). And, thankfully, there's never a hint of baked Alaska!

Good-quality table wines are included in the cruise fare for lunch and dinner. Real wine connoisseurs, however, will appreciate the availability of an extra wine list, of special vintages and premier crus (at extra cost). If you want to do something different with a loved one, you can also arrange to dine one evening on the open (but covered) deck, overlooking the swimming pool and stern – it can be a magical and very romantic setting.

A new, informal Topside Restaurant has been created from what used to be the outdoor cafe. Now it has glass sides and a glass roof. Informal dining is the theme here, whether for breakfast, lunch or dinner. Teak tables and chairs add another touch of class. And if you are hungry, no matter at what time of the day or night, you can "raid the pantry" and find something tasty to eat. Additionally, caviar (sevruga malossol) and champagne (Pommery) are always available whenever you want them.

ENTERTAINMENT. There is no evening entertainment as such, other than perhaps a solo musician to provide music for listening and dancing in the lounge. Dinner is the main event of the evening, and videos are available should you want to take one to your cabin.

SPA/FITNESS. The holistic approach to wellbeing plays a big part in relaxation and body pampering aboard *SeaDream II*. To this end, a new Asian Spa/Wellness Centre has been created, housed together with a small gymnasium, and beauty salon. There are three massage/body treatment rooms, a sauna, and small steam shower enclosure. The spa, located in a private area forward on Deck 4, is staffed and operated as a concession by Universal Maritime Services. SeaDream's Signature Massage (a combination of Eastern and Western massage techniques is featured ($150 for 80 minutes). Other types of massages offered include Shiatsu ($110 for 50 minutes), and Swedish Remedial Anti-Stress Massage ($110 for 50 minutes). Massage on the beach is featured when the ship operates its famous beach party.

Body scrubs such as Balinese Salt Glow, Honey Glow Polish, Javanese Lulur, and Papaya Body Polish (all are $190 for 140 minutes of lavish pampering) are also offered. For the ultimate in "pampership", there's a complete SeaDream Wellness Day (at a cost of $500), or a whole week (a five day programme with treatments of 90 minutes each day, for $700). The spa and wellness centre offerings can also be coordinated with an optional spa cuisine program (at least one of the dishes featured is Oriental, in keeping with the theme of the spa).

Meanwhile, golfers should enjoy the new electronic golf simulator, with a choice of several golf courses to play. For more recreational facilities, note that at the stern is a small, retractable, water sports platform. Equipment carried for sporting types include a water-ski boat, sailboat, two wave runners (jet skis), seven kayaks, wake boards, snorkeling equipment and two Zodiacs. The use of all this equipment is included in the price of your cruise. Note, however, the sea conditions have to be just right (minimal swell) for these items to be used, which, on average is once or twice in a 7-night cruise. You may also be allowed to swim off the stern platform if conditions permit. Ten mountain bikes are also carried, so you can pedal away when ashore.

Sea Bird
★★

Boutique Ship: . . . . .99.7 tons	Total Crew: 22	Cabins (with private balcony): 0
Lifestyle: . . . . .Standard	Passengers	Cabins (wheelchair accessible): 0
Cruise Line: . . . . .Lindblad Expeditions	(lower beds/all berths): 70/70	Cabin Current: . . . . .110 volts
Former Names: . . . . . . *Majestic Explorer*	Passenger Space Ratio	Elevators: 0
Builder: . . . . .Whidbey Island	(lower beds/all berths): 1.4/1.4	Casino (gaming tables): . . . . .No
(USA)	Crew/Passenger Ratio	Slot Machines: .No
Original Cost: .n/a	(lower beds/all berths): 3.1/3.1	Swimming Pools (outdoors): 0
Entered Service: 1981	Navigation Officers: . . . . . .Scandinavian	Swimming Pools (indoors): 0
Registry: . . . . .The Bahamas	Cabins (total): .36	Whirlpools: 0
Length (ft/m): 151.9/46.3	Size Range (sq ft/m): 73.0–202.0/	Self-Service Launderette: . . . . .No
Beam (ft/m): 30.8/9.4	6.7–18.7	Dedicated Cinema/Seats: . . . . .No
Draft (ft/m): 8.0/2.4	Cabins (outside view): 36	Library: . . . . .No
Propulsion/Propellers: diesel/2	Cabins (interior/no view): 0	Classification Society: . .American Bureau
Passenger Decks: 4	Cabins (for one person): 2	of Shipping

BERLITZ'S OVERALL SCORE: 938 (OUT OF A POSSIBLE 2,000 POINTS)

OVERVIEW. *Sea Bird* carries a fleet of motorized Zodiac landing craft for use as shore tenders and for up-close shore exploration. A number of sea kayaks are also carried. An open-bridge policy means you can go to the navigation bridge at any time. The vessel is small enough to operate in ports and narrow inlets inaccessible to larger ships. Lecturers and recap sessions are held daily.

This small craft (and sister ship *Sea Lion*) is adequate for looking at nature and wildlife close-up, in modest but comfortable surroundings that provide an alternative to big-ship cruising. Cruises visit Alaska, Baja California and the Sea of Cortes. Tipping is suggested at about $7 per person per day. The onboard currency is the US dollar.

In the cabins, the mattresses are enclosed in a wood frame with sharp corners, which you bang into constantly.

SUITABLE FOR: *Sea Bird* is best suited to older couples and single travelers who enjoy learning about nature, geography, history and other life sciences in casual, non-dressy surroundings without a hint of pretension. They are likely to be hardy, outdoors types who don't need entertainment or silly parlor games.

ACCOMMODATION. All the cabins aboard this little ship have an outside view through picture windows, except for

BERLITZ'S RATINGS		
	Possible	Achieved
Ship	500	182
Accommodation	200	83
Food	400	204
Service	400	212
Entertainment	N/A	N/A
Cruise	500	257

those on the lowest deck, which have portholes. Some cabins have double beds, some have twin beds (they can be pushed together to form a queen-sized bed), and some are for singles (at a surcharge of 150 percent). There is plenty of room to stow your luggage.

All cabins have a private bathroom, although it really is tiny. There is no room service for food or beverages.

CUISINE/DINING. The dining room (non-smoking), which has ocean-view picture windows, is large enough to accommodate all passengers in a single seating. The tables are not assigned, and so you can sit with whom you like. The food is unpretentious, good and wholesome, although its presentation is very plain, with no frills, and features regional specialties. The wine list is very limited, and is comprised mostly of wines from California.

ENTERTAINMENT. There is no formal entertainment, although dinner and after-dinner conversation with fellow passengers in the ship's lounge/bar really becomes the entertainment. So, if you're not in the mood to talk to your fellow passengers, take a good book, or go outside, where you'll find nature provides varied entertainment.

SPA/FITNESS. There are no spa or fitness facilities aboard this very small cruise vessel.

Sea Cloud
★★★★★

Boutique Ship: . . . . .2,532 tons	Sail Area (sq ft/m2): 32,292/3,000	Cabins (outside view): 34
Lifestyle: . . . . .Luxury	Main Propulsion: . . . . .sail power	Cabins (interior/no view): 0
Cruise Line: . . . . .Sea Cloud Cruises	Propulsion/Propellers: diesel (4,476kW)/2	Cabins (for one person): 0
Former Names: . . . . . .Sea Cloud of Grand	Passenger Decks: 3	Cabins (with private balcony): 0
Cayman, IX-99, Antama, Patria,	Total Crew: 60	Cabins (wheelchair accessible): 0
Angelita, Sea Cloud, Hussar	Passengers	Cabin Current: . . . . .220 volts
Builder: . . . . .Krupp Werft (Germany)	(lower beds/all berths): 68/69	Elevators: 0
Entered Service: . . . . Aug 1931/1979	Passenger Space Ratio	Casino (gaming tables): . . . . .No
(restored)	(lower beds/all berths): 37.2/36.6	Slot Machines: . . . . .No
Registry: .Malta	Crew/Passenger Ratio	Swimming Pools (outdoors): 0
Length (ft/m): 359.2/109.5	(lower beds/all berths): 1.1/1.1	Whirlpools: 0
Beam (ft/m): 48.2814.9	Navigation Officers: . . . . .European	Self-Service Launderette: . . . . .No
Draft (ft/m): 16.8/5.13	Cabins (total): 34	Library: . . . . .Yes
Type of Vessel: . . . . .barque	Size Range (sq ft/m): 102.2–409.0/	Classification Society: . . . . .Germanischer
No. of Masts: . . . .4 (17.7 meters)/30 sails	9.5–38.0	Lloyd

OVERALL SCORE: 1,704 (OUT OF A POSSIBLE 2,000 POINTS)

OVERVIEW. *Sea Cloud* is the oldest and most beautiful sailing ship in the world, and the largest private yacht ever built (at three times the size of Captain Cook's *Endeavour*). It is a beautiful, completely authentic 1930s barque whose three masts are almost as high as a 20-story building (the main mast is 178 ft/ 54 meters above the main deck). This was the largest private yacht ever built when completed in 1931 by E.F. Hutton for his wife, Marjorie Merriweather Post, the American cereal heiress. Originally constructed for $1 million as *Hussar* in the Krupp shipyard in Kiel, Germany, this steel-hulled yacht is immensely impressive when in port, but exhilarating when under full sail.

During World War II, the vessel saw action as a weather observation ship, under the code name *IX-99*. You can still see five chevrons on the bridge, one for each half-year of duty, serving as a reminder of those important years.

There is plenty of deck space, even under the vast expanse of white sail, and the promenade deck outdoors still has wonderful varnished sea chests. The decks themselves are made of mahogany and teak, and wooden "steamer"-style deck lounge chairs are provided. One of the most beautiful aspects of sailing aboard this ship is its "Blue Lagoon", located at the very stern of the vessel. Weather permitting, you can lie down on the thick blue padding and gaze up at the stars and night sky – it's one of the great pleasures – particularly when the ship is under sail, with engines turned off.

The original engine room (with diesel engines) is still in operation for the rare occasions when sail power can't be used. An open-bridge policy is the norm (except during

BERLITZ'S RATINGS

	Possible	Achieved
Ship	500	423
Accommodation	200	173
Food	400	348
Service	400	335
Entertainment	N/A	N/A
Cruise	500	425

times of poor weather or navigational maneuvers).

In addition to its retained and refurbished original suites and cabins, some newer, smaller cabins were added in 1979 when a consortium of German yachtsmen and businessmen purchased the ship. The owners spent $7.5 million refurbishing it. The interiors exude warmth, and are finely hand crafted. There is much antique mahogany furniture, fine original oil paintings, gorgeous carved oak paneling, parquet flooring and burnished brass everywhere, as well as some finely detailed ceilings. There is no doubt that Marjorie Merryweather Post was accustomed only to the very finest things in life.

Sea Cloud is, without doubt, the ultimate, most romantic sailing ship afloat. Although there are many imitations, there still is none better than this beautiful vintage vessel. The ship is still kept close to its original state when built. It operates under charter for much of the year, and sails in both the Caribbean and European/Mediterranean waters.

A cruise aboard *Sea Cloud* is, in summary, a truly exhilarating experience. This is really a ship like no other, for the discerning few to relish the uncompromising comfort and elegance of a bygone era. A kind of stately home afloat, *Sea Cloud* remains one of the finest and nicest travel experiences in the world. The activities are few, and so relaxation is the key, in a setting that provides fine service and style, but in an unpretentious way. Note that some staircases are steep, as they are aboard almost all sailing vessels.

The only "dress-up" night is the Captain's Welcome Aboard Dinner, but otherwise, smart casual clothing is all that is needed (no tuxedo). Note that mini-skirts would be impractical due to the steep staircases in some places – trousers are more practical. Also note that a big sailing vessel such as this can heel to one side occasionally (so take flat shoes rather than high heels).

The crew is of mixed nationality, and the sailors who climb the rigging and set the sails include females as well as males. On the last night of the cruise, the sailors' choir sings seafaring songs. Gratuities are suggested at $15 per person, per day, although these can be charged to your account. The US dollar is used as the onboard currency.

The German owner, Sea Cloud Cruises, also operates the rivercruise vessels *River Cloud* and *River Cloud II* for cruising along the rivers of Europe, and, in 2001 introduced a brand new companion sailing ship, *Sea Cloud II*.

Sea Cloud is, for part of each year, under charter to Hapag-Lloyd Cruises. On those occasions, white and red wines and beer are included for lunch and dinner; soft drinks, espresso and cappuccino coffees are also included at any time; shore excursions are an optional extra, as are gratuities. Details may be different for other charter operators (such as Abercrombie & Kent).

Passengers are not permitted to climb the rigging, as may be possible aboard some other tall ships. This is because the mast rigging on this vintage sailing ship is of a very different type to the more modern sailing vessels (such as *Royal Clipper, Star Clipper, Star Flyer*, and *Sea Cloud II*). However, passengers may be able participate occasionally in the furling and unfurling of the sails.

Although now more than 70 years old, *Sea Cloud* is so lovingly maintained and operated that anyone who sails aboard it cannot fail to be impressed and totally absorbed by the character of this beautiful tall ship. If you seek entertainment, casinos, bingo, horse racing and flashy resort cruising, this is not the ship for you. However, if you want to be part of one of the most exclusive communities at sea aboard a ship that is utterly graceful, serene and calming, you will love *Sea Cloud*. The food and service are good, as is the interaction between passengers and crew, many of whom have worked aboard the ship for many, many years. One really important bonus is the fact that the doctor on board is available at no charge for medical emergencies or seasickness medication.

In 2001, the ship suffered a fire while in Rijeka, which put it out of commission for many months. However, all necessary repairs have been painstakingly made and it is now in its beautiful original condition again.

Rigging: For the sailors among you, the sails are (in order, from fore to aft mast, top to bottom):
Fore Mast: flying jib, outer jib, inner jib, fore topmast staysail, fore royal, fore topgallant, fore upper-top sail, fore lower-top sail, foresail.
Main Mast: main royal staysail, main topgallant staysail, main topmast staysail, skysail, main royal, main topgallant, main upper topsail, main lower topsail, main sail.
Mizzen Mast: mizzen royal staysail, mizzen topgallant staysail, mizzen topmast staysail, mizzen royal topsail, mizzen topgallant, mizzen upper topsail, mizzen lower topsail, mizzen course.

Spanker Mast: spanker top mast staysail, spanker staysail, spanker-gaff topsail, spanker.

SUITABLE FOR: *Sea Cloud* is best suited to couples and singles (not children) who would probably never consider a "normal" cruise ship, but who enjoy sailing aboard a real tall ship but want the experience wrapped in a package that includes accommodation, good food, like-minded companions, interesting destinations, and don't want the bother of owning or chartering their own mega-yacht.

ACCOMMODATION. Because *Sea Cloud* was built as a private yacht, there is a wide variation in cabin sizes and configurations. Some cabins have double beds, while some have twin beds (side by side or in an L-shaped configuration) that are fixed and cannot be placed together. Many of the original cabins have a fireplace (now with an electric fire).

All of the accommodation is very comfortable, but those on Main Deck (Cabins 1–8) were part of the original accommodation aboard this ship. Of these, the two owner's suites (Cabins 1 and 2) are really opulent, and feature real, original Chippendale furniture, fine gilt detailing, a real fireplace, French canopy bed, and large Italian Carrara marble bathrooms with gold fittings.

The Owner's Cabin Number 1 is decorated in white throughout, and has a fireplace and Louis Phillippe chairs. Owner's Cabin Number 2, completely paneled in rich woods, retains the mahogany secretary used 60 years ago by Edward F. Hutton (Marjorie Post's husband).

Other cabins (both the original ones, and some newer additions) are beautifully furnished (all were refurbished in 1993) and are surprisingly large for the size of the ship. There is a good amount of closet and drawer space and all cabins have a personal safe and telephone. The cabin bathrooms, too, are quite luxurious, and equipped with everything you will need, including bathrobes and hairdryer, and an assortment of toiletries (there is a 110-volt AC shaver socket in each bathroom). The "new" cabins are rather small for two persons, so it's best to take minimal luggage.

There is no cabin food or beverage service. Also, if you occupy one of the original cabins on Main Deck you may be subjected to some noise when the motorized capstans are used to raise and lower or trim the sails. On one day each cruise, an "open-house" cocktail party is held on the Main Deck, with all cabins available for passengers to see.

CUISINE/DINING. The dining room, created from the original owner's living room/saloon, is located in the center of the vessel. It is exquisite and elegant in every detail (it also houses the ship's library) has beautiful wood paneled walls and a wood beam ceiling. There is ample space at each table, so there is never a crowded feeling, and meals are taken in an open-seating arrangement. German chefs are in charge, and the cuisine is very international, with a good balance of nouvelle cuisine and regional dishes featured (depending on which region the ship is sailing in). High quality food and cuisine are featured throughout, although there is little choice, due to the size of the galley. Place settings for dinner (often by candlelight) are navy blue, white and gold Bauscher china.

There is always excellent seafood and fish (this is purchased fresh, locally, when available, as are most other ingredients). For breakfast and lunch, there are self-serve buffets. These are really good, and beautifully presented (usually indoors for breakfast and outdoors on the Promenade Deck for lunch). Meal times are announced by the ship's bell. European wines are provided for lunch and dinner (vintages tend to be young, however). Soft drinks and bottled water are included in the price, while alcoholic drinks cost extra. On the last day of each cruise, homemade ice cream is produced.

ENTERTAINMENT. There is a keyboard player/singer for the occasional soirée, but nothing else (nothing else needed – the thrill of sailing is the entertainment). Dinner and after-dinner conversation with fellow passengers really becomes the entertainment each evening. So, if you are feeling anti-social and don't want to talk to your fellow passengers, take a good book (or two).

SPA/FITNESS. There are no spa or fitness facilities. However, for recreation (particularly at night), there is the Blue Lagoon, an area of seating (with blue cushioned pads) at the very aft of the ship, where you can lie down and watch the heavens.

A PASSENGER'S PRAYER

"Heavenly Father, look down on us, Your humble, obedient passengers who are doomed to travel the seas and waterways of this earth, taking photographs, mailing postcards, buying useless souvenirs, and walking around in ill-fitting swimwear.

"We beseech You, oh Lord, to see that our plane is not hijacked, our luggage is not lost, and that our oversized carry-ons go unnoticed.

"Protect us from surly and unscrupulous taxi drivers, avaricious porters, and unlicensed, English-speaking guides in foreign places.

"Give us this day Divine guidance in the selection of our cruise ships and our travel agents — so that we may find our bookings and dining room reservations honored, our cabins of generous proportions, that our luggage arrives before the first evening meal, and that our beds are made up.

"We humbly ask that our shower curtains and personal safes do not provoke us into meaningless frustration and destructive thoughts.

"We pray for art auction-free cruise ships, duty-free-free zones, and mobile phone-free restaurants and open decks.

"We pray that our cabin telephones work, the operator (human or electrical) speaks our tongue, and that there are no phone calls from our children forcing us to abandon our cruise early.

"Lead us, dear Lord, to good, affordable restaurants in the world ashore, where the food is superb, the waiters friendly, and the wine included in the price of a meal.

"Please grant us a cruise director who does not "cream" excessively from the spoils of bingo or horse racing, or does not stress only those jewelry stores from which he accepts an offering.

"Grant us the strength to take shore excursions – to visit the museums, cathedrals, spice stalls, and gift shops listed in Berlitz Pocket Guides.

"And if on our return journey by non-air-conditioned buses we slip into slumber, have mercy on us for our flesh is weak, hot, and tired.

"Give us the wisdom to tip correctly at the end of our voyage. Forgive us for under-tipping out of ignorance, and over-tipping out of fear. Please make the chief purser and ship's staff loves us for what we are and not for what we can contribute to their worldly goods or company comment forms.

"Dear God, keep our wives from shopping sprees and protect them from bargains they do not need or cannot afford. Lead them not into temptation in St. Thomas or Hong Kong for they know not what they do.

"Almighty Father, keep our husbands from looking at foreign women and comparing them to us. Save them from making fools of themselves in cafés and nightclubs. Above all, please do not forgive them their trespasses for they know exactly what they do.

"And when our voyage is over and we return home to our loved ones, grant us the favor of finding someone who will look at our home videos and listen to our stories, so our lives as tourists will not have been in vain. This we ask you in the name of our chosen cruise line, and in the name of American Express, Visa, MasterCard, and our banks.

"Amen."

Sea Cloud II
★★★★★

Boutique Ship: . . . . .3,849 tons	Main Propulsion: . . . . .sail power	Cabins (outside view): 48
Lifestyle: .Luxury	Propulsion/Propellers: diesel (2,500kW)/2	Cabins (interior/no view): 0
Cruise Line: . . . . .Sea Cloud Cruises	Passenger Decks: 4	Cabins (for one person): 0
Former Names: . . . . .none	Total Crew: 60	Cabins (with private balcony): 0
Builder: Astilleros Gondan, Figueras (Spain)	Passengers	Cabins (wheelchair accessible): 0
Original Cost: . . . . .DM 50 million	(lower beds/all berths): 96/96	Cabin Current: . . . . .110 and 220 volts
Entered Service: . . . . .Feb 2001	Passenger Space Ratio	Elevators: 0
Registry: . . . . .Malta	(lower beds/all berths): 40.0/40.0	Swimming Pools (outdoors): 0
Length (ft/m): 383.8/117.0	Crew/Passenger Ratio	Whirlpools: 0
Beam (ft/m): 52.9/16.15	(lower beds/all berths): 1.6/1.6	Self-Service Launderette: . . . . .No
Draft (ft/m): 17.7/5.4	Navigation Officers: . .American/European	Library: . . . . .Yes
Type of Vessel: . . . . .barque	Cabins (total): .48	Classification Society: . . . . .Germanischer
No. of Masts: . . . . .3 (24 sails)	Size Range (sq ft/m): 215.2–322.9/	Lloyd
Sail Area (sq ft/m2): 32,292/3,000	20.0–30.0	

BERLITZ'S OVERALL SCORE: 1,709 (OUT OF A POSSIBLE 2,000 POINTS)

OVERVIEW. This new, three-mast tall ship is slightly longer (and beamier) than the original *Sea Cloud*, and has the look, ambience and feel of a 1930s sailing vessel, but with all the latest high-tech navigational aids. The ship complements the company's beautiful, original, 1931-built *Sea Cloud* in almost every way, including its external appearance – except for a very rounded stern in place of the counter stern of sister ship *Sea Cloud*.

Despite some appallingly low standards in the original fitting out of its interiors and carpeting by a shipyard that needs to learn the meaning of the word "quality", Sea Cloud Cruises quickly acted to correct the irritating items, and can now satisfy those seeking the very best of luxurious comfort and surroundings inside a wonderful sailing vessel.

A small water sports platform is built into the aft quarter of the starboard side (with adjacent shower), and the ship carries four inflatable craft for close-in shore landings, as well as snorkeling equipment.

The interior designers have managed to continue the same beautiful traditional look and design as that of *Sea Cloud*. These design details and special decorative touches will make those who have been on the sister ship feel instantly at home. Whether the modern materials used will stand up to 70 years of use like those of the original *Sea Cloud* remains to be seen, although they are of a high quality. In any event, passengers who have sailed aboard the original ship will compare the original with the new.

The main lounge is truly elegant, with sofa and large individual tub chair seating around oval drinks tables. The ceiling is ornate, with an abundance of wood detailing, and an oval centerpiece is set around skylights to the open deck

BERLITZ'S RATINGS		
	Possible	Achieved
Ship	500	435
Accommodation	200	173
Food	400	344
Service	400	333
Entertainment	N/A	N/A
Cruise	500	424

above. A bar is set into the aft port side of the room, which has audio-visual aids built in – for lectures and presentations.

A treasured aspects of sailing aboard this ship is the "Blue Lagoon", at the very stern of the vessel – part of the outdoor bar and casual dining area. Weather permitting, you can lie on thick blue padding and gaze up at the stars and warm night sky – it's a huge pleasure, particularly when the ship is under sail, with the engines turned off.

Overall, *Sea Cloud II* is one of the most luxurious true sailing ships in the world, although it is not the largest (that distinction goes to competitor Star Clippers' *Royal Clipper*). However, in terms of interior design, degree of luxury in appointments, the passenger flow, fabrics, food and service, the ceiling height of public rooms, larger cabins, great open deck space, better passenger space ratio and crew to passenger ratio, there is none better than *Sea Cloud II*. If you sail both vessels (as I have), I am absolutely certain you would agree with me, and that your overall sail-cruise experience will be a truly memorable one.

Your personal experience will depend on which company is operating the ship under charter when you sail, and exactly what is to be included in the package. This is, however, as exclusive as it gets – sailing in the lap of luxury.

Rigging: This consists of up to 24 sails: flying jib, outer jib; inner jib; fore royal, fore topgallant, fore upper topsail, fore lower topsail, fore course; main royal staysail, main topgallant staysail, main topmast staysail, sky sail, main royal, main topgallant, main upper topsail, main lower topsail, main sail; mizzen topgallant staysail, mizzen topmast staysail; mizzen gaff topsail, mizzen upper gaff sail, mizzen lower gaff sail, middle gaff, upper gaff.

If you have sailed aboard the original *Sea Cloud*, you will probably be disappointed with the more limited space and decoration of the equivalent cabins aboard this ship.

SUITABLE FOR: *Sea Cloud II* is best suited to couples and singles (not children) who would probably never consider a "normal" cruise ship, but who enjoy sailing aboard a real tall ship and want this experience wrapped in a package that includes accommodation, good food, like-minded companions, interesting destinations, and don't want the bother of owning or chartering their own mega-yacht.

ACCOMMODATION. The decor in the cabins is very tasteful 1920s retro, with lots of bird's-eye maple wood paneling, brass accenting, and beautiful molded white ceilings. All cabins have a vanity desk, hairdryer, refrigerator (typically stocked with soft drinks and bottled water), and a combination TV/video player. All cabins have a private bathroom with shower enclosure (or bathtub/shower combination), and plenty of storage space for your personal toiletries. Note that the cabin electrical current is 220 volts, although all bathrooms also include a 110-volt socket for shavers.

There are two suites. Naturally, these have more space (but not as much space as the two owner's suites aboard *Sea Cloud*), and comprise a completely separate bedroom (with four-poster bed) and living room, while the marble-clad bathroom has a full-sized tub.

There are 16 junior suites. These provide a living area and sleeping area with twin beds that convert to a queen-sized bed. The marble-clad bathroom is quite opulent, and has a small tub/shower combination, with lots of little cubbyholes to store personal toiletry items.

CUISINE/DINING. The one-seating dining room operates an open-seating policy, so you can dine with whom you wish, when you wish. It is decorated in a light, modern maritime style, with wood and carpeted flooring, comfortable chairs with armrests, and circular light fixtures. The gold-rimmed plates used for the captain's dinner (typically a candlelit affair) has the ship's crest embedded in the white porcelain; it is extremely elegant (and highly collectible). The place settings for dinner (often by candlelight) are navy blue, white and gold Bauscher china.

There is always excellent seafood and fish (this is purchased fresh, locally, when available, as are most other ingredients). For breakfast and lunch, there are self-serve buffets. These are really good, and beautifully presented (usually indoors for breakfast and outdoors on the Promenade Deck for lunch). Meal times are announced by the ship's bell. European wines are typically provided for lunch and dinner (vintages tend to be young, however). Soft drinks and bottled water are included in the price, while alcoholic drinks cost extra. On the last day of each cruise, homemade ice cream is produced.

ENTERTAINMENT. There is a keyboard player/singer for the occasional soirée, but nothing else (nothing else needed – the thrill of sailing is the entertainment). Dinner and after-dinner conversation with fellow passengers really becomes the entertainment each evening. So, if you are feeling anti-social and don't want to talk to your fellow passengers, take a good book (or two).

SPA/FITNESS. There is a health/fitness area, with small gymnasium, sauna and steam room. Massage is available.

Sea Lion
★★

Boutique Ship: . . . . .99.7 tons	Total Crew: 22	Cabins (with private balcony): 0
Lifestyle: . . . . .Standard	Passengers	Cabins (wheelchair accessible): 0
Cruise Line: . . . . . . .Lindblad Expeditions	(lower beds/all berths): 72/76	Cabin Current: . . . . .110 volts
Former Names: . . . .*Great Rivers Explorer*	Passenger Space Ratio	Elevators: 0
Builder: . . . . .Whidbey Island	(lower beds/all berths): 1.3/1.3	Casino (gaming tables): . . . . .No
(USA)	Crew/Passenger Ratio	Slot Machines: . . . . .No
Original Cost: .n/a	(lower beds/all berths): 3.2/3.4	Swimming Pools (outdoors): 0
Entered Service: 1982	Navigation Officers: . . . . . .Scandinavian	Swimming Pools (indoors): 0
Registry: . . . . .The Bahamas	Cabins (total): 37	Whirlpools: 0
Length (ft/m): 151.9/46.3	Size Range (sq ft/m): 73.0–202.0/	Self-Service Launderette: . . . . .No
Beam (ft/m): 30.8/9.4	6.7–18.7	Dedicated Cinema/Seats: . . . . .No
Draft (ft/m): 8.0/2.4	Cabins (outside view): 37	Library: . . . . .No
Propulsion/Propellers: diesel/2	Cabins (interior/no view): 0	Classification Society: . .American Bureau
Passenger Decks: 4	Cabins (for one person): 2	of Shipping

OVERALL SCORE: 938 (OUT OF A POSSIBLE 2,000 POINTS)

OVERVIEW. *Sea Lion* carries a fleet of motorized Zodiac landing craft for use as shore tenders and for up-close shore exploration. A number of sea kayaks are also carried. An open-bridge policy means that you are allowed to go to the navigation bridge at any time.

The vessel is small enough to operate in ports and narrow inlets inaccessible to larger ships. Lectures and recap sessions are held each day.

This small craft (together with sister ship *Sea Bird*) is adequate for looking at nature and wildlife close up, in modest but comfortable surroundings that provide an alternative to big-ship cruising.

Cruises visit Alaska, Baja California and the Sea of Cortes. Tipping is suggested at about $7 per person per day. The onboard currency is the US dollar.

Note that in the cabins, the mattresses are enclosed in a wood frame with sharp corners, which you can all too easily bang into constantly.

SUITABLE FOR: *Sea Lion* is best suited to older couples and single travelers who enjoy learning about nature, geography, history and other life sciences, in casual, non-dressy surroundings without a hint of pretension. They are likely to be hardy, outdoors types who don't need entertainment or silly parlor games.

ACCOMMODATION. All the cabins aboard this little ship have

BERLITZ'S RATINGS

	Possible	Achieved
Ship	500	182
Accommodation	200	83
Food	400	204
Service	400	212
Entertainment	N/A	N/A
Cruise	500	257

an outside view through picture windows, except for those on the lowest deck, which have portholes. Some cabins have double beds, some have twin beds (they can be pushed together to form a queen-sized bed), and some are for singles (at a surcharge). There is plenty of room to stow your luggage.

All cabins have a private bathroom, although it really is tiny. There is no room service for food or beverages.

CUISINE/DINING. The dining room (non-smoking), which has ocean-view picture windows, is large enough to accommodate all passengers in a single seating. The tables are not assigned, and so you can sit with whom you like. The food is unpretentious, good and wholesome, although its presentation is very plain, with no frills, and features regional specialties. The wine list is very limited, and is comprised mostly of wines from California.

ENTERTAINMENT. There is no formal entertainment, although dinner and after-dinner conversation with fellow passengers in the ship's lounge/bar really becomes the entertainment each evening. So, if you don't want to talk to your fellow passengers, take a good book, or go outside, where you'll find nature provides the rest of the entertainment.

SPA/FITNESS. There are no spa or fitness facilities aboard this very small cruise vessel.

Sensation
★★★ +

Large (Resort) Ship: ....70,367 tons	Passenger Decks: 10	Cabins (for one person): 0
Lifestyle: ....Standard	Total Crew: 920	Cabins (with private balcony): 54
Cruise Line: ....Carnival Cruise Lines	Passengers	Cabins (wheelchair accessible): 20
Former Names: ....none	(lower beds/all berths): 2,040/2,594	Cabin Current: ....110 volts
Builder: ....Kvaerner Masa-Yards	Passenger Space Ratio	Elevators: 14
(Finland)	(lower beds/all berths): 34.4/26.7	Casino (gaming tables): ....Yes
Original Cost: ....$300 million	Crew/Passenger Ratio	Slot Machines: ....Yes
Entered Service: ....Nov 1993	(lower beds/all berths): 2.2/2.8	Swimming Pools (outdoors): 3
Registry: ....The Bahamas	Navigation Officers: ....Italian	Swimming Pools (indoors): 0
Length (ft/m): 855.0/260.6	Cabins (total): 1,020	Whirlpools: 6
Beam (ft/m): 104.0/31.4	Size Range (sq ft/m): 173.2–409.7/	Self-Service Launderette: ....Yes
Draft (ft/m): 25.9/7.9	16.0–38.0	Dedicated Cinema/Seats: ....No
Propulsion/Propellers: .....diesel-electric	Cabins (outside view): 618	Library: ....Yes
(42,240kW)/2	Cabins (interior/no view): 402	Classification Society: ...Lloyd's Register

OVERALL SCORE: 1,385 (OUT OF A POSSIBLE 2,000 POINTS)

OVERVIEW. *Sensation*, whose bows are extremely short, has the distinctive, large, swept-back wing-tipped funnel that is the trademark of Carnival Cruise Lines. The ship, which is almost vibration-free, has expansive open deck areas (sadly, there is no wrap-around open promenade deck), but they quickly become inadequate when it is full and everyone wants to be out on deck. There is a "banked" jogging track outdoors on the deck above a large, glass-enclosed health spa. A well-defined "topless" sunbathing area can be found around the funnel base on Verandah Deck.

Inside, the general passenger flow is good, and the interior design is clever, functional, and extremely colorful. A dramatic six-deck-high atrium, with cool marble and hot neon, is topped by a large colored glass dome, and has a spectacular artistic centerpiece. Leading off from an indoor double-width promenade there are public entertainment lounges, bars and clubs galore.

The interiors have a $1 million art collection, much of it bright and vocal. The library is a lovely room, but there are few books. The Michelangelo Lounge is a creative thinker's delight, while Fingers Lounge is sheer sensory stimulation. The casino has plenty of gaming tables and slot machines.

ACCOMMODATION. There are 13 price grades. The standard outside-view and interior (no view) cabins have decor that is rather plain and unmemorable. They are marginally comfortable, yet spacious enough and practical (most are of the same size and appointments), with good storage space and practical, well-designed no-nonsense bathrooms.

Those booking one of the outside suites will find more space, whirlpool bathtubs, and some fascinating, rather eclec-

BERLITZ'S RATINGS

	Possible	Achieved
Ship	500	395
Accommodation	200	151
Food	400	221
Service	400	270
Entertainment	100	81
Cruise	400	267

tic decor and furniture. These are mildly attractive, but nothing special, and they are much smaller than those aboard competitors' ships of a similar size.

If you book accommodation in one of the suites (Category 11 or 12 in the Carnival Cruise Lines brochure) you qualify for "Skipper's Club" priority check-in at any US homeland port – useful for getting ahead of the crowd.

CUISINE/DINING. There are two huge, noisy dining rooms (Ecstasy and Fantasy, both no-smoking) with the usual efficient, assertive service. Dining in each restaurant is now in four seatings, for greater flexibility: 6pm, 6.45pm, 8pm and 8.45pm (these times are approximate).

The Lido Cafe self-serve buffets are very basic, as is the selection of breads, rolls, fruit and cheeses. At night, the "Seaview Bistro", as the Lido Cafe becomes known, provides a casual (dress down) alternative to the main dining rooms, serving pasta, steaks, salads and desserts (typically between 6pm and 9pm). The Pizzeria is open 24 hours a day.

ENTERTAINMENT. The Fantasia Showlounge is the main venue for large-scale production shows and cabaret acts (although 20 pillars obstruct the views from several seats).

SPA/FITNESS. SpaCarnival, a large health, fitness and spa complex, consists of a gymnasium with ocean-view windows, an aerobics exercise room, men's and women's changing rooms, sauna and steam rooms, and beauty salon.

● **For more extensive general information on what a Carnival cruise is like, see pages 107–111.**

Serenade
★ +

Mid-Size Ship: . . . . .14,173 tons	Passenger Decks: 9	Cabins (with private balcony): 0
Lifestyle: . . . . .Standard	Total Crew: 320	Cabins (wheelchair accessible): 0
Cruise Line: . . . . .Louis Cruise Lines	Passengers	Cabin Current: . . . . .110 and 220 volts
Former Names: . . .Mermoz, Jean Mermoz	(lower beds/all berths): 600/739	Elevators: 2
Builder: . . . . .Chantiers de l'Atlantique	Passenger Space Ratio	Casino (gaming tables): . . . . .Yes
(France)	(lower beds/all berths): 23.6/19.1	Slot Machines: . . . . .Yes
Original Cost: .n/a	Crew/Passenger Ratio	Swimming Pools (outdoors): 2
Entered Service: . . . .May 1957/Sept 1999	(lower beds/all berths): 1.8/2.3	Swimming Pools (indoors): 0
Registry: .Cyprus	Navigation Officers: . . . . . . .Cypriot/Greek	Whirlpools: . . . . .Yes
Length (ft/m): 531.5/162.01	Cabins (total): 300	Self-Service Launderette: . . . . .No
Beam (ft/m): 65.0/19.82	Size Range (sq ft/m): . . . . .n/a	Dedicated Cinema/Seats: Yes/240
Draft (ft/m): 20.9/6.40	Cabins (outside view): 230	Library: . . . . .Yes
Propulsion/Propellers: . . . . .diesel	Cabins (interior/no view): 70	Classification Society: . . . .Bureau Veritas
(8,000kW)/2	Cabins (for one person): 0	

OVERALL SCORE: 771 (OUT OF A POSSIBLE 2,000 POINTS)

OVERVIEW. *Serenade* has traditional 1950s lines and now looks extremely dated (indeed, it is a bit of a floating museum). It was operated for many years by the now-defunct Paquet Cruises, who incorporated a number of whimsical French touches into the ship's interiors. Cyprus-based Louis Cruise Lines bought it in 1999, and now operates it in the Mediterranean. There is a decent amount of open deck and sunbathing space, although the white plastic deck furniture doesn't fit this traditional vessel at all (teak or other hardwood furniture would look so much nicer).

Inside, the ship has what can be best described as a reasonably chic art deco-style decor that is rather eclectic, with a pastel color scheme and a "colonial" ambience. The spa and solarium are good spaces and, while there are few large public spaces, there are lots of nooks and crannies. The Winter Garden is delightful, as is the aft-facing library and card room, and the modern-looking Salon Atlantique bar.

This ship has a fine, perhaps somewhat eclectic character, and is for those who enjoy being aboard an older ship, with all its quirks and idiosyncrasies, albeit for a moderate price. The dress code is casual throughout. The onboard currency is the Cyprus pound.

SUITABLE FOR: *Serenade* is best suited to passengers seeking a first cruise on a low budget as a way of getting to interesting destinations in a setting that provides accommodation, food, and very little entertainment.

ACCOMMODATION. There are several price grades, and a diverse range of cabin configurations. Most cabins are quite small and equipped with only basic facilities, but they are

BERLITZ'S RATINGS

	Possible	Achieved
Ship	500	196
Accommodation	200	88
Food	400	170
Service	400	168
Entertainment	N/A	N/A
Cruise	500	149

tastefully furnished, cozy and quite comfortable, with solid fixtures and lots of wood everywhere. There is a fair amount of closet and drawer space, but the cabin bathrooms are small (little space for toiletries). All cabins are equipped with lower beds, although many cabins also have third/fourth upper berths that pull down from their recessed position.

CUISINE/DINING. The 340-seat Masilia Restaurant is attractive, with pleasing, light decor. Seating is at tables for two, four, six, or eight. However, the plastic chairs are grossly uncomfortable. There is also a smaller 155-seat Grill Room, with tub chairs, a pleasing "colonial outpost" ambience, and good food. There are both à la carte and self-serve buffet-style meals, and the menu choice includes three entrées. There is a full vegetarian menu. The selection of breads and ice cream sundaes is good. In fact, the food is perhaps the best part of a cruise aboard this vessel – there is plenty of it. The service is friendly, but lacks polish. The wine list is adequate, and prices are low, but the wines are all young.

ENTERTAINMENT. Facilities for shows really are minimal (sightlines in the single-level showlounge are obstructed from a few seats by slim pillars) and the floor is flat. When cabaret acts are featured, they tend to be vocalists, magicians, ventriloquists, and comedians, among others. Live music for dancing or listening is provided in some of the bars and lounges, however.

SPA/FITNESS. There is no gymnasium, although there is a sauna, as well as a solarium, several massage treatment rooms and a small beauty salon.

Serenade of the Seas
★★★★

Large (Resort) Ship: ....90,090 tons	Total Crew: 858	Cabins (with private balcony): 577
Lifestyle: ....Standard	Passengers	Cabins (wheelchair accessible): 14
Cruise Line: .Royal Caribbean Internttional	(lower beds/all berths): 2,100/2,500	(8 with private balcony)
Former Names: ....none	Passenger Space Ratio	Cabin Current: ....110/220 volts
Builder: ....Meyer Werft (Germany)	(lower beds/all berths): 42.9/36.0	Elevators: 9
Original Cost: ....$350 million	Crew/Passenger Ratio	Casino (gaming tables): ....Yes
Entered Service: ....August 2003	(lower beds/all berths): 2.4/2.9	Slot Machines: ....Yes
Registry: ....The Bahamas	Navigation Officers: ....Norwegian	Swimming Pools (outdoors): 2
Length (ft/m): 961.9/293.2	Cabins (total): 1,050	Swimming Pools (indoors): 0
Beam (ft/m): 105.6/32.2	Size Range (sq ft/m): 165.8–1,216.3/	Whirlpools: 3
Draft (ft/m): 27.8/8.5	15.4/113.0	Self-Service Launderette: ....No
Propulsion/Propellers: .....gas turbine/2	Cabins (outside view): 813	Dedicated Cinema/Seats: Yes/40
azimuthing pods (20 MW each)	Cabins (interior/no view): 237	Library: ....Yes
Passenger Decks: 12	Cabins (for one person): 0	Classification Society: .Det Norske Veritas

OVERALL SCORE: 1,546 (OUT OF A POSSIBLE 2,000 POINTS)

OVERVIEW. This is the third Royal Caribbean International ship to use gas and steam turbine power (the others are sister ships *Brilliance of the Seas* and *Radiance of the Seas*) instead of the formerly conventional diesel or diesel-electric combination (two gas turbines, one steam turbine).

Podded propulsion power is also provided. Briefly, two pods, which resemble huge outboard motors, replace internal electric propulsion motors, shaft lines, rudders and their machinery, and are compact, self-contained units that typically weigh about 170 tons each. Although they are at the stern, pod units pull, rather than push, a ship through the water. As is common aboard all RCI vessels, the navigation bridge is of the fully enclosed type (good for cruising in cold-weather areas such as Alaska). In the very front of the ship is a helipad, which also acts as a viewing platform for passengers (good for up-close-and personal cruising in Alaska). One of two swimming pools can be covered by a large glass dome (a magrodome) for use as an indoor/outdoor pool.

Serenade of the Seas is a streamlined contemporary ship, and has a two-deck-high wrap-around structure in the forward section of the funnel. Along the starboard side, a central glass wall protrudes, giving great views (cabins with balconies occupy the space directly opposite on the port side). The gently rounded stern has nicely tiered decks, which gives the ship an extremely well-balanced look.

Inside the ship, the decor is contemporary, yet elegant, bright and cheerful, designed for young, active, hip and trendy types. The artwork is quite eclectic (so there should be something for all tastes), and provides a spectrum and a half of color works.

BERLITZ'S RATINGS

	Possible	Achieved
Ship	500	433
Accommodation	200	163
Food	400	259
Service	400	298
Entertainment	100	81
Cruise	400	312

The interior focal point is a nine-deck high atrium lobby with glass-walled elevators (on the port side of the ship only) that travel through 12 decks, face the sea and provide a link with nature and the ocean. The Centrum (as the atrium is called), has several public rooms connected to it: the guest relations (the contemporary term for purser's office) and shore excursions desks, a Lobby Bar, Champagne Bar, the Library, Royal Caribbean Online (an internet-connect center), the Concierge Club, and a Crown & Anchor Lounge. A great view of the atrium can be had by looking down through the flat glass dome high above it.

Other facilities include a delightful, but very small library and, in the atrium lobby, a Coffee Shop that also sells pastries and cakes – it's rather like a small Seattle coffee house. There's a Champagne Bar, and a large Schooner Bar (a popular favorite aboard RCI ships, with nautical riggings, ship replicas, maritime art and other nautically-themed ephemera). Gambling devotees should enjoy the rather large, noisy and very colorful Casino Royale. There's also a small dedicated screening room for movies (with space for two wheelchairs), as well as a 194-seat conference center, and a business center.

This ship has a Viking Crown Lounge (a Royal Caribbean International trademark) is a large structure set around the base of the ship's funnel. It is an observation lounge during the daytime (with views forward over the swimming pool). In the evening, the space transforms itself into a futuristic, high-energy dance club, as well as a more intimate and relaxed entertainment venue for softer mood music and "black box" theater.

For those who wish to go online, Royal Caribbean

Online, located in a semi-private setting, is a dedicated computer center with 12 stations providing high-speed internet access for sending and receiving email. Four more internet-access computer terminals are located in Books 'n' Coffee, a bookshop with coffee and pastries, located in an extensive area of shops.

Youth facilities include Adventure Ocean, an "edutainment" area with four separate age-appropriate sections for junior passengers: Aquanaut Center (for ages 3–5); Explorer Center (6–8); Voyager Center (9–12); and the Optix Teen Center (13–17). There is also Adventure Beach, which includes a splash pool complete with waterslide; Surfside, with computer lab stations with entertaining software; and Ocean Arcade, a video games hangout.

The onboard product delivery is more casual and unstructured than RCI has previously been delivering. *Serenade of the Seas* offers more space and more comfortable public areas (and several more intimate spaces), slightly larger cabins and more dining options than most of the larger ships in the RCI fleet.

There is also a grand amount of glass that provides more contact with the ocean around you; of course, more glass means more cleaning of glass. However, at the end of the day, the overall product is similar to that delivered aboard other ships in the fleet. In the final analysis, while the ship is quite delightful in many ways, the onboard operation is less spectacular, and suffers from a lack of service staff. The onboard currency is the US dollar, and 15% is added to all bar and spa bills.

Many of the "private" balcony cabins are not very private, as they can be overlooked by anyone standing in the port and starboard wings of the Solarium, and from other locations. There are no cushioned pads for the deck lounge chairs, and the deck towels provided are quite thin and small. Spa treatments are extravagantly expensive (as they are aboard most ships today, in line with land-based spa prices in the US). It is virtually impossible to escape background music anywhere aboard this ship. Standing in lines for embarkation, the reception desk, disembarkation, for port visits, shore tenders and for the self-serve buffet stations in the Windjammer Cafe is an inevitable aspect of cruising aboard this large ship.

SUITABLE FOR: *Serenade of the Seas* is best suited to young-minded couples and singles of all ages, families with toddlers, tots, children, and teenagers who like to mingle in a large ship setting with plenty of life and high-energy entertainment for everyone, with food that is acceptable quantity rather than quality (unless you are prepared to pay extra for dining in the "alternative" restaurant), all delivered with friendly service that lacks polish.

ACCOMMODATION. There is a wide range of suites and standard outside-view and interior (no view) cabins to suit different tastes, requirements, and depth of wallet, in 10 different categories and 19 different price groups. The price will depend on the grade, size and location you choose. Apart from the largest suites (six owner's suites), which

have king-sized beds, almost all other cabins have twin beds that convert to a queen-sized bed (all sheets are of 100% Egyptian cotton, although blankets are of synthetic fabric). All cabins have rich (but faux) wood cabinetry, including a vanity desk (with hairdryer), faux wood drawers that close silently (hooray), television, personal safe, and three-sided mirrors. Some cabins have a recessed ceiling, pull-down berths for third and fourth persons, although closet and drawer space would be extremely tight for four persons (even if two of them are children), and some have interconnecting doors (so families with children can cruise together, in separate, but adjacent cabins).

Audio channels are available through the television; however, if you want to go to sleep with soft music playing in the background you'll need to put a towel over the television screen, as it is impossible to turn the picture off. Data ports are provided in all cabins.

Most cabin bathrooms have tiled accenting and a terrazzo-style tiled floor, and a shower enclosure in a half-moon shape (it is rather small, however), 100% Egyptian cotton towels, a small cabinet for personal toiletries and a small shelf. In reality, there is little space to stow personal toiletries for two (or more).

The largest accommodation consists of a family suite with two bedrooms. One bedroom has twin beds (convertible to queen-sized bed), while a second has two lower beds and two upper Pullman berths, a combination that can sleep up to eight persons (this would suit large families).

Occupants of accommodation designated as suites also get the use of a private Concierge Lounge (where priority dining room reservations, shore excursion bookings and beauty salon/spa appointments can be made).

CUISINE/DINING. "Reflections" is the name of the ship's principal dining room. It spans two decks; the upper deck level has floor-to-ceiling windows, while the lower deck level has picture windows. It is a lovely, but inevitably noisy dining hall – reminiscent of those aboard the transatlantic liners in their heyday (however, eight huge, thick pillars obstruct the sightlines – the dining room would be much nicer without them). Reflections seats 1,104 hungry persons, and its decor features a cascading water theme. There are tables for two, four, six, eight or 10 in two seatings. Two small private dining rooms (Illusions with 94 seats and Mirage with 30 seats) are located off the main dining room. No smoking is permitted in the dining venues.

The cuisine is typical of mass banquet catering that offers standard fare comparable to that found in American family-style restaurants ashore. The menu descriptions make the food sound better than it is (the ship uses many mixes and pre-prepared items). However, a decent selection of light meals is provided, and a vegetarian menu is available. The selection of breads, rolls, fruit and cheese is quite poor, however, and could do with improvement. Caviar (once a standard menu item) now incurs a hefty extra charge. Menus typically include a "Welcome Aboard" Dinner, French Dinner, Italian Dinner, International Dinner, Captain's Gala Dinner. One thing this company does once each cruise is to put on a "Galley Buffet" whereby passengers go through a section of the galley picking up food for a midnight buffet. There is an adequate wine list, moderately priced.

Alternative Restaurants. There are two: Portofino, with 112 seats, featuring Italian cuisine (choices include: antipasti, soup, salad, pasta, main dish, dessert, cheese and coffee); and Chops Grill Steakhouse, with 95 seats and an open "show" kitchen, serving premium meats in the form of veal chops and steaks (New York Striploin Steak, Filet Mignon, and Prime Rib of Beef).

Both alternative dining spots have food that is of a much higher quality than in the main dining room, with extremely good presentation and experienced service. The menus do not change throughout the cruise. There is an additional charge of $20 per person (this includes gratuities to staff), and reservations are required for both dining spots, which are typically open 6pm–11pm. Be prepared to eat a lot of food (do justice to the cover charge). The dress code in the alternative dining spots is smart casual.

Casual Eateries: Also, casual meals (for breakfast, lunch and dinner) can be taken in the self-serve, buffet-style Windjammer Cafe, which can be accessed directly from the pool deck. It has islands dedicated to specific foods, and indoors and outdoors seating. Additionally, there is the Seaview Cafe, open for lunch and dinner. Choose from the self-serve buffet, or from the menu for casual, fast-food seafood items including fish sandwiches, popcorn shrimp, fish 'n' chips, as well as non-seafood items such as hamburgers and hot dogs. The decor, naturally, is marine- and ocean related.

ENTERTAINMENT. Facilities include the three-level Tropical Theater, with 874 seats (including 24 stations for wheelchairs) and good sight lines from most seats. Strong cabaret acts are also featured in the main showlounge.

A second entertainment venue is the Safari Club. This is where more casual cabaret shows, including late-night adult (blue) comedy, and live music for dancing are featured.

All of the entertainment throughout this ship is upbeat (in fact, it is virtually impossible to get away from music and noise), but is typical of the kind of resort hotel found in Las Vegas. There is even background music in all corridors and elevators, and constant music on the pool deck. If you want a quiet holiday, choose another cruise line.

SPA/FITNESS. The ShipShape Spa's health, fitness and spa facilities have themed decor, and include a 10,176 sq.-ft (945 sq.-meter) solarium with whirlpool and counter current swimming under a retractable magrodome roof, a gymnasium (with 44 cardiovascular machines), 50-person aerobics room, sauna and steam rooms, and therapy treatment rooms. All are located on two of the uppermost decks of the ship, forward of the mast, with access from the forward stairway.

A climate-controlled 10,176 sq. ft (945 sq. meters) indoor/outdoor Solarium (with magrodome sliding glass roof that can be closed in cool or inclement weather conditions) provides facilities for relaxation. It has fascinating Balinese-themed decor, and includes a whirlpool and counter current swimming under a retractable magrodome roof. One neat feature is the Temple Gate Falls, a carved wooden gateway with water cascading down its sides.

For the more sporting passengers, there is activity galore – including a rock-climbing wall that's 30-ft (9 meters) high, with five separate climbing tracks. It is located outdoors at the aft end of the funnel.

Other sports facilities include a 9-hole miniature golf course, and an indoor/outdoor country club with golf simulator, a jogging track, and basketball court. Want to play pool? Well, you can, thanks to two special tables (called STables), whose technology adjusts to the movement of the ship automatically (you can find the tables in the Bombay Billiard Room, part of the Colony Club).

● **For more extensive general information about the Royal Caribbean experience, see pages 128–131.**

Seven Seas Mariner
★★★★★

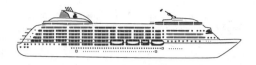

Mid-Size ship: . . . . .48,015 tons	Total Crew: 445	Cabins (with private balcony): 354
Lifestyle: . . . . .Luxury/Premium	Passengers	Cabins (wheelchair accessible): 6
Cruise Line: . . . . . . .Seven Seas Cruises	(lower beds/all berths): 708/752	Cabin Current: . . . . .110 volts
Former Names: . . . . .none	Passenger Space Ratio	Elevators: 5
Builder: Chantiers de l'Atlantique (France)	(lower beds/all berths): 67.8/63.8	Casino (gaming tables): . . . . .Yes
Original Cost: . . . .$240 million	Crew/Passenger Ratio	Slot Machines: . . . . .Yes
Entered Service: . . . . .Mar 2001	(lower beds/all berths): 1.6/1.7	Swimming Pools (outdoors): 1
Registry: . . . . .France	Navigation Officers: . . . . .French	Swimming Pools (indoors): 0
Length (ft/m): 713/217.3	Cabins (total): 354	Whirlpools: 3
Beam (ft/m): 95.1/29.0	Size Range (sq ft/m): 301.3–1,528.4/	Self-Service Launderette: . . . . .Yes (3)
Draft (ft/m): 21.4/6.5	28.0–142.0	Dedicated Cinema/Seats: . . . . .No
Propulsion/Propellers: . . .diesel-electric/2	Cabins (outside view): 354	Library: . . . . .Yes
azimuthing pods (8.5 MW each)	Cabins (interior/no view): 0	Classification Society: . . . .Bureau Veritas
Passenger Decks: 9	Cabins (for one person): 0	

OVERALL SCORE: 1,701 (OUT OF A POSSIBLE 2,000 POINTS)

OVERVIEW. This is presently the largest ship in the Seven Seas Cruises fleet, and the first to receive a "pod" propulsion system, replacing the traditional shaft and rudder system (the pods have forward-facing propellers that can be turned through 360°). For the technically minded, the ship was built in 32 blocks, using the same hull design as for Festival Cruises' *Mistral*, although the interior design is totally different. In the fitting out stage, for example, many changes were made to accommodate Seven Seas Cruises' need for all-outside-view suites. Consequently, its passenger space ratio is now the highest in the cruise industry, at just a fraction above those for *Europa*.

Seven Seas Mariner is operated by Seven Seas Cruises, although the ship is actually owned by a joint venture company established with ship managers V-Ships.

There is a wide range of public rooms to play in, almost all of which are located under the accommodation decks. Three sets of stairways (forward, center, aft) mean it is easy to find your way around the vessel. An atrium lobby spans nine decks, with the lowest level opening directly onto the tender landing stage.

Facilities include a delightful observation lounge, a casino, a shopping concourse (conveniently located opposite the casino) – complete with open market area, a garden lounge/promenade arcade, a large library with internet-connect computers, business center, card room and a conference room, a, cigar-smoking lounge (called the Connoisseur Club, for cigars, cognacs and other assorted niceties), and a photo gallery.

With the introduction of *Seven Seas Mariner*, Seven Seas Cruises moved into a new breed of larger ships that are

BERLITZ'S RATINGS

	Possible	Achieved
Ship	500	448
Accommodation	200	177
Food	400	334
Service	400	324
Entertainment	100	83
Cruise	400	335

more economical to operate, and provide more choices for passengers. However, the downside of a larger ship such as this is that there is a loss of the sense of intimacy that the company's smaller ships have previously been able to maintain. Thus, some of the former personal service of the smaller ships has been absorbed into a larger structure. Another downside is the fact that this ship is simply too large to enter the small harbors and berths that the company's smaller ships can, and so loses some of the benefits of small upscale ship cruising.

So, it's swings and roundabouts when it comes to scoring the ship. At present, it scores very highly in terms of hardware and software, but operationally may lose a few points if it is deemed that it can enter only mid-size ship ports. By comparison, this ship is a more upscale version of the eight ships in the former Renaissance Cruises fleet – with better food, more choices, and a staff that is more hospitality-conscious and generally better trained. *Seven Seas Mariner*, therefore, has ended up just a tad over the score base needed for it to join the "Berlitz Five Star" Club.

Gratuities are included, as are complimentary bar setups on embarkation and complimentary table wines for lunch and dinner (although premium and connoisseur selections are also available at extra cost). The onboard currency is the US dollar.

Service and hospitality are sometimes spotty and inconsistent – the result more of a multi-nationality crew mix provided by a maritime personnel supply agency that appears not to understand quality. The same carpeting is used throughout the public areas – with no relief or change of color or pattern on the stairwells. The decor is a little glitzy in places. Much of the intimacy and close-knit ambience of the smaller vessels is missing, and, because of all those cabins with balconies, the feeling of privacy and relaxation can also translate into less passengers and ambience in public rooms and for entertainment events, depending on the passenger mix.

SUITABLE FOR: *Seven Seas Mariner* is best suited to well traveled couples and single travelers (typically over 50) who seek excellent itineraries, fine food and good service, with some entertainment, all wrapped up in a contemporary ship which can best be described as elegant and quiet in its appointments and comfort levels.

ACCOMMODATION. There are 13 categories of cabins. The price you pay will depend on the grade, location and size you choose. *Seven Seas Mariner* is the cruise industry's first "all-suite, all-balcony" ship (terminology that marketing departments enjoy, although it is not actually correct, as not all accommodation has sleeping areas completely separated from living areas).

All grades of accommodation have private, marble-clad bathrooms with bathtub, and all suite entrances are neatly recessed away from the passenger hallways, to provide an extra modicum of quietness. In comparison with *Seven Seas Navigator*, the bathrooms aboard this ship are not as large in the lower grade of accommodation.

Master Suite: The largest accommodation (1,580 sq. ft/147 sq. meters), in two Master Suites, has two separate bedrooms, living room with TV/VCR and CD player, walk-in closet, dining area, large, two marble-clad bathrooms with bathtub and separate shower enclosure, and two private teakwood-decked balconies. These suites are located on the deck under the ship's navigation bridge, one balcony providing delightful forward-facing views, while a second balcony provides port or starboard views. Butler service is provided. To keep things in perspective, these two Master Suites are nowhere near as large as the two Penthouse Suites aboard the much larger Celebrity Cruises ships *Constellation, Infinity, Millennium* and *Summit* (which measure 2,350 sq. ft/218 sq. meters).

Mariner Suite: Six Mariner Suites (739 sq. ft/69 sq. meters), located on port and starboard sides of the atrium on three separate decks, have a separate bedroom, living room with TV/VCR and CD player, walk-in closet, dining area, large, marble-clad bathroom with bathtub and separate shower enclosure, and a good sized private balcony with either port or starboard views. Butler service is provided.

Grand Suites: Two Grand Suites (707 sq. ft/66 sq. meters) are located one deck above the ship's navigation bridge, and have a separate bedroom, living room with TV/VCR and CD player, walk-in closet, dining area, two marble-clad bathrooms with bathtub and separate shower enclosure, and a good sized private balcony with port or starboard views. Butler service is provided.

Seven Seas Suites: Six spacious suites (697 sq. ft/65 sq. meters) overlook the ship's stern (two suites are located on each of four decks) and have very generous private balcony space and good wrap-around views over the ship's stern and to port or starboard. However, the balconies are only semi-private and can be partly overlooked by neighbors in Horizon Suites as well as from above. Another two Seven Seas Suites are located just aft of the ship's navigation bridge and measure a slightly smaller 600 sq ft (56 sq. meters) and have balconies with either port or starboard views. These suites have a separate bedroom, living room with TV/VCR and CD player, walk-in closet, dining area, large, and marble-clad bathroom with a combination bathtub/shower.

Horizon Suites: There are 12 Horizon Suites (522 sq. ft/48 sq. meters) overlooking the ship's stern (three suites are located on each of four decks, sandwiched between the Seven Seas Suites) and have a good-sized balcony (though not as large as the Seven Seas Suites) and good views. These suites have a separate bedroom, living room with TV/VCR, walk-in closet, dining area, large, marble-clad bathroom with a combination bathtub/shower.

All Other Cabins: All other cabins (Categories A–H in the brochure, listed as Deluxe Suites and Penthouse Suites) measure 300 sq. ft (28 sq. meters) and have twin beds that can convert to a queen-sized bed (European duvets are standard), small walk-in closet, marble-lined bathroom with combination bathtub/shower, 100% cotton bathrobe and towels, vanity desk, hairdryer, TV/VCR, refrigerator (stocked with soft drinks and bar set-up on embarkation), personal safe. In these suites, the sleeping area is separated from the living area only by partial room dividers, and therefore is a cabin (albeit a good-sized one), and not a suite.

Six wheelchair-accessible suites are located as close to an elevator as one could possibly get, and provide ample living space, together with a large roll-in shower and all bathroom fittings located at the correct height.

CUISINE/DINING. There are four different dining venues, all operated on an open-seating basis, so that you can sit with whom you want, when you wish. In reality, this means that dining aboard ship is like dining on land – you can go to a different dining spot each night. The downside of this is that waiters don't get to know and remember your preferences. Reservations are required in two of the four dining spots. In general, the cuisine is very good, with creative presentation and a wide variety of food choices.

The main dining room is the 570-seat Compass Rose Restaurant, located in the center of the ship. It has a light, fresh decor, and seating at tables for two, four, six or eight. A large pre-dinner drinks bar is conveniently located adjacent on the starboard side. Fine Dudson china is used.

Off to the port side of the Compass Rose Restaurant is Latitudes – with 80 seats, the smallest of the specialty restaurants for alternative dining, with tableside preparation of dishes from all parts of the world (the decor, too, is an interesting, rather eclectic mix from several parts of the world). There is seating for two, four or six, and reservations are required.

A 120-seat "supper club", called Signatures – which has its own dedicated galley – is located one deck above the main galley (for convenient vertical supply and staff access), and has ocean views along the room's port side. It is directed and staffed by chefs wearing the white toque and blue riband of Le Cordon Bleu in Paris, the world's most prestigious culinary authority, and so the cuisine is classic French. Doors open onto a covered area outdoors, complete with stage and dance floor. Porsgrund china is used, as are silver show plates and the very finest silverware. Seating is at tables of two, four, or six, and reservations are required.

For more casual meals, La Veranda is a large self-serve indoor/outdoor cafe with seats for 450 (the teakwood-decked outdoor seating is particularly pleasant), and the decor is fresh and light. This eatery has several food islands and substantial counter display space. There is also an outdoor grill, adjacent to the swimming pool.

As another variation on the dining theme, you can also choose to dine in your cabin (most passengers do so for breakfast, for example, and some do for dinner instead of "going out" to the "public" restaurants). There is a 24-hour room service menu, and, during regular dinner hours, the full dining room menu is available.

ENTERTAINMENT. The Constellation Theater is the ship's main showlounge. It spans two decks and is quite stunning, and the sight lines are very good from almost all seats on both main and balcony levels. The proscenium stage is large enough to provide space for scenery changes and includes a "thrust" stage that is good for presenting more intimate cabaret acts. Seven Seas Cruises has an eclectic entertainment program that is tailored to each individual ship. Aboard *Seven Seas Mariner*, both production shows and cabaret acts are featured. The ship carries its own production show troupe of eight singers/dancers who perform the colorful shows (the cast is, however, small for the size of the stage). Cabaret acts tend to feature vocalists, magicians and comedy jugglers, among others).

There is also Stars nightclub, with an oval-shaped dance floor, and a Horizon Lounge – both rooms could be used for intimate late-night cabaret. A number of bands and small musical units and solo pianist entertainers can be found providing live music in several lounges and bars.

SPA/FITNESS. Health and fitness facilities include an extensive health spa with gymnasium and aerobics room, beauty parlor, and separate changing, sauna and steam rooms for men and women. The spa is located not at the top of the ship, as is common with many other ships today, but just off the atrium in the center of the ship.

Specialist Judith Jackson operates the spa and beauty services as a concession, and provides the staff. Here are some sample prices for treatments: European aromatherapy massage, $90 (50 minutes); four hand massage, $165 (60 minutes); reflexology session, $50 (30 minutes); rejuvenation facial, $110 (60 minutes); "fast fix" facial, $40 (20 minutes); neck-to-toe seaweed body wrap, $75 (50 minutes); micro-sea body scrub, $40 (30 minutes); aromatherapy bath and massage, $120 (60 minutes). Judith Jackson also has a range of beauty products for the body and well-being books for sale.

Sports devotees can play in the paddle tennis court, golf driving and practice cages.

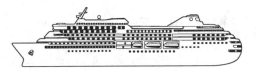

Seven Seas Navigator
★★★★ +

Mid-Size Ship: . . . . .28,550 tons	Total Crew: 325	Cabins (with private balcony): 196
Lifestyle: . . . . .Luxury/Premium	Passengers	Cabins (wheelchair accessible): 4
Cruise Line: . . . . . . .Seven Seas Cruises	(lower beds/all berths): 490/530	Cabin Current: . . . . .110 and 220 volts
Former Names: . . . . .none	Passenger Space Ratio	Elevators: 5
Builder: . . . . .T. Mariotti (Italy)	(lower beds/all berths): 58.2/53.8	Casino (gaming tables): . . . . .Yes
Original Cost: . . . .$200 million	Crew/Passenger Ratio	Slot Machines: . . . . .Yes
Entered Service: . . . . .Aug 1999	(lower beds/all berths): 1.5/1.6	Swimming Pools (outdoors): 1
Registry: . . . . .The Bahamas	Navigation Officers: . . . . .European/	Swimming Pools (indoors): 0
Length (ft/m): 559.7/170.6	International	Whirlpools: 2
Beam (ft/m): 71.5/21.8	Cabins (total): 245	Self-Service Launderette: . . . . .Yes
Draft (ft/m): 21.3.0/6.5	Size Range (sq ft/m): 301.3–1,173.3/	Dedicated Cinema/Seats: . . . . .No
Propulsion/Propellers: . . . . .diesel	28.0–109.0	Library: . . . . .Yes
(13,000kW/2	Cabins (outside view): 245	Classification Society: . . .Registro Navale
Passenger Decks: 8	Cabins (interior/no view): 0	Italiano (RINA)
	Cabins (for one person): 0	

OVERALL SCORE: 1,653 (OUT OF A POSSIBLE 2,000 POINTS)

OVERVIEW. *Seven Seas Navigator* was built using a hull that was already constructed in St. Petersburg, Russia, as the research vessel *Akademik Nikolay Pilyugin*. After launching the hull, the name *Blue Sea* was used for a short time. The superstructure was incorporated into the hull in an Italian shipyard – the result being that for all intents and purposes a new ship was delivered in record time. However, the result is less than handsome – particularly at the ship's stern. It is, however, large enough to be stable over long stretches of water, and there is an excellent amount of space per passenger.

The interiors have a mix of classical and contemporary Italian styling and decor throughout, with warm, soft colors and fine quality soft furnishings and fabrics. The Vista Lounge is the ship's forward-view observation lounge. At the opposite end of the ship is Galileo's, a large piano lounge with good views over the stern.

A Navigator's Lounge has warm mahogany and cherry wood paneling and large, comfortable, mid-back tub chairs. Meanwhile, next door, cigars and cognac (and other niceties) can be taken in the delightful Connoisseur's Club – the first aboard a Seven Seas Cruises vessel. The extensive library also has several computers with direct email/internet access (for a fee).

The ship is designed for worldwide cruise itineraries, and is one of the upscale ships in the diverse Seven Seas Cruises fleet. As with all ships in the fleet, all gratuities are included. The onboard currency is the US dollar.

There is no wrap-around promenade deck outdoors, although there is a jogging track high atop the aft section of

BERLITZ'S RATINGS

	Possible	Achieved
Ship	500	416
Accommodation	200	180
Food	400	332
Service	400	318
Entertainment	100	83
Cruise	400	324

the ship around the funnel housing. Two of the upper, outer decks are laid with green Astroturf, which cheapens the look of the ship – these decks would be better in teak. The ceilings in several public rooms (including the main restaurant) are quite low, which makes the ship feel smaller and more closed in than it is. The ship suffers from a considerable amount of vibration, which detracts from the comfort level when compared with other vessels of the same size. Service and hospitality are spotty and inconsistent.

SUITABLE FOR: *Seven Seas Navigator* is best suited to well-traveled couples and single travelers (typically over 50) who seek excellent itineraries, fine food and good service, with some entertainment, all wrapped up in a contemporary ship which can best be described as elegant and quiet in its appointments and comfort levels.

ACCOMMODATION. There are 11 price grades (the price will depend on the grade, location and size you choose). The company markets this as an "all-suite" ship. Even the smallest suite is quite large, and all have outside views. Almost 90 percent of all suites have a private balcony, with floor-to-ceiling sliding glass doors, while 10 suites are interconnecting, and 38 suites have an extra bed for a third occupant. By comparison, even the smallest suite aboard this ship is more than twice the size of the smallest cabin aboard the world's largest cruise ships, Royal Caribbean International's Voyager-class ships.

All grades of accommodation have a walk-in closet, European king-sized bed or twin beds, wooden cabinetry with nicely rounded edges, plenty of drawer space, mini-bar/refrigerator (stocked with complimentary soft drinks and bar set-up on embarkation), TV/VCR, personal safe and other accoutrements of fine living at sea in the latest design format. The marble-appointed bathroom has a full-size bathtub, as well as a separate shower enclosure, 100% cotton bathrobe and towels, and hairdryer.

The largest living spaces can be found in four master suites, with forward-facing views (all have double-length side balconies). Each suite has a completely separate bedroom with dressing table; the living room has a full dining room table and chairs for up to six persons, wet bar, counter and bar stools, large 3-person sofa and six armchairs, and an audio-visual console/entertainment center. Each suite has a large main, marble-clad, fully tiled bathroom with full-sized bathtub and separate shower enclosure, a separate room with bidet, toilet and washbasin, with plenty of shelf and other storage space for personal toiletries. There is a separate guest bathroom.

Next in size are the superb Navigator Suites, which have a completely separate bedroom, walk-in closet, large lounge with mini-bar/refrigerator (stocked with complimentary soft drinks and bar set-up on embarkation), personal safe, compact disc player, large TV/VCR player, and dining area with large table and four chairs. The marble-clad, fully tiled bathroom has a full-sized bathtub with hand-held shower, plus a separate shower enclosure (the door to which is only 18 inches/45 cm, however), large washbasin, toilet and bidet, and ample shelf space for personal toiletries.

It is unfortunate that the Navigator Suites are located in the center of the ship, as they are directly underneath the swimming pool deck. They are, thus, subject to noise attacks at 6am daily, when deck cleaning is carried out, and chairs are dragged across the deck directly over the suites. They are further subjected to noise attacks whenever pool deck stewards drag and drop deck lounge chairs into place. Despite these disadvantages, the Navigator Suites are delightful living spaces.

Four suites for the physically challenged have private balconies, and are ideally located adjacent to the elevators (correcting a mistake made when the company's *Radisson Diamond* was constructed, when they were located as far from any elevators as they possibly could be). However, while the suites are very practical, it is almost impossible to access the balcony, because of the "lip" or "threshold" at the bottom of the sliding glass door.

CUISINE/DINING. The Compass Rose Dining Room has large ocean-view picture windows and open-seating dining, which means that you may be seated when and with whom you wish. Complimentary wines are served during dinner, although a connoisseur wine list is available for those who prefer to choose a vintage wine (at extra cost). The company also features "heart healthy" cuisine. Although most of the dining room is non-smoking, a small section is available for smokers.

An alternative dining spot, Portofino Grill, has informal Italian dining for dinner (reservations are required). The Grill is part of a larger restaurant with indoor/outdoor seating. For fast-food items, there is also a small indoor/outdoor Grill, adjacent to the swimming pool.

You can also choose to dine in your cabin. There is a 24-hour room service menu; also, during regular dinner hours, you can choose from the full dining room menu.

ENTERTAINMENT. The Seven Seas Lounge is a two-deck-high showlounge, with reasonable sightlines from most seats on both main and balcony levels (although several pillars obstruct the views from some of the side balcony seats). Seven Seas Cruises has an eclectic entertainment program tailored to each ship. *Seven Seas Navigator* features both production shows and cabaret acts.

A number of bands and small musical units and solo pianist entertainers can be found providing live music in several lounges and bars throughout the ship.

SPA/FITNESS. The Spa is located just aft of the Vista Observation Lounge on the ship's uppermost deck, forward of the ship's mast. Facilities include a gymnasium, aerobics exercise area, sauna and steam rooms, changing area, showers, and treatment rooms. A beauty salon is located on the deck below.

Specialist Judith Jackson operates the spa and beauty services as a concession, and provides the staff. Here are some sample prices for treatments: European aromatherapy massage, $90 (50 minutes); four hand massage, $165 (60 minutes); reflexology session, $50 (30 minutes); rejuvenation facial, $110 (60 minutes); "fast fix" facial, $40 (20 minutes); neck-to-toe seaweed body wrap, $75 (50 minutes); micro-sea body scrub, $40 (30 minutes); aromatherapy bath and massage, $120 (60 minutes).

Judith Jackson also has a range of beauty products for the body and wellbeing books for sale.

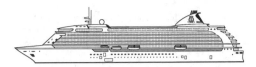

Seven Seas Voyager
★★★★★

Mid-Size Ship: . . . . .41,827 tons	Total Crew: 445	Cabins (with private balcony): 354
Lifestyle: . . . . .Luxury/Premium	Passengers	Cabins (wheelchair accessible): 4
Cruise Line: . . . . . . .Seven Seas Cruises	(lower beds/all berths): 708/752	Cabin Current: . . . . .110 volts
Former Names: . . . . .none	Passenger Space Ratio	Elevators: 6
Builder: .Chantiers de l'Atlantique (France)	(lower beds/all berths): 59.0/55.6	Casino (gaming tables): . . . . .Yes
Original Cost: . . . .$240 million	Crew/Passenger Ratio	Slot Machines: . . . . .Yes
Entered Service: . . . . .Mar 2003	(lower beds/all berths): 1.65/1.6	Swimming Pools (outdoors): 1
Registry: .France	Navigation Officers: . . . . .French	Swimming Pools (indoors): 0
Length (ft/m): 669.2/204.0	Cabins (total): 354	Whirlpools: 3
Beam (ft/m): 94.5/28.8	Size Range (sq ft/m): 356.0/1,399.3/	Self-Service Launderette: . . . . .Yes (3)
Draft (ft/m): 23.0/7.0	33.0–130.0	Dedicated Cinema/Seats: . . . . .No
Propulsion/Propellers: . . .diesel-electric/2	Cabins (outside view): 354	Library: . . . . .Yes
azimuthing pods (8.5MW each)	Cabins (interior/no view): 0	Classification Society: . . . .Bureau Veritas
Passenger Decks: 9	Cabins (for one person): 0	

OVERALL SCORE: 1,701 (OUT OF A POSSIBLE 2,000 POINTS)

OVERVIEW. Slightly narrower and smaller than *Seven Seas Mariner*, this latest ship allows Seven Seas Cruises to provide a central corridor for accommodation designated as suites (sister ship *Seven Seas Mariner* has two corridors – port and starboard). This is presently the second ship in the Seven Seas Cruises fleet to receive a "pod" propulsion system (the first being *Seven Seas Mariner*), replacing the traditional shaft and rudder system (the pods have forward-facing propellers that can be turned through 360°).

For the technically minded, the ship was built in 32 blocks, using the same basic hull design as for the company's *Seven Seas Mariner*, with a few modifications. The passenger space ratio is among the highest in the cruise industry, at about the same as the smaller, but better-built *Europa*. *Seven Seas Voyager* is operated by Seven Seas Cruises, although the ship is actually owned by a joint-venture company established between Seven Seas Cruises and ship managers V-Ships.

There is a decent range of public rooms in which to play, almost all of which are located below the accommodation decks. Three sets of stairways (forward, center, aft) mean it is easy to find your way around the vessel. An atrium lobby spans nine decks, with the lowest level opening directly onto the tender landing stage.

Facilities include a showlounge that spans two decks, an observation lounge (it's the only place aboard this ship where you can see the bows, a casino, a shopping concourse (conveniently located opposite the casino) – complete with an open "market" area, a large library, internet-connect center and business center (Club.com, and Coffee.com), card room and a small conference room.

BERLITZ'S RATINGS

	Possible	Achieved
Ship	500	449
Accommodation	200	177
Food	400	334
Service	400	324
Entertainment	100	83
Cruise	400	334

There is also a nightclub (Voyager) with an oval-shaped dance floor, a cigar-smoking lounge (the Connoisseur Club, for cigars, cognacs and other assorted niceties), and the usual photo gallery.

Seven Seas Cruises has clearly moved into a new breed of larger ships that are more economical to operate, provide better economies of scale, as well as more choices for passengers. However, the downside of a larger ship such as this is that there is a loss of the sense of intimacy that the company's smaller ships have previously been noted for. Thus, some of the former personal service of the smaller ships has been absorbed into a larger structure, although this does not always translate well.

Another downside is the fact that this ship is too large to enter the small harbors and berths that the company's smaller ships can, and so loses some of the benefits of the smaller upscale ships such as those of the more stylish Hapag-Lloyd, SeaDream, Seabourn and Silversea. So it's swings and roundabouts when it comes to scoring the ship.

At present, the ship scores well in terms of hardware (it's a combination of all the best of *Seven Seas Mariner* and *Seven Seas Navigator*) and software, but operationally may lose a few points if it is deemed that the ship can only enter mid-size ship ports. By comparison, this ship is a much more upscale version of the eight ships in the former Renaissance Cruises fleet – with better food, more choices, and a staff that is more hospitality-conscious and generally better trained.

Gratuities are included, as are complimentary stocked bar set-ups on embarkation (two bottles of spirits is the norm), as well as complimentary table wines for lunch and dinner (although premium and connoisseur selections are available at extra cost). The onboard currency is the US dollar. *Seven Seas Voyager*, therefore, has ended up just a tad over the score base needed for it to join the "Berlitz Five Star" Club.

Service and hospitality can be spotty and inconsistent – the result more of a multi-nationality crew mix provided by a maritime personnel supply agency that appears not to understand the highest quality. The decor is a little glitzy in places, very plain in others (beiges and browns are the prevailing colors). The ship is too large to get into some of the smaller ports of call that the smaller ships in the fleet can get into. Also, much of the intimacy and close-knit ambiance of the smaller vessels is missing. There is no wrap-around outdoor promenade deck. There is no forward-viewing exterior deck with views over the ship's bows. The white plastic deck lounge chairs should really be replaced by those made of teak, or stainless steel (plastic is not luxury).

SUITABLE FOR: *Seven Seas Voyager* is best suited to well-traveled couples and single travelers (typically over 50) who seek excellent itineraries, fine food and good service, with some entertainment, all wrapped up in a contemporary ship which can best be described as elegant and quiet in its appointments and comfort levels.

ACCOMMODATION. There are 12 accommodation price grades. The price you pay will depend on the grade, size and location you choose. As the ship was built with a central corridor design, this has allowed for larger suites (and much larger bathrooms) than aboard *Seven Seas Mariner*, with which many repeat passengers will no doubt compare it. This is Seven Seas Cruises' second "all-suite all-balcony" ship (terminology that marketing departments thoroughly enjoy, although not actually correct, as not all accommodation has sleeping areas that are completely separated from living areas). However, all grades of accommodation have private, marble-clad bathrooms with tub (although marble floors can be very cold on bare feet), walk-in closet with personal safe, and most suite entrances are neatly recessed away from passenger hallways (a central corridor), so as to provide an extra modicum of quietness. All have a "private" balcony, although all measure only 50 sq. ft (4.6 sq. meters) with the exception of those in the Master Suites and Grand Suites; however, they do have pleasing teak decking. All partitions are of the partial type, except for the Master Suites and Grand Suites, which have full floor-to-ceiling partitions, and are completely private.

Master Suites (1,162 sq. ft/108 sq. meters). The largest accommodation can be found in two Master Suites (1100 and 1001 each measure 1,403 sq. ft/130.3 sq. meters when added with one Grand Suite via an interconnecting door,) while (700 and 701 measure 1,335 sq. ft (124 sq. meters). Each has two separate bedrooms, living room with TV/DVD player, walk-in closet with personal safe, dining area, large, two marble-clad bathrooms with bathtub and separate shower enclosure, and private teakwood-decked balconies. These suites are located on the deck under the ship's navigation bridge, one balcony providing delightful forward-

facing views, while a second balcony provides port or starboard views. Butler service is provided. To keep things in perspective, these two Master Suites are nowhere near as large as the two Penthouse Suites aboard the much larger Celebrity Cruises ships *Constellation, Infinity, Millennium* and *Summit* (which measure 2,350 sq. ft/235 sq. meters). The bathrooms, which are open to the bedroom, feature a stand-alone tub with integral shower, separate shower enclosure, toilet, bidet and washbasin. The private balcony (the partitions are floor-to-ceiling, and, therefore, completely private) has teak decking and teak deck furniture (two chairs and drinks table).

Grand Suites (876 sq. ft/81.3 sq. meters). Two Grand Suites (1104, 1005) are located one deck above the ship's navigation bridge. They are very pleasant living spaces, and feature a separate bedroom, living room with TV/DVD player, walk-in closet, dining area, and two marble-clad bathing areas. One bathing area, which is open to the bedroom (a curtain can be used to close it off), has a large five-sided sit-in bathtub placed in a glass walled enclosure on the balcony (but with no access door to the balcony, which can only be accessed from the lounge/dining area). The second is a bathroom with separate shower enclosure, bidet, toilet and washbasin. The suites have a private balcony with port or starboard views. There is also an additional (guest) toilet. Butler service is provided. The private balcony (the partitions are floor-to-ceiling, and, therefore, completely private) has teak decking and teak deck furniture (two chairs and drinks table).

Voyager Suites (603 sq. ft/56 sq. meters). Eight Voyager Suites, located on port and starboard sides of the atrium on three separate decks, have a separate bedroom, living room with TV/DVD player, walk-in closet, dining area, large, marble-clad bathroom with bathtub and separate shower enclosure, and a good sized private balcony with either port or starboard views. Butler service is provided. The balcony has teakwood deck, part partitions, and white plastic deck furniture.

Seven Seas Suites (657 sq. ft/61 sq. meters) Aft. Six spacious suites overlook the ship's stern (two suites are located on each of four decks), and have a generous wrap-around balcony, and good views over the ship's stern and to port or starboard. However, the balconies are only semi-private and can be partly overlooked by neighbors in other suites as well as from above (they do have teak decking, but white plastic deck furniture). Butler service is provided.

Another four Seven Seas Suites are located amidships and measure a slightly smaller 545 sq. ft (50.6 sq. meters), and have small balconies with either port or starboard views. These suites have a separate bedroom, living room with TV/DVD player, walk-in closet, dining area, large, and marble-clad bathroom with a combination bathtub/shower. Butler service is provided.

Penthouse Suites (370 sq. ft/34.3 sq. meters). There are 32 Category "A" Penthouse Suites and 32 Category "B" Penthouse Suites (Category "A" Suites have the better location, but the size is the same). These have a sleeping area with dressing table and adjacent lounge area, walk-in closet, and bathroom with bathtub, washbasin, separate shower enclosure, and toilet. The balcony is accessed from the lounge. The balcony has teakwood deck, part partitions, and white plastic deck furniture. Butler service is provided.

Horizon Suites (522 sq. ft/48.4 sq. meters). There are 29 Horizon Suites overlooking the ship's stern (some are sandwiched between the larger Seven Seas Suites) and have a good-sized balcony (though not as large as those of the Seven Seas Suites) and delightful aft-facing views. These suites have a separate bedroom, living room with TV/DVD player, walk-in closet, dining area, large, marble-clad bathroom with a combination tub/shower. The balcony has teakwood deck, part partitions, and white plastic deck furniture.

All Other Cabins (356 sq. ft/33 sq. meters). All other cabins (Categories C–H in the brochure, listed as Deluxe Suites) are larger than those of the same grade aboard *Seven Seas Mariner*. They have twin beds that can convert to a queen-sized bed (European duvets are standard), small walk-in closet, marble-lined bathroom with combination tub/shower, 100% cotton bathrobe 100% cotton towels, vanity desk, hairdryer, TV/DVD player, refrigerator (stocked with soft drinks and bar set-up on embarkation), personal safe. In these suites, the sleeping area is separated from the living area only by partial room dividers, and therefore is a cabin (albeit a good-sized one), and not a suite.

Four wheelchair-accessible suites (761, 762, 859, and 860) are all located as close to an elevator as one could possibly get, and provide ample living space, together with a large roll-in shower and all bathroom fittings located at the correct height.

CUISINE/DINING. There are four different dining venues, all of which are operated on an open-seating basis, so that you can sit with whom you want, when you wish. In reality, this means that dining aboard ship is like dining on land – you can go to a different dining spot each night. The downside of this is that waiters do not get to know and remember your preferences. Reservations are required in two of the four dining spots. In general, the cuisine is very good, with creative presentation and a wide variety of food choices.

The main dining room is the 570-seat Compass Rose Restaurant, which is located in the center of the ship, has a light, fresh decor, and seating at tables for two, four, six or eight. A large pre-dinner drinks bar is conveniently located adjacent on the starboard side. Dudson china, from England, is used.

Off to the port side of the Compass Rose Restaurant is Latitudes – with 80 seats the smallest of the specialty restaurants for alternative dining, with tableside preparation of dishes from all parts of the world (the decor, too, is an interesting, rather eclectic mix from several parts of the world). There is seating for two, four or six, and reservations are required.

A 120-seat supper club, called Signatures – which shares a galley with Latitudes – is located one deck above the main galley (for convenient vertical supply and staff access), and has ocean views along the room's port side. It

is directed and staffed by chefs wearing the white toque and Blue Riband of Le Cordon Bleu in Paris, the most prestigious culinary authority in the world; hence the cuisine is classic French. Doors open onto a covered area outdoors, complete with stage and dance floor. Porsgrund china is used, as are custom-made silver show plates and the very finest silverware. Seating is at tables of two, four, or six, and reservations are required.

Latitudes, is the name of a reservations-only restaurant with a show business flair and an open "show" kitchen (also used for Le Cordon Bleu cooking classes). Dinner is at a set time (typically 7.30pm) and consists of a set menu (the only choice being the main course, which is fish or meat). Seating is in alcoves or at open tables. This restaurant provides an entertaining meal.

For more casual meals, La Veranda is a large self-serve indoor/outdoor cafe with seats for 450 (the teakwood-decked outdoor seating is particularly pleasant), and the decor is fresh and light. This eatery has a substantial amount of counter display space. There is also an outdoor grill, adjacent to the swimming pool, for fast food items.

For another variation on the dining theme, you can also choose to dine in your cabin. There is a 24-hour room service menu, and, during regular dinner hours, you can choose from the full (Compass Rose) dining room menu.

ENTERTAINMENT. The Constellation Showlounge spans two decks and is quite a stunning room; the sightlines are very good from almost all seats in both main and balcony levels.

A troupe of 10 singers/dancers provides colorful mini-Las Vegas-style revues and production shows that are entertaining. Additionally, cabaret acts (vocalists, illusionists, ventriloquists, comedians, and others) provide stand-alone evening shows. The ship carries a main showband, and several small musical units and soloists (such as a singer/harpist and singer/pianist).

SPA/FITNESS. Health and fitness facilities include a reasonably extensive (though not quite as large as one might expect) health spa with gymnasium (plenty of cardiovascular equipment) and aerobics room, beauty salon, and separate changing, sauna and steam rooms (small) for men and women. Specialist Judith Jackson provides the staff and spa and beauty services, which are located not at the top of the ship, as is common with many other ships today, but in the forward section of the ship, above the showlounge.

Here are some sample prices for treatments: European aromatherapy massage, $90 (50 minutes); four hand massage, $165 (60 minutes); reflexology session, $50 (30 minutes); rejuvenation facial, $110 (60 minutes); "fast fix" facial, $40 (20 minutes); neck-to-toe seaweed body wrap, $75 (50 minutes); micro-sea body scrub, $40 (30 minutes); aromatherapy bath and massage, $120 (60 minutes). Judith Jackson also has a range of beauty products for the body and wellbeing books for sale.

Sports devotees can play in the paddle tennis court, golf driving and practice cages.

Silver Cloud
★★★★★

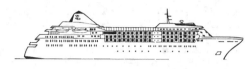

Small Ship:	16,927 tons	Total Crew:	210	Cabins (with private balcony):	110
Lifestyle:	Luxury	Passengers		Cabins (wheelchair accessible):	2
Cruise Line:	Silversea Cruises	(lower beds/all berths):	296/315	Cabin Current:	110 and 220 volts
Former Names:	none	Passenger Space Ratio		Elevators:	4
Builder:	Visentini/Mariotti (Italy)	(lower beds/all berths):	57.1/53.7	Casino (gaming tables):	Yes
Original Cost:	$125 million	Crew/Passenger Ratio		Slot Machines:	Yes
Entered Service:	Apr 1994	(lower beds/all berths):	1.4/1.5	Swimming Pools (outdoors):	1
Registry:	The Bahamas	Navigation Officers:	Italian	Swimming Pools (indoors):	0
Length (ft/m):	514.4/155.8	Cabins (total):	148	Whirlpools:	2
Beam (ft/m):	70.62/21.4	Size Range (sq ft/m):	240.0–1,314.0/	Self-Service Launderette:	Yes
Draft (ft/m):	17.3/5.3		22.2–122.0	Dedicated Cinema/Seats:	Yes/306
Propulsion/Propellers:	diesel	Cabins (outside view):	148	Library:	Yes
	(11,700kW)/2	Cabins (interior/no view):	0	Classification Society:	Registro Navale
Passenger Decks:	6	Cabins (for one person):	0		Italiano (RINA)

OVERALL SCORE: 1,722 (OUT OF A POSSIBLE 2,000 POINTS)

OVERVIEW. *Silver Cloud* has quite a handsome profile, with a sloping stern reminiscent of an "Airstream" trailer. The size is just about ideal for highly personalized cruising in an elegant environment. The vertical cake-layer stacking of public rooms aft and the location of accommodation units forward ensures quiet cabins. There is a synthetic turf-covered wrap-around promenade deck outdoors, and a spacious swimming pool deck with teak/aluminum deck furniture (little "Silversea" touches such as cold towels, water sprays and fresh fruit provide poolside pampering on hot days)..

The spacious interior is well planned, with elegant decor and fine quality soft furnishings throughout, accented by the gentle use of brass fittings (some of sub-standard quality and now showing blotchy patches in several places), fine woods and creative ceilings. Although the ship was given a multi-million dollar makeover in 2003, some parts show signs of aging (the spa and shore tenders need attention).

There is a useful business center as well as a CD-ROM and hardback book library, open 24 hours a day. There is an excellent amount of space per passenger and there is no hint of a line anywhere in this unhurried environment. Good documentation is provided before your cruise, all of which comes in a high-quality document wallet.

An elegant, announcement-free onboard ambience prevails, and there is no pressure, no hype, and an enthusiastic staff to pamper you, with a high ratio of Europeans. Insurance is now extra (it was included when Silversea Cruises first started). All drinks, gratuities and port taxes are included, and no further tipping anywhere on board is necessary (though it is not prohibited). This ship is perhaps ideal for those who enjoy spacious surroundings, excellent

BERLITZ'S RATINGS		
	Possible	Achieved
Ship	500	435
Accommodation	200	181
Food	400	342
Service	400	341
Entertainment	100	78
Cruise	400	345

food, and some entertainment. It would be difficult not to have a good cruise holiday aboard this ship, albeit at a fairly high price.

Silversea Cruises has come a long way since it began in 1994 and, after 10 years, has re-invented itself, with a more defined and refined product, and its Italian Heritage theme. The company's many international passengers react well to the ambience, food, service and the staff, most of whom will go out of their way to please. Most of the artwork is of poor quality.

Silversea Cruises has "all-inclusive" fares, including gratuities (they do not, however, include vintage wines, or massage, or other personal services), but they do include many things that cost extra aboard the ships of many other cruise lines. The passenger mix includes many nationalities, which makes for a more interesting experience, although the majority of passengers are North American (children are sometimes seen aboard, although they are not really welcomed by most passengers, who enjoy cruising without them). The onboard currency is the US dollar.

In 2002, Silversea Cruises introduced "Personalized Voyages" whereby you choose the port of embarkation and disembarkation and the length of cruise you want (minimum is five days). While this is a flexible feature, the onboard programming is already set, so you may be joining and leaving in the middle of a "normal" cruise.

Few ships make it to a five-star Berlitz rating today, but Silversea Cruises has earned an enviable reputation for high quality, particularly when it comes to cuisine. Although the ship is showing signs of wear, the actual onboard product delivered is very good, particularly with regard to the cuisine and its presentation. Shuttle buses are provided in most ports of call, and all the little extras that passengers receive aboard this ship makes it an extremely pleasant cruise experience, in surroundings that are very comfortable and contemporary without being extravagant, with open seating dining and drinks included, cold canapés and hot hors d'oeuvres served in the bars in the pre-dinner cocktail hour, a captain's welcome aboard and farewell cocktail party and other niceties.

Some vibration is evident when bow thrusters or the anchors are used, particularly in the forward-most cabins. Plastic deck lounge chairs and patio tables for the alternative dining spot do not signal a luxury product; these should be changed to teak or other sustainable hardwood variety. The self-service launderette is poor and not large enough for longer cruises, when passengers like to be able to do their own small items. Sadly, crew facilities are minimal, and so keeping consistency is difficult, as high crew turnover is a fact of life. The artwork is quite poor.

SUITABLE FOR: *Silver Cloud* is best suited to discerning, well-traveled couples (typically over 50) who seek a small ship setting (they wouldn't be seen dead aboard today's huge standard resort cruise ships), with excellent food that is approaching gourmet standards, and fine European-style service in surroundings that can best be described as bordering on the elegant and luxurious.

ACCOMMODATION. There are seven price grades in this "all suite" ship. The all-outside-view suites (75 percent of which have fine private teakwood balconies) have convertible queen-to-twin beds and are beautifully fitted out. They have huge floor-to-ceiling windows, large walk-in closets, dressing table, writing desk, stocked mini-bar/refrigerator (no charge), and fresh flowers. The marble floor bathrooms have a bathtub, fixed showerhead (this is not as hygienic as a hand-held unit), single washbasin, and plenty of high-quality towels. Personalized stationery, bathrobes, and a decent range of Bulgari amenities is provided in all suites.

All suites have televisions and VCR or DVD players (top grade suites also have CD-players). However, the walk-in closets do not actually provide much hanging space (particularly for such items as full-length dresses), and it would be better for the door to open outward instead of inward. The drawers themselves are poorly positioned, but several other drawers and storage areas are provided in the living area. Although the cabin insulation above and below each cabin is good, the insulation between cabins is not (a privacy curtain installed between entry door and sleeping area would be most useful), and light from the passageway leaks into the cabin, making it hard to achieve a dark room.

The top-grade suites feature teak balcony furniture, while all other suites have plastic deck furniture (but all balconies have teak floors) Suites with balconies on the lowest deck can suffer from sticky salt spray when the ship is moving, so the balconies require lots of cleaning. Each evening, the stewardesses bring plates of canapés to your suite – just right for a light bite with cocktails.

CUISINE/DINING. The main dining room (called, simply, "The Restaurant") provides open-seating dining in elegant surroundings. It has an attractive arched gazebo center and a wavy ceiling design as its focal point, and is set with fine Eschenbach china and well-balanced Christofle silverware. Meals are served in an open seating, which means you can eat when you like (within the given dining room opening times), and with whom you like. The dining is good throughout the ship, with a choice of three dining salons, and both the cuisine and its presentation have been improved substantially since the beginning of 2004. Standard table wines are included for lunch and dinner, but there is also a "connoisseur list" of premium wines at extra charge. All meals are now prepared as à la carte items, with almost none of the pre-preparation that existed previously).

For more informal dining, there's the Terrace Cafe for self-serve breakfast and lunch buffets (this has proved popular aboard all the company's ships), and informal themed dining at night.

An alternative dining salon, Saletta (adjacent to the main dining room), is more intimate (seating just 24 persons), and its smaller menu includes dishes contributed by Relais Gourmands (the cuisine-oriented division of Relais & Châteaux). Menus change every few days. Note that in spring 2005 Saletta will be transformed into an exclusive salon featuring upscale Italian cuisine.

The ship also provides 24-hour in-cabin dining service (full course-by-course dinners are available, although the balcony tables in the standard suites are rather low for dining outdoors).

ENTERTAINMENT. The Showlounge is the venue for all entertainment events and some social functions. The room spans two decks and has a sloping floor; both banquette and individual seating are provided, with good sightlines.

Although Silversea Cruises places more emphasis on food than entertainment, what is provided is quite tasteful and not overbearing, as aboard some larger ships. A decent array of cabaret acts does the Silversea circuit and small colorful production shows have been reintroduced. Most of the cabaret acts provide intelligent entertainment that is generally appreciated by the ship's well-traveled international clientele. Also, more emphasis is now placed on classical music ensembles. There is also a band, as well as several small musical units for live music in the evenings in The Bar, and Panorama Lounge.

SPA/FITNESS. The spa area is not large, and could do with some improvement; the tiled decor is bland and uninviting. In 2000, a new concession took over the health spa and improved upon the services and range of personal treatments available. The Mandara Spa (originating in Bali, now headquartered in Hawaii, but actually owned by Steiner Leisure) includes Ayurvedic treatments.

Fitness classes are usually free, and being aboard will give you an opportunity to try some of the more exotic treatments (some of which cost extra).

Silver Shadow
★★★★★

Small Ship: ....28,258 tons	Total Crew: 295	Cabins (with private balcony): 157
Lifestyle: ....Luxury	Passengers	Cabins (wheelchair accessible): 2
Cruise Line: ....Silversea Cruises	(lower beds/all berths): 388/400	Cabin Current: ....110 and 220 volts
Former Names: ....none	Passenger Space Ratio	Elevators: 5
Builder: ....Visentini/Mariotti	(lower beds/all berths): 72.8/70.6	Casino (gaming tables): ....Yes
(Italy)	Crew/Passenger Ratio	Slot Machines: ....Yes
Original Cost: ....$150 million	(lower beds/all berths): 1.3/1.3	Swimming Pools (outdoors): 1
Entered Service: ....Sept 2000	Navigation Officers: ....Italian	Swimming Pools (indoors): 0
Registry: ....The Bahamas	Cabins (total): 194	Whirlpools: 2
Length (ft/m): 610.2/186.0	Size Range (sq ft/m): 287.0–1,435.0/	Self-Service Launderette: ....Yes
Beam (ft/m): 81.8/24.8	26.6–133.3	Dedicated Cinema/Seats: ....No
Draft (ft/m): 19.6/6.0	Cabins (outside view): 194	Library: ....Yes
Propulsion/Propellers: diesel/2	Cabins (interior/no view): 0	Classification Society: ...Registro Navale
Passenger Decks: 7	Cabins (for one person): 0	Italiano (RINA)

OVERALL SCORE: 1,757 (OUT OF A POSSIBLE 2,000 POINTS)

OVERVIEW. *Silver Shadow* is the second generation of vessels in the Silversea Cruises fleet, and is slightly larger than the company's first two ships, *Silver Cloud* and *Silver Wind*, with a more streamlined forward profile and large, sleek single funnel. However, the stern section is not particularly handsome. There is a generous amount of open deck and sunbathing space, and aluminum/teak deck furniture is provided.

Silversea Cruises has come a long way since it began in 1994, ,and is re-inventing itself, with a more defined and refined product, and its Italian Heritage theme. The company's many international passengers react well to the ambience, food, service and the staff, most of whom will go out of their way to please. The cruise line has "all-inclusive" fares, including gratuities (they do not, however, include vintage wines, or massage, or other personal services), but they do include many things that are at extra cost compared aboard the ships of many other cruise lines. The passenger mix includes many nationalities, which makes for a more interesting experience although the majority of passengers are North American (children are sometimes seen aboard, although they are not really welcomed by most passengers, who enjoy cruising without them). The onboard currency is the US dollar.

Few ships make it to a five-star Berlitz rating today, but Silversea Cruises has earned an enviable reputation for high quality, and, although the ship is showing signs of wear, the onboard product is very good, particularly with regard to the cuisine and its presentation. Shuttle buses are provided in most ports of call, and all the little extras that passengers receive makes this an extremely pleasant cruise experience, in surroundings that are very comfortable and contempo-

BERLITZ'S RATINGS

	Possible	Achieved
Ship	500	454
Accommodation	200	180
Food	400	339
Service	400	349
Entertainment	100	86
Cruise	400	349

rary without being extravagant, with open seating dining and drinks included, cold canapés and hot hors d'oeuvres served in the bars in the pre-dinner cocktail hour, a captain's welcome aboard and farewell cocktail party. The swimming pool is surprisingly small, as is the fitness room.

In 2002, Silversea Cruises introduced "Personalized Voyages" whereby you choose the port of embarkation and dis-embarkation and the length of cruise (minimum is five days). While this is a flexible feature, the onboard programming is already set, so you may be joining and leaving in the middle of a "normal" cruise.

"The Humidor, by Davidoff," the cigar smoking lounge; has 25 seats and the style of an English smoking club. Other additions include a champagne bar and a computer-learning center, with four computer terminals.

SUITABLE FOR: *Silver Shadow* is best suited to discerning, well-traveled couples (typically over 50) who seek a small ship setting, with excellent food that is approaching gourmet standards, and fine European-style service in surroundings bordering on the elegant and luxurious.

ACCOMMODATION. There are eight price grades in this "all suite" ship. All suites have double vanities in the marble-floored bathrooms, which also have a bathtub and separate shower enclosure. Silversea-monogrammed Frette bed linen is provided in all grades, as are soft down pillows, 100% cotton bathrobes and a range of personal toiletries by Bulgari, and personalized stationery.

Vista Suites: These suites (287 sq. ft/27 sq. meters) do not have a private balcony. Instead there is a large window, twin beds that convert to a queen-sized bed, sitting area, television and VCR, refrigerator, writing desk, personal safe, cocktail cabinet, dressing table with hairdryer, and walk-in closet. The bathroom is marble-clad in gentle colors, and has two (his 'n' hers) washbasins, full-sized bathtub, separate shower enclosure, and toilet.

Veranda Suites: Each of the Veranda Suites (really a Vista Suite plus a veranda) measures 345 sq. ft (33 sq. meters) and have convertible twin-to-queen beds. They are well fitted out with just about everything you would need, including large floor-to-ceiling windows, large walk-in closet, dressing table, writing desk, stocked mini-bar/refrigerator (all drinks are included in the price of your cruise), and fresh flowers. The marble-clad bathrooms have two washbasins, full-sized tub, separate shower enclosure, and toilet.

Silver Suites: These measure 701 sq. ft (65 sq. meters). These are much wider than the Vista Suites or Veranda Suites and have a separate bedroom, an entertainment center with CD player, TV/VCR unit (in both bedroom and living room) and much more living space that includes a large dining area with table and four chairs. The marble-clad bathrooms have two washbasins, full sized tub, separate shower enclosure, and toilet.

Owner's Suites: The two Owner's Suites, each of which measures 1,208 sq. ft (112 sq. meters), are much larger units and includes an extra bathroom for guests, as well as more living space. There is a 200 sq.-ft (18 sq.-meter) veranda, two bedrooms (with queen-sized beds), two walk-in closets, two living rooms, two sitting areas, separate dining area, an entertainment center with flat-screen plasma television in the living room and TV/VCR player in each bedroom, telephones, refrigerators, cocktail cabinet, writing desk, dressing tables with hairdryers. There are two marble-clad bathrooms, one with a full sized whirlpool bathtub and two washbasins, separate toilet, and separate shower, as well as a powder room for guests. Owner's Suites can be either a one- or two-bedroom configuration.

Royal Suites: Stately accommodation can be found in two Royal Suites, which measure either 1,312 sq. ft (122 sq. meters) or 1,352 sq. ft (126 sq. meters). These are two-bedroom suites, with two teakwood verandas, two living rooms, sitting areas, dining area, queen-size beds, an entertainment center with flat-screen plasma television in the living room and TV/VCR player in each bedroom, telephones, refrigerators, cocktail cabinet, writing desk, two closets, dressing tables with hairdryers. There are two marble-clad bathrooms, one with a full-sized whirlpool bathtub and two washbasins, separate toilet, and separate shower, as well as a powder room for guests. Royal Suites can be either a one- or two-bedroom configuration.

Grand Suites: There are two of these, one measuring 1,286 sq. ft (119 sq. meters), and the other (including an adjoining suite with interconnecting door) 1,435 sq. ft (133 sq. meters). These have two bedrooms, two large walk-in closets, two living rooms, Bang & Olufsen entertainment centers, and large, forward-facing, private verandas that face forwards. These really are sumptuous apartments that have all the comforts of home, and then some.

Disabled Suites: There are two suites for the physically disabled (535 and 537), both of which are adjacent to a lift, as well as being next to each other. Measuring a generous 398 sq. ft (37 sq. meters), they are well equipped with an accessible hanging rail, and roll-in bathroom with roll-in shower unit.

CUISINE/DINING. The main dining room ("The Restaurant") provides open-seating dining in elegant surroundings. Three grand chandeliers provide an upward focal point, while you can dine when you want, and with whom you wish (within the given dining room opening times) in these refined surroundings. Meals can also be served, course-by-course, in your suite, although the balcony tables are rather low for dining outdoors. The dining is good throughout the ship, with a choice of formal and informal areas, although the cuisine and presentation doesn't quite match up to that of products such as the smaller Seabourn Cruise Line ships. Cristofle silverware is provided. Standard table wines are included for lunch and dinner, but there is also a "connoisseur list" of premium wines at extra charge. The house champagne is Moet & Chandon.

A poolside grill provides a casual alternative daytime dining spot, for fast food items.

For even more informal dining, there's the Terrace Cafe for self-serve breakfast and lunch buffets (this has proved popular aboard all the company's ships). In the evening this room has themed dinners and softer lighting. Adjacent to the cafe is a wine bar as well as a cigar smoking room. Once each cruise, there's a "Galley Brunch" in the ship's galley, transformed for the occasion into a large "chef's kitchen."

A new Relais et Châteaux dining spot (reservations may be necessary but there is no exra charge) enables diners to experience signature dishes created for Silversea Cruises by Joachim Koerper, owner of Girasol in Moraira, near Alicante, Spain. The menu is smaller than in the dining room, but more specialized. Wines are not included and must be ordered from the wine list.

ENTERTAINMENT. The Showlounge is the venue for all entertainment events and some social functions. The room spans two decks and has a sloping floor; both banquette and individual seating are provided, with good sightlines from almost all seats.

Although Silversea Cruises places more emphasis on food than entertainment, what is provided is quite tasteful. A decent array of cabaret acts does the Silversea circuit, and small, colorful production shows have been reintroduced. More emphasis is now placed on classical music ensembles. There is a band, and several small musical units for live music in the evenings in The Bar, and the Panorama Lounge.

SPA/FITNESS. The Mandara Spa operates the health spa facilities, and specializes in Ayurvedic treatments. Fitness classes are usually free. Massage and other body pampering treatments, facials, pedicures, and beauty salon treatments cost extra.

Silver Whisper
★★★★★

Small Ship: ....28,258 tons	Passengers	Cabin Current: ....110 and 220 volts
Lifestyle: ....Luxury	(lower beds/all berths): 388/400	Elevators: 5
Cruise Line: ....Silversea Cruises	Passenger Space Ratio	Casino (gaming tables): ....Yes
Former Names: ....none	(lower beds/all berths): 72.8/70.6	Slot Machines: ....Yes
Builder: ....Visentini/Mariotti	Crew/Passenger Ratio	Swimming Pools (outdoors): 1
(Italy)	(lower beds/all berths): 1.3/1.3	Swimming Pools (indoors): 0
Original Cost: ....$150 million	Navigation Officers: ....Italian	Whirlpools: 2
Entered Service: ....July 2001	Cabins (total): 194	Fitness Center: ....Yes
Registry: ....The Bahamas	Size Range (sq ft/m): 287.0–1,435.0/	Sauna/Steam Room: ....Yes/Yes
Length (ft/m): 610.2/186.0	26.6–133.3	Massage: ....Yes
Beam (ft/m): 81.8/24.8	Cabins (outside view): 194	Self-Service Launderette: ....Yes
Draft (ft/m): 19.6/6.0	Cabins (interior/no view): 0	Dedicated Cinema/Seats: ....No
Propulsion/Propellers: diesel/2	Cabins (for one person): 0	Library: ....Yes
Passenger Decks: 7	Cabins (with private balcony): 157	Classification Society: ...Registro Navale
Total Crew: 295	Cabins (wheelchair accessible): 2	Italiano (RINA)

OVERALL SCORE: 1,757 (OUT OF A POSSIBLE 2,000 POINTS)

OVERVIEW. *Silver Whisper*, which Russia's President Putin chartered in 2003 to host guests for the three-day celebrations of St. Petersburg's 300th anniversary, is the second generation of vessels in the Silversea Cruises fleet (its sister is *Silver Shadow*), and is slightly larger than the line's first two ships, *Silver Cloud* and *Silver Wind*, but with a more streamlined profile and large, sleek single funnel.

Silversea Cruises has come a long way since it began in 1994, and is re-inventing itself with a more defined and refined product, and its Italian Heritage theme. The company's many international passengers react well to the ambience, food, service and the staff, most of whom will go out of their way to please. The cruise line has "all-inclusive" fares, including gratuities (although additional grauities are not expected, they are not prohibited). The fares do not, however, include vintage wines, or massage, or other personal services, but they do include many things that are at extra cost compared aboard the ships of many other cruise lines. The passenger mix includes many nationalities, which makes for a more interesting experience, although the majority of passengers are North American (children are sometimes seen aboard, although they are not really welcomed by most passengers). The onboard currency is the US dollar.

Few ships make it to a five-star Berlitz rating today, but Silversea Cruises emphasis on quality has earned it an enviable reputation, particularly for cuisine, although the ship is showing signs of wear. Shuttle buses are provided in most ports of call, and all the little extras that passengers receive aboard this ship makes it an extremely pleasant cruise expe-

BERLITZ'S RATINGS

	Possible	Achieved
Ship	500	454
Accommodation	200	180
Food	400	339
Service	400	349
Entertainment	100	86
Cruise	400	349

rience, in surroundings that are very comfortable and contemporary without being extravagant, with open seating dining and drinks included, cold canapés and hot hors d'oeuvres served in the bars in the pre-dinner cocktail hour, a captain's welcome aboard and farewell cocktail party and other niceties.

In 2002, Silversea Cruises introduced "Personalized Voyages" whereby you choose the port of embarkation and disembarkation and the length of cruise (minimum is five days). But the onboard programming is set, so you may be joining and leaving in the middle of a cruise.

Aluminum/teak deck furniture is provided around the ship's swimming pool (although the pool itself is quite small). "The Humidor, by Davidoff," the 25-seat cigar smoking lounge, has been styled like an English smoking club. All the cigars are provided by Davidoff. Other facilities include a wine bar and computer learning center.

SUITABLE FOR: *Silver Whisper* is best suited to discerning, well-traveled couples (typically over 50) who are looking for a small-ship setting with excellent food approaching gourmet standards, and fine European-style service in surroundings bordering on the elegant and luxurious.

ACCOMMODATION. There are eight cabin price categories in this "all suite" ship. All grades have double vanities in the marble-floored bathrooms, which also have a tub and separate shower enclosure. Silversea-monogrammed Frette bed linen is provided in all grades, as are soft down pillows, 100% cotton bathrobes, a range of toiletries by Bulgari, and personalized stationery.

Vista Suites: These suites measure 287 sq. ft (27 sq. metes), and do not have a private balcony. Instead there is a large window, twin beds that convert to a queen-sized bed, sitting area, TV and VCR player, refrigerator, writing desk, personal safe, cocktail cabinet, dressing table with hairdryer, and walk-in closet. The bathroom is marble-clad in gentle colors, and has two (his 'n' hers) washbasins, full-sized tub, separate shower enclosure, and toilet.

Veranda Suites: Each of the Veranda Suites (really a Vista Suite plus a veranda) measures 345 sq. ft (32 sq. meters) and has convertible twin-to-queen beds. They are well fitted-out, and have large floor-to-ceiling windows, large walk-in closet, dressing table, writing desk, stocked mini-bar/refrigerator (drinks included in the cruise price), and fresh flowers. The marble-clad bathrooms have two washbasins, full-sized bathtub, separate shower enclosure, and toilet.

Silver Suites: The Silver Suites measure 701 sq. ft. (65 sq. meters). These are much wider than the Vista Suites or Veranda Suites and have a separate bedroom, an entertainment center with CD player, TV/VCR unit (in both bedroom and living room) and much more living space that includes a large dining area with table and four chairs. The marble-clad bathrooms have two washbasins, full-sized tub, separate shower enclosure, and toilet.

Owner's Suites: The two Owner's Suites, each 1,208 sq. ft (112 sq. meters), are much larger units and includes an extra bathroom for guests, as well as more living space. There is a 200 sq. ft (18 sq. meter) veranda, two bedrooms (with queen-sized beds), two walk-in closets, two living rooms, two sitting areas, separate dining area, an entertainment center with flat-screen plasma television in the living room and TV/VCR player in each bedroom, telephones, refrigerators, cocktail cabinet, writing desk, dressing tables with hairdryers. There are two marble-clad bathrooms, one with a full-sized whirlpool bathtub and two washbasins, separate toilet, and separate shower, plus a powder room for guests. Owner's Suites can be a one- or two-bedroom configuration.

Royal Suites: Stately accommodation can be found in two Royal Suites, which measure either 1,312 sq. ft (122 sq. meters) or 1,352 sq. ft (126 sq. meters). These are two-bedroom suites, with two teakwood verandas, two living rooms, sitting areas, dining area, queen-size beds, an entertainment center with flat-screen plasma television in the living room and TV/VCR player in each bedroom, telephones, refrigerators, cocktail cabinet, writing desk, two closets, dressing tables with hairdryers. There are two marble-clad bathrooms, one with a full-sized whirlpool bathtub and two washbasins, separate toilet, and separate shower, as well as a powder room for guests. Royal Suites can be either a one- or two-bedroom configuration.

Grand Suites: There are two Grand Suites, one 1,286 sq. ft (119 sq. meters), and the other (including an adjoining suite with interconnecting door) 1,435 sq. ft (133 sq. meters). These have two bedrooms, two large walk-in closets, two living rooms, Bang & Olufsen entertainment centers, and large, forward-facing, private verandas that face forwards. These really are sumptuous apartments that have all the comforts of home, and then some.

Disabled Suites: There are two suites for the physically disabled (535 and 537), both adjacent to an elevator, and next to each other. They measure a generous 398 sq. ft (37 sq. meters). The suites are well-equipped with an accessible hanging rail, and roll-in bathroom with roll-in shower unit.

CUISINE/DINING. The main dining room ("The Restaurant") provides open-seating dining in elegant surroundings. Three grand chandeliers provide an upward focal point, while you can dine when you want, and with whom you wish (within the given opening times). Meals can also be served, course-by-course, in your suite, although the balcony tables are rather low for dining outdoors. The dining is good throughout the ship, with a choice of formal and informal areas, although the cuisine and presentation doesn't quite match up to that of products such as the smaller Seabourn Cruise Line ships. Cristofle silverware is provided. Standard table wines are included for lunch and dinner, but there is also a "connoisseur list" of premium wines at extra charge. The house champagne is Moet & Chandon.

A poolside grill provides a casual alternative daytime dining spot. For even more informal dining, there's the Terrace Cafe for self-serve breakfast and lunch buffets (this has proved popular aboard all the company's ships). In the evening this room has themed dinners and softer lighting.

Adjacent to the cafe is a wine bar as well as a cigar smoking room. Once each cruise, there's a "Galley Brunch" in the ship's galley, transformed for the occasion into a large "chef's kitchen."

A new Relais et Châteaux dining spot (reservations may be necessary but there is no exra charge) offers signature dishes created for Silversea Cruises by Joachim Koerper, owner of Girasol in Moraira, near Alicante, Spain. The menu here is smaller than in the dining room, but more specialized. Wines are not included and must be ordered from the wine list.

ENTERTAINMENT. The Showlounge spans two decks and has a sloping floor; both banquette and individual seating are provided, with good sightlines from almost all seats.

Although Silversea Cruises places more emphasis on food than entertainment, what is provided is quite tasteful. A decent array of cabaret acts does the Silversea circuit, most of them providing intelligent entertainment, and colorful production shows have been reintroduced. More emphasis is now placed on classical music ensembles. There is a band, and small musical units for live music in the evenings in The Bar, and the Panorama Lounge.

SPA/FITNESS. The Mandara Spa (originating in Bali, but owned by the spa concession Steiner) operates the health spa facilities, much expanded when compared to smaller sisters *Silver Cloud* and *Silver Wind* (although the fitness center is miserably small), and specializes in Ayurvedic treatments.

Fitness classes are usually free. Massage and other body-pampering treatments, facials, pedicures, and beauty salon treatments cost extra.

Silver Wind
★★★★★

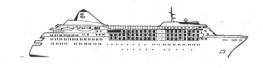

Small Ship: ....16,927 tons	Total Crew: 197	Cabins (with private balcony): 110
Lifestyle: ....Luxury	Passengers	Cabins (wheelchair accessible): 2
Cruise Line: ....Silversea Cruises	(lower beds/all berths): 296/315	Cabin Current: ....110 and 220 volts
Former Names: ....none	Passenger Space Ratio	Elevators: 4
Builder: ....Visentini/Mariotti (Italy)	(lower beds/all berths): 57.1/53.7	Casino (gaming tables): ....Yes
Original Cost: ....$125 million	Crew/Passenger Ratio	Slot Machines: ....Yes
Entered Service: ....Jan 1995	(lower beds/all berths): 1.5/1.5	Swimming Pools (outdoors): 1
Registry: ....Italy	Navigation Officers: ....Italian	Swimming Pools (indoors): 0
Length (ft/m): 514.4/155.8	Cabins (total): 148	Whirlpools: 2
Beam (ft/m): 70.62/21.4	Size Range (sq ft/m): 240.0–1,314.0/	Self-Service Launderette: ....Yes
Draft (ft/m): 17.3/5.3	22.2–122.0	Dedicated Cinema/Seats: Yes/306
Propulsion/Propellers: ....diesel	Cabins (outside view): 148	Library: ....Yes
(11,700kW)/2	Cabins (interior/no view): 0	Classification Society: ...Registro Navale
Passenger Decks: 6	Cabins (for one person): 0	Italiano (RINA)

OVERALL SCORE: 1,722 (OUT OF A POSSIBLE 2,000 POINTS)

OVERVIEW. *Silver Wind* has a quite handsome profile, with a sloping stern reminiscent of an "Airstream" trailer. The size is just about ideal for highly personalized cruising in an elegant environment. The vertical cake-layer stacking of public rooms aft and the location of accommodation units forward ensures quiet cabins. There is a synthetic turf-covered wrap-around promenade deck outdoors (this should be upgraded to teak or Bolidt), and a fairly spacious swimming pool and sunbathing deck, with teak/aluminum deck furniture (little "Silversea" touches such as cold towels, water sprays and fresh fruit provide poolside pampering on hot days).

Although the ship underwent a multi-million dollar makeover in 2003, some parts show signs of ageing (the spa and shore tenders need replacing). The spacious interior is well-planned, with elegant decor and fine-quality soft furnishings throughout, accented by brass fittings (some of which is of sub-standard quality and shows blotchy patches in several places), fine woods and creative ceilings.

There is an excellent amount of space per passenger and there is no hint of a line anywhere in this unhurried environment. Good documentation is provided before your cruise, all of which comes in a high-quality document wallet and presentation box. There is a useful internet center, a 24-hour library with hardback books, CD-ROMs and DVDs, and a cigar lounge.

An elegant, announcement-free onboard ambiance prevails, and there is no pressure, no hype, and an enthusiastic staff to pamper you, with a high ratio of Europeans. Insurance now costs extra (it was included when Silversea Cruises first started). All drinks, gratuities and port taxes

BERLITZ'S RATINGS

	Possible	Achieved
Ship	500	435
Accommodation	200	181
Food	400	342
Service	400	341
Entertainment	100	78
Cruise	400	345

are included, and no further tipping anywhere on board is necessary (though it is not prohibited). This ship is perhaps ideal for those who enjoy spacious surroundings, excellent food, and some entertainment. It would be difficult not to have good cruise holiday aboard this ship, albeit at a fairly high price. Silversea Cruises has come a long way since its inception in 1994, and continues to refine its product. The company's many international passengers like the ambiance, food, service and the staff, most of whom will go out of their way to please.

Silversea Cruises has "all-inclusive" fares, including gratuities (they do not, however, include vintage wines, or massage, or other personal services), but they do include many things that are at extra cost compared aboard the ships of many other cruise lines. The passenger mix includes many nationalities, which makes for a more interesting experience, although most passengers are North American (children are sometimes seen aboard, although they are not really welcomed by most passengers). The onboard currency is the US dollar.

After 10 years, Silversea Cruises re-invented itself, with a more defined and refined product and an Italian Heritage theme. The past few years saw the delivery of a tarnished Silver(sea) service; however, I am pleased that this has been recognized and that Silversea Cruises is now polishing the silver again). Few ships make it to a five-star Berlitz rating today, but, although the ship is showing signs of wear, Silversea Cruises has earned an enviable reputation for high quality, particularly when it comes to cuisine. Shuttle buses are provided in most ports of call, and all the little extras that passengers receive aboard this ship makes it an extremely pleasant cruise experience, in surroundings that are very comfortable and contemporary without being extravagant, with open seating dining and drinks included, cold canapés and hot hors d'oeuvres served in the bars in the pre-dinner cocktail hour, a captain's welcome aboard and farewell cocktail party and other niceties.

In 2002, Silversea Cruises introduced "Personalized Voyages" whereby you choose the port of embarkation and disembarkation and the length of cruise you want (minimum is five days). While this is a flexible feature, the onboard programming is already set, so you may be joining and leaving in the middle of a "normal" cruise.

Most of the artwork is of very poor quality. Some vibration is evident when bow thrusters or the anchors are used, particularly in the forward-most suites. The self-service launderette is poor and not large enough for longer cruises, when passengers like to wash their own small items.

Crew facilities are minimal, and so keeping consistency is difficult, thanks to a high crew turnover.

SUITABLE FOR: *Silver Wind* is best suited to discerning, well-traveled couples (typically over 50) who seek a small ship setting (they wouldn't be seen dead aboard today's huge standard resort cruise ships), with excellent food that is approaching gourmet standards, and fine European-style service in surroundings that can best be described as bordering on the elegant and luxurious.

ACCOMMODATION. There are seven price grades. The all-outside suites (75 percent of which have fine private teakwood-floor balconies) have convertible queen-to-twin beds and are nicely fitted out with just about everything one needs, including large floor-to-ceiling windows, large walk-in closets, dressing table, writing desk, stocked minibar/refrigerator (no charge), and fresh flowers. The marble floor bathrooms have a tub, fixed shower head (this is not as hygienic as a hand-held unit), single washbasin, and plenty of high-quality towels. Personalized stationery, bathrobes, and a decent range of Bulgari amenities is provided in all suites.

All suites have TV and VCR or DVD players (top-grade suites also have CD players). However, the walk-in closets don't actually provide much hanging space (particularly for such items as full-length dresses), and it would be better for the door to open outward instead of inward. The drawers themselves are poorly positioned, although several other drawers and storage areas are provided in the living area. Although the cabin insulation above and below each suite is good, the insulation between them is not (a privacy curtain installed between entry door and sleeping area would be useful), and light from the passageway leaks into the suite, making it hard to achieve a dark room.

The top grades of suites have teak balcony furniture, while all others have plastic furniture (but all balconies have teak floors). Suites with balconies on the lowest deck can suffer from sticky salt spray when the ship is moving, so the balconies need lots of cleaning. Each evening, the stewardesses bring plates of canapés to your suite – just right for a light bite with cocktails.

CUISINE/DINING. The main dining room (called, simply, "The Restaurant") provides open-seating dining in elegant surroundings. It has an attractive arched gazebo center and a wavy ceiling design as its focal point, and is set with fine Limoges china and well-balanced Christofle silverware. Meals are served in an open seating, which means you can eat when you like (within the given dining room opening times), and with whom you like.

The dining is good throughout the ship, with a choice of three dining salons. Standard table wines are included for lunch and dinner, but there is also a "connoisseur list" of premium wines at extra charge. All meals are now prepared as à la carte items, with almost none of the pre-preparation that existed previously (special orders are also possible).

An alternative dining salon, the 24-seat Saletta (adjacent to the main dining room) provides a more intimate setting, a smaller menu with dishes contributed by Relais Gourmands (the cuisine-oriented division of Relais & Châteaux). Menus change every few days. Note that in spring 2005 Saletta will be transformed into an exclusive salon featuring upscale Italian cuisine.

For more informal dining, there's the Terrace Cafe for self-serve breakfast and lunch buffets (this has proved popular aboard all the company's ships). In the evening this room features themed dinners and softer lighting.

The ship also provides 24-hour in-cabin dining service (full course by course dinners are available, although the balcony tables in the standard suites are rather low for dining outdoors).

ENTERTAINMENT. The Showlounge is the venue for all entertainment events and some social functions. The room spans two decks and has a sloping floor; both banquette and individual seating are provided, with good sightlines from almost all seats.

Although Silversea Cruises places more emphasis on food than entertainment, what is provided is quite tasteful and not overbearing, as aboard some larger ships. A decent array of cabaret acts does the Silversea circuit, and small, colorful production shows have been reintroduced. Most of the cabaret acts provide intelligent entertainment.

Also, more emphasis is now placed on classical music ensembles. There is also a band, as well as several small musical units for live music in the evenings in The Bar, and the Panorama Lounge.

SPA/FITNESS. The spa area is not large, and could do with some improvement; the tiled decor is bland and uninviting. In 2000, a new concession took over the health spa and improved upon the services and range of personal treatments available. The Mandara Spa (originating in Bali, now headquartered in Hawaii, but actually owned by Steiner Leisure) includes Ayurvedic treatments. A separate gymnasium (formerly the observation lounge) is located atop the ship and provides sea views.

Fitness classes are mostly free. Massage and other body pampering treatments, facials, pedicures, and beauty salon treatments cost extra.

Sovereign of the Seas
★★★ +

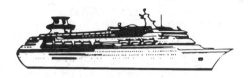

Large (Resort) Ship: ....73,192 tons	Passenger Decks: 11	Cabins (for one person): 0
Lifestyle: ....Standard	Total Crew: 825	Cabins (with private balcony): 62
Cruise Line: ....Royal Caribbean	Passengers	Cabins (wheelchair accessible): 6
International	(lower beds/all berths): 2,276/2,852	Cabin Current: ....110 volts
Former Names: ....none	Passenger Space Ratio	Elevators: 13
Builder: Chantiers de l'Atlantique (France)	(lower beds/all berths): 32.1/25.6	Casino (gaming tables): ....Yes
Original Cost: ....$183.5 million	Crew/Passenger Ratio	Slot Machines: ....Yes
Entered Service: ....Jan 1988	(lower beds/all berths): 2.7/3.4	Swimming Pools (outdoors): 2
Registry: ....The Bahamas	Navigation Officers: ....Norwegian	Swimming Pools (indoors): 0
Length (ft/m): 879.9/268.2	Cabins (total): 1,138	Whirlpools: 2
Beam (ft/m): 105.9/32.3	Size Range (sq ft/m): 118.4–670.0/	Self-Service Launderette: ....No
Draft (ft/m): 24.9/7.6	11.0–62.2	Dedicated Cinema/Seats: Yes-2/144 each
Propulsion/Propellers: ....diesel	Cabins (outside view): 722	Library: ....Yes
(21,844kW)/2	Cabins (interior/no view): 416	Classification Society: Det Norske Veritas

OVERALL SCORE: 1,386 (OUT OF A POSSIBLE 2,000 POINTS)

OVERVIEW. *Sovereign of the Seas* (sister to *Majesty of the Seas* and *Monarch of the Seas*) is a handsome ship with a well-balanced profile, nicely rounded lines and high superstructure, but the open deck space is not generous, considering the number of passengers carried. A Viking Crown Lounge is built around the funnel (this was the trademark of a Royal Caribbean International ship in the late 1980s and early 1990s) and has superb views. The ship has a wide wrap-around outdoors polished wood deck, and there is a basketball court. The interior layout is a little awkward, as it is designed in a vertical stack, with most public rooms located aft, and the accommodation located forward (this helps to keep the noise level down in accommodation areas).

There is an impressive array of spacious and elegant public rooms, although the decor definitely brings to mind the IKEA school of interior design. A five-deck-high Centrum lobby has cascading stairways and two glass-walled elevators, and a new Latin bar (Boleros) was added in the latest refit.

There is the inevitable array of shops, with lots of tacky merchandise. Casino gamers will find blackjack, craps, Caribbean stud poker and roulette tables, plus an array of slot machines. The former library, card room and champagne bar have been converted into a sophisticated business facility, with conference center and internet-connect center. The entertainment program is quite sound, and there is a good range of children's and teens' programs and cheerful youth counselors. Teen-only facilities now include a nightclub, a hangout lounge (The Living Room) and an open (aft) sundeck with open-air dance floor.

This floating resort provides a well tuned, yet very

BERLITZ'S RATINGS

	Possible	Achieved
Ship	500	381
Accommodation	200	141
Food	400	244
Service	400	286
Entertainment	100	73
Cruise	400	261

impersonal short cruise experience, for a lot of passengers. The dress code is very casual. The ship was extensively refurbished in 1997, when 220 new third and fourth berths were added to increase capacity to more than 2,800, and the shopping area was increased. More seats in the dining rooms were also added.

In the final analysis, you will probably be overwhelmed by the public spaces, and underwhelmed by the size of the cabins. However, this is basically a well-run, fine-tuned, highly programmed cruise product geared to those seeking an action-packed cruise vacation at a moderately good price, with lots of fellow passengers.

ACCOMMODATION. There are 17 cabin price grades. The price you pay will depend on the grade, location and size you choose. Some of the cabins have interconnecting doors (particularly useful for families with children). All bathrooms were given makeovers in the 2004 refit and private balconies were added to 62 cabins.

Suites: Thirteen suites on Bridge Deck (the largest is the Royal Suite) are reasonably large and nicely furnished, with separate living and sleeping spaces. They provide more space, with better service, and more perks than the standard-grade accommodation.

Standard Cabins: The standard outside-view and interior (no view) cabins are very small, although an arched window treatment and colorful soft furnishings do give the illusion of more space. Almost all cabins have twin beds that can be converted to a queen-sized or double-bed configuration, together with moveable bedside tables. All of the standard cabins have very little closet and drawer space (you will need some luggage engineering to stow your cases). You should, therefore, think of packing only minimal clothing, which is all you really need for a short cruise. All cabins have a private bathroom, with shower enclosure, toilet and washbasin.

CUISINE/DINING. The two dining rooms, Gigi and Kismet (on two different decks, one above the other and both non-smoking), provide seating at tables for four, six, or eight (there are no tables for two). There are two seatings.

For casual breakfasts and lunches, the Windjammer Cafe is the place to go, although there are often long lines at peak times, and the selection is extremely average. A new pizza parlor was created in the 2004 refit, as well as a Latte'Tudes coffee shop/ice cream parlor.

ENTERTAINMENT. The Follies Lounge is the name of the ship's principal showlounge; it has both main and balcony levels, with banquette seating. On the stage is a video wall with 50 screens – good for visual presentations.

Strong cabaret acts perform in the main showlounge. A second, smaller entertainment lounge, called Finian's Rainbow Lounge, is where cabaret acts, including late-night adult (blue) comedy are featured, as well as music for dancing.

SPA/FITNESS. The ShipShape Fitness Center and Sovereign Day Spa has a gymnasium with an expanded range of muscle-pumping machinery. There is also an aerobics studio offering classes in a variety of keep-fit regimes, a hair and nails salon, and a sauna, as well as 11 treatment rooms (including one for couples massages). While the facilities are not as extensive as those aboard the company's newer ships, they are adequate for the short cruises that this ship operates.

For the more sporting, there is activity galore – including a rock-climbing wall, with several separate climbing tracks. It is located outdoors at the aft end of the funnel.

● **For more extensive general information about the Royal Caribbean experience, see pages 128–131.**

Spirit of '98
★★ +

Boutique Ship: . . . . .99 tons	Total Crew: 30	Cabins (with private balcony): 0
Lifestyle: . . . . .Standard	Passengers	Cabins (wheelchair accessible): 1
Cruise Line: . . . . .Cruise West	(lower beds/all berths): 96/96	Cabin Current: . . . . .110 volts
Former Names: . . . .*Pilgrim Belle,*	Passenger Space Ratio	Elevators: 1
Victorian Empress	(lower beds/all berths): 1.0/1.0	Casino (gaming tables): . . . . .No
Builder: . . . . . .Bender Shipbuilding (USA)	Crew/Passenger Ratio	Slot Machines: .No
Original Cost: . . . . .n/a	(lower beds/all berths): 3.2/3.2	Swimming Pools (outdoors): 0
Entered Service: 1984/1993	Navigation Officers: . . . . .American	Swimming Pools (indoors): 0
Registry: . . . . .USA	Cabins (total): 49	Whirlpools: 0
Length (ft/m): 192.0/58.2	Size Range (sq ft/m): 80.0–510.0/	Self-Service Launderette: . . . . .No
Beam (ft/m): 40.0/12.1	7.4–47.3	Dedicated Cinema/Seats: . . . . .No
Draft (ft/m): 9.3/2.8	Cabins (outside view): 49	Library: . . . . .Some bookshelves
Propulsion/Propellers: diesel/1	Cabins (interior/no view): 0	Classification Society: . .American Bureau
Passenger Decks: 4	Cabins (for one person): 0	of Shipping

OVERALL SCORE: 997 (OUT OF A POSSIBLE 2,000 POINTS)

OVERVIEW. *Spirit of '98* is a distinctive-looking vessel built to resemble a late 1800s coastal cruising vessel. It is particularly suited to in-depth glacier spotting, and for close-in cruising along the coastline of Alaska. There is only one public room – the Grand Salon, although it is large. You are much closer to nature aboard a small cruise vessel such as this. There are no lines, no loud rap and rock music, no shows, no casino. There is a viewing area outdoors right at the ship's bow. There is an "open bridge" policy, and the company is concerned about protecting the natural environment.

The dress code is absolutely casual (not even a jacket for men, and no ties, please). However, do take comfortable walking shoes, as well as photographic materials for wildlife spotting. Smoking is permitted only on the outside decks. All tips are pooled by all staff, using the amounts recommended in the cruise line's brochure of $10 per passenger, per day (this is high for the services offered). The cruising areas are Alaska, the Pacific Northwest, and California's wine country. The onboard currency is the US dollar.

This ship is very small. There is an almost constant throbbing from the diesel engines/generator. There is no doctor on board (except for cruises in the Sea of Cortes). There are no cushioned pads for the deck lounge chairs.

SUITABLE FOR: *Spirit of '98* is best suited to couples and single travelers (mostly over 60) who enjoy nature and wildlife up close and personal. It would particularly suit those seeking an all-American crew and cruise experience, and those who don't need the kind of entertainment or vapid parlor games that some large ships provide.

BERLITZ'S RATINGS

	Possible	Achieved
Ship	500	201
Accommodation	200	118
Food	400	199
Service	400	212
Entertainment	N/A	N/A
Cruise	500	267

ACCOMMODATION. There are six grades of cabin. The Owner's Suite is the largest accommodation in the Cruise West fleet, and has large picture windows on three sides. It consists of two rooms; a lounge/living room with game table, TV/VCR, refrigerator and fully stocked complimentary bar. There is a separate bedroom with a king-sized bed, and large bathroom with Jacuzzi tub.

There are also four irregular-shaped deluxe cabins at the front of the vessel, with decent closet space, a queen-sized bed (or twin beds that convert to a double bed), and a bathroom with a separate shower enclosure. Two of the cabins also have an extra sofa bed. The other cabins are quite small, but are reasonably comfortable, and have a large picture window. While a few cabins have queen-sized or double beds, most have single beds that cannot be moved together. Each cabin has its own private bathroom, although these really are tiny, and have a wall-mounted shower. There is no room service for food or snack items.

CUISINE/DINING. The Klondyke Dining Room, decorated in the style of 100 years ago, is elegant. The cuisine is decidedly plain and simple (though tasty) American fare. Expect lots of seafood. The ingredients are mostly fresh, and local. Wine and full bar services are provided.

ENTERTAINMENT. There is no formal entertainment, although dinner and after-dinner conversation with fellow passengers in the ship's lounge/bar really constitutes the entertainment each evening.

SPA/FITNESS. There are no spa or fitness facilities.

Spirit of Alaska
★★

Boutique Ship: ....97 tons	Total Crew: 20	Cabins (wheelchair accessible): 0
Lifestyle: ....Standard	Passengers	Cabin Current: ....110 volts
Cruise Line: ....Cruise West	(lower beds/all berths): 78/78	Elevators: 0
Former Names: ......*Pacific Northwest*	Passenger Space Ratio	Casino (gaming tables): ....No
Explorer	(lower beds/all berths): 1.2/1.2	Slot Machines: ....No
Builder: ....Blount Marine (USA)	Crew/Passenger Ratio	Swimming Pools (outdoors): 0
Original Cost: ....n/a	(lower beds/all berths): 3.9	Swimming Pools (indoors): 0
Entered Service: 1980/1991	Navigation Officers: ....American	Whirlpools: 0
Registry: ....USA	Cabins (total): 39	Self-Service Launderette: 0
Length (ft/m): 143.0/43.5	Size Range (sq ft/m): ...80–128/7.4–11.6	Dedicated Cinema/Seats: ....No
Beam (ft/m): 28.5/8.6	Cabins (outside view): 27	Library: ....Some bookshelves
Draft (ft/m): 7.5/2.2	Cabins (interior/no view): 12	Classification Society: ..American Bureau
Propulsion/Propellers: diesel/1	Cabins (for one person): 0	of Shipping
Passenger Decks: 4	Cabins (with private balcony): 0	

OVERALL SCORE: 924 (OUT OF A POSSIBLE 2,000 POINTS)

OVERVIEW. *Spirit of Alaska* was was originally built for the American Canadian Caribbean Line, and is quite well suited to in-depth, in-your-face glacier spotting and for close in cruising along the coastline of Alaska. There is only one public room inside the ship – the Glacier View Lounge.

You are much closer to nature aboard a small cruise vessel such as this. There are no lines, no loud rap and rock music blaring, no shows, no cabaret, and no casino. There is a viewing area outdoors right at the ship's bow. One bonus is the fact that at the bow of the vessel, a "bow gangway" comes into its own for landing passengers. There is an "open bridge" policy, so you can visit the wheelhouse whenever you wish (except possibly during difficult maneuvers). The company has a genuinely caring attitude towards protecting the natural environment.

There is only one public room inside the ship – the Riverview Lounge. The dress code is absolutely casual (not even a jacket for men is needed, and no ties, please). However, do take comfortable walking shoes, as well as photographic materials for wildlife spotting. Smoking is permitted only on the outside decks.

All tips are pooled by all staff, using the amounts recommended in the cruise line's brochure of $10 per passenger, per day (this is high for the services offered). The ship cruises in Alaska and the Pacific Northwest. It was laid-up in 2002 due to the economic after-effects of the terrorist attacks on the United States, but began operating again in 2003. The onboard currency is the US dollar.

The ship is very small, and there are no nooks and crannies to hide away in (except for your cabin). There is an almost constant throbbing from the diesel engines/generator. There is no doctor on board, and so anyone with medical problems should really not consider this vessel. There are no cushioned pads for the deck lounge chairs.

SUITABLE FOR: *Spirit of Alaska* is best suited to couples and single travelers (mostly over 60) who enjoy nature and wildlife up close and personal in a small ship setting. It suits those who are seeking an all-American crew and cruise experience, and those who don't need entertainment or vapid parlor games to pass the time.

ACCOMMODATION. There are five grades of cabin. All are small when compared to most cruise ships, but are reasonably comfortable. A few have double beds, but most have single beds that cannot be moved together. Each cabin has its own private bathroom, although these really are tiny, and have a wall-mounted shower. Each cabin has a small sink. There is no room service for food or snacks.

CUISINE/DINING. The dining room has very plain decor, but the open-seating policy means that you can dine with whomever you wish, in one seating. The cuisine is decidedly plain though tasty American fare (expect lots of seafood). The ingredients are mostly fresh, and local. Wine and full bar services are provided.

ENTERTAINMENT. There is no formal entertainment. Dinner and after-dinner conversation with fellow passengers in the ship's lounge/bar becomes the entertainment each evening.

SPA/FITNESS. There are no spa or fitness facilities.

BERLITZ'S RATINGS

	Possible	Achieved
Ship	500	175
Accommodation	200	83
Food	400	199
Service	400	210
Entertainment	N/A	N/A
Cruise	500	257

Spirit of Columbia
★★

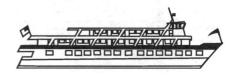

Boutique Ship: ....98 tons	Total Crew: 20	Cabins (with private balcony): 0
Lifestyle: ....Standard	Passengers	Cabins (wheelchair accessible): 0
Cruise Line: ....Cruise West	(lower beds/all berths): 78/82	Cabin Current: ....110 volts
Former Names: ....New Shoreham II	Passenger Space Ratio	Elevators: 0
Builder: ....Blount Marine	(lower beds/all berths): 1.2/1.1	Casino (gaming tables): ....No
(USA)	Crew/Passenger Ratio	Slot Machines: ....No
Original Cost: ....n/a	(lower beds/all berths): 3.9/4.1	Swimming Pools (outdoors): 0
Entered Service: 1979/1995	Navigation Officers: ....American	Swimming Pools (indoors): 0
Registry: ....USA	Cabins (total): 39	Whirlpools: 0
Length (ft/m): 143.0/43.5	Size Range (sq ft/m): 80–121.0/	Self-Service Launderette: 0
Beam (ft/m): 28.0/8.5	7.4–11.2	Dedicated Cinema/Seats: ....No
Draft (ft/m): 6.5/1.9	Cabins (outside view): 27	Library: ....Some bookshelves
Propulsion/Propellers: diesel/1	Cabins (interior/no view): 12	Classification Society: ..American Bureau
Passenger Decks: 4	Cabins (for one person): 0	of Shipping

OVERALL SCORE: 924 (OUT OF A POSSIBLE 2,000 POINTS)

OVERVIEW. *Spirit of Columbia* was originally built for the American Canadian Caribbean Line, and is quite well suited to in-depth, in-your-face glacier spotting and for close in cruising along the coastline of Alaska.

You are much closer to nature aboard a small cruise vessel such as this. There are no lines, no loud rap and rock music blaring, no shows, no cabaret, and no casino. There is a viewing area outdoors right at the ship's bow. One bonus is the fact that a direct access loading ramp can be opened up from the lounge, for landing passengers.

There is an "open bridge" policy, so you can visit the wheelhouse whenever you wish (except possibly during difficult maneuvers). The company genuinely cares about protecting the natural environment.

There is only one public room inside the ship – the Riverview Lounge. The dress code is absolutely casual (not even a jacket for men is needed, and no ties, please). However, do take comfortable walking shoes, as well as photographic materials for wildlife spotting. Smoking is permitted only on the outside decks.

All tips are pooled by all staff, using the amounts recommended in the cruise line's brochure of $10 per passenger, per day (this is high for the services offered). This ship features cruises in Alaska and the Pacific Northwest. The onboard currency is the US dollar.

This ship is very small, and there are no nooks and crannies to hide away in (except for your cabin). There is an almost constant throbbing from the diesel engines/generator. Remember that there is no doctor on board, so anyone with medical problems should not consider this vessel. There are no cushioned pads for the deck lounge chairs.

BERLITZ'S RATINGS

	Possible	Achieved
Ship	500	175
Accommodation	200	83
Food	400	199
Service	400	210
Entertainment	N/A	N/A
Cruise	500	257

SUITABLE FOR: *Spirit of Columbia* is best suited to couples and single travelers (mostly over 60) who enjoy nature and wildlife up close in a small-ship setting, and who would not dream of cruising in the mainstream sense aboard ships with large numbers of people. This is more suitable for those who are seeking an all-American crew and cruise experience, and for those who don't need entertainment or vapid parlor games to pass the time.

ACCOMMODATION. There are five grades of cabin. All are small when compared to most cruise ships, but they are reasonably comfortable. A few have double beds, but most have single beds that cannot be moved together (romantics please note). Each cabin has its own private bathroom, although these really are tiny, and feature a wall-mounted shower. Each cabin also has a small sink. There is no room service for food or snack items.

CUISINE/DINING. The dining room has minimal decor, but does have an open-seating policy. The cuisine is decidedly plain and simple American fare (expect good seafood), and quite tasty. This is because the ingredients are mostly fresh, and local. Wine and full bar services are provided.

ENTERTAINMENT. There is no formal entertainment, so dinner and after-dinner conversation with fellow passengers in the ship's lounge/bar really constitutes the entertainment each evening. So, if you don't want to talk to your fellow passengers, take a good book.

SPA/FITNESS. There are no spa or fitness facilities.

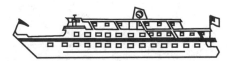

Spirit of Discovery
★★

Boutique Ship: . . . . .94 tons
Lifestyle: . . . . .Standard
Cruise Line: . . . . .Cruise West
Former Names: . . . . .Independence,
Columbia
Builder: . . . . .Blount Marine (USA)
Original Cost: . . . . .n/a
Entered Service: 1982/1992
Registry: . . . . .USA
Length (ft/m): 166.0/50.5
Beam (ft/m): 37.0/11.2
Draft (ft/m): 7.5/2.2
Propulsion/Propellers: diesel/1
Passenger Decks: 3

Total Crew: 20
Passengers
(lower beds/all berths): 84/84
Passenger Space Ratio
(lower beds/all berths): 1.1/1.1
Crew/Passenger Ratio
(lower beds/all berths): 4.2/4.2
Navigation Officers: . . . . .American
Cabins (total): 43
Size Range (sq ft/m): 64–126.0/
5.9–11.7
Cabins (outside view): 43
Cabins (interior/no view): 0
Cabins (for one person): 2

Cabins (with private balcony): 0
Cabins (wheelchair accessible): 0
Cabin Current: . . . . .110 volts
Elevators: 0
Casino (gaming tables): . . . . .No
Slot Machines: . . . . .No
Swimming Pools (outdoors): 0
Swimming Pools (indoors): 0
Whirlpools: 0
Self-Service Launderette: . . . . .No
Dedicated Cinema/Seats: . . . . .No
Library: . . . . .Some bookshelves
Classification Society: . .American Bureau
of Shipping

OVERALL SCORE: 924 (OUT OF A POSSIBLE 2,000 POINTS)

OVERVIEW. *Spirit of Discovery* was originally built for the American Canadian
Caribbean Line, and is quite well suited
to in-depth, close-up glacier spotting
and for cruising along the coastline of
Alaska. There is only one public room
inside the ship – the Glacier View
Lounge. Smoking is permitted only on
the outside decks.

You are much closer to nature aboard
a small cruise vessel such as this. There
is a viewing area outdoors right at the
ship's bow. There are no lines, no loud rap and rock music
blaring, no shows, no cabaret, and no casino. There is an
"open bridge" policy, so you can visit the wheelhouse
whenever you wish (except possibly during difficult
maneuvers). The company has a genuinely caring attitude
towards protecting the natural environment.

The dress code is absolutely casual (not even a jacket
for men, and no ties, please). However, do take comfortable
walking shoes, as well as photographic materials for
wildlife spotting. All tips are pooled by all staff, using the
amounts recommended in the cruise line's brochure of $10
per passenger, per day (this is high for the services offered).

This ship cruises in Alaska and the Pacific Northwest. It
is very small, and there are no nooks and crannies to hide
away in (except for your cabin). There is an almost constant throbbing from the diesel engines/generator. There is
no doctor on board, and so anyone with medical problems
should really not consider this vessel. There are no cushioned pads for the deck lounge chairs. The onboard currency is the US dollar.

SUITABLE FOR: *Spirit of Discovery* is best suited to couples
and single travelers who enjoy nature and wildlife up close

BERLITZ'S RATINGS

	Possible	Achieved
Ship	500	175
Accommodation	200	83
Food	400	199
Service	400	210
Entertainment	N/A	N/A
Cruise	500	257

in a small-ship setting, and who would
not dream of cruising in the mainstream
sense aboard ships with large numbers
of people. This is more suitable for
those who are seeking an all-American
crew and cruise experience, and for
those who don't need entertainment or
vapid parlor games.

ACCOMMODATION. There are six grades
of cabin. All are small when compared
to most cruise ships, but they are reasonably comfortable, and have a large picture window and
small clothes closet. A few have double beds, but most have
single beds that cannot be moved together. Each has its
own private bathroom, although these really are tiny, and
have a wall-mounted shower. Each cabin also has a small
basin. There is no room service for food or snack items.

CUISINE/DINING. The dining room has very plain decor,
but the open-seating policy means that you can dine with
whomever you wish, in one seating. The cuisine is decidedly plain and simple American fare (expect lots of
seafood), as is the cutlery (no fish knives are used, for example). The food is quite tasty. This is due to the fact that the
ingredients are mostly fresh, and local. Wine and full bar
services are provided.

ENTERTAINMENT. There is no formal entertainment, so dinner and after-dinner conversation with fellow passengers
in the ship's lounge/bar really constitutes the entertainment
each evening. If you don't want to talk to your fellow passengers, take a good book.

SPA/FITNESS. There are no spa or fitness facilities.

Spirit of Endeavour
★★

Boutique Ship: ....95 tons	Total Crew: 28	Cabins (with private balcony): 0
Lifestyle: ....Standard	Passengers	Cabins (wheelchair accessible): 0
Cruise Line: ....Cruise West	(lower beds/all berths): 102/107	Cabin Current: ....110 volts
Former Names: ....*Nantucket Clipper,*	Passenger Space Ratio	Elevators: 0
SeaSpirit	(lower beds/all berths): 0.9/0.8	Casino (gaming tables): ....No
Builder: ....Jeffboat (USA)	Crew/Passenger Ratio	Slot Machines: ....No
Original Cost: ....n/a	(lower beds/all berths): 3.6/3.8	Swimming Pools (outdoors): 0
Entered Service: 1983/1996	Navigation Officers: ....American	Swimming Pools (indoors): 0
Registry: ....USA	Cabins (total): 51	Whirlpools: 0
Length (ft/m): 217.0/66.1	Size Range (sq ft/m): 110.0–153.0/	Self-Service Launderette: 0
Beam (ft/m): 37.0/11.3	10.2–14.2	Dedicated Cinema/Seats: ....No
Draft (ft/m): 8.5/2.5	Cabins (outside view): 51	Library: ....Yes
Propulsion/Propellers: diesel/1	Cabins (interior/no view): 0	Classification Society: . .American Bureau
Passenger Decks: 4	Cabins (for one person): 0	of Shipping

OVERALL SCORE: 934 (OUT OF A POSSIBLE 2,000 POINTS)

OVERVIEW. *Spirit of Endeavour* was originally built for Clipper Cruise Line, and is the flagship of the Cruise West fleet, and is particularly suited to in-depth glacier spotting and for up-close cruising along the coastline of Alaska. There is only one public room inside the ship – the Explorer Lounge. Smoking is permitted only on the outside decks.

You are much closer to nature aboard a small cruise vessel such as this. There is a viewing area outdoors right at the ship's bow. An "open bridge" policy means that you can visit the wheelhouse whenever you wish (except possibly during difficult manoeuvres). The company genuinely cares about protecting the environment.

The dress code is absolutely casual (not even a jacket for men, and no ties, please). However, do take comfortable walking shoes, as well as photographic materials for wildlife spotting. All tips are pooled by all the staff, using the amounts recommended in the cruise line's brochure of $10 per passenger, per day (this is high for the services offered). The cruising areas are Alaska, the Sea of Cortes, and California's wine country.

This ship is very small. There is an almost constant throbbing from the diesel engines/generator. There is no doctor on board (except for the Sea of Cortes cruises), so anyone with medical problems should not consider this vessel. There are no cushioned pads for the deck lounge chairs. The onboard currency is the US dollar.

SUITABLE FOR: *Spirit of Endeavour* is best suited to couples and single travelers (mostly over 60) who enjoy nature and wildlife up close in a small-ship setting, and who would not dream of cruising in the mainstream sense aboard ships

BERLITZ'S RATINGS

	Possible	Achieved
Ship	500	185
Accommodation	200	83
Food	400	199
Service	400	210
Entertainment	N/A	N/A
Cruise	500	257

with large numbers of people. This is more suitable for those who are seeking an all-American crew and cruise experience, and for those who don't need entertainment or vapid parlor games to while away the time.

ACCOMMODATION. There are four grades of cabin. All are small when compared to most cruise ships, but they are reasonably comfortable for this small size of vessel, and have a large picture window (just four cabins on Main deck have a porthole), a clothes closet, television and VCR. A few cabins have twin beds that can convert into a queen-sized bed, but most have single beds that cannot be moved together. Each cabin has its own private bathroom, although these really are tiny, and have a wall-mounted shower. Several cabins have a Pullman-berth for a third occupant. Each cabin also has a small basin. There is no room service for food or snack items.

CUISINE/DINING. The Resolution Dining Room has plain decor, but an open-seating policy means that you can dine with whomever you wish. The cuisine is decidedly plain and simple American fare (expect lots of seafood), although it is quite tasty. This is because the ingredients are mostly fresh, and local. Wine and full bar services are provided.

ENTERTAINMENT. There is no formal entertainment, so dinner and after-dinner conversation with fellow passengers in the ship's lounge/bar really constitutes the entertainment each evening.

SPA/FITNESS. There are no spa or fitness facilities.

Spirit of Glacier Bay
★★

Boutique Ship: . . . . .97 tons	Total Crew: 15	Cabins (with private balcony): 0
Lifestyle: . . . . .Standard	Passengers	Cabins (wheelchair accessible): 0
Cruise Line: . . . . .Cruise West	(lower beds/all berths): 52/54	Cabin Current: . . . . .110 volts
Former Names: . . . . .Glacier Bay Explorer,	Passenger Space Ratio	Elevators: 0
New Shoreham I	(lower beds/all berths): 1.8/1.7	Casino (gaming tables): . . . . .No
Builder: . . . . .Blount Marine (USA)	Crew/Passenger Ratio	Slot Machines: . . . . .No
Original Cost: .n/a	(lower beds/all berths): 3.4/3.6	Swimming Pools (outdoors): 0
Entered Service: 1971/1990	Navigation Officers: . . . . .American	Swimming Pools (indoors): 0
Registry: . . . . .USA	Cabins (total): .27	Whirlpools: 0
Length (ft/m): 125.0/38.1	Size Range (sq ft/m): 55.0–72.0/	Self-Service Launderette: 0
Beam (ft/m): 28.0/8.5	5.1–6.6	Dedicated Cinema/Seats: . . . . .No
Draft (ft/m): 6.5/1.9	Cabins (outside view): 14	Library: . . . . .Some bookshelves
Propulsion/Propellers: diesel/1	Cabins (interior/no view): 13	Classification Society: . .American Bureau
Passenger Decks: 3	Cabins (for one person): 2	of Shipping

OVERALL SCORE: 910 (OUT OF A POSSIBLE 2,000 POINTS)

OVERVIEW. *Spirit of Glacier Bay* is quite suited to in-depth, in-your-face glacier spotting and for close-in cruising along the coastline of Alaska. There is only one public room inside the ship – the Glacier View Lounge. Smoking is permitted only on the outside decks.

You are much closer to nature aboard a small cruise vessel such as this. There is a viewing area outdoors right at the ship's bow. One bonus is the fact that at the bow of the vessel, a "bow gang-way" comes into its own for landing passengers. There is an "open bridge" policy, so you can visit the wheelhouse whenever you wish (except possibly during difficult manoeuvres). The company has a genuinely caring attitude towards protecting the natural environment. Cruising areas are Alaska and the Pacific Northwest.

The dress code is absolutely casual (not even a jacket for men, and no ties, please). However, do take comfortable walking shoes, as well as photographic materials for wildlife spotting. All tips are pooled by all staff, using the amounts recommended in the cruise line's brochure of $10 per passenger, per day (this is high for the services offered).

The ship is very small, and there are no nooks and crannies to hide away in (except for your cabin). There is an almost constant throbbing from the diesel engines/generator. Remember that there is no doctor on board, and so anyone with medical problems should really not consider this vessel. There are no cushioned pads for the deck lounge chairs. The onboard currency is the US dollar.

SUITABLE FOR: *Spirit of Glacier Bay* is best suited to couples and single travelers (mostly over 60) who enjoy nature and wildlife up close in a small-ship setting, and who would

BERLITZ'S RATINGS

	Possible	Achieved
Ship	500	166
Accommodation	200	75
Food	400	199
Service	400	214
Entertainment	N/A	N/A
Cruise	500	256

not dream of cruising in the mainstream sense aboard ships with large numbers of people. It suits those who are seeking an all-American crew and cruise experience, and those who don't need lots of entertainment laid on.

ACCOMMODATION. There are three grades of cabin. All are small when compared to most cruise ships, but they are reasonably comfortable, and most have a large picture window and small clothes closet. A few cabins have double beds, but most have single beds that cannot be moved together. Two cabins on the lowest deck, in the front of the ship have upper and lower berths. Each cabin has its own private bathroom, although these really are tiny, and there is a wall-mounted shower. Each cabin also has a small basin. There is no room service for food or snack items.

CUISINE/DINING. The dining room has really plain decor, but the open-seating policy means that you can dine with whomever you wish, in one seating. The cuisine is decidedly plain and simple American fare (expect lots of seafood), although it is quite tasty. This is because the ingredients are mostly fresh, and local. Wine and full bar services are provided.

ENTERTAINMENT. There is no formal entertainment, so dinner and after-dinner conversation with fellow passengers in the ship's lounge/bar really constitutes the entertainment each evening. If you don't want to talk to your fellow passengers, take a good book.

SPA/FITNESS. There are no spa or fitness facilities.

Spirit of Oceanus
★★★

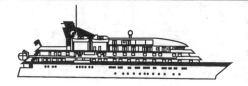

Boutique Ship: . . . . .4,200 tons	Total Crew: 55	Cabins (wheelchair accessible): 0
Lifestyle: . . . . .Standard	Passengers	Cabin Current: . . . . .110 volts
Cruise Line: . . . . .Cruise West	(lower beds/all berths): 114/127	Dining Rooms: 1
Former Names: . . . .MegaStar Sagittarius,	Passenger Space Ratio	Elevators: 1
Sun Viva, Renaissance Five	(lower beds/all berths): 37.5/33.0	Casino (gaming tables): . . . . .No
Builder: . . . . .Nuovi Cantieri Apuania	Crew/Passenger Ratio	Slot Machines: .No
(Italy)	(lower beds/all berths): 2.0/4.7	Swimming Pools (outdoors): 1
Entered Service: 1991/2001	Navigation Officers: . . . . .American	Swimming Pools (indoors): 0
Registry: . . . . .The Bahamas	Cabins (total): .57	Whirlpools: 1
Length (ft/m): 294.5/89.7	Size Range (sq ft/m): 215.0–353.0/	Self-Service Launderette: . . . . .No
Beam (ft/m): 50.1/15.30	20.0–32.7	Dedicated Cinema/Seats: . . . . .No
Draft (ft/m): 13.2/4.05	Cabins (outside view): 57	Library: . . . . .Yes
Propulsion/Propellers: . . . . .diesel	Cabins (interior/no view): 0	Classification Society: . .American Bureau
(5,000kW)/2	Cabins (for one person): 0	of Shipping
Passenger Decks: 5	Cabins (with private balcony): 12	

OVERALL SCORE: 1,218 (OUT OF A POSSIBLE 2,000 POINTS)

OVERVIEW. *Spirit of Oceanus* has a contemporary exterior, a private yacht-like look and handsome styling with twin, flared funnels. The navigation bridge is a well-rounded half-moon design. There is a teakwood promenade deck outdoors, and a reasonable amount of open deck and sunbathing space. The deck furniture is teak and the deck lounge chairs have thick cushioned pads. There is a teakwood water sports platform at the stern of the ship (not used in Alaska), plus a number of Zodiac inflatable rubber landing craft. Snorkeling gear is provided (not used in Alaska).

The main lounge, the focal point for social activities, has six pillars that destroy sightlines to the small stage area. There is a very small book and video library.

The ship was acquired by Cruise West in 2001 and is the only ocean-going vessel in its fleet. It cruises Alaska and British Columbia in summer, and sails to Tahiti, the Fijian Islands and other Pacific Ocean itineraries in winter. The onboard currency is the US dollar.

SUITABLE FOR: *Spirit of Oceanus* is best suited to couples and single travelers who enjoy nature and wildlife up close in a contemporary small-ship setting, and who would not dream of cruising in the mainstream sense aboard ships with large numbers of people.

ACCOMMODATION. There are six price categories. Fine all-outside-view cabins (called "suites" in the brochure) combine highly polished imitation rosewood paneling with lots of mirrors, and fine, hand-crafted Italian furniture. All suites have twin beds that can convert to a queen-sized bed, a sit-

BERLITZ'S RATINGS

	Possible	Achieved
Ship	500	339
Accommodation	200	150
Food	400	211
Service	400	237
Entertainment	N/A	N/A
Cruise	500	281

ting area with three-person sofa, one individual chair, coffee table, mini-bar/refrigerator (stocked with juices and bottled water), TV/VCR, direct-dial satellite telephone, and a bowl of fresh fruit on embarkation day. While closet space is good, space for stowing luggage is tight, and there is little drawer space. There are no music channels in the cabins, and there is no switch to turn off announcements in your cabin.

The marble bathrooms are compact units that have showers (no bathrooms have a tub) with fold-down (plastic) seat, real teakwood floor, marble vanity, large mirror, recessed towel rail , and built-in hairdryer. There is a high "lip" into the bathroom.

CUISINE/DINING. The Restaurant, which has an open-seating policy, is bright, elegant, welcoming, and non-smoking. It is on the lowest deck and has portholes rather than windows, due to international maritime construction and insurance regulations. There are tables for two, four, six, or eight. Dinners are normally sit-down affairs, although, depending on the itinerary and length of cruise, there could be an occasional buffet. Breakfast and lunch are typically self-serve buffets and can be taken at the poolside (weather permitting), in your cabin, or in the restaurant.

ENTERTAINMENT. There is no formal entertainment, so dinner and after-dinner conversation with fellow passengers in the ship's lounge/bar really constitutes the entertainment each evening.

SPA/FITNESS. Small fitness center. Massage is available.

Splendour of the Seas
★★★★

Large (Resort) Ship: ....69,130 tons	Passenger Decks: 11	Cabins (with private balcony): 231
Lifestyle: ....Standard	Total Crew: 720	Cabins (wheelchair accessible): 17
Cruise Line: ....Royal Caribbean	Passengers	Cabin Current: ....110 and 220 volts
International	(lower beds/all berths): 1,804/2,064	Elevators: 11
Former Names: ....none	Passenger Space Ratio	Casino (gaming tables): ....Yes
Builder: ....Chantiers de l'Atlantique	(lower beds/all berths): 38.3/33.4	Slot Machines: ....Yes
(France)	Crew/Passenger Ratio	Swimming Pools (outdoors): 2
Original Cost: ....$325 million	(lower beds/all berths): 2.5/2.8	(1 with sliding roof)
Entered Service: ....Mar 1996	Navigation Officers: ....Norwegian	Swimming Pools (indoors): 0
Registry: ....The Bahamas	Cabins (total): 902	Whirlpools: 4
Length (ft/m): 867.0/264.2	Size Range (sq ft/m): 137.7–1,147.4/	Self-Service Launderette: ....No
Beam (ft/m): 105.0/32.0	12.8–106.6	Dedicated Cinema/Seats: ....No
Draft (ft/m): 24.5/7.3	Cabins (outside view): 575	Library: ....Yes
Propulsion/Propellers: ....diesel	Cabins (interior/no view): 327	Classification Society: ....Det Norske
(40,200kW)/2	Cabins (for one person): 0	Veritas

OVERALL SCORE: 1,511 (OUT OF A POSSIBLE 2,000 POINTS)

OVERVIEW. *Splendour of the Seas* (sister to *Legend of the Seas*) has a contemporary profile that looks somewhat unbalanced (although it grows on you), and does have a nicely tiered stern. The pool deck amidships overhangs the hull to provide an extremely wide deck, while still allowing the ship to navigate the Panama Canal. With engines placed amidships, there is little noise and no noticeable vibration, and the ship has an operating speed of up to 24 knots.

The interior decor is very colorful, but perhaps a little too glitzy for European tastes. The outside light is brought inside in many places, with an extensive amount of glass area that provides contact with sea and air (more than 2 acres/8,000 sq. meters of glass). There's an innovative single-level sliding glass roof (not a magrodome) over the more formal setting of one of two swimming pools, providing a large, multi-activity, all-weather indoor/outdoor area, called the Solarium. The glass roof provides shelter for the Roman-style pool and adjacent health and fitness facilities (which are superb) and slides aft to cover the miniature golf course when required (both cannot be covered at the same time, however).

Golfers might enjoy the 18-hole, 6,000 sq.-ft (557 sq.-meter) miniature golf course, with the topography of a real golf course, complete with trees, foliage, grass, bridges, water hazards, and lighting for play at night. The holes are 155–230 sq. ft. (14–21 sq. meters).

Inside, two full entertainment decks are sandwiched between five decks full of cabins. The tiered and balconied showlounge, which covers two decks, is expansive and has excellent sightlines, and very comfortable seats. Several

BERLITZ'S RATINGS

	Possible	Achieved
Ship	500	426
Accommodation	200	163
Food	400	248
Service	400	302
Entertainment	100	78
Cruise	400	294

large-scale production shows are provided here, and the orchestra pit can be raised or lowered as required. A multi-tiered seven-deck-high atrium lobby, complete with a huge stainless steel sculpture, connects with the impressive Viking Crown Lounge via glass-walled elevators. The casino is really expansive, overly glitzy and absolutely packed. The library, outside of which is a bust of Shakespeare, is a fine facility, and has more than 2,000 books.

The casino could be somewhat disorienting, with its mirrored walls and lights flashing everywhere, although it is no different to those found in Las Vegas gaming halls. There is, sadly, no separate cinema. As with any large ship, you can expect to find yourself standing in lines for embarkation, disembarkation, buffets and shore excursions, although the company does its best to minimize such lines.

ACCOMMODATION. There are 17 cabin price grades, which is far too many. The price you pay will depend on the grade, location and size you choose.

Royal Caribbean International has realized that small cabins do not please passengers. The company therefore set about designing a ship with much larger standard cabins than in any of the company's previous vessels (except sister ship *Legend of the Seas*). Some cabins on Deck 8 also have a larger door for wheelchair access in addition to the 17 cabins for the disabled, and the ship is very accessible, with ample ramped areas and sloping decks. All cabins have a sitting area and beds that convert to double configuration, and there is ample closet and drawer space, although there is not much space around the bed (and the showers could have been better designed). Cabins with balconies have glass railings rather than steel/wood to provide less intrusive sightlines.

The largest accommodation, the Royal Suite, is a superb living space for those who can afford the best. It is beautifully designed, finely decorated, and has a baby grand piano and whirlpool bathtub. Several quiet sitting areas are located adjacent to the best cabins amidships. There are no cabins for singles.

CUISINE/DINING. The two-deck-high King and I dining room has dramatic two-deck-high glass side walls, so many passengers both upstairs and downstairs can see both the ocean and each other in reflection (it would, perhaps, have been even better located at the stern), but it is quite noisy when full (call it atmosphere). There are two seatings.

For casual meals, there are two informal options: a cavernous indoor-outdoor cafe, located towards the bow and above the bridge, and a good-sized snack area.

ENTERTAINMENT. The 42nd Street Theater seats 802 and is a single-level showlounge with tiered seating levels. The sightlines are generally good from almost all seats. Strong

cabaret acts are also featured in the main show lounge.

Other cabaret acts are featured in the Top Hat Lounge, and these include late-night adult (blue) comedy, as well as live music for dancing. A number of other bars and lounges have live music of differing types.

SPA/FITNESS. The ShipShape Fitness Center has a gymnasium (it is located on the port side of the ship, aft of the funnel), and has a small selection of high-tech muscle-pumping equipment. There is also an aerobics studio (classes are offered in a variety of keep-fit regimes), a beauty salon, and a sauna, as well as rooms for such pampering treatments as massages, facials, etc. While the facilities are quite small when compared with those aboard the company's newer ships, they are adequate for the short cruises that this ship operates. The spa is operated by Steiner, a specialist concession.

For the more sporting, there is activity galore – including a rock-climbing wall, with several separate climbing tracks. It is outdoors at the aft end of the funnel.

● **For more extensive general information about the Royal Caribbean cruise experience, see pages 128–131.**

WHERE WELL-KNOWN TERMS CAME FROM

Brass monkeys

Ever wondered where the expression "Cold enough to freeze the balls off a brass monkey" came from? Well, maritime history tells us that in the days when war ships and most freighters carried cannons (and round cannon balls) made of iron. In order to keep a supply of supply of cannon balls near each cannon, a method of keeping them from rolling around had to be found.

The best storage device consisted of a square-based pyramid. One cannon ball rested on top of four others, which rested on top of nine other, which rested on a base of sixteen. Thus, a supply of 30 cannon balls could be stacked in a small area. There

was, however, a small problem – how to prevent the bottom layer from rolling out from under the others on a moving ship. The solution was a metal plate called a "monkey." It had 16 round indentations – one for each of the 16 "base layer" of cannon balls.

If the "monkey" were made of iron, the cannon balls placed on it would rust to it; the solution was to make the "monkey" out of brass, of course. However, brass contracts more than iron when it is chilled. Unfortunately, when the temperature dipped too far, the brass indentations would shrink so much that the iron cannon balls would come adrift from the "monkey." It was, thus, really case of being "cold enough to

freeze the balls off a brass monkey."

He let the cat out of the bag

On board a square-rigger 150 years ago, this would have sent shudders through one's spine – for it meant that a sailor had committed an offense serious enough to have the "cat o' nine tails" extracted from its bag.

The "cat" was a whip made of nine lengths of cord, each being about 18 inches (45 cm) long with three knots at the end, all fixed to a rope handle. It could seriously injure, or even kill, the victim. It is no longer carried on today's tall ships, having been outlawed by the US Congress in 1850, and then by Britain's Royal Navy in 1879.

Boutique Ship:	2,298 tons	Sail Area (sq ft/m2):	36,221/3,365/
Lifestyle:	Standard		16 manually furled sails
Cruise Line:	Star Clippers	Main Propulsion:	sail power
Former Names:	none	Propulsion/Propellers:	diesel
Builder:	Scheepswerven van		(1,030kW)/1
	Langerbrugge (Belgium)	Passenger Decks:	4
Original Cost:	$30 million	Total Crew:	72
Entered Service:	May 1992	Passengers	
Registry:	Luxembourg	(lower beds/all berths):	170/180
Length (ft/m):	366.1/111.6	Passenger Space Ratio	
Beam (ft/m):	49.2/15.0	(lower beds/all berths):	13.5/12.7
Draft (ft/m):	17.7/5.6	Crew/Passenger Ratio	
Type of Vessel:	barkentine schooner	(lower beds/all berths):	2.3/2.5
No. of Masts:	4 (208 ft)	Navigation Officers:	European
		Cabins (total):	85

Size Range (sq ft/m):	.95.0–225.0/8.8–21.0
Cabins (outside view):	78
Cabins (interior/no view):	6
Cabins (for one person):	0
Cabins (with private balcony):	0
Cabins (wheelchair accessible):	0
Cabin Current:	110 volts
Elevators:	0
Casino (gaming tables):	No
Slot Machines:	No
Swimming Pools (outdoors):	2
Whirlpools:	0
Self-Service Launderette:	No
Library:	Yes
Classification Society:	Lloyd's Register

OVERALL SCORE: 1,402 (OUT OF A POSSIBLE 2,000 POINTS)

OVERVIEW. *Star Clipper* is one of a pair of almost identical tall ships (its sister ship is *Star Flyer*). It is, first and foremost a sailing vessel with cruise accommodation that evokes memories of the 19th-century clipper sailing ships. This is an accurate four-mast, barkentine-rigged vessel with graceful lines, a finely shaped hull and masts that are 206 ft (63 meters) tall. Breathtaking when under full sail, the ship displays excellent sea manners. This working sailing ship relies on the wind about 80 percent of the time. A diesel engine is used as backup in emergencies, for generating electrical power and for desalinating the approximately 40 tons of seawater each day for shipboard needs. The crew performs almost every task, including hoisting, trimming, winching and repairing the sails (helped by electric winches).

Water sports facilities include a water ski boat, sunfish, scuba and snorkel equipment, and eight Zodiac inflatable craft. Sports directors provide basic dive instruction (for a fee). The whole cruise experience evokes the feeling of sailing aboard some famous private yacht.

Some of the amenities of large modern cruise vessels are provided, such as air-conditioning, cashless cruising, occasional live music, a small shop, and two pools to "dip" in. Inside the vessel, classic Edwardian nautical decor throughout is clean, warm, intimate, and inviting. The paneled library has a fireplace, and chairs that are comfortable. A cruise aboard it means no lines, no hassle, and "Sailing a Square Rigger" classes are a part of every cruise.

Each morning, passengers typically gather for "captain's story-time" – normally held on an open deck area adjacent to

BERLITZ'S RATINGS

	Possible	Achieved
Ship	500	382
Accommodation	200	134
Food	400	249
Service	400	271
Entertainment	N/A	N/A
Cruise	500	366

the bar – which, incidentally, has a fine collection of single malt whiskies. The captain explains sailing maneuvers when changing the rigging or directing the ship as it sails into port, and notes the important events of the day. Passengers are encouraged to lend a hand, pulling on thick ropes to haul up the main sail. And they love it.

The vessel promotes total informality and provides a carefree sailing cruise experience in a totally unstructured setting at a modest price. Take minimal clothing: short-sleeved shirts and shorts for the men, shorts and tops for the women are the order of the day (and night). No jackets, ties, high-heeled shoes, cocktail dresses, or formal wear is needed. The deck crew consists of real sailors, brought up with yachts and tall ships – most wouldn't set foot aboard a cruise ship.

It is no exaggeration to say that to be sailing aboard either *Star Clipper* or *Star Flyer* is to seem to have died and gone to yachtsman's heaven, as there is plenty of sailing during the course of a typical one-week cruise. Even the most jaded passenger should enjoy the feel of the wind and sea close at hand. Just don't expect fine food to go with what is decidedly a fine sailing experience – which is what *Star Clipper* is all about. Note that 12.5% is added to all beverage purchases. The onboard currency is the US dollar.

The food, its quality, variety, presentation and service are adequate, but could be better. The steps of the internal stairs are steep, as in most sailing vessels. Tips are pooled (the suggested amount is $8 per passenger, per day).

SUITABLE FOR: *Star Clipper* is best suited to couples and singles who would probably never even consider a "normal" cruise ship, but who enjoy sailing and the thrill of ocean and wind, but want these things wrapped in a package that includes accommodation, food, like-minded companions, interesting destinations, and don't want the bother of owning or chartering their own yacht.

ACCOMMODATION. There are six cabin price grades. The price will depend on the grade, location and size chosen (generally, the higher the deck, the more expensive your cabin will be). The cabins are quite well equipped and comfortable; they have wood-trimmed cabinetry and wall-to-wall carpeting, two-channel audio, color TV, lockable personal safe and full-length mirrors. The bathrooms are very compact but practical units, and have gray marble tiling, a toiletries cabinet, some under-shelf storage space, washbasin, small shower stall and toilet. There is no "lip" to prevent water from the shower from moving over the bathroom floor. European duvets (a mix of 50% cotton and 50% polyester) are provided.

The deluxe cabins are larger, and additional features include a full-sized bathtub and mini-bar/refrigerator. There is no cabin food or beverage service.

The cabins in the lowest price grade are interior cabins with upper and lower berths, and not two lower beds – so someone will need to be agile to climb up to the upper berth (a ladder is provided, of course). A handful of cabins have a third, upper Pullman-style berth (note that closet and drawer space will be at a premium with three persons in a cabin, so do take only the minimal amount of clothing).

CUISINE/DINING. The dining room is quite attractive, and has lots of wood and brass accenting and nautical decor. There are self-serve buffet breakfasts and lunches, together with a mix of buffet and à la carte dinners (generally with a choice of two entrées). There is one (open) seating. The seating arrangement (mostly with tables of six, adjacent to a porthole) makes it difficult for waiters to serve properly. However, you can dine with whomever you wish, and this is supposed to be a casual experience. While cuisine aboard the Star Clippers ships is perhaps less than the advertised "gourmet" excellence (as far as presentation and choice are concerned), it is fairly creative, and one has to take into account the small galley provided (changed to a better layout in a recent refurbishment).

Perhaps fewer passenger cabins and more room in the galley would have enabled the chefs to provide a better dining experience than the present arrangement. There is a limited choice of bread rolls, pastry items, and fruit.

Tea and coffee should be, but is not, available 24 hours a day (now provided in china mugs), particularly in view of the fact that there is no cabin food service. Drinks prices include a service charge (presently 12.5%).

ENTERTAINMENT. There are no entertainment shows, nor are any expected by passengers aboard a tall ship such as this, where sailing is the main purpose of a cruise aboard *Star Clipper*. There is, however, live music, which is provided by a single lounge pianist/singer. Otherwise, dinner is the main evening event, as well as "captain's story-time", recaps of the day's events, and conversation with fellow passengers in the lounge or on deck (under the stars) provides engaging entertainment.

During the daytime, when the ship is sailing, passengers can learn about the sails, and the captain or chief officer will give briefings as the sails are being furled and unfurled. The closest this tall ship comes to any kind of "show" is when, one evening towards the end of each cruise, a "sailor's choir", comprised of the ship's crew, presents a nautical performance of sea songs, sea shanties, and other light diversions.

SPA/FITNESS. There are no fitness facilities, or beauty salon, or anything related to spa services aboard this tall ship. However, for recreation, the ship does have a water sports programme. Facilities include a water ski boat, sunfish, scuba and snorkel equipment, and eight Zodiac inflatable craft.

Star Flyer
★★★★

Boutique Ship: ....2,298 tons	Sail Area (sq ft/m2): 36,221/3,365/	Size Range (sq ft/m): .95.0–225.9/8.8–21.0
Lifestyle: ....Standard	16 manually furled sails	Cabins (outside view): 78
Cruise Line: ....Star Clippers	Main Propulsion: ....sail power	Cabins (interior/no view): 6
Former Names: ....none	Propulsion/Propellers: ....diesel	Cabins (for one person): 0
Builder: ....Sheepswerven van	(1,030kW)/1	Cabins (with private balcony): 0
Langerbrugge (Belgium)	Passenger Decks: 4	Cabins (wheelchair accessible): 0
Original Cost: ....$25 million	Total Crew: 72	Cabin Current: ....110 volts
Entered Service: ....July 1991	Passengers	Elevators: 0
Registry: ....Luxembourg	(lower beds/all berths): 170/180	Casino (gaming tables): ....No
Length (ft/m): 366.1/111.6	Passenger Space Ratio	Slot Machines: ....No
Beam (ft/m): 49.2/15.0	(lower beds/all berths): 13.5/12.7	Swimming Pools (outdoors): 2
Draft (ft/m): 17.7/5.6	Crew/Passenger Ratio	Whirlpools: 0
Type of Vessel: ....barkentine schooner	(lower beds/all berths): 2.3/2.5	Self-Service Launderette: ....No
No. of Masts: ....4 (208 ft)	Navigation Officers: ....European	Library: ....Yes
	Cabins (total): 85	Classification Society: ...Lloyd's Register

OVERALL SCORE: 1,402 (OUT OF A POSSIBLE 2,000 POINTS)

OVERVIEW. *Star Flyer* is one of a pair of almost identical tall ships (its sister ship is *Star Clipper*). It is, first and foremost, a sailing vessel with cruise accommodation that evokes memories of the 19th-century clipper sailing ships. This is an accurate four-mast, barkentine-rigged vessel with graceful lines, a finely shaped hull and masts that are 206 ft (63 meters) tall. Breathtaking when under full sail, the ship displays excellent sea manners. This working sailing ship relies on the wind about 80 percent of the time. A diesel engine is used as backup in emergencies, for generating electrical power and for desalinating the approximately 40 tons of seawater each day for shipboard needs. The crew performs almost every task, including hoisting, trimming, winching and repairing the sails (helped by electric winches).

The whole cruise experience evokes the feeling of sailing aboard some famous private yacht a century ago. *Star Flyer*, the first clipper sailing ship to be built for 140 years, became the first commercial sailing vessel to cross the North Atlantic in 90 years.

Some of the amenities of large modern cruise vessels are provided, such as air-conditioning, cashless cruising, occasional live music, a small shop, and two pools to "dip" in. Inside the vessel, classic Edwardian nautical decor throughout is clean, warm, intimate, and inviting. The paneled library has a fireplace, and chairs that are comfortable. A cruise aboard it means no lines, no hassle, and "Sailing a Square Rigger" classes are a part of every cruise.

Each morning, passengers typically gather for "captain's story-time" – normally held on an open deck area adjacent

BERLITZ'S RATINGS

	Possible	Achieved
Ship	500	382
Accommodation	200	134
Food	400	249
Service	400	271
Entertainment	N/A	N/A
Cruise	500	366

to the bar – which, incidentally, has a fine collection of single malt whiskies. The captain also explains sailing maneuvers when changing the rigging or directing the ship as it sails into port, and notes the important events of the day. Passengers are encouraged to lend a hand, pulling on thick ropes to haul up the main sail. And they love it.

The vessel promotes total informality and provides a carefree sailing cruise experience in a totally unstructured setting at a modest price. Take minimal clothing: short-sleeved shirts and shorts for the men, shorts and tops for the women are the order of the day (and night). No jackets, ties, high-heeled shoes, cocktail dresses, or the slightest hint of formal wear is needed. The deck crew consists of real sailors, brought up with yachts and tall ships – and most would not set foot aboard a cruise ship.

It is no exaggeration to say that to be sailing aboard either *Star Clipper* or *Star Flyer* is to seem to have died and gone to yachtsman's heaven, as there is plenty of sailing during the course of a typical one-week cruise. Even the most jaded passenger should enjoy the feel of the wind and sea close at hand – just don't expect fine food to go with what is decidedly a fine sailing experience. Note that 12.5% is added to all beverage purchases. The onboard currency is the US dollar.

The food, its quality, variety, presentation and service are adequate, but could be better. The steps of the internal stairs are steep, as in most sailing vessels. Tips are pooled (the suggested amount is $8 per passenger, per day).

SUITABLE FOR: *Star Flyer* is best suited to couples and singles who would probably never even consider a "normal" cruise ship, but who enjoy sailing and the thrill of ocean and wind, but want these things wrapped in a package that includes accommodation, food, like-minded companions, interesting destinations, and don't want the bother of owning or chartering their own yacht.

ACCOMMODATION. There are six price grades. The price will depend on the grade, location and size you choose. (generally, the higher the deck, the more expensive your cabin will be). The cabins are quite well-equipped and comfortable; they have wood-trimmed cabinetry and wall-to-wall carpeting, two-channel audio, color television, lockable personal safe and full-length mirrors. The bathrooms are very compact but practical units, and have gray marble tiling, a toiletries cabinet, some under-shelf storage space, washbasin, small shower stall and toilet.

There is no "lip" to prevent water from the shower from moving over the bathroom floor. European duvets (a mix of 50% cotton and 50% polyester) are provided. A handful of cabins have a third, upper Pullman-style berth (note that closet and drawer space will be at a premium with three persons in a cabin, so do take only the minimal amount of clothing you can).

The deluxe cabins are larger, and additional features include a full-sized bathtub and mini-bar/refrigerator. There is no cabin food or beverage service.

The cabins in the lowest price grade are interior cabins with upper and lower berths, and not two lower beds – so someone will need to be agile to climb up to the upper berth (a ladder is provided, of course). A handful of cabins have a third, upper Pullman-style berth (note that closet and drawer space will be at a premium with three persons in a cabin, so do take only the minimum amount of clothing).

CUISINE/DINING. The dining room is quite attractive, and has lots of wood and brass accenting and nautical decor. There are self-serve buffet breakfasts and lunches, together with a mix of buffet and à la carte dinners (generally with a choice of two entrées). There is one (open) seating. The seating arrangement (mostly with tables of six, adjacent to a porthole) makes it difficult for waiters to serve properly. However, you can dine with whomever you wish, and this is supposed to be a casual experience. While cuisine aboard Star Clippers' ships is perhaps less than the advertised "gourmet" excellence (as far as presentation and choice are concerned), it is fairly creative, and one has to take into account the small galley provided (changed to a better layout in a recent refurbishment).

Perhaps fewer passenger cabins and more room in the galley would have enabled the chefs to provide a better dining experience than the present arrangement. There is a limited choice of bread rolls, pastry items, and fruit.

Tea and coffee should be, but is not, available 24 hours a day (now provided in china mugs), particularly in view of the fact that there is no cabin food service. Note that drinks prices include a service charge (presently 12.5%).

ENTERTAINMENT. There are no entertainment shows, nor are any expected by passengers aboard a tall ship such as this, where sailing is the main purpose of a cruise aboard *Star Flyer*. There is, however, live music, which is provided by a single lounge pianist/singer. Otherwise, dinner is the main evening event, as well as talks by the captain. Conversation with fellow passengers in the lounge or on deck (under the stars) provides engaging entertainment.

During the daytime, when the ship is sailing, passengers can learn about the sails, and the captain or chief officer will give briefings as the sails are being furled and unfurled. The closest this tall ship comes to any kind of "show" is when, one evening towards the end of each cruise, a "sailor's choir", comprised of the ship's crew, presents a nautical performance of sea songs, sea shanties, and other light diversions.

SPA/FITNESS. There are no fitness facilities, or beauty salon, or anything related to spa services aboard this tall ship. However, for recreation, the ship does have a water sports programme. Facilities include a water ski boat, sunfish, scuba and snorkel equipment, and eight Zodiac inflatable craft. Water sports directors provide basic dive instruction (for a fee).

Star Pisces
★★★

Large (Resort) Ship: ....40,012 tons	Total Crew: 750	Cabins (with private balcony): 0
Lifestyle: ....Standard	Passengers	Cabins (wheelchair accessible): 6
Cruise Line: ....Star Cruises	(lower beds/all berths): 1,394/1,900	Cabin Current: ....220 volts
Former Names: ....*Kalypso*	Passenger Space Ratio	Elevators: 5
Entered Service: 1990	(lower beds/all berths): 28.7/21.0	Casino (gaming tables): ....Yes
Builder: ....Wartsila (Finland)	Crew/Passenger Ratio	Slot Machines: ....Yes
Original Cost: ....SEK650 million	(lower beds/all berths): 1.8/2.5	Swimming Pools (outdoors): 1
Registry: ....Panama	Navigation Officers: ......Scandinavian	Swimming Pools (indoors): 1
Length (ft/m): 579.3/176.6	Cabins (total): 718	Whirlpools: 3
Beam (ft/m): 97.1/29.6	Size Range (sq ft/m): 67.8–145.3/	Self-Service Launderette: ....No
Draft (ft/m): 20.3/6.2	6.3–13.5	Dedicated Cinema/Seats: ....No
Propulsion/Propellers: ....diesel	Cabins (outside view): 303	Library: ....Yes
(23,760kW)/2	Cabins (interior/no view): 415	Classification Society: ......Det Norske
Passenger Decks: 12	Cabins (for one person): 42	Veritas

OVERALL SCORE: 1,247 (OUT OF A POSSIBLE 2,000 POINTS)

OVERVIEW. This ship, formerly a Baltic car-passenger ferry, is wide and squat looking. Although the outdoor deck and sunbathing space is limited, it is little used by its Asian passengers. There is a helipad, a huge duty-free shopping center and a supermarket. The Regal Casino (essentially for VIPs) is large and has a high, detailed ceiling. There is a second casino for general use. There are many meeting rooms, conference auditoriums and a business center. The extensive facilities for children include computers and educational rooms, play areas and a huge video machine section. There is free ice cream for kids.

Skillfully converted into a cruise vessel for the Asian family market, *Star Pisces* is normally based on Hong Kong. The ship offers short cruises, with lots of good Asian hospitality, wide choice of dining, lots of karaoke and gambling, all in a modern ship with colorful surroundings. The initial ticket price is extremely low, but almost everything on board costs extra. All gratuities are included.

Many of the public rooms are always crowded. The cabins (and bathrooms) are very small – particularly when occupied by three or four persons. Standing in line for embarkation, disembarkation, shore tenders and for buffet meals is inevitable when cruising aboard all large ships.

SUITABLE FOR: *Star Pisces* is best suited to Mandarin- and English-speaking passengers wanting a cruise in a casual, yet comfortable environment with a range of foods and dining spots, as an introduction to cruising, at low cost.

ACCOMMODATION. There are six grades. Except for some large "imperial" suites, almost all cabins are extremely

BERLITZ'S RATINGS

	Possible	Achieved
Ship	500	277
Accommodation	200	123
Food	400	275
Service	400	265
Entertainment	100	56
Cruise	400	251

small, with just the basic facilities, and very little closet and drawer space. Many cabins have third- and fourth-person upper berths – good for families who don't mind tight quarters. The cabin insulation is quite poor, and the bathrooms are really tiny. The largest suites are very spacious, and are decorated in luxurious, richly lacquered materials, have two bathrooms, butler service, a private club meeting room, private sun deck and spa.

CUISINE/DINING. There are seven restaurants. A Chinese restaurant has live fish tanks from which to select your seafood. A Japanese restaurant includes a sushi bar, waitresses in kimonos, and private tatami rooms. An Italian restaurant has candlelight dining. A Spice Island buffet restaurant has items such as laksa, satay and hawker delights. In addition, there are three other snack cafes. The cruise fare includes only the basic buffet restaurants.

ENTERTAINMENT. Because this ship operates short cruises for the local Southeast Asian market, the entertainment actually consists of the casino, and onboard shopping, with the occasional cabaret act taking center stage (particularly during special celebration, holiday or themed cruises). There is also live music for listening or dancing to, in several of the lounges and bars.

SPA/FITNESS. There's a decent health club for men (some "extra" services are available, even if they are not listed on the rate card). Facilities include a gymnasium with high-tech muscle-pumping equipment, sauna, steam room, and massage/treatment rooms.

Star Princess
★★★★

Large (Resort) Ship:	.......108,977 tons	Total Crew:	1,200	Cabins (wheelchair accessible):	28	
Lifestyle:	..................Standard	Passengers		(18 outside/10 interior)		
Cruise Line:	..........Princess Cruises	(lower beds/all berths):	.....2,602/3,102	Cabin Current:	...............110 volts	
Former Names:	.................none	Passenger Space Ratio		Elevators:	14	
Builder:	...................Fincantieri	(lower beds/all berths):	........41.8/35.1	Casino (gaming tables):	............Yes	
	(Italy)	Crew/Passenger Ratio		Slot Machines:	....................Yes	
Original Cost:	.............$460 million	(lower beds/all berths):	..........2.3/2.8	Swimming Pools (outdoors):	4	
Entered Service:	.............Feb 2002	Navigation Officers:	.....British/European	Swimming Pools (indoors):	0	
Registry:	..................Bermuda	Cabins (total):	1,301	Whirlpools:	9	
Length (ft/m):	...........951.4/290.0	Size Range (sq ft/m):	.....161.4–1,314.0/	Self-Service Launderette:	..........Yes	
Beam (ft/m):	...............118.1/36.0		15.0–122.0	Dedicated Cinema/Seats:	..........No	
Draft (ft/m):	.................26.2/8.0	Cabins (outside view):	935	Library:	.........................Yes	
Propulsion/Propellers:	.....diesel-electric	Cabins (interior/no view):	366	Classification Society:	...Registro Navale	
	(42,000kW)/2	Cabins (for one person):	0		Italiano (RINA)	
Passenger Decks:	13	Cabins (with private balcony):	711			

OVERALL SCORE: 1,545 (OUT OF A POSSIBLE 2,000 POINTS)

OVERVIEW. The design for this large cruise ship, whose sister ships are *Golden Princess* and *Grand Princess* (and slightly larger half-sister *Caribbean Princess*), presents a bold, forthright profile, with a racy "spoiler" effect at its galleon-like transom stern that I (and others) do not consider handsome (the "spoiler" acts as a stern observation lounge by day, and a stunning discotheque by night). *Star Princess* is quite a ship. With a beam of 118 ft/36 meters, including the navigation bridge wings and with many balcony cabins overhanging the ship's hull, it is too wide – by more than 13 ft/3.9 meters – to transit the Panama Canal. When the ship was delivered by the shipyard in Italy, *Star Princess* went through the Suez Canal (the largest passenger ship ever to do so), then sailed to Singapore for its maiden voyage, before going to Los Angeles; thus the ship did half an around-the-world sailing before commencing service on the US west coast.

A few changes (compared with *Golden Princess* and *Grand Princess*) have been incorporated, including a substantially enlarged and much improved children's area (the Fun Zone) at the stern of the vessel. Also different (and improved) is the layout of the Lotus Spa (particularly the placement of the saunas/changing rooms).

There is a good sheltered teakwood promenade deck, which almost wraps around (three times round is equal to one mile) and a walkway which goes right to the (enclosed, protected) bow of the ship. The outdoor pools have various beach-like surroundings. One lap pool has a pumped "current" to swim against.

Unlike the outside decks, there is plenty of space inside

BERLITZ'S RATINGS

	Possible	Achieved
Ship	500	432
Accommodation	200	168
Food	400	256
Service	400	293
Entertainment	100	82
Cruise	400	314

the ship (but there are also plenty of passengers), and a wide array of public rooms to choose from, with many "intimate" (this being a relative word) spaces and places to play. The passenger flow has been well thought-out, and works with little congestion. The decor is attractive, with lots of earth tones (well suited to both American and European tastes). In fact, this is a culmination of the best of all that Princess Cruises has to offer from its many years of operating what is now a well-tuned, good-quality product.

Four areas center on swimming pools, one of which is two decks high and is covered by a magrodome, itself an extension of the funnel housing. High atop the stern of the ship is a ship-wide glass-walled disco pod. It looks like an aerodynamic "spoiler" and is positioned high above the water, with spectacular views from the extreme port and starboard side windows.

An extensive collection of art works has been chosen, and this complements the interior design and colors well. If you see something you like, you will be able to purchase it on board – it's almost all for sale.

Like sister ships *Golden Princess* and *Grand Princess*, *Star Princess* also has a Wedding Chapel (a live web-cam can relay ceremonies via the internet). The ship's captain can legally marry (American) couples, thanks to the ship's Bermuda registry and a special dispensation (which should be verified when in the planning stage, according to where you reside). Princess Cruises offers three wedding packages – Pearl, Emerald, Diamond. The fee includes registration and official marriage certificate. However, to get married and take your close family members and entourage with you on your honeymoon is going to cost a lot of money. The "Hearts & Minds" chapel is also useful for "renewal of vows" ceremonies.

For children, there is a two-deck-high playroom, teen room, and a host of specially trained counselors. Children have their own pools, hot tubs, and open deck area at the stern of the ship, thankfully away from adult areas. There are good netted-in areas; one section has a dip pool, while another has a mini-basketball court.

Gamblers should enjoy what is one of the largest casinos at sea (Grand Casino), with more than 260 slot machines; there are blackjack, craps and roulette tables, plus newer games such as Let It Ride Bonus, Spanish 21 and Caribbean Draw Progressive. But the highlight could well be the specially linked slot machines that provide a combined payout.

Other features include a decent library/CD-Rom computer room, and a separate card room. Ship lovers should enjoy the wood-paneled Wheelhouse Bar, finely decorated with memorabilia and ship models tracing part of parent company P&O's history (this ship highlights the 1950-built cargo ship *Ganges*. A sports bar, Shooters, has two billiard tables, as well as eight television screens.

A high-tech hospital is provided, with live SeaMed telemedicine link-ups with specialists at the Cedars-Sinai Medical Center in Los Angeles available for emergency help.

The ship is a stunning, grand resort playground in which to roam when you are not ashore. Princess Cruises delivers a consistently fine, well-packaged vacation product, with a good sense of style, at an attractive, highly competitive price, and this ship will appeal to those that really enjoy a big city to play in, with all the trimmings and lots of fellow passengers. The ship is full of revenue centers, however, designed to help part you from your money. As cruising aboard large ships such as this has become increasingly an onboard revenue-based product, you can expect to be subjected to a stream of flyers advertising daily art auctions, "designer" watches and other promotions, while "artworks" for auction are strewn throughout the ship.

The dress code has been simplified – reduced to formal or smart casual (which seems to be translated by many as jeans and trainers). Gratuities to staff are automatically added to your account, at $10 per person, per day (gratuities for children are charged at the same rate). If you want to pay less, you'll need to go to the reception desk to have these charges adjusted (that could mean lining up with many other passengers wanting to do the same). The onboard currency is the US dollar.

Whether this really can be considered a relaxing holiday is a moot point, but with so many choices and "small" rooms to enjoy, the ship has been extremely well designed, and the odds are that you'll have a fine cruise vacation.

If you are not used to large ships, it will take you some time to find your way around, despite the company's claim that this vessel offers passengers a "small ship feel, big ship choice." The cabin bath towels are small, and drawer space is very limited. There are no butlers – even for the top-grade suites (which are not really large in comparison similar suites aboard some other ships). Cabin attendants have too many cabins to look after (typically 20), which does not translate to fine personal service.

The automated telephone system is frustrating, and luggage delivery is inefficient.

ACCOMMODATION. There are six principal types of cabins and configurations: (a) grand suite, (b) suite, (c) mini-suite, (d) outside-view double cabins with balcony, (e) outside-view double cabins, and (f) interior (no view) double cabins. These come in 35 different brochure price categories (the price you pay will depend on the grade, location and size chosen). The choice is quite bewildering for both travel agents and passengers; pricing will depend on two things, size and location.

(a) The largest, most lavish suite is the Grand Suite (B748, which is located at the ship's stern – a different position to the two Grand Suites aboard Grand Princess). It has a large bedroom with queen-sized bed, huge walk-in (illuminated) closets, two bathrooms, a lounge (with fireplace and sofa bed) with wet bar and refrigerator, and a large private balcony on the port side (with hot tub that can be accessed from both balcony and bedroom).

(b/c) Suites (with a semi-private balcony) have a separate living room (with sofa bed) and bedroom (with a television in each). The bathroom is quite large and has both a tub and shower stall. The mini-suites also have a private balcony, and a separate living and sleeping area (with a television in each). The differences between the suites and mini-suites are basically in the size and appointments, the suite being more of a square shape while mini-suites are more rectangular, and have few drawers. Both suites and mini-suites have plush bathrobes, and fully tiled bathrooms with ample open shelf storage space. Suite and mini-suite passengers receive greater attention, including priority embarkation and disembarkation privileges. What is not good is that the most expensive accommodation has only semi-private balconies that can be seen from above and so there is little privacy (Suites C401, 402, 409, 410, 414, 415, 420, 421, 422, 423, 424 and 425 on Caribe Deck in particular). Also, the suites D105 and D106 (Dolphin Deck), which are extremely large, have balconies that are overlooked from above.

(d/e/f). Both interior (no view) and outside-view (the outsides come either with or without private balcony) cabins are of a functional design, although almost no drawers are provided. They are quite attractive, with warm, pleasing decor and fine soft furnishing fabrics; 80 percent of the outside-view cabins have a private balcony. Interior (no view) cabins measure 160 sq. ft (14.4 sq. meters), while the standard outside-view cabins measure 228 sq. ft (21 sq. meters).

The 28 wheelchair-accessible cabins measure 250–385 sq. ft (23.2–35.7 sq. meters). Surprisingly, there is no mirror for dressing, and no full-length hanging space for long dresses (yes, some passengers in wheelchairs do also use mirrors and full-length clothing). Additionally, two family suites consist of two suites with an interconnecting door, plus a large balcony. These can sleep up to 10 (if at least four are children) or up to eight people (if all are adults).

All passengers receive turndown service and chocolates on pillows each night, bathrobes (on request), and toiletry amenity kits (larger for suite/mini-suite occupants). A hairdryer is provided in all cabins, sensibly located at the vanity desk unit in the living area. All bathrooms have tiled floors, and there is a decent amount of open shelf storage space for personal toiletries, although the plain beige decor is very basic and unappealing. Princess Cruises typically carries CNN, CNBC, ESPN and TNT on the in-cabin color television system (when available, depending on cruise area).

Most outside cabins on Emerald Deck have views obstructed by the lifeboats. There are no cabins for singles. Your name is placed outside your suite or cabin in a documents holder – making it simple for delivery service personnel but also making it intrusive as far as privacy is concerned. There is 24-hour room service (but some items on the room service menu are not available during early morning hours).

Some cabins can accommodate a third and fourth person in upper berths. However, in such cabins, the lower beds cannot then be pushed together to make queen-sized bed.

Almost all balcony suites and cabins can be overlooked both from the navigation bridge wing, as well as from the port and starboard sections of the ship's discotheque – located high above the ship at the stern. Cabins with balconies on Dolphin, Caribe and Baja decks are also overlooked by passengers on balconies on the deck above. They are, therefore, not at all private. However, perhaps the least desirable balcony cabins are eight balcony cabins located forward on Emerald Deck, as the balconies do not extend to the side of the ship and can be passed by walkers and gawkers on the adjacent Upper Promenade walkway (so occupants need to keep their curtains closed most of the time). Also, passengers occupying some the most expensive suites with balconies at the stern of the vessel may experience considerable vibration during certain ship maneuvers.

CUISINE/DINING. As befits the size of the ship, there is a variety of dining options. For formal meals there are three principal dining rooms (Amalfi, with 504 seats; Capri, with 486 seats; and Portofino, with 486 seats), and seating is assigned according to the location of your cabin. There are two seatings in one restaurant (Amalfi), while "anytime dining" (where you choose when and with whom you want to eat) is typically offered by the other two. All three are non-smoking and split into multi-tier sections in a non-symmetrical design that breaks what are quite large spaces into many smaller sections, for better ambiance. Each dining room has its own galley. While four elevators go to Fiesta Deck where the amalfi and Portofino restaurants are located, only two elevators go to Plaza Deck 5 where the Capri Restaurant is located (this can cause long wait problems at peak times, particularly for anyone in a wheelchair).

Specially designed dinnerware and high-quality linens and silverware are used in the main dining rooms; by Dudson of England (dinnerware), Frette Egyptian cotton table linens, and silverware by Hepp of Germany. Note that 15% is added to all beverage bills, including wines.

Alternative (Extra Charge) Dining Options: There are two: Sabatini's Trattoria and Tequila's. Both are open for lunch and dinner on days at sea. Sabatini's is an Italian eatery, with colorful tiled Mediterranean-style decor; it is named after Trattoria Sabatini, the 200-year old institution in Florence (where there is no cover charge). It has Italian-style pizzas and pastas, with a variety of sauces, as well as Italian-style entrées (including tiger prawns and lobster tail – all provided with flair and entertainment from by the staff of waiters (by reservation only, with a cover charge of $15 per person, for lunch or dinner on sea days only).

Tequila's has "southwestern American" food; by reservation only, with a cover charge of $8 per person, for lunch or dinner on sea days only. However, do note that Tequila's is spread over the whole beam (width) of the ship, and two walkways intersect it, which means that it's a very open area, with people walking through it as you eat – not a very comfortable arrangement. The cuisine in both of these spots is decidedly better than in the three main dining rooms, with better quality ingredients and more attention to presentation and taste.

A poolside hamburger grill and pizza bar (no additional charge) are dining spots for casual bites, while extra charges will apply if you order items to eat at either the coffee bar/patisserie, or the caviar/champagne bar.

Other casual meals can be taken in the Horizon Court, which is open 24 hours a day. It has large ocean-view on port and starboard sides and direct access to the two principal swimming pools and lido deck. There is no real finesse in presentation, however, as plastic plates are provided.

ENTERTAINMENT. The Princess Theater (showlounge) is the main entertainment venue; it spans two decks and has comfortable seating on both main and balcony levels. It has $3 million in sound and light equipment, plus a 9-piece orchestra, and a scenery loading bay that connects directly from stage to a hull door for direct transfer to the dockside).

The Vista Lounge is a second entertainment lounge. It has cabaret acts (magicians, comedy jugglers, ventriloquists and others) at night, and lectures, bingo and horse racing during the day. Explorers, a third entertainment lounge, can also host cabaret acts and dance bands. A variety of other lounges and bars feature live music, and Princess Cruises has a number of male dance hosts as partners for women traveling alone.

SPA/FITNESS. The Lotus Spa has Japanese-style decor, and surrounds one of the swimming pools (you can have a massage or other spa treatment in an ocean-view treatment room). It is unfortunate, however (perhaps a lack of knowledge or respect on the part of the interior designer), that the Japanese symbol on the door of the steam inhalation rooms means insect – not a nice thing to call passengers. Note also that some of the spa (massage) treatment rooms are located directly underneath the jogging track.

● **For more extensive general information about the Princess Cruises experience, see pages 124–127.**

Statendam
★★★★

Large (Resort) Ship:	.55,451 tons	Total Crew:	.557
Lifestyle:	.Premium	Passengers	
Cruise Line:	.Holland America Line	(lower beds/all berths):	.1,266/1,627
Former Names:	.none	Passenger Space Ratio	
Builder:	.Fincantieri (Italy)	(lower beds/all berths):	.43.8/34.0
Original Cost:	.$215 million	Crew/Passenger Ratio	
Entered Service:	.Jan 1993	(lower beds/all berths):	.2.2/2.9
Registry:	.The Netherlands	Navigation Officers:	.Dutch
Length (ft/m):	.719.4/219.3	Cabins (total):	.633
Beam (ft/m):	.101.0/30.8	Size Range (sq ft/m):	.186.2–1,124.8/
Draft (ft/m):	.24.6/7.5		17.3–104.5
Propulsion/Propellers:	.diesel-electric	Cabins (outside view):	.502
	(34,560kW)/2	Cabins (interior/no view):	.131
Passenger Decks:	.10	Cabins (for one person):	.0

Cabins (with private balcony):	.150
Cabins (wheelchair accessible):	.6
Cabin Current:	.110 and 220 volts
Elevators:	.8
Casino (gaming tables):	.Yes
Slot Machines:	.Yes
Swimming Pools (outdoors):	.1
Swimming Pools (indoors):	.1
	(magrodome)
Whirlpools:	.2
Self-Service Launderette:	.Yes
Dedicated Cinema/Seats:	.Yes/249
Library:	.Yes
Classification Society:	.Lloyd's Register

OVERALL SCORE: 1,533 (OUT OF A POSSIBLE 2,000 POINTS)

OVERVIEW. *Statendam* is the first of a series of four almost identical ships in the same series – the others being *Maasdam*, *Ryndam* and *Veendam*. The exterior styling is rather angular (some would say boxy – the funnel certainly is), although it is softened and balanced somewhat by the fact that the hull is painted black.

There is a full wrap-around teakwood promenade deck outdoors – excellent for strolling, and, thankfully, there's no sign of synthetic turf. The deck lounge chairs on the exterior promenade deck are wood, and come with comfortable cushioned pads, while those at the swimming pool on Lido Deck are of white plastic. Holland America Line keeps its ships clean and tidy, and there is good passenger flow throughout the public areas.

In the interiors of this "S" -class ship, an asymmetrical layout helps to reduce bottlenecks and congestion. Most of the public rooms are concentrated on two decks, Promenade Deck, and Upper Promenade Deck, which creates a spacious feel to the ship's interiors. In general, a restrained approach to interior styling is taken, using a mixture of contemporary materials combined with traditional woods and ceramics. There is, fortunately, little "glitz" anywhere.

What is outstanding is the array of artworks throughout the ship (costing about $2 million), assembled and nicely displayed to represent the fine Dutch heritage of Holland America Line and to present a balance between standard itineraries and onboard creature comforts. Also noticeable are the fine flower arrangements throughout the public areas and foyers – used to good effect to brighten up what to some is dull decor.

Atop the ship, with forward facing views that wrap around the sides is the Crow's Nest Lounge. By day it makes a fine

BERLITZ'S RATINGS

	Possible	Achieved
Ship	500	418
Accommodation	200	162
Food	400	267
Service	400	299
Entertainment	100	77
Cruise	400	310

observation lounge, with large ocean-view windows, while by night it turns into a nightclub with extremely variable lighting. The atrium foyer is three decks high, although its sculptured center-piece (*Fountain of the Sirens*, a late 17th-century bronze piece by Willem de Groat) makes it look a little crowded, and leaves little room in front of the purser's office (called the Front Office). A hydraulic magrodome (glass) roof covers the reasonably sized swimming pool/whirlpools and central Lido area (whose focal point is a large dolphin sculpture) so that this can be used in either fine or inclement weather.

The ship has a large, relaxing library. There's also a card-room, an Explorer's Lounge (good for relaxing in, for after-noon tea, and after-dinner coffees), a Crows Nest (the ship's observation lounge that doubles as a late-night spot and discotheque), an intimate Piano Bar, and, of course, a casino. Adorning stairway landings are several oil paintings by Stephen Card (an ex-captain) showing former Holland America Line ships that bore the name *Statendam*.

Statendam is basically a well-built ship, and has fairly decent interior fit and finish. Holland America Line is constantly fine-tuning its performance as a cruise operator and its regular passengers (almost all of whom are North American – there are few international passengers) find the company's ships very comfortable and well-run. The company continues its strong maritime traditions, although the present food and service components let down the rest of the cruise experience. Perhaps the ship's best asset is its friendly and personable Filipino and Indonesian crew, although communication can prove frustrating at times. The onboard currency is the US dollar.

An escalator travels between two of the lower decks (one of which was originally planned to be the embarkation point), but it is almost pointless. The charge to use the washing machines and dryers in the self-service launderette is petty, particularly for occupants of expensive suites. The men's urinals in public restrooms are unusually high.

ACCOMMODATION. There are 17 cabin price grades. The price you pay will depend on the grade, location and size you choose. Cabins range from small interior (no view) cabins to a large penthouse suite (with ocean views). All cabin televisions carry CNN and TNT.

The interior (no view) and outside-view standard cabins have twin beds that can be converted to a queen-sized bed, and there is a separate living space with sofa and coffee table. However, although the drawer space is generally good, the closet space is very tight, particularly for long cruises (although more than adequate for a 7-night cruise). The bathrooms are tiled, and compact but practical. Bathrooms are also provided for all suites/cabins, as are hairdryers, and a small range of personal amenities (soap, conditioning shampoo, body lotion, shower cap, vanity kit). The bathrooms are quite well laid out, but the bathtubs are small units better described as shower tubs.

On Navigation Deck, 28 suites have accommodation for up to four persons. These also have in-suite dining as an alternative to the dining room, for private, reclusive meals. These are very spacious, tastefully decorated and well laid-out, and have a separate living room, bedroom with two lower beds (convertible to a king-size bed), a good size living area, dressing room, plenty of closet and drawer space, marble bathroom with whirlpool bathtub.

The largest accommodation of all is a penthouse suite. There is only one, located on the starboard side of Navigation Deck at the forward staircase. It has a king-sized bed, television and video player, and vanity desk. A large walk-in closet has superb drawer space. There is an oversize whirlpool bath (it could seat four) and separate shower enclosure, and a separate washroom with toilet, bidet and washbasin. The living room has a writing desk, a large television and a full set of audio equipment. The dressing room has a large private balcony (with teak lounge chairs and drinks tables, dining table and four chairs). The pantry has a large refrigerator, toaster unit, and full coffee/tea making facilities and food prepareation area, and a separate entrance from the hallway. There's a mini-bar/refrigerator, a guest toilet and floor to ceiling windows. Note that there is no bell push.

Passengers in accommodation designated as suites and mini-suites have the use of a private concierge club called the Neptune Lounge, where light breakfast and snacks throughout the day can be taken.

CUISINE/DINING. The Rotterdam Dining Room, with smoking and no-smoking sections, spans two decks. It is located at the stern of the ship, is quite dramatic, and has two grand staircases to connect the two levels, panoramic views on three sides, and a music balcony. It has open seating for breakfast and lunch, and four seatings for dinner (you must pre-select a time and stick with it) at 5.45pm, 6.15pm, 8pm and 8.30pm. There are tables for two, four, six or eight. The waiter stations in the dining room are very noisy for anyone seated adjacent to them. Fine Rosenthal china and cutlery are used (although there are no fish knives).

Alternative Dining Option: A small restaurant was added in 2002. Called the Pinnacle Grill, it is located just forward of the balcony level of the main dining room on the starboard side. The 66-seat dining spot has Pacific Northwest cuisine (Alaska salmon, halibut and other regional specialities, plus a selection of premium steaks). The new venue (reservations are necessary, and a cover/service charge of $20 applies) was created out of the the former private dining wing of the main dining room, plus a slice of the Explorer's Lounge. A Bulgari show plate, Rosenthal china, Reidel wine glasses, and Frette table linen are used. The Pinnacle Grill is a much better dining experience than the main dining room, and worth it for that special celebration.

For more casual evening eating, the Lido Buffet is open for dinners on all except the last night of each cruise, in an open-seating arrangement. Tables are set with crisp linens, flatware and stemware. A set menu is featured, and this includes a choice of four entrées.

The dual-line, self-serve Lido Buffet (one side is for smokers, the other side for non-smokers) is also the place for casual breakfasts and lunches. Again there is much use of canned fruits (good for dentally challenged older passengers) and packeted items, although there are several commercial low-calorie salad dressings. The choice of cheeses (and accompanying crackers) is very poor. The beverage station also lets it down, for it is no better than those found in family outlets ashore in the United States. In addition, a poolside grill provides basic American hamburgers and hot dogs.

Passengers will need to eat in the Lido Cafe on any days when the dining room is closed for lunch (typically once or twice per cruise, depending on the ship's itinerary).

ENTERTAINMENT. The Van Gogh Showlounge, located at the forward part of the ship, spans two decks, with banquette seating on both main and upper levels. It is basically a well-designed room, but the ceiling is low and the sightlines from the balcony level are quite poor.

SPA/FITNESS. The Ocean Spa is located one deck below the navigation bridge at the very forward part of the ship. It includes a gymnasium (with all the latest muscle-pumping exercise machines, including an abundance of treadmills) with ocean views, an aerobics exercise area, large beauty salon with ocean-view windows to the port side, several treatment rooms, and men's and women's sauna, steam room and changing areas.

● **For more extensive general information on what a Holland America Line cruise is like, see pages 118–122.**

Summit
★★★★ +

Large (Resort) Ship: ....91,000 tons	Total Crew: 999	Cabins (wheelchair accessible): 26
Lifestyle: ....Premium	Passengers	(17 with private balcony)
Cruise Line: ....Celebrity Cruises	(lower beds/all berths): 1,950/2,450	Cabin Current: ....110 and 220 volts
Former Names: ....none	Passenger Space Ratio	Elevators: 10
Builder: ....Chantiers de l'Atlantique	(lower beds/all berths): 46.6/37.1	Casino (gaming tables): ....Yes
(France)	Crew/Passenger Ratio	Slot Machines: ....Yes
Original Cost: ....$350 million	(lower beds/all berths): 1.9/2.4	Swimming Pools (outdoors): 2
Entered Service: ....Nov 2001	Navigation Officers: ....Greek	Swimming Pools (indoors): 1
Registry: ....The Bahamas	Cabins (total): 975	(with magrodome)
Length (ft/m): 964.5/294.0	Size Range (sq ft/m): 165.1–2,530.0/	Whirlpools: 4
Beam (ft/m): 105.6/32.2	15.34–235.0	Self-Service Launderette: ....No
Draft (ft/m): 26.2/8.0	Cabins (outside view): 780	Dedicated Cinema/Seats: Yes/368
Propulsion/Propellers: .....gas turbine/2	Cabins (interior/no view): 195	Library: ....Yes
azimuthing pods (39,000kW)	Cabins (for one person): 0	Classification Society: ...Lloyd's Register
Passenger Decks: 11	Cabins (with private balcony): 590	

OVERALL SCORE: 1,697 (OUT OF A POSSIBLE 2,000 POINTS)

OVERVIEW. *Summit* is a sister ship to *Constellation, Infinity* and *Millennium.* Jon Bannenberg (famous as a mega-yacht designer) designed the exterior that has a royal blue and white hull, and racy lines in red, blue and gold, although it has actually turned out to look extremely ungainly. This is the third Celebrity Cruises ship to be fitted with a "pod" propulsion system (and controllable pitch propellers) coupled with a quiet, smokeless gas turbine powerplant (two GE gas turbines provide engine power while a single GE steam turbine drives the electricity generators).

One neat feature is a conservatory which includes many seats set in a botanical environment of flowers, plants, tress, mini-gardens and fountains, designed by the award-winning floral designer Emilio Robba of Paris. It is located directly in front of the main funnel and has glass walls that overlook the ship's side.

Inside, the ship has the high-class decor and materials and public rooms that have made the existing ships in the fleet so popular and user-friendly. The atrium spans 11 decks. It is capped with a glass dome, and four glass elevators travel through the port side of the atrium.

Facilities include a combination Cinema/Conference Center, an expansive shopping arcade, with 14,500 sq. ft (1,300 sq. meters) of retail store space, a lavish four-decks-high showlounge with the latest in staging and lighting equipment, a two-level library (one level for English-language books; a second level for books in other languages), a card room, a music room, and a combination observation lounge/discotheque. Michael's Club (originally a cigar smoker's haven), is now a piano lounge/bar. Gaming facilities include the ship's

BERLITZ'S RATINGS

	Possible	Achieved
Ship	500	454
Accommodation	200	180
Food	400	327
Service	400	330
Entertainment	100	78
Cruise	400	328

overly large Fortunes Casino, with blackjack, roulette, and slot machines, and lots of bright lights and action. Families will appreciate the Fun Factory (for children) and The Tower (for teenagers). Children's counselors and youth activities staff provide a wide range of supervised activities.

After the business downturn following the 2001 terrorist attacks on America, new management was brought in to restore Celebrity Cruises to the premium product originally envisioned, and the improvements introduced in 2003 have restored the art of hospitality and provide a taste of luxury for all. The ship's two seating dining and two shows, sadly, detract from an otherwise excellent product, and this ship (with sisters *Constellation, Infinity* and *Millennium*) provides the very best of the ships in the Premium segment of the market, offering a taste of luxury to those who book the largest suites.

There is no wrap-around wooden promenade deck outdoors. There are cushioned pads for poolside deck lounge chairs only, but not for chairs on other outside decks. Trying to reach Cabin Service or the Guest Relations Desk to answer the phone (to order breakfast, for example, if you don't want to do so via the interactive television) is a matter of luck, timing and patience.

ACCOMMODATION. There are 20 different grades, giving you a wide choice of size and location (the price you pay will depend on the grade, location and size chosen).

Almost half the accommodation has a "private" balcony; approximately 80 percent are outside-view suites and cabins, and 20 percent are interior (no view) cabins. The accommodation is extremely comfortable throughout this ship, regardless of which grade you choose. Suites, naturally, have more space, butler service (whether you want it or not), more and better amenities and more personal service than if you choose any of the standard cabin grades. There are several categories of suites, but those at the stern of the ship are in a prime location and have huge balconies that are really private and not overlooked from above.

All suites and cabins have wood cabinetry and accenting, interactive television and entertainment systems (you can go shopping, book shore excursions, play casino games, interactively, and even watch soft-porn movies). Bathrooms have hairdryers, and 100% cotton towels.

Penthouse Suites: Two Penthouse Suites (on Penthouse Deck) are the largest accommodation aboard. Each occupies one half of the beam (width) of the ship, overlooking the ship's stern. Each measures a huge 2,530 sq. ft (235 sq. meters) – 1,432 sq. ft (133 sq. meters) of living space, plus a huge wrap-around balcony measuring 1,098 sq. ft (102 sq. meters) with 180° views, which occupies one-half of the beam (width) of the ship, overlooking the ship's stern (it includes a wet bar, hot tub and whirlpool tub); however, note that much of this terrace can be overlooked by passengers on other decks above.

Features include a marble foyer, a separate living room (complete with ebony baby grand piano – bring your own pianist if you don't play yourself) and a formal dining room. The master bedroom has a large walk-in closet; personal exercise equipment; dressing room with vanity desk, exercise equipment; marble-clad master bathroom with twin washbasins; deep whirlpool bathtub; separate shower; toilet and bidet areas; flat-screen televisions (one in the bedroom and one in the lounge) and electronically controlled drapes. Butler service is standard, and a butler's pantry, with separate entry door, has a full-sized refrigerator, temperature-controlled wine cabinet, microwave oven and good-sized food preparation and storage areas. For even more space, an interconnecting door can be opened into the adjacent suite (ideal for multi-generation families).

Royal Suites: Eight Royal Suites, each measuring 733 sq. ft (68 sq. meters), are located towards the aft of the ship (four each on the port and starboard sides). Each has a separate living room with dining and lounge areas (with refrigerator, mini-bar and Bang & Olufsen CD sound system), and a separate bedroom. There are two entertainment centers with DVD players, and two flat-screen televisions (one in the living area, one in the bedroom), and a large walk-in closet with vanity desk. The marble-clad bathroom has a whirlpool bathtub with integral shower, and there is also a separate shower enclosure, two washbasins and toilet. The teakwood decked balcony is extensive (large enough for on-deck massage) and has a whirlpool hot tub.

Celebrity Suites: Eight Celebrity Suites, each measuring 467 sq. ft (44 sq. meters), have floor-to-ceiling windows, a separate living room with dining and lounge areas, two entertainment centers with flat-screen televisions (one in the living room, one in the bedroom), and a walk-in closet with vanity desk. The marble-clad bathroom has a whirlpool

bathtub with integral shower (a window with movable shade lets you look out of the bathroom through the lounge to the large ocean-view windows). Interconnecting doors allow two suites to be used as a family unit (as there is no balcony, these suites are ideal for families with small children). These suites overhang the starboard side of the ship (they are located opposite a group of glass-walled elevators), and provide stunning ocean views from the glass-walled sitting/dining area, which extends out from the ship's side. A personal computer with wood-surround screen allows direct internet connectivity. Butler service is standard.

Sky Suites: There are 30 of these, each measuring 308 sq. ft (28.6 sq. meters), including the private balcony (some balconies may be larger than others, depending on the location). Although these are designated as suites, they are really just larger cabins that feature a marble-clad bathroom with bathtub/shower combination. The suites also have a VCR player in addition to a TV set, and have a larger lounge area (than standard cabins) and sleeping area. Butler service is standard.

Butler Service: Butler service (in all accommodation designated as suites) includes full breakfast, in-suite lunch and dinner service (as required), afternoon tea service, evening hors d'oeuvres, free espresso and cappuccino, daily news delivery, shoeshine service, and other personal touches.

Suite occupants in Penthouse, Royal, Celebrity and Sky suites also get welcome champagne; a full personal computer in each suite, including a printer and internet access (on request in Sky Suites); choice of films from a video library; personalized stationery; tote bag; priority dining room seating preferences; private portrait sitting, and bathrobe; and in-suite massage service.

Concierge Class: In 2003, Celebrity Cruises added a third service "class" to some of the accommodation grades aboard this ship. Positioned between the top grade suite grades and standard cabin grades, Concierge Class adds value to purchasers of these "middle-class" cabins.

Enhanced facilities include priority embarkation, disembarkation, tender tickets, alternative dining and spa reservations. Here's what you get in the Concierge Class cabins that others don't (except for the suites): European duvet; double bed overlay (no more falling "between the cracks" for couples); choice of four pillows (goose down pillow, isotonic pillow, body pillow, conformance pillow); eight-vial flower vase on vanity desk; throw pillows on sofa; fruit basket; binoculars; golf umbrella; leather telephone notepad; larger beach towels; hand-held hairdryer. The balcony gets better furniture. In the bathrooms: plusher Frette bathrobe; larger towels in sea green and pink (alternating days); flower in silver vase in bathroom. It all adds up to an excellent value for money, as well as better recognition from staff.

Standard Outside-View/Interior (No View) Cabins: All other outside-view and interior (no view) cabins have a lounge area with sofa or convertible sofa bed, sleeping area with twin beds that can convert to a double bed, a good amount of closet and drawer space, personal safe, mini-bar/refrigerator (extra cost), interactive television, and private bathroom. The cabins are nicely decorated with warm wood-finish furniture, and there is none of the boxy feel of cabins in so many ships, due to the angled placement of vanity and audio-video consoles. Even the smallest cabin has a good-sized bathroom and shower enclosure.

Wheelchair-Accessible Accommodation: This is available in six Sky Suites, three premium outside-view, eight deluxe ocean-view, four standard ocean-view and five interior (no view) cabins measuring from 347 to 362 sq. ft (32.2 to 33.6 sq. meters) and are located in the most practical parts of the ship and close to elevators for good accessibility. All have doorways and bathroom doorways and showers are wheelchair-accessible. Some cabins have extra berths for third or third and fourth occupants (note, however, that there is only one safe for personal belongings, which must be shared).

CUISINE/DINING. The 1,170-seat Cosmopolitan Restaurant, the ship's formal dining room. It is two decks high, has a grand staircase connecting the two levels, a huge glass wall overlooking the sea at the stern of the ship (electrically operated shades provide several different backdrops), and a musician's gallery on the upper level (typically for a string quartet/quintet). There are two seatings for dinner (open seating for breakfast and lunch), at tables for two, four, six, eight or 10. The dining room is a no-smoking area, and, you should note that, like all large dining halls, it can prove to be extremely noisy. The menu variety is good, the food has taste, and it is very attractively presented and served in a well-orchestrated operation that displays fine European traditions and training. Full service in-cabin dining is also available for all meals (including dinner). As a tribute to the French Line ship *Normandie*, a statue created by Leon-Georges Baudry, called "La Normandie", that once overlooked the ship's grand staircase and for the past 47 years graced the Fontainebleu Hotel in Miami, can now be seen in this dining room.

For casual eating, the Waterfall Cafe is a self-serve buffet area, with six principal serving lines and 754 seats. There is also a grill and pizza bar.

For champagne and caviar lovers, the Platinum Club has a platinum and silver art-deco decor that is reminiscent of a 1930s gentleman's club. It includes a diamond-pane reflective mirror wall. There's also a Martini Bar.

Alternative (Reservations-Only, Extra Cost) Dining Option: The Normandie Restaurant is an alternative dining room, adjacent to the conference center. It has gold lacquered paneling form the smoking room of the original French Line ship. Fine tableside preparation is the feature of this alternative dining room, whose classic French cuisine and service is outstanding (masterminded by Michel Roux, owner of a three-star Michelin restaurant near Windsor, England). This is haute cuisine at the height of professionalism. However, with just 134 seats, not all passengers can experience it even once during a one-week cruise (reservations are necessary, and a cover charge of $25 per person applies). There is a dine-in wine cellar (with more than 200 labels from around the world), and a demonstration galley. A team of 10 chefs prepares the cuisine exclusively for this restaurant. Tableside preparation is a feature of this alternative dining spot.

Cova Cafe di Milano: The Cova Cafe di Milano is a signature item aboard all Celebrity Cruises ships, and a seagoing version of the 200-year-old Cafe di Milano originally located next to La Scala Opera House in Milan. It is in a prominent position, on the second level of the atrium lobby, and several display cases show off the extensive range of Cova coffee, chocolates and alcoholic digestives; this is the place to see and be seen. It is a delightful setting (and meeting place) for those who appreciate fine Italian coffees (for espresso, espresso macchiato, cappuccino, latte), pastries and superb cakes in an elegant, refined setting. The breakfast pastries are really superb (the favorite seems to be the Italian pane con cioccolata – chocolate pastry).

ENTERTAINMENT. The 900-seat Celebrity Theater is the three-deck-high venue for the ship's production shows and major cabaret acts. It is located in the forward part of the ship, with seating on main, and two balcony levels. The large stage is equipped with a full fly loft behind its traditional proscenium.

SPA/FITNESS. Spa facilities include an AquaSpa (a multi-station thalassotherapy pool), 16 treatment rooms, plus eight treatment rooms with showers and one treatment room specifically designed for wheelchair passengers, aerobics room, gymnasium (complete with over 40 machines), large male and female saunas (with large ocean-view porthole window), a unisex thermal suite (containing several steam and shower mist rooms with different fragrances such as camomile, eucalyptus and mint, and a glacial ice fountain), and beauty salon.

Sports facilities include a full-size basketball court, compact football, paddle tennis and volleyball, golf simulator, shuffleboard (on two different decks) and a jogging track.

● **For more extensive general information on what a Celebrity cruise is like, see pages 111–115.**

Sun Princess
★★★★

Large (Resort) Ship: ....77,499 tons	Total Crew: 900	Cabins (with private balcony): 410
Lifestyle: ....Standard	Passengers	Cabins (wheelchair accessible): 19
Cruise Line: ....Princess Cruises	(lower beds/all berths): 1,950/2,250	Cabin Current: ....110 and 220 volts
Former Names: ....none	Passenger Space Ratio	Elevators: 11
Builder: ....Fincantieri (Italy)	(lower beds/all berths): 39.7/34.4	Casino (gaming tables): ....Yes
Original Cost: ....$300 million	Crew/Passenger Ratio	Slot Machines: ....Yes
Entered Service: ....Dec 1995	(lower beds/all berths): 2.0/2.5	Swimming Pools (outdoors): 4
Registry: ....Great Britain	Navigation Officers: ....Italian	Swimming Pools (indoors): 0
Length (ft/m): 857.2/261.3	Cabins (total): 975	Whirlpools: 5
Beam (ft/m): 105.6/32.2	Size Range (sq ft/m): 134.5–753.4/	Self-Service Launderette: ....Yes
Draft (ft/m): 26.5/8.1	12.5–70.0	Dedicated Cinema/Seats: ....No
Propulsion/Propellers: .....diesel-electric	Cabins (outside view): 603	Library: ....Yes
(28,000kW)/2	Cabins (interior/no view): 372	Classification Society: ...Registro Navale
Passenger Decks: 10	Cabins (for one person): 0	Italiano (RINA)

OVERALL SCORE: 1,539 (OUT OF A POSSIBLE 2,000 POINTS)

OVERVIEW. Although large, this all-white ship has a good profile, and is well balanced by its large funnel, which contains a deck tennis/basketball/volleyball court in its sheltered aft base. There is a wide, teakwood wrap-around promenade deck outdoors, some real teak steamer-style deck chairs (complete with royal blue cushioned pads), and 93,000 sq. ft (8,600 sq. meters) of space outdoors. An extensive glass area on the upper decks provides plenty of light and connection with the outside world.

The ship, while large, absorbs passengers well, and has an almost intimate feel to it, which is what the designers intended. The interiors are very pretty and warm, with attractive colors and welcoming decor that includes some very attractive wall murals and other artwork. The signs around the ship could be improved, however. There is a wide range of public rooms, with several intimate rooms and spaces so that you do get the feel of being overwhelmed by large spaces. The interior focal point is a huge four-deck-high atrium lobby with winding, double stairways, complete with two panoramic glass-walled elevators.

The main public entertainment rooms are located under three decks of cabins. There is plenty of space, the traffic flow is good, and the ship absorbs people well. There are two showlounges, one at each end of the ship; one is a superb 550-seat, theater-style showlounge (movies are also shown here) and the other is a 480-seat cabaret-style lounge, complete with bar.

The library is a very warm room with ocean-view windows, and has six large buttery leather chairs for listening to audio CDs. There is a conference center for up to 300, as well as a business center, with computers, photocopiers and

BERLITZ'S RATINGS

	Possible	Achieved
Ship	500	428
Accommodation	200	162
Food	400	266
Service	400	291
Entertainment	100	86
Cruise	400	306

fax machines. The collection of artwork is good, particularly on the stairways, and helps make the ship feel smaller than it is, although in places it doesn't always seem co-coordinated. The casino, while large, is not really in the main passenger flow and so it does not generate the "walk-through" factor found aboard so many ships.

The most traditional (many say the nicest) room aboard is the Wheelhouse Lounge/Bar, which is decorated in the style of a late 19th-century gentleman's club, complete with wood paneling and comfortable seating. Its focal point is a large ship model from the P&O archives.

At the end of the day, as is the case aboard most large ships today, if you live in the top suites, you will be well attended; if you do not, you will merely be one of a very large number of passengers. One nice feature is the captain's cocktail party; it is held in the four-deck-high main atrium so you can come and go as you please – and there's no standing in line to have your photograph taken with the captain if you don't want to.

There are a number of dead ends in the interior layout, so it's not as user-friendly as a ship this size should be. The cabin numbering system is extremely illogical, with numbers going through several hundred series on the same deck. The walls of the passenger accommodation decks are very plain (some artwork would be an improvement). The swimming pools are quite small for so many passengers, and the pool deck is cluttered with white, plastic deck lounge chairs, which do not have cushioned pads.

ACCOMMODATION. There are 28 different cabin grades: 20 outside-view and 8 interior (no view) cabins. Although the standard outside-view and interior (no view) cabins are a little small, they are well designed and functional in layout, and have earth tone colors accentuated by splashes of color from the bedspreads. Proportionately, there are quite a lot of interior (no view) cabins. Many of the outside-view cabins have private balconies, and all seem to be quite well soundproofed, although the balcony partition is not floor to ceiling type, so you can hear your neighbors clearly (or smell their smoke). Note that the balconies are very narrow, only just large enough for two small chairs, and there is no dedicated lighting.

A reasonable amount of closet and abundant drawer and other storage space is provided in all cabins – adequate for a 7-night cruise, as are a television and refrigerator. Each night a chocolate will appear on your pillow. The cabin bathrooms are practical, and come complete with all the details one needs, although they really are tight spaces, best described as one person at-a-time units. They do, however, have a decent shower enclosure, a small amount of shelving for your personal toiletries, real glasses, a hairdryer and a bathrobe.

The largest accommodation can be found in six suites, two on each of three decks located at the stern of the ship, with large private balcony (536–754 sq. ft./49.8–21.3 sq. meters, including balcony). These are well laid-out, and have large bathrooms with two basins, a Jacuzzi bathtub, and a separate shower enclosure. The bedroom has generous amounts of wood accenting and detailing, TV sets in both bedroom and lounge areas. The suites also have a dining room table and four chairs.

The 32 mini-suites (374–536 sq. ft./34.7–49.7 sq. meters) typically have two lower beds that convert into a queen-sized bed. There is a separate bedroom/sleeping area with vanity desk, and a lounge with sofa and coffee table, indented ceilings with generous amounts of wood accenting and detailing, walk-in closet, and larger bathroom with Jacuzzi tub and separate shower enclosure.

There are 19 wheelchair-accessible cabins, which measure 213–305 sq. ft (19.7–28.2 sq. meters.), and are a mix of 7 outside-view and 12 interior (no view) cabins.

BBC World, CNN, CNBC, ESPN and TNT are typically carried by the in-cabin color television system (when available, depending on cruise area).

CUISINE/DINING. There are two main dining rooms of asymmetrical design: Marquis, and Regency. Both are non-smoking, as are all dining rooms aboard the ships of Princess Cruises. They are located adjacent to the two lower levels of the four-deck high atrium lobby. Each seats around 500, has its own galley, and is split into multi-tier sections, which help create a feeling of intimacy, although there is a lot of noise from the waiter stations adjacent to many tables. Breakfast and lunch are provided in an open-seating arrangement, while dinner is in two seatings.

On any given 7-day cruise, a typical menu cycle will include a Sailaway Dinner, Captain's Welcome Dinner,

Chef's Dinner, Italian Dinner, French Dinner, Captain's Gala Dinner, and Landfall Dinner. The wine list is reasonable, but not good, and the company has, sadly, dispensed with wine waiters. Note that 15% is added to all beverage bills, including wines.

Alternative Dining (Extra Charge) Option: For some really good meat, however, consider the Sterling Steakhouse; it's for those that want to taste four different cuts of Angus beef from the popular "Sterling Silver" brand of USDA prime meats – Filet Mignon, New York Strip, Porterhouse, and Rib-Eye – all presented on a silver tray.

There is also a barbecue chicken option, plus the usual baked potato or French fries as accompaniments. This is available as an alternative to the dining rooms, between 6.30pm and 9.30pm only, at an additional charge of $8 per person. However, it is not, as you might expect, a separate, intimate dining room, but is located in a section of the Horizon Buffet, with its own portable bar and some decorative touches to set it apart from the regular Horizon Buffet.

The Horizon Buffet is open 24 hours a day, and, at night, has an informal dinner setting with sit-down waiter service; a small bistro menu is also available. The buffet displays are, for the most part, quite repetitious, but better than they have been in the past few years (there is no real finesse in presentation, however, as plastic plates are provided, instead of trays). The cabin service menu is very limited, and presentation of the food items featured is poor.

There is also a pâtisserie (for cappuccino/espresso coffees and pastries), a wine/caviar bar, and a pizzeria (complete with cobblestone floors and wrought-iron decorative features), and excellent pizzas (there are six to choose from).

ENTERTAINMENT. There are two showlounges (both theater and cabaret style). The principal showlounge, the Princess Theater, has a sloping floor, with aisle-style seating (as typically found in shore-side movie houses) that is well-tiered, and with good sightlines to the raised stage from most of the 500 seats.

The second showlounge (Vista Lounge), located at the aft end of the ship, has cabaret entertainment, and also acts as a lecture and presentation room. Princess Cruises has a good stable of regular cabaret acts to draw from, so there should be something for almost all tastes.

SPA/FITNESS. A glass-walled health spa complex is located high atop ship and includes a gymnasium with high-tech machines. One swimming pool is "suspended" aft between two decks (there are two other pools, although they are not large for the size of the ship).

Sports facilities are located in an open-air sports deck positioned inside the ship's funnel and adaptable for basketball, volleyball, badminton or paddle tennis. Joggers can exercise on the wrap-around open Promenade Deck.

● **For more extensive general information about the Princess Cruises experience, see pages 124–127.**

SuperStar Gemini
★★★ +

Mid-Size Ship: . . . . .19,093 tons	Passenger Decks: 9	Cabins (for one person): 0
Lifestyle: . . . . .Standard	Total Crew: 470	Cabins (with private balcony): 10
Cruise Line: . . . . .Star Cruises	Passengers	Cabins (wheelchair accessible): 4
Former Names: . . . . .Crown Jewel	(lower beds/all berths): 800/900	Cabin Current: . . . . .110 and 220 volts
Builder: . . . . .Union Navale de Levante	Passenger Space Ratio	Elevators: 4
(Spain)	(lower beds/all berths): 23.8/21.2	Casino (gaming tables): . . . . .Yes
Original Cost: . . . .$100 million	Crew/Passenger Ratio	Slot Machines: .Yes
Entered Service: . . . .Aug 1992/July 1995	(lower beds/all berths): 1.7/1.9	Swimming Pools (outdoors): 1
Registry: .Panama	Navigation Officers: . . . . . .Scandinavian	Swimming Pools (indoors): 0
Length (ft/m): 537.4/163.81	Cabins (total): .400	Whirlpools: . . . . .3 (2 outside/1 inside)
Beam (ft/m): 73.8/22.50	Size Range (sq ft/m): 139.9–349.8/	Self-Service Launderette: . . . . .No
Draft (ft/m): 17.7/5.40	13.0–32.5	Dedicated Cinema/Seats: . . . . .No
Propulsion/Propellers: . . . . .diesel	Cabins (outside view): 241	Library: . . . . .Yes
(13,200kW)/2	Cabins (interior/no view): 159	Classification Society: Det Norske Veritas

OVERALL SCORE: 1,322 (OUT OF A POSSIBLE 2,000 POINTS)

OVERVIEW. *SuperStar Gemini* is a handsome mid-sized cruise ship with smart exterior styling (the largest cruise vessel ever built in Spain). The ship has a sister in *Braemar* (operated by Fred Olsen Cruise Lines). There is a wrap-around promenade deck outdoors.

Although the fit and finish was originally poor, Star Cruises has made the ship's interiors much warmer and more colorful. Inside, the ship has a traditional layout that provides reasonable horizontal passenger flow, although the passageways are narrow. There are picture windows in almost all of the public rooms that connect passengers with the sea and the outside light. There is a reasonable amount of open deck and sunbathing space for the size of the ship, and this includes a neat area high atop the ship in front of a glass windbreak area – lovely for those balmy evenings outdoors, away from the crowds inside. Cushioned pads are provided for the deck lounge chairs.

Other features include a five-deck-high glass-walled atrium, and a karaoke/disco lounge. The decor is attractive, with upbeat art-deco color combinations and splashy, colorful soft furnishings. The artwork is fairly plain and simple and could be improved. The fitness center/spa area is decent but quite cramped.

This very informal ship caters to a mix of Australian, European (mainly British and German) as well as Southeast Asian passengers, and announcements may be in several languages. The ship presently operates Andaman Sea cruises. The dress code is totally casual.

All in all, the company provides really good value for money, cruising in a homey ship that is bright, contemporary, and very informal. The staff is young, though, and

BERLITZ'S RATINGS

	Possible	Achieved
Ship	500	348
Accommodation	200	132
Food	400	253
Service	400	265
Entertainment	100	58
Cruise	400	266

needs more training, experience and supervision in the arts of hospitality, service and flexibility. Gratuities are included and no further tipping is allowed. All in all, you should have an enjoyable, fun voyage for a destination-intensive week, with acceptable, but not memorable food and service. The onboard currency is the Taiwan dollar.

The staff could be better trained, and there is a high turnover. There are too many loud announcements. Music plays constantly in public spaces, hallways, and on open decks, making a relaxing cruise experience impossible.

SUITABLE FOR: *SuperStar Gemini* is best suited to couples, singles, and families with children of all ages who want to cruise aboard a contemporary ship with decent facilities that are really dedicated to Southeast Asians, at a very reasonable price.

ACCOMMODATION. There are six cabin price categories (the price you pay will depend on the grade, location and size chosen), which consists of executive suites (220.7–377.8 sq. ft/20.5–35.1 sq. meters), junior suites (225–258.3 sq. ft/20.9–24 sq. meters), ocean-view cabins with double bed (134.5–212 sq. ft/12.5–19.7 sq. meters), ocean-view cabins with twin beds (137.8 sq. ft/12.8 sq. meters), smaller ocean-view cabins with window (114.1–148.5 sq. ft/10.6–13.8 sq. meters), and interior (no view) cabins (127–150.7 sq. ft/11.8–14 sq. meters). There are four cabins for the disabled, and several cabins have interconnecting doors (good for families with children).

Eight of the Executive Suites have a private balcony, although the partitions are not of the floor-to-ceiling type –

so you can hear your neighbors clearly, or smell their smoke). Junior Suites are really little larger than standard and larger standard cabins, but with more closet space). Both types of suite are nicely furnished. The sleeping area can be curtained off from the living area. A tea/coffee making set, and laser disc player are provided (Executive Suites only).

The standard outside-view and interior (no view) cabins, almost all of which are the same size, are really quite small (they somehow remind me of caravan accommodation), although they are nicely furnished, and trimmed with blond wood cabinetry. Most of them have broad picture windows (some deluxe cabins on Deck 6 and Deck 7 have lifeboat-obstructed views). They are practical and comfortable, with wood-trimmed accents and multi-colored soft furnishings, but there is almost no drawer space, and the closet space is extremely small.

The bathrooms are reasonably decent considering the size of the ship, and each has two small toiletries cabinets, although the shower cubicle is small. The cabin sound-proofing is quite poor; the 100% cotton towels are thin; there is little room for luggage, so take only what is really necessary (casual clothing only, no formal attire needed – even the captain's gala dinner night asks for "smart casual" attire). Bathrobes, slippers and toiletry amenities are provided in all cabins, as well as a small color television, telephone, and bottled water.

None of the cabins has a bathtub. Hairdryers are not supplied for any cabin category, so take your own if you need to use one. Also, there is no room service for such items as coffee or tea, nor is there a menu for snacks. The cabin numbering system and signage is confusing.

CUISINE/DINING. The attractive Ocean Palace dining room is located aft and has large picture windows on three sides (although the accenting in the center of the ceiling makes the room appear round). There are two seatings. It is not open for dinner each night (it will depend on the itinerary being operated).

The ambiance is friendly (but very noisy), but there are few tables for two (most tables are for four, six or eight).

Meals feature international cuisine with an Oriental touch, and there is open seating for all meals, except for dinner on the one "formal" night of the cruise. On the six-day cruise, one night includes a barbecue outside on the pool deck (the main dining room is closed on this night).

The wine list is reasonable, but the wines themselves are all young and prices are high – the cost of wines and spirits in Southeast Asia is high due to high import duties, and champagne is incredibly expensive.

There is also an informal cafe, called Mariner's Buffet (a pork-free eatery). Breakfast here always includes some Southeast Asian dishes such as Nasi Lemak, and Fried Noodles, as well as western favorites. Lunch and dinner are also provided in this eatery. Australian passengers will appreciate the ample supply of Vegemite. There is a good selection of beer, including some regional varieties, and some draft lager.

ENTERTAINMENT. The Galaxy of the Stars Lounge is the venue for all entertainment events. There is often congestion between first- and second-seating passengers at the entrance to the room, which is poorly designed for passenger movement, 15 pillars obstruct the sightlines to the stage, and the seating arrangement is poor.

Cabaret acts (such as singers, magicians, ventriloquists, comedians, and comedy jugglers) are presented here as the main entertainment, although it should be said that Southeast Asian passengers prefer to be in the casino.

SPA/FITNESS. There is a health spa, although it is small, and has limited facilities. It includes a combined gymnasium/aerobics room, and separate rooms for men and women, with sauna, steam room and small changing area. Some fitness classes are free, while some may cost extra. However, being aboard will give you an opportunity to try some of the more indulgent treatments (particularly some of the massages available). Thai massage is a specialty of the spa. Do make appointments as early as possible, as treatment time slots do tend to go quickly, so the day you board is the best time to book your desired treatments.

SuperStar Virgo
★★★★

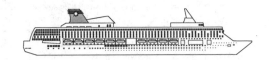

Large (Resort) Ship: . . . . .75,338 tons	Total Crew: 1,300	Cabins (with private balcony): 391
Lifestyle: . . . . .Standard	Passengers	Cabins (wheelchair accessible): 4
Cruise Line: . . . . .Star Cruises	(lower beds/all berths): 1,974/2,800	Cabin Current: . . . . .240 volts
Former Names: . . . . .none	Passenger Space Ratio	Elevators: 9
Builder: . . . . .Meyer Werft (Germany)	(lower beds/all berths): 38.1/26.9	Casino (gaming tables): . . . . .Yes
Original Cost: . . . .$350 million	Crew/Passenger Ratio	Slot Machines: . . . . .Yes
Entered Service: . . . . .Aug 1999	(lower beds/all berths): 1.5/2.1	Swimming Pools (outdoors): 2
Registry: . . . . .Panama	Navigation Officers: . . . . . .Scandinavian	Swimming Pools (indoors): 0
Length (ft/m): 879.2/268.0	Cabins (total): 987	Whirlpools: 4
Beam (ft/m): 105.6/32.2	Size Range (sq ft/m): 150.6–638.3/	Self-Service Launderette: . . . . .No
Draft (ft/m): 25.9/7.9	14.0–59.3	Dedicated Cinema/Seats: . . . . .No
Propulsion/Propellers: . . . . .diesel	Cabins (outside view): 608	Library: . . . . .Yes
(50,400kW)/2	Cabins (interior/no view): 379	Classification Society: . . . . . .Det Norske
Passenger Decks: 10	Cabins (for one person): 0	Veritas

OVERALL SCORE: 1,522 (OUT OF A POSSIBLE 2,000 POINTS)

OVERVIEW. *SuperStar Virgo* (sister to *SuperStar Leo*, now renamed *Norwegian Spirit*) was the second new ship ordered specifically for the Asian market. The all-white ship has a distinctive red/blue funnel with gold star logo. There is a wrap-around promenade deck outdoors, good for strolling. Inside, there are two boulevards, and a stunning, wide-open six-deck-high central atrium lobby, with three glass-walled elevators and ample space to peruse the shops and cafes that line its inner sanctum.

The casino complex is at the forward end of the atrium boulevard on Deck 7. This includes a large general-purpose, brightly lit casino, called Oasis, with gaming tables and slot machines. There's a smaller "members only" gaming club, as well as VIP gaming rooms, one of which has its own access to the upper level of the showlounge. The 450-seat Galaxy of the Stars Lounge is an observation lounge by day and a nightclub at night, with live music.

The decor aboard *SuperStar Virgo* has some distinctly European touches in its design, taste and color combinations, and the layout was modified and improved slightly from that of the sister ship (for a slightly different market). The lobby, for example, has become an Italian Piazza, with a stunning *trompe l'oeil* and multi-colored stained-glass ceiling. The decor mixes east and west, and public room names have been chosen to appeal to a mixture of Australian, European and Asian passengers. Three stairways are each carpeted in a different color, which helps new cruise passengers find their way around easily.

There is a business center (with six meeting rooms), a large library and writing room, as well as private mahjong and karaoke rooms, and a smoking room. A shopping con-

BERLITZ'S RATINGS

	Possible	Achieved
Ship	500	421
Accommodation	200	156
Food	400	293
Service	400	284
Entertainment	100	66
Cruise	400	302

course is set around the second level of the lobby, and includes a wine shop.

Teens have their own huge video arcade, while younger children get to play in a wet 'n' wild aft pool (complete with pirate ship and caves) and two whirlpool tubs. Plus there's all the fun and facilities of Charlie's childcare center (open 24 hours a day), which includes a painting room, computer learning center, and small cinema.

There's even a room full of cots for toddlers to use for sleepovers, and even the toilets are at a special low height. About 15,000 sq. ft (1,400 sq. meters) is devoted to children's facilities – all tucked well away from adult recreation areas.

Star Cruises has established a Southeast Asian regional cruise audience for its diverse fleet of ships. *SuperStar Virgo* is a fine ship for the active local market, and is certainly the most stunning and luxurious of any of the ships sailing year-round from this popular Southeast Asian region.

The passenger mix is international, although the local (regional) market has now been developed, so you can expect to find lots of families with children (who are allowed to roam around the ship uncontrolled), particularly on the weekend (Friday–Sunday) cruise.

More choices, more dining options, and Asian hospitality all add up to a very attractive holiday package that is particularly suitable for families with children, in a very contemporary floating leisure center that operates from Singapore. The dress code is casual – very casual (no jacket and tie needed), and the ship operates under a "no-tipping" policy. While the initial cruise fare seems very reasonable, the extra costs and charges soon mount up if you want to indulge in more than the basics. Although service levels and finesse remain inconsistent, hospitality is very good.

There are many extra cost items (in addition to the à la carte dining spots), such as for morning tea, afternoon tea, most cabaret shows (except a crew show), and childcare. There are some inevitable entertainment and activity announcements (in English and Mandarin). Finding your way around the many areas blocked by portable "crowd containment" ribbon barriers can prove frustrating.

SUITABLE FOR: *SuperStar Virgo* is best suited to couples, singles, and families with children of all ages who want to cruise aboard a real contemporary floating resort with decent facilities and many dining spots that are really dedicated to Southeast Asians, at a very attractive price.

ACCOMMODATION. There are seven types of accommodation, in 15 price categories. Three entire decks of cabins feature private balconies, while two-thirds of all cabins have an outside view. Both the standard outside-view and interior (no view) cabins really are very small (particularly since all cabins have extra berths for a third/fourth person), so take only the very smallest amount of clothing you can (there's almost no storage space for luggage).

All cabins have a personal safe, 100% cotton towels and 100% cotton duvets or sheets. Bathrooms have a good-sized shower enclosure, and include personal toiletries such as Burberry soap, conditioning shampoo and body lotion.

For more space, choose one of 13 suites. Each suite has a separate lounge/dining room, bedroom, and bathroom, and an interconnecting door to an ocean-view cabin with private balcony (with light). All cabinetry features richly lacquered woods, large (stocked) wet bar with refrigerator, dining table (with a top that flips over to reveal a card table) and four chairs, sofa and drinks table, and trouser press.

The bedroom is small, completely filled by its queen-sized bed; there is a reasonable amount of drawer space (but the drawers are very small), and the closet space is rather tight (it contains two personal safes). A large en-suite bathroom is part of the bedroom and open to it – as is the trend in high-cost, interior architect-designed bathrooms ashore, and has a gorgeous mosaic tiled floor, kidney bean-shaped whirlpool bathtub, two basins, separate shower enclosure (with floor-to-ceiling ocean-view window) and separate toilet (with glass door). There are TV sets in the lounge, bedroom and bathroom.

For even more space, choose one of the six largest suites (Boracay, Nicobar, Langkawi, Majorca, Phuket, and Sentosa) and you'll have a generous amount of private living space, with a separate lounge, dining area, bedroom, large bathroom, and private balcony (with light). All cabinetry features richly lacquered woods, large (stocked) wet bar with refrigerator, dining table (with a top that flips over to reveal a card table) and four chairs, sofa and drinks table, and trouser press. The bedrooms and large en-suite bathrooms are similar to those in the suites already described. There are televisions in the lounge, bedroom and bathroom.

A small room service menu is available (with a 15% service charge plus a gratuity).

CUISINE/DINING. There is certainly plenty of choice both for fine dining and informal trans-ethnic eating spots, with a total of eight venues (all non-smoking areas). You need to plan your venue in advance, or you may be disappointed. The following eateries are included in the cruise price:

● **Bella Vista** seats over 600 in an open-seating arrangement, although, in effect the restaurant operates two seatings. The aft section is two decks high, and huge cathedral-style windows are set in three sections overlooking the ship's stern.

● **Mediterranean Buffet:** this is a large self-serve buffet restaurant with indoor/outdoor seating for 400.

● **The Pavilion Room:** has traditional Cantonese Chinese cuisine, including dim sum at lunchtime.

The following are à la carte (extra-cost) dining spots:

● **Noble House:** a Chinese Restaurant, with traditional Hong Kong-themed decor and items such as dim sum (there are also two small private dining rooms).

● **Palazzo:** a beautiful, if slightly ostentatious Italian restaurant. It has fine food, and a genuine Renoir painting (well protected by cameras and alarms).

● **Samurai:** a Japanese restaurant and sushi bar (for sashimi and sushi). There are two teppanyaki grills, each with 10 seats, where the chef cooks in front of you.

● **The Taj:** an Indian/Vegetarian dining spot that offers a range of food in a self-serve buffet setup.

● **Blue Lagoon:** a casual 24-hour street cafe with noodle dishes, fried rice and other Southeast Asian dishes.

● **Out of Africa:** a casual karaoke cafe and bar, where coffees, teas and pastries are available.

ENTERTAINMENT. The Lido, with 973 seats, is two decks high, with a main and balcony levels (note that the balcony level is reserved for "gaming club" members only). The room has almost no support columns to obstruct the sightlines, and a revolving stage for Broadway-style reviews and other production shows (typically to recorded music – there is no live showband). The showlounge can also be used as a large-screen cinema, with superb surround sound.

In addition, local specialty cabaret acts are brought on board, as are revue-style shows (complete with topless dancers). Bands and small musical units provide plenty of live music for dancing and listening in the various lounges.

SPA/FITNESS. The Roman Spa and Fitness Center is located on one of the uppermost decks, just forward of the Tivoli Pool. It has a gymnasium full of high-tech muscle-toning equipment, and aerobics exercise room, hair and beauty salon, and saunas, steam rooms, and changing rooms for men and women, as well as several treatment rooms, and aqua-swim pools that provide counter-flow jets). There is an extra charge for use of the sauna and steam rooms.

Although there are several types of massages available, Thai massage is a speciality of the spa (you can have it in the spa, outdoors on deck, in your cabin or on your private balcony, space permitting). Sports facilities include a jogging track, golf driving range, basketball and tennis courts, and there are four levels of sunbathing decks.

Tahitian Princess
★★★★

Mid-Size Ship: . . . . .30,277 tons	Passengers	Cabin Current: . . . . . . .110 and 220 volts
Lifestyle: . . . . .Standard	(lower beds/all berths): 688/826	Elevators: 4
Cruise Line: . . . . .Princess Cruises	Passenger Space Ratio	Casino (gaming tables): . . . . .Yes
Former Names: . . . . .R Four	(lower beds/all berths): 44.1/36.6	Slot Machines: . . . . .Yes
Builder: Chantiers de l'Atlantique (France)	Crew/Passenger Ratio	Swimming Pools (outdoors): 1
Original Cost: . . . .$150 million	(lower beds/all berths): 1.8/2.2	Swimming Pools (indoors): 0
Entered Service: . . . . .Nov 1999/Dec 2002	Navigation Officers: . . . . .European	Whirlpools: 2
Registry: . . . . .Gibraltar	Cabins (total): 344	(+ 1 thalassotherapy)
Length (ft/m): 593.7/181.0	Size Range (sq ft/m): . . . . .145.3 – 968.7/	Fitness Center: . . . . .Yes
Beam (ft/m): 83.5/25.5	13.5 – 90.0	Sauna/Steam Room: . . . . .No/Yes
Draft (ft/m): 19.5/6.0	Cabins (outside view): 317	Massage: . . . . .Yes
Propulsion/Propellers: . . . . .diesel-electric	Cabins (interior/no view): 27	Self-Service Launderette: . . . . .Yes
(18,600kW)/2	Cabins (for one person): 0	Dedicated Cinema/Seats: . . . . .No
Passenger Decks: 9	Cabins (with private balcony): 232	Library: . . . . .Yes
Total Crew: .373	Cabins (wheelchair accessible): 3	Classification Society: . . . .Bureau Veritas

OVERALL SCORE: 1,487 (OUT OF A POSSIBLE 2,000 POINTS)

OVERVIEW. *Tahitian Princess* and sister ship *Pacific Princess* are of an ideal size for operating in the warm water regions of Tahiti and the Pacific Ocean islands. *Tahitian Princess* now has an all-white hull (when owned by the now defunct Renaissance cruises, it had a black hull with white superstructure). The all-white hull makes the ship appear larger. It has a large, square-ish white funnel.

The interior decor is stunning and elegant, a throwback to ship decor of the ocean liners of the 1920s and '30s. This includes detailed ceiling cornices, both real and faux wrought-iron staircase railings, leather- and cherry wood paneled walls, *trompe l'oeil* ceilings, rich carpeting in hallways with an Oriental rug-look center section, and many other interesting (and expensive-looking) decorative touches. The overall feel is of an old-world country club. The staircase in the main, two-deck-high foyer may remind you of the one in the 1998 blockbuster movie *Titanic*.

The public rooms are basically spread over three decks. The reception hall (lobby) has a staircase with intricate wrought-iron railings. The Nightclub, with forward-facing views, sits high in the ship and has Polynesian-inspired decor and furniture.

There are plenty of bars – including one in the entrance to each of the restaurants. Perhaps the nicest can be found in the casino bar/lounge, a beautiful room reminiscent of London's grand hotels and understated gaming clubs. It has an inviting marble fireplace and comfortable sofas and individual chairs. There is also a large Card Room, which incorporates an Internet Center, with eight stations.

The Library is a grand room, designed in the Regency

BERLITZ'S RATINGS		
	Possible	Achieved
Ship	500	406
Accommodation	200	155
Food	400	265
Service	400	287
Entertainment	100	72
Cruise	400	302

style (it was designed by Scottish ships interior designer John McNeece), and has a fireplace, a high, indented, *trompe l'oeil* ceiling, and an excellent selection of books, plus some comfortable wing-back chairs with footstools, and sofas you can easily fall asleep on (it's the most relaxing room aboard).

Tahitian Princess cruises year-round on three different 10-day itineraries in the warm water regions of Tahiti and the South Pacific. The value for money is extremely good, and will provide you with a chance to cruise in comfort aboard a mid-sized ship with some interesting dining choices. There's very little entertainment, but it is certainly not needed in these cruise areas. *Tahitian Princess* is much more about relaxation than the larger ships in the fleet, and would make a good child-free vessel.

In common with all ships in the Princess Cruises fleet, 15% is added to all bar and spa accounts (drink prices are moderate, while beer prices are high), and a standard gratuity (about $10 per person, per day) is automatically added to your onboard account. If you think this is too much and want to reduce the amount, you'll need to go to the reception desk to do so.

There is no wrap-around promenade deck outdoors (there is, however, a small jogging track around the perimeter of the swimming pool, and port and starboard side decks), and no wooden decks outdoors (instead, they are covered by Bollidt, a sand-colored rubberized material). There is no sauna. Stairways, although carpeted, are tinny. In order to keep the prices low, often the air routing to get to and from your ship is often not the most direct. There is a charge (tokens must be obtained from the reception desk) for using the machines in the self-service launderette (a change machine in the launderette itself would be better).

Note that getting to Tahiti is not easy (Princess Cruises mostly uses a charter airline, with very cramped seating), and flights are limited. If you make your own air travel arrangements, allow plenty of time for connections (preferably an extra day or so before your cruise).

SUITABLE FOR: *Tahitian Princess* is best suited to couples (both young and not so young), families with children and teenagers, and older singles who like to mingle in a mid-size ship setting with pleasing, sophisticated surroundings and lifestyle, reasonably good entertainment and fairly decent food and service, all wrapped up in one package, at an affordable price.

ACCOMMODATION. There is a variety of about eight different cabin types. All of the standard interior (no view) and outside-view cabins (the lowest four grades) are extremely compact units, and extremely tight for two persons (particularly for cruises longer than seven days). Cabins have twin beds (or queen-size bed), with good under-bed storage areas, personal safe, vanity desk with large mirror, good closet and drawer space (in rich, dark woods), and bathrobe. Color TVs carry a major news channel (where obtainable), plus a sports channel and several round-the-clock movie channels. The bathrooms, which have tiled floors and plain walls, are compact, standard units, and include a shower enclosure with a removable, strong hand-held shower unit, hairdryer, 100% cotton towels, toiletries storage shelves and a retractable clothesline.

The suites/cabins that have private balconies (66 percent of all suites/cabins, or 73 percent of all outside view suites/cabins) have partial, and not full, balcony partitions, sliding glass doors, and, due to good design and layout, only 14 cabins on Deck 6 have lifeboat-obstructed views. The balcony floor is covered in thick plastic matting (teak would be nicer), and some awful plastic furniture.

Mini-Suites: The 52 accommodation units designated as mini-suites are in reality simply larger cabins than the standard varieties, as the sleeping and lounge areas are not divided. While not overly large, the bathrooms have a good-sized bathtub and ample space for storing personal toiletry items. The living area has a refrigerated mini-bar, lounge area with breakfast table, and a balcony with two plastic chairs and a table.

Owner's Suites: The 10 Owner's Suites are the most spacious accommodation, and are fine, large living spaces located in the forward-most and aft-most sections of the accommodation decks (particularly nice are those that overlook the stern, on Deck 6, 7 and 8). They have more extensive balconies that really are private and cannot be overlooked by anyone from the decks above. There is an entrance foyer, living room, bedroom (the bed faces the sea, which can be seen through the floor-to-ceiling windows and sliding glass door), CD player, bathroom with Jacuzzi bathtub, as well as a small guest bathroom.

CUISINE/DINING. Flexibility and choice are what this mid-sized ship's dining facilities are all about. There are four different dining spots (one is a casual self-serve buffet):

● **The Club Restaurant** has 338 seats (all chairs have armrests), and includes a large raised central section. There are large ocean-view windows on three sides, several prime tables overlooking the stern, and a small bandstand for occasional live dinner music. The noise level in this dining room can be high, due to its single deck height ceiling. This restaurant is operated in two seatings (the others have an open dining hours); dinner is typically 6pm and 8.15pm.

● **Sabatini's Trattoria** is an Italian restaurant, with 96 seats (all chairs have armrests), windows along two sides, and a set "Bellissima" three-hour degustation menu. The cover charge is $15 per person.

● **The Sterling Steakhouse** is an "American steak house", has 98 seats (all chairs have armrests), and windows along two sides and a set menu (together with added daily chef's specials). The cover charge is $8 per person.

● **The Lido Cafe** has seating for 154 indoors and 186 outdoors (with white plastic patio furniture). It is open for breakfast, lunch and casual dinners. It is the ship's self-serve buffet restaurant (24 hours a day), and incorporates a small pizzeria and grill. Basic salads, a meat carving station, and a reasonable selection of cheeses are served daily.

All restaurants have open-seating dining, although reservations are necessary in Sabatini's Trattoria and Sterling Steakhouse, where there are mostly tables for four or six (there are few tables for two). There is a Poolside Grill and Bar for fast food items.

ENTERTAINMENT. The 345-seat Cabaret Lounge has a stage, and circular hardwood dance floor with banquette and individual tub chair seating, and raised sections on port and starboard sides. It is not large, and not really designed for production shows, so cabaret acts form the main focus, with mini-revue style shows presented by a troupe of resident singer/dancers in a potted version of what you might experience aboard the large ships of Princess Cruises. Inevitably, art auctions and bingo are pushed almost daily. The entertainment highlight for many, however, is a song and dance show put on by locals of all ages, so you become immersed in the art and culture of the islands.

A band, small musical units, and solo entertaining pianists provide live music for shows and dancing in the various lounges and bars before and after dinner.

SPA/FITNESS. There is a gymnasium (with ocean-view windows) with some high-tech muscle-toning equipment and treadmills, steam rooms (no sauna), changing areas for men and women, and a beauty salon with ocean views. The spa is operated by Steiner, a specialist concession.

A lido deck has a swimming pool, and good sunbathing space, while one of the aft decks has a thalassaotherapy pool. A jogging track circles the swimming pool deck (but one deck above). The uppermost outdoors deck includes a golf driving net and shuffleboard court.

The Emerald
★★★

Mid-Size Ship: . . . . .26,431 tons	Passenger Decks: 10	Cabins (with private balcony): 0
Lifestyle: . . . . .Standard	Total Crew: .412	Cabins (wheelchair accessible): 2
Cruise Line: . . . . .Louis Cruise Lines	Passengers	Cabin Current: . . . . .110 and 220 volts
Former Names: . . . .*Regent Rainbow,*	(lower beds/all berths): 990/1,198	Elevators: 3
Diamond Island, Santa Rosa	Passenger Space Ratio	Casino (gaming tables): . . . . .Yes
Builder: . . . . .Newport News Shipbuilding	(lower beds/all berths): 26.6/22.0	Slot Machines: . . . . .Yes
(USA)	Crew/Passenger Ratio	Swimming Pools (outdoors): 1
Original Cost: . . . .$25 million	(lower beds/all berths): 2.4/2.9	Swimming Pools (indoors): 0
Entered Service: . . . .June 1958/Apr 1997	Navigation Officers: . . . . .Greek/European	Whirlpools: 2
Registry: .Cyprus	Cabins (total): 500	Self-Service Launderette: . . . . .No
Length (ft/m): 599.0/182.57	Size Range (sq ft/m): 124.8–304.6/	Dedicated Cinema/Seats: . . . . .No
Beam (ft/m): 84.0/25.60	11.6–28.3	Library: . . . . .Yes
Draft (ft/m): 27.5/8.38	Cabins (outside view): 338	Classification Society: . .American Bureau
Propulsion/Propellers: . . . . .steam turbine	Cabins (interior/no view): 162	of Shipping
(16,400kW)/2	Cabins (for one person): 10	

OVERALL SCORE: 1,102 (OUT OF A POSSIBLE 2,000 POINTS)

OVERVIEW. After being laid up for more than 10 years, this solid, American-built, former ocean liner (originally built for Grace Line) underwent a great amount of reconstruction (costing a whopping $72 million) in Greece in 1992. Louis Cruise Lines spent more money on another refit in 1997, when the company bought the ship from its former operators, the now defunct Regency Cruises. With new upper decks added, the ship's profile is not exactly handsome, although, unlike new cruise ships, this does have a decent sheer along its waistline ("sheer" is a nautical term for a sweep that sags in the middle, intentionally, being a ship with a proper keel). The ship also benefits from a strong, riveted hull (all new ships are seam-welded).

The open deck and sunbathing space is quite limited when the ship is full, although there are a good number of deck lounge chairs. There is, however, a good wrap-around promenade deck outdoors, with plenty of chairs.

The ship's interiors are quite pleasant and surprisingly comfortable, and have a warm decor that is contemporary without being at all brash. Many of the public rooms have high ceilings, and the ship has a spacious ocean-liner feel. There are some fine wrought-iron railings on the stairways. The artwork, unfortunately, is low-budget stuff.

For short cruises, this ship provides a range of public spaces that, in turn, promote a good party ambiance and a number of bars for drinking in (five, actually). The casino is quite large, and has a high ceiling.

The ship, which is based in Corfu for the summer and operates Adriatic and Greek Isles cruises, is quite well suited for this task. Thomson's wholly owned airline (Britannia

BERLITZ'S RATINGS

	Possible	Achieved
Ship	500	259
Accommodation	200	114
Food	400	215
Service	400	242
Entertainment	100	50
Cruise	400	222

Airways) will probably fly you to your port of embarkation from a choice of almost a score of UK airports (you can have an extra wide seat for an additional £20 per person), while pre-booked meals cost £10 per person (£5 per child). Despite the minor criticisms, Thomson provides quite a decent cruise experience, and this ship therefore achieves a very respectable rating. Hotel add-ons can extend your vacation, and Thomson has a fine collection of them.

The high density of this vessel means that there is little room to move about when full (some operators call this "ambiance"). All gratuities are included in the cruise fare. The onboard currency is the British pound.

SUITABLE FOR: *The Emerald* is best suited to adult couples and singles who want a first cruise that provides very good value-for-money vacation in unpretentious, old-style (traditional) ship surroundings (typically 80 percent of passengers are over 45).

ACCOMMODATION. *The Emerald* has a varied mix of cabins both old and new that offer a wide range of configurations. These are now presented in six main categories: Premier, Superior Outside Plus, Superior Outside, Superior Inside (no view), Standard Outside, and Standard Inside (no view). Accommodation can be found on six of the ship's decks. If this is your first cruise, it would be wise to consider a cabin with a view (called an "outside" cabin) rather than one without a view, so that each morning when you get up, you'll be able to see what the weather is like and dress accordingly, and you will be less disoriented in an unfamiliar setting.

Cabins are not assigned until you are at the embarkation port for check-in unless you pay a supplement of $50 (£30) per cabin in order to pre-book (you can choose your preferred cabin from the deck plan – not that if you are cruising for the first time I would recommend you choose a cabin in or close to the center of the ship, where is likely to be less movement in case of inclement weather or poor sea conditions). This method of assigning cabins on the day of embarkation (unless you pre-book, which I would strongly recommend) means that those who book first, and those who arrive first at the embarkation port, probably will get the best cabins, in the best locations.

Many of the original cabins are quite spacious, with good closet and drawer space, while newer ones are a little more compact, and have poor insulation. Continental breakfast in your cabin will cost about $7.50 (£4.50) extra per person (each time). There is also a 24-hour cabin service menu for snacks, all of which cost extra.

CUISINE/DINING. The Chanterelle Dining Room is located in the center of the ship. It has large ocean-view windows and an interesting, rather neat little "orchestra" balcony. There are two seatings (you can request first or late seating when you make your booking; first seating for dinner is typically at 6.30pm, while second seating is at 8.30pm). The dining room is designated a non-smoking area.

A second restaurant, Le Bistro, is also located in the center of the ship, but two decks above the Chanterelle Dining Room. Although there are windows on two sides, the views are obstructed by the ship's lifeboats. This dining spot is also designated a non-smoking area.

While it won't win any awards, the food quality and its variety and presentation are actually quite decent considering the cost of a cruise, although you won't find many exotic dishes on the menu, and special orders are normally not available. Vegetarians should note that there is always a vegetarian entrée for lunch and dinner (as well as vegetarian appetizers and soups). The service is friendly and quite attentive, although you should not expect grand hotel-style service.

ENTERTAINMENT. The sight lines in the showlounge really are very poor (particularly from the port and starboard side seating areas, where there is obstruction from 12 thick pillars), and the entertainment is typical of what can be achieved or provided for a low budget.

Thomson does a good job of providing a range of entertainment to suit its clientele, and the shows, although not of the top professional variety, are, nonetheless fun and entertaining for the whole family. In addition, there is plenty of music for dancing, both live and recorded.

SPA/FITNESS. There is a small fitness center, although it is located low down in the ship and, without windows, is without natural light; there's also a sauna, while the ship's beauty salon is located on another deck – again in an interior position (there is no natural light, which makes tinting and coloring difficult). The range of services offered is quite basic (well, you are on vacation to relax and get away from it all!) and the facilities are quite limited. Sample treatment prices: Swedish Classic Massage/Indian Head Massage £30 (30 minutes) or £44 (45 minutes) or £52 (60 minutes); Cleansing Facial £36; Pedicure and Foot Massage £22; Exfoliating Body Polish £34.

The Iris
★★

Small Ship: . . . . .12,688 tons	Passenger Decks: 7	Cabins (with private balcony): 0
Lifestyle: . . . . .Standard	Total Crew: 170	Cabins (wheelchair accessible): 1
Cruise Line: . . . . .Mano Maritime	Passengers	Cabin Current: . . . . .220 volts
Former Names: . . . .*Francesca,*	(lower beds/all berths): 462/828	Elevators: 2
Konstantin Simonov	Passenger Space Ratio	Casino (gaming tables): . . . . .Yes
Builder: . . . . . .Szczesin Stocznia (Poland)	(lower beds/all berths): 27.4/15.3	Slot Machines: . . . . .Yes
Original Cost: . . . . .n/a	Crew/Passenger Ratio	Swimming Pools (outdoors): 1
Entered Service: . . . . .Apr 1982/Mar 2001	(lower beds/all berths): 2.7/4.8	Swimming Pools (indoors): 0
Registry: .Malta	Navigation Officers: . . . . .European	Whirlpools: 1
Length (ft/m): 452.7/138.0	Cabins (total): 231	Self-Service Launderette: . . . . .Yes
Beam (ft/m): 68.8/21.0	Size Range (sq ft/m): . . . . .n/a	Dedicated Cinema/Seats: . . . . .No
Draft (ft/m): 19.0/5.8	Cabins (outside view): 157	Library: . . . . .No
Propulsion/Propellers: . . . . .diesel	Cabins (interior/no view): 74	Classification Society: . .Russian Shipping
(12,800kW)/2	Cabins (for one person): 3	Register

OVERALL SCORE: 912 (OUT OF A POSSIBLE 2,000 POINTS)

OVERVIEW. *The Iris*, which was refurbished in 2001, has an angular profile with a boxy stern (complete with fold-down car ramps), stubby bow and a fat funnel placed amidships – otherwise it's a moderately handsome vessel. It has a fully enclosed bridge for all-weather operation. There is also a small helicopter landing deck, and the ship can also take about 20 private cars.

This vessel was placed under charter to Israel's Mano Maritime in 2001. Maintenance is generally sound, and the ship is clean and tidy. By international standards, though, its quality, facilities, fittings and fixtures only match ships of a low standard. It's the onboard product, however, and particularly the food, where Mano Cruises achieves some distinction.

Some cruises during Jewish holidays cost more. To the cost of your cruise, you need to add port charges, handling fees and administrative expenses.

Both interior and exterior staircases are quite steep, the ship having been originally built in Poland as a ro-ro/passenger ferry. There's a limited amount of open deck and sunning space (particularly if the ship is full) and a tiny swimming pool that is really a "dip" pool. Public rooms inlcude the Galaxy Piano Bar, a casino (with tables and slot machines), a discotheque, main lounge, a large duty-free shop, and a small children's playroom.

SUITABLE FOR: *The Iris* is best suited to Hebrew-speaking passengers seeking a first taste of cruising aboard a ship of very modest facilities and features, but with good food.

ACCOMMODATION. There are eight price grades. These include 20 Presidential Suites, 4 Royal Suites,, the other

BERLITZ'S RATINGS

	Possible	Achieved
Ship	500	219
Accommodation	200	95
Food	400	193
Service	400	195
Entertainment	100	41
Cruise	400	169

accommodation being a variety of outside-view and interior (no view) cabins. Except for the 13 large cabins classed as "suites," all are small and somewhat utilitarian in their fittings and furnishings. Cabin hallways are plain.

There is very little drawer space, the under-bed storage space for luggage is tight, and lighting is minimal. Some 33 cabins are fitted with upper two lower beds and two upper berths. All have a private bathroom, with shower, and a small cabinet for toiletry items (only soap is supplied).

The suites have a much larger bathroom, with bathtub and shower combination, and each has a television and video player. The two largest of the "luxe" cabins have a separate bedroom with plenty of closet and drawer space, and a large bathroom with bathtub and shower combination.

CUISINE/DINING. The Grand Restaurant and Topaz Restaurant have two seatings, and tables for four, six or eight. The food is surprisingly good, with lots of fresh salads and vegetables, as well as good meats and local fish. There is certainly plenty of variety. Kosher food can also be supplied for a surcharge of around $19 per passenger, per day.

ENTERTAINMENT. The shows in the L-shaped Palace Club are strictly geared to the Israeli cruise market, with visiting cabaret acts and a small troupe of resident dancers. There is live and recorded music for dancing and listening.

SPA/FITNESS. In 2004, a small spa/health club was created in a space previously part of the garage/storage area. The facilities include a small gym, sauna, and massage rooms.

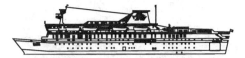

The Jasmine
★★

Small Ship:	12,637 tons	Passenger Decks:	7	Cabins (with private balcony):	0
Lifestyle:	Standard	Total Crew:	150	Cabins (wheelchair accessible):	1
Cruise Line:	Mano Maritime	Passengers		Cabin Current:	220 volts
Former Names:	Palmira, Natasha,	(lower beds/all berths):	450/750	Elevators:	2
	Lev Tolstoi	Passenger Space Ratio		Casino (gaming tables):	Yes
Builder:	Szczesin Stocznia (Poland)	(lower beds/all berths):	28.0/16.8	Slot Machines:	Yes
Original Cost:	n/a	Crew/Passenger Ratio		Swimming Pools (outdoors):	1
Entered Service:	1981/Mar 2002	(lower beds/all berths):	3.0/5.0	Swimming Pools (indoors):	0
Registry:	St. Vincent/Grenadines	Navigation Officers:	European	Whirlpools:	1
Length (ft/m):	452.7/138.0	Cabins (total):	225	Self-Service Launderette:	Yes
Beam (ft/m):	68.8/21.00	Size Range (sq ft/m):	118.4–322.9/11–30	Dedicated Cinema/Seats:	No
Draft (ft/m):	19.0/5.8	Cabins (outside view):	159	Library:	No
Propulsion/Propellers:	diesel	Cabins (interior/no view):	86	Classification Society:	Russian Shipping
	(12,800kW)/2	Cabins (for one person):	3		Register

OVERALL SCORE: 909 (OUT OF A POSSIBLE 2,000 POINTS)

OVERVIEW. *The Jasmine* has a square, angular profile with a boxy stern (complete with fold-down car ramps), stubby bow and a fat funnel placed amidships. There's a fully enclosed bridge for all-weather operation, and a small helicopter landing deck. The ship can carry up to 80 cars. Outdoors facilities include a small swimming pool, regulation volleyball court, and sun deck.

This Polish-built, soundly maintained vessel was designed for carrying both cars and passengers on line voyages, although it is now used solely as a cruise ship, having been extensively reconstructed and placed under charter to Israel's Mano Maritime in 2002. Inside, there is a range of public rooms, although the ceilings are quite low. These include a main lounge (The Palace), large duty-free store, casino with tables and slot machines, (very) small children's playroom, and beauty salon. In 2004, a new, enlarged health spa was created.

Some special cruises during Jewish holidays cost more. All passengers are provided with a photo ID/charge card (Mano Card). To the cost of your cruise, you need to add port charges, handling fees and administrative expenses.

Both interior and exterior staircases are quite steep. There is no observation lounge with forward-facing views over the ship's bows. This ship has a limited amount of open deck and sunning space, and a tiny swimming pool.

SUITABLE FOR: *The Jasmine* is best suited to Hebrew-speaking passengers seeking a first taste of cruising aboard a ship of very modest facilities and features, but with good food.

ACCOMMODATION. There are eight grades, spread over five decks. These include two large Royal Suites and 13 Presi-

BERLITZ'S RATINGS

	Possible	Achieved
Ship	500	216
Accommodation	200	95
Food	400	193
Service	400	195
Entertainment	100	41
Cruise	400	169

dential Suites; the other accommodation is a variety of outside-view and interior (no view) cabins.

Standard Outside-view/Interior (No View) Cabins: All regular cabins are very small and utilitarian in their fittings and furnishings. There is little drawer space, and the under-bed storage space for luggage is tight. Most cabins are fitted with one or two beds and one or two upper Pullman berths. All suites/cabins have a private bathroom, with shower, and a small cabinet for toiletries (only soap is supplied).

Royal Suites/Presidential Suites: The two Royal Suites have a separate bedroom with plenty of closet and drawer space, and a large bathroom with bathtub and shower combination. The Presidential suites have a much larger bathroom, with bathtub and shower combination, and each has a TV/VCR. The Presidential Suites with the best location are the two directly under the ship's navigation bridge.

CUISINE/DINING. The Grand Restaurant, which seats about 420, is operated in two seatings, with tables for four, six or eight, and the chairs have armrests. It has large picture windows on three sides, although the ceiling is quite low. The food is surprisingly good, with lots of fresh salads and vegetables, good meats and local fish. Kosher food can be supplied (surcharge of about $19 per passenger, per day).

ENTERTAINMENT. The entertainment is strictly geared to the local Israeli cruise market, with visiting cabaret acts providing the show. There is also live and recorded music for dancing and listening.

SPA/FITNESS. There is a sauna, and a small fitness room.

Thomson Celebration
NOT YET RATED

Large (Resort) Ship: ....33,930 tons	Passenger Decks: 10	Cabins (for one person): 0
Lifestyle: ....Standard	Total Crew: 520	Cabins (with private balcony): 0
Cruise Line: ....Thomson Cruises	Passengers	Cabins (wheelchair accessible): 4
Former Names: ....*Noordam*	(lower beds/all berths): 1,254/1,350	Cabin Current: ....110 and 220 volts
Builder: ....Chantiers de l'Atlantique	Passenger Space Ratio	Elevators: 7
(France)	(lower beds/all berths): 27.0/25.1	Casino (gaming tables): ....Yes
Original Cost: ....$160 million	Crew/Passenger Ratio	Slot Machines: ....Yes
Entered Service: .....Apr 1984/May 2005	(lower beds/all berths): 2.4/2.6	Swimming Pools (outdoors): 2
Registry: ....The Bahamas	Navigation Officers: ....European	Swimming Pools (indoors): 0
Length (ft/m): 704.2/214.66	Cabins (total): 627	Whirlpools: 1
Beam (ft/m): 89.4/27.26	Size Range (sq ft/m): 150.6–296.0/	Self-Service Launderette: ....Yes
Draft (ft/m): 24.2/7.40	14.0–27.5	Dedicated Cinema/Seats: Yes/230
Propulsion/Propellers: ....diesel	Cabins (outside view): 413	Library: ....Yes
(21,600 kW)/2	Cabins (interior/no view): 194	Classification Society: ...Lloyd's Register

OVERALL SCORE: NYR (OUT OF A POSSIBLE 2,000 POINTS)

OVERVIEW. *Thomson Celebration* (formerly Holland America Line's *Noordam*) and sister to *Thomson Spirit* (formerly Holland America Line's *Nieuw Amsterdam*), has a nicely raked bow and a contemporary transom stern, but overall the ship's angular exterior superstructure design makes it look squat and boxy. There is a good amount of open deck space, and the traditional teakwood decks outdoors include a wrap-around promenade deck. The ship, however, has a poor build quality and suffers from some vibration. Perhaps its best asset is its friendly and personable international crew.

The ship has a spacious interior design and layout, with most public rooms located aft in a vertical arrangement, while accommodation is positioned in the forward section, which keeps noise away from the accommodation areas. The soothing color combinations do not jar the senses; although they are rather dark and somber, with some new color splashes added during the ship's refurbishment in 2005. There is much polished teakwood and rosewood paneling throughout the interiors. Horizon's observation lounge, atop the ship, is a good retreat.

The main lounge, which has a small balcony level, is reminiscent of those found on former ocean liners, and is really more suited to cabaret entertainment, and not full production shows.

Children are well catered to, with their own play areas at the aft of Bridge Deck. There are several children's clubs: Tots is for 3–5-year-olds, Team is for 6–8-year-olds, while Tribe is for 9–12-year-olds. The clubs operate five days a week (not on embarkation or disembarkation days), and are supervised by qualified "Children's Hosts."

BERLITZ'S RATINGS		
	Possible	Achieved
Ship	500	NYR
Accommodation	200	NYR
Food	400	NYR
Service	400	NYR
Entertainment	100	NYR
Cruise	400	NYR

The ship is exclusive to Thomson Cruises, so your fellow passengers are likely to be British, and typically about 80 percent of passengers will be over 45. Refreshingly, all gratuities are included, and the onboard currency is the pound sterling. In the UK market, Thomson goes head to head with P&O's *Ocean Village* and Island Cruises' *Island Escape* cruise concept for those seeking a casual, utterly relaxed vacation. However, Thomson, like Island Cruises (part of First Choice) has a major advantage in that it owns its own airline (Britannia Airlines), and has much experience in operating fly-cruises to the Mediterranean (the company offers airlift from almost a score of UK airports). You can pre-book a window seat on Britannia for an extra £10 per adult (£5 for children), and a premium seat (more space than standard seats) for £25 per person, while pre-booked meals cost £10 per person (£5 per child).

Note that there are many interior (no view) cabins. There may be some vibration, particularly at the stern. Standing in line for embarkation, disembarkation, shore tenders and for self-serve buffet meals is an inevitable aspect of cruising aboard all large ships. Although not officially rated when this book was published, it is expected that the ship will be common rated with sister ship *Thomson Spirit*.

SUITABLE FOR: *Thomson Celebration* is best suited to adult couples and singles taking their first or second cruise, and for families with children of all ages, all seeking a modern (but not glitzy) ship with a wide array of public lounges and bars, and a middle-of-the-road lifestyle, with food and entertainment that is quite acceptable rather than fancy.

ACCOMMODATION. There is one suite grade, four grades of outside-view cabins (one designated Deluxe), two grades of interior (no view) cabins. There are four cabins for the disabled (these are large, and have great forward-facing views). You can pre-book your preferred cabin for a per cabin fee of £30 (around US$50).

In general, most cabins have a reasonable amount of space, although they are small when compared with those of many other ships. In general, they are adequately appointed and practically laid out, with some wood furniture and fittings, wood paneling, good counter and storage space (although there is very little drawer space), a large mirror, and a private bathroom very modest in size.

The top three categories of cabins (which are only marginally larger and should not really be called suites or mini-suites) have bathtubs while all others have shower enclosures only. Several cabins have king- or queen-sized beds, although most have twin beds (some, but not all, can be pushed together). In many cabins, particularly those that are interior (no view), the bed configuration is L-shaped, and the beds cannot be pushed together.

A number of cabins also have additional upper berths for a third/fourth person. Room service is provided 24 hours a day. All cabin televisions receive live news via satellite. The cabin insulation, however, is extremely poor, and bathroom towels are small. In addition, some cabins on Boat and Navigation Decks have obstructed views.

CUISINE/DINING. The Meridian Restaurant, which sits in the center of the ship, is reasonably large and attractive, with warm decor, and ample space. Breakfast and lunch and dinner (6pm–10.30pm) are served in an open-seating arrangement (so you may get a different table and different waiters for each meal). Although there are a few tables for two, most are for four, six or eight. Dinners typically include a choice of four entrées (a vegetarian entrée is also available daily). Children have their very own menu, with "home-from-home" dishes and small portions. Dessert and pastry items will typically be of good quality, and made specifically for British tastes, although there is much use of canned fruits and jellies.

Sirocco's A La Carte Restaurant is the ship's alternative dining spot (reservations are required and a per person cover charge applies). It seats only 45 and has superior food and service as well as a more refined, quieter atmosphere. It is located adjacent to the Meridian Restaurant, but is best entered from the aft stairway.

Instead of the more formal dining room, there is a Lido Restaurant for a more casual setting. This is open 24 hours a day in an open-seating arrangement. Tables are set with crisp linens, flatware and stemware for dinner, when a set menu includes a choice of four entrées. Each week a themed buffet (Chinese, Indian or Mexican, depending on the cruise itinerary) may be featured for dinner. On Lido Deck, the outdoor Terrace Grill provides fast-food grilled items and pizza during the day. All dining venues are non-smoking.

ENTERTAINMENT. The 600-seat Broadway Lounge is two decks high (with a main and balcony level) and is the principal venue for production shows and cabaret entertainment. There are many pillars in the show lounge, so sightlines are obstructed from some seats.

Thomson presents an array of production shows that are colorful, lively, and entertaining (aboard other ships chartered by Thomson, the young entertainment/cruise staff enthusiastically provide the shows), while cabaret acts provide entertainment on evenings when there are no production shows.

A second entertainment venue (High Spirits) is a multi-functional room for quizzes, dancing, and late-night discotheque. A number of bands and musical units provide live music for dancing and listening in several lounges and bars.

SPA/FITNESS. Oceans Health Club is atop the ship at the aft end. It has good ocean views, and overlooks the aft pool. Facilities include an aerobics exercise room, a decent size gymnasium (there are plenty of treadmills, exercycles, and other body-toning and muscle-pumping equipment), sauna (there is no steam room), and several treatment rooms. You can have massages, aromatherapy facials, body wraps, manicures, pedicures, and hair beautifying treatments. Note that the beauty salon is located in a completely different area (close to the Reception Desk on the port side) to the health and fitness facilities.

Sample treatment prices: Swedish Classic Massage/ Indian Head Massage £30 (30 minutes) or £44 (45 minutes) or £52 (60 minutes); Cleansing Facial £36; Pedicure and Foot Massage £22; Exfoliating Body Polish £34.

Thomson Destiny
NOT YET RATED

Large (Resort) Ship: . . . . .37,584 tons	Total Crew: 540	Cabins (with private balcony): 9
Lifestyle: . . . . .Standard	Passengers	Cabins (wheelchair accessible): 0
Cruise Line: . . . . .Thomson Cruises	(lower beds/all berths): 1,450/1,611	Cabin Current: . . . . .110 volts
Former Names: Sunbird, Song of America	Passenger Space Ratio	Elevators: 7
Builder: . . . . .Wartsila (Finland)	(lower beds/all berths): 25.9/23.3	Casino (gaming tables): . . . . .Yes
Original Cost: . . . .$140 million	Crew/Passenger Ratio	Slot Machines: .Yes
Entered Service: . . . .Dec 1982/May 2005	(lower beds/all berths): 2.6/2.9	Swimming Pools (outdoors): 2
Registry: . . . . .The Bahamas	Navigation Officers: . . . . . . .International	Swimming Pools (indoors): 0
Length (ft/m): 705.0/214.88	Cabins (total): .725	Whirlpools: 0
Beam (ft/m): 93.1/28.40	Size Range (sq ft/m): 118.4–425.1/	Self-Service Launderette: . . . . .No
Draft (ft/m): 22.3/6.80	11.0–39.5	Dedicated Cinema/Seats: . . . . .No
Propulsion/Propellers: . . . . .diesel	Cabins (outside view): 425	Library: . . . . .Yes
(16,480kW)/2	Cabins (interior/no view): 300	Classification Society: . . . . . . .Det Norske
Passenger Decks: 11	Cabins (for one person): 0	Veritas

---

OVERALL SCORE: NYR (OUT OF A POSSIBLE 2,000 POINTS)

OVERVIEW. Originally built for Royal Caribbean International, the ship was sold in 1999 to My Travel/Sun Cruises, which pulled out of cruise vacations and ship ownership towards the end of 2004. It is now the largest ship in the Thomson Cruises fleet. The all-white ship, now refurbished, is a smart-looking vessel with nicely rounded lines, sharply raked bow, and a single funnel with a cantilevered, wrap-around lounge called the Chart Room (a fine place from which to observe the world around and below you).

There is a decent amount of open deck and sunbathing space (but it will be crowded when the ship sails full, which is most of the time), and some nicely polished wooden decks and rails. There are two swimming pools – the aft pool designated for children, the forward pool for adults.

The interior decor is bright and breezy. There is a good array of public rooms, most of which have high ceilings, and are one deck above the dining room. These include the main show lounge, casino and nightclub. There is also a small conference center for meetings, as well as an internet cafe (with six computer terminals – but no cafe).

Thomson Cruises provides a consistent, well-tuned and well-packaged, fun product, in comfortable surroundings. As part of Thomson Holidays, it uses the Thomson-owned Britannia Airways and is therefore able to offer complete cruise-air-stay packages at such attractive rates. The company does a good job of getting you and your luggage from aircraft to ship without having to go through immigration (depending on itinerary) in foreign countries whenever possible – so your cruise holiday is relatively seamless. The company offers airlift from almost a score of UK airports via Britannia Airlines. You can pre-book a window seat for

BERLITZ'S RATINGS		
	Possible	Achieved
Ship	500	NYR
Accommodation	200	NYR
Food	400	NYR
Service	400	NYR
Entertainment	100	NYR
Cruise	400	NYR

an extra £10 per adult (£5 for children), and a premium seat (more space than standard seats) for £20 per person, while pre-booked meals cost £10 per person (£5 per child).

The company's brochures tell it like it is – so you know before you go exactly what you will get for your money. Like other ships in the Thomson Cruises fleet, the space per passenger (particularly on the open decks) is very tight when the ships are full. There is little choice of tea and coffee. There are no cushioned pads for the deck lounge chairs. Standing in line for embarkation, disembarkation, shore tenders and for self-serve buffet meals is an inevitable aspect of cruising aboard all large ships.

Your fellow passengers are likely to be British (typically about 80 percent of passengers will be over 45). During the summer a lot of families with children go cruising, so you can expect to find them everywhere. Perhaps the best part of cruising aboard *Thomson Spirit* lies in the destinations, and not the ship (although it is perfectly comfortable). Hotel add-ons can extend a cruise vacation, and Thomson has a fine collection, depending on your needs, budget, and whether you are traveling with children (or grandchildren). The onboard currency is the British pound.

SUITABLE FOR: *Thomson Destiny* is best suited to adult couples, singles, singles taking their first or second cruise, and families with children, all seeking a modern (but not glitzy) ship with a wide array of public lounges and bars, a middle-of-the-road lifestyle, with food and entertainment that is quite acceptable rather than fancy, and a British ambience. The company does not actively market or specialize in cruises for families with children because the children's and youth facilities are limited (there is also no evening babysitting service).

ACCOMMODATION. This is provided in five categories and nine price bands: Interior (no-view) Cabins (parallel or L-shaped bed arrangement), Outside View Cabins (parallel or L-shaped bed arrangement), Deluxe Cabins (with parallel twin beds that can be converted to a queen-sized bed), Suites and Grand Suites. You can now also book the exact cabin and location you want if you pay an extra charge of £50 per cabin (roughly US$85), which also lets you choose whether to dine at the early or late evening seating.

Most cabins are of a similar size (actually very small compared to today's newer ships) and the insulation between them is quite poor. The cabins also have mediocre closets and very little storage space, yet somehow everyone seems to manage. They are just about adequate for a one-week cruise, as you will need only a small selection of mainly casual clothes (you'll probably have to put your shoes – and luggage – under the bed).

Most bathrooms typically contain a washbasin, toilet, and shower, with very little space for your toiletry items. Although they are reasonably cheerful, the shower enclosure is small, and has a curtain that you will probably end up dancing with. Towels are 100% cotton.

In some cabins, twin beds are fixed in a parallel mode (some are moveable and can be made into a queen-sized bed), while others may be in an L-shape. Note that in almost all cabins there is a "lip" or threshold (of about 9 inches/23 cm) at the bathroom door to step over.

You can get more space and a larger cabin if you book one of the 21 slightly more expensive deluxe-grade cabins on Promenade Deck. These have twin beds that convert to a queen-sized bed, set diagonally into a sleeping area adjacent to outside-view windows. There is more drawer space, more closet space, and the bathroom has a half-size tub and shower combination – bathrobes are also provided. The largest of these deluxe-grade cabins is Cabin 7000.

For even more exclusivity, you can book one of nine Suites. All are located in a private area, have fine wood paneling and trim, and come with additional space and better, more personalized service.

The additional space includes a lounge area with sofa (this converts to a double bed – making it ideal for families with children), coffee table and two chairs, a vanity desk, combination TV/VCR, an abundance of drawers, illuminated closets (with both hanging space and several shelves), excellent storage space, king-sized bed, and bathrobes. The bathroom is fully tiled, and has a full-sized enamel bathtub (rare in ships today) with shower, pink granite-look washbasin, and plenty of storage space for toiletry items. Suite occupants also get a semi-private balcony (the door of which is extremely heavy and difficult to open) with drinks table and two teak chairs. You will also be able to eat in your suite from the full dining room menu for breakfast, lunch and dinner – although there is no dining table in the suite. Book one of the two Grand Suites, and you'll get even more room – plus views over the ship's bows and a larger balcony (these can be overlooked from the open deck above), more floor space, and a walk-in closet. Missing are a bedside telephone and a bathroom telephone.

The cabin voltage is 110 volts, so British passengers will need to take a US-style adapter for any electrical appliances such as a hairdryer. Note that the accommodation deck hallways are also very narrow on some decks.

CUISINE/DINING. The Seven Seas Restaurant, a large room, consists of a central main section and two long, narrow wings (the Magellan Room and Galileo Room) with large, ocean-view windows. The low ceiling creates a high level of ambient noise. There are two seatings, both no-smoking. There are tables for two (but only 14), four, six or eight (window tables are for two or six). The service is average.

The cuisine is basic, no-frills food. There is plenty of it, though; indeed, it is quantity, not quality, that prevails, but do remember that it is all provided at a low cost. Presentation is a weak point, and there are no fish knives. If you enjoy going out to eat, and enjoy being adventurous with your food and eating habits – then you could be disappointed. The menus are standard and deviation is difficult. Bottled water is offered, and costs extra; the ship's drinking water (for which there is no charge) is adequate.

There is an adequate, but limited, wine list, and the wines are almost all very young – typical of supermarket bottles. Wine prices are quite modest, as are the prices for most alcoholic beverages.

For casual, self-serve breakfasts and lunches, the Veranda Cafe is the alternative choice, although the tables and seats outdoors are of metal and plastic, and the buffets are basic and old-fashioned. The low cruise price dictates the use of plastic cups and plastic stirrers (teaspoons are unheard of). At night you can "dine" under the steel and canvas canopy, where the cafe becomes a pleasant, outdoors alternative to the dining room – and includes waiter service. Additionally, during lunchtime, baguettes are available at the bar forward of the forward swimming pool.

ENTERTAINMENT. The Can Can Lounge is the venue for all entertainment events and social functions, and has a stage and hardwood dance floor. It is a single-level room, designed more for cabaret acts than for large-scale production shows. The revue-style shows are typically of the end-of-pier variety type, with an energetic, well-meaning cast of young people who also double as cruise staff during the day, together with some professional cabaret acts.

Another, smaller room, the Oklahoma Lounge, has a stage and dance floor, and is often used to present late-night comedy and other acts.

SPA/FITNESS. Although the spa facilities are not exactly generous, there is a gymnasium, sauna (no steam room), changing rooms for men and women, and a beauty salon. Spa and beauty services are provided by Harding Brothers, who operate similar beauty services for a number of cruise lines. You can book a massage, an aromatherapy facial, manicure and pedicure, among other treatments.

Thomson Spirit
★★★ +

Large (Resort) Ship: . . . . . . .33,930 tons	Passenger Decks: 10	Cabins (with private balcony): 0
Lifestyle: . . . . .Standard	Total Crew: 520	Cabins (wheelchair accessible): 4
Cruise Line: . . . . .Louis Cruise Lines/	Passengers	Cabin Current: . . . . .110 and 220 volts
Thomson Cruises	(lower beds/all berths): 1,254/1,350	Elevators: 7
Former Names: . . . . . .*Nieuw Amsterdam,*	Passenger Space Ratio	Casino (gaming tables): . . . . .Yes
Patriot, Nieuw Amsterdam	(lower beds/all berths): 27.0/25.1	Slot Machines: . . . . .Yes
Builder: .Chantiers de l'Atlantique (France)	Crew/Passenger Ratio	Swimming Pools (outdoors): 2
Original Cost: . . . .$150 million	(lower beds/all berths): 2.4/2.6	Swimming Pools (indoors): 0
Entered Service: . . . .July 1983/May 2002	Navigation Officers: . . . . .European	Whirlpools: 1
Registry: . . . . .The Bahamas	Cabins (total): .627	Self-Service Launderette: . . . . .Yes (3)
Length (ft/m): 704.2/214.66	Size Range (sq ft/m): 150.6–296.0/	Dedicated Cinema/Seats: Yes/230
Beam (ft/m): 89.4/27.26	14.0–27.5	Library: . . . . .Yes
Draft (ft/m): 24.6/7.52	Cabins (outside view): 413	Classification Society: . . .Lloyd's Register
Propulsion/Propellers:	Cabins (interior/no view): 194	
diesel (21,600 kW)/2	Cabins (for one person): 0	

OVERALL SCORE: 1,311 (OUT OF A POSSIBLE 2,000 POINTS)

OVERVIEW. *Thomson Spirit* was originally built for and operated by Holland America Line. It has a nicely raked bow and a contemporary transom stern, but overall the ship's angular exterior superstructure design makes it look squat and quite boxy. The ship's exterior has a deep blue hull, with a white superstructure. There is a good amount of open teakwood deck space (particularly at the aft section of the ship), and the traditional outdoors teakwood decks include a wrap-around promenade deck. Unfortunately, the ship has always suffered from poor build quality (it was built in a French shipyard) and excessive vibration, particularly at the stern, since new.

As *Patriot*, the ship had a disastrous, short-lived liaison with United States Lines, following its sale by Holland America Line to the publicly funded United States Lines in 2000. That venture was short-lived, and United States Lines collapsed in a sea of debt owed to US taxpayers in October 2001. Carnival Corporation (owners of Holland America Line) repurchased the ship for the amount outstanding ($79.8 million), and then chartered it to Louis Cruise Lines, who in turn has sub-chartered it to Thomson Cruises for a three-and-a-half year period, to replace one of the older ships the company had previously chartered. *Thomson Spirit* has a sister ship in the slightly newer, 1984-built *Thomson Celebration* (formerly Holland America Line's *Noordam*).

Thomson first operated cruises in the 1970s, then abandoned them, only to start cruises operations again in the mid-1990s (it has proved a highly successful venture, offering extremely good value for money, particularly for adult couples, and occasionally families with children), using char-

BERLITZ'S RATINGS

	Possible	Achieved
Ship	500	330
Accommodation	200	137
Food	400	241
Service	400	261
Entertainment	100	64
Cruise	400	278

tered, rathered than wholly-owned ships.

Thomson Spirit has quite a spacious interior design and layout, with little crowding and almost no points of congestion, and most of the public rooms are located on a single deck. The color combinations do not jar the senses (most are pretty nondescript, although there are many splashes of color), and the decor was greatly changed and brightened during the change to its new owners. There is much polished teakwood and rosewood paneling throughout the interiors. For quieter moments, try the Horizon Lounge, atop the ship; it has a wooden dance floor. The main lounge, with a small balcony level, is reminiscent of the ocean liners of yesteryear.

Children are well catered to, with their own play areas at the aft of Bridge Deck. There are several children's clubs: Tots is for 3–5 year-olds, Team is for 6–8 year-olds, while Tribe is for 9–12 year-olds. The clubs operate five days a week (not on embarkation or disembarkation days), and are supervised by qualified "Children's Hosts."

It's good to see a tour operator like Thomson Cruises charter and operate this ship, particularly in light of the fact that the competition in the cruise industry is increasing. This ship is quite acceptable for passengers wanting pleasant surroundings and an all-British ambiance. However, many newer ships have more space, better facilities and more options, and these leave this ship losing a few points in relation to the increased competition in the international marketplace.

Perhaps the best part of cruising aboard *Thomson Spirit* lies in the destinations, and not the ship (although it is perfectly comfortable). Hotel add-ons can extend a cruise vacation, and Thomson has a fine collection, depending on your needs, budget, and whether you are traveling with children (or grandchildren). The ship is exclusive to Thomson Cruises, so your fellow passengers are likely to be British (typically about 80 percent of passengers will be over 45).

In the UK market, Thomson goes head to head with P&O's *Ocean Village* and Island Cruises' *Island Escape* cruise concept for the young at heart. However, Thomson, like Island Cruises (part of First Choice) appears to have a major advantage in that it owns its own airline (Britannia Airlines), and has much experience in operating fly-cruises to the Mediterranean (the company offers airlift from almost a score of UK airports). With Thomson, you only pay for what you want. As far as Britannia aircraft seats go, you can pre-book a window seat for an extra £10 per adult (£5 for children), and a premium seat (more space than standard seats) for £25 per person, while pre-booked meals cost £10 per person (£5 per child).

Standing in line for embarkation, disembarkation, shore tenders and for self-serve buffet meals is inevitable aboard all large ships.

SUITABLE FOR: *Thomson Spirit* is best suited to adult couples and singles taking their first or second cruise, families with children of all ages, all seeking a modern (but not glitzy) ship with a wide array of public lounges and bars, and a middle-of-the-road lifestyle, with food and entertainment that is quite acceptable rather than fancy.

ACCOMMODATION. There is one suite grade, four grades of outside-view cabins (one designated Deluxe), two grades of interior (no view) cabins. There are four cabins for the disabled (these are large, and have great forward-facing views). You can pre-book your preferred cabin for a per cabin fee of £30 (around US$50).

Most of the cabins are quite small (below the industry standard of 170 sq. ft/15.7 sq. meters). They are reasonably well appointed and practically laid out. Some have wood furniture, fittings, or accenting, good counter and storage space (but little drawer space), a large dressing mirror, and private bathrooms that are adequate, but no more. The top cabin categories (which are only marginally larger and should not really be called suites), have full-sized bathtubs while all others have showers. Several cabins have king- or queen-sized beds, although most have twin beds.

The largest accommodation is in the Presidential Suite (on Eagle Deck), a new suite created when United States Lines purchased the ship. Small by comparison to suites aboard many other ships, it measures 464 sq. ft (43.1 sq. meters) and is located on the uppermost accommodation deck. There is a king-sized bed, walk-in closet, wet bar, study and dining areas, television, VCR, and stereo system. The bathroom includes a whirlpool tub, double sink unit, and a separate powder room.

A number of cabins also have additional berths for a third/fourth person. Room service is provided 24 hours a day. All cabin TVs carry BBC World. The cabin insulation is extremely poor, and the bathroom towels are small.

CUISINE/DINING. The Compass Rose Restaurant is reasonably large and attractive, with warm decor and ample space. Breakfast, lunch and dinner (6pm–10.30pm) are served in an open-seating arrangement (so you may get a different table and different waiters for each meal). Although there are a few tables for two, most are for four, six or eight. Dinners typically include a choice of four entrées (a vegetarian entrée is also available daily). Children have their very own menu, with "home-from-home" dishes and small portions.

Dessert and pastry items will typically be of good quality, and made specifically for British tastes, although there is much use of canned fruits and jellies.

Sirocco's A La Carte Restaurant is the ship's alternative dining spot (reservations are required and a per person cover charge applies). It seats only 45 and has superior food and service as well as a more refined, quieter atmosphere. It is located adjacent to the Compass Rose Restaurant, but is best entered from the aft stairway.

Instead of the more formal dining room, there is a more casual Lido Restaurant. This is open 24 hours a day in an open-seating arrangement. Tables are set with crisp linens, flatware and stemware for dinner, when the set menu includes a choice of four entrées. Each week a themed buffet (Chinese, Indian or Mexican, depending on the cruise itinerary) may be featured for dinner. On Lido Deck, the outdoor Terrace Grill provides fast-food grilled items and pizza during the day. All dining venues are non-smoking.

ENTERTAINMENT. The 600-seat Broadway Showlounge is two decks high (main and balcony levels) and is the ship's principal venue for production shows and cabaret entertainment. Although Thomson is not generally known for high-quality shows, they are, in fact, good fun, and are professionally produced (aboard other ships chartered by Thomson the young entertainment/cruise staff enthusiastically provide the shows), while cabaret acts provide entertainment on evenings when there is no production show.

A second entertainment venue (High Spirits) is a multifunctional room for quizzes, dancing, and late-night discotheque. A number of bands and musical units provide live music for dancing and listening in several lounges and bars.

SPA/FITNESS. Oceans Health Club is atop the ship at the aft end. It has good ocean views, and overlooks the aft pool and hot tub, on Bridge Deck. Facilities include an aerobics exercise room, a decent size gymnasium (there are plenty of treadmills, exercycles, and other body-toning and muscle-pumping equipment), sauna (there is no steam room), and several treatment rooms. You can have massages, aromatherapy facials, body wraps, manicures, pedicures, and hair beautifying treatments. Note that the beauty salon is located in a completely different area (close to the Reception Desk on the port side) to the health and fitness facilities. Sample prices: Swedish Classic Massage/Indian Head Massage £30 (30 minutes) or £44 (45 minutes) or £52 (60 minutes); Cleansing Facial £36; Pedicure and Foot Massage £22; Exfoliating Body Polish £34.

Triton
★★ +

Mid-Size Ship: . . . . .14,155 tons	Passenger Decks: 7	Cabins (for one person): 0	
Lifestyle: . . . . .Standard	Total Crew: 265	Cabins (with private balcony): 0	
Cruise Line: . . . . . .Royal Olympia Cruises	Passengers	Cabins (wheelchair accessible): 0	
Former Names: . . . . . .*Cunard Adventurer,*	(lower beds/all berths): 756/945	Cabin Current: . . . . .110 and 220 volts	
Sunward II	Passenger Space Ratio	Elevators: 2	
Builder: Rotterdamsche Dry Dock (Holland)	(lower beds/all berths): 18.7/14.9	Casino (gaming tables): . . . . .Yes	
Original Cost: .n/a	Crew/Passenger Ratio	Slot Machines: . . . . .Yes	
Entered Service: . . . . .Oct 1971/May 1992	(lower beds/all berths): 2.8/3.5	Swimming Pools (outdoors): 1	
Registry: .Greece	Navigation Officers: . . . . .Greek	Swimming Pools (indoors): 0	
Length (ft/m): 491.1/149.70	Cabins (total): 378	Whirlpools: 0	
Beam (ft/m): 70.5/21.50	Size Range (sq ft/m): 118.4–131.3/	Self-Service Launderette: . . . . .No	
Draft (ft/m): 19.22/5.86	11.0–12.2	Dedicated Cinema/Seats: Yes/96	
Propulsion/Propellers: . . . . .diesel	Cabins (outside view): 236	Library: . . . . .No	
(19,860kW)/2	Cabins (interior/no view): 142	Classification Society: . . .Lloyd's Register	

OVERALL SCORE: 1,009 (OUT OF A POSSIBLE 2,000 POINTS)

OVERVIEW. *Triton* was originally built for Norwegian Cruise Line (then called Norwegian Caribbean Line). It was later bought by Royal Olympia Cruises and introduced in 1992 for informal cruises; it has a reasonably handsome profile, a deep clipper bow, and twin funnels. The ship has been fairly well maintained, although it is now showing its age. There is a wrap-around painted steel outdoors promenade deck of sorts, as well as a decent amount of open deck space for sunbathing, and a small "kidney-shaped" swimming pool, although space is extremely tight when the ship is full (which is most of the time). Much of the open space outdoors is covered by canvas awnings, much appreciated by many passengers as a shelter from the intensity of the summer sun.

Inside, a good general layout and passenger flow makes it easy to find your way around in a short time (it is a fairly small ship by today's standards). There is a decent choice of public rooms, most of which are dressed in cheerful, warm colors, although the ceiling height is quite low, and this provides quite a cramped feeling. The decor and artwork are eclectic, some left over from the ship's former days with Norwegian Cruise Line and Cunard, while the deck names are Greek.

There's a good (but small) nightclub with forward observation views. The showlounge is a single-level room, with sight lines obstructed by six pillars and the absence of a sloping floor, so only those passengers seated in the first few rows can see below waist level. There is no library (although there is a token gesture of two unkempt bookcases with a few old paperbacks).

On one of the upper decks, a dance floor is provided outdoors, with a bar called Jailhouse Rock – it's good for

BERLITZ'S RATINGS

	Possible	Achieved
Ship	500	253
Accommodation	200	93
Food	400	200
Service	400	226
Entertainment	100	50
Cruise	400	187

lively nights under the summer stars (but it is not used early and late in the season when the weather is cooler).

These destination-intensive itineraries (typically from April to November) are excellent for those who want to see many places in a short time (there are two ports of call on most days). But, be warned, they are extremely busy, particularly on the first day (there are no days at sea). In other words, these three- and four-night cruises are not for relaxing, but for sightseeing.

Triton is a decent down-home ship for short cruises around the Greek islands and Mediterranean. The dress code is very casual throughout (there are no formal nights), so leave your coats and ties and long dresses at home, as you simply don't need them. Gratuities (suggested at $8 per person per day) are pooled among the crew on the last day.

Forget about such things as chocolates on your pillow, and the other niceties associated with cruising aboard other cruise lines – this one will get you around the Greek islands in low-budget surroundings, with food that is more quantity than quality, and service that is mostly indifferent. Of course, with two sets of passengers each week, it is hard to provide friendly contact.

Triton really is a high-density ship with crowded public areas. Expect lines for buffets and shore excursions. There are many announcements for tours, in several languages, when in ports of call. The nature of the Greek island cruises means that crew contracts are seasonal, and, at the end of the season (end of October/beginning of November) most crew are tired and clearly want to go home – and it shows – to the detriment of the product. The onboard currency is the euro.

SUITABLE FOR: *Triton* is best suited to first-time passengers who simply want a ship to take them to a number of destinations in a modicum of comfort, with few facilities, and at a bargain price. You must be prepared for very small cabins, food and service that are best described as what the British would call "motorway cafe standard", and entertainment that is second-rate.

ACCOMMODATION. *Triton* has cabins in eight grades, the price depending on grade, location and size. Most of the cabins are very small and narrow, dimensionally challenged, and basic in appointments. The closet and drawer space (the drawers are rather tinny) is minimal, and cabin soundproofing is very poor. There are 32 cabins (in the two highest grades) with a bathtub/shower; otherwise the cabin bathrooms have very small shower units, and little space for personal toiletries (however, the ship operates short cruises, so you won't need to take much).

CUISINE/DINING. While the Horizon Dining Room is reasonably attractive and has contemporary colors and ambiance, it is also a noisy room. There are two seatings for dinner on most nights (typically it will be an open seating for the first night of the cruise), and open seating for breakfast and lunch. Dining room seating and table assignments for the cruise (except for the first night) are normally handled by the maître d' upon embarkation.

The cuisine is predominantly Continental, with many regional (Greek) specialties (there is much use of oil and salt). The presentation is spotty and inconsistent. Spa and vegetarian dishes are also available on lunch and dinner menus. Overall, however, the food has very little taste. There is a limited (repetitious) choice of bread rolls, fruits and cheeses, and desserts rely too much on canned fruits and jellies. The "old-world" service from the Greek dining room stewards adds to the experience, although it is not nearly as good as it used to be, and is far too hurried.

Casual breakfast and lunch (with limited choices) can also be taken outside on deck adjacent to the swimming pool, or in the main lounge when the weather is not good. Additional light refreshments are available indoors at the Cafe Brazil.

ENTERTAINMENT. The Sirenes Main Lounge is the venue for shows and entertainment events. It is a single level, rectangular-shaped room designed for cabaret acts, and not production-style shows. Banquette and individual seating is clustered around a "thrust" stage, but note that that several pillars obstruct the sightlines from some seats.

Entertainment has never been a strong point for Royal Olympia Cruises, and there is no cohesive plan for entertainment, other than filling in spots with whatever cabaret acts are available at low cost. As a result, shows tend to be an afterthought.

SPA/FITNESS. There is a small gymnasium located aft, close to the swimming pool (this can really only be considered a "dip" pool); adjacent is a sauna and massage room. A beauty salon is located indoors on another deck (there is no natural light, which makes tinting and coloring difficult). Massages, aromatherapy facials, manicures, pedicures, and hair beuatifying treatments are available.

WATERTIGHT CONTRACTS

Cruise lines are masters of small print when it comes to contracts. A clause in the ticket typically reads: "The Carrier's legal responsibility for death, injury, illness, damage, delay, or other loss or detriment of person or property of whatever kind suffered by the Passenger will, in the first instance, be governed by the Athens Convention relating to the Carriage of Passengers and their Luggage by Sea, 1974, with protocols and amendments, together with the further provisions of the International Convention on Limitation of Liability for Maritime Claims, 1976, with revisions and amendments (hereinafter collectively referred to as the "Convention"). The Carrier shall not be liable for any such death, injury, illness, damage, delay, loss, or detriment caused by Act of God, war or warlike operations, civil commotions, labor trouble, interference by Authorities, perils of the sea, or any other cause beyond the control of the Carrier, fire, thefts or any other crime, errors in the navigation or management of the Vessel, or defect in, or unseaworthiness of hull, machinery, appurtenances, equipment, furnishings, or supplies of the Vessel, fault or neglect of pilot, tugs, agents, independent contractors, such as ship's Physician, Passengers or other persons on board not in the Carrier's employ or for any other cause of whatsoever nature except and unless it is proven that such death, injury, illness, damage, delay, loss resulting from Carrier's act or omission was committed with the intent to cause such loss or with knowledge that such loss would probably result therefrom and in that event the Carrier's liability therefore shall not exceed the specified limitations per Passenger in Special Drawing Rights (S.D.R.) as defined in the applicable conventions or in any further revision and/or amendment thereto as shall become applicable."

Van Gogh
★★ +

Mid-Size Ship: . . . . .15,402 tons	Passenger Decks: 7	Cabins (wheelchair accessible): 0
Lifestyle: . . . . .Standard	Total Crew: 250	Cabin Current: . . . . .220 volts
Cruise Line: . . . . .TravelScope	Passengers	Refrigerator: . . . . .No
Former Names: . . . . . .Club I, Odessa Sky,	(lower beds/all berths): 506/795	Dining Rooms: .1
Gruziya	Passenger Space Ratio	Elevators: 1
Gross Tonnage: 15,402	(lower beds/all berths): 30.4/19.3	Casino (gaming tables): . . . . .Yes
Builder: . . . . .Wartsila (Finland)	Crew/Passenger Ratio	Slot Machines: . . . . .Yes
Original Cost: . . . .$25 million	(lower beds/all berths): 2.0/3.1	Swimming Pools (outdoors): 1
Entered Service: . . .June 1975/May 1999	Navigation Officers: . . . . .Ukrainian	Swimming Pools (indoors): 0
Registry: . . . .St. Vincent & the Grenadines	Cabins (total): 253	Whirlpools: 0
Length (ft/m): 512.6/156.27	Size Range (sq ft/m): . . .90–492/8.4–45.7	Self-Service Launderette: . . . . .Yes
Beam (ft/m): 72.3/22.05	Cabins (outside view): 148	Dedicated Cinema/Seats: Yes/140
Draft (ft/m): 19.4/5.92	Cabins (interior/no view): 105	Library: . . . . .Yes
Propulsion/Propellers: . . . . .diesel	Cabins (for one person): 0	Classification Society: . . . . . . .Det Norske
(13,430kW)/2	Cabins (with private balcony): 0	Veritas

---

OVERALL SCORE: 1,088 (OUT OF A POSSIBLE 2,000 POINTS)

OVERVIEW. This is a reasonably smart-looking vessel with a squarish 1970s profile and smart, but boxy funnel. There is a decent outdoor promenade area for strolling or relaxing in a deck lounge chair, although the open deck space is tight when the ship is full.

The ship was bought by the Dutch firm Eltek in 1998 and operated by Club Cruise specifically for short cruises from Rotterdam for Dutch passengers. Later, under charter, it provided comfortable, unpretentious cruises for French-speaking passengers.

The ship is now operated by other tour companies in the European market (such as Travelscope in the UK). Thus, the currency used on board will depend on the country of origin of the tour operator. Overall, the ship provides a decent range of public rooms, lounges and bars, with cozy, warm decor.

Inside, most of the few public rooms are on one horizontal deck. The nicest (for drinks and conversation) is the Captain's Bar (decorated in maritime paraphernalia) There is a casino with tables and slot machines, a small boutique, a small cinema and discotheque.

Communication with many staff can prove frustrating, although they are friendly. There are no cushioned pads for the deck lounge chairs. The gangway is narrow.

SUITABLE FOR: *Van Gogh* is best suited to adult couples and singles wanting a cruise holiday at rock-bottom prices to take them to interesting destinations in a modicum of comfort, with basic food and low-budget entertainment.

ACCOMMODATION. Four suites on Boat Deck offer the largest accommodation, with sweeping forward views.

BERLITZ'S RATINGS

	Possible	Achieved
Ship	500	270
Accommodation	200	112
Food	400	204
Service	400	232
Entertainment	100	53
Cruise	400	217

These provide very spacious accommodation for the size of the ship, with good closet and drawer space and have full-sized bathtubs. Another six suites are almost as large but don't have the fine forward-facing views. All other cabins are very small and sparingly furnished with merely adequate bathrooms. The insulation between cabins is poor.

One cabin has been "adapted" for the disabled, although it would be difficult to get even a junior collapsible wheelchair through the cabin door.

CUISINE/DINING. There is a rather plain (non-smoking) dining room, but it has nicely decorated soft furnishings, and is moderately comfortable. There are tables for four, six or eight, assigned for the cruise's duration. Dinner is in two seatings. Casual, self-serve breakfast and lunch buffets are available on the port side of the swimming pool, although the choice is limited. In the main, the food is wholesome.

ENTERTAINMENT. Cruise prices are low, so you should not expect entertainment to be of a high standard. However, what is presented in the main lounge are mini-revue shows, typically with wanna-be cabaret acts (vocalists, magicians, ventriloquists, comedians) as a main feature. In other words, the entertainment is entertaining and colorful, but provided on a shoestring budget. A band and small musical units provide live music for dancing or listening.

SPA/FITNESS. There is a sauna (this may cost extra), and a small gymnasium with a few bits of (mostly old, but solid) exercise equipment. Massage is also available.

Veendam
★★★★

Large (Resort) Ship: ....55,451 tons	Total Crew: 561	Cabins (with private balcony): 150
Lifestyle: ....Premium	Passengers	Cabins (wheelchair accessible): 6
Cruise Line: ......Holland America Line	(lower beds/all berths): 1,266/1,627	Cabin Current: ....110 and 220 volts
Former Names: ....none	Passenger Space Ratio	Elevators: 8
Builder: ....Fincantieri (Italy)	(lower beds/all berths): 43.8/34.0	Casino (gaming tables): ....Yes
Original Cost: ....$215 million	Crew/Passenger Ratio	Slot Machines: ....Yes
Entered Service: ....May 1996	(lower beds/all berths): 2.2/2.9	Swimming Pools (outdoors): 1
Registry: ....The Bahamas	Navigation Officers: ......British/Dutch	Swimming Pools (indoors): 1
Length (ft/m): 719.3/219.3	Cabins (total): 633	(magrodome)
Beam (ft/m): 101.0/30.8	Size Range (sq ft/m): 186.2–1,124.8/	Whirlpools: 2
Draft (ft/m): 24.6/7.5	17.3–104.5	Self-Service Launderette: ....Yes
Propulsion/Propellers: .....diesel-electric	Cabins (outside view): 502	Dedicated Cinema/Seats: Yes/249
(34,560kW)/2	Cabins (interior/no view): 131	Library: ....Yes
Passenger Decks: 10	Cabins (for one person): 0	Classification Society: ...Lloyd's Register

---

OVERALL SCORE: 1,533 (OUT OF A POSSIBLE 2,000 POINTS)

OVERVIEW. *Veendam* is one of a series of four almost identical ships in the same series – the others being *Maasdam, Statendam,* and *Ryndam.* The exterior styling is rather angular (some would say boxy – the funnel certainly is), although it is softened and balanced somewhat by the fact that the hull is painted black. There is a full wrap-around teakwood promenade deck outdoors – excellent for strolling, and, thankfully, no sign of synthetic turf anywhere. The deck lounge chairs one the exterior promenade deck are wood, and come with comfortable cushioned pads, while those at the swimming pool on Lido Deck are of white plastic.

In the interiors of this "S" -class ship, an asymmetrical layout helps to reduce bottlenecks and congestion. Most of the public rooms are concentrated on two decks, Promenade Deck, and Upper Promenade Deck, which creates a spacious feel to the ship's interiors. In general, a restrained approach to interior styling is taken, using a mixture of contemporary materials combined with traditional woods and ceramics. There is, fortunately, little "glitz" anywhere.

What is outstanding is the array of artworks throughout the ship (costing about $2 million), assembled and nicely displayed to represent the fine Dutch heritage of Holland America Line and to present a balance between standard itineraries and onboard creature comforts. Also noticeable are the fine flower arrangements throughout the public areas and foyers – used to good effect to brighten up what to some is rather dull decor.

Atop the ship, with forward-facing views that wrap around the sides is the Crow's Nest Lounge. By day it makes a fine observation lounge, with large ocean-view windows; by night it is a nightclub with extremely variable lighting.

BERLITZ'S RATINGS

	Possible	Achieved
Ship	500	418
Accommodation	200	162
Food	400	267
Service	400	299
Entertainment	100	77
Cruise	400	310

A three-deck high atrium foyer is quite appealing, although its sculpted centerpiece makes it look a little crowded, and leaves little room in front of the purser's office. A hydraulic magrodome (glass) roof covers the reasonably sized swimming pool/whirlpools and central Lido area (whose focal point is a large dolphin sculpture) so that this can be used in good or bad weather.

There is a large reference library, quite lovely and relaxing. The company keeps its ships very clean and tidy, and there is good passenger flow throughout.

Veendam is well-built, with fairly decent interior fit and finish. Holland America Line is constantly fine-tuning its performance and its regular passengers (almost all of whom are North American) find the company's ships very comfortable and well-run. The company continues its strong maritime traditions, although the present food and service components still let the rest of the cruise experience down.

The service staff is Indonesian, and, although they are mostly quite charming, communication often proves frustrating, and service is spotty and inconsistent.

An escalator travels between two of the lower decks (one was originally planned to be the embarkation point), but it is almost pointless. The charge to use the washing machines and dryers in the self-service launderette is petty, particularly for suite occupants, who pay high prices for their cruises. The men's urinals in public restrooms are unusually high.

ACCOMMODATION. The accommodation ranges from small interior (no view) cabins to a large penthouse suite, in 17 price categories (the price will depend on the grade, location and size chosen). All cabin televisions normally carry CNN and TNT programming.

The interior (no view) and outside-view standard cabins have twin beds that convert to a queen-size bed, and there is a separate living space with sofa and coffee table. However, although the drawer space is generally good, the closet space is actually very tight, particularly for long cruises (although more than adequate for a 7-night cruise). The bathrooms are tiled, and compact but practical. Bathrobes are also provided, as are hairdryers.

Bathrobes are also provided for all suites/cabins, as are hairdryers, and a small range of personal amenities (soap, conditoning shampoo, body lotion, shower cap, vanity kit). The bathrooms are quite well laid out, but the bathtubs are small units better described as shower tubs. Some cabins have interconnecting doors.

On Navigation Deck, 28 suites have accommodation for up to four. These also have in-suite dining as an alternative to the dining room, for private, reclusive meals. These are very spacious, tastefully decorated and well laid-out, and feature a separate living room, bedroom with two lower beds (convertible to a king-sized bed), a good-sized living area, dressing room, plenty of closet and drawer space, marble bathroom with Jacuzzi tub.

The largest accommodation of all is a penthouse suite. There is only one, located on the starboard side of Navigation Deck at the forward staircase. It has a king-sized bed (TV and video player) and vanity desk; large walk-in closet with superb drawer space, oversize whirlpool bath (it could seat four) and separate shower enclosure, separate washroom with toilet, bidet and washbasin; living room with writing desk, large TV and full set of audio equipment); dressing room, large private balcony (with teak lounge chairs and drinks tables, dining table and four chairs), pantry (with large refrigerator, toaster unit, and full coffee/tea making facilities and food preparation area, and a separate entrance from the hallway), mini-bar/refrigerator, a guest toilet and floor-to-ceiling windows. There is no bell push.

CUISINE/DINING. The Rotterdam Dining Room, with smoking and no-smoking sections, spans two decks. It is located at the stern of the ship, is quite dramatic, and has two grand staircases to connect the two levels, panoramic views on three sides, and a music balcony. It has open seating for breakfast and lunch, and four seatings for dinner (you must pre-select a time and stick with it), at 5.45pm, 6.15pm, 8pm and 8.30pm. There are tables for two, four, six or eight. The waiter stations in the dining room are very noisy for those seated adjacent to them. Fine Rosenthal china and cutlery are used (although there are no fish knives).

Alternative Dining Option: The intimate Pinnacle Grill, added in 2002, is located just forward of the balcony level of the main dining room on the starboard side. The 66-seat dining spot has Pacific Northwest cuisine (fresh Alaskan salmon and halibut, and other regional specialties, plus a selection of premium steaks such as filet mignon from Black Angus beef). The new venue (reservations are necessary, and a cover/service charge of $20 applies) was created out of the former private dining wing of the main dining room, plus a slice of the Explorer's Lounge. A Bulgari show plate, Rosenthal china, Reidel wine glasses, and Frette table linen are featured. The Pinnacle Grill is a much better dining experience than the main dining room and worth it for that special celebration.

Instead of the more formal dining room (or Pinnacle Grill), the Lido Buffet is open for casual dinners on all but the last night of a cruise, in an open-seating arrangement. Tables are set with crisp linens, flatware and stemware. A set menu includes a choice of four entrées.

For more casual evening eating, the Lido Buffet is open for casual dinners on all except the last night of each cruise, in an open-seating arrangement. Tables are set with crisp linens, flatware and stemware. A set menu is featured, and this includes a choice of four entrées.

The dual-line, self-serve Lido Buffet (one side is for smokers, the other side for non-smokers) is also the place for casual breakfasts and lunches. Again there is much use of canned fruits (good for dentally challenged older passengers) and packeted items, although there are several commercial low-calorie salad dressings. The choice of cheeses (and accompanying crackers) is very poor. The beverage station also lets it down, for it is no better than those found in family outlets ashore in the United States. In addition, a poolside grill provides basic American hamburgers and hot dogs.

Passengers will need to eat in the Lido Cafe on any days when the dining room is closed for lunch (typically once or twice per cruise, depending on the ship's itinerary).

ENTERTAINMENT. The Rubens Showlounge, located at the forward part of the ship, spans two decks, with banquette seating on both main and upper levels. It is basically a well designed room, but the ceiling is low and the sightlines from the balcony level are quite poor.

SPA/FITNESS. The Ocean Spa is located one deck below the navigation bridge at the very forward part of the ship. It includes a gymnasium (with all the latest muscle-pumping exercise machines, including an abundance of treadmills) with ocean views, an aerobics exercise area, large beauty salon with ocean-view windows to the port side, several treatment rooms, and men's and women's sauna, steam room and changing areas.

● **For more extensive general information on what a Holland America Line cruise is like, see pages 118–122.**

Vision of the Seas
★★★★

Large (Resort) Ship: ....78,491 tons	Total Crew: 765	Cabins (with private balcony): 229
Lifestyle: ....Standard	Passengers	Cabins (wheelchair accessible): 14
Cruise Line: Royal Caribbean International	(lower beds/all berths): 2,000/2,435	Cabin Current: ....110 and 220 volts
Former Names: ....none	Passenger Space Ratio	Elevators: 9
Builder: Chantiers de l'Atlantique (France)	(lower beds/all berths): 39.2/32.2	Casino (gaming tables): ....Yes
Original Cost: ....$275 million	Crew/Passenger Ratio	Slot Machines: ....Yes
Entered Service: ....May 1998	(lower beds/all berths): 3.0/3.6	Swimming Pools (outdoors): 1
Registry: ....The Bahamas	Navigation Officers: ....International	Swimming Pools (indoors): 1
Length (ft/m): 915.3/279.0	Cabins (total): 1,000	(inside/outside)
Beam (ft/m): 105.6/32.2	Size Range (sq ft/m): 135.0–1,270.1/	Whirlpools: 6
Draft (ft/m): 24.9/7.6	12.5–118.0	Self-Service Launderette: ....No
Propulsion/Propellers: .....diesel-electric	Cabins (outside view): 593	Dedicated Cinema/Seats: ....No
(50,400kW)2	Cabins (interior/no view): 407	Library: ....Yes
Passenger Decks: 11	Cabins (for one person): 0	Classification Society: Det Norske Veritas

OVERALL SCORE: 1,519 (OUT OF A POSSIBLE 2,000 POINTS)

OVERVIEW. This striking ship, sister to *Rhapsody of the Seas*, shares design features that make all Royal Caribbean International ships identifiable, including a Viking Crown Lounge (which is also the ship's disco). The Viking Crown Lounge is just aft of the center of the ship (above the central atrium lobby), with the funnel located well aft – a departure from all other RCI ships to date. The ship's stern is beautifully rounded. There is a reasonable amount of open-air walking space, although this can become cluttered with deck lounge chairs (which, incidentally, do not have cushioned pads).

Inside, the ship provides RCI's interpretation of a floating contemporary hotel, and presents the nicest mix of colors and decor of any of the Vision-class ships, with lots of warm beige and pink tones (particularly in the expansive atrium).

The artwork (which cost $6 million) is plentiful, colorful and very creative, with more previously blank wall space covered with interesting artworks of differing shapes and sizes. Most noticeable is the extensive use of glass (two beautiful glass sculptures stand out – one in the atrium (at the entrance to a Champagne Bar), one on the upper level of the Viking Crown Lounge). There are plenty of public rooms, bars and lounges, as well as a large, well-lit casino.

The Viking Crown Lounge is a multi-level nightspot (the music can be loud and overbearing, however, and so can cigarette smoke around the bar – one of few places where smokers can light up). Perhaps the best atmosphere is in the nautical-theme Schooner Bar. The Library has an excellent array of hardbacks, and a neat wooden sculpture of something that looks like the Tin Man from *The Wizard of Oz*.

BERLITZ'S RATINGS

	Possible	Achieved
Ship	500	428
Accommodation	200	166
Food	400	248
Service	400	302
Entertainment	100	81
Cruise	400	294

SUITABLE FOR: *Vision of the Seas* is best suited to young-minded couples and singles of all ages, families with toddlers, children, and teenagers who like to mingle in a large ship setting with plenty of life and high-energy entertainment, with food that is acceptable quantity rather than quality, all delivered with friendly service that lacks polish.

ACCOMMODATION. There are 18 cabin categories, in 11 pricing units (the price you pay will depend on the grade, location and size chosen).

The standard interior (no view) and exterior view cabins are of an adequate size, and have just enough functional facilities to make them comfortable for a one-week cruise, but longer might prove confining. The decor is bright and cheerful, although the ceilings are plain; colorful soft furnishings make one's home away from home look like the inside of a modern Scandinavian hotel – minimalist, yet colorful. Twin lower beds convert to queen-sized beds, and there is a reasonable amount of closet and drawer space (there is little room to maneuver between the bed and desk/television unit).

The bathrooms are small but functional, although the shower units are small, and there is no cabinet for personal toiletry items. The towels could be larger and thicker.

Choose a "C" grade suite if you want spacious accommodation that includes a separate (curtained-off) sleeping area, a good-sized outside balcony (with part, not full, partition), lounge with sofa, two chairs and coffee table, three closets, plenty of drawer and storage space, television and VCR. The bathroom is large and has a full-size tub, integral shower, and two washbasins/two toiletries cabinets.

For the ultimate accommodation aboard this ship, choose the Royal Suite, which resembles a Palm Beach apartment, and comes with a white baby grand (player) piano. It has a separate bedroom with king-sized bed, living room with queen-size sofa bed, refrigerator/mini-bar, dining table, entertainment center, and vanity dressing area. The decor is simple and elegant, with pastel colors, and wood accented ceiling treatments. Located just under the starboard side navigation bridge wing, it has its own private balcony.

CUISINE/DINING. The no-smoking Aquarius Dining Room is set on two levels with large ocean-view picture windows on two sides (rectangular windows on the upper level, large circular windows on the lower level) and a large connecting stairway. There are two seatings.

The Windjammer Cafe is the casual dining spot for self-serve buffets. The area is well-designed, with contemporary decor and colors, but the food is really basic fare and disappointing; the four-sided self-service buffet area is small for the number of passengers that use it. More money needs to be spent for better-quality ingredients and more variety is needed. Each evening, the room offers an alternative to the more dressy dining room. The evening buffets typically feature a different theme, something this company has been doing for more than 25 years – perhaps the time has come for more creativity.

A hamburger/hot dog grill counter in the Solarium, but typically you don't get a choice of how well done or not so well done you get your hamburgers – everything appears to be well done.

The company has introduced a drinks package (available at all bars, in the form of cards or stickers) that enables you to pre-pay for a selection of standard soft drinks and alcoholic drinks. The packages are not easy to understand.

ENTERTAINMENT. The Masquerade Theatre is the ship's principal showlounge, located in the forward section of the ship (accessed by the forward stairway/elevators), for production shows and other major cabaret shows. It is a large, but a well-designed room with main and balcony levels, and good sightlines from most of the banquette seats.

Other cabaret acts are featured in the Some Enchanted Eevening, located aft, and these include late-night adult (blue) comedy, as well as live music for dancing. A number of other bars and lounges have live music of differing types.

The entertainment throughout is upbeat (in fact, it is difficult to get away from music and noise). There is even background music in all corridors and elevators, and constant music outdoors on the pool deck. If you want a quiet relaxing holiday, choose another ship.

SPA/FITNESS. The spa, with its solarium and indoor/outdoor dome-covered pool, Inca- and Mayan-theme decor, sauna/steam rooms and gymnasium, provides a haven for the health-conscious and fitness buff (although there is a pizza bar forward of the pool area). A lovely "Mayan Serpent" sculpture is featured in the solarium.

For more sporting passengers, there is activity galore – including a rock-climbing wall, with several separate climbing tracks. It is located outdoors at the aft end of the funnel.

● **For more extensive general information about the Royal Caribbean cruise experience, see pages 128–131.**

Small Ship: ....7,478 tons	Passenger Decks: 6	Cabins (for one person): 5
Lifestyle: ....Standard	Total Crew: 110	Cabins (with private balcony): 11
Cruise Line: ....Plantours & Partners	Passengers	Cabins (wheelchair accessible): 0
Former Names: ....none	(lower beds/all berths): 299/320	Cabin Current: ....220 volts
Builder: ......Union Navale de Levante	Passenger Space Ratio	Elevators: 1
(Spain)	(lower beds/all berths): 25.3/23.3	Casino (gaming tables): ....No
Original Cost: ....$45 million	Crew/Passenger Ratio	Slot Machines: ....No
Entered Service: ....Sept 1989	(lower beds/all berths): 2.7/2.9	Swimming Pools (outdoors): 1
Registry: ....Spain	Navigation Officers: ....Spanish	Swimming Pools (indoors): 0
Length (ft/m): 396.9/121.00	Cabins (total): 152	Whirlpools: 0
Beam (ft/m): 55.1/16.82	Size Range (sq ft/m): 129.1–150.6/	Self-Service Launderette: ....No
Draft (ft/m): 14.9/4.55	12.0–14.0	Dedicated Cinema/Seats: ....No
Propulsion/Propellers: ....diesel	Cabins (outside view): 126	Library: ....Yes
(3,900kW)/2	Cabins (interior/no view): 26	Classification Society: ....Bureau Veritas

OVERALL SCORE: 1,232 (OUT OF A POSSIBLE 2,000 POINTS)

OVERVIEW. *Vistamar* has a moderately smart, reasonably contemporary, but rather squat small ship profile. The ship, which has an ice-hardened hull, also carries several inflatable rubber landing craft for close-up landings during certain itineraries that include the Arctic and Antarctic.

There is an "open bridge" policy, so you can join the captain and other navigation officers at almost any time (except during difficult maneuvers). There is a good open observation deck at the forward-most part of the ship – atop the navigation bridge, although the other open deck and sunbathing space is a little limited, particularly on the aft open deck around the small outdoor pool (it is really only a "dip" pool, although it has a large splash surround).

The interior layout has all the public rooms located aft, in a "cake-layer" stacking, with a single, central staircase that takes up most of the space in an atrium lobby that spans three decks (with a glass elevator shaped like half a cable car). Features include wood-trimmed interior decor, which is quite jazzy, attractive and warm, although the mirrored metallic ceilings are somewhat irritating.

A four-deck high atrium with a "sky dome" has a glass-walled elevator and a wrap-around staircase, and is the focal point of the ship's interior. The library has comfortable high wingback chairs, but there aren't many books. There is also a Card Room, and board games are available.

The ship's main lounge, Don Fernando, is named after Senor Don Fernando Abril Martorell, the president of the Union Navale de Levante shipyard that constructed *Vistamar* in 444 days (perhaps if more time had been taken, the ship would have been built better). Additionally, there is a

BERLITZ'S RATINGS

	Possible	Achieved
Ship	500	291
Accommodation	200	127
Food	400	244
Service	400	271
Entertainment	100	58
Cruise	400	241

rather jazzy nightclub/disco, with acres of glass, set around the base of the funnel, with a long bar, and dance floor, for the late-night set.

This ship has been under charter to Plantours & Partners, specifically for German-speaking passengers, since 1991, and the product is aimed at the inexpensive end of the market. The dress code is ultra-casual (no tuxedos, no ties). While the ship is not in the best condition, and maintenance is spotty (shoddy tenders, for example), there is a friendly ambiance, which attracts many repeat passengers. There is an abundance of greenery throughout the ship, which helps to make it feel warm, more comfortable and less clinical. The ship is quite small, and so passengers can enjoy interesting destination-intensive cruises, with many port calls that larger ships simply can't get into. Tipping is recommended at 5–6 euros (the onboard currency) per person, per day.

The tiny "dip" swimming pool is virtually useless. There is a distinct odor of diesel fuel at the upper level of the lobby, where there is also a complete lack of air-conditioning. The ship's hotel operation is rather sloppy and needs streamlining. There is no walking track or wrap-around promenade deck outdoors. The fit, finish and maintenance of this ship are all quite poor, and well below the standard expected. The sightlines in the single-level showlounge are very poor, and there is a lack of good stage lighting.

SUITABLE FOR: *Vistamar* is best suited to German-speaking couples and single travelers looking for a first cruise in the comfortable, contemporary, but not luxurious or pretentious surroundings of a small ship featuring interesting itineraries, and all at a low price.

ACCOMMODATION. The passenger accommodation areas are located forward, while the public rooms are positioned aft, which means there is a minimal amount of noise in the cabins – good if you're having an early night.

There are 11 cabin grades, but in just two different sizes: suites with private (covered) balcony and queen-sized bed; outside-view or interior (no view) cabins for two, three or four persons, all with fixed, wide single beds. All of the cabins are reasonably comfortable, although the bathrooms are extremely small and tight (there is a considerable "lip" to step over to access the bathroom), and both closet and drawer space is limited.

Cabins have twin beds with wooden headboard, small vanity/writing desk, color television, climate-control, telephone, and hairdryer. Most of the cabinetry is made with a wood finish.

There are 11 suites, each of which has a small, narrow, private, covered balcony outdoors. The suites are: Alboran, Algarve, Almeria, Armador, Cadiz, Cordoba, Granada, Huelva, Jaen, Malaga, Seville – all of which are regions of Andalucia. They also have a more spacious bathroom, with a large bathtub and integral shower. The living area s also larger, and comes with a sofa, coffee table, vanity/writing desk, and a larger color television. Note that Armador is the owner's suite, and comes with a circular bathtub with integral shower, set against large picture windows (wonderful for the Arctic and Antarctic cruises that this company typically operates in the appropriate season).

No matter what accommodation grade or location they choose, all passengers get personal amenities that include soap, shampoo, body lotion and bath/shower gel, and shoeshine mitt. Accommodation hallways are provided either in hospital green, powder blue, or hot pink.

CUISINE/DINING. The Andalucia Restaurant is quite warm and inviting, with contemporary colors and decor, and large picture windows, although the six pillars detract from the otherwise attractive room. The room's focal point is a model of a sailing vessel with an emerald green hull (about the same color as the fabrics on the dining room chairs. There is one seating for all passengers (so meals are leisurely), with assigned tables for four, six or eight (there are no tables for two). Window-side tables are for six, and all chairs have armrests.

The food is reasonably adequate, and quite sound, and dinners typically come with a choice of three entrées (plus a vegetarian selection). The selection of cooked green vegetables, breads, cheeses and fruits is limited, and the overall cuisine really is of quite a low standard (it could be said to be quite similar to that found aboard other ships operated for German-speaking passengers, such as *Albatros* and *Maxim Gorkiy*, which have two seatings for dinner). The service is adequate, no more, as is the wine list. Sekt (sweet sparkling wine) is provided for breakfast, while white and red table wines are provided for lunch and dinner.

ENTERTAINMENT. There is little entertainment apart from some cabaret acts and live music for dancing and listening.

SPA/FITNESS. There is no spa to speak of, although there is a fitness room, a sauna, a massage treatment room, and a small beauty salon.

Volendam
★★★★

Large (Resort) Ship: ....60,906 tons	Total Crew: 561	Cabins (with private balcony): 197
Lifestyle: ....Premium	Passengers	Cabins (wheelchair accessible): 23
Cruise Line: ....Holland America Line	(lower beds/all berths): 1,440/1,850	Cabin Current: ....110 volts
Former Names: ....none	Passenger Space Ratio	Elevators: 12
Builder: ....Fincantieri (Italy)	(lower beds/all berths): 42.2/32.9	Casino (gaming tables): ....Yes
Original Cost: ....$300 million	Crew/Passenger Ratio	Slot Machines: ....Yes
Entered Service: ....Nov 1999	(lower beds/all berths): 2.5/2.5	Swimming Pools (outdoors): 2
Registry:..............The Netherlands	Navigation Officers: ....Dutch	Swimming Pools (indoors): 1
Length (ft/m): 781.0/238.00	Cabins (total): 720	(magrodome cover)
Beam (ft/m): 105.8/32.25	Size Range (sq ft/m): 113.0–1,126.0/	Whirlpools: 2
Draft (ft/m): 25.5/7.80	10.5–104.6	Self-Service Launderette: ....Yes (2)
Propulsion/Propellers: .....diesel-electric	Cabins (outside view): 581	Dedicated Cinema/Seats: Yes/205
(37,500kW)/2	Cabins (interior/no view): 139	Library: ....Yes
Passenger Decks:..................10	Cabins (for one person): 0	Classification Society: ....Lloyds Register

OVERALL SCORE: 1,541 (OUT OF A POSSIBLE 2,000 POINTS)

OVERVIEW. The ship's name is derived from the fishing village of Volendam, located north of Amsterdam, Holland. The hull is dark blue, in keeping with all Holland America Line ships. Having been built to approximately the same size as the company's newest *Rotterdam*, the same layout and public rooms have been incorporated into the interiors. This carries on the same flow and comfortable feeling so that repeat passengers will quickly feel at home aboard almost any ship in the Holland America Line fleet.

Volendam has three principal passenger stairways, which is so much better than two stairways, particularly the viewpoints of safety, accessibility and passenger flow. There is a magrodome-covered pool on the Lido Deck between the mast and the ship's funnel. The main interior design theme is flowers, from the 17th to the 21st centuries. The interior focal point is a huge crystal sculpture, *Caleido*, in the three-deck-high atrium, by one of Italy's leading contemporary glass artists, Luciano Vistosi. Health spa facilities include more treatment rooms (each has a shower and toilet).

In the casino bar (also known as the ship's sports bar), a cinematic theme presents visions of Hollywood, and includes a collection of costumes, props, photos and posters of movies and the actors who starred in them.

At the Lido Deck swimming pool, leaping dolphins are the focal point. The pool itself is also one deck higher than the Statendam-class ships, with the positive result being the fact that there is now direct access between the aft and midships pools (not so aboard the S-class ships).

There is a charge to use the washing machines and dryers in the self-service launderette, although it really should be included for the occupants of high priced suites. Although

BERLITZ'S RATINGS		
	Possible	Achieved
Ship	500	430
Accommodation	200	165
Food	400	281
Service	400	276
Entertainment	100	77
Cruise	400	312

room service is adequate, it remains a weak point.

SUITABLE FOR: *Volendam* is best suited to older couples and singles (and their grandchildren) who like to mingle in a large ship, in an unhurried setting with fine quality surroundings, with plenty of eclectic antique artwork, decent (though not gourmet) food and service from a smiling Indonesian and Filipino crew that likes to serve, but lacks the finesse that might be expected.

ACCOMMODATION. The range is similar to that found aboard the similarly sized *Rotterdam*, and comprises 17 different categories. The price you pay will depend on the grade, location and size you choose. There is one penthouse suite, and 28 suites, with the rest of the accommodation a mix of outside-view and interior (no view) cabins, and many more balcony cabins ("mini-suites") aboard this ship than aboard the slightly smaller *Statendam*-class ships.

All standard interior and outside cabins are tastefully furnished, and have twin beds that convert to a queen-sized bed (space is tight for walking between beds and vanity unit). All cabin televisions carry CNN and TNT. The bathrooms (fully tiled) are disappointingly small (particularly for long cruises) and have small shower tubs, utilitarian personal toiletries cupboards, and exposed under-sink plumbing. Storage space is also small for long cruises.

There are 28 full Verandah Suites (Navigation Deck), and one Penthouse Suite. All suite occupants share a private Concierge Lounge (the concierge handles such things as special dining arrangements, shore excursions, private parties and special requests). Strangely, there are no butlers for these suites. Each Verandah Suite has a separate bedroom, dressing and living areas. Suite passengers get personal stationery, complimentary laundry and ironing, cocktail hour hors d'oeuvres and other goodies, as well as priority embarkation and disembarkation.

For the ultimate in accommodation and living space aboard this ship, choose the Penthouse Suite. It has a separate steward's entrance, a large bedroom with king-sized bed, separate living room (with baby grand piano) and a dining room, dressing room, walk-in closet, butler's pantry, and private balcony (though the balcony is no large than that of any other suite). Other facilities include an audio-visual center with television and VCR, wet bar with refrigerator, large bathroom with Jacuzzi bathtub, separate toilet with bidet, and a guest bathroom (with toilet and washbasin).

With the exception of the penthouse suite, located forward on the starboard side, the bathrooms in the other suites and "mini-suites" are a little disappointing – neither as spacious nor as opulent as one would expect. All outside-view suites and cabin bathrooms feature a bathtub/shower while interior (no view) cabins have a shower only. Also, note that the 23 cabins for the mobility-limited have a roll-in shower enclosure for wheelchair users (none have bathtubs, no matter what the category).

CUISINE/DINING. There is one main dining room, and one alternative dining spot (open for dinner only). The 747-seat Rotterdam Dining Room, with smoking and no-smoking sections, is quite a grand room, spread over two decks, with ocean views on three sides and a grand staircase connecting the upper and lower levels. There are two seatings for dinner (you must pre-select a time and stick with it, at 5.45pm, 6.15pm, 8pm and 8.30pm), open seating for breakfast and lunch.

Alternative Dining Option: The casual-dress Marco Polo Restaurant seats 88, and there is no charge, although reservations are required. It is created in the style of a California artists' bistro and provides Italian cuisine (this has a set menu together with nightly specials). Passengers thus have more choice and an occasional change of venue (anyone booking suite-grade accommodation get priority reservations).

The Lido Buffet is a self-serve cafe for casual breakfasts and luncheons. There is also an outdoor grill for those who enjoy hamburgers, hot dogs and other grilled fast-food items. The Lido Buffet is also open for casual dinners on each night except for the last one, in an open-seating arrangement. Tables are set with crisp linens, flatware and stemware. A set menu includes a choice of four entrées.

ENTERTAINMENT. The two-deck-high Frans Hals Show-lounge spans two decks, with banquette seating on both main and upper levels. It is basically a well-designed room, but the ceiling is low and the sight lines from the balcony level are poor.

SPA/FITNESS. The health spa facilities are quite extensive, and include a gymnasium (with good muscle-toning equipment), separate saunas and stean rooms for men and women, and more treatment rooms (each has a shower and toilet). Practice tennis courts can be fund outdoor, as well as the traditional shuffleboard courts, jogging track, and a full wrap-around teakwood promenade deck for strolling.

The Ocean Spa and onboard fitness classes are operated by Steiner, a specialist concession.

● **For more extensive general information on what a Holland America Line cruise is like, see pages 118–222.**

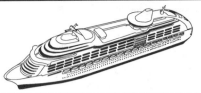

Voyager of the Seas
★★★★

Large (Resort) Ship: ....137,280 tons	Passenger Decks: 14	Cabins (for one person): 0
Lifestyle: ....Standard	Total Crew: 1,176	Cabins (with private balcony): 757
Cruise Line: Royal Caribbean International	Passengers	Cabins (wheelchair accessible): 26
Former Names: ....none	(lower beds/all berths): 3,114/3,838	Cabin Current: ....110 volts
Builder: ...Kvaerner Masa-Yards (Finland)	Passenger Space Ratio	Elevators: ....14 (6 glass-enclosed)
Original Cost: ....$500 million	(lower beds/all berths): 44.0/35.7	Casino (gaming tables): ....Yes
Entered Service: ....Nov 1999	Crew/Passenger Ratio	Slot Machines: ....Yes
Registry: ....The Bahamas	(lower beds/all berths): 2.6/3.2	Swimming Pools (outdoors): 3
Length (ft/m): 1,020.6/311.1	Navigation Officers: ......Scandinavian	Swimming Pools (indoors): 0
Beam (ft/m): 155.5/47.4	Cabins (total): 1,557	Whirlpools: 6
Draft (ft/m): 28.8/8.8	Size Range (sq ft/m): 151.0–1,358.0/	Self-Service Launderette: ....No
Propulsion/Propellers: .....diesel-electric	14.0–126.1	Dedicated Cinema/Seats: ....No
(42,000 kW)/3 azimuthing pods	Cabins (outside view): 939	Library: ....Yes
(14 MW each)	Cabins (interior/no view): 618	Classification Society: Det Norske Veritas

OVERALL SCORE: 1,537 (OUT OF A POSSIBLE 2,000 POINTS)

OVERVIEW. This is a large, stunning, floating resort (sister to *Adventure of the Seas*, *Explorer of the Seas*, *Mariner of the Seas* and *Navigator of the Seas*). The exterior design is not unlike an enlarged version of the company's Vision-class ships. The *Voyager*-class ships are, at present, the largest cruise vessels in the world in terms of tonnage measurement (except for Cunard Line's *Queen Mary 2*). After a difficult life in the shipyard, where a fire caused havoc and necessitated the replacement of some 80 cabins and the whole of the main restaurant, the ship debuted without further problems.

The ship's propulsion is derived from three pod units, powered by electric motors (two azimuthing, and one fixed at the centerline) instead of conventional rudders and propellers, in the latest configuration of high-tech systems.

With its large proportions, it provides more facilities and options, and caters to more passengers than any other Royal Caribbean International ship has in the past, and yet the ship manages to have a healthy passenger space ratio (the amount of space per passenger). It is too large to go through the Panama Canal, thus limiting itineraries almost exclusively to the Caribbean (where few islands can accept it), or for use as a floating island resort. Spend the first few hours wandering exploring all the many facilities and public spaces aboard this vessel and it will be time well spent.

Although *Voyager of the Seas* really is a large ship, the cabin hallways have an extremely warm and attractive feel to them, with artwork cabinets and wavy lines to lead you along and break up the monotony. In fact, there are plenty of colorful, even whimsical, decorative touches to help you avoid what would otherwise be a very clinical environment.

BERLITZ'S RATINGS

	Possible	Achieved
Ship	500	431
Accommodation	200	160
Food	400	252
Service	400	294
Entertainment	100	83
Cruise	400	317

At certain times, passengers are allowed to stand right at the bow of the ship at the observation point, perhaps with arms spread in an "eagle-like" position, just like the stars in the film *Titanic*. What a photo opportunity! However, for the best ones, as in in the film, you'll need to bring a helicopter. Those seeking a view of the navigation bridge can see what's happening from a special spot above the bridge.

Embarkation and disembarkation take place through two stations/access points, designed to minimize the inevitable lines at the start and end of the cruise (that's over 1,500 people for each access point). Once inside the ship, you'll need good walking shoes, particularly when you need to go from one end to the other – it really is quite a long way.

The four-decks-high Royal Promenade, the interior focal point of the ship, is a good place to arrange to meet someone. It is 394 ft (120 meters) long – the length of two football fields (American football, that is), and has two internal lobbies (atria) that rise through 11 decks, one at each end. There are 16 elevators in four banks of four. The entrance to one of three levels of the main restaurant, together with shops and entertainment locations are spun off from this "boulevard", while interior "with-view" cabins (with rather useless bay windows) look into it from above.

It houses a traditional English "pub" ("Pig 'n' Whistle), a Champagne Bar, the Promenade Cafe (for continental breakfast, all-day pizzas, sandwiches and coffees), Sprinkles (for round-the-clock ice-cream and yoghurt), Scoreboard (a sports bar), and a captain's balcony arched across the promenade. There are also several shops – jewelry shop, gift shop, liquor shop and a logo souvenir shop, as well as a bright red telephone kiosk that houses an ATM cash machine. Altogether, it's a nice place to see and be seen, and street performers complete the scene. It really is a cross between a shopping arcade and an amusement park (Florida's Aventura meets New York's Coney Island crowd). The chairman of Royal Caribbean International even donated his own beloved Morgan sports car *(see picture, page 129)* to grace the Royal Promenade (which is supposedly designed in the image of London's fashionable Burlington Arcade). Actually, by far the best view of the whole promenade is from one of the 138 premium-price cabins that look into it, or from a "captain's bridge" that crosses above it.

The ship's Casino Royale is large, and always noisy with action. Gaming includes blackjack, Caribbean stud poker, craps, and roulette (including the world's largest interactive roulette wheel that is activated by a roulette ball tower four decks high), as well as 300 slot machines.

A second showlounge (Studio B, a regulation-size ice-skating rink that has real, not fake, ice) has arena seating for up to 900, and the latest in broadcast facilities. A number of slim pillars obstruct the clear-view arena stage sightlines, however. An Ice Follies show is presented by a professional ice-skating show team each cruise. If ice-skating in the Caribbean doesn't particularly appeal, you might like to visit the stunning two-deck library (it's the first aboard any ship, and is open 24 hours a day). A whopping $12 million has been spent on permanent artwork.

Drinking places include a neat Aquarium Bar, with 50 tons of glass and water in four large aquariums (whose combined value is over $1 million), the small and intimate Champagne Bar, and the Connoisseur Club – for cigars and cognacs. Lovers of jazz might appreciate High Notes, an intimate room for cool music atop the ship within the Viking Crown Lounge, or the Schooner Bar piano lounge. Golfers might enjoy the 19th Hole, a golf bar, as they play the Voyager Links.

There is a large television studio, located adjacent to rooms that can be used for trade show exhibit space, with conference center that seats 400 and a multi-media screening room that seats 60. Lovers could tie the knot in a wedding chapel in the sky, the Skylight Chapel (it's located on the upper level of the Viking Crown Lounge, and even has wheelchair access via an electric stairway elevator). Meanwhile, outdoors, the pool and open deck areas provide a resort-like environment.

Families with children are also well catered to, as facilities for children and teenagers are quite extensive. "Aquanauts" is for 3–5-year-olds. "Explorers" is for 6–8-year-olds. "Voyagers" is for 9–12-year-olds. Optix is a dedicated area for teenagers, including a daytime club (with computers), soda bar, disk jockey and dance floor. Challenger's Arcade has an array of the latest video games. Virtual Submarine is a virtual reality underwater center for all ages. Computer Lab has 14 computer stations loaded with fun and games. Paint and Clay is an arts and crafts center for younger children. Adjacent to these indoor areas is Adventure Beach, an area for all the family to enjoy: it includes swimming pools, a water slide and game areas outdoors.

Royal Caribbean International has, since its inception, always been an innovator in the cruise industry, and will probably remain so with this new vessel, the first of five such ships to be placed into service by the company.

In terms of sheer size, this ship presently dwarfs all other ships in the cruise industry, but in terms of personal service, the reverse is the case, unless you happen to reside in one of the top suites. Royal Caribbean International does, however, try hard to provide a good standard of programmed service from its hotel staff. This is impersonal city life at sea, and a superb, well-designed alternative to a land-based resort, which is what the company wanted to build. Welcome to the real, escapist world of highly programmed resort living aboard ship. Perhaps if you dare to go outside, you might even be able to see the sea – now there's a novelty! Remember to take lots of extra pennies: you'll need them to pay for all the additional-cost items. The onboard currency is the US dollar.

The ship is large, so remember that if you meet someone somewhere, and want to meet them again you'll need to make an appointment – for this really is a large, Las Vegas-style American floating resort-city for the lively of heart and fleet of foot. The best advice I can give you is to arrange to meet somewhere along the Royal Promenade.

ACCOMMODATION. There is a wide range of 22 cabin categories, in four major groupings: Premium ocean-view suites and cabins, interior (atrium-view) cabins, Ocean-view cabins, and Interior (no view) cabins. Note that many cabins are of a similar size (good for incentives and large groups), and 300 have interconnecting doors (good for families). The price you pay will depend on the grade, location and size you choose.

A total of 138 interior (no view) cabins have bay windows that look into an interior horizontal atrium – a cruise industry first when the ship debuted. Regardless of what cabin grade you choose, however, all except for the Royal Suite and Owner's Suite have twin beds that convert to a queen-sized unit, television, radio and telephone, personal safe, vanity unit, hairdryer and private bathroom.

The largest living spaces includes luxuriously appointed penthouse suites (whose occupants, sadly, must share the rest of the ship with everyone else, except for their own exclusive, and private, concierge club). The grandest is the Royal Suite, positioned on the port side of the ship. It has a king-sized bed in a separate, large bedroom, a living room with an additional queen-sized sofa bed, baby grand piano (no pianist is included, however), refrigerator/wet bar, dining table, entertainment center, and large bathroom.

The 10 slightly smaller, but still highly desirable Owner's Suites (located in the center of the ship, on both port and starboard sides) and the four Royal Family suites have similar items. However, the four Royal Family suites, which have two bedrooms (including one with third/fourth upper Pullman berths) are located at the stern of the ship and have magnificent views over the ship's wash.

All cabins have a private bathroom, as well as interactive television and pay-per-view movies, including an X-rated channel, where you must enter a "pin" code to prevent children from watching. Some grades have a refrigerator/mini-bar, although there is no space left in the refrigerator, because it is stocked with "take-and-pay" items. Note that, if you take anything from the mini-bar/refrigerator on the day of embarkation in Miami, Florida sales tax will be added to your bill. Cabins with "private balconies" should be aware that they are not so private. The balcony decking is made of Bolidt – a sort of rubberized sand – and not wood, while the balcony rail is of wood.

If you have a cabin with a door that interconnecting door to another cabin, be aware that you'll be able to hear everything your next-door neighbors say and do. Bathroom toilets are explosively noisy

CUISINE/DINING. The main dining room is extremely large and is set on three levels, each with an operatic name and theme: Carmen, La Boheme and Magic Flute. A dramatic staircase connects all three levels, and huge, fat support pillars obstruct the sight lines from many seats. All three have exactly the same menus and food. The dining room is totally non-smoking, there are two seatings, and tables are for four, six, eight 10 or 12.

Alternative Dining Options: Alternative dining options for casual and informal meals at all hours (according to company releases) include:

● *Promenade Cafe:* for continental breakfast, all-day pizzas, sandwiches and coffees (provided in paper cups).

● *Windjammer Cafe:* for casual buffet-style breakfast, lunch and light dinner (except for the cruise's last night).

● *Island Grill* (this is actually a section inside the Windjammer Cafe): for casual dinner (no reservations necessary) featuring a grill and open kitchen.

● *Portofino:* this is the ship's "upscale" (non-smoking) Euro-Italian restaurant, open for dinner only. Reservations are required, and a $6 gratuity per person is charged). The food and its presentation are better than the food in the dining room, although the restaurant is not large enough for all passengers to try even once during a cruise. Choices include: antipasti, soup, salad, pasta, main dish, dessert, cheese and coffee. The menu does not change during the cruise.

● *Johnny Rockets*, a retro 1950s all-day, all-night diner-style eatery that has hamburgers, malt shakes, and jukebox hits, with both indoor and outdoor seating (all indoor tables have a mini-jukebox; dimes are provided for you to make

your selection of vintage records), and all-singing, all-dancing waitresses that'll knock your socks off, if you can stand the volume.

● *Sprinkles:* for round-the-clock ice cream and yoghurt, pastries and coffee.

ENTERTAINMENT. The 1,350-seat Showlounge is a really stunning space that could well be the equal of many such rooms on land. It is located at the forward end of the ship and spans the height of five decks (with only a few slim pillars and almost no disruption of sightlines from any seat in the house). The room has a hydraulic orchestra pit and huge stage areas, together with sonic-boom loud sound, and some superb lighting equipment.

In addition, the ship has an array of cabaret acts. Although many of these are not what you would call headliners (the strongest cabaret acts are featured in the main showlounge, while others are presented in the Cleopatra's Needle Lounge, also the venue for late-night adults-only comedy), they regularly travel the cruise ship circuit. The best shows aboard this ship, however, are the Ice Spectaculars.

There is also a television studio (in case you thought you'd need one aboard a cruise ship), located adjacent to rooms that could be used, for example, for trade show exhibit space (good for conventions at sea).

SPA/FITNESS. The ShipShape health spa is large, measuring 15,000 sq. ft (1,400 sq. meters). It includes a large aerobics room, fitness center (with the usual stairmasters, treadmills, stationary bikes, weight machines and free weights), treatment rooms, and men's and women's sauna/steam rooms. Another 10,000 sq. ft (930 sq. meters) is devoted to a Solarium (with magrodome sliding glass roof).

For the more sporting, there is activity galore – including a rock-climbing wall that's 32.8 ft high (10 meters), with five separate climbing tracks. It is located outdoors at the aft end of the funnel. You'll get a great "buzz" being 200 ft (60 meters) above the ocean while the ship is moving.

Other sports facilities include a roller-blading track, a dive-and-snorkel shop, a full-size basketball court and 9-hole, par 26 golf course.

● **For more extensive general information about a Royal Caribbean cruise experience, see pages 128–131.**

Westerdam
★★★★

Large (Resort) Ship: . . . . .81,769 tons	Total Crew: 842	Cabins (wheelchair accessible): 28
Lifestyle: . . . . .Premium	Passengers	Cabin Current: . . . . .110 volts
Cruise Line: . . . . . . .Holland America Line	(lower beds/all berths): 1,848/2,272	Elevators: 14
Former Names: . . . . .none	Passenger Space Ratio	Casino (gaming tables): . . . . .Yes
Builder: . . . . .Fincantieri (Italy)	(lower beds/all berths): 44.2/35.9	Slot Machines: . . . . .Yes
Original Cost: . . . .$400 million	Crew/Passenger Ratio	Swimming Pools (outdoors): 2
Entered Service: . . . . .Apr 2004	(lower beds/all berths): 2.1/2.6	+1 children's pool
Registry: . . . . .The Netherlands	Navigation Officers: . . . . .European	Swimming Pools (indoors): 1
Length (ft/m): 959.6/292.50	Cabins (total): 924	(indoor/outdoor)
Beam (ft/m): 105.6/32.25	Size Range (sq ft/m): 185.0–1,318.6/	Whirlpools: 5
Draft (ft/m): 25.5/7.80	17.1–122.5	Self-Service Launderette: . . . . .No
Propulsion/Propellors . . . .diesel-electric	Cabins (outside view): 788	Dedicated Cinema/Seats Yes/170
(34,000 kW)/2 pods, (17.6 MW each)	Cabins (interior/no view): 136	Library: . . . . .Yes
Passenger Decks: 10	Cabins (for one person): 0	Classification Society: . . .Lloyd's Register
	Cabins (with private balcony): 810	

OVERALL SCORE: 1,546 (OUT OF A POSSIBLE 2,000 POINTS)

OVERVIEW. *Westerdam* is another in the latest generation of new, larger ships for Holland America Line (its sister ships are *Oosterdam* and *Zuiderdam*), designed to appeal to younger, more vibrant cruise vacationers. *Westerdam* has two funnels, placed close together, one in front of the other, the result of the slightly unusual machinery configuration. The ship has, in effect, two engine rooms – one with three diesels, and one with two diesels and a gas turbine. Podded propulsion *(see page 151 for explanation)* is provided, powered by a diesel-electric system, with a small gas turbine located in the funnel for the reduction of emissions.

There's a complete wrap-around exterior teak promenade deck, and teak "steamer" style deck lounge chairs are provided. A jogging track is located around the mast and the forward third of the ship. Exterior glass elevators, mounted midships on both port and starboard sides, provide fine ocean views. There are two centrally located swimming pools outdoors, and one can be used in inclement weather due to its retractable sliding glass roof. Two whirlpool tubs, adjacent to the swimming pools, are abridged by a bar. Another smaller pool is available for children; it incorporates a winding water slide that spans two decks in height. There is an additional whirlpool tub outdoors.

You enter the ship through an intimate lobby than spans three decks, and is topped by a beautiful, rotating, Waterford crystal globe of the world. The interior decor is interesting; the ceilings are particularly noticeable in the public rooms. In terms of overall decor, the colours were toned down and refined when compared to sister ships *Oosterdam* and *Zuiderdam*. Maintaining its traditions, Holland America

BERLITZ'S RATINGS

	Possible	Achieved
Ship	500	430
Accommodation	200	163
Food	400	283
Service	400	280
Entertainment	100	77
Cruise	400	313

Line provides a large collection of artwork, including Dutch exploration, maritime history and art. The focal point of the ship is its soothing midnight blue atrium lobby (like a hotel lobby), containing a glass replica of a sailing ship.

There are two whole entertainment/public room decks. The most dramatic room is the showlounge, spanning four decks in the forward section.

Other facilities include a winding shopping street with boutique stores and logo shops, an internet center, library, card room, an art gallery, photo gallery, and several small meeting rooms. The casino is large (one has to walk through it to get from the restaurant to the show lounge on one of the entertainments decks), and has the usual gaming paraphernalia and slot machines. There's a basketball court, volleyball court, and golf simulator. Club HAL's KidZone is an area dedicated to kids' facilities and extensive programming for different age groups (5–17), with one counselor for every 30 children.

With this large ship, Holland America Line is trying to be all things to all people, although this reviewer is not convinced that the formula works well for the many loyal repeat passengers used to the smaller ships. However, this vessel does offer a range of public rooms that have a reasonably intimate feel to them and the overall feel of the ship and its eclectic decor is quite homely and comforting.

The information desk in the lobby is small and somewhat removed from the main passenger flow on the two decks above it. Many pillars obstruct the passenger flow and lines of sight throughout the ship. There are no self-service launderettes (something families with children might miss – although special laundry packages *are* available).

ACCOMMODATION. There are 24 price categories (16 outside-view/eight interior (no view). Some cabins on the lowest accommodation deck (Main Deck) have views obstructed by lifeboats. Some cabins that can accommodate a third and fourth person have very little closet space, and only one personal safe. Some cabins have interconnecting doors – good for families with children. Occupants of suites also get exclusive use of the Neptune Lounge and concierge service, priority embarkation and disembarkation, and other benefits (thus, in effect, making this a two-class ship). In many of the suites and cabins with private balconies the balconies are not really very private, as many can be overlooked from various public locations.

Penthouse Verandah Suites: These two suites have the largest accommodation (1,126 sq. ft/104.6 sq. meters). These have a separate bedroom with a king-sized bed; there's also a walk-in closet, dressing room, living room, dining room, butler's pantry, mini-bar and refrigerator, and private balcony (verandah). The main bathroom has a large whirlpool bathtub, two washbasins, toilet, and plenty of storage space for personal toiletries. Personalized stationery and complimentary dry cleaning are included, as are hot hors d'oeuvres daily.

DeLuxe Verandah Suites: Next in size are 60 of these suites (563 sq. ft/52.3 sq. meters). These have twin beds that convert to a king-sized bed, vanity desk, lounge area, walk-in closet, mini-bar and refrigerator, and bathroom with full-size bathtub, washbasin and toilet. Personalized stationery and complimentary dry cleaning are included, as are hot hors d'oeuvres and other goodies.

Verandah Suites: There are 100 of these Verandah Suites (actually they are cabins, not suites, and measure (284 sq. ft/26.3 sq. meters). Twin beds convert to a queen-sized bed; there is also a lounge area, mini-bar and refrigerator, while the bathroom has a tub, washbasin and toilet. Floor to ceiling windows open onto a private balcony (verandah).

Outside-view Cabins: Standard outside cabins (197 sq. ft/18.3 sq. meters) have twin beds that convert to a queen-sized bed. There's also a small sitting area, while the bathroom has a bathtub/shower combination. The interior (no view) cabins are slightly smaller (182.9 sq. ft/17 sq. meters).

CUISINE/DINING. Dining options range from full-service meals in the main dining room and à la carte restaurant to casual, self-serve buffet-style meals and fast-food outlets.

The Vista (main) Dining Room is two decks high, with seating provided on both main and balcony levels, and is located at the stern of the ship. It provides a traditional Holland America Line dining experience, with friendly service from smiling Indonesian and Filipino stewards. It has open seating for breakfast and lunch, and four seatings for dinner (you must pre-select a time and stick with it), at 5.45pm, 6.15pm, 8pm and 8.30pm. There are tables for two, four, six or eight, and both smoking and no-smoking sections. The waiter stations in the dining room are noisy for anyone seated adjacent to them. Fine Rosenthal china and cutlery

are used (but there are no fish knives). Live music is provided for dinner each evening; once each cruise, a Dutch Dinner is featured (hats are provided), as is an Indonesian Lunch. "Lighter option" meals are available for the nutrition-conscious. Holland America Line can provide Kosher meals, although these are prepared ashore, frozen, and brought to the table sealed in their original containers.

Alternative Dining Option: The 130-seat Odyssey Restaurant and Pinnacle Grill is a more upscale dining spot (with higher quality ingredients, and better presentation than in the larger main dining room). It is located on Lower Promenade Deck, and fronts onto the second level of the atrium lobby. Pacific Northwest cuisine is featured (with items such as sesame-crusted halibut with ginger-miso, Peking duck breast with blackberry sauce, and an array of premium quality steaks from hand-selected cuts of beef – shown to you at tableside). Fine table settings, china and silverware are provided, as are leather-bound menus. The wine bar offers mostly American wines. Reservations are required and there is a cover charge of $20 per person for service and gratuity.

Informal Eateries: For casual eating, there is an extensive Lido Cafe, which wraps around the funnel housing and extends aft. It includes a pizzeria counter, a salad bar, Asian stir-fry counter, deli sandwiches, and a separate dessert buffet. Movement around the buffet area can be very slow.

Additionally, there is an outdoor self-serve buffet (adjacent to the fantail pool), which serves fast-food items such as hamburgers and hot dogs, chicken and fries, as well as two smaller buffets adjacent to the midships swimming pool area, and a Windsurf Cafe in the atrium lobby (open 20 hours a day), for coffee, pastries, snack foods, deli sandwiches and liqueur coffees (evenings only) – all at extra cost.

ENTERTAINMENT. The 867-seat Vista Lounge is the ship's principal venue for Las Vegas-style revue shows and major cabaret presentations. It spans three decks in the forward section of the ship. The main floor level has a bar in its starboard aft section, while the upper two levels. Spiral stairways at the back of the lounge connect all levels. The upper levels have better sightlines.

SPA/FITNESS. The Greenhouse Spa, a large, two-decks-high health spa, is directly above the navigation bridge. Facilities include a solarium, hydrotherapy pool, unisex thermal suite – a unisex area incorporating a Laconium (gentle sauna), Hamman (mild steam), and Camomile Grotto (small aromatic steam room). There is also a beauty parlor, 11 massage/therapy rooms (including one for couples), and a large gymnasium with floor-to-ceiling windows on three sides and forward-facing ocean views, and the latest high-tech muscle-toning equipment.

● **For more extensive general information on what a Holland America Line cruise is like, see pages 118–122.**

Wilderness Adventurer
★★

Boutique Ship:	.89.5 tons	Total Crew:	.20	Cabins (wheelchair accessible):	.0
Lifestyle:	.Standard	Passengers (lower beds/all berths):	.68/76	Cabin Current:	.110 volts
Cruise Line:	.Glacier Bay Cruises	Passenger Space Ratio		Elevators:	.0
Former Names:	.Caribbean Prince	(lower beds/all berths):	.1.1/1.0	Casino (gaming tables):	.No
Builder:	.Blount Shipyards (USA)	Crew/Passenger Ratio:		Slot Machines:	.No
Original Cost:	.$6 million	(lower beds/all berths):	.3.4/3.8	Swimming Pools (outdoors):	.0
Entered Service:	.1983/1997	Navigation Officers:	.American	Swimming Pools (indoors):	.0
Registry:	.USA	Cabins (total):	.34	Whirlpools:	.0
Length (ft/m):	.156.6/47.7	Size (sq ft/m.):	.70.0–88.0/6.5–8.1	Self-Service Launderette:	.No
Beam (ft/m):	.38.0/11.0	Cabins (outside view):	.30	Movie Theater/Seats:	.No
Draft (ft/m):	.6.5/1.8	Cabins (interior/no view):	.4	Library:	.Yes
Propulsion/Propellers: diesel (1,472kw)/1		Cabins (for one person):	.0	Classification Society:	.American Bureau
Passenger Decks:	.3	Cabins (with private balcony):	.0		of Shipping

OVERALL SCORE: 905 (OUT OF A POSSIBLE 2,000 POINTS)

OVERVIEW. This vessel, originally built for the American Canadian Caribbean Line, is good for real in-depth, up-close cruising along the coastline of Alaska. One bonus is the fact that at the bow of the vessel, a "bow gangway" comes into its own for landing passengers. As the company says, this is a Sport Utility Vessel. The ship is also equipped with a retractable wheelhouse for passage under low bridges on inland waterways, and there is also a platform for those who want to swim off the stern. A fleet of two-person kayaks is carried, for up-close exploration of the Alaska shoreline. Water sports facilities include a glass-bottom boat/sunfish sailboat (not used on Alaska itineraries).

The dress code is absolutely casual (not even a jacket for men is needed, and no ties, please). There is an ample supply of snorkeling gear, so there is really no need to take your own (Mexico's Sea of Cortez itineraries only – from January through March). Make sure that you take comfortable walking shoes, as well as photographic materials for wildlife spotting (particularly in Alaska).

Glacier Bay Cruises was formerly known as Alaska's Glacier Bay Tours and Cruises. The cruises are very expensive (compared with other ships operating in the areas), and are for those who want to get close to nature and wildlife, in a small environment (but note that all shore excursions are included). Tips are pooled and shared among all the staff, using the amounts recommended in the cruise line's brochure of $8–$12 per passenger, per day, which is high for the services provided. The onboard currency is the US dollar.

There is an almost constant throbbing from the diesel engines/generator. There is no doctor on board, and so anyone with medical problems shouldn't consider this vessel.

BERLITZ'S RATINGS

	Possible	Achieved
Ship	500	181
Accommodation	200	76
Food	400	199
Service	400	204
Entertainment	N/A	N/A
Cruise	500	245

SUITABLE FOR: *Wilderness Adventurer* is best suited to couples and single travelers who enjoy nature and wildlife at close range, and who would not dream of cruising aboard ships with large numbers of people. This is for hardy, outdoors types who don't need entertainment or vapid parlor games, but who want to cruise with an all-American crew.

ACCOMMODATION. The cabins (there are only three types to choose from – one on each of three decks) really are utilitarian, ultra-tiny, no-frills units that are just about adequate if you are not used to, or do not want, anything better. While 14 cabins have a double bed, all others have two lower beds, and 8 also have an upper (Pullman) berth. Each cabin has a private bathroom, although these really are minuscule. There is no room service for food or snack items.

CUISINE/DINING. The dining room has minimal decor, but the open-seating policy means that you can dine with whomever you wish, in a single seating. The cuisine is decidedly plain and simple American fare, as is the cutlery (no fish knifes are used, for example), but it is rather tasty. This is because the ingredients are all fresh. A full-service bar provides a selection of wines and other alcoholic beverages.

ENTERTAINMENT. There is no formal entertainment, although dinner and after-dinner conversation with fellow passengers in the ship's lounge/bar really constitutes the entertainment each evening.

SPA/FITNESS. There are no facilities.

Wilderness Discoverer
★★

Boutique Ship: . . . . .99 tons	Total Crew: 22	Cabins (wheelchair accessible): 0
Lifestyle: . . . . .Standard	Passengers (lower beds/all berths): .84/98	Cabin Current: . . . . .110 volts
Cruise Line: . . . . .Glacier Bay Cruises	Passenger Space Ratio	Elevators: 0
Former Names: . . . . .Mayan Prince	(lower beds/all berths): 1.1/1.0	Casino (gaming tables): . . . . .No
Builder: . . . . .Blount Shipyards (USA)	Crew/Passenger Ratio:	Slot Machines: .No
Original Cost: . . . .$7.5 million	(lower beds/all berths): 4.2/4.4	Swimming Pools (outdoors): 0
Entered Service: . . . . . .June 1992/1998	Navigation Officers: . . . . .American	Swimming Pools (indoors): 0
Registry: . . . . .USA	Cabins (total): 42	Whirlpools: 0
Length (ft/m): 169.0/51.5	Size (sq ft/m.): 88.0–196.0/8.1–18.2	Self-Service Launderette: . . . . .No
Beam (ft/m): 38.0/11.5	Cabins (outside view): 37	Movie Theater/Seats: . . . . .No
Draft (ft/m): 6.7/2.0	Cabins (interior/no view): 5	Library: . . . . .Yes
Propulsion/Propellers: diesel (1,472kw)/1	Cabins (for one person): 0	Classification Society: . .American Bureau
Passenger Decks: 3	Cabins (with private balcony): 0	of Shipping

OVERALL SCORE: 905 (OUT OF A POSSIBLE 2,000 POINTS)

OVERVIEW. This vessel, originally built for the American Canadian Caribbean Line, based on the US east coast, is small and squat, has a shallow draft, being designed specifically for in-depth coastal cruising. It is equipped with a unique, retractable wheelhouse, although this is no longer used. In 2001 it acquired a floating dock, and a small fleet of kayaks and Zodiac landing craft. As the company says, this is a Sport Utility Vessel.

A cruise aboard the ship is for those who really appreciate camaraderie. There is very little service, and no entertainment. Indeed, unless you go to your cabin, there is no getting away from other passengers. Take only very casual clothing, as the attire is strictly non-dressy.

Glacier Bay Cruises was formerly known as Alaska's Glacier Bay Tours and Cruises. *Wilderness Discoverer* presently operates five-night round-trip cruises from Juneau, to Haines, Skagway, Sitka, Glacier Bay and Tracy Arm, Alaska during the summer. The cruises are very expensive (particularly when compared with other ships operating in the same areas), and are for those who want to be close to nature and wildlife in a small environment (note that all shore excursions are included, however).

Gratuities are expected, at about $8–$12 per person, per day. The onboard currency is the US dollar.

SUITABLE FOR: *Wilderness Discoverer* is best suited to couples and single travelers who enjoy nature and wildlife at close range, and who would not dream of cruising in the mainstream sense aboard ships with large numbers of people. This is for hardy, outdoors types who don't need entertainment or vapid parlor games to pass the time, but who

BERLITZ'S RATINGS		
	Possible	Achieved
Ship	500	181
Accommodation	300	76
Food	400	199
Service	400	204
Entertainment	N/A	N/A
Cruise	400	245

want to cruise with an all-American crew.

ACCOMMODATION. There are four cabin grades spread over three decks, and all are dimensionally challenged, so take only the most minimal amount of clothing and personal effects you possible can. There are six cabins on the lowest deck that do not have a window, and they are really tiny. While 7 cabins have a double bed, all others have two lower beds, and several also have an upper (Pullman) berth. There is no room service for food or snack items or beverages.

The air-conditioning consists of re-circulated air, much like that found aboard aircraft, and is, therefore, not very fresh. Each cabin has its own private bathroom, although these really are minuscule.

CUISINE/DINING. The dining room is mildly attractive and has a single, open-seating policy (so you can dine with whomever you wish). The food is reasonably sound American fare, with good presentation and decent creativity. Wines and other alcoholic drinks can be obtained from a full-service bar.

ENTERTAINMENT. There is no formal entertainment, although dinner and after-dinner conversation with fellow passengers in the ship's lounge/bar really constitutes the entertainment each evening. So, if you don't want to talk to your fellow passengers, take a good book.

SPA/FITNESS. No spa or fitness facilities are provided aboard this very small cruise ship.

Wind Spirit
★★★★

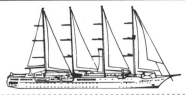

Boutique Ship: . . . . .5,350 tons	Sail Area (sq ft/m2): 21,489/1,996.4	Size Range (sq ft/m): 185.0–220.0/
Lifestyle: . . . . .Premium	Main Propulsion: . . . . . .a) engines/b) sails	17.0–22.5
Cruise Line: . . . . .Windstar Cruises	Propulsion/Propellers: . . . . .diesel-electric	Cabins (outside view): 74
Former Names: . . . . .none	(1,400kW)/1	Cabins (interior/no view): 0
Builder: . . . . .Ateliers et Chantiers	Passenger Decks: 5	Cabins (for one person): 0
du Havre (France)	Total Crew: 88	Cabins (with private balcony): 0
Original Cost: . . . .$34.2 million	Passengers	Cabins (wheelchair accessible): 0
Entered Service: . . . . .Apr 1988	(lower beds/all berths): 148/159	Cabin Current: . . . . .110 volts
Registry: . . . . .The Bahamas	Passenger Space Ratio	Casino (gaming tables): . . . . .Yes
Length (ft/m): 439.6/134.0	(lower beds/all berths): 36.1/33.6	Slot Machines: . . . . .Yes
Beam (ft/m): 51.8/15.8	Crew/Passenger Ratio	Swimming Pools (outdoors): . .1 (dip pool)
Draft (ft/m): 13.4/4.1	(lower beds/all berths): 1.6/1.8	Whirlpools: 1
Type of Vessel: . . . . . .computer-controlled	Navigation Officers: . . . . .European	Self-Service Launderette: . . . . .No
sail-cruiser	Cabins (total): 74	Library: . . . . .Yes
No. of Masts: . . . . . .4/6 self-furling sails		Classification Society: . . . .Bureau Veritas

OVERALL SCORE: 1,518 (OUT OF A POSSIBLE 2,000 POINTS)

OVERVIEW. *Wind Spirit*, when built, was one of three identical vessels (a fourth, *Wind Saga*, was planned but never built). One of the original three sister ships, *Wind Song*, suffered a fire and was declared a constructive total loss in Tahiti in 2002. *Wind Spirit* is a long, sleek-looking craft that is part-yacht, part-cruise ship, with four giant masts that tower 170 ft (52 meters) above the deck (they are actually 204 ft, or 62 meters) high, and fitted with computer-controlled sails; the masts, sails and rigging alone cost $5 million. The computer keeps the ship on an even keel (via the movement of a water hydraulic ballast system of 142,653 gallons/540,000 liters), so there is no heeling (rolling) over 6 degrees.

There is little open deck space when the ship is full, due to the amount of complex sail machinery. At the stern is a small water sports platform for those who enjoy all the goodies the ship offers (but only when at anchor and only in really calm sea conditions). Water sports facilities include a banana boat kayaks, sunfish sailboats, windsurf boards, water ski boat, scuba and snorkel equipment, and four Zodiacs. You will be asked to sign a waiver if you wish to use the water sports equipment.

The ship has a finely crafted interior with pleasing, blond woods, together with soft, complementary colors and decor that is chic, even elegant, but a little cold. Note that the main lounge aboard this ship is of a slightly different design than sister ship *Wind Star*.

No scheduled activities help to make this a real relaxing, unregimented "get away from it all" vacation. The Windstar ships will help you to cruise in very comfortable, contem-

BERLITZ'S RATINGS

	Possible	Achieved
Ship	500	382
Accommodation	200	164
Food	400	295
Service	400	300
Entertainment	N/A	N/A
Cruise	500	377

porary surroundings that are bordering on the luxurious, yet in an unstructured environment. They will provide a very relaxing, virtually unstructured cruise experience that is just right for seven idyllic nights in sheltered areas (but can be disturbing when a Windstar vessel is in small ports alongside several gigantic cruise ships).

This ship is ideal for couples who do not like large ships. The dress code is casual (no jackets and ties required), even for dinner (the brochure states casual elegance). There are no formal nights or theme nights.

You will probably be under sail for less than 40 percent of the time (conditions and cruise area winds permitting). Gratuities are "not required" by the friendly, smiling staff, according to the brochure, but passengers find they are always accepted. The onboard currency is the US dollar.

Note that there is very little open deck space, and the swimming pool is really only a tiny "dip" pool. Be prepared for the "whine" of the vessel's generators, which are needed to run the air-conditioning and lighting systems 24 hours a day. That means you will also hear it at night in your cabin (any cabin), and takes most passengers a day or two to get used to.

Beverage prices are high. The library is small, and needs more hardback fiction. The staff, though friendly, is casual and a little sloppy at times in the finer points of service.

SUITABLE FOR: *Wind Spirit* is best suited to young-minded couples and singles who want contemporary facilities and some watersports in a very relaxed but chic setting that is different to "normal" cruise ships, with good food and service, but with no entertainment, time-passing parlour games, structured activities, or ship's photographers.

ACCOMMODATION. Regardless of the category you choose, all cabins are nicely equipped, have crisp, inviting décor and a mini-bar/refrigerator (stocked when you embark, but all drinks are at extra cost), 24-hour room service, personal safe, television (with CNN, when available, for news) that rotates so that it is viewable from the bed and the bathroom, video player, compact disc player, plenty of storage space, and two portholes. The cabins all have two portholes with outside views, and deadlights (steel covers that provide a complete blackout at night and can be closed in inclement weather conditions). The decor is a pleasant mix of rich woods, natural fabrics and colorful soft furnishings, and hi-tech yacht-style amenities. However, note that some of the cabinetry is looking a little tired, and has that "I've been varnished many times" look. A basket of fruit is provided, and replenished daily.

The bathrooms are best described as compact units, designed in a figure of eight, with a teakwood floor in the central section. There is a good amount of storage space for personal toiletries in two cabinets, as well as under-sink cupboard space; a wall-mounted hairdryer is also provided. The shower enclosure (no cabins have bathtubs) is circular (like many of today's passengers), and has both a hand-held as well as a fixed shower (so you can wash your hair without getting the rest of your body wet). Soap, shampoo and after-sun soothing lotion are provided, as is a vanity kit and shower cap.

Note, however, that the lighting is not strong enough for women to apply make-up – this is better applied at the vanity desk in the cabin, which has stronger overhead (halogen) lighting. Bathrobes and towels are 100% cotton.

CUISINE/DINING. There is one rather chic and elegant dining room (The Restaurant), with ocean views from large, picture windows, a lovely wood ceiling and wood paneling on the walls. California-style nouvelle cuisine is served, with dishes that are attractively presented. Additionally, "sig-

nature" dishes, created by master chefs Joachim Splichal and Jeanne Jones, are offered daily. Open seating means you dine when you want and with whomever you wish to.

When the company first started, European waiters provided service with practiced European finesse. However, those waiters have been replaced by Indonesians and Filipinos, whose communication skills at times can prove inadequate, although the service is pleasant enough. The selection of breads, cheeses, and fruits could be better. There is a big push to sell wines, although the prices are extremely high, as they are for most alcoholic drinks (even bottled water is the highest in the industry, at $7 per liter bottle).

There is often casual dinner on the open deck under the stars, with grilled seafood and steaks. At the bars, hot and cold hors d'oeuvres appear at cocktail times.

ENTERTAINMENT. There is no showlounge, shows or cabaret. However, none are really needed, because a cruise aboard this high-tech sailing ship provides an opportunity to get away from all that noise and "entertainment". The main lounge (a corner of which is dedicated to a small casino) does have a small dance floor, and, typically, a trio is there to play for your dancing or listening pleasure. The main lounge is also used for cocktail parties and other social functions. Otherwise, it's down to more personal entertainment, such as a video in your cabin late at night – or, much more romantic, after-dinner hours spent outside strolling or simply lounging on deck.

SPA/FITNESS. A gymnasium (with a modicum of muscle-toning equipment, treadmills and exercycles) and sauna are located at the aft of the ship, adjacent to the Watersports platform. Special spa packages can be pre-booked through your travel agent before you arrive at the ship. Well-being massages, aromatherapy facials, manicures, pedicures, and hair beautifying treatments are all at extra cost (massage, for example, costs about $2 per minute, plus gratuity). The spa is operated by Steiner Leisure, a specialist concession, whose young staff may try to sell you Steiner's own-brand Elemis beauty products (spa girls have sales targets).

Wind Star
★★★★

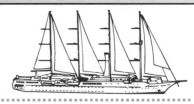

Boutique Ship: . . . . .5,350 tons	Sail Area (sq ft/m2): 21,489/1,996.4	17.0–22.5
Lifestyle: . . . . .Premium	Main Propulsion: . . . . . .a) engines/b) sails	Cabins (outside view): 74
Cruise Line: . . . . .Windstar Cruises	Propulsion/Propellers: . . . . .diesel-electric	Cabins (interior/no view): 0
Former Names: . . . . .none	(1,400kW)/1	Cabins (for one person): 0
Builder: . . . . .Ateliers et Chantiers	Passenger Decks: 5	Cabins (with private balcony): 0
du Havre (France)	Total Crew: 88	Cabins (wheelchair accessible): 0
Original Cost: . . . .$34.2 million	Passengers	Cabin Current: . . . . .110 volts
Entered Service: . . . . .Dec 1986	(lower beds/all berths): 148/168	Casino (gaming tables): . . . . .Yes
Registry: . . . . .The Bahamas	Passenger Space Ratio	Slot Machines: . . . . .Yes
Length (ft/m): 439.6/134.0	(lower beds/all berths): 36.1/33.6	Swimming Pools (outdoors): . .1 (dip pool)
Beam (ft/m): 51.8/15.8	Crew/Passenger Ratio	Whirlpools: 1
Draft (ft/m): 13.4/4.1	(lower beds/all berths): 1.6/1.8	Self-Service Launderette: . . . . .No
Type of Vessel: . . . . . .computer-controlled	Navigation Officers: . . . . .European	Library: . . . . .Yes
sail-cruiser	Cabins (total): .74	Classification Society: . . . .Bureau Veritas
No. of Masts: . . . . . .4/6 self-furling sails	Size Range (sq ft/m): 185.0–220.0/	

OVERALL SCORE: 1,518 (OUT OF A POSSIBLE 2,000 POINTS)

OVERVIEW. *Wind Star* is one of three identical vessels (a fourth, *Wind Saga*, was planned but never built). One of the original three sister ships, *Wind Song*, suffered a fire and was declared a constructive total loss in Tahiti in 2002. *Wind Star* is a long, sleek-looking craft that is part-yacht, part-cruise ship, with four giant masts that tower 170 ft (52 meters) above the deck (they are actually 204 ft, or 62 meters) high, and fitted with computer-controlled sails; the masts, sails and rigging alone cost $5 million. The computer keeps the ship on an even keel (via the movement of a water hydraulic ballast system of 142,650 gallons/540,000 litres), so there is no heeling (rolling) over 6 degrees. When the masts for Wind Star (first of the three original Windstar vessels) were lowered into position, a US silver dollar, dated 1889, was placed under mast number two (the main mast).

There is very little open deck space when the ship is full, due to the amount of complex sail machinery. There is a tiny dip pool. At the stern is a small water sports platform for those who enjoy all the goodies the ship offers (but only when at anchor, and only in really calm sea conditions). Water sports facilities include a banana boat kayaks, sunfish sailboats, windsurf boards, water ski boat, scuba and snorkel equipment, and four Zodiacs. You will be asked to sign a waiver if you wish to use the water sports equipment.

The ship has a finely crafted interior with pleasing, blond woods, together with soft, complementary colors and decor that is chic, even elegant, but a little cold. Note that the main lounge aboard Wind Star is of a different design than sister ship *Wind Spirit*.

No scheduled activities help to make this a real relaxing,

BERLITZ'S RATINGS

	Possible	Achieved
Ship	500	382
Accommodation	200	164
Food	400	295
Service	400	300
Entertainment	N/A	N/A
Cruise	500	377

unregimented "get away from it all" vacation. The Windstar ships will cruise you in extremely comfortable surroundings bordering on contemporary luxury, yet in an unstructured environment. They provide a very relaxing, virtually unstructured cruise experience just right for seven idyllic nights in sheltered areas (but can be disturbing when a Windstar vessel is in small ports alongside several huge cruise ships).

This ship is ideal for couples who do not like large ships. The dress code is casual (no jackets and ties required), even for dinner (the brochure states casual elegance). There are no formal nights or theme nights. You will probably be under sail for less than 40 percent of the time (conditions and cruise area winds permitting). Gratuities are "not required" by the friendly, smiling staff, according to the brochure, but passengers find they are always accepted. The onboard currency is the US dollar.

Note that there is very little open deck space, and the swimming pool is really only a tiny "dip" pool. Be prepared for the "whine" of the vessel's generators, which are needed to run the air-conditioning and lighting systems 24 hours a day. That means you will also hear it at night in your cabin (any cabin), and takes most passengers a day or two to get used to.

Beverage prices are high. The library is small, and needs more hardback fiction. The staff, though friendly, is casual and can be a little sloppy at times in the finer points of service.

SUITABLE FOR: *Wind Star* is best suited to young-minded couples and singles who want contemporary facilities and some watersports in a very relaxed but chic setting that is different to "normal" cruise ships, with good food and service, but with no entertainment, time-passing parlour games, structured activities or ship's photographers.

ACCOMMODATION. Regardless of the category you choose, all cabins are very nicely equipped, have crisp, inviting decor, and a mini-bar/refrigerator (stocked when you embark, but all drinks are at extra cost), 24-hour room service, personal safe, television (with CNN, when available, for news) that rotates so that it is viewable from the bed and the bathroom, video player, compact disc player, plenty of storage space, and two portholes. The cabins all have two portholes with outside views, and deadlights (steel covers that provide a complete blackout at night and can be closed in inclement weather conditions). The decor is a pleasant mix of rich woods, natural fabrics and colorful soft furnishings, and hi-tech yacht-style amenities. However, note that some of the cabinetry is looking a little tired, and has that "I've been varnished many times" look. A basket of fruit is provided, and replenished daily.

The bathrooms are best described as very compact units, designed in a figure of eight, with a teakwood floor in the central section. There is a good amount of storage space for personal toiletries in two cabinets, as well as under-sink cupboard space; a wall-mounted hairdryer is also provided. The shower enclosure (no cabins have bathtubs) is circular (like many of today's passengers), and has both a hand-held, as well as a fixed shower (so you can wash your hair without getting the rest of your body wet). Soap, shampoo and after-sun soothing lotion are provided, as is a vanity kit and shower cap.

Note, however, that the lighting is not strong enough for women to apply make-up – this is better applied at the vanity desk in the cabin, which has stronger overhead (halogen) lighting. Bathrobes and towels are 100% cotton.

CUISINE/DINING. There is one rather chic and elegant dining room (The Restaurant), with ocean views from large, picture windows, a lovely wood ceiling and wood paneling on the walls. California-style nouvelle cuisine is served, with dishes that are attractively presented. Additionally, "signature" dishes, created by master chefs Joachim Splichal and Jeanne Jones, are offered daily.

Open seating means you dine when you want and with whomever you wish to. Both smoking and no-smoking sections are provided.

When the company made its debut, European waiters provided service with practiced European finesse; those waiters are now from Indonesia and the Philippines, who provide friendly service but with less finesse. The selection of breads, cheeses, and fruits could be better. There is a big push to sell wines, although the prices are extremely high, as they are for most alcoholic drinks (even bottled water is the highest in the industry, at $7 per liter bottle).

There is often casual dinner on the open deck under the stars, with grilled seafood and steaks. At the bars, hot and cold hors d'oeuvres appear at cocktail times.

ENTERTAINMENT. There is no showlounge, shows or cabaret. However, none are really needed, because a cruise aboard this high-tech sailing ship provides an opportunity to get away from all that noise and "entertainment". The main lounge (a corner of which is dedicated to a small casino) does have a small dance floor, and, typically, a trio is there to play for your dancing or listening pleasure. The main lounge is also used for cocktail parties and other social functions. Otherwise, it's down to more personal entertainment, such as a video in your cabin late at night – or, much more romantic, after-dinner hours spent outside strolling or simply lounging on deck.

SPA/FITNESS. A gymnasium (with a modicum of muscle-toning equipment, treadmills and exercycles) and sauna are located at the aft of the ship, adjacent to the Watersports platform. Special spa packages can be pre-booked through your travel agent before you arrive at the ship. Well-being massages, aromatherapy facials, manicures, pedicures, and hair beautifying treatments are all at extra cost (massage, for example, costs about $2 per minute, plus gratuity). The spa is operated by Steiner Leisure, a specialist concession, whose young staff may try to sell you Steiner's own-brand Elemis beauty products (spa girls have sales targets).

Wind Surf
★★★★ +

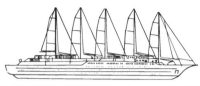

Small Ship: . . . . .14,745 tons	Sail Area (sq ft/m2): 26,910/2,500	Cabins (outside view): 154
Lifestyle: . . . . .Premium	Main Propulsion: . . . . . .a) engines/b) sails	Cabins (interior/no view): 0
Cruise Line: . . . . .Windstar Cruises	Propulsion/Propellers: diesel (9,120kW)/2	Cabins (for one person): 0
Former Names: . . . .*Club Med I*	Passenger Decks: 8	Cabins (with private balcony): 0
Builder: . . . . .Ateliers et Chantiers	Total Crew: 163	Cabins (wheelchair accessible): 0
du Havre (France)	Passengers	Cabin Current: . . . . .220 volts
Original Cost: . . . .$140 million	(lower beds/all berths): 308/308	Elevators: 2
Entered Service: . . . .Feb 1990/May 1998	Passenger Space Ratio	Casino (gaming tables): . . . . .Yes
Registry: . . . . .The Bahamas	(lower beds/all berths): 47.8/47.8	Slot Machines: . . . . .Yes
Length (ft/m): 613.5/187.0	Crew/Passenger Ratio	Swimming Pools (outdoors): 2
Beam (ft/m): 65.6/20.0	(lower beds/all berths): 1.8/1.8	Whirlpools: 2
Draft (ft/m): 16.4/5.0	Navigation Officers: . . . . .European	Self-Service Launderette: . . . . .No
Type of Vessel: . . . . .high-tech sail-cruiser	Cabins (total): 154	Library: . . . . .Yes
No. of Masts: . . . .5/7 computer-controlled	Size Range (sq ft/m): 188.0–375.6/	Classification Society: . . . .Bureau Veritas
sails	57.3–114.5	

OVERALL SCORE: 1,567 (OUT OF A POSSIBLE 2,000 POINTS)

OVERVIEW. One of a pair of the world's largest sail-cruisers, *Wind Surf* is part-cruise ship, part-yacht (its sister ship operates as *Club Med II*). This is a larger, grander sister to the original three Windstar Cruises vessels. Five huge masts of 164 ft/50 meters (these actually rise 221 feet, or 67.5 meters above sea level) carry seven triangular, self-furling sails (made of Dacron) with a total surface area of 26,881 sq. ft (2,497 sq. meters). No human hands touch the sails, as everything is handled electronically by computer control from the bridge.

A computer keeps the ship on an even keel (via the movement of a water hydraulic ballast system of 266,800 gallons/1 million liters), so there is no heeling (rolling) over 6 degrees. When the ship is not using the sails, four diesel-electric motors propel it at up to approximately 12 knots.

There is a large, hydraulic water sports platform at the stern (swimming from it is not allowed, however), and extensive water sports facilities include 12 windsurfers, 3 sailboats, 2 water-ski boats, 20 single scuba tanks, snorkels, fins and masks, and 4 inflatable Zodiac motorized boats (for water-skiing, etc), and all at no extra charge (except for the scuba tanks). Note that you will be asked to sign a waiver if you wish to use the water sports equipment.

There are two (saltwater) swimming pools (really little more than dip pools); one is located amidships on the uppermost deck of the ship, while the other is located aft, together with two hot tubs, and an adjacent bar.

In December 2000, the ship underwent further internal redesign, with enhancement of some features and the addition of new ones. A new gangway was installed, which has

BERLITZ'S RATINGS

	Possible	Achieved
Ship	500	422
Accommodation	200	166
Food	400	299
Service	400	289
Entertainment	N/A	N/A
Cruise	500	391

improved embarkation/disembarkation. A business center has been added; this incorporates a computer center (with 10 internet-access computer terminals, and a meeting room for between 30 and 60 persons. In the ship's casino/main lounge, which has an unusually high ceiling for the size of the ship, the dance floor has thankfully been relocated for better access and flow.

Other facilities include an integrated main lounge and enlarged casino (with 4 blackjack and one roulette table, and 21 slot machines).

Wind Surf is a good choice for couples seeking the "California Casual" dress code (no jackets or ties required) and informality found aboard this vessel, yet don't want the inconvenience of the workings of a real tall ship. The high quality of food and its presentation is a definite plus, as is the policy of no music in passenger hallways or elevators – in other words, it's a delightful, peaceful environment.

Wind Surf cruises from Barbados (November–March) and from Nice (May–October). However, the European itineraries are really port-intensive, which means you sail each night and are in port each day. With such itineraries, there seems little point to having the sails.

This ship has become a larger sister ship (with more space per passenger) to the two original Windstar Cruises vessels presently operating (*Wind Spirit, Wind Star*). All gratuities and port taxes are included in the brochure price (no additional gratuities are expected), which itself is considerably higher than those of the three smaller vessels in the fleet. The onboard currency is the US dollar.

There are no showers at either of the two swimming pools (they really are just dip pools for cooling off) –

passengers get into pool or hot tubs, while covered in oil or lotion, an unhygienic arrangement. Don't even think about purchasing a cigar from the onboard shop – because the air temperature in the shop is high, cigars will be dry and absolutely worthless (they should, of course, be sold from a properly kept humidor).

SUITABLE FOR: *Wind Surf* is best suited to young-minded couples and singles who want contemporary facilities and some watersports in a very relaxed but chic setting that is different to "normal" cruise ships, with good food and service, but with no entertainment, time-passing parlour games, structured activities or ship's photographers.

ACCOMMODATION. There are just three price categories, making your choice a simple one. Regardless of category, all cabins are very nicely equipped, have crisp, inviting decor, and a mini-bar/refrigerator (stocked when you embark, but all drinks are at extra cost), 24-hour room service, personal safe, a TV set (with CNN, when available) that rotates so that it is viewable from the bed and the bathroom, video player, compact disc player, plenty of storage space, and two portholes. Videos and compact discs are available from the library. There are six 4-person cabins; 35 doubles are fitted with an extra Pullman berth, and several cabins have an interconnecting door (good for families). Some of the cabinetry is looking a little tired.

The bathrooms are compact units, designed in a figure of eight, with a teakwood floor in the central section. There is a good amount of storage space for personal toiletries in two cabinets, as well as under-sink cupboard space, There's a wall-mounted hairdryer. The shower enclosure (no cabins have bathtubs) is circular, and has both a hand-held and a fixed shower (so you can wash your hair without getting the rest of your body wet). Soap, shampoo and after-sun soothing lotion are provided, as is a vanity kit and shower cap. The lighting is not strong enough for women to apply make-up – this is better applied at the vanity desk in the cabin. Bathrobes and towels are 100% cotton, while bed linen is of a mix of 50% cotton/50% polyester (with 100% cotton sheets available on request).

In 1998, 31 new suites were added to Deck 3 during an extensive refit (one Owner's Suite plus 30 suites that were created by using two former standard cabins for one suite). All except one of the new suites have two bathrooms, a separate living/dining area, sleeping area (this can be curtained off from the lounge), two writing desks (there is even enough room for you to have an in-suite massage), and four portholes instead of two.

There are two TV sets (one in the lounge, on in the sleeping area), VCR and CD player. However, note that movies cannot be watched from the bed – only from the sofa in the lounge area. Popcorn is available from room service.

CUISINE/DINING. The 272-seat Restaurant has tables for two, four or six, and open seating (with no pre-assigned tables), so you can sit with whom you wish, when you like. It is open only for dinner, which is typically between 7.30pm and 9.30pm. Both smoking and no-smoking sections are provided. California-style nouvelle cuisine is served, with dishes that are attractively presented. Additionally, "signature" dishes, created by master chefs Joachim Splichal and Jeanne Jones, are offered daily.

A 124-seat Bistro provides an alternative venue to the main restaurant (for dinner). The menus are basically the same, and the Bistro really provides an overflow – particularly when the ship is full. The Bistro is thus not a bistro at all. It is located high atop the ship (on Star Deck) and has picture windows on port and starboard sides, an open kitchen, and tables for two, four or six. This is a no-smoking dining spot. Reservations are required for dinner, and passengers are restricted to two visits per 7-day cruise.

The Veranda, amidships (on Star Deck), has its own open terrace for informal, self-serve breakfast and lunch buffets. It really is very pleasant to be outside, eating an informal meal on a balmy night. Do try the bread pudding – the ship is famous for it (available after lunch each day). Additionally, a permanent barbecue is also set up aft of the Veranda, for fresh grilled items for breakfast and lunch.

The Compass Rose, an indoor/outdoor bar, provides snack items plus some pastries and coffee for breakfast.

Windstar Cruises food is generally very good, although highly geared toward American tastes. Europeans and other nationals should note that items such as bacon is fried to death, and the choice of cheeses and teas is poor. The service is also fast, geared towards American impatience.

ENTERTAINMENT. There is no showlounge, shows or cabaret. However, none are really needed, because a cruise aboard this high-tech sailing ship provides an opportunity to get away from all that noise and "entertainment". The main lounge (a corner of which is dedicated to a small casino) does have a small dance floor, and, typically, a trio is there to play for your dancing or listening pleasure. The main lounge is also used for cocktail parties and other social functions. Otherwise, it's down to more personal entertainment, such as a video in your cabin late at night. One disturbing trend, however, is use of the lounge for art auctions after dinner, once or more each cruise. How sad that an otherwise pleasant, casual cruise experience is ruined in this way –they'll be selling used cars next! Better to retire to your cabin and take in a video, or spend it out on deck taking a stroll or lounging under the stars.

SPA/FITNESS. The Health Spa (with a staff of 10) has a co-ed sauna (bathing suits are required), beauty salon, and several treatment rooms for massage, facials and body wraps; there is also a decent gymnasium (on a separate deck – with ocean views), and an aerobics workout room. Unfortunately, the spa facilities are split on three separate decks, making them rather disjointed. Special spa packages can be pre-booked through your travel agent before you arrive at the ship. The spa is operated by Steiner Leisure, a concession. Well-being massages, aromatherapy facials, pedicures, and beauty salon treatments cost extra (massage, for example, costs about $2 per minute, plus gratuity).

World Renaissance
★★ +

Small Ship: . . . . .11,724 tons	Passenger Decks: 8	Cabins (with private balcony): 0
Lifestyle: . . . . .Standard	Total Crew: 204	Cabins (wheelchair accessible): 0
Cruise Line: . . . . . .Royal Olympia Cruises	Passengers	Cabin Current: . . . . .110 volts
Former Names: . . . . .Awani Dream,	(lower beds/all berths): 481/599	Elevators: 1
World Renaissance, Renaissance,	Passenger Space Ratio	Casino (gaming tables): . . . . .Yes
Homeric Renaissance	(lower beds/all berths): 24.3/19.5	Slot Machines: . . . . .Yes
Builder: Chantiers de l'Atlantique (France)	Crew/Passenger Ratio	Swimming Pools (outdoors): 2
Original Cost: .n/a	(lower beds/all berths): 2.2/2.9	Swimming Pools (indoors): 0
Entered Service: . . . .May 1966/Jan 1996	Navigation Officers: . . . . .Greek	Whirlpools: 0
Registry: .Greece	Cabins (total): 241	Self-Service Launderette: . . . . .No
Length (ft/m): 492.1/150.02	Size Range (sq ft/m): 110–270/10.2–25.0	Dedicated Cinema/Seats: Yes/110
Beam (ft/m): 69.0/21.06	Cabins (outside view): 178	Library: . . . . .Yes
Draft (ft/m): 22.9/7.00	Cabins (interior/no view): 63	Classification Society: . . .Lloyd's Register
Propulsion/Propellers: diesel(10,060kW)/2	Cabins (for one person): 1	

OVERALL SCORE: 1,091 (OUT OF A POSSIBLE 2,000 POINTS)

OVERVIEW. *World Renaissance* has traditional 1960s styling and profile topped by a pencil-slim funnel and white superstructure atop a royal-blue hull. There is a generous amount of open deck and sunbathing space. The interior layout, however, is disjointed and awkward, and signage could be better. The internal decor is both "colonial" and eclectic. Although the main lounge is comfortable, there are few other public rooms, and therefore the ship always feels busy (i.e. crowded). The friendly staff are Greek and there is good basic service, although there is not much refinement. The onboard currency is the euro.

The ship has a steep passenger gangway in most ports of call. There is no wrap-around promenade deck outdoors, and there are no cushioned pads for the deck lounge chairs.

SUITABLE FOR: *World Renaissance* is best suited to those taking a first cruise to interesting destinations, and who will accept an old ship with few facilities in order to cruise at a low price, with food and service that are very basic.

ACCOMMODATION. There are 10 price grades. While accommodation designated as suites, as well as a few other cabins, have a double bed, most have two lower beds (although some have one lower bed and one upper berth), so check the brochure carefully. Although the cabins are compact but "homey", they are certainly not luxurious. Cabin bathrooms are tiled, but are very small, with little space for toiletries.

Grades designated as suites have more space, and a lounge seating area. Bathrooms have a tub/shower combination,

BERLITZ'S RATINGS

	Possible	Achieved
Ship	500	241
Accommodation	200	105
Food	400	238
Service	400	241
Entertainment	100	50
Cruise	400	216

whereas non-suite grades have only a shower enclosure.

CUISINE/DINING. The dining room, which seats 300, is reasonably pleasant, although there are no tables for two, the tables are close together, and there are two seatings for dinner. Open seating for breakfast and lunch (a breakfast buffet is also set up in the dining room, but a regular à la carte breakfast menu is also available). The cuisine is predominantly Continental, with regional (Greek) specialties (there is much use of oil and salt). The presentation is spotty and inconsistent. Spa and vegetarian dishes are also available on lunch and dinner menus. Overall, however, the food has very little taste. There is a repetitious choice of bread rolls, fruits and cheeses, and desserts rely too much on canned fruits and jellies. Casual buffet breakfasts and lunches are unimaginative, relying too much on standard food items.

ENTERTAINMENT. The main lounge acts as a room for cabaret acts, which are low-budget. You can expect to find singers, magicians, and other visual acts that can appeal to a range of nationalities. The main entertainment is the ship's itinerary, and interesting lecturers. There is a ship's band and a couple of small musical units to provide live music for dancing or listening.

SPA/FITNESS. There is a small gymnasium (with some pretty old equipment), a sauna, and beauty salon. Massages, manicures, pedicures and aromatherapy facials are offered, together with hair beautifying services.

Yamal
★★★

Boutique Ship: . . . . .23,445 tons
Lifestyle: . . . . .Standard
Cruise Line: . . . . .Poseidon Arctic
Voyages
Former Names: . . . . .none
Builder: . . . . .Baltic Shipyard &
Engineering (Russia)
Original Cost: . . . .$150 million
Entered Service: . . . . .Nov 1992
Registry: .Russia
Length (ft/m): 492.1/150.0
Beam (ft/m): 98.4/30.0
Draft (ft/m): 36.0/11.0
Propulsion/Propellers: . .nuclear-powered
turbo-electric (55,950kW)/3
Passenger Decks: 4

Total Crew: 150
Passengers
(lower beds/all berths): 100/100
Passenger Space Ratio
(lower beds/all berths): 234.0/234.0
Crew/Passenger Ratio
(lower beds/all berths): 0.6/0.6
Navigation Officers: . . .Russian/Ukrainian
Cabins (total): 56
Size Range (sq ft/m): 130.0–300.0/
14.3–27.8
Cabins (outside view): 56
Cabins (interior/no view): 0
Cabins (for one person): 3
Cabins (with private balcony): 0
Cabins (wheelchair accessible): 0

Cabin Current: . . . . .220 volts
Dining Rooms: .1
Elevators: 0
Casino (gaming tables): . . . . .No
Slot Machines: . . . . .No
Swimming Pools (indoors): 1
Whirlpools: 0
Self-Service Launderette: . . . . .Yes
Lecture/Film Room: . . . . . .Yes (seats 100)
Library: . . . . .Yes
Zodiacs: 4
Helicopter Pad: . . . . .2 helicopters for
passenger use
Classification Society: . .Russian Shipping
Registry

OVERALL SCORE: 1,246 (OUT OF A POSSIBLE 2,000 POINTS)

OVERVIEW. The ultimate in technology accompanies this special ship, one of a fleet of four that comprise the world's most powerful icebreakers, with a 48mm-thick (about 3 inches) armored double hull. Propulsion power is provided by two nuclear-powered reactors (encased in 160 tons of steel), which provide the steam for propulsion via a pair of steam turbines. Each turbine operates three generators, and these in turn produce DC power for the electric propulsion motors that power the three powerful four-bladed propellers, each of which weighs about seven tons. The ship carries enough fuel for four years without refueling. Of the 150 crew, 50 are officers and engineers dedicated to the maintenance and operation of the highly specialized vessel.

Yamal is one of few surface ships ever to reach the North Pole, assisted by an air-bubbling system which delivers hot water through jets under the surface of the ice (rather like the feeling of being in a floating whirlpool bath). Two helicopters are carried for reconnaissance and passenger sightseeing use; their use is included in the expedition fare, and provide a bird's-eye view of the polar landscape. The ship carries a fleet of Zodiac inflatable landing craft.

Rugged yet surprisingly comfortable surroundings prevail inside. There are two lounges. A tiered lecture theater with stage is the setting for a team of biologists, scientists, geologists, and other lecturers. There is a heated indoor seawater pool. Light but warm parkas are provided for everyone.

Yamal is occasionally placed under charter to various operators (mostly the immensely experienced Quark Expeditions). This is one of the most exciting, seat-of-your-pants

BERLITZ'S RATINGS

	Possible	Achieved
Ship	500	307
Accommodation	200	120
Food	400	244
Service	400	250
Entertainment	N/A	N/A
Cruise	500	331

expedition cruise experiences available. The onboard currency is the US dollar.

SUITABLE FOR: This type of expedition cruising vessel is best suited to adventurous, hardy outdoors types who enjoy being with nature and wildlife in some of the most inhospitable places on earth and don't mind roughing it a little.

ACCOMMODATION. All of the cabins are generously sized (considering the type of specialized vessel this is), and all are outside, with private facilities, television (for in-house viewing), VCR (suites only), refrigerator and desk. There is, however, a limited amount of closet and drawer space in most cabins. The bathrooms are small and utilitarian, and you will need to take your own toiletry items.

CUISINE/DINING. The dining room is nicely appointed, and all passengers dine in one seating. The carbohydrate-rich food is hearty, with plenty of meat and potato dishes, but little fruit and cheese. When the ship is under charter to Western companies, Western rather than Russian chefs oversee the food operation, and the selection of foods is better.

ENTERTAINMENT. The expedition cruise itself, into unhospitable regions such as the Arctic and Antarctica is really the main diversion. However, each day, a recap of the day's events and experiences makes for a fascinating evening's conversation.

SPA/FITNESS. There is a small gymnasium, and a sauna.

Yankee Clipper
★★

Boutique Ship: ....327 tons	Main Propulsion: ....sail power	Cabins (interior/no view): 0
Lifestyle: ....Standard	Propulsion/Propellers: diesel/1	Cabins (for one person): 0
Cruise Line: ....Windjammer Barefoot	Passenger Decks: 3	Cabins (with private balcony): 0
Cruises	Total Crew: 24	Cabins (wheelchair accessible): 0
Former Names: ....*Pioneer, Cressida*	Passengers	Cabin Current: ....110 volts
Builder: ....Krupp (Germany)	(lower beds/all berths): 64/64	Elevators: 0
Entered Service: 1927/1965	Passenger Space Ratio	Casino (gaming tables): ....No
Registry: ....Equitorial Guinea	(lower beds/all berths): 5.1/5.1	Slot Machines: ....No
Length (ft/m): 197.0/60.0	Crew/Passenger Ratio	Swimming Pools (outdoors): 0
Beam (ft/m): 30.0/9.1	(lower beds/all berths): 2.6/2.6	Whirlpools: 0
Draft (ft/m): 17.0/5.1	Navigation Officers: ....International	Self-Service Launderette: ....No
Type of Vessel: ....schooner	Cabins (total): 32	Library: ....Yes
No. of Masts: 3	Size Range (sq ft/m): ..65.0–86.0/6.0–7.9	Classification Society: ....none
Sail Area (sq ft/m2): 8,000/743.2	Cabins (outside view): 32	

OVERALL SCORE: 902 (OUT OF A POSSIBLE 2,000 POINTS)

OVERVIEW. The ship was built as one of the only armor-plated private yachts in the world, for the German industrialist Alfred Krupp. Confiscated during World War II as a war prize, it was later acquired by the Vanderbilts. It joined the Windjammer Barefoot Cruises fleet in 1965. Aboard this fleet, you can let the crew do all the work, or you can lend a hand at the helm. One neat thing to do is just to sit or lie in the nets at the bows of the vessel, without a care in the world.

The mood is free and easy, the ships are equipped very simply, and only the most casual clothes are required (T-shirts and shorts). Shoes are optional, although you may need them if you go off in one of the ports. Quite possibly the most used item will be your bathing suit – better take more than one. Smoking is allowed only on the open decks.

Jammin' aboard a Windjammer is no-frills cruising in a no-nonsense, friendly environment, for the young at heart and those who don't need programmed activities. It's all about going to sea and the romance of being at sea under sail. Those who enjoy beaches, scuba diving and snorkeling around the Caribbean will be best suited to such a cruise. This ship can anchor in neat little Caribbean hideaways that regular cruise ships, being bigger, can't get near.

Although itineraries (well, islands) are provided in the brochure, the captain actually decides which islands to go to in any given area, depending on sea and weather conditions. The ship features year-round cruises in the British and US Virgin Islands. Brochure rates might seem inexpensive, but you'll need to add on the airfare in order to get the true cost.

Yankee Clipper sails in the Caribbean, from Grenada. Other tall ships in the fleet include *Flying Cloud, Legacy,*

BERLITZ'S RATINGS

	Possible	Achieved
Ship	500	219
Accommodation	200	79
Food	400	166
Service	400	188
Entertainment	N/A	N/A
Cruise	500	250

Mandalay, and *Polynesia.* Note that it's all extremely basic, and there's little space per passenger. Tips to the crew are suggested – at a whopping $50 per week per person. The onboard currency is the US dollar.

SUITABLE FOR: *Yankee Clipper* is best suited to young, carefree singles who enjoy beaches, scuba diving and snorkeling, and are happy with just the basic necessities, all in an ultra-casual setting of sails, sea and sun, with no pretension whatsoever.

ACCOMMODATION. There are four grades: Deck Cabin, Captain's Cabin, Captain's Double, and Standard Cabin. The cabins are dimensionally challenged (more for packages than people), however, particularly when compared to regular cruise ships. Remember, however, that this is a very casual cruise, so you won't need a lot of clothes anyway. All of the cabins are equipped with upper and lower berths, and most of them are quite narrow.

CUISINE/DINING. There is one dining room, and meals are all very simple in style and service, with little choice and only the most basic presentation. Breakfast is served on board, as is dinner, while lunch could be available either on board or at a beach, picnic-style. Wine is included for dinner, but don't expect it to be very good.

ENTERTAINMENT. Entertainment in the evenings consists of just you and the crew. You can put on a toga, take or create a pirate outfit and join in the fun.

SPA/FITNESS. No facilities are provided.

Yorktown Clipper
★★ +

Boutique Ship: . . . . .2,354 tons	Total Crew: 40	Cabins (with private balcony): 0
Lifestyle: . . . . .Standard	Passengers	Cabins (wheelchair accessible): 0
Cruise Line: . . . . .Clipper Cruise Line	(lower beds/all berths): 138/138	Cabin Current: . . . . .110 volts
Former Names: . . . . .none	Passenger Space Ratio	Elevators: 0
Builder: . . . .First Coast Shipbuilding (USA)	(lower beds/all berths): 17.0/17.0	Casino (gaming tables): . . . . .No
Original Cost: . . . .$12 million	Crew/Passenger Ratio	Slot Machines: . . . . .No
Entered Service: . . . . .Apr 1988	(lower beds/all berths): 3.4/3.4	Swimming Pools (outdoors): 0
Registry: . . . . .USA	Navigation Officers: . . . . .American	Swimming Pools (indoors): 0
Length (ft/m): 257.0/78.30	Cabins (total): 69	Whirlpools: 0
Beam (ft/m): 43.0/13.10	Size Range (sq ft/m): 121.0–138.0/	Self-Service Launderette: . . . . .No
Draft (ft/m): 8.0/2.43	11.2–12.8	Dedicated Cinema/Seats: . . . . .No
Propulsion/Propellers: . . . . .diesel	Cabins (outside view): 69	Library: . . . . .Yes
(1,044kW)/2	Cabins (interior/no view): 0	Classification Society: . .American Bureau
Passenger Decks: 4	Cabins (for one person): 0	of Shipping

OVERALL SCORE: 982 (OUT OF A POSSIBLE 2,000 POINTS)

OVERVIEW. *Yorktown Clipper* was built specifically to operate coastal and inland waterway cruises. The draft is shallow, and the ship has good maneuverability, and has been quite well maintained since new, although it is certainly showing signs of wear and tear, and needs some attention. There is a teakwood outdoor sun deck. Inflatable rubber Zodiac craft are used for close-in shore excursions.

Inside, there is a glass-walled observation lounge. This ship offers a decidedly American experience for those seeking to learn more about the coastal ports around the USA during the summer months, while Caribbean cruises are featured in winter.

The lifestyle is casual and unregimented – rather like a small, congenial country club. There are always one or two lecturers aboard, which enhances the learning experience. The price, however, is very high for what you get when compared to many other ships, and the air fare is extra. There is a no-smoking policy throughout all interior areas. The onboard currency is the US dollar.

This is a high-density ship, with only two public rooms: a dining room and a lounge. The engine noise level is high when the ship is underway. Although there is a wrap-around teakwood walking deck outdoors, it is quite narrow. The per diem price is steep, and the air fare is extra. There is no elevator (a disadvantage for older passengers).

SUITABLE FOR: The vessel is best suited to couples and single travelers who enjoy nature and wildlife at close range. This is for outdoors types who don't need constant entertainment, but do want an all-American cruise experience.

BERLITZ'S RATINGS

	Possible	Achieved
Ship	500	206
Accommodation	200	78
Food	400	220
Service	400	233
Entertainment	N/A	N/A
Cruise	500	245

ACCOMMODATION. The all-outside cabins are really quite small (think mobile home rather than cruise ship), but, with lots of wood-accented trim and restful colors, they are marginally comfortable and tastefully furnished. There are no cabins with private balconies, and the fixed windows cannot be opened. The bathrooms, too, are small, with little space for toiletries, but a night-light is provided, so you don't have to turn on bright lights in the middle of the night – a thoughtful touch. There is no room service for food and beverage items, as found aboard larger ships.

CUISINE/DINING. The dining room is warm and fairly inviting and has large picture windows, although there are no tables for two. There is one open seating, so you can dine with whom you wish. The service is provided by a young, all-American, mid-western team, whose friendly approach makes up for a lack of finesse..

The cuisine is generally of a good quality, and made from locally purchased fresh ingredients. There is little menu choice, but the food provided is nicely presented. There is an adequate but very limited selection of breads and fruits, and the wine list is generally limited to American wines.

ENTERTAINMENT. There is no formal entertainment, although dinner and after-dinner conversation with fellow passengers in the ship's lounge/bar really constitutes the main diversion each evening.

SPA/FITNESS. No facilities are provided.

Zaandam
★★★★

Large (Resort) Ship: . . . . .60,906 tons	Total Crew: 561	Cabins (with private balcony): 197
Lifestyle: . . . . .Premium	Passengers	Cabins (wheelchair accessible): 23
Cruise Line: . . . . . . .Holland America Line	(lower beds/all berths): 1,440/1,850	Cabin Current: . . . . .110 volts
Former Names: . . . . .none	Passenger Space Ratio	Elevators: 12
Builder: . . . . .Fincantieri (Italy)	(lower beds/all berths): 42.3/32.9	Casino (gaming tables): . . . . .Yes
Original Cost: . . . .$300 million	Crew/Passenger Ratio	Slot Machines: . . . . .Yes
Entered Service: . . . . .May 2000	(lower beds/all berths): 2.5/2.5	Swimming Pools (outdoors): 2
Registry: . . . . .The Netherlands	Navigation Officers: . . . . .Dutch	Swimming Pools (indoors): 1
Length (ft/m): 777.5/237.00	Cabins (total): 720	(magrodome cover)
Beam (ft/m): 105.8/32.25	Size Range (sq ft/m): 113.0–1,126.3/	Whirlpools: 2
Draft (ft/m): 25.5/7.80	10.5–104.6	Self-Service Launderette: . . . . .Yes
Propulsion/Propellers: . . . . .diesel-electric	Cabins (outside view): 581	Dedicated Cinema/Seats: Yes/205
(37,500kW)/2	Cabins (interior/no view): 139	Library: . . . . .Yes
Passenger Decks: 10	Cabins (for one person): 0	Classification Society: . . . .Lloyds Register

OVERALL SCORE: 1,541 (OUT OF A POSSIBLE 2,000 POINTS)

OVERVIEW. *Zaandam*'s hull is dark blue, in keeping with all Holland America Line ships. Although similar in size to *Rotterdam*, this ship has a single funnel, and is a sister ship to *Volendam*.

Zaandam has three principal passenger stairways, which is so much better than two stairways, particularly from the viewpoints of safety, accessibility and passenger flow. There is a magrodome-covered pool on the Lido Deck between the mast and the ship's funnel.

The interior decor is restrained, with much use of wood accenting, and the design theme of music incorporated throughout. Music memorabilia is scattered throughout the ship, in fabrics, posters, and – believe it or not – real instruments. The musical instruments and other memorabilia were acquired from the "Pop and Guitars" auction at Christie's in London in 1997. They include a Fender Squire Telecaster guitar signed by Mick Jagger, Keith Richards, Charlie Watts, Ronnie Wood and Bill Wyman of the Rolling Stones; a Conn Saxophone signed on the mouthpiece by former US President Bill Clinton; an Ariana acoustic guitar signed by David Bowie and Iggy Pop; a Fender Stratocaster guitar signed in silver ink by the members of the rock band Queen; a Bently "Les Paul" style guitar signed by various artists, including Carlos Santana, Eric Clapton, B.B. King, Robert Cray, Keith Richards and Les Paul (perhaps the ship should be called *Rockerdam*).

The decor is quite refined, with much traditional ocean liner detailing. Additions are children's and teens' play areas, although these are token gestures by a company that traditionally doesn't cater well to children. Popcorn is even available at the Wajang Theater for moviegoers (just like ashore), while adjacent is the popular Java Cafe. The casino has black-

BERLITZ'S RATINGS

	Possible	Achieved
Ship	500	430
Accommodation	200	165
Food	400	281
Service	400	276
Entertainment	100	77
Cruise	400	312

jack, roulette, stud poker and dice tables alongside the requisite rows of slot machines.

The ship's focal point is a three-deck-high atrium, around which the ship's main offices can be found (reception desk, shore excursions desk, photo shop, and photo gallery). It also houses a real showpiece – a fancy 22-ft (6.7-meter) high pipe organ that comes complete with puppets that move in time with the music; it is one of the largest such Dutch band organs ever built (it was custom-built in Hilversum in the Netherlands especially for Holland America Line).

As in *Volendam*, the Lido Deck swimming pool is located one deck higher than the *Statendam*-class ships, so that you can now have direct access between the aft and midships pools aboard this ship (not so aboard the S-class ships). This provided more space on the Navigation Deck below for extra cabins to be accommodated.

With one whole deck of suites (and a dedicated, private concierge lounge, with preferential passenger treatment), the company has in effect created a two-class ship. The charge to use the washing machines and dryers in the self-service launderette is petty and irritating, particularly for the occupants of suites, as they pay high prices for their cruises.

Communication (in English) with many of the staff, particularly in the dining room and buffet areas, can be frustrating. Room service is poor. Non-smokers should avoid this ship, as smokers are everywhere. Standing in line for embarkation, disembarkation, shore tenders and for self-serve buffet meals is inevitable aboard large ships.

ACCOMMODATION. The range is comparable to that found aboard the similarly sized *Rotterdam*, and comprises 17 different categories. The price will depend on the grade, location and size you choose. There is one penthouse suite, 28 suites, and 168 mini-suites, with the rest of the accommodation comprised of a mix of outside-view and interior (no view) cabins. However, there are many more balcony cabins (called "mini-suites") aboard this ship than aboard the slightly smaller *Statendam*-class ships (*Maasdam, Ryndam, Statendam,* and *Veendam*).

All standard interior and outside cabins are tastefully furnished, and have twin beds that convert to a queen-sized bed (space is tight for walking between beds and vanity unit). There is a decent amount of closet and drawer space, although this will prove tight for the longer voyages featured. All cabin televisions carry CNN and TNT. The bathrooms, which are fully tiled, are disappointingly small (particularly for long cruises) and have small shower tubs, utilitarian personal toiletries cupboards, and exposed under-sink plumbing. There is no detailing to distinguish them from bathrooms aboard the *Statendam*-class ships.

There are 28 full Verandah Suites (Navigation Deck), and one penthouse suites. All suite occupants share a private Concierge Lounge (the concierge handles such things as special dining arrangements, shore excursions and special requests). Strangely, there are no butlers for these suites, as aboard ships with similar facilities.

Each Verandah Suite has a separate bedroom, dressing and living areas. Suite passengers get personal stationery, complimentary laundry and ironing, cocktail hour hors d'oeuvres and other goodies, as well as priority embarkation and disembarkation. The concierge lounge, with its latticework teak detailing and private library, is accessible only by private key-card.

The ultimate in living space is the Penthouse Suite. It has a separate steward's entrance, and has a large bedroom with king-sized bed, separate living room (with baby grand piano) and a dining room, dressing room, walk-in closet, butler's pantry, private balcony (the balcony is no larger than the balcony of any of the other suites).

Other facilities include an audio-visual center with television and VCR, wet bar with refrigerator, large bathroom with Jacuzzi bathtub, separate toilet with bidet, and a guest bathroom (with toilet and washbasin).

With the exception of the penthouse suite, located forward on the starboard side, the bathrooms in the other suites and "mini-suites" are a little disappointing – not as spacious or opulent as one might expect. All outside-view suites and cabin bathrooms have a bathtub/shower while interior (no view) cabins have a shower only. Also, note that the 23 cabins for the mobility-limited have a roll-in shower enclosure for wheelchair users (none have bathtubs, no matter what the category).

CUISINE/DINING. The Rotterdam Dining Room, with smoking and no-smoking sections, is quite a grand room, and is spread over two decks, with ocean views on three sides with a grand staircase to connect the upper and lower levels. There are four seatings for dinner – you must pre-select a time and stick with it – at 5.45pm, 6.15pm, 8pm and 8.30pm, open seating for breakfast and lunch. There are tables for two, four, six or eight. The waiter stations are very noisy for anyone seated adjacent to them. Live music is provided for dinner each evening; once each cruise, a Dutch Dinner is featured (hats are provided), as is an Indonesian Lunch. "Lighter option" meals are available for the nutrition- and weight-conscious. Fine Rosenthal china and cutlery are used (although there are no fish knives). **Alternative Dining Option:** The casual-dress Marco Polo Restaurant (dinner only, with reservations required) seats 88, and there is no extra charge. It serves what is best described as California-Italian cuisine (this has a set menu together with nightly specials). Passengers thus have more choice and an occasional change of venue (anyone booking suite-grade accommodation gets priority reservations).

In addition, the Lido Buffet is a casual, self-serve cafe for casual breakfasts and luncheons, and a grill outdoors has the inevitable hamburgers, hot dogs and other fast-food items. The Lido Buffet is also open for casual dinners on several nights each cruise (typically three nights on a 7-night cruise), in an open-seating arrangement. Tables are set with crisp linens, flatware and stemware. The set menu includes a choice of four entrées.

ENTERTAINMENT. The Mondriaan Showlounge, located at the forward part of the ship, spans two decks, with banquette seating on both main and upper levels. It is basically a well-designed room, but the ceiling is low and the sight-lines from the balcony level are quite poor.

SPA/FITNESS. The health spa facilities are quite extensive, and include a gymnasium (with good muscle-toning equipment), separate saunas and steam rooms for men and women, and more treatment rooms (each has a shower and toilet). Practice tennis courts can be fund outdoor, as well as the traditional shuffleboard courts, jogging track, and a full wrap-around teakwood promenade deck for strolling.

● **For more extensive general information on what a Holland America Line cruise is like, see pages 118–122.**

Zenith
★★★★

Large (Resort) Ship: . . . . .47,255 tons	Total Crew: 670	Cabins (with private balcony): 0
Lifestyle: . . . . .Premium	Passengers	Cabins (wheelchair accessible): 4
Cruise Line: . . . . .Celebrity Cruises	(lower beds/all berths): 1,378/1,800	Cabin Current: . . . . .110 volts
Former Names: . . . . .none	Passenger Space Ratio	Elevators: 7
Builder: . . . . . . .Meyer Werft (Germany)	(lower beds/all berths): . . . . . . .34.2 /26.2	Casino (gaming tables): . . . . .Yes
Original Cost: . . . .$210 million	Crew/Passenger Ratio	Slot Machines: . . . . .Yes
Entered Service: . . . . .Apr 1992	(lower beds/all berths): 2.0/2.6	Swimming Pools (outdoors): 2
Registry: . . . . .The Bahamas	Navigation Officers: . . . . .Greek	Swimming Pools (indoors): 0
Length (ft/m): 681.0/207.59	Cabins (total): 689	Whirlpools: 3
Beam (ft/m): 95.1/29.00	Size Range (sq ft/m): 172.2–500.5/	Self-Service Launderette: . . . . .No
Draft (ft/m): 23.6/7.20	16.0–46.50	Dedicated Cinema/Seats: . . . . .No
Propulsion/Propellers: . . . . .diesel	Cabins (outside view): 541	Library: . . . . .Yes
(19,960kW)/2	Cabins (interior/no view): 148	Classification Society: . . .Lloyd's Register
Passenger Decks: 9	Cabins (for one person): 0	

OVERALL SCORE: 1,537 (OUT OF A POSSIBLE 2,000 POINTS)

OVERVIEW. This ship, now over 10 years old, has a smart, contemporary profile that gives the impression of power and speed owing to its blue paint striping along the sides, separating the hull from the superstructure, as in its two-years-older sister *Horizon*. The funnel is instantly recognizable in royal blue, with a white "X", the company's logo.

Inside, there is a similar interior layout to *Horizon* and elegant and restrained decor that most find a little warmer, and an enlarged and enhanced forward observation lounge with a larger dance floor that is a pleasant setting for cocktails and late-night dance music.

The feeling is one of uncluttered surroundings. Intelligent, well-chosen art works are provided, and soothing pastel colors and high-quality soft furnishings are used throughout the ship's interiors. The principal deck that houses many of the public entertainment rooms has a double-width indoor promenade. Facilities include an excellent showlounge, with main and balcony levels, and good sightlines from almost all seats (however, the railing at the front of the balcony level does impede viewing).

There is a good-sized library, which was relocated and enlarged in a 1999 refit. There is a good (seasonal) programme for children and teenagers, with specially trained youth counselors. The large, elegantly appointed casino has its own bar, while outside is a satellite-linked BankAtlantic ATM machine (with a $5 access charge) in case you didn't bring enough cash. An art deco-style hotel-like lobby (reminiscent of hotels in Miami Beach) has a two-deck-high ceiling and a spacious feel to it.

The 1999 refurbishment added a delightful "Michael's Club" cigar smoking lounge (complete with fireplace and

BERLITZ'S RATINGS

	Possible	Achieved
Ship	500	398
Accommodation	200	157
Food	400	298
Service	400	317
Entertainment	100	68
Cruise	400	299

bookshelves containing leather-bound volumes) in what was formerly an underused discotheque, as well as the enlarged library and a small business center. Also added was a popular martini bar, a room dedicated to the display of art (for art auctions), an expanded health spa (this now includes a rasul treatment room, AquaJet and dry flotation bath), and an enlarged beauty salon with ocean-view windows; and a Cova Cafe (the original Cova Cafe, located near the La Scala Opera House, opened in 1756).

This ship will provide a well-packaged cruise holiday in elegant, calming surroundings, with finely presented food in a formal dining room setting, and service from a well-trained service staff that includes a large percentage of Europeans. Almost all passengers feel that the company exceeds their expectations. The onboard currency is the US dollar.

Standing in line for embarkation, disembarkation, shore tenders and for self-serve buffet meals is inevitable when cruising aboard all large ships. Unlike the company's larger ships, no suites or cabins have private balconies. Trying to reach Cabin Services or the Guest Relations Desk to answer the phone (to order breakfast, for example, if you don't want to do so via the interactive television) is a matter of luck.

The doors to the public restrooms and the outdoor decks are rather heavy. The public restrooms are clinical and need some softer decor. There are cushioned pads for poolside deck lounge chairs only, but not for chairs on other outside decks.

Participation activities tend to be amateurish and should be upgraded. The officers have become more aloof lately, with far less contact with passengers than when the company first started. The production shows are quite poor.

SUITABLE FOR: *Zenith* is best suited to well-traveled couples and singles of 40 and above (but really cannot be recommended for children and teenagers) who are seeking a large ship with a sophisticated environment, good itineraries, fine food and good European-style service from a well trained crew that cares and delivers an onboard product that is well above average.

ACCOMMODATION. There are 12 grades, including outside-view suites and cabins, and interior (no view) cabins, but even the smallest cabin is considerably larger than most of the standard outside and interior (no view) cabins aboard the ships of sister company Royal Caribbean International. No suites or cabins have private balconies (they weren't in vogue when this ship was constructed). Also, most outside cabins on Bahamas Deck have lifeboat-obstructed views. **Standard Cabins:** All standard outside-view and interior (no view) cabins have good-quality fittings with lots of wood accenting, are tastefully decorated and of an above-average size, with an excellent amount of closet and drawer space, and reasonable insulation between cabins. All have twin beds that convert to a queen-sized bed, and a good amount of closet and drawer space. The cabin soundproofing is fair to very good, depending on location. All accommodation has interactive Celebrity Television, including pay-per-view movies. The bathrooms have a generous shower area, and a small range of toiletries is provided (typically soap, shampoo/conditioner, body lotion, and shower cap), although bathroom towels are a little small, as is storage space for toiletries. The lowest-grade outside-view cabins have a porthole, but all others have picture windows. **Royal Suites:** The largest accommodation can be found in two Royal Suites on Atlantic Deck (Deck 10). These have butler service, and have a separate bedroom and lounge, dining area with glass dining table (with CD player and VCR player in addition to the large television). The bathroom is also larger and has a whirlpool bathtub with integral shower. Butler service is standard.

Another 20 suites (also on Atlantic Deck) are very tastefully furnished, although they are really just larger cabins and shouldn't be called suites. They are not as large as the suites aboard the company's larger ships, *Century, Constellation Galaxy, Infinity, Mercury, Millennium,* and *Summit.* They do have a generous amount of drawer and other storage space, however, and a sleeping area (with European duvets on the beds instead of sheets and blankets) plus a lounge area. They also have good bathrooms. Butler service is standard.

All accommodation designated as suites do suffer from noise generated on the swimming pool deck directly above. No suites or cabins have private balconies (they weren't in vogue when this ship was built).

In early 2005, *Zenith* will undergo a major refit/reconstruction program that will move the navigation bridge forward so that additional cabins can be added. Plans include the addition of balconies to cabins on Bermuda Deck (9), while the spa/fitness area will be expanded, the Fleet Bar (observation) lounge will be expanded forwards;

a new "alternative" restaurant will be added, and public rooms and foyers will be completely redecorated. All cabins will be refurbished (new furniture will be introduced), and bathrooms will be completely renewed. Until this has been completed (and the ship re-inspected and evaluated), the present scores and rating remain in place.

CUISINE/DINING. The Caravelle Dining Room, which has a raised section in its center, has several tables for two, as well as for four, six or eight (in banquettes), although the chairs do not have armrests. There are two seatings for dinner (open seating for breakfast and lunch), at tables for two, four, six, eight or 10. The dining room is a totally no-smoking area. The cuisine, its presentation and service are really extremely good. There is a separate menu for vegetarians and children. An extensive wine cellar means that the wine list has a fine selection of vintage and non-vintage wines and champagnes from around the world. The wine sommeliers are knowledgeable, and wine suggestions are provided on all dinner menus.

For informal meals, the Windsurf Cafe (non-smoking) has good buffets for breakfast (including an omelet station) and luncheon (including a pasta station, rotissereie and pizza ovens). At peak times, however, the buffet is simply too small. At night, the area changes into an alternative dining spot for those who want good food but in a more casual setting than the main restaurant, with items such as grilled salmon, steaks, and rotisserie chicken, as well as specialities that change frequently.

The Grill, located outdoors adjacent to (but aft of) the Windsurf Cafe, serves typical fast-food items. And for those that cannot live without them, freshly baked pizzas (in a box) can be delivered, in an insulated pouch, to your cabin.

ENTERTAINMENT. The two-level Celebrity Showlounge/theater with side balconies is a good showlounge. It has a large stage (for this size of ship) and decent lighting and sound equipment. Unfortunately, the production shows are not nearly as lavish. In fact, compared to some of the other major cruise lines, the shows are a real let-down, and not in keeping with the elegant nature of the interior décor. Bar service, supplied continuously during shows, can prove irritating.

While there are some decent cabaret acts, they are the same ones seen aboard many ships of the major cruise lines. There are a number of bands, although there is very little music for social dancing, other than disco and pop music.

SPA/FITNESS. The AquaSpa health and fitness center is located aft of the funnel on Sun Deck. It has a gymnasium with ocean-view windows and the latest in high-tech muscle-pump equipment, an exercise area, several therapy treatment rooms, and men's/women's sauna.

The spa is operated by Steiner, whose staff will try to and sell you Steiner's own-brand Elemis beauty products. Some fitness classes are free, while some, such as yoga and kickboxing, cost $10 per class. Massage, facials, pedicures, and beauty salon treatments cost extra. as doing personal training sessions in the gymnasium.

Zuiderdam
★★★★

Large (Resort) Ship: . . . . .81,679 tons	Total Crew: 842	Cabins (wheelchair accessible): 28
Lifestyle: . . . . .Premium	Passengers	Cabin Current: . . . . .110 volts
Cruise Line: . . . . . . .Holland America Line	(lower beds/all berths): 1,848/2,272	Elevators: 14
Former Names: . . . . .none	Passenger Space Ratio	Casino (gaming tables): . . . . .Yes
Builder: . . . . .Fincantieri (Italy)	(lower beds/all berths): 43.6/35.9	Slot Machines: . . . . .Yes
Original Cost: . . . .$400 million	Crew/Passenger Ratio	Swimming Pools (outdoors): . . . . .2+1
Entered Service: . . . . .Dec 2002	(lower beds/all berths): 2.1/2.6	children's pool
Registry: . . . . .The Netherlands	Navigation Officers: . . . . .European	Swimming Pools (indoors): 1
Length (ft/m): 951.4/290.00	Cabins (total): 924	(indoor/outdoor)
Beam (ft/m): 105.6/32.25	Size Range (sq ft/m): 185.0–1,318.6/	Whirlpools: 5
Draft (ft/m): 25.5/7.80	17.1–122.5	Self-Service Launderette: . . . . .Yes
Propulsion/Propellers: . . . . .diesel-electric	Cabins (outside view): 788	Dedicated Cinema/Seats: Yes/170
(34,000 kW)/2 pods	Cabins (interior/no view): 136	Library: . . . . .Yes
(17.6 MW each)	Cabins (for one person): 0	Classification Society: . . .Lloyd's Register
Passenger Decks: 10	Cabins (with private balcony): 810	

OVERALL SCORE: 1,546 (OUT OF A POSSIBLE 2,000 POINTS)

OVERVIEW. *Zuiderdam* (sister to *Oosterdam* and *Westerdam*) shares a common platform and hull shape (*Zuiderdam* is pronounced Zider-dam), and is designed to appeal to younger, more vibrant, multi-generational family-oriented passengers. There are two funnels, placed close together, one in front of the other, and not side by side as aboard the smaller *Amsterdam* and *Rotterdam*. This placement is the result of the slightly unusual machinery configuration. The ship has, in effect, two engine rooms – one with three diesels, and one with two diesels and a gas turbine. A pod propulsion *(see page 151 for definition)* is provided, powered by a diesel-electric system, with a small gas turbine located in the funnel for the reduction of emissions.

A complete wrap-around exterior promenade deck is enjoyed by many. Exterior glass elevators, mounted midships on both port and starboard sides, provide fine ocean views. There are two centrally located swimming pools outdoors, and one of the pools can be used in poor weather due to its retractable magrodome (glass dome) cover. Two whirlpool tubs, adjacent to the swimming pools, are abridged by a bar. Another smaller pool is provided for children.

When you first walk into the ship's interior, you'll be greeted by the size of the lobby space that spans eight decks. The atrium lobby, with its two grand stairways, has a stunning wall decoration that is best seen from any of the multiple viewing balconies on each deck above the main lobby floor level. Alternatively, you could take a drink from the lobby bar and look upwards – the surroundings are quite stunning. In keeping with the traditions of Holland America Line, there is a large collection of artwork. The decor is

BERLITZ'S RATINGS

	Possible	Achieved
Ship	500	430
Accommodation	200	163
Food	400	283
Service	400	280
Entertainment	100	77
Cruise	400	313

extremely bright for a Holland America Line ship, and a rather eclectic mix of colors and patterns assails you from all directions.

There are two entertainment/public room decks, the upper of which has an exterior promenade deck – something new for this traditional cruise line. Although it doesn't go around the whole ship, it's long enough to do some serious walking on. Additionally, there is also a jogging track outdoors, located around the mast and the forward third of the ship.

The most dramatic public room is the Queens Lounge, the ship's showlounge; it spans three decks in the forward section of the ship. The main floor level has a bar in its starboard aft section. Other facilities include a winding shopping street with boutique stores and logo shops.

The casino is large (one has to walk through it to get from the restaurant to the showlounge), and this is equipped with all the gaming paraphernalia and array of slot machines you can think of – all designed, of course, to entertain you while you are relieved of your money.

Children have KidZone (an indoor/outdoor facility), and Cub Hal for ages 5–12 (sleepovers aren't allowed, though), with dedicated youth counselors. Teenagers get to use WaveRunner, which includes a dance floor, special lighting effects, and booming sound system. There's also a video game room, and big-screen television for movies.

The information desk in the lobby is small in comparison to the size of the lobby. Many of the private balconies are not so private, and can be overlooked from various public locations. Many pillars obstruct the passenger flow and lines of sight throughout the ship. Communication (in English) with many of the staff, particularly in the dining room and buffet areas, can prove very frustrating. It may be difficult to escape from smokers, and people walking around in unsuitable clothing, clutching plastic sport drinks bottles.

ACCOMMODATION. There are 19 price grades. In keeping with industry trends, there are more cabins with private balconies than aboard any other Holland America Line ship. **Penthouse Verandah Suites:** The largest accommodation (1,126 sq. ft/104.6 sq. meters) is in two Penthouse Verandah Suites. These have a separate bedroom with a king-sized bed; there's also a walk-in closet, dressing room, living room, dining room, butler's pantry, mini-bar and refrigerator, and private balcony (verandah). The main bathroom has a large whirlpool bathtub, two washbasins, toilet, and plenty of storage space for personal toiletries. Personalized stationery and complimentary dry cleaning are included, as are hot hors d'oeuvres and other goodies daily. **DeLuxe Verandah Suites:** Next in size are 60 DeLuxe Verandah Suites (563 sq. ft/52.3 sq. meters). These have twin beds that can convert to a king-sized bed, vanity desk, lounge area, walk-in closet, mini-bar and refrigerator, and bathroom with full-sized tub, washbasin and toilet. Personalized stationery and complimentary dry cleaning are included, as are hot hors d'oeuvres daily and other goodies. **Verandah Suites:** There are 100 of these (actually they are cabins, not suites, and measure 284 sq. ft/26.3 sq. meters). Twin beds can convert to a queen-sized bed; there is also a lounge area, mini-bar and refrigerator, while the bathroom has a tub, washbasin and toilet. Floor-to-ceiling windows open onto a private balcony (verandah). **Outside-view Cabins:** Standard outside cabins (197 sq. ft/18.3 sq. meters) have twin beds that convert to make a queen-sized bed. There's a small sitting area, while the bathroom has a bathtub/shower combination. The interior (no view) cabins are slightly smaller, at 182.9 sq ft/17 sq. meters.

A number of cabins on the lowest accommodation deck (Main Deck) have views obstructed by lifeboats. Some cabins that can accommodate a third and fourth person have very little closet space, and there's only one personal safe. There is no separate radio in each cabin – instead, audio channels are provided on the in-cabin TV system.

Each morning, an eight-page *New York Times* (Times Fax) is provided for each cabin. Fresh fruit is available on request, shoe shine service, and evening turndown service are also provided, as is a small range of bathroom toiletries including shampoo, bath and facial soaps, and body lotion.

CUISINE/DINING. The Vista (main) Dining Room, with smoking and no-smoking sections, is two decks high, and is quite stunning. Located at the stern, it seats 1,045. It is traditional Holland America Line in its operation, with friendly service from smiling Indonesian stewards, and has Rosenthal china (but no fish knives). There are four seatings for dinner (you must pre-select a time and stick with it), at 5.45pm, 6.15pm, 8pm and 8.30pm), open seating for breakfast and lunch. There are tables for two, four, six or eight.

The waiter stations in the dining room are noisy for anyone seated adjacent to them. Live music is provided for dinner each evening; once each cruise, a Dutch Dinner is featured (hats are provided), as is an Indonesian Lunch. "Lighter option" meals are always available for the nutrition-conscious and the weight-conscious.

Alternative Dining Option: The 130-seat Odyssey Restaurant is a slightly more upscale dining spot (with higher-quality ingredients and better presentation than in the larger main dining room). Located on Lower Promenade Deck, it fronts onto the second level of the atrium lobby. The cuisine is Pacific Northwest (with items such as sesame-crusted halibut with ginger-miso, Peking duck breast with blackberry sauce, premium quality steaks from hand-selected cuts of beef). Fine table settings, china and silverware are provided, as are leather-bound menus. The wine bar offers mostly American wines. Reservations are needed and there is a cover charge of $15 per person for service and gratuity.

Informal Eateries: For casual eating, there is an extensive Lido Cafe, which form an eatery that wraps around the funnel housing and extends aft; there are also some fine views over the ship's central multi-deck atrium. It includes a pizzeria counter, a salad bar, Asian stir-fry counter, deli sandwiches, and a separate dessert buffet, although movement around the buffet area is very slow (particularly at peak times, such as in the mornings in port before shore excursions), and requires you to stand in line for everything.

Additionally, there is an outdoor self-serve buffet (adjacent to the fantail pool), which serves fast-food items such as hamburgers and hot dogs, chicken and fries. There are two smaller buffets adjacent to the midships swimming pool area, and a Windsurf Cafe in the atrium lobby (open 20 hours a day), for pastries, snack foods, deli sandwiches and liqueur coffees (evenings only).

ENTERTAINMENT. The 1,045-seat Vista Lounge is the principal venue for Las Vegas-style revue shows and major cabaret presentations. It spans three decks in the forward section of the ship. The main floor level has a bar in its starboard aft section. Spiral stairways at the back of the lounge connect all levels. Stage shows are best seen from the upper levels, from where the sightlines are quite good.

SPA/FITNESS. The Greenhouse Spa is a large, two-decks-high health spa, located directly above the navigation bridge. Facilities include a solarium, unisex thermal suite – a unisex area incorporating a Laconium (gentle sauna), Hamman (mild steam), and Camomile Grotto (small aromatic steam room). There's also a beauty parlor, 11 massage/therapy rooms (including one for couples), and a large gymnasium with floor-to-ceiling windows on three sides and forward-facing ocean views, and the latest high-tech muscle-toning equipment.

● **For more extensive general information on what a Holland America Line cruise is like, see pages 118–122.**

Practical Information

BOOKING AND BUDGETING

Is it better to book cruises directly or through a travel agent?
And what hidden extras should you look for when calculating costs?

Booking Direct

In the 1960s, about 90% of all cruises were booked by passengers directly with cruise lines and about 10% were booked by travel agents. Then along came some enterprising travel agents. They saw a golden opportunity and started to act on behalf of the cruise lines, who were happy to accept such bookings because they could then reduce staff and overheads in their sales/booking offices. Established companies such as American Express and Thomas Cook booked cruises, as did many others, and received a commission for doing so. During the 1970s, that percentage quickly reversed. Today, about 80% of all cruises are booked by travel agents, and about 20% are booked direct (including internet bookings). However, I fully expect that the number of passengers booking cruises direct will increase substantially over the next few years.

The Internet

While the Internet may be a good *resource* tool, it is not the place to book your cruise, unless you know *exactly* what you want. Questions cannot be asked, and most of the information provided by the cruise companies is strictly marketing hype. Most sites providing cruise ship reviews have something to sell, and the sound-byte information provided can be misleading. Fewer than 5% of cruise bookings are made through the internet.

The Internet vs Travel Agents

So, you've found a discounted rate for your cruise on the net. That's fine. But, if a cruise line suddenly offers special discounts for your sailing, or cabin upgrades, or things go wrong with your booking, your internet booking service may prove very unfriendly. Your travel agent, however, can probably work magic in making those special discounts work for *you*. It's called personal service.

Travel Agents

Travel agents do not generally charge for their services, although they earn a commission from cruise lines. Consider a travel agent as your business advisor, not just a ticket agent. He/she will handle all matters relevant to your booking and should have the latest information on changes of itinerary, cruise fares, fuel surcharges, discounts, and any other related items, including insurance in case you have to cancel prior to sailing. Most travel agents are linked into cruise line computer systems and have access to most shipboard information.

There is *no* "Best Cruise Line in the World" or "Best

Cruise Ship" — only the ship and cruise that's right for *you*. Your travel agent should find exactly the *right ship* for *your needs* and *lifestyle*. Some sell only a limited number of cruises and are known as "preferred suppliers," because they receive special "overrides" on top of their normal commission (they probably know their limited number of ships well, however).

If *you* have chosen a ship and cruise, be firm and book exactly what you want, or change agencies. In the UK, look for a member of the Guild of Professional Cruise Agents. PSARA (Passenger Shipping Association of Retail Agents) provides in-depth agent training in the UK, as well as a full "bonding" scheme to protect passengers from failed cruise lines. In the US, look for a CLIA (Cruise Lines International Association) affiliated agency.

Questions to Ask a Travel Agent

● Is air transportation included in the cabin rate quoted? If not, what will be the extra cost?
● What other extra costs will be involved? These can include port charges, insurance, gratuities, shore excursions, laundry, and drinks.
● What is the cruise line's cancellation policy?
● If I want to make changes to my flight, routing, dates, and so on, will the insurance policy cover everything in case of missed or canceled flights?
● Does your agency deal with only one, or several different insurance companies?
● Does the cruise line offer advance booking discounts or other incentives?
● Do you have preferred suppliers, or do you book any cruise on any cruise ship?
● Have you sailed aboard the ship I want to book, or that you are recommending?
● Is your agency bonded and insured? If so, by whom?
● If you book the shore excursions offered by the cruise line, is insurance coverage provided?

Reservations

Do plan ahead and book early. After choosing a ship, cruise, date, and cabin, you pay a deposit that is roughly 10 percent for long cruises, 20 percent for short cruises (most cruise lines ask for a set amount). The balance is normally payable 45 to 60 days before departure. For a late reservation, you pay in full when space is confirmed (when booking via the internet, for example). Cruise lines reserve the right to change prices in the event of tax increases, fluctuating rates of exchange, fuel surcharges, or other costs beyond their control.

When you make your reservation, also make special dining requests known: seating preference, smoking or

---

LEFT: Windjammer Barefoot Cruises' *Mandalay*.

nonsmoking sections. It's useful to keep a note of them.

After the line has received full payment, your cruise ticket will be sent. Check all documents. Make sure the ship, date, and cruise details are correctly noted. Verify connecting flight times that seem suspiciously short.

Extra Costs

Cruise brochures boldly proclaim that "almost everything's included," but in most cases you will find this is not strictly true. In fact, for some cruises "all-exclusive" would be a more appropriate term. In the aftermath of the September 11, 2001, terrorist attacks in the USA, many cruise lines cut their fares dramatically in order to attract business. At the same time, the cost of many onboard items went up. So allow for extra onboard costs.

Your fare covers the ship as transportation, your cabin, meals, entertainment, activities, and service on board; it typically does not include alcoholic beverages, laundry, dry cleaning or valet services, shore excursions, meals ashore, gratuities, port charges, cancellation insurance, optional onboard activities such as gambling.

Expect to spend about $25 a day per person on extras, plus another $10–$12 a day per person in gratuities. Genuine exceptions can be found in some small ships

Typical Extra-cost Items
'Alternative' dining (cover charge) ...$15–$25 a person
Baby-sitting (per hour) $5
Bottled water ....$2.50–$7 (per bottle)
Cappuccino/espresso....................................$1.75–$3
Cartoon character bedtime "tuck-In" service..........$20
Wash one shirt..$1.50–$3
Dry-clean dress ....$3–$7.50
Dry-clean jacket ....$4–$8
Golf simulator ....$15 (30 minutes)
Group bicycling class ....$10 per class
Hair wash/set ....$20–$40
Haircut (men) $20
Ice cream ....$1–$3.75
In-cabin movies....................................$6.95–$12.95
Kick-boxing class...............................$10 per class
Laundry soap...$1–$1.50
Massage ....$1.50-plus a minute (plus tip)
Pottery class $40
Satellite phone/fax ....$4.95–$15 per minute
Send/receive e-mails ....$0.75 per minute
Sodas (soft drinks)..$1–$2
Souvenir photograph (8" by 6")......................$10–$12
Souvenir photograph (10" by 8")..............$20–$27.50
Trapshooting (three or five shots) $5, $8
Tuxedo rental (7-day cruise)................................$85
Use of Aqua Spa (*Queen Mary 2*) ....$25 per day
Video postcard..................................$4.95–$6.95
Wine/cheese tasting ....$10–$15
Wine with dinner...$7–$500
Yoga class..$10 per class

(those with fewer than 500 passengers) where just about everything *is* included.

Calculate the total cost of your cruise (not including any extra-cost services you might decide you want once on board) with the help of your travel agent. Here are the approximate prices per person for a typical seven-day cruise aboard a well-rated mid-size or large cruise ship, based on an outside-view two-bed cabin:

Cruise fare	*$1,200*
Port charges	*$100 (if not included)*
Gratuities	*$50*
Total per person	*$1,350*

This comes to less than $200 per person per day. For this price, you wouldn't even get a decent hotel room, without meals, in London, New York, Tokyo, or Venice.

However, your 7-day cruise can become expensive when you start adding on a few extra touches. For example, add two flight-seeing excursions in Alaska (at about $250 each), two cappuccinos each a day ($25), a scotch and soda each a day ($35), a massage ($100), 7 mineral waters ($28), 30 minutes' access to the internet for emails ($15), three other assorted excursions ($120), and gratuities $50). That's an extra $838 – without even one bottle of wine with dinner! So a couple will need to add an extra $1,576 for a 7-day cruise (plus the cruise fare, of course, and the cost of getting to and from your local airport, or ship port).

Discounts and Incentives

Book ahead to get the best discounts (discounts decrease closer to the cruise date).

You may be able to reserve a cabin grade, but not a specific cabin — "tba" (to be assigned). Some lines will accept this arrangement and may even upgrade you. It is useful to know that the first cabins to be sold out are usually those at minimum and maximum rates. Note: Premium rates apply to Christmas/New Year cruises.

Cancellations and Refunds

Take out full cancellation insurance (if it is not included), as cruises (and air transportation to/from them) must be paid in full before your tickets are issued. Otherwise, if you cancel at the last minute (even for medical reasons) you could lose the whole fare. Insurance coverage can be obtained from your travel agent, and paying by credit card makes sense (you'll probably get your money back if the agency goes bust) or through the internet. Beware of policies sold by the cruise lines – they may well be no good if the cruise line goes out of business.

Cruise lines usually accept cancellations more than 30 days before sailing, but all charge full fare if you don't turn up on sailing day. Other cancellation fees depend on the cruise and length of trip. Many lines do not return port taxes, which are not part of the cruise fare.

Medical Insurance

Whether you intend to travel overseas or cruise down a local river, and your present medical insurance does not cover you, you should look into extra coverage for your cruise. A "passenger protection program" may be offered by the cruise line, the charge for which will appear on your final invoice, unless you decline. It is worth every penny, and it typically covers such things as evacuation by air ambulance, high-limit baggage, baggage transfers, personal liability, and missed departure.

Port Taxes/Handling Charges

These are assessed by individual port authorities and are usually shown in the brochure. Port charges form part of the final payment, although they can be changed right up to the day of embarkation.

Air/Sea Packages

When your cruise fare includes "free air" (as in a one-way or round-trip air ticket), note that airline arrangements usually cannot be changed without paying a premium, as cruise lines often book group space on aircraft to obtain the lowest rates.

If you do make changes, remember that, if the airline cancels your flight, the cruise line is under no obligation to help you or return your cruise fare if you don't reach the ship on time. If flying to a foreign country, allow extra time (particularly in winter) for flight delays and cancellations.

Airlines often use a "hub-and-spoke" system, which can prove frustrating. Because of changes to air schedules, cruise and air tickets may not be sent to passengers until a few days before the cruise.

In Europe, air/sea packages generally start at a major metropolitan airport; some include first-class rail travel from outlying districts. In the United States, many cruise lines include connecting flights from suburban airports as part of the package.

Most cruise lines allow you to jet out to join a ship in one port and fly home from another. An advantage is that you only have to check your baggage once at the departure airport. The baggage transfer from plane to ship is handled for you. This does not include intercontinental fly/ cruises, where you must claim your baggage at the airport on arrival to clear it though customs.

Travel Insurance

Although I have mentioned Cancellation and Medical Insurance already, it would be wise to further consider the following: cruise lines and travel agents routinely sell travel cover policies that, on close inspection, appear to wriggle out of payment due to a litany of exclusion clauses, most of which are never explained. Examples:
● "Pre-existing" medical conditions.
● "Valuables" left unattended on a tour bus (even though the tour guide says it is safe and that the driver will lock the door).

How to get the best travel insurance deal:
● Allow time to shop around and don't accept the first travel insurance policy you are offered.

● Read the contract carefully and make sure you know exactly what you are covered for.
● Beware of the "box ticking" approach to travel cover, which is often done quickly at the travel agent's office in lieu of providing expert advice. However, watch out for questions relating to "pre-existing medical conditions" as this little gem alone could cost you dearly. Insurers should not, in reality, be allowed to apply exclusions that have not been clearly pointed out to the policyholder.
● Do ask for a detailed explanation of all exclusions, excesses, and limitations.
● Check out the procedure you need to follow if you are the victim of a crime (such as your wallet or camera being stolen while on a shore excursion). Incidentally, if anything does happen, *always* obtain a police report as soon as possible. Note that many insurance policies will only reimburse you for the *secondhand* value of an item that has been lost or stolen, rather than the full cost of replacement. You will also probably be required to produce the original receipt for any such items claimed.
● Watch out for exclusions for "hazardous sports." These could include things typically offered as shore excursions aboard ships. Examples: horse riding (there goes that horse riding on the beach excursion in Jamaica) or cycling (mountain biking excursions in Alaska, Antigua or Rhodes, for example), jet skiing (most beaches), or ziplining (Hawaii).
● If you purchase travel cover over the internet, do check the credentials of the company that is underwriting the scheme. It is best to deal with well-established names, and not to take what appears to be the cheapest deal offered.

Guaranteed Singles Rates

Although some singles travel with friends or family, many others like to travel alone. For this reason, cruise lines have established several programs to accommodate them. One is the "Guaranteed Single" rate, which provides a set price without having to be concerned about which cabin to choose. Some cruise lines have guaranteed singles' rates, but the line and *not* the passenger picks the cabin. If the line does not find a roommate, the single passenger may get the cabin to himself/herself at no extra charge.

Guaranteed Share Programs

A "Guaranteed Share" program allows you to pay the normal double-occupancy rate, but the cruise line will find another passenger of the same sex to share the double cabin with you. Some cruise lines do not advertise a guaranteed-share program in their brochures but will often try to accommodate such bookings, particularly when demand for space is light. You could book a guaranteed share basis cabin only to find that you end up with a cabin to yourself. As cruise lines are apt to change such things at short notice, it is best to check with your travel agent for the latest rates, and read the fine print. ❑

DON'T LEAVE HOME WITHOUT...

Cruise ships are well stocked for most people's everyday needs,
but there are certain things you need to take with you

Baggage

There is generally no limit to the amount of personal baggage you can take on your cruise (towels, soap, shampoo, and shower caps are provided aboard most cruise ships). Do allow extra space for purchases on the cruise.

Tag all luggage with your name, ship, cabin number, sailing date, and port of embarkation (tags are provided with your tickets). Baggage transfers from airport to ship are generally smooth and problem-free when handled by the cruise line.

Liability for loss or damage to baggage is contained in the passenger contract (part of your ticket). Do take out insurance (the policy should extend from the date of departure until two or three days after your return home).

Clothing

If you think you might not wear it, don't take it, as closet space aboard many ships is at a premium. So, unless you are on an extended cruise, keep your luggage to a minimum.

For cruises to tropical areas, where the weather is warm to hot with high humidity, casual wear should include plenty of lightweight cottons and other natural fibers. Synthetic materials do not "breathe" as well and often retain heat. Clothes should be as opaque as possible to counteract the sun's ultraviolet rays. Take a lightweight cotton sweater or windbreaker for the evenings, when the ship's air-conditioning will seem even more powerful after a day in the sun. Pack sunglasses and a hat. Rainstorms in the tropics are infrequent and don't last long, but they can give you a good soaking, so take inexpensive, lightweight rainwear for excursions you go on.

The same is true for cruises to the Mediterranean, Greek Isles, or North Africa, although there will be little or no humidity for most of the year. Certain areas may be dusty as well as dry. In these latitudes, the weather can be changeable and cool in the evenings from October to March, so take extra sweaters and a windbreaker.

For cruises to Alaska, the North Cape, or the Norwegian fjords, take some warm comfortable clothing layers, plus a raincoat or parka for the northernmost port calls. Cruises to Alaska and the Land of the Midnight Sun are operated during the peak summer months, when temperatures are pleasant and the weather less likely to be poor.

Unless you are traveling to northern ports such as St. Petersburg in winter, you will not need thermal underwear. However, you will need thermal underwear, and thick socks – and heavy sweaters – if you take an adventure cruise to the Antarctic Peninsula or through the Northwest Passage.

In destinations with a strong religious tradition, like Venezuela, Haiti, the Dominican Republic, Colombia, and countries in the Far East, shorts or bare shoulders may cause offense, so cover up.

Aboard ship, dress rules are relaxed by day, but in the evening what you wear should be tasteful. Men should take a blazer or sports jacket and ties for the dining room and for any "informal" occasions. Transatlantic crossings are normally more elegant and require formal attire.

For formal nights (usually two out of seven), women can wear a long evening gown, elegant cocktail dress, or a smart pants suit. Gentlemen are expected to wear either a tuxedo or dark business suit and tie. These "rules" are less rigid on short and moderately priced cruises. If you are the athletic type, pack sportswear (and gym shoes) for the gymnasium or aerobics classes.

No matter where you are going, comfortable low- or flat-heeled shoes are a must for women, except for formal nights. Light, airy walking shoes are best for walking. If you are in the Caribbean or Pan-Pacific region and you are not used to heat and humidity, your ankles may swell, so tight shoes are not recommended. Rubber soles are best for walking on the deck of a ship.

Formal: Tuxedo, dinner jacket or dark suit for men; evening gown or other appropriate formal attire for women.

Informal: Jacket and tie for men; cocktail dress, dressy pantsuit, or the like for women.

Casual (Elegant): While this is an oxymoron, it generally means long trousers (no shorts or jeans), proper collared and sleeved shirt (gentlemen); skirt or slacks and top for women.

Casual (Relaxed): Slacks over sweater or open shirt (no tie) for men (no beach wear or muscle shirts); a blouse with skirt, slacks, or similar comfortable attire for women. Shoes are required.

Documents

A passport is the most practical proof of your citizenship and identification. Visas are required for some countries (allow time to obtain these). On most cruises, you will hand in your passport to the purser on embarkation (it would be wise to keep a photostat of the main pages with you). This helps the ship to clear customs and immigration inspection on arrival in ports of call. It will be returned before you reach the port of disembarkation.

Flying...and Jet Lag

Several cruise lines have "air deviation" desks that allow you to change your flights and connections, for an fee (typically $25–$50 per person).

Air travel today is fast and efficient. But even experienced travelers find that the stress of international travel can persist long after the flight is over. Eastbound flights tend to cause more pronounced jet lag than westbound flights. Jet aircraft are generally pressurized to some 8,000 ft (2,400 meters) in altitude, causing discomfort in the ears and the stomach, and swollen feet. A few precautions should reduce the less pleasant effects of flying around the world. Plan as far in advance of your cruise as possible. Take a daytime flight, so that you can arrive at, or close to, your normal bedtime. Try to be as quiet as possible before flying, and allow for another five hours of rest after any flight that crosses more than five time zones.

Note: Babies and small children are less affected by changes in time because of their shorter sleeping and waking cycles. But adults generally need more time to adjust.

Medication

Take any medicine and other medical supplies that you need, plus spare eyeglasses or contact lenses. In many countries it may be difficult to find cer-

tain medicines. Others may be sold under different names. If you are taking a long cruise, ask your doctor for names of alternatives.

The ship's pharmacy will stock certain standard remedies, but do not expect a supply of the more unusual or obscure medicines. Remember to take along a doctor's prescription for any medication.

Also, be advised that if you run out of your medication and you need to get a supply aboard ship, most ships will require that you see the doctor, even if you have a prescription. There is a charge for each visit, plus the cost of any medication.

Let spouses/companions carry a supply of your medicine and medical supplies. Do not pack medication in any luggage to be checked in when flying, but take it in your carry-on.

Money Matters

Most ships operate primarily in US dollars or euros, but a few use other currencies (check with your travel agent or supplier). Major credit cards and traveler's checks are accepted on board (few lines take personal checks). You sign for drinks and other services, as part of "cashless cruising." Some large resort ships have ATM cash machines (although a "transaction fee" is assessed).

Pets

Pets are not allowed aboard cruise ships, with one exception: the regular transatlantic crossings aboard Cunard Line's *Queen Mary 2*, continuing the tradition of the *QE2*, which had air-conditioned kennels (plus a genuine British lamppost and New York fire hydrant) and cat containers. (The kennels were not in use during the *QM2*'s first crossings in 2004 because Cunard was assessing demand prior to introducing them.)

Photography

Use low-speed film in tropical areas such as the Caribbean or South Pacific (high-speed film is easily damaged by heat). Take plenty of film with you; standard sizes are available in the ship's shop, but the selection will be limited, particularly if you use slide film. If you buy film during a port visit, try to obtain it from an air-conditioned store, and check the expiration date.

Keep film cool, as the latent image on exposed film is fragile and easily affected by heat. There will be professional photographers on board who may develop print film for you, for a fee.

When taking photographs in ports of call, respect the wishes of local inhabitants. Ask permission to photograph someone close-up. Most will smile and tell you to go ahead. But some people are superstitious or afraid of having their picture taken and will shy away from you. Do not press the point. ❏

SIX FIRSTS

- In 1903 the British liner *Lucania* became the first ship to acquire wireless equipment, which enabled it to keep in touch with both sides of the Atlantic Ocean at the same time.
- The first ship-to-shore wireless telegraphy took place on the American passenger ship *St. Paul* in 1899.
- The first twin-screw passenger ship was the Compagnie Générale Transatlantique's 3,200-ton *Washington*, built in 1863 and converted in 1868.
- The first floating eclipse expedition was led by the US astronomer Ted Pedas in 1972, when 800 passengers sailed to a spectacular rendezvous with a total sun eclipse in the North Atlantic.
- The first passenger ship to exceed 80,000 tons was the Compagnie Générale Transatlantique's *Normandie*, which measured at 82,799 tons in 1936.
- The first gravity lifeboats were installed aboard the Compagnie Générale Transatlantique's *Ile de France* in 1928.

WHAT TO EXPECT

If you've never been on a cruise before, here is what you need

to know about a typical initial embarkation process

Testing the waters by taking your first cruise? Make sure sure you have your passport and any visas required (in some countries – such as the People's Republic of China, or Russia – you might go ashore on organized excursions under a group visa). Pack any medication you may need, and advise family members and friends where you are going.

You already have been sent your cruise tickets and documents by the cruise line or your travel agent. A typical document package might include:

- Air ticket
- Cruise ticket
- Luggage tags
- Embarkation card (to fill out before you get to the embarkation point)
- Discount coupons for the shops on board
- Bon Voyage gift selection form
- Shore excursion brochure
- Onboard credit account form
- Guide to services on board (including e-mail)
- Ship's telephone and fax contact numbers
- Coupon for tuxedo rental

Assume that you've arrived at the airport closest to your ship's embarkation point, and retrieved your luggage. It is probable that there will be a representative from the cruise line waiting, holding aloft the company's sign. You will be asked to place your luggage in a cluster together with those of other passengers. The next time you see your luggage should be aboard your ship, where it will be delivered to your cabin.

Go to the registration (check-in) area in the terminal building. For the large resort ships, numerous desks will be set up. Go to the desk that displays the first letter of your surname, wait in line (having filled out all embarkation, registration, and immigration documents), and then check in. If your accommodation is designated as a "suite," there should be a separate check-in facility (sometimes called gold card service).

If you are cruising from a US port and you are a non-US citizen or "Resident Alien," you will go to a separate desk to check in (*Note*: Do not buy duty-free liquor to take on board – it will not be allowed by the cruise line and will be confiscated until the last day of the cruise). You will be asked for your passport, which you deposit with the check-in personnel (be sure to ask for a receipt – it is, after all, a valuable document, and preferably have a photostat of the main pages to keep with you). If you are cruising from any other port in the world that is not a US port, be advised that each country has its own check-in requirements, setups, and procedures (passport control and inspection, for example).

Documents in hand, you will probably go through a security-screening device, for both your person and hand luggage (just like at airports). Next, you'll walk a few paces towards the gangway. This may be a covered, airport-type gangway, or an open one (hopefully with a net underneath it in case you drop something over the side). The gangway could be flat, or you may have to walk up (or down) an incline, depending on the location of the gangway, the tide, or other local conditions.

As you approach the gangway you will probably be greeted by the ship's photographers, a snap-happy team ready to take your photograph, bedraggled as you may appear after having traveled for hours. If you do not want your photograph taken, say "no" firmly, and proceed.

Once on the gangway, you will feel a heightened sense of anticipation. At the ship end of the gangway, you will find a decorated (hopefully) entrance and the comfortable feel of air-conditioning if the weather is hot. The ship's cruise staff will welcome you aboard. Give them your cabin number, and a steward should magically appear to take your carry-on luggage from you and take you directly to your cabin. At last you've arrived.

The door to your cabin should be open. If it is locked, ask the steward to obtain the key to open the door. Aboard the newest ships, you will probably be handed an electronically coded key card. Once inside the cabin, take a good look. Is it clean? Is it tidy? Are the beds properly made? Check under them to make sure the floor is clean (on one cruise I found a pair of red ladies shoes, but, alas, no lady to go with them). Make sure there is ice in the ice container. Check the bathroom, bathtub (if there is one), or shower. Make sure there are towels and soap. If all is clean and shipshape, fine.

If there are problems, bring them to the attention of your cabin steward immediately. Or call the purser's office (or reception desk), and explain the problem, then quietly, but firmly request that someone in a supervisory position see you to resolve it. The housekeeping in cruise ships is generally very good, but sometimes when "turnaround" time is tight, when passengers disembark in the morning and new passengers embark in the afternoon, little things get overlooked. They shouldn't, of course, but they do (just as in any hotel ashore).

One thing you also should do immediately is to remember the telephone number for the ship's hospital, doctor, or for medical emergencies, just so you know how to call for help if any medical emergency should arise.

Your luggage probably will not have arrived yet (if it is a ship carrying more than 500 passengers) so don't sit in the cabin waiting for it. Put your hand luggage away somewhere, and, deck plan in hand, take a walk.

Familiarize yourself with the layout of the ship. Learn which way is forward, which way is aft, and how to reach your cabin from the main stairways. This is also a good time to learn how to get from your cabin to the outside decks in an emergency. A Passenger Lifeboat Drill typically takes place *before* the ship sails. Regulations dictate that a drill *must* take place within 24 hours after the ship sails from the embarkation port.

After the drill (you'll find your lifejacket in the cabin and directions to your assembly station will be posted on the back of the cabin door), you can take off the lifejacket and *relax*. By now, your luggage probably will have arrived.

Unpack, then go out on deck just before the ship sails. It's always a magical moment, and a good time to meet some new faces. You'll soon be ready for that first night's dinner. It is simply amazing how the sea air gives you an appetite. ❑

CRUISE LINES BY MARKET CLASSIFICATION

Although there are four fairly distinctive divisions of cruise lines and their ships, some blurring between these divisions has occurred as companies have responded to changing passenger tastes and to the tougher market conditions created by the threat of international terrorism.

UTTERLY EXCLUSIVE
Hapag-Lloyd Cruises (5)
SeaDream Yacht Club

LUXURY
Crystal Cruises (4)
Cunard Line (4)
Hebridean Island Cruises (6)
Sea Cloud Cruises
Seabourn Cruise Line
Seven Seas Cruises (4)
Silversea Cruises

PREMIUM
Abercrombie & Kent
Asuka Cruise (NYK)
Celebrity Cruises
Club Mediterranée Cruises
Holland America Line
Lindblad Expeditions
Noble Caledonia
Ponant Cruises
Quark Expeditions
Saga Cruises
Society Expeditions
Swan Hellenic Cruises
Venus Cruise (Japan Cruise Line)
Windstar Cruises

STANDARD
Aida Cruises (3)
American Canadian Caribbean
  Line
American Cruise Lines
Carnival Cruise Lines
Canodros
Classic International Cruises (2)
Clipper Cruise Line
Costa Cruises
Cruise West
Delphin Seereisen
Disney Cruise Line
easyCruise
Elegant Cruises & Tours
First Choice Cruises
Fred Olsen Cruise Lines
Galapagos Cruises
Glacier Bay Cruiseline
Golden Star Cruises
Hansa Touristik
Hapag-Lloyd Cruises (4)
Holiday Cruises
Imperial Majesty Cruise Line
Island Cruises
Kleintours
Kristina Cruises
Louis Cruise Lines

MSC Italian Cruises
Majestic International Cruises
Mano Maritime
Mare Nostrum Cruises
Mitsui OSK Passenger Line
NCL America
New Paradise Cruises
Noble Caledonia
Norwegian Cruise Line
Orient Lines
P&O Cruises
P&O Cruises (Australia)
Phoenix Seereisen
Plantours & Partner
Princess Cruises
Pullmantur Cruises
Royal Caribbean International
Royal Olympia Cruises
Seetours (3)
Spanish Cruise Line
Star Cruises
Star Clippers
Star Line Cruises
Thomson Cruises
Transocean Tours
Travelplan Cruises
Viajes Iberojet
Windjammer Barefoot Cruises

Notes:
(1) This company operates under different brand
    names in Europe and North America.
(2) These companies are one and the same.
(3) Aida Cruises is marketed by Seetours

(4) This company has ships and onboard products that
    straddle the line between Luxury and Premium.
(5) *Europa* only
(6) *Hebridean Spirit* only

WHAT TO DO IF...

Twenty practical tips for a good cruise experience

❶ Your luggage does not arrive at the ship.
If you are part of the cruise line's air/sea package, the airline is wholly responsible for locating your luggage and delivering it to the next port. If you arranged your own air transportation it is wholly *your* problem. Always keep easy-to-read name and address tags both *inside* as well as *outside* your luggage. Keep track of claim documents and give the airline a detailed itinerary and list of port agents (usually included with your documents).

❷ *You* miss the ship.
If you miss the ship's departure (due to late or non-performing flight connections, etc), and you are traveling on an air/sea package, the airline will arrange to get you to the ship. If you are traveling "cruise-only," however, and have arranged your own air transportation, then *you* are responsible for onward flights, hotel stays, and transfers. Many cruise lines now have "deviation" desks, where (for a fee) you can adjust airline flights and dates to suit personal preferences. If you arrive at the port just as your ship is pulling away, see the ship's port agent immediately.

❸ Your cabin is too small.
Almost all cruise ship cabins are too small (I am convinced that some are designed for packages rather than people). When you book a cruise, you pay for a certain category and type of cabin but have little or no control over which one you actually get. See the hotel manager as soon as possible and explain what is wrong with the cabin (noisy, too hot, etc). If the ship is full (most are nowadays), it will be difficult to change. However, the hotel manager will probably try to move you from known problem cabins, although they are not required to do so.

❹ Your cabin has no air-conditioning, it is noisy, or there are plumbing problems.
If there is anything wrong in your cabin, or if there is something wrong with the plumbing in your bathroom, bring it to the attention of your cabin steward immediately. If nothing gets better, complain to the hotel manager. Some cabins, for example, are located above the ship's laundry, generator, or galley (hot); others may be above the disco (noisy). If the ship is full, it may be difficult to change.

❺ You have noisy cabin neighbors.
First, politely tell your neighbors that you can hear them brushing their hair as the cabin walls are so thin, and would they please not bang the drawers shut at 2am! If that does not work, complain to the purser or hotel manager, and ask them to attend to the problem.

❻ You have small children and the brochure implied that the ship has special programs for them, but when on board you find out it is not an all-year-round program.
In this instance, either the brochure was misleading, or your travel agent did not know enough about the ship or did not bother to ask the right questions. If you have genuine cause for complaint, then see your travel agent when you get home. Most ships generally will try to accommodate your young ones (the large resort ships – those carrying more than 1,200 passengers – have more facilities), but may not be covered by their insurance for "looking after" them throughout the day, as the brochure seemed to promise. Again, check thoroughly with your travel agent *before* you book.

❼ You do not like your dining room seating.
Most "standard" market ships operate two seatings for dinner (sometimes this applies to all meals). When you book your cruise, you are asked whether you want the first or second seating. The line will make every attempt to please you. But if you want second seating and are given first seating (perhaps a large group has taken over the entire second seating, or the ship is full), there may be little the restaurant manager can do.

❽ You want a table for two and are put at a table for eight.
Again, see the restaurant manager and explain why you are not satisfied. A little gratuity should prove helpful.

❾ You cannot communicate with your dining room waiter.
Dining room waiters are probably of a nationality and tongue completely foreign to yours, and all they can do is smile. This could prove frustrating for a whole cruise, especially if you need something out of the ordinary. See the restaurant manager, and tell him you want a waiter with whom

you can communicate. If he does not solve the problem, see the hotel manager.

⑩ The food is definitely not "gourmet" cuisine as advertised in the brochure.
If the food is not as described (for example, whole lobster in the brochure, but only cold lobster salad once during the cruise, or the "fresh squeezed" orange juice on the breakfast menu is anything but), inform the maître d' of the problem.

⑪ A large group has taken over the ship.
Sometimes, large groups have blocked (pre-booked) several public rooms for meetings (seemingly every hour on the hour in the rooms you want to use). This means the individual passenger (that is you) becomes a second-class citizen. Make your displeasure known to the hotel manager immediately, tell your travel agent, and write a follow-up letter to the line when you return home.

⑫ A port of call is deleted from the itinerary.
If you only took the cruise because the ship goes to the place you have wanted to go for years, then read the fine print in the brochure *before* you book. A cruise line is under *no* obligation to perform the stated itinerary. For whatever reason (political unrest, weather, mechanical problems, no berth space, safety, etc.), the ship's captain has the ultimate say.

⑬ You are unwell aboard ship.
Do not worry. There will be a qualified doctor (who generally operates as a concession, and therefore charges) and medical facilities, including a small pharmacy. You will be well taken care of. Although there are charges for medical services rendered, almost all cruise lines offer insurance packages that include medical coverage for most eventualities. It is wise to take out this insurance when you book.

⑭ You have a problem with a crew member.
Go to the hotel manager or chief purser and explain the problem (for single women this could be a persistent cabin steward with a master door key). No one will do anything unless you complain. Cruise ships try to hire decent staff, but, with so many crew, there are bound to be a few bad apples. Insist on a full written report of the incident, which must be entered into the ship's daily log by the staff captain (deputy captain).

⑮ You leave some personal belongings on a tour bus.
If you find you have left something on a tour bus, and you are back on board your ship, the first thing to do is advise the shore excursion manager or the purser's office. The shore excursion manager will contact the tour operator ashore to ascertain whether any items have been handed in to their office.

⑯ The cruise line's air arrangements have you flying from Los Angeles via Timbuktu to get to your cruise ship.
Fine if your cruise ship is in Timbuktu (difficult, as it is inland). Most cruise lines that have low rates also use the cheapest air routing to get you to your ship. That could mean flights from a central hub. Be warned: you get what you pay for. Ask questions *before* you book.

⑰ You fly internationally to take a cruise.
If your cruise is a long distance away from your home, then it usually makes good sense to fly to your cruise embarkation point and stay for at least a day or two before the cruise. Why? Because you will be better rested and you will have time to adjust to any time changes. You will step aboard your ship already relaxed and ready for a real vacation.

⑱ The ship's laundry ruins your clothes.
If any of your clothing is ruined or discolored by the ship's laundry, first tell your cabin steward(ess), and then follow up by going to the purser's office and getting it registered as a proper complaint. Take a copy of the complaint with you, so you can follow up when you get home. Unfortunately, you will probably find a disclaimer on the laundry list saying something to the effect that liability is limited to about $1 per item, which is not a lot. So, although the laundry and dry cleaning facilities generally work well, things can occasionally go wrong just like ashore.

⑲ You have extra charges on your bill.
Check your itemized bill carefully. Then talk to the purser's office and ask them to show you the charge slips. Finally, make sure you are given a copy of your bill, *after* any modifications have been made.

⑳ You're unhappy with your cruise experience.
You (or your travel agent) ultimately choose the ship and cruise. But if your ship does not meet your specific lifestyle and interests, or the ship performs less well than the brochure promises, then let your travel agent and the cruise line know as soon as possible. If your grievance is valid, many cruise lines will offer a credit, good towards a future cruise. But do be sure to read the fine print on the ticket. ❑

WHERE TO FIND THE MAJOR CRUISE LINES

NORTH AMERICA

Abercrombie & Kent
1520 Kensington Road
Oak Brook
IL 60523-2141. USA
www.aandktours.com

**American Canadian
Caribbean Line**
461 Water Street
Warren
RI 02885. USA
www.accl-smallships.com

American Cruise Lines
One Marine Park, Haddam
CT 06438. USA
www.americancruiselines.com

Carnival Cruise Lines
3655 NW 87 Avenue
Miami
FL 33178-2428. USA
www.carnival.com

Celebrity Cruises
1050 Port Boulevard
Miami
FL 33124. USA
www.celebrity-cruises.com

**Classical Cruises/Travel
Dynamics International**
132 East 70 Street
New York
NY 10021. USA
www.classicalcruises.com

Clipper Cruise Line
7711 Bonhomme Avenue
St. Louis
MO 63105. USA
www.clippercruise.com

Club Med Cruises
75 Valencia Ave.
Coral Gables
FL 33134. USA
www.clubmed.com

Costa Cruises
World Trade Center
80 SW 8 Street, 27th Floor
Miami

FL 33130-3097. USA
www.costacruises.com

Cruise West
2401 Fourth Avenue, Suite 700
Seattle
WA 98121-1438. USA
www.cruisewest.com

Crystal Cruises
2049 Century Park East,
Suite 1400, Los Angeles
CA 90067. USA
www.crystalcruises.com

Cunard Line
6100 Blue Lagoon Drive,
Suite 400
Miami
FL 33126. USA
www.cunard.com

Discovery World Cruises
1850 Eller Drive, Suite 402
Ft. Lauderdale
FL 33316, USA
www.discoveryworldcruises.com

Disney Cruise Line
210 Celebration Place,
Suite 400
Celebration
FL 33747-4600. USA
www.disney.com/
DisneyCruise

Elegant Cruises & Tours
24 Vanderventer Avenue
Port Washington
NY 10050. USA
www.elegantcruises.com

Glacier Bay Cruiseline
107 West Denny Way,
Suite 303, Seattle
WA 98101. USA
www.glacierbaytours.com

Holland America Line
300 Elliott Avenue West
Seattle
WA 98119. USA
www.hollandamerica.com

Lindblad Expeditions
720 Fifth Avenue, Suite 605
New York
NY 10019. USA
www.expeditions.com

MSC Italian Cruises
6750 North Andrews Avenue
Fort Lauderdale
FL 33309. USA
www.msccruisesusa.com

Norwegian Coastal Voyages
405 Park Avenue
New York
NY 10022. USA
www.coastalvoyage.com

**Norwegian Cruise Line/
NCL America**
7665 Corporate Center Drive
Miami
FL 33126. USA
www.ncl.com

Oceania Cruises
8120 NW 53rd Street,
Suite 100
Miami, FL 33166. USA
www.oceaniacruises.com

Orient Lines
7665 Corporate Center Drive
Miami
FL 33126. USA
www.orientlines.com

Princess Cruises
24305 Town Center Drive
Santa Clarita
CA 91355-4999. USA
www.princesscruises.com

Quark Expeditions
980 Post Road
Darien
CT 06820. USA
www.quark-expeditions.com

Radisson Seven Seas Cruises
600 Corporate Drive, Suite 410
Ft. Lauderdale
FL 33180. USA
www.rssc.com

Royal Caribbean International
1050 Caribbean Way
Miami
FL 33132-2096. USA
www.royalcaribbean.com

Royal Olympia Cruises
One Rockefeller Plaza
New York
NY 10020. USA
www.royalolympiacruises.com

Seabourn Cruise Line
6100 Blue Lagoon Drive
Suite 400, Miami
FL 33126. USA
www.seabourn.com

SeaDream Yacht Club
2601 South Bayshore Drive,
Penthouse 1B
Coconut Grove
FL 33133, USA
seadreamyachtclub.com

Silversea Cruises
110 E. Broward Boulevard
Suite 300
Ft. Lauderdale
FL 33301. USA
www.silversea.com

Star Clippers
4101 Salzedo Avenue
Coral Gables
FL 33146. USA
www.star-clippers.com

Windjammer Barefoot Cruises
1759 Bay Road
Miami Beach
FL 33119. USA
www.windjammer.com

Windstar Cruises
300 Elliott Avenue West
Seattle
WA 98119. USA
www.windstarcruises.com

REST OF THE WORLD

Aida Cruises
Am Seehafen 1
Siemenstrasse 90
63203 New Isenberg
GERMANY
www.aida.de

Canodros
Guayaquil
Ecuador
www.canodros.com

Costa Crociere (Costa Cruises)
Via Gabriele D'Annunzio, 2/80
16121 Genoa
ITALY
www.costacruises.com

Delphin Seereisen
Blumenstrasse 20
63004 Offenbach/Main
GERMANY
www:delphin-cruises.com

Discovery World Cruises
15 Young Street
London W8
ENGLAND
www.discoveryworldcruises.com

Fred Olsen Cruise Lines
Fred Olsen House
White House Road
Ipswich
Suffolk 1P1 5LL
ENGLAND
www.fredolsen.co.uk

Golden Star Cruises
85 Akti Miaouli
Piraeus
GREECE 185 38
www.goldenstarcruises.com

Hansa Touristik
Contrescarpe 36
28203 Bremen
GERMANY
www.hansatourstik.com

Hapag-Lloyd Cruises
Ballindamm 25
D-20095 Hamburg
GERMANY
www.hlkf.com

Hebridean Island Cruises
Griffin House
Broughton Hall
Skipton
North Yorkshire BD23 3AN
ENGLAND

Holiday Cruises
Graf-Adolf-Strasse 58
4000 Düsseldorf 1
GERMANY

Kristina Cruises
16 Kirkkokatu
Kotka 48100
FINLAND
www.kristinacruises.com

Louis Cruise Lines
54-58 Evangoros Avenue
(P.O. Box 1306)
Nicosia, CYPRUS
www.louiscruises.com

Mitsui OSK Passenger Line
Shuwa-Kioicho Park Building
Kioicho 3-6
Chiyoda-ku
Tokyo 192-8552
JAPAN
www.mopas.co.jp.com

NYK Line (Nippon Yusen Kaisha)
Yusen Building
3-2 Marunouchi 2-choime
Chiyoda-ku
Tokyo 100-0005
JAPAN
www.asukacruise.co.jp

New Paradise Cruises
P.O. Box 50157
3601 Limassol
CYPRUS
www.paradise.com.cy

Orient Lines
1, Derry Street
Kensington
London W8 5NN
ENGLAND
www.orientlines.com

P&O Cruises
Richmond House
Terminus Terrace
Southampton
Hants SO14 3PN
ENGLAND
www.pocruises.com

P&O Cruises (Australia)
P.O. Box 5287
Sydney 2001
New South Wales
AUSTRALIA
www.pocruises.com.au

Phoenix Seereisen
Kolnstrasse 80
53111 Bonn
GERMANY
www.phoenixreisen.com

Plantours & Partner
Obern Street 69
Bremen 28195
GERMANY

Ponant Cruises
60 Boulebard Marchal Juin
44100 Nantes
FRANCE
www.ponant.com

Saga Cruises
The Saga Building
Folkestone
Kent
ENGLAND
www.saga.co.uk

Sea Cloud Cruises
Ballindamm 17
D-200095 Hamburg
GERMANY
www.seacloud.com

Seetours
Frankfurterstrasse 233
63263 Neu-Isenburg
GERMANY
www.seetours.de

Star Cruises
Star Cruises Terminal
Pulau Indah
PO Box No. 288
42009 Pelabuhan Klang
Selangor Darul Ehsan
MALAYSIA
www.starcruises.com.my

Star Line Cruises
P.O. Box 81443
Mombasa
KENYA

Swan Hellenic Cruises
77 New Oxford Street
London WC1A 1PP
ENGLAND
www.swan-hellenic.co.uk

Thomson Cruises
Greater London House
Hampstead Road
London NW1 7SD
ENGLAND
www.thomson-holidays.com

Transocean Tours
Postfach 10 09 07
28009 Bremen
GERMANY
www.transocean.de

Venus Cruise
Umeda Hanshin Daiichi
Building
5-25, Umeda 2-chome
Kita-ku
Osaka 530-0001
JAPAN
www.venus-cruise.co.jp

SHIPS RATED BY SCORE

Ship	Score	Rating	Ship	Score	Rating
LARGE (RESORT) SHIPS			*Oriana*	*1,530*	*4*
(over 1,000 passengers)			*AIDAaura*	*1,528*	*4*
			AIDAvita	*1,528*	*4*
Queen Mary 2 (Grill Class)	*1,754*	*5*	*Norwegian Dawn*	*1,524*	*4*
Constellation	*1,697*	*4+*	*Norwegian Star*	*1,522*	*4*
Infinity	*1,697*	*4+*	*SuperStar Virgo*	*1,522*	*4*
Millennium	*1,697*	*4+*	*Enchantment of the Seas*	*1,521*	*4*
Summit	*1,697*	*4+*	*Grandeur of the Seas*	*1,521*	*4*
Queen Elizabeth 2 (Grill Class)	*1,687*	*4+*	*Oceana*	*1,519*	*4*
Century	*1,663*	*4+*	*Rhapsody of the Seas*	*1,519*	*4*
Galaxy	*1,663*	*4+*	*Vision of the Seas*	*1,519*	*4*
Mercury	*1,663*	*4+*	*AIDAcara*	*1,517*	*4*
Queen Mary 2 (Britannia Class)	*1,601*	*4+*	*Norwegian Sun*	*1,517*	*4*
Queen Elizabeth 2 (Caronia Class)	*1,599*	*4+*	*Legend of the Seas*	*1,511*	*4*
Diamond Princess	*1,548*	*4*	*Splendour of the Seas*	*1,511*	*4*
Sapphire Princess	*1,548*	*4*	*Disney Magic*	*1,504*	*4*
Caribbean Princess	*1,547*	*4*	*Disney Wonder*	*1,504*	*4*
Brilliance of the Seas	*1,546*	*4*	*Norwegian Spirit*	*1,497*	*4*
Jewel of the Seas	*1,546*	*4*	*Royal Princess*	*1,496*	*4*
Radiance of the Seas	*1,546*	*4*	*Carnival Legend*	*1,474*	*4*
Serenade of the Seas	*1,546*	*4*	*Carnival Miracle*	*1,474*	*4*
Oosterdam	*1,546*	*4*	*Carnival Pride*	*1,474*	*4*
Westerdam	*1,546*	*4*	*Carnival Spirit*	*1,474*	*4*
Zuiderdam	*1,546*	*4*	*Carnival Conquest*	*1,457*	*4*
Golden Princess	*1,545*	*4*	*Carnival Glory*	*1,457*	*4*
Grand Princess	*1,545*	*4*	*Carnival Destiny*	*1,455*	*4*
Star Princess	*1,545*	*4*	*Carnival Triumph*	*1,455*	*4*
Coral Princess	*1,544*	*4*	*Carnival Victory*	*1,455*	*4*
Island Princess	*1,544*	*4*	*MSC Opera*	*1,452*	*4*
Amsterdam	*1,542*	*4*	*MSC Lirica*	*1,451*	*4*
Rotterdam	*1,541*	*4*	*MSC Armonia*	*1,449*	*4*
Volendam	*1,541*	*4*	*Norwegian Crown*	*1,445*	*4*
Zaandam	*1,541*	*4*	*Costa Atlantica*	*1,438*	*4*
Aurora	*1,540*	*4*	*Costa Mediterranea*	*1,438*	*4*
Dawn Princess	*1,539*	*4*	*MSC Sinfonia*	*1,436*	*4*
Sun Princess	*1,539*	*4*	*Costa Fortuna*	*1,432*	*4*
Adonia	*1,537*	*4*	*Regal Princess*	*1,416*	*4*
Adventure of the Seas	*1,537*	*4*	*Costa Victoria*	*1,406*	*4*
Explorer of the Seas	*1,537*	*4*	*Costa Europa*	*1,394*	*3+*
Mariner of the Seas	*1,537*	*4*	*Majesty of the Seas*	*1,394*	*3+*
Navigator of the Seas	*1,537*	*4*	*Monarch of the Seas*	*1,394*	*3+*
Voyager of the Seas	*1,537*	*4*	*Paradise*	*1,390*	*3+*
Zenith	*1,537*	*4*	*Elation*	*1,387*	*3+*
Horizon	*1,536*	*4*	*Pride of Aloha*	*1,387*	*3+*
Maasdam	*1,533*	*4*	*Sovereign of the Seas*	*1,386*	*3+*
Ryndam	*1,533*	*4*	*Norwegian Majesty*	*1,386*	*3+*
Statendam	*1,533*	*4*	*Ecstasy*	*1,385*	*3+*
Veendam	*1,533*	*4*	*Fantasy*	*1,385*	*3+*

Ship	Score	Rating	Ship	Score	Rating
Fascination	*1,385*	*3+*	*Holiday Dream*	*1,400*	*3+*
Imagination	*1,385*	*3+*	*Albatros*	*1,367*	*3+*
Inspiration	*1,385*	*3+*	*Grand Latino*	*1,343*	*3+*
Sensation	*1,385*	*3+*	*Maxim Gorkiy*	*1,342*	*3+*
Norwegian Dream	*1,381*	*3+*	*Braemar*	*1,325*	*3+*
Norwegian Wind	*1,381*	*3+*	*SuperStar Gemini*	*1,322*	*3+*
Queen Elizabeth 2			*Costa Tropicale*	*1,237*	*3*
(Mauretania Class)	*1,370*	*3+*	*Marco Polo*	*1,232*	*3*
Costa Romantica	*1,369*	*3+*	*Costa Marina*	*1,224*	*3*
Costa Classica	*1,368*	*3+*	*Mona Lisa*	*1,218*	*3*
Norwegian Sea	*1,366*	*3+*	*Costa Allegra*	*1,206*	*3*
Ocean Village	*1,351*	*3+*	*MSC Rhapsody*	*1,177*	*3*
AIDAblu	*1,338*	*3+*	*Ocean Monarch*	*1,103*	*3*
Empress of the Seas	*1,313*	*3+*	*The Emerald*	*1,102*	*3*
Thomson Spirit	*1,311*	*3+*	*Princess Danae*	*1,101*	*3*
Island Escape	*1,258*	*3+*	*Van Gogh*	*1,088*	*2+*
Celebration	*1,252*	*3+*	*Ocean Majesty*	*1,054*	*2+*
Holiday	*1,252*	*3+*	*Sapphire*	*1,036*	*2+*
MSC Melody	*1,252*	*3+*	*New Flamenco*	*1,026*	*2+*
Pacific Sky	*1,251*	*3+*	*Triton*	*1,009*	*2+*
Star Pisces	*1,247*	*3*	*Ausonia*	*996*	*2+*
Oceanic	*1,093*	*2+*	*Bolero*	*988*	*2+*
Arcadia	*NYR*	*NYR*	*MSC Monterey*	*984*	*2+*
Carnival Valor	*NYR*	*NYR*	*Regal Empress*	*896*	*2*
Costa Magica	*NYR*	*NYR*	*Aegean I*	*820*	*2*
Pacific Sun	*NYR*	*NYR*	*Serenade*	*771*	*1+*
Pride of America	*NYR*	*NYR*	*Delphin Renaissance*	*NYR*	*NYR*
Thomson Celebration	*NYR*	*NYR*	*Deutschland*	*NYR*	*NYR*
Thomson Destiny	*NYR*	*NYR*	*Discovery*	*NYR*	*NYR*
			Grand Voyager	*NYR*	*NYR*
MID-SIZE SHIPS			*Saga Ruby*	*NYR*	*NYR*
(500–1,200 passengers)					
			SMALL SHIPS		
Crystal Serenity	*1,702*	*5*	(201–500 passengers)		
Crystal Symphony	*1,701*	*5*			
Seven Seas Mariner	*1,701*	*5*	*Europa*	*1,858*	*5+*
Seven Seas Voyager	*1,701*	*5*	*Silver Shadow*	*1,757*	*5*
Prinsendam	*1,691*	*4+*	*Silver Whisper*	*1,757*	*5*
Crystal Harmony	*1,666*	*4+*	*Silver Cloud*	*1,722*	*5*
Asuka	*1,616*	*4+*	*Silver Wind*	*1,722*	*5*
Pacific Venus	*1,601*	*4+*	*Seven Seas Navigator*	*1,653*	*4+*
Insignia	*1,553*	*4+*	*Paul Gauguin*	*1,645*	*4+*
Regatta	*1,553*	*4+*	*Radisson Diamond*	*1,591*	*4+*
Minerva II	*1,498*	*4*	*Wind Surf*	*1,567*	*4+*
Pacific Princess	*1,487*	*4*	*Royal Clipper*	*1,540*	*4*
Tahitian Princess	*1,487*	*4*	*Club Med 2*	*1,532*	*4*
Astor	*1,450*	*4*	*Clipper Odyssey*	*1,451*	*4*
Astoria	*1,433*	*4*	*Star Clipper*	*1,402*	*4*
Black Watch	*1,429*	*4*	*Star Flyer*	*1,402*	*4*
Saga Rose	*1,423*	*4*	*Nippon Maru*	*1,391*	*3+*

Ship	Score	Rating	Ship	Score	Rating
C. Columbus	1,383	3+	Yamal	1,246	3
Orient Venus	1,361	3+	Spirit of Oceanus	1,218	3
Explorer II	1,357	3+	Clipper Adventurer	1,175	3
Fuji Maru	1,346	3+	Kapitan Dranitsyn	1,164	3
Endeavour	1,242	3	Kapitan Khlebnikov	1,164	3
Vistamar	1,232	3	Monet	1,097	2+
Black Prince	1,093	2+	Polaris	1,071	2+
World Renaissance	1,091	2+	Andrea	1,062	2+
Funchal	1,089	2+	Kristina Regina	1,052	2+
Royal Star	1,069	2+	Legacy	998	2+
Calypso	1,062	2+	Spirit of '98	997	2+
Odysseus	1,042	2+	Yorktown Clipper	982	2+
Paloma I	947	2+	Nantucket Clipper	982	2+
The Iris	912	2	Niagara Prince	964	2+
The Jasmine	909	2	Grande Caribe	963	2+
Princesa Marissa	891	2	Grande Mariner	963	2+
Arion	859	2	Professor Molchanov	947	2
Atalante	645	1	Professor Multanovskiy	947	2
			Akademik Sergey Vavilov	942	2
BOUTIQUE SHIPS			Sea Bird	938	2
(50-200 passengers)			Sea Lion	938	2
			Spirit of Endeavour	934	2
SeaDream I	1,790	5	Spirit of Alaska	924	2
SeaDream II	1,790	5	Spirit of Columbia	924	2
Seabourn Legend	1,786	5	Spirit of Discovery	924	2
Seabourn Pride	1,785	5	Spirit of Glacier Bay	910	2
Seabourn Spirit	1,785	5	Wilderness Adventurer	905	2
Hanseatic	1,740	5	Wilderness Discoverer	905	2
Sea Cloud II	1,709	5	Flying Cloud	902	2
Hebridean Spirit	1,707	5	Mandalay	902	2
Sea Cloud	1,704	5	Polynesia	902	2
Hebridean Princess	1,701	5	Yankee Clipper	902	2
Orion	1,612	4+	American Glory	835	2
Le Levant	1,609	4+	American Eagle	827	2
Le Diamant	1,544	4	American Spirit	NYR	NYR
Le Ponant	1,540	4	Celebrity Xpedition	NYR	NYR
Wind Spirit	1,518	4	easyCruise I	NYR	NYR
Wind Star	1,518	4	Island Sky	NYR	NYR
Bremen	1,461	4	Island Sun	NYR	NYR
Galapagos Explorer II	1,365	3+			

NYR = Not Yet Rated

Index

Credits

Photography:
Carnival Cruise Lines 8, 9, 20, 29, 33, 42, 46, 55, 73, 113, 114, 115, 116
Celebrity Cruises 79, 118, 119, 120
Corbis 22, 23, 25L&R
Costa Cruises 16, 121, 122, 123, 139, 151
Cruise West 90
Cunard 18/19, 48, 58, 97, 137
Jon Davison 63
Delta Steamboat Company 89
Expedition Hanseatic 92
Glyn Genin 4/5, 6, 35, 39, 59

Hapag Lloyd 100, 146
Matthew Hawkins 3
Mary Ann Hemphill 12, 13
Holland America Line 30, 32, 70, 124, 125, 126, 127
Bob Krist 10, 11, 36, 41, 43, 45
Norwegian Cruise Line 56, 128, 129
P&O Cruises 99, 101, 153
Princess Cruises 69, 75, 130, 131, 132, 133
Regal China Cruises 87
Royal Caribbean International 15, 134, 135, 136
Seabourne Cruise Line 68, 98
SeaDream 14, 144, 147, 149
Topham Picturepoint 26, 27

V&A Picture Library 1
Douglas Ward 21, 34, 47, 51, 53, 71, 72, 76, 78, 83, 88, 94, 95, 96, 108, 111, 141
Windjammer Barefoot Cruises 636

Picture Editor: Hilary Genin
Art Director: Klaus Geisler
Production: Sylvia George
Cartography Editor: Zoë Goodwin

Map Production Tyne Mapping
Maps © 2005 Apa Publications GmbH & Co. Verlag KG (Singapore branch)

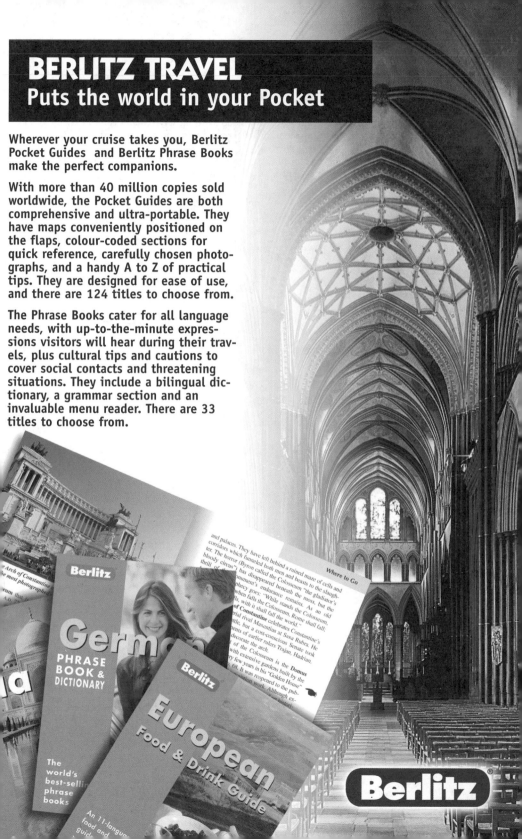

DEAR PASSENGER,

You are most welcome to send me your observations concerning any recent cruises taken. Please complete the following basic information when sending comments concerning your recent cruise experiences.

Although I cannot acknowledge receipt of this comment form, or any letters, because of my non-stop travel schedule, I do thank you for your input, and for purchasing this book.

Cruise Date . . . .   Ship Name . . . .

Cruise Line . . . .   Suite/Cabin Number . . . .

Dining Room Seating (tick box):   ❑ Open   ❑ First   ❑ Second

Your Comments . . . .

. . . .

. . . .

. . . .

. . . .

. . . .

Your Pet Peeves

(1) . . . .

. . . .

(2) . . . .

. . . .

(3) . . . .

. . . .

Your name . . . .

Address . . . .

. . . .

. . . .

Please send to the address below:
Mr Douglas Ward
The Maritime Evaluations Group
Canada House
1 Carrick Way
New Milton
Hampshire BH25 6UD
United Kingdom

Alternatively, please email these details to:
dw@berlitzcruising.com